GunDigest® 2021

CELEBRATING
75
EDITIONS
OF FREEDOM
& FIREARMS!

EDITED BY

Philip P. Massaro

Published by

Gun Digest® Books, an imprint of Caribou Media Group, LLC

Gun Digest Media
5600 W. Grande Market Drive, Suite 100
Appleton, WI 54913
www.gundigest.com

To order books or other products call 920.471.4522
or visit us online at www.gundigeststore.com

CAUTION: Technical data presented here, particularly technical data on handloading and on firearms adjustment and alteration, inevitably reflects individual experience with particular equipment and components under specific circumstances the reader cannot duplicate exactly. Such data presentations therefore should be used for guidance only and with caution. Caribou Media accepts no responsibility for results obtained using these data.

ISBN-13: 978-1-951115-07-4

Edited by Phil Massaro and Chuck Smock
Cover Design by Gene Coo
Interior Design by Dave Hauser, Jeromy Boutwell, & Jordan Matuszak

Printed in the United States of America

10 9 8 7 6 5 4 3 2 1

John T. Amber

LITERARY AWARD

The John T. Amber Literary Award is named for the editor of *Gun Digest* from 1950 to 1979, a period that could be called the heyday of gun and outdoor writing. Amber worked with many of the legends in the business during his almost 30 years with the book, including the great shooting and hunting writer Townsend Whelen. In 1967, Amber instituted an annual award, which he named for Whelen, to honor an outstanding author from the previous year's *Gun Digest* edition. In 1982, three years after Amber's retirement, the award was renamed in his honor.

I first noticed Joe Coogan's name when it was attached to a bunch of fantastic articles about hunting Africa, something I am extremely passionate about. Within a few paragraphs, I was absolutely hooked; Joe's life experiences and writing style, coupled with the fact that he had the privilege of working with the famous Professional Hunter Harry Selby, had my undivided attention. Little did I know that fate would allow me to proudly present Joe with the 39th Annual John T. Amber Literary Award, for his excellent article on the .700 Holland & Holland Nitro Express in the 2020 *Gun Digest* annual.

Growing up in East Africa with his family during the 1960s and 1970s, Florida-native Joe Coogan and his father, Joe Sr., experienced the unique adventure of hunting African big game as Kenya residents. An avid hunter, shooter and outdoorsman, Coogan's early Kenya experiences laid the groundwork that led him into safari work as a professional hunter in Botswana and Tanzania.

Coogan earned a degree in journalism from the University of South Florida in 1972, after which he returned to Africa to join the long-established safari firm, Ker, Downey & Selby (KDS) Safaris. Signing on to their Botswana operation under the leadership of the renowned Harry Selby, Coogan received his Botswana professional hunter's license under Selby's tutelage and guidance. For the next 20 years, Coogan conducted hunting and photo safaris throughout the Okavango Delta and Kalahari Desert

JOE COOGAN

areas of the southern Africa nation.

In 1991, Coogan traded the African bush for the asphalt jungles of Los Angeles, joining the editorial staff of *Petersen's HUNTING* magazine under the editorship of Craig Boddington. Coogan left LA in 1998 for the duck and deer woods of Arkansas' Grand Prairie, managing a wildlife project at the legendary duck mecca Wingmead, for owner and good friend, the late Frank Lyon, Jr. Coogan returned to his beloved Africa in 2001 when he joined Arusha-based Tanzania Game Tracker Safaris (TGTS), conduct-

ing hunting and photo safaris in East Africa for the next five years. Benelli USA then offered Coogan a position as its brand marketing manager, which brought him back to company headquarters in Accokeek, Maryland, in 2006. In that capacity, he was responsible for Benelli's brand names and products, as well as hosting *Benelli On Assignment*, a popular outdoor TV show, for six years.

"Receiving the John T. Amber Award is a real honor, and one for which I'm extremely proud," Coogan said. "Working with doyens of the industry such as *Gun Digest* former editor, the late Jerry Lee, and the current editor, Phil Massaro, makes the writing I do an absolute pleasure."

Today, Coogan writes for several gun and national outdoor magazines, including *Gun Digest*. He continues to travel between his home state of Florida and Africa, arranging and conducting safaris through his company, Africa All-Ways, Inc. (AAW) (www.africaallways.com and Africa All-Ways on Facebook). AAW is a U.S.-based outfitting agency specializing in planning and arranging all trip details for African sporting adventures, including hunting, fishing, climbing and photographic safaris.

Named in honor of John T. Amber, the long-time editor of this book and a staple in the firearms industry, this literary award is proudly given to Joe Coogan, who also represents a chapter in the history of hunting, firearms and the literature that surrounds it all. Congratulations, Joe!

Phil Massaro, Editor-in-Chief

GunDigest® 2021

2 0 2 1   F I R E A R M S   C A T A L O G

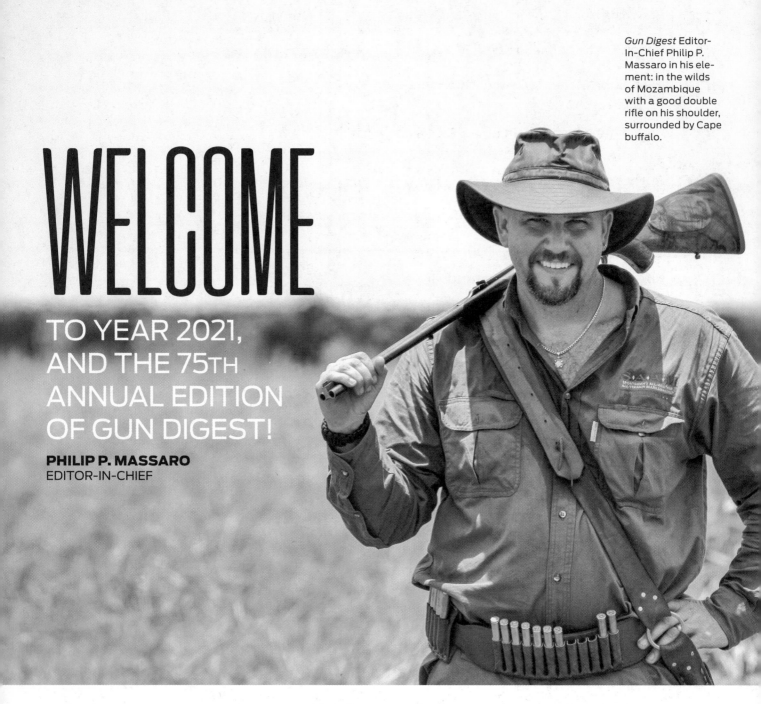

WELCOME

TO YEAR 2021, AND THE 75TH ANNUAL EDITION OF GUN DIGEST!

PHILIP P. MASSARO
EDITOR-IN-CHIEF

Gun Digest Editor-In-Chief Philip P. Massaro in his element: in the wilds of Mozambique with a good double rifle on his shoulder, surrounded by Cape buffalo.

And welcome to my first edition serving as editor-in-chief. To say that I'm honored to be here, is, well, a gross understatement, as the space in between the covers of this revered tome is certainly hallowed ground. It has been graced by names such as Elmer Keith, Warren Page, Jack O'Connor, Ned Roberts, Bob Bell, Townsend Whelen, Phil Sharpe and John T. Amber, who served as both author and editor for three decades, and that's just the tip of the iceberg. I have happily occupied the editor's seat for the Ammunition, Ballistics and Components section since the 70th Edition, under the leadership of the late Jerry B. Lee, who sadly passed away in November 2019 (see a tribute to Jerry, starting on page 284).

For as long as I can remember, the *Gun Digest* annual has been *THE* collectable book on firearms; each year, I would look forward to reading those feature pieces, which would cover a range of topics wide enough to keep my mind occupied for weeks. I'd pore over the catalog section, dreaming of hunting with some of those wonderful guns. But the *Gun Digest* was, is and always will be, more than just a wish book; the *Gun Digest* is a source of firearms wisdom. The long list of excellent writers who have imparted their knowledge over the decades reads like the Hall of Fame for the firearms industry, and as the seventh editor-in-chief of this excellent book, I have done my best to assemble a team of the best available. Some names you'll be very familiar with, names like Boddington, Spomer, van Zwoll, Tabor, Turpin, Weishuhn and Wieland; others might be new to you, but I can assure you this: They all have something wonderful to offer. There are African Professional Hunters, a Weatherby Award winner, decorated veterans, shooting instructors, and many of us who make a living writing about guns. And after all, the gun is the common denominator here; you are holding this book in your hands because of an interest in firearms.

The *Gun Digest* has long provided insight to the history of firearms, cartridges and their accoutrements, while simultaneously looking forward to new products destined to become game changers. In print since 1944, *Gun Digest* has seen many changes in the industry, from the development of so many of the cartridges we rely upon each season or shooting session, to the rise of the synthetic-stocked weather-proof firearms, to the polymer handguns that are now the norm. Here in the 75th Anniversary Edition, we continue that trend, both bringing new developments to the foreground while respecting and honoring the history of our industry.

INSIDE THE 75TH EDITION

Dave Campbell brings us the history of the venerable 1886 Winchester, Bryce Towsley traces the roots of the Remington Model 700, Wayne van Zwoll covers single-shot rifles and Ron Spomer weighs in on straight-pull bolt rifles. There are vintage snub-nosed revolvers, the new Glock Model 44 in .22 LR, and a dissertation on the equally loved and hated 6.5 Creedmoor cartridge. There are pieces on the vintage Browning Superposed shotgun and the modern Browning X-Bolt Hell's Canyon rifle, and from Joe

Coogan's classic Model 721 .300 H&H Magnum to the Tikka Model T3. Phil Shoemaker brings us the tale of his famous .458 Winchester Magnum – Old Ugly – which has had more adventures among the brown bears than any of us could imagine. And, on top of all this, Walther is celebrating its 90th anniversary, Nosler has introduced its new .27 Nosler cartridge, adding a new dimension to the .277-inch bore diameter, and Remington has partnered with the editors of the NRA's *American Hunter* magazine for a new Model 700. From long-range target guns, to rifles best suited to the Alaskan mountains, to handguns old and new, the 2021 *Gun Digest* has something for all.

IN MEMORIAM

Sadly, Jerry Lee was not the only member of the *Gun Digest* family to leave us since the last edition. Walter D. Hampton III passed away Jan. 8, 2020. Walt was a retired wildlife biologist and a gunsmith, as well as sharing his knowledge as an outdoor writer since 1990. Walt's contributions to the *Gun Digest* annual and

Gun Digest the Magazine, as well as his warm personality, will be missed.

LOOKING FORWARD

There might be some of you wondering "Who exactly is Phil Massaro?" Well, if I may, allow me to tell you a bit about myself. I hold no degree in journalism, nor did I start my career as a gun writer early in life; rather, it found me, and not until I was over 40. I am a land surveyor by trade, and a musician by choice, but for my entire life I have been an avid hunter and aficionado of firearms of all sorts. I am a passionate reloader, having spent an exorbitant amount of time loading for myself, and as the president of Massaro Ballistic Laboratories, my own custom ammunition shop, for clients. I am also highly passionate about hunting Africa, both plains game and dangerous game, and the cartridges and rifles of the Golden Age of safaris, though I love hunting just about anything. I have published five books, including Gun Digest titles: *Shooter's Guide to Reloading* and *Big Book of Ballistics*; and am the editor-in-chief of *Handloader's Digest, 19th Edition*, in addition to writing hundreds of articles, both on the web and in print. But, at the end of the day, I am just a passionate hunter who thinks guns of all sorts are fascinating.

"Variety is the spice of life," the old saying goes, and while I know there are those who enjoy the same topics that I do, there are those with completely different passions, and those passions should be addressed by those who are most knowledgeable about them. As the editor of such a revered title, I have done my best – and will continue to do so – to assemble the best team possible, to cover the wide range of gun topics.

So, with my fingers crossed and the greatest hope for the next generation of the *Gun Digest* annual, I present to you the 2021 Edition of the World's Greatest Gun Book. 𝗚𝗗

GUN DIGEST STAFF

JIM SCHLENDER | Group Publisher

PHILIP P. MASSARO | Editor-In-Chief

CHUCK SMOCK | Features Editor

DEPARTMENT CONTRIBUTORS

Wayne van Zwoll | Rifles
Todd Woodard | AR Rifles
Robert Sadowski | Semi-Auto Pistols
Max Prasac | Revolvers & Others
Kristin Alberts | Shotguns

Matthew Breuer | Muzzleloaders
Joe Arterburn | Optics
Jim House | Airguns
Philip P. Massaro | Ammo, Reloading & Ballistics
Tom Turpin | Custom & Engraved Guns

ATAC
DEFENSE
ENHANCED
RIFLE

The *Gun Digest 2021* cover gun is the ATAC Defense Enhanced Rifle (ADER 5.56; MSRP: $1,299). Numerous enhancements make this rifle fast to operate and a dream to shoot. **These enhancements include an** ambidextrous safety, ambi mag release with oversized mag button, oversized bolt release, oversized ambi charging handle, muzzle brake, a nickel-boron-coated bolt-carrier group, and a Mission First Tactical (MFT) Battlelink Minimalist Milspec Stock and MFT Engage Grip.

In addition to the Burnt Bronze Cerakote finish of the cover gun, these rifles are available in Black, Tungsten, Flat Dark Earth (FDE) and Olive Drab (OD) Green Cerakote finishes. Three different triggers are available: drop-in curved or straight with a 3.5-pound pull; or a two-stage trigger with a 1.5-pound pull in the first stage and a 2-pound pull in the second stage.

At ATAC Defense, quality, reliability, accuracy and fit and finish are of the greatest concerns. The company believes in holding a quality level that is far above Mil-Spec. All components are hand-picked and tested by the marksmen who design the rifles.

"One thing we chase is quality," said Monty Johnson, ATAC Defense co-owner. "Fit, finish and accuracy. We're not cranking out firearms for the masses. We were just trying to come up with something in a relatively affordable price range, but with quality that exceeds expectations. I won't send out a rifle I wouldn't use to defend my family in a bad situation." ATAC Defense was born in the custom car-parts shop of fellow co-owner Chris Johnson (no relation) in Lucedale, Mississippi. In 1999, Monty joined the team that fabricated everything from twin turbo kits, to custom super-charger kits, to complete intake manifolds. And the team just happened to include more than a few gun enthusiasts.

"We were hard-core gun guys," Monty said. "When we had any downtime, we would be tinkering with stuff, making parts. Being gun guys, it was a natural progression into making gun parts with all the equipment we had."

ADER rifles are also available with a Tungsten Cerakote finish.

(opposite and above) In addition to a Burnt Bronze Cerakote finish, these ATAC Defense rifles are available in Black, Tungsten, Flat Dark Earth (FDE) and Olive Drab (OD) Green Cerakote finishes.

ATAC Defense now supplies parts to more than 300 firearms manufacturers.

"Quality manufacturing is the very first step," Monty said. "And we have a lot of control over the quality because we do most of the manufacturing of the parts we use in our guns. We're just gun enthusiasts doing what we love to do, and doing it with quality."

And the end-results should be obvious considering the attention to detail and quality control that goes into the building of every ATAC Defense firearm.

The upper and lower receivers on the ADER 5.56 are machined in-house at company headquarters in Lucedale, to ensure proper fit, without slack and rattle. Each ATAC Defense Enhanced Rifle is hand assembled with the company's inspected, tested and approved components. After assembly, each firearm goes through a test-fire session and is re-inspected. Each firearm must pass a final inspection before it can be shipped to the customer.

An ADER lower receiver starts as a 7075 T6 aluminum forging that is machined to exact tolerances. After inspection, it moves through an in-house mag-well broaching process to ensure proper dimensions, and a straight, true mag well. Then it goes through a vibratory tumbler that uses ceramic media to deburr it. Additional, enhanced features include: threaded bolt catch pin, threaded (captured) rear detent pin and an upper-to-lower adjustment feature.

(below) The upper and lower receivers on the ADER 5.56 are machined in-house at company headquarters in Lucedale, Mississippi, to ensure proper fit, without slack and rattle. Each ATAC Defense Enhanced Rifle is hand assembled with the company's inspected, tested and approved components.

The upper receivers also start as a 7075 T6 aluminum forging. They also must pass inspection at every machining station they go through. They are then tumbled and deburred in a vibratory tumbler. During the machining process, ATAC chooses to leave the upper receiver lugs slightly oversized. Utilizing the oversized lugs, builders hand-fit each upper and lower receiver to ensure a proper, tight upper-lower fit.

The M4 contour 4150 CrMoV barrel starts life as a true gun-barrel steel blank that meets Mil-B-1159SE specifications, which cover alloys steel, bars and blanks under 2 inches in diameter for use in the manufacture of barrels for small firearms. All ADER barrels are precision-bored and button-rifled using a six-groove rifling at a 1:7

In addition to an ambidextrous charging handle, the ATAC Defense Enhanced Rifle has an ambidextrous safety and an ambidextrous magazine release.

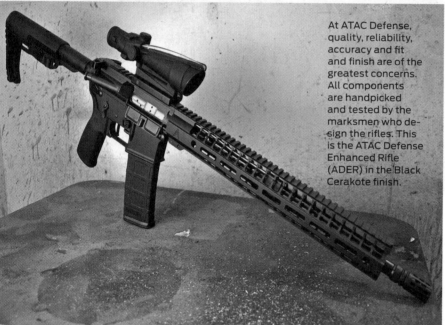

At ATAC Defense, quality, reliability, accuracy and fit and finish are of the greatest concerns. All components are handpicked and tested by the marksmen who design the rifles. This is the ATAC Defense Enhanced Rifle (ADER) in the Black Cerakote finish.

Leupold Freedom RDS 1x34

The optic on this year's cover gun is a Leupold Freedom RDS (Red Dot Scope) 1x34. It is built Leupold tough, performs in extreme conditions, and won't break the bank with an MSRP of $364.99, without mounts.

The Leupold Freedom RDS has a 34mm main tube that offers unparalleled windage and elevation adjustment travel (80 MOA, each), and the 1/4 MOA precision finger-click adjustments deliver absolute repeatability and dependability over a lifetime of extreme use.

The Freedom RDS has a 34mm main tube that offers unparalleled windage and elevation adjustment travel (80 MOA, each), and the 1/4 MOA precision finger-click adjustments deliver absolute repeatability and dependability over a lifetime of extreme use. The 1 MOA dot is ideal for precise shot placement. The scope is 5.3 inches long and weighs 7.2 ounces without mounts.

The Freedom RDS features Motion Sensor Technology, which extends battery life by automatically deactivating illumination after five minutes of inactivity, yet reactivates instantly as soon as any movement is detected. Leupold reports battery life (one 3V CR2032 lithium battery) of a minimum of 1,000 hours on brightness level four of eight.

This updated version will accept the Alumina Flip Back Objective Lens Cover and the Alumina Flip Back Eyepiece Cover. And it is backed by a Leupold lifetime warranty.

twist rate. Each chamber is cut to match the 5.56 caliber. After boring, rifling and chambering, the exterior of the barrel is cut to the M4 profile with a .750 gas-block diameter, and a 1/2 x 28 muzzle thread. The gas port is properly sized to achieve the right gas pressure for proper ejection. After final machining, inspection and testing, the barrel is then salt bath nitride coated and quenched to provide a durable lasting finish. At assembly, a muzzle brake is mated to the 1/2 x 28 threaded barrel.

Bolts are precision-machined from Carpenter 158 steel, a chrome-nickel al-loy steel with an analysis representing the best case-hardening steel known for parts subject to heavy shock and wear. After machining, the bolt is vibratory tumbled and deburred.

Carriers are machined from AISI 8620 alloy steel to full auto profile, then stress relieved, and case-hardened, which results in excellent wear characteristics. After the machining and hardening, they are nickel-boron coated. The gas key is machined from 4130 chromoly alloy, heat treated, and attached to the bolt-carrier group using grade-eight hardware torqued to the recommended spec. After the bolts are torqued, they are properly staked to mil-specifications. The bolt carrier group is assembled using stainless steel gas rings, a 4340 heat-treated cam pin, and an 8640 heat-treated firing pin. The extractor is heat-treated, precision-ground 4340, and a S7 heat-treated ejector is used.

"I hate sloppy, loose parts," Monty Johnson said. "We're holding to a better standard in everything we do. I just want every one of them to be good. Every time you pull the trigger, we want them to be accurate." GD

The Tikka T3 Hunter chambered in .308 Winchester is a gorgeous rifle, perfect for hunting all over North America.

Options abound for customizing these high-performance, budget-friendly rifles ›THOMAS GOMEZ

THE TIKKA T3
AND T3x

I n 1918, Finnish firearms company Tikkakoski started to manufacture firearms components. Sixty-three years later, Tikkakoski and another Finnish firearms company, Sako, collaborated on a prototype rifle. Sako then purchased Tikkakoski from Nokia in 1983. The companies merged to create Oy Sako-Tikka Ab, which later became Sako. A world-class manufacturer of hunting, law enforcement and military rifles, Sako positioned the Tikka brand as a "budget" class of rifles. The Beretta Holdings Group purchased Sako in 2000, and in 2003 the Tikka T3 rifle was released to the market. After over a decade of success with the Tikka T3, Tikka released an updated version, the Tikka T3x, which debuted in 2016.

Being Sako's budget brand does not mean these rifles are cheap or of poor quality. The Tikka T3 has been well-received by the U.S. market and is noted for its accuracy, versatility and excellent trigger. Tikka offers models for hunting, law enforcement, and precision-rifle applications.

Tikka offers the T3 and T3x exclusively as long-action rifles. The actions have a round bottom and calibers run from .204 Ruger up to .300 Winchester Magnum. Many gunsmiths will note that the Tikka action tends to be true and requires little blueprinting. Like the universal action size, Tikka uses one magazine size with internal magazine blocks to accommo-

date the different calibers. Bolt travel differs based on cartridge length, with Tikka using two different bolt stops, depending on the caliber.

The action is secured by two M6 metric thread action screws, and mates with the stock via an aluminum recoil lug.

Tikka offers rifles that have an integrated Picatinny scope base, and some with a plain dovetail that can accept proprietary scope rings. The single-stage trigger on the Tikka T3/T3x is user adjustable between 2 and 4 pounds. The trigger is crisp and noted as one of the best factory

(right) Top: Tikka T3. Bottom: Tikka T3x. Note the increased ejection port on the T3x. Tikka rifles are noted as having some of the smoothest actions on the market.

(below) This Tikka T3 is chambered in 6.5 PRC, mated to a Modular Driven Technologies ESS Chassis, and was custom-built by Bill Marr of 872 Custom Gunwerks. The factory Tikka trigger is excellent.

triggers available. Both Tikka and Sako barrels are cold hammer-forged and are made side by side in the same factory. Tikka guarantees a five-shot 1-MOA guarantee on its heavy barrel rifles, and a three-shot 1-MOA guarantee on its sporter barrel rifles.

The Tikka rifle receiver features broached raceways to accommodate the two lugs on the bolt. Bolt throw is 70 degrees, and the Tikka T3/T3x has one of the smoothest actions on the market. The bolt has a Sako-style extractor and a spring-and-plunger ejector. The bolt handle is dovetailed into the bolt and can easily be removed by the end-user. The shroud on the Tikka T3 bolt is polymer and, like the bolt handle, it can easily be customized with an aftermarket option. The Tikka T3x bolt shrouds are aluminum. The bottom metal is constructed of polymer on both the Tikka T3 and T3x.

Tikka launched the Tikka T3x in 2016 and made changes to both the receiver and the stock. On the receiver, Tikka opened up the ejection port, which allows users to easily feed one round at a time. Tikka replaced the polymer bolt shroud with an aluminum one and changed the aluminum stock lug to steel. The steel lug addressed deformation issues that had occurred with large-caliber rifles. The top of the receiver was drilled and tapped to accommodate a Picatinny rail; this modification was also possible with the Tikka T3, but Tikka felt there was room for improvement.

The most significant aesthetic change was the inclusion of a modular stock that features interchangeable pistol grips and fore-ends. Through the Beretta store, customers can purchase grips and fore-ends with different textures, sizes and colors. The stock is filled with foam inserts to dampen noise, and an enhanced recoil pad mitigates felt recoil.

ANALYSIS

Over the years, I have owned a suite of Tikka T3 and Tikka T3x rifles. To me, the Tikka T3/T3x is analogous to a Glock 19: It is an inexpensive, quality firearm that simply performs. I am not afraid to damage it and will modify it to suit my needs. I rarely get attached to my stock Tikkas and see them as tools to perform a given task. These tough rifles can be easily customized and tend to hold their value. I have never owned one that failed to hold MOA, given good factory ammunition and solid shooting fundamentals.

For years, I thought the Tikka T3 was good out of the box, but after owning a few Tikka T3x rifles, I appreciate the upgrade. A common complaint about the Tikka T3 bolt was the plastic bolt shroud. I never took issue with this or had one fail in the field, but I am glad Tikka addressed this issue by making an aluminum bolt shroud standard on the

Tikka's feed from a polymer magazine. Tikka uses blocks in the magazine to accommodate the various caliber configurations. Metal magazines do exist, though the author never had a problem with the factory polymer magazines.

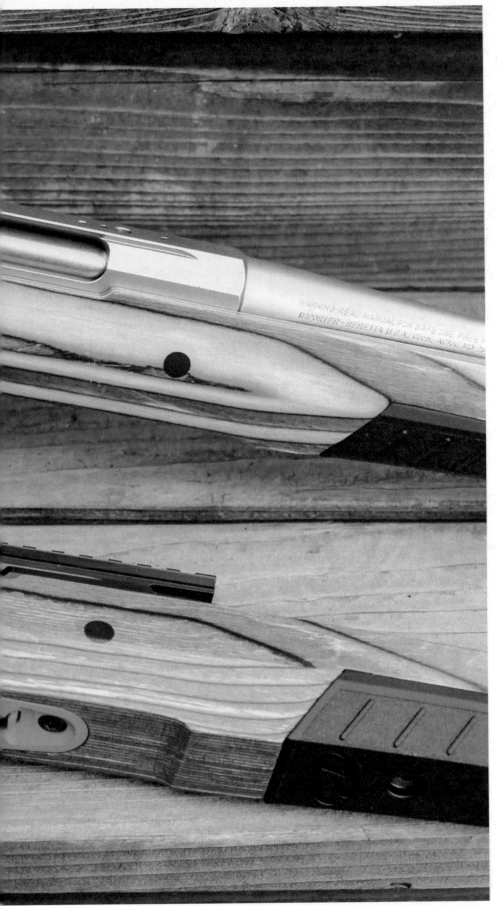

Tikka T3x series. The custom grip and fore-ends are a nice touch, and the larger ejection port does ease loading of single rounds. Did I ever have problems after attaching a Picatinny rail to my Tikka T3? No, but if user feedback demanded a more solid rail interface, I am glad Tikka took note and put its engineers to work upgrading this component on the Tikka T3x. Tikka offers both right- and left-handed models.

MODIFYING THE TRADITIONAL HUNTING RIFLE

Except for the Tikka T3x CTR, T3x UPR, T3x TACT A1, and the Tikka T3 Super Varmint, Tikkas do not have a Picatinny scope base. The rifles without scope bases use a specialized scope ring, which is readily available from a variety of manufacturers. These rings mount directly to the top of the receiver. In my experience, this is a lightweight, stream-lined way to install a scope. If you attach a Picatinny scope base, this modification will raise up your scope and you might need to raise your comb height to ensure a proper cheek weld. This subsequent adjustment is paramount if you train and shoot in the prone position. Raising the comb can be accomplished either by building up the comb with tape and pad-ding or by installing a nylon comb riser/ammo pouch. Kalix Teknik of Sweden makes a retrofit kit that looks like it was installed at the factory and requires only a slight modification to the rifle. The CR-1 has an adjustable comb, secured inside the rifle buttstock by an aluminum assembly. A knob on the stock allows the user to secure the comb at the desired height. In my opinion, the Kalix Teknik CR-1 is the best aftermarket accessory currently available for adjusting comb height.

Both of these semi-custom Tikka T3 and T3x rifles have an aluminum bottom metal from High Desert Rifle Works and are at-tached to Boyds At-One stocks. Simple upgrades make a good rifle even better.

The polymer bottom metal in the middle is off a factory Tikka. Unfortunately, in rare cases these bottom metals can crack. The orange and metallic guards are aluminum bottom metals from High Desert Rifle Works. If you hunt in extreme weather, an aluminum bottom metal is a good upgrade.

Except for the T3x TACT A1, Tikka rifles tend to be on the lighter side in terms of weight. A lightweight rifle is fantastic to carry around the woods all day. The only drawback of a lightweight rifle is increased recoil. The easiest way to decrease recoil on a lightweight hunting rifle is to add a muzzle brake and a recoil pad. If you do add a muzzle brake, hunting with hearing protection is absolutely mandatory. Training and getting proficient with a light rifle are easier when excessive recoil is mitigated. This adjustment is particularly important for small-statured or new shooters.

If I wanted to set up the optimal Tikka T3/T3x for a lightweight hunting rifle, I would start with a Tikka T3/T3x Lite and install a LimbSaver buttpad. Tikka did upgrade the buttpad on the T3x rifles,

A custom 6.5 PRC build by 782 Custom Gunwerks. This rifle features a 20 MIL prism from TACOM HQ that allows for shots past 1 mile.

but I think a LimbSaver is still superior to the factory product. If, after installing a Limbsaver recoil pad, I cannot comfortably zero a rifle and gather ballistic data out to 600 yards on an 8-inch steel plate, I will consider a muzzle brake. My 6.5 Creedmoor backcountry hunting rifle did not require a brake and was a joy to shoot, even in the prone position. My .308 Winchester and .300 Winchester Short Magnum both have muzzle brakes.

I also would replace the polymer bottom metal with an aluminum bottom metal from High Desert Rifle Works. An aluminum bottom metal mitigates fliers and increases the tension between the action and the stock. Though anecdotal, I believe that an aluminum bottom metal leads to a more accurate rifle by positively affecting barrel harmonics, and it will never crack. Unfortunately, I have had factory Tikka polymer bottom metals break, where the action screws interface with the bottom metal. In my home state of New Mexico, it can be near freezing in the morning and 95 degrees in the afternoon. This heating-and-cooling cycle is tough on polymers, and all my backcountry Tikkas have aluminum bottom metals.

One area where I don't mind weight

is in my rifle scope. Hunting in the West requires quality glass and, potentially, 400- to 500-yard, cross-canyon shots. For a scope, I would select a TRACT TORIC UHD 30mm. These top-of-the-line scopes use premium glass and feature a MIL-based reticle that allows you to hold for elevation and wind.

For a general-use rifle where weight is not a concern, I would install a muzzle

brake and look at a stock with more features, like adjustable length of pull and comb height, and modular interfaces for bipod and sling attachment. Suitable candidates would include the Boyds At-One Thumbhole Stock, Kinetic Research Group Bravo stock, and my new favorite, the Modular Driven Technologies XRS. I would also consider attaching a suppressor to the rifle.

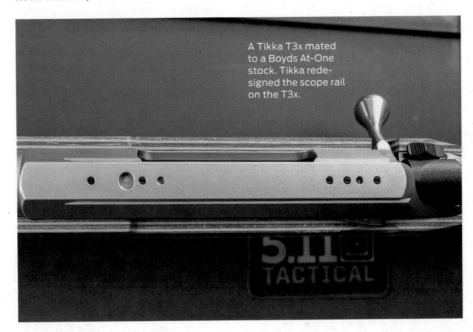

A Tikka T3x mated to a Boyds At-One stock. Tikka redesigned the scope rail on the T3x.

This Tikka T3 Lite is chambered in .308 Winchester, mated to a Boyds At-One rifle stock with a Nikon Black riflescope and an AMTAC Mantis P Suppressor. It is perfect for 800 yards and in.

CUSTOM RIFLES

Since the Tikka T3/T3x is a long action, it has a lot of versatility for caliber selection and is perfect for a custom rifle. About 10 years ago, I found a .300 WSM in a gun store being sold for $275. I asked the clerk why the rifle was so cheap, and he responded that the seller found the recoil to be hellacious and could not effectively use the rifle. Twenty minutes later, I was the new owner of a Tikka T3 chambered in .300 WSM. I threw the rifle in my safe and forgot about it. Fast forward to the 2018 SHOT Show, where I first saw the 6.5 PRC round from Hornady. When I got home from SHOT Show, I contacted Bill Marr at 782 Custom Gunworks and inquired about rebuilding my .300 WSM into a 6.5 PRC. Bill said it wasn't a problem, and noted that my request couldn't have come at a better time because he had just received a 6.5 PRC reamer. I shipped my Tikka T3 to Long Island, New York, and, several weeks later, received a custom Tikka rifle. The rifle featured a 26-inch 1:8-inch twist Shilen Select Match Barrel, and the barreled action was mated to a Kinetic Research Group Bravo chassis. The rifle launches 147-grain Hornady ELD-M rounds at 2,920 fps, and can easily hold five-shot, sub-.40-inch groups.

The rifle was immediately put to work dispatching coyotes at long range and has been used on several long-range antelope hunts. I can get consistent hits on a 24-inch plate at 2,000 yards and, besides long-range predator control, I use the rifle when I have to test optics and optical accessories past 1,800 yards. The only change I have made was swapping out the Kinetic Research Group Bravo chassis for a Modular Driven Technologies ESS Chassis. The Modular Driven Technologies chassis has better comb and buttpad adjustments and complements lights, lasers, and clip-on thermal and night-vision technology.

If you have an old Tikka T3/T3x that you want to rebuild or customize, contact 782 Custom Gunwerks, or Oregon Mountain Rifle Company. 782 Custom Gunwerks is one of the premier gunsmiths in the United States and has expertise in building custom Tikkas. Bill Marr, the owner and lead gunsmith, can do anything you want to a Tikka. Oregon Mountain Rifle Company offers a Tikka T3/T3x Upgrade Package, in which it installs a carbon-fiber barrel, muzzle brake and carbon-fiber stock.

CLOSING THOUGHTS

The Tikka T3/T3x are fantastic rifles. Tikka rifles start at around $550 for a Tikka T3x Lite model and go all the way to $1,800 for a chassis-style Tikka T3x TAC A1. These rifles can be purchased stock and immediately put to work, or

This 6.5 PRC owns everything out 1,400 yards.

The current configuration of the author's custom 6.5 PRC. The Kinetic Research Group stock was swapped out for a Modular Driven Technologies ESS, which is optimal for testing technology such as prisms, thermal and night-vision devices.

(below) This 6.5 PRC achieved a 60-percent hit rate on a 24-inch plate at 1,800 yards in 25-mph wind.

customized to meet a particular use. In the last several years, I have observed a robust aftermarket segment materialize.

At the 2018 SHOT Show, Tikka released the Tikka T1x MTR, a rimfire chambered in .22 LR and .17 HMR. These rifles are perfect for training and hunting, and are extremely popular in the NRL22, a .22-caliber-specific league of the National Rifle League. At the 2020 SHOT Show, Tikka released four new models. The T3x Lite Veil Wideland and Veil Alpine feature fluted barrels and bolts for weight reduction, muzzle brakes and a nice hydrographic camo pattern on the stock. The T3x Lite Roughtech is similar to the Veil in that it has a fluted barrel and bolt and a muzzle brake, but has a textured stock that provides extra grip in inclement weather conditions. The final rifle debuted was the Tikka T3x UPR, or Ultimate Precision Rifle. The UPR has a modern, but traditional, form factor, adjustable comb, threaded, medium-profile barrel, and a 0- or 20-MOA scope base. This rifle is optimal for precision-rifle applications. The Tikka lineage has been producing firearms and firearms components for over 100 years. Tikka's are my go-to rifles, and I am excited to see what this company does in the coming years. GD

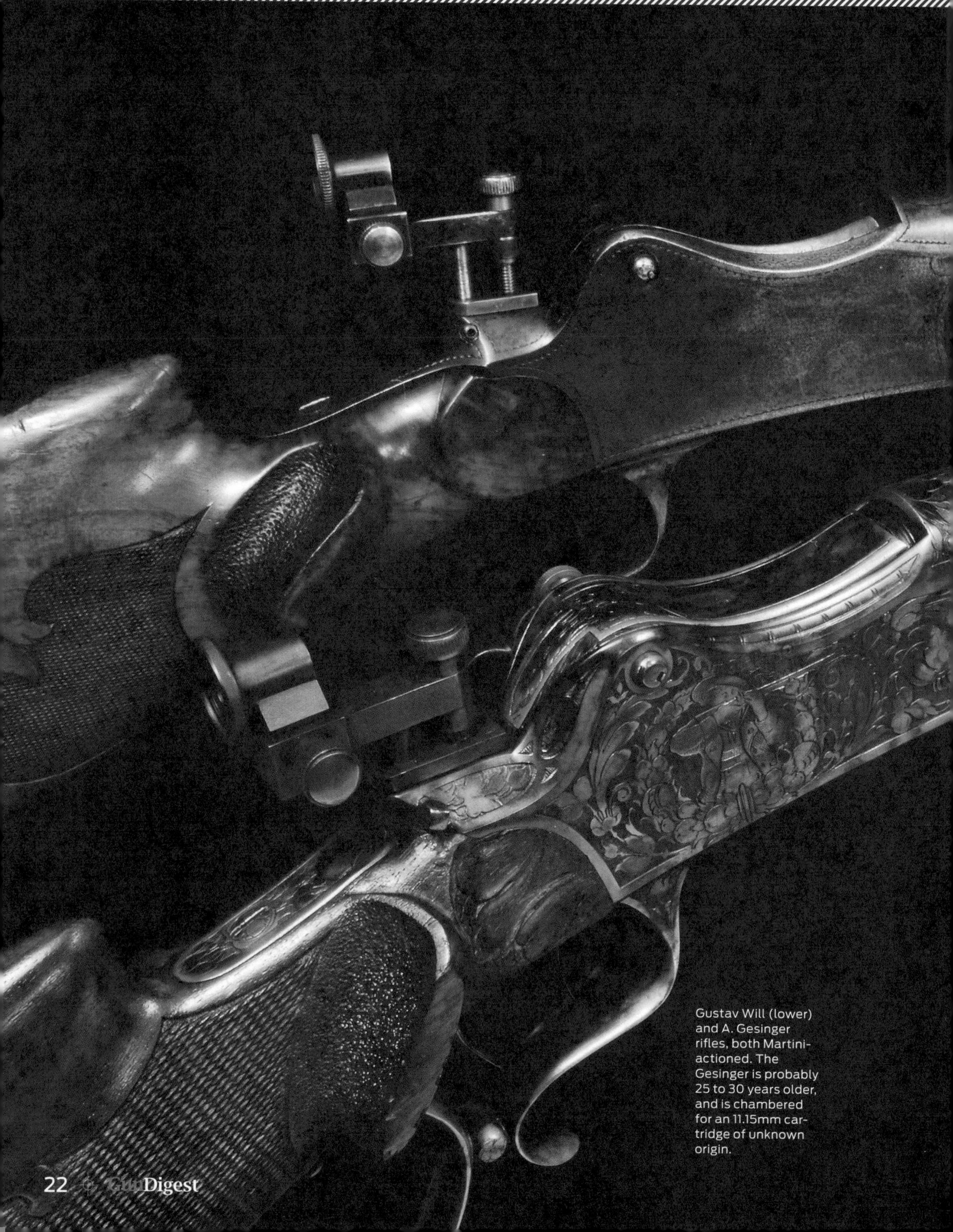

Gustav Will (lower) and A. Gesinger rifles, both Martini-actioned. The Gesinger is probably 25 to 30 years older, and is chambered for an 11.15mm cartridge of unknown origin.

ECHOES OF VALHALLA

German Schüetzen Rifles

›TERRY WIELAND

I t was preview day at the Rock Island Auction in early 2020, and a bunch of us were browsing through the vast display hall with its more than 11,000 guns. Lined up on one high rack were two dozen German Schuetzen rifles, easily distinguishable by their intricate curly-cue trigger guards, extra-long barrels and elaborately carved stocks.

I had one down off the rack, studying its intriguing falling-block mechanism, when a man and his teenage daughter

stopped to look. He was a gun dealer whose main interest was old Winchesters. His comment: "Those sure are funny looking, huh?" The young lady, whose life experience obviously included the world of fantasy games and Norse mythology, was more flattering. "I think it's pretty," she said, running her fingers over the dashing stag, carved into the stock. "And." she added, with a defiant glance at her father, "Really *interesting*." He shrugged and moved on down

the line. She lingered to look at more Schuetzens.

That, in a nutshell, reflects the status of traditional German Schuetzen rifles in the United States: Appreciated by a few, but a continuing mystery to most, which is unfortunate, because if you love fine guns, you will find more ingenuity, artistry, craftsmanship and intriguing variety in old German target rifles than anywhere else I can think of outside of the gun trade in Victorian England.

Martini-action Schuetzen rifle, probably built in the 1880s. It is chambered for an 11.15mm cartridge of unknown origin and nomenclature, which the author christened the 11.15x51R Kurz. It is based on the .43 Mauser case. The rifle's maker is identified on the barrel as A. Gesinger, Bremen, but he was probably the retailer. Who actually made the rifle is anyone's guess.

We should begin by explaining the name Schuetzen, because even though it's also used in the United States for a particular type of target shooting, here it doesn't mean quite the same thing. Properly, the word is *Schützen*, and it has a number of definitions, none of which really translate into English. For our purposes, we'll call it marksmanship, and give it the common American spelling, "Schuetzen."

In Germany, Schuetzen is, or was, until 1935, the highly formalized sport of shooting offhand at a target 300 meters away, using iron sights, with a rifle designed specifically for that activity and useless for anything else. Like the highly specialized American trap gun, the German Schuetzen does only one thing, but it does it exceedingly well.

It's impossible to discuss Schuetzen competition, or the rifles themselves, without getting into both the history and the elaborate traditions. For centuries, Schuetzen matches were a vibrant part of German cultural life, especially in Bavaria and the other southern regions, as well as in Austria and Switzerland. It

traces its roots to the year 1139 (almost 900 years ago, and 350 years before Columbus arrived in America) when the first recorded society was established to support target shooting as a pastime. They first used bows, then crossbows and, finally, with the arrival of gunpowder, firearms. From there, the societies expanded and flourished as guns evolved from matchlock to flintlock to percussion to centerfire breechloaders.

Gradually, *Schuetzenfests* (shooting tournaments) became huge and elaborate affairs, involving thousands of competitors in one place at one time. Cities were awarded the right to hold the national annual match, and built large shooting ranges and whole shooting villages for the occasion, similar to a city preparing for the Olympics. American Schuetzen, as it was around 1900, was certainly big, but never as big as it was in Germany.

The main interest of the German city fathers, from the Middle Ages to the 1800s, was defense of their territory against invaders, and the need for trained archers, and later riflemen, should an invading army appear on the horizon. The

German states were scattered, numbering in the hundreds and ranging from large kingdoms like Prussia and Bavaria down to small city states. Until Bismarck unified the country in the 1860s, there was no standing army to protect German territories from, mainly, the French.

For the better part of one thousand years, the French were free to invade, loot and pillage their immediate German neighbors, with the destruction reaching its depths in the Thirty Years' War. The dreadful carnage and destruction between 1618 and 1648 was never equaled until the mass bombings late in World War II. Under those circumstances, one can see how the existence of a skilled and well-armed militia would be a comfort to the citizens.

This story is told in a three-volume work, *Alte Scheibenwaffen*, written by a group of American Schuetzen enthusiasts. Volumes one and two were published in 1999, followed by volume three in 2004. The initial research and writing were done by Jesse Thompson, and his work was completed by editor Tom Rowe, with contributions from Bill Loos,

Martini-actioned Schuetzen rifle, engraved with the name "Gust. Will" of Zwickau. It is chambered for the 8.15x46R cartridge. The stock is Tyrolian. It was probably made before 1914.

Allen Hallock and Ron Dillon. This is the only attempt, in English, at a comprehensive treatment of the subject. Thompson became interested in Schuetzen rifles during his time with the U.S. Air Force in Germany in the 1940s, and continued his research into the 1970s. The others took up where he left off, and the result is a magnificent, 1,200-page effort covering every aspect of Schuetzen culture, from the rifles and actions, to the sights, medals, ornate beer steins and historical accounts of the great matches held over the years.

James J. Grant, the high priest of single-shots in America, who published five books on the subject between the 1940s and 1990s, dealt with German Schuetzen rifles only in passing. As he acknowledged, the subject was too vast to deal with adequately in a chapter or two, but he summed up his feelings by insisting that no single-shot rifle collection could possibly be complete without a couple of examples of the wondrous German Schuetzen.

During the years 1950 to 1985, one might have expected *Gun Digest,* under editor John T. Amber, to cover the subject, but little appeared in spite of the fact that Amber was a serious single-shot collector and owned some spectacular examples, including a couple that are shown in *Alte Scheibenwaffen.* Probably, no one proposed an article because there was so little information available.

Here is where we need to bring in some politics, because politics is what killed traditional Schuetzen in both its native Germany and in the United States, where it had been transplanted by German immigrants.

Gunmaking in America was widely influenced by German techniques and tastes, reflected in the elaborate long rifles from Pennsylvania, where the "Pennsylvania Dutch" or, more properly, *Deutsch*, or German, immigrants also brought with them their taste for competitive offhand shooting. Schuetzen parks became common from the northeast all the way to Texas, and as far west as San Francisco. This gave rise to the famous American single-shot target rifles: the Sharps, Ballard, Stevens and so on. This was a highly popular sport until 1914, following traditional German rules, and even using German nomenclature.

The Great War ended that. A combination of anti-German feeling after 1917, and interest in shooting the new and different Springfield .30-06 in military style, killed off both Schuetzenfests and Schuetzen rifles.

In Germany, Schuetzen managed to

The 11.15mm case is based on the 11mm Mauser (.43 Mauser) with its convex "Type A" head, cut down by about a quarter inch. The bullet is 370 grains.

survive the Great War, but it could not survive Adolf Hitler. After the National Socialists gained power in 1933, Nazification spread throughout Germany. Schuetzen shooting with traditional rifles was viewed as useless in terms of training for war. It was archaic, quaint and anti-Nazi. The ancient Schuetzen culture, already diminished by the inflation of the 1920s, and later by the Great Depression, finally disappeared. The last great Schuetzenfest was held in Leipzig in 1934. Henceforth, shooting matches in Germany were dominated by Mauser 98s and swastika armbands.

After 1945, the victorious Allies were determined to disarm the German populace, seizing or destroying any and all firearms, while individual soldiers engaged in wholesale looting. This was when most of the German Schuetzens we see today came to America, shipped or brought home by returning GIs. The

Russians were even more rapacious than the Americans, and thousands of guns disappeared behind the Iron Curtain.

Jesse Thompson and others estimated that between 1850 and 1935, about 150,000 Schuetzen cartridge rifles were made in Germany. This is compared to only about 15,000 high-quality single-shot target rifles in Britain during the same period, and a mere 5,000 in the United States. These are ballpark figures, of course, but one can see the relative numbers. They then estimated that of those 150,000, at least 75,000 were destroyed after 1945. Of the remainder, many went to Russia or the U.S. Add in natural attrition over the years, and relatively few were left.

It was many years before interest in Schuetzen began to revive in Germany, but by the 1990s, there were glimmerings of interest. Rifles that had been carefully hidden after 1945 began to emerge. When the Iron Curtain came down in 1990, German aficionados began searching out surviving specimens in Russia, and many old rifles came home, albeit mostly in dreadful shape. Visitors to the United States began to repatriate finer examples.

Unfortunately, many of these rifles were (and are) incomplete. The front, mid-barrel and diopter (tang) sights were both intricate and delicate, and the German custom was to detach and store them in a separate case. As a result, many looted rifles were sent to America lacking some or all of their sights, and since the vast majority were either custom or one-off designs, replacing them is not as simple as searching on eBay.

But now, what exactly were these rifles?

As the accompanying photographs show, the classic Schuetzen is a single-shot with a long barrel (30 to 34 inches), an elaborate combination triggerguard and lever, and a fantastic stock, with extravagant cheek rests and buttplates. The stocks are often carved and checkered from end to end, and the actions engraved with scenes that can defy belief.

These rifles were made to be shot offhand, with no rest of any kind (not even the American palm rest), and every feature is geared to that end. The usual target distances were 175 and 300

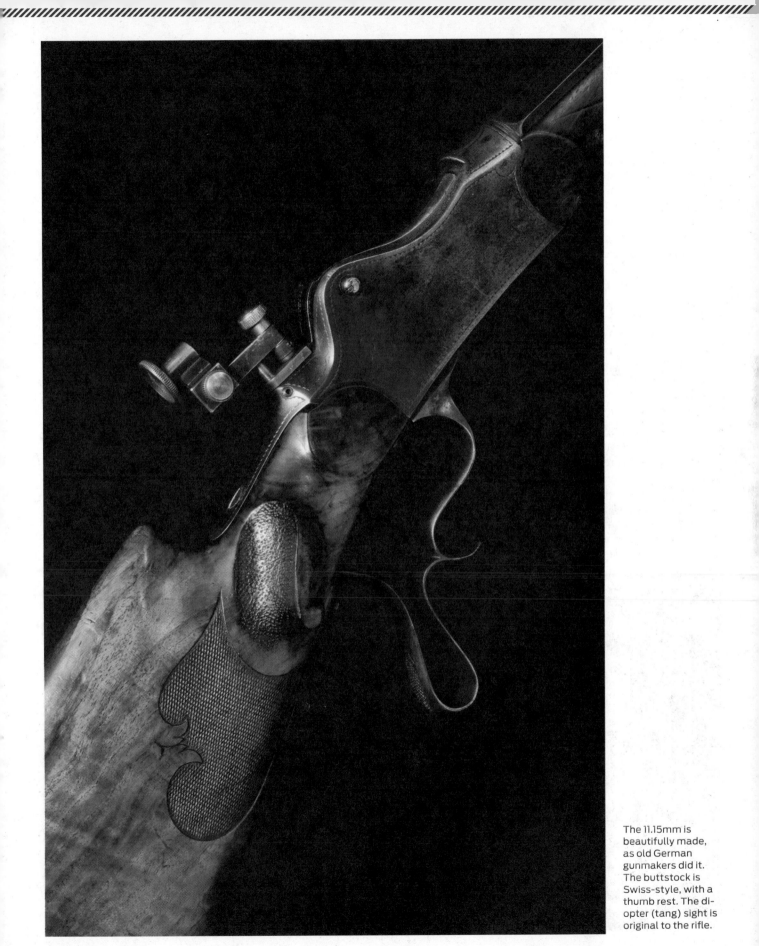

The 11.15mm is beautifully made, as old German gunmakers did it. The buttstock is Swiss-style, with a thumb rest. The diopter (tang) sight is original to the rifle.

meters (191 and 328 yards). A typical rifle weighed 12 to 14 pounds. Double set triggers were almost universal.

Jesse Thompson estimated there were more than 300 individual action designs, most of which were variations on other designs. Of these, about half were derived from the Peabody-Martini dropping-block, which originated in the United States, was modified in Switzerland, and then refined to unbelievable lengths by hundreds of independent German gunmakers. The other half were falling-blocks of one kind or another. The most famous of these is the Aydt action, in which the breechblock pivots on a pin located under the barrel. It bears some similarity to the Stevens 44 in that regard, except that the Stevens breechblock rocks to the rear, while the Aydt, with its longer arm, drops almost straight down.

Typical features include a double set trigger attached to a trigger plate that is easily removed without tools, and a breechblock and firing mechanism that can be removed the same way. They might employ a spring-powered striker or internal tumbler, but are rarely seen with an external hammer.

If there is no standard, universal action, the situation with the gunmakers themselves is even more chaotic. There was no dominant company like Win-chester. There were a few prominent makers, such as C.G. Haenel or Büchel, which supplied basic actions, but in the vast majority of cases, the name you see on the action or barrel is that of the retailer or a small-town gunmaker. This causes considerable confusion. At the same time, it's impossible to prepare the kind of listings of models, serial numbers and dates so beloved of gun collectors. It's a wide-open field, and the only real guide a buyer has is his own knowledge of what makes a fine firearm.

For example, the two rifles shown in the opening spread of this article are both Martinis, but who made the basic action is anyone's guess. The older of the two, dating from the 1880s, is marked "A. Gesinger, Bremen," but Bremen was not a gun-making hotbed, and no Gesinger is listed in Thompson's extensive directory of the German trade, included in volume two of *Alte Scheibenwaffen*. Similarly, the newer (probably made around 1912) is marked "Gust. Will, Zwickau." While there were many men in the trade with the surname Will, there is no Gustav listed. The actual origins of both rifles remain a mystery, as do the makers of the excellent set triggers with which both are equipped.

A word about stocks. Elaborate and individual as most Schuetzen stocks are, there were some established styles. The Will rifle has what is commonly called a Tyrol stock, with the large, cradling cheekpiece. The Viennese (Wien) style is similar but more elaborate. The Gesinger rifle has a Swiss stock, straighter, simpler and more angular. The fourth major style is the German, which is plainer still. These are guidelines only, as every stock maker and client had quirks and preferences.

Like American Schuetzens, Germans used pronounced hooks on the butt-plates. When shooting, the forward hand is positioned immediately in front of the triggerguard and acts as a fulcrum. The weight of the barrel pulls the muzzle down and gives stability. The hook fits under the arm, and this not only keeps the rifle from tipping too far, it means the forward hand is effectively relieved of much of the rifle's weight. With such heavy rifles, that is no small thing; as well, equal weight on both sides would create a seesaw effect that is difficult to control.

The average American, handed a German Schuetzen, tries to bring it to his shoulder in the normal way and finds it completely unmanageable. Instead, the body should be positioned almost parallel with the line to the target. The butt is not tucked into the shoulder, but

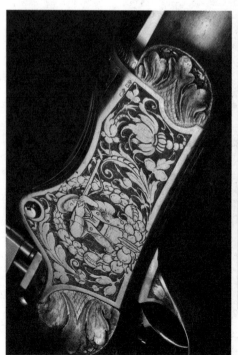
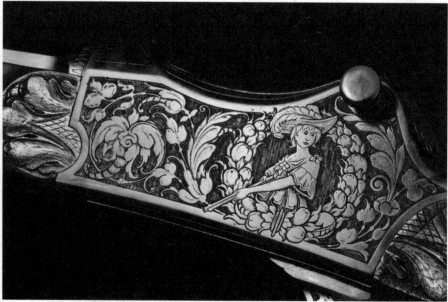

Engraving on the Gustav Will is typically Teutonic. The man is obviously a Schuetzen shooter. The young lady's identity is a mystery, but she's the author's kind of girl.

This sight was made for the rifle by Lee Shaver Gunsmithing, the single-shot specialist and maker of target sights for American Schuetzen rifles.

positioned slightly to the side with the hook under the armpit; similarly, the lead hand must be close to the triggerguard, with the upper arm braced against the body, otherwise the weight is too great. Shooting such a rifle is a skill that takes considerable practice, and while it might look odd in a world of AR-15s and combat-shooting techniques, it works beautifully for its purpose once you get the hang of it.

The sights on Schuetzen rifles are a world unto themselves. Like stocks and actions, there were some basic approaches, but the sights themselves display the ideas of myriad different makers. In the United States, you might get a Winchester High Wall, then order a Lyman tang sight to fit. In Germany, almost nothing was standardized in this way, and the array of sight variations is dizzying.

The basic principles were these: There

was a front sight, usually on a ramp that fit into a dovetail, often with interchangeable blades or rotating sights that offered several different posts or apertures. On the barrel in front of the action, there was an integral dovetail. The mid-barrel open sights were attached to this dovetail, and could be moved back and forth to suit the shooter's eyesight. Finally, there was the diopter (tang) sight, which was an aperture. This was not used as sight; aiming was done with the front and mid-barrel sight, while the diopter served only to sharpen the sight picture. This was an optical phenomenon Germans discovered early and used extensively.

Although Schuetzen was practiced in all the Teutonic regions of central Europe, the Swiss had considerable influence. Because Swiss matches were geared to military training, competitions often prohibited the use of a diopter sight. If you find a rifle with no provision for a

diopter, chances are it was made for the Swiss market. Similarly, the Swiss stock is more plain and functional than the Tyrol.

In Germany, matches could be either "two-sight" or "three-sight," allowing or disallowing the diopter. There was no variation calling for the front sight and diopter alone. This was one more reason to make the sights detachable. Unfortunately, when the Americans were ransacking western Germany's closets and gun racks, the sights had often been removed and stored separately. As a result, many Schuetzen rifles in America are found with only one sight, usually the front, or none at all.

In these instances, front sights are the easiest to find, since they generally depend on a simple dovetail. Mid-barrel sights are next. Although the dovetail rails vary in width, if you find a sight that is even close, a good gunsmith can usually make it fit. In both cases, however, the purist will give some thought to getting sights that are the right vintage for the rifle, as designs evolved over time.

Diopter sights are a whole different proposition. They are as elaborate, intricate and complicated as any iron sight ever devised, and were generally custommade for an individual rifle. One could devote several articles to German rifle sights, and still not come close to covering them all. Tangs are different, bases are different. Some have one post, some two. Some posts are round, others are square, and still others are combinations.

German sights were often housed in cases like jewel boxes, with carefully fitted compartments for bases, apertures and various accoutrements, and were often "liberated" separately from the rifles themselves. As a result, there are quite a few old German sights in collections around the United States, and an intrepid researcher can often find something that, even if it does not fit his rifle, can at least indicate what is required. One should be warned, however: The sights, beautiful mechanical implements that they are, can

be every bit as addictive as the rifles.

Over several years of watching these rifles come up for auction, I have noticed that those lacking sights almost always sell for a fraction of what they would bring if fully kitted out. Conversely, an old and battered beast, fully equipped with sights, will bring considerably more than might otherwise be expected.

This brings us to the question of caliber. German Schuetzens followed a path, from the beginning of the centerfire era up to 1900, that parallels Schuetzen in the United States. Early American rifles were chambered for .44 or .45 caliber, which shrank first to the .40s, then down to .38s, like the .38-55, then to the .32-40 and its ilk. American shooters were on their way to embracing the .28 by 1900, but by then the reign of blackpowder was pretty much at an end.

Germans used, first, 11.5mm and 11mm cartridges, then 10mm and 9.5mm, and finally settled on the 8mm in the early 1890s. There were so many variations of 11mm and 9.5mm that it's impossible to even begin to list and describe them, but many of the early ones were based on the famous 11mm (.43) Mauser case with its convex base, what came to be known in Germany as the "Type A" head.

In 1893, Adolf Frohn produced a radical new cartridge initially dubbed the 8.15x46½, and it took the shooting world by storm. In 1910, it was standardized as the 8.15x46R, and from that point until the effective end of Schuetzen in 1935, almost no other chamberings were used. It was, and is, extremely accurate, with virtually no recoil. It's worth noting that RWS still makes brass for it, which simplifies things con-

Trigger group from the 11.15mm. This is a three-blade set trigger. Designs ranged from one blade up to seven, each progressively more sensitive. Triggers were a separate gun-making skill (Stechermacher), with specialists supplying the companies that made the actions or barreled actions, either for completion themselves or for sale to small gunsmiths and retailers.

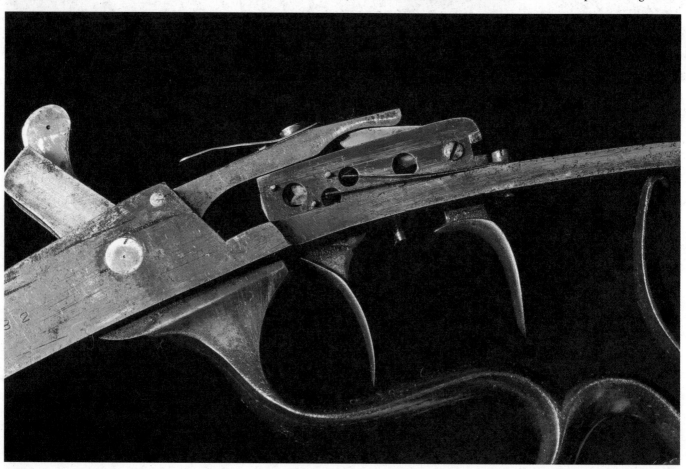

siderably. Of rifles made since 1895, you are more likely to find an 8.15x46R than anything else. At the Rock Island auction mentioned earlier, every single Schuetzen rifle was an 8.15, except for a handful in .22 LR.

German shooters generally loaded their own ammunition, but did so using factory brass and bullets. Compared to Americans, there was almost no experimentation and wildcatting by individual shooters. Since shooters traveled to distant matches by train, baggage weight and bulk were a concern. A match might call for several hundred rounds, so it was easier to carry components and only a few dozen cases, reloading them as needed. Instead of a powder measure, shooters took powder in pre-measured packets about the size of a cigarette filter. They were tucked whole into the case, and the nitro-paper wrapping was consumed by the powder burning. These powder charges were sold in boxes of 50 or 100. The standard bullet for the 8.15x46R was the pattern 16H, a 180-grain cast bullet with a belt about halfway between the base and the tip. It was hand lubed, then pushed down into the case using finger pressure. The belt prevented it going too far in and provided uniform overall length. Since cases were not resized, there was a saving in equipment at every step.

Although large companies did produce Schuetzen rifles and barreled actions, the whole nature of the German target-rifle industry was one of hundreds of small shops, individual craftsmen and specialist outworkers, not unlike the gun trade in England in the 1890s. One particularly important specialty was the making of the double-set triggers, which were the industry standard. These were multileafed affairs, with triggers denoted by the number of levers: three-lever, four-lever and so on, up to seven. The setting trigger did not count, so a three-lever trigger actually had four leaves, which is confusing. Most fine Schuetzen rifles had three-leaf triggers. As the number of leaves increased, triggers became so sensitive that only the most experienced shooter could fully appreciate and utilize the delicate touch.

Jesse Thompson tells the story of one *Stechermachermeister,* Emil Kommer,

Mid-barrel open sight on the Gustav Will. Adjustments are made using a clock key.

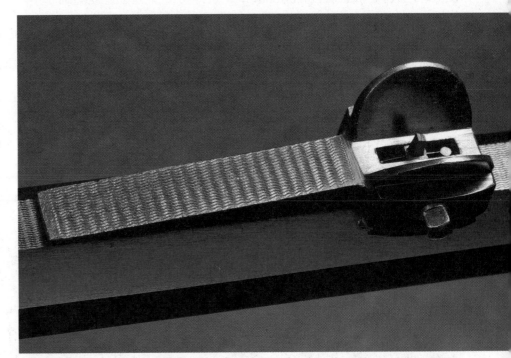

Front sight on the Gustav Will. There are four sights (one post, three blades with pinhead bead) which are rotated into place using a clock key.

who apprenticed to his father, opened his own shop in 1903, and produced his last trigger in 1966, when he was 87. His shop had only one "power" tool (a lathe powered by a foot pedal), yet he made five- and six-lever triggers of the finest quality. In fact, so competitive was the rifle industry, and so skilled the *Stechermachers,*

that (provided it had not been tampered with by morons) every German set trigger that Thompson encountered worked perfectly, a hundred or more years after it was made.

An obvious question regarding these rifles is: just how accurate were they? Indications are they were every bit as accurate as the best American offhand rifles. Some groups shot at 300 meters, offhand, are astounding. There are official verified photos of some groups, of 10, 20 or more shots, that are so small I would have difficulty duplicating them at 50 meters, much less 300. The official German 300-meter target had a 20-ring that was only 4cm (1 9/16 in.) in diameter, yet the best shooters could obliterate it with a string of shots.

Accuracy was certainly important to German shooters, but if the better surviving rifles are anything to go by, aesthetics were also a major consideration. Shooters were continuing an ancient tradition, and not only their clothing but their rifles reflected that. No German Schuetzen was complete without extensive engraving on the action, and comparable carving on the stock. The stocks resembled the later sculptures of Henry Moore in many ways, with deep-dished cheekpieces and sweeping curves. These stocks were so elaborate that most could not be carved from one stock blank. Instead, pieces were shaped separately and the wood grain matched so perfectly that they appeared to be one piece of wood.

When it came to engraving, the German craftsmen recognized no boundaries. Favorite themes were St. Hubertus and the stag, ancient fairy tales, scenes from Norse mythology, Wagner's *Ring of the Nibelungen*, and, in Switzerland, the legend of William Tell. A favorite was the *Schützenliesl*, a Bavarian barmaid in traditional costume wearing a target for a hat, with foaming steins of beer in her hands, dancing atop a rolling beer barrel. She really existed, immortalized by a famous painter in 1881, and her portrait still hangs in Munich. There were seemingly endless variations on this theme alone.

Engraving included oak leaves, forest glades, wild boars, stags, roe deer and every other Teutonic vision imaginable. The engravers were largely anonymous, treated by the industry not as artists but merely as craftsmen, but some of their creations are truly spectacular. Not surprisingly, the heights were reached with rifles created for presentation to crown princes and archdukes, but even the average Schuetzen rifle bore a level of ornamentation found only on very special-order rifles in the United States. It was all part of the ancient rite and culture, and the rifles were as much badges of honor as they were firearms.

At Rock Island, the young lady stayed with us for several minutes while we looked at one Schuetzen rifle after another. She studied the engraving, admired the wood carving, commented on the intricacy of the sights, and remarked about the mythological themes embedded in the steel. Obviously, these relics of ancient German culture intrigued her mightily. "It's like a fantasy," she smiled. When her father returned to reclaim her and drag her off to look at still more Marlins and Winchesters, she rolled her eyes, said goodbye to Wotan, Siegfried and the Schuetzenliesl and, with a wistful smile, walked away. Her father never gave the Schuetzens a second glance.

All of these rifles came up for auction on the third day. They were grouped singly, or in twos and threes. Not one of them was really complete; most were missing one or more sights, a couple had lost their breechblocks. All had been sorely neglected, and the scratches and grime reflected a rough life in the years since they were abducted in Germany and carried off to America. In a flight of fancy, I was reminded of captured Teutons in the first century B.C., dragged off to Rome in chains, paraded through the streets, and then torn apart by lions. Schuetzen rifles tend to encourage such flights of fancy.

At Rock Island the year before, I bought my two Schuetzens. Both are Martinis, and I was in the market for a Haenel "Original Aydt" or a Buchel *Meister*. Those two are considered the aristocrats of the non-Martini Schuetzens. One lot of three rifles included two Aydts and a Meister, all in 8.15x46R, all incomplete and grimy, but salvageable. I watched as they sold for twice what I was prepared to pay, but I didn't mind. They were going to someone who obviously appreciated them and would, I hoped, give them a good home.

Since the Berlin Wall came down in 1989, and the Soviet government fell two years later, there has been a revival of interest in Schuetzen in Germany, and quite a few looted rifles have gone home, both from Russia and the United States. Those coming back from Russia look like most refugees from Stalin, damaged almost beyond reclamation; those returning from America are sometimes better, but not always.

Interest shown here by visitors from Germany, seeking to locate their

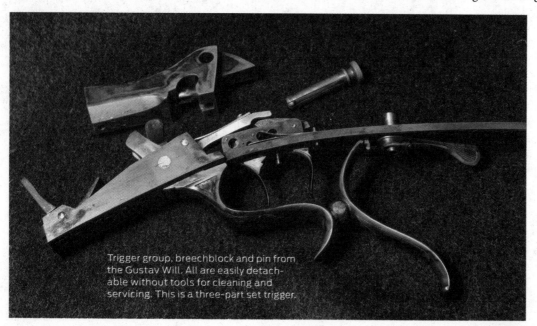

Trigger group, breechblock and pin from the Gustav Will. All are easily detachable without tools for cleaning and servicing. This is a three-part set trigger.

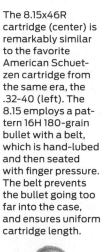

The 8.15x46R cartridge (center) is remarkably similar to the favorite American Schuetzen cartridge from the same era, the .32-40 (left). The 8.15 employs a pattern 16H 180-grain bullet with a belt, which is hand-lubed and then seated with finger pressure. The belt prevents the bullet going too far into the case, and ensures uniform cartridge length.

Alte Scheibenwaffen, the three-volume history of Schuetzen in Germany, by Jesse Thompson, Bill Loos, Ron Dillon and Allen Hallock, edited and compiled by Tom Rowe. They were published between 1999 and 2004, and are a comprehensive history, essential for anyone with even a moderate interest in these magnificent rifles.

lost children, has sparked more interest among shooters in America. It's an odd thing that many of the rifles were brought here purely as loot, by men with no interest in shooting, merely looking for something German to hang on the wall beside their campaign medals and old uniforms. Few rifles, it seems, were cared for and provided with the wherewithal to go to a range and do what they were made for.

In my experience, though, when you restore a rifle like my two Martinis, provide them with good sights, load proper ammunition, tune their set triggers, and put them in the hands of people who've never seen such a rifle before, it's a revelation. Sure, they're heavy. Sure, they're awkward at first. But when you hoist one to your shoulder, snuggle into the stock, caress that front trigger, and the heavy lead bullet hits a distant steel plate with a *Clang!* that resounds like Donner throwing open the gates to Valhalla, suddenly everyone seems to want one. They have that magic. GD

The 8.15x46R (left) was designed by Adolf Frohn in 1893, and swiftly took over the Schuetzen rifle world, relegating large old cartridges like the 11.15x51R Kurz to the status of "old iron." The 11.15 still shoots extremely well, and the 8.15 is every bit as accurate as the .32-40.

VINTAGE
Snubbies
(And why I like them)

SHOOTING

By J. Henry FitzGerald

The Fitz Special was the invention of John Henry FitzGerald, a burly, cigar-chomping ex-lawman and ex-hibition shooter who worked for Colt Patent Firearms Company. It facilitates a faster draw from his pants pockets, a preferred method of carrying for many in the 1920s and '30s. Among other things, Fitz bobbed the hammer and cut away a portion of the trigger guard. This Detective Special, from the 1930s, was turned into a Fitz Special for the author by the combined talents of Turnbull Restoration (www.turnbullmfg.com) and gunsmith Andy Horvath (440-458-4369).

Revolvers from another era still have appeal
> RICK HACKER

I guess you could say it all started with Phillip Marlowe, or at least as he was portrayed by Humphrey Bogart in the 1948 movie, *The Big Sleep*, when he reached for a Detective Special from the glove compartment of his car. Or maybe it was Jack Webb as Sergeant Joe Friday, in the long-running *Dragnet* TV series, who at various times carried a Smith & Wesson Chief's Special or a 2-inch-barreled Model 10. It might even have been the Hubley Colt Detective Special Cap Gun I had as a kid. Whatever the impetus, my fascination with snub-nosed revolvers has been with me throughout my entire life as a shooter, gun writer and collector. And I'm not referring to the current wave of short-barreled, globular CCW guns – as good as they might be. They just don't have the "it" factor for me.

Besides, although many of today's gun magazines seem more focused on the coverage of ever-smaller, pocket-sized semi-automatics, there's something the about snub-nosed revolvers; those squat, compact and graceful-looking little wheel guns from the 20th century, that I simply can't resist. I'm referring to those 2-inch-barreled Colts and Smith & Wessons that were slipped into the trench-coat pocket of a hard-boiled private dick (the early 20th century slang term for a detective) who was about to take a slow walk down a shadowy, rain-soaked alley late at night.

To be sure, it was the Film Noir motion pictures of the 1940s and '50s that really brought the snub-nosed revolver to the public's attention. But hard-hitting pocket pistols were on the scene long before the first snubbies made their debut on the silver screen. In the 19th century, Jesse James removed the entire barrel from a Colt Single Action Army in order to fit it into his pocket. And, of course, we have the ultra-rare, special-order 3-inch-barreled first-generation SAA Sheriff's Models (a modern term coined by collectors; Colt never used it in its contemporary advertising) of that era as well. But even before that, in 1866 to be exact, Remington had introduced its Double Derringer, a pocket-sized pistol with two stacked, 3-inch barrels, each chambered in .41 Short.

Eventually renamed the Model 95, it remained in the line until 1935. And in 1877, P. Webley & Son of London & Birmingham England brought out the British Bull Dog, a scaled-down version of Webley's Royal Irish Constabulary Model in 1872. Chambered for cartridges such as the .44 Webley, .450 C.F. and .455 Webley, it became one of the most popular pocket-sized double actions in Europe as well as in the United States, and was produced until 1914, when World War I caused arms making to be redirected to military endeavors.

So early on, there was a need for pocket pistols, but with the exception of certain derringer-styled handguns, the larger-bored revolvers were, of necessity given the technology of the time, all built on large frames, although when outfitted with shorter barrels, they were still easy to fit into the baggy pants pockets of the day. However, most of them came with barrel lengths that were more suitable for holsters than pockets. But it was the advent of the .32- and .38-caliber double actions, built on smaller frames than the .44s and .45s of the late 19th and early 20th centuries, that set the stage for the truly compact snub-nose revolver.

Specifically, it was the Colt Police Positive, a small-framed, six-shot revolver introduced in 1907 that started things rolling. Chambered in .32 Long/Short Colt, .32 Colt New Police (the same as .32 S&W Long), .38 Colt New Police (the same as .38 S&W), as well as the .22 rimfire cartridge, it was quickly adopted by numerous police departments, including plain-clothes detectives. Heeding their requests, just one year later, in 1908, Colt lengthened the Police Positive's frame and cylinder slightly so it could be chambered for the .32-20 cartridge as well as the much more effective .38 Special, which was favored by law enforcement. That gun, then, became the Police Positive Special, which ended up being one of the most popular revolvers in the Colt line. Although the Police Positive Special could also be ordered in .32 Colt New Police and .38 Colt New Police calibers, it was the .38 Special version that was adopted by countless police forces, express agencies and others across the country.

Unfortunately, as far as those who wanted a slightly more compact revolver for off-duty or concealed carry were concerned, the Police Positive Special only came with 4-, 5-, and 6-inch barrel lengths. Consequently, it was not uncommon for many individuals, law enforcement and civilians alike, to trim off the excess barrel, just even with the end of the ejector rod. And thus, the first "modern" snub-nosed revolvers were born. For years, I owned an early 1920s-era Colt Police Positive Special in .38 Special

Made by P. Webley & Son of London & Birmingham, England, this British Bull Dog was made in the 1880s and is chambered for the .44 Webley cartridge. It was a popular late-19th-century "carry gun" in both England and the United States.

This Colt Detective Special was shipped on Dec. 19, 1956 to the Washington D.C. Metropolitan Police Department.

caliber that had been carried by a Union Pacific Railroad detective who probably took it to the UPRR machine shop and had its factory 4-inch barrel shortened to 2 inches, unceremoniously lopping off part of the barrel's roll-stamped nomenclature in the process.

It was about this time that a Colt factory employee named John Henry FitzGerald, who was the head of the firearms testing department and was also an exhibition shooter, began experimenting with ways to alter the dimensions of the company's double-action revolvers to facilitate a faster draw from his pockets, which he had lined with leather. "Fitz," as he was called, was a big, husky fellow with beefy hands, but he ended up reducing the size of the Colt New Service by shortening the backstrap and grips, reducing the barrel to 2 inches – just even with the ejector rod, which he also trimmed – and grinding away the front portion of the trigger guard for quicker access to the trigger. He also bobbed off the hammer spur, which tended to hang up on clothing as the gun was being drawn. This then, coupled with a well-tuned action, became what is now known as the Fitz Special, one of the rarest variations of all double-action snubbies.

It is estimated that there are fewer than 100 authentic factory-documented Fitz Specials, those made by either FitzGerald or by other Colt workers as special-order guns. Of course, over the years, many more have been given the "Fitz" treatment by numerous gunsmiths outside of the factory.

Fitz also had these alterations performed on other Colt DAs as well, although not all of them had their backstraps reduced, especially the smaller D-framed Police Positives. Some had their hammers bobbed, but most did

There were two different grip styles on vintage Detective Specials. The gun on the right (c. 1933-1965) is an earlier "long-frame" version, with the metal frame extended to the bottom of the grip. The DS on the left (1966-1973) is the "short-frame" version, with the backstrap shortened to also fit grips for the Colt Agent and Cobra.

(below) A well-used Colt Detective Special, circa 1934.

not. However, almost all of them had their barrels shortened to 2 inches. Keep in mind that this was all prior to 1926, when cataloged snubbies did not exist; everything was custom ordered from the factory by gun owners or dealers, or performed for them by outside gunsmiths. Soon the executives at Colt began to realize that maybe Fitz was on to something. Bobbed hammer spurs and cut-away trigger guards were not for everyone and were not practical for the average pistolero, but plenty of shooters seemed to like the shortened barrels on Colt's medium-sized, D-frame double actions. Consequently, in 1926 Colt made its Police Positive Special available with a factory 2-inch barrel. One year later, this gun became re-branded as the Detective Special, which soon became one of the most popular revolvers in the Colt line.

Available in either blued or in a less-common nickel finish and fitted with two-piece checkered walnut grips, initially the "Dick Special" as it was nicknamed, was only chambered in .38 Special. But after 1946 the .38 Colt New Police, .38 S&W, .32 Colt, and .32 S&W chamberings were added, no doubt to appease those who were put off by the recoil of the .38 Special in the short-barreled snubbie. (There was also a very scarce variation of the Detective Special with a 3-inch barrel made for a short period after World War II, and from 1950 to 1981 an aluminum-framed variation, the Cobra, was produced.)

This, then, was the self-defense gun everybody had been waiting for, including the motion-picture industry, which was

The hump-backed S&W Model 49 still leaves the tip of its shrouded hammer spur exposed, should a cocked, well-aimed shot be necessary.

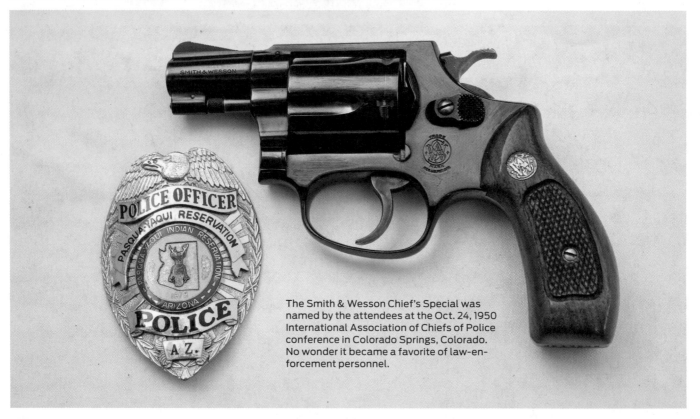

The Smith & Wesson Chief's Special was named by the attendees at the Oct. 24, 1950 International Association of Chiefs of Police conference in Colorado Springs, Colorado. No wonder it became a favorite of law-enforcement personnel.

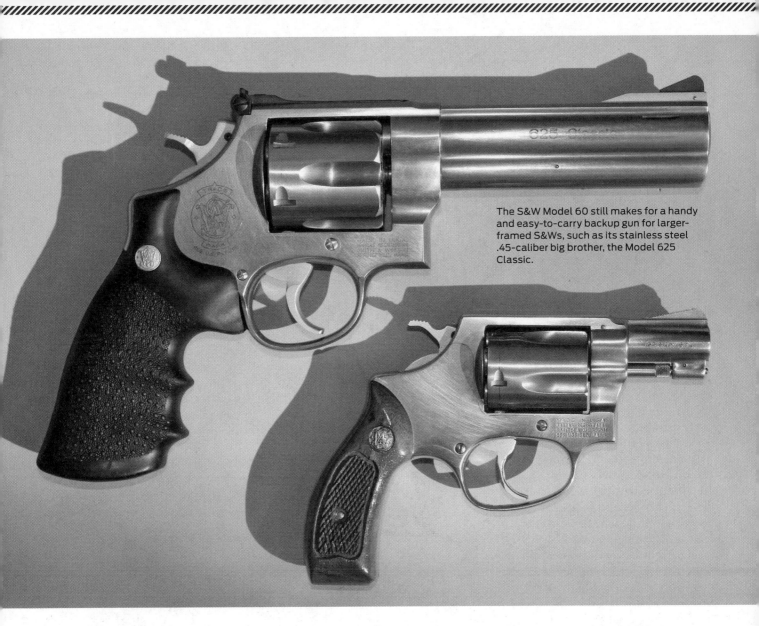

The S&W Model 60 still makes for a handy and easy-to-carry backup gun for larger-framed S&Ws, such as its stainless steel .45-caliber big brother, the Model 625 Classic.

quick to embrace the Detective Special for its popular gangster movies. That, of course, only added to its public appeal. Quoting from Colt's 1936 centennial catalog:

"More power is packed into the snub-nosed Colt Detective Special, than in any other arm of its size. This model is especially popular among Plain Clothes Detectives, Police Officers off duty, Bank Messengers and Payroll Clerks. The small size of the Detective Special – it is but 6 1/4 inches overall – makes it possible to carry it ready for instant action, in the pocket or shoulder holster….The Detective Special handles all .38 Special ammunition, including the High Speed. Although primarily for 'close quarters' service, the Detective Special is surpris-ingly accurate at distances of 25 yards and more."

Echoing this, and using Federal's 110-grain, .38 Special Hydra-Shoks, my 1950s-era Detective Special prints 3.5-inch groups at 25 yards, exhibiting more than adequate self-defense accuracy for a snub-nosed revolver, with which most shots would likely be fired at substantially closer distances. In the late 1920s and early '30s, FitzGerald bested this and wowed the crowds by shooting small wafers and wooden blocks out of the air with amazing speed, using a pair of Colt Detective Specials that had been given his "Fitz Special" treatment. His shooting feats, and that of others, only added to the allure of the Detective Special. To be sure, it was an extremely well-made gun,

exhibiting the quality of all pre-war Colt firearms, with polished and hand-fitted parts, a smooth action and outfitted with Colt's new Positive Safety Lock, which kept the hammer from contacting the frame unless the trigger was pulled.

The first Colt Detective Specials had an elongated, sharply defined square butt, however in 1933 that profile was changed to a more ergonomically rounded butt. Then, during what is referred to by collectors as the Second Issue, which ran from 1947 through 1972, the walnut grips were temporarily replaced with plastic, with the wood grips thankfully being brought back in 1954. The Third Issue, which ran from 1973 until 1986, effectively, in my opinion, takes the Detective Special out of the "vintage" class, as it

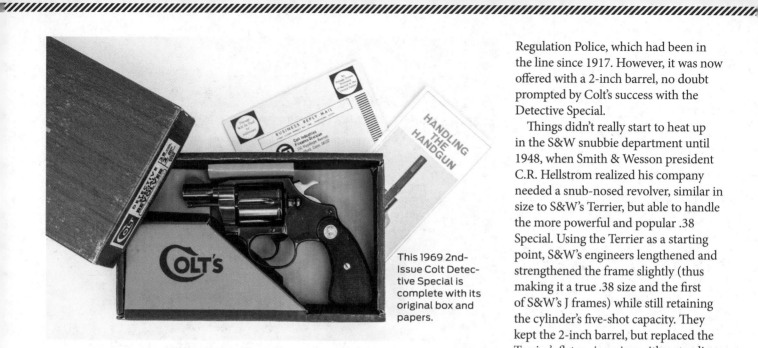

This 1969 2nd-Issue Colt Detective Special is complete with its original box and papers.

invoked a tweaking of the lock work, the unsightly (again, in my opinion) addition of modern-looking wraparound grips, a front sight with an elongated ramp that ran the length of the 2-inch barrel, and a more practical but less attractive shrouded ejector rod. A short-lived Fourth Series, which lasted from 1993 until 1995, included a last gasp for the little gun by offering it in stainless steel, **as well as** with an alloy frame, **plus** in a double-action-only mode with bobbed hammer (shades of Henry FitzGerald!). But for me, it is clearly the pre-1972 guns – the ones without the shrouded ejector rod and wraparound grips – that evoke the aura of a vintage Dick Special.

During the first decade of the Detective Special's existence, Smith & Wesson was sitting on the snub-nosed sidelines, even though its Military & Police had been offered with a 2-inch barrel ever since 1905, and with its .38 Special chambering, was a muscular-looking snubbie, yet its M&P frame presented some limitations as far as concealability was concerned. But the stocky S&W snubnose made up for its bulk by providing a little more recoil-absorbing ability. Besides, it just looked cool, with a hefty countenance that gives it a unique stature among vintage snubbies.

But it wasn't until 1936 that S&W finally brought out its first small-frame, five-shot snub-nosed revolver, which was later called the Terrier. Built on a

.32-caliber frame and chambered for the comparatively underpowered .38 S&W, .38 Colt Police Positive and the .38 S&W Super Police cartridges, the Terrier was basically a round-butt version of S&W's

Regulation Police, which had been in the line since 1917. However, it was now offered with a 2-inch barrel, no doubt prompted by Colt's success with the Detective Special.

Things didn't really start to heat up in the S&W snubbie department until 1948, when Smith & Wesson president C.R. Hellstrom realized his company needed a snub-nosed revolver, similar in size to S&W's Terrier, but able to handle the more powerful and popular .38 Special. Using the Terrier as a starting point, S&W's engineers lengthened and strengthened the frame slightly (thus making it a true .38 size and the first of S&W's J frames) while still retaining the cylinder's five-shot capacity. They kept the 2-inch barrel, but replaced the Terrier's flat mainspring with a sturdier coil spring. The first gun was completed on Oct. 24, 1950, and was shown that month at the International Association of Chiefs of Police conference in Colorado Springs, Colorado. There, in as shrewd a

From 1950 until 1966, the S&W Chief's Special was made with a "flat-latch" cylinder release (top). After that, it was changed to an easier-to-use concave checkered thumb latch (bottom).

marketing move as ever there was, Smith & Wesson invited the assembled chiefs of police to name the new revolver. No doubt inspired by the now-legendary Colt Detective Special, this newest snubnose on the block was overwhelmingly christened by the assembled lawmen as the Chief's Special.

Offered blued with case-hardened hammer and trigger, or nickeled, the Chief's Special came with rounded, two-piece checkered walnut grips, fixed sights and something that the Detective Special didn't have at the time: an under-barrel partial lug that shielded the tip of the ejector rod. And although it only had five shots compared to the Detective Special's six rounds, the Chief's Special was more compact. In summation, it not only looked good, it felt good in the hand, especially in small- to medium-sized hands like mine. It's a fun gun to carry and shoot, and I much prefer the original rounded-butt version to the square-butt variation, which was brought out in 1952 to satisfy those with larger mitts. A heavy barreled 3-inch version was introduced in 1955, along with limited runs with adjustable target sights.

The Chief's Special underwent a name change in 1957, when it became the Model 36, and I carry a popular varia-

The M&P Model 10 was given a new look when it was offered by Smith & Wesson with a 2-inch barrel. This particular chunky-looking snubnose was manufactured in December 1963.

tion of that gun, the Model 60, which was introduced in 1965 as the world's first stainless steel revolver. It makes a perfect "bathrobe gun" to clandestinely carry when sitting on my front porch late at night smoking a cigar. In fact, the newly christened Model 36 went on to inspire other vintage J-frame variations, includ-

ing the Chief's Special Airweight with an aluminum alloy cylinder and frame (warning: do NOT shoot these guns without having them factory-checked for safety beforehand), and the highly popular stainless steel Lady Smith. Other offshoots of the basic Model 36 are the shrouded-hammer Model 49 Bodyguard (a gun FitzGerald would have certainly approved, with its snag-proof, partially concealed hammer), and the hammerless Model 40 Centennial, with its squeeze-to-fire grip safety.

Today's .38 Special factory ammo, such as Federal's Personal Defense Micro loads and Hydra-Shoks, Hornady's Critical Defense line or the Black Hills offerings, even the Cowboy Loads, have made these vintage snubbies even more effective than they were in their heyday. But be forewarned: Do NOT shoot Plus-P ammo in these little belly guns; they were not designed for those higher pressures. But used within their limitations, they can evoke a refreshing and nostalgic return to the fog-shrouded streets of San Francisco or the rain-slicked sidewalks of New York, when a trench-coated figure, with his fedora pulled down and a snub-nosed revolver in his pocket, stalked the harbingers of crime while the rest of the city slept. GD

Small-framed snubbies such as this S&W Chief's Special owed their compact size to a smaller five-chambered cylinder.

DANGEROUS-GAME
RIFLES:
A MATTER OF
LIFE AND DEATH

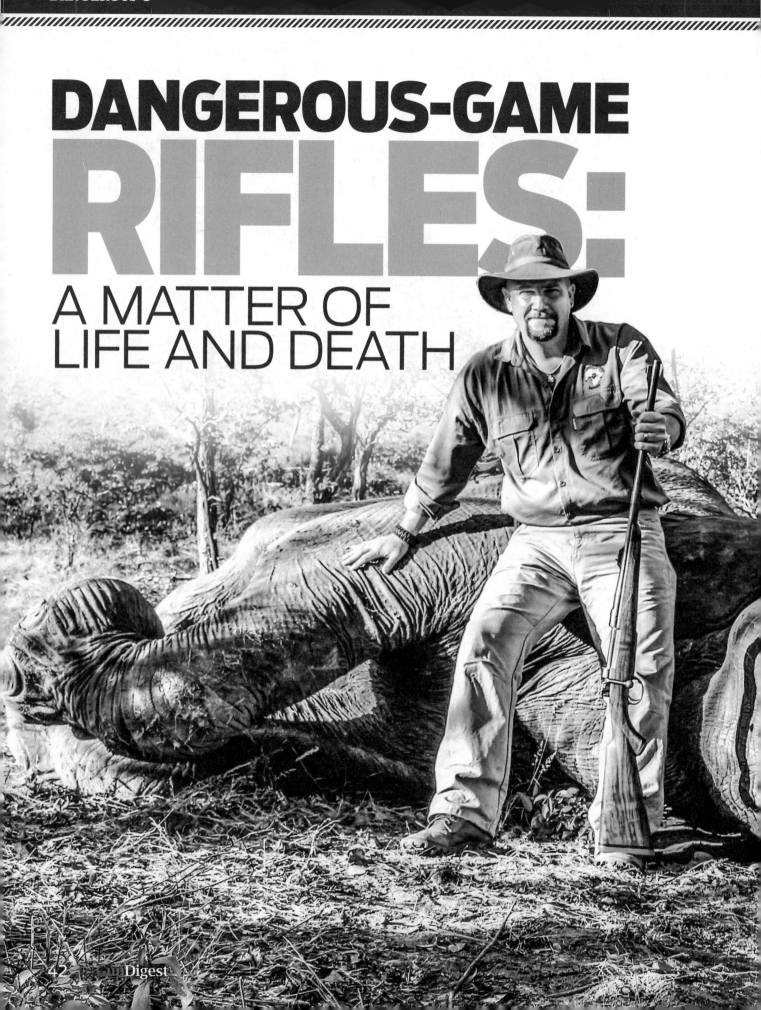

If you are up for pursuing dangerous game, buying the right rifle could be the most important hunting decision you ever make ❯PHIL MASSARO

I love the prospect of hunting dangerous game – on any continent – but the concept of a dangerous-game rifle warrants some special attention. A deer rifle can come in many different forms, from lever rifles to single shots to pumps, but if your deer rifle were to fail, odds are the worst thing that would happen is a cancelled hunt. Should your dangerous-game rifle go south, you might be in for a terrible experience, especially considering the locations and conditions under which dangerous-game hunts are conducted.

The term "dangerous game" is subjective; any game animal that has historically posed a threat to human life could easily be considered dangerous. A black bear will rarely kill a human, but under certain circumstances can pose quite the threat. Lions, leopards and cougars routinely kill people, yet can be taken cleanly with your favorite deer or elk rifle. So for the purpose of the dangerous-game rifle, I'd like consider those rifles (and cartridges) that are relied upon under the worst conditions, such as the recovery of a wounded dangerous-game animal or those used in the pursuit of an animal with the weight, height and girth – as well as horns, teeth or tusks – to end your life. Grizzly bear, brown bear and polar bear, and possibly the bison, are North America's dangerous game. Australia has the Asiatic water buffalo and banteng, and India's gaur, tiger and

When pursuing the largest and toughest game animals on Earth, you need a rifle you can bet your life on.

leopard certainly qualified as dangerous game. The European wisent (bison) and brown bear, as well as the huge wild boars, could lay a hurting on you, and the water buffalo imported to South America can be a cantankerous lot. And Africa has all sorts of stuff volunteering to end your existence on this planet, including, but not limited to elephant, Cape buffalo, lion, leopard, hippo, and crocodile; all can quickly ruin the mood. If you intend to pursue any of these species, a rifle of suitable caliber and design is most certainly warranted.

Most dangerous-game rifles are chambered for big-bore cartridges, though there were some hunters in the early days of jacketed bullets and smokeless powder that pushed the boundaries of what we all now consider to be the bottom end of the dangerous-game-cartridge spectrum. Sadly, not all walked away unscathed, but some happily lived out their days none the worse for wear. W.D.M. "Karamoja" Bell used a number of smaller-bore rifles, including the 6.5x54mm, the 7x57mm and the .318 Westley Richards to take a good percentage of the 1,011 elephants he took in his career. Col. Jim Corbett made a switch from the .450/400 Nitro Express to the .275 Rigby for his pursuit of man-eating tigers and leopards in northern India. Both lived to a ripe old

age, in spite of the use of smaller cartridges on dangerous game, but I surely wouldn't advise the adoption of their mindset. While Corbett's tigers are no longer a point of debate, the elephants of the 21st century have been exposed to hunters for well over a century, and the habitat in which they are hunted is thicker, with the shots generally closer than many of those who used the .275 Rigby, .318 Westley Richards and .350 Rigby Magnum for pachyderms. But many of the early hunters favored the sturdy bolt-action rifles based on proven military actions. Famous names like John Rigby & Co., Westley Richards, Holland & Holland, W.J. Jeffery and Griffin & Howe produced some fantastic big-game rifles, and many are still in service today.

The double rifle has long been a means of providing a quick second shot, and predates repeating rifles, smokeless powder and jacketed bullets. In many instances, the double rifle was relied upon for the speed of the follow-up shot, and in the hands of those exploring the yet-untouched corners of the wilds it represented two guns in one; the second barrel being kept in reserve for dire emergencies. With two barrels, two triggers and two locks, the adventurous hunter had what amounted to a spare rifle in hand. It was the preferred – if not most popular –

rifle of the African Professional Hunters, whether guiding clients or in pursuit of ivory.

The lever-action rifle led the way among the American repeating rifles, and for decades was one of the most popular choices for the hunter who wanted a fast-handling, quick-pointing rifle with plenty of firepower and knockdown power. All things being relative, the early models were chambered for anemic cartridges, but by the time the Winchester 1886, 1894 and 1895 arrived on the scene, there were some potent cartridges available. The classic scene of a hunter in grizzly country with a big-bore, lever-action rifle has graced the cover of many hunting magazines, and continues to capture the imagination.

The single-shot rifle was the pre-eminent style, and remains a popular choice to this day. Where once it was all that was available, in this modern era it is a prestigious choice, with many proponents of the single shot taking pride in the fact that they only need one shot. The design certainly hearkens back to the days when Samuel Baker and Frederick Courteney Selous would load up their two- and four-bore rifles in pursuit of ivory and horn. The Farquharson falling-block actions prevalent throughout England and her colonies, and the Ballard, Sharps

The Heym Model 89B double rifle in .470 NE is a classic combination for buffalo.

The Heym Express by Martini in .505 Gibbs is not for the faint of heart, but makes a dangerous-game stopper.

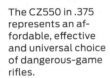

The CZ550 in .375 represents an affordable, effective and universal choice of dangerous-game rifles.

The Ruger No. 1 single-shot rifle can handle the dangerous-game cartridges, though you might have your guide firing backup shots

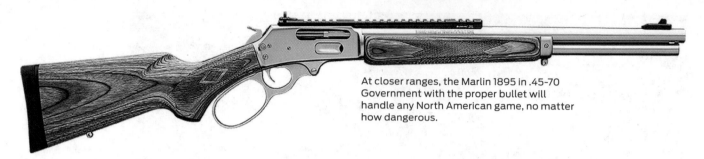

At closer ranges, the Marlin 1895 in .45-70 Government with the proper bullet will handle any North American game, no matter how dangerous.

and Winchester designs on this side of the pond accounted for an awful lot of game, including that of a dangerous nature. Of course, the single-shot rifle has its limitations and challenges, but that is part of the mystique. If the technological advances in rifle design made the flintlock and percussion-cap rifles nearly obsolete, the single-shot rifle survived the evolutionary purge; the Ruger No. 1 – introduced in 1967 – remains a popular choice among both hunters and collectors. It is available in a number of suitable dangerous-game cartridges, though it comes with a set of unique rules, which we'll address in just a bit.

SHOPPING FOR A DANGEROUS-GAME RIFLE

The search for a dangerous-game rifle requires an evaluation of your possible hunting scenarios. The big cartridges required will certainly preclude the rifle from being used for target purposes, though you'll certainly find that the big bores can be surprisingly accurate, so it's usually the species of game and the areas where they're hunted that influences your choice. A grizzly bear at 250 yards, certainly not an impossible scenario, requires a different mindset than does an elephant at 40 yards, though there are choices that will easily handle both.

Price will also be a factor, as there are choices that might fit the bill for under $1,000, and it wouldn't be difficult to spend $150,000 on a double rifle of British pedigree. I highly recommend that you buy the best dangerous-game rifle you can afford, while keeping in mind that no amount of engraving, color casehardening or fancy-figured walnut will matter to a dangerous-game animal. Only a bullet of proper weight, diameter and construction, placed into a vital organ, will get the job done. So, if you can

afford a dependable, yet plain bolt-action rifle, by all means book your hunt and enjoy those wild places left on this Earth. Should you feel the desire to enjoy the virtues of a double rifle, and are well-heeled enough to pull it off, I'll be the first to encourage you to do so, just make sure your rifle has the features you're comfortable with.

And touching briefly on the choice of cartridges, I can best put it this way: There are many good books on dangerous-game cartridges, which will highlight the pros and cons of many different cartridges. Choosing yours requires one of the most introspective exercises: admitting your own personal recoil limit. No matter how attractive a particular cartridge might be, if you don't shoot it well, it can be a recipe for disaster. For example, my pal and hunting partner Mike McNulty owns a beautiful Heym Express by Martini in .505 Gibbs, which he shoots very well. For me, that recoil level is just a bit too much; I can shoot it, but not nearly as well as my .404 Jeffery or .470 Nitro Express. Trust me, you're better off with a good .375 that you shoot well than with a .458 that causes a flinch. Try some different cartridges and find what works for you. Stock fit has quite a bit to do with felt recoil, but you'll have a better idea of your recoil limit in a real-world scenario rather than relying upon theoretical figures. Also pay attention to the availability of ammunition; if you handload the doors are wide open, but if not, you'll want to make sure you have access to good factory ammunition.

BOLT-ACTION DANGEROUS-GAME RIFLES

The bolt action represents the majority of dangerous-game rifles; they are among the strongest designs, they are rugged and reliable, as well as afford-

able. Any cartridge can be housed in a bolt-action (turnbolt for those of you across the pond), and the design has been with us since the end of the 19th century. The famous Mauser 98, and its modern clones, is still a perfectly viable choice, as its simplicity is a distinct part of the genius. Among these designs are the pre-'64 Winchester 70, the CZ550, the Dakota 76, the Ruger 77, the Heym Express by Martini and the Montana Rifle Company Model 1999; all have the large claw extractor and fixed-blade ejector of the Mauser design, and all control the cartridge from the time it comes out of the magazine until it is chambered, fired and ejected. I am a strong proponent of these controlled-round-feed, or CRF, designs on dangerous-game rifles, as opposed to the push-feed designs like the Remington 700, Savage 110, Weatherby Mark V and others. First, I want to reduce the possibility of a double feed or jam to nearly nil, as once the first shot is fired at a dangerous-game animal, the hunter might just be under the most stress of his or her life. Though it doesn't happen frequently, I've seen hunters short-stroke a push-feed rifle and end up with a mess in their hands (and possibly in their pants). Second, the extractors on the push-feed rifle are generally much smaller than their CRF counterparts – the Sako 85 does have a beefy extractor – and the ejector is often a spring-loaded plunger on the bolt face. Call me old fashioned, but I like fewer moving parts and I like them to be over-designed. The last thing I want to worry about when facing a wounded animal that can kill me is something breaking on my rifle. I have seen push-feed extractors fail, and I've seen those rifles jam a spent cartridge while being cycled.

If you insist on using a 700 or Mark V, or even the straight-pull Blaser R8, spend

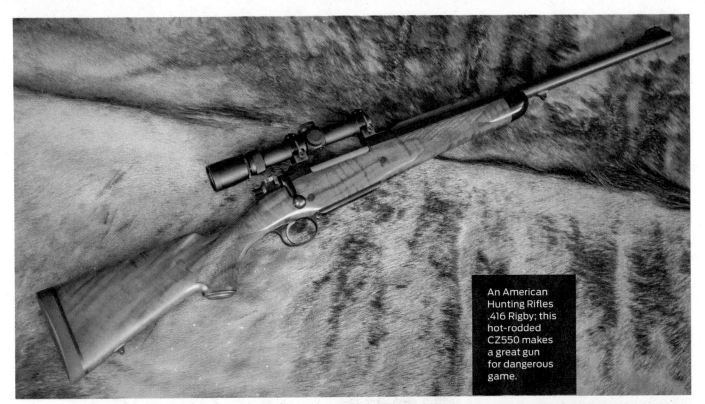

An American Hunting Rifles .416 Rigby; this hot-rodded CZ550 makes a great gun for dangerous game.

time at the range firing three rapid shots, working that bolt rearward hard to make sure to eject that spent case. I know many who use a push feed for dangerous-game work, but I also know my luck, and prefer to hedge my bets on all fronts, and use CRF actions nearly exclusively for dangerous game.

I have a few favorite bolt-action dangerous-game guns, and I think a brief overview will help demonstrate my way of thinking. They all have Leupold Optics, set in Talley detachable rings for quick access to the iron sights. I'll give the highlights of each.

The Heym Express by Martini in .404 Jeffery. This is, unequivocally, my favorite rifle. The Heym Express action is oversized (using a .780-inch diameter bolt, in comparison to the .750-inch magnum Mauser bolt), the magazine box is specifically engineered to each individual cartridge offered, and this rifle feeds a cartridge like no other I've ever used. The Krupp cold hammer-forged barrel is exceptionally accurate (this gun shoots sub-MOA with almost all loads), and the trigger is wonderfully crisp. But to me the best part of this rifle is the stock. Designed by famous gunmaker Ralf Martini, the stock is a work of art. With

The author's favorite dangerous game rifle: A Heym Express by Martini in .404 Jeffery

One of the classic dangerous-game combinations: A Winchester Model 70 Safari Express in .416 Remington Magnum, a great controlled-round-feed design

a 14-1/2-inch length of pull – which is stocked to my dimensions – the Express by Martini comes to the shoulder like a fine shotgun. The open, sweeping grip helps mitigate recoil, and the straight bolt is located in a natural spot, allowing the rifle to be cycled from the shoulder. Topped with a Leupold 2.5x Compact scope in Talley detachable rings, it is equally pleasurable to shoot with the optic or with the 50- and 100-yard leaves of the iron sights. If forced to keep just one rifle for the rest of my days, it would be this rifle.

The Winchester Model 70 Safari Express in .416 Remington Magnum. An iconic rifle in a universal cartridge, the rifle I call "Cocoa" is one of the last of the New Haven models, and has the pre-'64 CRF action. Cross-pinned stock of beefy dimensions, an adjustable trigger, three-position safety, good iron sights and a classic design all combine for an affordable and respectable, timeless design. Does it have the panache of the Heym? No, but it has its own appeal, and the price point makes it affordable. It has been the only rifle I've taken on a couple safaris, and it took my first Cape buffalo, as well as a good number of plains-game species in dangerous-game blocks. This gun puts three 400-grain Swift A-Frames into a one-inch group, and the Leupold VX-3 1.5-5x20 in detachable rings allows me to take the big gun out to 300 yards and a bit more.

The Bansner & Co. Custom Safari in .404 Jeffery. Mark Bansner makes an excellent, all-weather rifle, and the custom rifle he built me is no exception. This features one of Mark's fiberglass stocks and is built on the M704 action, a wonderful CRF design that doesn't use the Mauser side band and claw extractor, instead using a huge spring-loaded extractor which makes up nearly one-quarter of the bolt face. With a Timney trigger, fluted bolt, three-position M70-style wing safety and a 14 3/8-inch L.O.P, this rifle is perfectly suited to Alaska and other wet and salty climes. The Cerakote finish sheds moisture and even resists the acidity of my hands. It's been to the 49th state with me – having taken a good black bear in coastal grizzly country – and will return again. This gun loves the 450-grain Woodleigh

Using the M704 action, the author's Bansner & Co. .404 Jeffery is a sound choice for Alaskan dangerous game.

A 1916 Mauser Gewehr 98 in .318 Westley Richards; this cartridge was a popular dangerous-game choice a century ago.

The oversize (0.780-inch) bolt of the Heym Express.

load from Norma, putting three shots in three-quarters of an inch at 100 paces. The Leupold VX-5HD 1-5x24mm scope handles the cartridge's capabilities perfectly.

The Mauser Gewehr 98 in .318 Westley Richards. A quarter-century ago, I bought a 1916 Amberg Arsenal Gewehr 98 Mauser which had stood, muzzle-down, in the corner of a damp basement for who knows how long. Though I wished to keep it intact – all the parts had the same four-digit serial number – there was no saving the barrel. Nate Chesney and I turned that military 8x57 into a .318 Westley Richards, a cartridge very popular in East Africa a century ago, on its 100th anniversary. Driving a .330-inch, 250-grain bullet at 2,400 fps (a bit faster in my rifle), this was the all-around cartridge before the .375 H&H came on the scene, and while light for dangerous game by modern standards, it will cleanly take grizzly, polar bear, bison, lion and leopard. If legal, I would use it on Cape buffalo; that's how well the cartridge penetrates. I preserved the action – with the classic thumb groove and clip loading slot – magazine follower, and the bottom metal, installing a Kreiger barrel, NECG front and rear sights, and Timney trigger.

The Mauser "flag" safety was replaced with a Model 70-style three-position safety, and the rifle shoots very well. Topped with a Leupold VX-3i 1.5-5x20 in Talley detachables, it has the same feel as my other rifles, a point I feel important for dangerous-game rifles.

THE DOUBLE RIFLE

There is something very special about heading into the wild with a double rifle over your shoulder; it is an immediate connection to the past, and it evokes a bygone era. With it comes a hefty price tag, and the realization that some of the shot opportunities that a scoped rifle might be afforded will be off limits to an iron-sighted double. There are many different makes and models on the market, from over/under rifles to the classic side-by-side

The author's father enjoys this Browning 1886 in .45-70 Government, a great choice for North American dangerous game.

The Heym Model 89B in .450-400 3-inch NE, one of the best values in a double rifle today.

designs, with some bearing the names of companies that predate the United States itself, or they could be just one generation old. The classic British houses – John Rigby & Co., Holland & Holland, Boss, William Evans, Westley Richards, Purdey and more – make a great rifle, and can command a price well into six figures. There are more affordable companies, like Verney-Carron, Merkel, Kreighoff, and my own particular favorite: Heym.

The Heym Model 89B – I had the honor of taking the first Cape buffalo with the new rifle – uses the classic Anson & Deeley boxlock, with the added strength of a Greener crossbolt, and balances wonderfully. While some might prefer prestige of the sidelock models, I've found that the boxlock suits my needs just fine, though I appreciate the beauty and function of the sidelock rifles. After spending time with a Heym 89B in .450/400 3-inch NE and a .470 NE, I decided on the latter for my own double, and my gun shoots very well. Like the Heym Express, Ralf Martini was brought in to design the stock, and my rifle was stocked to my dimensions. It fits like a glove and is plenty accurate, with a right and left barrel printing under 2 inches apart at 100 yards. It has two triggers (I strongly prefer two triggers over one), a tang safety, a raised cheekpiece, and is wonderfully balanced. Carrying this rifle for hours on end is no problem – it

weighs in at just over 11 pounds – and with 26-inch barrels it settles down nicely for the shot, from all field positions.

The Krieghoff Big Five double rifle is another affordable and popular choice, what with its unique cocking/de-cocking safety, which seems to be either loved or hated among the populous. Personally, I prefer the traditional safety catch, as I find the Kreighoff cocking device a bit awkward, but there is a lid for every pot, and quite obviously there are a good number of hunters who are just fine with the design. It takes a significant amount of effort to run the safety forward (cocking the rifle) and I've seen more than one shooter struggle with it. Again, if it's good with you, so be it, but it is a point to consider.

Many of the double rifles are chambered for the big, rimmed, Nitro Express cartridges, and some for the belted and rimless cartridges. I personally prefer the rimmed cartridges, for the positive ejection and for the positive headspacing these cartridges afford. Lacking a magazine, the double rifle will be considerably shorter than its bolt-action counterpart, and easier to carry and swing in the thick vegetation. And, because there are no magazine restrictions, the longest cartridges can be housed in a double rifle without concern. Almost all modern double rifles come equipped with automatic ejectors, and I feel this is a good thing. You might read tales of elephant

hunters a century ago who insisted on rifles with extractors alone, as they preferred to manually eject the cases. Their belief was that in the midst of an elephant herd, once the initial shots had been fired, the remaining elephants would hear the sound of ejected brass cases and charge that sound. I don't believe that is the case, and at any rate, none of us are hunting ivory for profit. Automatic ejectors take one more high-dexterity function off the list while under the stresses of hunting dangerous game, and I'll attest that this is a good thing.

One of the greatest challenges that the double rifle presents is the need to use two triggers. I found myself doing it early on: I'd pull the right trigger, line up for the second shot, and pull the right trigger again. It just takes practice to get used to it, and practice you should. I make up a couple of dummy cartridges for my double, using sand or flour of the same weight as my powder charge in order to practice drawing two cartridges from my belt and loading the rifle quickly and smoothly. Once you spend some range time with your double rifle, you'll find it becomes an old friend. Make sure the rifle fits you properly – Chris Sells from Heym measured me like a tailor to ensure proper stock fit – and you'll find the recoil of even some of the biggest cartridges is manageable. If the barrels are too long or too short for your frame, the

The rifle of the late Professional Hunter Jay T. Carlson: a Ruger No. 1 Tropical chambered in .378 Weatherby Magnum. If only this rifle could talk...

A stellar dangerous-game combination: the Mauser 98 action on a Rigby rifle in .416 Rigby.

Your dangerous-game rifle must have good, strong iron sights for backup duty; shown here is the rear-sight island of the Heym Express by Martini.

A pair of Rigby bolt-action, dangerous-game rifles: single square bridge on the left and double square bridge on the right.

When pursuing an elephant bull, you'll want the best rifle you can afford, and the best cartridge you can shoot.

gun will feel either nose-heavy or butt-heavy; while it is certainly possible to find the perfect rifle off the rack, I like the bespoke experience, specifically regarding the stock dimensions. Invariably, you will be carrying your double rifle much more than you will be shooting it. Before you buy, hold the rifle in your hand and emulate a walk on safari. Is it comfortable in the hand? Does the weight bother you? After eight hours in the bushveldt anything can get heavy, but an overly heavy rifle can feel like a boat anchor. As nice as the Heym Model 88B (the predecessor to the Model 89B) is to shoot, the sharp, square edges of the receiver bother me. It's uncomfortable in the hand, and it's a big part of the reason I am so enamored with the 89B; when Heym engineers designed the 89B they rounded the edges, and gave the gun a better feel in all carry positions. While the double rifles might not be for everyone, I love my Heym .470, and am always eager to take it in the field.

Should you be in the position to order a Holland & Holland Royal or Rigby's Rising Bite, your rifle will be made to your specifications, and you'll certainly be in for a wonderful experience. As a gun writer, I am not in that financial position, so when we see each other at the conventions, please tell me about your experience.

LEVER-ACTION RIFLES FOR DANGEROUS GAME

Teddy Roosevelt helped lead the way for American hunters traveling to East Africa, as well as recording his exploits with the last of the bison on the Great Plains. While TR had a Holland & Holland Royal double – presented to him for his 1909-10 safari – he was a big fan of his Winchester 1895 lever gun in .405 Winchester, especially for lions; he preferred his "medicine gun" for soft-skinned game. The lever-action rifle is uniquely American, and it has been chambered in cartridges from the .22 LR and other rimfires up to the .50-110 and beyond.

Should you prefer to use a lever gun for dangerous game, I suggest two points to look at: How strong is the action, and can it handle a cartridge capable of delivering a bullet of appropriate weight, caliber and sectional density? The .38-55 Winchester is perfectly suitable for most black bears, yet is most certainly on the light side for any grizzly. The same can be reported for the .375 Winchester, the modern update of the .38-55. Rather than try to make a silk purse out of a sow's ear, I recommend looking to the strongest actions like the Winchester 1886, Winchester Model 71 and the Marlin Model 1895. Both the 1886 and 1895 can be chambered in the .45-70 Government (a worthy cartridge for all but the largest of animals), and the Model 71 came chambered in the .348 Winchester, a worthy cartridge of all North American game. Even better, I like Doug Turnbull's 1886 chambered in the .475 Turnbull; he has used that cartridge to take several Cape buffalo (including a bull in Namibia's Caprivi at 25 yards) and it is a sound big-game choice.

Having spent time with the .45-70 and .475 Turnbull in the '86, I know they can very accurate, and there are choices for the Browning and Marlin rifles that can be equally impressive. Browning's BLR comes chambered for the .450 Marlin (a shortened .458 Winchester case) and is a solid choice for bears in the thick stuff, and the Marlin Model 1895 in .444 Marlin has long been a favorite. Both of these will handle any North American game, yet are a bit lacking for African danger-

Three of the author's favorites: A Winchester 70 in .416 Remington Magnum, a Heym Express by Martini in .404 Jeffery and a custom Bansner & Co. in .404 Jeffery.

ous game. The same can be said for the Winchester 1895 in .405 Winchester; yes, it was TR's baby, but the .410-inch-diameter bullet at 300 grains lacks the sectional density to be a serious contender in the market. It will handle thin-skinned dangerous game, but I'd look elsewhere for the thick-skinned animals.

I like the Model 1886 in either .45-70 or .45-90, as it is one of the strongest lever-action rifles ever made. My dad – Ol' Grumpy Pants – has an excellent Browning 1886, made in 1986, in .45-70 Government, with octagon barrel and fine sights. The rifle is a shooter, and he's taken deer, coyotes and a nice bison in South Dakota with that rifle. It was, is and shall be a favorite of mine, though my quest for the Model 71 that's just right continues.

SINGLE-SHOT RIFLES FOR DANGEROUS GAME

The single-shot rifle has been with us for as long as safari has, and the idea of having just one shot is appealing to many hunters. However, in the world of dangerous-game hunting, it comes with a caveat: Using a single-shot rifle will greatly increase the odds of your Professional Hunter or guide firing at your animal. The need to back up your shots on dangerous game is a reality, and while one-shot kills aren't out of the realm of possibility, learning to reload a single shot quickly is imperative.

One of the beauties of the falling-block, single-shot rifle is that it can handle just about any cartridge, including the most powerful. There is no bolt face to worry about, nor magazine width,

length or depth. Ruger's famed No. 1 falling block includes a line chambered for (at one time or another) classic safari cartridges like the .450-400 3-inch NE, the 9.3x74R, the .450 NE, the .416 Rigby, .375 H&H Magnum and more. All can be used on even the African elephant – the largest of game animals – but again, your guide has a responsibility to see that you return home with your anatomy in its current configuration, and not stuffed in a mayonnaise jar, and might be required to fire backup shots.

The single-shot breech loader has no magazine, so, like the double rifle, it will tend to be shorter, and easier to maneuver in the brush. It too can handle the longest cartridges without any concern for the length of magazine. Rimmed cartridges are popular in the single-shot rifles for the same reason as doubles: they offer what I consider to be the easiest extraction. But as the Ruger No. 1 has shown us for over half a century, the rimless and belted cartridges function just fine as well. If you are a single-shot hunter, I won't tell you to avoid dangerous-game hunting, just please be aware of the concerns that your guide/PH has to deal with and be prepared to hear gunfire other than your own.

My only single-shot rifle belonged to my friend, the late Jay T. Carlson, who was a Professional Hunter on the island of Mindoro in the Philippines. The rifle began life as a Ruger No. 1 Tropical in .375 H&H Magnum, but Jay had the

chamber reamed out to hold the behemoth .378 Weatherby Magnum. Jay also cut down the fore-end, so he could grab the gun by the barrel, just behind the barrel band sling stud. Now, the .378 Weatherby will drive a 300-grain bullet at 3,000 fps, and I don't think that rifle weighs more than 7 1/2 pounds. I describe the recoil as "soul-crushing," but it is surprisingly accurate for an iron-sighted single shot. Jay relied on this gun in Africa and other places, and it didn't let him down; but I will report you need hang on to the old girl for dear life, as I've had that sling stud smash my left-hand knuckles, and the rifle has considerable muzzle jump. I've fired many other Ruger No. 1 rifles, including several of the big bores, but none had the recoil of Jay Carlson's beast.

IN CONCLUSION

Settling on the dangerous-game rifle that is right for you can be a difficult prospect, considering the wide range of choices. Whatever you decide upon, make sure it is utterly reliable, that it fits you well (I can't stress that point enough) and that it is chambered in a cartridge that you are honestly comfortable shooting repeatedly. Just as your Professional Hunter/Guide has an obligation to you and your safety, you have a responsibility to place your shots properly, and to make a clean kill. In order to do that, you need a rifle that you are completely confident in, capable of cleanly taking the largest species you intend to encounter. Buy the best rifle and optic you can afford, and enjoy your time among the dangerous-game animals. GD

The elegant Rising Bite rifle from John Rigby & Co. of London.

Ninety years ago, Walther established a defining influence on the design of concealed-carry firearms with the PPK, destined to become a cultural icon.

WALTHER'S TIMELESS PPK TURNS 90

Elegant lines and precision engineering have created an enduring appeal

› JOE COOGAN

In early James Bond novels, 007 carried a Beretta M418 semi-auto pistol concealed in a chamois shoulder rig. British firearms expert Geoffery Boothroyd observed that for someone "licensed to kill," Bond was woefully under-gunned with a diminutive .25-caliber pistol. Boothroyd's initial advice was to re-arm Bond with a British revolver, the bigger, the better, he believed. He offered his opinion of the .25-caliber pistol in a letter to author Ian Fleming, "This sort of gun is a lady's gun, and not a really nice lady at that." Appreciative of Boothroyd's polite criticism, Fleming responded, "As Bond's biographer, I am most anxious to see that he lives as long as possible and I shall be most grateful for any further technical advices you might like me to pass on to him."

Fleming acknowledged Boothroyd's gun savvy, but he still favored the smooth concealable lines of a semi-auto pistol, and so he re-armed Bond with a Walther PPK in its original 7.65mm (.32 ACP) chambering. As a "thank you" to the firearms expert, Fleming created the character "Major Boothroyd," who first appeared in *Dr. No* as Bond's service armorer and was later referred to as "Q" in subsequent Bond films.

The gun switch was initiated when the silencer of Bond's Beretta got caught in the waistband of his trousers at the end of *From Russia with Love*, an event that almost cost the secret agent his life.

When M, the head of MI6, ordered Bond to turn in his Beretta pistol, Bond argued unsuccessfully that because of the silencer, the incident would have happened with any kind of gun. Major Boothroyd replaced the Beretta with the "superior" Walther PPK and recommended that Bond stay away from silencers. Further to the real-life Boothroyd's advice, Fleming exchanged the chamois shoulder holster, which could hinder a quick draw, for a smooth-leather rig.

BACK TO THE FUTURE

By the time Bond holstered his sleek new pistol, the reputation of Walther's PPK was already firmly established, serving German military personnel, police and civilians with unfailing dependability since 1930. German gunmaker Carl Walther's greatest interest had been the design and development of self-loading pistols. In the early 1900s, he patented the world's first fixed-barrel semi-automatic pistol, which improved accuracy, even with compact barrels.

In 1929, Carl Walther Waffenfabrik AG introduced the groundbreaking PP (*Polizeipistole* or "Police Pistol"). The efficient, double-action semi-automatic pistol was adopted by the German military and the police under the Third Reich. Originally chambered for the 7.65x17mm caliber, the PP provided a muzzle-velocity of 950 fps. It accommodated a single-stack magazine holding eight rounds and, like most contemporary pistols of that period, featured a heel-catch magazine release. Following WWII, the heel-catch release was replaced by a frame-mounted, push-button magazine release. The PP's overall length was 6.8 inches with a barrel-length of 3.35 inches and an overall weight of 1.5 pounds. A loaded-chamber indicator in the form of a signal pin protruded through the rear of the slide when in contact with a chambered round. By glance or feel, the user would know if the gun was loaded.

Walther's PP was the first successful blowback operation of its kind, enabling both double-action and single-action capabilities. This was accomplished by way of a safety lever that served double duty, providing not only a safe mode, but also simultaneously de-cocking the hammer with a hammer block. This allows the hammer to drop without firing the gun. The external hammer is cocked when the slide is pulled rearward to chamber a round. Pushing the safety lever downward rotates the hammer block into position to separate the hammer and spring-loaded firing pin and "drops" the hammer. Moving the safety-lever upward takes the gun out of safe mode and al-

Prior to the Gun Control Act of 1968, PPKs were imported into the U.S. without restriction. A new PPK came in a lizard-skin embossed box, which included a factory target, an owner's manual, two magazines and a brass cleaning rod.

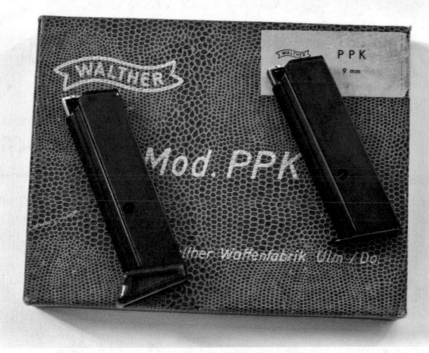

The PPK served German military personnel, police and civilians alike from 1930. The double-action pistol features brown plastic grips and comes with two magazines, one with a plastic finger-extension and one with a flush base for better concealability.

lows the pistol to be fired double action by simply pulling the trigger. The slide moves rearward with the energy of the fired shot and pushes the empty cartridge case and bolt to the rear by expanding gas created by the ignition of gunpowder. This action ejects the empty case, re-cocks the hammer and chambers another round to allow the following shots to be fired in single-action mode. The slide remains open with the last shot fired.

Takedown is accomplished by removing the magazine and making sure the gun is unloaded. The triggerguard is hinged at the rear and can be pulled downward from the front and secured against the frame. The slide can then be pulled fully rearward to disengage it from the frame and then lifted upward, which allows the slide to move forward and off the fixed barrel. The recoil spring can then be slipped off the barrel.

In 1930, the year after the PP's introduction, Walther released a smaller version of the PP, which was called the PPK (*Polizeipistole Kriminalmodell* or "Police Pistol Detective Model"). It featured a shorter grip, barrel, slide, frame and reduced magazine capacity. The PPK was more concealable than the original PP and more suited for plain-clothed police, intelligence agents and undercover work.

During and after WWII, PPKs were issued to the German military, the Luftwaffe and to various police agencies including the *SS* and *Gestapo*. In addition to the German Intelligence Service (BND), the PPK was also used by UK's MI5 and MI6, France's intelligence agency (SDECE), Israel's Mossad and Switzerland's Intelligence and Security Service. Protecting the United States president is the responsibility of the United States Secret Service and the actual bodyguards are a special unit called the Presidential Protective Detail. Over the years, they were allowed to carry a variety of firearms, which reputedly included the Walther PP during the 1980s.

The success of the PP and PPK as double-action semi-auto pistols was so well-regarded that the Chinese intelligence service issued a PPK clone. The PP series also inspired the design of other pistols, including the Soviet Makarov, the Hungarian FEG PA-63, the Polish P-64, the American Accu-Tek AT-380 II, and the Argentinian Bersa Thunder 380.

One of the most historic functions the PPK ever served was ending the life of Adolf Hitler when, on April 30, 1945, the Nazi dictator used his personal service pistol, a shiny gold-plated PPK, to commit suicide. The fate of the PPK that Hitler used to shoot himself, one of several PPs and PPKs that he owned, is uncertain.

Another world event unfolded when dictatorial rule in South Korea was ended with the assassination of Park Chung-hee on Oct. 26, 1979. Park was assassinated by his close friend Kim Jae-gyu, the director of the Korean Central Intelligence Agency using a PPK at a safe house in Seoul. Cha Ji-chul, chief of the Presidential Security Service, was also fatally shot by Kim. These PPK-assisted assassinations ultimately led to the start of democracy in South Korea.

Following World War II, the Soviet

The PPK/S (top left) differs from an original PPK (below), by utilizing the larger frame and grip of the PP, mated to the slide and barrel assembly of the smaller PPK. Magazine capacity of the PPK/S is increased by one round bringing the total to 7+1. The difference in grip size is noticeable when a PPK/S and PPK are placed next to each other. Otherwise the features of the two pistols are identical.

The PPK's fixed sights are easy to acquire after drawing the gun from a holster like Galco's S3H black-leather shoulder holster. The external hammer can be manually cocked by thumbing it rearward. Moving the safety lever downward releases the hammer and rotates the firing-pin block into position to separate the hammer and spring-loaded firing pin. Moving the safety lever upward takes the gun out of safe-mode and allows the pistol to be fired double-action by pulling the trigger.

SPECIFICATIONS

MANUFACTURER: **Walther Arms, Inc. Fort Smith, Arkansas**

MODEL: **PPK**

CALIBER: **.380 ACP**

ACTION: **Semi-automatic center-fire pistol**

METALWORK: **Stainless steel and black**

SAFETY: **Manual engaging firing-pin block**

SIGHTS: **Fixed front and rear sights**

BARREL LENGTH: **3.3˝**

TRIGGER PULL: **DA/SA   13.4 lbs./6.1 lbs.**

TRIGGER TRAVEL: **.04/.2˝**

MAGAZINE CAPACITY: **Single stack flat, 6 rounds (PPK); 7 rounds (PPK/S)**

OVERALL LENGTH: **6.1˝**

HEIGHT: **3.8˝**

WIDTH: **1˝**

WEIGHT EMPTY: **20.8 oz.**

ACCESSORIES: **Owner's manual, plastic case, extra magazine, cleaning rod**

MSRP: **$849**

(below) Walther released a smaller version of the PP, which it called the PPK. It featured a shorter grip, barrel, slide, frame and magazine, making it better-suited for plain-clothed police and undercover work. Ergonomically, the PPK is well-designed, offering a comfortable grip that makes it pleasant to shoot.

Union occupied East Germany, causing Walther to move its factory from Zella-Mehlis to Ulm. However, for several years following the war, the Allied powers prohibited any arms manufacture in Germany. With the prohibition of manufacturing, Walther decided to grant licenses for the production of its various products. In the early 1950s, Walther licensed production of its PP/PPK-series pistols to the French firm, *Manfacture de Machines de Haut-Rhin*, commonly known as "Manurhin." All postwar European-made PP-series pistols were manufactured by Manurhin until the 1960s, when Walther built a new plant at Ulm in West Germany. The contract PP/PPK series came to an end when Walther began production at the new plant.

In the United States, the assassinations of President John Kennedy in 1963 and, later, his brother Sen. Robert Kennedy, and Martin Luther King Jr. in 1968, prompted U.S. Congress to enact the Gun Control Act (GCA) of 1968, a federal law aimed at tighter gun laws for the firearms industry and firearms owners. The intent of this legislation was to limit interstate commerce in firearms by allowing only licensed manufacturers, dealers and importers to initiate and facilitate interstate gun transfers.

Limits were also placed on imported firearms coming into the U.S. based on their meeting several criteria. Under the GCA legislation, a pistol intended for import had to earn a certain number of points determined by various sporting features including size, weight and magazine capacity. Walther's PPK failed to meet the GCA's criteria and was prohibited from being imported for being an ounce too light and carrying too few rounds in the magazine.

In order to maintain PPK sales in the U.S., Walther overcame the restrictions by developing the PPK/S. To satisfy the weight requirements, Walther utilized the frame of the PP and teamed it with the slide and barrel of the PPK. This added 1.8 ounces, two-tenths of inch of length and an additional round in the magazine, which allowed the PPK/S to be legally imported into the U.S. It is presumed that the "S" added to the PPK designation stands for "Sporting."

The PPK takedown is accomplished by first pulling down the hinged triggerguard from the front. The slide can then be pulled rearward, which disengages it from the frame and allows it to slide forward and off the barrel. The recoil spring can then be slipped off the fixed barrel.

Interarms of Alexandria, Virginia, was the importer for Walther's PP and PPK series from 1968 when the PPK/S was introduced until the company closed in the late 1990s. For a few years, from 1978, Interarms also carried U.S.-made PPK/S pistols produced by Ranger Manufacturing in Gadsden, Alabama. In 1998, Walther's U.S. manufacturing and distribution licenses were transferred to the Smith & Wesson plant in Houlton, Maine. This allowed Walther to produce the lighter PPK for reintroduction to the American market. From 2002 until 2012, Smith & Wesson continued producing PPK/S models, due largely to the popularity of the James Bond films. During that time, 80 percent of the PPK/S pistols made were sold in the U.S., not counting government and police contracts.

For a time between Interarms going out of business in 1999 and S&W beginning manufacture in 2002, Ranger continued to make pistols for a new company named Walther USA LLC. This was not the current company, now headquartered in Fort Smith, Arkansas, but a separate Walther-controlled operation. These relatively few pistols are known as transitional models, also called "AAA Models" due to their unique serial numbers ending in AAA, or sometimes "Millennial" pistols due to their manufacture in 1999 to 2001. They have a unique roll stamp, Walther USA LLC, and the shortest production run of any of the series.

Walther Arms eventually took control of its U.S. operations, locating its headquarters and assembly facility in Fort Smith, Arkansas, in late 2012. Now, after a several-year absence from the market, the iconic PPK and PPK/S will once again be available to U.S. buyers. Assembled at the Ft. Smith facility, the PPK and PPK/S designs remain faithful to the originals manufactured in Germany with slides made at the Ulm factory and all other parts manufactured in the United States and assembled at the Fort Smith facility.

Like the originals, the PPK lineup features integrated front and rear sights, de-cocking safety, and a smooth DA/SA hammer-fired trigger system. They will be available in stainless (U.S. PPK and

Historical Correspondence

Author Ian Fleming, impressed by Geoffery Boothroyd's gun knowledge, wrote back to him:

KEMSLEY HOUSE, LONDON, W.C.1.
31st May, 1956
Dear Mr Boothroyd,

I really am most grateful for your splendid letter of May 23rd.

You have entirely convinced me and I propose, perhaps not in the next volume of James Bond's memoirs but, in the subsequent one, to change his weapons in accordance with your instructions.

Since I am not in the habit of stealing another man's expertise, I shall ask you in due course to accept remuneration for your most valuable technical aid.

Incidentally, can you suggest where I can see a .38 Airweight in London. Who would have one?

As a matter of interest, how do you come to know so much about these things? I was delighted with the photographs and greatly impressed by them. If ever there is talk of making films of some of James Bond's stories in due course, I shall suggest to the company concerned that they might like to consult you on some technical aspects. But they may not take my advice, so please do not set too much store by this suggestion.

From the style of your writing it occurs to me that you may have written books or articles on these subjects. Is that so?

Bond has always admitted to me that the .25 Beretta was not a stopping gun, and he places much more reliance on his accuracy with it than in any particular qualities of the gun itself. As you know, one gets used to a gun and it may take some time for him to settle down with the Smith and Wesson. But I think M. should advise him to make a change; as also in the case of the .357 Magnum.

He also agrees to give a fair trial to the Bern Martin holster, but he is inclined to favour something a little more casual and less bulky. The well-worn chamois leather pouch under his left arm has become almost a part of his clothes and he will be loath to make a change though, here again, M. may intervene.

At the present moment Bond is particularly anxious for expertise on the weapons likely to be carried by Russian agents and I wonder if you have any information on this.

As Bond's biographer I am most anxious to see that he lives as long as possible and I shall be most grateful for any further technical advices you might like me to pass on to him.

Again, with very sincere thanks for your extremely helpful and workmanlike letter.

Yours sincerely,

(Signed)
IAN FLEMING

G. Boothroyd, Esq.,
17, Regent Park Square,
Glasgow, S

PPK/S only) and black finishes, as well as several special-edition projects planned for the future. The standard caliber for the PPK and the PPK/S remains the .380 ACP or 9mm Kurz (Short).

"Having the PPK and PPK/S made by Walther allows us to have much better control over the quality of the pistol," said Bret Vorhees, director of product development for Walther Arms. "We are pleased to offer a higher quality product than what was previously available, which we feel the iconic PPK product line truly deserves. It is nothing less than legendary."

Clearly, the PPK established a defining influence on the design of concealed-carry firearms. Few guns have withstood the test of time like the reliably designed PPK and, to this day, the PPK is still one of the most sought-after concealed-carry pistols on the market. Walther Arms is justifiably proud of this series describing the PPK as one of the most iconic firearms still manufactured after 90 years. **GD**

Today, Walther Arms produces U.S.-made PPK and PPK/S models at its manufacturing facility in Fort Smith, Arkansas, allowing the company to maintain a consistent high quality for its products. Both models are available in stainless steel and black finishes and are chambered in .380 ACP or 9mm Short caliber.

DROPPING THE HAMMER: Perils and Pitfalls

The safety on the Walther PP/PPK is often referred to as a "hammer drop." It's common to simply thumb the safety and let the hammer snap downward. Most of the time, this leads to no obvious issues. The problem is that the hammer falls against a rigid piece of metal called the "safety spindle." Eventually, with enough stress, it's possible for the safety spindle to crack and break, which might cause the pistol to inadvertently fire. The problem is that there is no way to monitor this potential hazard from the outside. The safest method when you use the safety is to lower the hammer slowly.

(right) Hermann Goering's gold-plated Walther PPK, chambered for 7.65mm Browning (.32 ACP), is ornately engraved with a traditional Germanic oak leaf and acorn pattern. The gun, made in 1939, wears engraved ivory grips bearing Goering's initials on one side and his family crest on the other.

TWO
LEVER-ACTIONS
Tubular or box-magazine?

Picked up cheaply off a used-gun rack, this 60-plus-year-old Savage 99 in .300 Savage, "as is" with old 4X Redfield, groups plenty well enough for any likely purpose. Many thousands of well-worn lever-actions like this are still in use.

❯CRAIG BODDINGTON

Thanks to Christopher Spencer and B. Tyler Henry, the tubular-magazine lever-action was the world's first practical repeater. Spencer and Henry rifles were proved in the American Civil War. The self-contained metallic cartridge, initially rimfire, enabled the earliest lever-actions, and the centerfire cartridge enabled the greatly improved '73 Winchester. The tubular-magazine lever-action would be the dominant repeating action until about 1890, and would remain America's most popular sporting action for 50 years. The Model 1873 was manufactured continuously until 1923. Something like 720,000 were made, and copies are again manufactured today. Despite its obvious success, the "gun that won the West" had three design limitations, not all obvious in 1873.

This Marlin in .338 Marlin Express was one of the most accurate lever-actions the author has touched. Sighted 3 inches high at 100 yards, with 200-grain FTX bullets, it's a viable 300-yard elk rifle, which is really all you can ask of any lever-action.

NOT ENOUGH POWER!

First, action size. Winchester's .44-40 centerfire cartridge was a vast improvement over the mild .44 Henry rimfire, but it was still essentially a revolver cartridge, unable to compete with the large blackpowder cartridges developed for the big single-shot actions that dominated the last quarter-century of the blackpowder era.

Winchester's answer was the Model 1876 "Centennial," in many ways an enlarged 1873 action. The '76 action wasn't long enough to handle the .45-70 Government cartridge. Instead, Winchester developed a "family" of shorter-cased bottle-necked blackpowder cartridges sized to the 1876 action. First of these was the .45-75, which was similar in power to the .45-70, but loaded with a lighter 350-grain bullet because of action-length limitations. Other cartridges developed for the 1876 included the .40-60, .45-60 and .50-95 Winchester Express. The 1876 was a ground-breaking rifle in that it was the first repeater offering adequate power for large game, but its action was relatively weak and only 60,000 were manufactured.

A Colorado elk taken at about 200 yards with a .338 Marlin Express. The .338 ME didn't catch on, but it should have, and might yet. It's probably the most versatile cartridge ever developed for tubular-magazine lever-action rifles.

John Marlin's Model 1881 was actually the first lever-action strong enough and large enough to house the .45-70. More popular was the John M. Browning-designed Model 1886 Winchester. The rear-locking '86 was stronger than the toggle-action '76, and also larger. It was introduced in .45-70, .45-90 and .40-82, and was later chambered to the massive .50-110, which is the basis for Doug's Turnbull's .475 Turnbull. Still described as one of the smoothest of all lever-actions, the Model 1886 easily made the transition to smokeless powder. It was manufactured until 1935, and continued as the M71 in .348 Winchester until 1958.

Faithful copies of both the '86 and M71 are available today.

In North America few envisioned the lever-action as perfect for pachyderms, but the 1881 Marlin, the 1886 Winchester and the 1895 Marlin offered tubular-magazine lever-actions able to house cartridges suitable for anything in North America, and, with the right bullets and loads, anything else.

BLUNT BULLETS ONLY

Whether housed in the butt (like the Civil War Spencer) or under the barrel like most designs that followed, the tubular magazine seemed the answer. Even Peter Paul Mauser's first repeating bolt-action used a tubular magazine. So did France's 1886 Lebel in 8x50mmR, the first smokeless powder cartridge adopted by a major power.

Today the limitation seems obvious: In a tubular magazine, the nose of one cartridge rests against the base of the cartridge ahead of it. Detonation is thus possible with sharp-tipped bullets. Oddly, pointed bullets were virtually unknown until 1898. The generic term *spitzer* comes from German, but it was the French who first adopted a sharp-pointed bullet: *Balle D*, a homogenous-alloy brass boat-tail loaded in the 8x50R.

Detonation might have occurred during testing in the tubular-magazine Lebel. This was solved by a primer cover and a ring around the primer cup that caught the tip of the bullet behind it. The improved aerodynamics greatly improved long-range performance, especially for still-doctrinal volley fire and extreme-range machinegun fire. By the outbreak of WWI (in 1914) most major powers

had converted to spitzers, as did the U.S. in 1906. By then, most military rifles had box magazines, so the "French solution" wasn't necessary, but the inability to safely use aerodynamic bullets applied to all other tubular-magazine rifles past, present and future.

It was not solved until Hornady introduced its FTX (Flex-Tip eXpanding) bullet, 110 years after the development of the spitzer. FTX uses a compressible polymer tip that "squishes" sufficiently in the magazine to prevent detonation. The extension of this is the MonoFlex bullet, a homogenous-alloy version incorporating the compressible tip. Hornady's LeveRevolution factory ammo uses the tube-safe bullets and proprietary propellants that enhance velocity without increasing pressure. LeveRevolution ammo is now available in most traditional lever-action cartridges, and the bullets are also available as components.

On the one hand, these bullets solve the traditional problem of having to use blunt-nosed bullets in tubular magazines. However, it's not a complete solution because FTX and MonoFlex are just two bullet designs. You still can't use any projectile of your choice in a tubular magazine. Also, MonoFlex bullets are

currently only available in 140-grain, .30-caliber and 250-grain, .45-caliber. Here on the central coast of California we are in the "Condor Zone," mandating lead-free bullets for hunting since 2007.

A good California blacktail taken with a Winchester M88 in .308 Winchester. There isn't much that can't be done in North America with a .308 in any action type. The Winchester M88 sports a one-piece stock, rotary bolt and was chambered to versatile cartridges.

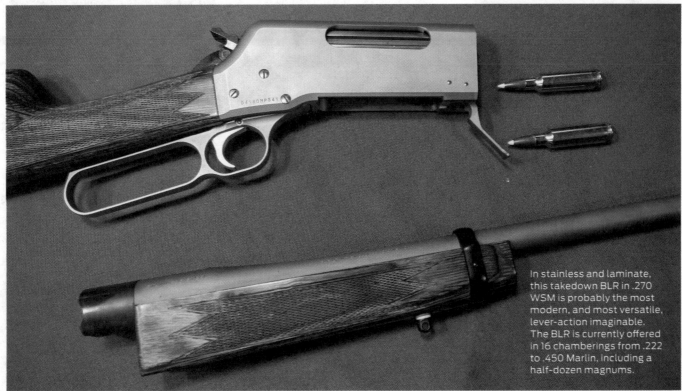

In stainless and laminate, this takedown BLR in .270 WSM is probably the most modern, and most versatile, lever-action imaginable. The BLR is currently offered in 16 chamberings from .222 to .450 Marlin, including a half-dozen magnums.

As of July 2019, unleaded projectiles must be used for all hunting in California. If you handload, there are flat-nosed copper bullets from Barnes and other specialty sources, but, for instance, there is no ready *unleaded* solution if I want to use my .25-35 for blacktails or my .348 for California wild hogs.

So, while Hornady's bullets and ammo are huge boons to lever-action fans, the problem of ammunition limitations still exists in tubular-magazine firearms. Thanks to the millions of Marlin and Winchester lever guns, most of us think of tubular-magazine rifles as the most traditional form. However, the tubular magazine is not a lever-action design requirement.

The problem was solved years before development of the spitzer bullet. Arthur W. Savage's rotary-magazine lever-action had been in development long before the introduction of his first production rifle, the Model 1895 Savage. The 1895 Savage was a success, leading with only minor modifications to the hundred-year run of the Savage 1899 and 99. The Savage design locked up via a massive bolt that mated into the rear of the action. It was very strong and would be chambered to cutting-edge smokeless cartridges: .250 Savage (1915), .300 Savage (1920). In later years it was chambered to the .243/.308 family of cartridges, and also to

the fast .284 Winchester. About 750,000 Savage 1899s and 99s were produced, with many still in use.

After the Model 1886, John Moses Browning designed Models 1892 and 1894 for Winchester, and then the Model 1895, with an in-line box magazine under the bolt. Both the Savage and the '95 were designed for smokeless powder. The 1895 chamberings included .30-40 Krag, .30-06, .35 Winchester and, of course, Teddy Roosevelt's "medicine gun" for lions, the .405 Winchester. Production continued until 1940, with numbers exceeding 425,000. However, this total includes some 300,000 7.62x54R rifles made for Imperial Russia.

So, there were two lever-actions suitable for all bullet types before spitzers were known. There would be more, but not many. Winchester's Model 88 was introduced in 1955 in .308 Winchester. It featured a rotary bolt and detachable-box magazine (as did later Savage 99s). Chamberings included .243, .358 and .284 Winchester. About 280,000 M88s were produced, so they are relatively available on the used-gun market. It was (and is) a good-looking, sweet-handling rifle. The only real drawback is the trigger mechanism is difficult to gunsmith.

I love Model 88s, but in the small world of "modern" lever-actions the Sako Finnwolf is even better. Among few non-

American lever-actions, the Finnwolf is a dandy, strong and accurate. It was manufactured between about 1959 and 1974, and chambered to .243 Winchester, .244 Remington and .308 and .358 Winchester. They're hard to find, but are excellent.

Savage 99s, Winchester Model 88s and Finnwolfs are only available on the used-gun market, with just two "modern" lever-action rifles currently in production. These are Henry's Long Ranger

All side-eject and angle-eject lever-actions can be readily scoped. Top, a new Marlin 1894 in .44 Remington Magnum with 1.5-6X Swarovski. Bottom, a vintage Savage 99 in .300 Savage wearing a 4X Redfield of similar vintage.

The author used a Doug Turnbull 1886 in .475 Turnbull to take this excellent Mozambique buffalo, using Barnes 400-grain flat-points. Lever-action rifles and cartridges are available that are suitable for just about any game, but the selection might be limited.

and Browning's BLR, which is probably the most versatile lever-action platform ever produced. Although never a huge seller, the BLR has been in production for more than 50 years. Variants include long-action and short, takedown models, pistolgrip and straight stock, stainless and blue. Current BLRs are chambered in 16 cartridges from .222 up to .450 Marlin. More interesting to me, the BLR is chambered to all the WSM cartridges, plus the 7mm Remington Magnum and

.300 Winchester Magnum. This suggests that the BLR could be rebarreled to any other standard-length belted magnum, including .458 Winchester Magnum. I don't know anyone who's done this, and since the BLR is pretty light, the result would be unpleasant, but I think it could be done with minimal gunsmithing. So, we can have lever-actions chambered to cartridges for just about any purpose, and we don't have to have lever-actions limited in the bullets they will digest.

NO SCOPES!

You don't know what you don't know. In 1895, I doubt Arthur Savage or John Browning knew that sharp-pointed bullets would soon come into widespread use. I doubt even more that they, or John Marlin, envisioned a time when optical sights would surpass iron sights for widespread use.

All the 19th century Winchester lever-actions, including the 1895, were top-eject, meaning they defied conven-

Despite range limitations, these two of the author's lever-actions will never wear optics. Top, a first-year production M71 .348 with bolt-mounted receiver sight. Bottom, a Savage 1899 .250-300 rifle with pop-up receiver sight. The M71 is top-eject; the 1899 could be drilled and tapped, but it was made 35 years before 99s were factory-prepped for optics.

tional over-the-receiver scope mounting. Telescopic sights were used in the Civil War, and some bison hunters used them. But it was well into the 20th century before manufacturers worried about facilitating scope mounting. To this day, you can't readily put a scope on a vintage Winchester.

I don't think John Marlin and Arthur Savage had better crystal balls than John Browning; I think they just got lucky. Marlin believed side-eject was better; all his lever-action designs from the Model 93 onward were side-eject, and Arthur Savage's lever-action also ejected to the right.

Older Savage and side-eject Marlins can be drilled and tapped for scope mounts. In time, this became a normal feature; in the 1950s, the Savage 99 was the first production rifle drilled and tapped for scope mounts as standard. About this time, and for the first time since 1894, Winchester started to see a decline in lever-action sales. The bolt-action, able to digest any bullet and just about any cartridge, was the new darling. Telescopic sights were coming into widespread use and soon would be almost universal.

A relatively simple engineering solution was close at hand but, inexplicably, Winchester didn't correct the situation until 1982, by which time lever-action sales were in the toilet and there was grim handwriting on the wall. The 1982 shift to "angle-eject" fixed the problem: The top-right receiver wall was dropped down, and ejection was directed up and right, enabling cases to clear a low-mounted scope. All 1894s since 1982 will

(left) Using tube-safe bullets with compressible polymer tips, Hornady's LeveRevolution line has given tubular-magazine lever-actions a new lease on life and is now available in most lever-action cartridges. Left to right: .25-35; .30-30 with both Monoflex and FTX bullets; .338 Marlin Express; .348 Winchester; .45-70 with both Monoflex and FTX bullets.

accept over-the-receiver scope mounts. All Mossberg 464s are angle eject, and all side-eject lever guns (starting with Savage and Marlin in the 1890s) are "scopeable."

Just as a thought: There have been 7.5 million 1894s sold, the most popular sporting rifle ever made. Imagine how many more there might be if Winchester had brought in angle-eject 30 years sooner, before lever-action sales really tanked.

RANGE

In any case, the only lever-actions that still resist conventional scope mounting are top-eject guns. These are mostly older, but include new remanufactured Winchesters. I didn't use to think this was a major drawback. Just about all cartridges top-eject rifles are chambered to are, in my opinion (and certainly for my use) at their best at short to medium range. For 40 years, I've generally put aperture sights on my top-eject lever-actions, and I've found them adequate *at the ranges I typically use these rifles*.

Well, that was when I could *see* iron sights! Recently, I discovered rather suddenly that I was having a terrible time resolving front sights. Time marches on. Light matters with all iron sights, but it

wasn't *that* long ago that I'd be confident to 200 yards with apertures, and something over 100 yards with open sights. Those days are *over*. A new eyeglass prescription helps tremendously, but, today, my range envelope is smaller with all iron sights.

Now, if you want more range you can put a scope on a Marlin or angle-eject rifle. And if you want a *lot* of range you can hunt up a Savage or Model 88 in a flatter-shooting cartridge, or get a BLR in a fast magnum. Thing is, we don't always need range. A little while back, I shot some Texas hogs with a Model 94 .30-30 using the traditional factory-issue buckhorn sights. I got within 60 yards, one shot per pig, no problems. At that range I'm still OK.

I have a takedown Savage 1899 .250-3000 with a pop-up receiver sight on the tang. This rifle is not drilled and tapped and will not be. I'll hunt with it this year, but I'll keep it close. My M71 .348 is also an aperture-sight rifle, and it's gonna stay that way. In my hands, it is no longer the 200-yard rifle it once was, but I'll hunt with it, I just need to get close and watch the light.

Those are both special rifles, but I don't have a thing about not putting optics on lever-actions. I have an Aimpoint on a

Mossberg 464 .30-30; it will do anything I need a .30-30 to do, in any light. I've used it for California hogs with Hornady's California-legal 140-grain MonoFlex load, and for my Kansas whitetail in 2019, an ancient cow-horn spike we've tried to get for three seasons. I've also used Aimpoints on Marlin .45-70s for our California hog hunting. Unlike aperture sights (especially these days), reflex sights are fine in bad light.

Depending on what I'm doing, I don't mind putting magnifying scope on lever-actions. I've been messing with a cute little 1894 Marlin .44 Magnum in stainless and synthetic. Accurate and very slick, it wears a 1.5-6X Swarovski. That probably sounds like too much scope for a little rifle, but I have it set up for first and last light on hogs, and it accounted for a nice Nebraska whitetail last fall just at sundown. We have another Savage 99 in .300 Savage, and this one wears a 4X scope, which is really plenty of scope for the rifle's purpose. This rifle was a good example of an ammo problem: I wanted to use it for California hogs, and although .300 Savage ammo remains available, *nobody* offers an unleaded load. I wasn't set up to load for it, so I called buddy Phil Massaro and he tightened me up with a batch of 165-grain GMX.

The Winchester M71 in .348 Winchester has been a favorite of the author for nearly 40 years. The .348 is fast, powerful and versatile, but the top-eject M71 defies conventional scope mounting. The author took this nilgai at nearly 200 yards, and admits he can no longer resolve iron sights well enough to reliably shoot that far.

ACCURACY

Lever-actions are not known for winning benchrest matches. Accuracy varies, but lever-actions have quite a bit going against them. Most have two-piece stocks, which makes bedding finicky. Rear-locking actions flex more than forward-locking actions. Although this is usually a minor factor in accuracy, rigid actions tend to group better. Then there's load variety, and load development. Other than Hornady's LeveRevolution, there hasn't been load development in cartridges like .25-35, .32 Winchester Special and .348 Winchester for genera-

tions. Even if LeveRevolution is fantastic, it's still just one load, likely to do better in one rifle than another. There is some selection in .30-30 and .45-70, but not much in other lever-action cartridges.

Of course, a "modern" box-magazine .308 lever-action can use the full range of .308 loads. Most of these rifles have two-piece stocks, but I expect all .308s to shoot well with something, and most of them do. Actually, whether tubular or box magazine, I've seen many lever-actions that group very well, but that depends somewhat on your expectations. How many of us shoot well enough to

know how accurate iron-sighted lever-actions really are? Usually they are accurate enough but, as with range, adequate accuracy depends on what you need. Most lever-actions shoot well enough, with some to spare.

When I use "modern" lever-actions such as Model 88s and BLRs I put "real scopes" on them. I expect them to shoot, and although I may need to work with the loads, they usually do. And sometimes lever guns surprise you. One of the most accurate lever guns I ever messed with was a stainless-and-laminate Marlin in .338 Marlin Express. It had everything going against it: tubular-magazine, two-piece stock and exactly one 200-grain FTX load to choose from. Didn't matter; it was a sub-MOA rifle and, if sighted 3 inches high at 100 yards, it was a 300-yard elk rifle. I should have bought it. I shot an elk and a Shiras moose with it and then, with some sobbing, I returned it.

A new Marlin "guide gun" in .45-70 with Aimpoint reflex sight easily passes the author's "paper-plate" test. The rifle is a great deal more accurate than this, but for the purposes he has for a .45-70 this is plenty good enough.

WHY A LEVER-ACTION?

If you find one that shoots like that Marlin, that's a silly question. But, realistically, most lever-actions don't shoot quite that well. Does it matter? Most lever-actions shoot plenty well enough to do their jobs, whether tubular or box magazines. If you want more you can keep messing with them and maybe they'll come around, but if you demand tack-driving accuracy, you might be better off with another action type.

Let's be honest: In part, I like lever-actions because they're fun. They're apple pie, motherhood and all those Western movies we grew up with. They also look good, feel good to carry and they're fast. Sort of. No lever-action is as fast as a semiauto or slide-action, and not much faster than a bolt gun worked properly, off the shoulder. But it's easier to learn to work a lever-action fast than it is a bolt gun, and after all, we've been trained watching all those Westerns. Within the capabilities of both the rifles and their cartridges, lever-actions work and make you feel good about using them. Maybe that's the best part of all. After decades of a very soft lever-action market, maybe that's why good old American lever guns are making a major comeback. 🄶🄳

An excellent Shiras moose, taken in snowy timber in northern Colorado with a Marlin in .338 Marlin Express and 200-grain FTX bullet.

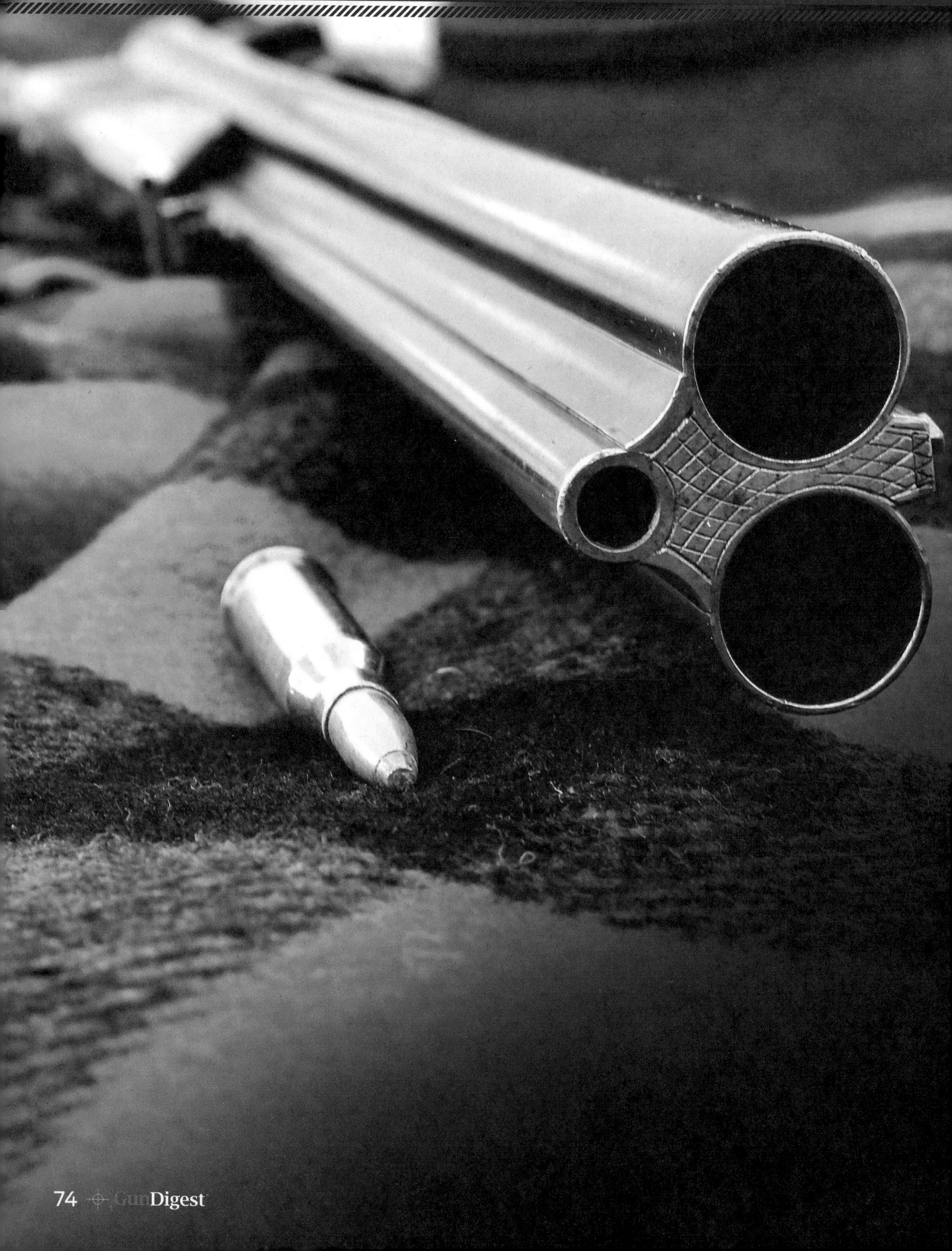

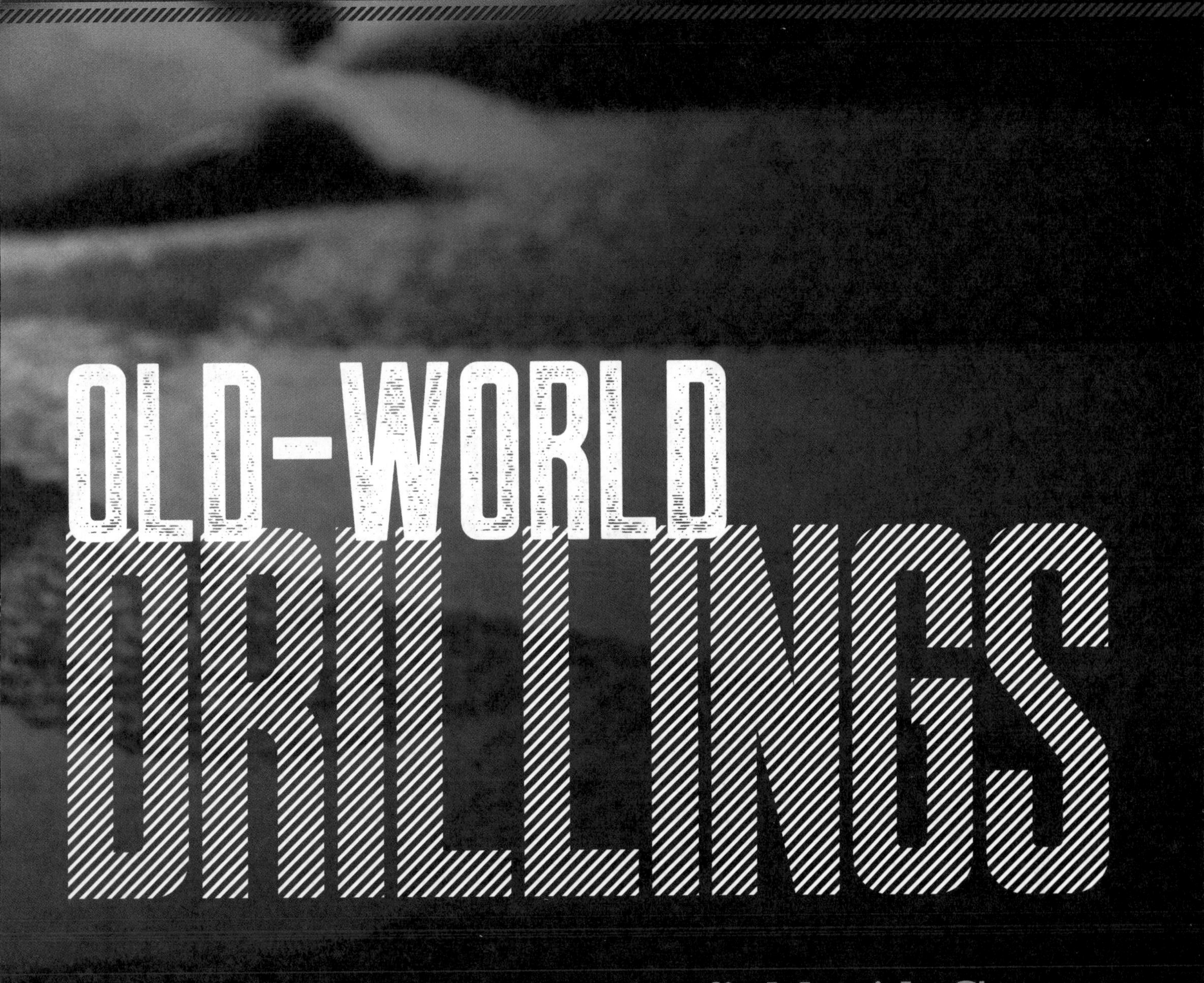

OLD-WORLD DRILLINGS

Back to the field with German-made, three-barrel long guns

> GARY LEWIS

Der *drelling*. The triplet. In hand, the three-barreled rifle/shotgun handled a bit like my favorite side-by-side shotgun, although heavier. Ahead of me, my 6-year-old Pudelpointer, a female descended from the old German line, cut back and forth. My hunting partners also carried drillings from the Old Country.

Two partridges skittered through the tall rye grass and flushed along the line of Russian olive trees. I rotated the safety through to "fire" and tried to pull the front trigger. It didn't fire. I looked down at the gun in my hands. Its front trigger was heavier than I had thought. I checked the barrel selector switch and it was set to "S" for shotgun. OK, then, try to do better.

We walked on about 50 yards and surprised a covey of California quail that erupted in front of the dog and passed over my partners on the other side of the tree line. Finney fired one barrel, tipping one bird; Chisel managed to fire the first barrel from his gun and forgot to change triggers for the second barrel.

We were learning.

AN INTRODUCTION TO DRILLINGS

Drillings were often custom-built and this one could have been custom-built for me. When it came to shoulder, the fine front bead was in perfect position over the plane of the sighting rib. But whoever this gun was built for might not have even used it much before he was shipped off to fight for the Kaiser.

Built in 1914, the drilling I carried came from Essen, the central and second largest city in the Ruhr, Germany's coal-mining and steel-producing powerhouse. The year 1914 was the first year of the Great War and it is probable that this was one of the last civilian market guns made until the cessation of hostilities in November 1918. The maker, Fr. Krupp, sold guns to Russia, Austria and the Ottomans and then later to Mexico, Spain, Greece and the Balkans.

As for the gun itself, it is not finished in as ornate a fashion as many drillings; it was probably used as a gamekeeper's gun or belonged to a working-class sportsman. The forearm is considerably darker than the buttstock wood, perhaps because that was where it was carried, or more likely it was made from another type of wood. Up top are two 16-gauge shotgun barrels with a rib equipped with rifle sights. The rifle barrel, chambered for 9.3x72R, is mounted beneath and between the shotgun barrels. Rather than using a Greener crossbolt, this box-lock gun relies on a "doll's head" locking lug with decorative scalloping on the breech face. Engraving is spare, save for an owl's face on the doll's head lug, decoration at the breech end of the barrels and around a pivot bolt head.

In the Fatherland, this gun might have accounted for partridge and roe deer, perhaps for wild boar and red deer. On stand, the hunter might have carried a Brenneke slug in one barrel and buck

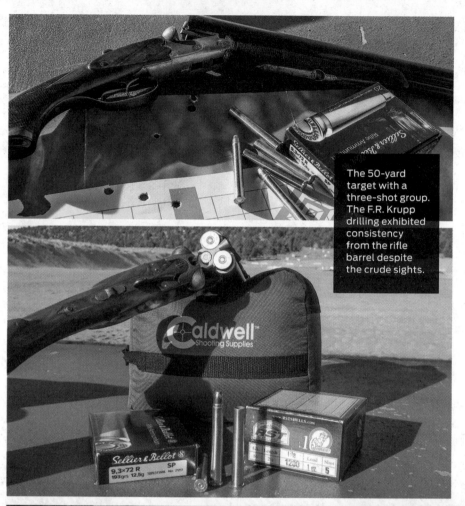

The 50-yard target with a three-shot group. The F.R. Krupp drilling exhibited consistency from the rifle barrel despite the crude sights.

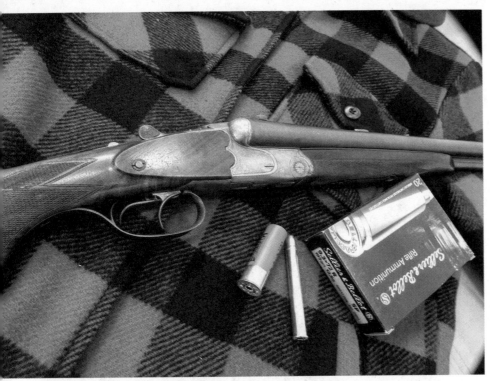

(above) Made with Essen steel in 1914, this F.R. Krupp drilling locks with a doll's head lug. Chambered for 16-gauge shotgun and the 9.3x72R cartridge, box lock exhibits sparse decoration. The rear sight must be flipped up manually when operating the rifle barrel using the K (Karabiner) setting.

(below) A Josef Just combination gun from the McFarland collection, this gun is equipped with a 16-gauge barrel and a rifle barrel chambered for the 7.72R cartridge. The gun is adorned with partridges and red deer on one side and rabbit and roe deer on the other.

shot in the other, while the rifle barrel would have been ready in case a longer shot was presented.

For this hunt, I used Sellier & Bellot ammunition loaded with a 193-grain bullet, in case there was a chance to shoot a badger, jack rabbit or coyote. The shotgun barrels were stoked with No. 5 RST loads for pheasant. If the tang-mounted selector switch is set to S, the shotgun barrels are controlled by the front trigger, which fires the right barrel, and the rear trigger, which fires the left barrel. Set the selector switch to K (Karabiner) and the front trigger fires the rifle barrel and the rear trigger fires the left shotgun barrel.

If the rifle barrel will be used, the shooter must remember to tip up the rear sight. On more expensive drillings, this feature is automatic to the operation of the barrel selectors. A safety switch, which arcs from safe (marked with an S) forward to fire, is positioned in the buttstock where a right-handed shooter might find it under the dominant thumb. On top of the lock, three cocking indicators protrude up from the action where the hunter can check the condition of the gun without looking at it. On top of the rib, integral scope mounts allow for mounting an optic. A sling swivel is mounted to the bottom of the rifle barrel and another swivel is in place in the stock.

While this might be a less-ornate gun than some drillings, it was certainly built for a discriminating hunter. And I appreciated the gun as I got to know it.

We hunted for partridge, pheasant, quail and jack rabbits on a preserve in southeast Oregon on a day when the mercury did not rise above freezing and the wind gusted up to 30 miles per hour. Seventeen-year-old Chisel McFarland carried a 16-gauge, 8x57JR Sauer made in 1936. Fifteen-year-old Finney McFarland was armed with a heavy three-barreled true 12-gauge shotgun drilling of modern manufacture by Chiappa and dubbed the Triple Crown. Twelve-year-old Katie, who has already hunted big game on two continents, did not carry a drilling because her dad is not willing to cut one off to a 12.5-inch length of pull. She hunted with a youth model semi-auto and was able to shoot her first pheasant on this hunt.

Matthew McFarland, the kids' father, and a collector of drillings and combination guns, sorted through his collection and selected for this trip a 16-gauge, 9.3x72R manufactured in 1925 after the war to end all wars. Each of the drillings on our hunt had its own characteristics with technology engineered to suit the individual gunmaker's vision of the best do-everything gun for the Germanic hunter.

Taking its name from the German word for triplet, the drilling (pronounce it "der drelling") is a break-action hunting gun with three (drei) barrels. Drillings might be any combination of shotgun and rifle barrels and are generally classed as shotgun drilling, over-and-under drilling or double-rifle drilling.

In its heyday, the drilling was a practical answer to a problem many hunters have encountered. Many types of game might be found in a hunting area, from partridge to rabbits to foxes to roe deer to wild boar to stags. On a stand or high sit in a Bavarian hunting reserve, a *jager* (hunter) might spend a day watching an opening and see all kinds of game pass by between dawn and dusk. With a proper all-purpose gun, the hunter could load a slug in one shotgun barrel, buckshot in another barrel and a big-game round in the rifle barrel. Another hunter on the same reserve might opt to load bird shot in one 16-gauge barrel, for pheasants or hares, load a 7x65R cartridge for deer and a rimfire .22 round for foxes.

The shotgun drilling has three shotgun barrels, perhaps with different gauges, but a shotgun drilling might also describe a double-barreled shotgun with a small rifle barrel between and below the shotgun muzzles.

An over-and-under drilling might employ a shotgun barrel above a rifle barrel with a small caliber barrel on one side. A common example might be a 12-gauge shotgun for shot with a .30-06 for big game and a .22 Magnum rimfire for smaller animals.

The double-rifle drilling is derived from a (side-by-side) double rifle with one shotgun barrel below. Various derivatives and versions of the drilling can be found in collections, but how they got to the United States is just as interesting.

Built sometime in the 1890s, this 16 gauge/43 Mauser drilling is marked H. Goez & CG Berlin. Opened via a Jones underlever, the barrels are Damascus steel. An elaborate horn is added behind the trigger guard. Engraving includes deer on one side and fox and partridges on the other.

This Blaser BD880 is of 1980s manufacture with a 16-gauge shotgun barrel, .30-06 barrel and another barrel sleeved for .22 Hornet. This variant is referred to as a Boch drilling. The barrel selector is on the side with a cocking device on the tang.

A post-war drilling manufactured in .30-06 caliber with twin 12-gauge barrels, this Franz Sodia, drilling is equipped with a Greener cross-bolt, tip-off scope mounts and automatic sight-in rifle mode.

When Germany surrendered to the Allies in 1945, wholesale confiscation resulted in thousands of privately owned firearms (yes, even hunting guns) being surrendered, and often turned to scrap. It was said hundreds of guns were lined up at a time and crushed by tanks. But many drillings were seized as war souvenirs and shipped home to the United States or Canada instead. It is likely some of the guns we hunted with on that cold day in January were "liberated" from their original owners in just this manner. These guns have histories that are hard for us to imagine until we take them back into the field.

Drillings were made by gun manufacturers in both Germany and Austria in times of peace when interest in hunting and target shooting was high and the economy was good. Austria's Ferlach, in the Klagenfurt-Land district, was home to gunmakers who specialized in drillings. Many German makers of drillings were associated with the neighborhoods of Suhl, which became part of communist East Germany after 1945.

Drillings represent a high point of the gunmaker's art. To build a pleasing combination gun or a drilling, or even a veirling (four barrels), requires the conjoining of steel, the integration of inner mechanisms and breeches and precise accurizing at hunting ranges. In addition, the guns are often built with the best wood available and engraved to a high degree, fitted to the customer's taste. To put the completed firearm in the hands of a hunter who will be happy to carry it afield is the ultimate test of the craftsman.

IN THE FIELD FOR PARTRIDGE AND PHEASANT

Muscle memory is a powerful force. While I am accustomed to shooting many different types of guns, the automatic reflexes take over when a bird is flushed. This gun, with a tang-mounted barrel selector in the spot I am accustomed to finding a safety switch, offered the distinct possibility I might switch from S to K and shoot the heavy rifle bullet at the pheasant instead of the shot. I found that as I approached the dog on point that to confuse my instincts, it helped to turn the gun on its side with my thumb on the knurled safety. With a bird in the air, it was a matter of a moment to slide the safety, orient the gun upright and find the bird over the bead.

After some trial and error, I was able to count a pheasant and a partridge to my score, while Chisel and Finney sorted out the issues of their guns and did at least as well, or better than I did. Their father, Matthew, who had hunted with drillings before, shot the birds we missed. The wind began to howl and pheasants and chukars going at least 20 mph, can be a hard target when they get a 30-mph wind gust behind them.

THE AMMUNITION

Drillings, and their kin, the combination guns and veirlings from Germany and Austria, can be found in private collections around North America. While the history of the individual firearm is a matter of conjecture, the gun can be taken back afield with a thought to its safety and condition, its collector value and the type of ammunition it was engineered to shoot. If it were not for a few companies that specialize in the proper care and feeding of these guns, ammunition would be very hard to come by.

Reed's Ammunition and Research (reedsammo.com), of Oklahoma City, offers loaded rifle ammunition in obscure metric and non-metric calibers. It is also a source for sub-caliber ammunition and 2- and 2-1/2-inch 12 gauge.

With a wide range of previously hard to find shotgun ammunition, RST Classic Shotshell Co. Inc. (rstshells.com), of Friendsville, Pennsylvania, can keep aficionados of antique shotguns in the field. Since many old shotguns and drillings are chambered for 2-1/2-inch cartridges, these guns are little more than wall-hangers unless ammunition can be found. Have a gun with Damascus steel barrels? There is a good chance RST has ammunition that will serve that old gun, too.

Similarly, Sellier & Bellot (sellierbellot.us), based in the Czech Republic, is keeping older calibers alive with a host of metric loads from the 6.5s to the 9.3s.

Another resource is Graf & Sons (grafs.com) with loaded ammunition for rifles and shotguns, as well as reloading components.

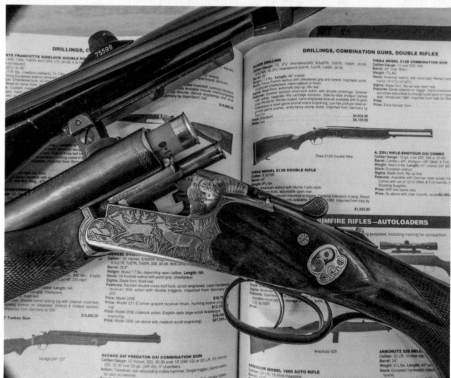

Jumping out of the pages of a past issue of *Gun Digest*, this Sauer Boch drilling is chambered for 16 gauge, 7.65R and .22 RF Magnum. Note tip-off scope mounts, tang-mounted barrel selector and side-mount safety selector.

This late-1940s manufacture Sauer drilling is chambered for twin 12 gauge and the 6.5x57R cartridge. One shotgun barrel is dedicated for a slug and one for buckshot.

This sparsely decorated circa-1936 Sauer was built in the Suhl district between the wars, chambered for 16 gauge and the 8x57JR cartridge. Note claw-mount scope and auto rear sight.

The owner or collector of drillings can learn quite a bit from reading the catalogs of these companies. In fact, these are the good old days for those who yearn to shoot their drillings. Just a few decades ago, it would have been difficult to find ammunition to feed a gun chambered for a 16-gauge chambered for 2-1/2-inch shells with a 7.72R or 9.3x72R rifle barrel.

CARE OF THE DRILLING

These guns are technologically more advanced than most other guns of their age. Blisters, loose rails and weak spots in the solder are indicators of possible problems. The inside of barrels and the muzzles are other places to check. Fitting of the wood might indicate issues with the gun and insertion tubes (if present) should be removed for detailed inspections. Can the gun be opened without problems after making a shot?

A good resource for the hunter or collector of drillings is *The Drilling*, by Norbert Klups (Schiffer Publishing Ltd, Pennsylvania, 2007). On the subject of care of the drilling, Klups recommends regular care of the barrels and shaft wood. The metal parts should always be wiped clean as hand sweat can work quick destruction on the old surface metal.

COLD-BARREL SHOOTING AT THE RANGE

In his book, Klups recommends shooting at least three-shot groups and always from a cold barrel. Matthew McFarland stressed the same thing because of the tendency of these guns to "string" their shots as the barrel heats up.

After our multi-species hunt, and without an opportunity to shoot a big-game animal or varmint with the 9.3x72R round, I took the drilling to the Central Oregon Shooting Sports Association range. Although the open sights on this drilling are crude by today's standards, the bead front sight is small and fine, the notch on the rear sight precise. The trigger must be set by nudging it forward. Then it breaks with a satisfactory touch.

To ascertain the fitness of the rifle for 100-yard shots with open sights, I shot the drilling from sandbags placed under the foregrip and under the butt, with the fingers of the left hand touching the wood only, and not the barrels. To maintain the integrity of the test, I loaded each of the shotgun barrels.

The first shot was at 25 yards where the bullet struck high and left out of a cold barrel. Determining the 50-yard shot would at least hit paper, I shot the next four rounds at 50 yards with a cooling gap of four to five minutes between each shot. At 50 yards, the shots grouped six inches high, an inch left of center. The four-shot group measured two inches. For my eyes and the crude sights, this did not seem too bad.

I waited five minutes before starting the next string and moved to the 100-yard target, which consisted of a two-inch orange dot against a whitetail deer paper target. At 100 yards, spacing the 193-grain shots four to five minutes apart, the bullets grouped 13 inches high and left. The shots grouped at a bit more than three inches. If I planned another hunt with this gun, the first task would be to mount rings and a scope. Or affix a bigger bead and an adjustable rear sight. I think the gun's inherent accuracy could be realized with a little work and a low-power optic.

The hunt in question? It would be somewhere in Germany or Austria. I would take a stand in a high *hochsitzen* and watch the edge of the *wald*. In the rifled barrel, I would load a 193-grain cartridge, while the shotgun barrels would be charged with a slug and double-ought buck. It would take practice at the range to develop the muscle memory to select the Karabiner barrel when the red stag showed at 120 meters along the tree line.

A gun for a multitude of purposes, the drilling might be tasked to shoot a roe or red deer, a partridge, a fox or a wild boar at any given moment. Beware the *jager* who owns only one *gewehr*. **GD**

With an old German drilling and a Pudel-pointer descended from the old German line, the author collected a couple of pheasants and helped to educate a few more.

A heavy three-barreled true shotgun drilling of modern manufacture by Chiappa and dubbed the Triple Crown.

To take his pheasant and a mallard, 17-year-old Chisel McFarland carried a 16-gauge X 8x57JR Sauer made in 1936.

(below) A German drilling, a Chinese rooster and a Himalayan chukar.

This rather plain drilling manufactured prior to the hostilities of 1914 proved to be a serviceable bird-hunting shotgun once the author grew accustomed to the stiff trigger and side-mounted safety. The rifle barrel was loaded in case a coyote or badger offered a shot.

In a hunting stand on the edge of the forest, a drilling might be loaded with a slug, shot and a rifle bullet

Sleeved with a shotgun, centerfire rifle and rimfire barrel, the 1950s Sauer drilling was ready for anything.

This picture was taken by Bill Strong on the hunt. From left, Hans De Young, Elmer Keith and H.L. Hart in 1919. This picture was included in Elmer Keith's book *Hell, I Was There!*, published in 1979.

ELMER KEITH'S DARKEST DAY

The famous gun writer experienced a tragic hunt as a young man

›FRED ZEGLIN

Before the United States joined the Great War, it was already obvious the U.S. would soon be involved. In May 1915, many prominent men in Helena, Montana, the state capitol, came together to restart the Helena Rifle Club, which took great pride in being associated with the National Rifle Association.

William R. Strong became secretary of the club. Members held matches and reported results to the local paper. Strong and his wife, Erma, were both active in the club. Results of matches frequently included H. L. Hart, Hans De Young, William Strong, Erma Strong and Elmer Keith among many others.

In the years just prior to World War I, Elmer Keith, who would become one of the most revered gun writers of all time, was avidly interested in all things to do with guns. He was acquiring, trading and shooting everything he could lay his hands on and, of course, he was hunting, too. This is testified to in his writings, particularly his 1974 autobiography, *Keith An Autobiography*.

Keith was 16 years old when that rifle club formed. Most of the members were older men and didn't want a kid hanging around. Bill Strong was one of the younger members, and he helped Keith convince others he would be a suitable member. It was agreed, if Keith qualified expert at the next annual match, he could join. He purchased a Krag rifle from the NRA for $1.50 and practiced.

At the annual match, Keith qualified expert using Bill Strong's Springfield 1903. Bill later helped Keith acquire a 1903 Springfield of his own. The military load in those years was a 150-grain flat-based bullet with a cupronickel jacket.

Bill became a close friend and mentor to Elmer. When Bill and his wife, Erma, had social events to attend, Elmer would sit with Bill's mother. She did not like to be alone.

In August 1917, Bill Strong, along with other Helena applicants, was selected for officers' training. They shipped off to the Presidio for the Third Officers' Training Camp in San Francisco, California, near the end of that month. Strong exited training at the Presidio with a commission as a first lieutenant of the infantry.

Belgian World War I Croix De Guerre (Cross of War). Awarded for bravery or other military virtue on the battlefield. Capt. William R. Strong received this medal for taking command when the officers of his unit were incapacitated.

Monture Creek Station as it appeared, circa 1920. Photo by Arthur M. Baum, Montana Historical Society Research Center Photograph Archives, Helena, Montana.

In the *Helena Independent Record*, Feb. 21, 1918, Strong credited his practice with the Helena Rifle Club as a major factor in his success. He qualified "expert" and came in sixth of a class of about 1,000 trainees. His first assignment was at Camp Lewis in Washington state, as the regimental range officer.

In April 1918, the Helena Rifle Club volunteered to train men at Fort Harrison, near Helena, where the club held matches. Keith spent Sundays on the range at the fort helping familiarize recruits with Springfield rifles. Time was limited so they focused on working with those who had little shooting experience.

When the 91st "Wild West" Division moved to the Atlantic coast in June 1918, Strong was the regimental supply officer for the 363rd Infantry. Soon they were shipped to France as part of the American Expeditionary Force.

During one battle, a company of Strong's regiment was moving forward under enemy fire. He went along, and all the officers of the command were shot down so Strong took command. For his actions in that battle, the Belgian government awarded him the Croix de Guerre (Cross of War). Strong saw action in the battles of the Meuse-Argonne, Saint-Mihiel, and others.

Strong received a field promotion to captain for his ability to move supplies to the men on the lines while under fire, and was cited for his actions. According to Keith, the promotion to captain came after the battle at Chateau-Thierry.

Keith said he wanted to volunteer for service, but his parents were dead set against it. So, he worked the ranch during the winter and in the summer of 1918 he ran pack trains for the United States Government Land Office, which in 1946 became part of the Bureau of Land Management.

Surveys Keith supplied were in what is now called the Bob Marshall Wilderness Area, starting from Ovando, Montana. Keith also packed for smoke chasers anytime a fire broke out in the backcountry. He mentions a large fire in the Babcock Creek drainage, so he was familiar with that country.

Strong returned to Helena in the summer of 1919. Keith's father had suggested

that he and his son (then 20) take Strong on an elk hunt along the South Fork of the Flathead River. Strong was set to go; then came to Elmer saying he had been approached by a couple of state officials to go hunting with them and he really couldn't refuse.

H. (Harlan) L. Hart, Montana state treasurer and Hans DeYoung, his chief clerk, were the men who were planning the hunt. Strong was listed in the 1917 Helena City Directory as a cashier for the state land office. Keith called Strong an accountant for the state. Strong made it clear he wanted Elmer on the hunt. The three agreed Elmer would pack the party for the hunt; DeYoung, Hart and Strong would split the cost of food and rental of additional pack animals.

Travel was different back then. They left Helena by train to Avon, then switched to stagecoach for Helmville and finally Ovando. They planned to head north up Monture Creek Trail to the Hahn Trail area and the Sullivan Cabin. From there, up Babcock Creek near the headwaters. On Oct. 15, they departed the Old McClain Ranch.

Keith said he and Strong both had premonitions of doom, saying there was something odd about how Hart kept talking about what to do, "if there were an accident." Over and over Hart talked about firing three fast shots to call for help. It was not long after leaving camp the first day Keith and Strong sat down and discussed the uneasy feelings they shared.

After talking, they set off separately hunting. Keith ran into a nice bull that afternoon. The story that ensues from the encounter is pure Keith. This was a 20-year-old with lots of youthful exuberance that clearly overshadowed any experience he might have had. A newspaper account reported: "Elmer Keith brought down one of the biggest bull elk ever brought out of the Ovando country and had a close call with the stunned bull before he finally brought down his meat."[1]

At about 75 yards, Keith raised his Springfield rifle, loaded with a 220-grain, soft-nosed bullets, and shot the elk. He heard the impact of the bullet hitting

---

1   *Helena Daily Independent*, October 24th, 1919

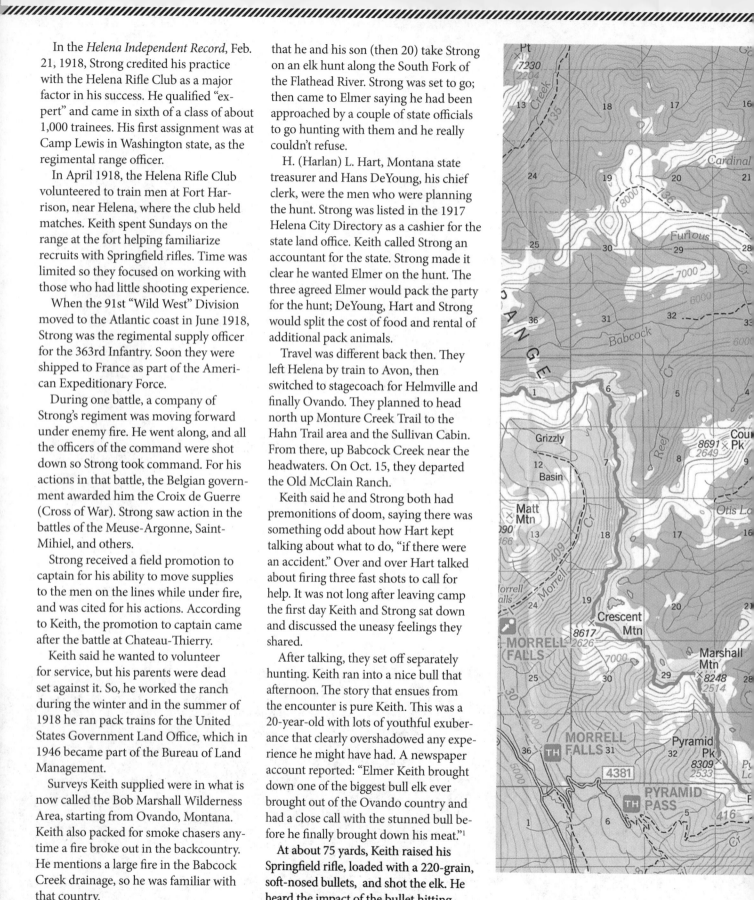

This map depicts the trail into the hunt area in what is today the southernmost part of the Bob Marshall Wilderness Area. Goat Mountain was mentioned in testimony as where H. L. Hart was hunting on the fateful day Strong lost his life. Elmer Keith and the others were north of Babcock Creek. (U.S. Forest Service Map)

the bull and saw him drop in deep snow. The big bull fell, head turned under his body. Keith approached and turned over the animal "like a fool." Suddenly, the big bull revived, stood up and charged him, rolling Keith down a steep hillside for at least 75 yards.

His rifle fell in the snow during the mix-up. Stunned by his tumble down the hillside, he recovered his senses seeing the bull stomping, as if trampling whatever had shot him. Keith pulled his Colt single action in .38-40, with alternating loadings of Remington factory nickel-primer, soft-nosed bullets, with smokeless powder, and his handloads containing a 260-grain .40-82 bullet sized down, over 40 grains of black.

Keith cocked the Colt, which drew the bull's attention. The first round up was a Remington factory round, he shot and hit the bull in the forehead. After shaking his head, the bull charged. The second round went in a little low, missing his brain, but it knocked him down. The bull slid to a stop next to Keith.

Ovando City Center in 1919. (Photo courtesy of Brand Bar Museum, Ovando, Montana)

Elmer Keith with a spike whitetail buck taken for camp meat on the hunt in 1919. Keith used this image in his 1974 book, *Keith An Autobiography*. Photo by William R. Strong.

The young hunter learned from his mistake. He backed away from the bull, reloaded his pistol and tied down his holster so it would not move around. Locating his rifle, Keith had to clear the snow from its bore, before reloading it. By now the elk had been down for a bit, head under the snow again. This time approaching from the rear, Keith poked the bull in the rump with the muzzle of his Springfield. The bull lashed out with its hind feet and sent Keith rolling.

He lost his rifle again, so when he came up, he pulled the .38-40 and started firing again. The first shot was one of those low-powered factory loads. The bull was unaffected. The next two shots were Keith's blackpowder loads. They penetrated. The third shot broke the bull's neck.

These events took place before Elmer Keith had written a single line. He was a cow puncher, guide and packer at the time. In short, his fame was still years away.

Plot twist. Rod Strong of Salmon, Idaho, the grand-nephew of Bill Strong, donated a letter from Keith to Gen.

George V. Strong (Bill's brother and Rod's grandfather) to the Brand Bar Museum, Ovando, Montana. Dated July 10, 1944, that letter is the source of details below.

The day after Keith killed his elk, he and Capt. Strong skinned and quartered the bull, by then it was late and spitting snow. Strong suggested they blaze trail for a horse. They moved straight downhill from the elk. On the flat, little more than a bog with a tangle of downed trees, they marked trees with a belt ax. Visibility was bad; maybe 60 yards. The ax made plenty of noise anyone could hear.

After some time blazing the trail, Strong stopped Keith and broke a chocolate bar in half for them to share. Strong stepped ahead of Keith as they passed a large spruce tree. He suggested he could pick a horse route while Elmer blazed behind, saving time.

As Strong was stepping ahead of him, Keith said he smelled the strong scent of elk. He started to whisper to Bill to get his rifle ready. Later, Keith said he found elk tracks not three feet from where Bill was standing. While he was whispering, Keith heard a bullet go between him and the spruce tree. He believed it was within a foot of him.

Strong was hit in the back, about center of his right lung. Strong gasped, doubled up and fell backward. Keith dove behind the spruce tree, drew his sixgun and fired three rapid shots in the air and began yelling to "Stop shooting! Someone killed my partner!" He said there was no answer even though he repeated yelling the warning.

Now Keith saw red, he took his rifle off his back and crawled, circling behind where he believed the shot originated. He thought perhaps an Indian had shot Bill for his rifle. He found the empty case from the cartridge that shot Bill at about 60 paces away. From that location, Keith said the shooter could not have seen more of Bill's back than a patch about the size of a man's hand.

It's hard to say from Keith's writings if the visibility was limited because of timber and brush or fog and rain, perhaps a combination. He spotted brush moving and held his sights on the spot waiting to see what or who emerged. To his surprise, out stepped Hans DeYoung. Keith yelled at him. When DeYoung saw that Keith had a rifle on him, he stopped.

Keith yelled, "You shot Bill."

DeYoung responded, "NO!"

Keith repeated, "You shot Bill."

Keith said DeYoung moved his rifle as if he planned to shoot himself. Approaching warily, he talked Hans out of harming himself. Keith said he had to force DeYoung go along to aid Bill. Keith stated he personally did all he could to care for his friend and try to stop the bleeding. Strong was still holding on to life.

Keith noted DeYoung appeared overcome with grief, yet, unwilling to touch Strong. Keith asked him to return to camp and bring back Strong's medicine kit, food, blankets and H. L. Hart. It was dusk and was raining. DeYoung said he couldn't do it. He agreed somewhat reluctantly, according to Keith, to care for Strong while Keith went for help.

It was about three miles to camp, the first mile through the bog. Keith fired three fast shots every five minutes or so along the way as Hart had been so careful to instruct daily. He found Hart cooking dinner and asked if he had heard the shots? Hart said, "Yes, but I supposed you had killed your elk and were celebrating." This angered Keith. He responded "I don't waste ammo, especially in game country."

Keith told Hart what had happened. He comments in the letter to Strong's brother, that even then it did not seem as though Hart showed much surprise. Keith gathered up the medicine kit, whiskey, blankets and an ax. He asked Hart to follow with more bedding and food. Hart said he could not make it up there in the dark, so Keith left without him, double-timing it back to DeYoung and Strong.

DeYoung had built a fire near Strong. Keith inquired, "How's Bill doing?" DeYoung responded, "He only lived a minute or so after you left." Keith asked, "Why didn't you get your rifle and call me back?" DeYoung didn't answer the question.

An hour later, Hart showed up with a flashlight. Neither man helped as Keith dragged their friend's body out of the logs so he could lay him out and wrap him in a blanket. The only aid they provided was to hold the flashlight. Keith was drenched in sweat and blood, so he dried out by the fire. Hart wanted to return to camp. Keith angered and said no man would leave there that night alive.

The next morning, they started the process of getting help and packing out. Keith wrangled horses and Hart offered to ride for Sullivan's Cabin. Hart said there was a phone there and the McKinnon hunting party might be able to help. Hart promised to return, instead he continued on to town after meeting McKinnon's party.

The packer for the McKinnon party, Earl Watts, a resident of Ovando, agreed to pack Strong's body. Keith said putting his friend on the pack horse and tying a three-quarter diamond hitch over him, "took about all the heart out of me." Watts took Strong's remains to Ovando with little rest along the way.

The Powell County coroner held an inquest at Ovando, taking testimony concerning transportation of the body, and its identification.

Hart testified: *"I came in from hunting Sunday evening about five o'clock and*

Sullivan's Cabin, circa 1920. Maps indicate this was the only phone line into the area at the time. Photo by Arthur M. Baum, Montana Historical Society Research Center Photograph Archives, Helena, Montana.

while cutting wood for the camp heard several shots in the direction I thought the rest of the boys were hunting in. Three of the shots came in rapid succession and then I heard a noise as if somebody were yelling or hollering; I didn't know what the shots were for because the party had already killed three elk. Unless is was that the boys were shooting to celebrate the killing of a fourth elk.

"A short time later Elmer Keith came rushing into camp and reported that Strong had been accidentally shot and wanted me to go for assistance. I sent what medicine we had in camp and a Red Cross First Aid Kit back with Keith. I knew he would get to the scene of the accident first and then I followed.

"When I arrived at the site, I found Keith crying and DeYoung in a nervous and much excited condition. It took a while to quiet Hans down so he could tell me what happened. Hans told me that he fired the shot that killed Strong and that he thought he was an elk. DeYoung said that Strong never spoke and was apparently never conscious after the hit."

Hart drew a diagram (not found in the files) for the inquest which showed that Keith and Strong were cutting trail on the same side of the creek that DeYoung was hunting on. Hart testified further that DeYoung told Hart: "I heard a noise below and seeing a light colored object in the brush fired at what I supposed to be an elk." Strong was wearing a buckskin shirt and had his gun slung over his shoulder, suspended by a strap, the gun barrel sticking up, which, to DeYoung looked just like the antlers of an elk.

Doughboy with a Springfield M1903, similar to the one Elmer Keith borrowed from Bill Strong to qualify as an expert and earn membership in the Helena Rifle Club in Montana. (Photo courtesy Library of Congress)

If you ever stop in Ovando, Montana, this little museum is worth your time.

Hart continued: "We had no outfit (vehicle) in camp. So, I went to Sullivan Cabin to seek help from the S. McKinnon party, I secured the services of his packer, Mr. Earl G. Watts, to bring the body to Ovando."

The inquest was continued until Keith and DeYoung packed out. It took three days for Keith and company to pack out, along with the remainder of McKinnon's camp.

Hart made a beeline for Helena. Keith and DeYoung were deposed at the coroner's inquest on Oct. 27. Keith testified first; his testimony raised no questions as to the suspicions Keith tells about in later writings. The questions were not designed to elicit new information.

DeYoung took the stand last. His statements contradict some details from Keith's telling, but not any testimony at the inquest. What follows is derived from that testimony, assembled for ease of reading. The questions asked of DeYoung did not push for any details that would check his story against Keith's or Hart's testimony.

"Sunday October 18th, I left camp before the others. I knew the country so I directed the others where to hunt. I sent Hart up in the direction of Goat Mountain and told Strong to go with Keith to help him with his elk.

"I should say, I thought I was hunting about three miles above Keith and Strong. My position above Babcock Creek was about a half mile up hill. There are some little parks there that I hunted. I saw several elk that day. I had shot at a bull on Saturday and thought I might have wounded him. Sunday I hunted higher; coming down the ridge I jumped two elk. I got a shot at one, and killed and gutted him and started after the other. I jumped him two or three times but never got a shot. Followed him again and took another shot at him.

"Just then, Elmer yelled that I had shot Bill. When I shot I was between fifty and seventy-five yards from him, I think. It was a heavy spruce and underbrush thicket. When I got to Bill I got him some water but saw there was no use as the wound would be fatal. I cut off a piece of my legging and tried to stop the blood but there was no use."

Ultimately the coroner's inquest jury found the shooting was an accident. No criminal charges were recommended.

Hart and DeYoung refused to pay for the expenses of the trip. They billed Capt. Strong's wife, who was five months pregnant, for the entire trip. She received an itemized bill that included the cost of packing out her husband's body from the wilderness. Keith intimated he learned things which convinced him something nefarious took place, as far as this writer could tell, he never told what it was that he learned beyond their act of refusing to pay for the trip.

Keith told of going to Hart and DeYoung about the bill they sent to Mrs. Strong, asking them to split it with him. Hart told him, "Oh, she's got insurance. She may just as well pay for part of it."

Keith responded, "Hell, it's all of it!" Hart and DeYoung never did pay, and Mrs. Erma Strong told Elmer she would not take his money, as he had done more than his share.

Capt. William R. Strong's daughter was born in December 1919, two months after her father's tragic death. Erma named her Billie; she sadly passed away at the tender age of five. According to Keith, Billie was born premature and was a tiny little wreck until her death. She is buried alongside her father in the Forestvale Cemetery in Helena, Montana.

Keith wrote to Gen. Strong, "The trip and its tragedy are one of the blackest pages in my life. Though I may be wrong, have never been able to reconcile myself on the accident angle, especially after what followed." GD

Forestvale Cemetery in Helena, Montana, where both William and Billie Strong are buried.

This fantastic rifle began as a desire from a client of Reto Buehler. The client had commissioned two big-game rifles from Reto previously and he expressed a desire to have Reto build him a full-sized rifle, but chambered for the diminutive .22 LR rimfire cartridge. Reto couldn't resist the challenge. He started with a Springfield M22 training rifle and transformed it into the magnificent rifle shown here. It has all the bells and whistles of an express rifle, but chambered for the rimfire cartridge. All work by Reto Buehler.

Photos by Brian Dierks

CUSTOM AND ENGRAVED GUNS

Our annual review of the finest examples of beauty and artistry in the world of custom guns

Reto Buehler

(right top & bottom) A typical Buehler British Express rifle, using a Granite Mountain Arms (GMA) small-ring action, Pac-Nor barrel and custom-machined quarter rib, front sight ramp and barrel band. Turkish walnut stock with 24 lpi checkering and light engravings done by John Todd. The GMA factory bottom metal was replaced with a Blackburn/Swift drop-box magazine.

Photos by Brian Dierks

Brian Powley

The Engravers' Choice Award of Merit at the annual Firearms Engravers Guild of America (FEGA) Exhibition of 2020 was presented to Brian Powley for his masterful engraving of this Colt Single Action, .38 caliber. Brian executed his engraving pattern in keeping with original factory Colt styling. He did an outstanding job.

Photos by Sam Welch

Brian Hochstrat

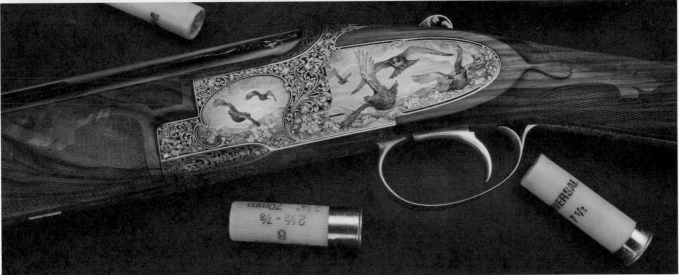

Brian Hochstrat knows his way around an engraving bench to be sure. A former professional bull rider, Brian learned early on there had to be a better way to make a living, and took up the art of engraving. This Browning O/U is an example of how he has mastered his art. To use the term magnificent is not strong enough to describe his work. This Browning was awarded the Best Engraved Shotgun prize and the Engravers' Choice Award of Merit by his peers.

Photos by Brian Hochstrat

Lee Griffiths

Lee Griffiths is one of the most talented and most unique engravers I know. It doesn't take a lot of experience viewing his artistry to be able to discern his work from across a big room. At the recently concluded FEGA Exhibition, Lee received two awards, the Artistic Uniqueness Award and the Best Engraved Single Shot Rifle Award.

Photos by Sam Welch

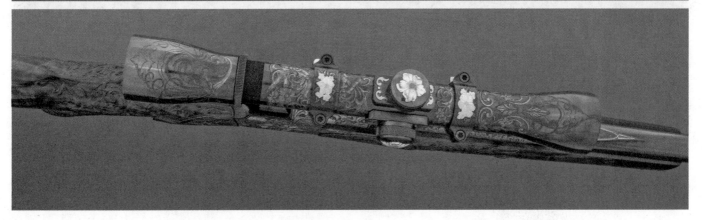

Gordon Alcorn

Gordon Alcorn was awarded the Best Engraved Knife Award at the 2020 Firearms Engravers Guild of America (FEGA) annual exhibition. He performed his highly talented magic on a Tom Buckner titanium beauty.

Photo by Sam Welch

Marty Rabeno

A typical example of Marty Rabeno's outstanding artistry on one of his favorite canvases, a Winchester Model 1876. I've seen quite a number of engravings done by Marty and most all have been on lever-action Winchesters. This exquisite '76 won the award for Best Engraved Rife and also the Engravers' Choice Award of Merit at the recently completed Firearms Engravers Guild of America (FEGA) Exhibition.

Photo by Sam Welch

Dale Bass

This Remington .45 ACP was beautifully engraved by Dale Bass of Amarillo, Texas. His work is new to me, but he is obviously turning out excellent engraving. This 1911 would look great in anyone's collection.

Photos by Sam Welch

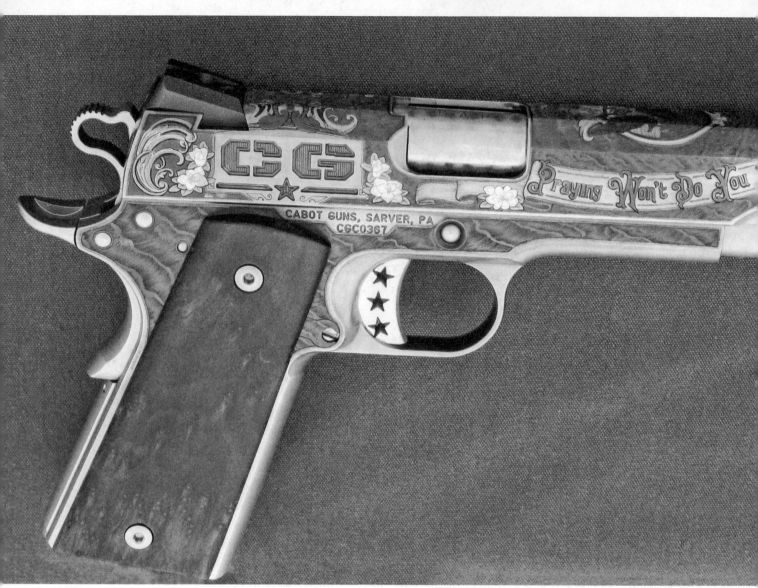

Melissa McMinn

Melissa McMinn is another engraver who is new to me. While I had not previously seen her work, I do know the engraver who mentored her, John Barraclough. Her unique styling is not often seen, but it is exceptionally well-executed. This Cabot 1911 that she embellished won the Best Engraved Handgun Award at the FEGA Exhibition.

Photos by Sam Welch

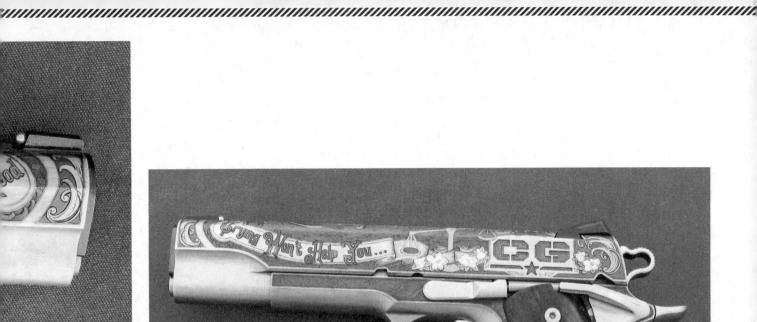

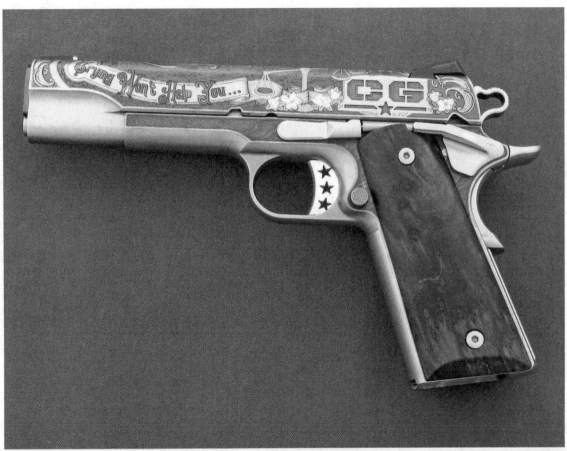

LOVE IT OR HATE IT, THE 6.5 CREEDMOOR IS HERE TO STAY

A big plus for the 6.5 Creedmoor is its ability to chamber in AR-platform rifles such as this CMMG Mk3 rifle, which has a 20-inch barrel, single-stage trigger and A2 furniture and compensator.

The popular caliber from Hornady continues to be a favorite with hunters and target shooters

❱ MIKE DICKERSON

I f you spend much time on social media, you've probably seen some of the memes portraying the 6.5mm Creedmoor cartridge as an effeminate or nerdy-looking guy. The unspoken implication is that anything that kicks less than an angry zebra is somehow unmanly.

I beg to differ, and when people ask me about the 6.5 Creedmoor, I respond with a much more accurate comparison. The 6.5 Creed, I tell them, is a lot like former New England Patriots quarterback Tom Brady.

Now, before you alert the authorities to come cart me away for a mental evaluation, allow me to explain. Brady was never the strongest or fastest quarterback in the NFL, but for most of his career he has been accurate, efficient and tough on the competition. So has the 6.5 Creedmoor. Some people are ready to crown Brady the greatest of all time, and more than a few people view the 6.5 Creedmoor as the greatest 6.5 cartridge ever. Of course, Brady also has more than his share of haters, often for reasons that have little logical basis, and so does the 6.5 Creedmoor.

No other cartridge in living memory has sparked such an explosion in popularity (or incited as much animosity) as the 6.5 Creedmoor, and no other cartridge with "mm" in its caliber has captured the hearts of American shooters like the 6.5 Creed. I became intrigued with the cartridge early on and have spent the last several years engaged in what amounted to a long, extended field test of the cartridge. That was partly by choice and partly because that's what rifle manufacturers were sending me. There was a time when new rifle models were almost always first chambered in .30-06 Springfield. Today, they're just as likely to be chambered in 6.5 Creedmoor, and I've spent so much time shooting guns in the chambering that one outdoor publisher joked that I was turning into the Elmer Keith of the 6.5 Creedmoor.

I suspect old Elmer would not have been a fan of the 6.5 Creed, as he preferred to punch very large holes in things, but you can't put as many rounds downrange and kill as much game as I have with this cartridge without forming some conclusions. Before we get to those, a quick review is in order.

The 6.5 Creedmoor was developed in 2007 by Hornady engineers Dave Emary and Joe Thielen for the specific purpose of winning competitive shooting matches, and that's exactly what it did, outperforming rounds like the .308 Win. As America's interest in long-range shooting blossomed, so did the fortunes of the 6.5 Creed, and it didn't take long for hunters to discover and take advantage of the cartridge's considerable attributes. Based on a modified .30 Thompson/Center case, the round holds a bit less powder than a .308 Winchester, but can seat long, high-ballistic-coefficient bullets in the magazines of short-action rifles without having to yield much in case capacity. Compared to the .308 Win., it has a flatter trajectory and better resistance to wind drift. It is, in a word, efficient.

ACCURACY IN SPADES

The 6.5 Creedmoor is also an inherently accurate cartridge. I didn't realize just how accurate it truly was until I looked at the data from the last dozen rifles I tested that were chambered for the cartridge.

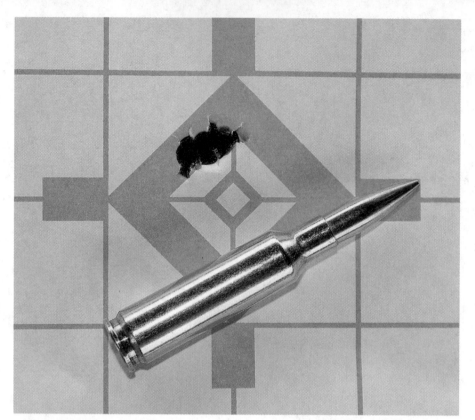

(top) The 6.5 Creedmoor is an inherently accurate cartridge, as demonstrated by this Nosler 140-grain load.

(above) One thing the 6.5 Creedmoor has going for it that previous 6.5 cartridges didn't is widespread availability of affordable factory ammo, and affordable rifles, that shoot with superb accuracy.

The 6.5 Creedmoor works as well on predators as it does on deer-size game. The author shot this 45-pound coyote in Texas with a Bergara B-14 BMP chassis rifle.

(below) The author's long-running field test of the 6.5 Creedmoor continued recently when he took this Axis deer in Texas with Hornady's 143-grain ELD-X Precision Hunter load.

With price tags ranging from as little as $300 to more than $3,000, these guns included models from Nosler, Savage, Mauser, Ruger, Mossberg, Remington, Bergara, Thompson/Center, CMMG, Smith & Wesson and Browning. All 12 guns were tested at the standard distance of 100 yards, with at least five different factory loads, shooting three groups per load.

When I crunched the numbers, I was somewhat stunned to discover that the average group size, for all loads tested for all rifles, was just 1.05 inches. That's an eye-popping number considering the odds against 12 different off-the-shelf factory rifles shooting that consistently well with a variety of factory loads.

But that tells only part of the story. When I computed the average group size for each load that each rifle liked best, the overall average shrank to 0.77 of an inch. Looking at only the best single groups turned in by all 12 rifles, the average shrinks to 0.52 inch of an inch, with seven of the rifles printing best groups measuring less than half an inch and four shooting best groups measuring 0.30 of an inch or less.

I can assure you I would be hard-pressed to duplicate that performance with factory ammo and a dozen factory rifles shooting other long-established cartridges intended for use on medium-sized game. Notably, only one of the tested rifles could be considered a match rifle. Two were AR-platform guns and the remainder were bolt-action hunting rifles.

The ability to readily chamber ARs for 6.5 Creedmoor is another big plus for the cartridge, and that fact has not escaped the attention of the U.S. military. U.S. Special Operations Command tested the 6.5 Creed in 2017, pitting it against the 7.62 NATO and .260 Rem. The 6.5 Creed came out on top, doubling hit probability at 1,000 meters over the 7.62 NATO, with less recoil and wind drift, and USSO-COM is adopting the round for use in a number of rifle types. The Department of Homeland Security is dumping all of its 7.62 NATO ammo and replacing it with 6.5 Creedmoor.

SOFT KICKER, SOLID HITTER

The 6.5 Creed is kind to barrels and easy on the shoulder with significantly less recoil than .308 rifles of the same weight. That mild recoil can enhance accuracy and enable hunters to place bullets precisely when it counts. It is, after all, not the size of the hole that matters, but where it's located. Bullets used in the 6.5 Creedmoor, optimally pushed through zippy 1-8 twist barrels for bullets in the 140-grain class, have a high ballistic coefficient, but they also have high sectional density, which translates into better penetration than lighter bullets with a lower sectional density. The result is impressive terminal performance on game. I have, to date, shot some large mule deer, whitetail deer, axis deer, hogs and coyotes with the 6.5 Creedmoor, and in every case where I did my job behind the trigger, the animals never took more than a few steps.

I suspect that one of the factors motivating the anti-Creedmoor crowd was the number of people who pronounced the 6.5 Creedmoor to be the .308 killer, or who asserted that it would hasten the demise of other cartridges. No one likes to hear their favorite cartridge is going to be replaced by a newcomer, and reactions were predictable. The 6.5 Creedmoor cer-

The well-appointed Ruger American Go Wild rifle was one of the more affordable 6.5 Creedmoor rifles the author tested, and one of the most accurate.

tainly hasn't killed off the .308, but it has cut into its sales and likely further marginalized some cartridges that weren't doing all that great to start with.

Some people will still tell you with a straight face that the 6.5 Creedmoor is just a fad. If so, as of this writing, that fad

This Hornady 143-grain ELD-X bullet performed perfectly and was recovered from the offside hide of an axis deer shot by the author at 150 yards.

Browning's X-Bolt Long Range Hunter in 6.5 Creedmoor was one of the rifles the author tested at the range. Four of five factory loads produced sub-MOA average groups, and the only one that didn't barely missed the mark.

is in its 13th year and shows no sign of diminishing. Ammo makers guard sales figures like the Crown Jewels, but several I spoke with confirmed the round's front-runner status. A Federal ammunition representative told me the 6.5 Creedmoor ranks among the firm's top-five-selling cartridges overall and is the number one short-action centerfire round. A Remington spokesman said the cartridge is selling at a pace two-to-three times greater than the .308 Win., and is holding steady. "We can't make enough of them," he said. As for Hornady, the originator of the cartridge, "We're in the same boat as the others," a spokesman said. "We technically

move more rounds of .223/5.56, but the 6.5 Creedmoor is our biggest centerfire round outside of that."

Part of the backlash against the 6.5 Creed might be viewed as a reaction to those who hailed the cartridge as the Holy Grail for long-range hunters. There's no doubt that the round excels at punching targets at 1,000 yards, but there are obviously more potent choices available if you are one of those who specializes in shooting game at truly long distances.

I am not one of them, and neither are the majority of American hunters. For most of us, normal shooting distance for medium-sized game is 300 yards or less. When you're taking game at this distance, or are competent enough behind the trigger to stretch your reach a few hundred yards farther, the 6.5 Creed shines.

Out of a 24-inch barrel, Hornady's 143-grain ELD-X bullet (an excellent hunting bullet) launches at 2,700 fps and will impact at 500 yards with a bit more than 1,300 ft-lbs of energy, which is well above the often-quoted minimum of 1,000 ft-lbs for deer-sized game. At 400 yards, the bullet hits with 1,475 ft-lbs of energy, which is just slightly below the 1,500 ft-lbs threshold quoted for elk. Of course, game animals don't read energy charts, and a lot of hunters have killed elk, black bears, moose and African plains game with the 6.5 Creed. The key to taking game cleanly, with any cartridge, is to place properly constructed bullets precisely where they are supposed to go, and the 6.5 Creed gives hunters the ability to do that thanks to its accuracy, mild recoil and ability to buck the wind.

The success of the 6.5 Creedmoor has arguably helped to inspire ammo makers in developing even newer 6.5 cartridges that can be viewed as the 6.5 Creedmoor on steroids. These include Hornady's 6.5 PRC, which exits the muzzle 260 fps faster with the same 143-grain ELD-X bullet; the 26 Nosler, which steps out at 3,300 fps with a 140-grain bullet; and the new speed king of 6.5 cartridges, the 6.5-300 Weatherby Magnum, which sizzles along at 3,395 fps with a 140-grain bullet. These cartridges all have their purpose, but they won't make deer any more dead at normal hunting distances, and they come with a corresponding increase in recoil and potentially shorter barrel life.

SUCCEEDING WHERE OTHERS HAVE FAILED

The 6.5 Creedmoor is, without question, the first 6.5 round to achieve the level of popularity it currently enjoys in the United States, and it has succeeded where others have failed. The 6.5x55 Swedish, for example, was quite popular in Europe, but was never embraced to the same extent by American shooters. Neither the 6.5 Rem. Mag. nor the .264 Win. Mag. set the world on fire with American shooters. Of the 6.5 cartridges that preceded the Creedmoor, the .260 Rem. was the most successful, particularly in competitive shooting, but it never caught on with hunters to the extent that the 6.5 Creedmoor has.

Some people will tell you the 6.5 Creed's success was the result of brilliant marketing, but Hornady has a ready response to that. "It's always entertaining to see people claim the 6.5 Creedmoor success is based off of Hornady marketing hype," said company spokesman Neal Emery. "We launched it in 2007 as an across-the-course cartridge and did a bit of advertising that year and the year after. It wasn't a huge, major launch by today's standards. It didn't immediately sell well. That took years. What made it popular was that it shot well in virtually all the guns it was chambered in. It was made to. Between the location of the bullet in the case to the chamber design, it was designed for accuracy and to utilize long, heavy-for-caliber bullets. With the increase in long-range shooting, it was a natural fit and offered a total package that out-performed many of the mainstream standards when you account for recoil, efficiency, accuracy and ability to stabilize the bullets people wanted to shoot."

There are plenty of faster cartridges and lower-recoiling cartridges, but the

While some say the 6.5 Creedmoor is only suitable for deer-sized game, plenty of people have taken larger game with the cartridge, such as this elk shot in Colorado this past season by Hornady's Sean McGee.

Creedmoor puts everything together in a way that makes it easy to shoot at longer range for everyone.

A closer look at the rounds the 6.5 Creedmoor is often compared to, the 6.5 Swede and .260 Rem, reveals some small but important differences. The Swede is less resistant to wind, has less retained energy at longer ranges and more bullet drop. With a 140-grain bullet, the .260 Rem. starts out with a slight velocity advantage over the 6.5 Creedmoor, but the 6.5 Creed has an advantage in seating longer ogive bullets, which translates into high B.C. values and downrange performance, and the 6.5 Creed starts to outshine the .260 Rem past 500 yards. That matters in long-range target shooting, but not so much at normal hunting distances. What does matter for hunters is the fact that it is a lot easier to find factory 6.5 Creedmoor ammo loaded with high B.C. bullets.

All of these factors make the 6.5 Creedmoor a very good cartridge, but detractors are quick to point out that similar "hunting ballistics" of some of the cartridges mentioned, using bullets with similar diameters, have been around for a very long time. That assertion is akin to stating that water is wet, but it also assumes, in some cases, that virtually everyone is a handloader. The masses are not, and they have embraced the 6.5 Creedmoor in stunning numbers.

"Had the .260 Rem been spec'd with a faster than 1:9 twist barrel and didn't require long streamlined bullets to be pushed far into the case for the max COL or to fit in a short-action rifle, it could have been extremely popular too, but it wasn't," Emery said. "Sure, handloaders can put a fast-twist barrel on their rifles, use a long action and seat heavy bullets out all they want, but that's not the same. Some rifle makers have brought out rifles in .260 with faster twists, but that's not going to prompt a major ammo company to load high-performance ammo when the vast majority of rifles on the market won't stabilize the bullets at sea level on a cold day."

In addition to the factors already mentioned, there's one more that nudges the 6.5 Creedmoor from being a merely good cartridge into the category of being a great one, and it's something that previous 6.5 cartridges never had. It is the widespread availability of affordable factory rifles that shoot relatively inexpensive and readily available 6.5 Creedmoor factory ammo with superb accuracy.

In 2020, Hornady offered 12 factory loads with bullets ranging from 95-grain varmint bullets to 147-grain match bullets. Federal matches that number with a similar range of bullet weights, and a quick survey of other major ammo makers reveals that virtually every significant manufacturer offers 6.5 Creed ammo. I quit counting when the number of factory options topped 60.

This doesn't mean everyone should throw away all other cartridges, fall on their knees and worship at the shrine of the 6.5 Creedmoor, but if the current level of enthusiasm for the round continues into the decades ahead, and there's no reason to believe it won't, the 6.5 Creedmoor will be viewed by history as one of America's greatest cartridge designs, metric or otherwise.

Given the 6.5 Creedmoor's track record to date, I wouldn't bet against it. GD

For hunters on a budget, the Thompson/Center Compass rifle hits the mark. The author used one in 6.5 Creedmoor to take this burly Wyoming mule deer.

A COWBOY THUMPER

When a cowboy needed serious stopping power, he reached for his Winchester Model 1886 ⟩DAVE CAMPBELL

Cowboy movies, stories and television almost always show our horseback heroes with a lever-action rifle chambered in a pistol-caliber cartridge. And in many cases, that's a factual rendition. Real cowboys rarely had the money for a truly big rifle that took advantage of the better ballistics of large-bore cartridges with a profile resembling a panatela. Some, of course, did, but a pistol like a Colt Single Action Army set him back $20. An 1873 Winchester started out at $18 for the carbine. The 1886 was $21 at the time of its first issue. At that time the typical cowboy made $20 to $25 a month. When you also realize that two calibers of ammo were needed to feed an 1886 and his pistol, the issue is not only just the money, but the very real logistical considerations as to how to pack all that plunder on a horse.

Nonetheless, when it came time to shoot a bear or elk, the .44-40 Winchester Center Fire (WCF) with its 212-grain, lead flat-point bullet at 1,100 to 1,300 fps, depending on whether it was fired from the revolver or rifle, often came up a bit shy on stopping and killing power. Too, not everything that needed shooting was on four legs, or out in the open for that matter. Desperados were not ashamed to hide behind doors, piles of firewood and such. Sometimes it's kind of handy to have a rifle that launches a bullet the size of your thumb with enough velocity to turn cover into concealment.

The Model 1873 Winchester was, and is, a slick, fast-handling rifle or carbine that can extract the most from its .44-40 WCF chambering. Yes, it was chambered in other cartridges, but 80 percent of them were chambered for the .44-40, according to George Madis' *The Winchester Book*. When Colt introduced the Single Action Army in the same caliber, it virtually guaranteed the popularity of that cartridge. But that power thing kept dogging Winchester. The company's first reply was the 1876 Winchester, essentially a scaled-up variation of the 1873 model. The 1876 was chambered in cartridges that nearly mimicked or, in a few cases, exceeded the also-popular .45-70 Government cartridge that was the darling of the single-shot crowd. While the 1876 model is a decent rifle, the receiver was too short to accommodate the .45-70 Government round.

As the 1880s blossomed, a young gunsmith out of Ogden, Utah, also came into his own. John Moses Browning had designed and built a working prototype of a single-shot, self-cocking, falling-block rifle that was sturdy, reliable and graceful in profile when he was just 19 years old. Oliver F. Winchester's son-in-law, Thomas Gray (T.G.) Bennett, who was also sales manager for Winchester Repeating Arms at the time, bought the design from Browning. While acquiring the rights to manufacture what would become known as the Model 1885, Bennett learned of the new lever-action rifle Browning was working on. Unlike the toggle-link lockup of the Model 1873 and 1876, this lever action had an opposing pair of vertically sliding locking bolts that combined the strength and camming abilities of a falling block with the room to accommodate a magazine and repeating-feeding mechanism.

Browning did not have anything like the machinery of Winchester. His guns and prototypes were handmade using files, saws and scrapers. While it took a week or more for a letter or small package to make the trip from Ogden to New Haven, Browning could often turn around a revision or improvement idea from Winchester in a day or two. He was clearly what we now call a workaholic. The result of his hard work came to frui-

Fortunately, the relief contour at the rear of the bolt clears the aftermarket aperture sight on the author's Model 1886. Browning's upsized levergun is one of the slickest operating rifles of that genre.

The steel buttplates on the Model 1886 were crescent shaped: wickedly good looking and equally wicked on the shoulder.

A simple blade is all that's needed for a front sight.

Prior to 1900, the receivers on the Model 1886 were color case hardened. Original color case hardening, like this on the author's rifle, is somewhat fragile and fades easily under the ultraviolet light of the sun.

tion on Oct. 14, 1884, in the form of U.S. patent 306,577. This rifle became known as the Model 1886, and it was one of the premier rifles made by Winchester.

No less than 19 separate chamberings were manufactured during the production of the '86. Leading popularity was the .45-70, but cartridges as large as the .50-100-450 also were made. Some cartridges like the .45-90-2.4 had to be loaded with shorter and lighter 300- and 350-grain bullets in order to function through the rifle. Such rounds were designated WCF (Winchester Center Fire) or Express loads. Barrel lengths ran from 20 inches up to 36 inches. Standard length for a rifle was 26 inches; carbines had a 22-inch barrel. An "Extra Light" carbine had a 22-inch round barrel and a half magazine.

When smokeless powder replaced blackpowder, this sturdy lever action was so far ahead of its time, the only change needed in the rifle was to use nickel-steel in the barrels. I have an 1895-vintage '86, chambered in .45-90 WCF, and although it is 125 years old it can still put three 350-grain bullets within 3 inches at 100 yards.

The Model 1886 was a massive rifle, averaging about 9 pounds. Stoked with seven or eight rounds of .45-70 or .45-90 W.C.F. ammo added more than an additional pound to the rifle. That weight was welcome when firing it, considering the cartridges it was chambered for. As with many guns of that period, Winchester was pretty accommodating in terms of extras and custom options.

In addition to the barrel lengths, double-set triggers were an option, as was engraving and a variety of sights. Stocks were typically straight-grained American walnut, sans checkering, but higher grades offered figured walnut and checkering. The stock configuration was typical for the era with the drop at comb and heel far greater that we are used to in modern rifles. Steel buttplates were crescent shaped (wickedly good looking and equally wicked on the shoulder), however military and shotgun-style buttplates were available. Some were stocked with a quarter pistol grip and a curved lever and called "Sporter" versions.

This large, powerful, yet fast-handling

rifle was an instant success in the West where large and often dangerous animals were common. Some of these animals had but two legs.

Commodore Perry Owens was sheriff of Apache County, Arizona Territory. On Sunday, Sept. 4, 1887, Owens rode to the home of Andy Blevins in Holbrook to serve an arrest warrant. In the home were Andy, along with brothers Cooper, John and Sam Houston Blevins, as well as several women and children. Owens had his 1886 Winchester in .45-70 Government in hand as he approached the front door. When Andy answered the door with a pistol in hand, Owens asked him to come outside, telling him he had a warrant for his arrest. Andy refused and started to close the door. With the rifle at his hip, Owens fired through the door wounding Andy in the belly. John Blevins, Andy's half-brother, pushed another door to his right open with a pistol and shot at Owens, missing him. Owens turned toward John and sent another .45-70 round his way, wounding him in the arm and taking him out of the fight.

To get a better view of the situation, Owens backed up to where he could see more of the house. He observed Andy crawling away from the door and loosed a third round at him through the side of the house, striking the felon in the right hip. At this point, Mose Roberts, a boarder with the Blevins family, jumped out of a window and upon spotting Owens, turned and ran. Owens shot him in the back, and Roberts collapsed at the back door. Then Sam Houston Blevins, who was 15 years old, grabbed Andy's Colt pistol and ran out to confront Owens. As the young man charged toward him, Owens fired another round killing Sam. Five rounds, four outlaws (three dead, one wounded) all in less than a minute.

On another occasion in 1891 at Leoncita Flats in Brewster County, Texas, one Fine Gilliland entered into a hostile negotiation with a gentleman, Henry Powe, concerning the ownership of a bull calf. Gilliland took exceptional umbrage during the discussion and shot Powe in the back, killing him. Sometime later, Gilliland was killed by an officer armed with another 1886 in .45-70 Government in the Glass Mountains near Marathon, Texas.

Though faded and a bit worn after 125 years, the .45-90 W.C.F. stamping on top of the barrel indicates this is a serious rifle meant for serious work. Unfortunately, however, bullets heavier than 350 grains will not work from the magazine because the overall length of the cartridge is too long.

Even after the automobile largely replaced the horse, many savvy lawmen kept an '86 handy to stop another vehicle. Those thumb-sized chunks of lead speak with authority. That same authority was also put to good use in game fields where elk, moose and bear were on the menu. Although I have not yet had my '86 in hand when elk have showed up, I did take a very nice B&C black bear in Alaska with another lever-action .45-70. I had to shoot quickly at the bear from about 90 yards, and he did not run 10 feet.

The Model 1886 even saw some military service during the early part of the Great War. Britain's Royal Flying Corps used '86s chambered in .45-90 with incendiary bullets to knock down German dirigibles filled with hydrogen gas.

The Model 1886 had a pretty good run of 50 years, yet just about 160,000 were made initially. Just prior to ceasing production, Winchester initiated a few modifications to it and renamed it the Model 71. Chambered exclusively in the .348 Winchester cartridge, the Model 71 extended the rifle's life an additional 23 years until it was discontinued in 1958 with some 47,254 being made. Like its predecessor, the Model 71 was quite popular with Northeastern woods hunt-

ers and in Canada.

Nearly all the 19th-century lever-action rifles have been replicated as the costs of the originals keep inching higher. The 1886 Winchester is no exception. Today, an original Model 1886 can fetch five figures. Uberti and Pedersoli have produced replica 1886 rifles for several years. Available only in .45-70 Government, the quality is excellent. Fit and finish rival that of the early Winchesters. Browning introduced a repro Model 1886 in the mid-1980s. Made by the Japanese gunmaker Miroku, these are also excellent in quality. Typically, these modern renditions of the 1886 cost $1,200 to a shade more than $2,000.

When Winchester was reborn from the ashes of New Haven as Winchester Repeating Arms, the original name of the company, it took over the production of newer Model 1886 rifles. The new WRA is still owned by FN Herstal, and as such continues to have its replicas manufactured by Miroku. I have a replica Model 1895 in .405 Winchester, and I'll match it against any original for fit, finish and reliability. All of the Miroku guns have a couple of features that cause purists like me to start gnashing our teeth. The hammers are of rebound design, and the

A peek into the inner workings of the receiver shows the complexity of machine work necessary to produce the Model 1886. Recall that this rifle was made by hand, long before computer-controlled machining centers.

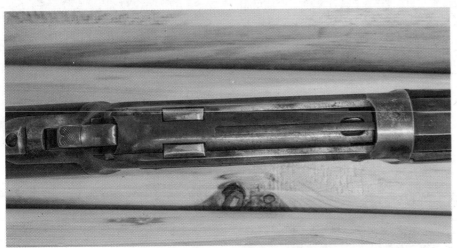

The dual locking lugs allow the Model 1886 to handle pressures greater than those found in prior leverguns. Yet with all that brawn, the rifle boasts clean lines and extraordinarily slick operation.

This simple stamp pushes the value of this rifle astronomically. Really pristine examples are in a somewhat forced retirement because of the risk of lowering their value, but the author enjoys taking this one out for a spin now and then.

rifles are equipped with tang-mounted safeties. This fly in the ointment is not the fault of Miroku. The blame rests solely on the brass at FN Herstal. Purists simply do not appreciate attorneys and engineers making our rifles idiot proof. We do not consider ourselves to be idiots, and everybody got along real fine without rebounding hammers and manual safeties for decades.

Winchester offers three different versions of the Model 1886: Deluxe, Deluxe Case Hardened, and Short Rifle. The Deluxe model features grade III/IV walnut in the pistol-grip configuration capped at both ends in steel. This rifle is chambered in .45-90 WCF with a sporter contour 24-inch barrel. Metal is blued except for the receiver, which is color case hardened and the bolt, which is brushed and left in the white. With an MSRP of $1,740, it is one of the least expensive current production rifles, and it won't break the bank to shoot, provided that you handload.

The Deluxe Case Hardened is nearly identical, except it is chambered in .45-70 Government, and more of the furniture, notably the crescent buttplate, fore-end cap, lever and lower tang, are color case hardened. It, too, will lighten your wallet $1,740. With the Short Rifle, you get a more utilitarian rifle but a handsome one, nonetheless. The Short Rifle is blued without any color case hardening and has a round 24-inch barrel. Wood is straight-grained American walnut. Doing without the frills and dressings will save you $400 off the MSRP. Davidson's Gallery of Guns has an exclusive variation, the Deluxe Takedown that, not surprisingly, is a takedown version of the Deluxe. It also features .45-90 WCF chambering and a 26-inch, half-round, half-octagon barrel. MSRP is $1,740.

Winchester's finest big-bore has had quite a run, and the run continues. If you want a firearm to last through the centuries, in this case, three, the first requirement is that it be designed by John Moses Browning. Granted, most of his designs required some tweaking to get them into manufacturing, but once there they did not need a Gen2, Gen3 or GenX revision to keep them marketable. They also did not need attorneys getting into the design business. **GD**

John Nosler, in 1973, with his signature product, the Partition bullet. (Photo courtesy Nosler family)

John Nosler at the drafting table in 1965. The self-taught engineer built a better bullet that is used by sportsmen around the world. (Photo courtesy Nosler family)

JOHN NOSLER:
SPORTSMAN AND INNOVATOR

John Nosler slid the Winchester Model 70 out of its soft case and pushed three rounds into the magazine. Puffy gray and white clouds hung in the blue sky. A breeze blew across the desert, riffling the tops of the sagebrush like wavelets on an inland sea. For most of the day, the three hunters covered ground, using binoculars and a spotting scope to probe the canyons and the shoulders of the buttes. Finally, they found what they were looking for. Three mule deer climbed toward the saddle. The biggest buck stopped to look back. It would be a long shot, but Nosler was used to long shots. Taking a steady rest, the hunter, who had turned 90 years old earlier that year, steadied the cross hairs and tightened his finger on the trigger. When the buck dropped, Nosler unloaded his rifle and put his hand on his grandson's shoulder. This was why he was here. Desert days like this one, with his grandson and a good friend, were what kept him coming back. The challenge and the promise of each new day drew him to the desert year after year.

The life of John A. Nosler is the uniquely American story of a young boy with a gun in his hand and grease under his fingernails. He grew to manhood in a world full of possibilities, in a country poised for greatness. Life on the ranch prepared him for the challenges he would face as an adult. Just as it did for thousands of others in his generation.

Nosler was born on April 4, 1913, into a home that smelled of honeydew melons, homemade bread and butter in the churn. The barefoot boy in overalls

"He built a better bullet"
❯ GARY LEWIS

learned fabrication and innovation at an early age. Before he had a driver's license, he had a working knowledge of auto mechanics. He bought his first car at the age of 8, sold it and traded his bicycle for a broken-down Ford Model T that he towed home with his dad's mules. Roaming the hills west of Los Angeles, he hunted rabbits and other small game with his .22 rifle. When the stock market crashed, his family's finances went with it. He quit school in his junior year and went to work.

His passion for automobiles led to a job as cleanup boy for a Ford dealership in Chino, California. Before long, he was a mechanic. When the shop foreman quit, he got the job. Soon he and a partner invested in a racecar and the duo took to the tracks. Nosler was the mechanic and he watched most of the races from the sidelines. He thought the Model B engine, with its heavy-duty crankshaft, would help their Model A stay ahead of the pack, but, under high rpm, it failed too often. The 19-year-old welded counter-balancing weights to the Model B crank and headed back to the tracks where everyone else ate their dust. After the racing season, Nosler loaned his crankshaft to employees at the Ford Assembly Plant. It wasn't long before

Dearborn retrofitted dealer stocks across the nation with the young mechanic's innovation. The men in Detroit recognized talent when they saw it, and Ford offered Nosler an engineering scholarship and a job when he graduated. But he turned them down. Someone else had noticed him. Her name was Louise, and they were married within the year.

John and Louise saved their money over the next few years. Nosler went back to Ford and asked if the company needed another agency. Ford sent them to Reedsport on the Oregon coast, where John put up his shingle and began selling cars and trucks. A sagging economy forced the Noslers to sell and move. John kept one truck and packed his wife and their new baby boy to another town and a new start.

The young couple, in the years before World War II, built a trucking business in Ashland, Oregon, and it was there, when John Nosler was in his mid-20s, that he killed his first big-game animal, a blacktail deer. Trucking was good for John and Louise and their fleet of Ford and Peterbilt trucks grew, while their deliveries took Nosler and his employees up and down the West Coast.

MOOSE AND MAGNUMS

In 1941, Nosler rewarded himself with a trip to British Columbia to hunt moose. At a diner in a crossroads town, he met a Canadian Mountie, who pointed him down an old trail to the coast. "If you can make it far enough," the Mountie said, "you'll find Indians who can show you where to hunt." John returned to

BC every year for almost a decade. In 1946, he carried a Winchester Model 70 chambered for the 300 H&H Magnum. Toward the end of the trip, hunting moose in a marsh, he found a bull feeding in a patch of willows.

The animal stood broadside. His polished antlers gleamed, and his body was black with caked mud. Nosler could hear the rasp of his breath and smell the sweat caked on his body. He raised the rifle, found the bull in his scope, pushed the safety to "fire" and squeezed the trigger. At the shot, the bull shook his head, and started forward. John cycled the bolt and fired again, putting the cross hairs on the animal's shoulder. The bull didn't stagger or fall or bellow or charge. Instead, he turned and trotted toward the cover of the trees. Nosler hit him again, then again and finally saw him stumble at the impact of the fourth bullet. John reloaded, pushing rounds from his pocket into the magazine. He knew his bullets had struck, but they didn't seem to be doing any damage. Now the bull was quartering away, and Nosler fired a raking shot that broke through the bull's armor.

John and his guide, working with their skinning knives, found that Nosler's bullets had splattered on the hard, mud-caked hide. His 300 H&H Magnum sent its bullets at such high speed that the projectile's thin copper jacket couldn't contain its soft lead core. Though John was shooting from close range, most of his shots didn't even penetrate to the vitals. His high-powered rifle was TOO powerful to kill a moose with the best bullets then available to hunters.

In B.C. in those days, a hunter could give his moose tag to another hunter. The Postmaster, who was blind, wanted Nosler to bring in a moose for him. The day before the end of the hunt, John went hunting again. Right away, he stumbled onto a nice bull. Thumbing the safety to fire, he steadied his aim and fired two quick shots that splattered on the bull's shoulder. The bull started forward and Nosler fired again, holding the crosshairs on the belly, raking forward through the vitals. The bullet fragmented in the internal organs and the moose dropped in his tracks.

Over-expansion was only one of the problems with the bullets that hunters used in the 1940s. Some bullets penetrated, but didn't kill cleanly. On another hunt in British Columbia, Nosler happened on a bull and a cow feeding together. The cow was between the bull and John, so he stalked from a different angle to shoot the bull without hitting the cow. A stick cracked under his boot and the bull turned to face him, giving Nosler a frontal shot. He took it, hitting the bull in the chest. The bullet traveled all the way through the animal and exited from the right hindquarter. Today's bullets would have dropped that animal. He had to track the moose for four hours before

John Nosler at work in his Ashland, Oregon, shop, where the first Partition bullets were made. (Photo courtesy Nosler family)

John Nosler and one of his longtime hunting partners, Jack James. (Photo courtesy Nosler family)

he caught up and finished him off. To Nosler, this kind of bullet performance was unacceptable on big game the size of moose. He realized he had a choice: Either he had to go back to hunting with his old, slow .30-40 Krag and .30-30 Winchester, or find a better bullet.

Back home, Nosler returned to target-shooting competition on Tuesday nights and weekends. Since many of the other shooters were hunters, he began his search among the people he knew to find a bullet that would stand up to high velocity. To compete at the highest levels, many shooters loaded their own ammunition to match-grade standards. As more people realized they could save a little money, while they tailored custom loads to fit their own rifles and handguns, interest grew in handloading.

Fred Huntington, Joyce Hornady, Bruce Hodgdon, the Speers and others like them were traveling around the country, putting on ammunition-loading seminars at police stations, gun clubs, sporting-goods stores, schools and anywhere else they could find shooters to listen. Nosler asked everyone he knew to be on the watch for a strong bullet that combined penetration with reliable expansion.

There were basically two types of bullets then available: Bullets that had tremendous penetration, but minimal expansion. And bullets that expanded quickly, but failed to penetrate. The first group would shoot clear through an animal, often without inflicting a fatal wound. The second would expand, but often wouldn't penetrate, resulting in the type of nonlethal wounds that weren't sufficient to bring down an elk or moose.

In his search for effective bullets, Nosler tried projectiles from around the world. The German H-Mantle bullets seemed like they might offer the performance he was after, but Nosler found that the front piece often broke off, leaving the small rear portion without enough weight to penetrate.

On one deer hunt, he used a .30-06 with 150-grain hollowpoint bullets manufactured by prisoners in San Quentin and distributed by the Western Tool and Copper Works. Before World War II, the inmates made and sold their bullets in

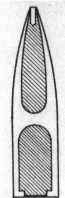
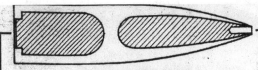
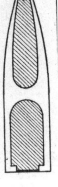

!! THANKS !!

Your orders and good letters commending our product convinced us you are looking for the best in bullets for big game hunting. Heavy demand for 150 and 180 gr. in 30 caliber has delayed production of other cal. & weights. Attention Elk Hunters: THIS BULLET IS DOING A WHALE OF A JOB THIS SEASON!

•

NOSLER PARTITION JACKET BULLET

John A. Nosler   382 Weightman St.   Ashland, Oregon

(above) The first advertisement John Nosler circulated in the sporting press.

(right) One of the early advertisements for the Nosler bullet.

NOSLER
PARTITION JACKET BULLET

We GUARANTEE our bullet to hold together better in heavy game than any other type of expanding bullet OR YOUR MONEY BACK.

All calibers 10¢ each shipped 50 per box 30 caliber, 150, 180 grain available now.

JOHN A. NOSLER

382 Weightman Street • Ashland, Oregon

John Nosler with a grizzly. (Photo courtesy Nosler family)

large numbers. Nosler thought they were pretty good compared to what was then available, but he knew there was a lot of room for improvement.

Up and down the West Coast on a regular basis, Nosler visited many of San Francisco's big sporting goods stores to see what they had in 7mm Magnum or 300 Magnum, 180-grain bullets. He found some 220-grain bullets that Winchester claimed made a good African load. When he tried them, he found they did a better job when velocity was held below 2,500 fps. On subsequent hunts, he used them with good effect on moose and other game, but he knew this bullet wasn't the answer because velocities had to be kept low for optimum performance.

He told himself there was an answer out there, a way to marry the qualities of penetration and expansion. He just had to keep searching until he found it.

At home that winter, Nosler continued to puzzle over the problem. It became clear that if he wanted a better bullet, he would have to build it himself. A bullet that combined good penetration with controlled expansion. In effect, he wanted two bullets in one. On a scrap of paper, he sketched his concept, a jacketed bullet with its lead cores separated by a copper partition.

BUILDING A BETTER BULLET

Nosler had plenty of room to work in his old garage when all the trucks were on the road. A lathe sat in the corner beside a milling machine he had picked up in San Francisco. Since he had the tools, he decided to try to rough out a bullet with a partition. With the lathe, he would build a jacket to contain the cores. The front core would mushroom while the rear core would carry the bullet's weight, allowing penetration while controlling expansion.

With his shop mechanic, Roy Banta, he went to work. They made a hand press, then brought a screw machine back from Los Angeles. Nosler bought some 5/16-inch copper rod and some lead wire. The copper rod came in 10- and 12-foot lengths. The rods were 5/16-inch (.3125) and a 30-caliber bullet was .308. So, they put the rod pieces into the lathe and machined the outside diameter. Then they

made a special drill to bore a hole in the front of the jacket. When they had a pan full of jackets, they put them in the lathe with the other end sticking out. They drilled it for the rear core and the Partition jackets were ready. The hard part was forming the jackets into bullets. Without any good way to get the lead inside, they had to melt the lead and let it drip in and harden.

Later, they built some crude dies then tamped lead in each end and pressed them into bullets. They shot some and when they were really careful they could keep them on a dinner plate. They were not match-grade bullets by any means, but Nosler thought he might be able to hit a moose with one.

In 1947, John took Clarence Purdie, owner of the Gopher Shooter Supply in Minnesota, with him to British Columbia. Nosler carried his 300 H&H, while Purdie shot a .30-06. Both hunters loaded their guns with Nosler's handcrafted ammunition.

Purdie had the honor of taking the first game with the new Nosler Partition bullet. One shot was all he needed.

John found his bull browsing in a stand of jack pines. When he was within 15 yards, he shouldered his rifle, centered the cross hair on the shoulder, and squeezed the trigger. The bull dropped in its tracks.

Both men found, under the offside hides of their moose, a perfectly expanded bullet. As crude as those first bullets were, they had held together. Nosler had proved the value of his bullet to himself. Now he had to prove it to the world. At the time, he didn't consider manufactur-

One of John's favorite calibers was the .280 Remington. (Photo courtesy Nosler family)

ing the bullets himself, but he did want to see them made available to the shooting public. Magnum rifles were becoming more popular and it was obvious that better bullets would have to be made.

IT WORKED. NOW WHAT?

Nosler paid a visit to Sierra Bullets in its Whittier, California, machine shop. After looking at his design and seeing his enthusiasm, Sierra executives asked John to join them as a partner. The bullets they were making were the cup-type and were most properly used for light hunting and target use. It was obvious to Nosler that Sierra was organized and would be a fine company to work with. However, the line of presses the workers used in production of their bullets was not adaptable to manufacturing Partition-type bullets.

Next, Nosler traveled to Lewiston, Idaho, to see Vernon Speer, who was making a line of bullets similar to Sierra's. He had an old Army press and was making Speer-cup bullets with it. His machines

(left) The converted truck garage in Ashland, Oregon, where John Nosler made the first Partition bullets. (Photo courtesy Nosler family)

After the stock market crash of 1929, John Nosler went to a work for a Ford dealership in Los Angeles. (Photo courtesy Nosler family)

Inside the shop where the first Nosler Partition was built.

could not be used for making Partition jackets.

While he looked for a manufacturer, Nosler began the process of study that would turn him into an engineer. He devoured books on metallurgy and manufacturing. His hometown library didn't have much to offer, so he began to stop in bookstores in Portland, San Francisco and Los Angeles and sent away for books other people told him about.

He flew to Washington D.C., to file a patent on his invention. While he was on the East Coast, he stopped at the Winchester plant in New Haven, Connecticut. Nosler explained his design and left a few samples behind. The engineers at Winchester were interested and John thought he had finally found someone to produce his bullet. He went home and waited for the letter to come that would tell him how much they liked it and how much they were going to pay him for his invention. When the letter finally arrived, it told him Winchester executives had decided not to spend the money. The Partition was too different from what they were making, and they had no machines with which to build it. The proposition of tooling up to produce Partitions sounded too expensive for Winchester.

Nosler was the only person in the world who believed in his concept enough to build it. He was fascinated with the idea and the more he researched, the more it looked like manufacturing the bullet might be profitable. A good mechanic and machinist, he knew he wasn't an engineer. But the engineers he'd met didn't know anything about bullets.

There are few products that require tighter manufacturing tolerances than bullets. The longest centerfire .22 bullets require one revolution of the bullet in the barrel every 7 inches. When that bullet is traveling above 3,000 fps, it is revolving at something near 6,000 revolutions per second. It is very hard for most mechanical engineers to understand the stress. The centrifugal force is so powerful that some bullets actually explode in the air.

Nosler thought he knew something about bullets, and he figured he could learn engineering and manufacturing. What followed were months of design, construction, trial and error and studying engineering texts late into the night. There were no machines to make a bullet like this. When he needed a piece of equipment, he had to design and build it himself.

He had been thinking about making the bullet from tubing. In San Francisco, he found a turret lathe and began to talk to his copper-tube supplier about the size of tubing available. Finally, he bought the minimum order of tubing required and went to work on designing a die system.

He bought a new 35-ton Niagara punch press, then two smaller presses. Then he bought a Diamond 14-ton. Nosler designed a set of dies and filed for a patent on his die system. Then he bought automatic screw machines made by Brown and Sharpe that would handle any bullet.

After running the tube through the dies, he found he could produce a very nice jacket that required no trimming and was ready for the lead cores. A little worried about sending that solid 90-percent copper through the rifling, he ran each bullet through an automatic machine that ran a groove called a "relief" around the bullet. The finished product looked good.

Nosler knew he had to automate every operation if he hoped to ever make a profit on his invention. After every step forward, he looked for another way to automate each step.

The next operation was to form the

John Nosler, in 2004.

jackets, with the front and rear lead cores in place, into bullet shapes. John tooled the 14-ton press so it would tamp the lead core, then press the bullet and eject. He hand-fed this press and was now able to make a few Partition bullets. Every operation was slow, so very few bullets were made in a day's work, but the fledgling company began to turn out .30 caliber 150-, 180- and 200-grain Partitions. With bullets in production, Nosler began sending them out to see what the gun writers thought of them. Warren Page, Jack O'Connor and Elmer Keith sampled some of those early bullets. Page and O'Connor, in particular were big boosters. Keith was very interested, and the two hunters became good friends over the next few years.

O'Connor later wrote in his book *The Art of Hunting Big Game*, "If I am in grizzly country I take with me a few cartridges loaded with the 150-grain Nosler bullet at around 2950, and either (rifle)

will put this heavier bullet to the same point of impact as the lighter ones to 200 yards. There are other combinations just as good for sheep, no doubt, but I can't think of a better one."

Herb Klein, a wealthy hunter from Texas, carried some of the first Partitions bullets to Africa. In his book *Lucky Bwana*, he called them, "the world's deadliest bullet."

Nosler was doing what he set out to do and soon the Nosler Partition Bullet Company was hard-pressed to keep up with demand. He had proved the Partition was needed and proved it could be built and hunters would buy it. By 1958, the company had outgrown the converted truck garage. John moved his family and operations to the small town of Bend in central Oregon.

In the years that followed, he worked to refine the process for making his Partitions, eventually settling on extrusion as the best method for bringing his prod-

uct to sportsmen at a price the average hunter could afford.

NOSLER BULLETS

Today, with over 70 years in production, the Nosler Partition bullet is the standard of the industry and is used by more hunters than any other bullet. Its design is unique in that much of the front lead is released to fragment, causing tissue damage by the flying bits of lead. The folded-back, mushroomed bullet penetrates enough to most often exit the animal or be found just under the skin on the off side.

Nosler Incorporated has stayed on the leading edge of innovation in the shooting sports. The Nosler Ballistic Tip is made for hunting varmints and thin-skinned game such as antelope and deer. Because of its excellent ballistics, it is a good choice for use on game when long shots are possible. It is a long bullet with a boat tail with its weight in the

John Nosler, in his early 90s at the Central Oregon Shooting Sports Association 1,000-yard range that now bears his name.

The Nosler
AccuBond.

Nosler E-Tip.

Nosler Ballistic Tip
Hunting.

Nosler Ballistic Tip Varmint.

rear. A sharp plastic tip resists deforming in magazines and retains its shape for utmost consistency, shot after shot.

In 2003, Nosler's engineers developed the AccuBond. The AccuBond employs an extruded jacket, which is thinner at the point and heavier in the midsection. The jacket is gilding metal, an alloy noted for its ability to smoothly pass through the gun barrel. Like the Ballistic Tip, it sports a polycarbonate tip. The lead core is bonded to the gilding metal jacket by a proprietary process developed over years of research and development.

On target, it expands readily as the jacket is forced back by the impact of the tip. A portion of the lead core is exposed by the opening jacket and released to cause tissue damage and bleeding for quicker kills. At expansion, the bullet retains 70 to 80 percent of its weight, never going beyond two times its original diameter.

Wide expansion is seldom good for deep penetration. The AccuBond keeps expansion to an optimum diameter to ensure deep penetration. Like the Ballistic Tip, the AccuBond has a very good ballistic coefficient, which means a minimum loss of velocity at long range. The bonded core works to tighten the group size for match-grade accuracy in a premium hunting bullet.

When California and other states began to mandate the use of lead-free ammunition, manufacturers developed projectiles to serve hunters in those parts of the country. Nosler's copper-free offering, the Expansion Tip was developed in 2007 with copper-alloy construction, a control ring, expansion chamber, a signature OD green polymer tip and a boat tail. While the Partition and AccuBond tend to retain 65 to 80 percent of their weight, the E-Tip is designed for 95-percent weight retention. The company recommends a minimum impact velocity of 1,800 fps.

The AccuBond Long Range (ABLR), identified by its gray polymer tip, was developed to serve the needs of hunters who employ top-level optics and ultra-high-velocity cartridges for targets which might be encountered at 500, 800 or 1,000 yards or more. For reliable expansion at extreme range, the ABLR was designed for a minimum impact velocity of 1,300 fps.

Today, the Nosler catalog includes offerings from the AccuBond, AccuBond Long Range, Partition, E-Tip, Ballistic Tip Hunting, Ballistic Tip Varmint, Ballistic Silvertip Hunting, Ballistic Silvertip Varmint, Custom Competition, Bonded Performance, BT Lead-Free, Nosler Solid, Varmageddon, Ballistic Tip Muzzleloader and Sporting Handgun. Beyond projec-

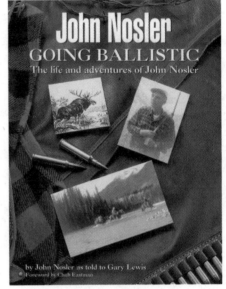

The book: *John Nosler Going Ballistic.*

tiles, the company offers loaded ammunition and custom rifles.

If John Nosler was still with us, he would be actively involved in the business. He loved the industry and the people he met along the way.

John Nosler continued to shoot well into his mid-90s, and he went to his office at the plant in Bend, Oregon, at least twice a week. He kept a 1929 Model A Ford in top running condition and did a lot of the work himself. He still had grease under his fingernails. He even drove the Model A once in a while on a sunny summer day, even after they took away his driver's license.

The young barefoot farm boy in overalls became a legendary sportsman and innovator. His life's work spawned the premium bullet industry that employs thousands across the country and satisfies sportsmen around the globe. **GD**

Gary Lewis is the author of 16 books, including John Nosler Going Ballistic – The Life and Adventures of John Nosler. *For a signed copy, send $25 to Gary Lewis Outdoors, P.O. Box 1364, Bend, OR 97709.*

The first generation of Nosler Partition packaging.

GLOCK
RIMFIRE PERFECTION

44:

The Glock G44 .22 LR includes two, single-stack 10-round magazines

Glock introduces its first rimfire pistol, in .22 LR

❯CLAY MARTIN

A t last, the long-awaited caliber addition to the lineup. In the last few months leading up to the announcement, a lot of us Glock fanboys felt like a dad in the maternity waiting room, circa 1950, waiting on the doctor to tell us what we got. Part of the job, as a both a gun writer and Glock aficionado, is staying up with the rumor train. Instead of following Gaston out of his garage or staking out the factory in Georgia, we scour the patent applications and website registrations.

When Glock registers a new number, we know we are six months, to a year, out from a new model. We might have no idea what that model is, but a new one is coming. Sometimes, it is obvious. A G43X would be a longer-handled G43, building on the G19/G19X relationship. But usually, it is an absolute mystery, which is further obscured by the fact that Glock numbers haven't made sense in any way since the original G17.

The Glock 17, it is rumored, was named such since it was the only model Glock made, and it held 17 rounds of 9mm. Then came the G19, a more compact version of the G17, with a capacity of 15. A Glock 45 is a 9mm gun, and a Glock 20, 29 or 40 is a 10mm gun. Confused? Good. More man hours than we can count have been spent trying to decipher the numbering system like it's the DaVinci Code of firearms, to no avail. My best guess is that it is actually a cultural habit of Glock Inc., based purely on design philosophy. Utility. Nothing more, nothing less. Pick a number we haven't used yet.

So, while we might have known a G44 was on the way, no one had any idea what it was. Glock is also notoriously good at guarding secrets. Speculation abounded. But I don't think any of us expected what we got: The first-ever, long-overdue rimfire Glock. Finally, the mighty "plastic fantastic" in .22 Long Rifle.

I actually heard rumors of a .22 LR Glock, at the Smyrna, Georgia, factory no less, as far back as 2013. Why, exactly, has it taken this long to get one? My belief is that this is a twofold set of factors. First, we saw a huge shortage of .22 LR around the same time. Many of you, I'm certain, remember the shortages of just a few years ago. It is not a great time to spend precious R&D resources on a gun, when ammunition can't be purchased. The second had to do with engineering challenges.

Building a rimfire is one thing. Building a rimfire that feels and functions like a "real" pistol is quite another. Given the look and feel of the Glock family of handguns, all a shared design scaled up or down for caliber, Glock needed one that fit the "real" category. You can't very well have 40 models of the same variation, and then a fixed-barrel blowback bolt one. It wasn't what we Glock guys wanted. We have seen some manufacturers create a .22-caliber version of their duty guns that are basically a plastic shell over an existing .22 pistol. Not Glock's style, fortunately. And don't get me started on the companies that make a reduced-size version of the duty gun to shoot .22 LR.

So, Glock needed a way to mimic the feel and function of its patented designs. How do you do that, with the reduced recoil of rimfire ammunition? Many of us have tried aftermarket aluminum-slide conversion kits for our Glocks, usually

The Glock G44 cycled reliably with a variety of ammunition brands and loads during the author's extensive testing.

with less-than-stellar results. Well, if you are Glock, you do something so simple it is brilliant: You make the slide out of polymer. The company that pioneered the polymer frame, managed to wow us with plastic again.

The G44 is exactly the same dimensions as a Generation 5 Glock 19, except for the weight. While I might have preferred a G17 size first, going to the G19 makes sense. The Glock 19 is the most popular handgun in the world, and I am quite sure that is for a reason. The G19 also gave Glock a decent size grip, while reducing slide weight via length from a full-size duty gun.

The slide on a G19 would still have been a problem, in steel. So how to really reduce the weight? As mentioned, Glock knows polymer like no one else. As we all know, polymer is tough as nails, but would have nowhere near the abrasion resistance of steel. Plastic rubbing on metal would quickly reduce the plastic to sawdust. But if you are Glock, how did you solve this the first time?

Easy, which is a word we can use only in retrospect, after someone else figured it out. Gaston molded steel rails into the top of the original polymer G17 frame, so that steel contacts steel. A quick look at any Glock pistol you own will show that in no area does the steel slide actually make contact with the polymer frame. So, some brilliant engineer obviously looked at the problem and asked, "What if we do it again on top of the gun?"

Which is exactly what happened. The new G44 polymer slide has an insert near the rear sight, which extends down to a set of full-length steel rails. We are back to steel on steel for all the moving parts. Why hasn't anyone done this before? I don't know. Probably the same reason no one made a pistol that set the standard for reliability by reducing the total number of parts to 34.

An obvious question then would be about durability. Will a polymer slide hold together? If you are young, you might not remember people asked the same thing about Glock frames in the 1980s. People swore that the guns couldn't hold together. No way. Metal frames back then often cracked around 50,000 rounds. How could plastic keep up with that?

The author shot more than 2,000 rounds through his new Glock G44 in .22 LR during testing.

It seems laughable now, with almost four decades of service to back it up. The polymer wonder set the standard for toughness, to a point it is called the AK-47 of pistols, in some circles. But it was true. And if you have ever seen a Glock frame under a high-speed camera, it offers another clue as to how it survives.

The polymer frame actually flexes and twists, albeit much faster than the human eye can perceive. A metal frame does not. I would like to ask Gaston Glock someday if he knew that during design, or if it was just a happy accident. But the movement seems to absorb some of the punishment of recoil, and gives Glocks a longer service life. Like the old proverb of Confucius: "The green reed which bends in the wind is stronger than the mighty oak which breaks in a storm." How do I know this? First-hand experience. One of the reasons I had admission to the Glock factory in 2013 was I was taking in a G34 with over 250,000 rounds through it (my competition gun) for the engineers to take a look at. The frame was still 100-percent serviceable and passed all their QC tests.

So, the same should hold true for a polymer slide. Especially at the reduced recoil of .22 LR. This makes the total package feel exactly like a G19, with 8.89 ounces shaved off the weight. Most of that is slide to slide, though a bit of metal

did get removed somewhere else. The barrel, as you can imagine, is significantly smaller in a .22 caliber. It is actually the only thing that looks out of place when you disassemble the gun. The chamber end of the barrel is still the same looking square Glock standard. This is then rapidly reduced to a tiny little rimfire barrel. I would venture to say it looks cute.

The truly amazing part of the G44 is when you take the slide off and look at the internals. This gun doesn't just look like a Glock. It is a Glock. Everything, every detail, is the same as another Gen-5 weapon. The ejector has its own angle for caliber, much like the difference in a 9mm to .40 S&W model, but it is all Glock standard. Looking at it next to my G19X, it is absolutely amazing. And this isn't just my un-calibrated eyeball. Apex Tactical, famous for its aftermarket triggers, has already reported that its current Gen-5 kit will also fit the G44.

The only two special considerations I can tell on the G44 are the sights and the magazines. The sights are very similar to typical Glock plastic sights, with the white-dot front and white-U rear. But the default for the G44 is that the rear is adjustable, which makes sense given the wide variety of rimfire ammunition available. The magazines have a capacity of only 10, but are the size and shape of a 15-round 9mm magazine. This was likely

The Glock G44 uses a single-stack, 10-round magazine that has the same dimensions as magazines used in the Glock G19.

The author believes the G44 in .22 LR absolutely lives up to the Glock name in terms of performance, reliability and accuracy.

done to increase reliability, as .22 LR can be a very finicky round, and it is safer to single stack them than try for staggered. Though even at 10 rounds, it looks like enough of the follower could be shaved down to make room for a few more. We will see what the future holds.

So, it looks and feels like a Glock. Does it perform like a Glock? This should be the first question on everyone's mind. The .22 LR, as many of us have seen, can be a fickle mistress. I've seen bolt actions jam on it, something that would be hard-pressed to see in any other caliber. And semi-autos can be very hit or miss. Glock made its reputation on reliability, and I would think we all expect the same from its rimfire offerings. Could it hold up to the standards set by its centerfire forefathers?

Off to the range we went. I was able to round up eight brands of .22 LR, from subsonic to hyper velocity, and everything in between. I went with as many weights and speeds as I could find, which was not made easy by the run on ammunition in spring 2020. Three flavors of

Federal, CCI, Blazer, Remington, Winchester and Gem Tech subsonic made the lineup.

I was very happy to find that my G44 not only worked fine, right out of the box, but that it would eat six out of eight loads with shocking reliability, even the subsonic, which I did not expect. With a reduced velocity and the same 40-grain bullet, subsonic doesn't work well in a lot of semi-autos. The G44 test model chewed up 100 in a row without a hitch.

In total, I shot a little over 2,000 rounds, consistently going back to the two brands my test gun malfunctioned with to see if some break-in would help. But no matter what I did, it never liked the Remington or Winchester, which to me isn't a deal breaker. Most .22s I own prefer one brand or another, so no big deal. It is also entirely possible that I got a box of those two brands that was missed at QC. With the astounding volume of .22 LR turned out every day in this country, it does happen.

For the vast majority of my test with Federal and Blazer, my G44 ran with bor-

ing reliability. For a rimfire, it was amazing to have one go bang that many times in a row. In my opinion, it absolutely lives up to the Glock name.

I was also impressed with accuracy. The G44 features what Glock calls the Marksman Barrel, introduced with the Generation-5 guns. This is a new barrel design Glock engineers say increases accuracy, though I never had a problem with the old ones. My G44 would consistently bang the 2-inch by 2-inch head on a mini USPSA steel target at 10 meters, point of aim, point of impact.

So, we covered the fact that the gun runs, and how it's made, but who is it for? I see this as Glock taking care of the heavy-use client, first and foremost. Glock makes duty weapons, not safe queens. If you just wanted to plink cans in the backyard, any .22 would do. You could even argue that other .22s on the market are lighter, have better triggers out of the box and are more configurable.

To me, that is largely missing the point. I see this gun as an engineered training tool, for people who carry Glocks for real

The Glock G44 has adjustable rear sights standard, which the author thinks is an excellent idea with rimfire pistols.

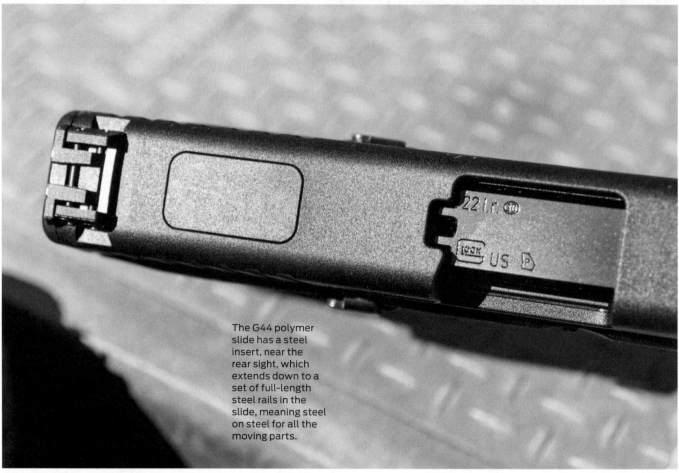

The G44 polymer slide has a steel insert, near the rear sight, which extends down to a set of full-length steel rails in the slide, meaning steel on steel for all the moving parts.

22 l.r.

GLOCK US

With the slide of the G44 removed, you can see this is all Glock.

work. Be that personal protection, law enforcement, or, where I did, as a soldier. A couple of things we have to admit as Glock guys. First, the feel of a Glock is like nothing else. Second, the Glock trigger is also unique. And both of those things matter when it comes to training repetitions.

Here is an example. I fell so in love with the Glock platform that I opted to use it in competitive shooting as well. Not only was it the feel of my duty piece, but the reliability factor would matter a few times. Now after matches, it is extremely common to hang out with your friends and shoot each other's guns. At the time, 3-Gun was absolutely dominated by high-capacity 1911s. That gun was pretty much purpose-made for competing: very tightly fit barrels, 1-pound triggers, and a starting price of about $3,000, up to $5,000. I was thinking about getting one, so I borrowed a friend's. The only target available was a long way off, say 80 to 100 yards. I shot a couple of magazines, magic trigger, blah blah, I was hitting about one out of eight times. I handed it back, and out of curiosity, pulled out my G34 and shot at the same target. All of a sudden, I was hitting one out of two or three, consistently.

That is the power of familiarity. I assure you, in a vice, that hi-cap 1911 would print a group that is amazing. But, in the real world, what you have thousands of reps with matters. And in the real world, I pick the gun that goes bang dirty, full of sand, neglected and possibly rusty. If you carry a Glock, you want to train on a Glock. The other part of this I've seen first-hand is the repetitions carry over across a family of weapons. A G19 and a G34 index the same during presentation. That is why the G44 is so game-changing.

If you want to be a good shooter, you have to shoot a lot. From an economic perspective, that is a lot easier with .22 Long Rifle. Now, you have one that fits your holsters and magazine pouches. For not only the armed citizen, but hopefully for LEOs, everyone can get in a lot more trigger time. If you have children, you can teach them on the same platform they might want to carry as adults. Shooting skills keep all of us safer, and this is the perfect tool to refine them. GD

The D Grade Parker was a favorite in its day and is a perfect example of the artistic beauty Parker Brothers Company was capable of. This one was built in the timeframe of 1897/98 and has a high degree of engraving, well-figured wood and nice checkering.

AMERICA'S Side-by-Side PRIDE

Parker Brothers, L.C. Smith and A.H. Fox produced some of the finest double-barrel shotguns made in the United States

› TOM TABOR

Over the decades there has clearly been a shift within the firearms industry away from the fine craftsmanship and high quality we once knew and expected, in favor of higher production rates and lower overall costs. Obviously there is some benefit with being able to purchase a centerfire rifle or repeating shotgun for a few hundred bucks, but when we sacrifice quality and workmanship solely for the sake of flooding the market with cheaply produced, low-quality firearms we are sacrificing considerably more than we are receiving. And nowhere is this trend more evident than it is in our side-by-side shotguns.

At one time a side-by-side was the preferred choice of most upland bird hunters, waterfowlers, and those shooting skeet and trap. But as pump and semi-automatics became more reliable, easier to build and cheaper to purchase, it resulted in a slow shift away from the side-by-side in favor of these cheaper single-barrel alternatives.

For centuries, Europe has justifiably been credited with producing some of the finest quality side-by-side shotguns. Names like Purdy, Holland & Holland, Jeffery, W.W. Greener and many others are often looked upon as some of the best and most prestigious of those. But the United States has its own legendary side-by-side manufacturers. The shotguns carrying the names of Parker Bros., L.C. Smith and A.H Fox are often considered some of the best of those and as such are often coveted and cherished worldwide by collectors.

PARKER BROTHERS

Parker Bros. began building shotguns in 1867 and continued until the mid-1930s, when those rights were sold to Remington Arms, which continued to produce the Parker Gun until the costs of production became too high, resulting in its discontinuance as WWII raged on in 1942.

Prior to becoming the founder of Parker Bros., Charles Parker worked as an apprentice casting buttons for the garment industry. From there he moved on to the manufacturing of steam engines, printing presses and the production of machining tools. The machining experience he was able to accumulate in those roles became very useful in his future endeavors within the firearms industry. Early in his gun-building career, he worked constructing Springfield rifles and in the production of some of the earliest repeating-rifle designs, which were sold under the company name of Parker, Snow and Company.

The first Parker shotguns were back-lock hammer designs, which came with either an under-lever release or a top-lever release. As the Parker Bros. Company evolved, the back-locks were ultimately dropped in favor of the box-lock hammerless design, which Parker Bros. became best known for. A wide variety of grades were offered starting with the very plain field-quality P, V and Trojan all the way up to the more adorned grades of G, D, C, B, A, AA, A-1 Special. And for the ultimate of high-quality engraving, inlay work, checkering, wood figure, there was the Invincible Grade. At this very top of the pinnacle, the Invincible was built to commemorate the company's 200,000-production milestone. It is commonly accepted that only two of these shotguns were produced. These were exquisite examples of the finest gunsmithing art and carried the serial numbers of 200,000 and 200,001. These were adorned with the most beautiful one-of-a-kind engraving, gold inlay work, very extravagant checkering and were stocked with the best highly figured walnut. Very little is known as to the whereabouts these two shotguns today, but a very interesting story involves one of them.

Sometime in the late 1940s or early 1950s, the 200,000-serialized Parker Bros. Invincible simply vanished, never to be seen publicly again. As an example of the Parkers Bros.' superb gun-building abilities, the Invincible was placed on display at the Kennedy Brothers sporting goods store in Minneapolis, Minnesota. After the show, the gun was to be transported to another locale, but it failed to reach that destination. The missing gun was written about in the local newspaper, but rather than reporting the gun was stolen it was written it had "disappeared."

The Parker Bros. D Grade was a middle-grade shotgun that came from the factory with an ample amount of engraving.

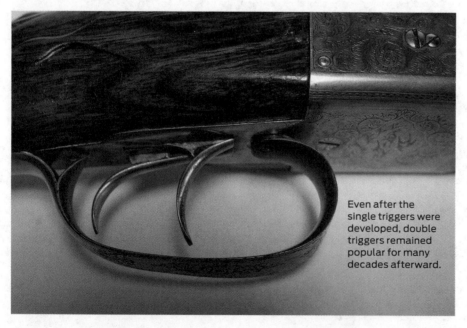

Even after the single triggers were developed, double triggers remained popular for many decades afterward.

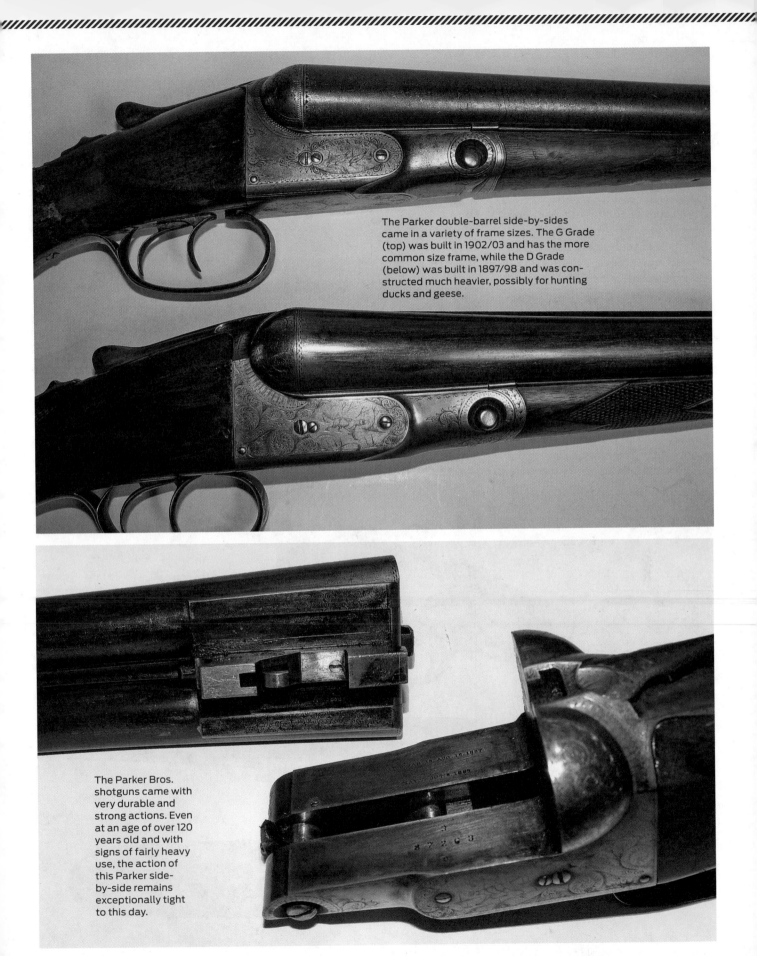

The Parker double-barrel side-by-sides came in a variety of frame sizes. The G Grade (top) was built in 1902/03 and has the more common size frame, while the D Grade (below) was built in 1897/98 and was constructed much heavier, possibly for hunting ducks and geese.

The Parker Bros. shotguns came with very durable and strong actions. Even at an age of over 120 years old and with signs of fairly heavy use, the action of this Parker side-by-side remains exceptionally tight to this day.

That wording resulted in a great deal of speculation as to what actually occurred and that mystery remains unsolved even today, with no one knowing for sure where that Invincible ended up.

I would be remiss if I didn't mention that there have been unsubstantiated rumors of a couple of other Invincible Grade Parkers. Most discriminating collectors however are very skeptical of those claims. Supposedly, the story goes that two additional Invincible grades were built, but only one of those has ever been seen. That gun was reported to have carried the serial number 230,329, but lacked the overall quality that would be expected with such a high-grade Parker. In all likelihood, the existence of these shotguns is simply a myth and will remain that way until someone comes forth to prove it to the contrary.

The model designation on Parker Bros. hammerless shotguns is sometimes followed by the letter "H" to indicate the barrels had been constructed of fluid steel as opposed to Damascus. Following that, an "E" would indicate ejectors are present

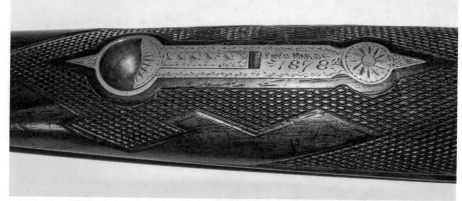

The Parker D Grade has extensive and beautiful metal engraving throughout.

To break down the L.C. Smith, you simply stick a finger under the end of the forearm stock and pull downward. That allows the removal of that portion of the stock. After that, the action should be opened to allow the barrels to rotate out of the frame.

For cleaning and/or storage, the L.C. Smith doubles can be easily broken down into to three main parts.

rather than the more common and less expensive extractors. In this case the entire designation might read something like: DHE Grade.

While the vast majority of the Parker Bros. shotguns consisted of double barrels in side-by-side formation, which most often were used by bird hunters, there were some designed specifically for shooting trap and skeet. In 1922, a single-barrel trap gun was offered, named the Flyer, which became available in the grades of: SC, SB, SA, SAA and SA-1 Special.

At the conclusion of the Parker Bros. reign in 1942, nearly 243,000 of these fine shotguns had been built in a wide variety of grades, gauges and styles.

L.C. SMITH

The roots of the L.C. Smith essentially date back to 1877, when Lyman Cornelius Smith, his brother Leroy, and William H. Baker entered into a partnership to produce the Baker three-barrel gun. Three years later, L.C. bought out his partners and dropped the W.H. Baker & Co. name. After that, those shotguns were marketed as: "L.C. Smith, Sole Maker of the Baker Gun." The years that followed from 1883 through 1888 brought substantial changes to the company, including dropping the production of the Three-Barrel Gun and adding the L.C. Smith Hammerless.

Over the last 100-plus years, the vast majority of the side-by-side shotguns have been box-lock designs. Box-lock actions are easier to construct and consequently cheaper to build. In that design, the hammers, springs, sears and firing pins are entirely housed inside the frame on the hammerless models. The side-lock hammerless shotguns differ in that some of those same parts are housed on the inside surface of the side-lock panels. Because these parts are mounted and held separately, it becomes extremely

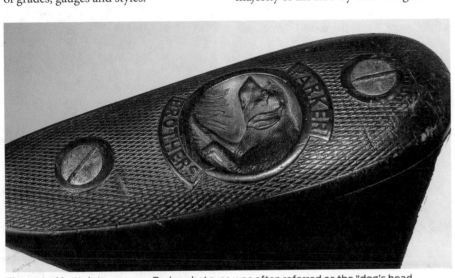

The typical buttplate on many Parker shotguns was often referred as the "dog's head buttplate."

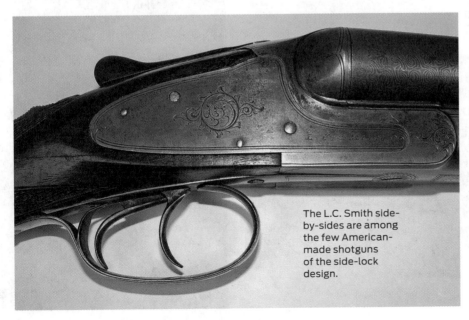

The L.C. Smith side-by-sides are among the few American-made shotguns of the side-lock design.

This Grade 2 L.C. Smith was built in 1920 and is a bit more visually embellished than the more common 0 and 00 grade field guns.

important the side-lock panels are precisely inlet in order to ensure the perfect matching of the parts. The production difficulty and challenges inherent in the production of the side-lock design makes this style of shotgun fairly rare, with L.C. Smith being one of the few U.S. manufacturers ever to build them. Nevertheless, this was the company's preferred shotgun design. It did, however, offer one box-lock design, a single-barrel trap gun first introduced 1917.

At the heart of L.C. Smith's design is a very strong, patented rotary bolt-locking system. Even though this design was patented by the company, it is said to have been copied by several other firearm manufacturers.

The first L.C. Smith side-by-sides were hammered designs and available in 8, 12, 16, 20 gauge and .410 bore, but before long the exterior hammer models became replaced with the new hammerless versions. All of the early shotguns came with Damascus barrels, but, as the 20th century was ushered in, fluid-steel barrels began to replace Damascus throughout the industry. Initially, however, some shooters were reluctant to accept this change and, recognizing that hesitancy, L.C. Smith's 1900 catalog attempted to assure prospective customers by reporting: "The new Armour Steel barrels are plain, but will stand the severest strain of nitro powder."

The L.C. Smiths were available in a wide variety of grades beginning with basic field grades of 0 and 00. These field guns were initially available at a cost of a little over $30. As the model numbers

The author's C Grade A.H. Fox 12-gauge double barrel is an elegant example of the craftsmanship of those shotguns carrying the Fox name. This one is in excellent condition, considering it was built in 1920. This was after A.H. Fox had left the company, but before Savage Arms took over.

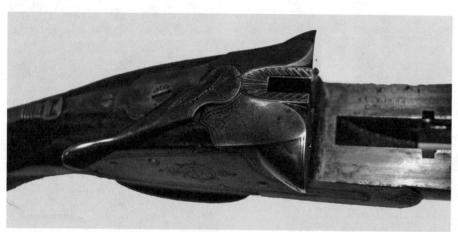

The L.C. Smith locking mechanism was at the heart of this company's fine shotguns.

Many of the earlier side-by-side doubles were made with exposed hammers, like this 10-gauge Ithaca.

increased beyond 0, so did the fanciness of the engraving, checkering and wood quality. Various options were available at increased cost including a few different stock designs, single triggers (which in some cases were selectable) and automatic ejectors. In 1904, the option of a single trigger over the more traditional double trigger would cost the purchaser an additional $25. But even after the single trigger was offered, double triggers remained very popular with shooters. Eventually various higher-grade models became available, including the Crown, Monogram, Pigeon, Specialty and the heavily engraved, much-coveted, gold-inlayed Deluxe Grade. Over time, skeet and trap models were added as well as guns specifically designed for use by waterfowlers and lightweight versions for the upland bird hunter.

I once owned a Model 3E L.C. Smith double barrel that was built in 1902. This particular gun was designed specifically for shooting trap and came with fluid-steel barrels and ejectors. What made this shotgun unique was the fact it had come from the factory with no safety. While many of the modern-era trap guns lack a safety, all the L.C. Smith side-by-side trap guns I have encountered since that time had a safety in the typical location on the tang of the receiver.

There was even a custom-built presentation L.C. Smith double barrel built specifically for Annie Oakley. This gun was engraved with Ms. Oakley's signature on the trigger guard and very detailed facial profiles of her on each of the side-locks. It is not clear, however, whether this shotgun came engraved in this way from the factory, or whether it was engraved later.

A.H. FOX

By the mid-1890s, Ansley H. Fox, had established himself within the Baltimore area as a very prominent and capable live-pigeon and trap shooter. That interest in shooting and firearms eventually led to the development of The Fox Gun Company in July 1898. Customer demand quickly overpowered the operational capabilities of that plant, leading to its closure only six months later. The assets of The Fox Gun Company were then transferred to a new company called the Baltimore Arms Co.

Being equipped with fluid-steel barrels, the author's C Grade A.H. Fox is perfectly safe for use shooting modern-era smokeless ammo.

Damascus steel barrels are beautiful in their own right, yet not recommended for use with the modern-day, smokeless-powder ammunition.

FROM DAMASCUS TO FLUID-STEEL BARRELS

Most shotguns produced in the 1800s up until the early 20th century were made with Damascus barrels. Even though Damascus steel is very attractive, fluid-steel barrels are far superior for strength. Producing Damascus is an elaborate and time-consuming process that requires literally thousands of welds. The process begins by twisting and welding small pieces of metal rod together (sometimes alternating iron and steel) in order to form larger ones. Those bars are then flattened and spiral-coiled around a mandrel then forge-welded. The end result is an eye-catching beautiful work of gunsmithing art containing a swirl pattern of light and dark metal. But while stunningly beautiful in appearance, Damascus generally lacks strength and durability that is needed to withstand the pressures generated by the smokeless-powder ammunition of today.

Aside from being stronger and more reliable, the fluid-steel barrels came with the advantage of being cheaper to produce. But the move away from Damascus wasn't readily accepted by all shooters, many of whom continued to cling to their belief that Damascus was still superior to the then newly offered alternative. Because of this hesitancy, some manufacturers even resorted to the unscrupulous action of imprinting the outer surface of their fluid-steel barrels with a faux swirl pattern, believing it might fool their customers into thinking the barrels were actual Damascus. I don't believe Parker Brothers, L.C. Smith or A.H. Fox ever resorted to doing this, but some other manufacturers did.

If you are ever in doubt as to whether your barrels are actually made of Damascus steel, there is an easy way to verify the authenticity. Simply locate an area that is normally out view then use a piece of fine sandpaper, or a small amount of muriatic acid to etch the surface. If it is true Damascus, you won't be able to eliminate the swirl pattern.

The deep-cut engraving on this A.H. Fox C Grade has a great deal of eye-appeal.

But even then, the years that followed continued to be volatile and unstable for A.H. In 1904, A.H. left Baltimore Arms to form a new firearms company called the Philadelphia Gun Company, which also was short-lived. In the meantime, Winchester had taken A.H. on as a professional shooter, which likely helped his reputation. Possibly the most important milestone to his career occurred in July 1905 when the Philadelphia Gun Company announced the release of his A.H. Fox Gun. Production records are a bit sketchy during these early years, but it is believed that fewer than 2,000 shotguns were produced by the Philadelphia Gun Company before the operation was sold and renamed the A.H. Fox Gun Company.

Initially five grades of Fox shotguns were offered: A, B, C, D and F, which were only available in 12 gauge, but in 1912 those offerings were expanded to include the 16 and 20 gauge. All of the varying grades were similar in overall construction, but varied in the amount of engraving, inlays, checkering and the degree of wood figure. In order accommodate the lower-end market in 1910, the Fox Sterlingworth was offered in 20, 16 and 12 gauge and priced at only $25. These guns came with genuine Sterlingworth Fluid Compressed Steel barrels and were available in a choice of barrel lengths from 26 to 32 inches.

Unique features of the A.H. Fox shotguns include their barrel extension and

horizontal axis rotary fastener, which differed from all other box-lock style shotguns. The Fox Sterlingworth shotguns did not incorporate this design, but used through-lump barrels instead. The "lump" in this name applies to a piece of steel which is machined separately and then brazed to the bottom of the barrels. While this design is perfectly functional and less costly to produce, its appearance is less elegant. Because of its lower production cost, lump-barrel construction is commonly found on the less-expensive British and American double guns.

In later years the A.H. Fox grading nomenclature became a bit more confusing. The grades of AE through FE escalated in fanciness as the letters progressed higher,

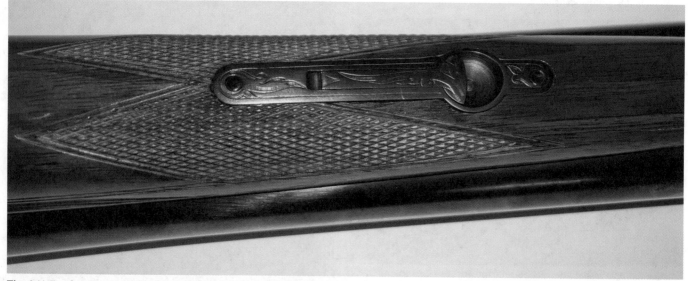

The A.H. Fox forearm stock is released in the traditional manner by using the inlayed metal release in the forearm.

but upon reaching the HE grade those embellishments seemed to decrease. Then there were even fancier models like the XE Grade, which came with exceptional checkering, engraving, gold inlays and the highest degree of figure in its stocks.

Even though A.H. Fox's reputation within the side-by-side shotgun industry is quite noteworthy, his actual involvement within those ranks was short-lived. In 1912, company investors bought out his interest in the company. After that, The Fox Shotgun Company continued to produce the fine-quality A.H. Fox shotguns under the same name until late in 1929. In that year, Savage acquired the company, essentially ending the high-quality legacy of the A.H. Fox shotgun. Savage continued producing Fox-named shotguns in the years to come, but they were cheaper versions of considerably lesser quality.

After leaving the shotgun-building business, A.H. Fox went on to form the Fox Motor Company in 1919, but after only a few autos were built, that venture abruptly came to an end two years later.

THE WAY I SEE IT

I have a real love affair with our high-quality, American-built, side-by-side shotguns. If you are lucky enough to find and buy any of these legendary works of gunsmithing art today they might come to you with a few dents or scratches, which are simply reflections of their age; the bluing might be warn in places; and the checkering could be starting to disappear. But, to me, those marks only amount to signs of an active lifestyle from a colorful past when life was often simpler, and quality was appreciated to a higher degree than it is today. If you question the quality of any of these old favorites, I would suggest that you simply open the action then close it again. Hear that resounding "thug" as the heavy, well-built action locks into place? To me that is the sound of quality that is seldom found in the doubles of today. 🔘

The author's collection of American-built, side-by-side doubles grows whenever he can locate an appropriate addition.

M O U N T

Three things to consider when hunting at higher elevations: weight, weather protection and accuracy

› TYLER FREEL

Although a cheeky definition of a mountain rifle is: "any rifle you are willing to carry up a mountain," the reality is that an entire genre of hunting rifles has grown and separated itself from your everyday deer or elk rifle. Sure, in the early days of mountain sheep and goat hunting, typical hunting rifles had to suffice, but I have no doubt that since the first sheep hunters carried a rifle up the mountain, they have been working to make them lighter and more effective.

AIN RIFLES

On a mountain hunt, your rifle is always either in your hand or strapped to your pack. Sheep and goat hunters are always looking for ways to maximize performance and minimize weight.

Don't Over-Scope

We go out of our way to look for lighter options in a mountain rifle. Many folks immediately negate that weight savings by installing too much scope. For any reasonable shot, 7x or 8x magnification is plenty adequate, and a mountain hunter rarely needs a large, light-gathering objective. ideal mountain riflescope is a Leupold V 2.5-8x36mm with the CDS turret, which will take all the elevation guesswork ou your shots, helping to ensure that shot a lifetime gets to the right spot. You ge the performance you need, and any big scope, frankly, is just worthless extra w Also consider your mounting system. L weight rings and bases like those from are a great way to securely mount you scope, but save on weight.

Sheep camp consists of the bare essentials. Not only do you have to pack everything in, you also have to be able to pack out your gear and a sheep.

An experienced mountain hunter is often meticulous about what everything weighs. That's because every piece of gear or food must be carried into the backcountry, and any place a hunter can cut weight in gear allows him or her to be more efficient. Weight saved in other areas can also be replaced with food, buying valuable extra time in the field. A rifle is no exception to that rule, and on a sheep or goat hunt, it's usually ideal to have the lightest rifle possible, without sacrificing accuracy or reliability.

A properly used mountain rifle is sure to endure some of the worst treatment and conditions any hunting rifle will have to. We're not talking about a walk from the truck to a treestand. Impact, abrasions, temperature swings, and often constant, unrelenting moisture are par for the course on a sheep or mountain goat hunt, and your rifle needs to withstand it.

WEIGHT

By far, the most talked about characteristic of a mountain rifle is its weight, or lack thereof. That's easy to understand, being that during 99 percent of a mountain hunt, that rifle is either strapped to a backpack or being carried by hand. Day after day, climbing mountain after mountain can really take a toll, and every bit of weight a hunter can cut is a welcome blessing. Sure, a 10-pound rifle will get the job done if you're willing to tolerate it, but in today's world, we can do much better.

This is packed for a 14-day hunt. The weight of your rifle plays a big part in your overall pack weight, so you don't want it to be excessive, but it needs to be absolutely dependable.

Another factory rifle that will get by in the mountains is the Winchester XPR. It's not expensive or fancy, but it gets the job done. This particular XPR in 6.5 Creedmoor has killed six Dall rams.

The stock is probably the most significant component that weight can be cut from on a rifle. We're not suggesting shaving wood off your old Mauser or Springfield either. Modern materials and designs have given us rifle-stock options that are lighter, stronger, and more functional than ever before. "Synthetic" no longer means only plastic, as other options abound. On the cheaper end, you'll still find hollow or foam injected plastic stocks, and typically they are a good value for the price. Moving up from there, foam-filled fiberglass brings a stronger and slightly lighter option to the table, and on some of the lightest models, you'll find foam-core, carbon-fiber stocks. Don't let the "foam" part throw you off, these are some of the most rugged, durable and accurate stocks, especially considering how lightweight they are. You can even give your beat-up hunting rifle a makeover by ordering an aftermarket stock, many times cutting your rifle's weight by a pound or more, especially if it's wearing wood.

After the stock, the most common place to see weight shaved is the barrel. A pencil-thin barrel contour is expected, and excess steel is certainly a good place to cut the weight. Fluted barrels are also common, removing material, but leaving a larger overall diameter. This does help in cooling by creating more surface area, and can help with barrel rigidity, but it's often still tough to get the weight down as much as an overall thinner profile will. On many rifles, you'll also see the barrels cut down in length slightly. This saves a few ounces and typically has no relevant effect on performance. Rather than 24- to 26-inch barrels, you'll typically see 20- to 22-inch barrels on mountain guns. This will cause a slight loss in velocity with some chamberings, particularly large, slow-burning magnums, but not so much that it hurts performance at reasonable hunting ranges. Some of the more nimble cartridges, like the 6.5 Creedmoor, tend to be hardly affected at all by a shorter barrel, and there's no reason to carry metal you don't need.

Carbon-wrapped barrels are also a good option for cutting weight on a mountain rifle, while maintaining a larger barrel profile. On custom jobs, and

Factory rifles like this Ruger M77, an early rifle offered in 6.5 Creedmoor, have been toted around the mountains for decades. If your budget doesn't allow for an expensive custom rifle, these will do just fine.

Sheep and goat hunts demand a rifle withstand heat, cold, moisture and, sometimes, salt water, and still get the job done. The author took this mountain goat with a Browning X-Bolt Pro in .300 Win Mag. (Photo courtesy John Whipple)

even some production models, you will see excess metal removed or replaced with some titanium components. Drilled out bolt handles, ventilated extractors, and fluted bolts are all effective manifestations of weight reduction you'll commonly find on specialized mountain rifles. After all, we are talking about hunters who will cut their toothbrush handle in half to save weight.

WEATHER PROTECTION

There was a point in time when Parkerizing and bluing were the standard for corrosion protection on rifles. This seems a little laughable to us these days, but if you think blued rifles rust easily, try the steel by itself. Still, in those days, sheep hunters used it because it's what they had. This required quite a bit of extra effort to keep the rifles corrosion-free and functioning properly when exposed to the elements. Even something as simple as condensation in the tent will give a rifle a coating of surface rust overnight, and it's even worse if you're in

coastal regions hunting mountain goats. This isn't to say you cannot use blued rifles. They do work, but require lots of extra care, and you're basically guaranteed to get some corrosion if you use one enough.

As stainless steel barrels, receivers and other weather-resistant components became much more widely available, they largely replaced blued steel, for good reason. Stainless can still rust, but requires much less babying during the course of a hunt, and in that way, it gives us a more effective tool for the job. You'd hear people knock stainless with a variety of complaints, especially as it became more and more prominent. Claims that stainless wasn't as accurate due to the nickel content and barrel-cutting procedures, and that it didn't cool as fast might have had some clout, but no longer. There are innumerable fantastic-shooting stainless barrels available, and for a mountain rifle, it's silly to go without. Corrosion-resistant materials are thankfully becoming much more commonplace throughout

a rifle, in bolt assemblies and trigger groups as well as barrels and receivers, making a mountain hunter's life much easier.

Although a major attribute of a modern mountain rifle's stock is its reduced weight, weather protection is a major area in which these synthetic materials shine. As a general rule, synthetics are not only lighter, but tougher and much more moisture-resistant than their wood counterparts. The generally abrasive nature of everything encountered on a mountain hunt doesn't play well with walnut and fine finishes, but that's the least of your worries. When conditions are chronically wet, as they often are on mountain hunts, the wood in a stock has the tendency to absorb moisture and swell slightly. This will change the pressure on the action and potentially the barrel, which can play hell with your point of impact. I've seen big rams missed and hearts broken because of this. If you like a pretty wood stock on a rifle, that stock is likely not to be so pretty

Many custom (and now also factory) rifles have fluted bolts and hollowed bolt handles to help reduce the weight, and Cerakote finishes to improve corrosion resistance. That, with a lightweight scope and CDS dial, is a great combination.

Over the years, the author has trimmed down the gear on his rifle by using a smaller scope, ditching the sling, and using a lighter weight bipod. Ounces add up to pounds.

Mountain hunters love wildcat cartridges, and fast, medium-sized cartridges are perfect for sheep. Pictured is a 27 O'Connor, essentially a .280 Ackley Improved necked down to .270, with slightly more case capacity than a .270 Winchester A.I.

after you beat the hell out of it for 10 days in the rocks. That, coupled with moisture issues, makes going synthetic for this purpose a no-brainer.

The final piece of the weather-protection pie is coatings. Gun coatings have come a long way in just the past few years, and although Cerakote is likely the most popular option, there are a variety of good coatings that will protect your rifle and keep it functioning in the elements even better. Adding a quality coating to already weather- and scratch-resistant materials provides a superior level of protection and requires very little maintenance. As an added benefit, it's possible to keep that dark/blued rifle look and coloring with a completely superior performing system. These options are now becoming more available and even standard in many factory offerings.

ACCURACY

It's very easy to get wrapped up in details like weight, or the most technologically advanced, good-looking coatings, but it's all for nothing if your rifle isn't also accurate. Mountain hunting is expensive in many ways, in dollars and in effort. Shot opportunities are always hard-earned, and often very hard to come by, so you need to know that your rifle is going to be able to hold up its end of the deal. In a mountain rifle, what we'd call accuracy is a little bit more complex than just the rifle's ability to punch holes in paper off a bench. Before actually putting a number on it, there are a few things that need to be understood about the types of shots you'll likely be taking.

Many of your shots on animals like sheep and mountain goats will be steep-angle shots from improvised positions, most commonly resting on a backpack. A lightweight mountain rifle tends to be much less forgiving and less stable to aim than your 11-pound precision rifle. You might be told to expect extreme long-range shots, but in reality, there's typically no need to shoot more than 300 yards. And with the 13 rams I've taken, I've shot more than 400 yards only twice. Also considering the often extremely difficult-to-read wind and atmospheric conditions, you shouldn't be overly concerned with taking long shots.

Most high-end, "ultra-light" mountain rifles will have some sort of action bedding to improve accuracy, and some of them will shoot absolutely lights-out. However, as far as accuracy itself is concerned, a rifle that will shoot three-shot groups less than 1.5 MOA is completely adequate for a mountain rifle, which is typically easy to attain, even in more generic, non-bedded factory rifles. If you can find a load that will shoot less than 1 MOA, you're golden, and anything more is getting nitpicky. Although some prefer the five-shot group for their standard of accuracy, I believe in a practical application. Three-shot groups are adequate for gauging accuracy in mountain rifles. Even premium, ultralight rifles will often start throwing flyers after three or four rounds due to barrel heat. The trade-off for removing lots of mass from barrels is that they get hot quickly, and each barrel will react differently. My custom sheep rifle will consistently hold 1-inch groups at 200 yards for the first three shots, but if I keep shooting or don't let my barrel cool completely between groups, watch out. It's rare in the field

Rifle Accessories and Additional Weather Protection

Your basic rifle and optic setup should be very weather resistant, however there are a few extra steps you should take to both minimize corrosion and ensure that your rifle will be ready to get the job done, even in the absolute worst conditions.

Muzzle Tape: In my opinion, your muzzle should be taped at all times in the field. This prevents dirt, debris and moisture from contaminating your bore and causing corrosion, a wet-bore miss, or even your gun to blow up. It's one of the easiest things you can do. Keep extra tape wrapped around the barrel in front of the fore-end, and just shoot through the tape. The air pressure will blow the tape off before the bullet ever gets there and you will see zero point of impact shift.

Scope Caps: A few different styles of flip-up scope caps are available, and you should get them. They are great at keeping your lenses free of moisture and debris and are easily flipped open when it's time to shoot. Also, it's not a bad idea on mountain hunts also to use a neoprene sleeve to protect your scope when it's in your backpack.

ChapStick: Use ChapStick to fill in the screw heads on your rifle and optics mounts and rings. Screw heads are one of the first places you'll see corrosion and the ChapStick will keep moisture out and is easily washed away with any basic solvent.

Bipods: I've packed bipods while sheep hunting for years, and I highly recommend them. On mountain hunts, you'll often have plenty of time to set up your shot, and bipods often offer a much more stable rest than a backpack. Currently, the Javelin and Javelin Lite bipods from Spartan Precision Equipment are probably the best-suited to mountain hunting. They are extremely light, and the bipod is stowed in a pocket until ready to shoot, then easily popped into a magnetic socket. They are fantastic.

Slings: A rifle sling is up to personal preference, but over the years I've found them to be just dead weight. On a sheep hunt, my rifle is either strapped to my pack or in my hand, and almost never slung over my shoulder, so I quit taking one and haven't looked back.

It's a good idea to step up in cartridge size for mountain goats, as they are both notoriously tough to put down, and have a tendency to throw themselves off cliffs if they are not anchored quickly. However, the author's .25-06 did a fine job on this big billy.

Mountain Cartridges

Don't let yourself get too hung up on caliber, but here are some great, proven sheep cartridges.

.243 Win.
.270 Win.
.25-06 Rem.
.280 Ackley Imp.
6.5mm Creedmoor

For mountain goats, all of the previous will work, but I would generally recommend slightly more punch, as big billys are typically much tougher to put down than sheep, and tend to be in more precarious spots.

300 Win. Mag.
.30-06 Springfield
7mm Rem. Mag.
.340 Wby.
.338 Win. Mag.

to need to shoot more than two or three times in short succession, so it's extremely unlikely to cause you any issues.

PICKING YOUR MOUNTAIN RIFLE

Knowing how and why a mountain rifle is built the way it is can give you a much better idea of what to look for in your own rifle selection. You can weigh all the factors as well as price to come up with the best option for you. Some folks can afford to invest $3,000 to $5,000 into an absolute top-of-the-line rifle, but most of us have to prioritize what we want and find something we can afford, and that's OK.

If you're able to travel to do this kind of hunting, chances are you can afford a rifle on the upper end of the spectrum, but a lot of folks live in places with fantastic hunting opportunities, but aren't exactly rolling in the dough. If that's you, don't fret, there are still plenty of good options out there. When I was 18, I killed my first Dall ram with a Remington Model 710, which I had saved up for a few years earlier when they first came out. The rifle was on the heavier side, with an atrocious

polymer-lined action, but the thing did shoot well, and I killed a lot of animals with that rifle over the years. Now, I wouldn't go as far as to say it was a great mountain rifle, and there are much better options available on the affordable end of the spectrum. If that's where you're at, just keep in mind that you're going to have to put up with a little extra weight on your rifle.

I would consider the starting point to be something like the Winchester XPR. It's a no-frills, medium-weight factory rifle you can get in many calibers for around $500. They tend to shoot under 1 MOA, and in my experience, are very dependable. It has a polymer stock, coated barrel and receiver and although it's definitely not going to win any popularity contests in the sheep world, it quietly gets the job done. One that I have had for a few years in 6.5 Creedmoor has killed six rams, as well as several deer and caribou. When we're talking about purpose-built mountain rifles, it's hard to squeeze in ones like this, but for someone on a tight budget, a more generic rifle like the XPR will get the job done and provides a great baseline.

The midrange subset of production mountain rifles is probably where most of us tend to look when it comes to getting a new one. There is a large diversity of options, and although rifles in this category tend to be slightly more expensive, they are also a bit more specialized and refined. Most of these rifles will weigh 6 to 7.5 pounds and cost between $700 and $1,200. They aren't ultralight, but most hunters (including myself) would consider them very tolerable to tote up the mountain. An underrated option that is very popular here in Alaska is the Tikka T3x (and its variants). These rifles have a reputation of being very dependable, and consistently shoot very well. Their stainless models hold up great to foul conditions, the Superlite model weighs around 6 pounds, and you can usually find them for less than $800. All these factors have made them a solid go-to for resident sheep hunters in Alaska and Canada for years.

You'll also have your Remington 700s,

Winchester M70s and Ruger Hawkeyes, all fairly standard rifles that fit a similar price, weight and accuracy range. If you're looking at this range of rifles, one relative newcomer that should not be overlooked is Bergara. Although these rifles have started hitting the shelves in the U.S., they haven't really established themselves in the mountain hunting game. With just a few variations of the B14 model, you're not looking at infinite options, but in my experience, these are smooth, fine and very accurate rifles. The B14 Hunter is probably the most ideal option, weighing right around 7 pounds with a price tag of $825, give or take. It's a fine rifle for the price, and definitely one to consider.

Topping out what I'd call the midrange production category would have to be the Browning X-Bolt, in stainless or Hell's Canyon configuration, at around $1,200. Both are going to hold up to the elements very well. It's accurate, well-put-together and

ergonomic rifle that will serve you well in the mountains. The short action will come in at around 6.5 pounds, which is getting pretty light for this category, and from experience, is a pleasure to handle on a mountain hunt.

Where we really start to see the cream rise to the top is in the high-end production mountain rifles. As you cut weight and increase precision, the price goes up, and most of these will range from $1,800 to $3,000. Most of these rifles incorporate features that were present only on custom rifles in years past. They offer the most optimal performance, weight and dependability money can buy in a factory rifle these days and are truly made for the mountains.

This topic can't be covered without mentioning one rifle in particular: the Kimber Mountain Ascent. Now, Kimber also has several other very adequate mountain rifle models, but this one is its flagship. In a short action, this factory gun is incredibly light

There are several different ballistic-turret systems out there for hunting riflescopes, and you should consider getting one. Taking out all the guesswork and holdover for shots across a variety of ranges gives much-needed confidence.

at just under 5 pounds. The 84M action is very popular with custom mountain rifle builders, and although this model has been around for a few years, it really sets the standard in this world. They are handy, comfortable to carry and shoot, and use a dependable Mauser-claw extractor. The Kimbers have been rumored to be either very accurate, or very inaccurate in past years, depending on the barrel you got, and I know folks who have had troubles finding loads that would shoot well. That seems to be in the past, however, and the Mountain Ascent carries a sub-MOA guarantee and $2,050 price tag.

Another staple, high-end production rifle is the Fieldcraft by Barrett. Ranging from 5.2 to 5.6 pounds, it's slightly heavier than the Ascent, but a couple hundred dollars cheaper as well, and most folks wouldn't be able to tell the difference in weight anyway. Complexity often results in chaos on the mountain, and this handy, and accurate push-feed-action rifle has a simplicity that perfectly fills the needs of a sheep or goat hunter.

If you're interested in carbon-wrapped barrels, don't overlook Christensen Arms, which has been hitting the market pretty hard and has a reputation for producing extremely accurate rifles. The Ridgeline Titanium model features a titanium action and a large-profile, carbon-wrapped match barrel. It carries a sub-MOA guarantee, but you should expect to find loads that will do much better than that. It's on the heavy side for this category, at just under 6 pounds, but still a very reasonable weight, and with a better point of impact holding, quicker cooling and a threaded muzzle.

You should be able to pick one up for around $2,500.

For all the Weatherby fans out there, there's a great option for you as well. Weatherby's MK V actions are dependable and heavy duty, and typically Weatherby rifles shade toward the heavy side, but the MK V Backcountry TI comes in at just 4.8 pounds in its standard-length action. It's just about as light as anything out there, and it delivers the high level of quality and craftsmanship you'd expect from a Weatherby. When chambered in the company's new 6.5 WBY RPM cartridge, it's probably the fastest and lightest cartridge and rifle combination you can get in a production rifle. You'll be looking at spending $3,500 for this rifle, but along with performance on the mountain, you're buying an heirloom. **GD**

Sheep hunting is unbelievably hard work, and in very remote country. Your rifle is just one part of the equation, but it's an important one if you want to have a heavy pack coming out.

A PAIR OF
COLD WAR
MAKEOVERS

Two cool considerations for communist-bloc firearms collectors

❯ GEORGE LAYMAN

The fall of the Iron Curtain saw countless numbers of former communist handguns and rifles, which were compliant with the Gun Control Act of 1968, arriving to the United States, well before the Berlin Wall had completely crumbled. However, a couple more surprises of two once-unobtainable Eastern-bloc submachine guns showed up in the 2000s, that is, after a complete about-face with some mechanical and cosmetic modifications to boot.

By 2006, the greater majority of surplus firearms from the old communist bloc had reached U.S. shores aside from a few late-comers. Eastern bloc leftovers or not, there were still several special-purpose firearms that were destined to become, or were already, obsolete, but were still taboo commodities for the average American shooter or collector. Numerous Class III, or fully automatic, former

Soviet or Eastern European arms that were declared surplus a few years after or even before the fall of the Berlin Wall and its successive domino effect, were anxiously awaiting disposal. Aside from current communist countries such as Cuba, North Korea, Laos or even China, which still maintains quantities of antiquated, fully automatic arms such as the old Russian PPSh-41, Czech M48, and the

Romanian Orita M 41 submachine guns, many were simply not importable to the United States, aside from deactivated parts kits and the like. By the mid-2000s, the BATFE provided some leeway in this regard, with specific instructions that some former communist submachine guns COULD be allowed into the U.S. re-classified as pistols, providing they follow strict guidelines and modifications that

The Vz 61 semi-automatic pistol appears to function best with European CIP-spec 7.65mm (.32 ACP) ammunition. However, most U.S. ammo will feed as well, providing it is of a round-nosed jacketed type. The double-staggered magazine finds that flat-nosed fodder will cause jams and hang-ups.

would meet government approval. Three major steps had to be adhered to: a) none would have selective automatic-fire capability, b) the arms had to be redesigned to fire from a closed bolt, and c) those with barrels 16 inches or less with folding or collapsible buttstocks, had to be welded or pinned to the frame permanently, or be removed altogether.

Going back in time, many of us remember when the first Israeli Military Industries Uzi 9mm semi-automatic classified as carbines were imported in the 1980s, both with a 16-inch barrel, and closed breech, however it did have a folding stock because the barrel met overall legal length requirements. In the same vein, a stockless, and a "mini-Uzi" version with the original submachine gun barrel length legally classified as a pistol, came later. In a nutshell, this concept was nothing new, especially as the Auto Ordnance 1927 A5 Thompson Semi-Auto Pistol pioneered the entire idea. By 2005, it appears the ball began rolling on introducing legal-to-own versions of former communist-bloc submachine guns. Two of the most well-known examples took the giant step. In the late 2000s, the first to make a showing that was completely BATFE-approved as a semi-automatic pistol, was a modified variation of the world-renowned Czechoslovakian 7.65mm (.32 ACP) Samopal Vzor 61 Submachine Gun, known more commonly as the Vz 61 Skorpion. Just before 2010, it would be followed by the previously licensed, Polish-made copy of the Russian Pistolet Pulemyot Sudaeyeva 43, or PPS 43. Marketed as a semi-automatic pistol coined the PPS 43c, this 7.62x25mm arm was additionally produced in a non-original 9mm Luger caliber as well. With each of these exciting new entries using several original surplus submachine gun parts and com-

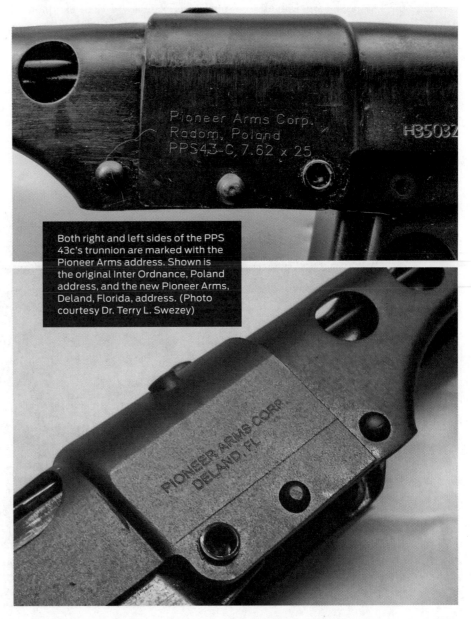

Both right and left sides of the PPS 43c's trunnion are marked with the Pioneer Arms address. Shown is the original Inter Ordnance, Poland address, and the new Pioneer Arms, Deland, Florida, address. (Photo courtesy Dr. Terry L. Swezey)

ponents, both ushered in a new concept for shooters and fans of communist-bloc military arms.

THE CZECHPOINT VZ 61 SKORPION PISTOL

Originally designed in 1959 by Miroslav Rybar, a Czech arms engineer, the Samopal Vz 61 submachine gun, much like the Russian AK-47 rifle, the Makarov and Tokarev pistols, is one of the most recognizable and well-known arms of the Cold War era. This closed-breech blowback submachine gun was produced from 1961 through 1979 and uses double-staggered 10- and 20-round curved box magazines. Chambered for the 7.65mm Browning (.32 ACP) pistol cartridge, the 2.87-pound arm with its 4.5-inch barrel makes the Czech Skorpion a fairly compact submachine gun that was specifically intended for armor, recon and special-operations groups requiring a compact but efficient arm that could be carried in a conventional belt or shoulder holster. As it was initially chambered for

a low-powered, subsonic cartridge, this also made the Vz 61 ideally adaptable to a suppressor. The configuration of its wire folding stock, which when closed, and positioned above the barrel, contributed to the weapon's "Skorpion" moniker.

Practically every communist-bloc country has used the Skorpion for one capacity or another. The Vz 61 was also made under license in Serbia for some years and was coined the M 84 and 84a. Serving four long tours in the 1970s and 80s in the Republic of Korea, I quickly learned of another regular user, following the attendance of counter intelligence after action briefings of captured or killed North Korean infiltrators. Shown on several occasions were static displays of numerous examples of Vz 61 Skorpion sub guns, some complete with silencers with others having the folding wire stock removed entirely. It is quite apparent that the DPRK has been a regular user of the Skorpion for clandestine operations and intrusions into the south since the late 1960s. At about age 16, when thumbing

through W.H.B. Smith's Small Arms of the World, I learned it wouldn't be long before the Vz 61 Skorpion would become one of my favorite modern firearms of all time, but during the Cold War they were an impossible item to obtain at any cost; even if one applied for a Class III license. Thus, it was during my 21-year career in the Army did I finally have an unlimited access to them as, being in military intelligence, captured examples abounded, and were many times taken to the firing ranges during my years when tasked with providing instruction and familiarization fire of opposing forces small arms. Of course, at the end of a class day, all were turned back into the armorer of the foreign-weapons section of the arms room in our battalion.

About 2006, things began to change when a BATFE-approved version of the Vz 61 Skorpion began to be imported. Manufactured in Jablunka, Czech Republic, the new approved semi-automatic pistol was manufactured with a completely modified lower receiver that had

Both the surplus holster (opposite) and original magazine pouch show Czech-inspector markings, along with a previous owner's name from the Cold War years. OTK stands for Office of Technical Control, an equivalent to our US MILSPEC marking.

two positions for its selector lever: "O" for Safe, and "1" for Semi-Automatic fire. The submachine gun version has a number "20" in the middle for fully automatic fire. In addition, the folding buttstock and its mount on the flat rear base of the upper frame was also eliminated to qualify it as a pistol, as the wire stock would constitute it as a "short-barrel rifle" requiring the $200 tax and registration as with a machine gun. Furthermore, inside the grip on the selective-fire version also includes an RPM regulator, or rate reducer, which keeps the action firing 850 rounds per minute; without it, the rate of fire would climb to 1,000 rounds per minute. On the new semi-auto version this device is unnecessary and omitted. In October 2008, CzechPoint, the firm that handled sales of the new Vz 61, obtained its Type 08 FFL import license. Prior to this, TGI of Knoxville, Tennessee, and Waffen Werks imported the Vz 61. According to Dan Brown of CzechPoint, the manufacturer in the

Czech Republic additionally changed its name from D-Technik to Czech Small Arms in order to better represent the company. It deserves to be mentioned that CZ Uhersky Brod, which once produced the Vz 61 submachine gun, has never manufactured the Vz 61 for the U.S. market, nor is there any connection of the legal-to-own Skorpion to CZ USA. Dan noted that monthly shipments of the Vz 61 are regularly received, but sell out rather quickly.

Noteworthy is that the new U.S.-legal Vz 61 is also available in both .380 ACP and 9mm Makarov, neither of which was ever used by the Czech military or police. CzechPoint offers a complete line of parts and accessories for the Vz 61 as well as complete guns and parts for the Vz 58 rifle and the older CZ 52 pistols. For those who wish to apply and modify their Vz 61 into a short-barrel rifle, Czech-Point also carries both the wire stock and adapter, the latter of which should be installed by a gunsmith.

I found that the Vz 61 semi-auto pistol handles like a charm and is a very intriguing representation of the original, and maintains accurate fire at 15 to 20 yards with a two-hand hold using the magazine as a hold or a rest. Unlike most other submachine guns, the Vz 61 Skorpion was originally made to fire from a closed bolt and functions smoothly without issue. This is one of the rare cases where such a weapon does not use a fixed firing pin from an open bolt to slam-fire the cartridge. As a result, no BATFE modification of the action was required, as we shall later see was the case with the Polish PPS 43c. For ammunition, it appears to function best with European CIP-spec brands such as Fiocchi, Sellier & Bellot or Serbian Privian Partizan. Using U.S.-made ammunition of SAAMI specs, especially with flat-nosed bullets or anything other than a full-metal jacketed, round-nosed projectile can lead to feeding problems. CzechPoint's Vz 61 is an out-of-sight addition to the arsenal of

any communist-bloc shooter or collector, and are available with both black plastic, or light beech wood grips; the former was used by Czech police with the latter supplied on the army-issue versions. Aside from the two cocking knobs, fire indicator and selector, which are made of a durable, glass-filled nylon, all parts are of milled or stamped metal. It was a 45-year wait, but well worth it.

PIONEER ARMS PPS 43C SEMI-AUTOMATIC PISTOL

Born during the 872-day siege of Leningrad, the PPS 43 Sudaeyev was one of the most efficient and simple subma-chine guns used during World War II. Developed in 1942 by Alexei Sudaeyev, it was based on the open-bolt submachine gun principle similar to the older PPSh 41, but was equipped with a folding stock with basic intentions for issue to vehicle crews, recon personnel and support troops. Early on, it was made at the Se-stroyetsk factory in the Kurotny district during the desperate battles in the Lenin-grad region and many were handed out the factory windows to soldiers, along with workers firing back at the attack-ing Germans. This 7.62x25mm arm was basically produced of stamped sheet steel, aside from the barrel, bolt and a few oth-er small components, and used a remov-able, but stationary, nub-type firing pin that slam-fired each cartridge. Supplied with a perforated cooling shield like the PPSh 41, the 35-round curved magazine serves as the fore grip. The PPS 43 went on to be used by numerous different communist and third-world coun-tries during the Cold War and even to the present, but was phased out of Russian service completely by 1960, used in the end by the Soviet navy. I had viewed fair numbers

of them at the captured-weapons dump at Long Binh Depot in Vietnam in 1971, however many of these might have been the Chinese copy known as the Type 54. On today's collector market, a transfer-able, fully automatic PPS 43 can sell for anywhere from $8,000 to $10,000.

It was in about 2008 to 2009 that a legal-to-own version of the famed PPS 43 was approved for import into the United States. Pioneer Arms of Radom, Poland, received the green light from the BATFE that its new PPS 43c Semi-Automatic Pistol would be available through its first importer, Inter Ordnance

The Vz 61 semi-automatic pistol appears to function best with round-nosed jacketed-type ammunition. The double-staggered magazine finds that flat-nosed fodder will cause jams and hang-ups.

The introduction of a former legal-to-own Russian submachine gun licensed to Poland was a great boon to communist-bloc firearms aficionados. The Pioneer Arms PPS 43c, when first imported, was an instant must-have for many. Re-engineered to fire semi-automatically from a closed bolt with permanently fastened, non-movable folding stock, it was introduced in the late 2000s. Nicely boxed, the PPS 43c includes a cleaning rod, three magazines and a manual. Magazine pouches, oiler and other components have to be purchased separately. (Photo courtesy Dr. Terry L. Swezey)

of Monroe, North Carolina. The "c" was added to distinguish it from the full-auto version. I.O. has since relocated to Palm Bay Florida and, up until three years ago, was the sole importer of the Pioneer Arms PPS 43c. Poland was licensed to manufacture the original PPS 43 in 1951, and produced some 111,000 pieces from 1952 to 1955.

In reality, the Pioneer Arms version is a reverse-engineered variation that has a completely redesigned fire-control group that uses a conventional hammer to strike the two-piece firing pin housed in the reworked, closed bolt. The Russian PPS 43 had a finger-operated, flat steel plate ahead of the trigger guard which serves as the safety, but did not act as a selector because the weapon was originally full-automatic only. In addition, the folding stock is permanently locked in place to qualify it as a legal pistol. If wishing to convert to a short-barrel rifle, a gunsmith would have to perform the task of releasing it to function. This and many other surplus Polish parts left over from the original 1950s production run are used on the Pioneer Arms offering. Looking closely at several components, one might see various inspector's cartouches and numerals on such original parts, which give it a touch of partial originality. Much like the PPSh 41, the PPS 43c disassembles like a break-open shotgun by pushing a spring loaded latch at the rear of the frame, and the internals consist of only two components: carrier-spring assembly and the breech block, simplicity at its best. Fit and finish are what would be expected from a partially surplus-built, military-grade submachine gun; blued finish, polished bolt, a few rough edges and black hard-plastic checkered grips.

Inter Ordnance offered these with two 35-round magazines, original Polish military oiler can, cleaning rod, with some having a sling included. I live not far from Palm Bay, Florida, and spoke some time ago with Michael Rivera, who oversaw I.O.'s marketing and was told the last known shipment of the PPS 43c Semi-Auto pistols arrived in early 2015. The good news is that Pioneer Arms Corporation, in 2017, began independently importing them once again. Its new U.S. location is now in South Daytona Beach, Florida, as of late 2018. It is, however,

The size of the holster is far larger than conventional pistol holsters. All in all, the PPS 43c is a very well-balanced pistol that is as close as possible to the real deal. (Dianna Kelly photo)

The author found that rapid firing the Pioneer PPS 43c is a real gas. It runs perfectly with new commercial 7.62x25mm ammunition without a hitch. The simple, but crude, folded steel muzzle brake blows all muzzle flash out to the sides. At 15 yards, two-handed accuracy from shoulder level isn't bad either. (Shawn Kelly photo)

interesting that the Pioneer Arms PPS 43c was once offered in 9mm Luger caliber, but has since been discontinued. I have owned the 7.62mm-version for some years now and find it quite intriguing as, aside from the closed bolt and the semi-automatic fire mode, it's as close to

Unlike most of the world's submachine guns, the Vz 61 fires from a closed bolt, which required no mechanical modification aside from reworking the selector to semi-automatic only. The open bolt shows position of the loaded magazine.

owning the real deal as legally possible.

It must be emphasized that, in the beginning, distributors and online video bloggers stated that they are suitable for use with all 7.62x25mm Eastern European surplus ammunition. I beg to differ with this. Personal experience and consulting with other owners have proved that soft strikes and misfires are a common occurrence with some varieties of old communist mil-surp fodder. Reason being, the primers on older communist-bloc surplus ammo have very hard metal primers and were intended to be used with a conventional pistol, or the forceful, slamming effect of open-bolt submachine guns. This is especially true with some lots surplus cartridges of Bulgarian and Polish origin, which often find 20, or more, out of a full 35-round magazine will misfire. Since the PPS 43c has a two-piece firing pin and a small hammer activated by a spiral main spring, the results can be frustrating, and especially rough on the nose or the entire firing pin altogether. Some owners have complained of broken firing pins on this pistol, which is a direct result of continual contact with hard primers of the older 1950-vintage surplus ammo. Personally, I have learned through experience that the

best course of action is to use commercial ammunition such as Sellier & Bellot, PPU and even Winchester's Metric Line, which is actually Czech-made 7.62x25mm ammunition and allows the PPS 43c to run like a clock. Perfect, and no light strikes or misfires.

For those who would be interested in the PPS 43c, we are fortunate that Pioneer Arms has recommenced importation. Keep in mind that there are countless original PPS 43 parts kits available online, which include both Polish- and Russian-made original components.

If you would like to spruce up your communist-bloc pistol or rifle inventory, both the CzechPoint Vz 61 Skorpion and the Pioneer Arms PPS 43c are perhaps the most legal and economically practical way to go for it. **GD**

(I wish to thank Dan Brown of Czech-Point, and CJ Johnson of Pioneer Arms Corporation for their assistance and advice.)

The Remington 700

The author shot this Cape buffalo with a .416 UMT rifle built on a Remington Model 700 action while hunting the Selous Reserve in Tanzania.

The greatest of all time?

› BRYCE M. TOWSLEY

"*How ya gonna keep 'em down on the farm After they've seen Paree*'"

This popular song is illustrative of the huge demographic changes resulting from World War I. So many of our doughboys were ripped from rural Americana and dumped into "the rest of the world" that something had to happen.

The concept spilled over into hunting rifles as well. Those guys fought and won a war with bolt-action rifles. How would they be content with anything less for hunting? They had "seen the elephant and heard the owl" and the status quo would never be good enough again.

Remington answered with its Model 30 rifle, introduced in 1921. Using leftover Enfield parts and chambered in the .30-06 cartridge, it was a sporting version of the rifle soldiers carried in war. In 1926, the Model 30 Express replaced it. It was a lighter rifle that cocked on opening and was offered in many variations and in a multitude of cartridges. It showed American hunters the future of sporting rifles and paved the way for today's rifles.

World War II killed off this rifle, as it did so many great firearms. Following that war, Remington introduced the Model 721 bolt-action rifle in 1948. It was a gun meant for the times. Using different manufacturing techniques and the engineering genius of Mike Walker, who was an avid benchrest shooter, the rifle was inexpensive and outstandingly functional. By using a cylinder-type action, manufacturing costs were reduced and accuracy improved. The 721 and the later short-action 722 rifles were just what the returning GIs needed: affordable performance.

The only flaw, if it might be called that, was the guns were rather plain. As the country prospered in the post-war boom, shooters' tastes evolved, and they began looking for form as well as function. Remington was losing market share to the prettier Winchester Model 70. In 1962, Remington addressed that problem with the introduction of the Model 700 rifle, along with a hot new cartridge, the 7mm Remington Magnum. The duo helped launch the magnum mania that followed.

The 700 retained the basic design of the 721, but with improvements and in a slicker, better-looking package. As they say, the rest is history. With more than 5 million sold, the Remington Model 700 rifle is arguably the best-selling, bolt-action sporting rifle in history. The models and variations that followed in the next 58 years are mind boggling, but they all have a common theme, the Model 700 action.

While elk hunting in Colorado in 2012, the author shot this bull at long range with Barnes Vor-Tx ammo and a Remington Model 700 rifle in .300 RUM.

The Remington Model 700 action is better than a high-dollar custom action. At least for a hobby gunsmith.

A Remington Model 700 XCR in .375 RUM on a Cape buffalo hunt in Tanzania in 2005. Note that this Remington XCR rifle has a synthetic stock. The stability of synthetics is important in this high-humidity area.

When it comes to rifles, everything is round. The cartridge is round, the bullets are round, the barrels are round, the bore is round, the bolts are round and so it stands to reason that the action should be round. If we are able to keep all these round things to a common center, accuracy is ensured. That, in a nutshell, is the success of the Remington 700 action. Because it's round, it's also less expensive to manufacture with far less machining needed than with other action designs. It's much easier to hold precision, which is one key factor in the Model 700's legendary accuracy.

The Model 700 comes in two lengths, short and long. One or the other will fit any cartridge from .17 Fireball through .375 RUM. The Model 700 bolt maintains the two-forward-lugs lockup style popularized with the Mauser action. This is a very strong action and, again, it's easier to maintain accuracy. Two lugs are easier to machine precisely than three, six or nine.

One component of accuracy is that all lugs support the bolt equally. The more lugs there are, the harder it is to achieve this goal.

The 700 bolt has a recessed bolt face that fits into another recess in the barrel and when you add the action, this creates the legendary "three rings of steel" surrounding the cartridge. This is considered to be much safer in the event of a cartridge failure as it helps isolate the gasses and particles from the shooter. There is some merit to the theory that this recessed bolt face helps keep the cartridge aligned in the chamber to enhance accuracy. Again, the more centered everything is, the better the accuracy. The recessed bolt supports the rear of the cartridge and helps keep it centered with the bore.

The Model 700 has a very fast lock time, which is the time from when the trigger releases until the firing pin strikes the primer. The theory is that the faster this happens, the less chance of the gun moving and having a negative effect on accuracy. While this does not mechanically improve accuracy, in the real world it makes it easier for the shooter to access the inherent accuracy in the rifle.

The Model 700 uses a separate recoil lug, which fits like a washer between the barrel and the receiver. Again, this keeps costs down as it's much less expensive to make than to machine the recoil lug integral to the action, as seen with some other rifle designs.

There are two complaints we often hear from rifle nerds about the Remington Model 700. First is that it is a push-feed rifle. That means that once the cartridge is free from the magazine it is not mechanically supported as it is pushed by the bolt for the short remaining distance into the chamber. In contrast, a controlled-round-feed (CRF) rifle captures the cartridge behind the extractor as it exits the magazine and against the bolt face while it is fed into the chamber.

The author built this custom .358 Winchester rifle on a Remington Model 700 action. This rifle was built with hand tools using a short-chambered barrel.

The Remington Model 700 in .338 RUM is one of the author's favorite rifles for big game.

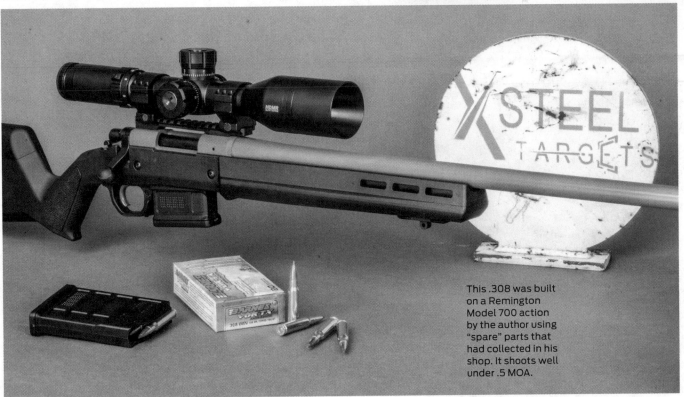

This .308 was built on a Remington Model 700 action by the author using "spare" parts that had collected in his shop. It shoots well under .5 MOA.

"Blueprinting" a Remington 700 action. Note how the front of the action is round. The tap must be below the surface to allow truing the front of the action with a lathe.

This barrel is being prepared for a Remington 700 action. Note the recess where the bolt will fit in to create the "three rings of steel."

The author built this custom .300 Winchester precision rifle on a Remington action. It is extremely accurate and capable of shooting very long range.

In reality, this is probably only important when hunting dangerous game. Even there, it might be more myth and tradition than truth. I have hunted dangerous game including Cape buffalo, brown bear, grizzly bear, black bear, leopard, hippo and several other large and surly critters with push-feed rifles. I once had a large, wounded, wild boar charge me while I was hunting in Hungary. I had a push-feed rifle and I killed him with the second shot, so close that he blew snow all over my boots as he skidded to a stop.

On the other hand, I have also hunted Cape buffalo, elephant, Asian buffalo, wild boar and brown bear with CRF rifles. Both designs have served me well.

One downside of using a CRF rifle is that most cannot be fed single cartridges. If the rifle is dry and things are happening fast, the option of tossing a cartridge into the loading port and slamming the bolt shut is comforting. Most push-feed designs allow this while most CRF rifles do not.

The other side of the argument is that the push-feed design seems to be a bit more accurate. The tension of the extractor on the cartridge in a controlled-round feed can influence the cartridge position in the chamber in a negative way. Most precision rifles are push-feed design because when accuracy is measured in tenths of an inch, the push-feed seems to have the advantage.

The other common complaint about the Remington Model 700 design is the extractor. Every armchair expert out there will tell you "It's no damn good!" The dangerous-game hunting guys and the tactical guys all claim it's a huge problem that will get you killed in the "real" world.

I'll be honest: It's a fragile looking little thing that looks like it should be a problem. But it's not. I should note that this extractor style has been used by Remington going back to at least 1948 with the 721 and 722 model rifles. There are almost 7 million rifles out there with the "horrible" extractors and yet there are virtually no reports of them failing during a critical time and getting somebody killed.

I have been a fan of Remington rifles all my life. I bought the first one, a Model

788, in 1968. Over the years, I have had a lot of Model 700 rifles and its relatives that use the same extractor system, such as the Model 788, Model Seven, Model 721 and Model 722, pass through my gun vault. I have used a few hundred different rifles with the Remington-style extractor, in a lot of cartridges and in a lot of places and I have never had an extractor problem.

If we followed up on most of the reports of extractor failures, we likely would find that an overpressure handload was stuck in the chamber and somebody beat the hell out of the bolt to remove it, which is gun abuse. The truth is, I did that myself, back before I knew better, and still never had an extractor fail. I have seen the bolt handle break off when a guy was beating on it with

The Remington Model 722 shown here in .300 Savage is a predecessor to the famous Remington Model 700 rifle.

The author shot this trophy red stag in Argentina in 2004, hunting with a Remington 700 CDL in .300 RUM.

I have installed both style extractors on custom rifles I have built, and I have left the original factory extractor in other custom rifles I have built. The number of problems with any of the extractors so far is zero. A couple of the rifles have been used for long-range target shooting and for a lot of ammo testing for magazine articles, so the round count is getting seriously high.

I built a 9.3x62 custom rifle for my buddy Tony Kinton expressly to take on a Cape buffalo hunt. We elected to stick with the Remington extractor. I trust it and so does Tony. The buffalo was un-available for comment.

Speaking of custom rifles, the Model 700 action is a long-time favorite of custom-gun builders, both professional and hobbyists. It's one of the few produc-tion rifle actions available on the current market as the action only. It also has a huge number of aftermarket parts and accessories available. When it comes to building bolt-action rifles, nothing matches the Model 700 in terms of the gadgets and goodies made to fit. It is the "kit" rifle of bolt actions.

The Remington 700 is extremely easy for hobby and professional gunsmiths to work with and it can produce outstand-ing results. Before I had a lathe, I custom-ized several rifles using only hand tools. I would lap bolt lugs for even contact, true the bolt face and then fit a short-cham-bered barrel. A short-chambered barrel comes with 90 percent of the work done. The threads are cut and the chamber is left .010-inch short so that once it's on the action you can finish cutting the chamber to the correct headspace. This provides a viable option for a hobby gunsmith with only hand tools. By cutting the last of the chamber by hand you can make the perfect minimum spec chamber.

How well does that work? I have a .308 Winchester I built that way that will shoot .5 MOA all day long. This is a great way to get started building your own rifles without spending your kid's college fund on expensive power tools.

Of course, most serious builders will eventually want a lathe, which is more af-fordable than you might suspect. I cover how to get started in my book *Gunsmith-ing Modern Firearms*. In that book, I have

a chunk of firewood to extract a stuck handload, but the extractor held.

I am sure the extractors wear out like any other piece of machinery and that they break now and then, but I just can't find any evidence that the Remington extractor is a true problem.

There are certain "facts" in the gun world that lazy gun writers, loud-mouth range rats and incompetent gun-store salesmen just keep repeating as truth and as far as I can tell, "Model 700 extractors suck" is one of them.

I have probably used guns with the 700-style extractor more than any other style of rifle. I have trusted them on dan-gerous game on multiple occasions. I

have carried a Remington on some very extreme hunts from Alaska to Africa and I have put thousands and thousands of rounds through Model 700 rifles in just about every imaginable cartridge, yet I have never seen an extractor fail from nor-mal use or from shooting the rifle. I know it happens, but either I am very lucky or it happens far less than all the hysteria would suggest that it does. Sure, I have replaced a few, but those I have replaced were all damaged by abuse, not use.

However, if you are concerned, it's easy enough to have a gunsmith replace the Remington extractor with a Sako or M-16-style extractor. This is a com-mon "upgrade" to the Model 700 rifle.

Remington's 2006 Limited Edition Model 700 Stainless CDL celebrating the 100-year anniversary of the .30/06 Springfield.

The bolt on the left has an M-16 extractor, compared to the Remington-style extractor on the other bolt.

The author built this custom 6mm Creedmoor precision rifle on a Remington action. It is capable of extraordinary accuracy.

chapters on building several rifles. Most are on a Remington 700 action.

Why?

The boom in custom rifles has inspired an entire industry of custom actions, most of those actions use the Model 700 basic design. So why do a lot of builders, particularly hobby guys, use the Model 700 action? These custom actions are outstanding, but they are expensive. I did a quick check on the Internet and found that the average high-end action costs about 2.8 times as much as a new Remington Model 700 action from Brownells. It's often even cheaper to prowl local gun shops to find old beater Model 700 rifles that you can buy for less than the price of a new action. I have a standing order in with a few local gun shops for beater guns I can use for projects.

The author shot this Mississippi buck on the last morning of his 2015 hunt with a Remington Model 700 CDL Limited Edition Rifle in .35 Whelen.

The author shot this Wyoming whitetail with a Remington 700 .300 RUM at 428 yards. This was the longest shot the author ever took on a whitetail deer. The .300 Ultra Mag is a good choice in cartridges and the new TTSX 200-grain bullet is a good match with that cartridge.

The author with a Coues deer he shot in the Sierra San Antonio Mountains in Sonora, Mexico. The range was 368 yards, the rifle was a 700 Remington in 7mm RUM. Hunting Coues deer here is always a long-range shooting situation.

With custom-rifle builders today, the choice is simple. Time is money. Back in the day, gunsmiths had to work with the rifle actions that were available. Often that meant a donor rifle that was cannibalized to get the action or, at best, buying an action, usually a Remington Model 700, Winchester Model 70 or a surplus Mauser. Today, things have changed and there are a lot of very good shovel-ready rifle actions on the market.

Skilled professional gunsmiths at the top of their games and in demand have only so much time available. The only way they can increase their income is to increase the amount of money they are paid per hour worked, or to streamline productivity. The best of the best are paid well for their time, so when it comes to a paid custom build, it's actually less expensive for most customers to buy a high-end action than it is to pay the gunsmith's time to blueprint and tune an existing action. That alone is motivation for most customers to buy a ready to rock, high-end action.

But, in terms of accuracy, a skilled gunsmith will produce a rifle that's every bit as accurate by blueprinting a factory Model 700 action. "Blueprinting" is nothing more than a fancy term for trueing everything to the common center. That means trueing the threads, bolt lugs, bolt face and the receiver face to the center line of the action. Finally, the bolt lugs will be lapped for a perfect mate to the action lugs.

I enjoy building guns and it's a hobby thing for me. So, if it takes me a bit longer to complete a project because I have to blueprint the action, I see that as more time with concrete under my feet and contentment in my heart. Most of my builds are for my own use or are for friends and family, so we try to keep the cost reasonable. That means, more often than not, a Remington 700 action.

Results? I have a precision rifle in 6mm Creedmoor rifle I built on a Remington 700 Short action that I would put up against any similar rifle on any action. I have lots of five shot groups that are .2-inch or a bit smaller. I think the limiting factor is my shooting ability, not the rifle.

On the other end of the spectrum, I built myself a 9.3x62 for hunting. It is capable of .5 MOA with factory loads and it runs as fast and smooth as any rifle I own. I have used it on elk and whitetail deer with great results. I would not hesitate to use it on dangerous game.

The Remington Model 700 rifle design is almost six decades old and it's still an industry leader. In that time, Remington has changed almost nothing in the basic design. That says a lot about the enduring legacy of the world's most popular bolt-action, sporting rifle. GD

The author with a Yukon Dall sheep taken in 2006. Also shown is guide Chris McKinnon. The rifle is the first Model 40XTi rifle ever produced by the Remington Custom Shop. It is in .280 Remington and has a Swarovski 3-10x42 scope.

From the lowest Grade 1 (top) to the most elaborate Midas Grade on the bottom, Browning always gave the purchaser the best it had for the money spent. Take note of the checkering patterns and the hint of the extra fancy wood on the Midas gun.

BROWNING'S FABULOUS SUPERPOSED SHOTGUN

The last of John Browning's many excellent and innovative designs

❯ STAN TRZONIEC

Deep down, the only shotgun I ever dreamed of owning was the Browning Superposed, but my timing was off. In the period I was going through the wants of having one, I was just married, had an entry-level job as a photographer and there were other more important things to buy than a high-grade shotgun. So said my wife!

For a dedicated bird hunter, the Superposed 20-gauge was the only way to go for upland game. However, that was not to be for me, for as soon as I could afford a nice Superposed, they were being discontinued with prices sharply increasing at all retail levels. Some were still available, but Browning was now going into production for a new gun called the Citori. In the meantime, the Superposed was going the route of custom guns made only on special order.

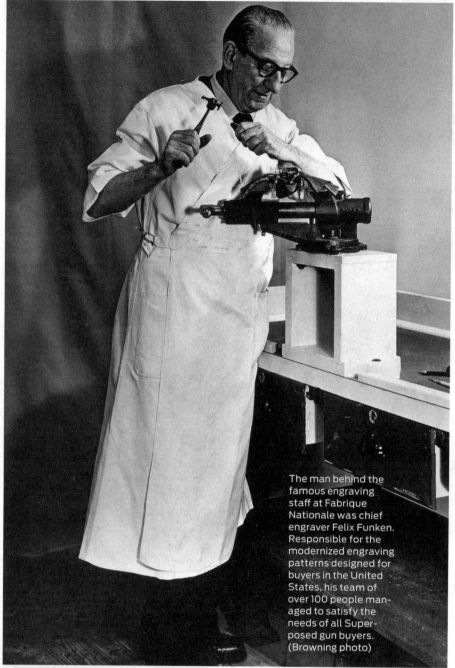

The man behind the famous engraving staff at Fabrique Nationale was chief engraver Felix Funken. Responsible for the modernized engraving patterns designed for buyers in the United States, his team of over 100 people managed to satisfy the needs of all Superposed gun buyers. (Browning photo)

blow-back, gas or recoil operated. At 23, he created his first weapon, a single-shot, lever-operated, breech-loading rifle. Later, his Model 1885 was one of 43 gun designs he sold to Winchester in both lever and pump, to fill the growing needs of a growing country. In his lifespan of some 71 years, he designed guns to suit every purpose for the likes of Winchester, Colt, Remington, Fabrique Nationale and Browning, plus Savage, Stevens, Ithaca and, of course, the military with the famed Model 1911, the BAR and the Model 1895 Automatic Machine Gun.

Browning died in November 1926, while working on his newest creation, the Browning Superposed shotgun, without the gun being finished. And, this is where we begin.

In sporting arms, this gun was probably his greatest achievement. To begin, it was the first over-and-under shotgun to be produced with a selective trigger (although the prototype had double triggers) and numerous other innovations for a gun at the time. The idea came from the thinking of a "super-imposed" shotgun, meaning one barrel laid (or mated) on top of the other, complete with a ventilated rib to dissipate heat during extended shooting sessions. The gun had only 70 parts, installed in 170 different steps, and, according to many, was "impossible to jam" simply because of the lack of moving parts.

On the tang, the operating lever moved to open the action that was supported by a full-length hinge pin. When this lever was moved, the barrels would tip up at the receiver, allowing the extractors to pull on the empty shell, expelling it out of the barrel. Rather than having a double-trigger arrangement to control barrel selection, the Superposed had a single, selective trigger that, with the movement of a thumb lever, could control which barrel (or choke) to use first and second on game. According to research material, the most popular shotgun shell at the time was the 16-gauge. As Bill Ruger did later going against tradition with his 20-gauge introduction of the Red Label shotgun, Browning decided to introduce his new gun in 12-gauge only.

After Browning died, his son Val continued with production of the gun.

Still part of the Browning heritage, hand engraving is the hallmark of the higher-grade shotguns. This is a Custom Shop photo showing a deft hit of the hammer is required for excellent work. You can't erase steel once the cut has been made. (Browning photo)

Regardless of its status either before or after the 1970s, the Superposed was a gun to be reckoned with especially with famous inventor John Browning involved in the design. Born in 1855, Browning designed a host of firearms never known to the world before. He designed guns ranging from the petite .22 Short to military weapons using a 37mm projectile, having them function perfectly no matter their size. His semi-automatic and automatic weapons would operate without problems regardless if they were

Prior to shipping, all Superposed shotguns underwent function tests, were inspected for quality and then passed for shipment. (Browning photo)

According to the original photo caption, this man is using a polishing lathe to put the finishing touches on the barrels of a Browning Superposed. In the beginning, full and full were the only chokes you could get on this shotgun. (Browning photo)

Try as he might, he could not sell the gun or its design to any United States manufacturer so final production went to Fabrique Nationale of Belgium. In 1928, the gun was introduced to the world as the Browning Superposed shotgun and from 1931 to 1948 this shotgun was only available in 12-gauge models. Later in 1949, Val had a hand in miniaturizing the receiver to handle the 20-gauge, some 13 years later in 1962, the 28-gauge and .410-bore were listed among the various model variations.

With the help of Browning's public relations man Paul Thompson, his staff, the fine work of Ned Schwing with his book on *Superposed*, and numerous periodicals, I managed to gather catalog sheets and information from the gun's introduction to it being discontinued in the 1970s. In addition, I was able to quote various manufacturing and design details from other printed material, namely specification sheets dealing with just the Superposed, its various models, features and other important details. One of these catalogs published in 1966 offered some good insights on the gun and its variations. While the history of the Superposed is so broad and varied, for

the purpose of this article and the space allowed, I will touch on what I think matters most with this fine shotgun.

To start, at its apex, the Superposed offered 50 different models with over 400 individual specifications for hunting, trap and skeet shooters. Guns were offered in 12-, 20-, 28-gauge and .410-bore, with the 12-gauge also available in the 3-inch Magnum. From here, there are four ascending grades (Grade I, Pigeon, Diana and Midas) with various combinations of barrel lengths and chokes. Both the 12- and 20-gauge are listed in two weights, Standard and Lightning for field use, while the 28-gauge and .410-bore were produced in one weight only.

Twenty-two different types of steel were used in the production and manufacture of the gun, with 84 individual parts that undergo 794 precise machining operations holding minimum tolerances for that just-right fit. In addition, over 60 of its components received heat-treating, and 1,500 different gauges monitored quality control in 2,310 separate operations to test and retest the various mechanisms that went into this gun.

Aside from all this, you have to account for the primary work and effort

that makes the Superposed. For example, custom fitting of all the parts to very close tolerances, hand-checkering, bluing, extra barrels, engraving on higher-grade guns, selection of the wood for the stock and forearm and finally, range testing to include pattern and high-pressure tests. Not finished yet, the builders used 155 different manual operations, making sure the gun was perfect in every respect before being shipped with a lifetime guarantee to the original owner.

In all probability, the things that set the Browning Superposed apart from others in its ilk were the four grades of finish to include wood selection, checkering and engraving. The most popular gun was the Grade I, not because of its price, but because it appealed to the average hunter. The receiver was true Superposed, but the stock, checkering and a very modest amount of scroll and rosette-designed engraving on the side of the receiver just meant this gun was made to work. For comparisons in various grades and in 12-gauge only, let's use the prices from the introductory year of 1931 [in brackets] and 1970 price as a benchmark as we were getting close the Superposed being dropped from the Browning line completely. Here we note the Standard Grade I gun retailed at $440 [$107.50]

If you wanted to move up to a high-grade gun in the Standard Grade, you had to order the Lightning model. The Pigeon grade would run you $675 [$175], the Diana grade $895 [$277], and my favorite, the Midas would top out at $1,255 [$374].

One interesting fact in the Superposed series is that around 1956 you could order "Super Tubes" in same-gauge barrel sets that would convert your 12-gauge field or target gun to shoot 20- or 28-gauge or .410-bore shotshells. With the "Three Gauge Set," ejection would remain intact and the change from one set to the other would take less than five minutes. Balance remained close to the original barrels, as did the employment of chokes and patterns with or without the tube inserted into the barrels. The tubes were shipped in a handsome luggage-type case, and the buyer would get two tubes for each gauge, a tap-out and cleaning rod, pin punch and a can

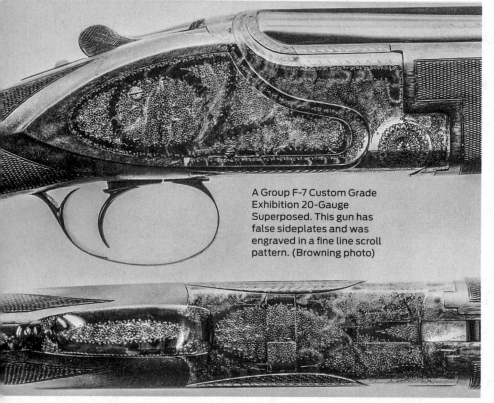

A Group F-7 Custom Grade Exhibition 20-Gauge Superposed. This gun has false sideplates and was engraved in a fine line scroll pattern. (Browning photo)

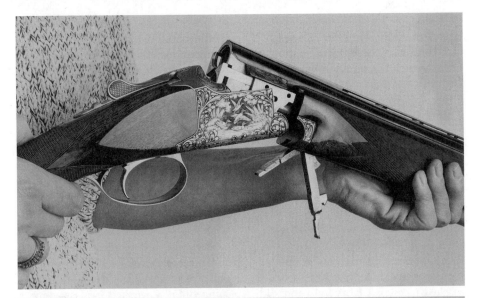

of gun oil. As a side note, you could also purchase a "Single Gauge Set" complete with two tubes in the desired gauge, along with accessories in a vinyl case.

When it came to specific models, Browning had the field well-covered with most available right up to the fabulous Midas Grade. The Standard hunting grade was, for the most part, relegated to field duty without much attention to engraving or the high quality of the wood. With a popular price point, they satisfied most of the hunters out there, but if you wanted something for competition or with bragging rights, you had to move up the model scale. Available from 12-gauge to .410-bore, barrel lengths and chokes listed gave a wide selection for those with specific hunting needs in the field. Stocks were traditional in design with ample checkering coverage and included a deluxe recoil pad and a full grip contour on the forearm, all covered with a "hand-rubbed weather-resistant lacquer" formulated to bring out the best in the wood on any gun. During my time scouting gun shops, I never saw a Superposed I did not like. From the Grade 1 up to the Midas, wood was impressive on the lower grades and utterly spectacular as you moved up to the higher grades. All grades included the gold-plated trigger, selective barrel control, tang-mounted safety and sighting beads on the ventilated rib.

The Lightning Superposed is next on the list and followed the general profile of the Standard models; however, the overall weight of the guns did change. For example, on the 12-gauge model with

(top) This photo shows the assembly-disassembly levers on the Superposed that allow the forearm to slide forward releasing the barrels from the receiver. While the procedure is too lengthy to describe here, the system does make for a complete and secure locking of the barrels and forearm to the receiver.

(middle) With the gun open, we can see the fine detailing of this Pointer Grade Superposed. While not as deep as the higher grades, any pattern from Browning was impressive. Workmanship abounds as noted by fit and finish and cleanly cut checkering.

(bottom) Closer in, we can see the fine detailing of the Diana Grade as photographed in the author's studio years ago. With a grayed receiver and fine checkering, this is another fine example of Browning workmanship.

26 1/2-inch barrels, the weight averaged 7 pounds; with the 28-inch tubes, you were looking at 7 pounds, 4 ounces. This was done with the application of special steels while keeping the balance the same as the Standard Grade. Receivers on the Lightning Grade were engraved, hand-checkered and were available in all grades. For hunting, one could pick barrels with full, improved-modified, modified-improved cylinder, skeet or cylinder bore.

Moving up, we come to the Superlight models that joined the lineup in 12-gauge only in 1967, followed two years later in 20-gauge. With 26 1/2-inch barrels and checking in at 6 pounds for the 20-gauge gun (12-gauge guns weigh only 6 ounces more) it was available in all the four grades. Both models had a solid tapered rib, a slim forearm and minimal engraving around the edges of the receiver.

When it came to competition models, Browning was on top of its game in both trap and skeet shooting. According to Browning literature, the Superposed Trap models "have been designed to satisfy the most exacting requirements in handling qualities and performance." To this end, the company had a pair of guns with different shooter preferences dealing with the overall weight of the gun and the sighting plane. While both models are the same when it comes to stock design, they feature a full pistol grip with a longer, semi-beavertail forearm for a consistent hold shot after shot and a deluxe recoil pad. Ivory front and mid-barrel beads were standard, and a choice of chokes was available from improved-modified to full.

Trap models included the famous BROADway (Browning's way of identification and trademark) model, which features an extra-wide top ventilated rib that measures five-eighths of an inch wide. Chambered only for 12-gauge, barrel lengths were 30 or 32 inches with special orders entertained for 26 1/2 or 28 inches with extra barrel sets in either 12- or 20-gauge. The Lightning model has a standard width rib measuring five-sixteenths of inch.

Skeet models were offered in 12-, 20- and 28-gauge and .410-bore for those interested in four-gauge shooting competition. Since skeet is a fast-action game, there were differences in stock

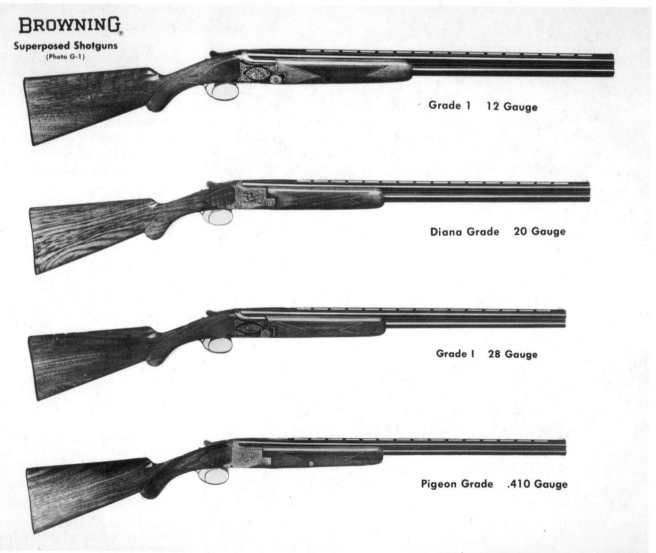

For the potential customer, Browning always seemed to do the right thing when it came to product identification. This sales sheet shows the different grades in four gauges to show barrel configurations and engraving patterns. (Browning photo)

(below) Shown here is the forearm for the Pointer Grade. Every part of the Superposed was done in the spirit of quality as one can see here on the sharply executed checkering with no mistakes and complete with a border. Finish is hand rubbed and toward the glossy side to accent the select wood used on all guns, no matter the grade.

(bottom) As promoted by Browning, this is the top-of-the-line Midas Grade with great wood and an elaborate and extended checkering pattern. Although various Midas guns might look the same, different engravers put their own style into each gun, thus making each a one of a kind. (Browning photo)

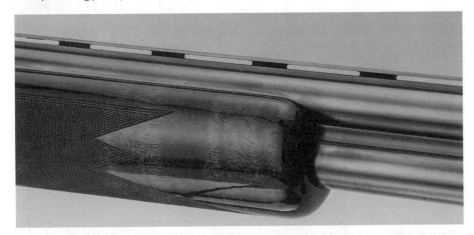

design to accommodate handling in the shooting field. There was no recoil pad to facilitate mounting the gun, the pistol grip was rounded and the forearm was shorter. In view of this, the guns retained their famous Browning balance by providing a choice of 26 1/2- or 28-inch barrels, with specially designed skeet chokes, a ventilated rib and the option for multi-barrel sets in 20- or 28-gauge, or .410-bore. Both Trap and Skeet guns, like others in the line, were available in Grade I, Pigeon, Diana and Midas grades.

When it came to specially engraved models, at the time the Superposed was in its prime, Browning led the pack from mild to wild engraving patterns. In its peak, Browning did all the work by hand, engraving steel in intricate patterns with a field of well-qualified engravers with Louis Vrancken and Andre Watrin at the

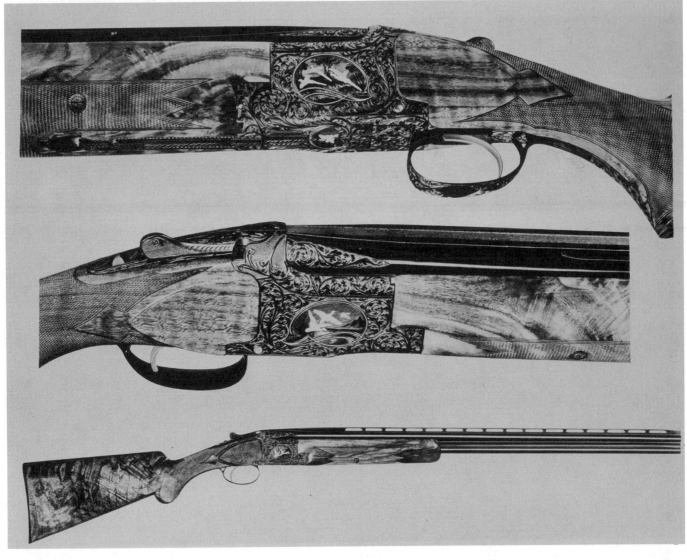

helm. Even the lower-priced Standard Grade Browning Superposed has a bit of engraving on the receiver. Moving up the scale, the Pointer and Pigeon Grade were next and although these patterns were discontinued in 1966 and 1975, respectively, simply because of the cost to produce, they were still available on special order.

Deeper-engraved patterns were used on the Diana and Midas guns in all gauges and models. Going with the Diana Grade, the purchaser received a silver-colored receiver complete with both floral and wildlife images in a heavier relief. The Midas was definitely a class act. Recently on a trip up to the Orvis flagship store in Vermont, I saw a mint Midas Skeet gun for sale with a price tag of $10,000. Maybe in my next life…

Of course, engraving of the Browning Superposed went much further than that and looking at research material shows that it could be covered in full article by itself. Because of declining sales from 1970 to 1977, when the Midas grade was discontinued, Fabrique Nationale offered several high-grade guns to Browning at a better-than-fair price. They were made for the European market, but with a declining market in this

Back in the days when you could still get a Superposed on consignment from Browning, the author had one to use on a weeklong quail hunt in Georgia. This was a Superlight in 20 gauge with fancy wood, and it tracked like radar on anything that flew.

A prime example of a pistol-grip cap engraved by a master engraver, from the new Custom Shop brochure. (Browning photo)

Since all Super-posed shotguns are now custom made, you have the right to expect the best in hand-cut engraving. Note the detail, especially around the eyes. (Browning photo)

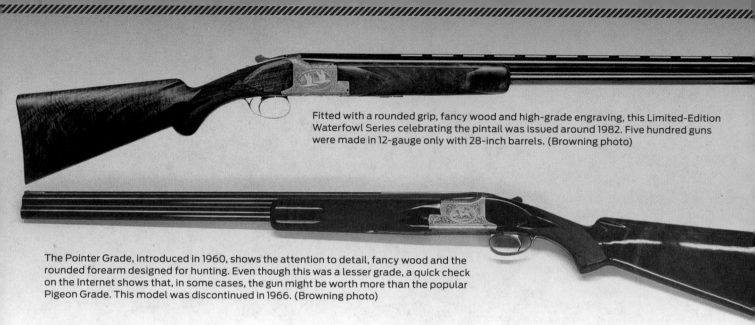

Fitted with a rounded grip, fancy wood and high-grade engraving, this Limited-Edition Waterfowl Series celebrating the pintail was issued around 1982. Five hundred guns were made in 12-gauge only with 28-inch barrels. (Browning photo)

The Pointer Grade, introduced in 1960, shows the attention to detail, fancy wood and the rounded forearm designed for hunting. Even though this was a lesser grade, a quick check on the Internet shows that, in some cases, the gun might be worth more than the popular Pigeon Grade. This model was discontinued in 1966. (Browning photo)

part of the world, these "C" Grade (C was the prefix of the serial numbers) Exhibition Superposed guns were grouped into special categories. Group letters and numbers including A, B, C, D, F and G with prices going from around $4,300 to $6,250, depending upon the wide variety of embellishment, wood and checkering patterns. Surprisingly just 256 of these special C Grade guns were made; only 231 were sold in the United States as production was coming to the end of the Superposed era.

During this same period from 1970 to 1977, catalog prices were rising while offerings in the Superposed line were declining. Seems prices were spiraling out of control with the Grade 1 retailing for around $435, depending on the dealer. In 1973, as to counteract the prices, Browning brought out an economy version of the Superposed called the "Liege." At only $30 or so below the Grade I gun, the interest was not there for deep-rooted Superposed fans and it was dropped from the line a year later.

From here, the next step was the Presentation or "P" series guns that moved the Superposed from a production to a custom gun only available on special order from 1977 up to (according to my catalogs) at least 1986. Looking at my 1978 catalog, the Presentation guns were available in hunting, trap and skeet guns. In four different and distinct grades, they were meant to keep the gun alive, however with prices starting at $2,990 for a Presentation 1 gun and going up to

$6,850 for the Presentation 4 gun; they were certainly a cut above the ordinary in a fine shotgun. Keep in mind that prices did moderate in among these four grades, as the potential owner did have more choices in blued, grayed or gold-inlaid receivers with models for hunting, trap and skeet.

In addition, P-1 (Presentation 1) buyers had a choice of six animal scenes to grace the receiver along with gold inlays and a blued or grayed receiver. P-2 guns had three sets of wildlife along with a more elaborate engraving pattern. P-3 had three scenes also, but with more of an elaborate engraving pattern with gold accents similar to the older Midas model. Finally, the P-4 gun had full sideplates, fantastic wood and the finest fleur-de-lis engraving money could buy. Later, these $6,800 shotguns would top $10,400, and for those who wanted to personize their guns to the ninth degree, options ran the gamut from special stock dimensions to a checkered wood butt (instead of a recoil pad), Schnabel forearm, hand-matted vent rib or an inlaid stock oval with their initials.

Through all this time, Browning seemed still interested in tapping the Superposed market with other offerings in the form of special editions with an over-and-under rifle/shotgun it called the Superposed Continental. Based on a 20-gauge, fully engraved frame, these 500 guns featured two barrels with one chambered for the .30-06 Springfield, the other for the 20-gauge shotgun shell. All poised in a

deluxe walnut case, this indeed was a special, special edition celebrating 100 years of the Browning company. After that came the Browning Express Rifle with a pair of 24-inch barrels chambered for the .270 Winchester and the.30-06 Springfield. Still later, the Superposed was out with the American Mallard, Pintail and Bottom Black Duck editions with specially designed straight grip and Schnabel forearms. Also in the mix was a specially designed trap gun called the Super Trap One-Hundred, complete with an "impact adjustment wedge" to sight in your shotgun for your personal style of shooting. In addition, the gun was equipped with a floating under barrel, selective trigger and a high post, and an extra-wide rib, obviously a design feature taken from the famous BROADway model.

In looking through my pile of catalogs, I take note that the Superposed was back on line in 1983 with a Grade I model in Lightning or Superlight in 12- or 20-gauge with a price point of under $2,000 for a gun built in Belgian. With the Citori getting stronger and stronger with new models, the famed Browning Superposed was moving toward the end of its productive life.

Not to be outdone by time or the lack of it, the Browning Superposed is now the B25 and the newer B15 Beauchamp shotguns. From the famed Custom Shop, the B25 can be ordered in just about any configuration, engraving pattern, hunting or competition model. The B15 is the next generation of John Browning's masterpiece and includes all the latest in technology with four outstanding grades for the discriminating shooter. Those who still want to own the best can access all the information at www.johnmbrowningcollection.com for the latest in pricing and delivery dates.

For an ending to this, I thought it would be only fair to peruse a bit on the original Superposed offering dated 1931, one page on one piece of paper that started it all. Even at that time, John Browning had a good product. As mentioned before, he did have the Standard Grade with guns working up to the Midas Grade. However, the interesting part of all this is that looking at the options, much did not change throughout the production life of the gun. For example, Browning offered stocks with special measurements at an additional cost and

offered extra pairs of barrels at half the retail price of the guns. While the guns were originally only made in 12-gauge, additional barrels could be ordered in 28, 30 and 32 inches with chokes from full to improved cylinder.

Automatic ejectors were standard with coil springs throughout and all the stocks were profiled from European walnut with a luster finish and fine checkering. Engraving started with the rosette pattern on the upper part of the frame followed

by an "artistic" border around the side and bottom of the frame. Gun cases could be purchased for specific guns, and were handmade and covered with cowhide leather.

Looking at the Superposed as it was made in 1931 showed it did not vary much over the life of this shotgun. Seems in all the years the gun was in production, only minor changes were made, leading to the fact that John Browning made it right from the start. GD

When the author was in Georgia, another hunter had a Superlight in 12 gauge, on the right. His gun was a grade lower than the author's, and you can see it in the quality of the wood. Nevertheless, both men were happy with the results of the hunt.

On the bottom of the receiver, there is no part of the metal not touched by the engraver on this Midas Grade. Note the details of the quail in gold overlay and his surroundings within the small circle and the deep relief on the trigger guard.

TALES OF A CUSTOM-RIFLE FANATIC

One man's lifelong journey in pursuit of customized excellence

› TOM TURPIN

I have been a fan of custom rifles for a very long time. I was introduced to custom rifles when I was but a rosy-cheeked lad in bib overalls, growing up in Kentucky. Earl "Rob" Robbins, a family friend, had returned home from his tour of duty as a merchant seaman supporting the war efforts in World War II. He was 11 years my senior in age, but a couple lifetimes ahead of me in world experiences. He had traveled the globe, whereas I had barely left Estill County at that stage of my life. I treasured his friendship, which lasted almost 70 years.

The author inherited the makings for this nice rifle when a dear friend passed away. It has a 09 Argentine action that came fitted with a .338 barrel. The author had no need for another .338, so he had Danny Petersen pull the barrel and fit one of his great barrels and chamber it for the .416 Ruger cartridge. Gary Goudy stocked it with a stick of European walnut the author provided.

My dad had been stricken with polio as a youngster, long before Jonas Salk developed the vaccine. Thankfully, dad recovered nicely, but was left with an impaired foot, preventing him from doing much walking. On the other hand, I was full of energy and had developed a serious interest in hunting and shooting. As dad was physically unable to take me hunting, Rob stepped up and took on the responsibility for that part of my education. During those days, Kentucky had no huntable numbers of big game, if any at all. I spent the vast majority my daylight hours either in school or in the woods. I suspect that few others matched my woods forays and I never saw so much as a track or any other sign of big game. I made do with hunting rabbits, squirrels, quail and, once in a great while, ruffed grouse, not that I felt left out.

I joined Rob on many hunts in Kentucky, but he also made an annual trek to Colorado to hunt mule deer. Years later, when deer became scarce and elk numbers increased dramatically, he switched to hunting elk. After a year or two hunting with various factory rifles, Rob took a war memento he had picked up somewhere, a military Model 98 Mauser, and gave it to a local gunsmith with instructions to "customize" it. I don't remember how long the 'smith had the rifle in his shop, but it wasn't more than a couple months. During that time, he replaced the 8mm military barrel with a commercial one in .30 caliber and chambered it for the .30-06 cartridge. He replaced the military two-stage trigger with a commercial single-stage one, did some re-styling to the action and bottom metal, honed and generally slicked up everything, and finally whittled out a very nice sporter stock using a stick of black walnut he obtained locally. The finished rifle was a sight for my young eyes to behold.

My memory is a bit foggy on the scope fitted to the rifle, but I believe it was initially a Weaver K-4. Rob later replaced that initial scope with a Bausch & Lomb BalVar 8. That was the first variable-power scope I had ever seen. Rob hunted with that rifle for most of the remainder of his life. He eventually sold the old Mauser to his Colorado pal to use as a gift for his friend's grandson. That rifle has taken a couple 18-wheeler loads of game and, as far as I know, it is still in use by the grandson today.

Rob's custom Mauser planted a seed in me which has never left. I made do with factory guns for my hunting and, truthfully, I was not handicapped by doing so. Still, I looked upon that situation as an interim solution until I could scratch the custom-rifle itch that was always with me.

I built my first custom rifle while I was still in college. A classmate of mine and I each purchased a surplus Springfield 1903 A3 rifle through the NRA. We each

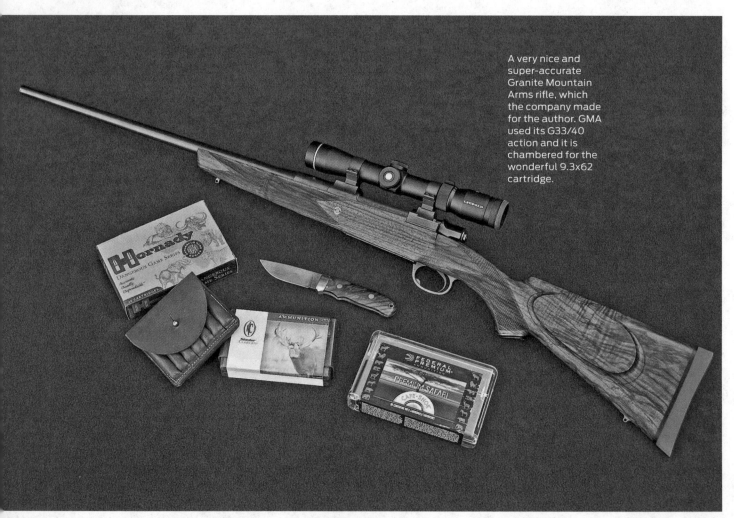

A very nice and super-accurate Granite Mountain Arms rifle, which the company made for the author. GMA used its G33/40 action and it is chambered for the wonderful 9.3x62 cartridge.

This rifle is a .280 Remington with a Danny Petersen barrel. It was built for the author by Gary Goudy.

These two rifles, both by Gary Goudy, are, in the author's view, the prettiest rifles he has ever had crafted. The Model 70 is a .300 Winchester Magnum and the Mauser is a .30-06.

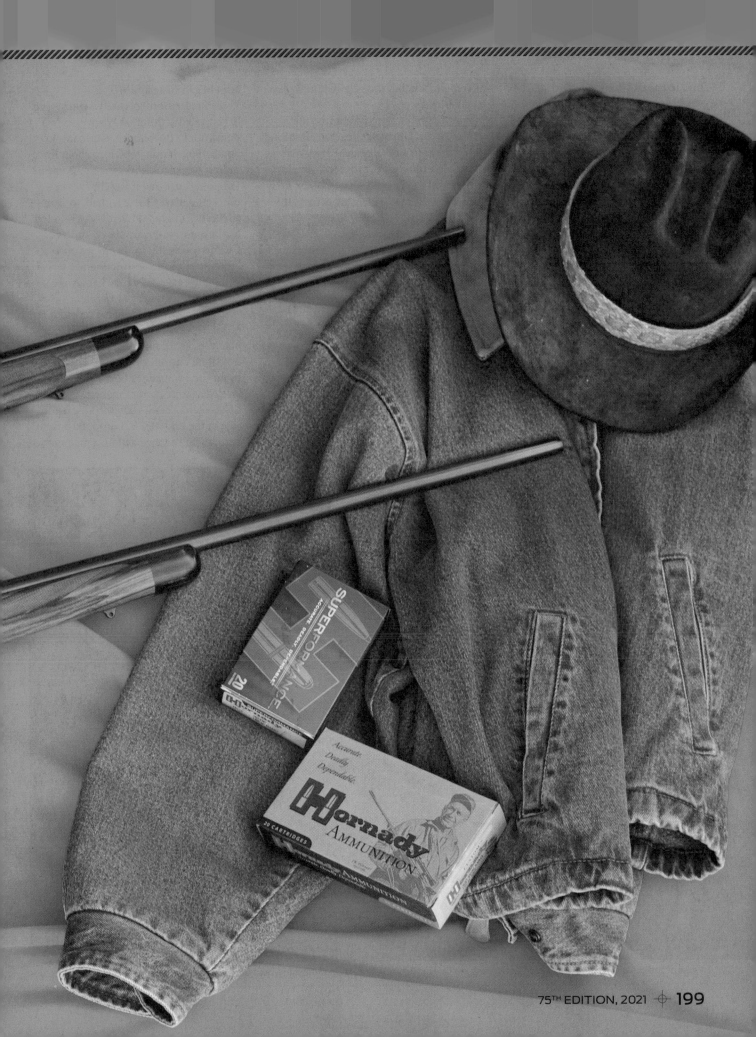

ordered a semi-finished sporting-style stock from either Fajen or Bishop, I've long since forgotten which. We then turned the bits and pieces into what passed for a rifle. My pal was a much more talented craftsman than I was, and his rifle was vastly better looking than mine. My efforts were pretty pitiful by comparison, but the rifle shot as well as my friend's.

After graduation, I went into the U.S. Army. During college, in addition to pursuing a BA degree, I also went through the ROTC program, which required me to serve two years on active duty after I graduated. My active duty stint began in early 1960.

My first custom job used a Springfield '03 barreled action that I delivered to a gunsmith in Boeblingen, Germany, in about 1962. It only took him about three or four weeks to deliver the finished rifle. I'm pretty sure that it was, by far, the quickest delivery I've ever had, for sure a record. I might add that it was also the least expensive custom I ever ordered. Germany was still in the throes of rebuilding after the destruction of the war, and the Deutsch Mark exchange rate for a U.S. dollar was very favorable.

In addition to holding the record for quick delivery time, I suspect that I also hold the record for the longest delivery time for a custom rifle. Slow delivery is by far the complaint I hear most often leveled against custom makers. Even so, I placed an order for my second custom rifle in the mid-1960s. I dropped off a '03 Springfield barreled action, a nice stick of

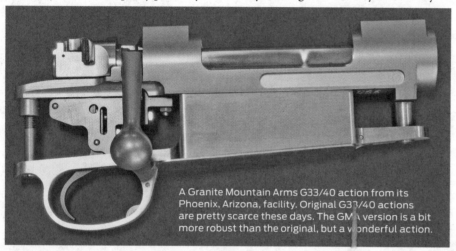

A Granite Mountain Arms G33/40 action from its Phoenix, Arizona, facility. Original G33/40 actions are pretty scarce these days. The GMA version is a bit more robust than the original, but a wonderful action.

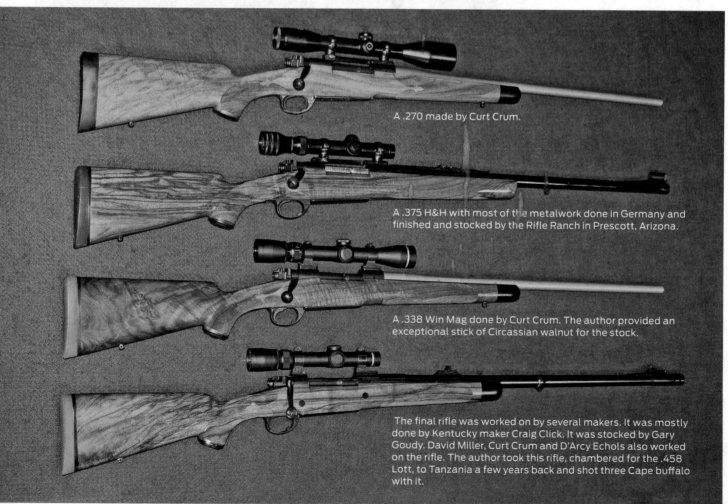

A .270 made by Curt Crum.

A .375 H&H with most of the metalwork done in Germany and finished and stocked by the Rifle Ranch in Prescott, Arizona.

A .338 Win Mag done by Curt Crum. The author provided an exceptional stick of Circassian walnut for the stock.

The final rifle was worked on by several makers. It was mostly done by Kentucky maker Craig Click. It was stocked by Gary Goudy. David Miller, Curt Crum and D'Arcy Echols also worked on the rifle. The author took this rifle, chambered for the .458 Lott, to Tanzania a few years back and shot three Cape buffalo with it.

A few of the custom jobs in the author's safe, built over a number of years. All four rifles are built on pre-64 Winchester Model 70 actions.

walnut, a scope and mounts and instructions to turn the bits and pieces into a nice sporter chambered for the .308 Norma cartridge. As I write this in 2020, my rifle still has not been delivered!

Presently I am thinking of packing up the makings of what would be my last custom rifle. I am reminded by my friends that I have now made pronouncements several times that a particular rifle on order was my last one, only to order another, and then another, and yet another. This one, however, for sure if I do it, will be my last. It will also be very special.

I am also very fond of single-shot rifles. When Bill Ruger came out with the No. 1, I thought I had gone to heaven. I've owned quite a few No. 1 rifles over the years, in both factory and custom guise. Some years back, I did some trading with my pal and colleague Terry Wieland, ending up with a new No. 1 chambered

for the .270 Weatherby cartridge. Another friend, David Miller of custom-rifle fame, had on hand a very nice two-piece blank of English walnut, which he no longer needed. He gave it to me. After aging in Arizona for well over 30 years, probably closer to 40, walnut does not get drier or more stable than that stick.

A year or two later, I talked gunmaker supreme D'Arcy Echols into putting his Hoenig duplicator to good use and turning my blank to his No. 1 pattern. In my "goodie box," I had a new Leupold VX-6 2-12x42mm scope, and a set of Talley 30mm scope rings. Now, all I needed was a maker.

More time passed and my advanced age began catching up with me. I made it 79-1/2 years before spending my first night in a hospital. Seventeen days and one surgery later, they let me go home. At that point, I began thinking seriously that my hunting and shooting days were

rapidly coming to a close. I seriously considered discontinuing the Ruger No. 1 project. More on that subject later. In addition, I started listing some of my rifles on the market. The last thing I wanted to do was to leave my wife with a safe full of expensive guns to dispose of.

I learned in short order that custom rifles were not the hottest ticket on the used-gun market. At the few gun shows I attended after deciding to "thin the herd," I noticed some very nice custom rifles changing hands for very low prices, sometimes less than the cost of the components used in the build. That was pretty shocking news. One excuse I had often used when trying to convince my wife that I simply had to have another custom job, was that she should consider another custom rifle in my safe as a worthy investment.

Early in my acquisition phase, that excuse was pretty much valid. However,

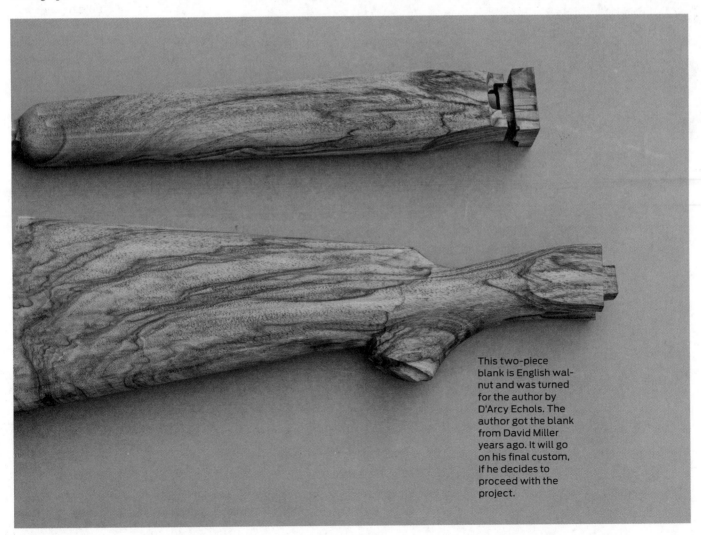

This two-piece blank is English walnut and was turned for the author by D'Arcy Echols. The author got the blank from David Miller years ago. It will go on his final custom, if he decides to proceed with the project.

most of six decades later it is about as true as a politician's promise. I contacted a few friends in the business of marketing quality used guns for clarification and advice. Mostly, they all told me the same story. They all related that the custom-gun trade was mostly built by my generation and the one that preceded it. As my generation passes on, our successors do not have the same interests.

That is true in many aspects, but seems particularly so when it comes to custom guns. I have three sons and two step-sons. Only one has an interest in custom guns. Most of the dealers I contacted had plenty of used custom guns in stock. All related that the market for custom guns was soft, resulting in bargain prices.

Several had rifles in inventory crafted by top makers with impeccable reputations at very reasonable prices. They were not flying off the shelves.

I also contacted several of my custom-maker friends for information. I wanted to learn what I could about the status of new orders coming into their shops. The information I collected was not all that rosy. None who I spoke with were ready to close their shops, but none were talking about expanding either.

Another item of interest that does not bode well for the trade in the future is that about 10 years or so back, the executive director of the American Custom Gunmakers Guild (ACGG) did a survey of the guild's members. Among other interesting findings was that the average age of the members was in the mid-60s! As mentioned, that data is from about 10 years, or so, back, but I doubt that it has changed all that much.

I do believe we have more top-notch custom makers in the trade today than at any point in my lifetime. The work several makers are turning out today is so good it is scary. Thankfully, some of the best makers are relatively young. I have seen numerous examples of the work of the legendary makers revered from the past. Some of them were truly outstand-

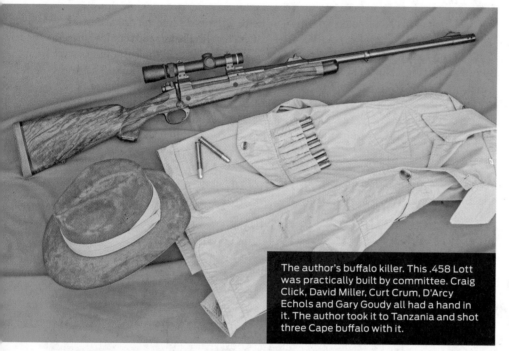

The author's buffalo killer. This .458 Lott was practically built by committee. Craig Click, David Miller, Curt Crum, D'Arcy Echols and Gary Goudy all had a hand in it. The author took it to Tanzania and shot three Cape buffalo with it.

A lovely rifle with a G33/40 action, Danny Pedersen .25-06 barrel and a Gary Goudy stock.

ing. None outshines work available from several markers today though, and much of it is not nearly as good.

I don't recall exactly how many custom guns I've commissioned over the years, but I'd guess somewhere around 20 to 25 rifles, 10, or so, shotguns and perhaps five handguns. As of this writing, I have either sold or traded all the custom handguns and shotguns. However, I still have a number of rifles remaining in my safe. They represent the work of several different makers although Gary Goudy has done more for me than anyone else. He did one rifle each year for me for several years.

Now back to the subject of my final custom rifle. A few months back, I was talking with one my favorite makers about several items. As we hadn't chatted for quite some time, it was a lengthy conversation catching up. Somewhere in our discussion, I mentioned that I had the makings of my final custom rifle in my safe, but that my advanced age and health issues were causing me to rethink the project. He told me such thoughts were folly and to please send the components to him and he'd see what could be done. It has been a dream of mine for a long time to have one of his rifles.

Alas, my taste for champagne, but budget for beer have never permitted that to happen. I will not mention his name here for several reasons, primarily because I haven't yet decided to follow through with the project. That, and the fact that I've not discussed the project in detail with the maker, give me reasons to hesitate.

However, rest assured that if I do proceed with the project, and our *Guns Digest* Executive Editor can be persuaded to run it, I will write a yarn about the rifle when it is finished. Let's keep our fingers crossed.

In the interim, I must confess that the term "investment" will not play a role in my decision. Rather, I am reminded of something Jack O'Connor wrote that explains my feelings on guns far better than I ever could. In his introduction to his classic, *The Rifle Book*, he wrote in part, "I like a handgun. I hold a shotgun in high regard; but rifles, well, I love the darned things." GD

This custom Springfield is, the author believes, the third rifle Al Biesen ever built for famous gun writer Jack O'Connor. Al once told the author he thought he made about 25 customs for O'Connor. Biesen engraved on the barrel of this rifle, "Custom Made for Jack O'Conner." Biesen didn't tell the author how Jack reacted to his misspelled name.

THE ONE-SHOT IMPERATIVE

Some rifles insist you make the first bullet count. That is not an unreasonable demand.

❯WAYNE VAN ZWOLL

A four-bore round dwarfs a .30-06. African explorers like Baker used such loads in single-shot rifles.

Greased by October frost, the scree rasped and slid underfoot, keen to rush me downhill. A rock bounced from basalt rubble above. Scrambling upright, I swung the Ruger. A buck powering to ridgetop bobbed through the scope. The rifle fired as crosswire met rib. The deer vanished behind a chimney.

Silence. Then, heart-shot, the heavy animal tumbled forth, riding the scree down, dead.

One bullet was all I had. Hunters have been so-limited for centuries, many by choice since the advent of breech-loaders. Africa, land of double guns, was settled by men with single shots.

Beginning around 1650, the Dutch colonized the Cape of Good Hope. British explorers probed to the north. The huge beasts they encountered fell only to out-size bullets from ponderous rifles. In 1840, when Samuel Baker was 19, he commissioned a 4-bore from Bristol gunmaker George Gibbs. Its 4-ounce (1,750-grain) silk-patched bullet, driven by 16 drams (437 grains) black powder, loped from a 2-groove, 36-inch barrel. That rifle scaled 21 pounds. In 1869, Holland & Holland built Baker a 3-bore that hurled a 5-ounce (2,187-grain) bullet. The exploits of Sir Samuel, who died in 1893 at 72, helped tobacconist Harris Holland and his nephew Henry grow their gun business, established in 1837.

In 1856, James Purdey came up with .450 and .500 Black Powder Express cartridge rifles, sending slender, lightweight bullets at high speeds. Twin barrels of reasonable weight and profile followed.

Double rifles were costly, and rare on the frontier stateside. But the Civil War in the 1860s pointed out the advantages of repeaters. Soldiers of that day carried the likes of the 1863 Springfield, a muzzleloader whose vulnerabilities appeared in a post-war government report:

Of 27,574 guns collected after battle "… we found at least 24,000 of these loaded; about one half of these contained two loads each, one fourth from three to ten loads each…. In many of these guns, from two to six balls have been found with only one charge of powder. In some, the balls have been found at the bottom of the bore with the charge of powder on top of the ball. In some, as many as six paper … cartridges have been found … without being torn or broken. Twenty-three loads were found in one Springfield rifle-musket."

Oliver Winchester's new breech-loading .44 Henry repeater saw limited action in the Civil War. But the Henry and its early progeny fired anemic rounds ill-suited to big beasts. In the raw West, hunters held to more powerful, more reliable single shots.

Young New Jersey gunsmith Christian Sharps was apprenticing under John Harris Hall, who had patented a breech-loading rifle in 1811. Sharps then set out on his own. In 1848, he patented a vertically sliding breech block, cycled by an under-lever/trigger guard. The resulting action was better engineered than promoted, and Sharps floundered. He secured a $500 loan and a rifle contract in 1849, as Walter Hunt developed the Volitional Repeater that sired the Henry. The Sharps Rifle Manufacturing

Co. incorporated in the fall of 1851. Robbins & Lawrence, then the largest of U.S. firearms manufacturers, would produce its rifles. When R&L went defunct in 1856, the Sharps organization assumed factory operations.

Christian Sharps left the company. After the Civil War, he converted percussion guns in arsenals to fire metallic cartridges. He died young of tuberculosis. The Sharps Rifle Manufacturing Co. soldiered on with dropping-block rifles. The New Model 1869 was its first in metallic chamberings, preceding the 1870 debut of the New Model 1874. The '74 Sharps lasted 12 years, spanning the height of the market-hunting era. Buffalo hunters appreciated the reach and power of its cartridges. The popular .50 sent a 473-grain paper-patched bullet ahead of 100 grains black powder from a 2 1/2-inch case. Muzzle velocity was a listed 1,350 fps, muzzle energy 1,920 ft-lbs. Alas, proprietary Sharps rounds gave the rifles little support. Indian raids left smashed Sharps rifles with dead settlers and hunters. But Winchesters and

Springfields were treasured, as .44-40 and .45-70 ammo was everywhere.

Sharps target rifles excelled in long-range matches. A custom-built, 22-pound '74 match rifle in .44-90 with factory-installed scope fetched $118! Still, the 1874 had flaws: Long hammer travel and lock time punished shooters who didn't follow through. The extractor was weak; cartridges could be inserted ahead of it. But changing times drew the curtain on the '74. By 1880, so many bison had been killed that human scavengers would glean 3 million *tons* of bones from the plains.

The vacant prairie also affected sales of Remington's Rolling Block. Rushed into production in 1866 to offset truncated military contracts after Appomattox, this single shot vied with the Sharps for the hunter's dollar. It was so quick to load a practiced shooter could send 20 shots a minute. Strength? One Rolling Block was loaded with 40 balls and 750 grains of powder, the charge filling 36 inches of its 40-inch barrel. Upon firing, "nothing extraordinary occurred."

Available in hunting, target and military versions and myriad chamberings, .22 rimfire to .50-70 and .44-100, this single-shot rifle would stay in production until 1933. Arguably, it rescued Remington from financial ruin.

The Rolling Block proved itself its first year, when 30 cowboys led by Nelson Story herded 3,000 cattle through Wyoming. Attacked by Sioux under Red Cloud and Crazy Horse, the cowhands fired with deadly effect, their barrels becoming so hot they had to cool them from canteens. Retreating warriors felt the Remingtons' sting from afar. At trail's end, after two more attacks, Story had lost only one man.

Rolling Blocks served buffalo hunters who raked in as much as $10,000 a year selling hides for up to $50 each. "Brazos" Bob McRae claimed 54 buffalo with as many shots at one stand with a .44-90 Remington and a Malcolm scope. Though it faced competition from Winchester's lever-action 1873 (in .44-40), the Remington was more powerful, more accurate. In 1873, George Custer reported,

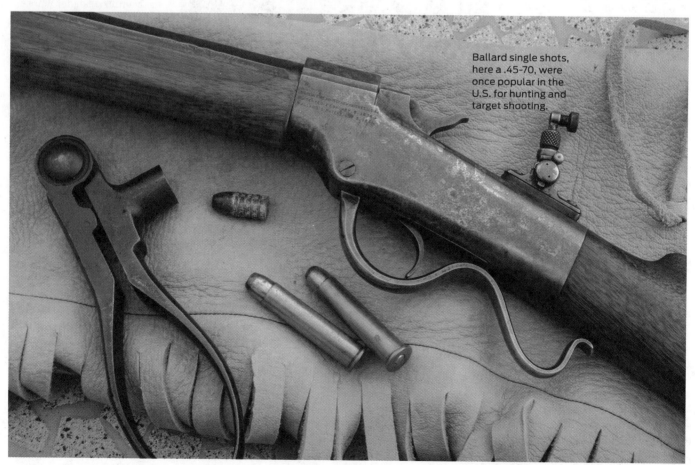

Ballard single shots, here a .45-70, were once popular in the U.S. for hunting and target shooting.

This elegant, accurate 6.5x57 *kipplauf* stalking rifle hails from Austria's gun-making center, Ferlach.

John Farquharson of Daldhu, Scotland, patented his single-shot rifle in 1872. A lovely specimen here.

Ruger's stout, comely No. 1 shows clear Farquharson influence. It sold for $265 at its 1966 debut.

The No. 1's investment-cast receiver boasts an adjustable trigger. The tang safety appeals to lefties.

The No. 1 has been barreled to 52 cartridges, big and small. Many, like this .475, had short tenures.

475 Turnb[ull]
Bullet: 400 Barnes
Muzzle velocity: 2,[...]
Muzzle energy: 4,[...]0

after a hunt: "With your rifle I killed far more game than any other single party... at longer range."

In 1874, Remington's L.L. Hepburn developed a rifle to beat the Irish in long-range competition at Wimbledon. Each team would comprise six men, shooting three rounds at 800, 900 and 1,000 yards, 15 shots per round. A newly formed National Rifle Association, with the cities of New York and Brooklyn, each put up $5,000 to build a venue on Long Island's Creed's Farm, provided by the state of New York.

In September, a favored Irish team lost to the Americans firing Remington .44-90s with 550-grain bullets. Sharps rifles contributed to the winning score: 934 to 931, with one Irish crossfire.

Off-shore military sales underpinned most of Rolling Block production. Thousands of rifles were bored to .43 Egyptian and .43 Spanish. In 1878, infantry versions listed at $16.50, Sporting models at $30.

Fitting a stock to a Ruger No. 1 requires careful handwork to ensure snug seams, and prevent tang splits.

That year in Ogden, Utah, firearms prodigy John M. Browning turned 23. He filed his first patent request May 12, 1879. Then John and his four brothers built a small factory to manufacture his dropping-block rifle. In 1883, a Winchester salesman came upon a second-hand Browning single shot and took it east to show company president Thomas Bennett. While Winchester's lever actions dominated the rifle market, none fired the huge cartridges used in Sharps 1874s and Remington Rolling Blocks. Browning's rifle did. Bennett quickly made the six-day rail trip from New Haven to Ogden, where he asked John to sell all rights. "The price is $10,000," replied the lad. A daunting sum. Astonished but unfazed, Bennett offered $8,000 and clinched the deal. Winchester would later produce its version as the Model 1885.

Other notable U.S. single-shots of that era came from Ballard, Stevens and Maynard.

In Europe, rifle evolution followed a different path. Austria's storied gun-

The author aligns this No. 1's excellent safari sights quickly, thanks to the Len Brownell-designed stock.

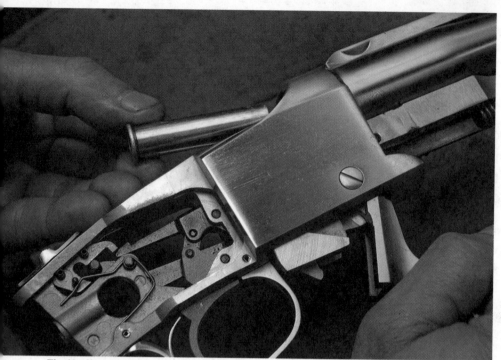

The No. 1's extractor is adjustable. Choose smart ejection or a gentle shove to pluck brass by hand.

making center, Ferlach, dates to 1246. The first gunsmith of record there appeared in 1551 registries of the Hollenburg Estates, which would furnish the Ljubljana Armory with 400 arquebuses. By 1732, area gun-makers were sending rifles to the Austrian Army. One family still building guns there, Fanzoj (*Fanzoy*), opened shop in 1790.

"Then the bottom fell out," Daniela Fanzoj told me. "Ferlach craftsmen held to traditional ways and were slow to adopt machine-driven manufacture of firearms, even parts. Military contracts shifted to factories in Steyr and Vienna. Ferlach remained a hub for hand-built sporting guns."

At this writing, Daniela and her brother Patrick manage the Fanzoj shop, succeeding their father Johann. She explained that, after brisk sales to wealthy German clients in the 1960s, prosperity in Russia and China buoyed firearms sales there, "where guns are status sym-

Ruger's No. 1B and V in small-bore chamberings have delivered tight groups with modern loads.

VARMINT EXPRESS™
Hornady
#83204 204 RUGER
32 gr V-MAX

VARMINT EXPRESS™
Hornady
#8336 22-250 REM
50 gr V-MAX™

The Ruger No. 1 action accepts big cartridges, not just belted magnums, but the husky .416 Rigby.

Remington
PREMIER A-FRAME™
416 REMINGTON MAGNUM
400 GR. SWIFT A-FRAME PSP   RS416RA

CUSTOM™
Hornady
#8265 416 RIGBY
400 gr. FMJ/ENC

bols." Still, many Ferlach shops failed to evolve with the times. In Daniela's youth "56 families built guns in Ferlach. Now there are five."

Many hunters in Europe still favor single-shot rifles from old-world shops. During the 1960s, the Fanzojs shipped as many as 150 rifles a year, a frenetic pace by local standards. "About 70 percent of the work in a Fanzoj rifle is skilled hand labor," said Patrick. "Only 10 people work here. They build firearms from scratch, now with the assistance of five-axis CNC and wire EDM machines." A signature

This classy modern Lyman rifle has the profile of an 1874 Sharps. It is scaled for the .38-55 cartridge.

Shoot It!

Stateside, single-shot rifles include economical hinged-breech models from the likes of Savage, H&R and T/C, and classy Sharps replicas from Dakota and Shiloh Sharps. My scaled-down Lyman Ideal .38-55 is fine rifle, modestly priced. The Model 10 Dakota, a Don Allen original, is the Ferrari of rifles, with an elegance of line to make any enthusiast weak-kneed. Mine, in .280, has figured French walnut, NECG sights and a petite 6x scope Leupold built briefly on the old Lyman Alaskan pattern. Dakota also markets Miller rifles, with silky cycling, vault-tight lock-up and head-turning wood.

Jim Boyd owns one of Ralf Martini's custom-built single shots, a .300 H&H on the lovely Hagn mechanism, with British detailing. "I'd like you to use it," he told me at an industry convention. Sure. To my surprise, UPS soon delivered a box big enough for a side of beef. It was Jim's rifle, with a terse note: "Shoot it." Jim had won the stock blank — stout, plain, perfectly laid out Turkish walnut — in a raffle by the American Custom Gunmakers Guild. After Ralf shaped and fitted the wood; Jim gave it an oil finish. Doug Turnbull case-colored the receiver. The rust-blued Krieger barrel wears Martini's front sight and quarter rib, a barrel band from New England Custom Guns.

Of course, I fired it. The block slid like a piston in a race engine, snapping shut on cartridge rims as if sealing a vacuum. The trigger read my mind. The first three-shot delta on paper miked .8 of an inch. Returning this rifle took all my resolve. "You haven't killed anything with it," Jim protested, when I stopped by his Montana digs, box in hand. I said it was too lovely to risk scarring, then drove off to escape seduction.

Listed for just a year, the No. 1 in .303 was a fine pairing. The author shot his first deer with that round.

The full-stocked No. 1 RSI has been offered in few chamberings. The author likes the way it handles.

Fine modern single shots include Miller rifles (here) and Dakota's Model 10, from the same shop.

This prairie whitetail fell to one 180-yard shot from the author's full-stocked No. 1RSI in .303 British.

product is the *kipplauf,* or hinged-breech stalking rifle. Lithe and lightweight, "it's an extension of a hunter's eye and hand. Its Swiss-watch precision and single-shot design reflects our hunting culture. Many *kipplaufs* are now fitted with scopes, but traditionalists take pride in getting close for a first-shot kill with open sights."

Early *kipplaufs* were chambered for cartridges like the 8x50R Austrian Mann-licher, introduced in 1888. The Great War vetted rimless rounds, but the .303 British and rimmed versions of other European favorites – 6.5x57R, 7x57R,

7x65R – endure. The 8x60R emerged from post-WWI sanctions on German military cartridges. A spin with a chamber reamer made an 8x60 or 8x60R from an 8x57.

"You must try my 6.5x57R," urged Patrick. "The range is close." Rifle fire echoes over Ferlach daily, evidence firearms remain the lifeblood of this community. Dating to 1906, the clubhouse is barely on its outskirts. I sandbagged the *kipplauf* on a window bench that had steadied rifles for over a century. The trigger broke like a thin icicle. Three shots yielded a

group the size of a quarter.

"There was no call for your last two bullets," Patrick deadpanned. "Our *kipplaufs* kill with the first."

As metallic cartridges were redefining stalking rifles in Austria, John Farquharson of Daldhu, Scotland, patented a dropping-block single shot. Shortly after the 1872 debut, he sold part interest in the rifle to George Gibbs, who manufactured it until the patent expired in 1889. Evidently fewer than 1,000 left Gibbs' shop before the last Farquharson was delivered in 1910. But the mechanism found its way into other rifles. Auguste Francotte of Herstal, Belgium, copied it. So did British maker W.J. Jeffery & Co., as early as 1895. In 1904, Jeffery announced an oversize version for the .600 Nitro Express. Farquharson actions produced after the Gibbs era bore a "PD" stamp to show the design had become "public domain."

A second mortgage might bring you a Gibbs-Farquharson. But as Browning resurrected the 1885 Winchester (in 1973 as the Model B-78, then in 1985 as the Model 1885), Bill Ruger gave Farquharson's action new life, and a trimmer profile. The lovely, affordable Ruger No. 1 appeared in 1966, elegant and classy, but with lean, taut lines that begged time afield. A graceful stock (of highly figured walnut on early No. 1s) and a more open guard than the Farquharson's gave the Ruger a clean look. All No. 1s, with and without sights, wore an artfully sculpted quarter-rib, notched for Ruger's scope rings. Chamberings would grow to include a host of cartridges, from the .22 Hornet and .218 Bee to the .416 Rigby. Listed initially at $265, the No. 1 has risen steadily in price, to $1,899 at this writing. Meantime, wood quality has fallen, and Ruger has pruned the No. 1 line. Excluding distributor specials, just one or two versions/chamberings are cataloged each year, to be discontinued the next.

Soon after snaring my first No. 1, a 7x57 in 1973, I began saving for more. Later, in an ill-advised fit of fiscal responsibility, I sold several, including rare specimens with gorgeous walnut.

Ace stock maker Len Brownell designed the No. 1's stock. The countless shapes of human faces, necks and

(top) The No. 1 breech block accommodates big cartridge heads and high pressures. It requires hand fitting.

(above) Hand assembly has pushed the price of No. 1s to $1,899. Meanwhile, wood quality has diminished.

shoulders argue against dimensions that satisfy everyone, but Brownell worked his magic to make this stock suit a wide range of body types. Its straight comb without cheek rest satisfies both right- and left-handed shooters (as does the rifle's tang safety). Comb height is perfect for me, aligning my eye with iron sights quickly and naturally. Scopes in low rings sit just a tad above that plane, promising a full field at a glance. The conservatively capped grip and the thin rubber pad hew to English tradition without compromising utility. Checkering patterns on No. 1s were spare and functional to start. Upscale versions later featured full-wrap fore-end checkering, with higher-grade wood.

For most hunters stateside, the No. 1 is the archetypal modern single shot, with a fetching profile, clever design and Spartan functionality. The breech-block slides like greased glass in its race. The trigger is adjustable, also the extractor, for smart ejection or to nudge cases free for the plucking. A dropping-block mechanism excels with rimmed cartridges, but Bill Ruger fashioned the No. 1 to work as well with rimless hulls. I've never had a No. 1 fail to pull a case, even with frothy handloads. The safety is easy to use and, while not recessed, properly unobtrusive. The short breech, with no bolt knob to snare scabbard or rifle case, shaves inches from overall length. Compared to bolt actions, it gives you roughly 4 inches more barrel for a given OAL. You get more of a cartridge's ballistic zip in a shorter rifle. For example, hand-loaded 180-grain Partitions leave the 26-inch barrel of my No. 1B in .300 Winchester at 3,040 fps. Factory-loaded Power-Points exit at 3,006. In a 24-inch-barreled M70, those loads clock 2,985 and 2,945.

Not all cartridges need that much barrel. No. 1 chamberings include the likes of the .308 Winchester, the 6.5 Creedmoor, Ruger Compact Magnums and other carbine-friendly rounds. Hornady's 6.5 Creedmoor loads thrust 129-grain SST and 140-grain A-Max bullets from the 24-inch barrel of my T/C Icon at 2,939 and 2,647 fps. They clock 2,910 and 2,603 from my 22-inch-barreled No. 1A, whose OAL is 6 inches shorter.

The No. 1 was designed as a hunting rifle, not a one-hole target rifle. Ac-

curacy varies from OK to excellent. My first 7x57 dashed my hopes. "Groups are big as baseballs!" I wailed to a fellow competitive shooter who, like me, was accustomed to half-minute knots from prone rifles. Seeking a solution, I seated a 175-grain bullet as far out as possible and chambered it to check throat length. It emerged with no land marks. Long throats were evidently the rule in early No. 1 7x57 barrels.

The fore-end hanger on a No. 1 doesn't ensure a "free-float" condition or consis-

tent barrel contact when you snug a sling or press the rifle hard onto a bipod. Not wishing to add a set screw to my No. 1B in .300 Winchester, I installed a rubber hose washer near the rear of the hanger, and a brass shim at fore-end's tip. This rifle had shot into 1 1/4 MOA. But at 200 yards, groups fired prone with a sling printed 9 inches below sandbag groups. The rubber washer would, I hoped, maintain steady barrel/fore-end contact up front, with mild pressure on the hanger. It worked. Disparities at 200 yards shrank

At the last minute, the author took this Idaho bull at 330 yards with his hunting partner's No. 1 in 7mm WSM.

to 4 inches, about what I'd come to expect from bolt rifles with barrels contacting stocks.

A cosmetically endearing feature of No. 1s is the barrel-mounted front swivel stud on A, H and S models. But sling tension on a barrel affects its vibration during bullet passage, shifting impact. Checking zeros on hunting rifles, I fire prone, with a sling.

My friend Ken Nagel is a savvy rifle enthusiast. He re-barreled a No. 1 to 7mm WSM. When we saddled up for an Idaho elk hunt, he raised an eyebrow at my iron-sighted 71 Winchester in .450 Alaskan. "For bulls in thickets," I beamed. Alas, we found just one bull so disposed, and he ran off. That evening, the Frank Church River of No Return Wilderness yawned wide below us, with towering ranks of jagged rock marching to the doors of dawn.

Next morning, we climbed back. In bleached grass on a distant bench, a herd of elk sifted toward a timbered hole. "We'll have to hurry," Ron said.

In the mid-1970s, Oregon's Wallowa Mountains yielded this fine buck to the author's 7x57, at 20 steps.

Ken shoved his No. 1 into my hand; I protested; Ron took the rifle: "*Now.*" We plunged downhill, across scree, over deadfall. The spine funneled us to an old burn. Nearly a quarter mile off, elk filed over the crest and down through the charred boles. "Time's up," hissed Ron. I grabbed the Ruger, scooted ahead on knees and elbows, snugged the sling. Antlers winked between trees. Shading for 350 yards, I crushed the trigger, flipping the lever in recoil as the "*whuck*" of the strike floated back.

Ken's generosity had given me that six-point bull. I was more than pleased when, the last morning of our hunt, he dropped a bull at 380 steps with that No. 1.

Ruger's light and medium sporters with Alex Henry fore-ends and open sights (No. 1A and No. 1S) appeal most to me. A No. 1A with a 3x Leupold accounted for one of my biggest mule deer, shot offhand at 20 yards on a cold north face at timberline as the buck jumped from his bed. A full-stocked No. 1RSI in .303 British with a 4x Zeiss reached 180 yards to drop a South Dakota whitetail. Credit fabulous fortune for the 7/8-inch knot a 7x57 printed on paper through open sights at 100 yards.

Incidentally, the .303 British lasted only a year in the No. 1, albeit I was told it topped sales charts during that short tenure. At this writing, Ruger has chambered its No. 1 for 52 cartridges, not all cataloged.

Recently I visited the Ruger factory and spoke with people building the company's popular 10/22 autoloading rifle. "We can produce one every 30 seconds," said Ron Nelson, 10/22 production supervisor. *Every 30 seconds?* "Yep. At full throttle, it's two per minute, what we *must* ship to meet peak demand." The 10/22 cell operates 20 hours daily but doesn't always steam at such a clip.

In another, distant aisle, I found the No. 1 cell. There, two technicians were assembling rifles on padded steel tables. "They're not as easy to build as bolt-actions," smiled one of the men. "Each requires hand fitting." He was timing the close of a No. 1 lever, while his colleague mated a buttstock to a tang. I came away wondering how Ruger could once have sold such a rifle in figured walnut for $265. GD

THREE CUSTOM REVOLVERS

These double-action revolvers were tuned up for defensive duty ›JIM WILSON

About a year ago, I decided to start spending more time with double-action revolvers. After all, that's what I started out with more years ago than I care to write about. When I went into police work, in the late 1960s, the double-action revolver was king. The only real decision to make was whether to carry a Colt or a Smith & Wesson. If a fellow could shoot, he got the job done in a workmanlike fashion.

The author reports
the Tiger McKee
Chopper conversion
of this S&W Model
10 is a real pleasure
to shoot.

And, I have noticed lately that more and more shooters are taking up the double-action revolver for defensive purposes. Social media is full of comments and articles as shooters rediscover the old guns and start getting experience with the new DA guns that have come on the market.

I'll save the pros and cons of defensive revolvers for another time. The main thing is that all of this has rekindled my interest in revolvers. And, over the past year, I've come up with some custom projects that have proved quite interesting and useful. I'll share with you three of those projects I am very pleased with.

SMITH & WESSON MODEL 19

The first of these is a Smith & Wesson Model 19-3 with a 2-1/2-inch barrel. I bought my first 2-1/2-inch Mod. 19 about 1970, and wore it as an off-duty gun. When I made detective, about 1972, it became my everyday carry gun. We had some adventures together.

However, the particular gun I am writing about is one I acquired about 10 years ago. I found that it shot well and so

The Sourdough Pancake holster snugs the Smith & Wesson Model 19 into the shooter's side for comfort and conceal- ment. In the au- thor's view, the S&W 2-1/2-inch Model 19 is one of the truly clas- sic American revolvers.

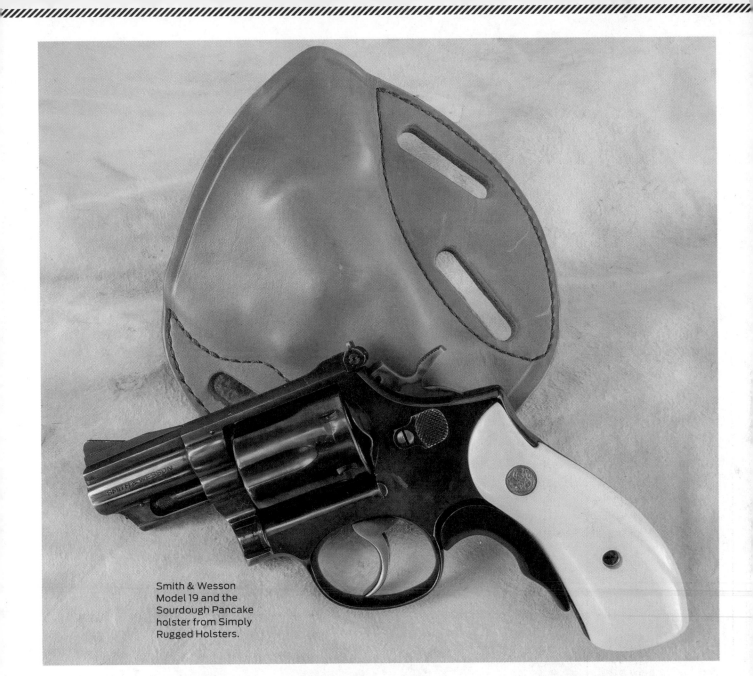

Smith & Wesson
Model 19 and the
Sourdough Pancake
holster from Simply
Rugged Holsters.

it was a sure candidate when I decided to have it slicked up a bit. I carried the gun to Vang Comp Systems (vangcomp.com) in Chino Valley, Arizona. Hans Vang's gunsmiths smoothed up the action and installed the smooth, narrow trigger I prefer on a double-action revolver.

When the gun was returned, I ordered a set of smooth-bonded ivory stocks from Altamont Company (altamont. com). At about the same time, I ordered a grip adapter from BK Grips (bkgrips. com) to also go on the gun. It is important that revolver grips fit the shooter's hand and I have found that the smooth magna stocks, with a grip adapter, are ex-

actly what I need. That a gun's stocks are also nice looking is really an afterthought since pretty stocks don't win gunfights.

When casting around for a holster, I knew I wanted one to wear on my belt, as in-the-pants rigs just don't suit me. One of the best I had ever found was the original Pancake holster that was made by the Roy Baker Holster Company, which is long out of business. This rig consisted of two circular pieces of leather stitched together, with three belt slots so a person could wear it on the strong side or as a crossdraw.

Fortunately, my friend Rob Leahy liked the old Baker Pancake as much as I did.

His Simply Rugged Holster company (simpyrugged.com) offers the Sourdough Pancake, which was exactly what I wanted. The Sourdough is built with good, thick leather, properly stitched, and fitted to a particular handgun. The holster rides high on the belt and snugs the gun into the side very nicely. Altogether, it is the perfect mate for my Model 19.

TIGER MCKEE CHOPPER

My second gun is the brainchild of Tiger McKee, the founder and owner of the Shootrite Firearms Academy (shootrite.org) in Alabama. And, while he teaches the Modern Technique of the

The mark of a good defensive revolver-and-holster combination is that it should be snug on the belt and comfortable to carry. The Chopper is shown here in the Urban Companion rig from Barranti Leather.

The Chopper from Tiger McKee at Shootrite Academy and the Urban Companion holster from Barranti Leather Co.

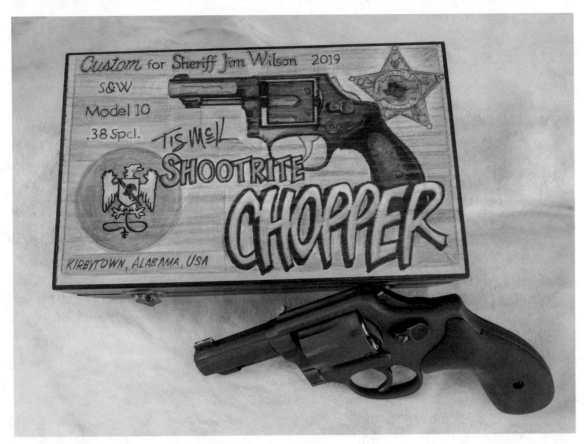

The Shootrite Academy delivers every Chopper in its own personalized box.

Pistol for all kinds of firearms, he enjoys DA revolvers as much as I do. The custom design he has come up with is called the Chopper.

The gun I sent to Tiger started life as a Smith & Wesson Model 10-8 4-inch, in .38 Special. It was probably a police trade-in gun as it showed a lot of external wear, but appeared to have been shot very little. It was the perfect candidate for being turned into a very smooth concealed-carry piece.

McKee began the conversion by cutting the barrel from 4 inches to 3 inches. He then milled the sides of the barrel flat to further reduce weight. An XS front sight was then installed to replace the original. XS makes a Big Dot sight and a Standard Dot front; I requested the latter. This white-dot front sight quickly forces the shooter's attention to the front sight, which is important in defensive shooting.

Turning his attention to the revolver frame, McKee did what he calls a frame melt, smoothing all of the sharp edges. In addition, he narrowed and smoothed the front portion of the trigger guard. This is a procedure that is often done on defensive handguns to aid in a quick

pistol presentation. Impacting a sharp edge during a quick draw, in a defensive situation, might slow the shooter down just a bit. And that is not a good thing when a person's life is on the line.

At my request, the revolver's action was smoothed. The hammer was bobbed to avoid it snagging on a concealment garment. This also encourages the defensive shooter to use only the double-action mode in firing his revolver in practice or in a serious situation. This is the safest and most dependable method for deploying the DA revolver as a defensive weapon. Based upon my preference for double-action guns, a smooth, narrow trigger was also installed.

As a standard part of the Chopper conversion, McKee usually converts a square-butt gun to round-butt configuration. However, since my S&W Model 10-8 was already a round-butt gun this was not necessary. A set of dark, synthetic combat stocks were installed that fit the gun very nicely and are an aid to fast double-action shooting.

Tiger offers several finishes from which the customer can choose. At his suggestion, I went with a dark Parkerized finish

with a black finish on the trigger, hammer and cylinder release. The result was a revolver with a very businesslike appearance as well as being quite durable.

The Chopper conversion also resulted in a revolver that shoots as well as I can hold it. When I do my part, it delivers +P .38 Special hits to the vital zone of the target, out to 25 yards, with regularity. The shortened barrel and frame melt also make it a gun that is quick to get into action. Try as I might, I can't find anything to criticize about the Chopper conversion, and find that it sure suits my needs in a defensive revolver.

Selecting a holster for my Chopper Smith & Wesson was an easy task for me. I asked Doc Barranti (barrantileather.com) for one of his Urban Companion holsters. This rig is a variation of the type of holster that was first designed by Bruce Nelson years ago. It rides high on the belt and, in addition to the standard belt loop, has a second belt loop at the back edge of the holster. This second belt loop causes the holster and gun to snug in close to the body for good concealment. Barranti includes a second piece of leather at the top of the holster pouch to reinforce that

area and make one-handed re-holstering easier. At my request, this holster was built with just a bit of a forward tilt to it, which is often called the FBI cant. Altogether, a fitting and serviceable rig for my Chopper .38 Special.

The final gun in my trio is more about history and nostalgia than modern defensive technique. As a life-long student of history, I have always been interested in stories of the old gunfighters, including those in the first half of the 20th century. And one of the most interesting fighting guns of that era was the FitzGerald Special.

THE FITZ SPECIAL

J. H. FitzGerald (1876-1945) was a Colt employee for over 20 years. As part of his job, he did a lot of exhibition shooting, taught police-firearms techniques, and attended all of the major shooting matches where he interacted with shooters and tuned and repaired their Colt guns. A big man, and quite flamboyant, I guess you could say during that period of time he was "Mr. Colt."

FitzGerald also had some very definite

Tyler Gun Works did an exceptional job converting the Colt Detective Special to a Fitz Special, one of the classic double-action revolvers of days gone by.

ideas about fighting revolvers. For some reason, during that time, Colt did not offer a 2-inch-barreled, double-action revolver. For his own use, FitzGerald decided to convert a pair of Colt Police Positive revolvers into his idea of what fighting guns ought to be. He began by cutting the barrels to 2 inches and replacing the front sight. He also bobbed the hammers and smoothed the actions quite a bit.

But the most interesting thing FitzGerald did was to completely cut away the front of the trigger guards. Being a big man, with big hands, this might have given him quicker access to the triggers for fast double-action work. It has also been suggested that, being from up North, he felt this allowed the shooter to run his guns even while wearing gloves. Being somewhat of a showman, it is also possible that FitzGerald just thought this would give his guns a unique appearance.

After working up the pair of .38 Special Colts, FitzGerald also converted a pair of the big Colt New Service guns in .45 Colt. Regardless of his motivations, FitzGerald's conversions quickly became quite popular and he built quite a few of them, possibly as many as 200. The Fitz Special became a favorite of shootists such as Col. Rex Applegate, Charles Askins, Jr., many FBI agents and numerous lawmen across the country.

Since those days, we have learned it is not necessary to cut away the trigger guard on a DA revolver. If a man has really big hands, it might be necessary to thin the trigger guard as Tiger McKee does on his Chopper conversions. Some folks even think cutting away the trigger guard makes it dangerous, although that is more of a training issue than an actual design flaw. Regardless, I find it an interesting revolver conversion that represents a bygone era. Put simply, I have wanted one for quite some time.

My chance came when, about a year ago, I traded for a Colt Detective Special, made in 1962, that was in good, but not pristine, condition. I took my gun and my idea to Bobby Tyler (tylergunworks.com) in Friona, Texas. Tyler Gun Works has quickly built a reputation for custom work on all manner of firearms, especially historic pieces. Tyler is especially known for his gun-bluing and color-

A.E. Nelson's upside-down shoulder holster is a very close replica of the old Berns/Martin Lightning holster, which comes from the same era as the Fitz Special.

casehardening work.

Since my Detective Special already had a 2-inch barrel, it was not necessary to do any barrel work. In keeping with the Fitz Special work, Tyler cut away the front portion of the trigger guard. He then bobbed the hammer. I suspect Tyler must have referred to photos of FitzGerald's personal guns during this process because he matched that work exactly.

At Tyler's urging, I agreed to let him

have the gun engraved with one-third coverage of very nice scroll engraving. At the same time, he fitted the gun with some very nice elk horn stag stocks. Finally, the gun was re-blued with the old-style, deep-blue finish Colt was known for back in FitzGerald's day. The hammer and trigger were also color casehardened. Altogether a very attractive gun that I'm sure FitzGerald would have approved of.

I was at somewhat of a loss to decide

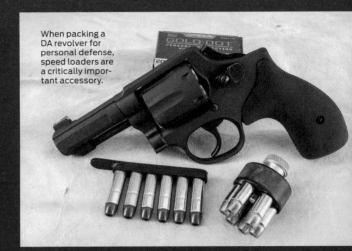

When packing a DA revolver for personal defense, speed loaders are a critically important accessory.

AMMO CONSIDERATIONS

For defensive purposes, with these type of revolvers, I prefer using +P .38 Special ammo. Frankly, that's also what I shoot in my Model 19 2-1/2-inch gun, though it's chambered for the magnum cartridge, for fast double-action work.

We are blessed that, in this day and time, the ammunition companies are making some very good defensive ammunition in .38 Special. The 125- to 130-grain JHP +P loads from any reputable manufacturer are an excellent choice. I particularly like Speer's Gold Dot Short Barrel loading. Another good choice is the 129-grain Hydra-Shok JHP from Federal.

Out of respect for the age and size of my Colt Fitz Special, I often select standard velocity .38 Special ammo for general practice. The 148-grain wadcutter target ammunition is pleasant to shoot in this little Colt. And I happen to have a stash of Federal 125-grain Nyclad hollowpoint ammo, in standard velocity.

When carrying my S&W Model 19 afield, where shots might be longer and I might have to deal with animals, it is generally loaded with Double Tap's 158-grain Hardcast Solid in +P configuration. This is a very accurate load and one that gives a bit more penetration in the target.

Shooters of double-action revolvers are also well-advised to acquire speedloaders for their defensive revolvers. I prefer the HKS loader, but there are a number of different types for shooters to choose from. A couple of speed-strips are good for times when a person has to replace only a few spent cartridges instead of the entire cylinder. Again, several types of speedstrips are available.

Even in this day of autoloaders, a lot of ammunition and accessories are available for the double-action revolver. The DA shooter is advised to experiment a bit and find what works best for the individual.

on a period-type holster to go with this fancy Colt. At a loss, that is, until I discovered the A.E. Nelson Holster Company (nelsonleather.com), which makes a very close reproduction of the old Berns/Martin Lightning shoulder holster. It is the No. 57 Upside-Down Shoulder Holster.

Berns/Martin was a pre-war holster company that incorporated an open front, using a V-shaped flat spring to retain the handgun. The gun was essentially pushed out the front of the holster as opposed to being drawn out the top, as with most other rigs. The Lightning shoulder holster incorporated the same design and is, I believe, the first upside-down shoulder rig ever to be produced. After World War II, Safariland and Bianchi holster companies produced shoulder holsters based upon the Berns/Martin design.

What becomes apparent with this whole revolver project of mine is that we are truly blessed with a number of excellent gunsmiths throughout the country who can meet just about any need, or desire, the shooter has. Thanks to them, I have two serious defensive revolvers and one very nice piece of gunfighting history. All that is required now is to load up with some ammo and hit the gun range. GD

STRAIGHT-P

With its wide selection of barrel lengths and chamberings, the Blaser R8 is extremely versatile, equally at home on the plains, and in the mountains, canyons and safari camps around the world.

ULL RIFLE

Modern straight-pull, bolt-action rifles perform reliably, smoothly and accurately

❯RON SPOMER

By most accounts, Peter Paul Mauser perfected the turn-bolt action in 1898. But that hasn't stopped other designers from introducing other bolt-actions. Some of the best are straight-pulls in several permutations. Heym's SR 30 (1988), Blaser's R8 (2008), and Merkel's RX (2010) are three straight-pulls in today's market, but don't let their recent vintage fool you. Straight-pulls have been around for a long, long time.

One of the first straight-pull, bolt-action rifles was the Lee Model 1895 chambered for the 6mm Lee Navy cartridge. As the model number indicates, it was adopted by the U.S. Navy in 1895. The Lee action wasn't purely a straight-pull because it rocked upward slightly at the rear of the receiver. When pushed forward to close, the mechanism picked a fresh round from the magazine, cocked the firing pin, and cammed a locking lug into the receiver. The Navy claimed the Lee's rate-of-fire bested all the turn-bolts it tested. Both rifle and ammunition proved quite accurate, too, many reportedly shooting MOA. Despite containing chamber pressures of 60,000 psi and being used effectively by U.S. Marines in the Philippines and Cuba, this rifle and cartridge faded quickly, particularly once the Springfield M1903 turn-bolt appeared. The action was never offered in a civilian hunting rifle, but many civilian sporting rifles were chambered for the 6mm Lee Navy cartridge. Ammunition manufacturing ceased around 1935 and no other 6mm (.243) cartridges appeared until the .244 Remington and .243 Winchester in 1955.

A slightly older and longer-lived straight-pull was the Swiss Schmidt-Rubin. It started in 1891, saw extensive military service, and was tweaked and perfected until emerging in its final form as the K31 in 1931. It proved so smooth, fast and effective that the Swiss retained it until 1958. Quite a few were modified and used as sporting arms, but apparently no major manufacturer picked up

A straight-pull rifle's action is in line with aiming and bullet flight, making it easier to stay on target throughout the recharging cycle.

Straight-pull rifles perform reliably, smoothly and incredibly quickly. And they are capable of delivering impressive accuracy.

the design and put it into production as a commercial hunting rifle. The K31 straight-pull locks via twin lugs, but they are turned into their locking recesses by the camming action of a sleeve with a helical groove activated by the straight pulling and pushing action of the bolt handle. It's similar to the locking action of many pump and autoloading shotguns and rifles.

Yet another successful military straight-pull no longer manufactured is the Steyr-Mannlicher M1895. Some 3.5 million were built and used by Austrian, Hungarian and Bulgarian armies. This action also used helical grooves in the bolt body to turn the two locking lugs on the bolt head into battery. A negative of this Mannlicher for sporting purposes was its en-bloc clip loading system. The handy block of five cartridges could be quickly shoved into the rifle from above, but this meant a scope could not be centered above the loading port. Neither could rounds be single-fed because the

en-bloc clip functioned as the feeding lips in the magazine, guiding the large rims of the 8mm cartridges under the extractor, which, like the controlled-round-feed extractor of the Mauser M98, could not ride over those rims.

Perhaps the best known and most successful of the older straight-pulls is the 1903 Canadian Ross, a military action that was chambered for the .303 British and later the relatively well-known .280 Ross of 1906. Mechanically, it was a near copy of the Mannlicher until a 1910 upgrade converted the twin locking lugs to an interrupted-thread system. That proved problematic in World War I because the thread grooves (three on the left lug, two on the right) too easily plugged with sand and dirt. Hard bolt manipulations even deformed the narrow threads, preventing lock up. Despite these shortcomings, snipers loved the Ross for its accuracy.

The Ross became a popular military-surplus hunting rifle in Canada. The

sporterized Mk III Ross rifles in .280 Ross won many international matches. With ballistics on par with today's .280 Remington, it was one of the fastest of its day.

STRAIGHT-PULL ADVANTAGES

A straight-pull, bolt-action rifle is self-identifying: The name describes the motion. A shooter merely pulls straight back on the bolt handle to eject a fired round, then pushes straight forward to pick up a fresh cartridge and lock it into battery. No lifting. No turning.

What's so special about that? Speed. "Smooth" speed. A straight-pull's action is in line with aiming and bullet flight. Many practiced turn-bolt shooters can cycle through four or five shots amazingly quickly, but they're always faced with compensating for vertical motion counter to the linear action of aiming at and delivering a bullet toward the target. Lifting a bolt against a slightly "sticky" round while simultaneously cocking a heavy firing pin spring further disrupts

While straight-pull rifles have been around since the late 1800s, modern versions combine high-tech designs and quality components built to exacting tolerances to produce excellent hunting rifles.

the sight picture, sometimes to such a degree that the shooter lowers the rifle to gain more leverage to complete the task. A straight-pull eliminates that.

Anyone familiar with the operation of a pump shotgun or rifle can appreciate this. All the action is in line with the barrel, making it easier to keep pointing at the target throughout the recharging cycle. Given the need for speed in wing shooting, this might be a major reason why pump-action shotguns flourished while lever- and bolt-action shotguns languished.

In-line action and cycling speed, then, are straight-pull advantages, and our three modern, straight-pull sporting rifles take full advantage.

HEYM SR30

The Heym SR30 is unique. This is the only centerfire rifle that uses ball bearings as locking lugs. Instead of two, three, six or nine right-angle lugs at or near the front of the bolt, the SR30 employs six ball bearings arrayed around the circumference of the bolt body near the head. These lock into recesses in the front receiver ring when the bolt handle is pushed forward, driving an internal sleeve under the balls, forcing them outward. At first blush, this might seem a weak link, but this locking system has been tested to 155,000 psi without failing. Some of the highest SAAMI chamber pressures allowed in cartridges like .300 Win. Mag. and .416 Rem. Mag. are just 65,000 psi.

The Heym SR30 bolt face is the recessed, push-feed type, but instead of a plunger ejector, it utilizes the rear standing ejector blade that slides through a groove in the bolt face.

Here are three of the six ball bearings set in the bolt body of the Heym SR30. An internal tube rammed forward by the straight-pull bolt slides under these balls to lock them out and firmly into recesses within the front receiver ring.

Because the ball-bearing lock-up requires no camming force to turn lugs into recesses, it requires less force to operate, enhancing the speed already enhanced by the straight-pull action. Because circles and balls are geometrically perfect, they contribute to precision, too. So long as

Heym builds its SR30 rifles with traditional blued steel and walnut stocks of varying grades, but also with handlaid, stiff synthetic stocks and carbon-wrapped barrels.

receiver threads are cut "square" and barrels are screwed on straight, there is no need to lap lugs and blueprint these actions. Heym guarantees its SR30 rifles will group 3/4 MOA. Any tested at the factory that do not meet this accuracy standard are not shipped.

In addition to its unique locking system, the SR30 action includes an unusual safety and cocking system. With the bolt pushed fully forward and the safety switch at the back of the bolt shroud disengaged, the rifle is ready to fire. Engage the safety switch and it locks both the trigger and bolt handle. However, there is an additional stage that can be employed with the safety disengaged: pull the bolt handle back just slightly and it de-cocks the striker. Combine this with the safety and not only is the trigger blocked and bolt locked, but the striker is de-cocked. You can't get much safer than that unless the chamber is empty and/or the bolt is removed. An alternative safety position for fast action is to disengage the safety switch, but pull the handle back to de-cock the striker. The bolt handle can then be nudged forward (and quite quietly when done slowly) to make ready to fire.

BLASER R8

Blaser had considerable success with its earlier straight-pull, the R93. In 2008, the company released the R8 as a beefed-up version with stronger radial locking lugs tested to withstand 210,300 psi pressure. That's the pressure the locks can hold, not necessarily the barrel and chamber.

Looking at the R8's bolt head, you might doubt this claim. Instead of the thick two or three locking lugs on most bolt-actions, the Blaser's radial lugs are 14 rather insubstantial bumps on the ends of integral splines cut into a steel tube or collet that rides inside the bolt

With scope mounts atop its interchangeable barrels, Blaser's R8 can be set up with pre-zeroed scopes for each barrel, making in-field swaps quick and easy. Blaser's quick-release scope mounts return to zero so reliably they can even be carried off the barrel. The twin barrel studs beneath the barrel extension mate with captured nuts inside the fore-end wood.

carrier. Another steel tube slides within this splined tube. When the bolt handle is pushed forward to chamber a round, it pushes the innermost "plunger" tube toward the tapered rear of the bolt head. This forces the surrounding splines to expand outward and lock into a radial recess inside the barrel extension. The result is a 360-degree radial lock up of the bolt head in the barrel. Despite the small surface area of each of these locking bumps, added together their locking surface area actually exceeds that of the Mauser 98 by about 40 percent.

A bonus to this solid lock up is that, under the pressure of ignition, any back-thrust on the bolt head only further presses the locking splines outward, increasing the locking tension.

A concern of many is that the R8's action might be a bit fragile. It looks the part because the bolt carrier rides on

Here is the R8 bolt pulled from the striker and firing pin on right. The stiff, strong twin rails are what the bolt carrier glides on along the lower action walls. While each locking lug at the end of the cylinder of splines is small, in aggregate they provide more locking surface area than a typical two-bolt Mauser-style.

What appears to be a classic tang safety on the R8 is really a cocking lever. This permits perfectly safe carry with a round in the chamber with no spring pressure on the striker.

The Blaser R8 features a traditional-looking push-feed bolt face with a large extractor hook and plunger ejector. But there is something different behind it, the multi-segmented circumference of locking lugs.

Turn off the captured nuts within an R8's fore-end and the two attachment screws are free. Just lift, and the barrel with sights comes free, the stocked action ready to receive the replacement.

At first glance, the R8 trigger group with integral magazine box looks questionable, but it proves to be a reliable, strong system with a simple, straight pin connection from trigger shoe to sear. The trigger group can be locked into position. When removed, the rifle cannot be fired.

twin triangular bars screwed to its bottom, outside edges. These bars, just 5/16th of an inch wide, protrude 5 inches in front of the carrier and glide within raceways milled into the lower half of the receiver. It looks as if they might easily bind or even bend, but in practice they are extremely strong, durable, smooth and reliable without even a hint of binding. The R8 has one of the smoothest, quickest-cycling actions in the world.

Because the R8's bolt body does not ride within a traditional receiver with an ejection port cut open between front and rear rings, it completely covers the action, magazine and trigger group when closed. While it looks a bit bulky, it does not feel or function that way. As a bonus, it's an effective cover against dust, debris and light precipitation.

The R8 "safety" is really a cocking lever at the back of the bolt carrier. Until it is pushed forward, the striker is not cocked. A round can be carried in the chamber in complete safety. The downside to this cocking system is that it is more difficult to operate than a simple trigger/sear safety. Considerable thumb pressure is required to shove the cocking lever forward. With practice, however, it can be reliably done even by older shooters with small hands and limited hand strength. Still, I wouldn't consider it optimum for a dangerous-game encounter requiring split-second shooting to stop a charge.

The rest of the rifle is cleverly engineered with virtually all parts modular and interchangeable, lock, stock and barrel. Two captured screws in the fore-end can be turned loose to release the barrel. Because the open sights and/or scope mounts are on the barrels, not the action, each newly mounted barrel is already zeroed. The quick-release scope mounts are so precise that optical sights can be removed and replaced without changing point of impact. Even the bolt head is modular. It can be swapped out in the field with no tools other than a fingernail. You can literally reconfigure an R8 from a .500 Jeffery to a .204 Ruger in the field in a minute or two.

While the removable trigger group is universal, nylon inserts must be changed out to fit various cartridge groups. They pop in and out in a second. The trigger group is held in the action via dual spring clamps that can be locked into place via a button slide accessible through the top of the magazine box. When the trigger group is detached from the receiver, the rifle cannot be fired. R8 triggers break at about 2.5 pounds and push straight up against the sears for a simple, direct connection.

The R8 bolt head is the familiar, recessed, push-feed type with a single plunger ejector inset within the bolt face and a large, spring-activated extractor hook riding on the outer rim. Blaser R8s are offered in a wide range of stocks, from traditional, high-grade walnut to synthetics, including thumb holes.

MERKEL RX HELIX

Merkel's straight-pull RX Helix wins the speed competition thanks to a 1:2 ratio bolt travel. The roughly 2.3-inch slide of the handle converts to enough bolt-head travel to easily eject and reload

A lean, mean, straight-pull machine. The Helix bolt rides entirely within its receiver. A camming helix transfers twice the bolt handle's movement to the bolt itself for the quickest cycling action in the business. The wood isn't hard on the eyes, either.

3.34-inch .300 Winchester Magnum cartridges. This is accomplished via a helical (spiral) mechanical linkage Merkel calls a transmission system. The slim bolt handle slides cartridges out of battery smoothly and easily while remaining completely within the receiver "garage." Yes, unlike most bolts that slide out of their receivers and back toward your eye, the Merkel Helix bolt remains entirely inside the receiver. This provides a little extra overhead debris protection as well as an exceptionally effective gas block in event of an unlikely case failure. The only openings are a bolt handle groove and ejection port on the side, the magazine port on the bottom, and a small slit on the rear to accommodate the sliding cocking lever which itself acts as a shroud against any escaping gases.

As the Helix bolt handle moves, it engages helical contacts on the bolt body, turning it forward twice the linear distance of the handle travel itself. As the

bolt head reaches the barrel chamber, it turns to engage its six stacked lugs into recesses within the barrel extension. It's all very clever, slick and fast. The push-feed bolt head is recessed with the usual plunger ejector and a small, inset, spring-activated extractor hook mounted in the head.

Like so many European rifles, the Helix is cocked by shoving forward what appears to be an oversized safety lever at the rear of the receiver. These are never as easy to flick off as most traditional safeties, but they are certainly safer since the rifle cannot possibly fire if the striker spring isn't even compressed. With a bit of practice, one can train to manipulate this cocking device reliably and quickly for just about any event short of an unexpected charge from hidden tigers or lurking buffalo.

As if the helical bolt travel wasn't special enough, the Helix also features quick-detach barrels. Truly quick. Press a button in the belly of the fore-end and it slides off the hanger bar projecting from the bottom of the receiver. Neither this hanger nor the fore-end touches the barrel, so this is essentially a free-floating barrel setup. To detach the barrel, pull down a barrel-locking lever protruding from the bottom left of the receiver. This releases the barrel/receiver connection. Lift the barrel out. If the bolt is closed during this operation, the bolt head will slide off the firing pin and bolt body and

remain inside the locking recesses of the barrel. If you are switching from, say, a .243 Winchester barrel to a .30-06 barrel, you use the same bolt head. If you're stepping up to a cartridge with a larger diameter head, like the 7mm Remington Magnum, you must attach a magnum sized head.

Merkel builds its Helix action with integral Picatinny rail mounts. Barrels are offered in three lengths and diameters with or without open sights in a dozen popular chamberings with or without threaded muzzles for suppressors. Stocks are offered in a variety of configurations from traditional in high-grade walnut to synthetic with Soft-Touch grip inlays, adjustable combs and radical pistol grips. Drop-box magazines are standard with extended versions holding up to five rounds.

CONCLUSION

Although straight-pull bolt-action rifless are nothing new, they have never approached the mass appeal of turn-bolts. Exactly why might be due to some loading and ejection issues with early, military models. Straight-pulls don't enjoy quite the same strong, camming force of turn-bolts, but hot loads and oversized cartridges are a thing of the past. Today's straight-pulls perform reliably, smoothly and incredibly quickly. Add their impressive accuracy and you have a great option for your next bolt-action hunting rifle. **GD**

With its fore-end slipped off, the Helix reveals its barrel release/lock lever on the lower left of the receiver, right behind the fore-end mounting bar. An easy swing down unlocks the indexed barrel, which then slips forward and out.

The Helix bolt head rotates via an internal cam on the bolt to lock rounds into battery. Note the solid receiver top and integral scope mount bases.

The Helix is a versatile, quick break-down, switch-barrel, straight-pull rifle that is fast, sleek, strong, reliable and delightfully accurate. Note the index groove on the silver barrel extension.

Extensive testing with a variety of factory ammunition convinced the author Merkel's Helix was no gimmick. It digested any and every load tried and clustered most of them 1.5 MOA or better. Often much better.

REMINGTON'S CELEBRATED SPANISH MODEL

An international peacemaker

› GEORGE LAYMAN

Surrounded by a collage of Argentine and Bolivian currency, this Remington Spanish Model was once a .58 Berdan-caliber Transformed Model, that was declared surplus by the French following the Franco-Prussian War, and sold to Belgium. It was re-barreled to .43 Spanish caliber and is one of thousands sold independently to numerous South American countries by the Belgians. (Author's Collection, Stuart Mowbray Photo)

This left view is the first-contract Spanish Model in its earliest configuration with the screw-retained bar extractor and the Dodge Patent screw-retained firing pin, which entered from the left side of the breech block. Later Spanish contract models omitted the latter not long after 1870. (Roy Marcot Photo Remington Arms Company Collection)

"Over 1,600,000 Sold." That was the boast in 1902, in the last Remington Arms Company catalog to feature its revered Spanish Model rolling-block rifle. From the first 10,000 sold to Spain from 1869 to 1870 to the last 2,000 rifles that left the factory to various foreign customers in 1910, the Remington Spanish Model was truly a blue-chip commodity. First mention of Spain's interest in the revolutionary new Remington-Rider breech-loading rifle was in a letter just prior to May 1868, sent to the Remington company from Spanish army Major Joaquin Buega y Peruela, about obtaining samples. What created the sensational, long-lived popularity of this single-shot rifle from the blackpowder era that gracefully blended into the smokeless times? Perhaps it was a reputation for strength and reliability, a quality that, for more than five decades, saw it in steady use by more than 20 countries, many of which were located in the Spanish-speaking Americas. By true definition, the Spanish Model was any Remington rolling-block that was chambered for the .43 Spanish cartridge, but there were several variations from a

(below) This beautifully preserved .58 Transformed Alteration musket re-barreled in Belgium to .43 Spanish is typical of many such conversions sold to Argentina in the mid-1870s. Originally Franco-Prussian War surplus, they were made from cut-down .58-caliber Civil War Springfield muzzle-loading rifles, their original short-range .58-caliber centerfire cartridge left much to be desired, hence they were converted to the more efficient .43 Spanish cartridge. This example is profusely marked with Belgian proofs and inspector markings. (Jude Steele Collection, Stuart Mowbray Photo)

cosmetic standpoint. The nickname "roll-ing-block" was a term coined by shooters and collectors in the mid-20th century and was never used by the factory as an official term.

The story of this successful breech-loading rifle that rescued E. Remington & Sons of Ilion, New York, from the post Civil War arms glut is, indeed, an interesting one. Following Denmark and Sweden, the first two countries to purchase large quantities of the new breech-loader, Spain made arrangements to evaluate the Remington-Rider in a series of trials that commenced on June 24, 1868. Conducted both in Spain and the colonial territory of Cuba, a series of abusive tests in sand, salt water and tropical climates saw the "Systema Remington" outperform other breech-loading systems. The first known contract of 10,000 Remington rolling-block rifles was shipped to the colonial Spanish army garrison in Cuba. Spanish authorities were impressed with the Remington and resultingly conducted a second set of trials from April 30, 1869, through Aug. 24, 1870. This was appar-

The early two-line Remington address and basic Rider/Geiger patent-date tang markings are encountered only on the first- and second-contract Spanish rifles. Note the early, direct, square shoulder fit where the stock meets the frame. On later Remington Spanish Models sold after Spain's contracts were fulfilled, the new, improved frame offered mortises where the buttstock and forearms met the frame. (Author's Collection)

This close-up of a first-contract Spanish Model frame shows the "Crown over B" cartouche known as the Barcelona acceptance proof. The top of the chamber on this early Spanish Model has a deeply stamped rack number of 45. It can also be seen here that the open breech exposes the concave-type breech-block axis, a feature not found on the later second- and third-contract Spanish rolling-blocks. Remington replaced the concave breech-block axis to the more well-known straight type after August 1870. The early first-contract Spanish Model rifles are rather scarce due to lower production numbers and high attrition rates (Chris Lener Collection)

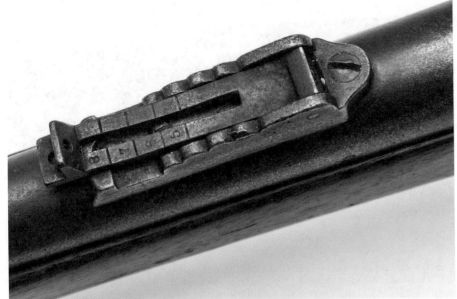

ally replaced by the new 7mm Mauser Model 1893 repeating rifle.

From 1868 to 1878, Spain had its hands full in Cuba during the Ten Years War, dealing with an independence movement. In addition, a recurring Carlist War on the Iberian Peninsula was in full swing by the early 1870s and saw Spain's army taxed to the utmost in controlling anti-government elements. A shortage of military arms soon existed. Thus, the Spanish Legislative Branch in 1873 presented the following request to deal with the ordnance shortfall:

By order of the Governor General of the Republic on 16 September 1873 it has been determined that an additional 30,000 Remington rifles be procured to fulfill the

Though the leaf is missing, this is the basic design of the Remington Spanish Model rear sight. Earlier versions incorporated a peep sight aperture as shown, however as a cost-saving measure, later generic Spanish Model Remingtons were supplied with an open "V" notch replacing this. (Stuart Mowbray Photo)

ently a confirmation trial, which resulted in a second order of 50,000 rifles placed late in 1870.

The 11.15x58mm cartridge, known commonly today as the .43 Spanish Remington, was specially designed for the Spain's ground forces and was nothing more than a modification of the .42 Russian Berdan cartridge with an increased bullet diameter expanded from .429" to .439", meaning that the neck of the case was merely re-formed to meet this requirement. Furthermore, it was a powerfully efficient cartridge that was well-suited for use on flat, long-range terrain, as well as having the capability to smash through dense jungle foliage. The successful completion of the second Spanish trials lead the Remington "North American Model" to become officially adopted by Spain through a national decree on Feb. 24, 1871. The Spanish government also acquired licensing rights to domestically manufacture the Remington in its own government armories one year prior to official adoption. Spain began production of the Remington rolling-block at the Oviedo national arsenal in mid-1870 and continued until early1894, when the Remington system was gradu-

Here we have the straight-axis-type breech block, which was common to the second- and third-contract Spanish rifles, as well as to all future Spanish Model Remington rolling-block rifles up until production was terminated in the late 1890s. (Author's Collection)

emergency order for the current call up of reserves, because the national factory is unable to meet its prerogatives and delivery schedule. Through legal bidding in the search to find a supplier for rifles, the Spanish Model of 1871 as manufactured by Remington has been selected by a hands down, favorable proceeding. After meeting all legal proceedings, the acquisition of 30,000 Remingtons with bayonets and maintenance accoutrements to be ordered immediately as this vignette is the only model firearm considered satisfactory."

Our military has been using several different classes of models of rifles and carbines such as the Berdan Model 1867, but most important of all the Remington Spanish Model 1871 rifles and carbines have been deemed the primary arms and nearly declared to be the official small arm. Several branches of service have relied upon the factory at Oviedo for various arms and it has been determined insufficient for production at this time. Due to the urgent situation at present, we are compelled to obtain our rifles from foreign sources once again and it has been verified that it will be the Remington company in the United States. We have satisfactorily celebrated two contracts from them, one for 10,000 that was received , and another for 50,000, which has now concluded that a total of 30,000 more are necessary to be issued here on the Peninsula by the end of the year.

The factory at Oviedo is producing 9,000 rifles and 2,000 carbines, construction which began on 12 Sept which will be continued until completed. The factory has been ordered to produce 40,000 arms annually, but the numbers are overwhelming and have forced us in this time of contingency to procure from foreign sources to meet armament goals. The inadequacy of this finds it necessary to overhaul manufacture plans and goals until abundant quantities and schedules can be met to rapidly arm the military.

Readers should be aware that all three Remington Spanish contracts saw two minor cosmetic features on all three contract rifles that are differences collectors should be on guard to identify. These features include:

The FB cartouche over the chamber indicates this rifle was re-chambered to use the improved .43 Reformado cartridge, replacing the earlier .43 Remington Spanish cartridge in 1889. They are the initials Lt. Colonel Freire and Captain Brulle, who jointly developed this higher-velocity cartridge, which used a brass-jacketed projectile. (Chris Lener Photo and Collection)

First Spanish Contract Remington: Early New Model Remington action with flat, non-mortised metal-to-wood flat frame shoulder, concave breech block, horizontal extractor, 35-1/4-inch barrel, tang marking of: Remington's Ilion, N.Y. U.S.A.

Pat May 3rd Nov 16th 1864, April 17th 1866. In addition, the first contract Remington Spanish Model rifles and carbines often, if not always, have a Crown over a letter "B" which is known as the "Barcelona Cartouche." This is typically found on the upper left frame side, and is practically never seen on the second or third contract model rifles.

Second Spanish Contract Remington: Mechanically identical to the first contract with the exception of having a flat, non-concave breech-block base.

Third Spanish Contract Remington: Identical to second contract aside from the following tang markings: REMINGTONS ILION, NY, USA

Pat. May 3rd 1864, May7th, June 11th Nov 12th, Dec 24th 1872,

Dec 31st 1872, Sept 8th 1873, Jan 12th, March 10th,1874

A great number of Spanish Model Remingtons issued in Spain are often discovered with provincial inspection markings. An example of which is the Bourbon Fleur-de-Lis marking on the left chamber flat showing such rifles

were procured and issued to local forces by the province of Cadiz. As domestic manufacture of Spanish-made variations of the Remington began to catch up with demand, at both Oviedo arsenal and at the Euscalduna Planencia, as well as by private manufacturers such as Orbea Hermanos, thousands of the Remington-made rifles were eventually released for issue to the overseas army garrisons or volunteer units of the Ejercito Ultramar in Cuba, Puerto Rico, and the Philippine Islands. An important note for collectors is that the bold, large marking of "FB" on the chamber or receiver on Remington-made Spanish Model rolling-blocks indicates such rifles were reamed out/rechambered for the improved 71/89, or .43 Reformado, cartridge, which used a brass-jacketed projectile and was a straight-cased cartridge as opposed to the earlier, bottleneck .43 Spanish Remington.

The markings FB are the first initials of two Spanish ordnance officers: Freire and Brulle, who were responsible for developing the ballistically efficient new cartridge that replaced the older .43 Spanish Remington cartridge in 1889. In addition, both Remington Spanish Model rifles and carbines might also have a Crown stamped over the letters "RV." This cartouche indicates such arms were overhauled and re-issued to pro-Spanish "Reglamento Voluntarios" or Volunteer

Among the most intriguing of all of Remington Spanish Model rolling-block rifles, are those with features that do not appear in the factory literature of the day. An example is the Egyptian/Spanish conversion shown. Completely overhauled new rifles re-chambered from .43 Egyptian to .43 Spanish caliber are a variety the author unearthed documentation on in 2010. This example from Ecuador shows the 1-3/4-inch repositioning of the rear sight due to shortening the barrel to 33-3/4 inches in order to allow enough steel to re-ream the chamber from the larger based .43 Egyptian to .43 Spanish. This version of the Spanish Model was sold to at least four known Latin American nations. (Keith Doyon Collection)

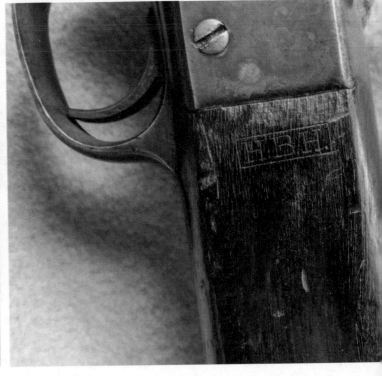

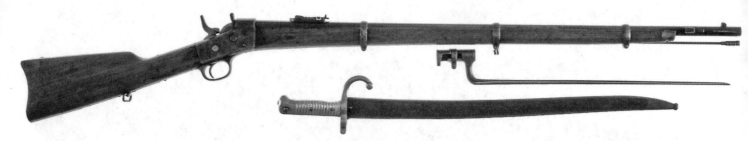

Shown is a special-order Spanish Model Remington with the combination bayonet lug. As an example, it displays both the socket and saber bayonets it was adapted to. This rifle is in like-new condition. (James Julia Auction Co. Photo)

Regiments, and most with this cartouche are chambered for the newer .43 Reformado. One more note, many Spanish-contract Remington rolling-block rifles shipped to Cuba have a Cuban armory cartouche found on the buttstock. The most common of these marks is a nickel-size roundel marked, "MTZA" over "HABANA" usually with a year, such as 1888 or 1889, beneath. MTZA is an abbreviation of "Maestranza" an old term for the Spanish royal arsenal with the year indicating when transferred to the Spanish armory at Havana. Many were older, refurbished Remington rifles reissued to pro-Spanish, Cuban military units.

The tremendous success of the Remington Spanish Model did not end with the 90,000-plus rolling-block rifles sold to Spain. It was just the beginning of one of the Remington rolling-block rifle's greatest success stories.

It is apparent that practically every

nation in the Spanish-speaking Americas, though having gained independence years earlier, culturally and militarily followed the former mother country in more ways than one, including the footsteps of arms procurement. The survival of the sales records of one of E. Remington & Sons' chief agents, the famed military arms dealer of Schuyler Hartley and Graham, indicate that as early as 1870, the company had already begun taking orders from the governments of countries in Central and South America for the soon to be tremendously popular, Remington "Spanish Model."

By summer of 1870, the Remington factory was working three shifts 24 hours a day to keep up with the demand for rolling-block rifles. This was escalated by the outbreak of the Franco-Prussian War of 1870-71, which took nearly all priority of rolling-block production. Much of this saw Remington purposely turning

down or canceling pre-existing contracts. In spite of this, several smaller nations somehow succeeded in receiving their orders without a hitch. One of the examples of this was a purchase from Ecuador for 2,000 Remington Spanish Rifles and 2,000 socket bayonets, which shipped on June 20, 1870. Guatemala ordered 1,000 rifles and bayonets that were shipped on Sept. 3, 1870. Panama ordered 300 rifles and bayonets on May 29, 1871. This proves Remington was indeed meeting the needs of several countries in South America and Central American while fulfilling Spanish contracts.

Schuyler Hartley & Graham records show that from Jan. 30, 1877, through March 8, 1885, some 9,450 .43-caliber Spanish Model Remingtons were received in Panama for both transshipment and/or domestic purchase for this one-time satellite state of Colombia. In addition, 800 rifles among this lot were

A late generic Spanish Model with all of the latest features has but one oddity, a Model 1879 Argentine Model rear sight. This was simply a case of Remington using surplus parts from previous contracts. It is a fact that there were hundreds of remaining components from the Argentine contract, as the last complete rifles were sold off in 1892 and could perfectly have qualified in the catalog as Spanish Models. This example appears to be either from Colombia or Costa Rica, as these two countries were known to domestically stamp serial numbers on the right side of the frame. This particular specimen would be of interest to the collector for the two features. (Alex Alexandrovich Photo)

equipped with saber bayonet lugs, the remainder utilizing socket bayonets. Sales of the Spanish Model were seemingly nonstop.

The last Spanish contract of 30,000 rifles might not have been delivered in its entirety, with several thousand forfeited by Spain, a reason why many of the early pattern Spanish Models were sold to Latin American customers. Proof of this was seen in the 1950s and '60s when thousands of the early Spanish Models of the type purchased by Spain were mixed in with military surplus shipments arriving from Colombia, Argentina, El Salvador and other Latin American countries. Following the December 1872 Remington patents that offered the new rotary extractor, the Spanish Model took on a new appearance, which also included screw-fit barrel bands, and other, more contemporary improvements. Currently, some of the most common, but well-designed, Spanish Model Remington rifles, are those of the special-order contract from Argentina in 1879. This was one of the highest quality variations of its ilk, and the most recognizable of all Spanish Models to the modern-day collector and shooter. Equipped with a 35-1/2-inch barrel, the 1879 Argentine Model was equipped with a special-order, 2-5/8-inch octagonal chamber, an Austrian Werndl-type rear sight, the long-type saber bayonet lug and naturally featured the positive rotary extractor.

Argentine ordnance authorities specifically requested these unique additions following their 1877-78 trials in search of a new breech-loading rifle. From an ordnance standpoint, Argentina was one of the more progressive nations in Latin America and thoroughly evaluated many breech-loading systems, including both American and European designs. In the end, a combination of Austrian Werndl-styled features coupled with the basic Remington design made for what was felt to be the satisfactory choice. Slightly over 50,000 rifles and carbines were sold under contract to Argentina directly by Remington between 1879 and 1882, and practically the entire order had returned to the United States military surplus arms importers between 1959 and 1962, at the height of the great military bargain boom. The Spanish Model Remington rolling-block remained in production long enough to outlast every other military rolling-block variation in factory literature, and by 1880 Remington already noted that more than "1,000,000 have been sold" (implying, perhaps, rolling-block rifles of all varieties).

With the exception of Mexico, Argentina and Guatemala, or those countries having a locally stamped circular ownership cartouche in the buttstock, few Spanish Model Remington rolling-blocks give today's collector an indication of which nations they were shipped to. It appears that one of the more prolific customers of the Remington Spanish Model was the Republic of Colombia, of which Schuyler Hartley & Graham records reflect that over 37,000 were shipped to that country from 1869 to 1890. Of course, many of these might have been destined for transshipment to other countries, especially, perhaps, to neighboring Peru during its struggle with Chile. Some of the last Remington Spanish Model rolling-block rifles that can be positively identified were those sold

This flower-like cartouche is commonly found on many third-contract Spanish Remington rolling-block rifles, usually on the right side of the chamber flat. It signifies a property mark indicating the arm was transferred to a Spanish colonial area, most often Cuba or the Philippines. (Chris Lener Collection and Photo)

to Guatemala and are marked as such over the barrel, with "Ejercito de Guatemala." (Army of Guatemala.) Most of the Guatemalan-marked rolling-blocks arrived at the piers of surplus arms import mogul Sam Cummings' Hunters Lodge, sometime between 1957 and 1959. They were among the first .43 Spanish-caliber rolling-blocks arriving from Latin America. However, due to the humid climate, they are rarely found in anything but good-plus condition and because of this, many were re-blued, and re-barreled to more common calibers.

There is a true oddity that is a hybrid version that could be considered a "factory" Spanish Model, but its existence can only be conjectured. There are at least five known examples of the Remington

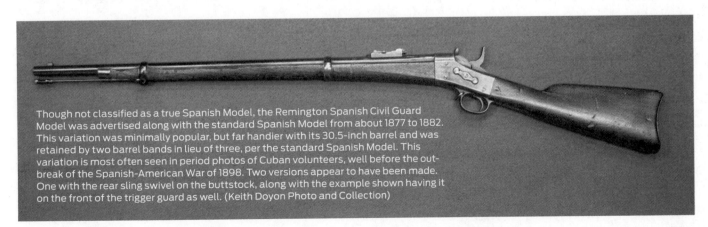

Though not classified as a true Spanish Model, the Remington Spanish Civil Guard Model was advertised along with the standard Spanish Model from about 1877 to 1882. This variation was minimally popular, but far handier with its 30.5-inch barrel and was retained by two barrel bands in lieu of three, per the standard Spanish Model. This variation is most often seen in period photos of Cuban volunteers, well before the outbreak of the Spanish-American War of 1898. Two versions appear to have been made. One with the rear sling swivel on the buttstock, along with the example shown having it on the front of the trigger guard as well. (Keith Doyon Photo and Collection)

Perhaps one of the most unique of all Spanish Models is this .43 Spanish Remington rifle, which was built on the early 1872 vintage New York State Model action. Shown is the Republic of Mexico liberty cap over the initials of RM, both on the right frame and on the chamber. Whether this particular configuration was solely associated with Mexico is unknown, as no other nation is reported to have purchased such a variation. It can also be seen that the arsenal admittance date 5.99 (May 1899) is deeply struck on the left lower frame. Only five examples of this hybrid Spanish Model have surfaced. (Chris Lener Collection)

From left to right, Cuban-arsenal-produced .43 Spanish, .43 Reformado and 400-grain .43 Spanish cartridge. At far right is a 375-grain Union Metallic Cartridge .43 Spanish cartridge, of which millions were sold between 1870 and 1915. (Stuart Mowbray Photo)

(below) Aside from the Model 1879 Argentine Model, and some Mexican versions, the Guatemalan Army Model, as shown, was the only other post-1879 Spanish Model to have national ownership markings. It appears Guatemala ordered some 3,500 such rifles after the Remington Arms Company reorganization, as all such marked examples reflect post 1888 tang markings. (Stuart Mowbray Photo)

.50-caliber New York State Model actions mated with .43 Spanish-caliber barrels. All have the Republica Mexicana logo of RM topped by a Gorro Frijo, Mexican Liberty Cap, marked on the top of the barrel and the right frame. The author believes Remington appears to have used up leftover New York State actions and coupled them with .43-caliber barrels to gainfully dispose of them, or they could have been sold to Mexico as actions only and subsequently re-barreled in Mexico's national FNDA armory. In any case, most show a Mexican overhaul date stamped on the lower bevel of the frames.

For the collector of military Remington rolling-block rifles, the Spanish Model in its several variations is one that might be considered an entire collecting theme all to its own, with perhaps more variety than any other rolling-block ever manufactured. In addition, they are great shooters, with cases and components readily available. The bottom line is if your .43 Spanish-caliber rolling-block is made by Remington and regardless of barrel length, rear-sight variation, or any other unusual feature, you can be sure you have an example of Remington's Celebrated Spanish Model: the peacemaker of Spain and Latin America. **GD**

BIBLIOGRAPHY

Schuyler Hartley and Graham, Shipping and Warehouse Registers 1868-1905

Shipping Registers of Hartley and Graham, and various research data from Remington author Edward Hull

The All New Collector's Guide to Remington Rolling Block Military Rifles of the World, George Layman, 2010, Mowbray Publishing, Woonsocket, RI 02895

This piece of Spanish-Remington history is what was issued to Spanish troops as a maintenance and tactical manual. Known as an Instructional Handkerchief, these were common issue to European soldiers in the 19th century as a "field manual." It didn't fall apart in rain like a paper book, and could serve many uses as well. Printed on this colorful cloth are instructions on maintaining the Model 1871 Remington and explanation of tactics for the Spanish soldier. It is of course printed in Spanish, but is a rare find for the collector. (Stuart Mowbray Photo)

The Browning X-Bolt Max Long Range isn't ideal for stalking in steep country, but it is a great option when making long shots from a stationary position in open country. The author was on a spot-and-stalk hunt for bear in Idaho when he carried the Max Long Range, and it proved to be a great gun for those conditions.

THE NEW GENERATION OF
HYBRID
HUNTING
RIFLES

Part tactical gun, part sporter, the latest trend toward hybrid hunting rifles is changing the sport

❯ BRAD FITZPATRICK

The annual SHOT Show in Las Vegas showcases the latest trends in the shooting and hunting industry. In recent years, the show has been dominated AR rifles and concealed-carry pistols, but in 20 several firearms companies rolled out brand-new hybrid hunting rifles, and it seems the market f these guns is only continuing to grow.

So, what exactly is a hybrid hunting rifle? In short, these guns offer features that have been b rowed from serious long-range competition an tactical guns and incorporate them into huntin rifles. The resulting guns blend accuracy-enhan ing features with the practicality of a sporter.

Benelli's new Lupo is essentially a chassis rifle dressed as a sporter. The stock design allows the shooter to adjust the gun to fit his or her body, and that enhances the gun's already outstanding accuracy.

The author used the Benelli Lupo to take this roan antelope in South Africa's Karoo Desert. The Benelli offers target-gun features, like an adjustable chassis with minimal mass to create the ultimate hybrid sporting rifle.

Most competitive shooters prefer rifles that offer adjustable stocks that can be customized to fit each individual shooter, and while that might not be essential when hunting whitetails at 200 yards, it's a real benefit when the distances are long and you might find yourself shooting from any number of practical field positions. Rifles that bear target-gun DNA in their design generally have stocks with elevated or adjustable combs, but also dual front sling studs (primarily used to mount a bipod and a sling separately)

and flat forearms for shooting off bags. A few new hunting rifles have even gone to chassis systems. Target and competition guns also tend to have heavier contour barrels, which maximize velocity figures (depending upon caliber), reduce barrel heating and recoil, and provide a stable platform for accurate shooting. Most hybrid rifles have all-steel barrels, but a few offer titanium or carbon-fiber-wrapped barrel options. Invariably, these guns have threaded muzzles. Do you need a muzzle device on a hunting rifle? No, but

a factory threaded muzzle offers the option to add a suppressor, muzzle brake, or another device easily and quickly.

Naturally, target shooters want good triggers, so virtually every hybrid hunting rifle is going to offer a light, crisp trigger with a clean break. What's more, most of these triggers are adjustable. Again, that's not a feature that hunters must have, but it's a benefit, nonetheless. Good triggers shrink group sizes, and that's something every hunter wants.

Tactical rails are another feature that have found their way onto hunting rifles. While some traditionalists might not like the look, rails do provide a very stable platform for mounting an optic. What's more, these rails often have elevation built into them (usually 20 MOA) and that built-in elevation affords shooters the ability to make holdover corrections for long-range shots. Rails are also capable of taking a real beating without shifting point of zero, and if you've ever carried your hunting rifle halfway around the world (and trusted baggage handlers to be gentle with your fine firearm) or had to ride into remote areas on horseback, you know just how severely a rifle can be beaten during transport. Rails, particularly those that are integral to the receiver, are extremely durable. They also allow shooters to quickly remove and replace optics in the field.

Perhaps you're looking for a hunting rifle that doesn't stray too far from the look and feel of a traditional sporting

The Browning Hunter Long Range combines the X-Bolt's proven three-lug action with a wood stock with adjustable cheek piece. The stock looks great and yet it can be quickly customized to fit individual shooters.

(above and below) Browning's X-Bolt Max Long Range looks more like a target gun than a field gun with its precision-adjustable composite stock, dual sling studs and fluted heavy barrel, but it's also well-suited for hunting because it's accurate, durable and not excessively heavy.

Browning's Rafe Nielsen with a huge Idaho bear he harvested with the X-Bolt Max Long Range rifle in .300 WSM. Rafe's long shot came at last light, and a rifle with target-gun DNA offers a distinct advantage when precision shooting is required.

rifle. If so, there are plenty of new rifles that offer just a few target-gun features while maintaining a more traditional look and feel. If, on the other hand, you want a serious long-range rifle that serves double duty as a PRS match gun and a hunting weapon, those are available as well. What's more, many of these guns offer features found on dedicated target guns at a price that's not out of line with more traditional hunting rifles.

A BUYER'S GUIDE TO WHAT'S NEW

Many hunting rifles have a few upgrades that make them better for long-range shooting without radically new styling, and one of those is the new Browning X-Bolt Hunter Long Range, a turn-bolt rifle that includes a wood stock with an adjustable comb and a heavy-contour barrel with a muzzle brake. Minus the comb, the Hunter Long Range

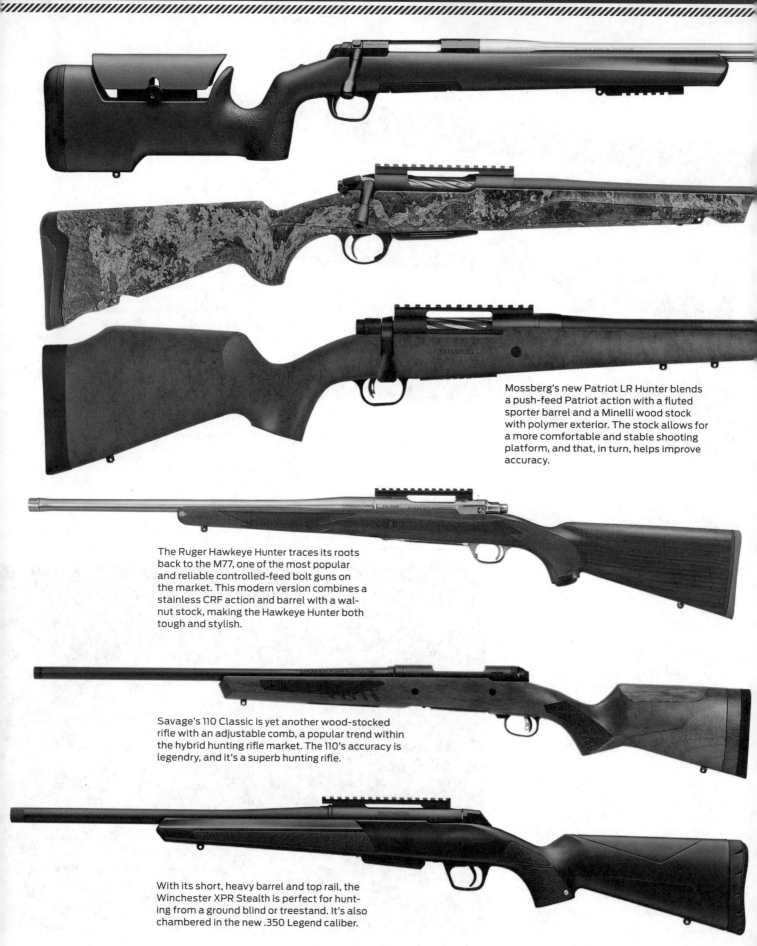

Mossberg's new Patriot LR Hunter blends a push-feed Patriot action with a fluted sporter barrel and a Minelli wood stock with polymer exterior. The stock allows for a more comfortable and stable shooting platform, and that, in turn, helps improve accuracy.

The Ruger Hawkeye Hunter traces its roots back to the M77, one of the most popular and reliable controlled-feed bolt guns on the market. This modern version combines a stainless CRF action and barrel with a walnut stock, making the Hawkeye Hunter both tough and stylish.

Savage's 110 Classic is yet another wood-stocked rifle with an adjustable comb, a popular trend within the hybrid hunting rifle market. The 110's accuracy is legendry, and it's a superb hunting rifle.

With its short, heavy barrel and top rail, the Winchester XPR Stealth is perfect for hunting from a ground blind or treestand. It's also chambered in the new .350 Legend caliber.

Part precision rifle, part hunting gun, the Browning X-Bolt Max Target Varmint blurs the lines between target and sporting rifles. The adjustable stock allows for an ideal gun fit and the long, heavy barrel helps wring every bit of velocity from each round. What's more, the heavy barrel dissipates heat more quickly than a sporter barrel.

Following on the heels of last year's Franchi Momentum rifle, the Momentum Elite offers different color options and includes a top rail and muzzle brake. These few extra touches add very little to the price, making the Momentum Elite the best buy in the Franchi lineup.

looks very much like the standard wood-stocked X-Bolt Hunter with a heavier barrel, and with the thread cap in place even the most die-hard traditionalists will like the look of this gun.

Also new this year is Winchester's XPR Stealth, an affordable push-feed bolt-action rifle that incorporates a short (16.5-inch) sporter-profile barrel with a threaded cap and comes with a top rail for mounting optics. Weighing in at 6.5

pounds, the XPR Stealth offers some of the features found on larger tactical and long-range rifles in a short, light package that's ideal for hunting big game in thick cover or for anyone who wants an affordable hunting rifle with a short barrel on which to mount a suppressor.

Mossberg's new Patriot LR Hunter rifle is a dressed-up version of the company's affordable Patriot bolt-action. The LR hunter version comes with a top rail, threaded, fluted barrel and a high-comb stock with a wood core and polymer exterior. And, like the guns listed above, it offers all these features in a relatively light (6.5 to 7 pounds), sporter-style profile.

Franchi has also expanded its Momentum line to include rifles that offer target-gun features. The new Momentum Flat Dark Earth comes with a muzzle brake and a top rail, but in other respects it's very similar to the standard Momentum that has won many hunters' hearts with its blend of accuracy-enhancing features and an affordable price point.

Ruger's new Hawkeye Hunter rifle looks and feels very much like the traditional sporter and includes an American-style walnut stock and a trim barrel profile. It also incorporates Ruger's time-tested controlled-feed action and

an internal box magazine with a hinged floorplate. The "target" features are few, a top rail and a threaded muzzle, and so this gun is good for those who don't want a deer rifle that looks as though it was designed to ring steel at a half-mile (though the Ruger can certainly do just that).

Benelli introduced its first bolt-action hunting rifle this year, and although the Lupo looks like most any sporter on the market, the Benelli incorporates some features found on the top target rifles in a clever, shooter-friendly package. The tubular receiver is mated with a two-piece aluminum chassis that is disguised as a synthetic sporter stock. While the Lupo is light and trim, the chassis and action are similar in concept to what you'll find on dedicated, high-end long-range rifles. That technology makes the Lupo exceedingly accurate. The one I tested and hunted with in Africa grouped around a half-inch with factory loads and kept five shots under an inch (the most accurate .30-06 factory gun I've tested).

Savage's 110 bolt actions are also known for being extremely accurate, and the company continues to roll out new rifles that blend elements from target guns and sporters. This year, the company launched its Ultralite model that mates the 110 action with a PROOF Research carbon-fiber-wrapped precision barrel with threaded cap. The Savage is very light, 6 pounds or less, but it comes with length-of-pull and comb-height inserts that allow you to custom fit the rifle to your exact dimensions, as well as a factory blueprinted action. Savage also offers its 110 Classic rifle, which comes with a well-figured walnut stock with an adjustable comb.

For those who want a hunting rifle that has all the features of a dedicated long-range gun, there are plenty of options. Browning's X-Bolt Max Long Range (new in 2019) and Max Varmint/Target (new for 2020) both include target-style stocks with wide pistol, steep grips and adjustable combs. They also come with heavy fluted barrels and muzzle brakes. Weighing between 8.25 and 9.5 pounds, these rifles aren't built for climbing mountains, but they're both target-style bolt guns that will work in the field. Ruger's American Rifle Hunter is another field gun that

The Mossberg Patriot LR Hunter doesn't just look the part of a target rifle, but it also offers the accuracy needed to make long shots on game. That consistent accuracy is due, at least in part, to the LBA trigger.

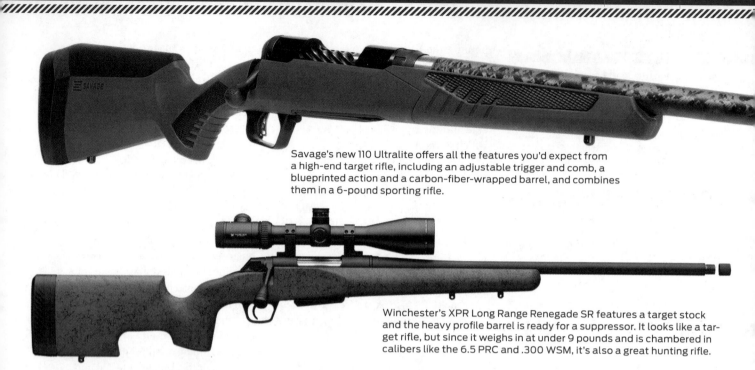

Savage's new 110 Ultralite offers all the features you'd expect from a high-end target rifle, including an adjustable trigger and comb, a blueprinted action and a carbon-fiber-wrapped barrel, and combines them in a 6-pound sporting rifle.

Winchester's XPR Long Range Renegade SR features a target stock and the heavy profile barrel is ready for a suppressor. It looks like a target rifle, but since it weighs in at under 9 pounds and is chambered in calibers like the 6.5 PRC and .300 WSM, it's also a great hunting rifle.

has a decidedly target-rifle profile and comes with a top rail, Magpul adjustable stock, detachable box magazine, and a 20-inch barrel with brake. Despite all its accuracy-enhancing features, the American Rifle Hunter weighs in around 9 pounds and is affordably priced. Winchester is releasing a Renegade Long Range SR (Suppressor Ready) version of its popular XPR rifles. The new Renegade comes with a target-style stock, oversized bolt handle, detachable box magazine,

dual sling studs and a threaded barrel. Weighing in at about 8.5 pounds, the Renegade is primarily designed to be a target rifle, but it will also serve dutifully as a hunting gun.

Perhaps the most radical of all the new hybrid rifles is Sig Sauer's new CROSS rifle, which was built from the ground up to be a precision hunting weapon. There's very little about this gun that looks traditional. With its Sig Precision multi-adjustable folding stock, its AR-style

handguard and dust cover the CROSS looks like purebred tactical/target rifle. The kicker, however, is these rifles weigh less than 7 pounds and offer a level of refinement that makes them an ideal backcountry hunting gun. The safety selector is positioned in the same place as an AR rifle and there's a threaded muzzle and top rail, as you might expect. Multiple caliber options are available, including 6.5 Creedmoor, .308 Win and the new .277 Sig Fury, and CROSS rifles come in

The Sig Sauer CROSS rifle blends features commonly found on tactical and target rifles (a free-floating handguard, folding stock) with the light weight and portability of a sporter. The Sig might look unconventional, but it works great as a hunting rifle and is available in the exciting new .277 Sig Fury round.

NEW HYBRID HUNTING/TARGET RIFLES

RIFLES	CALIBERS	MSRP
BENELLI LUPO	.270 WIN, .30-06, .300 WIN MAG	$1,700
BROWNING X-BOLT HUNTER LONG RANGE	6.5 CREEDMOOR, 6.5 PRC, .270 WIN, 7MM REM MAG, .308 WIN, .30-06, .300 WIN MAG	$1,300-$1,330
BROWNING X-BOLT MAX LONG RANGE	6MM CREEDMOOR, 6.5 CREEDMOOR, 6.5 PRC, 7MM REM MAG, .28 NOSLER, .308 WIN, .300 WIN MAG, .300 WSM, .300 RUM, .30 NOSLER	$1,300-$1,360
BROWNING X-BOLT MAX VARMINT/TARGET	.204 RUGER, .223 REM, .22-250, 6.5 CREEDMOOR, .28 NOSLER, .308 WIN, .300 WIN MAG	$1,340-$1,400
FRANCHI MOMENTUM FDE	.243 WIN, 6.5 CREEDMOOR, .270 WIN, .308 WIN, .30-06, .300 WIN MAG	$609
MOSSBERG PATRIOT LR HUNTER	6.5 CREEDMOOR, 6.5 PRC, .308 WIN, .300 WIN MAG	$721
RUGER AMERICAN RIFLE HUNTER	6.5 CREEDMOOR, .308 WIN	$799
RUGER HAWKEYE HUNTER	.204 RUGER, 6.5 CREEDMOOR, 6.5 PRC, 7MM REM MAG, .308 WIN, .30-06, .300 WIN MAG	$1,100
SAVAGE 110 CLASSIC	.243 WIN, 6.5 CREEDMOOR, .270 WIN, 7MM-08 REM, 7MM REM MAG, .308 WIN, .30-06, .300 WIN MAG	$999
SAVAGE 110 ULTRALITE	6.5 CREEDMOOR, 6.5 PRC, .270 WIN, .280 ACKLEY, .28 NOSLER, .308, .30-06, .300 WSM	$1,499
SIG SAUER CROSS	6.5 CREEDMOOR, .277 SIG FURY, .308 WIN	$1,779
WINCHESTER XPR RENEGADE LONG RANGE SR	.243 WIN, 6.5 CREEDMOOR, 6.5 PRC, .270 WSM, 7MM-08 REM, .308 WIN, .300 WSM	$1,069
WINCHESTER XPR STEALTH	.243 WIN, 6.5 CREEDMOOR, 6.5 PRC, .270 WSM, 7MM-08 REM, .308 WIN, .300 WSM	$1,069

either anodized black or camo. They're built with the crossover shooter in mind and they might provide a glimpse of what future hunting rifles will look like.

CARTRIDGE AND BULLET SELECTION

As rifles have evolved so have cartridges and bullets, and some of the new crop of factory hunting loads perform extremely well for hunters who like to expand their maximum effective range. The much-vaunted 6.5 Creedmoor and the newer 6.5 PRC and 6mm Creedmoor are all designed for maximum long-range accuracy. So is the new .300 PRC, another fine new round that's proved to be quite effective in game fields around the globe. These cartridges push heavy-for-caliber bullets, and that improves downrange performance and terminal ballistics. All four are catching fire, and all of them make great big-game cartridges.

There are plenty of new cartridges that were designed with big-game hunters in mind, and some of them have become very successful. The whole Nosler family of cartridges, which has now grown to include the .22, .26, .27, .28, .30 and .33 Nosler rounds, are high-speed performers that work well on game. The .28 Nosler, in particular, seems to have gained the largest following and is available in rifles from a wide range of manufacturers. Weatherby also unveiled its 6.5-300 recently, and its hot new 6.5 RPM cartridge is ballistically superior to the .264 Winchester Magnum, and it

utilizes Weatherby's light, dependable six-lug action.

Regardless of whether you choose a rifle in one of these new calibers or stick with your reliable .270 Winchester, .308 or .30-06 (all of which still kill game as effectively and efficiently as before), selecting a good hunting bullet is key. The good news is that today's bullets are better than ever, and some new bullets, like Hornady's ELD-X and Federal's Terminal Ascent, are terrific performers at a wide range of velocities, which makes them ideal for hunting where shots might be close or very far.

DO YOU REALLY NEED A NEW RIFLE?

The new hunting rifles that blend target and sporting features into a single gun have become very popular, and there are no signs that the trend is slowing. Rather, it seems that the evolution of the long-range hunting rifle has carried over into the hunting market. That's a good thing because it offers shooters with varying budgets, tastes and needs a gun that suits them perfectly. That's not to say that traditional sporters won't work, but if you want a gun that offers the best features from both realms there are plenty of options available to you today. **GD**

A look back at
a time when
Koreans hunted
tigers, and
tigers hunted
Koreans ›NICK HAHN

THE
LAND OF
TIGERS

In the past, Korea was first known to the West as the "Hermit Kingdom" during the Chosun, or Yi, Dynasty (1392-1897), then in the more modern period as the "Land of the Morning Calm." However, long before that, Korea was known regionally as "The Land of Tigers." It seems Korea had tigers and leopards in abundance. The tigers in Korea were the same as the Amur or Manchurian/Siberian tigers, and the leopards were also the same found in Manchuria and Siberia.

Today, it is unlikely there is any sort of a viable population of tigers left on the Korean Peninsula. There have been reports of sightings of leopards occasionally, especially around the DMZ where human presence has been restricted for more than a half a century and wildlife is thriving. However, the rest of South Korea is unlikely to have any big cats, especially tigers. But there was a time when the tiger population in Korea was high; higher than anywhere else in the region according to many sources, including the official records of the Chosun Dynasty. In fact, tigers and leopards were so numerous the Chinese had a saying: "Koreans hunted tigers for six months of the year and the tigers hunted Koreans for the other six months!" The reason for the "split" period is because most tiger hunters had to tend to their other means of livelihood to survive. Tiger hunting was mostly done in the colder months, especially when tracking was easier in the snow and the foliage was sparse or had fallen off, making it easier to see the tiger.

Although there are different names for tigers and leopards in Korean language (tiger is *horangi* and leopard *pyobom*), most Korean peasants simply lumped the two together, calling them both *horangi*. The only distinction that was made was that one was called the large tiger while the other called the small tiger. To most Korean peasants, it really made no difference since one was just as dangerous as the other, and in many cases, the leopard was even more dangerous since it was more numerous and often found in populated areas.

The Chosun Dynasty was pretty strict about weapons ownership, and, generally, commoners couldn't even own swords or bows and arrows. But apparently common folks could own weapons if they needed them for their living, like hunting. The very early Korean tiger hunters used spears, then crossbows. Around the 15th century, matchlocks came into use, and much later breechloaders.

Because of the serious problem with man-eaters, the tiger hunters became very important in the

Korean society. A separate caste of tiger hunters emerged. I don't believe there was another culture or country in the world that had a special class of people identified as tiger hunters (*horangi sanyankun*). It was a unique situation that developed a very unique caste within a very highly stratified society, where to this day, rank and title play an immensely important role. In general, peasants and most commoners had very low status in the old Korean society and were often abused and mistreated by the ruling class, the *yang ban*. Slaves (*nobi*) existed in Chosun Dynasty right up to the late 19th century when slavery was supposedly finally abolished in 1894. But in reality, slavery, under different guises (as indentured servants, etc.), continued surreptitiously, right on through the period of Japanese occupation in the 1930s. However, even in the past, a *nobi* or a peasant who developed skills as a tiger hunter, could become someone special with a rank and a title of the tiger hunter and shed their commoner or slave status.

Korean culture is probably the only culture in the world in which the tiger plays a central role. The tiger touches almost every aspect of Korean culture. The tiger appeared as a mascot both in the 1988 Seoul Summer Olympics and the 2018 Pyeongchang Winter Olympics which were held in South Korea. The tiger is possibly the most popular subject for art in Korea, be it silk screens, paintings, sculptures or ceramics. No other country in the world has such ties to the tiger. Korean folklore and mythology are full of tales and accounts of tigers and tiger hunting. Perhaps one of the oldest and best-known Korean children's folktales is about a great white tiger. It is a story of revenge in which the daughter of a famous tiger hunter who was killed and eaten by the tiger, disguises herself in her father's clothes to fool the tiger. She catches the beast off guard in her disguise, and gets close enough to kill it with a spear. The tale of "*Paek Horangi*" (*The White Tiger*) is well known to Korean children.

Toward the mid-19th century, modern firearms began to appear, and, it seems, that firearms in Korea went from matchlocks to the more modern muzzleloaders only briefly, and then jumped right to breechloaders. The most popular and common gun for Korean tiger hunters was the double-barreled shotgun. It made sense, since shotguns were used for all game and even tiger hunters had to shoot other game for a living. Naturally, to kill a tiger with a shotgun the hunter had to get very close. So, skill at stalking on foot became very important for the Korean tiger hunter. Some did use dogs that tracked the tiger silently, but packs were not used mainly because it was costly to maintain a pack of dogs. Good firearms were prized, and it was not uncommon for a tiger hunter to own a good quality European gun. Most tiger hunters saved their money to buy an imported (usually Belgian or German) gun, but Russian-made guns were also popular because they were more easily obtained. Although Japanese guns were available, most Koreans preferred European or Russian guns.

As already stated, during the Chosun Dynasty, despite strict controls, a

This 19th-century painting depicting man-eating tigers attacking a Korean family in their home, titled *"The Reign of the Tiger in Korea"* was published in 1909 in the *Le Petit Journal* newspaper in Paris. The *Le Petit Journal* was a popular conservative publication with a circulation of over 1 million at that time.

A Japanese hunter in Korea with what appears to be a double-barrel shotgun and the tiger he shot in 1922.

commoner could own a gun, but things changed dramatically at the turn of the century with Japan's occupation of Korea from 1910 to 1945. Although Japanese occupation officially began in 1910, in reality, control began after the Japanese assassination of Queen Min in 1895, when all sorts of very strict laws were passed, including forbidding Koreans to own firearms. But soon, Japan discovered that the tiger and leopard populations were getting out of control. Killings by man-eaters became rampant, and even in the capital city of Seoul, leopards were found preying on dogs and attacking people, especially small children.

An article appeared in the history section of *Korea Times* on May 6, 2007, titled "When Tigers Stalked Korea" by Robert Neff. He wrote his article based on information he gathered from old newspaper and magazine articles, as well as official records. Neff wrote that, in the late 19th century, a member of the British Legation, Alfred Burt Stripling, shot a leopard in the city limits of Seoul. He also quoted an article which appeared in a leading U.S. newspaper in the early 20th century describing the tiger problem in Korea:

"It appears that since the Japanese occupation of Korea natives have been forbidden to carry firearms and as a consequence, tigers have multiplied to an extraordinary extent. It is not safe to go out shopping after dusk in some of the inland villages, and as many as 30 or 40 luckless natives have been devoured in certain districts within a week. The authorities will not raise the embargo on firearms. How then, is the number of these dreaded beasts to be reduced?"

Neff wrote that in the 1890s British explorer/writer Arnold Henry Savage Landon visited Korea and described the country as being full of enormous tigers that were "fond of human flesh" and terrorized the population. He also said that the German Legation had to be evacuated because a large leopard was found in its compound.

Japan had problems with Korean Freedom Fighters even before the official annexation in 1910, so the strict laws on firearms restrictions never changed. But to solve the big-cat problem, firearm ownership was allowed for some of the known

Korean tiger hunters. The other solution Japan had was to cut down forests on the hills surrounding major cities and towns. This supposedly served a dual purpose for Japan. The denuded countryside deprived the tigers and leopards of their habitat, at the same time the lumber was shipped to Japan where it was needed for construction projects. The deforestation approach to solving the tiger problem was supposedly attempted before, during the earlier Chosun Dynasty, when the Korean peninsula experienced an unusual spike in man-eating tiger activity. However, it apparently only worked to some extent. It was still up to tiger hunters to try and control the man-eating tiger population. The early 20th century saw professional Korean tiger hunters, some Japanese sportsmen and a sprinkling of foreigners who were allowed to own firearms to hunt tigers, especially in the southern part of the peninsula. Many big cats were killed, and by midcentury, the tiger and leopard population in Korea was dramatically reduced. In the northern part, along the Manchurian border, it was a bit different story.

One interesting facet of tiger hunting in Korea was the presence of Russian hunters in northern part of Korea. At the start of the 20th century, Russia's interest in the region clashed with Japan's ambitions, which led to the Russo-Japanese War of 1905. The war ended with Russia's loss of concessions and control in the Far East, including its access to warm-water ports in Korea and Port Arthur in Manchuria. But, Russia had gained some foothold earlier in Manchuria when its laborers built the South Manchuria Railway to connect with the Trans-Siberian. Russia had been in the region for only about a half century, having acquired a big chunk of real estate known as Outer Manchuria in 1860. Outer Manchuria was about the same size as present Manchuria, so it was a lot of land that included the port city of Vladivostok (formerly called *Haisenwa* in Manchu and Chinese) and the Sakhalin Island. This was known as Amur Acquisition, or Annexation, which took place after Russia forced the weak and corrupt Ching Dynasty China to sign a treaty at the Convention of Peking in 1860, giving up all that territory. Some 35 years later,

Russia decided to try and expand its borders even more. Russia moved into the remaining Manchuria, built (modernized and Westernized) the city of Harbin, which was a small Manchu fishing village, and started the South Manchuria Railway. There were over 250,000 Russian military and civilians in Manchuria at the turn of the century.

Many Russians hired on as professional hunters for the South Manchuria Railway to provide meat for the workers and also to control the man-eating tiger problem that became a major issue. Their pursuit of game often took Russian hunters across the border into Korea. The Japanese allowed Russian hunters to continue to hunt in Korea to shoot tigers. Russians had been crossing into Korea since the 19th century, before the Japanese occupation, and some had developed reputations as successful tiger hunters.

After the railway was completed, many of these hunters remained in Manchuria and continued to hunt for a living. Some of these early Russian hunters in Manchuria gained fame for their tiger hunting prowess. One in particular became well-known to the outside world because he was a writer and his writings were translated and published in Europe in several languages. His name was Nikolai Baikov, and for all practical purposes, he was the best-known tiger hunter of Manchuria and Korea from about 1900 to the early 1920s. He published several books on hunting in the region and some of his books today, translated into English, are eagerly sought by collectors.

Baikov used a 12-gauge hammerless double-barrel shotgun for most of his tiger hunting. His technique was to stalk the tiger on foot in the snow, and approach it very closely. He apparently shot quite a few tigers in this manner, including a few man-eaters. Baikov often crossed the border into the northern part of Korea to hunt tigers, and, according to him, the tiger population in the early 20th century in Korea was very high.

Baikov's accounts of his tiger hunting are fascinating, for he was a talented writer. However, there were some who claimed that Baikov was more of a writer than a hunter. Besides his written accounts, there are photographic records of

Baikov with tigers, so no one is disputing the fact that he had hunted tigers. But his critics claim that although he did kill tigers, he wasn't quite the great tiger hunter that he portrayed himself in his writing. No doubt there was jealousy involved in this case, since Baikov gained fame while most Russian hunters lived in obscurity. By and large, the professional hunters in Manchuria were much like the buffalo hunters in the 19th century North America. They were not exactly refined as a group and tended to have somewhat of a questionable reputation, except for Baikov, whom the world owes much to for what little is known about tiger hunting in Manchuria and northern Korea in the early 20th century.

Perhaps the most successful and best-known tiger hunter or hunters of that region was a family of professional hunters that established an enclave in northern Korea, in a "Swiss Family Robinson" fashion, a homestead called "Novina" (new land). This Russian family, the Yankovskys, moved to northern Korea to escape the Bolsheviks during the Russian Revolution. They settled in northern Korea along the east coast, south of the Manchurian border near the town of Chongjin, where they built a large estate. It was a large family, a clan that combined with some smaller families and individuals for a total of about two dozen, or so, Russians. The number fluctuated since people used to come and go frequently. Some stayed briefly, before leaving for other places like the United States, Canada, Europe, Australia,

South America and even other destination within Asia. But the core group of the immediate and extended Yankovsky family members stayed on, and the entire colony was led by the patriarch, Yuri (George) Yankovsky.

The Yankovskys employed Korean farmers to tend fruit orchards and grow crops and farm animals for food. They also raised deer, like domesticated animals, and sold the antlers for medicinal purposes. However, their main occupation and livelihood was hunting. George Yankovsky accompanied by his three sons, Valery, Arseny and Yuri, spent at least six months of the year hunting. They shot boar, deer and elk for meat and other animals for fur. This wild game was either sold on the market or sold to the Japanese army. They also shot pheasant and waterfowl for the market and the Japanese. But their biggest money makers were tigers, leopards and bears, which the Chinese prized for medicinal purposes and paid an extraordinarily high price. The Yankovskys hunted as a family group of father and sons most of the time, and sometimes with other members of extended family and friends. In fact, one rare photograph shows their friend, a Russian-Korean hunter, posing with a very large tiger that he shot near the headwaters of Sungari River in Manchuria, just across the border from Korea. There is a fascinating story involved with this particular hunt, and the tiger, which was known as the "Dream Tiger." It was big, measuring 11 feet, 6 inches, over the curves. For comparison, Jim Corbett's

huge Bengal tiger, the "Bachelor of Powalgarh" measured out at 10 feet, 7 inches, over the curves.

The Yankovskys were without a doubt the most successful tiger and leopard hunters in Korea of all times, and they hunted from around the 1920s until the 1940s, roughly a 20-year span. In short, they took over where Baikov left off. They were also the best known of all tiger hunters in Korea to the outside world. Two months after the end of World War II, the October 1945 issue of *The National Geographic Magazine* had a lengthy, 21-page article on Korea. The author, Willard Price, was very thorough in his coverage of Korea of that era and even visited Novina, to interview and photograph George Yankovsky. *The National Geographic* photograph of George Yankovsky was possibly the very last one taken of him, before he was arrested by the Soviets, allegedly for his collaboration with the Japanese army, and hauled off to prison where he was killed.

The Yankovskys were well off, and the five children, daughters Muza and Victoria, and sons Valery, Arseny and Yuri, were tutored at home and later attended international boarding schools in Shanghai, and learned English. Actually, the Yankovskys had established a school in Novina where the children were taught by tutors brought in from Harbin and Shanghai until they reached about high-school age, at which point they were sent to Shanghai to boarding school to complete their formal education. They became multilingual, learned Korean and Japanese, which they all spoke at native fluency level. They learned Japanese because they had Japanese nannies and they also learned Chinese on the side. All of the Yankovskys were accomplished multilinguals.

The Yankovskys had an arsenal of various hunting arms. They tried out just about all of the available sporting arms, which they imported from Europe or bought directly from Shanghai or Harbin. The Mauser and Mannlicher sporting rifles were popular, especially in 7x57mm caliber, and they even had some German, three-barreled drillings and two-barreled combination guns they used occasionally. The lever-action Win-

Russian hunters with four large tigers and boars shot in northern Korea around 1920. They appear to be armed with the Russian service rifles, the Mosin-Nagant.

chester Model 95 was a popular choice because it offered rapid repeat shots and was chambered for cartridges like the .30/06, .303 British and 7.62 Russian, and not the usual lever-action calibers for tubular magazines, which tended to have inferior ballistics. However, the rifle that was a favorite with them was the British Lee-Enfield service rifle converted into a lighter sporting rifle. Some American hunters tend to look down on the .303, thinking of it as only marginally more powerful than the .30/30. Canadians, on the other hand, think otherwise and possibly more game has been shot in Canada with the .303 than any other, with the exception of the .30/30. The Yankovskys were perfectly satisfied with the power of .303 and shot most of their tigers with this rifle. The main reason for their preference of the Lee-Enfield was its 10-shot magazine capacity, which was important when they encountered large herds of animals. They were able to get off more shots and down more animals, before the herds scattered. More deer or boar down meant more money. They were market hunters, first, after all.

For shotguns, their unanimous choice was the Browning humpbacked autoloader. They did like some of the other guns, like the German J.P. Sauer double and some of the Belgian doubles, especially the Francotte. Of the British guns, they particularly liked the W.W. Greener for its durability. But for shooting game for the market, and even for sport, the Browning autoloader was their hands-down favorite. In fact, the Browning autoloader was the favorite for all of the Yankovskys, including the women. No doubt the Browning's five-shot capability was a factor in their choice of the autoloader over the two-shot double barrel. They also liked the Browning because of its durability and dependability.

Looking at the old photographs with huge piles of game animals the Yankovskys shot, some might feel sickened and repulsed by it. But, keep in mind this was at a different time. There was very little awareness of game conservation/preservation in that part of the world. Most thought the game would remain forever in large numbers. Yes, it was very short-sighted, foolish and politically incorrect by today's yardstick. But back then, it was a different world.

Some of these photographs of the Yankovskys with tigers were displayed in the Eddie Bauer store in San Francisco when it opened in 1968. The San Francisco store on Post Street was the first Eddie Bauer store to open outside of Seattle, where it originally started in 1920. Back in the day, Eddie Bauer stores sold firearms; and the photographs of Yankovskys with tigers were prominently displayed in the San Francisco store's firearms section. It is not clear how these photographs ended up in the Eddie Bauer store. They might have been sold by one of the Yankovsky family members, more than likely one of the daughters, Muza or Victoria, who lived in San Francisco Bay Area. Muza and Victoria avoided Soviet imprisonment and managed to reach the U.S. in somewhat of a circuitous manner by way of South America.

All of the Yankovsky men were arrested and imprisoned by the Soviets, except for Arseny, who managed to escape to South Korea and ultimately ended up in the U.S., also settling in the San Francisco Bay Area, in the late 1960s. Yuri was killed by the Soviets about the same time the father was killed, shortly after they were arrested. Valery survived imprisonment and remained in Russia after he was released. But those photographs of Yankovskys are no longer displayed, and, of course, Eddie Bauer doesn't sell firearms anymore, not in the San Francisco store or any other store for that matter. The world has indeed changed, not just for people, but for tigers as well.

Korea, once known as "The Land of Tigers" would be hard-pressed to produce any tigers on its land outside of those in captivity. Perhaps, only in some of the remote stretches along the Manchurian and Siberian border in North Korea do tigers still roam. Perhaps. But the days when tigers roamed freely on the Korean peninsula and even became a great danger to human population will never occur again. After all, the entire world population of tigers is in danger of extinction, not just the Amur or Manchurian/Siberian tiger, which at one time was known as the "Korean Tiger." GD

An early photo (1919) of Yankovsky family with game shot by adult members. The two younger Yankovsky sons were still too young at this time to participate in hunting with their father, Yuri (George), who is standing in the center. Valery, who was the oldest, did accompany his father, who is standing in the center.

Yuri (George) Yankovsky the patriarch, with his sons and the leopard shot by the oldest son Valery, who is on the left, holding a Winchester Model 95, Yuri, the youngest is holding what appears to be a .22 rifle, standing next to his father, and Arseny, the middle son, is holding a 7mm Mauser sporting rifle that he favored at that time.

Three early 20th-century (circa 1903) Korean tiger hunters armed with what appear to be double-barrel hammer shotguns. The cheek-piece on stock of the gun held by the hunter in the middle indicates it is probably of European origin, possibly Belgian or German. Japanese guns were available, but Koreans preferred European firearms.

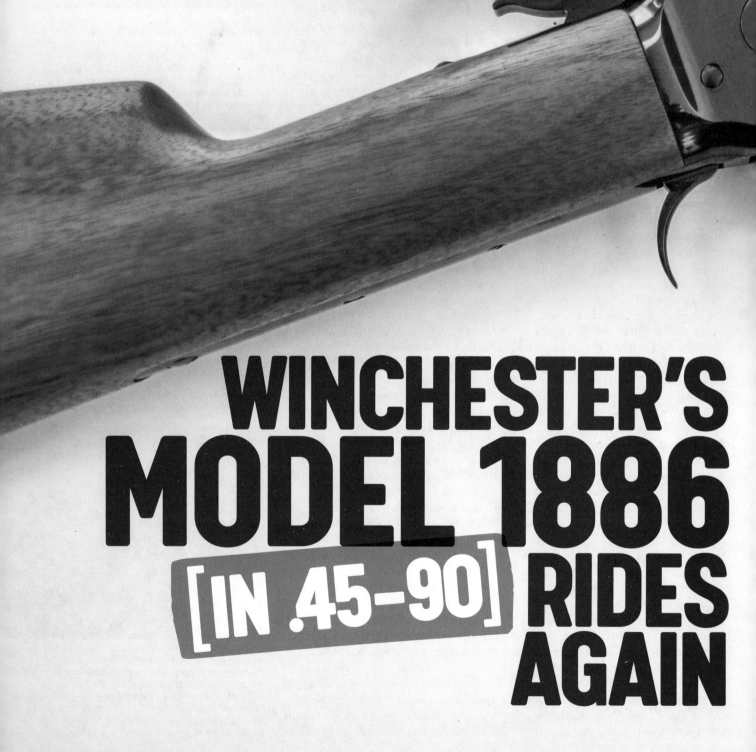

WINCHESTER'S
MODEL 1886
[IN .45-90] RIDES AGAIN

The M-1886 was the first of John M. Browning's lever guns to feature the stout locking bars at the rear of the action that made it much stronger than the toggle-actions of the Model 1873 and 1876.

Nostalgia buffs rejoice: Winchester delivers another modern piece of history ›STEVE GASH

The Model 1886 was the first lever-action repeater designed by John M. Browning and, of course, many more followed. The M-1886's patent was approved in October 1884, and in that same month, John and his brother Matt journeyed to New York and then on to New Haven, Connecticut, to demonstrate the new gun to Winchester vice president and general manager T. G. Bennett.

The evening before their meeting with Bennett, John and Matt were entertained by a Winchester sales representative who had met John in Ogden. After a night of modest revelry, John invited the salesman up to his hotel room to look at the new lever-action rifle. After a careful examination, the salesman stated that it "was the future of the Winchester Company." Winchester purchased the rifle the next day, and production started in 1886.

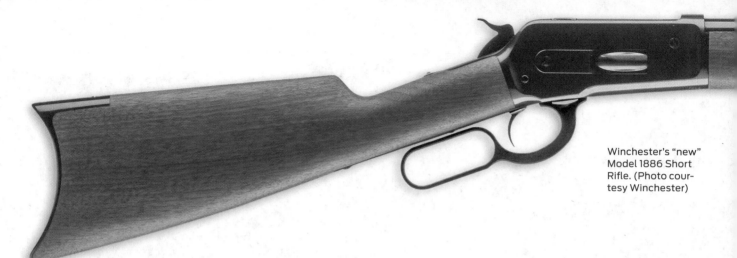

Winchester's "new" Model 1886 Short Rifle. (Photo courtesy Winchester)

The Model 1886 lever action was built by Winchester in various forms (for blackpowder cartridges) until it was discontinued in 1935, a span of 49 years, during which 159,994 were produced. In its time, the M-1886 was not as popular as earlier lever guns that fired pistol cartridges, but it still appeals to many shooters to this day.

The new M-1886 was a real step up in terms of power and strength. Gone were the relatively weak toggle-link actions of the Model 1873 and 1876. The Browning-designed M-1886 had two locking bolts that were raised up and closed behind the breechblock as the lever was raised, locking the breechblock in place. This feature was carried over to the later M-1892 and 1894 rifles.

The new locking system made the M-1886 very strong, so the rifle could chamber much more powerful cartridges. The initial chamberings were the .40-82, .45-70 and today's subject, the .45-90. A year later, the .38-56, .40-65 and .50-110 Express were added.

Winchester designed the .45-90 as what it called an "express" cartridge, i.e., one with a lighter and faster bullet. Consequently, the .45-90s were cut with a much slower 1:32-inch twist, as compared to the .45-70's 1:20-inch twist. Winchester loaded the .45-90 Express with a 300-grain, lead-alloy bullet at a listed velocity in 1899 of 1,480 fps, pretty darn fast for blackpowder cartridges of the day. Interestingly, an "express" version of the .50-110 was added in 1894 that also fired a 300-grain bullet, and with a slower twist.

In 1903, the .33 Winchester was introduced. It was the only Winchester cartridge for the M-1886 that was originally designed for smokeless powder. A brief synopsis of the M-1886 cartridge's pertinent features is provided in Table 1. As can be seen, Winchester used just two basic cartridge lengths for all (2.1 or 2.4 inches), and all but the .50-caliber round were based on the .45-70 case diameter.

TABLE 1. MODEL 1886 CARTRIDGES

CARTRIDGE	YEAR INTRO.	YEAR DISC.	CASE LNG. (IN).	RIFLING TWIST (IN.)
.40-82	1886	1910	2.4	28
.45-70	1886, ~1920S	1919 1932	2.1	20
.45-90	1886 2019	1919	2.4	32 20
.38-56	1887	1910	2.1	22(?)
.40-65	1887	1910	2.1	26
.50-110	1887	1919	2.4	54 OR 60
.38-70	1894	1919	2.4	22
.40-70	1894	1919	2.4	20
.33 WIN.	1903	1932	2.1	12

The M-1886 was not only chambered for a wide array of cartridges, but also, as was the custom in those days, in many versions and barrel lengths and rifling twists. The new Model 71 was a slightly redesigned M-1886, and was chambered for the equally new .348 Winchester cartridge. The M-71 was introduced in January 1936, and the M-1886 was discontinued then, or in 1932, depending on the reference at hand.

HISTORY REPEATS ITSELF

But just because something is old doesn't mean it's forgotten. So, it is with iconic lever actions. In the 1970s, Browning brought out new M-1892s that were made in Japan. They were chambered for the smokeless powder .357 and .44 Magnums, which were very popular. In 1985, Browning reintroduced the M-1886 in – what else? – .45-70. This M-1886 had a 26-inch octagon barrel. But, alas, Browning announced that it was going to make only 5,000 of them, and stuck to that

The new M-1886 features a crescent buttplate with the traditional "widow's peak." It is perfectly inletted.

promise to collectors. Howls of anguish were heard across the land. So, in the 1990s, Browning found a way around this problem. Another run of M-1886s was made, also in .45-70, but this time they were saddle-ring carbines.

By 1997, the Winchester name had been licensed to U.S. Repeating Arms Co., which released yet another M-1886. This version had a pistol-grip stock, a crescent rifle-style buttplate, a rebounding hammer and a tang safety. It also featured a 26-inch, octagon barrel, and was chambered to .45-70. A takedown version followed in 1999.

Winchester has for several years had what it calls the "Historic" production line of (at least nine) historically significant guns that are produced from time to time. In the line are models 1966, 1873, 1885 high and low walls, 1886, 1892, 1894, 1895 and 71.

At the 2019 SHOT Show in Las Vegas, Nevada, I learned that four Historic Winchester models were to be produced in 2019. They are the (1) M-1892 Short rifle in .44-40 Winchester; (2) M-1892 Large Loop in .357 and .44 Magnums, .44-40 Winchester and .45 Colt; and (3) M-1894

The fore-end has a steel cap of the short-rifle configuration.

.30-30 Winchester in a High Grade Anniversary edition.

The fourth gun is the one that caught my eye, and is indeed historic. It is the M-1886, this time in the "short rifle" configuration, with a steel fore-end cap, rather than the "carbine's" barrel band. It is chambered for the .45-70 and another of the model's original cartridges, the unique .45-90 Winchester. I was given no idea as to when each model was to be produced, but to my amazement, the .45-90 M-1886 became available in early 2019. I wasted no time in putting in my order for one.

THE MODERN M-1886

At long last, my "new" M-1886 arrived, and it is a blast from the past. The metal is brightly polished, and with a beauti-

ful bright blue-black finish. The round barrel is 24 inches long, and as noted, has a 1:20-inch twist. The tubular magazine holds eight rounds.

The hammer has a half-cock notch, and there is an unobtrusive two-position safety on the tang. While this addition might offend the sensibilities of purists, it is unobtrusive, works well and can be conveniently ignored. The trigger pull is crisp, with a pull weight of 3 pounds, 13.6 ounces.

I took a peek down the barrel with my Hawkeye Bore Scope, and the bore looked smooth, with no extraneous gouges or tool marks visible, and the rifling looked cleanly cut. And I am happy to report that the bore didn't foul much at all over the course of shooting many test rounds.

Ten .45-caliber bullets were tested in the .45-90 (from left, listed vertically for easier reference):
Hornady 300-grain InterLock Hollow Point
Hornady 350-grain InterLock Round Nose
Sierra 300-grain Hollow Point Flat Nose
Speer 300-grain Hollow Point
Speer 400-grain Flat Point
Laser Cast 300-grain Flat Point
Laser Cast 405-grain Flat Point
Laser Cast True Shot 430-grain Flat Point Gas Check
Laser Cast 500-grain Flat Point
Bushwhacker Bullet Co. 330-grain Flat Point

The front sight is a Marble brass bead, and the rear sight is a period-correct semi-buckhorn. It is adjustable for elevation with a metal elevator. For windage, you have to drift it in its dovetail. Fortunately, the receiver is drilled and tapped for the addition of a receiver sight. My eyes haven't been on speaking terms with open sights for many years, so I ordered a Lyman #66WB (for "Winchester Browning") from Brownells, and installed it on the M-1886. The .040-inch aperture provides a perfect sight picture with the brass bead front and an 8-inch bull's-eye target. The #66WB comes with two apertures, a .040 and .093 inch. And, should you wish to practice shooting your new iron at running jackrabbits, you can remove the aperture, and you have a gaping .220-inch "ghost ring" to see through.

The buttstock and fore-end are of American walnut, with nice straight grain, and are not checkered. The buttstock has a straight grip, and is finished off with a traditional crescent steel buttplate, with a "widow's peak" at the toe. Being a "short rifle," the fore-end has a steel cap.

THE AMMO DILEMMA

The .45-90 cartridge is sort of an odd duck. As noted previously, its case is exactly the same as the .45-70, except for a length of 2.4 inches, versus 2.1 inches for the .45-70. Winchester envisioned the round as what was called an "express" cartridge, i.e., a lightweight bullet at the highest velocities then possible with blackpowder, and .45-90 rifles had a twist of 1:32 inches appropriate for this lighter bullet.

But times change, and today not only are much heavier .45-caliber bullets available, their velocities in older cartridges with smokeless powders far exceed those of blackpowder, so Winchester cut the new M-1886 barrels with a steep 1:20-inch twist, just like original and modern-day .45-70s. This opens a

The Marble front sight has a brass bead, and is dovetailed into the barrel.

Handloading the .45-90 Winchester

Straight-walled cases like the .45-90 are a pure delight to handload with modern smokeless powders, blackpowder substitutes or original blackpowder, the "one true way" of purists. A huge selection of suitable .45-caliber bullets, both cast and jacketed, is available due to the immense and enduring popularity of the .45-70. The M-1886 is a strong action, and most loading manuals have plenty of pressure-tested load data for the .45-70. An expert ballistician of my acquaintance reports that "standard" smokeless-powder loads for the .45-70 can be cautiously increased about 3 to 5 percent for use in the .45-90, and I judiciously used this approach with good results.

However, a modicum of pressure-tested load data for the .45-90 is available in the Lyman Blackpowder Loading Manual for several types of blackpowder, as well as Pyrodex RS and Pyrodex Select with five different weights of cast bullets. Lyman used a 29.5-inch pressure barrel with a 1:20-inch twist. However, note that only two of these loads, the 292- and 405-grain bullets, are suitable for the lever-action M-1886, since close attention to the overall cartridge lengths (a maximum of 2.88 inches) is required for proper functioning. In addition, Western Powders lists five pressure-tested loads for cast bullets in the .45-90 with its blackpowder substitute, Blackhorn 209.

Remember the standard admonitions for blackpowder loads: powder up to the base of the bullet, light compression and no air space.

Loads with smokeless powders seem to work fine with standard (non-magnum) large-rifle primers. The substitutes and real blackpowder are harder to ignite, so magnum caps get the nod here.

As noted, Starline makes top-notch cases for the .45-90, but the company states that they are made "quite hard" to withstand higher pressures. Thus, they will probably not expand enough on firing to seal with blackpowder loads. Starline recommends annealing the cases for blackpowder loads, although I skipped this step, and had no "sealing" problems.

I can heartily recommend two excellent books by my buddy Mike Venturino. They are: *Shooting Lever Guns of the Old West* and *Shooting Buffalo Rifles of the Old West*. Mike is an expert on anything blackpowder, and a wealth of background and technical information is available on the M-1886 and the .45-90. Gobs of fascinating information are found on every page. Another specialty reference is the *Black Powder Cartridge Primer* by Steve Garbe and Mike Venturino.

In addition, .45-90 loaders should check out the excellent technical paper by Brett Olin and Alan Jones in the Speer Reloading Manual No. 14, pages 163-175. These experts used modern pressure-testing equipment to assess the nature and limits of blackpowder ammunition, and provide tips for loading top-grade ammunition.

The fascinating history of John M. Browning and the Browning company is deftly conveyed in *John M. Browning, American Gunmaker*, by John Browning (son of John M.) and Curt Gentry.

Our sport is greatly enriched by the information in all of these tomes. So, fellow hull-stuffing nostalgia buffs, rejoice! Read up, gear up and enjoy Winchester's "new" M-1886 in .45-90.

GOOD ACCURACY WAS OBTAINED WITH BOTH SMOKELESS AND BLACKPOWDER LOADS. HERE ARE FIVE EXAMPLES:

(right) The Laser Cast 405-grain cast bullet over 30 grains of AA-5744.

(below) Two cast bullet loads with Hodgdon's Trail Boss: 300-grain Laser Cast Flat Point with 23.4 grains (top), and the Bushwhacker Bullet Co. 330-grain Flat Point with 22.7 grains (bottom). Both are mild, low-recoil practice loads.

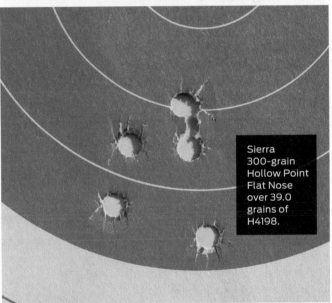

Sierra 300-grain Hollow Point Flat Nose over 39.0 grains of H4198.

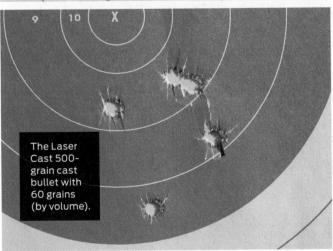

The Laser Cast 500-grain cast bullet with 60 grains (by volume).

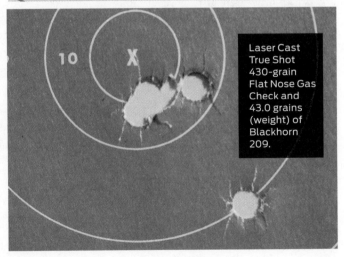

Laser Cast True Shot 430-grain Flat Nose Gas Check and 43.0 grains (weight) of Blackhorn 209.

wide window for the use of heavy bullets in the new .45-90.

I have been informed that Winchester Ammunition has no plans to make .45-90 ammo, although a few smaller, semi-custom outfits do. However, Starline Brass makes excellent .45-90 cases with the proper headstamp, and Lyman, RCBS, Redding and others make dies. Actually, one can readily load .45-90 ammo with .45-70 dies by simply readjusting them for the longer case. In fact, the M-1886 is a strong action, and most loading manuals have plenty of pressure-tested load data for the .45-70, which gives us a basis for .45-90 loads (see sidebar).

After reading everything I could on the rifle and cartridge, I gathered up dies and the necessary components, and put the new M-1886 to work on the range. This was a rewarding experience.

I used RCBS dies for the smokeless-powder loads, and Lyman dies for the blackpowder ammo. Both sets were excellent. Starline forwarded a supply of its well-made .45-90 cases, which have the correct headstamp. I used standard large-rifle primers for the smokeless powders, and magnum caps for blackpowder and substitute propellants.

I conducted the testing in essentially three phases. First were loads with smokeless powders with jacketed and cast bullets; I used the "plus 3 to 5 percent" suggestion for these loads. I used a lot of different smokeless powders just to see how modern-day components fared in this longer case. Next up were then various blackpowder substitutes, and finally the real stuff. The substitutes and blackpowder were just a nostalgic, if frustrating, jump back into the past.

Before we cover the shooting results, I must offer a caution. The loads I used worked fine in my rifle, but I make no representation that they will in yours. Use caution. Check everything at least twice. And watch for pressure signs.

SHOOTING RESULTS

OK, here's the CliffsNotes version of the shooting results, shown in Table 2. The dimensions of the cast bullets I used are in Table 3. I shot several loads with the issued open sights before the Lyman peep sight arrived. The average group size

with jacketed bullets for the open buck-horn rear sight was 1.47 inches, and for the Lyman peep sight, 1.03 inches. Thus, the peep sight (with the .040-inch aperture) improved groups for the jacketed bullet loads approximately 30 percent, so I split those group sizes into two columns on the load table, "open sight" and "peep."

Virtually all of the smokeless loads, with either jacketed or cast bullets, shot acceptably well, with one exception. The M-1886 didn't cotton to the Hornady 350-grain RN. No matter, as this bullet is built a little tough for .45-90 velocities, anyway. (Hornady lists a minimum muzzle velocity of 1,800 fps for best performance.)

As expected, cast bullets were right at home in the M-1886. I have used Laser Cast bullets from Oregon Trail for many years, and have always been pleased with their results. The other bullet brand I used was from the now defunct Bushwhacker

TABLE 3. DIMENSIONS OF CAST BULLETS

BULLET	ACTUAL WEIGHT (GRAINS)	DIAMETER (INCHES).
LASER CAST 300-GRAIN FP	300.6	.459
BUSHWACKER 330-GRAIN RN	337.2	.458
LASER CAST 405-GRAIN FP	408.1	.460
LASER CAST 430-GRAIN FP GC	429.8	.460
LASER CAST 500-GRAIN FP	498.4	.460

TABLE 2. WINCHESTER MODEL 1886 LOAD TABLE
.45-90 WINCHESTER, 24-INCH BARREL, 20-INCH TWIST

Bullet	POWDER (TYPE)	(GRS.)	CASE	PRIMER	COL (IN.)	VEL. (FPS)	S.D. (FPS)	RECOIL (FT-LB.)	ME (FT-LB.)	50-YD. ACC. (IN.) Open sight	Peep sight
Jacketed Bullet Loads											
Speer 300-grain HP	H4198	46.0	S-L	Fed 215	2.844	1,593	8	13.4	1,691	1.10	
Speer 300-grain HP	H4198	51.0	S-L	Fed 215	2.835	1,872	7	19.4	2,335		1.16
Speer 300-grain HP	Viht. N133	47.0	S-L	Fed 210	2.844	1,457	n.r.	11.3	1,414	n.r.	
Speer 300-grain HP	Viht. N133	49.0	S-L	Fed 210	2.844	1,477	n.r.	11.9	1,454	n.r.	
Speer 300-grain HP	Reloder 10	45.0	S-L	Fed 215	2.835	1,554	19	12.7	1,609	1.57	
Speer 300-grain HP	Reloder 7	44.5	S-L	Fed 215	2.835	1,534	30	12.3	1,568		0.98
Sierra 300-grain HP/FN	H4198	36.0	S-L	Fed 210	2.844	1,347	13	8.7	1,209	1.28	
Sierra 300-grain HP/FN	H4198	38.0	S-L	Fed 210	2.844	1,440	14	10.2	1,382	1.61	
Sierra 300-grain HP/FN	H4198	39.0	S-L	Fed 210	2.844	1,473	28	10.7	1,446	1.30	
Sierra 300-grain HP/FN	Reloder 7	38.0	S-L	Fed 210	2.844	1,214	29	7.2	982	1.93	
Sierra 300-grain HP/FN	Reloder 7	42.0	S-L	Fed 210	2.844	1,303	19	8.7	1,131	1.33	
Sierra 300-grain HP/FN	Reloder 7	43.0	S-L	Fed 210	2.844	1,312	21	8.9	1,147	1.35	
Sierra 300-grain HP/FN	Varget	57.0	S-L	Fed 215	2.844	1,618	36	15.3	1,744		0.88
Speer 300-grain HP	Reloder 10	45.0	S-L	Fed 215	2.835	1,554	19	12.7	1,609	1.57	
Speer 300-grain HP	Reloder 7	44.5	S-L	Fed 215	2.835	1,534	30	12.3	1,568		0.98
Hornady 300-grain HP	Trail Boss	24.2	S-L	Fed 215	2.845	1,269	26	6.9	1,073		1.10
Hornady 350-grain FP	Varget	54.0	S-L	Fed 215	2.840	1,527	11	16.8	1,813	2.36	
Speer 400-grain FP	AR-Comp	47.5	S-L	Fed 210	2.865	1,341	24	15.3	1,598	1.29	
Speer 400-grain FP	AR-Comp	51.0	S-L	Fed 210	2.865	1,505	26	19.8	2,012	1.32	
Speer 400-grain FP	PP Varmint	48.0	S-L	Fed 210	2.865	1,379	20	16.3	1,689	1.40	
Speer 400-grain FP	PP Varmint	52.0	S-L	Fed 210	2.865	1,518	25	20.3	2,047	1.41	
Speer 400-grain FP	H4895	49.0	S-L	Fed 210	2.865	1,382	22	16.5	1,697	1.38	
Speer 400-grain FP	H4895	53.0	S-L	Fed 210	2.865	1,627	27	23.5	2,352	1.40	
Speer 400-grain FP	Varget	49.0	S-L	Fed 215	2.865	1,312	16	14.8	1,529		0.55
Speer 400-grain FP	H4198	44.0	S-L	Fed 215	2.865	1,630	7	22.1	2,360		1.24
Speer 400-grain FP	Viht. N133	47.5	S-L	Fed 215	2.865	1,535	26	20.1	2,093		1.30
									averages	1.48	1.02
FTX Loads, full length .45-70 Cases											
Hornady 250-grain MonoFlex	Reloder 7	40.7	Fed.	Fed 210	2.652	1,512	35	8.6	1,269		1.65
Hornady 325-grain FTX	Reloder 7	38.6	Fed.	Fed 210	2.644	1,400	21	11.0	1,415		1.63
Cast Bullet Loads											
Laser Cast 300-grain Flat Point	Trail Boss	23.4	S-L	WLR	2.810	1,363	17	7.9	1,238		1.81
Bushwacker Bullet 330-grain FP	Trail Boss	22.7	S-L	WLR	2.825	1,278	10	8.2	1,197		1.88
Bushwacker Bullet 330-grain FP	H4198	47.0	S-L	WLR	2.825	1,712	14	18.2	2,148		1.08
Laser Cast 405-grain Flat Point	AA-5744	24.0	S-L	WLR	2.840	1,017	9	7.5	930		0.92
Laser Cast 405-grain Flat Point	AA-5744	30.0	S-L	WLR	2.840	1,247	17	11.9	1,399		1.88
Bushwacker Bullet 330-grain RN	Black Horn 209	50.0	S-L	Fed 215	2.825	1,629	16	16.9	1,945		1.85
Laser Cast 405-grain Flat Point	Black Horn 209	44.0	S-L	Fed 215	2.815	1,440	9	17.6	1,865		1.57
Laser Cast 430-grain Flat Point GC	Black Horn 209	43.0	S-L	Fed 215	2.810	1,399	10	18.2	1,869		1.77
Laser Cast 500-grain Flat Point	Black Horn 209	40.0	S-L	Fed 215	2.832	1,294	14	19.9	1,859		1.69
									avg.		1.61
Blackpowder Substitute and Blackpowder Loads, Cast bullets, Charges by volume											
Bushwacker Bullet 405-grain FP	Pyrodex RS	71.0	S-L	CCI 250	2.840	1,253	4	16.1	1,412		1.84
Laser Cast 500-grain Flat Point	Pyrodex RS	70.0	S-L	CCI 250	2.844	1,094	3	16.9	1,329		1.08
Bushwacker Bullet 330-grain FP	Olde Elmsford 2f	76.0	S-L	CCI 250	2.825	1,466	10	16.8	1,575		2.32
Laser Cast 405-grain Flat Point	Olde Elmsford 2f	74.0	S-L	CCI 250	2.840	1,355	1	19.2	1,652		1.01
Laser Cast 430-grain Flat Point GC	Olde Elmsford 2f	66.0	S-L	CCI 250	2.810	1,266	7	17.4	1,531		1.10
Laser Cast 500-grain Flat Point	Olde Elmsford 2f	60.0	S-L	CCI 250	2.832	1,199	7	19.2	1,596		1.12
									avg.		1.41

Notes: A Winchester Model 1886 Short rifle with a 24-inch barrel and a 20-inch twist was used for all testing. Sights were a Buckhorn open or a Lyman #66WB aperature rear and Marble bead front sight. Velocity is at 10 feet. Accuracy is the average of three, three-shot groups at 50 yards from an indoor bench rest. Range temperature was 37 to 58 degrees F.

Abbreviations: HP, Hollow Point; FN, Flat Nose; FP, Flat Point; GC, Gas Check; n.r., not recorded.

Bullet Co. Weights varied from 300 to 500 grains and one, the L-C 430-grain, carried a gas check.

Hornady bullets with the FTX tip are great for most lever guns, but you need to use shorter cases with them, as their ogives are too long for proper functioning. Well, if you simply must use these fine bullets in your .45-90, there is a super easy solution. Grab up some readily available *standard length* (2.1 inch) .45-70 cases, and have at it. I tried one load each with the 250-grain MonoFlex and the 325-grain FTX. Both averaged around 1.6 inches, so this is an itch you can easily scratch, if you need to.

I have used Hodgdon's H4198 for decades in my .444 Marlin and .45-70s, so I leaned on it for the .45-90, too, with good results. It produced the highest velocity cast-bullet load with 47.0 grains and the BBC 330-grain bullet. At 1,712 fps, muzzle energy was 2,148 ft-lb., serious horsepower for a cartridge introduced 134 years ago. Other good powders turned out to be Varget and Reloder 7.

Overall, the cast bullet loads averaged 1.61 inches, and can cover rabbits to bison, and most game in between. A case full of Hodgdon's Train Boss lobbed 300- and 330-grain cast slugs at 1,363 and 1,278 fps, respectively, effectively duplicating the .45-90's original "express" load. Groups were comfortably under 2 inches, and recoil was a measly 8 ft-lb. A charge of 24 grains of AA-5744 also shot well with 405-grain cast bullets at 1,017 fps.

At the other end of the scale, the 405-, 430- and 500-grain bullets from Laser Cast also shot well, overall averaging 1.57 inches.

SPECIFICATIONS: WINCHESTER MODEL 1886 SHORT RIFLE

ACTION TYPE: **Lever-action repeater**

CALIBER: **.45-90 Winchester centerfire**

MAGAZINE: **Tubular beneath barrel, capacity eight rounds**

BARREL: **24 inches, button rifled with recessed crown**

RIFLING TWIST: **1:20 inches**

OVERALL LENGTH: **42 inches**

WEIGHT: **8 pounds, 11 ounces**

METAL FINISH: **Polished blue**

SAFETY: **Two position on tang**

TRIGGER: **Trigger pull weight: 3 pounds, 13.6 ounces**

SIGHTS: **Marble Arms front brass bead, adjustable rear sight with elevator; receiver drilled and tapped for optional receiver-mounted peep sight**

STOCK: **American walnut, satin-oil finished, straight grip, crescent steel buttplate; length of pull 13.25 inches; drop at comb 1.25 inches, at heel, 2 inches**

ACCESSORIES: **Owner's manual, locking device**

MSRP: **$1,339.99**

MAKER: **Winchester Repeating Arms Co., winchesterguns.com**

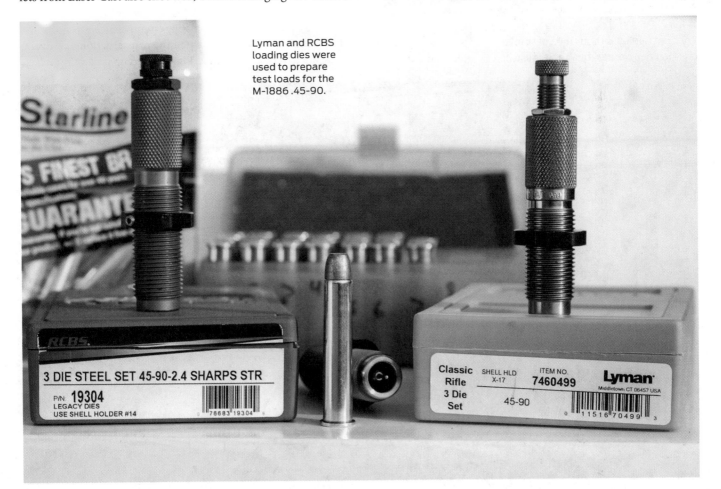

Lyman and RCBS loading dies were used to prepare test loads for the M-1886 .45-90.

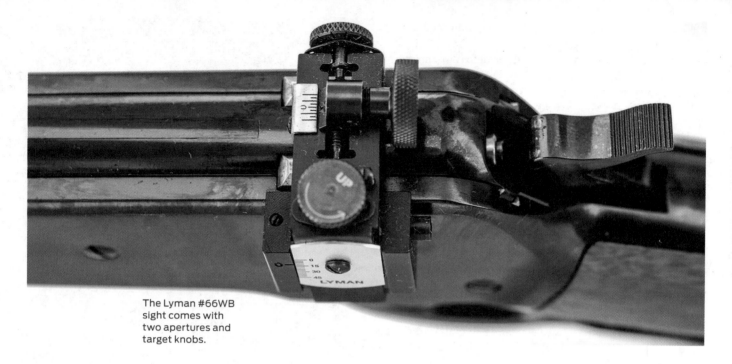

The Lyman #66WB sight comes with two apertures and target knobs.

All of the cast bullet loads with near-maximum loads of Blackhorn 209 produced good groups and plenty of power, with the Laser Cast 430-grain FP-GC and the 500-grain FP each produced over 1,850 ft-lb.

I have reloaded thousands of smokeless-powder rounds, but am less learned with blackpowder loads. Thus, it's a wonder that those .45-90 loads turned out as well as they did. I know serious blackpowder shooters will snicker at these groups, but I wasn't preparing for the BPCR Nationals, just trying to see what I could achieve with this fine new, old rifle. I thought the group sizes were quite acceptable for my purposes. Note the SDs. All but one is in the single digits, and the SD for one three-round group actually registered "0" on the Oehler M-35P tape.

This happy circumstance was not without hair-tearing consternation, however. At first, I just loaded up the test rounds

The author shooting the M-1886 from the shooting building.

The Lyman #66WB rear sight made shooting much easier, and groups with it were about one-third smaller than with the original rear sight.

Blackpowder only!

On the barrel of the new M-1886 in .45-90 is the warning "FOR BLACK POWDER ONLY." This is at first puzzling, as no such notation appears on M-1886s chambered for .45-70. So, what gives? Actually, it has a perfectly logical basis.

In 1996, Browning introduced a specialized version of the Model 1885 falling-block, single-shot rifle, made by Miroku in Japan. It was called the "BPCR Rifle," made for the Black Powder Cartridge Rifle silhouette game, and chambered for .45-70 and .40-65. (See the 1997 edition [51st] of the *Gun Digest* annual, page 348, for a description of this rifle.)

The Sporting Arms and Ammunition Manufacturers' Institute (SAAMI) is the voluntary regulatory body of the U.S. firearms industry that "approves" standards for both guns and ammo. A SAAMI-approved cartridge is considered a "factory" cartridge, and chambers, specs and ammo must conform to the prescribed pressure limits.

Even in 1996, there were dozens of pressure-tested loads for the .45-70, but none for the .40-65. While the M-1885 single shot is a very strong action, a cautious Browning lawyer rightfully foresaw the prospect of a nasty lawsuit if some nimrod blew himself up using a smokeless powder load in the new .40-65. Thus, this warning originated.

That is also the same reason this warning is on today's Winchester M-1886 in .45-90, as there are no pressure-tested, smokeless-powder loads for the round. Winchester had to protect itself, and I don't blame the company one bit. (An interesting side note: Early in the 20th century, Winchester sold a smokeless powder load for the .45-90, which was not dropped until 1919.)

with either Pyrodex RS 2F and Olde Elmsford 2f Black Powder, sat down in my shooting building, and fired them, one after another. OK, you know the results. After just a few rounds, the bullets started landing sideways on the target, and about 6 to 8 inches apart. So, I repeated the test loads, but then swabbed the bore after each shot, using the "Windex With Vinegar" recommended by Mike Venturino. Bingo! Flyers disappeared, and groups shrank. This was more like it. Holy relief. I also cleaned the rifle bore with Windex with Vinegar, and cleaned the cases fired with blackpowder with hot soapy water. So now I am ready for that bison hunt, should it ever materialize. And it's fun waiting until the blackpowder smoke cloud waifs off to see if you hit the target!

We shooters owe Winchester a round of thanks for making this, and the other Historic rifles available, for us hardcore nostalgia buffs. With them, we can jump back to the 1870s and 1880s, and vicariously relive those thrilling days of yesteryear and marvel again at the genius of John M. Browning.

AFTERWORD

As the saying goes, "Can we talk?" The logical question is

The new Winchester M-1886 is potent medicine for medium- to large-sized big game, and conjures up visions of hunting in the Old West.

whether a shooter needs a .45-90 if he or she is going to shoot nothing but modern-day smokeless-powder loads, since one can get the same maximum velocities out of the .45-70 as with the .45-90 with the same bullets. The obvious answer is "*of course!*" Every true nostalgia buff *needs* a unique piece of history called the Winchester Model 1886 .45-90.

ACKNOWLEDGEMENTS

I must express my heartfelt thanks to Lee Shaver, master gunsmith and world-champion blackpowder shooter (he builds his own muzzleloaders), and Ron Rieber, the CPW (Chief Powder Wizard) at Hodgdon Powder Company. Without the technical information and support I received from these two fine folks, this project would have been a tough row to hoe. My hat's off to them. GD

Shorter
barrels
deliver
stopping
power and
are easier
to conceal
and carry

›DICK WILLIAMS

THINK SHORT FOR BIG-BORE REVOLVERS

The author suspects two-legged predators will focus on the big bore and never notice the short barrel.

When the U.S. Army issued the .45-caliber 1873 Colt single action (and the .45 Schofield) to the troops, standard barrel lengths were 7.5 inches. Western settlers and lawmen tended to favor the same size guns and ammo as they were easier to master, and neither group was concerned with concealability. Some 60 years later, when Smith & Wesson introduced the first .357 Magnums, guns were offered in barrel lengths from 3.5 to more than 8 inches with the three longest barrel lengths dominating sales. Twenty-one years later (and some 80 years after the introduction of the Peacemaker,) S&W began production of the .44 Magnum with barrel lengths ranging from 4 to 8 3/8 inches. Unfortunately, there weren't many guys besides noted gun writer Elmer Keith who could comfortably handle the shorter barrel lengths with magnum loads and sales languished until the 1970s when Detective Dirty Harry Callahan hit the silver screen with "the world's most powerful handgun" sporting a 6.5-inch barrel. Sales skyrocketed, with primary demand being for the longer barrel

lengths. In between the 1956 introduction of the .44 Magnum and the incredibly successful publicity campaign provided by Clint Eastwood in 1971, the .41 Magnum arrived on the scene, and while the caliber and gun developed an almost cult following over the ensuing years, initial reception of the middle magnum was lukewarm, at best. And yes, barrel length options for the S&W .41 Magnum revolvers were the same 4 to 8-plus inches.

From the 1970s well into the new millennium, I spent a lot of time handgun hunting big game and shooting metallic silhouettes with the .44 Magnum using both S&Ws and Rugers. During that time frame, concealed carry became a reality for millions of "average" American citizens rather than just a bureaucratic designated privilege for the politically connected few. The vaunted power of the magnum handguns was obviously more than what was needed for self-protection despite the defensive achievements realized by big-bore users like Clint Eastwood in various movies. In addition, carrying a reasonably accessible 6.5-inch, large-frame revolver concealed is not an easy feat for the average citizen. Given the necessity of keeping a handgun completely concealed in many states, user interest focused on smaller, lighter handguns. Such handguns are much gentler on the shooter when they're chambered in smaller calibers with less recoil.

Like my fellow citizens, I followed the trend and went to more compact hardware when carrying concealed. Yet, after a lifetime appreciating the ballistic performance of big-bore cartridges, it was difficult, almost impossible, for me to simply ignore the great revolvers that chambered them. Even as my aging body raised increasing objections to a sustained diet of magnum calibers, I still appreciate the special capabilities of large, heavy, slower moving bullets. Factor in a decades-long love affair with large single- and double-action revolvers, and I couldn't even consider the prospect of an abrupt and permanent separation. Interestingly, the solution was found by a trip back in time rather than an adaptation of emerging technology. Given my history with various forty-fours, I'll start there.

When S&W began making titanium revolvers, the company chambered one in .44 Magnum. At the risk of appearing less-than-manly, I couldn't begin to handle the recoil, even with moderate loads like the .44 Special. Clearly, I had to stay with steel guns and deal with their added weight as best I could. Having spent a great deal of time hunting with Model 29s equipped with the longer barrels, this wasn't as difficult as I expected. A well-designed, high-riding belt holster provides good carry comfort, and with a shorter barrel, the gun can easily be concealed by an untucked lightweight shirt or sport coat. I've tried a pair of .44 Magnum revolvers, a S&W factory model 629 with a 3-inch barrel and a Ruger Super Blackhawk with a 3.75-inch barrel. While both performed well, I wanted something less bulky and more compact. The simple, if rather expensive, solution is to find a good custom pistol smith and tell him what you want.

I traveled a different path and shopped extensively for a discontinued S&W Model 24 or 624 chambered in .44 Special and wearing a 3-inch barrel. In time and with luck, I found one of each with the slightly tapered barrel rather than the bull barrels of the S&W magnums. Dropping from a magnum to a special posed no performance problems; everything I might ever want to do with a handgun can be done with a variety of factory-loaded .44 Special ammo with bullet weights ranging from 180-grain JHPs to heavy, hardcast bullets that produce muzzle velocities of 900 to 1,000 fps. Admittedly, this is not what one would consider a proper 200-meter gun for metallic silhouette shooting, but you might

The author runs his classic 3-inch-barreled S&W Model 24 through some Predator Defense drills at the famed Gunsite Academy.

Two excellent examples of short-barreled S&W big-bore revolvers; the Model 625, with cylinder, will handle either .45 ACP or .45 AR, while the holstered Model 624 works with .44 Special, .44 Russian and .44 Colt. Custom carry rig is from Erik Little at Rafter-L Combat Leather.

At 7 yards, the Model 624 in .44 Special has everything you need for a defensive handgun.

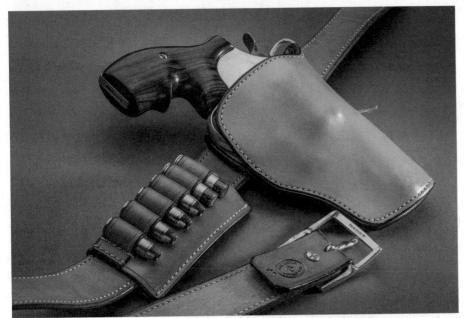

Whether your trails take you through urban or rural surroundings, the Model 624 carries a variety of viable ammo including a couple of CCI shot shells for predators with no legs.

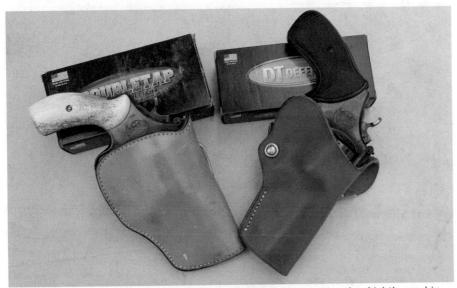

Custom holsters from Rafter-L Combat Leather (left) and Barranti Leather (right) carry big-bore, snub-nose handguns comfortably high on the hip and are easily concealed beneath an outer garment.

Ruger's Vaquero can be had with a 3.75-inch barrel in .45 Colt, which also fires the shorter case .45 Schofield.

surprise yourself on how effective it can be on man-size silhouettes out to 100 yards and perhaps beyond. While carrying my Model 624 in Texas, I had the opportunity to take a couple of rabbits and a whitetail doe, after which I carried the gun concealed on my drive home. Is that solution either fashionable or trend-setting? Perhaps not, but definitely useful, and that's a much more important word in my dictionary.

I mentioned above the variety of effective factory .44 Special ammo available today. Less well-known is the ability of a .44 Special revolver to effectively shoot two other factory loads, the .44 Colt and .44 Russian. Both these cartridges are smaller and less powerful than a typical .44 Special round, but they offer an interesting advantage should you need to use your revolver in a defensive application. The Colt and Russian cases are shorter than the .44 Special, which means the case mouth on a spent round that's being ejected will clear the cylinder breach face sooner (and perhaps more reliably) than a longer .44 Special case. No particular advantage in a tactical (or partial) reload, but when the gun is empty and you're more than a little anxious to refill it with live ammo, anything that might reduce the possibility of a malfunction is something to consider. As a lifelong shooter of big-bore handguns, I still find that reduced recoil provides a real incentive to practice and improve my skills. When we have a writers' shoot at Gunsite Academy that involves revolvers, no one uses full-power, magnum ammo.

Until fairly recently, the shortest factory barrel lengths I'd seen on Colt, S&W and Ruger revolvers chambered in .45 Colt were 4 inches for the S&W and 4.75 inches for the Colts and Rugers. I had read of Colt offering shorter Peacemakers on special order for serious shootists of the Old West, and I'd heard of "Sheriff Model" single-action Colt clones being available from some of the European manufacturers. Perhaps it was the movie *Tombstone* showing Doc Holliday's short-barrel, single-action revolver that motivated Ruger to shorten the barrel length on its Vaquero from 4.75 to 3.75 inches, but whatever the reason, the resulting gun is fast-handling and easy to carry and conceal. Cutting the barrel to 3.75 inches necessitated shortening the ejector rod and ejector-rod housing, which meant empty cases did not clear the cylinder and had to be manually extracted from each chamber after the rod pushed the case rim partially out of the cylinder. A shorter barrel would have resulted in eliminating the ejector system, and who wants to look for a ball-point pen to use as an ejector when it's time to reload? And while any handgun that chambers .45 Colt can also shoot .45 Schofield ammo, using the shorter round doesn't completely solve the partial-ejection issue, at least in a shortened single action.

While both .45 Colt and .45 Schofield ammo were issued to the U.S. Army in the 1870s, only the Peacemaker revolver was able to shoot both cartridges. I'm unaware of any earlier occasion where a duty-issue weapon was able to shoot two different factory rounds. The situation originated from the Army issuing two different handguns. The Colt, with its solid topstrap, was the kind of rugged gun you expect to see issued to soldiers, while the Schofield, with its capability to simultaneously eject six empty cases, was the improved (but less rugged) solution we like to provide our warriors.

World War I caught the United States with an insufficient number of new-issue handguns to equip all the troops we were sending to the front. So, our large-frame revolvers were modified to accept special clips that held three rounds of the new .45 ACP ammo, thus allowing the rimless cases to be fired and properly ejected by a double-action revolver. This gun/cartridge combination worked well (as witnessed by the fact they are still made today), but they didn't allow a tactical reload. After the war, ammo manufactures created the .45 AR, basically a .45 ACP round with a thick rim that could be used in the surplus .45 ACP revolvers without needing the half-moon clips. *[Editor's Note: This cartridge is more commonly known as the .45 Auto Rim]* The new round duplicated .45 ACP performance, but allowed you to reload single rounds as you fired. Factory .45 AR is still available, including a round loaded with a 255-grain lead bullet, a serious fight-stopper that allows you to load as you

Barranti's holster allowed a clean, smooth presentation of the author's Model 24.

For a full-blown, custom magnum revolver, check out this .41 Magnum from Ken Kelly at Magnaport. It features a 3.25-inch barrel, Magnaport slots to help tame recoil, and a complete action job that lets you shoot the same small groups with double action as you do with single action.

If your backyard is sometimes visited by brown bears, don't compromise. Get a full-power, compact .44 Magnum S&W or Ruger with heavyweight ammo from Garrett Cartridges of Texas.

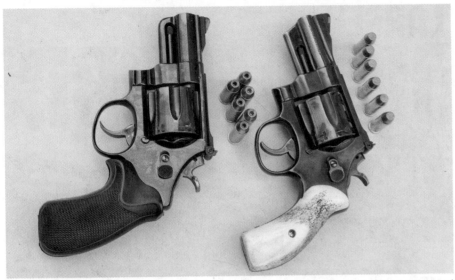

Ammo capacity of Smith & Wesson's "N" frame revolvers might seem substandard compared to today's semi-autos, but they launch big slugs and can be reloaded quickly with either speedloaders or full moon clips, depending on what caliber you're carrying.

Think "Betty Crocker" instead of "Boone & Crockett." The author's Model 624 did double duty as defensive handgun and meat supplier on a trip to West Texas.

shoot. I haven't seen a .45 ACP/.45 AR steel revolver wearing anything shorter than a 4-inch barrel, so once again we're back to the custom gunsmith approach.

At first glance, the .41 Magnum offers fewer short factory options than the other big bores, but again you might be surprised. S&W's Model 57 can be purchased with the standard heavy 4-inch barrel, but S&W also made a run of Model 57 Mountain guns with a tapered 4-inch barrel. Not long ago, I carried the Mountain gun through five days of training at Gunsite Academy and concluded it's a pretty nice self-defense weapon as issued. The only downside was that I had to load my own ammo in order to keep velocities under 1,000 feet per second. The revolver is quite manageable with magnum-level loads, but I didn't want to put myself through five days of magnum recoil. When S&W introduced its "Classics series," the company also made a run of Model 58 .41 Magnums, a lighter gun with fixed sights, a skinnier barrel and small grip panels. This model was originally envisioned and marketed as the ultimate police duty gun, but that was just before semi-automatic pistols became dominant in law enforcement. The factory grips are a little smaller than I like on a gun producing this level of performance, but installing slightly larger after-market grips is a simple change that can offer much enhanced comfort. If you would prefer a shorter barrel, it's time to call your favorite pistol smith.

OK, so maybe it was gamblers and gunslingers who originally popularized the concept of compact, concealable big-bore revolvers. Regardless of where the idea originated, the result is an intriguing creation. Big bores have a proven history of stopping threats, and they can only do that if they are with you when you need them. Gunsite Academy has a class called Predator Defense that deals with attacks from both two-legged and four-legged threats. My most recent visit there included a bunch of seriously credentialed and well-vetted gun writers. During the drills oriented toward more rural scenarios, i.e. potentially large critters, all participants were using bigger-bore handguns, and I don't recall seeing any revolvers with a barrel over 4 inches long. GD

THE SCHULTZ & LARSEN
RIGSPOLITIKARBIN
MD 42

A well-made, rugged carbine used by Danish police during World War II

›PAUL SCARLATA

PHOTOS BY JAMES WALTERS
AND BECKY SCARLATA

In April 1940, a Danish motorcycle unit armed with Krag-Jørgensen M.1889/24 Fodfolkskarabin.

The most common rifle in use with Danish police during the German occupation was the Krag-Jørgensen M.1889/24 Fodfolkskarabin. (Photo courtesy Rock Island Auction Co.)

The Schultz & Larsen Rigspolitikarbin Md 42 was made in German-occupied Denmark to provide police with a weapon that would not "threaten" the Nazi occupiers.

The necessity of producing regular columns on firearms can be a trying chore, forcing me to search constantly for something different that will, I hope, entertain my readers. A few months ago, I was discussing this with Noel Schott, my fellow collector of oddities, who inquired: "How about a Danish Rigspolitikarbin M.42?" When I discovered that he owned one, I was thrilled to say the least.

I'm sure many of our readers have some knowledge of Schultz & Larsen rifles. In 1889, Danish gunsmith Hans Schultz established a shop to build competition rifles. He was an ardent target shooter and hunter, but found that the quality he required was only available in costly custom-built guns. He decided to start producing hunting and target-shooting rifles where the emphasis was on first-class craftsmanship and a high degree of accuracy without the expenditure of large amounts of Kroner.

Niels Larsen entered the story in 1909, married Schultz's daughter in 1911, and, eight years later, became Hans' partner, resulting in the firm being renamed the Schultz & Larsen Geværfabrik og Dansk Ammunitionsfabrik A/S in Otterup (let's just call it S&L).

The firm prospered, becoming the country's premier private firearms and ammunition manufacturer and the former is still producing quality firearms to the present day (http://schultzlarsen.com/home-3). Of course, in a small, densely populated nation such as Denmark there

Hans Schultz the founder of the Schultz & Larsen Geværfabrik og Dansk Ammunitions-fabrik A/S in Otterup.

was limited demand for civilian firearms and most of their products consisted of high-end, rimfire target rifles.

With the end of World War I, there was plenty of German machinery available and Schultz and Larsen acquired additional equipment for manufacturing rifles and started producing small-caliber target rifles. Their dropping-block .22-caliber Model Number 24 rifle was introduced in 1923 and was intended for serious competition. It is also the first rifle in which every component was manufactured at the factory in Otterup.

Hans, Niels and Niels' son, Uffe, all competed in Olympic shooting, and in 1924 Niels took the bronze in the 600-meter free-rifle event.

In the 1920s and '30s, the company

also acted as a subcontractor to the German firm of Bergmann Waffenfabrik, producing, among other things, prototypes of the Maschinenpistole 35 submachine gun and the barrels to the Maschinengewehr 15 machine gun.

Niels' experience at the Olympics inspired him to construct a centerfire rifle action that utilized four lugs on the rear of the bolt that not only locked the bolt securely in the receiver, but provided a much shorter bolt lift allowing faster repeat shots.

Their first centerfire rifle, the Jagtriffel System Schultz & Larsen Md 38, was marketed as a hunting rifle and it was also the first to use the four-rear-lug, bolt-action rifles Schultz & Larsen rifles became famous for. It aped the appearance and styling of the popular Mannlicher-Schönauer with a medium-length barrel and full-length, pistol-grip stock of quality walnut. It had dual set triggers, utilized a single-column, three-round magazine with a detachable magazine floorplate to allow fast, safe unloading.

The Md 38 could be ordered chambered for the 8x58R Krag (see below) or the 6.5x58RD. The latter utilized the same 58mm rimmed case as the 8x58R Krag necked down to hold a 6.5mm, 139-grain soft-point bullet traveling at approximately 2,500 fps. It was widely used in Denmark as a target-shooting and hunting cartridge.[1]

---

1 Schultz & Larsen also re-barreled Krag-Jorgensen Gevær M.89 military rifles to 6,5mm for Danish target shooters.

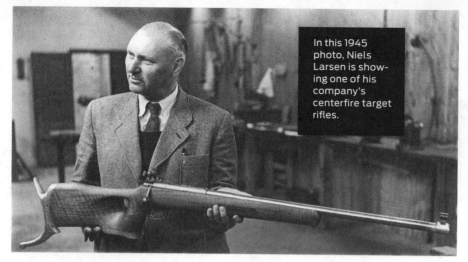

In this 1945 photo, Niels Larsen is showing one of his company's centerfire target rifles.

As has been the practice in a number of European countries, officers of the Danish Rigspolitiet (National Police) were typically equipped with little more than a truncheon (baton) and a pair of handcuffs. During the 19th century, whenever firearms were required, European police were often issued some type of long gun; and while this was often the standard military musket or rifle, by the 20th century lightweight carbines purpose-built for police service were becoming more common.

Since the 1860s, the Kingdom of Denmark had managed to remain neutral during its European neighbors' periodic bloodlettings. In April 1939, officials signed a non-aggression treaty with Nazi Germany, but their idyllic hopes for peace were rudely shattered on the morning of April 9, 1940, when the Wehrmacht rolled across the border. Against

such overwhelming forces, the small Danish army was capable of putting up only token resistance and, after less than 24 hours, King Christian X ordered them to stand down so as to avoid civilian casualties.

Hitler had hoped to convince the Danes, whom he regarded as "fellow Aryans," to cooperate with Germany. The Danish government and monarchy would remain intact, and Denmark's newspapers would continue to operate, albeit under strict censorship. Germany also allowed Denmark to maintain a small army, the Hæren, which it did not consider a threat to German forces. In return, the Danes were forced to provide Germany with large quantities of desperately needed agricultural and industrial products.

When the Wehrmacht took over the running of Denmark, they issued an order that all civilian-owned firearms, which were registered with the police, were to be handed over to the Rigspolitiet, and any weapons chambered in 9mm Parabellum or 8x58R Krag were purchased for a nominal sum and used by the police, all others were taken and stored in the local prisons. Apparently, the police soon "forgot" where the keys were kept and the Frihedskæmpere (Danish resistance fighters) often removed the weapons in the dark of night.[2]

According to Erik Troldhuus of the Danish Firearms Collectors Association, the Danish police were equipped with three different carbines during the German occupation of 1940-1945. The special police unit guarding the Amalienborgvagten (the royal palace) and King Christian X, were equipped with the KragJørgensen M.1889/24 Fodfolkskarabin (infantry carbine) while the Danish Coast Guard Police were equipped with the Krag Jørgensen M.1889/24 Artillerkarabin (artillery carbine). Both of these carbines were also issued to the Hæren.

2 https://shootingshed.co.uk/wp/2012/05/the-schultz-larsen-rplt42-rifle/

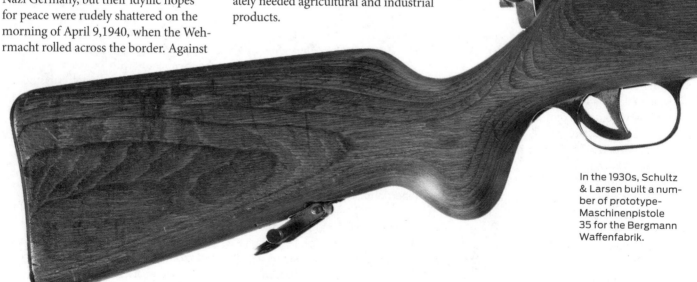

In the 1930s, Schultz & Larsen built a number of prototype-Maschinenpistole 35 for the Bergmann Waffenfabrik.

This close-up of the tubular receiver shows the long bolt handle and oval ejection port.

My good friend, fellow gun collector and historian Jørgen Christensen kindly provided the following information:

"In the fall of 1941 the German Wehrmacht in Denmark created a new police unit that was intended to keep spies out and the Danish Jews from escaping to neutral Sweden. The police unit was named Kystpolitiet (Coastal Police)"

Note: The Germans had decided to remove all Jews from Denmark to exter-mination camps. But, thanks to information leaked by a German diplomat and swift action by Danish civilians, 7,220 of Denmark's 7,800 Jews were transported to safety in Sweden by fishing boats and motorboats operating at night.

"At start, the new unit was equipped with M.1889.24 carbines but the Luftwaffe seized most of the available Danish military rifles for issue to their ground units and the Geværfabrikken (state arsenal) in Copenhagen were ordered to manufacture new ones. The arsenal could not make new rifles fast enough, so it was decided to order hunting rifles from Otterup Geværfabrik, (S&L), which were equipped with a heavier stock and marked with RPLT (Rigspolitiet) 1942 and a number series starting from num-

ber 100 (highest known number is 1396 and lowest is 426). A total of 1,200 rifles were delivered. The known examples of the rifles have all been numbered within this number range."

"*Note: When the RPLT 1942 were being produced there was a shortage of steel alloys, and their r eceivers were produced from carbon steel, the hardening made them so hard, that it was not unusual to see them crack during firing. A number of rifles have been seen with cracks to the left of the magazine weld, these rifles obviously have been shot frequently, but caution must given when choosing powder and bullet weight when loading for these old rifles. Do not get close to the max load and be careful when shooting old military ammunition, as they are often quite heavy loaded.*"[3]

Markings on a Jagtriffel System Schultz & Larsen Md 38 indicate it is chambered for the 6.5x58RD cartridge.

3 Source: Fritz and Uffe Schultz Larsen, Rigspolitets Våbeneftersynsprotokoller.

Some units of the Rigspolitiet were armed with a special carbine manufactured by Schultz & Larsen with the permission of the German occupation authorities, the RPLT Md 42 System Schultz & Larsen.[4]

Md 42s were also issued to the railway police, who were referred to as the "Svelletaelleren," which means "tracks counter" and probably refers to the monotony of walking the tracks while on duty.

They were also used to guard Danish government property and, perhaps, German prisoners and Danish collaborators after the liberation of the country by the Allies.

The RPLT Md 42 carbine was an interesting amalgam of features from military and sporting rifles. It was based upon a simple tubular receiver and a two-piece, cock-on-closing bolt similar to that used on the Md 38 sporting rifle. The non-rotating, front section of the bolt contained the firing-pin mechanism and a simple extractor, while the rear section, which is rotated by a turned-down bolt handle, had four lugs that mate with mortises at the rear of the receiver. An ejector was mounted in the bottom of the bolt way and runs in a slot in the bottom of the front section of the bolt. A Mauser-type wing safety on the bolt head is rotated 90 degrees to the right to lock the firing pin (Note: the bolt can be opened even when the safety is applied).

---

4 RPLT stands for Rigspolitikarbin (National Police Carbine).

8mm Krag ammunition (l to r): custom reloaded 8x58R cartridge, a round of 8mm skarp Gevaerpatron M.1908 and a .30-06 for comparison.

(top, midle and bottom) Danish Frihedskæmpere patrolling Copenhagen in 1945. Note the mixture of arms including M1 Carbines, Swedish Suomi submachine guns, Krag-Jørgensen rifles and even an ancient Remington Rolling Block rifle.

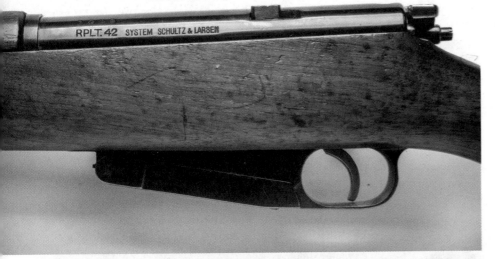

The square lever at the top of the receiver is the bolt-release catch.

The single-column magazine was loaded by opening the floor plate and dropping in four rounds.

To remove the bolt, it was opened and retracted about one-third of the way and a catch on the upper, left side of the receiver was rotated 90 degrees to the rear, allowing the bolt to be pulled from the receiver. Before reinserting the bolt, the trigger had to be pulled, lowering the sear.

A single-column, four-round magazine extended under the stock. No doubt influenced by that of the KragJørgensen, opening the floorplate compressed the follower, allowing cartridges to be manually loaded. Closing the floorplate released the follower, elevating the cartridges so they could be picked up by the forward moving bolt.

A full-length, hardwood stock with a metal muzzle cap was fitted with a hand-guard running from the receiver ring to the single barrel band. As befitting a carbine intended for paramilitary service, sling swivels were located on the barrel band and the heel of the butt, while a steel buttplate graced the end of the stock.

Sights were simple and rugged in the extreme: a plain blade front sight mounted on a sporting-style serrated ramp, while the rear sight was a simple U-notch fixed for 200 meters. Both were adjustable for windage.

The Rigspolitikarbin Md 42 was chambered for the standard Danish army cartridge, the 8mm skarp geværpatron M.1908. Better known as the 8x58R or 8mm Danish Krag, it had been developed in the late 1880s for the Gevær M.1889 Krag-Jørgensen rifle. Originally loaded with blackpowder, in 1890 smokeless propellant was substituted and in 1908 the 237-grain, round-nosed bullet was replaced with a Spitzer-style projectile weighing 196 grains, traveling at 2,460 fps.

As Scandinavian rifles go, the Md 42 is one of the rarest around. Most factory records disappeared during the occupation, and Danish collectors don't really know how many were finished before production ended. By 1943, most Danish factories producing war materials were being sabotaged daily and this is given as the reason why production on the Md 42 was limited.

Danish Frihedskæmpere broke into the S&L factory at Otterup and stole the final deliveries of rifles and, after the war, some

RPLT Md 42s were rebuilt to Jagtriffel specifications by the Otterup Factory, the suggestion is that either S&L brought them back from the state police or the saboteurs who stole them, but there are no records either way.[5]

During World War II Schultz & Larsen was "required" to perform work for the Germans, including repairing

5 https://shootingshed.co.uk/wp/2012/05/the-schultz-larsen-rplt42-rifle/

weapons for the occupation forces. The German authorities had a habit of periodically disarming the Danish police, as well as confiscating stores of Danish military rifles.

Mr. Troldhuus conveyed an interesting vignette to me regarding the M.42. *"I spoke with an elderly gentleman, who had participated in the resistance during the German occupation. He informed me that he and his colleagues, who operated in a group called Holger Danske near Elsinore, a city north of Copenhagen, from time to time held up Danish policemen guarding the waterfront and beaches of the sound between Denmark and Sweden to prevent Danes from fleeing to Sweden, only a few kilometers away. The policemen who were held up readily handed over their M.42 rifles without hesitation, as they knew that the freedom fighters needed weapons. So despite the information I have gathered for you from other sources about the M.42 rifles being stored and never used, this gentleman, who was there on the scene, is a living evidence that they were actually in use, at least to some small degree."*

He further explained: *"The German army confiscated about 50,000 rifles from Denmark, mostly M.1889/24 KragJørgensen carbines, but it is possible that some M/42s were among them as well. It is still a mystery where all these rifles went. Most likely they went into the mill, but some concentration-camp prisoners have claimed that they saw some German guards equipped with M.1889/24 carbines."*

According to a pamphlet published in Denmark 1995 by the Frihedsmuseets Venners Forlags Fond: *"On September 19, 1944 the Germans disbanded the Danish police in order not to be attacked from behind in the event of an Allied invasion. About 1,900 policemen in Copenhagen, Aarhus, Odense, and Aalborg were arrested and sent to concentration camp along with 141 Border Guards. About 80 policemen and 41 Border Guards died."*

"The police unit guarding the Amalienborg Palace had a fight with a German unit lasting some hours until the Germans withdrew. The police continued to guard the Amalienborg Palace until liberation.

About 7,000 policemen went into...the underground army. One of their tasks was to investigate informers and prepare the postwar internments."

While obtaining material for this report, I received the following regarding the use of the Md 42 from a Scandinavian collector.

"The Md 42 was used by the Danish Police executioners and firing squads, of 46 of the 76 collaborating Danes, sentenced to death after WW2, who in many cases had killed other Danes during WW2. About 400 Danes died, due to

The two-piece bolt had four locking lugs on the rear section, while the non-rotating, front section of the bolt contained the firing-pin mechanism and a simple extractor.

The front sight, Mannlicher-style stock and muzzle cap are all reminiscent of European sporting rifles.

The rear sight was a simple U-notch, fixed for 200 meters.

various reasons of the WW2 German occupations of Denmark. The last of the Danish collaborators were executed in 1950, and the remaining death sentences were commuted to prison terms."

"Before every execution of Danish Nazi collaborators, by the Danish police firing squads, which happened in the wee hours of the night, the Danish police executioners were treated to lavish dinners with lots of liquor, which did not do much for them, since many of them, actually ended up as alcoholics, and unable to cope with their deeds for their otherwise fairytale Kingdom, ending up committing suicide."

TEST FIRING

After assuring Noel that I would treat his *lidt dansk skønhed* (little Danish beauty) very carefully, he agreed to loan it to me to photograph and test fire.

Noel's Md 42 was in excellent condition and mechanically perfect. Aside from a few handling/storage dings the stock was unmarred and the bore was mirror bright, leading me to believe it had never been issued. The left side of the tubular receiver bore the markings *"RPLT. 42 System Schultz & Larsen"* surmounted by a four-digit serial number. With its full-length stock, muzzle cap, and slim lines it reminded me more of a European sporting carbine than a police firearm. Balance was excellent and the simple, fixed sights provided a sharp sight picture.

Test firing consisted of firing a series of five-shot groups from a sandbag rest at 75 yards. A friend who indulges in such alchemy, kindly assembled a supply of 8x58R ammunition from resized and reformed .45-70 brass loaded with 200-grain Speer soft-point bullets.

As a longtime collector of Krag-Jørgensen rifles, I found loading the magazine more or less second nature. While the bolt worked with a "new gun" stiffness and required a hefty shove to move rounds from the magazine to the chamber, the trigger had a very short take up and crisp let off. Despite weighing a hefty 8.65 pounds, the Md 42 proved to be a heavily recoiling, if accurate, carbine. In fact, all three of my groups were in the 3-inch range with the best a quite presentable (considering the rather basic sighting equipment) 2.75 inches in diameter.

I fired the remaining five rounds across my chronograph and obtained an average velocity of 2,136 fps, which was a bit below the published specs for the 8mm skarp geværpatron M.1908, but, considering the M.42's short barrel, can be considered in the ballpark.

In conclusion, it would appear that the Rigspolitikarbin M.42 was a well-made, rugged carbine suitable for use by police of that time and place. But, I have little doubt that most Danish police officers were very happy when they were replaced with M1 Carbines in the 1950s. As it is, having obtained an example of this rare police weapon to test fire, I now feel that I am a member of a very small, and fortunate, fraternity. Not that I'm bragging…

I would like to thank Noel Schott, Galen Burgett, Jørgen Christensen, Jonas Faber, Erik Troldhuus, Vince DiNardi, Troels Hojer, Torben Ohms, Lars Böttcher and Rock Island Auction Co., for supplying materials used to prepare this report. GD

SPECIFICATIONS SCHULTZ & LARSEN RIGSPOLITIKARBIN MD 42

CALIBER: **8mm skarp geværpatron M.1908**

OVERALL LENGTH: **43.6 inches**

BARREL LENGTH: **22.65 inches**

WEIGHT: **8.65 pounds**

MAGAZINE: **Four rounds, manually loaded**

SIGHTS, FRONT: **Blade**

SIGHTS, REAR: **U-notched, fixed for 200 meters**

BAYONET: **None**

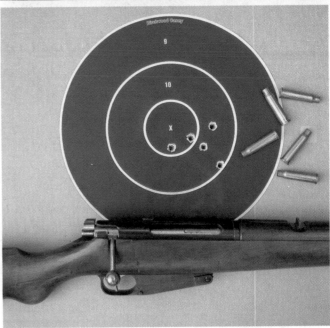

(top) The author test-fired the M.42 carbine from a sandbag rest on his club's 75-yard range.

(above) It proved to be an accurate rifle, with the author's best five-shot group measuring exactly 2.75 inches.

A TRIBUTE TO JERRY B. LE[E]

Former *Gun Digest* editor-in-chief pass[es] away in November

PHIL MASSARO

Jerry Lee and I got to know one another just a few yea[rs] as I had entered the firearms industry later in life, and introduced to him by way of the *Gun Digest the Maga[zine]* and the company's books department. He had asked [me to] take over the Ammunition, Ballistics and Components se[ction] of the *Gun Digest* annual book, in addition to giving me a [fea]ture article each year. To say I was honored doesn't quite c[apture] the emotions.

We'd discuss the parameters each fall, usually in late October or early November, settling on the feature-article topic and spending a bit of time conversing about families, firearms and just life in general. For five years I'd look forward to our annual telephone conversations, and brief face-to-face chats at the SHOT Show. Perhaps I worked too efficiently, as Jerry would just send me "good work" emails after everything was submitted in the springtime.

The fall of 2019 saw me hunting quite a bit, and with the workload I carry, time certainly flew by; before I knew it, November was upon us. My mind had turned to thinking of a topic for the *2021 Gun Digest* annual, when I received the terrible news: My friend Jerry passed away, unexpectedly (at least to us in the firearms industry) on Nov. 1, at the age of 82.

I didn't have a chance to say goodbye, or to tell him that though I deal with a healthy number of editors, and work with, and for, some great folks in this industry, working with him was an absolute pleasure. Jerry, in spite of his vast knowledge and experience in the industry, told me he was a fan of my work, and how he'd followed my stuff in other publications. Point being, Jerry Lee knew how to work with a writer, especially one who was as wet behind the ears as I was, to get the most from him or her, and those editions of the *Gun Digest* annual that featured him as editor-in-chief certainly reflect that.

Our time together was brief, and to be honest I knew very little of the man's personal life or history. I do know that Jerome Beauchamp Lee (Jerry to us) was born Aug. 12, 1937, in Maynard, Texas, a son to the late G.Y. Lee and Maud Magill Lee. In addition to a lengthy career in the gun-writing industry, he was a radio announcer and disc jockey, managed a radio station and was a musician who (I sadly found out posthumously, as I am as well) was an aficionado of vintage guitars. Professionally, he spent time as a writer, and at the helm of *Guns and Ammo*, *Shooting Times* and *Guns Magazine*, as well as serving as the editor of the *Gun Digest* annual from 2013 through the 2020 edition. He was a proud Life Member of the National Rifle Association and

a firearms enthusiast for his entire life.

Though Jerry was my friend, I didn't know him as long or as well as some of my colleagues did, especially those who worked with him in other publications. I feel that the measure of a man's life is the mark and influence he had on those who knew him, and the outpouring of sentiment regarding Mr. Jerry B. Lee is remarkable. I would like to share the memories and anecdotes of those who knew him better than I did, as a means of remembering Jerry's life within this industry.

Craig Boddington, a man I'm proud to call a friend and colleague, as well as a staple in our industry, had this to say about Jerry: "On the 'gun floor' at the old (and final) Petersen Publishing building on Wilshire Boulevard, Jerry Lee had the southwest corner office. In a workplace often tense with conflicting deadlines, Jerry's space was a small piece of calm, efficient tranquility! He was that increasingly rare editor, a quiet man whose only interest was to do the best job he possibly could, taking care of both his publications and his readers…and steadfastly remaining true to both. Jerry Lee had no interest in personal attention or self-promotion, and no hidden agendas; he was a true professional, totally and completely competent and confident. As a writer, and as a fellow editor, Jerry Lee was always a joy to work for, and to work with.

"Jerry always had a uniquely clear vision for the publications in his charge; he made clear assignments with brief and concise direction, which, of course, he expected to be followed!

"His editorial changes were never whimsical, but always based on the practical concept of right and wrong, correct or incorrect. Yep, he caught me making some bone-headed errors! He was thorough and knew his stuff. And, as a writer, I always felt he had my back (and I hope vice versa). Jerry Lee was not well-known to his readers, but that's the way he wanted it, the editor behind the scenes. Professionals of his caliber are uncommon today. He deserves to be well-remembered for his long contribution to the shooting and sporting press. I started missing him the day he began his short retirement, and I miss him more today."

Kevin Steele also worked with Jerry

at Petersen's and offered this: "I worked with Jerry for at least a decade as I recall. When I was the editor of GA, Todd Smith hired Jerry away from FMG. Jerry was a great person, kind and interesting. When he lived down in Orange County we would carpool occasionally before he moved to an apartment in Beverly Hills, closer to the Petersen building on Wilshire.

"Jerry was a bit of an enigma, not really being either a passionate shooter or hunter. He was a good editor with a workable knowledge of firearms, which I assumed he had picked up in the course of his life. He loved O'Connor, which, being a Keith man myself, always aroused my suspicions. He was an older gentleman when he came to work for us, in his late 50s or perhaps early 60s. He had a great voice and I was not surprised when he told me he had a career for many years as a radio DJ. Jerry loved talking to Steve Fjestad, with whom he shared an interest in music and classic guitars.

"I had not seen nor spoken to Jerry in nearly a decade when he turned up in our booth at this last year's SHOT Show. Knowing what I do now, I believe he had made the decision to say 'goodbye' to his friends and colleagues in the industry. We spent nearly an hour, late one afternoon, talking about the old days at Petersen, the folks in the industry and the state of the current market. I was glad to see him and for the opportunity to chat with him again. Looking back now, I wish I had known him better."

Kevin, I think we all share that last sentiment.

Patrick Sweeney credits Jerry for his introduction to the gun industry. "I am a successful gun writer in no small part because of Jerry Lee. I had a lot of knowledge, a lot of experience and a lot of ambition, but as far as getting all that in an entertaining and informative form, I might as well have been writing in cuneiform. As it turned out, both Jerry and I had come from radio broadcasting backgrounds, but in different parts of the country. Phone calls ostensibly scheduled for editing and gun-article idea generation often devolved into trading stories of radio stations and the people we had known 'back then.' One of the best bits of

Noted gun writers and editors (left to right) Rick Hacker, Garry James, Jerry Lee and George Wait pause for a photo during a weekend hunt in the Alabama Hills outside of Lone Pine, California, where many of the old Westerns were filmed. Jerry Lee was a very private man, making a photo such as this extremely rare.

advice Jerry gave me was to work harder on my photography. 'I can edit text, and make you sound like the new Hemingway,' he told me, 'but even a Photoshop genius can't correct a fuzzy photo. And I'm not a genius.'

"Always friendly, always approachable, always straight up about what he needed, wanted and could sell to the bosses, Jerry was the editor every writer wishes to have. I'll miss him terribly."

Few have had a run in the *Gun Digest* annual longer than Terry Wieland, who was also very close with Jerry Lee. Terry offered the following: "Undoubtedly, you will read here that Jerry Lee was a 'complete professional,' a 'writer's editor,' and that 'no one in the business was better liked.' And it's all true.

"Even more, what set Jerry apart was the fact that he was interested in guns of all kinds. If he didn't know about something, he wanted to learn, and believed his readers would, too. In 23 years of working with Jerry Lee, I never once heard him say 'nobody's interested in those' or 'our readers can't afford that.' He felt that if I was enthusiastic, and could convey that enthusiasm in an article, people would read the story and appreciate it.

"As a teenager, John Amber's *Gun Digest* introduced me to English double rifles, which I could not afford, and to Lucian Cary's stories about American

Schützen rifles, of which I knew nothing. But they were in *Gun Digest,* so I read the articles and was hooked.

"Like Mr. Amber, Jerry believed we should widen our readers' horizons by offering them stories about things they might never have thought about, whether it was the history of James Purdey & Sons or the labyrinthine world of Stevens target rifles. In every issue, he gave them some of what he knew they wanted, but then gave them much more besides. It was a formula that worked for John Amber, Jerry Lee carried on that tradition, and the *Gun Digest* of today shows that he succeeded."

Gun Digest Group Publisher Jim Schlender reflected on his relationship with Jerry: "My only regret about meeting Jerry Lee is that it wasn't sooner. It was April 2011, and the Gun Digest business was in desperate need of someone to step up and help carry the torch. My friend, *Gun Digest* books editor Dan Shideler, had died unexpectedly, leaving us with a gaping hole in our publishing plans.

"Jerry and I arranged to meet at the NRA convention in Pittsburgh, and by the time we were done talking about his family, his beloved home state of Texas, deer hunting, publishing and, of course, firearms, I was confident that 'The World's Greatest Gun Book' would continue in more-than-capable editorial

hands, as strong as ever. Every time Jerry and I spoke, I was reminded that whatever I thought I knew about gun history, pricing and collecting was still only a fraction of the many things this soft-spoken gentleman had already learned. And I always felt as if I had gained something valuable just for having taken the time to chat with my new friend.

"Jerry Lee stepped up at a time when *Gun Digest* needed the help of someone special to continue its legacy as the industry's most storied brand. I'm grateful for that, but even more so for the example he set and what he taught me during the few short years I knew him."

To have such prestigious names in our industry speak so highly of Jerry's work ethic, warm personality and the lasting effect he had on those around him surely affirms a life well-lived. Jerry, you are sorely missed, and I sincerely hope this 75th Edition of the World's Greatest Gun Book would've made you proud. GD

With its heavy fluted barrel, Cerakote finish and A-TACS AU camo stock, the Hell's Canyon Long Range is a good-looking rifle. And despite its heavy barrel profile the rifle is still relatively light, weighing less than 8 pounds.

GOING LONG

Part sporter, part target rifle, Browning's new Hell's Canyon Long Range is the hybrid hunting rifle you'll want to own

› **BRAD FITZPATRICK**

The Browning Hell's Canyon Long Range utilizes a three-lug bolt design. This gives the X-Bolt a shorter bolt throw than two-lug rifles.

The Hell's Canyon Long Range uses Browning's X-Bolt proven action. That and proper headspacing of the premium barrel make these rifles very accurate.

Browning's X-Bolt has been around since 2008, and since that time these guns have been refined and tuned to near perfection. You could claim these guns are the best hunting rifles Browning has ever built, and you certainly wouldn't get any argument from me. I've tested five different X-Bolts and have been impressed by all. But the company's new Hell's Canyon Long Range version is my personal favorite of the bunch. Here's why.

First, the Long Range model is a modified version of the company's superb Hell's Canyon sporter, a rifle that blends light weight with superb accuracy and the type of durability you need when you're hunting in really rough country. Like the original Hell's Canyon rifle, the Long Range version comes with a composite stock with A-TACS AU camo. The stock is mated with an X-Bolt action and

The Hell's Canyon Long Range is the heavy-barreled version of Browning's Hell's Canyon Speed rifle. Both guns are good, and both have their advantages: The Speed rifle has a shorter overall length and lighter weight, but the Long Range rifle's heavy barrel helps keep the barrel cool when firing and the added mass reduces recoil.

free-floating Browning barrel, but the primary difference between the two Hell's Canyon guns is the new Long Range version comes with a heavy sporter fluted barrel that's longer than those you'll find on the standard Hell's Canyon rifle. Both guns come with the same stylish Burnt Bronze Cerakote finish on the exposed metalwork so you won't have to worry about corrosion in the field.

With the addition of a heavy sporter barrel, the Hell's Canyon Long Range could be classified as a hybrid hunting rifle. Over the last couple years, these guns have grown in popularity, and there are more and more hunting rifles that have features borrowed from heavy tactical and PRS guns. The goal is improved accuracy (especially at long ranges), which certainly isn't a bad thing. But the romance of carrying a 10-pound rifle, with a heavy chassis or oversized adjustable stock, high into the mountains and making long shots on elk, mule deer and sheep fades at around 4,000 feet elevation. The higher you climb the heavier a heavy rifle feels, and when the air is thin and you realize the elk you're chasing is one canyon and a mile of steep hiking away you'll learn to detest every extraneous ounce of gun weight.

That's why the Hell's Canyon Long Range is so appealing. Yes, it has a relatively heavy contour barrel, but it is not so heavy that you'll hate it if you have to hike. Unloaded weights range from 7 pounds, 3 ounces to 7 pounds, 8 ounces, so it doesn't weigh much more than your average pencil-barrel sporter. This is a gun you can carry into the high country.

There's no fancy (read: heavy) stock, either. The straight comb profile and lightweight, yet durable, construction make this a long-range gun you can live with.

WHAT'S INSIDE

Browning got it right with the X-Bolt, and there's a good reason it's the company's flagship hunting rifle. For starters, the X-Bolt utilizes a push-feed bolt with three locking lugs up front, which shortens bolt lift and allows for faster cycling. A ring of steel on the front of the bolt surrounds the base of the cartridge and adds an extra level of security. The receiver itself is sculpted and contoured to shave unnecessary weight, and it is mated with a button-rifled, air-gauged barrel made by Miroku in Japan. Perhaps most importantly, all X-Bolt rifles are hand chambered so headspacing is perfect. The barreled action is then glass bedded at the front and rear of the action, further enhancing accuracy potential.

Browning designers raised some

eyebrows when they added a bolt-unlock button to their guns, but the system is functional and easy to use. The two-position tang-mounted safety locks the bolt in the SAFE position. To cycle the action, simply press down on the bolt-release button located at the top of the bolt handle and the X-Bolt can be loaded and unloaded safely. It's an intuitive system that's beneficial not only because of its added layer of security, but also because the bolt won't open while you're walking through brush. In really thick stuff, a non-locking bolt has the potential to open, and it can be a real nuisance. That's not an issue with the X-Bolt.

The Hell's Canyon Long Range comes with Browning's detachable rotary box magazine. I'm a fan of detachable box mags, but you can tell many of them were a cost-saving afterthought because they're finicky to load, hard to seat, and generally built to pretty low standards. The Browning's mag is the exception. It fits into the action securely and locks in place with a confidence-inspiring click. Feeding rounds into the magazine is easy, and I think it's wise to spend a few extra bucks to carry a spare magazine because it allows for faster reloads and doesn't reduce your hunting rifle to a single-shot gun if you happen to misplace a magazine. I've never had feeding issues with any cartridge out of an X-Bolt magazine, and the Hell's Canyon Long Range was no exception.

The X-Bolt draws its name from the X-Lock scope-base system that secures the base in four places instead of two. I've been burned by hunting rifles with loose scope bases and I'm borderline phobic (*loosebaseaphobia* is the clinical name, I

The detachable box magazine allows for faster reloads, but it is possible to top load the rifle thanks to the Browning's generous ejection port.

think) about optic security. I want a system that offers me the reliability of the X-Lock design, especially when I'm traveling for a hunt. There's nothing worse than flying halfway around the world only to find your scope has somehow shimmied loose. And you don't want to waste time at home or abroad tightening your scope and re-zeroing when you could be hunting.

All great hunting rifles, especially those designed for making long shots, must have a decent trigger. The X-Bolt's Feather Trigger is far above decent, and the three-lever design virtually eliminates creep. Hard-chromed steel components ensure this trigger will hold up, and it is user-adjustable from 3 to 5 pounds. Most X-Bolt triggers are factory set at 3.5 pounds, and I don't think I've ever shot one of these rifles that was more than a quarter pound off that mark when it came out of the box.

Add it all up and you have a superb hunting rifle that's built to make long shots and last for years. Fit and finish of the Hell's Canyon Long Range is excellent, and the action cycles smoothly with a tight, positive lockup. Added touches include a functional forearm design with a comfortable finger groove, stylish, but functional, texturing on the grip surfaces, an easy-to-see cocking indicator beneath the enclosed rear bolt shroud, and a detachable muzzle brake with an included thread cap.

MSRP for the Hell's Canyon Long Range rifle runs from $1,279.99 to $1,349.99. It isn't a budget rifle, but if you want a gun that is both accurate and well-constructed from premium components, you won't find it for less. There are 11 different caliber options, and the list of available chamberings reads like a who's who of hot long-range hunting rounds, including the 6mm and 6.5 Creedmoor, the .270 and .300 WSM, 6.5 PRC, 7mm Rem. Mag., 28 Nosler, .300 Win. Mag., .300 Remington Ultra Mag, .30 Nosler and the .300 PRC. That's a cartridge list that'll cover everything from red fox to brown bear.

SHOOTING THE HELL'S CANYON LONG RANGE

The Hell's Canyon Long Range I tested was chambered in 6.5 Creedmoor, and with the muzzle brake in place it was a real

ACCURACY RESULTS: BROWNING HELL'S CANYON LONG RANGE 6.5 CREEDMOOR

LOAD	GRAIN	VELOCITY (avg)	SMALLEST GROUP	AVERAGE GROUP
HORNADY AMERICAN GUNNER OTM	140	2,662	.55	.67
HORNADY PRECISION HUNTER ELD-X	143	2,685	.77	.91
WINCHESTER DEER SEASON COPPER IMPACT XP	125	2,841	.89	1.07

Accuracy results are based on three-shot groups at 100 yards from a fixed rest. Velocity figures are the average of 10 shots measured 10 feet from the muzzle using a Competition Electronics chronograph.

pussycat to shoot. All these rifles come equipped with 26-inch barrels regardless of caliber, and that only serves to further dampen recoil of the mild Creedmoor. Browning includes an Inflex recoil pad, and with so much protection against the evils of recoil this gun is pleasant. I love having the ability to switch to the included thread protector in the field, too. Your guides and PHs will appreciate that feature as well.

The Feather Trigger is excellent, both in its function (break weight was 3.6 pounds with no creep) and its architecture. I like the wide, flat trigger face and the roomy trigger guard allows you to shoot this gun while wearing gloves.

What's most important, though, is accuracy. Cool camo patterns and modern aesthetics won't make up for a gun that shoots poorly, and the X-Bolt didn't disappoint. Browning claims 1.5 MOA is its standard, but most of these guns will shoot better than that. The Hell's Canyon Long Range I tested certainly did. It managed to group and inch or better at 100 yards with the three different loads tested, and the 1:7"-twist barrel performed well with loads ranging from 125 to 143 grains. The best three-shot, 100-yard group measured .55-inches, and that came courtesy of Hornady's American Gunner 140-grain OTM load. But it's worth noting that both of the other rounds tested, Winchester's Deer Season Copper Impact XP and Hornady's Precision Hunter, both managed at least two groups at or below an inch at 100 paces. The average hunter doesn't need that type of accuracy to hunt deer-sized game, honestly, but this rifle was designed to do extraordinary things at extended distances. The Hell's Canyon Long Range also happens to shoot the best of any X-Bolt I've tested. Some credit

for the gun's impressive accuracy results has to be awarded to the optic, though. I mounted a Leupold VX-3i 4.5-14x40 with CDS and Zero-Lock on the X-Bolt, and that's an ideal rifle/optic combo because the Leupold offers superb light management and a wide magnification range yet doesn't add a lot of bulk to an otherwise trim hunting rifle. The rifle and optic together weighed in at just under 8 pounds.

It's true that you can find rifles that cost less and shoot about as well as an X-Bolt, but this gun warrants its price tag in terms of its reliability, intelligent design features and fit and finish. All X-Bolt rifles are good, but I think the Hell's Canyon Long Range is a standout because it is target-gun accurate and hunter friendly. It might be the brightest star in a very successful family of rifles. GD

BROWNING HELL'S CANYON LONG RANGE SPECIFICATIONS

ACTION: **Bolt-action centerfire**

CALIBER: **6.5 Creedmoor (10 other options available)**

WEIGHT: **7 lbs., 3 oz.**

LENGTH: **46 in.**

CAPACITY: **4+1**

TRIGGER: **3.6 lbs.**

SIGHTS: **Drilled and tapped**

BARREL: **Heavy sporter, fluted, detachable brake**

SAFETY: **Two position**

STOCK: **Composite, A-TACS AU camo**

FINISH: **Burnt Bronze Cerakote**

MSRP: **$1,279.99 as tested**

CONTACT: **Browning, browning.com**

Benelli's 3-inch, 28-gauge Ethos, right, did the deed at Strait Lake Lodge in Arkansas. It performed well next to 20-gauge magnums.

The author tested the new Backridge 28-gauge loads in the Benelli Ethos before the shells were available for retail sales.

THE
BENELLI
ETHOS RAFFAELLO

Testing a 28-gauge, 3-inch magnum shotgun, and new Backridge Ammunition shotshells

› **L.P. BREZNY**

It was a phone call from Major Adam Ziegler, 101st Airborne, and owner/president of Backridge Ammunition in Tennessee, that got the ball rolling. Backridge offers special custom loading for clubs and individuals who want ammunition that is not associated with the mainstream runs being marketed by the big three. It seemed that Ziegler was putting together a research test event regarding the development of a 3-inch, 28-gauge magnum shotshell that would involve several thousand miles of travel, and gunning warm targets from states ranging from the Mississippi Delta on the Gulf Coast, then inland as far as Tennessee.

This waterfowl hunter was totally in on the deal.

As a major part of this event, Benelli had offered the use of its new 28-gauge magnum Ethos Raffaello shotgun, thinking this would be a good test in terms of finding any flaws in the gunning system.

Even though several different 3-inch shotguns, and also a paired 20-gauge magnum group of guns were being included for comparative ballistics results, the Benelli 28-gauge magnum would be the star of the show, and up front and center regarding my field evaluation of the shotgun.

In the Benelli Ethos, we have a lightweight (5.3 pounds), autoloading,

3-inch magnum shotgun that is designed for a generation of shooters today who are older than 55 years.

Considering the loads developed by Backridge carried a full ounce of bismuth, or a paired load at one ounce of ITX shot, one could expect the gun could produce some recoil. As a point in fact, there was no problem in this area, as the Benelli 28 packs a buttstock anti-recoil system referenced as the "Progressive Comfort" design. In the field, shooting the heavy loads of one-ounce nontoxic loads, Benelli's system worked well. No recoil effects were observed as the gun's balance points, stocking and that special recoil-absorption system canceled those

PATTERN PERFORMANCE: BENELLI ETHOS 3-INCH MAGNUM, 28 GAUGE

LOADS	CHOKE	3 ROUNDS, 30-INCH CIRCLE (pellet percentages)		
BACKRIDGE 3 IN. MAG. 1 OZ. ITX #6	FULL	92	86	85
BACKRIDGE 3 IN. MAG. 1 OZ. ITX #6	MOD	88	84	79
BACKRIDGE 3 IN. MAG. 1 OZ. BISMUTH #6	FULL	84	96	81
BACKRIDGE 3 IN. MAG. 1 OZ. BISMUTH #6	MOD	74	77	73
BACKRIDGE 2 3/4 IN. 7/8 OZ. ITX #6	FULL	90	83	93
KENT BISMUTH 2 3/4 IN. 7/8 OZ. #6	FULL	83	79	90

BENELLI ETHOS 28 MAGNUM SPECIFICATIONS

TYPE: **Semi-auto, inertia-driven**
GAUGE: **28 ga.**
CHAMBER: **3 in.**
RECEIVER: **Nickel plated engraved**
STOCK: **AA-grade satin walnut**
BUTTSTOCK: **Progressive Comfort recoil-reduction system**
BARREL: **26 in.**
OVERALL LENGTH: **47 in.**
LENGTH OF PULL: **14 3/8 in.**
WEIGHT: **5.3 lbs.**
SIGHTS: **Interchangeable fiber-optic (red, yellow, green)**
SAFETY: **Right side rear trigger guard**
RIB: **Carbon fiber**
MSRP: **$2,199**
CONTACT: **www.benelliusa.com**

elements from the big picture. Second-shot recovery on follow-up shots, or fresh targets, due to the positive gun control, was as smooth as silk.

Because the Benelli 28 carries the traditional inertia-driven system, the same one used in the Benelli SBE and others in the gun builder's line, basic operational controls were second nature to me. Even for a shooter new to this gun, the right-side bolt release, and shotshell elevator control at the trigger guard make this autoloader simple to operate. I could load the magazine, chamber and bring the gun to mount without even looking down at the receiver's surface. Mind you, all this was while standing hip-deep in flooded timber, or balancing on a small piece of mud bog in the quicksand of the Mississippi Delta.

At Strait Lake Lodge in Arkansas, we left mud boats behind and walked into the timber and looking for the "X." This meant finding the location where the mallards wanted to feed, and then setting up directly under their approach routes. Here the new 28-gauge autoloader showed its true ability to match the 20-gauge magnum regarding payload, and with its outstanding pointing ability, cut down greenheads with precise accuracy as the ducks darted between the tree limbs toward the water.

Considering the set of five choke tubes, I elected to use a modified choke in the timber, but moved to the tight-patterning

full choke when shooting over open-water decoys, both in the Mississippi Delta, and later at Tennessee Lake, Tennessee. In terms of exact performance characteristics, you can refer to the two pattern tables illustrated in this article. Traditionally the 28 gauge will maintain wonderful patterns based on the bore size, versus payload weight and pellet-count balance. Backridge has worked very hard to offer custom loads that gain the very best performance out of this shotgun, as well as a handful of other 3-inch-chambered 28s.

With the shotgun designers making use of bright and engraved receiver metal, deep-luster bluing and AA-grade walnut stocks, we took great care of these guns, both on the salt-marsh areas of the delta, and farther north when hunting flooded timber. With the recoil system used in the gun's design, the fore-ends on the 28s are as slim as a high-powered rifle. The whole gun is more like a full-size pump-action .410 bore than a larger-frame 20 or 12 gauge. This gun will go into service here in my native Black Hills during spring when hunting turkeys. However, because of its bright appearance, the gun will be dressed in a camo jacket in the field.

After heavy use, this shotgun cleans up with ease. Being recoil operated (not a gas system) the parts list is low regarding the shotgun's receiver. Pull and swab the barrel with the stripping of the front magazine cap. Wash out the bolt assembly with a flushing spray (I prefer Liquid

Wrench). Wipe down surface areas, and you're ready to go back to work. One of our two test guns was shot for almost two weeks without any cleaning save for light surface oiling, and during that time no malfunctions were observed.

Thanks to the folks at Backridge Ammunition, Cajun Adventures in Louisiana, Haydel's Game Calls, Strait Lake Lodge in Arkansas, and the gun crew at Tennessee Lake. The gun was tested enough to show off a well-designed hybrid among sub-gauge, smooth-bore gunning systems. I can report for a fact that this shotgun, based on its firepower as an autoloading system, and the new 3-inch, 1-ounce, nontoxic loads designed by Backridge, is a total winner. As for my test gun? I am already searching for what I can sell to buy it outright. **GD**

FEDERAL CARTRIDGE VITAL OVERLAY* OF 30-INCH CIRCLE.

LOADS, BACKRIDGE 3 IN. MAG.	CHOKE	% IN CIRCLE	VITAL HITS
BACKRIDGE ITX	FULL	92	8
BACKRIDGE ITX	MOD	85	5
BACKRIDGE BISMUTH	FULL	96	7

*Overlay target is system that measured only the vitals of a large duck or small goose. In general, this represents the average hits on a passing duck at 35 to 40 yards.

DISTANCE: **40 yards**
ALTITUDE: **3,400 feet above sea level**
TEMPERATURE: **63 F**
WIND: **0 mph**
FIRING CONDITIONS: **Bench, shooting off bags.**
FOULING SHOTS PRIOR TO PATTERN TEST: **Three**

Editors from the NRA's *American Hunter* magazine worked with Remington designers to develop the Remington Model 700 American Hunter rifle in 6.5 Creedmoor.

REMINGTON MODEL 700
AMERICAN HUNTER

NRA editors and Remington designers collaborate to build a perfect rifle for hunting whitetail deer

❯BRYCE M. TOWSLEY

My only question was, "what took so long?"

It was after hours at the NRA Annual Meeting and I was sipping some amber amazement with Scott Olmsted, the editor in chief of the NRA's *American Hunter* magazine, in some forgotten bar. Scott had just told me about the rifle he and his staff were designing in conjunction with Remington.

"This is going to be a rifle designed by

Remington Model 700 American Hunter rifle in 6.5 Creedmoor. The muzzle of this barrel is threaded 5/8x24 to allow the easy installation of a suppressor or brake.

SHOOTING DATA COURTESY OF *AMERICAN HUNTER* MAGAZINE.

AMMO	WEIGHT (grains)	VELOCITY (fps)	GROUP SIZE (inches)		
			SMALLEST	AVG.	LARGEST
HORNADY SUPERFORMANCE	120	2,943	.89	1.02	1.10
BARNES VOR-TX LR LRX	127	2,741	.68	.87	.93
REMINGTON CORE-LOKT PSO	140	2,628	1.04	1.12	1.22

Range test results for three, three-shot groups at 100 yards. Sandbag rest.

hunters for hunters," Olmsted said.

That simple sentence sounds like a throw-away, but it's actually profound. Too many of the rifles hitting the market each year are designed by engineers or marketing people who don't hunt or shoot much. I know of one major company in the hunting world at which none of the top-level management hunts or shoots at all; they play golf. It's about time we had a rifle designed by the guys who are out there shivering in the cold, sweating in the sun, enduring the pain from hours of sitting still on stand or sucking air as they hike up a mountain so steep they slide back two steps for every three they take forward.

NRA's *American Hunter* is the largest hunting magazine in the world, with more than a million readers each month. As part of the job, the staff editors at *American Hunter* (full disclosure: I am a field editor for *American Hunter*) use and hunt with most all of the new guns that hit the market. They see the flaws in the designs, and they see what works. Remington is America's oldest firearms manufacturer and it makes the most popular bolt-action hunting rifle on earth, the Model 700. So, it made sense

to pair up and design a rifle.

The concept was a rifle designed for hunting the most popular big-game animal, the whitetail deer, but that would work equally well for a wide range of big game. The mythical "do-all" rifle does not exist, but this one comes close, while remaining true to the whitetail baseline.

Remington used this opportunity to launch some new manufacturing techniques that will mimic the way custom gun builders modify the 700 action to optimize performance. The action is the foundation of any rifle. If it's true and precise, the rifle will perform. Remington trues the action and the bolt lugs to a common center. These are steps taken by custom builders to make a 700 action perform best. The difference is that a custom builder will do it on a lathe, spending hours blueprinting the action, where Remington does it on a production level with CNC machines that do multiple actions at once. The bottom-line goal is the same: a precise and perfect action.

The bolt features an oversize bolt knob. Not one of those giant blobs as seen on a lot of precision rifles, but a nice, elegant, well-portioned knob that's

a good fit for a hunting rifle. The bolt is "jeweled" but in an odd, half-done way that I must admit is growing on me. I wasn't a fan at first, but the more I use the gun the more I appreciate that it's a good match with a hunting rifle as it is almost a camo look.

The heart of any rifle is the barrel. Remington uses a hammer forged, chrome-moly steel barrel with 5R rifling, which uses five grooves so that a groove opposes a land, rather than lands opposing lands. This is thought to create less bullet distortion and better accuracy. Also, the 5R style of rifling is designed with different, less radical radii in the corners to promote less fouling and easier cleaning.

The barrel is a moderately heavy contour measuring .731-inch at the muzzle behind the threads. It is fluted to cut weight a bit without sacrificing rigidity. Designers decided to go with a shorter 20-inch barrel, a concept that is seeing a lot of interest, particular with younger hunters. From a hunting standpoint this makes sense. A shorter barrel is much easier to use in a hunting blind. Anybody who has ever spooked a buck by hitting the blind wall with the rifle as they were trying

The logo of the NRA's *American Hunter* magazine is laser engraved on the surface of the floor plate.

to get it out the window probably has nightmares about long barrels. The shorter barrel is easier to use in thick brush and it's easier to carry. Many hunters who have used guns with long barrels have stuck the muzzle in the mud a time or two. With an overall length of just 39-3/8 inches, this gun is handy to use and carry. Weighing in at 6-3/4 pounds its light enough to carry all day hunting and just hefty enough to soak up the recoil so you can shoot it all day at the range.

Also, because the younger hunters are demanding it, the muzzle of this barrel is threaded 5/8x24 to allow the easy installation of a suppressor. Like it or not, the use of suppressors is growing in popularity with hunters. It protects the hunter's hearing and it helps keep game from pinpointing your location. I witnessed this a while ago while hunting in Texas for hogs. With our suppressed rifles, the hogs had trouble locating us and it resulted in more shooting opportunities. If you

don't want to use a suppressor or add a muzzle brake, the gun comes with a thread protector installed.

The rifle is, of course, chambered in 6.5 Creedmoor. I think it's a law these days that all new guns must be in that cartridge. No matter, it makes sense as this currently is the most popular hunting cartridge on the market. The 6.5 Creedmoor cartridge was spawned by long-range target shooting and is inherently accurate. This rifle has a 1:8-inch rifling twist rate that works well with the range of bullet weights that are appropriate for hunting or target shooting. I suspect that these rifles will see some offseason use smacking targets so far off that the steel will ring with a different accent.

The metal surfaces are finished in black Cerakote. This looks great and protects against wet weather. The composite stock is by Bell and Carlson, a company that has perfected the art of the synthetic rifle stock and is my first choice on the custom rifles I build. It uses a full-length aluminum bedding block and has the fore-end tip pressure on the barrel that has helped make Remington famous for out-of-the-box accuracy. There are sling swivel studs installed and a Pachmayr Decelerator

recoil pad fitted to the butt. The stock has a cheek piece and an open pistol grip that fits any hand, with or without gloves.

The magazine uses a hinged floor plate which has the *American Hunter* logo laser engraved on the surface. The magazine holds four cartridges.

The rifle features an enhanced version of the Remington X-Mark Pro adjustable trigger, factory set to break at 3.5 pounds. The receiver is drilled and tapped for the larger 8-40 screws, which is another upgrade found on custom rifles. The gun comes with Leupold Mark 4 scope bases, so all you need to mount a scope is rings. I fitted mine with Leupold rings and a Leupold VX-3i 3.5-10x40mm scope. This scope is designed for dial up and features a return to zero stop. The rifle shoots sub-MOA with hunting ammo and I feel confident in shooting out to any ethical range with this setup.

The rifle has a serial number starting with 19AH, indicating the year it was made and American Hunter. This is a limited-edition rifle with only 1,500 being made. Street price is running under $1,000 for this unique hunting rifle. But remember, supplies are limited. **GD**

REMINGTON MODEL 700 AMERICAN HUNTER SPECIFICATIONS

TYPE: **Bolt-action centerfire rifle**

CALIBER: **6.5 Creedmoor**

BARREL: **20 in.; cold-hammer-forged, chrome-moly steel; 5R rifling, 1:8-in. RH twist; 5/8x24 threaded muzzle. Protective cap included.**

MAGAZINE: **Internal box, hinged; 4-round capacity**

TRIGGER: **Single-stage, adjustable X-Mark Pro; 3.5-lb. advertised pull weight**

SAFETY: **Two-position toggle. Does not lock the bolt shut.**

SIGHTS: **Leupold Mark 4 bases installed**

STOCK: **Bell and Carlson composite; LOP 13.63-inches**

METAL FINISH: **Black Cerakote; jeweled bolt w/black oxide**

OVERALL LENGTH: **39-3/8 inches**

WEIGHT: **6-3/4 lbs.**

MSRP: **$1,349**

STREET PRICE: **Less than $1,000**

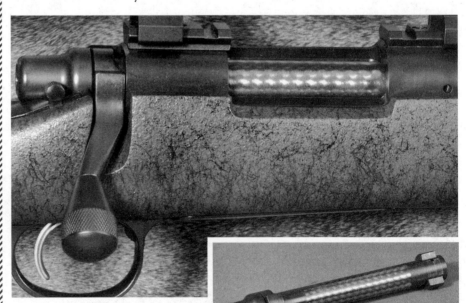

The Remington Model 700 American Hunter rifle in 6.5 Creedmoor has an oversize bolt handle and unique jeweling on the bolt.

The Remington Model Seven SS HS Precision rifle was designed with the hunter in mind, and is both attractive and versatile.

FAST & LIGHT
BY REMINGTON

Model Seven SS HS Precision

› **TOM TABOR**

I must admit I was slow in accepting the benefits associated with lightweight hunting rifles. Like many shooters, I assumed I would simply be trading a degree of my shooting accuracy in exchange for just a little less carrying burden. But after decades of facing long days afield, pursuing some of the most challenging species, often in the most difficult terrain, I decided to take a closer look at the concept and my views began to evolve. This change in attitude largely took shape on a Texas whitetail hunt where I used one of Remington's newest additions to its Model Seven lineup: the SS HS Precision.

THE RIFLE'S UNIQUE FEATURES

For the most part, the Remington Model Seven is a scaled down version of that company's time-proven and popular Model 700, with both rifles sharing a similar three-piece bolt design. This newest sub-model comes in a stainless steel construction with all of the metal surfaces glass-bead blasted to produce a satin matte finish. Its durable, weather-resistant synthetic H.S. Precision stock is flat black in color but attractively highlighted with spruce-green spider-web accents. Four cartridge choices are currently available,

The review of the Model Seven SS HS Precision .308 Winchester began on the bench prior to heading afield for a little hunting action.

including: 6.5 Creedmoor, 7mm-08 Remington, .243 Winchester and .308 Winchester, each having a four-cartridge fixed magazine.

Many shooters naturally view short, lightweight rifles as being primarily suited to long days afield, but I discovered they are equally at home inside the confines of a blind. Oftentimes space and free movement within a blind are severely limited, making the handling and use of longer rifles a bit clumsy. In this case, however, the short-barreled little Model Seven SS HS Precision, being only 39-1/4 inches long and weighing a mere 6 pounds, worked out perfectly for my Texas hunt.

For shooting accuracy, the rifle comes with its action aluminum bedded and equipped with the very desirable Remington X-Mark Pro trigger. The internal parts of this trigger are nickel plated to not only protect them from corrosion, but also to encourage a near frictionless environment. Typically, these triggers come from the factory set at a consistent 3-1/2 pounds, but they can easily be adjusted externally from 3 to 5 pounds.

A SHAKY BEGINNING FOR THE NEW RIFLE

Sometimes things don't move as smoothly as we all would prefer, and that was certainly the case of the first prototype Model Seven SS HS Precision

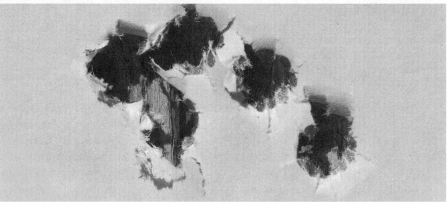

Five-shot, 100-yard groups like this one, measuring only around 1.25 inches, ended the author's concerns about accuracy.

rifles. Even though outwardly the rifle came out beautiful, when it came time to prove its worth on the rifle range those first prototypes lacked the level of accuracy company officials were looking for. The barrels on the prototypes were free-floating (no barrel-to-stock contact), which usually encourages a higher degree of accuracy, but that didn't prove to be the case in this situation. After considerable consultation within Remington and with stock manufacturer H.S. Precision, eventually a change in stock design was tried. In this case, the complete free-floated-barrel concept was abandoned in favor of modifying the stock mold to produce a small barrel-to-stock contact point near the end of the forearm. While that approach was initially questioned by some of the officials involved, the result was a very

favorable one, resulting in squeezing the groups down to very acceptable levels.

ON THE RANGE

For this review, I chose the popular deer-hunting caliber of .308 Winchester. And with a Leupold Vari-X III 3-9x scope mounted, I headed to the range. For both the range and the hunt to follow I shot the same ammunition, Barnes VOR-TX Premium Hunting ammo, which was loaded with 150-grain TTSX BT bullets. These Barnes solid-copper bullets are considered a premium hunting bullet and I have used them for many years. In that time, I have always found them to produce deep penetration, near perfect mushrooming and frequently retain 100 percent of their original weight.

It didn't take long on the range before

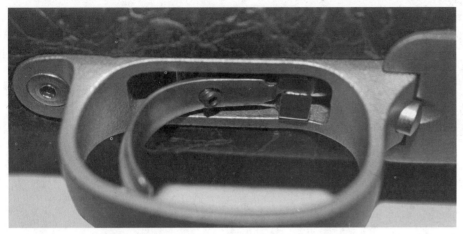

Remington's Model Seven SS HS Precision is equipped with the company's fine X-Mark Pro trigger, which can be easily adjustable externally, from 3 to 5 pounds pull weight, using the included tool.

The SS HS Precision's recessed target-style crown helps protect this vulnerable area from potential damage that could adversely affect the accuracy of the rifle.

I realized my little Model Seven SS HS Precision's accuracy was at least on par with most of my favorite larger and heavier hunting rifles. With groups consistently measuring around one inch at 100 yards, there was no doubt this rifle was clearly up to the task at hand.

IN THE FIELD

The game on the Texas ranch was completely free-range, with plenty of mature whitetail bucks to select from. My license allowed me to take one whitetail buck, one doe and as many feral hogs as I could find to shoot. On the days that followed, I put "brown on the ground" in the form of a trophy-quality eight-point buck and a fat doe for the freezer, each with a precisely placed shot to the lungs. When it came to hogs, however, I was only presented with a single opportunity for a shot. I suppose in that case you could say I put "black and white on the ground" with an unusually marked hog that became known as "Oreo" back at camp due to its contrasting white stripe around its belly. The result was three shots and three animals down.

THE WAY I SEE IT

While longer and heavier rifles certainly have a place in much of today's hunting, the scaled-down Remington Model Seven SS HS Precision certainly worked great on this occasion. Having an opportunity to use it both on the range as well as under actual hunting conditions gave me a perspective on its potential use and certainly opened my eyes to its advantages. I didn't encounter a single negative issue pertaining to its functionality or use. In my opinion, this is a well-constructed, accurate rifle that proved the benefits of light and short versus heavy and cumbersome. For an MSRP of $1,149, you currently have a selection of four calibers to choose from, all which are covered by a limited lifetime warranty. **GD**

The author's test rifle was responsible for taking this trophy whitetail buck, which fell to a single shot from the Model Seven SS HS Precision .308 Win.

A shot from the test rifle added this feral hog, affectionately called Oreo due to its coloration, to the author's Texas bag. Three shots, three clean kills. How could the rifle perform any better?

BACK TO BASICS:
RUGER'S WRANGLER

The Wrangler revolver is an everyday tool for outdoorsmen

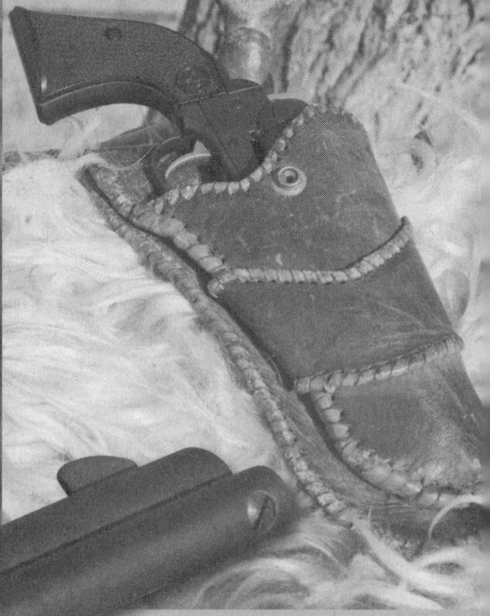

Ruger's Wrangler entry-level revolver is a robust and accurate handgun for those on a budget. Newer pistoleros should consider using the savings to buy ammo for practice.

› DAVE CAMPBELL

I've known a few cowboys in my time. These guys are not the pressed shirt and starched jeans over ostrich-skin boots types. No sir, I am referring to the man who wears a wrinkled chambray shirt, torn jeans that have patches on top of older patches with run-over boots and a sweat-stained hat. His hands have what seems to be a half-inch of rough calluses, and after you shake hands you wonder if he could file metal with them bare. He spends his days outdoors tending cows. His nights are an extension of his days. If he's lucky, he gets perhaps four or five hours under a leaky cabin roof to eat and sleep. Many nights are spent outside, regardless of the weather. And, if given an option, he'd certainly choose this life over steering a desk in a corner office at the corner of Wall and Broad streets.

His tools are as roughshod as he is. He rides a saddle with fenders so badly scratched from barbwire that it looks like hieroglyphics. The pistol he carries, at first look, probably dates back to the 19th century. Metal parts are gray, often with rust pits, and the stocks are smooth from wear, perhaps with a few chips. Cowboys like this, with rare exceptions, don't give a damn what a gun looks like. All they care is that it goes bang when they want it to and puts a hole in something. And, oh yeah, it doesn't cost them an arm and a leg to buy or shoot.

Ruger's Wrangler .22 LR, introduced in the spring of 2019, is made for these cowboys or anyone else interested in a rugged, dependable, entry-level sixgun. It provides the latest in single-action revolver technology without frills and dressing.

Bill Ruger kept alive what was thought to be a diminishing market for single-action revolvers when he introduced the Single-Six in 1953. Ruger was a brilliant engineer and designer, as well as being something of a renaissance man in terms of style. The Single-Six mimicked the lines of Colt's famous Single Action Army, but it was scaled to rimfire calibers. Ruger used coil springs instead of the flat springs of the Colt. Coil springs are far easier to make in quantity while maintaining quality and consistency. As most know now, Ruger pioneered the use of precision investment castings in the production of his guns. These qualities allowed Ruger to offer a well-made, accurate and rugged revolver at a competitive price point. The first Single-Sixes carried an MSRP of just $57 and change. Today, however, a new Single-Six carries an MSRP of $629. While it might be worth every penny, it's still a tough bite for a beginning pistolero or anyone on a tight budget.

The Wrangler steps up with an MSRP of $249, or about 40 percent the cost of a Single-Six. No, there's no spare cylinder in .22 WMR. To paraphrase Henry Ford, you can get any barrel length you want as long as it's 4-5/8 inches. The metal parts are not polished, they're Cerakoted, but you do get a choice of finish: black,

silver or burnt bronze. Its cylinder is finished in a black oxide. The only steel in the Wrangler is the barrel, cylinder and lockwork components. Those lockwork components, by the way, are metal injected molded. The frame and grip frame are investment-cast aluminum. Sights are fixed: a blade up front and a groove in the topstrap for a rear. Grips are composite, but the grip frame dimensions follow the XR-3, therefore aftermarket shoes should fit.

Arguably the best feature on this revolver, or any newer Ruger single action, is what Ruger calls its loading gate interlock. With the hammer down, open the loading gate. This lowers the cylinder-locking bolt and allows the cylinder to spin freely in either direction (very handy for topping off a cylinder when all the rounds have not been expended). In this condition, the hammer is prevented from moving. Conversely, if the hammer is cocked, the loading gate cannot be opened. Along with Ruger's transfer bar that prevents the hammer from touching the inertia-driven firing pin unless the trigger is fully pulled, these are among the safest of all single-action revolvers. You can carry it safely with all six rounds in the cylinder, and the only way it can discharge is to bring the hammer to full cock and press (and hold) the trigger completely.

The only issue I had was an occasional tie up of the lockwork when cocking the hammer. This was quickly solved with a few drops of gun oil in the cutouts on the side of the hammer and the loading gate pivot. It also helps to put a couple of drops of oil on the cylinder base pin. We have come far in

RUGER WRANGLER SPECIFICATIONS

TYPE: Single-action revolver

CALIBER: .22 LR

BARREL LENGTH: 4-5/8 inches

CAPACITY: Six rounds

TRIGGER: 5 pounds, 8 ounces

RIFLING: 1:14 RH

SIGHTS: Topstrap groove rear; fixed-blade front

SAFETY: Transfer bar and loading gate interlock

GRIPS: Black composite

OVERALL LENGTH: 10.25 inches

WEIGHT: 30 ounces

METAL FINISH: Cerakote; black oxide on cylinder

MSRP: $249

CONTACT: www.ruger.com

firearms design, but the damn things still need lubrication to function.

Something that gave me pause, but is probably not of any consequence in the grand scheme of things, is that the muzzle is not crowned. Muzzle crowns were done to protect the rifling at the muzzle and preserve accuracy. While the Wrangler certainly is no target pistol, it still has quite serviceable accuracy. As the table shows, I was able to wrangle 2-1/2 inches as an average at 25 yards. This kind of revolver is more likely to pot a rabbit at 10 to 15 yards or worry a tin can at the same distance.

Interestingly, the barrel-cylinder gap in my sample was a rather tight .0015-inch. I suspect that is to protect the aluminum frame from flame cutting, but if you are shooting some of the dirtier .22 LR ammo, plan on spraying that area after every 100 rounds or so, to wash away the gunk. I didn't have a problem with it, but someone who shoots this revolver a lot might find the gunk makes it a little tougher to cock and shoot.

No, Ruger's Wrangler is not a fine revolver with all the little tweaks to make it top of the line. It's a rough-and-tumble gun designed to punch holes in stuff reliably. In that regard, it's a winner. **GD**

SHOOTING RESULTS (25 YDS.)

.22 LR CARTRIDGE	VEL. @ 10 FT. (fps)	ENERGY (ft.-lbs.)	GROUP SIZE (inches)		
			SMALLEST	LARGEST	AVG.
WINCHESTER SUPER X 40-GR. HOLLOW POINT	946 AVG. 24 SD	93	1.775	2.75	2.21
CCI STANDARD VELOCITY 40-GR. LRN	894 AVG. 32 SD	71	2.625	3.25	3.08
CCI MINI MAG 40-GR. HOLLOW POINT	903 AVG. 22 SD	73	2.375	2.75	2.46
AVERAGE EXTREME SPREAD					2.58

Measured average velocity for 10 rounds from a 4 5/8-inch barrel. Range temperature: 30 F. Humidity: 49 percent. Accuracy for five-consecutive, five-shot groups at 25 yards from sandbags. Abbreviations: LRN (Lead Round Nose), SD (Standard Deviation).

The author reports the Henry Side Gate Lever Action Rifle handles like a good lever action should, springing naturally to the shoulder.

The Henry Side Gate Lever Action Rifle, with its brass receiver and nicely checkered American walnut stock and forearm, is an attractive lever action that handles and shoots very well.

HENRY'S
SIDE GATE
LEVER ACTION RIFLE

This replica of an Old-West icon is a real shooter

› SHANE JAHN

The lever-action rifle is uniquely American and "punchy" to boot. We see them as a connection to the Old West, where they were used in gun fights between lawmen and outlaws and on both sides of the Indian and bandit wars that tempered pioneers' steel. The lever action is equally at home in the heavily timbered hunting woods, where shots can be close and fast follow-ups a real necessity.

Henry (www.henryusa.com) started producing lever-action .22-caliber rifles in 1996. The growing business now offers multiple lever-action-rifle configurations in a variety of calibers, along with single shots, pumps and bolt actions. Henry even has shotguns in lever-action and single-shot models and an auto-loading survival rifle.

My first experience handling a Henry was a slick-actioned .22 rifle years ago and my personal Henry is chambered in .45-70 Government that is loaded from the magazine tube. I must admit, like many of you, I wondered why Henry only offered its lever guns with a tube-fed magazine. Well hold on, Henry's

customers asked for a side-loading rifle and the good folks there listened to those requests.

FIRST IMPRESSIONS

It was a cold winter day in west Texas when I stopped by Dodson Guns to pick up the test rifle, a model H024-3030, the Henry Side Gate Lever Action Rifle. Several of the local gun guys were gathered there to stay warm, catch up on the latest gossip and talk guns. I unboxed the Henry, opened the action and handed it to a well-known Big Bend cowboy and firearms aficionado. He admired the nicely checkered, dark, American walnut stock, polished brass receiver and smooth action. Another patron swaggered in, took hold of the lever action and gave his approval.

This new Henry is equipped with both the side-loading gate and the tube magazine. If you have the side gate, why do you need the magazine tube you ask? Simple, that makes the lever action much safer to unload. Instead of cycling the lever to eject loaded rounds you simply dump the magazine tube.

However, you need to pay close attention when unloading the rifle in this fashion. I found that the last round will be held in place by the cartridge rim, so when you dump your loaded rounds via the magazine tube while unloading, you will still have a live round in the magazine. Slightly opening the lever will release it and allow it to slide out of the tube. The folks at Henry aware of this and tell me they will likely be working on a fix to make that last cartridge slide out a bit more smoothly.

As with any gun, check it. Then check it again.

This rifle is chambered in the classic .30-30 Winchester and handles like a good lever action should, springing to your shoulder for fast shots and rapid follow-ups.

I did notice one imperfection in the test rifle that involved the rear sight. It is ever so slightly crooked, not in true line with the barrel. It appears that either the dovetail is cut a bit off-center or the base of the sight is not completely square, causing the rear sight to sit at an angle. I informed Henry and immediately received a phone call from Daniel Clayton-Luce, who took time from his busy schedule, while attending a hunting trade show, to contact me. He let me know the company stands behind its products with a lifetime guarantee for all customers and asked me to return the rifle ASAP so it could be re-barreled and quickly shipped back to me. That shows what a stand-up company Henry is, and this one flaw does not detract from a fine rifle in my mind. Sometimes imperfec-

LOAD VELOCITY (ADVERTISED)

		ACCURACY (60 YDS)
BUFFALO BORE HEAVY .30-30 WIN. 190 GR. JFN	2,100 FPS	0.75
BUFFALO BORE HEAVY .30-30 WIN. 150 GR. BARNES TSX	2,350 FPS	1.65
HORNADY LEVEREVOLUTION 160 GR. FTX	2,400 FPS	1.56
HORNADY AMERICAN WHITETAIL 150 GR. INTERLOCK	2,390 FPS	2.9
WINCHESTER DEER SEASON XP 150 GR.	2,390 FPS	1.95

tions are missed by quality control, that's life. The important thing is a good company will make it right and that is exactly what Henry is committed to do.

SKINNER SIGHTS

The semi-buckhorn rear sight supplied on the rifle is fine, but Andy Larsson, owner of Skinner Sights (www.skinnersights.com) sent me one of his excellent Black Gold Express rear sights for the Henry. This quality, American-made sight only added to a well-made rifle. I've always been fond of the "ghost-ring" style rear sight and shoot them comfortably. The ivory bead front sight that came on the rifle is quick to pick up and makes for fast sight acquisition. The Skinner sight is simple to install and comes with easy to follow instructions.

AT THE RANGE

The folks at Buffalo Bore, Winchester and Hornady supplied samples of their quality ammunition for the test.

At the range, I fired three shots with each load at 60 yards to get a feel for the overall accuracy of the rifle. The best group in this rifle came from Buffalo Bore's 190-grain load, measuring three-quarters of an inch. The others were acceptable for an open-sighted lever action averaging around 2 inches.

Things got a bit wider at 110 yards, with groups opening to 3.5 to 4 inches. I used blue industrial tape in an "X" pattern on white cardboard for my target. To me, the center of the 2-foot "X" gives a nice aiming point, especially with open sights. To put things in perspective as far as group sizes, the longer-distance groups can easily be covered by my hand.

The trigger scale I have access to only goes to 4.5 pounds and this rifle's trigger would not break within that limit. I would guess its trigger is 5 to 6 pounds. I

think a little trigger work by a competent gunsmith should cut these groups in half and I intend to test that theory soon. I'm told that the Henry's trigger components are really good, and a little extra work typically results in a safe, crisp 3.5- to 4-pound trigger pull. My statement is not to fault Henry. It's a fact that many stock guns from a variety of manufacturers can stand a tuned trigger.

After shooting from the bench, I took on the torso-shaped steel target off-hand at 60 yards and had no problem hitting it with rapid follow-ups. Out of curiosity, I shot an off-hand group at 25 yards after loading one round of each of the five loads supplied and was able to keep it in 3.5 inches, which is a fist-sized group.

As an afterthought, I decided to load the rifle via the magazine tube. This can be a little frustrating, as the cartridge rims can catch on the inner magazine tube as you slide them in. Good news, turning the inner tube while inserting it eventually works the cartridges into the tube. Better news, Federal and Henry recently collaborated on HammerDown ammunition that is specifically designed for lever actions. Along with other improvements, the rims are chamfered to ease loading in tube-fed rifles. This new ammo was not yet available for testing.

This rifle retails at the suggested price of $1,045. I gauge most gun prices off Gunbroker.com and it can be found there in the $850- to $900-range.

Henry Repeating Arms donates firearms and money to a variety of causes, including recognizing heroes, supporting the 2nd Amendment and caring for sick children. It is a consumer-oriented company that listens to its customers, provides quality firearms, great customer service, and the guns are made right here in the U.S.A. That's hard to beat. GD

All brands of ammunition tested in the Henry gave adequate results, but this rifle really liked Buffalo Bore's 190-grain JFN. This group measured three-quarters of an inch.

CLASSIC, CLASSY AND DEADLY

A beautiful Ruger No. 1, in .280 Ackley Improved, shoots even better than it looks

› LARRY WEISHUHN

"She was sleek and fun to handle." Words to the old George Jones song fleeted through my mind when Lee Newton handed me a Ruger No. 1, Joe Clayton Classic, chambered in Joe's favorite round, the .280 Ackley Improved. I was totally smitten. Love at first sight!

When Sturm, Ruger initially released the classy single-shot Ruger No. 1 rifle in 1967, I was in college at Texas A&M University studying wildlife science. Ads for the Farquharson-style, internal hammer, falling-block action showed a truly classic and sleek looking rifle, one of blued steel and finely figured walnut. I dreamed of owning and hunting with a Ruger No. 1. Alas, dreaming was all I could do. Every cent my wife and I garnered was destined for rent, food, college tuition and books. After all, I already had hunting guns; a .30-30 Winchester, a single-shot .22 rimfire,

The author with an ancient desert mule deer taken in the Trans Pecos area of Texas while hunting with Greg Simons with Wildlife Systems, and a Ruger No. 1, Joe D. Clayton limited edition in .280 Ackley Improved, topped with a Trijicon 4-16x50 AccuPoint scope, shooting Hornady's 162-grain ELD-X Precision Hunter.

The author's Ruger No. 1 JDC with Trijicon scope. Notice the quality of the wood.

a single-shot 12-gauge and .357 Mag Ruger Blackhawk. Still, I could dream.

In time, life changed, and I bought my first Ruger No. 1 Tropical in .375 H&H Mag to someday take to Africa. The die was cast. I would always be a fan of the Ruger single shot.

In my gun safe today are numerous Ruger No. 1s, chambered from .450-400 NE 3-inch to .257 Roberts. Over the years, I have had numerous favorite No. 1s, depending whether I hunted Africa for dangerous game, or other big-game species. Quality of wood and accuracy played heavily into my "favorite" equation. I dearly love and appreciate "pretty" wood stocks. However, I am a bit of an accuracy freak. Beauty and accuracy are two requirements I insist upon when it comes to my hunting guns.

Enter Lee Newton, friend and president of the Ruger Owners & Collectors Society, today's quintessential authority on Ruger No. 1s. "I'm working on a project," said Lee while I was at his Classic Sporting Arms (www.classicsportingarms.com) buying a No. 1 RSI chambered in .375 Ruger. "You know Joe Clayton, wrote the book on Ruger No. 1s. Working on a No. 1 to honor Joe and his favorite round, the .280 Ackley Improved." I had indeed known Joe for years as collector of Ruger No. 1s, hunter and friend. I loved Lee's new project. Clayton's *Ruger No. 1* was edited by John T. Amber (longtime editor of *Gun Digest*), published by Blacksmith Corporation and released in 1983. A collector's item, hardback editions demand, today, as much as

$950 per copy.

In the Introduction of *Ruger No. 1* Amber wrote, "Prejudiced as I am in favor of single-shot rifles, I hope this comprehensive treatment of the Ruger No. 1 will induce the reader to acquire and use the single-shot rifle, to accept the challenge that such rifles offer the discerning, knowledgeable individual, whether collector, shooter or hunter."

The book and the Ruger No. 1s had done just that for me, and many others.

Over the years, I hunted dangerous game in Africa with No. 1s chambered in.450-400 NE 3-inch and .405 Winchester, as well as plains game with my .300 H&H Mag. and .275 Rigby. I also used the latter on ibex and roe deer in Spain. Back home in North America, I hunted numerous species with Ruger No. 1s chambered in .257 Roberts, .270 Win., .275 Rigby, .280 Win., .300 Win. Mag., .300 H&H Mag., .300 PRC, .375 H&H Mag., .375 Ruger, .405 Win. and .450-400 NE 3-inch. Moving forward…

A mature whitetail and a Ruger No. 1, .280 Ackley Improved, taken by Joe D. Clayton, after whom the special-edition Ruger No. 1 JDC was named. The .280 Ackley Improved has long been Joe's favorite hunting round.

The Joe Clayton Classic Ruger No. 1 was released in October 2019. I was on my way home for a whitetail hunt in the Texas Panhandle using a Ruger No. 1 in .300 PRC when I spoke with Lee Newton on the phone. "Just got the first JDC Classic No. 1s." he said. "They've got 1-A, 25-inch barrels with an 8.5-inch twist rate. Joe, Tom (Hutton, Lee's brother-in-law) and I have chosen our rifles. If you stop by on your way home, you'll get choice number four. Some of the prettiest wood I've ever seen on any guns." I told Lee I would be there by six o'clock.

At his doorstep, Lee handed me a No. 1, indeed stocked with the most attractive wood I had ever seen. "Not suggesting you choose this one, but it'll likely be in the running." He continued, "We graded the wood. All are exceptional but some are indescribable. We've put aside eight of those for you to look at. If you don't like any of those, we'll look farther."

Lee explained the JDC Classic was limited to 125 rifles. Wood, not serial number, would determine my choice. I knew the third rifle I looked at was the one I wanted even though I looked at the other seven. It was the same one Lee initially handed me. Words could

not define the beauty of the wood, both buttstock and fore-end. "This one!" I said, showing the rifle to Joe, then Tom. Both nodded their approval as did Lee. Serial number JDC 120 it was! Moments later I filled out paperwork. Lee called in the information. I was approved for purchase and wrote Classics Sporting Arms a check.

Late that night, I woke my wife to show her my latest Ruger No. 1

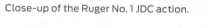

Close-up of the Ruger No. 1 JDC action.

acquisition. She, like me, appreciates finely figured wood and blued steel. Her smile showed her approval.

The following morning, I bought three boxes of .280 Ackley Improved, Hornady Precision Hunter, 162-grain ELD-X. Back home I removed the Trijicon AccuPoint 4-16x50 scope from my .300 PRC No. 1 (only one of two I am aware of) and mounted it on my .280 Ackley Improved.

That afternoon, I headed to my range. After bore-sighting and one shot at 25-yards, I shot the 100-yard target. My first two shots struck the target 2 inches high and 2 inches to the left. I made adjustments, 2-MOA right, 1/2-MOA down. Such a sight-in of 1 1/2-inches high at 100 yards should put my shots essentially dead-on at 200 yards (two shots confirmed this) and 7 inches low at 300 yards.

I love the challenge of getting as close as possible to game before pulling the trigger. I shoot long range at steel at ranges out to 1,000 yards and beyond to gain confidence in my ability with a rifle/scope/ammo combination, and it is fun. Then, when I stalk to within 200 yards or less of the animal, I can precisely place my bullet in the vitals. The challenge of getting close, to me, out-weighs shooting animals at long range.

The author selected his Ruger No. 1, serial number JDC - 120, based on the quality of the wood, but also with the help of both Joe Clayton and Lee Newton.

Sighted in 1 1/2-inches high at 100 yards, I was ready for desert mule deer with Wildlife Systems and whitetails with Bar None Hunts. I planned to use a mouth-blown Burnham Brothers Jack Rabbit in Distress call to entice mule deer to within 100 yards, and, to rattle in my whitetail to less than 50 yards. Coyotes were a different matter, fair game at any distance.

Before leaving the range, I shot three-shot groups at 100 and 200 yards with Hornady's Precision Hunter from my shooting sticks, as I would likely do when hunting. All three shots at both distances grouped 2 inches or less.

As a "hunting writer" for many years, I have had the opportunity to shoot a fair number of hunting guns, calibers, rounds and ammo at the range and hunting a wide variety of big game on six different continents. As a wildlife biologist, I have shot lots of deer and similar-sized animals for research purposes. Nearly every animal I have taken, as well as those taken by hunting partners, I personally have eviscerated to determine shot placement and terminal bullet performance. On deer and other game up to 1,000 pounds, Hornady's ELD-X bullets are, in my opinion, the deadliest I have ever used.

Years ago, I might have considered customizing a load for my .280 Ackley Improved. Frankly, with the precise accuracy and terminal performance of the commercially available Hornady Precision Hunter 162-grain ELD-X load, I do not think I could improve upon the commercial ammo.

I have long been a fan of 7mm, .284, rounds, particularly the 7x57 and .280 Remington. Only on occasion have I shot or hunted with the 7mm Magnums. Interestingly, with several custom loads, the .280 Ackley Improved duplicates the ballistics of a 7mm Rem. Mag. using the same bullets and does so with essentially 10-percent less propellant.

As most know, the .280 Ackley Improved was developed by P.O. Ackley. The round started as the 7mm-06 Improved, essentially a .30-06 Springfield case necked down to .284 and fire-formed to have less case taper,

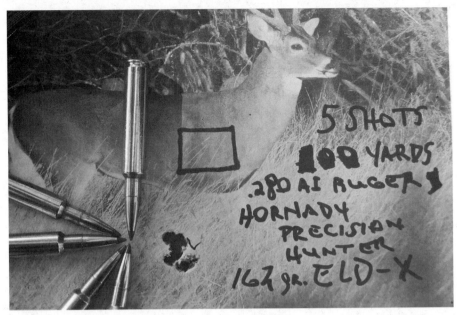

The author's five-shot group at 100 yards, with a Ruger No. 1 JDC, .280 Ackley Improved, Trijicon AccuPoint scope, shooting Hornady's 162-grain ELD-X Precision Hunter.

The author's three-shot group at 200 yards, two in nearly the same hole, and one the author pulled slightly high.

but with a 40-degree shoulder angle. R.C.B.S.'s Fred Huntington improved the case's configuration to a minimal body taper and changed the shoulder angle to 35 degrees. Huntington called his creation the .280 RCBS. Ackley then took that case and changed the shoulder angle back to 40 degrees, creating the .280 Ackley Improved as we know it today. In 2007, Nosler registered the .280 Ackley Improved with Sporting Arms and Ammunition Manufacturers' Institute (SAAMI) and started

producing factory ammo, the only Ackley Improved round ever approved by SAAMI.

My first hunting experience with the .280 Ackley Improved occurred in northern Mexico when I borrowed a friend's to shoot a nice whitetail. In South Africa during 1997, I used a custom rifle on a gemsbok. I was impressed and longed to own a rifle chambered for the round.

I finally got my own .280 Ackley Improved late October 2019, the fancy-wood-stocked Ruger No. 1 JDC Classic purchased from Lee Newton's Classic Sporting Arms. Lee asked if I was going to take mine hunting. He knew the answer. Indeed, I would. The wood might be the most beautiful I have ever seen, but the No. 1 is a hunting gun no matter how handsome!

The first hunting opportunity with my Ruger No. 1 Joe Clayton Classic occurred in the Trans Pecos of Texas with Greg Simons and his Wildlife Systems (www.wildlifesystems. com) for desert mule deer. Earlier in the year, I had taken a 17 1/2-inch pronghorn with my Ruger No. 1 (1A) .280 Remington topped with the same Trijicon AccuPoint scope (now on the Ackley Improved) and shooting Hornady Precision Hunter, 150-grain ELD-X ammo.

First afternoon in mule deer camp, we saw several impressive young bucks.

We were looking for a mature 2x2 or 3x3. Second morning as we headed to a distant ridge, we spooked a coyote. "Three hundred five yards!" said Greg looking through his Swarovski rangefinder binocular. I settled into a comfortable shooting position then held 7-inches above where I wanted the bullet to strike. I allowed a half-minute of left-to-right wind, then gently pulled the trigger. The bullet struck the coyote squarely in the shoulder.

Following morning after the fog lifted, I shot a second coyote, this one 200-yards distant. It too, dropped in its tracks. Mature management bucks continued to elude us.

With an hour remaining last afternoon, we spotted a mature buck with three points on one side and two on the other, plus brow tines. After a quarter-mile stalk, I set up the shooting sticks and prepared for a 125-yard

shot. The buck quartered toward me. The Trijicon's crosshairs settled on the front of the buck's shoulder. I gently pulled the trigger. At the shot, the buck jumped forward and disappeared behind underbrush.

While I watched, Greg walked to where the buck was last seen, then waved me forward. The ancient buck was down. Hearty congratulations followed. I loved my No. 1 JDC Classic .280 Ackley Improved.

A week later, I hunted the Bar None Ranch (www.barnonehunts.com), west of San Angelo, Texas. My gorgeously wood-stocked Ruger No. 1, .280 Ackley Improved, definitely now my favorite rifle, was the perfect rifle for the special hunt.

First evening in camp, Bar None's Tuffy Wood, Justin Wegner (my *DSC's Trailing the Hunter's Moon* cameraman) and I spotted a huge buck. Unfortunately, he was over 1,000 yards

The author's Ruger No. 1 JDC on Joe D. Clayton's classic book on the Ruger No. 1.

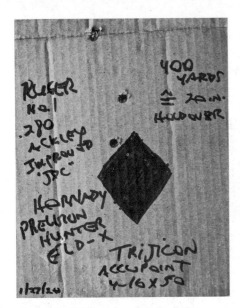

Shooting at 400 yards, using Hornady Precision Hunter, the author used a hold-over of approximately 20 inches to shoot this three-shot group.

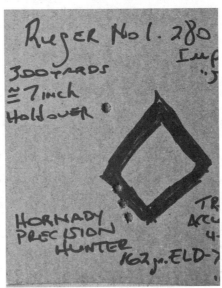

The author held over approximately 7 inches to shoot this group at 300 yards. After pulling the first shot, he settled down and shot a tight three-shot group.

A .280 Ackley Improved cartridge going into the chamber.

away, quickly disappearing into thick stands of mesquite. The next days we hunted hard and walked many miles. We spent hours each day rattling. Every time Tuffy (the ranch's foreman and hunt manager) hit rattling horns together, bucks responded; young bucks, good bucks and mature bucks with broken antlers, but not the monster we were looking for.

Last afternoon, less than an hour remaining, we rattled in four bucks at the same time. A tall-tined buck appeared on a distant ridge. He came charging in. I waited for him to stop, at 12 yards, then pulled the trigger. My favorite hunting rifle dropped the tall 7-year old, 9-point in his tracks!

I am proud to report my mule deer was the fifth animal taken with the Joe Clayton Classic .280 Ackley Improved Ruger No 1. As it should be, Clayton shot the first two taken with his namesake rifle, one an extremely handsome 10-point Texas whitetail. Third and fourth animals were taken appropriately by Lee Newton, who was responsible for the special edition No. 1. One of those bucks was a monstrous mid-180s Boone & Crockett, free-range Texas whitetail. Proper rifle for such an impressive buck.

Back home after hunting seasons closed, I had the opportunity to spend range time seriously shooting my Joe Clayton Classic No. 1. I used the same Hornady 162-grain ELD-X Precision Hunter ammo I had hunted with and the same Trijicon AccuPoint scope. Temperature was 62 degrees and no wind, perfect conditions. At 100 yards, my first shot was a little low and to the left. I started to make adjustments, but decided to shoot a five-shot group. My second shot barely increased the size of the first hole. I shot three more, waiting about five minutes between shots. All five created one .75-inch connected hole, measured outside to outside. I was impressed. I then adjusted the scope so I should be dead-on at 200 yards.

I shot three times at the 200-yard target. The first two, nearly in the center, measured 3/8-inch outside to outside. I pulled the third shot upward and called it as such. It hit 1 3/8-inches above the other two, still a 1 6/8-inch group.

Next up, 300 yards. To duplicate hasty shots at distant game, I held over what should be 7 inches above the center of the target. I pulled the first shot, so decided to shoot three more times at 300. They were one to one-half inches to the left, and from one-fourth to three-fourths of dead center. The outside-to-outside measurement of the group was 1 2/8 inches. Now I was really impressed!

At 400-yards, I knew the bullet, dead-on at 200 yards, should drop essentially 20 inches. Again, I decided to hold over rather than make a turret adjustment. My first shot hit the target 5/8-inch left and 1-inch high of dead center. My second shot struck the target 2 1/2 inches high of dead center. The third shot with a warm-to-the-touch barrel hit the target essentially 4 inches high and a half inch of dead center, a 3 1/2-inch group.

After shooting those groups, I wanted "to blow the smoke out of the end of the barrel" and put my rifle away quickly and act like I shot that way all the time!

This coming year, I have hunts planned in Spain for ibex, mule deer and pronghorn in Texas and whitetails from near Mexico to Canada. Want to guess which rifle I am going to be using? You got it. The .280 Ackley Improved, Ruger No. 1, Joe Clayton Classic, serial number JDC 120! Classy and deadly! ⊕

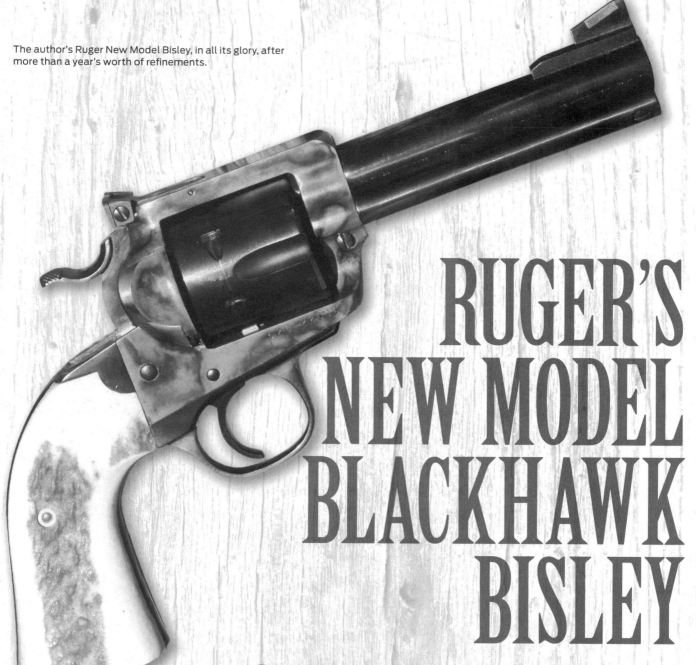

The author's Ruger New Model Bisley, in all its glory, after more than a year's worth of refinements.

RUGER'S NEW MODEL BLACKHAWK BISLEY

Making a good gun better

›**RICK HACKER**

S amuel Clemens (a.k.a. Mark Twain) once said, "Continuous improvement is better than delayed perfection." My particular "enhanced" Ruger Bisley is a prime example of this axiom, but to see how this gun got to be what it is, it might help to know where it came from, and, of course, it all started with the late William Batterman Ruger.

Bill Ruger was not one to rest on his laurels, mainly the resounding success of his seven-eighths scale, vastly improved .22-version of the Single Action Army, a gun that had been discontinued by Colt and had subsequently left a void in the shooting world. Ruger's Single Six admirably filled that void when it was introduced in 1953.

However, two years later, no doubt spurred on by the knowledge that, motivated by the burgeoning TV Western craze, Colt was planning to reintroduce its famed SAA, Ruger brought out his own version of the Peacemaker. But the sixgun Bill Ruger created was nothing like any single-action revolver that had come before it. Introduced in August 1955 (ironically, the same year Colt reintroduced its

Single Action Army), the new Ruger Blackhawk, named by classic motorcar collector Ruger after the racy Stutz roadster of the 1920s, was somewhat akin to the older and rarer pre-war Colt flattop. Only it wasn't.

With a noticeably thick 4140 chrome molybdenum steel top strap and frame, a one-piece cast aluminum trigger guard and backstrap, two-piece black checkered Butapreme grips (changed to walnut in 1960), 4 5/8-inch barrel, and a Micro click-adjustable rear sight teamed with a Baughman-style ramp front sight, the Blackhawk, true to its name, was anodized in black. Internally, Ruger's full-sized sixgun sported a spring-loaded, frame-mounted firing pin rather than a fixed firing pin, and a practically unbreakable coil mainspring, doing away with the somewhat fragile flat mainspring of the Colt. But the crowning glory for the new Ruger Blackhawk was that it was chambered for the powerful .357 Magnum, the most popular pistol cartridge in America at the time.

Over the years, Ruger continued to improve upon his ever-popular Blackhawk. In 1962, what had become known as the Flat Top was recontoured to incorporate protective "ears" on

either side of the rear sight. By that time, the frame had also been slightly enlarged and fitted with a non-fluted cylinder to better handle a newer .44 Magnum version. But the most significant change occurred in 1973, when Ruger revamped the Blackhawk, as well as the rest of its single-action lineup, to eliminate the half-cock notch. Instead, a revolutionary new transfer-bar safety design permitted the Ruger single-action revolver to be safety carried with a full payload of six rounds in the cylinder. To load these New Models, as they were called, the loading gate was flipped open, which freed the cylinder, allowing it to rotate for loading.

But true to Twain's words, Ruger wasn't finished looking for new ways to improve his Blackhawk design. While the Super Blackhawk was a beefier attempt to adapt his single action to the .44 Magnum (although most shooters ended up resorting to .44 Specials during extended range sessions in order to be spared the punishing recoil), Ruger once again looked to the Colt single action as inspiration for the next Blackhawk evolution: the Bisley.

Back in 1894, flush with the success of their Single Action Army, Colt

designers came out with a target version of their Peacemaker, which they dubbed the Bisley, after the famous English shooting range where Britain's international matches were held annually. Visually distinctive from the SAA, the Colt Bisley featured a slightly swept-under grip that enabled the gun to "hang" more naturally in the hand. In addition, the trigger guard was enlarged and encompassed a wide, curved and elongated trigger, which provided more surface area for better let-off control. Another Bisley characteristic was the hammer spur, which was lowered and given a graceful contour to bring it closer to the thumb to facilitate easier cocking. In 1985, Bill Ruger incorporated all of these features on his new Bisley, introduced in both Single Six and Blackhawk configurations.

I immediately gravitated toward the Ruger New Model Blackhawk Bisley, which was offered in .357 Magnum, .41 Magnum, .44 Magnum and .45 Colt. I ended up testing the Bisley in .45 Colt and .44 Magnum, which I wrote about and then returned to the factory. After all, I already had more than a few Peacemakers in .45 Colt and, frankly, the shape of the .44 Magnum's Bisley-styled backstrap was punishing to my medium-sized hands when firing .44 Magnum loads. But I found the gun to be quite pleasant when stoked with .44 Specials. If only Ruger would chamber its Bisley in that great Elmer Keith favorite, that would be the perfect gun, I wistfully thought.

In 2009, my wish was granted. That year, at the industry's Shooting, Hunting, Outdoor Trade (SHOT) Show, Jason Cloessner, vice president and product development manager of Lipsey's, one of Ruger's largest Distributors, showed me a limited run his company was launching of the Ruger Blackhawk Bisley chambered in .44 Special and built on Ruger's midsized XR-3 frame. It was one of those "I gotta have it" moments. I bought my Lipsey's .44 Special test gun. This version subsequently proved to be so popular it became a part of the regular Ruger line. Built on the original

Power Custom's Ruger Power Hammer & Trigger kits, which enable a New Model to be loaded via a traditional half cock, and Hamilton Bowen's Ruger Rough Country Rear Sight, with a white outline notch, give the author's Bisley individuality, as does the Turnbull case-colored frame.

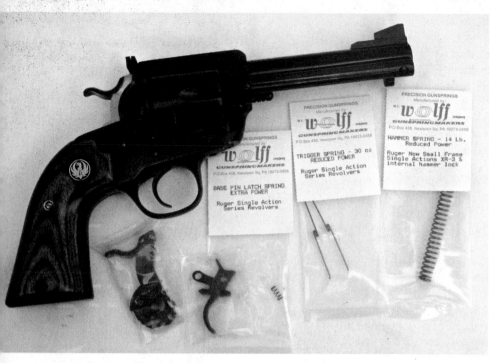

The author's stock Lipsey's .44 Special Bisley, before the makeover, is shown with the Wolff springs and Power Custom Ruger Power Hammer & Trigger kit that helped turn it into a "perfect" single action.

.357 Magnum frame and accented with laminated rosewood grips, it was a handsome six-shooter indeed. But even after putting a few hundred rounds through it, I realized something was missing – for me, at least.

For one thing, the action was a little bit rougher than I would have liked. For another, my aging eyes were having a tough time properly settling the all-black front sight into the all-black rear sight notch. And even though I was able to get some respectable 2 1/2-inch groups at 25 yards, I felt the gun could do better (my own shooting shortcomings notwithstanding, of course). Plus, like many of us who have reached "a certain age," after so many decades of shooting a Colt single action, muscle memory still tripped me up occasionally when trying to load my New Model Ruger SA, as I attempted to put the hammer on half cock, which, of course, didn't exist.

My first step to remedy these little hiccups was to order a Wolff 30-ounce reduced power trigger spring, a Wolff 14-pound reduced power hammer spring and a Wolff extra power pin latch spring from John Andrews of Wolff Gunsprings (www.gunsprings.com). The

hammer and trigger springs were to help smooth out the cocking and trigger pull of the Bisley Blackhawk, and the extra

power pin latch spring was an added bit of insurance against the cylinder base pin moving forward in the frame when shooting pumped-up loads – a phenomena I had already experienced with a few other single actions.

To solve my half-cock issue, I contacted Randall Power at Power Custom, which has since changed its name to Grand Masters LLC (www. powercustom.com), and ordered one of his Ruger Power Hammer & Trigger kits, which enables a New Model to either be loaded in the New Model's gate-open manner, or can actually be put on a traditional half cock for loading, thus giving me the best of both worlds. I made sure to state that this kit was for a Ruger Bisley, as other New Model trigger and hammer kits were available.

It should be noted that these kits normally come with the required Wolff springs, but as they were out of stock (as were Midway and Brownells, at the time) I ordered the springs separately from Wolff. I should also mention that, as the instructions state,

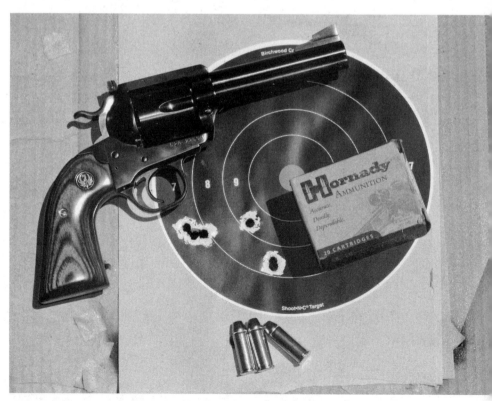

Out of the box, the Lipsey's Bisley performed well, but the author felt it could do better with a little tweaking.

"Due to manufacturing tolerances, gunsmithing is required for correct timing…" In fact, in my opinion, gunsmithing is required for the entire installation. So, inasmuch as the only tool I use on a regular basis is a corkscrew, I began a search for a competent, reliable and trustworthy gunsmith who not only knew guns, but also knew Rugers.

Through a lot of Internet sleuthing and receiving a number of recommendations, I ended up choosing an under-the-radar guy in La Grange, Ohio, named Andy Horvath, who had done some very satisfactory work for me before on a Colt Detective Special, but never on a Ruger. Yet, I found out, that was one of his specialties. However, Andy does not have a website and doesn't believe in email (did I mention he was under the radar?). Thus, the only way to contact him is by phone, which he thankfully does have: (440) 458-4369.

I dutifully overnighted the Ruger, Wolff springs and Grand Masters hammer and trigger kit to Andy, and I'd like to report things went smoothly, but unfortunately,

The Colt Bisley was the inspiration that motivated Bill Ruger to create the New Model Blackhawk Bisley.

that wasn't the case. Even for a skilled gunsmith like Andy, it took a couple of tries to get things right, noting to me that the Grand Masters replacement hammer had slightly different dimensions than the factory Bisley hammer, which complicated things. In the process of getting everything to function correctly, Andy also installed a reverse pawl, which permitted the cylinder to spin either clockwise or counter-clockwise for loading, an ultra-convenient feature.

Then there was the matter of the sights. To solve this problem, I first had Andy install a thick brass insert on the front sight ramp (gold was too expensive), as the look it provided somehow made me think of Alaska, and I was now seriously thinking of packing this Bisley as a camp gun on my next big-game hunt. For the other end of my sighting problem, I turned to the legendary expertise of Hamilton S. Bowen and his Bowen Classic Arms Corporation (www.bowenclassicarms.com) and ordered his Ruger Rough Country Rear Sight with a square white outline notch, a rugged and easy-to-see product that can't get knocked out of whack.

With all these parts installed, I then had Andy tune and time the action, polish the forcing cone and cylinder chambers, re-crown the barrel, and adjust the trigger pull to a crisp 2 1/2 pounds. But I wasn't quite finished yet. With the Bisley now functioning smoothly, it had to look the part. So I sent it to Doug Turnbull at Turnbull Restoration (www.turnbullrestoration.

com) to caseharden the frame. From there it went to Raj Singh at Art Jewel (www.eaglegrips.com) to be custom-fitted with a pair of elk-horn grips, which, besides being distinctive, stay anchored in the hand much better than the laminated rosewood, especially in times of stress when you have sweaty paws.

At last my Bisley had achieved perfection. Or had it? The only way to find out was to give it a baptism of fire. So I took it to Gunsite Academy in Paulden, Arizona, (www.gunsite.com), an internationally acclaimed, privately run firearms training facility for law enforcement, military and civilians who wish to become more proficient with their firearms. I had taken Gunsite's basic 250 self-defense pistol course numerous times, but always with either a 1911 or a double-action revolver, never with a single action. As you might imagine, my tricked-out Ruger Bisley received admiring glances from my fellow shooters, and, after three days and 350 rounds of Black Hills and Hornady .44 Special factory loads, the gun proved it could shoot, too.

Although it had taken me more than a year and I had spent far more than the original cost of the gun, I now had, in Mark Twain's words, the end result of "continuous improvement." But had I finally achieved perfection? All of which got me to thinking how a brass backstrap and trigger guard might offset those elk horn grips, and then, perhaps a little engraving…. GD

The Micro rear sight on the factory Bisley was somewhat fragile, in the author's opinion, and difficult to see with his aging eyes.

A quick flick of the wrist in a well-polished .458 is all that is required to chamber a new round.

After more than 35 years of unfailing performance, Old Ugly is the author's favorite rifle.

OLD UGLY

Three decades with a deadly serious rifle

›PHIL SHOEMAKER

American frontier icon Davy Crockett referred to his 42-bore flintlock long rifle as "Ole Betsy." Famous Western frontiersman, trapper and scout William "Buffalo Bill" Cody named his .50-70 Allin conversion "trapdoor" Springfield buffalo rifle "Lucretia Borgia." Hal Waugh, Alaska's first Master hunting guide, named his favorite brown-bear rifle, a Winchester M-70 re-chambered to .375 Weatherby, "Big Nan."

Having hunted around the globe and guided Alaskan hunters for well over four decades, I have grown attached to a fair number of rifles, but have never been much for naming inanimate objects. However, my all-time favorite .458 Winchester Magnum backup rifle, "Old Ugly," acquired a name by default. I doubt there has been a single season over the past four decades that at least one of my visiting hunters

hasn't felt obligated to comment disparagingly on its lack of aesthetics. The normal scenario happens just after they have proudly shown me their shiny new, high-dollar custom rifle, of which they are inordinately proud. Naively assuming such discerning connoisseurs of fine armament will recognize and appreciate real virtue, I haul out my favorite rifle; the one that their life might ultimately depend on. Thirty-seven years of use have honed its action to the consistency of polished ice. And, flicking open its bolt, I'll offer the rifle for their inspection.

I have learned to anticipate their reaction. It is usually as if I was offering them a dismembered body part from a leper colony. Recoiling in disgust, their inevitable comment is "That's ugly!" There have only been a handful of hunters who have actually taken it from me for even a polite, cursory look.

Webster defines ugly as "unpleasing to look at; aesthetically offensive." Over the years, I have grown quite fond of the rifle and personally find it rather attractive in a utilitarian sort of way. Beauty is as beauty does, they say. Webster also defines ugly as "threatening or ominous" and to my mind that describes it perfectly. It is intended to be threatening and ominous.

I began assembling Old Ugly in 1984 after a seriously close escapade with a vindictive brown bear that had been previously wounded by a client. I had been happy with my .30-'06 Springfield and 200-grain Nosler partition bullets, but, at my wife's insistence, decided a bit more persuasion could be comforting if I planned on dealing with many more wounded brown bears.

Since my new backup rifle was to be a working gun, I saw no reason to compromise reliability for aesthetics. Delicate elegance can be a fragile and costly extravagance in tools, as well as in friends. Like the weapons I had used in Vietnam, my rifle was built strictly for "go," not for show, and its sole purpose was to protect me, and my clients, from oversized brown bears.

I described its inception and construction in an article in the September-October 1985, issue number 101, of *Rifle* magazine. A few years later, I did a follow-up piece in the July 2003 issue. Over the years I made a few minor changes and modifications, like a filed-in thumb cut to speed reloading and Picatinny fore-end rail for a Surefire light, but my original concept has proved sound. The rifle weighs 9.25 pounds fully loaded and has been carried thousands of miles and used to stop four decades worth of irate, wounded brown bears. It has earned my trust and sits beside the door of our hunting lodge. Day or night, it is the one I grab when things look serious.

I chose the Mk X action due to the Mauser Model 98's well-earned reputation for durability and reliability. Polished and honed by years of use, the fat, wicked little .458 rounds positively slither into the chamber. When I push the two-position safety forward and mash back on the 5-pound trigger pull,

Clearly Accurate

Penetration difference in damp magazines between the .404 Jeffery with 400-grain Swift A-Frame and 500-grain Hornady in the .458 Win. The .404 was stopped on this page at 17 inches, and the .458 continued to penetrate 24 inches.

I can count on ignition. I have come to appreciate a slightly heavier, crisp trigger pull on larger caliber rifles. They typically weigh more and require a firmer grip when firing and, when under stress, one never notices a couple extra pounds of pull. As a long-time, double-action revolver shooter, I am used to steadily applying trigger pressure until the gun discharges. I also feel a heavier pull offers a bit more safety.

The two-position safety was another feature I added. The Yugoslavian built Mk X comes with a solid, reliable steel trigger and a sliding safety on the right side that blocks only the trigger. I much prefer a rugged shroud-mounted safety that blocks the striker and firing pin. The original military flag safety that swings over 180 degrees does that but is incompatible with scopes. I initially installed a low, flag-style safety

The author took Old Ugly to Zimbabwe for a Cape buffalo hunt for his 70th birthday present from his son. Cape buffalo are no larger than big brown bears.

Beauty and the Beast. Old Ugly lying on the fall tundra.

mounted on the left side of the shroud, rather than the more common right-side rendition. I felt, and still do, that this is the quickest safety of all to use for a right-hand gunner. I remained quite happy with this setup for years until I started testing different rifles and calibers that utilized the more common M-70-style swing safety mounted on the right side of the shroud. In stressful situations, fine coordination deteriorates, and familiar muscle memory becomes dominant.

In 1999, after a summer of testing a few customized Winchester Model 70-style rifles with the safety mounted on the right side, I was guiding Bob Gibbs, a bear hunter from Missouri. We were looking for an absolutely massive old boar that I had seen two weeks previously during moose season. We finally caught up with him on day three of the hunt as he was working up a little stream full of silver salmon. We were out of sight on a small bluff above

the creek and he came into view, 40 yards directly in front of us. Bob aimed and fired once with his 300 Weatherby. As the bear lunged across the creek toward the thick pucker brush, I vividly remember fumbling to find the safety on Old Ugly as the bear disappeared into the thicket of willows and alders. Fortunately, Bob's 180-grain Partition had been well-placed, and we found the bear within 30 yards, face down in a small pond. It turned out to be the largest bear I have ever seen, and we were fortunate it had turned out so well. After that incident, I vowed to make sure all my serious-use rifles had similar and familiar safeties and I replaced the left-side wing safety on Old Ugly with the more common M-70-style swinging safety on the right side.

Although the exterior finish of my .458 shows innumerable, well-worn layers of varying hues of Rust-Oleum paint and wraps of electrical and glow-in-the-dark duct tape, the bore is still

dime bright and the factory cold bluing that occasionally shows through the paint appears undamaged. The old Brown Precision fiberglass stock that I cut, chopped and built up with multiple layers of fiberglass cloth and resin to fit me, has proved to be as stable and rugged as the action.

When I built the .458, my original intent was to use a Redfield peep sight. After a season with the peep, I decided to do testing of the speed and accuracy between it, a barrel mounted V sight and a 2.5X scope at 5, 15 and 50 yards.

In the iron-sight category, the open V was marginally faster than the peep on large close targets, while the peep was noticeably more accurate as the range increased. Due to the well-fitting stock, I was able to shoot equally well out to 20 yards by simply pointing and firing instinctively. That was also markedly the quickest. As distances increased, the peep sight proved both faster and noticeably more accurate than an

Hal Waugh's famous M-70 .375 Weatherby, "Big Nan," and Old Ugly. Even though Hal was four inches taller than the author, both rifles have a short 13.25-inch length of pull, which is important for quick use when wearing layers of clothing.

open V sight and beyond 50 yards the advantages of the little 2.5X Leupold compact scope became obvious. Not only was it faster and more accurate, at dusk and in thick brush it enables me the ability to accurately place a killing shot. A scope also facilitates bullet placement at longer ranges.

The Redfield dovetail mounts with the Pilkington quick-release lever that I initially used eventually wore enough to need replacement. I found the steel Leupold cross-slot bases with lightweight Weaver rings a simpler, more reliable setup. With just a coin or pocketknife, the scope can be removed and replaced with no change in impact. The little Leupold 2.5X compact scope remained on the rifle and has worked superbly for three and a half decades!

When I began looking for something larger than my .30-06, I talked with Andy Runyon, a friend and famous Kodiak bear guide. Andy was a serious student of rifles and had experienced mixed results stopping bears with the .375 H&H. He considered his wildcat 404 BJ Express (very similar to the .416 Taylor) the ideal mixture of long-range ability and short-range power. But, because there were no factory cartridges available, and I was living in remote hunting camps, I did not want the hassle of building all my ammunition. Had the stainless steel Ruger .416 M-77 been available at the time, I am sure both Andy and I would have owned one. My best option at the time was the .458 Win.

Introduced by Winchester-Western in 1956, the .458 Win. Mag. was first in a long line of short, belted magnum cartridges designed to fit in standard-length actions, yet deliver the ballistics of the oversized, cordite filled, African dangerous-game rounds. Due to price, availability and the outstanding M-70 "African" rifle, the .458 quickly became the dominant dangerous-game-stopping cartridge in Africa. I knew a few Alaskan brown bear and polar bear hunters who adopted it as well. Its advertised ballistics of 2,130 fps from a 25-inch barrel matched those of the popular English large-bore rounds, and Winchester's superb 500-grain steel-

The author filed a thumb slot in Interarms MkX action in order to quickly reload.

jacketed solids possessed an astounding sectional density of .341, which assured deep penetration. An independent laboratory report by H.P. White was reported in the February 1961 issue of *American Rifleman* magazine and showed a velocity of 2,087 fps at 20 feet from the muzzle, verifying the accuracy of Winchester's original ballistics.

For two decades, all seemed well with the .458. Professional hunters, game rangers and hunters across the African continent traded in their .404s, .416s, .425s, various .450s, .465s and .470s (for which ammo was becoming difficult to find or was unreliable) for Winchester's

original short magnum.

Winchester's marketing people and ballistics engineers, however, failed to anticipate the long-term conditions that unfired cartridges would have to endure on the Dark Continent. The long, heavy bullets in the abbreviated case of the .458 required that the powders available at the time be heavily compressed. After a few years of banging around in Land Rovers and being baked in the equatorial sun, a few disturbing reports of less-than-adequate penetration began to surface. Various theories were postulated, including sub-diameter and loose bullets, but eventually hunter and

The author had to track this bear an hour through thick brush after it was wounded. Even with the .458 it took four additional shots before the bear quit.

A close-up of the action showing Redfield "Little Bo Peep" flip-up sight fitted to steel Leupold cross-slot scope base, two-position safety and Devcon liquid-steel coating to the bolt handle.

Doug Turnbull's 1886 Win., chambered in .475 Turnbull, and Old Ugly during Doug's Alaskan Peninsula bear hunt.

gun writer Jack Lott discovered that if you pulled the bullets on the original loads the powder was so compressed that it often failed to fully ignite. His answer, which eventually resulted in the .458 Lott, was simply to lengthen the case three-tenths of an inch in order to relieve the compression of the powder.

Considering the status of quality control at Winchester after the 1954 merger between Olin/Winchester and the giant Mathieson Chemical Corporation, it is a wonder problems hadn't surfaced earlier. This was the same time period that the company introduced the push-feed M-70, impressed checkering and the abysmal, gilded, flat-nosed "solids" for the .375 H&H.

Winchester eventually acknowledged a problem existed with the .458, reduced the powder and relisted muzzle velocities to 2,040 fps. Although not quite up to the advertised velocities of the revered English nitro rounds, it was certainly adequate. Probably because the advertised velocities of the famous Kynoch loads were given for overly long 28-inch barrels and were likely inflated as well, and cordite is also susceptible to age deterioration.

As the situation stands today, the .458 WM with modern bullets and powders, easily achieves the originally advertised ballistics and remains the standard by which all others big-bore rifles are measured. A tough 500-grain bullet, traveling at an honest 2,150 fps, was the goal of numerous English

Nitro calibers and, even today, nothing more is needed if the shooter is up to the task.

Although primarily designed for Africa's prehistoric mega-fauna, the .458 is not out of place in Alaska. Ever since its introduction, it was recognized by those of us who hunt the world's largest land carnivores as offering better stopping power than any of the smaller bores. A number of American gun writers have claimed that the .458 is unnecessary for any game in North America, although I will wager not a one of them ever faced a charging 1,200- to 1,500-pound bruin in the thick-alder hell wounded bears instinctively head for. For that purpose, the .458 Win. has proved to be ideal.

With modern propellants like AA 2230. RL-7. H-335 and IMR 3031 and super-premium bullets from North Fork, Kodiak, Swift and Woodleigh, its performance on game has to be seen to be believed. I have carried Old Ugly now for over 35 years and have more faith in it than any rifle I have ever owned. It fits like a glove, feeds and operated with 100-percent reliability and, with adequate shot placement, puts down big bears with the authority of a crane falling on them.

For most of the time I have carried Old Ugly, I relied on one version or another of Hornady's excellent 500-grain, round-nose bullets. In the abbreviated 21-inch barrel, 70 grains of IMR 3031 powder gave a muzzle velocity that matched the factory-claimed 2,040 fps. Results were always immediate and impressive. Any bear I ever tagged with a solid hit went down immediately. Some occasionally got back up, but did so noticeably slower than if they had been hit with a .375 or .416.

There are numerous other great bullets available for the .458 and I have tried most of them from 350 grains up to 510. The late Jack Carter sent me one of his first boxes of 500-grain Trophy Bonded bullets, which I promptly loaded over the same powder charge. That fall moose season, I had an opportunity to test one. I was sitting

Old Ugly earned its keep backing up the author's clients hunting for massive Alaskan Peninsula bruins. Few gun writers have dealt with 1,200-pound-plus bears.

ammo was back in camp and asked me to take the shot. The bull appeared to have been hit and I agreed.

With 500-grain bullets, I keep Old Ugly sighted in dead on at 100 yards. My trajectory table, while not exact, is simple, quick and easy to remember and satisfactory for the large animals I am hunting: 1-foot drop at 200 yards, 3 feet at 300, 6 at 400 and 12 at 500. Figuring the bull's body was a good 3-feet deep I held 4-feet high and fired. The 1,800 pound-bull gave a violent shudder. We heard the bullet whack and he collapsed where he stood.

Upon butchering, we found that two of John's bullets had struck low in the bull's chest, but failed to expand and had done very little damage. My single 500-grain Trophy Bonded bullet had taken out one rib going in, completely removed the top of the animal's heart, removed two ribs on the way out and was found under the hide on the offside. It had expanded to over an inch in diameter and, considering the distance, its velocity had to have been down somewhere around 1,100 fps. It was impressive performance.

Comforting, I suppose, is the adjective that best describes Old Ugly. I've used other rifles and calibers. My .505 Gibbs certainly hits with more authority and my .404 Jeffery, .416 Rigby and .375 H&H shoot flatter and offer more versatility. But in my extensive testing the 500-grain bullets in the .458 penetrate as well or better and all the others require a longer action. The extra little quarter inch of bolt throw never seems like much on the range, but under stress I consciously have to pull the bolt all the way rearward on a long action where as a slick M-98 seems to work with just a flick of the wrist. Under worst-case scenarios, when things really get tight and serious, and the world drops into slow motion, except for that rapidly advancing nightmare at the end of your tunnel vision, that extra motion can seem like an eternity. That is when the stubby .458 Winchester, in a well-honed, standard-length, rugged Mauser that fits like a glove is just beautiful. It's one good gun. GD

on a small knoll with John Nash, a moose-hunting client from Oregon, one evening when an absolute massive, 74-inch bull moose stepped out of a stand of willows a half-mile away and began ambling toward us. The terrain was open tundra and there was nothing we could do but sit and wait. There was a small pond about 400 yards from us and when the bull reached it, he stopped. It was almost dark, there was no way to stalk closer, and we were afraid we would miss an opportunity of a lifetime. John was

shooting a .411 KDF and thought he could make the shot. Lying prone and using my backpack for a rest, he held the cross hairs over the bull's withers and fired. I was watching through my binoculars and the bull never moved. I saw a splash of water behind and apparently above the bull and called the shot high. He held lower and shot again and this time I saw water splash in front of the bull. His third and final shot again made a splash behind the bull, but appeared to have hit him. John then told me his remaining

FROM SPAIN, WITH LOVE

The Richland Model 200 has traveled far and accomplished much in its 50-year journey afield.

The M-200 was made by Zabala in Eibar, Spain, in (about) 1970 or 1971, and imported to Blissfield, Michigan, before immigrating to Kansas.

MADE FOR RICHLAND ARMS Co — MADE IN SPAIN
BLISSFIELD, MICHIGAN MODEL 200

G. ZABALA Y Cª S.A.   20 GA — 3"

This Richland Model 200 shotgun has journeyed thousands of miles, hunting across the United States

› **STEVE GASH**

The phrase "One Good Gun" can mean different things to different people, depending on the gun's history, type and style. After all, a gun is just an inanimate object, a machine designed and built to perform certain functions. Right?

But, as all of us gunny types know, a gun isn't just a "thing." Over time, with use, travel and many hunting trips, a gun gradually acquires character, a personality, a life of its own, as molded by the owner's interpretation. So it is with the history and

The M-200 has bushed firing pins; note the index marks for the bushings.

automatic tang safety and bushed firing pins. The stock and fore-end are of walnut (Spanish?), and are nicely checkered fore and aft. The SxS models included the Model 711 Magnum, which was available in 12-gauge, 3-inch Magnum, and 10-gauge, 3 1/2-inch Magnum, made from 1963 to 1985. The similar M-707 Deluxe was available in 12 or 20 gauge.

The Model 200 Field Grade offered something for almost every scattergunner. It was made in 12, 16, 20 and 28 gauges and .410 bore, with barrel lengths of 22, 26 or 28 inches, depending on the gauge and bore. It was also made in the same 1963 to 1985 time period. A neat variation was the M-202 All Purpose, which came with two sets of barrels, one each in 12 and 20 gauge.

The O/Us were represented by the M-41 Ultra (20 and 28 gauge and .410 bore), models 747 (12 or 20 gauge), 757, 787 and 808 (12 gauge only), 810 (10 gauge), and 828 (28 gauge). Actions were either boxlock or Greener crossbolt, depending on the model.

heritage of my Richland Model 200 20-gauge side-by-side shotgun.

Let's start at the beginning. My gun was made by Zabala in Spain in about 1971. Richland Arms Co. was founded in Blissfield, Michigan, in the mid-1960s by Thomas Hoagland, Jr., who also owned Richland Furs. Mr. Hoagland had recently toured some firearms manufacturers in Spain. One of them was Zabala Hermanos S.A., located in Eibar, in the province of Gipuzkoa. Eibar is the heart of the Spanish gun-making industry, and various types of guns have been made there since

the 1500s. In fact, the Spanish Proof House, which oversees CIP standards, is located there. Right after this visit, Mr. Hoagland founded Richland Arms, which operated until 1986.

The line of guns imported by Richland Arms was a diverse assemblage of sturdy field shotguns. There were side-by-side doubles, over-unders, and one single-shot. The side-by-sides were similar in design and construction, and featured Anson & Deeley boxlock actions, and one-piece extractors. As far as I've been able to determine, all had double triggers, an

My first Richland Arms gun is a unique version of the Model 200 in 20 gauge. Its 22-inch barrels have 3-inch chambers, and fixed improved cylinder (right), and modified (left) chokes. With a weight of 6 pounds, 1 ounce, it handles well, and is on target in a jiffy. The crisp trigger pulls of about 4 1/2 pounds are delightful for a shotgun. A single brass bead is at the end of the solid middle rib. The walnut buttstock has a nicely curved pistol grip with a *gin-u-wine* plastic cap and a slim cheekpiece, and the fore-end is a semi-beavertail.

My M-200 has an extensive travel history and has had its share of both successful hunts as well as mishaps. As noted, it started its journey in Spain in about 1971, and from there it went west across the Atlantic to Richland Arms Co. in Blissfield, Michigan. Next, it went south to John's Sport Center in Pittsburg, Kansas. John's is still a gun-lover's mecca in southeast Kansas with a huge inventory.

In 1971, I had finally escaped the clutches of two universities with three degrees, and had accepted a job in southeastern Pennsylvania. We were

The barrels are silver-soldered together in the traditional manner. The front sight is a simple brass bead.

The one-piece extractor elevates empty cases for easy removal. The fore-end iron is shown at right.

moving east to the new job, but en route stopped off in Pittsburg to spend some time with my parents. Of course, I had to check out the gun rack at John's while I was in town. It was there that I spied the Richland. I was smitten, and my wife, Rosielea, already familiar with subtle hints, bought it for me on Aug. 15, 1971. The price was only $105. She called it a "new job" present.

So, the Richland went east with us to Pennsylvania. I hunted quail and ring-necked pheasants with it that fall; I even hit some birds, but the results weren't great. (Now I realize that it was not the gun, but the nut at the end of the stock.)

The next August, we were again in Pittsburg. I was still convinced my poor shooting with the Richland was the gun's fault, so asked my wife if I could sell it to our good friend Bob Westervelt, and she agreed. It was a decision I soon regretted. But Bob was a serious gunny guy, if there ever was one, so we knew he would give it a good home. (You can read about Bob and his exploits in the 2012 *Gun Digest,* 66th Edition, page 332.)

Bob and the Richland seemed to get along together just fine. There were still quite a few quail in southeast Kansas then, and Bob terrorized them with the Richland, clobbered pheasants in western Kansas and ambushed ducks with his trusty lab, Jack, at his side.

But Bob's son, Dan, also took a shine to it, and Bob, thoughtful father he was, loaned (or gave, it was a flexible agreement) the gun to Dan. In those days, Dan lived in Wichita, Kansas, so the gun next went west from Pittsburg. Kansas was still a great state for pheasant hunters back then, and Dan harvested his share with the Richland. Over the next 10 or so years, Bob and Dan traded it back and forth from Wichita to Pittsburg, and back again; its possession changed according to their whims and the hunting seasons.

Dan recently told me he had great success hunting with the Richland in its new environs, and that he shot "clay birds quite a lot." His shooting chums all wanted to buy it, he said. But of course, there was no sale.

Dan recalled that on one hunt he closed the action and both barrels discharged! He took it to a gunsmith, but the fellow never worked on it, so Dan retrieved it, unaltered. The cause of this malady remains a mystery, because the gun never malfunctioned again.

In December 2008, Bob passed away. Shortly thereafter, we visited the family in Pittsburg, and Bob's wife Bethel was anxious to move nearer their daughter Connie and her husband, Steve, and asked me to help take care of selling Bob's guns. Bob was like many of us: He wasn't a "collector," he was an "accumulator." It wasn't an extensive assemblage, but he had some neat ones. As we inventoried and cataloged, we all reminisced about the fine trips we'd been on together, the snowy Kansas milo fields, and shots made and missed with

Virtually any 20-gauge shell is appropriate for the M-200, including 3-inch magnums.

The buttstock has a raised cheekpiece, but no Monte Carlo comb. The Pachmayr recoil pad replaced the original, which ultimately deteriorated.

The top tang safety is automatic.

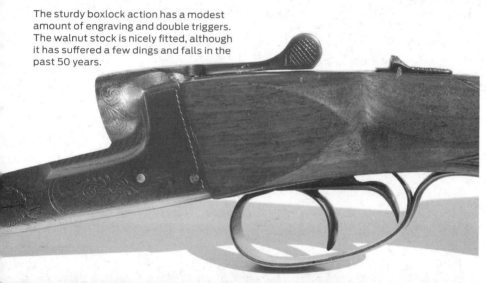

The sturdy boxlock action has a modest amount of engraving and double triggers. The walnut stock is nicely fitted, although it has suffered a few dings and falls in the past 50 years.

A pheasant, chukar and bobwhite quail all harvested with the Richland at a southwest Missouri shooting preserve.

some of the guns as we came to them.

When we were nearing the end of the inventory, we came to the Richland. I remembered the good times we had with it, and how much I regretted selling it. I felt a pang. To my delight, Dan said: "Here, I think it's time this went home," and handed me the little double. It was like seeing an old friend after a long separation. I was delighted, and I'm sure Bob was looking down, grinning ear-to-ear, too.

The gun was in excellent shape, except for the original red recoil pad, which had deteriorated into mush over the decades. The installation of a Pachmayr Decelerator pad fixed that. Recalling, the "doubling" problem, I test-fired it with each barrel, then both, and it functioned perfectly. In the 12 years since the Richland came home, I have hunted quail, ducks and doves on my acreage in southwest Missouri. I've even harvested a few turkeys with the M-200, some flying. It seems partial to Federal 3-inch, No. 6s for turkeys.

Unfortunately, I have added my share of nicks and bruises to the gun. Once, while crossing my creek en route to the duck pond, I slipped on the wet rocks and fell, hard, right on the M-200. The fore-end received a serious ding on its left side, but the buttstock was cracked inside the action, and I could wiggle the broken stock out of the right side of the action; it looked bad.

I found and studied an exploded-parts diagram for the M-200, and carefully removed the stock. I had never taken such a gun apart before, so this was a nerve-racking experience. Thankfully, the crack was not too serious, and easily fixed with Elmer's Wood Glue and an overnight rest in a large C-clamp. I refinished the fore-end damage and reassembled the gun. It's as good as new, mechanically, if a bit worse for wear, and it again goes "bang" every time I pull either trigger.

In the past 50 years, the M-200 has journeyed thousands of miles back and forth across the country, in the hands of folks who appreciate its unique utility and history, and has earned its title as "One Good Gun." The Richland Model 200 is home for good. GD

The author's early hunts in Kenya included a Remington Model 721 rifle chambered in .300 Holland & Holland Magnum and Winchester Silvertip ammunition. Other gear included a Buck Skinner Knife, compass, belt-type leather cartridge holder and 7X binoculars. Gerenuk horns are among the author's favorite trophies.

REMINGTON'S REMARKABLE MODEL SEVEN-TWENTY-ONE

The author's Remington Model 721, chambered in .300 Holland & Holland Magnum, spent many years in the African bush

› JOE COOGAN

A simple, iron-sighted Model 721 Remington rifle provided unfailing reliability for the hunting my father and I did in Kenya more than 50 years ago. Considered a plain vanilla rifle by most, our Model 721 accounted for many excellent trophies and contributed to memories I treasure even more with each passing year. My father purchased the rifle in 1956 at the Navy Base Exchange on Guam where he was attached to a Navy photo recon squadron. He bought the rifle, likely for less than $100, with the thought of hunting wild boar in the Philippines and seledang (a wild gaur) in Malaya. Those hunts never progressed beyond the talking stages, so the Model 721 was relegated to the back of coat closets until a flying job with Pan Am took my father and our family to Kenya 10 years later.

Getting the rifle to Africa was easy. It was just a matter of carrying it in a soft gun bag aboard a Pan Am flight from New York to Nairobi as hand baggage, and handing it over to a stewardess who carefully stood it in the cockpit with the pilots. No paperwork required this side and no raised eyebrows in those so much simpler times.

The Remington Model 721 rifle, chambered in .300 Holland & Holland Magnum, was the rifle we used for a majority of our hunting in Kenya and became the mainstay of our African battery in the early years. The .300 H&H cartridge was introduced by Holland & Holland in June 1925 and quickly established itself as a popular round for African hunting. Holland & Holland named it the Super .30, basing the case on the .375 H&H Magnum case. The Super .30 case featured a narrow slope rather than an actual shoulder and was belted for easier headspacing. Winchester was the first U.S. rifle company to chamber the British cartridge in its Model 70 in 1937. By then it was called the .300 Holland & Holland Magnum and was included in the original lineup of calibers available for Remington's Model 721, 10 years later.

The predecessor of Remington's Model 721 was the Model 720, an improved version of the previous Model 30 that was a Mauser 98-style action built as the flagship bolt-action rifle for Remington. But WWII brought a halt to the production of the Model 720 when Remington was called upon to build numerous military arms for the war effort. During the war, Remington's manufacturing methods and technology advanced to a point where the arms company faced a major decision after the war: resume the more complex production of an expensive rifle or update the design, utilizing modern production techniques and thus lowering cost. Remington chose a redesign and introduced the new Model 721 rifle in 1948. The last one was sold

The elegant, spiral-horned lesser kudu is one of the author's favorite African game animals. Accompanied by his father, Joe Sr., and tracker Dana, the author collected this fine lesser kudu in Kenya in the late 1960s with the iron-sighted Remington Model 721 rifle in .300 Holland & Holland Magnum.

sometime around 1962.

Prior to the war, Model 720 receivers were made from a billet-machined piece of steel, whereas after the war, the Model 721 incorporated a cost-cutting round profile that could be produced on a lathe rather than a mill. The Model 721 breech embodied the concept of "three-rings-of-steel" for greater strength and safety. The recessed bolt-face encircled the cartridge head, while the chamber and barrel surrounded the cartridge, all of which were contained within the receiver.

The bolt's redesign involved combining several separate pieces. A smaller, but effective extractor was mounted within the wall of the recessed bolt face, while a plunger-type ejector, located on the bolt face, replaced the old Mauser-style blade mounted in the receiver. The solid magazine floor plate lacked a hinge, so loading and unloading the rifle was accomplished strictly through the top of the receiver.

During 14 years of Model 721 production, 118,000 rifles were made in several calibers, including .264 Winchester Magnum, .270

The author's father bought this Remington Model 721 rifle new in the mid-1950s. To maximize its range potential, the author mounted a Redfield 4X Widefield scope on the rifle in the mid-1970s. The rifle was used for more than 26 years of African hunting.

The graceful, long-necked gerenuk was common in the Kenya bush country where the author and his father hunted in the 1960s and '70s. For game of this size, Winchester's Silvertip 180-grain load proved to be an efficient and accurate round. Using iron-sights meant having to stalk close to game.

Winchester, .280 Remington, .30-06 Springfield and .300 H&H Magnum. All calibers in the lineup exhibited excellent accuracy. In 1962, with the Model 721 having served as the basis for development, the highly successful Model 700 series of rifles was introduced. They are still in production today with no anticipated changes in sight.

ON SAFARI

We were fortunate indeed to live near classic African big-game country, located only a couple of hours drive from our home in Mombasa. It was hard, rugged terrain favored by black rhino, Cape buffalo and home to some of the largest tuskers in Africa. It was also prime habitat for lesser kudu, gerenuk, eland and fringe-eared oryx, while lions and leopards thrived on plentiful prey species such as impala, Peter's gazelle, Coke's hartebeest (kongoni), common waterbuck,

warthog, wildebeest and zebra.

The first African animal I took with the Model 721 was an impala ram. Other game followed, including kongoni, Peter's gazelle, zebra and warthog, but of all the plains game I hunted, the elegant, spiral-horned lesser kudu was unquestionably my favorite with the graceful, long-necked gerenuk a close second. I found *tendala ndogo* (Swahili for lesser kudu) fascinating from the first moment I saw the curl of nut-brown horns and the flash of white tail as one bounded away from us and into thick bush. Collecting my first lesser kudu stands out as one of my most memorable hunts.

I was freshly back in Kenya from my first year of college and on a wonderfully clear June morning my father and I, accompanied by two trackers, hiked up Kisoli Hill for a look at the surrounding countryside. Kisoli was located in southeastern Kenya, not far from the Tsavo West NP boundary. We had

topped the hill and walked a short distance down the other side when we suddenly spotted a magnificent lone lesser kudu bull on the slope below. The kudu was busily browsing on an acacia bush and was completely unaware of us. I carried the Model 721 and was immediately gripped by a classic case of buck fever. I unslung the rifle and racked a round into the chamber and in great haste managed to whistle an offhand shot over the kudu's back. I quickly cycled the bolt and repeated the miss. The kudu remained unaware of us and seemingly untroubled by the loud bangs.

"Son, settle down! The shots are high, bring your aim down," my father implored. I got a grip on myself with enough composure to forcefully and consciously lower my aim.

It was not the rifle's fault. Hurrying to get off the shots, I'd failed to allow for the sharp downward angle of the shots and hadn't lowered my point-of-aim. Unbelievably, the kudu still had not spotted us, for if he had, there certainly would not have been a third-shot opportunity. The kudu bucked and kicked his hind legs at the report of my final shot and bounded out of sight. One of the trackers raced back to the vehicle for more ammo, before we began tracking the kudu. There was plenty of blood to follow from where he'd been standing and we found him lying in the grass a short distance away. If there was only one trophy to keep from my years of hunting in Africa, it would certainly

Remington's Model 721 rifle, chambered in .300 Holland & Holland Magnum, provided the mainstay of the author's initial African battery. He carried it during his early years of hunting in Kenya and later in Botswana during his safari years as a PH.

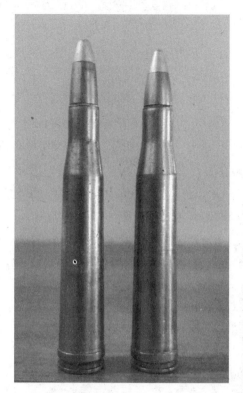

Originally called the "Super .30," the .300 Holland & Holland Magnum cartridge was introduced in June 1925, and soon established itself as a popular round for African hunting. Winchester Silvertip cartridges were offered in (from left) 220-grain and 180-grain loads.

The author and his tracker, Kiribai, with a fringe-eared oryx, a species unique to East Africa. Winchester's 220-grain Silvertip load was an effective round for heavier-bodied antelope like the oryx, which could be aggressive when wounded.

be that lesser kudu.

Trading the Kenya bush for Botswana's Okavango Delta and Kalahari Desert in 1972, both the Model 721 and my Winchester Model 70 .458 Win. Mag. were right by my side. For the new demands of professional safari work, I mounted a Redfield Widefield 4X scope on the Model 721, enabling it to comfortably reach out and tag game at 200 yards or more. Always in the gun rack while on safari, the Model 721 frequently was used by my clients when they had not brought a rifle of their own. Several new species were added to its lengthening list of accomplishments, including even Cape buffalo when I was able to acquire some 200-grain solids in .300 H&H Mag.

On one memorable occasion, I was hunting in the Kalahari with a Venezuelan client who happened to be using my Model 721. It was midday when we topped a slight rise to glass a flat stretch of country across a dry pan. I saw a small bump in the distance

that I confirmed with binoculars to be a lone springbok, which were few in this particular area and difficult to approach when you did find them. We crept down to the edge of the pan, which was as close as we could expect to get to the springbok.

I suggested to the client that he take a shot with the Model 721, to which he agreed and settled into a stable, steady shooting position. He asked what the distance was, and I guessed the springbok to be, at a minimum, more than 300 yards away. I advised that he should hold at least a foot or two over the animal's back and watched him raise the muzzle and squeeze off a shot. I then turned my attention to the springbok which, to my absolute astonishment, suddenly and silently collapsed in his tracks. Driving to the downed animal and using the Land Cruiser's odometer, we measured the

distance at roughly a half-a-kilometer (that's more than 500 yards) from where the shot was taken. I don't think anyone was more surprised by the hit than the client himself. Not only had he hit the animal, but the bullet struck the point of the shoulder at the exact spot where you would want to place a shot. What a rifle!

After logging more than 26 safari years in Africa, I semi-retired the Model 721, bringing her back to the States. I place great value on this venerable old rifle based on her early hunting history and the many memorable days we shared on safari. She now stands proudly in a rack among a row of other respected and accomplished rifles, ready to be taken out and held and admired as I tell the stories and brag about the long shots and the lengthy list of game credited to this "ordinary, but unique" Model 721. GD

The Bergara B-14 line comprises six models, with honed barrels that are true to .0002 inch.

NEW RIFLES

Chassis? Carbon-fiber barrels? Yes, but walnut, iron sights and case-colored steel, too!

WAYNE VAN ZWOLL

The changing face of sporting rifles is hard to ignore. Preoccupation with long-range shooting affects the design of bolt-actions that will never ring a steel plate or kill game more than a football field away. From suppressor-ready barrels to oversize bolt knobs to Picatinny rails with 20 minutes of gain, even hunting rifles reflect a seismic shift in shooter habit and expectations. Offhand marksmanship has acceded to the bipod. Sub-minute accuracy, once a lofty standard, is now ordinary, at least in print. Bullets with the ballistic coefficients of knitting needles carry it furlongs beyond the effective range of traditional round-nose soft-points. Bluetooth wizardry in riflescopes with six-times power ranges show you where bullets should hit at distance, if you can hold the rifle still.

But not all is rocket science. Absence may indeed make the heart grow fonder, as walnut stocks are creeping back into favor. Might iron sights be next? New loads for old hunting cartridges are popping up in thickets of sharp-shouldered hotrods. The bloom is not yet off the 6.5 rose, but one of the most impressive bolt rifles I've fired lately was a Remington in 7mm Magnum. Can it be that both the Model 700 and its belted wonder will soon be ripe for Social Security? Amid the seasonal flurry of fresh rifles and loads, it's useful to remember that some of the most useful of both appeared before the Depression.

And the allure of a fine rifle far outlives all attempts to describe it.

ASHBURY PRECISION ORDNANCE

The Saber Sport Utility series, on Remington 700 barreled actions, feature modular chassis and Rifle Basix triggers, and a host of options. The $2,750 Saber M700 Tactical Rifle in 6.5 Creedmoor and .308 is new in Ashbury's stable, where accuracy joins the disparate elements of tactical and hunting rifles. Enthusiasts mind the details; so does Ashbury.

ashburyprecisionordnance.com

BERGARA

New for 2020, Bergara's B-14 Wilderness Series (from $899), in Sniper Grey Cerakote, bridges the gap between the company's affordable family of B-14 rifles and its more expensive Premier Series rifles. Hunter and Ridge models have internal magazines, SoftTouch stock finishes. Chamberings: 6.5 Creedmoor to .28 Nosler and .300 Winchester. Wilderness Terrain and HMR rifles feature a "mini-chassis" and a brake, and AICS detachable boxes.

bergarausa.com

BLASER

The straight-pull action of Blaser's incomparable R8 will now fire .22 rimfire ammo, with a new Blaser barrel and magazine assembly. It's much harder to explain than to understand with the barrel and breech in hand. Since its 2008 debut, the R8 has

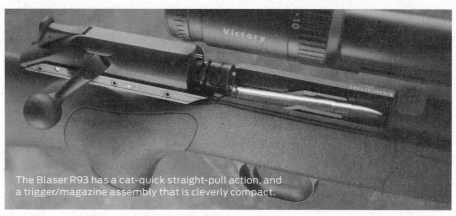

The Blaser R93 has a cat-quick straight-pull action, and a trigger/magazine assembly that is cleverly compact.

undergone few changes. It doesn't beg any. The radial-head bolt has an expanding collet that locks into the barrel. The straight-pull bolt telescopes, keeping the receiver short. A flick of your hand cycles the action, which can brook 120,000 psi of pressure. The R8's tang-mounted thumb-piece is a cocking switch, not a safety. Uncocked, the rifle is safe with the chamber loaded. Plasma nitriding on hammer-forged barrels ensures perfect return to zero with Blaser's exquisitely machined QD scope mounts. A feather-light, aramid-reinforced magazine resides in a trigger group that's easily detached or locked in place. The R8 comes in several versions, with barrels in chamberings to .338 Lapua and .500 Jeffery. Barrels (and mag assemblies) interchange easily. Choose synthetic stocks or walnut. You can even visit Blaser and select your blank from stacks of stunners.

blaser-usa.com

BROWNING

The X-Bolt series, maturing as Browning's replacement for the A-Bolt, includes a growing clan of specialized rifles. Last year, the Max Long Range Hunter appeared, with adjustable stock and threaded, fluted, heavy 26-inch barrel. It's bored for nine cartridges, 6mm Creedmoor to .300 UltraMag, including the .26 and .28 Nosler. For 2020, Browning adds the 6.5 PRC and

.30 Nosler. Prices start at $1,299. New as well: The X-Bolt Max Varmint/Target, with a heavy fluted stainless barrel that adds a pound. The gray textured stock is that of the Max Long Range, without speckling. Seven chamberings range from .204 to .28 Nosler and .300 Winchester. MSRP: from $1,339. The X-Bolt Tungsten announced last year is now available in 6.5 PRC, .30 Nosler and .300 RUM as well as its charter cartridges. Ditto the Burnt Bronze, Burnt Bronze Long Range, Hell's Canyon Long Range and Hell's Canyon Long Range McMillan. The Target McMillan A3-5 Ambush with fluted bull barrel, 20-minute Picatinny rail and muzzle brake should be a long-range champ. This 10-pound rifle in 6.5 Creedmoor, 6.5 PRC, .28 Nosler and .300 Winchester lists between $3,139 and $3,199.

There's new camo for Hell's Canyon Speed rifles. The 6.5 PRC, .30 Nosler and .300 Winchester bring chambering options to 15. Price: from $1,260. Threaded muzzles with brakes are standard on these Brownings, and on the new wood-stocked Hunter Long Range. The adjustable comb is useful without detracting from the checkered walnut and matte-blued steel. At $999 the Hunter, also in walnut, is $300 cheaper, but lacks comb adjustment and muzzle threads. It comes in a left-hand version. The Composite Stalker is similar, with

The "stainless thumbhole" Eclipse Hunter (from $1,269) is one of many Browning X-Bolt rifles.

black synthetic stock. More walnut? The Micro Midas compact rifle, and upscale Medallion and White Gold Medallion wear it well. The Eclipse Hunter ($1,269 to $1,299) has a threaded stainless, sporting-weight barrel with a laminated thumbhole stock. For the budget-conscious, Browning lists the AB3 bolt rifle, in Hunter (with walnut) and Stalker (synthetic) guises, $700 and $600. Four versions of the BLR lever rifle remain in the Browning stable, with seven BAR self-loaders. Browning has not changed its rimfire offerings for 2020. The BL-22, SA-22 and T-Bolt endure.

browning.com

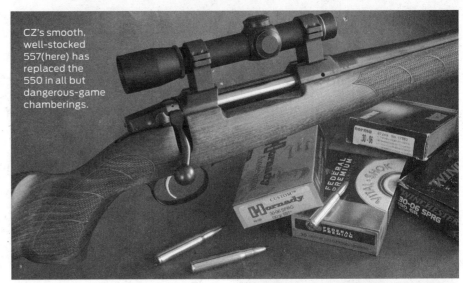

CZ's smooth, well-stocked 557(here) has replaced the 550 in all but dangerous-game chamberings.

CVA

Also in 2020 headlines: CVA is rolling out its first centerfire rifle. The bolt-action Cascade, announced in 6.5 Creedmoor, 7mm-08 and .308, is now available in .350 Legend too. The three-lug bolt has a short 70-degree lift, the 22-inch barrel a threaded muzzle. The stock is a gray synthetic material with SoftTouch finish. In blued and Cerakoted steel, the Cascade retails for $499 to $599. Accuracy trials show it shoots above its pay grade.

cva.com

CZ

The 557 bolt-action has replaced the 550 on CZ's centerfire rifle roster, save for Safari Magnum rifles. The 550's Mauser-style non-rotating claw will be missed by the faithful, but the bolt-face extractor on my two 557s work just fine. The short-action 557 in .308 has a detachable box; the long-action model wears a floorplate. All 557 receivers are machined to accept CZ rings. The walnut stocks are both better looking and more comfortable than those on early 550s. You can get synthetic versions. A walnut prone stock on a "varmint" edition and a left-hand 557 American rifle in walnut are also options. Choose from six popular chamberings, .243 to .30-06, from $792. CZ's lovely 527 is one of my favorite rifles, scaled to its petite chamberings: .17 and .22 Hornet, .204, .222, .223, 6.5 Grendel and 7.62x39. Choose from six models, two with iron sights. The

Varmint MTS has a stiff threaded barrel, a prone-style stock; all save the Synthetic Suppressor-Ready 527 wear walnut. All have adjustable single-set triggers and detachable boxes. My .17 Hornet is wonderfully accurate. Prices: $747 to $787.

In rimfire news, the 457 replaces the 455, which introduced interchangeable barrels to mothball the 452. The 457 receiver is shorter, with new two-piece bottom metal, a fully adjustable trigger. Priced from $365 (for a Scout model proportioned for young shooters), the 457 comes in .22 LR, .22 WMR and .17 HMR. Barrels can be changed quickly and easily. Besides predictable configurations like the walnut-stocked American and a synthetic-stocked Varmint Pro, the 457 comes in new Varmint Precision Chassis form, with an alloy chassis and adjustable AR-type stock with M-LOK slots. Like the new 457 Varmint Precision Trainer and ProVarmint with Manners carbon-fiber and painted-laminate stocks, respectively, the Chassis model has a threaded barrel. Ditto the 457 Varmint At-One, in an adjustable laminated prone-style stock from Boyds. The 457 Royal is a sporter-weight rimfire with 20 1/2-inch threaded barrel, figured walnut. The 457 Premium, also fresh for 2020, is a deluxe rifle in European fashion, with Schnabel-tipped walnut and iron sights on the 24 1/2-inch barrel, an upgrade of the 457 Training Rifle. A new 457 Jaguar, stocked in

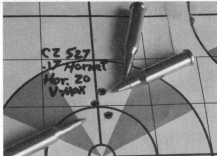

The author's CZ 527 in .17 Hornet nips three-quarter-minute groups. A superb light varmint rifle, with no recoil.

beech, carries its adjustable irons on a 28 1/2-inch threaded barrel. Unknown to many shooters, CZ has a 512 self-loading .22 WMR, one of few reliable, affordable autos in that chambering.

cz-usa.com

DAKOTA

Don Allen had an eye for elegance. His Dakota 76 was essentially an early Winchester M70 with refinements and stunning European walnut. In my view it's still the supermodel of semi-custom sporting rifles, with the M70 trigger and bolt, a more handsome profile and uncanny "pointability." The 76s I've shot have functioned silkily and drilled tiny groups. So, Dakota's shop would be foolish to alter this rifle. It hasn't, though new versions have joined this exclusive clan. Lightweight Alpine, sleek Mannlicher, take-down Traveler and synthetic-stocked Professional Hunter, like burly Safari and Africa models, hew to the highest cosmetic

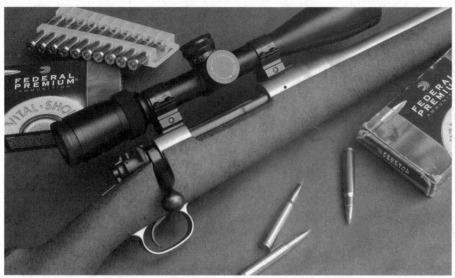

Dakota's 97 Outfitter isn't as pretty or costly as its 76 in fine walnut. Still, the 97 is beautifully built.

and functional standards. Yeah, they're expensive. For those of us who check the price of coffee at gas stations, there's the Model 97 Series, Outfitter, Stainless and Classic, with round receivers and synthetic stocks. The walnut-stocked Model 10 is a dropping-block single-shot whose lines, with those of Dakota's Baby Sharps, have sent enthusiasts to their knees in spasms of ecstasy. Nesika actions have infiltrated the Dakota line as a Varminter series, three of the four models in walnut. Remington's acquisition of the Dakota Shop brought new projects. It now must produce Custom Shop Remington and Marlin rifles too.

dakotaarms.com

HOWA

Two rifles with 24-inch carbon-fiber-wrapped barrels in 6.5 Creedmoor, and stocks by H-S Precision, have joined the stable of Howa bolt actions at Legacy Sports International. (They're identical save the stock colors: gray and OD green, each with black spider webbing.) The stocks feature full-length alloy bedding blocks. At 7 3/4 pounds, rifle weight reflects the heft of the Howa actions, each fed by an internal box with hinged floorplate. MSRP: $1,819. Another new pair of Howa rifles, with Cerakote "Tactical Gray" metal finish, feature pillar-bedded Hogue stocks in Verde and Vias camo. Available in

nine chamberings, .22-250 to .300 Winchester, they're priced from $759. New GamePro 2 models in gray and OD green boast these Hogue stocks and internal box magazines. Threaded barrels come in 11 chamberings (blued, gray stock), including the 6.5 and .300 PRC, at $699. OD green versions with stainless steel in 6.5 Creedmoor and .308 retail for $769. Legacy Sports International includes 3-10x44 Nikko Stirling scopes with both new Cerakote and GamePro 2 models.

Traditionalists have zeroed in on Howa's new Walnut Series announced at January's 2020 SHOT Show at a starting price of $619. Nicely checkered stocks on the Walnut Hunter, stainless and blued, are fitted with black rubber recoil pads. The blued version comes in seven standard and four magnum chamberings; stainless rifles are available only in 6.5 Creedmoor and .308. There's also a Mini Action Walnut Hunter in .223, 6.5 Grendel, 7.62x39 and .350 Legend. Unlike its siblings, this rifle has a detachable box. So do two new full-size Howa TSP X Folding Chassis rifles in 6.5 Creedmoor, 6.5 PRC, .300 Creedmoor. All Howa rifles are push-feeds, with twin-lug bolt, two-stage trigger, three-position safety. The cylindrical receiver is very stout. I'm pleased to see a swing back to traditional magazines on new Howas. Detachable boxes I've used afield made earlier Howas unwieldy; and the latches were easily snagged or bumped, dropping the magazine. Detachable boxes have a place in rifles used in combat and competition, and appear on the new 6 3/4-pound Hardy Hybrid rifle, with switchable, 24-inch, carbon-wrapped barrel in 6.5 PRC. Trigger pull adjusts down to 1 pound. Two new rimfire rifles, with green and gray synthetic stocks and stiff 18-inch barrels, come in .22 LR, .22 WMR and .17 HMR. Their starting price of $699 includes a 3.5-10x44 Nikko Stirling scope.

legacysports.com

KIMBER

Established by Australian Jack Warne to build high-quality .22 rimfire rifles, Kimber has become a major manufacturer of 1911 pistols.

Sturdy Howa rifles from Legacy Sports International include this small-action, detachable-box .223.

Kimber rifles have trim actions. The stiff barrel of a Kimber LPT in .308 held this group to .38 inch.

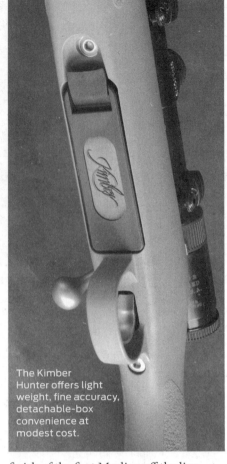

The Kimber Hunter offers light weight, fine accuracy, detachable-box convenience at modest cost.

Its centerfire rifles, sired by the trim 84M, now feature four action sizes (including the 84SM for short rimless magnums, the 84L for the .30-06 family of cartridges and the 8400LM for belted magnums). Chamberings range from .204 Ruger to .375 H&H. Lightweight sporters, the Montana, Adirondack and Mountain Ascent, have synthetic stocks. So do Open Range models with stiffer fluted barrels in 6.5 Creedmoor and .308. For 2020, Kimber shaves 12 ounces from its Open Range rifles. Both Granite and Open Country camo versions now come with Proof Research's threaded, carbon-fiber-wrapped barrels. Single-point cut rifling limits barrel stress in production. (At the Proof facility in northwest Montana, I fired a .2-inch, five-shot group with a Proof barrel in 6mm Creedmoor.) Kimber's Hunter, the company's first rifle with a detachable box, is one of the best bargains available for hunters wanting a lightweight Kimber at modest cost. It has the 84M mechanism, pillar-bedded to a well-shaped stock of molded polymer. Introduced in .243, .257 Roberts, 6.5 Creedmoor, 7mm-08 and .308, the 6 1/2-pound Hunter now comes in a long-action version for the .270, .280 A.I. and .30-06. Walnut stocks still grace Kimber Traditional and SuperAmerica rifles, and the Dangerous Game Caprivi in .375, with iron sights.

kimberamerica.com

MARLIN

The year 2020 marked Marlin's 150th in the firearms industry. The Model 444 Anniversary lever rifle with half-octagon barrel and curved grip terminus, sports fancy checkered walnut, Skinner sights and receiver engraving. A product of the Custom Shop in Sturgis, South Dakota, it retails for $1,899 and reflects the quality of components and the attention to fit and finish that have marked CS Marlins since Remington bought the company. Last year, Marlin revived the .444 round in "factory"1895 rifles built in Remington's Ilion, New York, plant, which also produces 336, .30-30 and short-action 1894 rifles. Shuttering Marlin's North Haven, Connecticut, plant and bringing its projects in-house when Ilion's staff had no experience building lever rifles was a perilous leap. Few Marlin employees who'd fitted the mechanisms made the move. The fit and finish of the first Marlins off the line there didn't pass muster with aficionados who'd teethed on "real" Marlins. But quality is improving. I've been assured that progress will continue.

Meanwhile, new rifles have appeared. The Dark Series comprises 1895, 336 and 1894 rifles with Picatinny rails and XS sights, threaded muzzles, black-painted hardwood stocks and oversize lever loops wrapped in parachute cord. Braided cord slings are part of

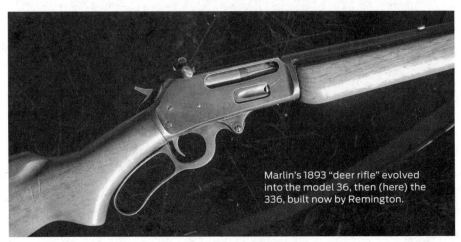

Marlin's 1893 "deer rifle" evolved into the model 36, then (here) the 336, built now by Remington.

the package. Special loops, rails and sights appear on other Marlins too. Traditional walnut-stocked models remain, including the 1895 and 1895CB (Cowboy) in .45-70, and the 1895 .410 bored for .410 shotshells ($847, or $934 if you want the version with interchangeable chokes). Stocks of gray laminate are an option for all action sizes, and Marlin lists a 336 in curly maple. In rimfires, the autoloading Model 60 survives, a sleek 5 1/2-pound rifle popular for decades. A 150th anniversary edition of the 60 has appeared, in stainless steel. Alas, the Model 39 lever-action .22, whose forebearers date to the 19th century, issues only from the Custom Shop. When I was a wee lad, you could buy a 39 at retail for $61. Now they're well into four figures. But Marlin's CS crew does a fine job building them.

marlinfirearms.com

MOSSBERG

The Patriot series of Mossberg bolt rifles has added the .350 Legend to its list of long- and short-action chamberings. New walnut- and synthetic-stocked models have 24-inch threaded barrels in 7mm, .300 and .338 Magnum. (There's a comely new .300 Magnum in walnut with iron sights.) Mossberg has put those three magnums in its Combo scoped-rifle stable too. After the MVP Light Chassis rifle in .223, 6.5 Creedmoor and .308 joined the MVP Precision last year, MVP Scout,

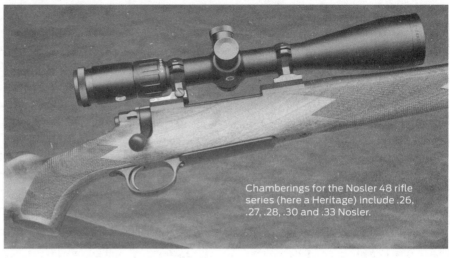

Chamberings for the Nosler 48 rifle series (here a Heritage) include .26, .27, .28, .30 and .33 Nosler.

Patrol and Predator versions arrived, with more traditional stocks but the same detachable AR magazines. The MVP LR has a heavier prone-style stock with an adjustable comb. That stock profile, but in "Spider Gray" and sans adjustable comb, now appears on a new Patriot LR Hunter in 6.5 Creedmoor and .300 Winchester. The 22- and 24-inch fluted, sporting-weight barrels are threaded, as are an increasing number of bolt rifles under every shingle. Patriot Predator rifles, with stocks in Flat Dark Earth and True Timber Strata camo, now include a .450 Bushmaster with FDE stock and a threaded 16 1/4-inch barrel under iron sights. Other Predators soon will be chambering the 6.5 PRC. The Revere is a tastefully gussied-up Patriot, with skip-checkered walnut stock and rosewood caps. All Patriots feature Mossberg's LBA trigger,

which adjusts down to 2 pounds. The Patriot series is modestly priced (from $396) and punches above its weight. My rifle, in .375 Ruger, cycles smoothly, points naturally and shoots accurately. Mossberg still catalogs a trio of traditional 464 lever-actions in .30-30, including the SPX with adjustable synthetic stock.

mossberg.com

NOSLER

The Model 48 bolt rifle comes in two new versions for 2020. Both Mountain Carbon and Long Range Carbon 48s were rumored last year; I have it on good report both are now available. Both feature carbon-wrapped barrels long enough to accelerate bullets from Nosler's high-octane cartridges. The Mt. Carbon weighs just 6 pounds in .26, .28, .30, and now .27 Nosler (you can specify other popular rounds too). The Long Range Carbon is 2 inches longer, with 26-inch CF barrel. Its stock has more beef at grip and fore-end, and two front swivel studs. Other 48s: The Long Range with Tactical Hunter Carbon/ Aramid Fiber stock, but a stainless steel barrel; the Liberty with a slimmer synthetic stock; the Heritage in walnut. Best-selling to date is the Liberty, in 14 chamberings, .22 Nosler to .33 Nosler (including 6mm and 6.5 Creedmoor). The new .27 Nosler, essentially on the same case as the .30 Nosler, has a longer neck and shorter torso to ensure Nosler .28s don't enter a .27 chamber. All 48 rifles feature a pillar-bedded, push-feed action with a two-position thumb safety

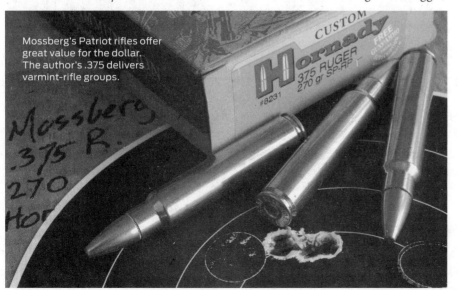

Mossberg's Patriot rifles offer great value for the dollar. The author's .375 delivers varmint-rifle groups.

and adjustable trigger. The lapped twin-lug bolt has a recessed bolt face, Sako-style extractor, plunger ejector. The flat-bottomed receiver accepts Remington 700 scope bases. Nosler's Custom Shop offers myriad options.

nosler.com

REMINGTON

To shiver saucepan-size plates 800 yards off, you need an accurate barrel, with stock, trigger and sight to match. These blessings arrived in one package last fall. The 700-X in 7mm Magnum is a Custom-Shop product, bedded with MarineTex in a McMillan stock. The Badger-knobbed bolt with M16-style extractor and twin ejectors cycled like a race-engine piston. The trigger broke at a wish. The 5 1/2-contour Shilen barrel, rifled 1-in-8, wore an AAC suppressor. A Swarovski Z8 3.5-28x50 scope helped me direct bullets from this nail-driver. But Remington's CS manager Carlos Martinez says "factory" 700s are slated to get the standout features of the 700-X, "receiver, bolt and barrel trued so they're coaxial and the bolt face squared with that axis. To better anchor heavy scopes, we'll change 6-48 base holes to 8-40s." He shied from schedules for installing on factory rifles the 700-X's claw extractor and dual ejectors.

Various renditions of the 700 remain Remington's bread-and-butter centerfires, the Model Seven a compact alternative, the 783 for shooters on brutal budgets. Three new 783s popped up last year. The Varmint, in .223, .22-250, .243, 6.5 Creedmoor and .308, comes in at $625. The HBT, or Heavy Barrel Threaded, lists at $459. For the same money you can also get a 783 in .450 Bushmaster, a straight-walled round popular in deer-hunting units previously under "shotgun-only" restriction. The 6.5 Creedmoor was added to the 783 Black Synthetic roster. Fresh for 2020: The Model 700 PCR (Precision Chassis Rifle) Enhanced in .308, 6mm and 6.5 Creedmoor has a fluted, threaded 24-inch barrel with 5R rifling. The alloy chassis accepts five- or 10-shot Magpul detachable boxes. M-LOK-ported, the handguard has a Pic rail up front, plus a bridge-to-handguard rail in the rear. A Magpul grip and

One of several forms of Ruger's Hawkeye chambers the 9.3x62, a superb hunting round since 1905.

threaded, oversize bolt knob, with the stock's adjustable comb and length of pull, help you shoot from any position. With a heft of over 11 pounds, the PCR serves best on a bipod. More agile in cover: the Remington Model Seven Synthetic Mossy Oak. Charitably, the rifle is shorter than the name. Its 20-inch threaded barrel in 6.5 Creedmoor (and a 16 1/2-inch in .300 Blackout) doesn't seem to justify the 20-minute rail. The SuperCell recoil pad is an asset, the stock well-shaped for catch-as-catch-can shooting. It joins four other Model Sevens, all with 20-inch barrels. The CDL boasts an American walnut stock.

remington.com

ROCK RIVER ARMS

Well-known for its excellent AR-style rifles, Rock River has opened a new decade with a chassis-based bolt-action rifle. The RBG in 6.5 Creedmoor and .308 comes in two versions, both with proprietary stainless steel actions fitted with 20-, 22- or 24-inch Wilson fluted stainless barrels, threaded, air-gauged and cryo-treated. They're rifled 1-in-10 and fed by AICS Magpul-compatible detachable boxes. Oversize bolt knobs, Triggertech triggers and 20-minute rails are standard. With adjustable KRG stock in black or tan, the 10 1/4-pound (20-inch barrel) RBG lists for $4,150. A "Tactical" version with McMillan A-6 stock is available too.

rockriverarms.com

RUGER

Of refinements that distinguish the Hawkeye from its M77 predecessor,

I especially like the lean, predatory profile of Standard and African rifles. The Hawkeye Hunter, in seven chamberings, .204 Ruger to .300 Win. Mag. is new this year. A stainless rifle, it also has a stock of traditional shape and checkered walnut. That Spartan form, modified by an adjustable butt, appears as well on the Long-Range Hunter. Its stock is not checkered walnut, but hardwood under the "speckled black/brown" paint of the Hawkeye Long-Range Target trotted out a year ago (this year with the .204 Ruger and .308 on its cartridge roster).

Newest in Ruger's Hawkeye stable: The nimble Long-Range Hunter in 6.5 PRC.

Like all Hawkeyes, the new L-R Hunter boasts a non-rotating Mauser extractor and fixed ejector, a three-detent safety. Unlike early M77s, feeding is truly controlled, follower to chamber. All Hawkeyes except the Long-Range duo have internal staggered-stack magazines with hinged floorplates. The A1 detachable boxes of LR Target and Hunter rifles hold five standard rounds, three of magnum diameter.

I hunted with a Long-Range Hunter last autumn, in 6.5 PRC (Precision Rifle Cartridge). Based on Hornady's .300 Ruger Compact Magnum, the 6.5 PRC has the .532 head of common belted magnums. Its 30-degree shoulder is set farther back than the 35-degree slope of WSMs, so the neck won't over-run the shanks of missiles with Pinocchio noses when they're seated to suit short-action magazines. The 6.5 PRC beats the 6.5 Creedmoor at the gate by about 250 fps. Hornady's 143-grain ELD-X from the Creedmoor clocks 2,700 fps. The PRC kicks it out at 2,960. Distance narrows that gap, as faster bullets endure more drag. But at 500 yards the 6.5 PRC still has an edge of 225 fps. The Hawkeye L-R Hunter I've used shot extremely well, its 1-in-8 rifling evidently ideal for Hornady's 143-grain ELD-X bullets. The threaded, stainless barrel, 22 inches long, is of "sporter" profile. Ruger indicates it might rethink the supplied 20-minute Pic rail, a holdover from the L-R Target, where it belongs. With the Hunter's standard comb, the rail puts a scope too high for quick aim. Also for 2020, Ruger has added a Rimfire Long-Range Target to its American series. This 8-pound rifle has the look and stock features of the Hawkeye L-R Target. You'll note this year all five bolt rifles in the 77-Series feature threaded muzzles. Bored to .17 WSM as well as .17 and .22 Hornet, plus.357 and .44 Magnum, 77-Series rifles include three with open sights on their 18 1/2-inch barrels.

ruger.com

SAUER

Now in its 269th year, J.P. Sauer & Sohn is Germany's oldest manufacturer of sporting arms. The company is now owned by the L&O Group that also

Impressed by Sauer's 101 rifle during a tour of Sauer's plant in Isny, Germany, the author bought one in 9.3x62.

controls Mauser and Blaser brands. The three share a campus in Isny, Germany. Sauer's rifle series, the 100 and 101 and switch-barrel 404 have sleek, box-fed bolt actions, with low-lift, multiple-lug, full-diameter bolts. Iron sights are standard on most 404 and 101 barrels. Triggers are adjustable or installed to break cleanly at 2 pounds. You can choose from a variety of stock materials and styles (including thumbhole and stutzen). The 303 is a self-loader with many of the same features. New S100 Pantera and Fieldshoot rifles boast fresh, attractive stock profiles especially well-adapted to prone shooting. They're lithe, not clubby. These two Sauers were the first rifles commercially bored for Hornady's 6.5 PRC round, new last year.
sauer.de

Sauer's upscale, switch-barrel 404 also features interchangeable bolt heads for different case sizes.

SAVAGE

Few pages in Savage's 2020 catalog have escaped new models. Five

versions of the flagship 110 bolt rifle, introduced in 1958, are fresh. Short years ago, that total might have accounted for all 110s. Now there are 25. All, even the new walnut-stocked Classic and braked, skeleton-stocked Precision and Elite Precision chassis rifles, have AccuFit-adjustable butt and comb, and a three-position tang safety. The new Ridge Warrior in Mossy Oak

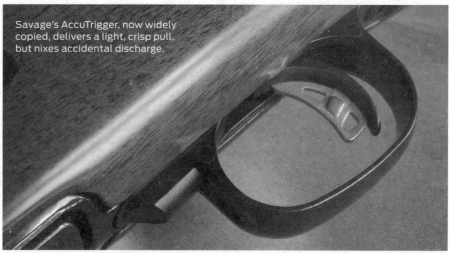
Savage's AccuTrigger, now widely copied, delivers a light, crisp pull, but nixes accidental discharge.

Overwatch camo comes in .308 and 6.5 Creedmoor. The 6-pound Ultralite offers eight chamberings for its carbon-fiber barrel, including the .280 Ackley, 6.5 PRC and .28 Nosler. Threaded muzzles are popping up on 110s of all profiles. Nearly all sub-models feature detachable box magazines. Prices range from $600 for the Hog Hunter and Engage Hunter to $1,500 for chassis rifles. Savage has added the .350 Legend to the cartridge rosters of four 110s. It also appears in seven of the 14 entry-level Axis rifles (from $375). The only Axis priced above $570 is the Axis II Precision chassis rifle with adjustable stock and 20-minute rail. Long-range competitors can choose from eight 9- to 13-pound rifles, .243 to .338 Lapua. Half are synthetic-stocked; the others wear gray laminated wood. A quartet of new rail-equipped, bolt-action slug guns boast Savage's AccuTrigger. Rifling twist for 12-gauge versions: 1-in-35. For 20-bores it's 1-in-24. There are few changes in Savage's rimfire family, which includes five B.Mag rifles in .17 WSM.

savagearms.com

THOMPSON/CENTER

Owned by Smith & Wesson, Thompson/Center has evolved from a blackpowder rifle company to a manufacturer of centerfire bolt rifles. Its Compass and Venture have supplanted the walnut-stocked Icon. The Compass retails from $359 in six short-action chamberings. A cheap, but serviceable, rifle. The three-lug Venture arrived in

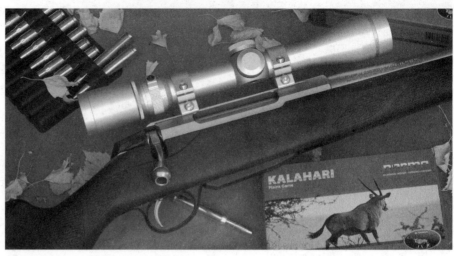

Tikka's T3 rifle, manufactured in the Riihimaki, Finland, plant producing Sakos, has given way to the T3x.

2009, with a tubular receiver, washer-style recoil lug and injection-molded stock to keep a lid on price. It has the Icon's 5R rifling: five grooves with angled groove-land junctures. The trigger is adjustable. The polymer magazine is a champ. Available now in nine chamberings to .300 Winchester (including .350 Legend), it came to me first in .270 and drilled half-inch knots with 53 grains IMR 4064 and 100-grain Hornadys at 3,465 fps. With 61 grains RL-22 and 130 Speers it shot into .6. My one criticism: a stubby bolt handle that made for hard lift from the shoulder. Still, this is a fine value in a durable, accurate rifle. The Venture II lists for just $525. T/C (and S&W's Performance Center) also lists a new, chassis-style LRR Long Range Rifle. In .243, 6.5 Creedmoor and .308, it features an alloy stock in tan or black, with Magpul

M-Lok accessory cuts and a 20-minute Picatinny rail. The trigger adjusts down to 2 1/2 pounds.

tcarms.com

TIKKA

New T3x rifles for 2020: The Lite Veil Alpine and Lite Veil Wideland differ only in stock camo and Cerakote colors on the steel. They come in 10 chamberings, with braked 22 1/2- and 24 1/2-inch barrels and weigh 6 1/2 to 7 pounds. The Lite Roughneck is physically identical, but with blued steel and a Roughtech stock in tan or black. A Polyfade rifle in digital camo, with a modular stock, comes in 20 chamberings and weighs from 6 to 6 1/2 pounds. In a nod to the long-range market, Tikka has trotted out its UPR (Ultimate Precision Rifle), in .308, .260 and 6.5 Creedmoor. Its prone-style, carbon-fiber/fiberglass stock is adjustable at comb and butt. Rail, threaded muzzle, 10-shot magazine and oversize bolt knob are standard. Specify single-stage or set trigger. Rimfire enthusiasts find the 10-shot T1x, in .22 LR and .17 HMR, looks and handles like a T3x.

tikka.fi

WEATHERBY

With California in the rearview mirror, Weatherby has ramped up rifle production in its Sheridan, Wyoming, facility. The new 6.5 RPM (Rebated Precision Magnum) headlines 2020

Thompson/Center's serviceable entry-level Compass rifle starts at just $359 in short-action form.

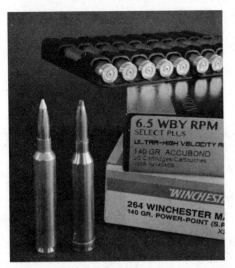

Weatherby's new 6.5 RPM (left) fits six-lug Mark V actions, but rivals the .264 Winchester in flight.

offerings. "The RPM takes advantage of every bit of space in our slim six-lug Mark V action," said Weatherby's chief, Adam Weatherby. "This 6.5 sends 127-grain bullets at over 3,200 fps, 140s at over 3,000." With close to a ton and a half of muzzle energy, those bullets deliver 1,500 ft-lbs nearly 500 yards. Unlike other Weatherby rounds, the RPM has no belt or radiused shoulder junctures. Like the .284 Winchester, its body is bigger in diameter than its .473 rim, so it holds lots of powder but fits standard bolt faces. Another distinction is in the rifle. It has no extended "freebore," the long throat Roy Weatherby paired with his hot cartridges to keep a lid on breech pressures. The RPM was designed without the freebore imperative. Adam told me that while Norma is loading Weatherby-branded belted cartridges, RPM ammunition will come from the Sheridan facility. A Backcountry rifle bored for this 6.5 weighs just 6 pounds. Price: $2,499. Weatherby has added to its Accumark (6- and 9-lug actions) Pro and Elite versions with prone-style stocks suited for long-range shooting. Carbon-fiber stocks hold weight to between 7 and 8 1/2 pounds. The Accumark series retails for $1,999 to $2,799. Carbonmark rifles, with threaded BSF carbon-fiber barrels tack $500 onto those prices. The Cerakoted Weathermark line marries traditional barrels with fiberglass stocks for as

little as $1,499. Walnut aficionados can still buy a Deluxe Mark V for $2,349. The Camilla Deluxe, stocked for women, now comes in an Ultra Lightweight version with synthetic stock. It weighs 5 3/4 pounds, lists for $2,399. A Camilla Wilderness has joined other Howa-based Vanguard rifles at $799. The Weatherguard, Multicam and Laminate complete the Vanguard line for standard (and some Weatherby) cartridges.

weatherby.com

WINCHESTER

Mossy Oak Break-Up Country camo adorns Winchester's latest XPR Hunter rifle and a Compact sibling. The Compact comes in eight short-action chamberings, like the standard XPR Compact in black polymer. Add five long-action rounds (.270, .30-06 and 7mm, .300 and .338 belted magnums) for Hunter, Hunter Strata, Hunter Highlander and walnut-stocked XPR and XPR Sporter versions. The .350 Legend is now on the cartridge roster for all XPR bolt-action rifles, priced at $550 for the XPR and XPR Compact, $600 for the others. All have a button-rifled barrel secured by a nut ensuring precise headspace. The full-diameter, three-lug bolt affords 60-degree lift and is nickel Teflon-coated for buttery travel in a receiver machined from bar stock. It has a lug-mounted extractor and

plunger ejector. The port is big enough for occasional top feed, when you've no time to charge the single-stack detachable box. A two-detent thumb safety locks the bolt; a tab lets you cycle it safely. The M.O.A. trigger adjusts for weight and over-travel. My XPR in .325 WSM came with a smooth, crisp, consistent 3-pound trigger. Scope-mount holes accept stout 8-40 screws, to anchor heavy scopes. A steel bar in the stock is the recoil lug, engaging a receiver slot. The stock's "Inflex Technology" buttpad has internal ribs that direct the comb away from your face. Fore-end cross-members limit flex. Textured panels fore and aft keep cold wet hands from slipping. GD

winchesterguns.com

Reinforcing ribs inside the fore-end make this lightweight XPR stock rigid. Note the inset recoil lug.

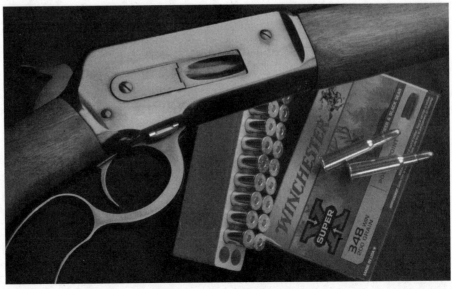

Winchester's Miroku plant in Japan builds faithful reproductions of classic lever rifles – here a 71.

NEW AR-STYLE RIFLES

Springfield Armory
SAINT Victor

› TODD WOODARD

As I write this, I'm looking at entries for AR-15 rifles on BudsGunShop.com, where I've bought several auto-loader rifles in the past year for examination in *Gun Tests* magazine. The most expensive is listed as a model from 2A Armament, model number 2A-CRP-16CFMLCBN. Buds has it for the low, low price of $3,415. Uh. I look down the specs list to see why it's so spendy. Has a .223 Wylde chamber to handle both 5.56 NATO and .223 Remington rounds without any function issues. Loading a diet of 5.56 rounds into a .223 SAAMI-spec chamber might cause some problems, but the compromise chambering solves that and isn't that costly. I bounce over to the 2A site (2A-Arms.com) and see a pretty standard Tier 1 listing of the guts of the gun, and all that un-obtainium adds up. Then I look at the Buds listing again and saw the number that mattered: 5.5 pounds.

Ahhh. Then I looked at the barrel spec

and saw, "PROOF RESEARCH, Carbon Fiber, Mid-length." Those are usually $500 net upgrades to most any AR-15 price. Being skinny never goes out of fashion, it seems.

These rifle types have been selling well for years now, but the market seems to have reached its fill, unless you're in a state (hello, Virginia) that is threatening to take them away, then everyone rushes to buy one or two, price be damned. Or unless there's a virus-created run.

What's amazing is how specific the build quality has become for the price point. By that I mean, anyone who's considering buying an AR can dip his or her toe in the market for not a lot of dollars; or, conversely, another buyer with a lot of money can buy an AR with the best components, from several high-end makers. The range of choices is

truly staggering, which places a burden on the novice buyer to know how to vet a list of components and find the things that truly matter.

Many shooters follow the same strategy: buy the best major components you can afford (receivers, barrels, bolt-carrier groups), then put the modularity of the AR platform into play to upgrade your rifle from the outside in (buttstocks, handguards, triggers), on whatever pace you desire.

In the following, I'll list some current commercial builds, at varying price points, to help you figure out what AR-15 or AR-10 you might want to invest in.

ANDERSON MANUFACTURING

The Hebron, Kentucky, builder made its name as a value-priced rifle supplier, as well as in parts and accessories. Also,

Anderson Manufacturing AM-9

Anderson promotes its "RF85 nano-technology," which Anderson reports makes its rifles the only ones in the world that require zero lubrication. The proprietary RF85 process permanently injects calcium into the molecular fabric of the metal, reducing friction while forming a lasting protective barrier that eliminates the need for any lubrication, according to the company. RF85-treated items sell for a pretty hefty premium: $140-plus on a basic optics-ready 5.56 rifle, or about 25 percent, but maybe having a "no-lube rifle" is worth the extra dollars. For some shooters, it absolutely would be worth it.

Anderson offers standard chamberings (5.56 in the AR-15 frame and .308 Win. in the AR-10 frame), as well as the 7.62x39 in the -15 line and 6.5 Creedmoor and .450 Bushmaster in its -10 line. You can get into the AR-10 complete rifles for as little as $1,100 (.308 Win., 18-inch barrel). Its AM-15 M4 Optic Ready (aka no sights) line in 5.56 can be had for about half that, $560.

For those who are finding out about the joys of pistol-claiber carbines, AM has a couple of offerings differentiated by different handguards. The AM-9 rifles have 16-inch Parkerized M4 Medium contour tubes with 1:10 twist rate. The lower receiver features a flared mag well, oversized magazine release, and bolt stop to speed up reloading time. One model has a 12-inch Keymod handguard while the other is an M-LOK design. $720.

andersonmanufacturing.com

ARMALITE

Former vice president and presidential candidate Joe Biden blurted out that he would confiscate "AR-14s" and other assault weapons if he became president. This is amusing because Armalite,

Armalite Rifles

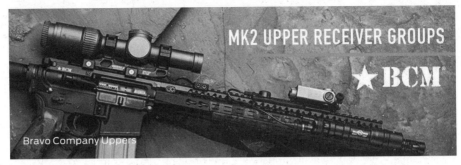
Bravo Company Uppers

MK2 UPPER RECEIVER GROUPS

★ **BCM®**

the original name in M16 and AR-15 development, actually built a precursor "AR-14" sporting rifle back in the 1950s. That's how long Armalite has been in the game, and the company continues to innovate in the segment. Example: The AR10 TAC 6.5 is the company's latest thinking in putting together an AR-10 that accuracy shooters will enjoy. Chambered in 6.5 Creedmoor (CM), which has a few more rounds of capacity (25) in the same space as a 20-round .308 magazine, the TAC 6.5 has a 22-inch medium-heavy stainless steel barrel to maximize the performance of VLD bullets. Many shooters are choosing the CM over its Winchester parent case because its .264-caliber bullets are more aerodynamic than .30-caliber projectiles in the .308 Win. In October 2017, U.S. Special Operations Command tested the performance of 7.62×51mm NATO, .260 Remington, and 6.5mm Creedmoor cartridges out of SR-25, M110A1 and Mk 20 Sniper Support Rifle rifles. SOCOM determined the 6.5 Creedmoor performed the best, doubling hit probability at 1,000-plus yards, substantially increasing effective range, reducing wind drift and producing less recoil than 7.62×51mm NATO rounds. Elsewhere on the rifle, there's a Magpul PRS buttstock with adjustable length-of-pull and comb height and an Armalite two-stage trigger. Pretty well-outfitted for $2,099.

armalite.com

BRAVO COMPANY MFG.

Bravo Company Mfg. (BCM) started in the garage of a veteran United States Marine in Hartland, Wisconsin, shortly after Operation Iraqi Freedom in 2003. BCM builds professional-grade weaponry manufactured, reinforced and tested to meet the unforgiving

needs of professional soldiers, law enforcement and responsible citizens in some of the highest-threat environments in the world.

For 2020, the bulk of BCM's new products are components, major components you can install by removing a couple of pins. For instance, there are several new upper-receiver groups that feature the company's patent-pending MK2 Upper Receiver, which BCM claims has enhanced rigidity over the USGI product. Less flex reduces premature damage, wear and failure of bolt lugs from misalignment. A gas expansion chamber is machined above the charging handle track, combined with dual vents machined at the rear (each side, above charging handle latch) help to redirect and vent gas away the shooter's face. Uppers with stainless steel barrels are machined from SS410 stainless steel, hand lapped, and have 1:7 or 1:8 twist rates, button rifling, and M4 feed ramps barrel extensions. In developing the USGI M4 carbine as one of the primary weapons for today's infantry, some modifications were performed to the original M16 platform to enhance the reliability of the shorter-barreled carbines. With the shorter carbine gas system and the increased gas port pressure, the carbine cycled faster, and at times the cycle rate could be faster than the magazine would feed ammunition. One of the modifications done to increase reliable feeding included enhancing the angle and the length of the feed ramps. This USGI modification was done to both the barrel extension and the upper receiver, creating a longer and steeper feed ramp. These Mil-Spec M4 feed ramps are part of the original CNC manufacturing process. Elsewhere, all of the BCM flat top uppers feature a USGI-type laser-etched T-marks to provide addressing for the remounting of tactical accessories such as optics, laser sights, etc. The chambers are 5.56 NATO Match Chamber (USMC SAM-R Chamber) styles, a precision version of the 5.56 NATO chamber. Barrel lengths include 14.5- (with permanent brakes), 16- and 18-inch lengths. Varying handguards and gas systems are available. And .300 Blackout uppers are available. Prices for the uppers start around $635.

bravocompanymfg.com

BROWNELLS

Brownells has had a lot of fun going "Back to the Future" with its Retro line of rifles, such as the BRN-10 .308 Winchester and BRN-605 5.56 Carbine. Now, Brownells, in collaboration with InRange TV and KE Arms, has announced the launch of the "What Would Stoner Do" (WWSD) 2020 Rifle Project. Inspired by the original InRange TV WWSD rifle project from 2017, WWSD 2020 further explores the question of what AR rifle designer Eugene Stoner might do, were he still around and had access to modern, lightweight materials and manufacturing methods.

Paul Levy, Brownells' director of product management said, "The collaboration on the WWSD 2020 was initiated after InRange TV posted a recap of the first WWSD Project. Brownells stocked a lot of those components, and it made sense to us to reach out to see if they'd be interested in building out a complete rifle for resale. KE Arms stepped up to assemble and manufacture the Mk3 Lower, and here we are."

The heart of the WWSD 2020 rifle is the one-piece polymer Mk3 Lower from KE Arms. The result is a very lightweight rifle with a polymer one-piece lower and a pencil barrel. Listed as #100-037-291 at Brownells.com, the WWSD 2020 rifle retails for $1,700. WWSD 2020 Rifles became available in Spring 2020.

It features several improvements over previous one-piece polymer lowers, including an improved magazine well optimized for P-Mags and D-60 drums, modernized pistol grip angle

and texture, and an already-installed ambidextrous PDQ bolt-release lever. The stock will have integral M-LOK slots and QD socket points for sling-attachment flexibility, along with an internal storage compartment for a cleaning kit or other small parts. Not only can customers buy complete WWSD 2020 rifles, they can also shop a line of stripped and completed lowers, as well as other components for their own lightweight builds.

brownells.com

CMMG

CMMG introduced three Resolute models (100, 200 and 300) that would fire the new .350 Legend straight-walled cartridge the day after the round was officially announced in 2019. For 2020, CMMG jumped on the bandwagon of a much older round, the 5.7x28mm, which until this year had mainly been chambered in the FN FiveseveN handgun and that company's personal defense weapon (PDW).

Based in Boonville, Missouri, CMMG has taken 5.7x28mm to a whole new level with the release of the 5.7 AR Conversion Magazine. This innovative new magazine holds 40 rounds of 5.7x28mm and is designed to fit and function in a Mil-Spec AR-15 lower receiver when paired with CMMG's 5.7x28mm Radial Delayed Blowback upper receiver. The appeal of 5.7x28mm is that it is a small caliber with high velocity designed for a handgun and PDW. The cartridge was developed in response to NATO's request for a replacement for the

9x19mm cartridge.

CMMG offers a complete line of firearms in Banshee and Resolute models that are designed for 5.7 AR Conversion Magazines. Each is built with CMMG's Mk4 lower receiver and a dedicated 5.7x28mm Radial Delayed Blowback upper receiver and ships with one 5.7 AR Conversion Magazine.

CMMG also offers complete 5.7x28mm upper receivers in Banshee and Resolute models that are made with three different barrel lengths: 5, 8 and 16 inches. Each complete upper receiver uses CMMG's patented Radial Delayed Blowback operating system and is compatible with 5.7 AR Conversion Magazines.

For gun builders, CMMG will also offer 5.7x28mm bolt and barrel kits in 5-, 8- and 16-inch barrel lengths. The bolt and barrel kits will be compatible with CMMG Mk57 lower receivers, as well as Mk4/AR-15 lower receivers (when used with CMMG 5.7 AR Conversion Magazines).

CMMG's 5.7 AR Conversion Magazine are sold both as a single unit and in packs of three. The MSRP for the 5.7 AR Conversion Magazine is $39.95 and the three-pack is $99.95.

cmmginc.com

DANIEL DEFENSE

The company's new DDM4 PDW Pistol and SBR are two variations the home-defender can look at if he or she wants a versatile, low-recoil platform. The Black Creek, Georgia, company's

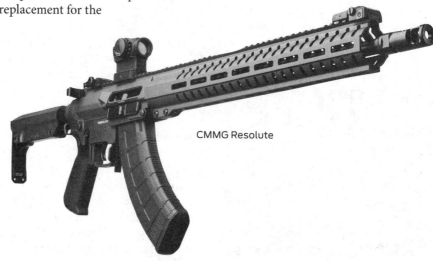

CMMG Resolute

President and CEO Marty Daniel said, "I believe our new DDM4 PDW is the absolute best gun you can buy to protect your family. And protecting our families is the most important thing any of us can ever do. It's accurate, easy to shoot and compact. I couldn't be any prouder of this groundbreaking product."

Featuring an overall length of 20.75 inches, the DDM4 PDW easily fits into a backpack for convenient transport. Its 7-inch .300 Blackout 1:7-twist cold-hammer-forged barrel keeps subsonic loads subsonic and provides great ballistics for a shorter barrel. The DDM4 PDW pistol comes equipped with the Maxim Defense CQB Pistol Brace with enhanced buffer system that functions reliably suppressed or unsuppressed. Other key features include a 6-inch MFR XL flat front rail, SLR M-Lok MOD2 Handstop, so you don't shoot your fingers off, a linear compensator to direct muzzle blast forward, and independently ambi GRIP-N-RIP Charging Handle with anti-gas features. MSRP for the DDM4 PDW pistol is $1,865 and $1,935 for the SBR. Both began shipping to dealers in February 2020.

danieldefense.com

F-1 FIREARMS

This Texas-based manufacturer makes more than 90 percent of each firearm using brand-new, state-of-the-art machines. Having this machining capability in-house allows F-1 Firearms to control critical tolerances for each component across all of platforms for top function, accuracy and dependability. Also, it produces 416 stainless steel barrels on an innovative barrel cell, which holds tolerances up to 0.0001 inch. The latest culmination of the gunmaker's art are two products, the BDRX-15 and BDRX-10 Skeletonized Rifles. The smaller-frame BDRX-15 has barrels chambered in .223 Wylde chamber for 5.56 NATO or .223 Rem., and also comes in .300 AAC, 7.62x39mm and .224 Valkyrie versions. The DuraBolt direct-impingement, full-auto-rated M16/M4 bolt carrier group fits AR-15 Mil-Spec receivers and associated components. The available DuraBolt Black DLC is enhanced with

H-K USA MR762A1
Long Rifle Package II

a Chemical Vapor Disposition (CVD) coating, which gives it an extremely durable and corrosion-resistant, black-mirror finish. This coating also offers unmatched lubricity with a 0.01 coefficient of friction, the best in the industry. The BDRX-10 is chambered in .308 Win. and 6.5 Creedmoor. The receivers and handguards on most models are meticulously engineered to be as light as possible, while remaining rigid and cosmetically pleasing. All areas not inherent to functionality have been stripped away, leaving a beautiful base for any build. Each set is hand-finished and matched in-house.

f-1firearms.com

FRANKLIN ARMORY

In 2020, Franklin Armory expanded its model lines to include chamberings for the .350 Legend cartridge, offering three new models, the M4-HTF-R3 XTD, XO-26 R3 and CA12. As with the existing models, the newest variants will be available in state-specific models for California, Connecticut, New Jersey and other restrictive jurisdictions. The M4-HTF R3 comes with one 10- or 20-round magazine. The barrel is a 16-inch M4 Contour with a 1:12 RH twist, the SAAMI standard for the Legend's bullets. The .350 Legend was designed for use in a number of U.S. states that have specific regulations for deer hunting with straight-walled centerfire cartridges. It has the same rim diameter as a 5.56 case (0.378 in.), so it can use the same bolt. Rounds will fit in a modified AR magazine. MSRP is $1,299.99.

franklinarmory.com

HK-USA

Notable among the company's 2020 offerings is the MR762A1 Long Rifle Package II (LRP II), an essentially standard MR762A1 (caliber 7.62x51mm NATO) semi-automatic rifle to which Heckler & Koch USA adds a Leupold 3-9VX-R Patrol 3-9x40mm scope and mount, HK G28 adjustable cheekpiece buttstock and LaRue Tactical BRM-S bipod. A semi-automatic rifle originally developed from the fully automatic HK417, the MR762A1 LRP employs the same HK proprietary gas-piston operating system found on current HK rifles and carbines, using a "pusher" rod in place of the gas tube normally found in AR15/M16/M4-style firearms. This method of operation virtually eliminates malfunctions that are common to direct-impingement gas systems, because hot carbon fouling and waste gases do not enter the receiver area. The barrels are manufactured in Germany and finished in the USA. Additional accessories and add-ons for the LRP variant of the MR762A1 include an ERGO Pistol Grip from Falcon Industries, the same Blue Force Gear sling used on the HK M27 IAR supplied to the USMC and an OTIS cleaning kit. The rifle package, complete with one 20- and one 10-round magazine, is shipped ready to use with the scope attached in a compact 42-inch Model 1720 Pelican case. Like its 5.56mm counterpart, the MR762A1 is a direct descendent of the HK416/417 series, only in a semi-automatic rifle configuration developed for civilian users. The MIL-STD-1913 Picatinny-type rail systems/handguards allow all current accessories, sights, lights and aimers used on M4/M16-type weapons to be fitted to the MR series. The HK rail systems can be removed without special tools by the user and ensures 100 percent return to zero when reinstalled. With both the HK Modular Rail System (MRS) and the Free Floating Rail System (FFRS), the barrel does not touch the handguard, ensuring the barrel/handguard relationship is free-floating for maximum accuracy. The MRS handguard was added in 2016 and has many of the features found on the FFRS, but with a more ergonomic design. It uses an HK proprietary keyhole design to allow the attachment on Picatinny rail segments to the handguard for the installation of accessories. Ambidextrous operating controls are standard on the MR762A1, including a convertible charging handle and an ambidextrous selector lever.

hk-usa.com

LWRCI

The REPR MKII Rapid Engagement Precision Rifle is a full-spectrum weapon system designed to deliver ultimate power and precision for a variety of real-world shooting applications. It has recently been chambered in 6.5 Creedmoor, in addition to the more-standard 7.62 issue. The REPR MKII platform was developed to meet the requirements of the U.S. Army's solicitation for a more Compact Semi Auto Sniper System (CSASS), which should have been named KICKASS, but they didn't ask me. The REPR MKII answered the call with significant improvements in dependability, accuracy and aesthetics that made the original REPR model a major success. The heart and soul of the REPR MKII is the

proprietary short-stroke, gas-piston operating system with 20-position gas block, allowing precise tuning to match exact shooting conditions, suppression or ammunition choice. The rifle is available with either LWRCI's non-reciprocating side-charge, which I really enjoy and prefer, or ambidextrous rear-charge configurations. The REPR MKII 6.5 Creedmoor is built with a Proof Research 22-inch stainless steel or carbon-fiber barrel on the Elite model. The 7.62 REPR MKII models are available in 12.7-, 16.1- and 20-inch barrel lengths and Proof Research stainless steel or carbon-fiber materials. Other features include a Geissele SSA-E trigger, Magpul UBR or PRS Stock, LWRCI Skirmish BUIS, Ultra Static Brake 4 Port Enhanced Muzzle, fully ambidextrous lower receiver, monoforge upper receiver and nickel-boron-coated bolt carrier.

lwrci.com

PATRIOT ORDNANCE FACTORY

Introduced in 2020, Patriot Ordnance Factory's Project "Rogue" was an exercise to turn the Revolution platform into the lightest .308 semi-auto rifle on the market, and to do it without lightening cuts while making the rifle available at a price point affordable to serious shooters. The result is a sub-6-pound, .308 rifle packed with proprietary and patented innovations. Thanks to its light weight, carrying this semi-auto .308 in the field seems like a more realistic option than humping a 10-pounder around. The Rogue features a stylized forged receiver set, stainless steel match-grade barrel, ambidextrous selector, oversized

heatsink barrel nut and a Micro B muzzle brake. Other features include an 11-inch M-LOK Renegade free-floating rail with four integrated QD sling mounts. E2 dual-extraction technology helps dislodge cartridge cases. There's also a one-piece, high-phosphorus, nickel-coated, direct-impingement bolt carrier with mechanical key built into the body and positioned behind the cam pin, as well as a chrome-plated bolt, extractor and firing pin. KNS Precision stainless steel non-rotating anti-walk pins, Mil-Spec aluminum anti-tilt buffer tube, and patented roller cam pin with NP3-coated roller head round out the goodies. MSRP $1,800. Pistol version also available.

pof-usa.com

RADICAL FIREARMS

This company was busy in 2020, rolling out several AR-style rifles in .350 Legend, .308 Winchester, and 6.5 Creedmoor. There are two Legend chamberings, both with 16-inch barrels and 15-inch handguards. The MHR handguard is a free-float M-Lok-style Hybrid Rail. The Radical Rail System offers a larger inside diameter designed to accommodate your suppressor or for those who like the feel of a full-sized quad rail. At 1.8 inches inside diameter, most suppressors easily fit inside and the cutouts on the rail aid in rapid cooling. In .308, Radical issued five models, three of which had TMS handguards and newly designed billet 7075 T6 matching upper and lower receivers starting at $1,050. The 15-inch TMS low-profile M-Lok rail is a free-float system for increased accuracy, keeping your hands cool and giving you plenty of room for accessories. These models were offered with 18-, 20- and 24-inch .308 tubes. Two similar rifles, $1100, were chambered in 6.5 Creedmoor with 20- and 24-inch barrels.

radicalfirearms.com

ROCK RIVER ARMS

In 1996, brothers Mark and Chuck Larson founded Rock River Arms (RRA) in an 1,800-square-foot shop in Cleveland, Illinois. Rock River Arms soon developed a reputation as one of the finest builders of hand-fitted custom

LWRCI REPR MKII

Sig Sauer 716i Tread

1911 pistols, and the brothers soon turned their manufacturing expertise into producing custom .223-caliber AR-style rifles. Today, operating out of a 50,000-square-foot facility in Colona, Illinois, the company produces a full line of custom rifles, parts and accessories. For 2020, RRA introduced its BT-6 in .338 Lapua Magnum, and updated LAR-15M's in .350 Legend, .450 Bushmaster and .204 Ruger. The BT-6 in .338 Lapua Magnum is a step up for most shooters used to the .308 Win. in this platform. This item comes with a 24-inch, black-nitride stainless steel barrel with 1:10 twist, and, thankfully, a four-port muzzle device. The trigger is RRA's Ultra Match Two Stage device. The RRA LAR-15M .450 Bushmaster produces new advantages for modern hunters using straight-wall cartridges. Delivering the same accuracy (1-MOA at 100 yards) expected from RRA's precision rifles, the .450 Bushmaster features a 16-inch stainless steel cryo-treated barrel with smooth rifling (1:24 twist) and equipped with an RRA Operator Brake. The RRA two-stage trigger provides a crisp break and is housed in the RRA winter trigger guard, allowing full dexterity while wearing gloves. The RRA LAR-15M .450 Bushmaster comes standard with a six-position Operator CAR stock, over-molded A2 pistol grip and 13-inch extended lightweight free-float handguard covering a low-profile gas block and mid-length gas system. The full-length top rail configuration fits all quality optic systems while the M-LOK compatibility provides for accessory attachments, such as a bipod and light source. A hard-plastic, five-round polymer magazine, owner's manual and warranty are included with the rifle. Specs for the .350 Legend

are similar. Also, RRA built new LAR-15 RRAGE Carbines in .223/5.56mm. The RRAGE Carbine builds on Rock River Arms' new extruded flat-top upper receiver. Made of 6061T aluminum, this receiver exhibits the clean lines and defined angles commonly associated with more expensive billet uppers.

rockriverarms.com

SIG SAUER

Introduced in 2020, the Tread 716i 16 is a 7.62x51 NATO-chambered variant in the company's lightweight big-bore AR platform. Featuring an ambidextrous lower receiver, a precision carbon-steel barrel and a free-floating M-LOK handguard, the 716i provides a versatile platform for long-range hunting and shooting while maintaining a lightweight design for easy carry. The new version is compatible with Tread accessories.

sigsauer.com

SPRINGFIELD ARMORY

Introduced midyear 2019, the SAINT Victor series of 5.56 rifles and pistols from Springfield Armory are designed to give you everything you need on a premium defensive firearm, right out of the box. The lower receiver on the SAINT Victor Rifle is Accu-Tite tension-bonded to a flat-top forged upper receiver and features a 16-inch CMV barrel that is Melonite-finished inside and out for corrosion resistance. The M-LOK free-float 15-inch handguard provides plenty of space for accessory attachment. Unlike many other AR rifles on the market today, SAINT

Victor rifles feature a pinned, low-profile gas block. Also included are spring-loaded, flip-up sights, a nickel-boron-coated, single-stage flat trigger and Springfield Armory's proprietary muzzle brake. The staked receiver end plate features a QD mount for sling attachment. Inside is an M16 bolt carrier group that is also Melonite-finished, HPT/MPI-tested, shot-peened and houses a 9310 steel bolt. The SAINT Victor rifle is also available in a California-approved model with a Strike Industries Featureless Grip and Magpul MOE fixed stock. An 11.5-inch SBR configuration is also available for LE and civilian use.

Springfield Armory's heavy-hitting addition to the new SAINT Victor family, also introduced mid-2019, comes chambered in .308 Win., the line's first AR-10 platform. Weighing in at 7.8 pounds, this rifle features a 16-inch, lightweight-profile CMV barrel that is Melonite-coated inside and out, and is partnered with an M-LOK free-float 15-inch handguard that protects the mid-length gas system. The Victor .308 also features a pinned, low-profile gas block, high-quality spring-loaded, flip-up sights, and a Springfield Armory-designed muzzle brake that eliminates barrel rise and softens recoil. An enhanced nickel-boron-coated, single-stage flat trigger provides more surface area for improved trigger contact. The end plate on the rifle features a QD mount for sling attachment. Inside is an enhanced bolt carrier group that is also Melonite-finished, with a 9310 steel bolt that is MPI-tested and shot-peened for the utmost reliability. A 20-round Magpul Gen M3 PMAG is included. **GD**

springfield-armory.com

Rock River Arms BT-6 .338 Lapua Magnum

NEW SEMI-AUTO PISTOLS

› **ROBERT SADOWSKI**

Smith & Wesson Performance Center M&P380 Shield EZ

For 2021, the trend I see in the latest semi-automatic pistols is more conceal-carry models, particularly in new variations from established models from Smith & Wesson, Mossberg, Sig and FN, to name a few. More conceal-carry, optic-ready pistols are being produced, too. AR-15-style pistols continue to be released with CMMG, Springfield Armory and Sig offering models in powerful calibers and stripped-down entry models and well-equipped versions. While those types of pistols make up the majority of new semi-automatics introduced, the real surprise is .22-caliber pistols. Both Ruger and Diamondback Firearms have breathed new life into the 5.7x28mm caliber, and Glock and Ruger have refreshed the .22 LR rimfire pistol. Walther has also rebooted a line, ignoring the decades-old trend of polymer-frame pistols to steel-frame models. Here is a look at new semi-automatic pistols this year.

CZ-USA

Competition shooters should check out the new Shadow 2 SA (MSRP: $1,349). This Shadow variant features a light, crisp single-action-only trigger. Plus, it has a swappable magazine release that allows users to extend the button to one of three settings. The grip is the thing with the Shadow. Thin aluminum grips have toothy checkering as do the front and rear grip straps. Target sights consist of a fiber-optic front and

CZ 75 B 45th Anniversary

a serrated, black HAJO rear. The iconic CZ 75 has been in production for 45 years and the CZ 75 B 45th Anniversary (MSRP: $1,720) celebrates that milestone. This limited-edition pistol (only 1,000 will be produced) features all-steel construction in a high-gloss blued finish with the deep engraving on the slide and frame. Wood grips have matching engraving. Controls contrast with a glossy silver finish.

cz-usa.com

DAN WESSON

The DWX series is a hybrid pistol that uses the single-action fire-control group of a Dan Wesson 1911 and combines it with the ergonomics and capacity of a CZ 75 pistol. The full-size DWX (MSRP: $1,799) features a 5-inch bushing-less, match-grade bull barrel and double-stack magazine. In 9mm, it holds 19 rounds and in .40 Auto the magazine capacity is 15 rounds. The full-size variant is compatible with CZ P-09/P-10 F magazines. The DMX C (MSRP: $1,799) features a 4-inch barrel that combines features of a 1911 with a CZ 75 Compact. Both feature a forged-aluminum frame. The cool thing about the new DWX pistols is all the aftermarket parts available for CZ 75 and 1911 pistols, so users can fine-tune their DWX to their exact needs. The Valor

Dan Wesson DWX

1911 series now features a Stan Chen SI mag well, tapered grip, a tactical ambidextrous safety, serrated U-notch rear and front tritium sight, GI-style cocking serrations, and is chambered in .45 Auto. The Valor comes in a matte stainless (MSRP: $1,864) or black (MSRP: $2,181) finish. The 1911-style Kodiak (MSRP: $2,349) is a long-slide 10mm outfitted with a 6-inch bushing-less bull barrel, fully adjustable fiber-optic sights, accessory rail on the dustcover, G10 textured grips and an ambidextrous safety. Available in two finishes: Black version has bronzed controls and barrel, and Tri-Tone with a matte gray slide.

danwessonfirearms.com

DIAMONDBACK FIREARMS

Diamondback DBX

Diamondback AM2

The DBX57 (MSRP: $1,299) is a locked-breech, dual-gas-system mechanism chambered in the small, but fast, 5.7x28mm cartridge. This pistol features a left-side charging handle, 8-inch barrel with DBX muzzle device and M-Lok handguard. It uses FN Five-seveN 20-round magazines and can be equipped with an arm brace. The DB9 (MSRP: $279) is now in its fourth generation with striker-fire, double-action trigger, 6+1 round capacity, and 3.1-inch barrel. The AM2 (MSRP: $339) is Diamondback's first full-size 9mm pistol offering a 3.5-inch barrel, striker-fire trigger, and 17+1 round capacity.

diamondbackfirearms.com

FN 509 Compact MRD

FN

New to the FN 509 striker-fire series of 9mm pistols is the FN 509 Compact MRD (MSRP: $799) designed as a conceal-carry option with a 3.7-inch barrel, 10+1 capacity in a flush-fit magazine, and a slide with FN's Low-Profile Optics Mounting System that accepts nearly all reflex and red-dot optics. The sights on the MRD models feature tall, blackout iron sights that co-witness with the red-dot. The shortened grip allows for easier concealment and features two interchangeable back straps for a perfect grip. Plus, a new flatter-faced trigger allows for more controllable trigger press and cleaner break. With an overall length of 6.8 inches and weight of 25.5 ounces, this FN is well-suited for everyday carry. Available in FDE or black finish.

fnamerica.com

GLOCK

I was invited to the launch of the G44 (MSRP: $430) when Glock shocked the shooting world with the introduction of a .22 LR. This is Glock's first rimfire and it was designed to match the dimensions of Glock's most popular pistol, the G19. The G44 uses a blowback mechanism and features a hybrid slide made of polymer and steel. Includes 10-round load-assist magazines, Marksman Barrel and adjustable sights. This pistol makes

Glock G44

a great training gun for new shooters as well as experienced shooters. Since it is similar to the G19, the transition from the G44 to G19 is nearly seamless. Plus, the G44 uses the same holster and magazine pouches as the G19.

us.glock.com/en

KAHR

Kahr K9 25th Anniversary

To celebrate 25 years of the iconic K9 pistol, the "25th Anniversary" limited-edition K9 (MSRP: $1,649) was developed. This limited-edition 9mm is made of stainless steel and is custom engraved with front and rear slide serrations, slide porting and a commemorative "25 Years" logo. The barrel and trigger are brightly polished. The finish is Sniper Grey Cerakote, and Hogue aluminum grips are custom engraved with aggressive stippling and the new Kahr logo. TruGlo tritium sights add the final and functional touch.

kahr.com

KEL-TEC

Kel-Tec P17

Another new .22 LR pistol designed for plinking fun is the P17 (MSRP: $199). At 14 ounces and only 6.7 inches long, this 16+1 capacity pistol offers a lot at a low cost. The P17 is made with a polymer frame that sandwiched together

the steel barrel and slide. Like most .22 LR pistols it uses a simple blowback action.

keltecweapons.com

KIMBER

The Collector Edition Raptor family consists of the full-size 1911 (MSRP: $1,524), Micro 9 (MSRP: $951), and EVO SP (MSRP: $999). These limited-edition pistols wear a unique two-tone finish, accented with a special patterned G10 grip, and night sights. Collector Series marking on the left side of the

Kimber Raptor

Kimber EVO SP

Kimber Micro 9 Triari

slide have special serial number prefixes. The Two-Tone finish treatment, blue slide and stainless frame, is now available with rosewood Crimson Trace green-laser Lasergrips. Variants available in this configuration include Ultra Carry II (MSRP: $1,177), Pro Carry II (MSRP: $1,136), Custom II (MSRP: $1,136), Micro (MSRP: $734), and Micro 9 (MSRP: $788). The Micro 9 Triari (MSRP: $788) has unique deep-relief, laser-engraved, stacked-cube front and rear cocking slide textures, plus Stiplex front strap pattern, and black linen Micarta grips with stacked-cube pattern for positive grip. Sights are a red fiber-optic front and green fiber-optic rear.

kimberamerica.com

MOSSBERG

Mossberg MC2c

The MC1sc 9mm subcompact line now includes an FDE finish (MSRP: $428) and two-tone finish (MSRP: $421). The new MC2c striker-fire series is a 9mm double-stack pistol with a 13-round flush-fit magazine and 15-round extended magazine. These compact pistols feature a 3.9-inch barrel, overall length of 7.1 inches, weight of 29 ounces loaded, and an accessory rail is built into the glass-reinforced polymer frame. Available in five variants: standard (MSRP: $490), cross-bolt safety version (MSRP: $490), stainless two-tone finish (MSRP: $490), stainless two-tone with cross-bolt safety (MSRP: $490), and a TruGlo tritium Pro sight model (MSRP: $595).

mossberg.com

NIGHTHAWK CUSTOM

The Agent2 Commander (MSRP: $4,499) resulted from a collaboration between Nighthawk and Agency Arms. Agency Arms took care of the

Nighthawk Agent2 Commander

Nighthawk Bull Officer

Heine sights, carbon-fiber grips and an Elite Smoke Cerakote finish. Thunder Ranch teamed up with Nighthawk on the Thunder Ranch Combat Special (MSRP: $3,399). This is Clint Smith's idea of an ultimate 1911. Features include course front and rear cocking serrations, lanyard loop mainspring housing, GI-Style thumb safety, custom engraving, gold-bead front sight, Smoked Nitride finish, and green linen/Micarta scale grips. Nighthawk takes a Series 70 1911 and transforms it into its Colt Series 70 (MSRP: $2,599). Sure, it looks a lot like a Colt Series 70, but inside it is fully tweaked and equipped with a new trigger system for optimal functionality.

nighthawkcustom.com

RUGER

The new Ruger-57 (MSRP: $799) revives the 5.7x28mm cartridge in a new pistol design with ergonomics that offer an easy trigger reach, 1911-style ambidextrous manual safety, rugged slide release and reversible magazine-release latch. It is available with either a 20- or 10-round magazine. It is equipped with adjustable rear and fiber-optic front sights and is drilled and tapped for easy mounting of optics with available optic-adapter plate. The new subcompact LCP II (MSRP: $349) is chambered in .22 LR and features the Lite Rack system with refined slide serrations, pronounced cocking ears and a lighter recoil spring, allowing for easy slide manipulation. Additional features include a 10-round magazine and Secure Action safety trigger with a short, crisp break. The Security-9 Pro (MSRP: $549) in 9mm features a 4-inch barrel, 15+1 round capacity in a rugged, no-nonsense design. The Security-9 Compact Pro

bad-attitude slide cuts and Nighthawk gun-smithed the rest to create a 1911 Commander with a unique look and flawless function. Features a match barrel in either 9mm or .45 Auto, crowned flush-cut barrel, custom trigger, ultra-high-cut front grip strap and whole lot more. The newest member of Nighthawk's Boardroom Series is the Vice President (MSRP: $4,199). The VP is chambered in 9mm and features heavy angle cuts in the slide with windows cut in the slide to show off the Gold Titanium Nitride crowned barrel. Sights consist of a Heinie Ledge rear sight and an 18k gold-bead front sight. Grips are Railscale Ascend G10.

The Bull Officer (MSRP: $3,699) uses an officer-sized frame with an Everlast Recoil System that can go up to 5,000 rounds before replacement. Other features include a 3.8-inch bull barrel,

Ruger-57 PC Charger

(MSRP: $549) is similar, but with a 3.4-inch barrel and 10+1 round capacity in a compact package. Ruger has taken its popular PC Carbine and reconfigured it into a pistol. The PC Charger (MSRP: $799) features a 6.5-inch barrel and a glass-filled polymer chassis system that allows mounting of standard AR grips. Overall length is 16.5 inches and it weighs 5.2 pounds. It also comes optic-ready and has interchangeable magazines wells to accept SR-Series, Security-9 and Glock pistol magazines. An additional magazine well accepting Ruger American Pistol magazines is also available.

ruger.com

SIG SAUER

Sig Sauer M18

The popular P365 series now includes an XL model (MSRP: $580) with a 3.7-inch barrel and slide cut for a Romeo Zero red-dot. It also includes X-RAY night sights. The XL Romeo Zero (MSRP: $680) comes with a Romeo Zero red-dot installed. All the XL models have a longer grip that holds a 12-round magazine and an XSeries flat trigger. The SAS (Sig Anti Snag) (MSRP: $580) has all the sharp edges rounded, 10-round magazine and a ported slide with a custom flush-fit tritium sight. This P365 is designed for deep conceal carry. The P320-M18 (MSRP: $600) is the civilian version of the U.S. military's M18 compact sidearm. Like Uncle Sam's, the P320-M18 comes with a Coyote Tan Cerakote finish, night sights, is optic-ready and has a manual thumb safety. The Legion Series expands with the new X5Legion pistol (MSRP: $899), which features the Legion Gray finish, flat skeletonized trigger, TXG grip module, 5-inch bull barrel,

Sig Sauer XL Romeo Zero

and fiber-optic front and adjustable rear sights. There is also a new P320 series. The RXP series offers a factory mounted red-dot in a Full-Size RXP (MSRP: $899), Compact RXP (MSRP: $899), XCompact RXP (MSRP: $899). All come out of the box with a Romeo red-dot mounted to the slide, and suppressor-height sights. New to the entry-level M400 Tread series of AR15 platforms is the Tread Pistol (MSRP:

$951). Wisely, Sig decided to equip this 5.56 NATO chambered pistol with an 11-inch barrel to get the best ballistic performance in most 5.56 NATO ammo. Comes with a Shockwave brace and M-Lok handguard.

sigsauer.com

SMITH AND WESSON

The new Performance Center M&P380 Shield EZ pistols (MSRP:

Smith & Wesson C.O.R.E. M&P9

Smith& Wesson
M&P9 Compact FDE

Springfield Armory Ronin Operator

$502) feature easy-to-use features of the M&P380 Shield EZ like an easy-to-rack slide, easy-to-load magazine and easy-to-clean design. These pistols feature a 3.8-inch ported barrel to reduce muzzle flip, lightening cuts in the slide for reduced weight, an 8+1 round capacity and HI-VIZ Litewave H3 Tritium/Litepipe sights. Available with a matte-black frame and a choice of black, silver or gold accents. Also coming out of the Performance Shop are full-size M&P9 and M&P40 models with 4.25- or 5-inch ported barrels and slides, larger slide stops, tuned actions and adjustable fiber-optic sights. These full-size pistols in 9mm and .40 Auto are also available in C.O.R.E., Competition Optic Ready, slides that allow easy mounting of red-dot optics, with ported barrels (MSRP: $735) and without ported barrels (MSRP: $721). The compact M&P9 Shield EZ M2.0 (MSRP: $559) is chambered in 9mm with a 3.6-inch barrel, 8+1 capacity and with a manual thumb safety or without. Both models are also available with a Crimson Trace Red Laserguard (MSRP: $575). Also new to the M&P9 Compact lines are an FDE-finish model (MSRP: $569) and a threaded-barrel model (MSRP: $569) with suppressor-height sights.
smith-wesson.com

SPRINGFIELD ARMORY

The Ronin Operator (MSRP: $849) is a 1911 pistol configured as a full-size 5-inch-barrel pistol with a two-tone finish, with a stainless steel forged frame and a forged slide of blued carbon steel. The flats of both the slide and frame are thoroughly polished. Sights consist of Tactical Rack rear and fiber-optic front. The trigger is a Gen 2 Speed Trigger that offers a crisp press and fast reset. Available in 9mm and .45 ACP variants.
springfield-armory.com

STOEGER

Stoeger STR-9 Compact

The STR-9 9mm striker-fire pistol line now has a Compact model (MSRP: $329 to $449, depending on configuration) designed for conceal carry. The compact model features a 3.8-inch barrel for easy concealment and an overall length of 6.9 inches. It weighs 24 ounces. The STR-9 is available with one or three 13-round magazines, different size back straps for a custom grip, and 3-dot sights or tritium night sights.
stoegerindustries.com

WALTHER

The Q4 Steel Frame pistol (MSRP: $1,399) is Walther's latest steel-frame pistol designed for conceal carry. The Q4 weighs 40 ounces and effectively distributes the weight to reduce felt recoil. The pistol features Performance Duty Texture designed to provide a functional grip with non-abrasive characteristics. The Quick Defense Trigger is two-stage trigger with a crisp break and short reset. The beavertail is optimized for optimal shooter grip and maximum concealability. There is also an Optics Ready variant (MSRP: $1,499) that allows mounting a red-dot reflex sight. GD
waltherarms.com

Walther Q4
Steel Frame

NEW REVOLVERS & OTHERS

› MAX PRASAC

Two new revolver releases this year have given me, an admitted handgun junkie, reason to rejoice. The first one should be obvious as this revolver has graced the cover of every recent major firearms publication and has been the subject of nonstop speculation, conjecture, declaration and various nonstop opining since the news was first leaked out, and that is the new release of an icon, the Colt Python. The news has clearly created quite a buzz, but it has also drawn some criticism from the always vocal party-pooper brigade, as well. The chief complaint is that it is a Python "in name only!" If that complaint had an

ounce of merit, we would have to rename every subsequent generation of virtually every product. Think Ford Mustang, and then think absurd. Once you get past the noise, we have a new, improved, accurate revolver that damn well looks like a Python, albeit only in polished stainless steel. But boy it looks good. I for one am happy to see Colt make this bold and gutsy move and cannot wait to get my paws on one.

Number two is the new Taurus Raging Hunter in .454 Casull. Anyone who has read my byline before will know that I am an avid and singularly obsessed handgun hunter, particularly with big-bore revolvers. More than a hobby, it is a way of life. I was elated to see Taurus release a dedicated hunting revolver last year in both .44 and .357 Magnum, but this year the Brazilian gun maker gave us a true powerhouse in .454 Casull. This is significant to the handgun hunter in that this revolver is purpose-built for handgun hunting. It's a big deal for the oft ignored hunter who likes to do things the hard way. But more on this later.

There have been other notable releases to include Ruger's new Super GP100 in 9mm, a revolver bred purely for competition from Ruger's own custom shop. The one example I have shot is last year's .357 Magnum version. It was smooth, accurate and a real pleasure to shoot. I have no reason to believe the new 9mm iteration will be anything less.

So, there you have it. The plastic "Tupperware" guns that have been all the rage continue to be produced in droves, but the revolver refuses to go down. New purpose-built revolvers are making their way down the assembly lines with bold resolve. Revolvers are here to stay.

They're seemingly outdated, singularly simplistic, boringly reliable and they *just won't go away.* So, with no further delays, I give you the new.

BOND ARMS

Bond Arms Rowdy

For more than 20 years, Bond Arms has been in the business of building high-quality derringers, in the great state of Texas. From the beginning, Bond Arms set out to create what was once considered a symbol of the Old West into a modern, safe and dependable defensive handgun for predators of all kinds imaginable.

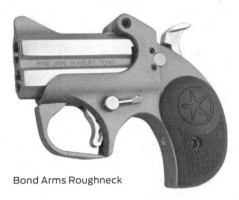

Bond Arms Roughneck

Three new derringers are being produced this year in the new Rough Series line. This was an attempt by Bond Arms to create a more affordable derringer option without compromising in quality. The name of the series was derived from the streamlined finishing process consisting of a quick cleanup and deburring, and then a bead blasting giving them a rough finish. The finish is functional and all business. Like all Bond double-barreled derringers, the Rough series guns are fitted with stainless steel barrels and frames, cross-bolt safety, retracting firing pins, a spring-loaded cam-lock lever and a rebounding hammer.

The Roughneck features 2 1/2-inch barrels, a blade front sight and a fixed rear site. Three chamberings are offered: 9mm, .357 Mag/.38 Spl, and .45 ACP. The Roughneck is finished with a textured rubber grip. The second Rough Series gun is the Rough N Rowdy, the biggest derringer of the series at 5-inches long. This one has 3-inch barrels with fixed sights and is chambered in .45 Colt and 2 1/2-inch

.410-bore shotshells.

The last in the series is the Grizzly, offering a number of upgrades over its Rough N Rowdy cousin to include larger rosewood grips engraved with grizzly bear artwork, and a matching leather holster embossed with a grizzly bear. This derringer also comes with 3-inch barrels chambered in .45 Colt and 2 1/2-inch .410 bore.

Lastly, there is an all-new offering from Bond Arms that redefines the term "lightweight," called the Stinger. This is a new slim-line derringer with an aluminum frame and steel barrels that comes in two chamberings: 9mm or .38 Special. The Stinger tips the scales at a feather-like 12 ounces.
bondarms.com

CHARTER ARMS

Founded in 1964, Charter Arms is headed by the third generation of Ecker family members, staying true to the spirit of this truly all-American firearms company known for producing double-action revolvers for more than half a century in the heart of New England's "Gun Valley." Charter Arms entered the gun-building fray with the Undercover, a five-shot .38 Special that weighed in at only 16 ounces. Today, continuing with that theme, Charter Arms produces a full line of double-action revolvers for many purposes. Charter Arms revolvers feature one-piece frames (stronger than screw-on side-plate designs), a safe and completely blocked hammer system, and three place cylinder lock-up. Another plus is that Charter Arms revolvers are 100-percent American made.

Charter Arms Undercover Lite

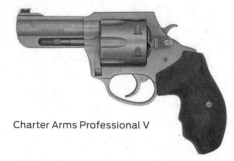

Charter Arms Professional V

Charter Arms offers 10 new models this year starting with the Undercover Lite of the Undercover Lite series, an aluminum six-shot .38 Special with a 2.2-inch barrel and an anodized finish. Another new member of the Undercover Lite series is the Pink Lady, sharing the same configuration as the Undercover Lite, but finished in pink and stainless steel.

The newest member of the Mag Pug series is the Target Magnum built on the XL frame, with a stainless steel finish and a 6-inch barrel. This six-shot is chambered in .357 Magnum. The Target Magnum is fitted with fully adjustable sights.

The PROFESSIONAL series has five new models to choose from starting with the PROFESSIONAL II, a .357 Magnum six-shot revolver built on the large frame with wood grips, a black nitride finish and a 3-inch barrel (and fixed sights). The PROFESSIONAL III is made on the XL frame, a black nitride finish covers the revolver that is a six-shot .357 with a 4.2-inch long barrel and adjustable sights. Like the PROFESSIONAL II, this one features wood grips. The PROFESSIONAL IV is a departure from its siblings in that it is chambered in .32 Magnum with a seven-shot cylinder, built on the large frame with a 3-inch barrel (fixed sights), wood grip and a stainless steel finish. The PROFESSIONAL V has fixed sights, a 3-inch barrel, wood grips, a six-shot cylinder in .357 Magnum, and a stainless steel finish. Lastly is the PROFESSIONAL VI, and like the PROFESSIONAL III, it is built on the XL frame and fitted with a 4.2-inch barrel and equipped with adjustable sights. This one is also stainless steel, fitted with wood grips and has a six-shot cylinder and is chambered in .357 Magnum.

There are two new Retriever/Starter Pistols in the lineup this year, the first being the Pro 209, that uses a 209 primer, is built on the small frame and has a six-shot capacity, a wood grip and a black finish. The second, the Pro 22 that takes a .22 blank and also features a six-shot capacity and is built on a small frame with wood grips and a black finish.

charterarms.com

CIMARRON

One thing I find remarkable about Cimarron is the constant evolution and expansion of the company's product line. Cimarron imports its revolver line from both Uberti and Pietta and offers a complete line of replica Single-Action Army revolvers as well as blackpowder percussion revolvers, open-top revolvers and conversion revolvers as well as shotguns. This is an impressive lineup that offers something for every enthusiast.

This year brings a new model to the appropriately named Bad Boy series, where the Old West meets the New West. The Bad Boy is a classic Single Action Army Pre-War frame with an 1860 Army-style, one-piece walnut grip. The six-shot cylinder is unfluted and chambered in the resurging and powerful 10mm. The 8-inch barrel is octagonal and fitted with adjustable target sights, but a Picatinny rail is available for an optic mount. The high-performance, carbon-alloy steel frame, cylinder and barrel are finished in classic blue.

cimarron-firearms.com

COLT

The company that really started it all still produces a version of the famous Single Action Army (SAA) to which virtually all modern single-action revolvers share DNA with Colt's classic yet timeless design. One of the most iconic pieces of Americana, the Colt Single Action Army is probably the most recognizable gun in American film history.

While the Single-Action Army is available today in a number of differing configurations to include the adjustable-sight version, the New Frontier, there is nothing new on the single-action front for 2020. However…

Colt Python

The big news for 2020, as I mentioned in my introduction, is the return of the all-new Colt Python. This American icon is back, this time only in stainless steel and better than ever. Originally debuting in 1955, the Python is back with a vengeance. Like its progenitor, the new Python is a six-shot double-action revolver with the easily identifiable ribbed barrel and, of course, chambered in .357 Magnum. Handsome walnut grips adorn the new Python and as of this writing, two barrel lengths are available: 4.25 and 6 inches.

colt.com

Cimarron Bad Boy 10mm

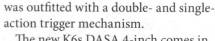

FREEDOM ARMS

Freedom Arms has the distinction of making some of the finest single-action revolvers in the industry, period. Demand and refinement are so high in Freedom, Wyoming, that Freedom Arms currently isn't releasing anything new on the revolver front.

These revolvers are the Rolls Royce of the single-action revolver world, and though a traditionally styled single-action revolver, the FA 83 is all modern on the inside and produced of 17-4PH stainless steel, in a five-shot configuration. Freedom Arms prides itself on hand-assembling each and every unit to tight and exacting tolerances. This is true "custom-built" production revolver.

Freedom Arms also produces a smaller-framed revolver, more in line with the size of the Colt Single-Action Army, the Model 97, for those who wish for a trimmer package on their hip. This revolver is a departure from the Model 83 mechanically, in that it features a transfer-bar safety system which allows for safe carry with a round under the hammer. Also of note is the size difference between the 97 and the 83.

Freedom also produces fine break-open, single-shot pistols designated the Model 2008. Available in a variety of calibers, and three different barrel lengths, 10, 15, and 16 inches, the Model 2008 defines practical. All barrels are interchangeable, making caliber switches simple, and they feature the excellent grip frame borrowed directly from the FA Model 83, a grip that lends itself well to heavy recoil. Non-catalog barrel lengths are available for a fee.

While the barrels are interchangeable, they need fitting, a service that Freedom Arms provides. In all, Freedom Arms produces true modern-day classics.

freedomarms.com

KIMBER

Known for quality semi-automatics, and not really known for revolvers, Kimber surprised the industry and the shooting world in 2016 with the introduction of the Kimber K6s double-action revolver: Purportedly the world's lightest small-frame, six-shot .357 Magnum revolver for concealed carry defense.

Kimber K6s
DASA Target

Fast forward to 2020, and the K6s model line has been expanded to include four new models. The K6s DASA (Double Action Single Action) is the next evolution of the successful K6s product line where the K6s system was outfitted with a double- and single-action trigger mechanism.

The new K6s DASA 4-inch comes in two flavors, the Target and the Combat models, both .357 Magnums. The 4-inch Target is fitted with extended oversized grips, a target-adjustable rear sight and a fiber-optic front sight. The 4-inch Combat model wears extended three finger grips for better control and white-dot sights.

The third new member of the K6s DASA family is the Texas Edition with a 2-inch barrel, cut scroll engraving and special ivory G10 grips with the Texas state moto, name and flag. The Texas Edition .357 Magnum revolver is fitted with white-dot sights.

A new K6s revolver called the Royal features a 2-inch barrel, ivory G10 grips, dovetailed white-dot rear sight with a brass-bead front sight. Visually, the new Royal has a stunning finish consisting of a high shine hand-polished finish with Dark Oil DLC applied.

kimberamerica.com

MAGNUM RESEARCH

Born in 1999, Magnum Research entered the revolver-building business with the introduction of the BFR, the Biggest Finest Revolver, chambered in the old warhorse .45-70 Government. Magnum Research has since redesigned its revolvers and today, Magnum Research produces both long- and short-frame revolvers in a range of calibers to suit just about everyone's needs. In this author's humble opinion, there is no wider assortment of hunting calibers offered under one roof than that of Magnum Research. There is something for everyone.

A subsidiary of Kahr Arms, Magnum Research of Minneapolis, Minnesota, offers a whole line of long-frame and short-frame stainless steel single-action revolvers in both standard caliber/configurations and a plethora of custom Precision Center offerings.

Six-shot revolvers are taking center stage this year with a .357 Magnum and a .44 Magnum being offered in the short-framed revolvers, and a six-shot .350 Legend rounding out the long-framed offerings. With a cylinder

Freedom Arms 2008

Magnum Research
.350 Legend

boasting the BFR's proportions, the engineers at Magnum Research decided to give the consumer an extra round in the cylinder. A welcome addition, for sure.

Also recently added to the custom lineup out of Magnum Research's Precision Center is the Number 5. This is a tribute to the Number 5 custom revolver that Elmer Keith wrote about many decades ago that featured an innovative base-pin latch that set it apart from all other single-action revolvers. Magnum Research has reproduced the latch and is offering it as a custom option. Also new to the custom catalog are wooden grips for both the standard plow handle and Bisley grip frames.

These are big, no-compromise, well-built revolvers that offer unparalleled accuracy and strength at a reasonable price point.

magnumresearch.com

NIGHTHAWK CUSTOM/ KORTH-WAFFEN

Nighthawk Custom was established in 2004 by four talented individuals who all shared a true passion for the ubiquitous 1911. The company has grown over the years to become a premier custom 1911 manufacturer/ builder, offering more than 40 unique versions of the 1911. Nighthawk also offers a line of tactical shotguns based on the Remington 870.

However, in the context of this chapter, Nighthawk offers a line of revolvers as well. The legendary German firearms manufacturer, Korth-Waffen, has partnered with Nighthawk Custom to produce a line of high-performance revolvers, the latest being the NXR.

The NXR is a six-shot .44 Magnum double-action revolver with a 6-inch barrel (stainless steel) inside a futuristic looking shroud. The rear sight is fully adjustable while the front sight is interchangeable. The whole revolver is black DLC finished. An innovative feature the NXR is equipped with is the removable under-barrel balancing lug/ weight. As expected, the double- and single-action pulls are as smooth as a baby's backside. Another unusual feature is the indent at full hammer extension. The trigger can be squeezed to that indent point and then held there until the shooter is ready to drop the hammer. The action can be ordered with one of five different indent settings so you can tailor the action to your needs/wants. The single-action pull is set at 2.5 pounds and the contoured walnut grip feels great in the hand. Picatinny rails top and bottom allow the shooter to accessorize with minimal hassle. With an MSRP of $5,299, the NXR doesn't come cheaply, but what you do get is a fine machine with many custom touches you can easily tune to perfection.

nighthawkcustom.com

SMITH & WESSON

Smith & Wesson has the distinction of building some of the finest double-action revolvers in the world, bar none, as well as numerous high-quality semi-automatic pistols. There is something for everyone in S&W's extensive catalog. Known for their quality fit and finish as well as their superb actions, Smith & Wesson firearms have a legacy of quality.

New from Smith & Wesson is the Model 610, or rather new once again with this popular reintroduction. Built on the large N-frame (same as the Model 29/629 .44 magnums), the Model 610 is chambered in the popular 10mm (a round enjoying a resurgence in popularity).This stainless steel revolver is available with a 4-inch or 6.5-inch barrel making it well-suited for personal protection or for hunting. The 610 has a six-round capacity and is designed to be used with moon clips, which are included with the revolver. The white-outlined rear sight is adjustable for elevation and windage and the front sight has a black blade that is interchangeable. The package is rounded out with black synthetic finger groove grips.

The other new revolver is also a reintroduction, the Model 648. This popular midsized K-frame revolver is a

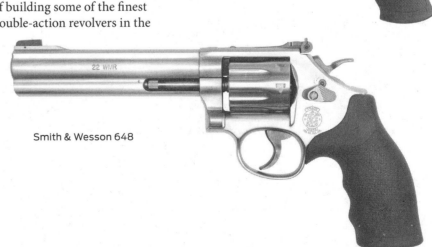

Smith & Wesson 610

Smith & Wesson 648

stainless steel eight-shot .22 Magnum. The 648 first made the scene in 1989 and was produced until 2005. This is the ideal small-game hunting or target revolver available only with a 6-inch barrel. The Model 648 is equipped with a Patridge front sight and a fully adjustable rear sight. The new 648 tips the scales at 46.2 ounces.

smith-wesson.com

STANDARD MANUFACTURING

Standard Manufacturing
Single Action

Known for its double-barreled pump shotguns, Standard Manufacturing is also in the revolver game and recently announced the introduction of an all-time American classic in handgun design, the Standard Single Action revolver, a facsimile of the Colt Single Action Army. It began chambered in the venerable .45 Colt and was made available with a 4 3/4-, 5 1/2-, or 7 1/2-inch barrel, and color casehardened frame and a deep-blued cylinder and barrel. These were also available with engraving if the customer so chose.

This year, the line has expanded to include nickel plating and nickel plating with engraving as well as more caliber options with the addition of the .38

Standard Manufacturing
Single Action Nickel

Special. The same barrel length options mentioned above are available. Soon to be introduced is a Storekeeper model that is ejector-less and is fitted with a 3-inch barrel. We are truly excited about this one.

Another interesting firearm from Standard Manufacturing is its innovative S333 Thunderstruck personal-protection handgun. The S333 is a double-barrel, double-action revolver that fires two rounds of .22 Magnum with each pull of the trigger, with an eight-round capacity. Constructed of lightweight aluminum, with a comfortable polymer grip, the S-33 weighs in at a feather-like 18 ounces.

stdgun.com

STURM, RUGER & COMPANY

The big news for last year was the introduction of Ruger's Custom Shop. How is that significant this year? The news was too late to include in last year's *Gun Digest* annual. However, and as the name implies, Ruger's Custom Shop is producing a number of really special firearms not restricted to this chapter on revolvers. And the introduction of the all-new Super GP100 has definite significance.

The Super GP100 Competition Revolver is essentially a Super Redhawk with its nose cut off. By nose, I mean

Ruger Super
GP100 9mm

the barrel extension of the standard models. In its place is a shrouded two-piece barrel of 5 1/2-inches with a half-lug, making case ejection fast. The Super GP100 utilizes the superior Super Redhawk two-spring action and grip frame. The rear sight is fully adjustable while the front is fiber optic and replaceable. The first Super GP was chambered in .357 Magnum (eight-shot cylinder) and obviously able to shoot .38 Special as well. The black PVD coating is slick and tough. The Hogue hardwood grip is comfortable and good looking to boot. The sample I tested was exceedingly accurate and featured by far the best trigger I have felt on a stock Ruger, ever.

New for this year is the Super GP100 Competition Revolver in 9mm. Also an eight-shot, the new Super GP features similar specifications to the .357 version, but this one is easily identified by the stainless steel finish, yet the cylinder is PVD coated. The cylinder and extractor are cut for moon clips and this Super GP includes with three of them.

Last year also ushered in the all-new Wrangler series of revolvers. This is a small, lightweight, inexpensive .22 LR single-action six-shooter. The frame is made from aluminum, the

Standard Manufacturing
S333 Thunderstruck

Ruger Super GP100 .357

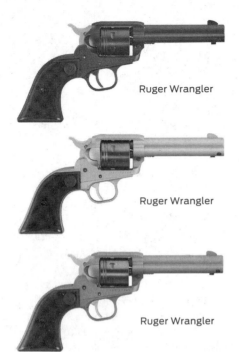

Ruger Wrangler

Ruger Wrangler

Ruger Wrangler

Taurus Defender 856

Taurus 942

grip frame of a zinc alloy wrapped in classic "gunfighter" style grips (Single Six stocks fit the Wrangler). The cylinder and barrel are made from steel with fixed sights front and rear, and the whole thing is covered in tough Cerakote. The cylinder is counter-bored, and Ruger opted for a free-wheeling pawl, making the loading and unloading of the Wrangler a snap. Like all Ruger revolvers, the Wrangler is equipped with a transfer-bar safety system. Three models are available in three different finishes: Black, Silver and Burnt Bronze Cerakote. The Wrangler comes in at a svelte 30 ounces and at $249 MSRP. Every member of the family should have at least two.

Many Distributor Exclusives are also new, but there are too many to mention here, many are cosmetic departures from the standard models offered by Ruger. I would recommend you go to Ruger's website for more details.

ruger.com

TAURUS

Taurus offers a wide range of revolvers for personal defense, recreational shooting and hunting. There is something in its catalog for any handgun endeavor you choose. Made in Brazil, Taurus offers a full line of

revolvers of differing frame sizes and calibers. At Taurus, variety is the spice of life.

Taurus' extensive revolver line was expanded with the addition of the new Defender 856. This six-shot, double-action defensive revolver is equipped with a 3-inch barrel and is chambered in .38 Special +P. All Defenders come equipped with a front sight post with an integrated tritium vial, enabling quick acquisition in low light. There are four standard models to include a stainless steel frame with matte finish, an ultralight aluminum alloy frame with matte finish, a stainless steel frame with black Tenifer finish, and an aluminum alloy frame with hard coat black anodized finish. All four are equipped with a Hogue rubber grip.

Taurus also offers two upgrade versions of the Defender featuring special finish treatments and grips. The two-tone version has a matte stainless steel finish on the frame and barrel with a black cylinder that is matched to the textured gray and black VZ grip. The other has a Tungston Cerakote finish (frame, barrel and cylinder) with Altamont walnut grips.

The all-new Taurus 942 is a short-barreled double-action revolver based

on the Taurus 856 revolver, chambered in .22LR and featuring an eight-shot cylinder. Since the 942 feels similar to larger caliber snubnosed revolvers, the 942 makes for a lower cost to shoot alternative, making it ideal for high-volume training. Eight models are available: 2- and 3-inch barrel with steel alloy frame and cylinder with matte black finish, 2- and 3-inch barrel models with an ultralight aluminum alloy frame in a black anodized finish, 2- and 3-inch barrel models with stainless steel frame and cylinder in a matte finish,

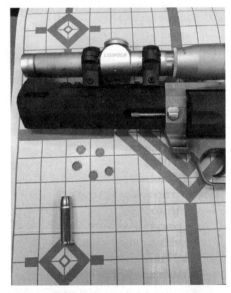

Taurus Raging Hunter

and 2- and 3-inch barrel models with an ultralight aluminum alloy frame in a stainless matte finish. All 942s come with finger-grooved grips, a serrated front ramp sight and a drift-adjustable (for windage) rear sight.

There is a new Raging Hunter in the lineup this year, chambered in the mighty .454 Casull. In a nutshell, the Raging Hunter is a double-action, five-shot revolver with integral Picatinny rail built into the top of the barrel shroud, making the addition of a scope or red-dot-type sight simple.

I really like this system as it allows the end-user to equip his/her Raging Hunter with an optic without disrupting the iron adjustable sites. If your optic dies for some reason in the field, you can simply remove it and your iron sights are ready to go. The barrel system is unique in that it features a steel sleeve inserted into an aluminum housing that cuts down on weight significantly. The cushioned insert grips and porting cut down on felt recoil, the porting actually reducing muzzle rise. For the handgun hunter, this one appears to be a winner. Three barrel lengths are available, 5.12, 6.75 and 8.37 inches, so there is something for pretty much everyone. The Raging Hunter comes in two finishes, a positively sinister Matte Black and the two-tone Matte Stainless.

taurususa.com

UBERTI

Uberti, a subsidiary of Benelli, offers a whole line of reproduction Colt 1873 Single Action Army and

Uberti Dalton

other Western reproduction revolvers, made of modern materials. These fine reproductions are economical, pleasing to look at, and of high quality.

Uberti is taking Cowboy Mounted Shooting (CMS) to the next level with two new offerings. These stainless steel revolvers are an expansion of its Short Stroke CMS Pro line. They are made for fast, one-handed shots while mounted on a horse, and both share a 3 1/2-inch barrel, a custom-grade main spring, and a low-profile, short-stroke hammer (20-percent less travel) that is extra wide and deeply grooved.

The first of the two is the Uberti USA Stainless Steel Short Stroke CMS Pro, a Single Action Army-style revolver in .45 Colt (six-shot cylinder) with the aforementioned 3 1/2-inch barrel with a "traditional" grip, finished in stainless steel.

The second of the CMS series revolvers is the Uberti USA Stainless Steel Short Stroke CMS KL Pro that is the result of the partnership between Uberti USA and legendary

CMS competitor Kenda Lenseigne, a six-time Overall National Champion Cowgirl winner. This stainless revolver is fitted with a 3 1/2-inch barrel, a low-lying, short-stroke hammer, a six-shot cylinder in .45 Colt, and a modified bird's-head grip. It also features Lenseigne's brand on the grip and her signature on the barrel.

Uberti is also expanding its Outlaws & Lawmen series with the addition of the Dalton revolver; a purportedly historically correct rendition of the famous six-shooter found on Bob Dalton's dead body. Bob was the Dalton Gang leader. This replica of the Colt Single Action Army carried by Bob Dalton is chambered in .45 Colt and is fitted with a 5 1/2-inch barrel. The receiver, grip frame, cylinder and barrel feature hand-chased engraving from the renowned Italian engraving company Atelier Giovanelli. Simulated pearl grips round out the package that accentuates the gorgeous color-cased frame. **GD**

uberti.com

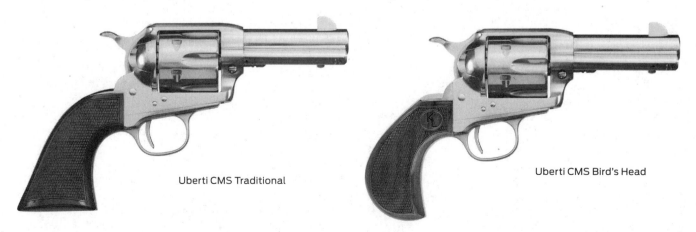

Uberti CMS Traditional

Uberti CMS Bird's Head

NEW SHOTGUNS

›KRISTIN ALBERTS

Lighter, faster, stronger. The sub-gauge craze continues to boom into the roaring 2020s. While Browning and others continue to crank out 10 gauges and magnum-length 12-gauge chambers, many shotgun makers are downsizing their collective bores.

Featherweight rifles are all the rage for ounce-counting mountain hunters, so why should serious ground-pounding shotgunners be left out? Gnash your teeth no longer, as more and more manufacturers are finding ways to reinforce lightweight alloy receivers for

strength, as well as weight savings, while beefing up the hinges and including steel blocks as receiver reinforcements.

This is also the age of customization, with the majority of manufacturers now offering not only adjustable-comb models, but also including multiple spacers for fitting length of pull as well as shims for both drop or cast.

And, there's a whole new category of shotguns not seen in *Gun Digest* for many decades: lever actions, and they're back in a big way with the tiniest of bores. Henry Repeating Arms leads the

way with not one, not two, but no less than five models of .410 shotguns. Not to be left in the dust, Marlin throws down with a revival of its traditional 1895 rifle-turned-shotgun for a true old Western style scattergun duel.

Turkey and waterfowl hunters have more specialty options now than ever before, covering every platform from single shots to semi-autos, slides to doubles. Clay busters and competition shooters are in the same metaphorical boat with a fine mix of upscale models and budget buys all built to powder the

Benelli Ethos BE.S.T.

Benelli SBE3 BE.S.T.

orange flyers. And for once, American-made options are back in the limelight with options from Savage, Remington, Henry and others, though there are steals and fine manufacturing to be found at shotgun manufacturers around the globe. Without wasting any more range time, let's get to the heart of the new 2020 scattergun matter.

BENELLI

All the Benelli hype at the 2020 SHOT Show centered around the company's first bolt-action rifle with the Lupo. Yet, it was a tank full of saltwater with a submerged pair of shotgun barrels, one rusted solid and the other seemingly new that should hold the greatest interest for hunters and foul-weather shotgunners. Benelli quietly debuted its BE.S.T. Series, at first glance a seemingly mis-dotted acronym, but the shortcut is for BEnelli Surface Treatment. This proprietary coating is advertised to form an armor over steel, using nanotechnology and diamondlike carbon particles to halt rust and corrosion, sworn enemies of hardcore hunters who don't always have the time to baby the tools of their trade.

Parts treated with BE.S.T. were tested by immersing them in saltwater, like that tank at SHOT Show, for three months with no signs of rust or corrosion while untreated parts, from competitors no doubt, went orange with rust in much less time. Benelli is so confident in the new coating that treated parts are backed with a 25-year warranty against those dangers of moisture on metal. BE.S.T. will debut on several Super Black Eagle III (SBE3) and Ethos models, all 12 gauge for now. While there's no excuse for not cleaning your guns, sometimes it's nice for hunters to focus more on the hunt than mollycoddling the gun, and to that

end, BE.S.T. looks ready to hit the duck blinds and provide some peace of mind. *benelliusa.com*

BERETTA

While Beretta's new pistols generated the majority of the buzz during SHOT Show 2020, several shotgun additions made their way to market under the Italian-maker's Trident branding. A fresh O/U competition platform emerged with the moniker Beretta 694. Designed with collaboration from Beretta's Shooting Team, the 694 is a serious O/U for seriously competitive clay dusters most in tune with the most intricate build details. There's a slightly decreased drop, more aggressive checkering on both the safety and pistol grip, wider comb for better cheek weld, and more ergonomic anti-glare-finish top lever suitable for both right- and left-handed shooters. The 694 is available in 12 gauge with either

30- or 32-inch barrels. Retail prices start at $4,500, with options to add the adjustable B-Fast stock system.

The 686 Silver Pigeon collection of Beretta O/U shotguns has long been regarded as one of its most popular with hunters and target shooters alike. This year's upgrade is branded with a Roman numeral to now become the 686 Silver Pigeon I. New features include improved Steelium Optima HP barrels, deeper laser engraving on the receiver of elegant floral motifs, and a MicroCore recoil pad. The 686 Silver Pigeon I is available in 12, 20, 28 gauge and .410 bore with 26-, 28- or 30-inch barrels for an MSRP of $2,350. The oil-finished walnut is classy, with shooters having a choice of either left- or right-handed versions as well as Schnabel or more plainly rounded fore-ends. There's little doubt the new 686 class will find a welcome home with Beretta followers and fans of fine O/Us in general. *Beretta.com*

BROWNING

The Buckmark-ed company somehow manages to add a slew of models and variants year after year, and the dawning of our new decade is no exception. While there are no big splashes of grandiose announcements,

Browning Cynergy Wicked Wing

Browning Cynergy Turkey

Browning Cynergy Feather

Browning Citori CXS White

Browning Citori CXT White

additions abound. Browning's Cynergy family of O/U shotguns debuted years ago as the company's lowest-profile double, with the lines of sleek racer. Now, however, the sporty model goes both feet into the hunting space as well as targeting specialty shooters with the respected Reverse Striker ignition system, mechanical trigger, VectorPro backboring and an aggressively angled Inflex recoil system designed to eat as much as 25 percent of felt recoil.

The Cynergy Ultimate Turkey cemented its place as one of the most upscale magnum-chambered O/U gobbler getters last year, and now the Cynergy takes its rightful place in the bird blinds. Hardcore hunters who dig Browning's Wicked Wing package on existing models like the A5 and Maxus will gravitate to the Cynergy Wicked Wing with its Burnt Bronze Cerakote metalwork, fully chromed bore, adjustable comb and a choice of several Mossy Oak and Realtree patterns. In addition to an adjustable comb, there are also quarter-inch length-of-pull spacers for customizing fit, especially helpful when wearing layers of waterfowling gear. Barrel lengths include 26-, 28-, and 30-inchers, each topped with an ivory front bead and threaded for the included Invector Plus choke tubes. Not only does the Cynergy Wicked Wing just plain look the part, but that double shoulders like a dream and would spice up any hunter's arsenal.

While weight might be welcome for its role in negating recoil in the magnum hunting market, toting a hefty double through the woods and fields is no longer a concern with additions like Browning's Feather series. Both the Cynergy Feather and 725 Feather use an aluminum alloy receiver to shave weight, while a steel breech face and similarly durable hinge reinforce the areas of greatest wear. While the Cynergy chambers only 12s at this time, it remains sub-7 pounds. The latter 725 Feather includes both 12 and 20 gauges weighing in from svelte high 5 pounds to the low 6s. Both are truly lightweight guns that balance well and swing surprisingly nicely.

Lovers of the more-traditionally built Citori family will appreciate the ever-expanding lineage with multiple silver-nitride receivers in CX, CXS and CXT White variants, each with an adjustable-stocked sub-option. Browning doesn't forget smaller-framed shooters either, especially for clay busters. The single barrel trap BT-99 goes Micro with an adjustable length of pull using a Graco buttpad system, the same as that debuted simultaneously on the Citori CX and CXT Micro.

Browning's Gold 10-gauge production continues into this age of smaller bores with little fanfare, but the fact that the magnum 10s hold their place in the catalog speaks to a remaining demand. The biggest news and highest-dollar additions, however, indicate a changing specialty market.

browning.com

CHARLES DALY

A name now synonymous with affordable scatterguns offers an updated trio of handy new models: the Model 202 O/U, Model 500 SxS and Model 101 Single Shot. The 202 O/U, with its silver receivers engraved with a hunting-dog scene, are actually built of an aluminum alloy. Available in either 12 or 20 gauge or .410 bore, they use a single selective mechanical trigger, fixed fiber-optic front sight, and extractors. The 202 ships with a set of five extended choke tubes with an MSRP from $499.

Likewise, the Model 500 side-by-sides in .410 might just be the best-looking Charles Daly doubles yet. There's a black engraved pistol-grip model with a 28-inch barrel, but it's the black engraved with gold accents and an English-style straight stock that wows in both appearance and balance. At first glance, I fully expected to see the name of a higher-dollar brand on the little beauty. Think double triggers, extractors, a manual safety and brass front bead. The slim baby bore weighs a scant 4.4 pounds and includes a set of five Mobil chokes for prices ranging from $725 to $875.

Though not as noteworthy, the Charles Daly Model 101 gets a bit of a makeover, with the price coming down lower than ever. The company now offers choices of checkered walnut or black synthetic in 12 and 20 gauges and .410 bore, all sub-$130 on the retail scale. These types of easily stowable single shots make ideal truck guns at a price that doesn't spur anxiety over rough handling.

charlesdaly.com

CZ USA

Instead of introducing a new model here or variant there, CZ blanketed its most successful lines of hunting

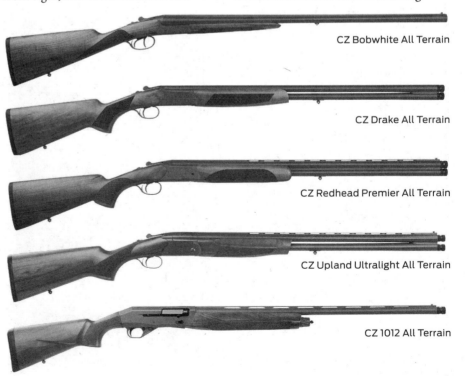

CZ Bobwhite All Terrain

CZ Drake All Terrain

CZ Redhead Premier All Terrain

CZ Upland Ultralight All Terrain

CZ 1012 All Terrain

CZ All Terrain

shotguns from each of the major families of actions, SxS, O/U, and semi-auto, with what the company calls the All-Terrain Series. Exterior appearance is readily identifiable with upgraded walnut stocks and field-practical full OD Green Cerakote coverage on both the barrels and receivers.

What truly sets the All-Terrain doubles apart (all models save the autoloading 1012) is the inclusion of a set of rare-earth magnets added to the extractors or ejectors. What for, you ask? Those accustomed to working with dogs in the duck blind or standing knee deep in the marshy bottoms might just appreciate the magnets knack for keeping shells from dropping out of an opened action while the hunter focuses on other tasks. Have you ever bent over to grab a duck from the pup and had your shells drop into the muck? No longer.

The new CZ All-Terrain Series includes the inertia-driven semi-automatic 1012, which runs the lightest target loads to the heaviest 3-inch magnums with ease. The side-by-side Bobwhite G2 exudes class, pairing double triggers with an English-style stock. Affordability meets the O/U market in the Drake, while the all-around Redhead Premier O/U is built for everything from birding to clay shooting. Last, and least only in weight, comes CZ's Upland Ultralight which is a full 2 pounds lighter than CZ's other steel-receiver O/U models. Regardless of the selection, each of the All-Terrain

ships with five choke tubes, either flush or extended depending on the model.

Those not yet familiar with CZ's foray into the inertia driven semi-automatic line best investigate the 1012. Though introduced in 2019, CZ continues to add new finishes, camos and options to the platform. Compare prices on CZ's inertia guns, packed with practical features and finishes, alongside those of competitors, and the difference is astonishing, and that's not because the 1012 doesn't shoot. We've had it out in the field in some harsh wintry conditions and it runs a mix of loads just as fast as the gunner can pull the trigger. With an MSRP of $659 to $749, including $690 for the 1012 All-Terrain, these Czech-made autoloaders are in the running for a best-buy award.

cz-usa.com

EUROPEAN AMERICAN ARMORY

The European American Armory Corporation (EAA) announced a fresh lineup of Turkish import shotguns in both O/U and SxS under the classy Churchill name. These Akkar-built doubles include both Field and Sporting variants. With a flooded O/U market, the 812 Churchills set themselves apart with features and feel not commonly found on the more budget-conscious brands. Where the Field has a silver receiver, the Sporting shows off an engraved and nicely case-colored housing partnered with a hand-rubbed oil finish on the walnut stocks. Though the Sporting is 12-gauge only at this

time, it is a tempting new name in a rather crowded class. If a variety of gauges is more your forte, the 812 Field includes 12, 20, 28 gauges and .410 bores. The Sporting shows off more features and subsequently higher prices than most from the region, with retail numbers on the pair of 812s running from $1,286 to $2,760.

At a time with fewer and fewer side-by-side models making a debut, the EAA 512 Churchill comes with a Nitride-finish receiver, chrome-lined barrels, single mechanical gold-plated trigger, front bead, extractors and standard Turkish walnut. Best of all, the 512s can be had in a full range of chamberings, including 12, 20, 28 gauges and .410 bore. MSRP is $1,355 and the EAA Churchill 512 ships with three choke tubes.

Shifting gears from doubles to semi-automatics, EAA expands its line of imports from Girsan with another Turkey model, this time the bird as well as the country. The EAA MC312 Gobbler is a 12-gauge, 3.5-inch-magnum-chambered hunter with a shorter 24-inch barrel desired by many turkey hunters. There's also a mid-bead, Picatinny top rail, Cerakote finish, camo synthetic pistol-grip stocks and front fiber-optic sight. In a thoughtful move, the company includes what it calls a "field-tested reflex optic" that fits into an integral rail atop the receiver. The combo should be well-received as more turkey hunters choose to go with optics over irons. The MC312 Gobbler retails for $607.

eaacorp.com

HENRY REPEATING ARMS

Who among us would have thought that traditional lever-gun rifle manufacturer Henry would warrant its own shotgun section of a catalog? The lever-action design has been America's great offering to the world of firearms design, and none personify that USA spirit today quite like Henry Repeating Arms with its "Made in America or Not Made at All" motto.

While Henry has produced single-shot shotguns for several years, in a variety of chamberings, the .410-bore

Henry Side Gate .410

Henry Axe .410

lever-gun market is booming. Whether for hunting, plinking or even home defense, Henry has nearly a half dozen models to scratch each itch, from long guns to a fresh shotgun version most closely related to the short Mare's Leg sidearm.

Henry designers prove time and again they actually listen to customer suggestions (they have an engaging online suggestion box to prove it) and their H024 line of Side Gate rifles was in direct response to shooters seeking a quicker way to load Henrys rather than the traditional magazine tube port. Henry engineers made what could be described as the greatest lever-action design improvement in decades by managing to add a side-loading gate in addition to keeping the existing tubular port, which allows for safer unloads. While this modification has put Henry back in the SASS conversation with quick top-offs via the side gate, the improvement also made its way to the shotgun world. Three models of .410 shotguns sporting side-loading gates hit

the market in 2020.

The first H024 Side Gates ever built wear Henry's recognizable polished-brass frame mated to exceptional American-walnut stocks embellished with deep scroll and floral checkering. The .410 is fitted with sights just like the rifles: adjustable semi-buckhorn rear with a diamond insert and ivory bead ramp front. A fixed cylinder bore choke is the only option as of publication and an MSRP is set the same as all the rifles at $1,077.

The latest is Henry's X-Model, its first synthetic-stocked, blacked-out lever action which sneaked into the SHOT Show at Federal's booth as part of the partnership with the Hammer Down ammunition launch. In addition to all the centerfire rifle calibers, a large-loop .410 shotgun is among the initial launch. The 7.5-pound gun holds six 2.5-inch shells. With a 20-inch round barrel, fiber-optic front sight, lower Picatinny accessory rail, M-LOK fore-end attachment points and interchangeable chokes, the X-Model

.410 is surprisingly practical and retails for $970, though nobody would balk at a 3-inch chamber.

Henry's Axe .410 is so named for its axe-handle-shaped short stock, with an overall length of 26.4-inches and barrel length just over 15-inches, dimensions keeping it completely legal and free from NFA regulation. The Axe is threaded for interchangeable chokes and wears an oversized lever loop. MSRP on the Axe is steep at $970, but the thing is built like a tank at 5.75-pounds, American-made down to the last screw and nicely figured American walnut, yet even with its diminutive stature holds only one round less than the full-size shotguns. *henryusa.com*

MARLIN

While Marlin produced lever-action .410 shotguns as much as 90 years ago, it had been slow to rejoin the baby-bore craze, but 2020 is the year. In response to Henry's lengthening scroll of .410-bore shotguns, Marlin shows off a new 1895 scattergun built on what has become the company's large-bore rifle frame. Dressed in an American black-walnut stock with a 22-inch round barrel, the 1895 shotgun chambers 2.5-inch shells and comes in a choice of two models, one has a fixed cylinder bore and the other ships with three flush mount interchangeable chokes. The Marlin 1895 shotguns retail from $847 to $934. Just like with the Henry lever guns above, hunting cottontails and other small

Henry Axe .410

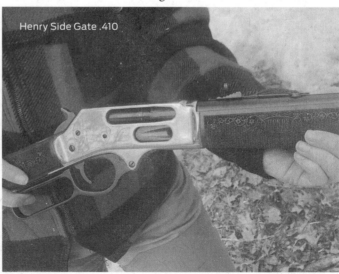

Henry Side Gate .410

Marlin 1895 .410

game with a .410 shotgun takes on a whole new level of enjoyment with a handsome lever action in the field.

marlinfirearms.com

MOSSBERG

What happens when you let the Miculek family, led by patriarch and fastest trigger finger Jerry Miculek, have the say in designing the best possible factory production shotgun for competition shooting? You get the high-capacity, ultra-fast cycling Mossberg 940 JM Pro.

The new 940 autoloader is essentially the heir to the throne of Miculek's own 930 JM Pro, making both internal and external changes for the discerning competitive shooter. Most notably, this upgraded iteration of speed is fitted with better-built internals ready for the wear and tear of high-volume shooting, along with a redesigned gas system that is intended to run much longer between cleanings. Mossberg is said to have put 1,500 rounds through the gun without maintenance.

The 940 JM Pro holds 9+1 rounds in the extended magazine tube, has a 3-inch chamber and wears a sporty 24-inch barrel. Length of pull is adjustable from 13 to 14.25 inches with the included spacers. The enlarged and beveled magazine port is one of the best of its kind coming off a factory line and allows for Miculek's preferred quad-loading style, something not accommodated on many, if any, production guns. A set of extended

Briley choke tubes is icing on the 3-gun cake. Run-and-gunners will have a choice of two models, the first black synthetic with gold accents and the other done in Black Multicam, sans the bling, both at the same MSRP of $1,015.

The diminutive .410 bore again makes a splash, with Mossberg now offering multiple options. While the fully camouflaged Model 500 Turkey debuted previously, Mossberg now shifts gears from pumps to semi-autos with a pair of SA-410s, one Field and one Turkey. Both wear a 26-inch, ventilated-rib barrel, have a 4+1 round capacity, and weigh only 6.5-pounds. Where the SA-410 Field is matte blued with black synthetic stocks, the SA-410 Turkey has complete Mossy Oak Bottomland coverage along with an XX-Full Extended Turkey choke. MSRPs run from $616 to $735.

Mossberg's Maverick budget-brand fills the home-defense niche with a more cost-effective pump in the Maverick 88 Cruiser. Spinning off the inexpensive black synthetic Maverick 88 pump actions, the 88 Cruiser initially launched in a six-shot, 18.5-inch-barreled hand cannon. The hot new eight-shot Cruiser ups the ante with a 20-inch barrel, a fixed cylinder bore choke and black synthetic pistol-grip stock. The non-NFA, 12-gauge handheld weighs in at 6 pounds empty with an MSRP of $231, putting it less than half cost, albeit with fewer frills, than Mossberg's own brand of Cruiser.

Those wanting to stick with Mossberg's door-sweeping, bedside

wonder and NFA-compliant Shockwave will find a new-for-2020 Model 590 Shockwave Laser Saddle version in 20 gauge. When Crimson Trace introduced its aftermarket side-saddle laser mounts for Mossbergs, it was only a matter of time before one came straight from the factory, at a dandy cost savings over buying separately. Mossberg offers the combo rig for $613 along with the Raptor grip and corncob fore-end with a grip strap.

mossberg.com

REMINGTON

While the Remington Outdoor Company is seemingly shuttering some of its other brands, including the more tactical-centric Bushmaster, DPMS and Tapco, Big Green keeps moving forward with American-made guns, including a healthy class of model additions to its shotgun arsenal. Remington spices up the existing V3, VersaMax and 870 families.

The V3's soft-recoiling system runs on Remington's self-regulating VersaPort gas system, with this iteration chambering up to 3-inch shells. While the existing lines targeted all-around shooting, from hunting to clay shooting, the new models are more tailored. The V3 Field Sport NWTF reveals a partnership with the National Wild Turkey Federation and uses Mossy Oak Obsession camo along with a 26-inch barrel at a $1,025 retail price point.

The V3 makes its move into the competitive shooting world with the V3 Competition Tactical. With 3-gun-friendly features like a 22-inch barrel, Hi-Viz front sight, flared loading port, oversized controls and extended 8+1 magazine-tube capacity, the Competition Tactical carries a price tag of $1,128. The standard V3 Tactical wears an 18.5-inch barrel, bead sights, similarly oversized workings and holds two fewer rounds for roughly $100 less.

While the V3 shotguns get upgrades, the VersaMax group makes itself more accessible to the average hunter with the VersaMax Sportsman, which goes more bare bones on frills in exchange for a lower price. Though introduced earlier, 2020 sees additions in both Mossy Oak Bottomland and Realtree Edge

Mossberg 940 JM Pro

Mossberg SA-410 Turkey

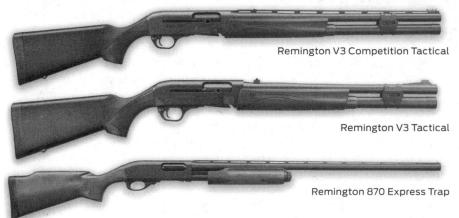

Remington V3 Competition Tactical

Remington V3 Tactical

Remington 870 Express Trap

coverage, both with a 26-inch barrel and the same VersaPort technology that chews through 2-3/4-inch on up to 3.5-inch magnum rounds. Though the Sportsman sacrifices some of the bells and whistles, and interior metal part coatings, MSRP on the Sportsman is $1,247, a more welcome number than the $1,665 to $1,765 of other camo VersaMax gas guns.

Hunters and shooters with a more modest disposable-income budget will gravitate to the pump-action 870 shotguns, continually expanding since their introduction in the early 1950s. Many things have changed, but what remains the same is a simple and affordable platform. While the 870 Trap has been around almost as long, the new Express Trap makes things more cost-effective, albeit plainer in appearance and without the frills one might find on the 870 Wingmaster line. The 870 Express Trap features a Monte Carlo wood stock, matte metalwork, mid-bead with ivory front sight, gold-plated trigger and three chokes for $609 retail.

If the goose blind is more your home than the trap range, check out the new 870 SuperMagnum Waterfowl with its 3.5-inch chamber and full Realtree Max-5 camouflage coverage. The SuperMag Waterfowl includes Hi-Viz sights and ships with a sling and "Over Decoys" Rem-choke for an MSRP of $661.

remington.com

RETAY

Just when we thought all Turkish-made shotguns fell into the cookie-cutter budget category, Retay Arms swoops in with inertia-driven semi-autos for hunters and do-all shooters seeking higher-dollar features at more reasonable than average prices. The Konya, Turkey, company has its USA headquarters in Easton, Maryland, and puts out two major shotgun lines, the Masai Mara and the Gordion. The Masai Mara offers a sweet, quick-release trigger group which comes free without tools and allows for both safe storage and quick clearing of debris in the duck flats. Both the Masai Mara and the Gordion use an Easy Unload system that allows the magazine tube to be cleared in seconds without racking live rounds through the action. In another sweet turn of engineering, Retay's Inertia Plus floating-bolt system is intended to eliminate misfires.

Gobbler hunters will want to look at the forthcoming XT Turkey Masai Mara as well as the already launched, and quite appealing, Gordion Turkey. Both come dressed in full coverage of the latest Mossy Oak and Realtree patterns. Additions to Retay's Waterfowl editions make life easier for duck and goose chasers wanting in on the inertia market with all the features, but significantly lower price points than larger competitors. The 3.5-inch magnum Masai Mara Air King edition looks the part with full Cerakote coverage, a host of camouflages and oversized controls, then backs up those good looks with smooth, fast cycling of the hardest hitting high-brass loads.

Retay designers cut their collective teeth in the upland and do-all shotgun market with fine-looking walnut-stocked models, as well as standard black synthetic. In a move to appeal to all types of shooters, Retay adds a smaller gauge to the Masai Mara, covering every model from camo woods guns to fine-looking uplanders and clay breakers.

Retay has, heretofore, been all 12 gauge, all the time, but 2020 marks the company's addition of 20-gauge models to the majority of its existing platforms. They are true, scaled-down 20s and not merely built on the larger frame, chambering 3-inch shells and

Retay Gordion

Savage Renegauge Waterfowl

available with either 26- or 28-inch barrels in the same variety of finishes and furniture. The 20s retain all the same features from the Masai Mara line, including the easily removeable trigger group and oversized controls on the synthetic models. Retay's retail pricing varies depending upon model but spans $1,099 to $2,100.

retayusa.com

SAVAGE

Every year, there are a few firearms announced that generate the greatest excitement, and the new Savage Renegauge autoloader is one such gun. Marking the company's first entry into the semi-automatic shotgun market (not counting the Browning Auto-5 spinoff M720 some 70 years back) the aptly named Renegauge is the product of years of internal engineering and design work at Massachusetts-based Savage Arms. The shotgun's launch comes hot on the heels of firearms manufacturer Savage parting ways with the Vista Outdoor family of brands.

What is traditionally a rifle company with an ever-expanding stable of centerfires with tailored and user-friendly advancements now takes some of that technology to the shotgun market. The Renegauge's appearance is slightly different from other competitors on the market, with the buttstock wearing a new iteration of Savage's adjustable AccuFit stock system that found wild success on the 110 bolt-action rifles. Everything from length of pull to comb height and drop at the heel can be customized to the individual shooter with the use of included and interchangeable gel cheek pads as well as LOP spacers. A fluted barrel is something seldom seen on scatterguns, also no doubt arising from the success of the rifles, and in the case of the Renegauge, barrels are coated with durable Melonite.

Savage's patented Dual Regulating Inline Valve (D.R.I.V.) gas system improves upon other gas-driven semi-autos by negotiating a way for excess gasses to vent forward toward the front of the fore-end and away from the action before it drives the bolt, resulting in, as the company reports "more consistent ejection, less felt recoil and a lightning fast cyclic rate for dependably fast split times." Dependability is addressed with chrome-plated reciprocating components and a single-piece, chromed action-bar assembly. Oversized controls and a flared, competition-ready magazine port will be welcomed by hunters and speed shooters alike.

Following the trend of downsizing the chamber even on hunting guns, the Renegauge will run everything from the lightest 2-3/4-inch target loads to the heaviest 3-inch high-brass hunting rounds, but forgoes the magnum 3.5-inch options. With the advent and perfection of numerous specialty metal shots like tungsten and related alloys, in many cases hunters are finding both superior patterns and knockdown power with the 3-inch loads.

The Savage Renegauge is made in the United States, making it one of very few USA-produced semi-automatic shotguns. The initial launch includes multiple models that can do it all, from hunting to competition to clays with SKUs specific to both turkey and waterfowl. A standard black synthetic comes with either a 26- or 28-inch barrel. A pair of Renegauge Turkey variants have shorter, wieldier 24-inch barrels and are dressed in Mossy Oak Bottomland or Obsession

camo. Waterfowlers will want to opt for either of the duo dressed in Mossy Oak Shadow Grass Blades. That makes a half-dozen versions for the initial 2020 launch, with more slated for the future, including a Compact option. Each will include a hard case and three chokes with an MSRP ranging from $1,449 to $1,549.

savagearms.com

STEVENS

There's too much going on with both Savage and Stevens to lump them together, though Stevens is a direct branch of the Savage Arms family tree.

Stevens breathed new life into the languishing single-shot scattergun platform with its break-action Model 301 .410 bore specialty turkey shotgun with an extended extra-full turkey choke. With an MSRP of just $204 and real-world prices closer to $175, local gun shops couldn't keep those 5-pound babies in stock. Even those seeking the budget appeal but wanting more pellets were pleased with the 301 in 20 gauge, each with a 26-inch barrel, brass front bead and the 20 weighing less than a

Stevens 301

Stevens 301 XP Turkey

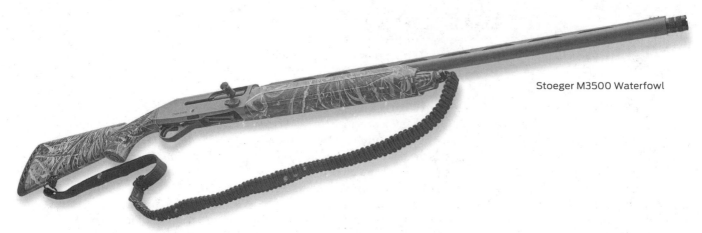

Stoeger M3500 Waterfowl

pound more than the .410 while being no less wieldy.

For 2020, Stevens by Savage adds a mounted and bore-sighted Tasco 1x30 red-dot optic to a detachable Picatinny top rail and tacks less than the cost of a plain optic onto the MSRP. The Stevens 301 XP is a lightweight, Mossy Oak-covered, affordable turkey reaper. The guns are optimized for use with Federal Premium TSS turkey loads.

Stevens enters into the specialty market with the introduction of the 555 Single Barrel Trap. Seldom seen in affordable trap guns, the 555 Trap is available not only in 12 gauge, but 20 gauge as well, with the receiver scaled to gauge. There's a 3-inch chamber, raised ventilated rib, manual safety and extractor and chrome-lined barrel. The lightweight aluminum receiver, now even seen on competition-grade scatterguns from bigger-name companies, is reinforced with a steel insert to maximize strength while also minimizing weight. Turkish-walnut stocks are oil-finished and feature an adjustable comb and 14.75-inch length of pull with the 30-inch barrel. The 555 Trap is simultaneously launching a Compact with a 13.75-inch LOP and 26-inch barrel. The new 555 Trap retails for only $689 and includes three chokes, making it one of the most affordable trap guns with those features.

savagearms.com

STOEGER

There might be flashier introductions from other companies, but Stoeger stays its course with a pair of critter-specific hunting additions to its inertia-driven M3500 semi-auto lineup. The M3500 Turkey/Predator uses a shortened 24-inch barrel and rubberized pistol grip intended to be more maneuverable in the gobbler woods as when hunting fast-moving coyotes. Rapid target acquisition is the name of the game when seconds count, with a red bar fiber-optic front sight as well as a receiver drilled and tapped for easy optics mounting. A set of five extended choke tubes includes the specialty MOJO Predator and MOJO Turkey. The use of Mossy Oak's Overwatch pattern is one of the first times that camouflage is fitted for the hunting woods. MSRP is $929.

Like the Predator/Turkey, the M3500 Waterfowl is tailor-made for hardcore hunters, with features like an enlarged trigger guard for gloved hands, chambered for 3.5-inch magnums, yet still able to cycle lighter loads in the inertia action. Flat Dark Earth Cerakote dresses for both durability and good looks, especially when partnered with a choice of Realtree, Mossy Oak or TrueTimber camo stocks. Ported barrels on both models help tame recoil, while a set of included stock shims allow hunters to customize the fit. MSRP on the Waterfowl is $849.

stoegerindustries.com

TRISTAR

If there was an award for most new shotgun models, TriStar would walk off stage with an armload of trophies and a mic drop. The self-proclaimed "value experts" restructure existing lines, create new ones and add more pizzazz to their all-Turkish-made lineup than seen in the past. Headlining the launch is a new family of O/U shotguns called Trinity.

The Trinity Series is comprised of two distinct builds: the all-steel Trinity and the alloy-framed Trinity LT. TriStar's heavily built Trinity is the best-looking of the bunch, the company's first with 24-karat gold detail on the deeply

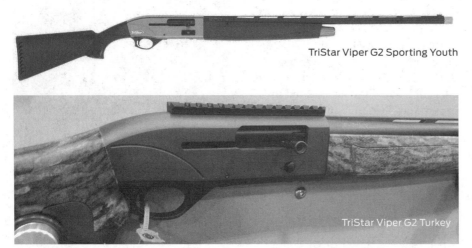

TriStar Viper G2 Sporting Youth

TriStar Viper G2 Turkey

Winchester 101 Light

Winchester 101 Deluxe Field Maple

Winchester SXP Extreme Defender

laser-engraved receiver. The LT version sacrifices the gold trim work for its aluminum-alloy receiver, which greatly shaves weight. The 5.3- to 6.3-pound weight, depending on gauge, makes the Trinity LT "one of the lightest O/ Us in the world," at least according to a company press release. Chamberings on the standard Trinity include 12, 20 and 16 gauge with an MSRP of $685, while the Trinity LT forgoes the 16 gauge, but adds the .410 bore and 28 gauge for an MSRP of $685 to $700. Each uses a single selective trigger, chrome-lined chamber and barrel, Turkish-walnut furniture, fiber-optic front sight, dual extractors, and ships with five Mobil-style chokes.

TriStar swaps out gold and engraving for a combination of camouflage stocks and Cerakote metalwork on its updated line of 3.5-inch-chambered Hunter Mag II O/U hunting shotguns. Bird blasters can choose from Mossy Oak Shadow Grass Blades with Bronze Cerakote or Mossy Oak Bottomland with Midnight Bronze Cerakote. If all-over camo coverage rather than Cerakote floats your duck boat, TriStar retains the existing pair of Mossy Oak Duck Blind and Mossy Oak Break-Up blanketed Hunter Mags. The solid frame and steel mono-block barrel construction ooze durability, and like the Trinity series before, come with TriStar's five-year warranty.

Shifting from magnum size to baby gauge, TriStar downsizes its Viper G2 Camo Turkey line of shotguns. What was previously limited to either 12 or 20 gauge with the pistol-grip stocks now adds .410 bore to the fray of 24-inch-barreled, rubberized pistol-grip gobbler getters with a top Picatinny rail. The updated, gas-driven semi-automatic Viper G2 Camo Turkey is dressed in Mossy Oak Bottomland synthetic stocks with a Bronze Cerakote receiver and barrel, extended turkey choke and weighs 6 to 6.8 pounds. MSRPs run from $685 to $715.

TriStar's TT-family of break-action shotguns comes full circle in 2020 with all models in stock and ready to ship. That includes not only the older TT-Trap, which has expanded to include a full contingent of adjustable Trap guns, but also the TT-Sporting with its wide

target rib, ported barrels, extended color-coded chokes and TT-Field lines. The Trap includes Mono, Top Single, Unsingle, DTA Adjustable, CTA Deluxe, as well as combo sets, all now with not only the adjustable comb, but fully adjustable buttpad system. The TT-Field in 12, 20 and 28 gauges and .410 bore, is built of steel, weighing from 5.5 to 7.0 pounds, and retailing for $855.

Sometimes, getting youngsters interested in shooting is as simple as catching their attention with color, and few guns do that as well as TriStar's G2 Sporting line with the red and blue anodized-aluminum receiver and magazine cap against the black synthetic stocks. TriStar expands the G2 Youth lineup to include these two eye-catching colors in 20 gauge with compact-sized stocks and a 26-inch barrel, weighing only 6.2 pounds and including a set of three extended choke tubes for $580.

tristararms.com

WINCHESTER

Winchester SXP Extreme Defender
There are no new or earth-shattering Winchester shotgun lineups, but there are plenty of eye-catching additions to existing collections. The 20-gauge chamberings are the biggest news, with that smaller bore finally being added to the semi-automatic SX-4 gas guns, heretofore only chambered in 12 gauge.

The SX-4 in 20 gauge continues to run Winchester's Active Valve gas system to cycle all loads, from the lightest 2-3/4-inch, 7/8 ounce loads to the heaviest 3-inch high brass with ease. By swapping out some of the steel or

aluminum alloy parts from the SX-3 shotguns with polymer on the SX-4, the guns are now lighter as well as more trim, though still maintaining the chrome-lined chamber and bore.

Over-under fans will embrace the options in Winchester's long-lived line of 101s. Most notable is the 101 Light model with its aluminum-alloy receiver, weighing in at only 6 pounds with 26-inch barrels or 6 pounds, 5 ounces with the 28-inchers. This fine field gun is engraved with quail, pheasants and a springer spaniel on its sides and bottom with Grade II Select walnut stocks. The 101 Light comes in with an MSRP of $1,870.

For a flavor more unique, and following Winchester's penchant to put beautifully figured AAA-grade maple on some of its heritage rifles, 2020 sees a Model 101 Deluxe Field Maple variant that nearly induces drool. The intricate engraving is delightful as well. The 101 Deluxe Field with its Grade III European walnut is equally as pleasant, albeit more toned down, but with the same features. Both of the Deluxe Field variants retail for $1,999.99.

The SXP Extreme Defender FDE has Flat Dark Earth coverage, a Picatinny rail with ghost-ring rear sight, pistol-grip buttstock, and side Picatinny accessory rails. The 18-inch barrel is topped with a heat shield and wears a hard-chromed chamber and bore for durability. The Door Breacher choke brings attitude, but there's also a flush-mount Invector Plus Cylinder choke. MSRP on the new SXP Extreme Defender FDE is only $529. **GD**

winchesterguns.com

Federal FireStick

›MATTHEW BREUER

NEW MUZZLELOADERS

Muzzleloaders have been around for ages and keep improving with time. This year we saw everything from a revolutionary new inline that will change the way we look at percussion guns forever, to a beautiful kit gun that is about as traditional as they come. Notable improvements in accuracy have developed over the past several years, and now manufacturers are starting to really refine the appearance and durability of their guns. Eliminating breech plugs and dynamic finishes are just a couple of things that have refined the market in 2020. This year was a bit stale on the mass of new offerings in blackpowder, with nothing new from Thompson/Center, and Lyman announcing a partnership

with Pedersoli that halted any information about updates to the Great Plains Rifle. However, the new stuff that did hit the market is noteworthy.

CONNECTICUT VALLEY ARMS

CVA has been trying to perfect the bond between Nitride and Cerakote

and the company succeeded. This bond makes CVA rifles the most weather-resistant muzzleloaders on the market. Plus, the barrels look amazing with the burnt-bronze finish.

The Accura models are CVA's top sellers, and the improvements to that line make them very attractive. The V2

CVA Accura V2

CVA Paramount Pro Colorado

model features a 27-inch Bergara barrel and comes with a thumbhole stock and the Veil camo pattern.

The Paramount was CVA's push into long-range muzzleloading. The Paramount rifles are designed to handle super-magnum charges and are reliable, in the hands of a competent shooter, out to 300 yards. The new Paramount Pro is an upgrade that is built on a Grayboe fiberglass stock, features a TriggerTech trigger and a Cerakote finish.

Also offered in 2020 is a Colorado version of the Paramount Pro, which includes a set of Williams peep sights.

PEDERSOLI

Pedersoli Howdah Hunter

Italian company Davide Pedersoli & C. manufactures some of the most elegant reproduction firearms on the market. New for this year in its muzzleloading line, engineers made tweaks to an existing replica. The Howdah is based on the famous 1920 Ithaca Auto & Burglar pistol, and new for this season the Howdah Hunter is available. This double-barrel, smoothbore flintlock pistol is chambered in 20 gauge and has no chokes, making it viable for birdshot as well as buckshot. Other features include a walnut pistol grip and handguard, a double trigger, a recoil-soaking endcap, and an elegant brass-bead front sight. The pistol weighs 4.85 pounds overall and sports a nice opaque finish on all metal surfaces.

TRADITIONS

The new NitroFire from Traditions is possibly the most innovative and game-changing product in the hunting industry this year. The NitroFire utilizes Federal's FireStick with self-contained propellant. The polymer casing loads into the rear of the barrel, eliminating the need for a breech plug. This makes for one of the cleanest, safest and most consistently accurate muzzleloaders out there. The FireStick uses Hodgdon Triple 8 powder and is available in 100- and 120-grain charges. The new NitroFire muzzleloader comes in .50 caliber and has a 26-inch, ultralight chromoly steel fluted and tapered barrel, 1:28-inch-twist rifling, dual safety system and much more. The NitroFire is also equipped with the new Elite XT trigger system, which is designed with a rebounding hammer, a captive half-cock, and a manual cross-block trigger safety. The Elite XT trigger allows the action to be broken open with the cross-bolt safety engaged, which allows you to load or unload your muzzleloader and view the chamber.

The NitroFire is available in four color patterns and can be purchased with or without a scope. All guns are drilled and tapped. The instructions are simple for this system: load the bullet from the muzzle, break open the barrel and insert the FireStick into the breech area, put a 209 primer in the primer pocket, close the barrel. That's it. This system is so simple it might just bring in a pile of new shooters to the blackpowder side of things.

Traditions stands by its name, and still makes traditional rifles that are very popular. The new Kentucky Deluxe takes the traditional Kentucky Rifle up several notches. The Kentucky Deluxe features a double-set trigger as well as a brass patch box. The new Kentucky Deluxe is available as a beautiful finished gun or can be purchased as a DIY kit. For anyone who is new to muzzleloading, and has never built a kit gun, this would be a great project and would transform into a beautiful muzzleloader that you built with your own two hands.

The new Mountain Rifle from Traditions is based off a Jacob and Samuel Hawken design. While the original had a rust-brown finish on the barrel, Traditions has selected a brown Cerakote finish, which replicates the original finish while providing increased corrosion resistance. The patch box, custom-scrolled trigger guard and many other features make this a gun you'll want to add to your collection. Available in both percussion and flintlock chambered in .50 caliber.

The new Pennsylvania model from Traditions might be the prettiest of all the guns on this list. This historically accurate rifle, holder of the enviable status of "authentic for re-enactment use" from the American Revolutionary Brigade, re-creates the finest features of the classic long rifles. In flintlock and percussion models, it features a full-length walnut stock with cheekpiece, solid brass patch box, stock inlay ornamentation and toe plate, double-set triggers, adjustable primitive-style rear sight and custom detailing throughout, without custom cost.

Two new revolvers can be found in the 2020 lineup from Traditions, as well. The new Wildcard and U.S. Marshall blackpowder revolvers chambered in .36 caliber are add-ons to the already popular line of 1851 Yankee Revolvers.

Unfortunately, no new cannons were found in the 2020 lineup from Traditions. GD

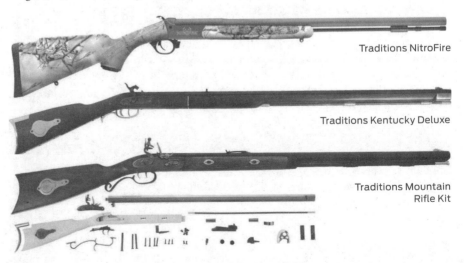

Traditions NitroFire

Traditions Kentucky Deluxe

Traditions Mountain Rifle Kit

Styrka S5

NEW OPTICS

›JOE ARTERBURN

Advances in optics happen fast, at the speed of technological advancements. No sooner are new technologies developed, new materials and new processes created than they are incorporated in optics, such as binoculars, riflescopes, spotting scopes and rangefinders, used by shooters and hunters.

Advanced prisms and lenses, lens coatings, night- and thermal-vision, laser rangefinders, rangefinding binoculars, rangefinders communicating with riflescopes and now a rangefinder that reads wind conditions downrange.

Think how far we've come from the days of simple field glasses. Imagine where optics will be in two, three, five years. It seems we are at a point that if it can be imagined, it can be built.

Here is a look at the new and new-and-improved optics companies have introduced for your consideration. But don't for a moment think it ends here. Technology is changing and none of these companies is content to sit still. But, for now, this is the latest and greatest.

CARSON OPTICAL

In addition to sports optics, Carson Optical, founded in 1990, produces optics in numerous categories, including telescopes, magnifiers, microscopes and digiscopes, but got its start with binoculars. With the new full-size 10x42mm RD-042MO model, Carson is targeting hunters and shooters, for sure, but also hikers, birdwatchers, campers, anyone engaging in outdoor activities. The "MO" in the model

Carson RD-042MO

designation references the Mossy Oak camo pattern of its protective body armor. The BAK-4 prisms and fully multicoated lenses provide a clear, bright image. The waterproof and fog-proof design holds up in inclement weather. Weight: 1.29 pounds. MSRP: $245. *carson.com*

German Precision Optics RangeGuide

FLIR

FLIR has extended the viewing capability of its Scion Outdoor Thermal Monocular (OTM) and Professional Thermal Monocular (PTM) series, increasing the range so users can quickly detect objects even at extreme distances and in challenging environments. With FLIR's high-performance Boson thermal core, the OTM model, with 25mm lens, extends viewing capability to 700 meters; the PTM model, with 36mm lens, to 1,000 meters.

Designed to provide smooth, unwavering vision and with a new manual focus, the new series is packed with more features than any other FLIR commercial thermal handheld device. Both the OTM and PTM series are available with 9 hertz or 60 hertz refresh rate and include Wi-Fi and Bluetooth connectivity. They also have two gigabytes of internal storage and a micro SD card slot to record video or still images. A new Lock Span Mode creates highly detailed images within a locked temperature range, effectively eliminating unwanted temperature

detection. Plus, they are GPS capable. MSRPs: OTM, $3,495; PTM, $3,995. *flir.com*

GERMAN PRECISION OPTICS

German Precision Optics is making its name for quality optics at reasonable prices, thanks to a corporate mindset different than many large manufacturers that price products to support massive corporate infrastructure. Without that level of expense, GPO established a model to match or beat those companies' products in quality and/or price. Toward that end, GPO introduced the RangeGuide, joining the trend for combining binoculars and rangefinders. RangeGuide is a compact 10x50 binocular with rangefinding capability out to 3,000 yards. Plus, it features true-range angle technology that measures the angle to your target and calculates

proper distance. On scan mode, you'll get three readings per second to keep up with a shifting view. The OLED display can be adjusted to nine brightness levels. The lenses feature GPObright high-transmission lens coatings to provide bright viewing in low light and the armored magnesium body is built to handle rough-and-tumble field use. MSRP: $1,700.

Even with rangefinding binoculars gaining popularity, there is still a need for, and those who prefer, stand-alone handheld rangefinding units, like the RangeTracker 1800, which can range as close as 6 yards for bowhunters to 1,800 yards for long-range rifle hunters. GPO puts all its proprietary expertise and technology in these 6x units, such as GPObright lens coating, Hyperscan that provides three readings per second for fast-changing scenarios and both line-of-sight and True-range angle-adjusted distance readings. Also, Target-seeker technology provides best laser hit or last laser hit, to better fit your situation. Also reads outside temperature. Price: $400.

In the riflescope category, GPO has come out with its Passion 5X, with a 30mm tube, double high-definition objective lens technology, GPObright lens coating and iControl microfiber optic illumination technology. MSRPs: 3.5-18x56i, $1,180; 1-5x24i, $880.

The Passion 4X 6-24x50 is GPO's best-selling long-range riflescope, thanks to specialty features such as second-focal-plane ballistic MOA reticle calibrated at 24x, full 70 inches of vertical adjustment and a free individualized Kenton turret to customize to your ammunition. It

FLIR Scion PTM 36mm

features a 30mm tube, bubble level, sunshade extension and double HD objective lens with GPO's multicoatings. MSRP: $1,150.

The 12.5x50 Passion HD binoculars join GPO's flagship line of products, boasting high-quality components and technology that produces 99.7-percent light transmission. GPObright lens coating on every optical surface, of course, and Passiondrop hydrophobic coating to help shed moisture, dirt and grime. There's a lot of magnification, field of view and eye relief in this binocular, which sells for $1,300. There are four other models in the Passion HD series. MSRPs: 10x50, $1,280; 8.5x50, $1,260; 10x42, $1,000; 8x42, $980.

gpo-usa.com

KAHLES

Kahles, with 120 years of optics experience, is one of the oldest riflescope manufacturers in the world, which is why when it introduces new products, savvy hunters and shooters notice. For instance, take the new Helia 1x26 red-dot sight, designed to deliver speed and precision in close-quarters scenarios. The highly visible red 2 MOA dot is easy to pick up, even in full daylight, plus it's adjustable for low-light situations. A low profile helps prevents snag for quick, efficient deployment. A unique Anti-Reflexion coating enhances clarity in the large 26mm window. Includes a Picatinny/Weaver mount or adapter plate and easy-to-adjust 1 MOA impact point correction. MSRP: $610.

And, IPSC and 3-gun competitors will want to take note of the new Kahles K18i 1-8x24 riflescope, which

Kahles Helia Red-Dot

Leica PRS Riflescope

has been optimized for competitive shooters with specialized reticles in an ultra-wide field of view, high-contrast image, Max Light extra-bright illuminated reticle and adjustable throw lever that can be operated with gloved hands. MSRP: $2,777.

The new Helia RF-M 7x25 rangefinding monocular is designed for simple, intuitive handling and is capable of ranging up to 2,000 yards while delivering exceptional clarity and a wide field of view and enhanced angle compensation, all in an ergonomic, easy-handling package. It has five brightness settings match changing ranging conditions, simple menu navigation and scan mode to track moving targets. Provides temperature and air pressure readings, too. Expect 4,000 measurements out of one CR2 battery. MSRP: $610.

kahles.at/us

LEICA

When introduced in 1992, Leica's Geovid started waves in the optics industry that have continued to build. Since that first commercially available rangefinding binocular, Geovid has continued to evolve, now with the 3200.COM, which features Bluetooth connectivity and an effective range to 3,200 yards on non-reflective targets. (Think deer and other "soft" targets.) In any weather conditions. On-board sensors also give air pressure, temperature and angle readings. It can be managed with the new Leica Hunting app, and linking to a Kestrel Elite weather meter allows you to use Applied Ballistics,

incorporating personalized ballistics for instant shooting solutions. It will also connect with your Apple Watch via smartphone for convenient, silent communication. Yes, Leica's quality optics throughout, in three models. MSRPs: 8x42, $2,949; 10x42, $2,999; 8x56, $3,299.

For the hunter or shooter who prefers a standalone rangefinder (with full ballistics functionality), Leica's new Rangemaster CRF 3500. COM is even more precise and is now Bluetooth enabled. You can create individual ballistics profiles with the Leica Hunting app and get reliable readings up to 3,500 yards, even in difficult weather conditions and on targets of all ranges of reflectivity. Can also be linked to a Kestrel Elite and, with Applied Ballistics, provide even more precise shooting information. Like the Geovid, it can connect with your Apple Watch to silently transmit info to your fingertips, well, wrist. MSRP: $1,199.

The new PRS 5-30x56i is Leica's first long-range riflescope with 6x zoom, ideal for a host of competitive situations as well as long-range hunting and sport shooting. Expect Leica's legendary optical performance, including high (greater than 90 percent) light transmission, high-contrast imaging and color fidelity. The first-focal-plane reticle's large adjustment range provides consistency through the zoom range. Tool-free zeroing of the turret means you can react quickly to fluid shooting situations. Choice of three reticle designs. MSRP: $2,699.

leicasportoptics.com

Leupold VX-Freedom

LEUPOLD

Leupold added four new models to its versatile VX-3i line of riflescopes, for the first time featuring the ZeroLock CDS dial, a premium feature at a nice price. (It's the first time Leupold made ZeroLock available at a price below its popular, high-end VX-5HD line.

Two of the new models have 30mm tubes, two have 1-inch tubes, and come in magnification ranges from 3.5-10 to 4.5x14 with Duplex or Wind-Plex reticles.

But back to the ZeroLock, a feature that prevents unintended adjustments or other mishaps and ensures quick and accurate return to zero. It's a low-profile, one-revolution system that's Custom Dial System (CDS) ready. One CDS dial, customized to match an exact load, velocity and average atmospheric conditions, is included with the purchase of each scope. The dial allows you to easily compensate for bullet drop and make quick adjustments for varying ranges. Price range: $650 to $975.

Leupold has also beefed up its VX-Freedom riflescope line, adding five new illuminated-reticle models. All have a version of a FireDot illuminated Models include: 1.5-4x20 with a MOA-Ring reticle; 3-9x40 with a TriMOA; 4-12x50 CDS with Duplex; VX-Freedom AR 1.5-4x20 with 223 MILRing; and 3-9x50 with the brand-new Twilight Hunter, which will be of special interest to deer hunters. They all have 30mm tubes and military-spec lens coatings to protect against abrasions and the elements.

Filling a need for hunters and recreational shooters, Leupold also added a model with milliradian (MIL) to the previously MOA-based VX-5HD riflescope. You get MIL-based adjustments and a Tactical Milling Reticle (TMR) without having to go through a custom shop order. The TMR reticle utilizes hash marks instead

of dots for increased ranging and hold-over precision, while providing aiming points for wind and bullet-drop compensation. It also features Leupold's Twilight Max HD Light Management, which combines enhanced light transmission and glare management, for better performance early and late in the day. Price range: $520 to $780.

With the SX-4 Pro Guide HD Spotting Scope, Leupold is offering a midrange-priced spotting scope that features its Twilight Max HD light management system, which the company contends is capable of adding up to 30 extra minutes of glassing light at dawn and dusk and will eliminate 90 percent more glare-producing stray light than its competitors. There are two models, a 20-60x85mm and a 15-45x65mm; both available in a straight- or angled-eyepiece design. Price range: $1,040 to $1,300.

leupold.com

MAVEN

Maven takes a different approach than other optics companies, cutting out middlemen and selling directly to customers. There's no distributor profit margin added to the consumer price, and no retail markup because you won't find Maven products in stores. And since Maven designers are not trying to hit a specific price point or performance category, they aren't limited in research, technology or material quality. And, because they don't have to operate in standard product categories, they can offer customized optics, where customers build binoculars, spotting scopes or riflescopes to fit their style and needs.

Maven's latest stock offerings include its new S.2 compact spotting scope. Measuring only 11 inches long and weighing just 34 ounces, this scope packs a lot, including a large 56mm objective lens that promises more light-gathering capability than traditional 50mm lenses on many other spotters. Magnification range is 12x to 27x, not as wide or high a range as bigger scopes, but what you lose in magnification you make up for in carrying convenience. Think backcountry hunters or others who hike miles carrying everything they need in a pack. You'll be able to scout long distances with the S.2, without having to lug a monster spotter.

The Abbe-Koenig roof-prism system (prized for its ability to reflect 100 percent of light that hits it, and longer

Maven B.5 Binoculars

focal length that reduces color and spherical aberrations) and premium crystal fluorite objective lens provide crisp, clear images without distortion at a decent price, $950, that gets you into the spotting-scope game in a big – make it compact – way.

Maven's B.5 binoculars are high magnification, either 15x or 18x, with big 56mm objective lenses for gathering light in the first- or last-light magic hours when animals are most likely to be on the move. Essentially, Maven engineers paired the lightweight magnesium frame and Abbe-Koenig prisms of their popular B.2 binoculars with the crisp fluorite glass of their S Series spotting scopes to create this best-of-both-worlds, tripod-mountable, easy-handling beauty for glassing and picking out detail at long distance. Weighing 43 ounces, they are a good choice for those wanting binocular performance and handling, yet spotting-scope-like capability when it's time to zero in. MSRPs: 15x, $1,500; 18x, $1,550.

With the RS.3, Maven set out to build a lightweight long-range hunting riflescope. It comes in at just 26.9 inches long, so it is one of the lightest, and features a wide 5x to 30x magnification range for most hunting situations you're likely to encounter. They come with either the SHR-W or MOA-2 reticle. The first, the Simplified Holdover Reticle adds windage measurements for those who prefer to dial elevation, but hold for wind. The MOA-2 features a floating dot to allow for precise holds. Both are first focal plane, so they are consistently accurate at any zoom range. Priced at $1,600, it features ED glass for true color rendering and a 50mm objective lens to maximize light transmission in low-light hunting situations.

mavenbuilt.com

MEOPTA

Meopta, which for more than 85 years has produced high-end European optics, continues the tradition with two lines of riflescopes, the Optika5 with 1-inch tubes and the Optika6 with 30mm tubes. The Optika5 features 5x zoom; the Optika6, a 6x zoom.

Starting with the Optika5, it comes in six models, the 2-10x42RF (rimfire), 2-10x42, 3-15x44, 4-20x44, 4-20x50 and 4-20x50 RD, all with reticles in the second focal plane; all with hunting turrets made of rubber-armored metal. MSRPs: $350 to $550.

The Optika6 models are available in first- or second-focal-plane reticle options, including DichroTech reticles, which feature battery-free illumination. The first-focal-plane Shooting series is available in 1-6x24, 3-18x50, 3-18x56, 4.5-27x50, plus a 34mm 5-30x56 model with ED glass to eliminate chromatic aberration at high magnification. The second-focal-plane Hunting series comes in 1-6x24, 2.5-15x44, 3-18x50, 3-18x56 and 4.5-27x50. All feature rubber-armored target turrets.

All the new Meopta scopes feature one-piece tubes; MeoBright lens coating for edge-to-edge clarity and bright, sharp image; zero-reset setting for quick return to zero; and zoom ring with multi-position throw lever. A well-thought-out feature is the rear-facing magnification display that allows quick, easy viewing of the power setting from behind the scope, so you don't have to peer at the top of the scope to see the setting. Expect retail pricing for Optika6 to be in the $499 to $899 range.

With its new MeoPro Air binocular, Meopta raises the bar of the popular MeoPro line with a lightweight magnesium-alloy chassis and ergonomic open-hinge design. Meopta's proprietary lens coating on the ED glass helps deliver clarity and bright, sharp images with virtually no chromatic aberration, meaning colors are true

and vivid and the resultant enhanced contrast makes it easier to pick out specific details, even in low light. For protection, the lenses are coated with anti-abrasion MeoShield and rain-, dust- and grease-repelling MeoDrop. MSRPs: 8x42, $980; 10x42, $1,000.

Meopta also added a straight-body version of its popular MeoPro HD 80 spotting scope, which features a fixed 20-60x eyepiece and a large 80mm fluoride objective lens, which delivers maximum light transmission and sharp resolution. The armored magnesium-alloy body protects Meopta's quality optics with MeoBright ion-assisted multicoatings to eliminate glare and reflection while delivering color fidelity. MeoDrop and MeoShield coatings provide protection from contaminants and abrasion. It has a Centric-Drive midbody focus control that is easy and fast to use, even with gloves on. Retail price is $1,600; add $100 to get the carbon-fiber tripod kit.

meoptasportsoptics.com

NIGHTFORCE

Nightforce's new NX8 riflescopes evolved from its classic NXS series, which have been used for 20 years by hunters, competitive shooters and the U.S. military. The wide 8x magnification range of the new two new NX8 models (2.5-20x50 F1 and 4-32x50 F1) sets them apart from most other variable-power scopes with modest magnification ranges, usually in the 5x to 6x range. Nightforce solved the problem of delivering clarity, resolution and brightness with an 8x scope at every setting, which for years was a

Nightforce NX8

puzzle for optical designers. On the low end of the magnification range, you can deal with up-close or moving targets; at the high end, zoom in on even small targets at longer distances. So, you have one riflescope with the versatility to function in virtually any shooting environment, at virtually any distance. Includes advanced DigIllum reticle illumination and Nightforce's ZeroStop technology. Comes in your choice of MOA or MIL adjustments. Measures just 13.4 inches and weighs less than 29 ounces. MSRPs: NX8 2.5-20, $1,950; NX8 4-32, $2,150.

nightforceoptics.com

Primary Arms GLx

NIKON

Nikon expanded its flagship Monarch HG line of binoculars by adding 8x30 and 10x30 models, which are smaller, more compact and portable binos. Both of the new Monarchs have the same great ED (extra-low dispersion) glass of the 42mm big-brother models, which reduces color aberration and enhances contrast. Fully multicoated optics with multiple layers of anti-reflective coating are par for the course for Nikon and its Field Flattener Lens System delivers sharp edge-to-edge images in the full field of view. The lightweight but tough magnesium alloy bodies are waterproof, and O-ring sealed. MSRPs: 8x30, $950; 10x30, $970.

Nikon has a heck of line of rangefinders, and have now brought out the Prostaff 1000 and Prostaff 1000i to provide more economical options. Both have a wide effective ranges, 6 to 1,000 yards and they'll display either

Nikon Prostaff 1000i

a single or continuous measurement. And, Tru Target technology allows you to pick between First Target and Distant Target modes. The difference between the two models is Prostaff 1000i has ID Technology which accounts for inclining or declining shooting angles, delivering the one number you need for the best shot. The Prostaff 1000 is priced at $150; the 1000i, $180.

nikonsportoptics.com

PRIMARY ARMS

Primary Arms Optics beefed up its lines this year with updates to existing favorites and additions to its GLx and SLx series, including new prism sights for each series. The new GLx 2X prism, the first fixed-power in the GLx line, is an original design engineered at HQ in Houston. Weighing 11 ounces (no heavier than holographic sights, but improved visibility and precision), its low magnification and large eye box provide clarity and balance for both close- and long-distance targeting; it is quick in close-quarters situations; and with the ACSS CQB-M5 reticles, it also offers intuitive long-distance holds for common cartridges, like the 5.56 and 7.62. MSRP: $370.

The SLx 3X and 5X Gen III compact prism scopes come in two reticle options, one calibrated for 5.56/.308/5.45x39 and the other for 7.62x39/300 Blackout. Improvements of this third generation include high-strength rugged mounting hardware to assure zero is maintained even in

tough environments. They also feature a removable top-mounted Picatinny rail and a built-in removable spacer so you can tailor scope height to AR-15 and AK-47 platforms. Weight: 16 ounces. MSRPs: $290, 3X; $330, 5X.

The new SLx-MD-25 splits the difference between micro and full-size red-dot sights, measuring 3 inches long and weighing 6.5 ounces. The 25mm aperture offers wide field of view even in a small unit. Choice of 2 MOA dot or ACSS reticle. MSRP: $170.

Both the SLx 1-8x24FFP and GLx 2.5-10x44FFP riflescopes feature reticles in the first focal plane. Primary Arms said the SLx 1-8x24FFP came about because customers asked for something between the SLx 1-6x24FFP and its popular but pricier PLx 1-8x24FFP. The new SLx comes in at $480 (versus $1,300 for the PLx model). The new GLx model fits in the medium-magnification category that'll hit a note with precision shooters and long-range hunters, especially with the ACSS Raptor M2 reticle geared for 5.56. Both the SLx and GLx additions feature the patent-pending turret design and AutoLive motion-sensing reticle illumination.

primaryarmsoptics.com

SIG SAUER

Sig Sauer Electro-Optics has upgraded its much-heralded Ballistic Data Xchange (BDX) rangefinder and riflescope system to make it easier to use right out of the box. Essentially, Sierra BDX riflescopes now come pre-loaded

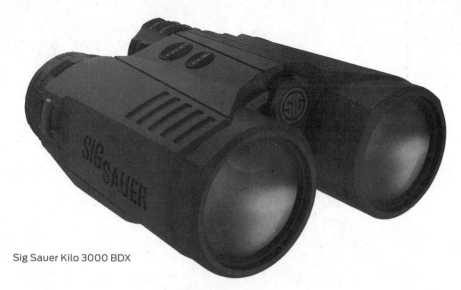

Sig Sauer Kilo 3000 BDX

with nine user-selectable Ballistic Drop Compensation reticles, and Kilo BDX rangefinders are pre-loaded with eight ballistic groups, plus the QuickBond feature, as the name implies, quickly bonds rangefinders and scopes so they function as a ballistics system. The ballistics groups cover most centerfire rifle cartridges, as well as crossbows and muzzleloaders. On your Sierra BDX riflescope, you select the best group based on cartridge, muzzle velocity and projectile weight, set the scope accordingly and the reticle will display five active hold points from zero to 500 yards. You can also create a custom ballistic profile through the free app. Kilo BDX rangefinders use the same ballistic groups, which you select on the same criteria, and when bonded to your scope it will measure the range and communicate ballistic holdover to the scope. Sierra 3 BDX scopes are available in eight configurations from 2.5-8x32 to 5-30x56, with prices ranging from $520 to $1,690. There are six Kilo BDX rangefinder models ranging from a 5x20 1,000-yard model, priced at $520, to a 7x25 2,400-yard model priced at $1,039. Kilo 3000 BDX rangefinding binoculars, which combine 3,000-yard rangefinding capability with 10x42 binoculars, have an MSRP of $1,560.
sigsauer.com

STYRKA

For not a lot of money, Styrka can get you in the caliber-specific game with its new S3 Series 3-9x40 riflescopes in two popular straight-wall caliber configurations, the .350 Legend and .450 Bushmaster.

Both configurations carry an MSRP of $310, but, if you keep your eyes open, you might find them advertised for as low as $239, a heck of a price for custom ballistic turrets that help you quickly get on target at various ranges. These are one-piece 1-inch aircraft-grade aluminum tubes, machined to maintain accuracy and point of impact even under tough hunting conditions. Lenses are coated multiple times with Styrka's SXL anti-reflective coatings to enhance brightness, color transmission, sharpness and contrast.

Styrka's S5 Series 10x42 binocular is an upgraded version of its previous model of the same name, designed to deliver high-contrast images and enhanced clarity, resolution and light transmission.

Styrka loads these binoculars with top features, such as multiple SXL-MAX anti-reflective broadband coatings and phase- and dielectric-coated BaK-4 prisms for increased light transmission. MSRP: $500, but expect to see them advertised for as much as $100 less.

Styrka's S3 Reflex Sight series comes with either 3- or 6-MOA red dot, targeting hunters and shooters looking for a quality optics that won't break the bank. Priced at $310 (but watch for $239, or so, advertised pricing), these sights weigh in at only 2.3 ounces, but are packed with features, including a double-lens optical system to enhance viewing while virtually eliminating parallax; dot-color-indexed coating to specifically match the wavelength of the red dot to help eliminate point-of-aim errors; strong, lightweight aluminum construction; unlimited eye relief; 10 brightness settings; and auto shut-off.

If you worry about buying optics at these prices, don't. Styrka will repair or replace damaged or malfunctioning optics at no charge, without a bunch of questions, registration or receipt requirements. And, the company will clean and tune your optics once a year if you send them in.
styrkastrong.com

SWAROVSKI OPTIK

Illumination being a hit in Swarovski's 30mm riflescopes, it has been added to the company's 1-inch Z5 line of scopes, designated Z5i. The Z5 series (first released in 2009), and now the Z5i, are known for lightweight, top-end optical performance, including high resolution and clarity and repeatable accuracy. Illumination allows quick target acquisition and improved visibility in low-light hunting situations with these 5x-zoom scopes.

Illumination comes in 64 brightness levels (32 for day; 32 for night) as well as SwaroLight technology that automatically turns off illumination if the firearm is tilted laterally more than 30 degrees or more than 70 degrees vertically, so it'll shut off and save battery if you lay it down or stand it upright in a rack or in the field.

You get a choice of three reticle designs, all in the second focal plane, and an optional ballistic turret, which works hand in hand with the four-point coil spring system to provide easy adjustability and repeatable accuracy. Available in 2.4-12x50; 3.5-18x44 and 5-25x52 models, with prices ranging from $1,588 to $1,921.

Swarovski also brought out the new Z8i 3.5-28x50 riflescope, targeting hunters looking for a slim, lightweight, long-range scope. The illuminated Z8i line has been a hit since introduced in 2016 in four magnification ranges. This latest addition features 8x zoom and will accept Swarovski's Turret Flex for elevation and windage adjustment, so you can dial up 70 clicks. Or you can order a custom ballistic ring for your specific ballistics. It weighs only 23.5 ounces and comes in your choice of three illuminated reticles. MSRP: $3,877.

swarovskioptik.com

Trijicon Huron

TRIJICON

With the Ventus, Trijicon is rattling the shooting world by adding wind-reading capability to a rangefinder, addressing two of the major concerns of hunters and shooters everywhere: How far is the shot and what is the wind doing between here and my target?

The Ventus, so new it was not available for testing in early 2020, measures three-dimensional wind velocities at multiple distances out to 500 yards and ranges non-reflective targets up to 5,000 yards. Without getting overly technical, the handheld Ventus uses Doppler LIDAR and four collimated lasers to measure wavelength interaction with dust particles at up to six different distances, so you can read variations and calculate for head, tail, cross and vertical winds. And, yes, it will work through dust, fog, sleet, snow and other less-than-favorable weather conditions. It features 9x magnification and center cross-dot reticle to help you get on target, as well as simple, oversized-button controls.

And, as though that's not enough, the further-advanced Ventus X model has a user-configurable on-board ballistic calculator that pairs with the Bluetooth-capable Trijicon Ballistic Calculator app you can customize to your ammo, so you can view specific ballistic solutions and wind map displays, as well as store shooter and target geographic locations. MSRP wasn't released by press time.

News of the Ventus has somewhat overshadowed the introduction of two new Trijicon riflescopes, the Huron and Credo series.

The Huron, priced at $650 to $699, comes in four models: 1-4x24, 2.5-10x40, 3-9x40 and 3-12x40, and in 30mm or 1-inch tube configurations. The reticle, on the second focal plane, is available in Standard Duplex, German

#4 and Trijicon's new BDC Hunter Holds reticle.

The Credo and Credo HX series gives you a plethora of choices, including 2-10x36 or 2.5-15x42 models; nine matte finishes; and nine LED-illuminated milling, holdover, and BDC reticles. They are also available in either first- or second-focal-plane models; and 30mm and 34mm tubes. With that many choices, prices range from $799 to $1,799.

Both the Huron and Credo models feature fully multicoated broadband anti-reflective glass for clarity and enhanced light transmission and distortion-free detail and color.

trijicon.com

VORTEX

Vortex addresses the need for a tactical riflescope that can handle anything from point-blank to long-range with the Razor HD Gen III. It ranges from 1x for point-blank operations to 10x for putting hits on target at longer ranges. And, the first-focal-plane optical system, coupled with Vortex's all-new EBR-9 MRAD or EBR-9 BDC MOA reticles, ensure all hold points are consistent and usable throughout the entire zoom range. Compact, stout and built on a 34mm aircraft-grade aluminum tube,

with 24mm objective lens, it features stay-out-of-the-way low-profile capped windage and elevation turrets for a sleek profile. Daylight-bright reticle illumination (11 intensity levels) provides red-dot functionality on 1X and full use of the data-rich, glass-etched reticle on the upper end, no matter the light conditions. MSRP: $2,900.

Quickly acquiring accurate distance readings and judging targets, two of the most important aspects of hunting and shooting, come together in the Fury HD 5000 10x42 rangefinding binocular. Right-side button controls allow you to manipulate it with one hand, leaving your other hand available to hold your rifle, bow or critter call. Expect accurate ranging out to 5,000 yards on reflective targets. Features angle compensation for uphill or downhill shots. Scan Mode provides readings as you track a moving target. Fully multicoated prisms and lenses deliver clear edge-to-edge views. Rubber armored housing protects while providing a comfortable, solid grip. Before you kick at the $1,599 price, consider it's pretty reasonable for a high-definition binocular and rangefinder in one. Price those separately and see where you end up. **GD**

vortexoptics.com

Vortex HD Razor Gen III

NEW

AIRGUNS

›JIM HOUSE

From the shelves of stores to the catalogs of suppliers, one thing is certain: The airgun industry is alive and well. Never has such a wide range of products been available. From low-powered plinkers to the high-powered hunters there is a model for every purpose. Among those in the former category are models that mimic numerous popular firearms and among the latter are the large-caliber rifles that fire .35-, .45- or even .50-caliber projectiles.

Power sources continue to be compressed air, nitrogen and CO2. The compression of air can take place in a series of pump strokes (a multi-pump pneumatic) or in a single stroke of either the barrel itself (a break-action) or a separate lever (the under-lever). If nitrogen in a cylinder is compressed rather than a strong spring, the rifle is known as a gas-piston model. Such rifles are usually quieter, can be left cocked for longer periods of time, and do not involve the rapid expansion of a strong, heavy spring when fired. With a pre-charged pneumatic (PCP) rifle, a reservoir is filled to a high pressure, which enables several shots to be fired without having to refill the tank.

Each type of power source has its advantages and disadvantages. Variable power is readily available with a multi-pump model. Much higher power is available with a PCP, but a separate compression source (a special pump, filled scuba tank or an air compressor) must be available.

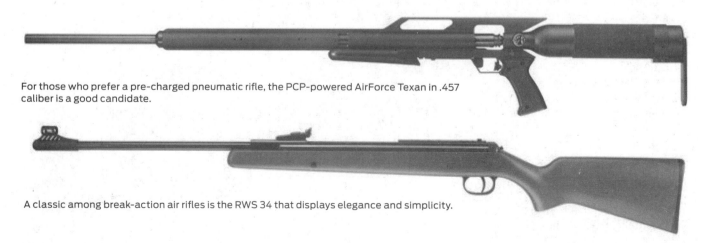

For those who prefer a pre-charged pneumatic rifle, the PCP-powered AirForce Texan in .457 caliber is a good candidate.

A classic among break-action air rifles is the RWS 34 that displays elegance and simplicity.

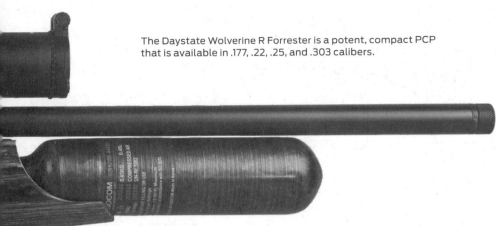

The Daystate Wolverine R Forrester is a potent, compact PCP that is available in .177, .22, .25, and .303 calibers.

One of the current trends in fun guns is the use of fully automatic models such as this Umarex Steel Strike.

Break-action air rifles that utilize drawing in and compressing air are sensitive to altitude because there is less air (lower atmospheric pressure) the higher the altitude. When high power is required, that dictates that a PCP model is in order, whereas a high rate of fire requires the use of CO2 cylinders. The earlier type of power production is suitable for rifles used for hunting and the latter is generally used for pistols. Airgun models that utilize all of these power sources are available in a high state of refinement.

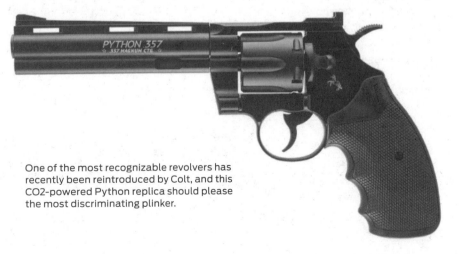

Multi-pump airguns have long been popular and the Crosman 1322 pistol is a potent pistol.

Airguns now carry names of famous firearm manufacturers such as Colt, Glock, Beretta, Smith & Wesson, Walther, Browning, Remington, Ruger, Winchester, H&K and others. In many cases, especially with handguns, the models replicate the appearance of particular firearms from the firearm manufacturers. This realism has resulted in tragedy in some cases when someone with a pellet- or BB-firing pistol was believed to be in possession of a firearm. Discretion in the use of any airgun is vitally important, and especially so when the device looks like a firearm.

A second general trend is toward expansion in the market of air rifles of large caliber that are intended for hunting game of medium to large size. These models utilize the PCP power Photosource. Most come without sights with the realization that hunters must place projectiles very accurately and that means some sort of auxiliary sighting equipment, usually a scope.

The enormous number of models of guns that utilize compressed gas for power is amazing. It is not possible to mention all of the large retail suppliers, but in order to get an overview of the market, the reader is encouraged to look at websites for companies such as Umarex, Pyramid Air, Airguns Arizona, Gamo USA/Daisy, Velocity Outdoors/Crosman, Airguns Depot, Cabela's, Scheels, Sportsman's Warehouse and others.

Two general trends in airguns can be readily discerned. First, there is an increase in the number of models that emphasize realistic appearance and function. The second is that models are introduced that have high-tech features. One high-end PCP rifle even has an LCD panel that displays the number of shots fired, number of pellets remaining in the magazine and the remaining pressure in the reservoir, and it is Bluetooth-ready to receive software updates.

PLINKERS

One of the developments in airguns sure to excite many is availability of models that fire BBs in a full-auto mode. With a firing rate of up to 1,400 rounds per minute, a 25-round magazine will be emptied in a flash. Specifications of various models are given in the catalog section of this book, so only a brief description of general characteristics of these guns will be given.

One such model, the DPMS, loosely resembles a submachine gun with an adjustable stock. Other full-auto models of the submachine gun type include the Crosman Bushmaster MPW, Umarex Steel Strike and the H&K MP5 K-PDW, which utilizes a 40-round magazine. These models are generally

One of the most recognizable revolvers has recently been reintroduced by Colt, and this CO2-powered Python replica should please the most discriminating plinker.

powered by two 12-gram CO2 cylinders and typically give velocities up to approximately 400 ft/sec.

The Uzi BB Submachine gun is designed for one-hand use. It features a 25-round magazine and is powered by two 12-gram CO2 cylinders. Umarex offers the Steel Storm full-auto pistol and, like some others, it can also be fired in a semi-automatic mode. Although of questionable use for target practice, these lively full-auto BB guns have interesting uses. Additional training and safety precautions are advised.

For the enjoyable practice of popping pine cones or bouncing a pop can, it is hard to beat shooting a CO2 pistol. Fortunately, there are many types available, both revolvers and semi-automatics.

HEAVY-HITTING HUNTERS

That hunting with airguns is on the rise can be seen from publications such as *Predator Xtreme* and *Airgun Hobbyist* that have regular sections devoted to hunting with airguns. The editorial content covers hunting pests, small game and large game. From the early days of airgunning, the use of airguns for pest control and small-game hunting has been common. However, the more recent introduction of large-caliber airguns having sufficiently high power to take large game has changed things. A most useful source of information on the use of airguns for hunting can be found on the website www.pyramydair.com/airgun-map. The site is sponsored by Pyramid Air and shows a map of the United States. By clicking on either the big-game or small-game icon, the map shows states that allow the use of airguns for species in those categories.

Although hunting small game

Among PCP rifles for hunting, the Daystate Huntsman provides plenty of performance.

with airguns is widely permitted, the regulations need to be considered. Some states, Kentucky being one of them, specify that airguns of certain caliber be used for specific species. For example, airguns of .177 caliber or larger may be used to hunt rabbits, but those of .22 caliber or larger are required for hunting opossum or raccoon. Other states have regulations that are similarly caliber-specific, so it is necessary to determine what regulations apply in the area of interest.

On some occasions, there come to mind those days from long ago when, as the designated shooter, it was my opportunity to initiate the preparation of farm animals being processed into food. The rifle of choice was an old Winchester Model 90 pump chambered for the .22 Short. Moreover, as a youngster I carried that rifle for countless hours and many miles along the river bottoms. When my father passed on, that .22 eventually became truly mine although in practice it was mine many years earlier. I came to appreciate the capability of a 29-grain bullet from a .22 Short even on a large animal when it was placed exactly right in the most lethal zone. However, it was necessary that the conditions were exactly right. In many ways, that is the situation with the use of airguns for hunting. To hunt ethically with an airgun, it is necessary that the hunter take only shots in which the projectile

can be placed with great accuracy.

The .22 Short fires a 29-grain bullet at over 1,000 ft/sec producing approximately 65-70 ft/lbs of energy whereas a .22-caliber airgun might fire a 14-grain pellet at 800 to 900 ft/sec, producing about 25 ft/lbs of muzzle energy. The difference between a .22-caliber firearm shooting even a .22 Short and a .22-caliber airgun is considerable. Such irrefutable facts must be kept in mind.

Specifications for airguns that may be used to hunt large game species vary widely with most specifying PCP rifles. For regulations on hunting particular species it is necessary to consult the regulations for each state.

For example, in Idaho, to hunt deer, pronghorn or wolf, the airgun must be of .35 caliber or larger and generate at least 350 ft/lbs of energy at the muzzle. For larger species, the requirement is for airguns to be of .45 caliber or larger. Arkansas requires airguns to be of at least .40 caliber and generate at least 400 ft/lbs of energy at the muzzle. Other states have different requirements, but those stated serve to illustrate that only large-caliber, high-powered airguns are suitable for use on large game species. The aspiring nimrod who wishes to use an airgun for hunting should consult the detailed information provided by the game and fish department of the areas to be hunted.

Several PCP rifles in .35 caliber can

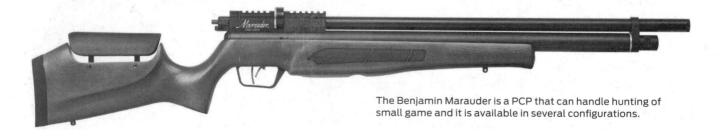

The Benjamin Marauder is a PCP that can handle hunting of small game and it is available in several configurations.

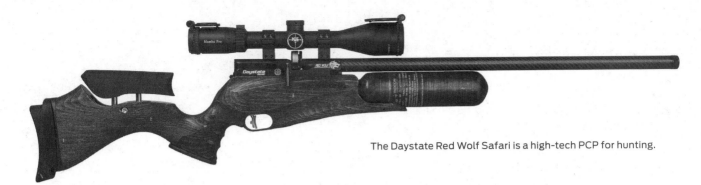

The Daystate Red Wolf Safari is a high-tech PCP for hunting.

launch a projectile weighing about 150 grains with a muzzle of velocity of approximately 800 to 900 ft/sec, which just about duplicates the ballistics of a .38 Special revolver. Will a well-placed bullet from a .38 Special dispatch medium-size game quickly and reliably? Certainly, if the bullet is placed correctly, and the same situation applies to a .35-caliber air rifle.

Does a .45 Auto produce greater effect that a .38 Special? Of course, it does, and a .45-caliber PCP air rifle produces greater effect than does one of .35 caliber. But a .45-caliber projectile fired from an air rifle is a far cry from a 240-grain bullet fired from a .44 Magnum rifle. Many PCP rifles will produce groups of one inch or less at 50 yards, so the accuracy potential is there. Whatever the air rifle used, it is necessary for the hunter to make sure the equipment used is approved for the species being hunted and he or she has the required shooting ability.

With the increasing extent of urban sprawl and other land-utilization modes, hunting with airguns is becoming a more attractive proposition. Many modern airguns have shrouded barrels and moderators to reduce sound levels. Regulations about the use of airguns are updated rather frequently as the whole sport changes. In some jurisdictions, high-powered airguns are considered to be firearms and the same regulations apply.

AIRFORCE AIRGUNS

Long known as a producer of high-powered PCP rifles, AirForce Airguns has models that should satisfy the shooter who wants maximum performance. The Texan series

includes rifles in .257, .308, .357 and .457 calibers that have a base price of $1,084.95. However, the .457 caliber version can launch a projectile at up to 1,000 ft/sec and deliver energy of over 600 ft/lbs. Power of the .257 model is impressive as a result of it being able to give a projectile weighing 100 grains a velocity of approximately 900 ft/sec. The TexanSS comes with the features of the regular Texan but includes a special release valve. A rifle in the Texan series can meet the needs of any hunter who uses an airgun. A shorter PCP model is the TalonP Carbine which comes in .25 caliber.

DAYSTATE

Daystate rifles have been produced for many years. The brand is most noted for PCP rifles that are some of the favorites of hunters who use air power. One of the flagship models is the Red Wolf Safari that is truly a high-tech wonder.

It utilizes a rotary magazine that holds 10 .22-caliber pellets and an electronic firing system. On an LCD screen are displayed such information as the shot count for the tank charge, reservoir pressure and magazine contents. It should come as no surprise that the MSRP for this marvel is $2,999.99.

Less laden with gadgets, but still highly capable rifles from Daystate include the Huntsman Regal that is available in four versions, and the

Wolverine Pulsar that is a bull-pup model. A new offering is the Delta Wolf model. The Tsar is a high-tech rifle for field-target competition, and it features adjustments in stock dimensions and many other refinements.

GAMO USA–DAISY

The merger of Daisy Outdoors and Gamo a couple of years ago has resulted in an airgun company that markets an enormous range of products. As has been the case for more than a century, the Daisy label appears on several BB guns and rifles that fire pellets. Currently the pellet-firing Daisy rifles are .177-caliber models, and the Model 880 continues as the flagship model in that group. For those seeking a first BB gun, the Model 105 Buck is a scaled down BB gun and the single pump Grizzly/Boy Scout that can fire either BBs or .177 pellets are popular.

The always-popular Red Ryder is available in several versions including a model that features a pink stock and forearm (guess the intended group of users) and in traditional finish with a large loop cocking lever. Daisy's least expensive and smallest BB gun is the 105 Buck. Target rifles for intermediate competition include the CO2-powered 887 and the single-cocking-stroke 753. Daisy also markets one multi-pump model that bears the Winchester label,

The Daisy 887 is a good choice for those seeking an entry-level air rifle for target shooting.

Among the most popular break-action rifles from Gamo are those in the Swarm series.

the Model 1977 XS, which can be used as a single-shot, .177-caliber pellet rifle or a repeater using BBs.

Gamo products include a wide range of break-action rifles, most notably the Swarm series that is available in at least a dozen variations as a result of different calibers, accessories, stock material,

etc. For hunters, Gamo also offers the PCP Coyote Whisper Fusion in .177 and .22 calibers. For bigger game, the Big Bore TC-35 and TC-45 models provide strong medicine. A wide range of CO_2 pistols that offer realistic appearance and versatility will delight the plinker.

HATSAN

Hatsan produces several PCP rifles, some of which are high-powered models intended primarily for hunting applications. These include the Neutron Star, Vectis, Galatian and Gladius models that are available in various versions and combinations

The Hatsan Bullmaster is a PCP that is suitable for hunting.

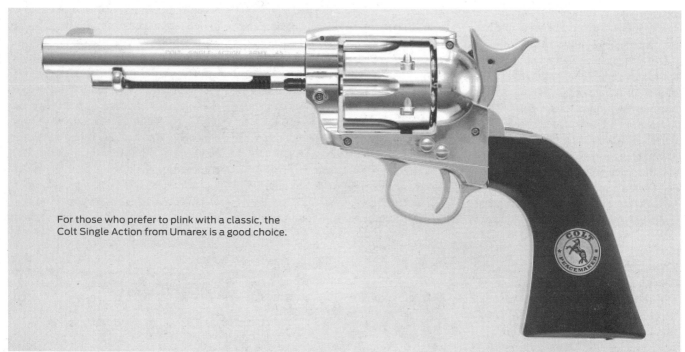

For those who prefer to plink with a classic, the Colt Single Action from Umarex is a good choice.

A classic among air rifles is this Benjamin 392 multi-pump .22, which has been available for many years.

with accessories. For those who prefer a short air rifle, the Bullmaster is an excellent choice.

Break-action models include the Edge, Striker and Alpha Youth rifles. The Proxima is a rifle that is cocked by means of a lever located under the barrel.

UMAREX

An enormous range of airguns and related products is offered by Umarex USA. Plinking pistols are available that mimic numerous firearms in both name and function including single-action revolvers and semi-automatics. Some have features that also make them suitable for training and target practice.

Long a purveyor of many break-action rifles, Umarex markets the Browning Leverage, Ruger Airhawk and other models, some of which are available with various options. Some of the most famous break-action rifles are the RWS 34 and 350 Magnum, both of which are still available. Also, the side-lever Models 48 and 54 are available, as is the Model 460 under-lever-cocking rifle. The Octane and Torq are break-action rifles offered by Umarex. In the PCP category, is the Gauntlet, which is available in both .177 and .22 calibers. Umarex also markets the NXG APX multi-pump rifle that is available with accessories, as well as the Legends Cowboy Lever Action Rifle.

VELOCITY OUTDOORS

Known as Crosman for many years, the name change was made to reflect the fact Velocity Outdoors markets a range of products that includes not only airguns, including those that carry the Benjamin label, but also optics, archery equipment and other items. Gone are the airguns that carried the Sheridan label.

However, many of the famous Crosman and Benjamin airguns remain in production. These include the Crosman 760 and 2100 multi-pump rifles, the multi-pump single shot pistols and the classic Benjamin 397 and 392 rifles in .177 and .22 calibers, respectively. Also available are the single-shot, CO2-powered Model 2240 and special 2300 Target and 2300 Silhouette versions. Crosman also produces several CO2 pistols that fire either BBs or .177-caliber pellets.

In the high-powered PCP rifle category, the Benjamin Marauder is available in several versions, including short bull pup and pistol models, in .177, .22, .25 and .35 calibers.

A higher-priced rifle known as the Armada that utilizes a rotary magazine is also available in .22 and .25 calibers. The Benjamin Discovery was a no-frills single shot PCP rifle that was one of the favorites of the author, but it has been replaced by the Maximus. A wide range

of break-action rifles is also available, with most utilizing the Nitro Piston power plant, in which cocking the rifle compresses a gas rather than a spring.

ALTERNATIVE SOURCES

In addition to the companies that market a broad range of airguns and ancillaries, there are numerous smaller producers who offer a limited number of products. Some of them produce only one or two models. For example, PBBA produces the Pro 20, a 20-gauge shotgun, and the Pro .308 rifle. Jefferson State markets rifles known as the Hawk and Raptor models. Rapid Air Weapons produces the HM1000X Long Range Target Rifle (LRT) and the HM1000X Chassis Rifle. American Air Arms produces two models, the Evol Classic Carbine and the Slayer High power bull pup. Edgun Leshiy produces the Gen 2 PCP rifle, and Western Big Bore manufactures the Bushbuck PCP rifle. These and other specialty shops add to the comprehensive selection of airguns available this year.

Today, there is an airgun for every appropriate use and the myriad products range in price from less than $20 to well over 100 times that figure. However, with the increase in airgun types, availability and capability will come an increase in regulations. **GD**

The Benjamin Maximus is a PCP single shot that can serve many purposes.

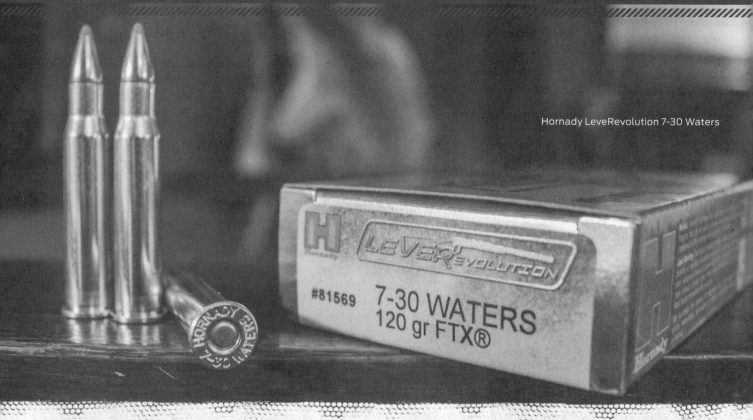

Hornady LeveRevolution 7-30 Waters

NEW AMMUNITION

› **PHIL MASSARO**

Among the most radically changing aspects of our industry is factory ammunition. I'm almost afraid to report it, but the factory ammunition of today absolutely gives handloaded stuff a run for its money, sometimes superseding the performance of even the best handloads. The consistency of the factory ammunition, the efficiency of the designs, and the results shown both on target and on game animals have proved we have the best factory ammo we've ever had. The long-range rifle bullets and cartridges continue to lead the way in new product department, as we continue to push the envelope of rifle, cartridge, optic and even the shooter. The 1,000-yard shot, which might have seemed nothing short of miraculous just a couple decades ago, has become much, much easier, and the ammunition is no small part of the equation.

Our projectile designs are constantly improving, and the cartridges are as well. We are seeing the versatility of our existing cartridges increase, and the newly released cartridges are designed with a new mindset. Rifles aren't the only area where advances are being made, as our handgun cartridges have seen many of the same upgrades: The projectile performance is constantly improving, our propellants give more uniform results, and the terminal performance continues to improve. Let's take a look at what's new this year.

BROWNING RIFLE AMMUNITION

New for 2020, Browning has extended its excellent

rifle ammunition line to include three newer cartridges: the .28 Nosler, the 6mm Creedmoor and the .350 Legend. Many feel the .28 Nosler is the flagship of the fleet, and the finest of the Nosler developments. Browning has offered the .28 with its 139-grain BXS at 3,350 fps and 155-grain BXC bullet at 3,250 fps,

Browning Rifle Ammo

as well as its Long Range Pro line with the 160-grain Sierra Tipped MatchKing at 3,200 fps. The 6mm Creedmoor is offered with the 97-grain BXR (designed for rapid expansion) at 3,210 fps and the 95-grain Long Range Pro at 3,285 fps. The .350 Legend ammo uses the 124-grain FMJ at 2,500 fps and the 155-grain BXR at 2,300 fps. Loaded in premium nickel cases, the Browning ammunition has been nothing but excellent, and I have no doubt it will continue to be so.

browningammo.com

BROWNING WICKED WING SHOTSHELLS

Browning Wicked Wing

Also new for 2020, Browning released its Wicked Wing waterfowl shotshells. Building on the success of the Browning BXD Waterfowl line, Browning has retained the BXD wad system, which increases pattern density at a variety of ranges, for the Wicked Wing shotshell line, and the new shotshells feature a proprietary round steel shot that is corrosion resistant for optimum performance. Available in 12-gauge, 3-inch magnum, Browning offers the serious waterfowler two loads to choose from: 1 1/4 ounces of No. 2 steel shot or 1 1/4 ounces of No. 4 steel shot. Both loads leave the muzzle at 1,450 fps, to reach out and touch those birds on the edge of the decoys. While steel is an excellent alternative to lead, especially over water, it certainly comes with its own set of unique challenges, and Browning's shotshells have maximized the effectiveness of steel. The Aerodynamically Stabilized Wad keeps that shot column tight through the bore, and continues to hold a tight pattern longer, putting more pellets on the bird instead of around it. While a highly respected name in the firearms industry, Browning entered the ammunition game late in life, but I will admit that all of the company's ammunition products have been impressive performers.

browningammo.com

CCI CLEAN-22 STEEL CHALLENGE RIMFIRE AMMUNITION

CCI Clean-22 Steel Challenge

Lead .22 LR bullets are affordable, readily available and plenty accurate, but they do come with their drawbacks. Barrel fouling is one of them, and, should you be running a suppressor, the lead residue will certainly build up in there as well. CCI has released its CCI Clean-22 Steel Challenge ammunition, built around a polymer-coated, 40-grain, round-nose lead bullet, at 1,235 fps. The polymer coating keeps both fouling and residue to a minimum, and the Clean-22 will minimize lead vapors in the air, as well run perfectly through the various semi-automatic actions. CCI is also donating a portion of the proceeds of this ammunition sold until Dec. 31, 2021, to the United States Practical Shooting Association (USPSA) to help promote participation in steel-shooting competition.

cci-ammunition.com

CHOICE AMMUNITION

Want the handloaded experience without handloading the ammunition yourself? Reach out to the folks at Choice Ammunition and tell them what you're looking for. Choice has an ever-expanding lineup of cartridge and bullet combinations, and I've used the stuff with great results, from the .22-250 Remington varmint loads, to the 6.5 Creedmoor target loads and even the .470 Nitro Express stuff. For 2020, Choice Ammunition has new loads for the .224 Valkyrie, the 6.5-284 Norma, 6.5 PRC, the .300 PRC, .300 Norma Magnum, .378 Weatherby Magnum, .416 Weatherby Magnum and all of the Nosler cartridges. Choice Ammunition is one of those companies you want to keep on the favorites bar of your computer, should you find that rifle chambered for an obscure cartridge. With a wide selection of cartridges and bullets, Choice most likely has what you're after.

choiceammunition.com

FEDERAL FIRESTICK

Perhaps this isn't exactly ammunition, per se, but this new muzzleloading "case" certainly warrants inclusion in this list. The new FireStick from Federal is a polymer capsule, which holds a 209 shotgun primer and is charged with a load of Hodgdon's new Triple Eight powder. Available in 100- and 120-grain loads, the Federal FireStick gives not only the consistency any hunter will appreciate, but is the most weatherproof system of charging a muzzleloading rifle ever been developed. The FireStick is inserted from the breech, while the bullet is loaded from the muzzle, and sits on a special shelf built into the barrel, to prevent the FireStick from being crushed. Should you wish to unload the firearm and make it safe, the FireStick can be removed; no longer does the rifle need to be fired to remove the powder charge, and with the FireStick removed, the rifle is completely inert. Climbing a fence, or into your favorite treestand has never been safer, and your powder charge has never been more resistant to the elements. Developed in conjunction with Traditions, in its new NitroFire rifle, this new system has proved to be incredibly accurate. I'm absolutely certain Federal has a winner here.

federalpremium.com

Federal Fire Stick

FEDERAL HAMMERDOWN

Federal HammerDown

Partnering with Henry Repeating Arms, Federal has announced the release of its HammerDown ammunition line, optimized to perform in lever-action repeating rifles. Using its nickel-plated cases to minimize corrosion, Federal has chamfered all the sharp edges on the case rims, in order to reduce drag in the lever-action rifles and give the smoothest feeding possible. If you've ever owned a lever gun that didn't like certain types of ammunition, you've probably experienced that "hard" feeding. Federal has chosen a quartet of pistol cartridges, .327 Federal, .357 Magnum, .44 Remington Magnum and .45 Colt, as well as two of the most popular centerfire rifle cartridges: .30-30 Winchester and .45-70 Government, all featuring a bonded-core bullet. Using Federal's Gold Medal primers, both the bullet weight and muzzle velocity have been designed for the best performance in a rifle-length barrel. Available in 20-count boxes in .327 Federal 127 grains, .357 Magnum 170 grains, .44 Remington Magnum 270 grains, .45 Colt 250 grains, .30-30 Winchester 150 grains and .45-70 Government 300 grains.

federalpremium.com

FEDERAL HYDRA-SHOK DEEP .380 AUTO

For those who enjoy the smaller handguns, the .380 Auto has been a viable choice for a cartridge. Federal just enhanced the capabilities of the .380 Auto by loading its 99-grain Hydra-Shok Deep, the one with the center post to enhance terminal performance, in the .380 Auto case, at 1,000 fps. In fact, the combination is so effective this is the first .380 load to make the FBI-requirement of 12-inches of penetration in both bare ballistic gelatin and through heavy clothing.

Loaded in Federal's nickel-plated cases, with the signature primer-sealant, the .380 Auto Hydra-Shok Deep comes in 20-count boxes.

federalpremium.com

FEDERAL PRACTICE & DEFEND PACKS

I have no problem reporting that my favorite defensive handgun bullets come from Federal. The Hydra-Shok and HST are among the best designs ever developed. Practicing with your chosen defensive ammunition in order to ensure you are familiar with its handling characteristics (recoil, feeding, ejection, etc.) can become rather costly if done on a routine basis. Federal solved the cost issue when it released its SynTech line of polymer-coated lead handgun bullets; the coating minimizes the exposed lead vapors, barrel fouling and splash on steel targets. The Federal Practice & Defend Packs give the shooter the combination of SynTech and HST projectiles in one box; 50 of each come in the 100-count box. Federal is offering the Practice & Defend Packs in 9mm Luger (124- and 147-grain bullets), .40 S&W (180-grain bullets) and .45 ACP (230-grain bullets).

federalpremium.com

FEDERAL PUNCH

Premium ammunition can be expensive, and though you need to trust your chosen bullet, not all great bullets will break the bank. Federal's Punch is a shining example of just that: A premium bullet that is easy on the wallet. Offering a jacketed-hollowpoint design with a skived jacket, for reliable expansion, Punch is all about value. Loaded in nickel cases, with Federal's famous primer sealant for consistent and reliable expansion, Federal Punch is available in the most popular defensive handgun calibers, including .380 Auto (85-grain), .38 Special +P (120-grain), 9mm Luger (124-grain), .40 S&W (165-grain), and .45 ACP (230-grain). If you want the consistent expansion and penetration of the premium bullets without the price tag, try Federal Punch in your handgun.

federalpremium.com

Federal Punch

FEDERAL SOLID CORE HANDGUN AMMUNITION

Hard-cast lead bullets have long been relied upon for both hunting purposes and for a self-defense choice; they hold together very well, offering reliable penetration on thick hides and tough bones. But hard-cast lead requires wax rings or gas checks, which can be messy and difficult, and still there is all that fouling to scrub out of the bore. Federal has solved that issue, and its new Solid Core line offers a viable choice for your sidearm, for the encounter with dangerous game animals. Extending the line of Syntech ammunition, which uses a proprietary polymer jacket to greatly reduce fouling in the bore, as well as minimize exposure to lead vapors, Federal's new Solid Core uses a hard-cast bullet fully wrapped in that polymer jacket, with a flat nose for increased energy transfer. Designed for those requiring a bullet for self-defense against dangerous game animals (problem bears on a stream while fishing comes immediately to mind) Federal has offered the Solid Core in common defensive calibers. Included are 9mm Luger +P (147-grain Solid Core), .357 Magnum (180-grain Solid Core), .40 S&W and 10mm Auto (200-grain Solid Core), .45 ACP +P (240-grain Solid Core) and .44 Remington Magnum (300-grain Solid Core).

federalpremium.com

FEDERAL'S TERMINAL ASCENT AMMUNITION

Since Federal engineers picked up Jack Carter's Trophy Bonded Bear Claw bullet, they've used the principle of that design for some excellent offshoots. The Trophy Bonded Bear Claw is still an excellent bullet, as is its oldest son, the Trophy Bonded Tip, but the latest iteration, Federal's Terminal Ascent, combines the proven terminal ballistics of the Trophy Bonded series with a sleek, high B.C. design. Terminal Ascent gives bonded-core performance, fully capable of even magnum-level impact velocities at close quarters, and still expands when impact velocities are low, as low as 200 fps lower than other comparable designs. The SlipStream Tip maintains the bullet's high B.C. throughout flight, and the AccuGroove channels on the shank reduce fouling and bearing surface, without sacrificing velocity. Terminal Ascent is offered in 11 different cartridges: 6.5 Creedmoor and 6.5 PRC 130-grain, .270 Winchester and .270 WSM 136-grain, 7mm Remington Magnum, .280 Ackley Improved and .28 Nosler 155-grain, .308 Winchester and .30-'06 Springfield 175-grain, .300 Winchester Magnum and .300 WSM 200-grain; all in 20-count boxes.

federalpremium.com

HORNADY HANDGUN HUNTER

Hornady Handgun Hunter

Using the proven Hornady MonoFlex bullet, a copper alloy monometal design, with a hollowpoint filled flush with a pliable elastomer material, the Handgun Hunter line offers an excellent choice for those who prefer to hunt with a handgun. The lead-free design is legal in all 50 states, and the strong construction of the MonoFlex ensures deep penetration. That elastomer filler in the bullet's hollowpoint compresses upon impact, driving the sidewalls outward, guaranteeing expansion. Combine these two attributes and you have a winner, especially when loaded in the excellent Hornady cases. Hornady's Handgun Hunter is available in 9mm Luger (a neat 115-grain +P

load), .40 S&W and 10mm Automatic (135-grain) for those who prefer to hunt with the semi-automatics, and in .357 Magnum (130-grain), .44 Remington Magnum, .454 Casull and .460 S&W (200-grain) for the revolver crowd. The .357 Magnum and 9mm Luger come in boxes of 25, and all the others come in boxes of 20.

hornady.com

HORNADY LEVEREVOLUTION 7-30 WATERS AMMO

I first heard of the 7-30 Waters when I was a teenager beginning to hunt deer. My dad had given me a brand-new Winchester Model 94 AE XTR in .30-30 Win, but he was upset because the 94 wasn't available in a long-barrel/.30-30 combination. The longer "rifle" variant was available in a cartridge called 7-30 Waters, the brainchild of Mr. Ken Waters, the famous cartridge wildcatter. While Ken's famous two-volume set "Pet Loads" would become a favorite of mine, his cartridge would become a favorite of T/C Encore fans, and those who embraced that Winchester rifle, in production from 1984 to 1997. Hornady has extended its LeveRevolution line to include a 120-grain FTX bullet in the 7-30 Waters, leaving the muzzle at 2,700 fps. The Flex Tip spitzer has a G1 B.C. of 0.320, making the downrange trajectory and striking energy higher for this Hornady load. When zeroed at 200 yards, the 120-grain bullet will hit 2.2 inches high at 100 yards, and will strike

only 9.7 inches low at 300 yards. The Winchester 94 AE XTR allows the use of a low-mounted scope over the center of the bore, so the classic lever gun just became a 300-yard deer gun.

hornady.com

HORNADY OUTFITTER AMMO

Based on the successes of last year's release of Hornady's Outfitter ammunition line, the Big Red H has expanded the offering. The combination of nickel-plated cases (made thoroughly waterproof) and the lead-free, polymer-tipped Hornady GMX bullet proved to be a winner, and for 2020 it is now available in four new loads. The .257 Weatherby Magnum, which is, to many shooters, the greatest of Roy Weatherby's cartridges, is available with a 90-grain GMX at 3,625 fps. The .300 Weatherby, the most popular of Roy's cartridges, is offered with the 180-GMX at 3,100 fps, and the .300 Remington Ultra Magnum is available with the same bullet at a muzzle velocity of 3,200 fps. Lastly, Hornady has (wisely, in my opinion) introduced the .338 Winchester Magnum with the 225-grain GMX, at a muzzle velocity of 2,600 fps, for a load that is capable of taking any North American game animal, and all of Africa's game except the true heavyweights. The Outfitter line is California compliant, as the GMX (Gilding Metal eXpanding) bullet has no lead core at all.

hornady.com

Hornady Outfitter

NORMA BONDSTRIKE
6.5MM AMMUNITION

The BONDSTRIKE bullet is the third in the Strike series from Norma, and has proved to be a sound choice for numerous big-game species. With a polymer tip, boat tail and bonded core, the BONDSTRIKE can handle the high impact velocities that close shots from a magnum cartridge will deliver, and yet still deliver the goods on distant shots, when velocities have dropped off. I had the opportunity to test the .30-caliber variants in the field last year, in both .308 Winchester and .300 Winchester Magnum, so you can imagine my excitement when Norma announced that the line would be extended to 6.5mm. The 143-grain bullet has a Sectional Density of 0.293 (compared to the 180-grain .308's S.D. of 0.271) and the 6.5mm BONDSTRIKE has a G1 B.C. of .600, so this load is poised to be a winner in the game fields. Norma is making the bullet available in the 6.5mm Creedmoor at 2.660 fps, the 6.5x55 at 2,690 fps and (my personal favorite) the 6.5-284 Norma at 2,825 fps. Loaded in Norma's excellent brass cases, the 6.5mm BONDSTRIKE series is certain to be a winner in the field.

norma-ammunition.com

Norma BONDSTRIKE
6.5 Creedmoor

NOSLER EXPANSION TIP
AMMUNITION

Nosler, long famous for its premium component projectiles, continues to develop loaded ammunition lines, and for 2020 has vastly expanded its Expansion Tip line. Using a copper-

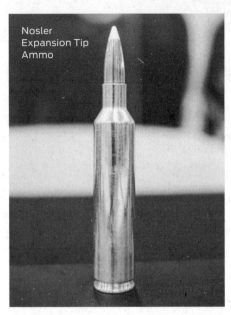

Nosler Expansion Tip Ammo

alloy, lead-free, boat-tail bullet, with a signature O.D. green polymer tip, the Expansion Tip ammunition can be used anywhere, including those states where leaded ammunition is forbidden. It has proved to be an accurate bullet, holding together well even when impact velocities are high, yet doesn't put all sorts of copper in the bore. For 2020, Nosler announces the following additions to the Expansion Tip ammo line: .223 Remington 55-grain, .260 Remington 120-grain, 6.5mm PRC 120-grain, .270 WSM 130-grain, .300 WSM and .300 RUM 180-grain, .325 WSM 180-grain and .338 Winchester Magnum 225-grain. I have found the Nosler loaded ammunition to be as good as the company's time-proven projectiles, and would recommend giving them a try in your rifle.

nosler.com

27 NOSLER

Fifth in Nosler's series of proprietary rifle cartridges, based on a blown-out .404 Jeffery case and shortened to fit on a .30-'06 length action, the 27 Nosler takes on the time-honored .277-inch bore diameter, and the king-of-the-hill, Jack O'Connor's beloved .270 Winchester. Rather than follow the "simply a larger case for greater speed" formula (many feel the velocity of the .270 Winchester is just fine) Nosler has coupled a boost in velocity with a faster than normal twist rate, allowing the 27 to use the standard 130-, 140- and 150-grain bullets, and the heavier 165-grain AccuBond Long Range bullet. This lends considerable versatility to the .277 bore, and that bonded core, sleek ABLR will take the caliber to where I have always felt it should be. No more questioning or even debating whether this 27 will cleanly take elk, moose and bear; it's an emphatic yes. This beltless magnum uses a 35-degree shoulder for good headspacing, and provides a 400 fps increase over the .270 Winchester with 150-grain bullets, and a 300 fps increase over the .270 WSM with the same projectile. Both loaded ammunition and component brass is available from Nosler, as are M48 rifles chambered for the new cartridge. I'd bet this one will garner some attention.

nosler.com/27-nosler

.416 RIGBY NO. 2

John Rigby & Co. has introduced the rimmed version of its world-famous big-game cartridge: the .416 Rigby No. 2. Maintaining the same 45-degreee shoulder, the .416 No. 2 gives the same velocity, ballistics and performance that the .416 Rigby has been giving us since 1911, but the rimmed version is better suited to double and single-shot rifles; driving a 400-grain bullet of nominal diameter, to a muzzle velocity of 2,400 fps, for more than 5,000 ft-lbs of muzzle energy. John "Pondoro" Taylor discussed the need for this cartridge back in the 1940s in his book *African Rifles and Cartridges*, and I can't argue with his assessment. I expect the first Rigby Rising Bite double rifles in .416 No. 2 to arrive on the scene shortly, so expect to be reading some successful hunting stories shortly thereafter.

johnrigbyandco.com

SIERRA PRAIRIE ENEMY
VARMINT AMMUNITION

Sierra broke into the loaded ammunition market last year with its GameChanger line, and now for 2020 the company is introducing its Prairie Enemy line, built around its excellent BlitzKing varmint bullet. The BlitzKing features a thin jacket for high frangibility, and a green polymer tip for

Sierra Prairie Enemy

devastating expansion. Sierra is offering four popular varmint cartridges for the initial run of ammunition: the .204 Ruger (36-grain), .223 Remington (55- and 69-grain), .224 Valkyrie (69-grain) and .243 Winchester (70-grain). Want to ruin a prairie dog's day? Intent on ending a coyote's career? Trying to outfox a fox? Grab a box of Sierra's Prairie Enemy, and just shoot straight.

sierrabullets.com

SIG SAUER .277 FURY

Breaking tradition with a two-piece case combining brass and stainless steel, the new .277 Fury uses a higher-than-normal pressure of 80,000 psi to launch a 140-grain .277-inch-diameter bullet to a muzzle velocity of 3,000 fps, from (and here's the hook) a 16-1/2-inch barrel in its new Cross rifle. Typical ammunition usually tops out at right around 65,000 psi, hence the harder steel base to the cartridge case, but the .277 Fury might be ushering in a new phase in cartridge development. The Fury uses a .473-inch case head, the same as the .30-'06 Springfield, .308 Winchester and 6.5 Creedmoor, and though it will certainly fit in a standard short-action receiver, only the Sig Cross rifle has been especially designed to handle the high pressures generated by the new cartridge. Keep your eye on this cartridge; it might just be the next step forward.

sigsauer.com

SPEER GOLD DOT 5.7X28MM

Speer has developed the first cartridge for the 5.7x28mm specifically designed for self-defense. Using the Speer Uni-Cor

bonding method, the jacket and core won't separate upon impact, ensuring that the high impact velocity won't pose an issue from the small-caliber round. Optimized for performance through a number of barriers, the Speer Gold Dot 40-grain load comes in 50-count boxes. With the number of handguns chambered for the little 5.7x28 increasing, it's no surprise that Speer has answered the call for a defensive round.

speer-ammo.com

WEATHERBY 6.5 RPM

Weatherby's 6.5mm Weatherby RPM (Rebated Precision Magnum) is a proprietary beltless cartridge based on an elongated .284 Winchester case. Its rebated rim (the same .473-inch as the 7x57/.30-'06 family) and resulting larger body diameter and minimal taper, coupled with a forward-situated, 35-degree shoulder, give the cartridge plenty of powder capacity. Weatherby's six-lug action allows the 6.5 RPM to be housed in a compact, light rifle; and the cartridge gives both respectable velocities and trajectory. Weatherby lists three different loads for the RPM: a 140-grain Nosler AccuBond bonded-core at 3,075 fps, a Hornady InterLock softpoint at 2,975 fps, and a 127-grain Barnes LRX at 3,225 fps. According to the published figures, the RPM will beat the velocities of the 6.5 Creedmoor by nearly 375 fps and the 6.5-284 Norma by 300 fps, putting the new cartridge in the 6.5 PRC class, without needing the longer/heavier receiver. Mated with the lightweight Mark V Backcountry

rifle, you'll have a combination that is easy on the shoulder and back, yet powerful enough to take any game animal you'd sensibly use a 6.5mm bullet for. Personally, I find the 6.5 Weatherby RPM makes much more sense than the 6.5-300 Weatherby Magnum does, and, probably because of my highly positive experiences with the 6.5-284 Norma, I'm intrigued by the new design.

weatherby.com

WINCHESTER DEER SEASON COPPER IMPACT

Winchester Deer Season Copper Impact

Winchester's Deer Season line of ammunition, and especially its Copper Impact variant, has become a popular choice among deer hunters. Expanding the line for 2020, Winchester has three new offerings: the .270 WSM 130-grain, the .300 WSM 150-grain and the ever-popular 6.5 Creedmoor 125-grain. With its oversize red polymer tip sitting over a large hollowpoint cavity, the Deer Season Copper Impact boasts quick energy transfer and deep penetration, perfect for deer hunting anywhere. **GD**

winchester.com

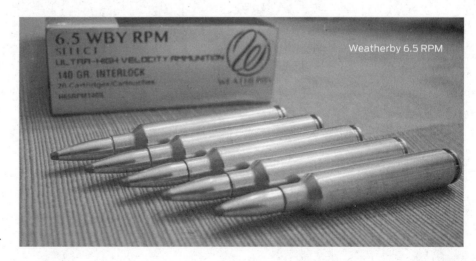

Weatherby 6.5 RPM

NEW RELOADING COMPONENTS AND SUPPLIES

› **PHIL MASSARO**

For as long as the centerfire metallic cartridge has existed, the desire to be able to reload that cartridge has existed. When I was younger, the majority of reloading was centralized around repurposing spent metallic cases or shotshells, adding a new powder charge, primer and projectile or payload and creating cost-effective ammunition. In the last five or six years, there has been a definite shift from reloading for quantity, to the practice of handloading for quality. With that shift comes a wave of precision tools, making the handloaded cartridge more effective than it ever has been.

In addition to the tools, the components are constantly being refined, what with the projectiles giving better downrange performance, powders are delivering the most uniform results we've yet to experience, across a wide range of temperatures, and the consistency of some of the brass cases produced today would have been unimaginable two or three decades ago.

So, in order to help keep your reloading bench up to date and allow you to make the best ammunition possible, let's look at what's new for reloading components and tools.

RCBS MatchMaster Dies Set

RCBS.

MATCHMASTER FL BUSHING SET 7MM-08 REMINGTON

P/N 13908
MATCHMASTER
USE SHELL HOLDER #3

BARNES

This year, Barnes has extended its LRX (Long Range X bullet) line to include three new bullets: a .22-caliber, 77-grain, a 6mm, 95-grain and a .30-caliber, 190-grain. The LRX line has the best B.C. values of the Barnes lead-free bullets, using a longer ogive and an alloy designed to expand reliably at a lower velocity than any of its other bullets. I have found them to be the most accurate of the Barnes lineup, and having hunted with them both here in North America and in Africa for plains game, can attest to the terminal performance of the bullet. For those who enjoy the .224 Valkyrie, 6mm Creedmoor and .243 Winchester, and .300 Winchester Magnum and .300 PRC, these new offerings will help take advantage of the trajectories those cases (and their like) can generate.

barnesbullets.com

Barnes LRX Bullets

BERGER

New for 2020, Berger announces its Long Range Hybrid Target line of bullets, designed for excellent performance on distant targets. The Hybrid design uses a blend of two different ogive curves, to best handle the stresses of the impact of the bullet into the lands, as well as to give the best B.C. for retained energy and wind-deflection values. Berger has

Berger Long Range Hybrid Target Bullets

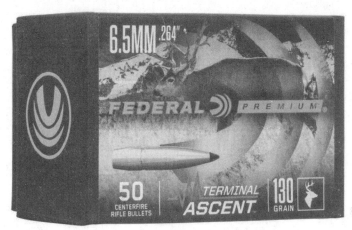

Federal Terminal Ascent

verified the B.C. values of its new bullets via Doppler Radar, and indicates a variation of less than 1percent; part of the consistency is the Meplat Reduction Technology System that puts consistent pressure along the ogive during production to keep the bullet profile as uniform as possible. The Long Range Hybrid Target is available in: .22-caliber, 85.5-grain; 6mm-caliber, 109-grain; 6.5mm-caliber, 144-grain; 7mm-caliber, 190-grain; .308-caliber, 208- and 220-grain.

bergerbullets.com

FEDERAL AMMUNITION

Federal's proprietary bullet line has long been successful, and its latest offering, the Terminal Ascent bullet, is no different. It is the latest in the family of the time-proven Trophy Bonded Bear Claw, with a lead core in front of the bullet chemically bonded to the rear copper shank. Terminal Ascent, however, has the highest B.C. of the bunch (Bear Claw, Trophy Copper, Trophy Bonded Tip) and was specifically designed as a long-range hunting bullet. Using the Slipstream polymer tip, and the patented AccuChannel grooves on the bullet shank, the Terminal Ascent is a hunting bullet designed to fly like a match bullet, yet give a fantastic range of weight retention and expansion at ranges from up-close-and-personal to that-deer-is-in-the-next-zip-code. I've tested this bullet at the range in a couple of different calibers and I am quite impressed, though based on my experiences with the Trophy Bonded

Tip, itself a fantastic hunting bullet, I am not surprised. For the hunter who wants a bullet that is excellent in the wind, is truly capable of pinpoint accuracy, and will provide wonderful terminal ballistics, the Terminal Ascent is one of the best choices a reloader could ask for. Available bullets: 6.5mm-caliber, 130-grain; .277-caliber, 136-grain; 7mm-caliber, 155-grain; and .308-caliber, 175- and 200-grain.

federalpremium.com

FORSTER PRODUCTS

As bullet technology continues to evolve, and the ogive of target bullets continues to grow, the potential for jacket deformation during the seating process grows. Few things bother me more than trying to seat a sleek target bullet, only to see that tell-tale ring where the seater stem has distressed the jacket. Forster now offers a custom polishing service for its seater stems, which will eliminate this problem. You'll need to send three or four cases and bullets to allow Forster to get things just right, but in the end, you'll have a perfectly seated bullet, free of any deformation. Modern problems require modern solutions.

Forster Stem Polishing

forsterproducts.com

HORNADY

Bullet technology is evolving at a rapid pace, what with the extreme long-range shooting sports exploding in popularity and the participants in precision shooting competitions increasing each year. Hornady set the target world on its ear with the polymer tipped ELD-Match bullet, a design that has been wonderfully accurate in a number of my rifles, and has upped its game with the introduction of the aluminum-tipped A-TIP Match Bullets. While the idea of an aluminum tip isn't new (it has been used before by Hornady), this bullet represents a radical advance in match bullets. Hornady has machined this tip, a costly procedure, and chosen the perfect blend of ogive, boat-tail angle, and bearing surface for each particular

bullet weight and caliber. Hornady packages these bullets just as they come off the press, sequentially in boxes of 100; they still have the lubricant on them, and Hornady provides a cleaning rag to remove it. This packaging procedure ensures the most consistent projectiles possible, and, having spent time with these bullets in 6.5mm, 135-grain and .308-caliber, 230-grain, I can report their accuracy and long-range performance is nothing shy of excellent. They aren't cheap, but they are worth the price. Hornady has a winner here. Available calibers/grains: .22/90, 6mm/110; 6.5mm/135 and 153; 7mm/166 and 190; .30/176, 230 and 250; .338/300; .375/390; and .416/500. Hornady also offers specialized seating stems, required for properly seating the A-TIP Match bullets.

Hornady's component brass cases have come a long way since the days when they bore the Frontier headstamp; these cases are relied upon for some of the most accurate handloaded ammunition made today. For 2020, Hornady has extended its line to include some new cartridges, both rifle and pistol. Included in the new product lineup are the 5.45x39mm, 7-30 Waters, .284 Winchester and .350 Legend in the rifle realm (50-count package), and .32 H&R Magnum, .327 Federal (200-count package), and .41 Remington Magnum

Hornady Precision
Measurement Station

(100-count package) in the handgun world. I use Hornady's brass for a number of my rifles and pistols, and have been nothing but happy with the results.

Measuring the varying dimensions of our ammunition has taken on a much different role, especially as the ranges continue to get longer and longer. Hornady has seen the light, introducing its Precision Measurement Station, which will measure case length, headspace location, bullet runout and

Hornady A-TIP
Match Bullets

Hornady Brass Cases

other case/cartridge variations. A dial indicator gives an immediate visual reading of the varying measurements, and the eight-pound base keeps things nice and steady. Adjustable feet will keep the unit perfectly level, and there are five bushings and seven bullet comparators included with the unit. This handy tool can be used for measuring both handloaded and factory loaded ammunition, and handloading components as well.

hornady.com

LYMAN

For any semi-auto handgun to run smoothly, its ammunition must be of proper dimension, and if your handloads aren't correct, the resulting mayhem will be nothing shy of a nightmare. Lyman has come up with a handy little tool that quickly and easily checks large volumes of ammunition: the 9mm 100-Hole Ammo Checker Block. Simply slide your loaded ammo into the block, and if it fits, you're good to go. Lyman has had the holes in the block manufactured to the minimum SAAMI spec., so if your loaded ammo fits in the hole, it'll chamber in your handgun. It's a perfect tool for the progressive press crowd; it'll check your ammo quickly and easily, and save the embarrassing feeding malfunctions associated with improperly sized ammunition.

lymanproducts.com

NOSLER

Nosler engineers have been very busy over the last decade, what with the expansion of their already famous bullet line, their brand of component brass, and not least the line of proprietary cartridges. New for 2020, Nosler has announced its .27 Nosler cartridge, and in addition to excellent loaded ammunition, the company is offering component brass and the .277-inch-diameter, 165-grain AccuBond Long Range bullet. The RDF bullet line now incorporates a 6mm, 115-grain HPBT, and the Varmageddon line has a .22-caliber, flat-base bullet (woodchucks, beware!). The Expansion Tip (E-Tip) lead-free, polymer-tipped boat-tail line now includes a 250-grain

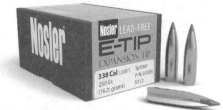

Nosler Component Bullets

offering in .338-caliber, a great choice for the big bears of the north, and moose and elk alike.

nosler.com

RCBS

I've long been a fan of the RCBS digital powder dispensers, from the ChargeMaster 1500, which still has a place on my bench, and probably always will, to the simple-to-use ChargeMaster Lite. As I write these words, I'm just home from a tour of the RCBS factory on Oroville, California, where RCBS unveiled its latest digital powder dispenser: the MatchMaster Powder Dispenser. Using "dual tube dispense technology," the MatchMaster is one of the most universal tools for dispensing powder I've ever seen. In standard mode, it is much faster than either of the previous designs, dispensing many common load weights in less than 20 seconds. In match mode, it won't dispense as fast, but it will measure down to 0.04-grain. The user can customize the performance of the unit to optimize the

throw time, depending on the powder grain structure. Oh, and the entire unit can be run via Bluetooth from an app on your smartphone, storing your favorite presets. Lastly, and perhaps one of my favorite features, is has an open drain alarm. If you've used any of the RCBS units, I'd be willing to wager that, like me, you've left the drain open while dumping a half-pound of powder into the hopper, and then watched it pour all over the bench. With an aluminum chassis, a level bubble in the front and quick-leveling feet, the RCBS MatchMaster is a worthy investment; you will invariably produce more consistent ammunition with this unit.

Designed to accompany the MatchMaster dispenser, the MatchMaster reloading dies incorporate many features of RCBS's previous designs into what might be the best dies RCBS has offered yet. The resizing dies are bushing dies, so they will help to extend your brass life. For those not familiar, there are bushings of varying sizes, usually .002 to .003 of an inch smaller than the final OD of your cartridge, which will prevent the reloader from unnecessarily overworking the case neck. The resizing dies are offered in both full-length and neck-sizing variants, with a Titanium Nitride expander ball designed to reduce wear and friction. The seater

RCBS MatchMaster Powder Dispenser

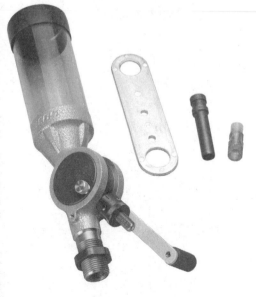

RCBS Uniflow III Powder Measure

dies have a couple of really cool features: one, an accurate micrometer adjustment for obtaining an accurate seating depth, and two, RCBS has cut a window into the die body so the bullet can be fed from the top, rather than from underneath the die body, and the free-floating bullet stem keeps things concentric. The RCBS MatchMaster dies are producing some wonderfully accurate ammunition and are available in a wide selection of calibers from the .204 Ruger to the 8x57mm Mauser.

RCBS has hailed its Uniflow III Powder Measure as the most accurate mechanical powder dispenser on the market. Using one precision metering screw, reloaders can now throw a powder charge from as low as half a grain, to as much as 120 grains, covering nearly all conceivable powder charges, from pistol to magnum rifle. The large hopper will hold a full pound of extruded powder or a half pound of flake powder. If you want just one powder thrower on your bench, take a good look at the RCBS Uniflow III.

rcbs.com

REDDING RELOADING COMPANY

The concentricity of your ammunition most definitely plays a role in the accuracy of your rifle, and the ability to measure concentricity and bullet run out will make your loads more consistent. Redding has long been famous for its precision tools, dies and other reloading gear, and the Slant Bed Concentricity

Redding Slant Bed Concentricity Gauge

Redding 6.5 RPM Dies

Gauge continues the legacy. Set up to be the most ergonomic design possible, the Slant Bed Concentricity Gauge will measure both case-neck variations as well as bullet run out, and the 30-degree slant is both comfortable to the hand as well as aiding in a proper reading of the dial indicator. Bearing sliders mounted on stainless steel guide ways will accurately measure cartridges between .17 Remington and .408 CheyTac, and the flexible unit can be quickly adjusted for left-hand use. If you've put the time and effort into setting up a respectable long-range rig, you owe it to yourself to have the tools to help feed that rifle the best ammunition possible, and the Slant Bed Concentricity Gauge should be on that list.

The standard resizing die relies on the SAAMI specifications for that particular cartridge. While this isn't technically incorrect, it does, rather routinely, work the neck and case mouth of your brass more than it needs to be worked. Using a bushing inside the resizing die, sized about 0.001 or 0.002 of an inch larger than a loaded cartridge's neck O.D., you will invariably see an extended case life. If you want to help keep your cases more concentric, and custom-dimensioned for your chamber, a neck-sizing die will give the necessary neck tension, without moving the shoulder or reducing the

body radius of your fired cartridge. Neck sizing, while not as popular as it once was, remains a popular choice for enhancing accuracy. When seating bullets, the addition of a micrometer adjustment to establish precise seating has made an undeniable difference in the consistency of the ammunition we produce. Combine these three ideas, and mate them with the Redding reputation for very tight tolerances, and what you have is the Redding Type-S Elite die set. Full-length and neck-sizing bushing dies, and a Competition Seating die combine to give reloaders all sorts of flexibility in the way they handle their handloaded ammo. These dies are shipped without bushings; you'll need to measure a few sample loaded cartridges and order the specific bushing size.

redding-reloading.com

ROBERSON CARTRIDGE COMPANY

If you have an obscure rifle or pistol, one for which ammunition is nearly impossible to obtain, you are limited in your resources. As a handloader, I have learned to lean upon those sources of quality components that can fuel those rifles and handguns. The Roberson Cartridge Company is certainly a company that provides brass cases for nearly any need you could imagine, including some of the most obscure specimens you could think of. I have relied on Roberson for cases for my beloved .318 Westley Richards, and more recently, the .350 Rigby Magnum I'm having built. Its lineup continues to expand and evolve, and, considering Roberson cases are lathe turned and not drawn, you have an incredibly uniform source for your obscure gun. The Roberson lineup has expanded this year to include a good number of cartridges, including the .470 Capstick, the .350 Rigby Magnum No. 2, the .450/400 2-3/8-inch NE, the .277 Fury, .22-3000 and more. If you have the need for properly head-stamped brass cases for nearly any centerfire (and some rimfire and shotgun) cases, contact the folks at Roberson and I bet they'll solve your problem.

rccbrass.com

Roberson Cartridge Company

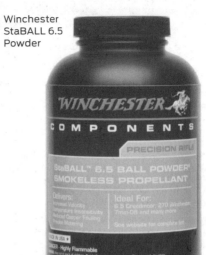

Winchester
StaBALL 6.5
Powder

SIERRA BULLETS

When I learned how to reload, all we had was Dad's 1st Edition Sierra manual from 1971; I read the ink off the pages, and he still has it on the reloading shelf. Sierra is now onto its 6th Edition, and I'm happy to report the company still retains the three-ring-binder format. This edition covers cartridge history and information, a glossary of reloading and ballistic terms, a full description of the reloading process, tools and equipment. Sierra has also included a question-and-answer section, with questions both common and unusual, as taken by its customer-service department. It is 1,368 pages, covering many of the most popular rifle and handgun cartridges.

sierrabullets.com

VIHTAVUORI

Vihtavuori's new N555 powder has been optimized for performance in the 6.5 Creedmoor, .260 Remington, .284 Winchester and similar-sized cases, giving consistent performance across a wide range of temperatures. This new powder has shown excellent results in both the 6mm and 6.5mm Creedmoor and has also shown unprecedented lot-to-lot consistency. Included in the new powder is an anti-fouling agent, to reduce the need for cleaning you barrel, and N555's short grain structure will aid in even metering in powder dispensers.

vihtavuori.com

Vihtavuori N555
Powder

WINCHESTER

Winchester's new StaBALL 6.5 is the first temperature-insensitive ball powder, optimized for use in cartridges like the 6.5 Creedmoor, 7mm-08 Remington and .270 Winchester. The spherical conformation works very well in nearly all powder dispensers, giving better results in the progressive presses, and takes up less room in the case compared to the extruded stick powders. A copper-fouling eliminator has been built into the formula, and StaBALL 6.5 has proved to give a definite velocity advantage over extruded powders. Hodgdon, which makes Hodgdon, IMR and Winchester powders, has provided data for this powder in cartridges as small as the .223 Remington and .22-250 Remington, to cartridges as large as the .375 Holland and Holland Magnum, .416 Remington Magnum and .416 Rigby. For those who use their rifles in varying environments, from precision competitions which change from cool in the morning to hot in the afternoon, to hunters who find themselves in the heat of Africa and the frozen North country in the same season, the temperature stability of StaBALL 6.5 will appeal to you. It has a burn rate a bit slower than Accurate 4350, making it a very useful choice. **GD**

wwpowder.com

Sierra
Reloading Manual

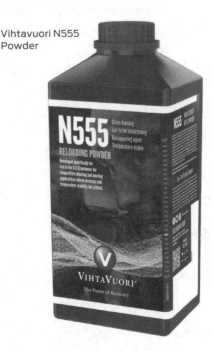

AUTO-ORDNANCE 1927A-1 THOMPSON
Caliber: .45 ACP. **Barrel:** 16.5 in. **Weight:** 13 lbs. **Length:** About 41 in. overall (Deluxe). **Stock:** Walnut stock and vertical fore-end. **Sights:** Blade front, open rear adjustable for windage. **Features:** Recreation of Thompson Model 1927. Semi-auto only. Deluxe model has finned barrel, adjustable rear sight and compensator; Standard model has plain barrel and military sight. Available with 100-round drum or 30-round stick magazine. Made in USA by Auto-Ordnance Corp., a division of Kahr Arms.
Price: Deluxe w/stick magazine......................................$1,551.00
Price: Deluxe w/drum magazine.....................................$2,583.00
Price: Lightweight model w/stick mag..............................$1,403.00

AUTO-ORDNANCE 1927 A-1 COMMANDO
Similar to the 1927 A-1 except has Parkerized finish, black-finish wood butt, pistol grip, horizontal fore-end. Comes with black nylon sling. Introduced 1998. Made in USA by Auto-Ordnance Corp., a division of Kahr Arms.
Price: T1-C...$1,479.00

AUTO ORDNANCE M1 CARBINE
Caliber: .30 Carbine (15-shot magazine). **Barrel:** 18 in. **Weight:** 5.4 to 5.8 lbs. **Length:** 36.5 in. **Stock:** Wood or polymer. **Sights:** Blade front, flip-style rear. **Features:** A faithful recreation of the military carbine.
Price: $1,036.00
Price: Folding stock.. $1,137.00

BARRETT MODEL 82A-1 SEMI-AUTOMATIC
Calibers: .416 Barret, 50 BMG. **Capacity:** 10-shot detachable box magazine. **Barrel:** 29 in. **Weight:** 28.5 lbs. **Length:** 57 in. overall. **Stock:** Composition with energy-absorbing recoil pad. **Sights:** Scope optional. **Features:** Semiautomatic, recoil operated with recoiling barrel. Three-lug locking bolt; muzzle brake. Adjustable bipod. Introduced 1985. Made in USA by Barrett Firearms.
Price: From...$9,119.00

BARRETT M107A1
Caliber: 50 BMG. **Capacity:** 10-round detachable magazine. **Barrels:** 20 or 29 in. **Sights:** 27-in. optics rail with flip-up iron sights. **Weight:** 30.9 lbs. **Finish:** Flat Dark Earth. **Features:** Four-port cylindrical muzzle brake. Quick-detachable Barrett QDL Suppressor. Adjustable bipod and monopod.
Price: $12,281.00

BERETTA ARX 100
Caliber: 5.56 NATO. **Capacity:** 30-round. Accepts AR magazines. **Barrel:** 16 in. with flash suppressor and quick changeability. **Features:** Ambidextrous controls, Picatinny quad rail system.
Price: $1,950.00

BERETTA CX4 STORM CARBINE
Calibers: 9mm, 40 S&W, .45 ACP. **Barrel:** 16.6 in. **Stock:** Black synthetic with thumbhole. **Sights:** Ghost ring. **Features:** Blowback single action, ambidextrous controls, Picatinny quad rail system. Reintroduced in 2017.
Price: $700.00

BROWNING BAR SAFARI AND SAFARI W/BOSS SEMI-AUTO
Calibers: Safari: .25-06 Rem., .270 Win., 7mm Rem. Mag., .30-06, .308 Win., .300 Win. Mag. Safari w/BOSS: .270 Win., 7mm Rem. Mag., .30-06 Spfl., .300 Win. Mag., .338 Win. Mag. **Barrels:** 22–24 in. round tapered. **Weights:** 7.4–8.2 lbs. **Lengths:** 43–45 in. overall. **Stock:** French walnut pistol grip stock and fore-end, hand checkered. **Sights:** No sights. **Features:** Has new bolt release lever; removable trigger assembly with larger trigger guard; redesigned gas and buffer systems. Detachable 4-round box magazine. Scroll-engraved receiver is tapped for scope mounting. BOSS barrel vibration modulator and muzzle brake system available. Mark II Safari introduced 1993. Made in Belgium.
Price: BAR MK II Safari, From $1,230.00
Price: BAR Safari w/BOSS, From $1,400.00

BROWNING BAR MK III SERIES
Calibers: .243 Win., 7mm-08, .270 Win., .270 WSM, 7mm Rem., .308 Win, .30-06, .300 Win. Mag., .300 WSM. **Capacities:** Detachable 4 or 5-shot magazine. **Barrel:** 22, 23 or 24 in.es. **Stock:** Grade II checkered walnut, shim adjustable. Camo stock with composite gripping surfaces available. Stalker model has composite stock. **Weight:** 7.5 lbs. **Features:** Satin nickel alloy with high relief engraving, stylized fore-end.
Price: $1,240.00
Price: Camo..$1,380.00
Price: Stalker...$1,270.00

BROWNING BAR MK 3 DBM
Caliber: .308 Win. **Capacity:** 10-round detachable magazine. **Barrel:** 18 in. **Stock:** Black composite. Other features similar to standard BAR MK III.
Price: $1,530.00

CENTURY INTERNATIONAL AES-10 HI-CAP
Caliber: 7.62x39mm. **Capacity:** 30-shot magazine. **Barrel:** 23.2 in. **Weight:** NA. **Length:** 41.5 in. overall. **Stock:** Wood grip, fore-end. **Sights:** Fixed notch rear, windage-adjustable post front. **Features:** RPK-style, accepts standard double-stack AK-type mags. Side-mounted scope mount, integral carry handle, bipod. Imported by Century Arms Int'l.
Price: AES-10, From $450.00

CENTURY INTERNATIONAL GP WASR-10 HI-CAP
Caliber: 7.62x39mm. **Capacity:** 30-round magazine. **Barrel:** 16.25 in. 1:10 right-hand twist. **Weight:** 7.2 lbs. **Length:** 34.25 in. overall. **Stock:** Wood laminate or composite, grip, fore-end. **Sights:** Fixed notch rear, windage-adjustable post front. **Features:** Two 30-rd. detachable box magazines, cleaning kit, bayonet. Version of AKM rifle; U.S. parts added for BATFE compliance. Threaded muzzle, folding stock, bayonet lug, compensator, Dragunov stock available. Made in Romania by Cugir Arsenal. Imported by Century Arms Int'l.
Price: GP WASR-10, From $670.00

CENTURY INTERNATIONAL M70AB2 SPORTER
Caliber: 7.62x39mm. **Capacity:** 30-shot magazine. **Barrel:** 16.25 in. **Weight:** 7.5 lbs. **Length:** 34.25 in. overall. **Stocks:** Metal grip, wood fore-end. **Sights:** Fixed notch rear, windage-adjustable post front. **Features:** Two 30-rd. double-stack magazine, cleaning kit, compensator, bayonet lug and bayonet. Paratrooper-style Kalashnikov with under-folding stock. Imported by Century Arms Int'l.
Price: M70AB2, From..$480.00

Prices given are believed to be accurate at time of publication however, many factors affect retail pricing so exact prices are not possible.

DSA SA58 STANDARD
Caliber: .308 Win. **Barrel:** 21 in. bipod cut w/threaded flash hider. **Weight:** 8.75 lbs. **Length:** 43 in. **Stock:** Synthetic, X-Series or optional folding para stock. **Sights:** Elevation-adjustable post front, windage-adjustable rear peep. **Features:** Fully adjustable short gas system, high-grade steel or 416 stainless upper receiver. Many variants available. Made in USA by DSA, Inc.
Price: From...$1,700.00

DSA SA58 CARBINE
Caliber: .308 Win. **Barrel:** 16.25 in. bipod cut w/threaded flash hider. **Features:** Carbine variation of FAL-style rifle. Other features identical to SA58 Standard model. Made in USA by DSA, Inc.
Price: $1,700.00

DSA SA58 TACTICAL CARBINE
Caliber: .308 Win. **Barrel:** 16.25 in. fluted with A2 flash hider. **Weight:** 8.25 lbs. **Length:** 36.5 in. **Stock:** Synthetic, X-Series or optional folding para stock. **Sights:** Elevation-adjustable post front, windage-adjustable match rear peep. **Features:** Shortened fully adjustable short gas system, high-grade steel or 416 stainless upper receiver. Made in USA by DSA, Inc.
Price: $1,975.00

DSA SA58 MEDIUM CONTOUR
Caliber: .308 Win. **Barrel:** 21 in. w/threaded flash hider. **Weight:** 9.75 lbs. **Length:** 43 in. **Stock:** Synthetic military grade. **Sights:** Elevation-adjustable post front, windage-adjustable match rear peep. **Features:** Gas-operated semiauto with fully adjustable gas system, high-grade steel receiver. Made in USA by DSA, Inc.
Price: $1,700.00

EXCEL ARMS X-SERIES
Caliber: .22 LR, 5.7x28mm (10 or 25-round); .30 Carbine (10 or 20-round magazine). 9mm (10 or 17 rounds). **Barrel:** 18 in. **Weight:** 6.25 lbs. **Length:** 34 to 38 in. **Features:** Available with or without adjustable iron sights. Blow-back action (5.57x28) or delayed blow-back (.30 Carbine).
Price: .22 LR $504.00
Price: 5.7x28 or 9mm................................ $795.00–$916.00

FNH FNAR COMPETITION
Caliber: .308 Win. **Capacity:** 10-shot magazine. **Barrel:** 20 in. fluted. **Weight:** 8.9 lbs. **Length:** 41.25 in. overall. **Sights:** None furnished. Optical rail atop receiver, three accessory rails on fore-end. **Stock:** Adjustable for comb height, length of pull, cast-on and cast-off. Blue/gray laminate. Based on BAR design.
Price: $1,767.00

HECKLER & KOCH MODEL USC
Caliber: .45 ACP. **Capacity:** 10-round magazine. **Barrel:** 16 in. **Weight:** 6.13 lbs. **Length:** 35.4 in. **Features:** Polymer construction, adjustable rear sight, ambidextrous safety/selector, optional Picatinny rail. Civilian version of HK UMP submachine gun.
Price: $1,499.00

INLAND M1 1945 CARBINE
Caliber: .30 Carbine. **Capacity:** 15 rounds. **Barrel:** 18 in. **Weight:** 5 lbs. 3 oz. **Features:** A faithful reproduction of the last model that Inland manufactured in 1945, featuring a type 3 bayonet lug/barrel band, adjustable rear sight, push button safety, and walnut stock. Scout Model has 16.5-in. barrel, flash hider, synthetic stock with accessory rail. Made in the USA.
Price: $1,299.00
Price: Scout Model $1,449.00

KALASHNIKOV USA
Caliber: 7.62x39mm. **Capacity:** 30-round magazine. AK-47 series made in the USA in several variants and styles. **Barrel:** 16.25 in. **Weight:** 7.52 lbs.
Price: KR-9 Side-folding stock $1,249.00
Price: US132S Synthetic stock $799.00
Price: US132W Wood carbine $836.00

RUGER PC CARBINE
Caliber: 9mm, .40 S&W. **Capacity:** 17 rounds (9mm), 15 (.40). Interchangeable magazine wells for Ruger and Glock magazines. **Barrel:** 16.12-in. threaded and fluted. **Stock:** Glass-filled nylon synthetic. **Sights:** Adjustable ghost-ring rear, protected-blade front. **Weight:** 6.8 lbs. **Features:** Reversible magazine release and charging handle. Dead-blow action reduces felt recoil. Receiver has integrated Picatinny rail. Available with aluminum free-floating handguard.
Price: $649.00
Price: With handguard...$729.00

RUGER MINI-14 RANCH RIFLE
Calibers: .223 Rem., .300 Blackout (Tactical Rifle). **Capacity:** 5-shot or 20-shot detachable box magazine. **Barrel:** 18.5 in. Rifling twist 1:9 in. **Weights:** 6.75–7 lbs. **Length:** 37.25 in. overall. **Stocks:** American hardwood, steel reinforced, or synthetic. **Sights:** Protected blade front, fully adjustable Ghost Ring rear. **Features:** Fixed piston gas-operated, positive primary extraction. New buffer system, redesigned ejector system. Ruger S100RM scope rings included on Ranch Rifle. Heavier barrels added in 2008, 20-round magazine added in 2009.
Price: Mini-14/5, Ranch Rifle, blued, wood stock $999.00
Price: K-Mini-14/5, Ranch Rifle, stainless, scope rings $1,069.00
Price: Mini-14 Tactical Rifle: Similar to Mini-14 but with 16.12 in. barrel with flash hider, black synthetic stock, adjustable sights $1,019.00

SIG-SAUER MPX PCC
Caliber: 9mm. 30-round capacity. **Barrel:** 16 in. **Features:** M-LOK handguard, 5-position folding telescoping stock. **Weight:** 6.6 lbs. **Sights:** none.
Price: From $2,016.00

Prices given are believed to be accurate at time of publication however, many factors affect retail pricing so exact prices are not possible.

75TH EDITION, 2021 ⊕ **397**

SPRINGFIELD ARMORY M1A

Caliber: 7.62mm NATO (.308). **Capacities:** 5- or 10-shot box magazine. **Barrel:** 25.062 in. with flash suppressor, 22 in. without suppressor. **Weight:** 9.75 lbs. **Length:** 44.25 in. overall. **Stock:** American walnut with walnut-colored heat-resistant fiberglass handguard. Matching walnut handguard available. Also available with fiberglass stock. **Sights:** Military, square blade front, full click-adjustable aperture rear. **Features:** Commercial equivalent of the U.S. M-14 service rifle with no provision for automatic firing. From Springfield Armory.

Price: SOCOM 16.. **$1,987.00**
Price: Scout Squad, From **$1,850.00**
Price: Standard M1A, From **$1,685.00**
Price: Loaded Standard, From **$1,847.00**
Price: National Match, From **$2,434.00**
Price: Super Match (heavy premium barrel) about **$2,965.00**
Price: Tactical, From .... **$3,619.00–$4,046.00**

ALEXANDER ARMS AR SERIES

Calibers: .17 HMR, 5.56 NATO, 6.5 Grendel, .300 AAC, .338 Lapua Mag., .50 Beowulf. This manufacturer produces a wide range of AR-15 type rifles and carbines. **Barrels:** 16, 18, 20 or 24 in. Models are available for consumer, law enforcement and military markets. Depending on the specific model, features include forged flattop receiver with Picatinny rail, button-rifled stainless steel barrels, composite free-floating handguard, A2 flash hider, M4 collapsible stock, gas piston operating system.

Price: .17 HMR From	$1,097.00
Price: 5.56 NATO From	$1,155.00
Price: 6.5 Grendel From	$1,425.00
Price: .300 AAC From	$1,275.00
Price: .50 Beowulf From	$1,425.00

ALEXANDER ARMS ULFBERHT

Caliber: .338 Lapua Mag. Custom-designed adjustable gas-piston operating system. **Barrel:** 27.5-in. chrome moly with three-prong flash hider. **Stock:** Magpul PRS. **Length:** 41.25 in. (folded), 50 in. (extended stock). **Weight:** 19.8 lbs.
Price: From $6,090.00

ANDERSON MANUFACTURING AM-15 RIFLES

Calibers: 5.56 NATO, .300 Blackout, 7.62x39, .450 Bushmaster. This manufacturer produces a range of AR-15-type rifles and carbines. Barrels: 16, 18, 24 in. Models are available for consumer, law enforcement and military markets. Builds include CNC-machined 7075 T6 aluminum forgings for uppers and lowers, which are machined to military specifications and marked "Multi-Cal" to be used with multiple **calibers** on the AR-15 platform. The company offers its proprietary RF85 metal treatment on some rifles, which the company bills as needing "zero lubrication."

Price: AM-15 M4 Optic Ready 5.56	$559.00
Price: AM-15 M4 Optic Ready 5.56, RF85	$800.00
Price: AM-15 M4 Optic Ready 7.62x39	$689.00
Price: AM-15 M4 Optic Ready 7.62x39, RF85	$862.00

ANDERSON MANUFACTURING AM-10 RIFLES

Calibers: .308 Win., 6.5 Creedmoor. Barrels: 16, 18, 20, 24 in.

Price: AM-10 EXTSP-RT2, .308 Win.,18 in.	$1,100.00
Price: AM-10 EXTSP-RT2, 6.5 Creedmoor, 20 in.	$1,222.00

ARMALITE AR10 TAC 6.5

Caliber: 6.5 Creedmoor. **Capacity:** 25 rounds, windowed PMAG. **Barrel:** 22 in., med-heavy 1:8 stainless steel, black nitride finish. **Stock:** Magpul PRS with adjustable length-of-pull and comb height. **Sights:** Magpul MBUS front and rear. **Weight:** 10 lbs. Overall **Length:** 44 in. **Features:** ArmaLite Two-Stage Trigger, AR10 15 in. tactical handguard, ATB762 muzzle brake. New 6.5 CM chambering is superbly accurate for match shooting. Introduced 2020.
Price: $2,099.00

ARMALITE AR10 (3GN13/3GN18)

Caliber: 7.62x51/.308 Win. **Capacity:** 25 rounds, windowed PMAG. **Barrel:** 13.5 in., pinned and welded, or 18 in., stainless steel, 1:10 twist. **Stock:** MBA-1 Light Weight Precision with adjustable length-of-pull and comb height. **Sights:** Mil-Std 1913 top rail. **Weight:** 8.8-9.9 lbs. Overall lengths: 36.25, 40.25, 41.25 in. **Features:** Timney 4-lb. single-stage trigger, ArmaLite Tunable Competition Muzzle Brake, ambidextrous safety and Raptor charging handle, 12 in. free-floating, tactical Key-Mod handguard, ERGO wide grip. Introduced 2020.
Price: $2,199.00

ARMALITE EAGLE-15 VERSATILE SPORTING RIFLE – 15EAVSR

Caliber: .223 Rem., 5.56x45 (.223 Wylde chamber). **Capacity:** one 30-round Magpul PMAG. **Barrel:** 16 in., HB, chrome moly, 1:8 RH twist, flash suppressor. **Stock:** 6-position collapsible stock. **Sights:** Mil-Std 1913 rail section. **Weight:** 6.6 lbs. Overall **Length:** 31.1 in. collapsed, 34.5 in. extended. **Features:** Carbine length gas system, 15 in. Versatile Sporting Rifle Key-Mod handguard, forged flat top with Mil-Std 1913 rail, 7075-T6 aluminum upper receiver, forged 7075-T6 aluminum lower receiver.
Price: $818.00

ARMALITE M-15 LIGHT TACTICAL CARBINE

Calibers: .223 Rem., 6.8 SPC, 7.62x39mm. **Capacity:** 30-round magazine. **Barrel:** 16 in. heavy chrome lined; 1:7 in. twist, flash suppressor. (10.3 and 11.5 in. available. NFA regulations apply) **Weight:** 6 lbs. **Length:** 36 in. overall. **Stock:** Green or black composition. **Sights:** Standard A2. **Features:** Forged flattop receiver with Picatinny rail, 10-in. aluminum KeyMod handguard, anodize aluminum supper/lower receiver, flip-up sights. Introduced in 2016.
Price: ......$999.00-$2,099.00

ARMALITE AR-10 3-GUN COMPETITION RIFLE

Calibers: 7.62x1mm/.308 Win. **Capacity:** 25-round magazine. **Barrel:** 18-in. stainless steel. **Weight:** 8.9 lbs. **Features:** MBA-1 buttstock with adjustable comb and length of pull, 15-in. free-floating 3-Gun handguard, Raptor charging handle, Timney trigger, ambidextrous safety.
Price: $2,199.00

ARMALITE EAGLE-15 VERSATILE SPORTING RIFLE (VSR)

Caliber: .223 Rem/5.56x45 NATO (.223 Wylde chamber). **Capacity:** 30-shot Magpul PMAG. **Barrel:** 16-in. chrome moly with flash suppressor. **Stock:** 6-position collapsible with free-float rail system, rubberized grip. **Weight:** 6.6 lbs. **Features:** Carbine length gas system, 15-in. handguard with Key Mod attachments, forged lower and flat-top upper, Picatinny rail.
Price: $800.00

BRAVO COMPANY MFG. BCM M4 CARBINE MOD 0

Caliber: 5.56mm NATO. **Capacity:** 30 rounds. **Barrel:** 16 in., standard government profile, 1:7 twist, M4 feed ramp barrel extension. USGI chrome-lined bore and chamber. Mil-Spec 11595E barrel steel, manganese phosphate finish. **Stock:** BCM Gunfighter. **Sights:** Flat-top rail, post front. **Weight:** 6.3 lbs. Overall **Length:** 32.5 to 35.5 in. **Features:** Upper and lower receivers machined from aluminum forgings 7075-T6 and hard-coat anodized per MIL-A-8625F, Type III, Class 2. Upper has M4 feed ramp flat top with laser

Prices given are believed to be accurate at time of publication however, many factors affect retail pricing so exact prices are not possible.

75TH EDITION, 2021 ✦ 399

T-markings. Standard carbine gas system. BCM bolt carrier group. Machined from Mil-Spec Carpenter No. 158 steel, HPT/MPI, shot peened, tool steel extractor w/BCM extractor spring, chrome-lined carrier (full auto profile).
Price: **$1,202.00**

BRAVO COMPANY MFG. BCM RECCE-16 KMR-A CARBINE
Caliber: 5.56mm NATO. **Capacity:** 30 rounds. **Barrel:** 16 in., USGI profile, 1:7 twist, M4 feed ramp barrel extension. USGI chrome-lined bore and chamber. Mil-Spec 11595E barrel steel, manganese phosphate finish. **Stock:** BCM. **Sights:** M4 feed ramp flat top with laser T-markings. **Weight:** 6.1 lbs. Overall **Length:** 32.5 to 35.5 in. **Features:** Upper and lower receivers machined from aluminum forgings 7075-T6 and hard-coat anodized per MIL-A-8625F, Type III, Class 2. Mid-length gas system. BCM bolt carrier group, Mil-Spec Carpenter No. 158 steel, HPT/MPI, shot peened, tool steel extractor w/BCM extractor spring, chrome-lined carrier (full auto profile).
Price: **$1,500.00**

BARRETT MODEL REC7 GEN II
Calibers: 5.56 (.223), 6.8 Rem. SPC. **Capacity:** 30-round magazine. **Barrel:** 16 in. **Sights:** ARMS rear, folding front. **Weight:** 28.7 lbs. **Features:** AR-style configuration with standard 17-4 stainless piston system, two-position forward venting gas plug, chrome-lined gas block, A2 flash hider, 6-position MOE stock.
Price: **$2,759.00**

BROWNELLS "WHAT WOULD STONER DO" 2020 RIFLE
Caliber: 5.56 NATO or .223 Rem (.223 Wylde chamber). **Capacity:** 30-round Magpul P-Mag. **Barrel:** 14.5 in., with titanium flash hider for OAL of 16 in., 1/2-28 tpi muzzle threads. Upper/Lower Receivers: KE Arms MK3 polymer receiver. **Weight:** NA. **Trigger:** SLT-1 Sear Link Technology. Overall **Length:** NA. **Features:** One-piece polymer lower with an improved mag well that's been optimized for use with Magpul P-Mags and D-60 drum mags. Ambidextrous selector, ambi mag release, ambidextrous charging handle, PDQ lever, JP Silent Capture Spring System, carbon-fiber handguard. The Mk3 lower will also be available separately either stripped or with Mil-Spec internals.
Price: **$1,700.00**

BROWNELLS BRN-10 RETRO RIFLE
Caliber: .308 Winchester. **Capacity:** one supplied 20-round Brownells aluminum magazine. Compatible with metal DPMS/SR-25 magazines. **Barrel:** 20 in., 1:10 RH twist, 5/8-24 tpi muzzle threads, QPQ Nitride finish, 3-prong Dutch-style flash hider, .750-in. diameter at the gas block. Direct impingement. Upper/Lower Receivers: Machined from 7075 T6 aluminum billet. **Stock:** Type D, no trap door. **Sights:** Rear enclosed by the carry handle. A2-style horizontal thumbwheel adjusts elevation. Windage is changed by loosening a setscrew and drifting the rear peep. Standard AR-15-style front sight base. **Weight:** 8.6 lbs. **Trigger:** AR-15 style. Overall **Length:** 40.5 in. **Features:** Re-creation of Eugene Stoner's original lightweight .308 caliber battle rifle, Armalite AR-10. Slab-sided lower with straight magazine well. Serrated takedown pins, selector lever, magazine release and bolt release. No forward assist and shell deflector. "Trigger"-style charging handle located under the carry handle. Carrier has flats and two stabilizing flanges at the rear found on early carriers, and the entire bolt/carrier group is chrome plated. Bolt machined from 9310 carbon steel and magnetic particle inspected (MPI). Functional heavy fluting on the barrel under the handguard. Brown furniture. Many components are compatible with modern DPMS/SR-25 parts or AR-15 parts. The BRN-10B is inspired by later export rifles and has a closed-prong, Portuguese-type flash hider, later-style black furniture, and a lightweight barrel. **Weight:** 7.8 lbs. **Length:** 40.75 in.
Price: BRN-10A **$1,260.00**
Price: BRN-10B **$1,186.00**

BROWNELLS BRN-605 5.56 CARBINE
Caliber: 5.56 NATO. **Capacity:** one 20-round metal. **Barrel:** 15.5 in.; 1:12 RH twist, A1-profile, standard 3-prong "duckbill" flash hider. Upper/Lower Receivers: Machined 7075 T6 aluminum receivers. XBRN16E1 lower has partial "fence" around the magazine release. Upper has forward assist, but no shell deflector. **Stock:** Fixed "Type D" buttstock. **Sights:** Windage-adjustable A1-type rear sight drum. **Weight:** 7.5 lbs. Overall **Length:** 34 in. **Features:** Colt's first carbine variant of the M16 rifle. The Model 605 reproduction is a standard M16 with 4.5 in. lopped off the A1 barrel, retaining the rifle-length gas tube. Chrome-plated bolt/carrier group. Enlarged gas port, M193-type ammunition with 55-grain bullets recommended. No steel case or underpowered ammunition. Black furniture of reinforced polymer, triangular cross-section handguard.
Price: **$967.00**

CMMG MK SERIES
Calibers: 5.56 NATO, .308 Win., 7.62x39, .300 BLK. This company manufactures a wide range of AR and AK style rifles and carbines. Many AR/AK options offered. Listed are several variations of CMMG's many models. Made in the USA.
Price: MK4 LEM .223 .... **$995.00**
Price: MK3 .308 .... **$1,595.00**
Price: MK47 AKS8 7.62x39 (shown) **$1,650.00**
Price: MK4 RCE .300 BLK **$1,500.00**

CMMG MKW ANVIL
Caliber: .458 SOCOM. **Barrel:** 16.1 in. CMMG SV Muzzle Brake. **Weight:** 7.5 lbs. **Stock:** M4 with A2 pistol grip, 6 position mil-spec receiver extension. Introduced in 2017.
Price: From **$1,850.00**

CMMG MK4 DTR2
Caliber: .224 Valkyrie. **Capacity:** 10-round magazine (6.8 magazine). **Barrel:** 24 in. threaded. CMMG SV Muzzle Brake. **Weight:** 9.2 lbs. **Stock:** Magpul PRS with MOE Pistol grip4 with A2 pistol grip. **Features:** Model is engineered to deliver on this new cartridge's promise of long-range accuracy and high-energy performance.
Price: From **$1,699.95**

CMMG RESOLUTE 100 RIFLES AND CARBINES
Calibers: 5.7x28mm (Conversion), 9mm (Conversion), .350 Legend, .458 SOCOM, .22 LR, .300 Blackout, .308 Win., .40 S&W, .45 ACP, 5.56x45mm, 5.7x28mm (FN), 6.5 Grendel, 7.62x39mm, 9mm (Colt), 9mm (Glock). **Capacity:** 30-round Magpul PMAG (5.56). **Barrel:** 16.1, 16.6, or 17 in. (varies by chambering), 1:7 twist, medium taper, 4140CM, SBN (5.56). **Stock:** CMMG M4 with 6-position receiver extension. **Sights:** Flat-top rail. **Weight:** 6.3 lbs. Overall **Length:** 32.5 to 35.5 in. **Features:** Forged 7075-T6 AL M4-type upper, AR-15-type lower, Type III hard-coat anodize finish, CMMG single-stage Mil-Spec trigger, integrated or CMMG triggerguard, Mil-Spec charging handle, A2-style pistol grip, CMMG RML15 M-LOK free-floating handguard, M4-style buttstock, salt bath nitride barrel finish, M4 Mil-Spec receiver end plate, A2 Comp, threaded 1/2-28, standard safety selector.
Price: .... **$950.00-$1,500.00**

CMMG RESOLUTE 200 RIFLES AND CARBINES

Calibers: 5.7x28mm (Conversion), 9mm (Conversion), .350 Legend, .458 SOCOM, .22 LR, .300 Blackout, .308 Win., .40 S&W, .45 ACP, 5.56x45mm, 5.7x28mm (FN), 6.5 Grendel, 7.62x39mm, 9mm (Colt), 9mm (Glock). **Capacity:** 30-round Magpul PMAG (5.56). **Barrel:** 16.1, 16.6, or 17 in. (varies by chambering), 1:7 twist, medium taper, 4140CM, SBN (5.56). **Stock:** CMMG Ripstock. **Sights:** Flat-top rail. **Weight:** 6.3 lbs. **Overall Length:** 32.5 to 35.5 in. **Features:** Forged 7075-T6 AL M4-type upper, AR-15-type lower, Type III hard-coat anodize finish, CMMG single-stage Mil-Spec trigger, integrated or Magpul MOE triggerguard, Mil-Spec charging handle, Magpul MOE pistol grip, CMMG RML15 M-LOK free-floating handguard, M4-style buttstock, salt bath nitride barrel finish, M4 Mil-Spec receiver end plate, CMMG SV muzzle device threaded 1/2-28, standard safety selector.
Price: .... $1,125.00-$1,675.00

CMMG RESOLUTE 300 RIFLES AND CARBINES

Calibers: 5.7x28mm (Conversion), 9mm (Conversion), .350 Legend, .458 SOCOM, .22 LR, .300 Blackout, .308 Win., .40 S&W, .45 ACP, 5.56x45mm, 5.7x28mm (FN), 6.5 Grendel, 7.62x39mm, 9mm (Colt), 9mm (Glock). **Capacity:** 30-round Magpul PMAG (5.56). **Barrel:** 16.1, 16.6, or 17 in. (varies by chambering), 1:7 twist, medium taper, 4140CM, SBN (5.56). **Stock:** CMMG Ripstock. **Sights:** Flat-top rail. **Weight:** 6.3 lbs. **Overall Length:** 32.5 to 35.5 in. **Features:** Forged 7075-T6 AL M4-type upper, AR-15-type lower, laser-engraved "Resolute" on lower receiver. Premier Cerakote finish (10 color options), Geissele SSA two-stage trigger, integrated or Magpul MOE triggerguard, CMMG ambidextrous charging handle, Magpul MOE pistol grip, CMMG RML15 M-LOK free-floating handguard, M4-style buttstock, salt bath nitride barrel finish, M4 Mil-Spec receiver end plate, CMMG SV muzzle device threaded 1/2-28, CMMG ambidextrous safety selector.
Price: Mk4 5.56 .... $1,450.00-$2,000.00

COLT LE6920 M4 CARBINE

Caliber: 5.56 NATO. **Barrel:** 16.1-in. chrome lined. **Sights:** Adjustable. Based on military M4. **Features:** Magpul MOE handguard, carbine stock, pistol grip, vertical grip. Direct gas/locking bolt operating system.
Price: From .... $849.00–$1,099.00

COLT LE6940

Caliber: 5.56 NATO. Similar to LE1920 with Magpul MBUS backup sight, folding front, four accessory rails. One-piece monolithic upper receiver has continuous Mil-Spec rail from rear of upper to the front sight. Direct gas (LE6940) or articulating link piston (LE6940P) system.
Price: LE6940 .... $1,399.00

COLT L36960-CCU

Caliber: 5.56 NATO. **Capacity:** 30-round magazine. **Barrel:** 16-in. **Stock:** Magpul MOE SL with pistol grip. **Weight:** 6.7 lbs. **Features:** Combat Unit Carbine with 30-shot magazine. Aluminum receiver with black finish, mid-length gas system, optics ready.
Price: $1,299.00

COLT EXPANSE M4

Caliber: 5.56 NATO. **Capacity:** 30 rounds. **Barrel:** 16.1 in. **Sights:** Adjustable front post. Comes optics ready. **Weight:** 6.4 lbs. Flattop Picatinny rail. **Stock:** Adjustable M4 with A2-style grip. Economy priced AR. Introduced in 2016.
Price: $799.00

DANIEL DEFENSE DD5V3 RIFLE

Calibers: 7.62x51mm/.308 Win. **Capacity:** 20-round Magpul PMAG. **Barrel:** 16 in., 5/8x24 tpi muzzle thread, S2W barrel profile, 1:11 twist. **Stock:** Daniel Defense Buttstock. **Sights:** Full-length top rail. **Trigger:** Daniel Defense Mil-Spec. **Handguard:** Daniel Defense DD5 Rail 15.0, 6061-T6 aluminum, M-LOK. **Weight:** 8.3 lbs. **Overall Length:** 33.375 to 37 in. **Features:** Intermediate gas system, two-position adjustable gas block, DLC-coated bolt carrier group, cold hammer chrome-lined forged barrel, Mil-Spec heavy phosphate coated. 4-Bolt Connection System, ambidextrous controls (bolt catch, magazine release, safety selector, furniture, GRIP-N-RIP charging handle). Lower Receiver: Enhanced flared magazine well and rear receiver QD swivel attachment point. CNC machined of 7075-T6 aluminum, Type III hard-coat anodized. Upper Receiver: CNC machined of 7075-T6 aluminum, Type III hard-coat anodized. Daniel Defense Superior Suppression Device, 6-position Mil-Spec 7075-T6 aluminum receiver extension. Daniel Defense Pistol Grip, accepts all SR-25 magazines.
Price: DD5V3 .... $2,499.00
Price: DD5V4 (7.62mm, 6.5 CM, 18-in. barrel) $2,499.00
Price: DD5V5 (6.5 CM, .260 Rem., 20-in. barrel) $2,499.00

DANIEL DEFENSE AR SERIES

Caliber: 5.56 NATO/.223. **Capacity:** 20-round Magpul PMAG magazine. **Barrels:** 16 or 18 in.es. Flash suppressor. **Weight:** 7.4 lbs. **Lengths:** 34.75–37.85 in. overall. **Stock:** Glass-filled polymer with Soft Touch overmolding. Pistol grip. **Sights:** None. **Features:** Lower receiver is Mil-Spec with enhanced and flared magazine well, QD swivel attachment point. Upper receiver has M4 feed ramps. Lower and upper CNC machined of 7075-T6 aluminum, hard coat anodized. Shown is MK12, one of many AR variants offered by Daniel Defense. Made in the USA
Price: From $1,599.00
Price: DD5VI 7.62/.308 .... $3,044.00
Price: DDM4V7 .... $1,729.00
Price: DDM4ISR .300 Blackout $3,135.00
Price: DDM4V11 .... $1,729.00–$1,999.00
Price: DDM4V9 .... $1,826.00–$1,999.00
Price: MK12 .... $2,162.00
Price: Ambush Camo $1,946.00

DSA ZM4 AR SERIES

Caliber: .223/5.56 NATO. **Weight:** 9 pounds. **Features:** Standard Flattop rifle features include 20-in., chrome moly heavy barrel with A2 flash hider. Mil-Spec forged lower receiver, forged flattop or A2 upper. Fixed A2 stock. Carbine variations are also available with 16-in. barrels and many options. WarZ series has premium match barrel, 5.56 match chamber developed by Marine Corps, and upgraded fire control group.
Price: Standard Flat-Top $820.00
Price: MRC Multi-Role Carbine $1,275.00
Price: Mid Length Carbine $834.00
Price: Flat-Top with rail $850.00
Price: WarZ Series .... $865.00–$1,150.00

Prices given are believed to be accurate at time of publication however, many factors affect retail pricing so exact prices are not possible.

75TH EDITION, 2021 ✛ **401**

DSARMS AR15 ZM4 WARZ SERIES 5.56 RIFLE

Caliber: 5.56 NATO. **Capacity:** Magpul Custom G2 MOE 30-round magazine, black with Flat Dark Earth ribs. **Barrel:** 16 in., lightweight mid-length, 1:8 twist, M4 feed ramps on both barrel extension and upper receiver. **Stock:** B5 Systems Custom SOPMOD Stock, Flat Dark Earth, B5 Systems QD end plate. **Sights:** Full-length top rail. **Weight:** 6.9 lbs. **Trigger:** ALG Defense Advanced Combat Trigger. **Overall Length:** 33 to 35 in. **Features:** Premium match barrel machined from either 416-R Stainless Steel or 4150-11595 Mil-Spec material, 5.56 match chamber. Enhanced A3M4 upper receiver, upgraded fire control group, ambidextrous selector switch and WarZ triggerguard, bolt catch and charging handle. Low-mass sand-cut bolt carrier group with nitride finish. DuraCoat finish in Flat Dark Earth over the hard-coat anodized lower receiver, upper receiver and handguard. 4140-steel MK12-style low-profile, set-screw gas block, stainless steel mid-length gas tube. Midwest Industries 15-in. Combat Series M-LOK free-float handguard. Magpul Custom MIAD Modular Pistol Grip, Flat Dark Earth with black two-tone. DSArms Enhanced FDE alloy triggerguard, SureFire Pro Comp (1/2x28 tpi).

Price: FDE **$1,150.00**
Price: Titanium **$1,150.00**

DSARMS AR15 SERVICE SERIES 5.56X45 NATO BLOCK 1 CARBINE - KNIGHT'S ARMAMENT UPGRADES

Caliber: 5.56 NATO. **Capacity:** ASC 30-round gray alloy magazine. **Barrel:** 14.5 in., with permanently affixed A2 Bird Cage Flash Hider for 16 in. barrel OAL, M4-profile, chrome-lined chamber and bore, 4150 - 11595E Mil-Spec barrel steel, 1:7 twist. **Stock:** Mil-Spec, M4-style, 6-position Mil-Spec buffer tube. **Sights:** Top rail segments, forged front sight tower (F-Marked). **Weight:** 6.9 lbs. **Features:** Carbine-length gas system, M4 feed ramps on both barrel extension and upper receiver. Stainless steel carbine-length gas tube, Knight's Armament Co. M4 RAS carbine-length handguard assembly. Knight's forward vertical grip. DSArms forged A3M4 Mil-Spec upper receiver, DSArms forged lower receiver, both hard-coat anodized per MIL-A-8625F, Type III, Class 2 finish. Mil-Spec M16 complete bolt carrier group. Mil-Spec A2-style pistol grip.

Price: **$1,200.00**

F-1 FIREARMS BDRX-15 SKELETONIZED RIFLE

Caliber: .223 Wylde chamber for 5.56 NATO or .223 Rem. .300 AAC, 7.62x39mm, .224 Valkyrie. **Capacity:** 30-round magazines standard. **Barrel:** 16 (standard) or 18 in., light, medium, fluted contours, 1:8 twist, F-1 Firearms Flat-Face, Angle-Face, or F-1 Firearms Slay-AR compensator, 1:10 twist on 7.62x39mm, stainless and black-nitride finishes. **Upper/Lower Receivers:** 7075-T6511 BDRx-15 billet receiver matched set, skeletonized. Black Type III hard anodizing. **Stock:** Magpul MOE standard. **Handguard:** C7K 12.75-in., 7-series aluminum lightweight free-float rail system. Options available. **Sights:** None, scalloped partial top rail. **Weight:** 8 lbs. **Trigger:** Hiperfire EDT Heavy Gunner standard. Velocity and Geisselle brands available as options. **Length:** 33-37.5 in. **Features:** Introduced 2019. Modular build; user selects options on almost all components. 60-degree beveled mag well.

Price: **$2,050.00**

F-1 FIREARMS BDRX-15 RIFLE SPECIAL EDITION STEAMPUNK

Similar to BDRX-15, but with specific feature set. **Barrel:** 16-in., .223 Wylde Proof Research carbon-fiber barrel, Slay-AR brake in rose gold. F-1 Firearms grip and foregrip, minimalist stock, Hiperfire EDT2 trigger, ambi charging handle.

Price: **$3,410.00**

F-1 FIREARMS BDRX-10 SKELETONIZED RIFLE

Calibers: .308 Win., 6.5 Creedmoor. **Capacity:** 20-round magazines. **Barrel:** 16, 18, 20 in., 1:10 twist, medium contour (.308, 416 stainless steel), 22-in. Criterion (6.5 CM). Proof Research carbine-fiber barrels offered as upgrades (add ....$500). **Upper/Lower Receivers:** 7075-T6511 BDRx-15 billet receiver matched set, skeletonized. Large-frame DPMS High-Profile-style compatible, 60-degree beveled mag well. Black Type III hard anodizing. **Stock:** Magpul MOE standard. **Handguard:** C7K 14-in., 7-series aluminum lightweight free-float rail system. **Sights:** None, scalloped partial top rail. **Weight:** 8.4 lbs. **Trigger:** Hiperfire EDT Heavy Gunner standard. **Length:** 33-37.5 in. **Features:** Accepts all Mil-Spec (DPMS) patterned parts as well as SR25 patterned mags.

Price: **$2,950.00**

F-1 FIREARMS BDRX-10 RIFLE SPECIAL EDITION STEAMPUNK

Similar to BDRX-10, but with specific feature set. **Barrel:** 16-in., Proof Research, Slay-AR brake in black DLC. F-1 Firearms grip and foregrip, Magpul CTR stock, Hiperfire EDT2 trigger, ambi charging handle.

Price: **$4,255.00**

FN 15 SERIES

Caliber: 5.56x45. **Capacity:** 20 or 30 rounds. **Barrels:** 16 in., 18 in., 20 in. **Features:** AR-style rifle/carbine series with most standard features and options.

Price: Tactical II (also in .300 BLK) **$1,599.00**
Price: Standard rifle **$1,149.00**
Price: Sporting **$1,749.00**
Price: DMR II **$1,999.00**
Price: Carbine **$1,149.00**
Price: Competition.. **$2,240.00**
Price: Military Collector **$1,749.00**

FN 15 TACTICAL CARBINE FDA P-LOK

Caliber: 5.56x45mm. **Capacity:** 30-shot PMAG. **Barrel:** 16-in. free-floating and chrome-lined with FN 3-prong flash hider. **Stock:** B5 Systems buttstock and grip. **Weight:** 7.2 lbs. **Finish:** Flat Dark Earth. **Features:** P-LOK handguard, M-LOK accessory mounting system, hard anodized aluminum flat-top receiver with Picatinny rail, forward assist.

Price: **$1,499.00**

FN 15 SRP G2

Caliber: 5.56 NATO. **Capacity:** One 30-round magazine. **Barrel:** 11.5 and 16 in., 1:7 RH twist, alloy steel, button-broached, chrome-plated, A2-style flash hider. **Stock:** 6-position, collapsible. **Sights:** Low-profile, folding metal front and rear sights. Full-length 12 o'clock Picatinny rail with five built-in QD points. **Weight:** 5.6 lbs. (11.5 in.); 6.25 lbs. (16 in.). **Trigger:** FN Combat Trigger, 4.75-7.75 lbs. **Overall Length:**

27.5-30.75 in. (11.5 in.); 31.9-35.2 in. (16 in.) **Features:** Law-enforcement models have lightweight design, extended handguards and sight-ready configuration. Multiple M-LOK and quick-detach (QD) points, chrome-lined barrel with pinned low-profile gas block, MPI-inspected and marked M16-style bolt carrier. Free-floated handguard (10.5-in. long with 11.5-in. barrel, or 15-in. long with 16-in. barrel.)
Price: 11.5-in. barrel...**Agency Request**
Price: 16-in. barrel..**Agency Request**

FNH SCAR 16S
Caliber: 5.56mm/.223. **Capacities:** 10 or 30 rounds. **Barrel:** 16.25 in. **Weight:** 7.25 lbs. **Lengths:** 27.5–37.5 in. (extended stock). **Stock:** Telescoping, side-folding polymer. Adjustable cheekpiece, A2 style pistol grip. **Sights:** Adjustable folding front and rear. **Features:** Hard anodized aluminum receiver with four accessory rails. Ambidextrous safety and mag release. Charging handle can be mounted on right or left side. Semi-auto version of newest service rifle of U.S. Special Forces.
Price: **$3,299.00**

FNH SCAR 17S
Caliber: 7.62x51 NATO/.308. **Capacities:** 10 or 30 rounds. **Barrel:** 16.25 in. **Weight:** 8 lbs. **Lengths:** 28.5–38.5 in. (extended stock). **Features:** Other features the same as SCAR 16S.
Price: **$3,499.00**

FNH SCAR 20S
Caliber: 7.62x51mm. **Capacities:** 10. **Barrel:** 20 in. **Weight:** 11.2 lbs. **Lengths:** 40.6-42.5 in. (extended stock). **Stock:** Precision adjustable for LOP, adjustable cheek piece, Hogue rubber pistol grip with finger grooves. **Features:** Hard anodized aluminum receiver with four accessory rails, two-stage match trigger, Semi-auto version of newest service rifle of U.S. Special Forces.
Price: **$4,499.00**

FRANKLIN ARMORY 3 GR-L
Caliber: 5.56mm/.223. **Capacities:** 10 or 30 rounds. **Barrel:** 18 in. fluted with threaded muzzle crown. **Weight:** 7.25 lbs. **Stock:** Magpul PRS. Adjustable comb and length of pull. **Features:** Hard anodized Desert Smoke upper receiver with full-length Picatinny rail. One of many AR type rifles and carbines offered by this manufacturer. Made in the USA.
Price: **$2,310.00**

FRANKLIN ARMORY F17-L
Caliber: .17 Winchester Super Magnum Rimfire. **Capacity:** One 10- or 20-round magazine. **Barrel:** 20 in., full contour, 1:9 RH twist, 11-degree target crown. **Stock:** Magpul MOE. **Sights:** Optic ready 12 o'clock Picatinny rail. **Weight:** NA. Trigger: FN Combat Trigger, 4.75-7.75 lbs. Overall **Length:** 30.75 in. **Features:** Gas piston rimfire rifle, F17 Piston. Rotating locking bolt and piston design, 12-in. TML M-LOK Handguard/Upper, .17 WSN Salt Bath Nitride bolt carrier, Ergo Sure Grip. Libertas lower.
Price: **$1,900.00**

FRANKLIN ARMORY F17-SPR
Similar to F17-L. Barrel: 18-in., lightweight profile. Lower Receiver: FAI. **Stock:** MFS Battlelink Minimalist. **Grip:** MFT EPG16. **Weight:** 6.6 lbs.
Price: **$1,450.00**

FRANKLIN ARMORY F17-M4
Similar to other F17-Series models. Barrel: 16-in., M4 Contour. Lower Receiver: FAI. Handguard/Upper: 7-in. TML M-LOK. **Stock:** M4. **Grip:** A2. **Weight:** NA.
Price: **$1,380.00**

FRANKLIN ARMORY F17-VS4
Similar to other F17-Series models. Barrel: 20-in., full contour. Lower Receiver: FAI. Handguard/Upper: 12-in. TML M-LOK. **Stock:** A2. **Grip:** A2. **Weight:** NA.
Price: **$1,480.00**

FRANKLIN ARMORY F17-X
Similar to other F17-Series models. Barrel: 16-in., M4 Contour. **Sights:** Fixed front and MBUS. Lower Receiver: FAI. Handguard/Upper: Magpul MOE SL M-LOK Gray. **Stock:** Magpul SL. **Grip:** Magpul K2. **Weight:** NA.
Price: **$1,480.00**

FRANKLIN ARMORY BFS III M4
Caliber: 5.56 NATO. **Capacity:** One 10- or 20-round magazine. **Barrel:** 16 in., LTW Contour, 1:7 RH twist, A2 muzzle device. **Stock:** M4. **Sights:** Optics ready 12 o'clock full-length Picatinny rail. **Weight:** NA. **Trigger:** BFSIII Binary Trigger. **Overall Length:** NA. **Features:** Standard charging handle, low-profile gas block, 15-in. FST Handguard/Upper, salt bath nitride bolt carrier, A2 Grip. FAI-15 lower.
Price: **$1,000.00**

FRANKLIN ARMORY M4-HTF R3
Caliber: .350 Legend. **Capacity:** One 10- or 20-round magazine. **Barrel:** 16 in., M4 Contour, 1:12 RH twist, Aura XTD muzzle device. **Stock:** B5 Bravo. **Grip:** B5. **Handguard:** 15-in., FSR. **Sights:** Optics ready 12 o'clock full-length Picatinny rail. **Weight:** NA. **Trigger:** BFSIII Binary Trigger or custom tuned. **Overall Length:** NA. **Features:** .350 Legend was designed for use in a number of American states that have specific regulations for deer hunting with straight-walled centerfire cartridges. It has the same rim diameter as a 5.56 case (0.378 in.), so it can use the same bolt. Rounds will fit in a modified AR magazine. MFT EVOLV charging handle, mid-length gas system, low-profile gas block, salt bath nitride bolt carrier, FAI-15 lower.
Price: **$1,300.00**

Prices given are believed to be accurate at time of publication however, many factors affect retail pricing so exact pricing are not possible.

75TH EDITION, 2021 ⊕ **403**

HECKLER & KOCH MODEL MR556A1
Caliber: .223 Remington/5.56 NATO. **Capacity:** 10+1. **Barrel:** 16.5 in. **Weight:** 8.9 lbs. **Lengths:** 33.9–37.68 in. **Stock:** Black synthetic adjustable. **Features:** Uses the gas piston system found on the HK 416 and G26, which does not introduce propellant gases and carbon fouling into the rifle's interior.
Price: **$3,399.00**

HECKLER & KOCH MODEL MR762A1
Caliber: Similar to Model MR556A1 except chambered for 7.62x51mm/.308 Win. cartridge. **Weight:** 10 lbs. w/empty magazine. **Lengths:** 36–39.5 in. **Features:** Variety of optional sights are available. Stock has five adjustable positions.
Price: **$3,999.00**

HK-USA MR762A1 LONG RIFLE PACKAGE II
Caliber: 7.62x51mm. **Capacity:** 10- or 20-round magazines. **Barrel:** 16.5 in., four lands and grooves, right twist, 1:11. **Stock:** Fully adjustable G28 buttstock. **Sights:** Leupold 3-9VX-R Patrol 3-9x40 mm scope, base, mounts. **Weight:** 10.42 lbs. Trigger: Two stage. Overall **Length:** 36.5 to 40.5 in. **Features:** MR762 semi-auto rifle with LaRue/Harris bipod, new long 14.7-in. Modular Rail System (MRS) handguard, Blue Force Gear sling and sling mount, one 10-round and one 20-round magazine, OTIS cleaning kit, HK multi-tool, and Pelican Model 1720 case.
Price: **$5,999.00**

JP ENTERPRISES LRP-07
Calibers: .308 Win., .260 Rem., 6.5 Creedmoor, .338 Federal. **Barrels:** 16–22 in., polished stainless with compensator. **Buttstock:** A2, ACE ARFX, Tactical Tactical Intent Carbine, Magpul MOE. **Grip:** Hogue Pistol Grip. **Features:** Machined upper and lower receivers with left-side charging system. MKIII Hand Guard. Adjustable gas system.
Price: From..**$3,299.00**

JP ENTERPRISES JP-15
Calibers: .223, .204 Ruger, 6.5 Grendel, .300 Blackout, .22 LR. **Barrels:** 18 or 24-in. **Buttstock:** Synthetic modified thumbhole or laminate thumbhole. **Grip:** Hogue Pistol grip. Basic AR-type general-purpose rifle with numerous options.
Price: From..**$1,999.00**

JP ENTERPRISES SCR-11 RIFLE
Calibers: .223, 6.5 Grendel, .224 Valkyrie, .22 LR. **Capacity:** Magazines vary by chambering. Receiver: Machined from billet 7075-T6 upper/lower receiver set with left-side charging system on upper receiver. Matte black hard-coat anodizing on aluminum components. **Barrel:** JP Supermatch 416R air-gauged,

button-rifled, cryogenically treated barrel Thermo-Fit to receiver, polished stainless, JP Compensator. **Stock:** Hogue OverMolded, Magpul MOE, Magpul CTR, LUTH-AR "Skullaton," or Mission First Tactical BATTLELINK. Handguard: JP MK III system. **Grip:** Hogue pistol grip. **Sights:** Optics ready top rail. **Weight:** NA. Trigger: JP Fire Control Package available in weights of 3.0 to 4.5 lbs. Overall **Length:** NA. **Features:** Scaled-down version of the LRP-07 available with the same caliber, barrel, handguard, metal finishing and stock options as the CTR-02. Exaggerated bevel on the magazine well. JP adjustable gas system; choice of JP Low Mass Operating System or JP Full Mass Operating System.
Price: **$2,699.00**

JP ENTERPRISES LRI-20 SEMI-MONOLITHIC LONG RANGE PRECISION RIFLE
Calibers: 6mm and 6.5 Creedmoor, .260 Rem. and .308 Win. **Capacity:** Magazines vary by chambering. Receiver: Machined from billet 7075-T6 upper/lower receiver set with left-side charging system on upper receiver. Matte black hard-coat anodizing on aluminum components. **Barrel:** JP Supermatch 416R air-gauged, button-rifled, cryogenically treated barrel Thermo-Fit to receiver, polished stainless, JP Compensator. **Stock:** Hogue OverMolded, Magpul MOE, Magpul CTR, LUTH-AR "Skullaton," or Mission First Tactical BATTLELINK. Handguard: JP MK III system (Signature or Rapid configuration). Grip: Hogue pistol grip. **Sights:** Optics ready top rail. **Weight:** NA. Trigger: JP Fire Control Package available in weights of 3.5 to 4.5 lbs. Overall **Length:** NA. **Features:** Scaled-down version of the LRP-07 available with the same caliber, barrel, handguard, metal finishing and stock options as the CTR-02. Exaggerated bevel on the magazine well. New integral handguard nut stabilizes the barrel mount and front pivot-pin joint. MicroFit Takedown Pins, lightened military-style upper design, dust cover and forward assist paired with dedicated side-charging handle. Thermo-Fit installation. LRI-20 upper assemblies pair with any existing LRP-07 side-charge lower. JP adjustable gas system; JP .308 Low Mass Operating System with JP High Pressure EnhancedBolt.
Price: **$3,499.00**

KEL-TEC RFB
Caliber: 7.62 NATO/.308. 20-round FAL-type magazine. **Barrel:** 18 in. with threaded muzzle, A2-style flash hider. **Weight:** 8 lbs. **Features:** A bullpup short-stroke gas piston operated carbine with ambidextrous controls, reversible operating handle, Mil-Spec Picatinny rail.
Price: **$1,927.00**

KEL-TEC SU-16 SERIES
Caliber: 5.56 NATO/.223. **Capacity:** 10-round magazine. **Barrels:** 16 or 18.5 in. **Weights:** 4.5–5 lbs. **Features:** Offering in several rifle and carbine variations.
Price: From..**$682.00–$900.00**

LARUE TACTICAL OBR
Calibers: 5.56 NATO/.223, 7.62 NATO/.308 Win., .260 Rem. **Barrels:** 16.1 in., 18 in. or 20 in. **Weights:** 7.5–9.25 lbs. **Features:** Manufacturer of several models of AR-style rifles and carbines. Optimized Battle Rifle (OBR) series is made in both NATO calibers. Many AR-type options available. Made in the USA
Price: OBR 5.56..**$2,245.00**
Price: OBR 7.62, .260..**$3,370.00**

LEWIS MACHINE & TOOL (LMT)
Calibers: 5.56 NATO/.223, 7.62 NATO/.308 Win. **Barrels:** 16.1 in., 18 in. or 20 in. **Weights:** 7.5–9.25 lbs. **Features:** Manufacturer of a wide range of AR-style carbines with many options. SOPMOD stock, gas piston operating system, monolithic rail platform, tactical sights. Sharpshooter Weapons System includes Harris Bipod and case, eight 20-shot magazines, FDE finish. Made in the USA by Lewis Machine & Tool.
Price: Standard 16..**$1,649.00**
Price: Comp 16, flattop receiver..**$1,685.00**
Price: CQB Series from..**$2,399.00**
Price: Sharpshooter Weapons System..**$6,499.00**
Price: Valkyrie..**$2,299.00**
Price: 6.5 Long Range..**$2,999.00**

Prices given are believed to be accurate at time of publication however, many factors affect retail pricing so exact prices are not possible.

LWRC INTERNATIONAL M6 SERIES
Calibers: 5.56 NATO, .224 Valkyrie, .6.5 Creedmoor, 6.8 SPC, 7.62x51mm, .300 BLK. **Capacity:** 30-shot magazine. **Features:** This company makes a complete line of AR-15 type rifles operated by a short-stroke, gas piston system. A wide variety of stock, sight and finishes are available. Colors include black, Flat Dark Earth, Olive Drab Green, Patriot Brown.
Price: M6-SPR (Special Purpose Rifle)...............................**$2,479.00**
Price: REPR (Shown)..**$5,139.00**
Price: SIX8 A5 6.8 SPC...**$2,600.00–$2,750.00**
Price: IC-DI 224 Valkyrie **$1,995.00**

LWRC INTERNATIONAL IC-ENHANCED
Caliber: 5.56 NATO. **Barrel:** 12.7, 14.7, 16.1 in. **Features:** Includes a Picatinny rail at 12 o'clock, a bayonet lug, and is compatible with accessories like the M320 grenade launcher and the M26 shotgun.
Price: **$2,549.00**

LWRC INTERNATIONAL IC-SPR
Caliber: 5.56 NATO. **Capacity:** Magpul PMAG 5.56. **Barrel:** 14.7, 16.1 in., 1:7 in. RH twist, 1/2x28 tpi muzzle threads, cold hammer forged, spiral fluted, NiCorr treated. **Stock:** LWRC adjustable compact stock. **Sights:** Low-profile, flip-up Skirmish Sights. **Weight:** 7 lbs., 7.3 lbs. Trigger: LWRC Enhanced Fire Control Group. Overall **Length:** 32-35.25 in. **Features:** Individual Carbine has ambi controls, SPR modular rail system, low-profile, fixed-gas block, 12-inch user-configurable modular rail system. Ambidextrous sling mount, charging handle, lower receiver, MOE+ grip; can be fired suppressed.
Price: **$2,396.00**

LWRC INTERNATIONAL SIX8
Caliber: 6.8 SPC II. **Capacity:** Magpul 20-round PMAG. **Barrel:** 14.7, 16.1 in., 1:10 in. RH twist, 5/8x24 tpi muzzle threads, cold hammer forged, spiral fluted, NiCorr treated. **Stock:** LWRC adjustable compact stock. **Grip:** Magpul MOE+. **Sights:** Low-profile, flip-up Skirmish Sights. **Weight:** 6.95 lbs., 7.25 lbs. Trigger: LWRC Enhanced Fire Control Group. Overall **Length:** 32-35.25 in. **Features:** LWRCI proprietary upper and lower receivers optimized for 6.8 SPC II cartridge; adjustable 2-position gas block, Birdcage (A2) Flash Hider; 12-in. user-configurable rail system; ambidextrous charging handle and lower receiver.
Price: **$2,549.00**

LWRC INTERNATIONAL REPR MKII SC 6.5 CREEDMOOR ELITE
Caliber: 6.5 Creedmoor. **Capacity:** Magpul 20-round PMAG 6.5 Creedmoor. **Barrel:** 22 in., Proof Research carbon-fiber or stainless steel barrel, 1:8 in. RH twist, 5/8x24 tpi muzzle threads. **Stock:** Magpul PRS. **Grip:** Magpul MOE+. **Sights:** Low-profile, flip-up Skirmish Sights. **Weight:** 10.5 lbs. Trigger: Geissele SSA-E 2-Stage Precision. Overall **Length:** 43.5 in. **Features:** Rapid Engagement Precision Rifle. Non-reciprocating side charging handle, 20-position tunable gas block, short-stroke gas piston system, Monoforge upper receiver with integrated rail-base, removable top rail design, removable barrel, fully ambidextrous lower receiver controls include bolt catch and release, magazine release and safety selector. LWRCI Advanced Triggerguard, Skirmish Back-Up Iron Sights, Enhanced 4-port Ultra Static muzzle brake.
Price: **$4,670.00**

LWRC INTERNATIONAL IC-A5
Similar to IC-SPR. Caliber: 5.56 NATO. **Barrel:** 10.5, 12.7, 14.7, 16.1 in. **Features:** Has a low-profile, two-position adjustable gas block allowing the shooter to compensate for running a suppressor and a longer modular rail system.
Price: **$2,651.00**

MIDWEST INDUSTRIES COMBAT RAIL SERIES
Caliber: .300 AAC Blackout. **Capacity:** AR-15-pattern magazines. **Barrel:** 16 in., Criterion 1:8 twist, stainless-nitride finish, A2 flash hider, .625 in. diameter. **Upper/Lower Receivers:** Forged 7075 aluminum, M16/M4 specs. **Stock:** Magpul CTR buttstock. **Grip:** Magpul MOE. **Sights:** Optics-ready top rail, laser engraved T-marks. **Weight:** 6.2 lbs. for MI-FC300CRM12. Trigger: NA. Overall **Length:** NA. **Features:** MI-CRM Combat series handguards, M-LOK compatible. Hard-coat anodized Mil 8625 Type 3, Class 2 finish, M4 feed ramps, .250-in. takedown pins, M16 bolt carrier group. Works with standard AR-15 components and magazines, receiver rear takedown pin detent hole threaded for a 4-40 set screw. Models denote handguard lengths.
Price: MI-FC300CRM12 .... **$1,225.00**
Price: MI-FC300CRM14 .... **$1,230.00**
Price: MI-FC300CRM15 .... **$1,235.00**

LWRC INTERNATIONAL IC-PSD
Caliber: 5.56 NATO. **Barrel:** 8.5 in. **Capacity:** Magpul PMAG 30-round magazine. **Stock:** LWRC adjustable compact stock. **Sights:** Low-profile, flip-up Skirmish Sights. **Weight:** 5.9 lbs. Trigger: LWRC Enhanced Fire Control Group. Overall **Length:** 25-28 in. **Features:** Part of the Individual Carbine series of rifles. NFA item. LWRCI Monoforge upper receiver with modular 7-in. rail system. Nickel-boron coated bolt carrier, LWRCI High Efficiency 4-Prong Flash Hider.
Price: **$2,396.00**

Prices given are believed to be accurate at time of publication however, many factors affect retail pricing so exact prices are not possible.

75TH EDITION, 2021 ✦ **405**

MIDWEST INDUSTRIES SLH FIREARMS

Caliber: .300 AAC Blackout. **Capacity:** AR-15-pattern magazines. **Barrel:** 16 in., Criterion 1:7 twist, stainless-nitride finish, A2 flash hider, .750 in. diameter. **Upper/Lower Receivers:** Forged 7075 aluminum, M16/M4 specs. **Stock:** Magpul CTR buttstock. **Grip:** Magpul MOE. **Sights:** Optics-ready top rail, laser engraved T-marks. **Weight:** 6.2 lbs. for MI-FN300SLH12. **Trigger:** NA. **Overall Length:** NA. **Features:** MI-SLH 12-in. Slim Line Handguards, M-LOK compatible. Hard-coat anodized Mil 8625 Type 3, Class 2 finish, M4 feed ramps, .250 in. takedown pins, M16 bolt carrier group. Works with standard AR-15 components and magazines, receiver rear takedown pin detent hole threaded for a 4-40 set screw. Models denote handguard lengths.
Price: MI-FN300SLH12 .... **$1,125.00**
Price: MI-FN300SLH14 .... **$1,130.00**

MIDWEST INDUSTRIES MI-10F-16M

Caliber: .308 Win. **Capacity:** one Magpul 10-round magazine; accepts SR-25 pattern magazines. **Barrel:** 16, 18, 20 in., Criterion 1:10 twist, stainless-nitride finish. **Upper/Lower Receivers:** Forged 7075 aluminum. **Stock:** Magpul Gen 3 PRS buttstock. **Grip:** Magpul MOE. **Sights:** Optics-ready top rail. **Weight:** 8.2 lbs. for MI-10F-16M. **Trigger:** NA. **Overall Length:** NA. **Features:** Midwest Industries 308 bolt-carrier group, 12-in. M-LOK handguard, two-chamber-enhanced muzzle brake, mid-length gas system, .750 in. gas block, MI-HDEP heavy-duty quick-detach end plate.
Price: MI-10F-16M **$1,700.00**
Price: MI-10F-18M **$1,775.00**
Price: MI-10F-20M **$2,075.00**

MOSSBERG MMR SERIES

Caliber: 5.56 NATO. **Capacity:** 10 or 30 rounds. GIO system. **Barrel:** 16 or 18 in. with A2-style muzzle brake. **Features:** Picatinny rail, black synthetic stock, free-floating stainless barrel. Offered in several variants. Pro and Optics Ready have JM Pro match trigger. Optics Ready has 6-position stock with FLEX pad, Magpul MOE grip and trigger guard. Introduced in 2016.
Price: MMR Carbine..**$938.00**
Price: MMR Tactical Optics Ready....................................**$1,253.00**
Price: MMR Pro..**$1,393.00**

PATRIOT ORDNANCE FACTORY ROGUE

Caliber: 7.62x51mm NATO (.308 Win.). **Capacity:** one Magpul 20-round magazine. **Barrel:** 16.5 in., 1:8 twist, 5/8x24 tpi muzzle threads, match-grade stainless steel, Micro-B muzzle brake. **Stock:** Mission First Tactical. **Sights:** None, optics ready with top Picatinny rail. **Weight:** 5.9 lbs. **Trigger:** 4.5-lb. POF-USA drop-in trigger system with KNS anti-walk pins. **Length:** 34 in. **Features:** 11-in. M-LOK Renegade free-floating rail with four integrated QD sling mounts. E2 dual-extraction technology helps dislodge cartridge cases. One-piece, high-phosphorus nickel coated direct impingement bolt carrier with mechanical key built into the body and positioned behind the cam pin. Chrome-plated bolt,

extractor and firing pin. Oversized heat-sink barrel nut, KNS Precision stainless steel non-rotating anti-walk pins. Mil-Spec aluminum anti-tilt buffer tube. Patented roller cam pin with NP3-coated roller head. Introduced 2020.
Price: **$1,800.00**

RADICAL FIREARMS .350 LEGEND

Caliber: .350 Legend. **Capacity:** .350 Legend magazine. **Barrel:** 16 in., 1:14 twist, 4140 chrome-moly vanadium steel, Melonite finish, Big Bore Contour, A2 flash hider, 5/8x32 tpi muzzle thread. **Upper/Lower Receivers:** Forged 7075 T6, M4 Mil-Std upper with oversized ejection port, forward assist and dust cover. Type III anodizing. **Stock:** B5 Bravo, 6-position. **Handguard:** Free-float M-LOK hybrid rail, 15 in. **Sights:** None, full length top rail. **Weight:** NA. **Trigger:** Mil-Std. **Length:** 33-37.5 in. **Features:** Carbine-length gas system, low-profile gas block, Mil-Std charging handle, carbine Mil-Std buffer tube.
Price: $850.00

RADICAL FIREARMS .308 WINCHESTER

Caliber: .308 Win. **Capacity:** 20-round, .308 magazines. **Barrel:** 18 in., 1:10 twist, 5/8x24 tpi muzzle threads, RF-MS Compensator. **Upper/Lower Receivers:** 7075 T6 billet aluminum, DPMS Pattern High, Type III anodizing with forward assist and dust cover. **Stock:** Mission First Tactical Minimalist. **Sights:** None, full length top rail. **Weight:** NA. **Trigger:** Mil-Std. **Length:** 33-37.5 in. **Features:** Mid-length gas system, M-LOK Thin Rail Handguard, 15 in.
Price: 18- and 20-in. barrel...**$1,050.00**
Price: 24-in. barrel..**$1,100.00**
Price: 20- and 24-in. barrel, 6.5 CM **$1,100.00**

ROCK RIVER ARMS LAR SERIES

Calibers: 204 Ruger, .223/5.56, .243 Win., 6.5 Creedmoor, .300 AAC Blackout, 7.62x39mm, .308/7.62, 6.8 SPC, .450 Bushmaster, .458 SOCOM, 9mm and .40 S&W. **Features:** These AR-15 type rifles and carbines are available with a very wide range of options. Virtually any AR configuration is offered including tactical, hunting and competition models. Some models are available in left-hand versions.
Price: ....**$760.00–$2,200.00**

ROCK RIVER ARMS LAR SERIES

Chamberings in .350 Legend were added in 2020. RRAGE 3G Rifles and Carbines with skeletonized handguards were added in 2020.
Price: RRAGE 3G Rifle **$820.00**
Price: RRAGE 3G Carbine..**$760.00**

ROCK RIVER ARMS ENHANCED MID-LENGTH A4 BT-3

Caliber: .308/7.62x51mm. **Capacity:** 20. **Barrel:** 16 in., 1:10 twist, 5/8-24 tpi muzzle threads, fluted stainless steel heavy, cryogenically treated, A2 flash hider. **Upper/Lower Receivers:** RRA BT-3 Billet A4 Upper; RRA BT-3 Billet lower. **Stock:** RRA 6-position Operator CAR. **Sights:** None, optics-ready full-length top rail. **Weight:** 8.2 lbs. **Trigger:** RRA Two-Stage. **Length:** 35 to 37.5 in. **Features:** Low-profile gas block, mid-length gas system, RRA lightweight free-float rail, 13-in. extended, M-LOK compatible. Introduced 2020.
Price: Starting at...**$1,500.00**

Prices given are believed to be accurate at time of publication however, many factors affect retail pricing so exact prices are not possible.

ROCK RIVER ARMS PRECISION RIFLE BT-3
Similar to Enhanced Mid-Length A4. Barrel: 18 in. **Weight:** 8.5 lbs. **Length:** 36.5 to 39 in. Introduced 2020.
Price: Starting at **$1,550.00**

ROCK RIVER ARMS VARMINT RIFLE BT-3
Similar to Enhanced Mid-Length A4. Barrel: 20 in., 1:10 twist, fluted stainless steel heavy, cryogenically treated. **Stock:** RRA 6-position NSP-2 CAR. **Grip:** Hogue Rubber. **Sights:** None, optics-ready full-length top rail. **Weight:** 9.8 lbs. **Trigger:** RRA Two Stage. **Length:** 37 to 39.75 in. **Features:** RRA lightweight free-float rail, 17-in. extended, M-LOK compatible. Introduced 2020.
Price: Starting at.. **$1,500.00**

ROCK RIVER ARMS 20-INCH SELECT TARGET RIFLE BT-3
Similar to Enhanced Mid-Length A4. Barrel: 20 in. **Weight:** 8.6 lbs. **Length:** 42 in. **Stock:** Magpul Gen3 Precision Rifle. Hogue Grip. Introduced 2020.
Price: Starting at.. **$1,800.00**

RUGER AR-556
Caliber: 5.56 NATO, .350 Legend, .450 Bushmaster. **Capacity:** 30-round magazine (5.56), 5 rounds (.350 and .450). **Features:** Basic AR M4-style Modern Sporting Rifle with direct impingement operation, forged aluminum upper and lower receivers, and cold hammer-forged chrome-moly steel barrel with M4 feed ramp cuts. Other features include Ruger Rapid Deploy folding rear sight, milled F-height gas block with post front sight, telescoping 6-position stock and one 30-round Magpul magazine. Introduced in 2015. MPR (Multi Purpose Rifle) model has 18-in. barrel with muzzle brake, flat-top upper, 15-in. free-floating handguard with Magpul M-LOK accessory slots, Magpul MOE SL collapsible buttstock and MOE grip.
Price: **$799.00**
Price: MPR (5.56) **$899.00**
Price: MPR (.350 Legend, .450 Bushmaster) **$1,099.00**

ROCK RIVER ARMS BT-6
Caliber: .338 Lapua Magnum. **Capacity:** two 10-round magazines. **Barrel:** 24 in., 1:10 twist, black-nitride stainless steel. Upper/Lower Receivers: BT-6 billet aluminum. **Stock:** Magpul Gen3 Precision Rifle. RRA Overmolded A2 pistol grip. **Sights:** None, optics-ready full-length top rail. **Weight:** 13.5 lbs. **Trigger:** RRA Ultra Match Two Stage. **Length:** 48 in. Introduced 2020.
Price: **$5,050.00**

SAVAGE MSR 15/MSR 10
Calibers: AR-style series chambered in 5.56 NATO (Patrol and Recon), 6.5 Creedmoor or .308 Win. (MSR 10 Hunter and Long Range). **Barrels:** 16.1 in. (Patrol and Recon), 16 or 18 in. (Hunter), 20 or 22 in. (Long Range). Wylde chamber on Patrol and Recon models. Hunter and Long Range models have muzzle brake.
Price: Patrol **$869.00**
Price: Recon (shown) **$994.00**
Price: MSR 10 Long Range **$2,284.00**
Price: MSR 10 Hunter.. **$1,481.00**

SIG SAUER M400 TREAD
Caliber: 5.56 NATO/.223 Rem. **Capacity:** one 30-round magazine, compatible with AR-15 types. **Barrel:** 16 in., 1:8 RH twist, stainless steel. Upper/Lower Receivers: Forged aluminum, hard-coat anodized finish. **Stock:** Magpul SL-K 6-position telescoping stock. **Sights:** None, optics ready. **Weight:** 7 lbs. Trigger: Single-stage, polished hard-coat trigger. Overall **Length:** 30.8 in. **Features:** Direct-impingement operating system, integral QD mount, ambi safety selector, charging handle, free-floating 15-in. MLOK handguard, mid-length gas system.
Price: **$799.99**

SIG SAUER M400 TREAD COIL
Similar to M400 Tread, but with popular features: Matchlite Duo Trigger, 13-in. lightweight M-LOK handguard, Tread Romeo5 red-dot sight, vertical foregrip.
Price: **$999.99**

SIG SAUER 716i TREAD
Caliber: .308 Win. **Capacity:** one 20-round magazine, compatible with SR-25 magazines. **Barrel:** 16 in., 1:10 RH twist, stainless steel. Upper/Lower Receivers: Forged aluminum, hard-coat anodized finish. **Stock:** Magpul SL-K 6-position telescoping stock. **Sights:** None, optics ready. **Weight:** 8.5 lbs. Trigger: Two-stage match. Overall **Length:** 33.8 to 37 in. **Features:** Direct-impingement operating system, integral QD mount, ambi safety selector, charging handle, free-floating 15-in. M-LOK handguard.
Price: **$1,299.99**

SIG-SAUER MCX VIRTUS PATROL
Calibers: 5.56 NATO, 7.62x39mm or .300 Blackout. **Features:** AR-style rifle. Modular system allows switching between calibers with conversion kit. Features include a 16 in. barrel, aluminum KeyMod handguards, ambi controls and charging handle, choice of side-folding or telescoping stock, auto-regulating gas system to all transition between subsonic and supersonic loads.
Price: **$2,233.00**

SIG 516 PATROL
Caliber: 5.56 NATO. **Features:** AR-style rifle with included 30-round magazine, 16-in. chrome-lined barrel with muzzle brake; free-floating, aluminum quad Picatinny rail, Magpul MOE adjustable stock, black anodized or Flat Dark Earth finish, various configurations available.
Price: From... **$1,888.00**

Prices given are believed to be accurate at time of publication however, many factors affect retail pricing so exact prices are not possible.

75TH EDITION, 2021 ⊕ 407

SIG-SAUER SIG716 TACTICAL PATROL

Caliber: 7.62 NATO/.308 Win., 6.5 Creedmoor. **Features:** AR-10 type rifle. Gas-piston operation with 3-round-position (4-position optional) gas valve; 16-, 18- or 20-in. chrome-lined barrel with threaded muzzle and nitride finish; free-floating aluminum quad rail fore-end with four M1913 Picatinny rails; telescoping buttstock; lower receiver is machined from a 7075-T6 Aircraft grade aluminum forging; upper receiver, machined from 7075-T6 aircraft grade aluminum with integral M1913 Picatinny rail. DMR has free-floating barrel, two-stage match-grade trigger, short-stroke pushrod operating system.
Price: $2,385.00
Price: Designated Marksman (DMR) $3,108.00

SIG-SAUER M400

Caliber: 5.56 NATO. AR-style rifle with Direct Impingement system, 20-in. chrome-lined barrel with muzzle brake; free-floating M-LOK handguard with lightening cuts, 3-chamber compensator, Magpul SLK 6-position adjustable stock, various configurations available.
Price: $900.00

SIG-SAUER MCX VIRTUS PATROL

Calibers: 5.56 NATO, 7.62x39mm or .300 Blackout. **Features:** AR-style rifle. Modular system allows switching between calibers with conversion kit. Features include a 16 in. barrel, aluminum KeyMod handguards, ambi controls and charging handle, choice of side-folding or telescoping stock, auto-regulating gas system to all transition between subsonic and supersonic loads.
Price: $2,233.00

SMITH & WESSON M&P15

Caliber: 5.56mm NATO/.223. **Capacity:** 30-shot steel magazine. **Barrel:** 16 in., 1:9 in. twist. **Weight:** 6.74 lbs., w/o magazine. **Lengths:** 32–35 in. overall. **Stock:** Black synthetic. **Sights:** Adjustable post front sight, adjustable dual aperture rear sight. **Features:** 6-position telescopic stock, thermo-set M4 handguard. 14.75 in. sight radius. 7-lbs. (approx.) trigger pull. 7075 T6 aluminum upper, 4140 steel barrel. Chromed barrel bore, gas key, bolt carrier. Hard-coat black-anodized receiver and barrel finish. OR (Optics Ready) model has no sights. TS model has Magpul stock and folding sights. Made in USA by Smith & Wesson.
Price: Sport Model..$739.00
Price: OR Model..$1,069.00
Price: TS model $1,569.00

SMITH & WESSON M&P15-300

Calibers: .300 Whisper/.300 AAC Blackout. **Features:** Other specifications the same of 5.56 models.
Price: $1,119.00

SMITH & WESSON MODEL M&P15 VTAC II

Caliber: .223 Remington/5.56 NATO. **Capacity:** 30-round magazine. **Barrel:** 16 in. **Weight:** 6.5 lbs. **Length:** 35 in. extended, 32 in. collapsed, overall. **Features:** Six-position stock. Surefire flash-hider and G2 light with VTAC light mount; VTAC/JP handguard; Geissele Super-V trigger; three adjustable Picatinny rails; VTAC padded two-point adjustable sling.
Price: $1,949.00

SMITH & WESSON M&P15PC CAMO

Caliber: 223 Rem/5.56 NATO, A2 configuration. **Capacity:** 10-round magazine. **Barrel:** 20 in. stainless with 1:8 in. twist. **Weight:** 8.2 lbs. **Length:** 38.5 in. overall. **Features:** AR-style, no sights but integral front and rear optics rails. Two-stage trigger, aluminum lower. Finished in Realtree Advantage Max-1 camo.
Price: $1,589.00

SMITH & WESSON M&P10

Caliber: .308 Win., 6.5 Creedmoor. **Capacity:** 10 rounds. **Barrel:** 18-20 in. **Weight:** 7.7 pounds. **Features:** Magpul MOE stock with MOE Plus grip, 15-in. free-float Troy M-LOK handguard, black hard anodized finish. Camo finish hunting model available w/5-round magazine.
Price: .308..$1,619.00
Price: 6.5 Creedmoor.......................................$2,035.00

SPRINGFIELD ARMORY SAINT

Caliber: 5.56 NATO. **Capacity:** 30-round magazine. **Barrel:** 16 in., 1:8 twist. **Weight:** 6 lbs., 11 oz. **Sights:** AR2-style fixed post front, flip-up aperture rear. **Features:** Mid-length gas system, BCM 6-position stock, Mod 3 grip PMT KeyMod handguard 7075 T6 aluminum receivers. Springfield Armory's first entry into AR category. Introduced 2016. In 2020, several models with M-LOK handguards were added. The Bravo Company handguards have an internal aluminum heat shield.
Price: $899.00
Price: ST916556BM $972.00

SPRINGFIELD ARMORY SAINT VICTOR RIFLES

Caliber: 5.56 NATO. **Capacity:** Includes one 30-round Magpul PMAG Gen M3. **Barrel:** 16-in., CMV, 1:8 twist, Melonite-finished barrels, Springfield Armory proprietary muzzle brake. **Upper/Lower Receivers:** Lowers are Accu-Tite tension-bonded to a flat-top forged upper receiver with Melonite finish. **Stock:** BCMGUNFIGHTER Mod 0. **Pistol Grip:** BCMGUNFIGHTER Mod 3. **Sights:** Spring-loaded, flip-up iron sights adjustable for windage and elevation. **Weight:** 6.9 lbs. **Trigger:** Enhanced nickel-boron-coated, single-stage flat trigger. **Overall Length:** 32.25 to 35.5 in. **Features:** Introduced 2019. Direct-impingement mid-length gas system. M16 bolt carrier group that is also Melonite finished, HPT/MPI tested, shot peened, and houses a 9310 steel bolt. 15-in. M-LOK free-float handguard, pinned, low-profile gas block. QD mounts built into the end plate and stock.
Price: Starting at...$1,073.00

SPRINGFIELD ARMORY SAINT VICTOR RIFLE .308

Caliber: .308 Win. **Capacity:** one 20-round Magpul Gen M3. **Barrel:** 16 in., 1:10 twist, lightweight profile, CMV Melonite finish, SA muzzle brake. **Upper/Lower Receivers:** Forged Type III hard-coat anodized, 7075 T6 Aluminum. Lower has Accu-Tite Tension System. **Stock:** Bravo Company 6-Position. **Pistol Grip:** Bravo Company Mod. 3. **Sights:** Spring-loaded, flip-ups. **Weight:** 7.8 lbs. **Trigger:** Enhanced nickel-boron-coated, single-stage flat trigger. **Overall Length:** 34.5 to 37.5 in. **Features:** Introduced 2019. Gas system is direct-impingement, mid-length, pinned gas block. Bolt carrier group is MPT, Melonite finish with a 9310 steel bolt; handguard is 15-in. M-LOK aluminum free-float with SA locking tabs.
Price: $1,399.00

STAG ARMS AR-STYLE RIFLES

Calibers: 5.56 NATO/.223, 6.8 SPC II. **Capacities:** 20- or 30-round magazine. **Features:** This manufacturer offers many AR-style rifles or carbines with many optional features including barrel length and configurations, stocks, sights, rail systems and both direct-impingement and gas-piston operating systems. Left-hand models are available on some products.
Price: Stag 15 Tactical 16 ....$1,000.00
Price: Stag 15 M4 ....$900.00
Price: Stag 15 Retro $950.00
Price: Stag 15 Bones $800.00
Price: Stag 15 O.R.C. $760.00
Price: Stag 15 Super Varminter (6.8) $1,050.00
Price: Stag 15 LEO $1,050.00
Price: Stag 15 Tactical SBR 10.5 ....$900.00
Price: Stag 15 3Gun Elite $1,400.00

Prices given are believed to be accurate at time of publication however, many factors affect retail pricing so exact prices are not possible.

STAG ARMS AR-10 STYLE RIFLES
Similar to AR-15 models, but chambered in .308 Win. or 6.5 Creedmoor.
Price: Stag 10 Creedmoor Bones **$1,575.00**
Price: Stag 10 LR **$2,050.00**
Price: Stag 10 Creedmoor S **$1,950.00**
Price: Stag 10 .308 M-LOK **$1,800.00**
Price: Stag 10 Creedmoor **$2,200.00**

STONER SR-15 MOD2 LPR
Caliber: .223. Capacity: 30-round magazine. Barrel: 18 in., free-floated inside M-LOK URSx handguard. Weight: 7.6 lbs. Length: 38 in. overall. Stock: Mag-Pul MOE. Sights: Post front, fully adjustable rear (300-meter sight). Features: URX-4 upper receiver; two-stage trigger, 30-round magazine. Black finish. Made in USA by Knight's Mfg.
Price: **$2,700.00**

STONER SR-25 ACC E2
Caliber: 7.62 NATO. Capacities: 10- or 20-shot steel magazine. Barrel: 16 in. with flash hider. Weight: 8.5 lbs. Features: Shortened, non-slip handguard; drop-in two-stage match trigger, removable carrying handle, ambidextrous controls, matte black finish. Made in USA by Knight's Mfg. Co.
Price: **$4,900.00**

WILSON COMBAT TACTICAL
Caliber: .204 Ruger, 5.56mm NATO, .223 Wylde, .22 Nosler, .260 Rem., 6.8 SPC, .300 Blackout, .300 Ham'r, 7.62x40mm WT, .338 Federal, .358 Win. Capacity: Accepts all M-16/AR-15 Style Magazines, includes one 20-round magazine. Barrel: 16.25 in., 1:9 in. twist, match-grade fluted. Weight: 6.9 lbs. Length: 36.25 in. overall. Stock: Fixed or collapsible. Features: Free-float ventilated aluminum quad-rail handguard, Mil-Spec Parkerized barrel and steel components, anodized receiver, precision CNC-machined upper and lower receivers, 7075 T6 aluminum forgings. Single-stage JP Trigger/ Hammer Group, Wilson Combat Tactical muzzle brake, nylon tactical rifle case. Made in USA by Wilson Combat.
Price: Protector, Ranger **$2,000.00**
Price: Recon Tactical from **$2,225.00**
Price: Hunter from **$2,365.00**
Price: Ultimate, Ultralight Hunter **$3,210.00**
Price: Super Sniper **$3,020.00**
Price: Urban Sniper **$2,200.00**
Price: Ultralight Ranger **$2,750.00**

WINDHAM WEAPONRY VEX-SS WOOD STOCK SERIES
Caliber: .223 Rem. Capacity: 5+1, ships with one 5-round magazine (accepts all standard AR-15 sizes). Barrel: 20 in., 1:8 RH twist, fluted 416R stainless steel, matte finish. Upper/Lower Receivers: A4-type flat-top upper receiver with optics riser blocks, forged 7075 T6 aircraft aluminum with aluminum triggerguard. Electroless nickel-plated finish. Stock/Fore-end: laminated wood. Pistol Grip: Hogue OverMolded rubber pistol grip. Sights: None, optics ready, Picatinny rail partial top rail. Weight: 8.35 lbs. Length: 38.1875 in. Features: Gas-impingement system, Carpenter 158 steel bolt. Compass Lake chamber specification with matched bolt. Wood-stock series includes Pepper and Nutmeg.
Price: **$1,480.00**

WINDHAM WEAPONRY 20 VARMINT
Caliber: .223 Rem./5.56mm NATO. Capacity: 5+1, ships with one 5-round magazine (accepts all standard AR-15 sizes). Barrel: 20 in., 1:8 RH twist, fluted 416R stainless steel, matte finish. Upper/Lower Receivers: A4-type flattop upper receiver, forged 7075 T6 aircraft aluminum with aluminum triggerguard. Electroless nickel-plated finish. Forend: 15-in. Windham Weaponry Aluminum M-LOK Free Float. Pistol Grip: Hogue OverMolded rubber pistol grip. Sights: None, optics ready, Picatinny top rail. Weight: 8.4 lbs. Length: 38.1875 in. Features: Gas-impingement system, Carpenter 158 steel bolt. Compass Lake chamber specification with matched bolt. LUTH MBA-1 stock. Comes with hard-plastic gun case with black web sling.
Price: R20FSSFTTL **$1,432.00**

WINDHAM WEAPONRY A1 GOVERNMENT
Caliber: .223 Rem./5.56mm NATO. Capacity: 30+1, ships with one 30-round magazine (accepts all standard AR-15 sizes). Barrel: 20-in., A2 profile, chrome-lined with A1 flash suppressor, 4150 chrome-moly-vanadium 11595E steel with M4 feed ramps. Rifling: 1:7 RH twist. Receivers: A1 upper with brass deflector and teardrop forward assist. Forend: Rifle-length triangular handguard with A1 Delta Ring. Pistol Grip: A1 Black Plastic Grip. Rear Sight: A1 dual aperture rear sight. Front Sight: Adjustable-height square post in A2 standard base. Trigger: Standard Mil-Spec Trigger. Stock: A2 Solid Stock with Trapdoor Storage Compartment. Weight: 7.45 lbs. Length: 39.5 in.
Price: R20GVTA1S-7 .... **$1,160.00**

WINDHAM WEAPONRY .223 SUPERLIGHT SRC
Caliber: .223 Rem./5.56mm NATO. Similar to A1 Government internally. Barrel: 16 in., Superlight with Melonite QPQ Finish and A2 flash suppressor, M4 Feed Ramps, 1:9 rifling. Flattop-type upper receiver. Forend: Single-layer Heat Shield Handguard, A2 black plastic grip. Sights: None, optics ready. Six-position telescoping buttstock. Weight: 5.85 lbs. Length: 32.5-36.25 in.
Price: R16SLFTT **$968.00**

WINDHAM WEAPONRY DISSIPATOR M4
Caliber: .223 Rem./5.56mm NATO. Similar to Superlight SRC. Barrel: 16 in., M4 profile, chrome lined with A2 flash suppressor. Flattop-type upper receiver with A4 detachable carry handle. Rifle-length heat-shielded handguards. A2 black plastic grip. Rear Sight: A4 dual-aperture elevation and windage adjustable for 300–600m. Front Sight: adjustable-height square post in A2 standard base. Six-position telescoping buttstock. Weight: 7.2 lbs. Length: 32.375-36.125 in.
Price: R16M4DA4T **$1,192.00**

WINDHAM WEAPONRY SRC-308
Caliber: .308 Win. Capacity: 20+1, ships with one 20-round Magpul PMag magazine. Barrel: 16.5-in., medium profile, chrome lined with A2 flash suppressor; 4150M chrome-moly-vanadium 11595E steel; 1:10 right-hand-twist rifling, 6 lands and grooves. Upper/Lower Receivers: A4-type flattop upper receiver, forged 7075 T6 aircraft aluminum with aluminum trigger guard. Fore-end: Midlength tapered shielded handguards. Pistol Grip: Hogue OverMolded rubber pistol grip. Sights: None, optics ready, Picatinny top rail. Weight: 7.55 lbs. Length: 34.1875-38 in. Features: Gas-impingement system, Carpenter 158 steel bolt. Compass Lake chamber specification with matched bolt. Six-position telescoping buttstock. Comes with hard-plastic gun case with black web sling.
Price: R16FTT-308 .... **$1,413.00**

BIG HORN ARMORY MODEL 89 RIFLE AND CARBINE

Caliber: .500 S&W Mag. **Capacities:** 5- or 7-round magazine. **Features:** Lever-action rifle or carbine chambered for .500 S&W Magnum. 22- or 18-in. barrel; walnut or maple stocks with pistol grip; aperture rear and blade front sights; recoil pad; sling swivels; enlarged lever loop; magazine capacity 5 (rifle) or 7 (carbine) rounds.
Price: $2,424.00

BIG HORN ARMORY MODEL 89B RIFLE AND CARBINE

Caliber: .475 Linebaugh. **Capacities:** 7-round magazine. **Barrel:** 16, 18 or 22-in. barrel. **Stock:** walnut or laminate buttstock and fore-end with pistol grip. **Sights:** Aperture rear and blade front. **Features:** Color case hardened finish.
Price: $3,699.00

BIG HORN ARMORY MODEL 90 SERIES

Calibers: .460 S&W, .454 Casull. **Features** similar to Model 89. Several wood and finish upgrades available.
Price: .460 S&W $2,849.00
Price: .454 Casull, .45 Colt $3,049.00
Price: .500 Linebaugh $3,699.00

BROWNING BLR

Features: Lever action with rotating bolt head, multiple-lug breech bolt with recessed bolt face, side ejection. Rack-and-pinion lever. Flush-mounted detachable magazines, with 4+1 capacity for magnum cartridges, 5+1 for standard rounds. **Barrel:** Button-rifled chrome-moly steel with crowned muzzle. **Stock:** Buttstocks and fore-ends are American walnut with grip and forend checkering. Recoil pad installed. **Trigger:** Wide-groove design, trigger travels with lever. Half-cock hammer safety; fold-down hammer. **Sights:** Gold bead on ramp front; low-profile square-notch adjustable rear. **Features:** Blued barrel and receiver, high-gloss wood finish. Receivers are drilled and tapped for scope mounts, swivel studs included. Action lock provided. Introduced 1996. Imported from Japan by Browning.

BROWNING BLR LIGHTWEIGHT W/PISTOL GRIP, SHORT AND LONG ACTION; LIGHTWEIGHT '81, SHORT AND LONG ACTION

Calibers: Short Action, 20 in. Barrel: .22-250 Rem., .243 Win., 7mm-08 Rem., .308 Win., .358, .450 Marlin. **Calibers: Short Action, 22 in. Barrel:** .270 WSM, 7mm WSM, .300 WSM, .325 WSM. **Calibers: Long Action 22 in. Barrel:** .270 Win., .30-06. **Calibers: Long Action 24 in. Barrel:** 7mm Rem. Mag., .300 Win. Mag. **Weights:** 6.5–7.75 lbs. **Lengths:** 40–45 in. overall. **Stock:** New checkered pistol grip and Schnabel forearm. Lightweight '81 differs from Pistol Grip models with a Western-style straight grip stock and banded forearm. Lightweight w/Pistol Grip Short Action and Long Action introduced 2005. Model '81 Lightning Long Action introduced 1996.
Price: Lightweight w/Pistol Grip Short Action, From.....................$1,040.00
Price: Lightweight w/Pistol Grip Long Action $1,100.00
Price: Lightweight '81 Short Action $990.00
Price: Lightweight '81 Long Action $1,040.00
Price: Lightweight '81 Takedown Short Action, From $1,040.00
Price: Lightweight '81 Takedown Long Action, From $1,120.00
Price: Lightweight stainless $1,120.00
Price: Stainless Takedown $1,260.00

CHIAPPA MODEL 1892 RIFLE

Calibers: .38 Special/357 Magnum, .38-40, .44-40, .44 Mag., .45 Colt. **Barrels:** 16 in. (Trapper), 20 in. round and 24 in. octagonal (Takedown). **Weight:** 7.7 lbs. **Stock:** Walnut. **Sights:** Blade front, buckhorn. Trapper model has interchangeable front sight blades. **Features:** Finishes are blue/case colored. Magazine capacity is 12 rounds with 24 in. bbl.; 10 rounds with 20 in. barrel; 9 rounds in 16 in. barrel. Mare's Leg models have 4-shot magazine, 9- or 12-in. barrel.
Price: From $1,329.00
Price: Takedown $1,435.00
Price: Trapper $1,329.00
Price: Mare's Leg, from $1,288.00

CHIAPPA MODEL 1886

Caliber: .45-70. **Barrels:** 16, 18.5, 22, 26 in. Replica of famous Winchester model offered in several variants.
Price: Rifle $1,709.00
Price: Carbine $1,629.00
Price: Kodiak $1,909.00

CHIAPPA 1886 LEVER-ACTION WILDLANDS

Caliber: .45-70. **Capacity:** 4. **Barrel:** 18.5-in., stainless steel, Cerakote dark gray finish, heavy, threaded. **Stock:** Laminate. **Sights:** Fixed fiber-optic front, skinner peep rear. **Weight:** 9.5 lbs. **Features:** Take-down style, 38.3 in. overall length.
Price: $2,099.99

CHIAPPA 1892 LEVER-ACTION WILDLANDS

Caliber: .44 Mag. **Capacity:** 5. **Barrel:** 16.5 in., stainless steel, Cerakote dark gray or color case finish, heavy. **Stock:** Wood laminate or hand-oiled walnut. **Sights:** Fixed fiber-optic front, Skinner peep rear. **Weight:** 6.3 lbs. **Features:** Takedown and solid-frame configurations, mag tube fed.
Price: ....$1,434.99-$1,689.99

CIMARRON 1873 SHORT RIFLE

Calibers: .357 Magnum, .38 Special, .32 WCF, .38 WCF, .44 Special, .44 WCF, .45 Colt. **Barrel:** 20 in. tapered octagon. **Weight:** 7.5 lbs. **Length:** 39 in. overall. **Stock:** Walnut. **Sights:** Bead front, adjustable semi-buckhorn rear. **Features:** Has half "button" magazine. Original-type markings, including caliber, on barrel and elevator and "Kings" patent. Trapper Carbine (.357 Mag., .44 WCF, .45 Colt). From Cimarron F.A. Co.
Price: $1,299.00
Price: Trapper Carbine 16-in. bbl. $1,352.00

CIMARRON 1873 DELUXE SPORTING

Similar to the 1873 Short Rifle except has 24-in. barrel with half-magazine.
Price: $1,485.00

CIMARRON 1873 LONG RANGE SPORTING

Calibers: .44 WCF, .45 Colt. **Barrel:** 30 in., octagonal. **Weight:** 8.5 lbs. **Length:** 48 in. overall. **Stock:** Walnut. **Sights:** Blade front, semi-buckhorn ramp rear. Tang sight optional. **Features:** Color casehardened frame; choice of modern blued-black or charcoal blued for other parts. Barrel marked "Kings Improvement." From Cimarron F.A. Co.
Price: $1,385.00

EMF 1866 YELLOWBOY LEVER ACTIONS

Calibers: .38 Special, .44-40, .45 LC. **Barrels:** 19 in. (carbine), 24 in. (rifle). **Weight:** 9 lbs. **Length:** 43 in. overall (rifle). **Stock:** European walnut. **Sights:** Bead front, open adjustable rear. **Features:** Solid brass frame, blued barrel, lever, hammer, buttplate. Imported from Italy by EMF.
Price: Rifle $1,175.00

EMF MODEL 1873 LEVER-ACTION

Calibers: .32/20, .357 Magnum, .38/40, .44-40, .45 Colt. **Barrels:** 18 in., 20 in., 24 in., 30 in. **Weight:** 8 lbs. **Length:** 43.25 in. overall. **Stock:** European walnut. **Sights:** Bead front, rear adjustable for windage and elevation. **Features:** Color casehardened frame (blued on carbine). Imported by EMF.
Price: $1,250.00

HENRY ORIGINAL RIFLE

Caliber: .44-40, .45 Colt. **Capacity:** 13-round magazine. **Barrel:** 24 in. **Weight:** 9 lbs. **Stock:** Straight-grip fancy American walnut with hardened brass buttplate. **Sights:** Folding ladder rear with blade front. **Finish:** Hardened brass receiver

Prices given are believed to be accurate at time of publication however, many factors affect retail pricing so exact prices are not possible.

with blued steel barrel. **Features:** Virtually identical to the original 1860 version except for the caliber. Each serial number has prefix " BTH" in honor of Benjamin Tyler Henry, the inventor of the lever-action repeating rifle that went on to become the most legendary firearm in American history. Introduced in 2014 by Henry Repeating Arms. Made in the USA.
Price: **$2,415.00**
Price: Deluxe Engraved Edition **$3,670.00**
Price: Silver Deluxe Engraved Edition **$3,817.00**

HENRY .45-70
Caliber: .45-70. **Capacity:** 4-round magazine. **Barrel:** 18.5 in. **Weight:** 7 lbs. **Stock:** Pistol grip walnut. **Sights:** XS Ghost Rings with blade front.
Price: **$850.00**

HENRY HENRY SIDE GATE LEVER ACTION
Caliber: .30-30, .35 Rem., .38-55. **Capacity:** 5-round magazine. **Barrel:** 20 in. **Weight:** 7 lbs. **Stock:** Pistol grip walnut. **Sights:** Semi-buckhorn rear, ivory bead front. Removable tube magazine plus side loading gate.
Price: **$1,045.00**

HENRY BIG BOY LEVER-ACTION CARBINE
Calibers: .327 Fed. Magnum, .357 Magnum/.38 Special, .41 Magnum, .44 Magnum/.44 Special, .45 Colt. **Capacity:** 10-shot tubular magazine. **Barrel:** 20 in. octagonal, 1:38 in. right-hand twist. **Weight:** 8.68 lbs. **Length:** 38.5 in. overall. **Stock:** Straight-grip American walnut, brass buttplate. **Sights:** Marbles fully adjustable semi-buckhorn rear, brass bead front. **Features:** Brasslite receiver not tapped for scope mount. Available in several Deluxe, engraved and other special editions. All Weather has round barrel, hardwood stock, chrome satin finish. Made in USA by Henry Repeating Arms.
Price: **$945.00**
Price: All Weather **$1,050.00**
Price: Engraved Special Editions from **$1,470.00**

HENRY BIG BOY X MODEL
Calibers: .45 Colt, .357/.38 Spl, .44 Mag/.44 Spl. **Capacity:** 7. **Barrel:** 17.4 in., round blue steel. **Stock:** Synthetic. **Sights:** Fiber optic. **Weight:** 7.3 lbs. **Features:** Robust and versatile, solid rubber buttpad, M-LOK Picatinny rail optional.
Price: **$970.00**

HENRY .30/30 LEVER-ACTION CARBINE
Same as the Big Boy except has straight grip American walnut, .30-30 only, 6-shot. Receivers are drilled and tapped for scope mount. Made in USA by Henry Repeating Arms.
Price: H009 Blued receiver, round barrel **$893.00**
Price: H009B Brass receiver, octagonal barrel **$998.00**

HENRY LEVER ACTION X MODEL
Caliber: .45-70. **Capacity:** 4. **Barrel:** 19.8 in., round blue steel. **Stock:** Synthetic. **Sights:** Fiber optic. **Weight:** 7.4 lbs. **Features:** Large loop lever, swivel studs, 5/8x24 threaded barrel.
Price: **$970.00**

HENRY LONG RANGER
Calibers: .223 Rem., .243 Win., 6.5 Creedmoor, 308 Win. **Capacities:** 5 (.223), 4 (.243, .308). **Barrel:** 20 in. **Stock:** Straight grip, checkered walnut with buttpad, oil finish, swivel studs. **Features:** Geared action, side ejection, chromed steel bolt with 6 lugs, flush fit detachable magazine.
Price: **$1,066.00**
Price: Deluxe Engraved model **$1,850.00**

MARLIN MODEL 336C LEVER-ACTION CARBINE
Calibers: .30-30 or .35 Rem. **Capacity:** 6-shot tubular magazine. **Barrel:** 20 in. Micro-Groove. **Weight:** 7 lbs. **Length:** 38.5 in. overall. **Stock:** Checkered American black walnut, capped pistol grip. Mar-Shield finish; rubber buttpad; swivel studs. **Sights:** Ramp front with wide-scan hood, semi-buckhorn folding rear adjustable for windage and elevation. **Features:** Hammer-block safety. Receiver tapped for scope mount, offset hammer spur; top of receiver sandblasted to prevent glare. Includes safety lock. The latest variation of Marlin's classic lever gun that originated in 1937.
Price: **$635.00**
Price: Curly Maple stock **$899.00**

MARLIN MODEL 336SS LEVER-ACTION CARBINE
Caliber: .30-30 only. **Capacity:** 6-shot. **Features:** Same as the 336C except receiver, barrel and other major parts are machined from stainless steel. receiver tapped for scope. Includes safety lock.
Price: **$779.00**

MARLIN MODEL 336W LEVER-ACTION
Similar to the Model 336C except has walnut-finished, cut-checkered Maine birch stock; blued steel barrel band has integral sling swivel; no front sight hood; comes with padded nylon sling; hard rubber buttplate. Introduced 1998. Includes safety lock. Made in USA by Marlin.
Price: **$548.00**

MARLIN 336BL
Caliber: .30-30. **Capacity:** 6-shot full-length tubular magazine. **Barrel:** 18-in. blued with Micro-Groove rifling (12 grooves). **Features:** Lever-action rifle. Finger lever; side ejection; blued steel receiver; hammer block safety; brown laminated hardwood pistol-grip stock with fluted comb; cut checkering; deluxe recoil pad; blued swivel studs.
Price: **$667.00**

MARLIN MODEL 1894C
Caliber: .44 Special/.44 Magnum, 10-round tubular magazine. **Barrel:** 20 in. Ballard-type rifling. **Weight:** 6 lbs. **Length:** 37.5 in. overall. **Stock:** Checkered American black walnut, straight grip and fore-end. Mar-Shield finish. Rubber rifle buttpad; swivel studs. **Sights:** Wide-Scan hooded ramp front, semi-buckhorn folding rear adjustable for windage and elevation. **Features:** Hammer-block safety. Receiver tapped for scope mount, offset hammer spur, solid top receiver sandblasted to prevent glare. Includes safety lock.
Price: **$789.00**

MARLIN MODEL 1894 COWBOY
Calibers: .357 Magnum, .44 Magnum, .45 Colt. **Capacity:** 10-round magazine. **Barrel:** 20 in. tapered octagon, deep cut rifling. **Weight:** 7.5 lbs. **Length:** 41.5 in. overall. **Stock:** Straight grip American black walnut, hard rubber buttplate, Mar-Shield finish. **Sights:** Marble carbine front, adjustable Marble semi-buckhorn rear. **Features:** Squared finger lever; straight grip stock; blued steel fore-end tip. Designed for Cowboy Shooting events. Introduced 1996. Includes safety lock. Made in USA by Marlin.
Price: **$1,093.00**

MARLIN 1894 DELUXE
Caliber: .44 Magnum/.44 Special. **Capacity:** 10-shot tubular magazine. **Features:** Squared finger lever; side ejection; richly polished deep blued metal surfaces; solid top receiver; hammer block safety; #1 grade fancy American black walnut straight-grip stock and fore-end; cut checkering; rubber rifle buttpad; Mar-Shield finish; blued steel fore-end cap; swivel studs; deep-cut Ballard-type rifling (6 grooves).
Price: **$950.00**

MARLIN 1894 SBL
Caliber: .44 Magnum. Capacity: 6-round tubular magazine. Features: 16.5-in. barrel, laminated stock, stainless finish, large lever, accessory rail, XS Ghost Ring sights.
Price: $1,146.00

MARLIN 1895 444 150TH ANNIVERSARY
Caliber: .444 Marlin. Capacity: 6. Barrel: 24 in., half-octagon/half-round, blued. Stock: C-grade American black walnut, pistol grip. Sights: Skinner ladder. Weight: 7 lbs. Features: Engraved receiver with gold inlay, commemorative box, historical checkering.
Price: $1,899.99

MARLIN MODEL 1895 LEVER-ACTION
Caliber: .45-70 Govt. Capacity: 4-shot tubular magazine. Barrel: 22 in. round. Weight: 7.5 lbs. Length: 40.5 in. overall. Stock: Checkered American black walnut, full pistol grip. Mar-Shield finish; rubber buttpad; quick detachable swivel studs. Sights: Bead front with Wide-Scan hood, semi-buckhorn folding rear adjustable for windage and elevation. Features: Hammer-block safety. Solid receiver tapped for scope mounts or receiver sights; offset hammer spur. Includes safety lock.
Price: $745.00

MARLIN MODEL 1895 TRAPPER
Similar to Model 1895 with deep-cut Ballard-type rifling, threaded muzzle, pistol-grip black synthetic stock with large-loop lever, matte black finish. Barrel: 16.5 in. Overall length: 35 in. Weight: 7 lbs. Sights: Skinner peep, blade front..
Price: $1,123.00

MARLIN MODEL 1895 DARK SERIES
Similar to Model 1895 with deep-cut Ballard-type rifling; pistol-grip synthetic stock with large-loop lever, matte stainless finish, full length magazine. Barrel: 16.25 in. Overall length: 34.5 in. Weight: 7.65 lbs. Sights: XS lever rail with ghost-ring receiver sight.
Price: $949.00

MARLIN MODEL 1895 SBLR
Caliber: .45-70 Govt. Features: Similar to Model 1895GS Guide Gun but with stainless steel barrel (18.5 in.), receiver, large loop lever and magazine tube. Black/gray laminated buttstock and fore-end, XS ghost ring rear sight, hooded ramp front sight, receiver/barrel-mounted top rail for mounting accessory optics. Chambered in .45-70 Government. Overall length is 42.5 in., weighs 7.5 lbs.
Price: $1,232.00

MARLIN 1895GBL
Caliber: .45-70 Govt. Features: Lever-action rifle with 6-shot, full-length tubular magazine; 18.5-in. barrel with deep-cut Ballard-type rifling (6 grooves); big-loop finger lever; side ejection; solid-top receiver; deeply blued metal surfaces; hammer block safety; pistol-grip two-tone brown laminate stock with cut checkering; ventilated recoil pad; Mar-Shield finish, swivel studs.
Price: $786.00

NAVY ARMS 1873 RIFLE
Calibers: .357 Magnum, .45 Colt. Capacity: 12-round magazine. Barrels: 20 in., 24.25 in., full octagonal. Stock: Deluxe checkered American walnut. Sights: Gold bead front, semi-buckhorn rear. Features: Turnbull color case-hardened frame, rest blued. Full-octagon barrel. Available exclusively from Navy Arms. Made by Winchester.
Price: $2,500.00

NAVY ARMS 1892 SHORT RIFLE
Calibers: .45 Colt, .44 Magnum. Capacity: 10-round magazine. Barrel: 20 in. full octagon. Stock: Checkered Grade 1 American walnut. Sights: Marble's Semi-Buckhorn rear and gold bead front. Finish: Color casehardened.
Price: $2,300.00

NAVY ARMS LIGHTNING RIFLE
Calibers: .45 Colt, .357 Magnum. Replica of the Colt Lightning slide-action rifle of the late 19th and early 20th centuries. Barrel: Octagon 20 or 24 in. Stock: Checkered Grade 1 American walnut. Finish: Color casehardened.
Price: $2,200.00

ROSSI R92 LEVER-ACTION CARBINE
Calibers: .38 Special/.357 Magnum, .44 Magnum., .44-40 Win., .45 Colt. Barrels: 16 or 20 in. with round barrel, 20 or 24 in. with octagon barrel. Weight: 4.8–7 lbs. Length: 34–41.5 in. Features: Blued or stainless finish. Various options available in selected chamberings (large lever loop, fiber-optic sights, cheekpiece).
Price: Blued $624.00
Price: Stainless $659.00

UBERTI 1873 SPORTING RIFLE
Calibers: .357 Magnum, .44-40, .45 Colt. Barrels: 16.1 in. round, 19 in. round or 20 in., 24.25 in. octagonal. Weight: Up to 8.2 lbs. Length: Up to 43.3 in. overall. Stock: Walnut, straight grip and pistol grip. Sights: Blade front adjustable for windage, open rear adjustable for elevation. Features: Color casehardened frame, blued barrel, hammer, lever, buttplate, brass elevator. Imported by Stoeger Industries.
Price: Carbine 19-in. bbl. $1,309.00
Price: Trapper 16.1-in. bbl. $1,329.00
Price: Carbine 18-in. half oct. bbl. $1,379.00
Price: Short Rifle 20-in. bbl. $1,339.00
Price: Sporting Rifle, 24.25-in. bbl. $1,339.00
Price: Special Sporting Rifle, A-grade walnut $1,449.00

UBERTI 1866 YELLOWBOY CARBINE, SHORT, RIFLE
Calibers: .38 Special, .44-40, .45 Colt. Barrel: 24.25 in. octagonal. Weight: 8.2 lbs. Length: 43.25 in. overall. Stock: Walnut. Sights: Blade front adjustable for windage, rear adjustable for elevation. Features: Frame, buttplate, fore-end cap of polished brass, balance charcoal blued. Imported by Stoeger Industries.
Price: 1866 Yellowboy Carbine, 19-in. round barrel......................$1,269.00
Price: 1866 Yellowboy Short Rifle, 20-in. octagonal barrel $1,269.00
Price: 1866 Yellowboy Rifle, 24.25-in. octagonal barrel $1,269.00

UBERTI 1860 HENRY
Calibers: .44-40, .45 Colt. **Barrel:** 24.25 in. half-octagon. **Weight:** 9.2 lbs.
Length: 43.75 in. overall. **Stock:** American walnut. **Sights:** Blade front, rear
adjustable for elevation. Imported by Stoeger Industries.
Price: 1860 Henry Trapper, 18.5-in. barrel, brass frame **$1,499.00**
Price: 1860 Henry Rifle Iron Frame, 24.25-in. barrel **$1,499.00**

WINCHESTER MODEL 94 SHORT RIFLE
Calibers: .30-30, .38-55, .32 Special. **Barrel:** 20 in. **Weight:** 6.75 lbs. **Sights:**
Semi-buckhorn rear, gold bead front. **Stock:** Walnut with straight grip.
Fore-end has black grip cap. Also available in Trail's End takedown design in
.450 Marlin or .30-30.
Price: **$1,230.00**
Price: (Takedown) **$1,460.00**

WINCHESTER MODEL 94 CARBINE
Same general specifications as M94 Short Rifle except for curved buttplate
and fore-end barrel band.
Price: **$1,200.00**

WINCHESTER MODEL 94 SPORTER
Calibers: .30-30, .38-55. **Barrel:** 24 in. **Weight:** 7.5 lbs. **Features:** Same
features of Model 94 Short Rifle except for crescent butt and steel
buttplate, 24 in. half-round, half-octagon barrel, checkered stock.
Price: **$1,400.00**

WINCHESTER 1873 SHORT RIFLE
Calibers: .357 Magnum, .44-40, .45 Colt. **Capacities:** Tubular magazine
holds 10 rounds (.44-40, .45 Colt), 11 rounds (.38 Special). **Barrel:** 20 in.
Weight: 7.25 lbs. **Sights:** Marble semi-buckhorn rear, gold bead front.
Tang is drilled and tapped for optional peep sight. **Stock:** Satin finished,
straight-grip walnut with steel crescent buttplate and steel fore-end cap.
Tang safety. A modern version of the "Gun That Won the West."
Price: **$1,300.00**
Price: Deluxe Sporting Rifle **$1,800.00**

WINCHESTER MODEL 1886 SHORT RIFLE
Caliber: .45-70. **Barrel:** 24 in. **Weight:** 8.4 lbs. **Sights:** Adjustable buckhorn
rear, blade front. **Stock:** Grade 1 walnut with crescent butt.
Price **$1,340.00**

WINCHESTER MODEL 1892 CARBINE
Calibers: .357 Magnum, .44 Magnum, .44-40, .45 Colt. **Barrel:** 20 in.
Weight: 6 lbs. **Stock:** Satin finished walnut with straight grip, steel fore-end
strap. **Sights:** Marble semi-buckhorn rear, gold bead front. Other features
include saddle ring and tang safety.
Price: **$1,260.00**
Price: 1892 Short Rifle **$1,070.00**

Prices given are believed to be accurate at time of publication however, many factors affect retail pricing so exact prices are not possible.

75TH EDITION, 2021 ✦ **413**

ARMALITE AR-30A1 TARGET

Calibers: .300 Win. Mag., .338 Lapua. **Capacity:** 5 rounds. **Barrel:** 26 in., target-grade chrome moly. **Weight:** 12.8 lbs. **Length:** 46 in. **Stock:** Standard fixed with adjustable cheek piece. **Sights:** None. Accessory top rail included. **Features:** Bolt-action rifle. Muzzle brake, ambidextrous magazine release, large ejection port makes single loading easy, V-block patented bedding system, bolt-mounted safety locks firing pin. AR-31 is in .308 Win., accepts AR-10 double-stack magazines, has adjustable pistol grip stock.
Price: **$3,460.00**
Price: AR-31..**$3,460.00**

ARMALITE AR-50A1

Caliber: .50 BMG, .416 Barrett. **Capacity:** Bolt-action single-shot. **Barrel:** 30 in. with muzzle brake. National Match model (shown) has 33-in. fluted barrel. **Weight:** 34.1 lbs. **Stock:** Three-section. Extruded fore-end, machined vertical grip, forged and machined buttstock that is vertically adjustable. National Match model (.50 BMG only) has V-block patented bedding system, Armalite Skid System to ensure straight-back recoil.
Price: **$3,359.00**

ANSCHUTZ 1782

Calibers: .243 Win., 6.5 Creedmoor, .308 Win., .30-06, 8x57, 9.3x62. **Capacity:** 3. **Barrel:** 20.5 to 23.8 in., blued, threaded. **Stock:** Walnut. **Sights:** Integrated Picatinny rail. **Weight:** 8 lbs. **Features:** Solid-steel milled action, 60-degree bolt lift, sliding safety catch.
Price: **$2,795.99**

BENELLI LUPO

Calibers: .30-06, .300 WSM, .270 Win. **Capacity:** 5. **Barrel:** 22 to 24 in., Crio-treated, free-floating attached to a hardened steel extension. **Stock:** Synthetic. **Sights:** None, drilled and tapped. **Weight:** 7 lbs. **Features:** Shims allow the stock to be set in 36 different positions, progressive comfort system.
Price: **$1,699.99**

BARRETT FIELDCRAFT HUNTING RIFLE

Calibers: .22-250 Rem., .243 Win., 6mm Creedmoor, .25-06, 6.5 Creedmoor, 6.5x55, 7mm-08 Rem., .308 Win. .270 Win., .30-06. **Capacity:** 4-round magazine. **Barrel:** 18 (threaded), 21 or 24 inches. **Weight:** 5.2-5.6 lbs. **Features:** Two-position safety, Timney trigger. Receiver, barrels and bolts are scaled for specific calibers. Barrels and action are made from 416 stainless steel and are full-length hand bedded.
Price: ....**$1,879.00-$1,929.00**

BARRETT MODEL 99 SINGLE SHOT

Calibers: .50 BMG., .416 Barrett. **Barrel:** 33 in. **Weight:** 25 lbs. **Length:** 50.4

in. overall. **Stock:** Anodized aluminum with energy-absorbing recoil pad. **Sights:** None furnished; integral M1913 scope rail. **Features:** Bolt action; detachable bipod; match-grade barrel with high-efficiency muzzle brake. Introduced 1999. Made in USA by Barrett Firearms.
Price: From..**$3,999.00-$4,199.00**

BARRETT MRAD

Calibers: .260 Rem., 6.5 Creedmoor, .308 Win., .300 Win. Mag., .338 Lapua Magnum. **Capacity:** 10-round magazine. **Barrels:** 20 in., 24 in. or 26 in. fluted or heavy. **Features:** User-interchangeable barrel system, folding stock, adjustable cheekpiece, 5-position length of pull adjustment button, match-grade trigger, 22-in. optics rail.
Price: ....**$5,850.00-$6,000.00**

BERGARA B-14 SERIES

Calibers: 6.5 Creedmoor, .270 Win., 7mm Rem. Mag., .308 Win., .30-06, .300 Win. Mag. **Barrels:** 22 or 24 in. **Weight:** 7 lbs. **Features:** Synthetic with Soft touch finish, recoil pad, swivel studs, adjustable trigger, choice of detachable mag or hinged floorplate. Made in Spain.
Price: **$825.00**
Price: Walnut Stock (Shown, Top) **$945.00**
Price: Premier Series, From **$2,190.00**
Price: Hunting and Match Rifle (HMR)(Shown, Bottom), From **$1,150.00**

BERGARA BCR SERIES
Calibers: Most popular calibers from .222 Rem. to .300 Win. Mag **Barrels:** 18, 22, 24 or 26 in. Various options available.
Price: BCR23 Sport Hunter from **$3,950.00**
Price: BCR24 Varmint Hunter from **$4,100.00**
Price: BCR25 Long Range Hunter from **$4,350.00**
Price: BCR27 Competition from **$4,950.00**

BERGARA MOUNTAIN 2.0

Calibers: 6.5 Creedmoor, 6.5 PRC, .308 Win., 28 Nosler, .300 Win. Mag., .300 PRC. **Capacity:** 2 to 4. **Barrel:** 22 to 24-in., No. 3 stainless steel. **Stock:** Carbon fiber. **Sights:** None, drilled and tapped. **Features:** Trigger tech trigger, two-lug action, Cerakote finished metal.
Price: **$2,250.00**

BLASER R-8 SERIES

Calibers: Available in virtually all standard and metric calibers from .204 Ruger to .500 Jeffery. Straight-pull bolt action. **Barrels:** 20.5, 23, or 25.75 in. **Weights:** 6.375–8.375 lbs. **Lengths:** 40 in. overall (22 in. barrel). **Stocks:** Synthetic or Turkish walnut. **Sights:** None furnished; drilled and tapped for scope mounting. **Features:** Thumb-activated safety slide/cocking mechanism; interchangeable barrels and bolt heads. Many optional features. Imported from Germany by Blaser USA.
Price: From.. **$3,787.00**

BROWNING AB3 COMPOSITE STALKER

Calibers: .243, 6.5 Creedmoor, .270 Win., .270 WSM, 7mm-08, 7mm Rem.

Prices given are believed to be accurate at time of publication however, many factors affect retail pricing so exact prices are not possible.

Mag., .30-06, .300 Win. Mag., .300 WSM or .308 Win. **Barrels:** 22 in, 26 in. for magnums. **Weights:** 6.8–7.4 lbs. **Stock:** Matte black synthetic. **Sights:** None. Picatinny rail scope mount included.
Price: **$600.00**
Price: Micro Stalker **$600.00**
Price: Hunter **$670.00**

BROWNING X-BOLT HUNTER
Calibers: .223, .22-250, .243 Win., 6mm Creedmoor, 6.5 Creedmoor, .25-06 Rem., .270 Win., .270 WSM, .280 Rem., 7mm Rem. Mag., 7mm WSM, 7mm-08 Rem., .308 Win., .30-06, .300 Win. Mag., .325 WSM, .338 Win. Mag., .375 H&H Mag. **Barrels:** 22 in., 23 in., 24 in., 26 in., varies by model. Matte blued or stainless free-floated barrel, recessed muzzle crown. **Weights:** 6.3–7 lbs. **Stocks:** Hunter and Medallion models have black walnut stocks; Composite Stalker and Stainless Stalker models have composite stocks. Inflex Technology recoil pad. **Sights:** None, drilled and tapped receiver, X-Lock scope mounts. **Features:** Adjustable three-lever Feather Trigger system, polished hard-chromed steel components, factory pre-set at 3.5 lbs., alloy trigger housing. Bolt unlock button, detachable rotary magazine, 60-degree bolt lift, three locking lugs, top-tang safety, sling swivel studs. Introduced 2008.
Price: Standard calibers **$900.00**
Price: Magnum calibers **$950.00**
Price: Left-hand models......................**$940.00–$980.00**

BROWNING X-BOLT HUNTER LONG RANGE
Calibers: 6.5 Creedmoor, 6.5 PRC, .308 Win., .270 Win., .30-06, 7MM Rem. Mag., .300 Win. Mag. **Capacity:** 3 to 4. **Barrel:** 22 to 26 in., blued sporter, heavy. **Stock:** Satin finish checkered walnut. **Sights:** None, drilled and tapped. **Weight:** 7.6 to 8 lbs. **Features:** Ambidextrous adjustable comb, muzzle brake with suppressor threads.
Price: **$1,300.00**

BROWNING X-BOLT MAX LONG RANGE
Calibers: 6mm Creedmoor, 6.5 Creedmoor, .308 Win., .300 WSM, 7MM Rem. Mag., 28 Nosler, .300 Win. Mag., .300 RUM, 6.5 PRC, 30 Nosler, .300 PRC. **Capacity:** 3 to 4. **Barrel:** 26 in., satin gray stainless steel sporter, heavy. **Stock:** Composite black, gray splatter. **Sights:** None, drilled and tapped. **Weight:** 8.2 to 8.6 lbs. **Features:** Adjustable comb, extended bolt handle, three swivel studs for sling and bipod use.
Price: .... **$1,300.00-$1,340.00**

BROWNING X-BOLT MAX VARMINT/TARGET
Calibers: .204 Ruger, .223 Rem., .22-250 Rem., 6.5 Creedmoor, .308 Win., 28 Nosler, .300 Win. Mag. **Capacity:** 3 to 5. **Barrel:** 26 in., stainless steel heavy bull, fluted. **Stock:** Composite. **Sights:** None, drilled and tapped. **Weight:** 9 to 9.5 lbs. **Features:** Quarter-inch and two-thirds-inch LOP spacers, extended bolt handle, gray textured stock, suppressor ready.
Price: .... **$1,340.00-$1,400.00**

BROWNING X-BOLT MICRO MIDAS
Calibers: .243 Win., 6mm Creedmoor, 6.5 Creedmoor, 7mm-08 Rem., .308 Win., .22-250 Rem. .270 WSM, .300 WSM. **Barrel:** 20 in. **Weight:** 6 lbs.,1 oz. **Length:** 37.625–38.125 in. overall. **Stock:** Satin finish checkered walnut or composite. **Sights:** Hooded front and adjustable rear. **Features:** Steel receiver with low-luster blued finish. Glass bedded, drilled and tapped for scope mounts. Barrel is free-floating and hand chambered with target crown. Bolt-action with adjustable Feather Trigger and detachable rotary magazine. Compact 12.5 in. length of pull for smaller shooters, designed to

fit smaller-framed shooters like youth and women. This model has all the same features as the full-size model with sling swivel studs installed and Inflex Technology recoil pad. (Scope and mounts not included).
Price: **$860.00**

BROWNING X-BOLT MEDALLION
Calibers: Most popular calibers from .223 Rem. to .375 H&H. **Barrels:** 22, 24 or 26 in. free-floated. **Features:** Engraved receiver with polished blue finish, gloss finished and checkered walnut stock with rosewood grip and fore-end caps, detachable rotary magazine. Medallion Maple model has AAA-grade maple stock.
Price: **$1,040.00**
Price: Medallion Maple **$1,070.00**

BROWNING X-BOLT ECLIPSE HUNTER
Calibers: Most popular calibers from .223 Rem. to .300 WSM. Same general features of X-Bolt series except for its laminated thumbhole stock. Varmint and Target models have 26-in. bull barrels.
Price: **$1,200.00**
Price: Varmint and Target models........................ **$1,430.00**

BROWNING X-BOLT HELL'S CANYON
Calibers: .22 Nosler, 6mm Creedmoor, .243 Win., 26 Nosler, 6.5 Creedmoor, .270 Win., .270 WSM, 7mm-08 Rem., 7mm Rem. Mag., .308 Win., .30-06, .300 Win. Mag., .300 WSM. **Barrels:** 22–26-in. fluted and free-floating with muzzle brake or thread protector. **Stock:** A-TACS AU Camo composite with checkered grip panels. **Features:** Detachable rotary magazine, adjustable trigger, Cerakote Burnt Bronze finish on receiver and barrel.
Price: .... **$1,260.00–$1,320.00**

BROWNING X-BOLT WHITE GOLD
Calibers: Eighteen popular calibers from .223 Rem. to .338 Win. Mag. Same general features of X-Bolt series plus polished stainless steel barrel, receiver, bolt and trigger. Gloss-finished finely checkered walnut Monte Carlo-style stock with rosewood grip and fore-end caps.
Price: .... **$1,420.00–$1,540.00**

BROWNING X-BOLT PRO SERIES
Calibers: 6mm Creedmoor, 6.5 Creedmoor, 26 Nosler, 28 Nosler, .270 Win., 7mm Rem. Mag., .308 Win., .30-06., .300 Win. Mag. Detachable rotary magazine. **Barrels:** 22–26 in. Stainless steel, fluted with threaded/removable muzzle brake. **Weights:** 6–7.5 lbs. **Finish:** Cerakote Burnt Bronze. **Stock:** Second generation carbon fiber with palm swell, textured gripping surfaces. Adjustable trigger, top tang safety, sling swivel studs. Long Range has heavy sporter-contour barrel, proprietary lapping process.
Price: X-Bolt Pro....................................**$2,070.00–$2,130.00**
Price: X-Bolt Pro Long Range ....**$2,100.00–$2,180.00**
Price: X-Bolt Pro Tungsten ....**$2,070.00–$2,130.00**

Prices given are believed to be accurate at time of publication however, many factors affect retail pricing so exact prices are not possible.

75TH EDITION, 2021 **415**

CHEYTAC M-200
Calibers: .357 CheyTac, .408 CheyTac. **Capacity:** 7-round magazine. **Barrel:** 30 in. **Length:** 55 in. stock extended. **Weight:** 27 lbs. (steel barrel); 24 lbs. (carbon-fiber barrel). **Stock:** Retractable. **Sights:** None, scope rail provided. **Features:** CNC-machined receiver, attachable Picatinny rail M-1913, detachable barrel, integral bipod, 3.5-lb. trigger pull, muzzle brake. Made in USA by CheyTac, LLC.
Price: From...$11,700.00

CHRISTENSEN ARMS MESA TITANIUM EDITION
Calibers: 6.5 Creedmoor, 6.5 PRC, .308 Win., .300 Win. Mag. **Capacity:** 3 to 4 **Barrel:** 22 to 24 in., 416R stainless steel, threaded. **Stock:** Carbon-fiber composite, sporter style. **Sights:** None, drilled and tapped. **Weight:** 6.1 lbs. **Features:** LimbSaver recoil pad, nitride-treated bolt, match-grade trigger.
Price: $1,795.99

CHRISTENSEN ARMS RIDGELINE TITANIUM EDITION
Calibers: 6.5 Creedmoor, 6.5 PRC, .308 Win., .300 Win. Mag. **Capacity:** 3 to 4. **Barrel:** 22 to 24 in., 416R stainless steel, carbon-fiber wrapped. **Stock:** Carbon-fiber composite, sporter style. **Sights:** Picatinny rail. **Weight:** 5.8 lbs. **Features:** Titanium radial brake, M16-style extractor, LimbSaver recoil pad.
Price: $2,495.99

COOPER FIREARMS OF MONTANA
This company manufacturers bolt-action rifles in a variety of styles and in almost any factory or wildcat caliber. Features of the major model sub-category/styles are listed below. Several other styles and options are available. Classic: Available in all models. AA Claro walnut stock with 4-panel hand checkering, hand-rubbed oil-finished wood, Pachmayr pad, steel grip cap and standard sling swivel studs. Barrel is chrome-moly premium match grade Wilson Arms. All metal work has matte finish. Custom Classic: Available in all models. AAA Claro walnut stock with shadow-line beaded cheek-piece, African ebony tip, Western fleur wrap-around hand checkering, hand-rubbed oil-finished wood, Pachmayr pad, steel grip cap and standard sling swivel studs. Barrel is chrome-moly premium match grade Wilson Arms. All metal work has high gloss finish. Western Classic: Available in all models. AAA+ Claro walnut stock. Selected metal work is highlighted with case coloring. Other features same as Custom Classic. Mannlicher: Available in all models. Same features as Western Classic with full-length stock having multi-point wrap-around hand checkering. Varminter: Available in Models 21, 22, 38, 52, 54 and 57-M. Same features as Classic except heavy barrel and stock with wide fore-end, hand-checkered grip.

COOPER MODEL 21
Calibers: Virtually any factory or wildcat chambering in the .223 Rem. family is available including: .17 Rem., .19-223, Tactical 20, .204 Ruger, .222 Rem., .222 Rem. Mag., .223 Rem, .223 Rem AI, 6x45, 6x47. Single shot. **Barrels:** 22–24 in. for Classic configurations, 24–26 in. for Varminter configurations. **Weights:** 6.5–8.0 lbs., depending on type. **Stock:** AA-AAA select claro walnut, 20 LPI checkering. **Sights:** None furnished. **Features:** Three front locking-lug, bolt-action, single-shot. Action: 7.75 in. long, Sako extractor. Button ejector. Fully adjustable single-stage trigger. Options include wood upgrades, case-color metalwork, barrel fluting, custom LOP, and many others.
Price: Classic $2,495.00
Price: Custom Classic...$2,995.00
Price: Western Classic. $3,795.00
Price: Varminter...$2,495.00
Price: Mannlicher $4,395.00

COOPER MODEL 22
Calibers: Virtually any factory or wildcat chambering in the mid-size cartridge length including: .22-250 Rem., .22-250 Rem. AI, .25-06 Rem., .25-06 Rem. AI, .243 Win., .243 Win. AI, .220 Swift, .250/3000 AI, .257 Roberts, .257 Roberts AI, 7mm-08 Rem., 6mm Rem., .260 Rem., 6x284, 6.5x284, .22 BR, 6mm BR, .308 Win. Single shot. **Barrels:** 24 in. or 26 in. stainless match in Classic configurations. 24 in. or 26 in. in Varminter configurations. **Weight:** 7.5–8.0 lbs. depending on type. **Stock:** AA-AAA select claro walnut, 20 LPI checkering. **Sights:** None furnished. **Features:** Three front locking-lug bolt-action single shot. Action: 8.25 in. long, Sako-style extractor. Button ejector. Fully adjustable single-stage trigger. Options include wood upgrades, case-color metalwork, barrel fluting, custom LOP, and many others.
Price: Classic $2,495.00
Price: Custom Classic...$2,995.00
Price: Western Classic. $3,795.00
Price: Varminter...$2,495.00
Price: Mannlicher $4,395.00

COOPER MODEL 38
Calibers: .22 Hornet family of cartridges including the .17 Squirrel, .17 He Bee, .17 Ackley Hornet, .17 Mach IV, .19 Calhoon, .20 VarTarg, .221 Fireball, .22 Hornet, .22 K-Hornet, .22 Squirrel, .218 Bee, .218 Mashburn Bee. Single shot. **Barrels:** 22 in. or 24 in. in Classic configurations, 24 in. or 26 in. in Varminter configurations. **Weights:** 6.5–8.0 lbs. depending on type. **Stock:** AA-AAA select claro walnut, 20 LPI checkering. **Sights:** None furnished. **Features:** Three front locking-lug bolt-action single shot. Action: 7 in. long, Sako-style extractor. Button ejector. Fully adjustable single-stage trigger. Options include wood upgrades, case-color metalwork, barrel fluting, custom LOP, and many others.
Price: Classic $2,225.00
Price: Custom Classic...$2,595.00
Price: Western Classic. $3,455.00
Price: Varminter...$2,225.00
Price: Mannlicher $4,395.00

COOPER MODEL 52
Calibers: .30-06, .270 Win., .280 Rem, .25-06, .284 Win., .257 Weatherby Mag., .264 Win. Mag., .270 Weatherby Mag., 7mm Remington Mag., 7mm Weatherby Mag., 7mm Shooting Times Westerner, .300 Holland & Holland, .300 Win. Mag., .300 Weatherby Mag., .308 Norma Mag., 8mm Rem. Mag., .338 Win. Mag., .340 Weatherby V. Three-shot magazine. **Barrels:** 22 in. or 24 in. in Classic configurations, 24 in. or 26 in. in Varminter configurations. **Weight:** 7.75–8 lbs. depending on type. **Stock:** AA-AAA select claro walnut, 20 LPI checkering. **Sights:** None furnished. **Features:** Three front locking-lug bolt-action single shot. Action: 7 in. long, Sako style extractor. Button ejector. Fully adjustable single-stage trigger. Options include wood upgrades, case-color metalwork, barrel fluting, custom LOP, and many others.
Price: Classic. $2,495.00
Price: Custom Classic...$3,335.00
Price: Western Classic. $3,995.00
Price: Jackson Game $2,595.00
Price: Jackson Hunter $2,595.00
Price: Excalibur. $2,595.00
Price: Mannlicher $4,755.00
Price: Open Country Long Range $3,795.00-4,155.00
Price: Timberline, Synthetic Stock $2,595.00
Price: Raptor, Synthetic tactical stock $2,755.00

COOPER MODEL 54
Calibers: .22-250, .243 Win., .250 Savage, .260 Rem., 7mm-08, .308 Win. and similar length cartridges. Features are similar to those of the Model 52.
Price: Classic. $2,495.00
Price: Custom Classic...$3,355.00
Price: Western Classic. $3,995.00
Price: Jackson Game $2,595.00
Price: Jackson Hunter $2,595.00
Price: Excalibur. $2,595.00
Price: Mannlicher $4,995.00

Prices given are believed to be accurate at time of publication however, many factors affect retail pricing so exact prices are not possible.

CZ 527 LUX BOLT-ACTION
Calibers: .17 Hornet, .204 Ruger, .22 Hornet, .222 Rem., .223 Rem. **Capacity:** 5-round magazine. **Barrels:** 23.5 in. standard or heavy. **Weight:** 6 lbs., 1 oz. **Length:** 42.5 in. overall. **Stock:** European walnut with Monte Carlo. **Sights:** Hooded front, open adjustable rear. **Features:** Improved mini-Mauser action with non-rotating claw extractor; single set trigger; grooved receiver. Imported from the Czech Republic by CZ-USA.
Price: Brown laminate stock...**$733.00**
Price: Model FS, full-length stock, cheekpiece **$827.00**

CZ 527 AMERICAN BOLT-ACTION
Similar to the CZ 527 Lux except has classic-style stock with 18 LPI checkering; free-floating barrel; recessed target crown on barrel. No sights furnished. Introduced 1999. Imported from the Czech Republic by CZUSA.
Price: From...**$733.00**

CZ 527 AMERICAN SUPPRESSOR READY
Calibers: .223 Rem., 6.5 Grendel, .300 Blackout, 7.62x39mm. 5-shot capacity. **Barrel:** 16.5 in. **Stock:** Synthetic American style. **Weight:** 5.9 lbs. No sights furnished. Integrated 16mm scope bases.
Price: From **$766.00**

CZ 550 SAFARI MAGNUM/AMERICAN SAFARI MAGNUM
Similar to CZ 550 American Classic. **Calibers:** .375 H&H Mag., .416 Rigby, .458 Win. Mag., .458 Lott. Overall length is 46.5 in. **Barrel:** 25 in. **Weight:** 9.4 lbs., 9.9 lbs (American). **Features:** Hooded front sight, express rear with one standing, two folding leaves. Imported from the Czech Republic by CZ-USA.
Price: Safari Magnum **$1,215.00**
Price: American Safari Field ....**$1,215.00–$1,348.00**

CZ 550 MAGNUM H.E.T.
High Energy Tactical model similar to CZ 550 American Classic. **Caliber:** .338 Lapua. **Length:** 52 in. **Barrel:** 28 in. **Weight:** 14 lbs. **Features:** Adjustable sights, satin blued barrel. Imported from the Czech Republic by CZ-USA.
Price: **$3,929.00**

CZ 550 ULTIMATE HUNTING
Similar to CZ 550 American Classic. **Caliber:** .300 Win Mag. **Length:** 44.7 in. **Barrel:** 23.6 in. **Weight:** 7.7 lbs. **Stock:** Kevlar. **Features:** Nightforce 5.5-20x50 scope included. Imported from the Czech Republic by CZ-USA.
Price: **$3,458.00**

CZ 557
Calibers: .243 Win., 6.5x55, .270 Win., .308 Win., .30-06. **Capacity:** 5+1. **Barrel:** 20.5 in. **Stock:** Satin finished walnut or Manners carbon fiber with textured grip and fore-end. **Sights:** None on Sporter model. **Features:** Forged steel receiver has integral scope mounts. Magazine has hinged floorplate. Trigger is adjustable. Push-feed action features short extractor and plunger style ejector. Varmint model (.243, .308) has 25.6-in. barrel, detachable box magazine.
Price: Sporter, walnut stock **$832.00**
Price: Synthetic stock **$779.00**
Price: Varmint model...**$865.00**

FIERCE FIREARMS CARBON FURY
Calibers: .300 PRC, 6.5 Creedmoor, 6.5 PRC, 7MM Rem. Mag, .300 Win. Mag, .300 RUM, .300 WSM, 28 Nosler. **Capacity:** 4 to 5. **Barrel:** 24 to 26 in., stainless steel liner, carbon-fiber overlay. **Stock:** Carbon-fiber Monte Carlo. **Sights:** None, drilled and tapped. **Weight:** 6.6 lbs. **Features:** Guaranteed half-inch three-shot group at 100 yards; target crown for accuracy.
Price: **$2,740.00**

FIERCE FIREARMS RIVAL
Calibers: 6.5 Creedmoor, 6.5 PRC, 7mm Rem., 28 Nosler, .300 Win., .300 PRC, .300 RUM. **Capacity:** 4 to 5. **Barrel:** 20 to 26 in., spiral-fluted, match-grade stainless steel or carbon fiber. **Stock:** Fierce Tech C3 carbon fiber. **Sights:** None, drilled and tapped. **Weight:** 6.4 to 7 lbs. **Features:** Cerakote finish, Trigger Tech trigger, built-in bipod rail.
Price: ....**$2,295.99-$2,795.99**

FRANCHI MOMENTUM ELITE
Calibers: 6.5 Creedmoor, .308 Win., .223 Rem. **Capacity:** 3+1, 4+1. **Barrel:** 22 to 24 in., threaded, free-floating with Cerakote finish. **Stock:** Synthetic, ergonomic. **Sights:** One-piece Picatinny rail. **Weight:** 7.1 to 7.5 lbs. **Features:** TSA recoil pad, hinged floorplate, multiple camo stock options.
Price: ....**$849.99-$899.99**

FRANCHI MOMENTUM
Calibers: .243 Win., 6.5 Creedmoor, .270 Win., .308 Win., .30-06, .300 Win. Mag. **Barrels:** 22 or 24 in. **Weights:** 6.5–7.5 lbs. **Stock:** Black synthetic with checkered gripping surface, recessed sling swivel studs, TSA recoil pad. **Sights:** None. **Features:** Available with Burris Fullfield II 3-9X40mm scope.
Price: Varminter..**$609.00**
Price: With Burris 3-9X scope...**$729.00**

HEYM EXPRESS BOLT-ACTION RIFLE
Calibers: .375 H&H Mag., .416 Rigby, .404 Jeffery, .458 Lott, .450 Rigby. **Capacity:** 5. **Barrel:** 24 in., Krupp steel, hammer-forged. **Stock:** Custom select European walnut. **Sights:** Iron, barrel-banded front. **Weight:** 9 to 10.5 lbs. **Features:** Caliber-specific action and magazine box, classic English sporting rifle, three-position safety.
Price: From..**$12,000.00**

HOWA MINI ACTION FULL DIP
Calibers: .223 Rem., 6.5 Grendel, 7.62x39. **Capacity:** 5. **Barrel:** 20 in., threaded, heavy. **Stock:** Hogue pillar-bedded. **Sights:** 3.5-10x44 scope. **Weight:** 10 lbs. **Features:** Full-dipped camo, forged, one-piece bolt with locking lugs.
Price: **$769.99**

CENTERFIRE RIFLES Bolt Action

HOWA HS CARBON FIBER
Caliber: 6.5 Creedmoor. **Capacity:** 4. **Barrel:** 24 in., carbon-fiber wrapped. **Stock:** Synthetic, CNC-machined aluminum bedding block. **Sights:** None, drilled and tapped. **Weight:** 7.8 lbs. **Features:** Lightweight, hand-finished stock, scope optional.
Price: **$1,819.99**

HOWA/HOGUE KRYPTEK RIFLE
Calibers: Most popular calibers from .204 Ruger to .375 Ruger. **Barrel:** 20, 22 or 24 in., blue or stainless. **Stock:** Hogue overmolded in Kryptek Camo. **Features:** Three-position safety, two-stage match trigger, one-piece bolt with two locking lugs.
Price: **$672.00**
Price: Magnum calibers **$700.00**
Price: Stainless from **$736.00**

HOWA ALPINE MOUNTAIN RIFLE
Calibers: .243 Win., 6.5 Creedmoor, 7mm-08, .308 Win. **Barrel:** 20 in. **Weight:** 5.7 lbs. **Stock:** OD Green synthetic. **Features:** Two-stage HACT trigger, Cerakote finish on barrel and action, Pachmyr Decelerator pad.
Price: Stainless, From **$1,188.00**

H-S PRECISION PRO-SERIES 2000
Calibers: 30 different chamberings including virtually all popular calibers. Made in hunting, tactical and competition styles with many options. **Barrels:** 20 in., 22 in., 24 in. or 26 in. depending on model and caliber. Hunting models include the Pro-Hunter Rifle (PHR) designed for magnum calibers with built-in recoil reducer and heavier barrel; Pro-Hunter Lightweight (PHL) with slim, fluted barrel; Pro-Hunter Sporter (SPR) and Pro-Hunter Varmint (VAR). Takedown, Competition and Tactical variations are available. **Stock:** H-S Precision synthetic stock in many styles and colors with full-length bedding block chassis system. Made in USA
Price: PHR **$3,795.00**
Price: PHL **$3,895.00**
Price: SPR **$3,495.00**
Price: SPL Sporter **$3,595.00**
Price: VAR **$3,595.00**
Price: PTD Hunter Takedown... **$3,595.00**
Price: STR Short Tactical **$3,895.00**
Price: HTR Heavy Tactical **$3,895.00**
Price: Competition... **$3,895.00**

KENNY JARRETT RIFLES
Calibers: Custom built in virtually any chambering including .223 Rem., .243 Improved, .243 Catbird, 7mm-08 Improved, .280 Remington, .280 Ackley Improved, 7mm Rem. Mag., .284 Jarrett, .30-06 Springfield, .300 Win. Mag., .300 Jarrett, .323 Jarrett, .338 Jarrett, .375 H&H, .416 Rem., .450 Rigby, other modern cartridges. Numerous options regarding barrel type and weight, stock styles and material. **Features:** Tri-Lock receiver. Talley rings and bases. Accuracy guarantees and custom loaded ammunition. Newest series is the Shikar featuring 28-year aged American Black walnut hand-checkered stock with Jarrett-designed stabilizing aluminum chassis. Accuracy guaranteed to be .5 MOA with standard calibers, .75 MOA with magnums.
Price: Shikar Series **$10,320.00**
Price: Signature Series... **$8,320.00**
Price: Long Ranger Series **$8,320.00**
Price: Ridge Walker Series... **$8,320.00**
Price: Wind Walker **$8,320.00**
Price: Original Beanfield (customer's receiver) **$6,050.00**
Price: Professional Hunter... **$11,070.00**
Price: SA/Custom **$7,000.00**

KIMBER MODEL 8400
Calibers: .25-06 Rem., .270 Win., 7mm, .30-06, .300 Win. Mag., .338 Win. Mag., or .325 WSM. **Capacity:** 4. **Barrel:** 24 in. **Weights:** 6 lbs., 3 oz.–6 lbs., 10 oz. **Length:** 43.25 in. **Stocks:** Claro walnut or Kevlar-reinforced fiberglass. **Sights:** None; drilled and tapped for bases. **Features:** Mauser claw extractor, two-position wing safety, action bedded on aluminum pillars and fiberglass, free-floated barrel, match-grade adjustable trigger set at 4 lbs., matte or polished blue or matte stainless finish. Introduced 2003. Sonora model (2008) has brown laminated stock, hand-rubbed oil finish, chambered in .25-06 Rem., .30-06, and .300 Win. Mag. Weighs 8.5 lbs., measures 44.50 in. overall length. Front swivel stud only for bipod. Stainless steel bull barrel, 24 in. satin stainless finish. Made in USA by Kimber Mfg. Inc.
Price: Classic **$1,223.00**
Price: Classic Select Grade, French walnut stock (2008) **$1,427.00**
Price: SuperAmerica, AAA walnut stock **$2,240.00**
Price: Patrol Tactical **$2,447.00**
Price: Montana **$1,427.00**

KIMBER MODEL 8400 TALKEETNA
Similar to Model 8400. **Caliber:** .375 H&H. **Capacity:** 4-round magazine. **Weight:** 8 lbs. **Length:** 44.5 in. **Stock:** Synthetic. **Features:** Free-floating match-grade barrel with tapered match-grade chamber and target crown, three-position wing safety acts directly on the cocking piece for greatest security, and Pachmayr Decelerator. Made in USA by Kimber Mfg. Inc
Price: **$2,175.00**

KIMBER MODEL 84M
Calibers: .22-250 Rem., .204 Ruger, .223 Rem., .243 Win., 6.5 Creedmoor, .257 Roberts., .260 Rem., 7mm-08 Rem., .308 Win., .300 AAC Blackout. **Capacity:** 5. **Barrels:** 22 in., 24 in., 26 in. **Weight:** 4 lbs., 13 oz.–8 lbs. **Lengths:** 41–45 in. **Stock:** Claro walnut, checkered with steel grip cap; synthetic or gray laminate. **Sights:** None; drilled and tapped for bases. **Features:** Mauser claw extractor, three-position wing safety, action bedded on aluminum pillars, free-floated barrel, match-grade trigger set at 4 lbs., matte blue finish. Includes cable lock. Introduced 2001. Montana (2008) has synthetic stock, Pachmayr Decelerator recoil pad, stainless steel 22-in. sporter barrel. Adirondack has Kevlar white/black Optifade Forest camo stock, 18-in. barrel with threaded muzzle, weighs less than 5 lbs. Made in USA by Kimber Mfg. Inc.
Price: Classic **$1,223.00**
Price: Varmint **$1,291.00**
Price: Montana **$1,427.00**
Price: Mountain Ascent.. **$2,040.00**
Price: SuperAmerica **$2,240.00**

KIMBER MODEL 84M HUNTER
Calibers: .243 Win., .257 Roberts., 6.5 Creedmoor, 7mm-08, .280 Ackley Imp., .308 Win. **Capacity:** 3 + 1, removable box type. **Barrel:** 22 in. **Weight:** 6.5 lbs. **Stock:** FDE Polymer with recoil pad, pillar bedding. **Finish:** Stainless. Other features include Mauser-type claw extractor, M70-type 3-position safety, adjustable trigger.
Price: **$973.00**

KIMBER MODEL 84L CLASSIC
Calibers: .270 Win., .30-06. **Capacity:** 5-round magazine. **Features:** Bolt-action rifle. 24-in. sightless matte blue sporter barrel; hand-rubbed A-grade walnut stock with 20 LPI panel checkering; pillar and glass bedding; Mauser claw extractor; 3-position M70-style safety; adjustable trigger.
Price: **$1,427.00**

KIMBER ADVANCED TACTICAL SOC/SRC II
Calibers: 6.5 Creedmoor, .308 Win. SRC chambered only in .308. **Capacity:** 5-round magazine. **Barrel:** 22-in. (SOC) stainless steel, (18 in. (SRC) with threaded muzzle. **Stock:** Side-folding aluminum with adjustable comb. **Features:** Stainless steel action, matte black or Flat Dark Earth finish. 3-position Model 70-type safety.
Price: **$2,449.00**

KIMBER OPEN RANGE PRO CARBON
Calibers: 6.5 Creedmoor, .308 Win. **Capacity:** 4. **Barrel:** 24 in., carbon-fiber wrapped, Proof Research. **Stock:** Carbon fiber. **Sights:** None, drilled and tapped. **Weight:** 6 lbs. **Features:** Sub-MOA accuracy, 84M stainless controlled-round-feed action, three-position safety.
Price: **$3,099.99**

Prices given are believed to be accurate at time of publication however, many factors affect retail pricing so exact prices are not possible.

CENTERFIRE RIFLES Bolt Action

MAUSER M-03 SERIES
Calibers: .243, 6.5x55SE, .270 Win., 7x64mm, 7mm Rem. Mag., .308 Win., .30-06, .300 Win Mag., 8x57mm IS, .338 Win. Mag. 9.3x62mm. **Capacity:** 5-round magazine. **Barrels:** 22 in., 18.5 in. (Trail Model). **Stock:** Grade 2 walnut with ebony tip, or synthetic. **Features:** Classic Mauser design with Mag Safe magazine lock, adjustable rear and ramp front sights.
Price: Extreme (synthetic) $3,745.00
Price: Pure (walnut) $4,941.00
Price: Trail (polymer w/orange pads) $4,410.00

MAUSER M-12 PURE
Calibers: .22-250, .243, 6.5x55SE, .270 Win., 7x64mm, 7mm Rem. Mag., .308 Win., .30-06, .300 Win Mag., 8x57mm IS, .338 Win. Mag. 9.3x62mm. **Capacity:** 5-round magazine. **Barrel:** 22 in. **Sights:** Adjustable rear, blade front. **Stock:** Walnut with ebony fore-end tip.
Price: $1,971.00

MAUSER M-18
Calibers: .243, .270 Win., 7mm Rem. Mag., .308 Win., .30-06, .300 Win Mag. **Capacity:** 5-round magazine. **Barrel:** 21.75 or 24.5 in. **Weight:** 6.5 lbs. **Stock:** Polymer 2 with grip inlays. **Features:** Adjustable trigger, 3-position safety, recessed 3-lug bolt head chiseled from full diameter body.
Price: $699.00

MERKEL RX HELIX Calibers: .223 Rem., .243 Rem., 6.5x55, 7mm-08, .308 Win., .270 Win., .30-06, 9.3x62, 7mm Rem. Mag., .300 Win. Mag., .270 WSM, .300 WSM, .338 Win. Mag. **Features:** Straight-pull bolt action. Synthetic stock on Explorer model. Walnut stock available in several grades. Factory engraved models available. Takedown system allows switching calibers in minutes.
Price: Explorer, synthetic stock, From $3,360.00
Price: Walnut stock, From $3,870.00

MOSSBERG MVP SERIES
Caliber: .223/5.56 NATO. **Capacity:** 10-round AR-style magazines. **Barrels:** 16.25-in. medium bull, 20-in. fluted sporter. **Weight:** 6.5–7 lbs. **Stock:** Classic black textured polymer. **Sights:** Adjustable folding rear, adjustable blade front. **Features:** Available with factory mounted 3-9x32 scope, (4-16x50 on Varmint model). FLEX model has 20-in. fluted sporter barrel, FLEX AR-style 6-position adjustable stock. Varmint model has laminated stock, 24-in. barrel. Thunder Ranch model has 18-in. bull barrel, OD Green synthetic stock.
Price: Patrol Model $732.00
Price: Patrol Model w/scope $863.00
Price: FLEX Model $764.00
Price: FLEX Model w/scope $897.00
Price: Thunder Ranch Model $755.00
Price: Predator Model $732.00
Price: Predator Model w/scope $872.00
Price: Varmint Model $753.00
Price: Varmint Model w/scope $912.00
Price: Long Range Rifle (LR) $974.00

MOSSBERG PATRIOT
Calibers: .22-250, .243 Win., .25-06, .270 Win., 7mm-08, .7mm Rem., .308 Win., .30-06, .300 Win. Mag., .38 Win. Mag., .375 Ruger. **Capacities:** 4- or

5-round magazine. **Barrels:** 22-in. sporter or fluted. **Stock:** Walnut, laminate, camo or synthetic black. **Weights:** 7.5–8 lbs. **Finish:** Matte blued. **Sights:** Adjustable or none. Some models available with 3-9x40 scope. Other features include patented Lightning Bolt Action Trigger adjustable from 2 to 7 pounds, spiral-fluted bolt. Not all variants available in all calibers. Introduced in 2015.
Price: Walnut stock $438.00
Price: Walnut with premium Vortex Crossfire scope $649.00
Price: Synthetic stock $396.00
Price: Synthetic stock with standard scope $436.00
Price: Laminate stock w/iron sights $584.00
Price: Deer THUG w/Mossy Oak Infinity Camo stock $500.00
Price: Bantam, From $396.00

MOSSBERG PATRIOT LONG RANGE HUNTER
Calibers: .308 Win., 6.5 Creedmoor, 6.5 PRC, .300 Win. Mag. **Capacity:** 3 to 5. **Barrel:** 22 to 24 in., blued, fluted. **Stock:** Monte Carlo. **Sights:** Picatinny rail. **Weight:** 6.5 to 7.5 lbs. **Features:** Dual swivel studs, aluminum pillar bedding, bench rest-type fore-end.
Price: $721.00

MOSSBERG PATRIOT NIGHT TRAIN
Calibers: .308 Win. or .300 Win. Mag. **Features:** Tactical model with Silencerco Saker Muzzle brake, 6-24x50 scope with tactical turrets, green synthetic stock with Neoprene comb-raising kit. **Weight:** 9 lbs.
Price: Night Train with 6-24x50 scope $811.00

NESIKA SPORTER RIFLE
Calibers: .260 Rem., 6.5x284, 7mm-08, .280 Rem., 7mm Rem. Mag., 308 Win., .30-06, .300 Win. Mag. **Barrels:** 24 or 26 in. Douglas air-gauged stainless. **Stock:** Composite with aluminum bedding block. **Sights:** None, Leupold QRW bases. **Weight:** 8 lbs. **Features:** Timney trigger set at 3 pounds, receiver made from 15-5 stainless steel, one-piece bolt from 4340 CM steel. Guaranteed accuracy at 100 yards.
Price: $3,499.00
Price: Long Range w/heavy bbl., varmint stock $3,999.00
Price: Tactical w/28î bbl., muzzle brake, adj. stock $4,499.00

NEW ULTRA LIGHT ARMS
Calibers: Custom made in virtually every current chambering. **Barrel:** Douglas, length to order. **Weights:** 4.75–7.5 lbs. **Length:** Varies. **Stock:** Kevlar graphite composite, variety of finishes. **Sights:** None furnished; drilled and tapped for scope mounts. **Features:** Timney trigger, hand-lapped action, button-rifled barrel, hand-bedded action, recoil pad, sling-swivel studs, optional Jewell trigger. Made in USA by New Ultra Light Arms.
Price: Model 20 Ultimate Mountain Rifle $3,500.00
Price: Model 20 Ultimate Varmint Rifle $3,500.00
Price: Model 24 Ultimate Plains Rifle $3,600.00
Price: Model 28 Ultimate Alaskan Rifle $3,900.00
Price: Model 40 Ultimate African Rifle $3,900.00

NOSLER MODEL 48 SERIES
Calibers: Offered in most popular calibers including .280 Ackley Improved and 6.5-284 wildcats. **Barrel:** 24 in. Long Range 26 in. **Weight:** 7.25–8 lbs. **Stock:** Walnut or composite. Custom Model is made to order with several optional features.
Price: Heritage $2,035.00
Price: Custom Model from $2,595.00
Price: Long Range $2,675.00

Prices given are believed to be accurate at time of publication however, many factors affect retail pricing so exact prices are not possible.

75TH EDITION, 2021 ✦ **419**

REMINGTON MODEL 700 CDL CLASSIC DELUXE

Calibers: .243 Win., .270 Win., 7mm-08 Rem., 7mm Rem. Mag., .30-06, .300 Win. Mag. **Barrels:** 24 in. or 26-in. round tapered. **Weights:** 7.4–7.6 lbs. **Lengths:** 43.6–46.5 in. overall. **Stocks:** Straight-comb American walnut stock, satin finish, checkering, right-handed cheekpiece, black fore-end tip and grip cap, sling swivel studs. **Sights:** None. **Features:** Satin blued finish, jeweled bolt body, drilled and tapped for scope mounts. Hinged-floorplate magazine capacity: 4, standard calibers; 3, magnum calibers. SuperCell recoil pad, cylindrical receiver, integral extractor. Introduced 2004. CDL SF (stainless fluted) chambered for .260 Rem., .257 Wby. Mag., .270 Win., .270 WSM, 7mm-08 Rem., 7mm Rem. Mag., .30-06, .300 WSM. Left-hand versions introduced 2008 in six calibers. Made in U.S. by Remington Arms Co., Inc.
Price: Standard Calibers, From .... **$1,029.00–$1,089.00**
Price: CDL SF, From **$1,226.00**

REMINGTON MODEL 700 BDL

Calibers: .243 Win., .270 Win., 7mm Rem. Mag., .30-06, **Barrels:** 22 in., 24 in., 26-in. round tapered. **Weights:** 7.25–7.4 lbs. **Lengths:** 41.6–46.5 in. overall. **Stock:** Walnut. Gloss-finish pistol grip stock with skip-line checkering, black forend tip and grip cap with white line spacers. Quick-release floorplate. **Sights:** Gold bead ramp front; hooded ramp, removable step-adjustable rear with windage screw. **Features:** Side safety, receiver tapped for scope mounts, matte receiver top, quick detachable swivels.
Price: Standard Calibers **$994.00**

REMINGTON MODEL 700 SPS

Calibers: .22-250 Rem., 6.8 Rem SPC, .223 Rem., .243 Win., .270 Win., .270 WSM, 7mm-08 Rem., 7mm Rem. Mag., 7mm Rem. Ultra Mag., .30-06, .308 Win., .300 WSM, .300 Win. Mag., .300 Rem. Ultra Mag. Barrels: 20 in., 24 in. or 26 in. carbon steel. **Weights:** 7–7.6 lbs. **Lengths:** 39.6–46.5 in. overall. **Stock:** Black synthetic, sling swivel studs, SuperCell recoil pad. Woodtech model has walnut decorated synthetic stock with overmolded grip patterns. Camo stock available. **Sights:** None. **Barrel:** Bead-blasted 416 stainless steel. **Features:** Introduced 2005. SPS Stainless replaces Model 700 BDL Stainless Synthetic. Plated internal fire control component. SPS DM features detachable box magazine. SPS Varmint includes X-Mark Pro trigger, 26-in. heavy contour barrel, vented beavertail fore-end, dual front sling swivel studs. Made in U.S. by Remington Arms Co., Inc.
Price: From .... **$724.00–$838.00**

REMINGTON 700 SPS TACTICAL

Calibers: .223 .300 AAC Blackout and .308 Win. **Features:** 20-in. heavy-contour tactical-style barrel; dual-point pillar bedding; black synthetic stock with Hogue overmoldings; semi-beavertail fore-end; X-Mark Pro adjustable trigger system; satin black oxide metal finish; hinged floorplate magazine; SuperCell recoil pad.
Price: From .... **$788.00–$842.00**

REMINGTON MODEL 700 VTR SERIES

Calibers: .204 Ruger, .22-250, .223 Rem., .260 Rem., .308 Win. **Barrel:** 22-in. triangular counterbored with integrated muzzle brake. **Weight:** 7.5 lbs. **Length:** 41.625 in. overall. **Features:** FDE stock with black overmold strips and carbon steel barrel, or with black stock with gray grips and stainless barrel. ented semi-beavertail fore-end, tactical-style dual swivel mounts for bipod, matte blue on exposed metal surfaces.
Price: From **$930.00**

REMINGTON MODEL 700 VARMINT SF

Calibers: .22-250, .223, .220 Swift, .308 Win. **Barrel:** 26-in. stainless steel fluted. **Weight:** 8.5 lbs. **Length:** 45.75 in. **Features:** Synthetic stock with ventilated forend, stainless steel/trigger guard/floorplate, dual tactical swivels for bipod attachment.
Price: **$991.00**

REMINGTON MODEL 700 MOUNTAIN SS

Calibers: 6.5 Creedmoor, .25-06, .270 Win., .280 Rem., 7mm-08, .308 Win., .30-06. **Barrel:** 22 in. **Length:** 40.6 in. **Weight:** 6.5 lbs. **Features:** Satin stainless finish, Bell & Carlson Aramid Fiber stock.
Price: From... **$1,152.00**

REMINGTON MODEL 700 XCR TACTICAL

Calibers: .308 Win., .300 Win. Mag., 338 Lapua Mag. Detachable box magazine on Lapua model. **Barrel:** 26-in. varmint contour, fluted and free floating. **Features:** Tactical, long-range precision rifle with Bell & Carlson Tactical stock in OD Green, full-length aluminum bedding, adjustable X-Mark Pro trigger. Muzzle brake on .338 Lapua model.
Price: **$1,540.00**
Price: .338 Lapua **$2,515.00**

REMINGTON MODEL 700 AWR

Calibers: .270 Win., .30-06, .300 Win. Mag., .300 Rem. Ultra Mag., .338 RUM, .338 Win. Mag. **Barrel:** 24- or 26-in. free floating. **Features:** Adjustable trigger, fiberglass stock. American Wilderness Rifle.
Price: **$1,150.00**

REMINGTON MODEL 700 LONG RANGE

Calibers: .25-06 Rem., 7mm Rem. Mag., .30-06, .300 Win. Mag., .300 Rem. Ultra Mag. **Barrel:** 26-in. heavy contour with concave target-style crown. **Weight:** 9 lbs. **Features:** Bell and Carlson M40 tactical stock, externally adjustable trigger, aluminum bedding block.
Price: **$880.00**

REMINGTON MODEL 783

Calibers: .223 Rem., .22-250, .243 Win., .270 Win., 7mm Rem. Mag., .308 Win., .30-06, .300 Win. Mag. **Barrel:** 22 in. **Stock:** Synthetic. **Weight:** 7–7.25 lbs. **Finish:** Matte black. **Features:** Adjustable trigger with two-position trigger-block safety, magnum contour button-rifle barrel, cylindrical receiver with minimum-size ejection port, pillar-bedded stock, detachable box magazine, 90-degree bolt throw.
Price: **$399.00**
Price: Compact with 18.25- or 20-in. bbl........................... **$399.00**

REMINGTON MODEL SEVEN CDL

Calibers: .243, .260 Rem., 7mm-08, .308 Win. **Barrel:** 20 in. **Weight:** 6.5 lbs. **Length:** 39.25 in. **Stock:** Walnut with black fore-end tip, satin finish. **Features:** Lightweight barrel has 16.5-in. barrel with threaded muzzle, synthetic camo stock, is available in .300 AAC Blackout chambering.
Price: CDL.. **$1,039.00**
Price: Synthetic stock **$731.00**
Price: Synthetic stock/stainless.. **$838.00**
Price: Lightweight/threaded **$795.00**

REMINGTON 40-XB TACTICAL

Caliber: .308 Win. **Features:** Stainless steel bolt with Teflon coating; hinged floorplate; adjustable trigger; 27.25-in. tri-fluted 1:14 in. twist barrel; H-S Precision Pro Series tactical stock, black color with dark green spiderweb; two front swivel studs; one rear swivel stud; vertical pistol grip. From the Remington Custom Shop.
Price: **$3,195.00**

REMINGTON 40-X TIR

Caliber: .308 Win. **Features:** Adjustable trigger, 24-in. match-grade, hand-lapped barrel, AAC 51T muzzle brake adaptor, H-S Precision PST tactical stock with adjustable length-of-pull and cheek piece, vertical pistol grip, clip-slotted Picatinny rail. Target Interdiction Rifle from the Remington Custom Shop.
Price: **$4,095.00**

Prices given are believed to be accurate at time of publication however, many factors affect retail pricing so exact prices are not possible.

REMINGTON 40-XB RANGEMASTER

Calibers: Almost any caliber from .22 BR Rem. to .300 Rem. Ultra Mag. Single-shot or repeater. **Features:** Stainless steel bolt with Teflon coating; hinged floorplate; adjustable trigger; 27.25-in. tri-fluted 1:14 in. twist barrel; walnut stock. From the Remington Custom Shop.

Price: **$2,595.00**
Price: Repeater **$2,717.00**

REMINGTON 40-XS TACTICAL SERIES

Caliber: .338 Lapua Magnum. **Features:** 416 stainless steel Model 40-X 24-in. 1:12 in. twist barreled action; black polymer coating; McMillan A3 series stock with adjustable length of pull and adjustable comb; adjustable trigger and Sunny Hill heavy-duty, all-steel trigger guard; Tactical Weapons System has Harris bi-pod with quick adjust swivel lock, Leupold Mark IV 3.5-10x40 long range M1 scope with Mil-Dot reticle, Badger Ordnance all-steel Picatinny scope rail and rings, military hard case, Turner AWS tactical sling. From the Remington Custom Shop.

Price: .308 Win. **$4,400.00**
Price: .338 Lapua **$4,995.00**
Price: Tactical Weapons System, From **$7,695.00**

ROCK ISLAND ARMORY TCM

Caliber: .22 TCM. **Capacity:** 5-round magazine, interchangeable with .22 TCM 17-round pistol magazine. **Barrel:** 22.75 in. **Weight:** 6 lbs. **Features:** Introduced in 2013. Manufactured in the Philippines and imported by Armscor Precision International.

Price: **$450.00**

RUGER HAWKEYE LONG-RANGE HUNTER

Calibers: 6.5 Creedmoor, 6.5 PRC. **Capacity:** 3 to 5. **Barrel:** 22 in., stainless steel, threaded. **Stock:** Speckled wood laminate. **Sights:** 20 MOA Picatinny rail. **Weight:** 7.2 lbs. **Features:** Three position safety, non-rotating Mauser-type controlled-round-feed extractor.

Price: **$1,279.99**

RUGER PRECISION RIFLE

Calibers: 6mm Creedmoor, 6.5 Creedmoor, 6.5 PRC, .300 PRC, .308 Win., .300 Win. Mag., .338 Lapua Mag. **Capacity:** 10-round magazine. **Barrel:** Medium contour 20 in. (.308), 24 in. (6mm, 6.5), 26 in. (PRC & Magnums). **Stock:** Folding with adjustable length of pull and comb height. Soft rubber buttplate, sling attachment points, Picatinny bottom rail. **Weight:** 9.7–11 lbs. **Features:** Three lug one-piece CNC-machined bolt with oversized handle, dual cocking cams; multi-magazine interface works with Magpul, DPMS, SR-25, M110, AICS and some M14 magazines; CNC-machined 4140 chrome-moly steel upper; Ruger Marksman adjustable trigger with wrench stored in bolt shroud; comes with two 10-round Magpul magazines. Introduced in 2016.

Price: .308, Creedmoor and PRC calibers **$1,599.00**
Price: With muzzle brake **$1,799.00**
Price: Magnum calibers **$2,099.00**

RUGER AMERICAN RIFLE

Calibers: .22-250, .243, 7mm-08, .308, .270 Win., .30-06, .300 Win. Mag, .350 Legend, .450 Bushmaster. **Capacity:** 4-round rotary magazine. **Barrels:** 22 in. or 18 in. (Compact). **Length:** 42.5 in. **Weight:** 6.25 lbs. **Stock:** Black composite. **Finish:** Matte black or matte stainless (All Weather model). **Features:** Tang safety, hammer-forged free-floating barrel. Available with factory mounted Redfield Revolution 4x scope. Ranch model has Flat Dark Earth composite stock, Predator has Moss Green composite stock, both chambered in several additional calibers to standard model.

Price: Standard or compact.. **$489.00**
Price: With scope... **$639.00**
Price: Ranch or Predator model **$529.00**
Price: .300 Win. Mag. **$699.00**

RUGER GUNSITE SCOUT RIFLE

Caliber: .308 Win. **Capacity:** 10-round magazine. **Barrel:** 16.5 in. **Weight:** 7 lbs. **Length:** 38–39.5 in. **Stock:** Black laminate. **Sights:** Front post sight and rear adjustable. **Features:** Gunsite Scout Rifle is a credible rendition of Col. Jeff Cooper's "fighting carbine" scout rifle. The Ruger Gunsite Scout Rifle is a platform in the Ruger M77 family. While the Scout Rifle has M77 features such as controlled round feed and integral scope mounts (scope rings included), the 10-round detachable box magazine is the first clue this isn't your grandfather's Ruger rifle. The Ruger Gunsite Scout Rifle has a 16.5-in. medium contour, cold hammer-forged, alloy steel barrel with a Mini-14 protected nonglare post front sight and receiver mounted, adjustable ghost ring rear sight for out-of-the-box usability. A forward-mounted Picatinny rail offers options in mounting an assortment of optics, including scout scopes available from Burris and Leupold, for "both eyes open" sighting and super-fast target acquisition.

Price: **$1,139.00**
Price: (stainless) **$1,199.00**

RUGER MODEL 77 SERIES

Calibers: .17 Hornet, .22 Hornet, .357 Magnum, .44 Magnum. **Capacities:** 4–6 rounds. **Barrel:** 18.5 in. (.357 and .44 Mag,), 20 or 24 in. (.17 Hornet and .22 Hornet). **Weight:** 5.5–7.5 lbs. **Stock:** American walnut, black synthetic, Next G1 Vista Camo or Green Mountain laminate.

Price: 77/17, Green Mtn. laminate stock........................... **$969.00**
Price: 77/22, Green Mtn. laminate stock **$969.00**
Price: 77/22, walnut stock **$939.00**
Price: 77/357, 77/44, black synthetic stock....................... **$999.00**
Price: 77/44, Next G1 Vista camo **$1,060.00**

RUGER GUIDE GUN

Calibers: .30-06, .300 Win. Mag., .338 Win. Mag., .375 Ruger, .416 Ruger. **Capacities:** 3 or 4 rounds. **Barrel:** 20 in. with barrel band sling swivel and removable muzzle brake. **Weights:** 8–8.12 pounds. **Stock:** Green Mountain laminate. **Finish:** Hawkeye matte stainless. **Sights:** Adjustable rear, bead front. Introduced 2013.

Price: **$1,269.00**

Prices given are believed to be accurate at time of publication however, many factors affect retail pricing so exact prices are not possible.

75TH EDITION, 2021 ⬦ **421**

RUGER HAWKEYE

Calibers: .204 Ruger, .223 Rem., .243 Win., .270 Win., 6.5 Creedmoor, 7mm/08, 7mm Rem. Mag., .308 Win., .30-06, .300 Win. Mag., .338 Win. Mag., .375 Ruger, .416 Ruger. **Capacities:** 4-round magazine, except 3-round magazine for magnums; 5-round magazine for .204 Ruger and .223 Rem. **Barrels:** 22 in., 24 in. **Weight:** 6.75–8.25 lbs. **Length:** 42–44.4 in. overall. **Stock:** American walnut, laminate or synthetic. FTW has camo stock, muzzle brake. Long Range Target has adjustable target stock, heavy barrel. **Sights:** None furnished. Receiver has Ruger integral scope mount base, Ruger 1 in. rings. **Features:** Includes Ruger LC6 trigger, new red rubber recoil pad, Mauser-type controlled feeding, claw extractor, 3-position safety, hammer-forged steel barrels, Ruger scope rings. Walnut stocks have wrap-around cut checkering on the forearm, and more rounded contours on stock and top of pistol grips. Matte stainless all-weather version features synthetic stock. Hawkeye African chambered in .375 Ruger, .416 Ruger and has 23-in. blued barrel, checkered walnut stock, windage-adjustable shallow V-notch rear sight, white bead front sight. Introduced 2007.

Price: Standard, right- and left-hand $939.00
Price: Compact $939.00
Price: Laminate Compact $999.00
Price: Compact Magnum $969.00
Price: VT Varmint Target $1,139.00
Price: Predator $1,139.00
Price: African with muzzle brake $1,279.00
Price: FTW Hunter $1,279.00
Price: Long Range Target $1,279.00

SAKO TRG-22 TACTICAL RIFLE

Calibers: 6.5 Creedmoor, .308 Winchester (TRG-22). For TRG-22A1 add .260 Rem. TRG-42 only available in .300 Win. Mag., or .338 Lapua. **Features:** Target-grade Cr-Mo or stainless barrels with muzzle brake; three locking lugs; 60-degree bolt throw; adjustable two-stage target trigger; adjustable or folding synthetic stock; receiver-mounted integral 17mm axial optics rails with recoil stop-slots; tactical scope mount for modern three-turret tactical scopes (30 and 34 mm tube diameter); optional bipod. 22A1 has folding stock with two-hinge design, M-LOK fore-end, full aluminum middle chassis.

Price: TRG-22 .... $3,495.00
Price: TRG-22A1 .... $6,725.00
Price: TRG-42 .... $4,550.00

SAKO MODEL 85

Calibers: .22-250 Rem., .243 Win., .25-06 Rem., .260 Rem., 6.5x55mm, .270 Win., .270 WSM, 7mm-08 Rem., 7x64, .308 Win., .30-06; 7mm WSM, .300 WSM, .338 Federal, 8x57IS, 9.3x62. **Barrels:** 22.4 in., 22.9 in., 24.4 in. **Weight:** 7.75 lbs. **Length:** NA. **Stock:** Polymer, laminated or high-grade walnut, straight comb, shadow-line cheekpiece. **Sights:** None furnished. **Features:** Controlled-round feeding, adjustable trigger, matte stainless or nonreflective satin blue. Offered in a wide range of variations and models. Introduced 2006. Imported from Finland by Beretta USA.

Price: Grey Wolf $1,725.00
Price: Black Bear $1,850.00
Price: Kodiak $1,950.00
Price: Varmint Laminated $2,025.00
Price: Classic $2,275.00
Price: Bavarian .... $2,200.00–$2,300.00
Price: Bavarian carbine, Full-length stock $2,400.00
Price: Brown Bear $2,175.00

SAKO 85 FINNLIGHT

Similar to the Model 85 but chambered in .243 Win., .25-06, .260 Rem., 6.5 Creedmoor, .270 Win., .270 WSM, .300 WSM, .30-06, .300 WM, .308 Win., 6.5x55mm, 7mm Rem Mag., 7mm-08. **Weights:** 6 lbs., 3 oz.–6 lbs. 13 oz. **Features:** Stainless steel barrel and receiver, black synthetic stock. Finnlight II has composite stock with carbon fiber bedding, adjustable comb.

Price: $1,800.00
Price: Finnlight II $2,475.00

SAVAGE MODEL 110 ULTRALITE

Calibers: .308 Win., .270 Win., 28 Nosler, .280 AI, .30-06, .300 WSM, 6.5 Creedmoor, 6.5 PRC. **Capacity:** 2 to 4. **Barrel:** 22 to 24 in., matte-black, carbon-wrapped stainless steel. **Stock:** Synthetic, AccuFit. **Sights:** None, drilled and tapped, no scope included. **Weight:** 6 lbs. **Features:** Spiral-fluted bolt, detachable box magazine, Proof Research rifled barrel.

Price: $1,499.99

SAVAGE MODEL 110 PRECISION

Calibers: .308 Win., .300 Win. Mag., .338 Lapua, 6.5 Creedmoor. **Capacity:** 5, 8/10. **Barrel:** 20 to 24 in., carbon steel, heavy, threaded. **Stock:** Aluminum chassis. **Sights:** Picatinny rail. **Weight:** 8.9 lbs. **Features:** BA muzzle brake, skeletonized stock with adjustable comb height and LOP.

Price: $1,499.99

SAVAGE AXIS II PRECISION

Calibers: .243 Win., .223 Rem, .270 Win., .30-06, .308 Win., 6.5 Creedmoor. **Capacity:** 5 to 10. **Barrel:** 22 in., carbon steel, button-rifled heavy, threaded w/cap. **Stock:** Aluminum MDT chassis. **Sights:** Picatinny rail. **Weight:** 9.9 lbs. **Features:** AccuTrigger, adjustable comb height and LOP spacers, AICS magazine.

Price: $949.99

SAVAGE AXIS SERIES

Calibers: .243 Win., 6.5 Creedmoor, 7mm-08 Rem., .308 Win., .25-06 Rem., .270 Win, .30-06, .223 Rem., .22-250 Rem. **Barrel:** 22 in. **Weight:** 6.5 lbs. **Length:** 43.875 in. **Stock:** Black synthetic or camo, including pink/black Muddy Girl. **Sights:** Drilled and tapped for scope mounts. Several models come with factory mounted Weaver Kaspa 3-9x40 scope. **Features:** Available with black matte or stainless finish

Price: From .... $363.00–$525.00

SAVAGE CLASSIC SERIES MODEL 14/114

Calibers: .243 Win., 7mm-08 Rem., .308 Win., .270 Win., 7mm Rem. Mag., .30-06, .300 Win. Mag. **Capacities:** 3- or 4-round magazine. **Barrels:** 22

Prices given are believed to be accurate at time of publication however, many factors affect retail pricing so exact prices are not possible.

in. or 24 in. **Weight:** 7–7.5 lbs. **Length:** 41.75–43.75 in. overall (Model 14 short action); 43.25–45.25 in. overall (Model 114 long action). **Stock:** Satin lacquer American walnut with ebony fore-end, wraparound checkering, Monte Carlo comb and cheekpiece. **Sights:** None furnished. Receiver drilled and tapped for scope mounting. **Features:** AccuTrigger, matte blued barrel and action, hinged floorplate.
Price: From...$979.00

SAVAGE MODEL 12 VARMINT/TARGET SERIES
Calibers: .204 Ruger, .223 Rem., .22-250 Rem. **Capacity:** 4-shot magazine. **Barrel:** 26 in. stainless barreled action, heavy fluted, free-floating and button-rifled barrel. **Weight:** 10 lbs. **Length:** 46.25 in. overall. **Stock:** Dual pillar bedded, low profile, black synthetic or laminated stock with extra-wide beavertail fore-end. **Sights:** None furnished; drilled and tapped for scope mounting. **Features:** Recessed target-style muzzle. AccuTrigger, oversized bolt handle, detachable box magazine, swivel studs. Model 112BVSS has heavy target-style prone laminated stock with high comb, Wundhammer palm swell, internal box magazine. Model 12VLP DBM has black synthetic stock, detachable magazine, and additional chamberings in .243, .308 Win., .300 Win. Mag. Model 12FV has blued receiver. Model 12BTCSS has brown laminate vented thumbhole stock. Made in USA by Savage Arms, Inc.
Price: 12 FCV...$780.00
Price: 12 BVSS...$1,146.00
Price: 12 Varminter Low Profile (VLP)....................$1,181.00
Price: 12 Long Range Precision..............................$1,288.00
Price: 12 BTCSS Thumbhole stock..........................$1,293.00
Price: 12 Long Range Precision Varminter.............$1,554.00
Price: 12 F Class...$1,648.00
Price: 12 Palma..$2,147.00

SAVAGE MODEL 10 GRS
Calibers: 6.5 Creedmoor, .308 Win. **Stock:** Synthetic with adjustable comb, vertical pistol grip. **Sights:** None. Picatinny rail atop receiver. **Features:** Designed primarily for Law Enforcement. Detachable box magazine.
Price: $1,450.00

SAVAGE MODEL 10FP/110FP LAW ENFORCEMENT SERIES
Calibers: .223 Rem., .308 Win. (Model 10), 4-round magazine; .25-06 Rem., .300 Win. Mag., (Model 110), 3- or 4-round magazine. **Barrel:** 24 in.; matte blued free-floated heavy barrel and action. **Weight:** 6.5–6.75 lbs. **Length:** 41.75–43.75 in. overall (Model 10); 42.5–44.5 in. overall (Model 110). **Stock:** Black graphite/fiberglass composition, pillar-bedded, positive checkering. **Sights:** None furnished. Receiver drilled and tapped for scope mounting. **Features:** Black matte finish on all metal parts. Double swivel studs on the fore-end for sling and/or bipod mount. Right- or left-hand. Model 110FP introduced 1990. Model 10FP introduced 1998. Model 10FCP HS has HS Precision black synthetic tactical stock with molded alloy bedding system, Leupold 3.5-10x40 black matte scope with Mil Dot reticle, Farrell Picatinny Rail Base, flip-open lens covers, 1.25-in. sling with QD swivels, Harris bipod, Storm heavy-duty case. Made in USA by Savage Arms, Inc.
Price: Model 10FCP McMillan, McMillan fiberglass tactical stock..$1,591.00
Price: Model 10FCP-HS HS Precision, HS Precision tactical stock ...$1,315.00
Price: Model 10FCP $925.00
Price: Model 10FLCP, left-hand model, standard stock
    or Accu-Stock $975.00
Price: Model 10FCP SR $785.00
Price: Model 10 Precision Carbine $952.00

SAVAGE 110 BA STEALTH
Calibers: .300 win, Mag., or .338 Lapua Mag. **Capacities:** Detachable 5- or 6-round box magazine. **Barrel:** 24 in. with threaded muzzle. **Stock:** Fab Defense GLR Shock buttstock, M-LOK fore-end. **Weight:** 11.125 lbs.

Features: Adjustable AccuTrigger, Picatinny rail. Stealth Evolution has fluted heavy barrel, 10-round magazine, adjustable length of pull stock, Flat Dark Earth finish.
Price: Stealth..$1,484.00
Price: Stealth, .338 Lapua....................................$1,624.00
Price: Evolution...$1,999.00
Price: Evolution, .338 Lapua................................$2,149.00

SAVAGE MODEL 10 PREDATOR HUNTER
Calibers: .204 Ruger. .223, .22-250, .243, .260 Rem., 6.5 Creedmoor, 6.5x284 Norma. **Barrel:** 22 in. medium-contour. **Weight:** 7.25 lbs. **Length:** 43 in. overall. **Stock:** Synthetic with Mossy Oak Max-1 Camo coverage. **Features:** AccuTrigger, oversized bolt handle, right or left-hand action.
Price: $999.00

SAVAGE MODEL 110 PREDATOR
Calibers: .204 Ruger. .223, .22-250, .243, .260 Rem., 6.5 Creedmoor. **Capacity:** 4-round magazine. **Barrels:** 22 or 24 in. threaded heavy contour. **Weight:** 8.5 lbs. **Stock:** AccuStock with Mossy Oak Max-1 camo finish, soft grip surfaces, adjustable length of pull.
Price: $899.00

SAVAGE MODEL 110 HUNTER SERIES
Calibers: .204 Ruger. .223, .22-250, .243, .25-06, .260 Rem., 6.5 Creedmoor, .270 Win., 7mm-08 Rem., .280 Ackley Imp., .308 Win., .30-06, .300 Win. Mag. **Capacities:** 3- or 4-round magazine. **Barrels:** 22 or 24. in. **Weight:** 8.5 lbs. **Stock:** AccuStock with gray finish, soft-grip surfaces, adjustable length of pull.
Price: Hunter $749.00
Price: Bear Hunter (.300 WSM, .338 Fed., .375 Ruger $999.00
Price: Hog Hunter (20 in. bbl. open sights) $594.00
Price: Brush Hunter (20-in. bbl., .338 Win., .375 Rug.) ...$784.00
Price: Long Range Hunter (26 in. bbl., muzzle brake) ...$1,099.00

SAVAGE MODEL 110 TACTICAL
Caliber: .308 Win. **Capacity:** 10-round magazine. **Barrels:** 20 or 24 in. threaded and fluted heavy contour. **Weight:** 8.65 lbs. **Stock:** AccuStock with soft-grip surfaces, AccuFit system. **Features:** Top Picatinny rail, right- or left-hand operation.
Price: $784.00
Price: Tactical Desert (6mm, 6.5 Creedmoor, FDE finish ...$769.00

SAVAGE MODEL 12 PRECISION TARGET SERIES BENCHREST
Calibers: .308 Win., 6.5x284 Norma, 6mm Norma BR. **Barrel:** 29-in. ultra-heavy. **Weight:** 12.75 lbs. **Length:** 50 in. overall. **Stock:** Gray laminate. **Features:** New Left-Load, Right-Eject target action, Target AccuTrigger adjustable from approx. 6 oz. to 2.5 lbs. oversized bolt handle, stainless extra-heavy free-floating and button-rifled barrel.
Price: $1,629.00

SAVAGE MODEL 12 PRECISION TARGET PALMA
Similar to Model 12 Benchrest but in .308 Win. only, 30-in. barrel, multi-adjustable stock, weighs 13.3 lbs.
Price: $2,147.00

SAVAGE MODEL 12 F CLASS TARGET RIFLE
Similar to Model 12 Benchrest but chambered in 6 Norma BR, 30-in. barrel, weighs 13.3 lbs.
Price: $1,648.00

Prices given are believed to be accurate at time of publication however, many factors affect retail pricing so exact prices are not possible.

75TH EDITION, 2021 ✛ 423

SAVAGE MODEL 12 F/TR TARGET RIFLE
Similar to Model 12 Benchrest but in .308 Win. only, 30-in. barrel, weighs 12.65 lbs.
Price: **$1,538.00**

SAVAGE MODEL 112 MAGNUM TARGET
Caliber: .338 Lapua Magnum. Single shot. **Barrel:** 26-in. heavy with muzzle brake. **Stock:** Wood laminate. **Features:** AccuTrigger, matte black finish, oversized bolt handle, pillar bedding.
Price: **$1,177.00**

STEYR PRO HUNTER II
Calibers: .223 Rem., 7mm-08 Rem., 6.5 Creedmoor, .308 Win. **Capacity:** 4 to 5. **Barrel:** 20 in., hammer-forged stainless steel. **Stock:** Wood laminate, Boyds. **Sights:** None, drilled and tapped. **Weight:** 7 lbs. **Features:** Three-position safety, crisp 3-lb. trigger.
Price: **$1,199.99**

STEYR SSG08
Calibers: .243 Win., 7.62x51 NATO (.308Win), 7.62x63B (.300 Win Mag)., .338 Lapua Mag. **Capacity:** 10-round magazine. **Barrels:** 20, 23.6 or 25.6 in. **Stock:** Dural aluminum folding stock black with .280 mm long UIT-rail and various Picatinny rails. **Sights:** Front post sight and rear adjustable. **Features:** High-grade aluminum folding stock, adjustable cheekpiece and buttplate with height marking, and an ergonomical exchangeable pistol grip. Versa-Pod, muzzle brake, Picatinny rail, UIT rail on stock and various Picatinny rails on fore-end, and a 10-round HC-magazine. SBS rotary bolt action with four frontal locking lugs, arranged in pairs. Cold-hammer-forged barrels are available in standard or compact lengths.
Price: **$5,899.00**

STEYR SM 12
Calibers: .243, 6.5x55SE, .270 Win., 7mm-08 Rem., .308 Win., .30-06, .300 Win. Mag, .300 WSM, 9.3x62mm. **Barrels:** 20-in. blue or 25-in. stainless. **Stock:** Walnut with checkered grip and fore-end. Available in half or full-length configurations. **Sights:** Adjustable rear, ramp front with bead. Stainless barrel has no sights. **Features:** Sling swivels, Bavarian cheekpiece, hand-cocking system operated by thumb manually cocks firing mechanism.
Price: Standard-length stock............................**$2,545.00**
Price: Full length (Mannlicher) **$2,750.00**

STRASSER RS 14 EVOLUTION STANDARD
Calibers: .222 Rem., .223 Rem., .300 AAC Blackout, .22-250 Rem., .243 Win., 6 XC, 6.5 Creedmoor, .284 Norma, 6.5x55SE, 6.5x65RWS, .270 Win., 7x64, 7mm-08 Rem, .308 Win., .30-06, 8x57 IS, 8.5x63, 9.3x62, 9.3x57, 7mm Rem. Mag., .300 Win. Mag., .375 Ruger, .338 Win. Mag., .458 Win. Mag., 10.3x68. **Capacity:** 3 to 7. **Barrel:** 22 to 24 in., blued. **Stock:** Grade-1 wood, grade-2 wood, standard or thumbhole. **Sights:** Integrated Picatinny rail. **Weight:** 6.75 to 7.725 lbs. **Features:** Barrel-exchange system, adjustable trigger with trigger set, plasma-hardened bolt.
Price: ....**$3,452.99-$4,033.99**

STRASSER RS 14 EVOLUTION TAHR
Calibers: .222 Rem., .223 Rem., .300 AAC Blackout, .22-250 Rem., .243 Win., 6 XC, 6.5 Creedmoor, .284 Norma, 6.5x55SE, 6.5x65RWS, .270 Win., 7x64, 7mm-08 Rem., .308 Win., .30-06, 8x57 IS, 8.5x63, 9.3x62, 9.3x57, 7mm Rem. Mag., .300 Win. Mag., .375 Ruger, .338 Win. Mag., .458 Win. Mag., 10.3x68. **Capacity:** 3 to7. **Barrel:** 22 to 24 in., blued. **Stock:** Laminate, standard or thumbhole. **Sights:** Integrated Picatinny rail. **Weight:** 6.75 to 7.725 lbs. **Features:** Barrel-exchange system, adjustable trigger with trigger set, plasma-hardened bolt.
Price: ....**$3,452.99 to $4,033.99**

THOMPSON/CENTER COMPASS II
Calibers: .223 Rem., 5.56 NATO, .243 Win., .270 Win., .300 Win. Mag., .308 Win., .30-06, 6.5 Creedmoor, 7mm Rem. Mag. **Capacity:** 5 to 6. **Barrel:** 21.625 to 24 in., blued. **Stock:** Composite. **Sights:** Weaver bases or Crimson Trace scope combo. **Weight:** 8 lbs. **Features:** Threaded muzzle, three-lug bolt design, three-position safety.
Price: ....**$405.99 to $575.99**

THOMSON/CENTER COMPASS II COMPACT
Calibers: .223 Rem., 5.56 NATO, .243 Win., .308 Win., 6.5 Creedmoor. **Capacity:** 6. **Barrel:** 16.5 in., blued. **Stock:** Composite. **Sights:** Weaver bases or Crimson Trace scope combo. **Weight:** 6.5 lbs. **Features:** 5R rifling, compact size, Generation II trigger.
Price: ....**$405.99 to $575.99**

THOMPSON/CENTER COMPASS UTILITY
Calibers: .223 Rem., 5.56 NATO, .243 Win., .270 Win., 6.5 Creedmoor, .308 Win., .30-06. **Capacity:** 6. **Barrel:** 21.625 in., blued. **Stock:** Composite. **Sights:** Weaver bases or T/C scope combo. **Weight:** 8 lbs. **Features:** 5R rifling, flush-fit rotary magazine, three-stage trigger.
Price: ....**$359.99 to $459.99**

THOMPSON/CENTER VENTURE II
Calibers: .223 Rem., 5.56 NATO, .243 Win., .270 Win., 6.5 Creedmoor, .308 Win., .30-06, 7mm Rem. Mag., .300 Win. Mag., .350 Legend. **Capacity:** 4. **Barrel:** 22 to 24 in., Weather-Shield stainless steel. **Stock:** Composite with Hogue panels. **Sights:** None. **Weight:** 7.3 lbs. **Features:** American made, Generation II trigger.
Price: **$525.99**

THOMPSON/CENTER VENTURE MEDIUM ACTION
Calibers: .204, .22-250, .223, .243, 7mm-08, .308 and 30TC. **Capacity:** 3+1 detachable nylon box magazine. **Features:** Bolt-action rifle with a 24-in. crowned medium weight barrel, classic-styled composite stock with inlaid traction grip panels, adjustable 3.5- to 5-pound trigger along with a drilled and tapped receiver (bases included). **Weight:** 7 lbs. **Length:** 43.5 in.
Price: **$537.00**

THOMPSON/CENTER VENTURE PREDATOR PDX
Calibers: .204, .22-250, .223, .243, .308. **Weight:** 8 lbs. **Length:** 41.5 in. **Features:** Bolt-action rifle similar to Venture medium action but with heavy, deep-fluted 22-in. barrel and Max-1 camo finish overall.
Price: From..**$638.00**

Prices given are believed to be accurate at time of publication however, many factors affect retail pricing so exact prices are not possible.

THOMPSON/CENTER LONG RANGE RIFLE
Calibers: .243 Win., 6.5 Creedmoor, .308 Win. **Capacity:** 10-round magazine. **Barrel:** 20 in. (.308), 22 in. (6.5), 24 in. (.243). Fluted and threaded with muzzle brake. **Weight:** 11-12 lbs. **Stock:** Composite black with adjustable cheek piece and buttplate, built-in Magpul M-LOK accessory slots. **Finish:** Black or Flat Dark Earth. **Features:** Picatinny-style rail, adjustable trigger, Caldwell Pic Rail XLA bipod. From the T/C Performance Center.
Price: **$1,211.00**

THOMPSON/CENTER COMPASS
Calibers: .204 Ruger, .223 Rem, .22-250 Rem., .243 Win., 6.5 Creedmoor, .270 Win., 7mm-08 Rem., 7mm Rem. Mag., .308 Win., .30-06, .300 Win. Mag. **Capacity:** 4-5-round detachable magazine. **Barrel:** Match-grade 22 in., (24 in. magnums.) with threaded muzzle. **Weight:** 7 ¼-7 1/2 lbs. **Stock:** Composite black with textured grip panels.
Price: From.. **$399.00**

TIKKA T3X SERIES
Calibers: Virtually any popular chambering including .204 Ruger .222 Rem., .223 Rem., .243 Win., .25-06, 6.5x55 SE, .260 Rem, .270 Win., .260 WSM, 7mm-08, 7mm Rem. Mag., .308 Win., .30-06, .300 Win. Mag., .300 WSM. **Barrels:** 20, 22.4, 24.3 in. **Stock:** Checkered walnut, laminate or modular synthetic with interchangeable pistol grips. Newly designed recoil pad. **Features:** Offered in a variety of different models with many options. Left-hand models available. One minute-of-angle accuracy guaranteed. Introduced in 2016. Made in Finland by Sako. Imported by Beretta USA.
Price: Hunter from.. **$875.00**
Price: Lite from (shown) **$725.00**
Price: Varmint from **$950.00**
Price: Laminate stainless.. **$1,050.00**
Price: Forest... **$1,000.00**
Price: Tac A1 (shown).. **$1,899.00**
Price: Compact Tactical Rifle, From.................................... **$1,150.00**

WEATHERBY MARK V
This classic action goes back more than 60 years to the late '50s. Several significant changes were made to the original design in 2016. Stocks have a slimmer fore-end and smaller grip, which has an added palm swell. The new LXX trigger is adjustable down to 2.5 lbs. and has precision ground and polished surfaces and a wider trigger face. All new Mark V rifles come with sub-MOA guarantee. Range Certified (RC) models are range tested and come with a certified ballistic data sheet and RC engraved floorplate. Calibers: Varies depending on model. Barrels: 22 in., 24 in., 26 in., 28 in. Weight: 5 3/4 to 10 lbs. Stock: Varies depending on model. Sights: None furnished. Features: Deluxe version comes in all Weatherby calibers plus .243 Win., .270 Win., 7mm-08 Rem., .30-06, .308 Win. Lazermark same as Mark V Deluxe except stock has

extensive oak leaf pattern laser carving on pistol grip and fore-end; chambered in Wby. Magnums .257, .270 Win., 7mm., .300, .340, with 26 in. barrel. Sporter is same as the Mark V Deluxe without the embellishments. Metal has low-luster blue, stock is Claro walnut with matte finish, Monte Carlo comb, recoil pad. Chambered for these Wby. Mags: .257, .270 Win., 7mm, .300, .340. Other chamberings: 7mm Rem. Mag., .300 Win. Introduced 1993. Six Mark V models come with synthetic stocks. Ultra Lightweight rifles weigh 5.75 to 6.75 lbs.; 24 in., 26 in. fluted stainless barrels with recessed target crown; Bell & Carlson stock with CNC-machined aluminum bedding plate and tan "spider web" finish, skeletonized handle and sleeve. Available in .243 Win., .25-06 Rem., .270 Win., 7mm-08 Rem., 7mm Rem. Mag., .280 Rem, .308 Win., .30-06, .300 Win. Mag. Wby. Mag chamberings: .240, .257, .270 Win., 7mm, .300. Accumark uses Mark V action with heavy-contour 26 in. and 28 in. stainless barrels with black oxidized flutes, muzzle diameter of .705 in. No sights, drilled and tapped for scope mounting. Stock is composite with matte gel-coat finish, full-length aluminum bedding block. Weighs 8.5 lbs. Chambered for these Wby. Mags: .240, .257, .270, 7mm, .300, .340, .338-378, .30-378. Other chamberings: 6.5 Creedmoor, .270 Win., .308 Win., 7mm Rem. Mag., .300 Win. Mag. Altitude has 22-, 24-, 26-, 28-in. fluted stainless steel barrel, Monte Carlo carbon fiber composite stock with raised comb, Kryptek Altitude camo. Tacmark has 28-in. free floated fluted barrel with Accubrake, fully adjustable stock, black finish. Safari Grade has fancy grade checkered French walnut stock with ebony fore-end and grip cap, adjustable express rear and hooded front sights, from the Weatherby Custom Shop. Camilla series is lightweight model designed to fit a woman's anatomy. Offered in several variations chambered for .240 Wby. Mag., 6.5 Creedmoor, .270 Win., .308 Win., .30-06. Arroyo is available in Weatherby Magnums from .240 to .338-378, plus 6.5 Creedmoor, .300 Win. Mag., and .338 Lapua Mag. Finish is two-tone Cerakote with Brown Sand and FDE added flutes. Carbonmark has 26in. Proof Research carbon fiber threaded barrel and is chambered for .257 and .300 Wby. Mags. Outfitter is chambered for .240-.300 Wby. Magnums plus most popular calibers. Stock has Spiderweb accents. KCR model comes with Krieger Custom Match-grade barrel in .257, 6.5-300, .300 and .30-378 Wby. Magnums. Altitude is lightweight model (5 ¾-6 ¾ lbs.) and comes in Wby. Magnums from .240 to.300, plus 6.5 Creedmoor, .270 Win., .308, .30-06. Dangerous Game Rifle is offered in all Wby. Magnums from .300 to .450, plus .375 H&H. Hand laminated Monte Carlo composite stock. All Weatherby Mark V rifles are made in Sheridan, Wyoming.
Price: Mark V Backcountry **$2,499.99**
Price: Mark V Deluxe **$2,700.00**
Price: Mark V Lazermark... **$2,800.00**
Price: Mark V Sporter **$1,800.00**
Price: Mark V Ultra Lightweight **$2,300.00**
Price: Mark V Accumark .... **$2,300.00–$2,700.00**
Price: Mark V Altitude .... **$3,000.00–$3,700.00**
Price: Mark V Safari Grade Custom............................ **$6,900.00–$7,600.00**
Price: Mark V Tacmark **$4,100.00**
Price: Mark V Camilla Series..................................... **$2,300.00–$2,700.00**
Price: Mark V Arroyo **$2,800.00**
Price: Mark V Carbonmark **$4,100.00**
Price: Mark V Outfitter .... **$2,600-$2,800.00***
Price: Mark V Krieger Custom Rifle (KCR)................... **$3,600-$4,100.00***
Price: Mark V Altitude **$2,700.00***
Price: Mark V Dangerous Game Rifle **$3,600.00**
***Add .... $500 for optional Range Certified (RC) model with guaranteed sub-MOA accuracy certificate and target.**

WEATHERBY VANGUARD II SERIES
Calibers: Varies depending on model. Most Weatherby Magnums and many standard calibers. **Barrels:** 20, 24, or 26 in. **Weights:** 7.5–8.75 lbs. **Lengths:** 44–46.75 in. overall. **Stock:** Raised comb, Monte Carlo, injection-molded composite stock. **Sights:** None furnished. **Features:** One-piece forged, fluted bolt body with three gas ports, forged and machined receiver, adjustable trigger, factory accuracy guarantee. Vanguard Stainless has 410-Series stainless steel barrel and action, bead blasted matte metal finish. Vanguard Deluxe has raised comb, semi-fancy-grade Monte Carlo walnut stock with maplewood spacers, rosewood fore-end and grip cap, polished action with high-gloss blued metalwork. Sporter has Monte Carlo walnut stock with satin urethane finish, fineline diamond point checkering, contrasting rosewood fore-end tip, matte-blued metalwork. Sporter SS metalwork is 410 Series bead-blasted stainless steel. Vanguard Youth/Compact has 20 in. No. 1 contour barrel, short action, scaled-down nonreflective matte black hardwood stock with 12.5-in. length of pull, and full-size, injection-molded composite stock. Chambered for .223 Rem., .22-250 Rem., .243 Win., 7mm-08 Rem., .308 Win. Weighs 6.75 lbs.; OAL 38.9 in. Sub-MOA Matte and Sub-MOA Stainless models have pillar-bedded Fiberguard composite stock (Aramid, graphite unidirectional fibers

Prices given are believed to be accurate at time of publication however, many factors affect retail pricing so exact prices are not possible.

75TH EDITION, 2021 — 425

and fiberglass) with 24-in. barreled action; matte black metalwork, Pachmayr Decelerator recoil pad. Sub-MOA Stainless metalwork is 410 Series bead-blasted stainless steel. Sub-MOA Varmint guaranteed to shoot 3-shot group of .99 in. or less when used with specified Weatherby factory or premium (non-Weatherby calibers) ammunition. Hand-laminated, tan Monte Carlo composite stock with black spiderwebbing; CNC-machined aluminum bedding block, 22 in. No. 3 contour barrel, recessed target crown. Varmint Special has tan injection-molded Monte Carlo composite stock, pebble grain finish, black spiderwebbing. 22 in. No. 3 contour barrel (.740-in. muzzle dia.), bead blasted matte black finish, recessed target crown. Back Country has two-stage trigger, pillar-bedded Bell & Carlson stock, 24-in. fluted barrel, three-position safety.

Price: Vanguard Synthetic **$649.00**
Price: Vanguard Stainless **$799.00**
Price: Vanguard Deluxe, 7mm Rem. Mag., .300 Win. Mag..............**$1,149.00**
Price: Vanguard Sporter **$849.00**
Price: Vanguard Youth/Compact..**$599.00**
Price: Vanguard S2 Back Country **$1,399.00**
Price: Vanguard RC (Range Certified)...............................**$1,199.00**
Price: Vanguard Varmint Special **$849.00**
Price: Camilla (designed for women shooters) **$849.00**
Price: Lazerguard (Laser carved AA-grade walnut stock) **$1,199.00**
Price: H-Bar (tactical series) from ....**$1,149.00–$1,449.00**
Price: Weatherguard **$749.00**
Price: Modular Chassis **$1,519.00**
Price: Dangerous Game Rifle (DGR) .375 H&H **$1,299.00**
Price: Safari (.375 or .30-06) **$1,199.00**
Price: First Lite Fusion Camo **$1,099.00**
Price: Badlands Camo **$849.00**
Price: Accuguard **$1,099.00**
Price: Select **$599.00**
Price: Wilderness **$999.00**

WINCHESTER MODEL 70 SUPER GRADE

Calibers: .270 Win., .270 WSM, 7mm Rem. Mag., .30-06, .300 Win Mag., .300 WSM, .338 Win. Mag. **Capacities:** 5 rounds (short action) or 3 rounds (long action). **Barrels:** 24 in. or 26 in. blued. **Weights:** 8–8.5 lbs. **Features:** Full fancy Grade IV/V walnut stock with shadow-line cheekpiece, controlled round feed with claw extractor, Pachmayr Decelerator pad. No sights but drilled and tapped for scope mounts.
Price: ....**$1,440.00–$1,480.00**

WINCHESTER MODEL 70 ALASKAN

Calibers: .30-06, .300 Win. Mag., .338 Win. Mag., .375 H&H Magnum. **Barrel:** 25 in **Weight:** 8.8 lbs. **Sights:** Folding adjustable rear, hooded brass bead front. **Stock:** Satin finished Monte Carlo with cut checkering. **Features:** Integral recoil lug, Pachmayr Decelerator recoil pad.
Price: **$1,400.00**

WINCHESTER MODEL 70 COYOTE LIGHT SUPRESSOR READY

Calibers: .22-250, .243 Win., .308 Win., .270 WSM, .300 WSM and .325 WSM. **Capacities:** 5-round magazine (3-round mag. in .270 WSM, .300 WSM and .325 WSM). **Barrel:** 22-in. fluted stainless barrel (24 in. in .270 WSM, .300 WSM and .325 WSM). **Threaded for suppressor or other muzzle device. Weight:** 7.5 lbs. **Length:** NA. **Features:** Composite Bell and Carlson stock, Pachmayr Decelerator pad. Controlled round feeding. No sights but drilled and tapped for mounts.
Price: ....**$1,270.00–$1,310.00**

WINCHESTER MODEL 70 FEATHERWEIGHT

Calibers: .22-250, .243, 6.5 Creedmoor, 7mm-08, .308, .270 WSM, 7mm WSM, .300 WSM, .325 WSM, .25-06, .270, .30-06, 7mm Rem. Mag., .300 Win. Mag., .338 Win. Mag. **Capacities:** 5 rounds (short action) or 3 rounds (long action). **Barrels:** 22-in. blued (24 in. in magnum chamberings). **Weights:** 6.5–7.25 lbs. **Length:** NA. **Features:** Satin-finished checkered Grade I walnut stock, controlled round feeding. Pachmayr Decelerator pad. No sights but drilled and tapped for scope mounts.
Price: **$1,010.00**
Price: Magnum calibers.................................**$1,050.00**
Price: Featherweight Stainless ....**$1,210.00–$1,250.00**

WINCHESTER MODEL 70 SPORTER

Calibers: .270 WSM, 7mm WSM, .300 WSM, .325 WSM, .25-06, .270, .30-06, 7mm Rem. Mag., .300 Win. Mag., .338 Win. Mag. **Capacities:** 5 rounds (short action) or 3 rounds (long action). **Barrels:** 22 in., 24 in. or 26 in. blued. **Weights:** 6.5–7.25 lbs. **Length:** NA. **Features:** Satin-finished checkered Grade I walnut stock with sculpted cheekpiece, controlled round feeding. Pachmayr Decelerator pad. No sights but drilled and tapped for scope mounts.
Price: **$1,010.00**

WINCHESTER MODEL 70 SAFARI EXPRESS

Calibers: .375 H&H Magnum, .416 Remington, .458 Win. Mag. **Barrel:** 24 in. **Weight:** 9 lbs. **Sights:** Fully adjustable rear, hooded brass bead front. **Stock:** Satin finished Monte Carlo with cut checkering, deluxe cheekpiece. **Features:** Forged steel receiver with double integral recoil lugs bedded front and rear, dual steel crossbolts, Pachmayr Decelerator recoil pad.
Price: **$1,560.00**

WINCHESTER RENEGADE LONG RANGE SR

Calibers: .243 Win., 6.5 Creedmoor, 7mm-08 Rem, .308 Win., .270 WSM, .300 WSM, 6.5 PRC. **Capacity:** 3. **Barrel:** 22 to 24 in., stainless steel, sporter. **Stock:** Composite Grayboe. **Sights:** None, drilled and tapped. **Weight:** 8.5 lbs. **Features:** Recessed target crown, Inflex Technology recoil pad, enlarged bolt knob.
Price: **$1,069.99**

WINCHESTER XPR HUNTER TRUE TIMBER STRATA

Calibers: .243 Win., 6.5 Creedmoor, 7mm-08 Rem., .308 Win., .270 WSM, .300 WSM, .325 WSM, .270 Win., .30-06, 7mm Rem. Mag., .300 Win. Mag., .338 Win. Mag., .350 Legend, .223 Rem, 6.5 PRC. **Capacity:** 3 to 5. **Barrel:** 22 to 26 in., steel sporter, with Permacote finish. **Stock:** Composite, True Timber Strata camo. **Sights:** None, drilled and tapped. **Weight:** 6.75 to 7 lbs. **Features:** Inflex Technology recoil pad, sling swivel studs.
Price: **$599.99**

WINCHESTER XPR

Calibers: .243, 6.5 Creedmoor, 270 Win., .270 WSM, 7mm-08, 7mm Rem. Mag., .308 Win., .30-06, .300 Win. Mag., .300 WSM, .325 WSM, .338 Win. Mag.,.350 Legend. **Capacities:** Detachable box magazine holds 3 to 5 rounds. **Barrels:** 24 or 26 in. **Stock:** Black polymer with Inflex Technology recoil pad. **Weight:** Approx. 7 lbs. **Finish:** Matte blue. **Features:** Bolt unlock button, nickel coated Teflon bolt.
Price: **$549.99**
Price: Mossy Oak Break-Up Country camo stock...........................**$600.00**
Price: With Vortex II 3-9x40 scope......................................**$710.00**
Price: XPR Hunter Camo (shown) **$600.00**
Price: Sporter w/Grade 1 walnut stock..................................**$600.00**
Price: True Timber Strata Camo **$600.00**
Price: Thumbhole Varmint Suppressor Ready **$800.00**

WINCHESTER XPC

Caliber: .243, 6.5 Creedmoor, 308 Winchester. **Capacity:** 3. **Barrel:** 20 in., free floating with target crown, threading for suppressor or muzzle brake. **Stock:** Cerakote fully machined alloy chassis frame, Magpul PRS Gen III fully adjustable buttstock. **Weight:** 10 lbs. **Length:** 40 in. **Features:** MOA Trigger System, two-position thumb safety. Full length Picatinny rail, M-LOK on fore-end and buttstock for attaching accessories.
Price: **$1,600.00**

ARMALITE AR-50
Caliber: .50 BMG **Barrel:** 31 in. **Weight:** 33.2 lbs. **Length:** 59.5 in. **Stock:** Synthetic. **Sights:** None furnished. **Features:** A single-shot bolt-action rifle designed for long-range shooting. Available in left-hand model. Made in USA by Armalite.
Price: $3,359.00

BALLARD 1875 1 1/2 HUNTER
Caliber: Various calibers. **Barrel:** 26–30 in. **Weight:** NA **Length:** NA. **Stock:** Hand-selected classic American walnut. **Sights:** Blade front, Rocky Mountain rear. **Features:** Color casehardened receiver, breechblock and lever. Many options available. Made in USA by Ballard Rifle & Cartridge Co.
Price: $3,250.00

BALLARD 1875 #3 GALLERY SINGLE SHOT
Caliber: Various calibers. **Barrel:** 24–28 in. octagonal with tulip. **Weight:** NA. **Length:** NA. **Stock:** Hand-selected classic American walnut. **Sights:** Blade front, Rocky Mountain rear. **Features:** Color casehardened receiver, breechblock and lever. Many options available. Made in USA by Ballard Rifle & Cartridge Co.
Price: $3,300.00

BALLARD 1875 #4 PERFECTION
Caliber: Various calibers. **Barrels:** 30 in. or 32 in. octagon, standard or heavyweight. **Weights:** 10.5 lbs. (standard) or 11.75 lbs. (heavyweight bbl.) **Length:** NA. **Stock:** Smooth walnut. **Sights:** Blade front, Rocky Mountain rear. **Features:** Rifle or shotgun-style buttstock, straight grip action, single- or double-set trigger, "S" or right lever, hand polished and lapped Badger barrel. Made in USA by Ballard Rifle & Cartridge Co.
Price: $3,950.00

BALLARD MODEL 1885 LOW WALL SINGLE SHOT RIFLE
Calibers: Various calibers. **Barrels:** 24–28 in. **Weight:** NA. **Length:** NA. **Stock:** Hand-selected classic American walnut. **Sights:** Blade front, sporting rear. **Features:** Color casehardened receiver, breechblock and lever. Many options available. Made in USA by Ballard Rifle & Cartridge Co.
Price: $3,300.00

BALLARD MODEL 1885 HIGH WALL STANDARD SPORTING SINGLE SHOT
Calibers: Various calibers. **Barrels:** Lengths to 34 in. **Weight:** NA. **Length:** NA. **Stock:** Straight-grain American walnut. **Sights:** Buckhorn or flattop rear, blade front. **Features:** Faithful copy of original Model 1885 High Wall; parts interchange with original rifles; variety of options available. Introduced 2000. Made in USA by Ballard Rifle & Cartridge Co.
Price: $3,300.00

BALLARD MODEL 1885 HIGH WALL SPECIAL SPORTING SINGLE SHOT
Calibers: Various calibers. **Barrels:** 28–30 in. octagonal. **Weight:** NA. **Length:** NA. **Stock:** Hand-selected classic American walnut. **Sights:** Blade front, sporting rear. **Features:** Color casehardened receiver, breechblock and lever. Many options available. Made in USA by Ballard Rifle & Cartridge Co.
Price: $3,600.00

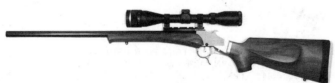

BROWN MODEL 97D SINGLE SHOT
Calibers: Available in most factory and wildcat calibers from .17 Ackley Hornet to .375 Winchester. **Barrels:** Up to 26 in., air-gauged match grade. **Weight:** About 5 lbs., 11 oz. **Stock:** Sporter style with pistol grip, cheekpiece and Schnabel fore-end. **Sights:** None furnished; drilled and tapped for scope mounting. **Features:** Falling-block action gives rigid barrel-receiver matting; polished blue/black finish. Hand-fitted action. Standard and custom made-to-order rifles with many options. Made in USA by E. Arthur Brown Co., Inc.
Price: Standard model $1,695.00

C. SHARPS ARMS 1874 BRIDGEPORT SPORTING
Calibers: .38-55 to .50-3.25. **Barrel:** 26 in., 28 in., 30-in. tapered octagon. **Weight:** 10.5 lbs. **Length:** 47 in. **Stock:** American black walnut; shotgun butt with checkered steel buttplate; straight grip, heavy fore-end with Schnabel tip. **Sights:** Blade front, buckhorn rear. Drilled and tapped for tang sight. **Features:** Double-set triggers. Made in USA by C. Sharps Arms.
Price: $1,995.00

C. SHARPS ARMS NEW MODEL 1885 HIGHWALL
Calibers: .22 LR, .22 Hornet, .219 Zipper, .25-35 WCF, .32-40 WCF, .38-55 WCF, .40-65, .30-40 Krag, .40-50 ST or BN, .40-70 ST or BN, .40-90 ST or BN, .45-70 Govt. 2-1/10 in. ST, .45-90 2-4/10 in. ST, .45-100 2-6/10 in. ST, .45-110 2-7/8 in. ST, .45-120 3-1/4 in. ST. **Barrels:** 26 in., 28 in., 30 in., tapered full octagon. **Weight:** About 9 lbs., 4 oz. **Length:** 47 in. overall. **Stock:** Oil-finished American walnut; Schnabel-style fore-end. **Sights:** Blade front, buckhorn rear. Drilled and tapped for optional tang sight. **Features:** Single trigger; octagonal receiver top; checkered steel buttplate; color casehardened receiver and buttplate, blued barrel. Many options available. Made in USA by C. Sharps Arms Co.
Price: From $1,975.00

C. SHARPS ARMS 1885 HIGHWALL SCHUETZEN RIFLE
Calibers: .30-30, .32-40, .38-55, .40-50. **Barrels:** 24, 26, 28 or 30 in. Full tapered octagon. **Stock:** Straight grain American walnut with oil finish, pistol grip, cheek rest. **Sights:** Globe front with aperture set, long-range fully adjustable tang sight with Hadley eyecup. **Finish:** Color casehardened receiver group, buttplate and bottom tang, matte blue barrel. Single set trigger.
Price: From $2,875.00

CIMARRON BILLY DIXON 1874 SHARPS SPORTING
Calibers: .45-70, .45-90, .50-70. **Barrel:** 32-in. tapered octagonal. **Weight:** NA. **Length:** NA. **Stock:** European walnut. **Sights:** Blade front, Creedmoor rear. **Features:** Color casehardened frame, blued barrel. Hand-checkered grip and fore-end; hand-rubbed oil finish. Made by Pedersoli. Imported by Cimarron F.A. Co.
Price: From $2,141.70
Price: Officer's Trapdoor Carbine w/26-in. round barrel.................$2,616.00

CIMARRON ADOBE WALLS ROLLING BLOCK
Caliber: .45-70 Govt. **Barrel:** 30-in. octagonal. **Weight:** 10.33 lbs. **Length:** NA. **Stock:** Hand-checkered European walnut. **Sights:** Bead front, semi-buckhorn rear. **Features:** Color casehardened receiver, blued barrel. Curved buttplate. Double-set triggers. Made by Pedersoli. Imported by Cimarron F.A. Co.
Price: From $1,740.00

DAKOTA ARMS SHARPS
Calibers: Virtually any caliber from .17 Ackley Hornet to .30-40 Krag. **Features:** 26-in. octagon barrel, XX-grade walnut stock with straight grip and tang sight. Many options and upgrades are available.
Price: From $4,490.00

EMF PREMIER 1874 SHARPS
Calibers: .45-70, .45-110, .45-120. **Barrel:** 32 in., 34 in.. **Weight:** 11–13 lbs. **Length:** 49 in., 51 in. overall. **Stock:** Pistol grip, European walnut. **Sights:** Blade front, adjustable rear. **Features:** Superb quality reproductions of the 1874 Sharps Sporting Rifles; casehardened locks; double-set triggers; blue barrels. Imported from Pedersoli by EMF.
Price: Business Rifle $1,585.00
Price: Down Under Sporting Rifle, Patchbox, heavy barrel $2,405.00
Price: Silhouette, pistol-grip...$1,899.90
Price: Super Deluxe Hand Engraved $3,600.00
Price: Competition Rifle...$2,200.00

H&R BUFFALO CLASSIC
Calibers: .45 Colt or .45-70 Govt. **Barrel:** 32 in. heavy. **Weight:** 8 lbs. **Length:** 46 in. overall. **Stock:** Cut-checkered American black walnut. **Sights:** Williams receiver sight; Lyman target front sight with 8 aperture inserts. **Features:** Color casehardened Handi-Rifle action with exposed hammer; color casehardened crescent buttplate; 19th-century checkering pattern. Introduced 1995. Made in USA by H&R 1871, Inc.
Price: Buffalo Classic Rifle...$479.00

KRIEGHOFF HUBERTUS SINGLE-SHOT
Calibers: .222, .22-250, .243 Win., .270 Win., .308 Win., .30-06, 5.6x50R Mag., 5.6x52R, 6x62R Freres, 6.5x57R, 6.5x65R, 7x57R, 7x65R, 8x57JRS, 8x75RS, 9.3x74R, 7mm Rem. Mag., .300 Win. Mag. **Barrels:** 23.5 in. Shorter lengths available. **Weight:** 6.5 lbs. **Length:** 40.5 in. **Stock:** High-grade walnut. **Sights:** Blade front, open rear. **Features:** Break-open loading with manual cocking lever on top tang; takedown; extractor; Schnabel forearm; many options. Imported from Germany by Krieghoff International Inc.
Price: Hubertus single shot, From....................................$7,295.00
Price: Hubertus, magnum calibers $8,295.00

MERKEL K1 MODEL LIGHTWEIGHT STALKING
Calibers: .243 Win., .270 Win., 7x57R, .308 Win., .30-06, 7mm Rem. Mag., .300 Win. Mag., 9.3x74R. **Barrel:** 23.6 in. **Weight:** 5.6 lbs. unscoped. **Stock:** Satin-finished walnut, fluted and checkered; sling-swivel studs. **Sights:** None (scope base furnished). **Features:** Franz Jager single-shot break-open action, cocking/uncocking slide-type safety, matte silver receiver, selectable trigger pull weights, integrated, quick detach 1 in. or 30mm optic mounts (optic not included). Extra barrels are an option. Imported from Germany by Merkel USA.
Price: Jagd Stalking Rifle $3,795.00
Price: Jagd Stutzen Carbine $4,195.00
Price: Extra barrels $1,195.00

MILLER ARMS
Calibers: Virtually any caliber from .17 Ackley Hornet to .416 Remington. Falling block design with 24-in. premium match-grade barrel, express sights, XXX-grade walnut stock and fore-end with 24 LPI checkering. Made in several styles including Classic, Target and Varmint. Many options and upgrades are available. From Dakota Arms.
Price: From $5,590.00

ROSSI SINGLE-SHOT SERIES
Calibers: .223 Rem., .243 Win., .44 Magnum. **Barrel:** 22 in. **Weight:** 6.25 lbs. **Stocks:** Black Synthetic Synthetic with recoil pad and removable cheek piece. **Sights:** Adjustable rear, fiber optic front, scope rail. Some models have scope rail only. **Features:** Single-shot break open, positive ejection, internal transfer bar mechanism, manual external safety, trigger block system, Taurus Security System, Matte blue finish.
Price: $238.00

RUGER NO. 1 SERIES
This model is currently available only in select limited editions and chamberings each year. Features common to most variants of the No. 1 include a falling block mechanism and under lever, sliding tang safety, integral scope mounts machined on the steel quarter rib, sporting-style

recoil pad, grip cap and sling swivel studs. Chamberings for 2018 and 2019 were .450 Bushmaster and .450 Marlin. In addition, many calibers are offered by Ruger distributors Lipsey's and Talo, usually limited production runs of approximately 250 rifles, including .204 Ruger, .22 Hornet, 6.5 Creedmoor, .250 Savage, .257 Roberts, .257 Weatherby Mag. and .30-30. For availability of specific variants and calibers contact **www.lipseysguns.com** or **www.taloinc.com.**
Price: ....$1,899.00-$2,115.00

SHILOH CO. SHARPS 1874 LONG RANGE EXPRESS
Calibers: .38-55, .40-50 BN, .40-70 BN, .40-90 BN, .40-70 ST, .40-90 ST, .45-70 Govt. ST, .45-90 ST, .45-110 ST, .50-70 ST, .50-90 ST. **Barrel:** 34-in. tapered octagon. **Weight:** 10.5 lbs. **Length:** 51 in. overall. **Stock:** Oil-finished walnut (upgrades available) with pistol grip, shotgun-style butt, traditional cheek rest, Schnabel fore-end. **Sights:** Customer's choice. **Features:** Re-creation of the Model 1874 Sharps rifle. Double-set triggers. Made in USA by Shiloh Rifle Mfg. Co.
Price: $2,059.00
Price: Sporter Rifle No. 1 (similar to above except with 30-in. barrel, blade front, buckhorn rear sight) $2,059.00
Price: Sporter Rifle No. 3 (similar to No. 1 except straight-grip stock, standard wood) $1,949.00

SHILOH CO. SHARPS 1874 QUIGLEY
Calibers: .45-70 Govt., .45-110. **Barrel:** 34-in. heavy octagon. **Stock:** Military-style with patch box, standard-grade American walnut. **Sights:** Semi-buckhorn, interchangeable front and midrange vernier tang sight with windage. **Features:** Gold inlay initials, pewter tip, Hartford collar, case color or antique finish. Double-set triggers.
Price: $3,533.00

SHILOH CO. SHARPS 1874 SADDLE
Calibers: .38-55, .40-50 BN, .40-65 Win., .40-70 BN, .40-70 ST, .40-90 BN, .40-90 ST, .44-77 BN, .44-90 BN, .45-70 Govt. ST, .45-90 ST, .45-100 ST, .45-110 ST, .45-120 ST, .50-70 ST, .50-90 ST. **Barrels:** 26 in. full or half octagon. **Stock:** Semi-fancy American walnut. Shotgun style with cheek rest. **Sights:** Buckhorn and blade. **Features:** Double-set trigger, numerous custom features can be added.
Price: $2,044.00

SHILOH CO. SHARPS 1874 MONTANA ROUGHRIDER
Calibers: .38-55, .40-50 BN, .40-65 Win., .40-70 BN, .40-70 ST, .40-90 BN, .40-90 ST, .44-77 BN, .44-90 BN, .45-70 Govt. ST, .45-90 ST, .45-100 ST, .45-110 ST, .45-120 ST, .50-70 ST, .50-90 ST. **Barrels:** 30 in. full or half octagon. **Stock:** American walnut in shotgun or military style. **Sights:** Buckhorn and blade. **Features:** Double-set triggers, numerous custom features can be added.
Price: $2,059.00

Prices given are believed to be accurate at time of publication however, many factors affect retail pricing so exact prices are not possible.

SHILOH CO. SHARPS CREEDMOOR TARGET
Calibers: .38-55, .40-50 BN, .40-65 Win., .40-70 BN, .40-70 ST, .40-90 BN, .40-90 ST, .44-77 BN, .44-90 BN, .45-70 Govt. ST, .45-90 ST, .45-100 ST, .45-110 ST, .45-120 ST, .50-70 ST, .50-90 ST. **Barrel:** 32 in. half round-half octagon. **Stock:** Extra fancy American walnut. Shotgun style with pistol grip. **Sights:** Customer's choice. **Features:** Single trigger, AA finish on stock, polished barrel and screws, pewter tip.
Price: $3,105.00

THOMPSON/CENTER ENCORE PRO HUNTER PREDATOR RIFLE
Calibers: .204 Ruger, .223 Remington, .22-250 and .308 Winchester. **Barrel:** 28-in. deep-fluted interchangeable. **Length:** 42.5 in. **Weight:** 7.75 lbs. **Stock:** Composite buttstock and fore-end with non-slip inserts in cheekpiece, pistol grip and fore-end. Realtree Advantage Max-1 camo finish overall. Scope is not included.
Price: $882.00

THOMPSON/CENTER G2 CONTENDER
Calibers: .204 Ruger, .223 Rem., 6.8 Rem. 7-30 Waters, .30-30 Win. **Barrel:** 23-in. interchangeable with blued finish. **Length:** 36.75 in. **Stock:** Walnut. **Sights:** None. **Weight:** 5.5 pounds. Reintroduced in 2015. Interchangeable barrels available in several centerfire and rimfire calibers.
Price: $769.00

UBERTI 1874 SHARPS SPORTING
Caliber: .45-70 Govt. **Barrels:** 30 in., 32 in., 34 in. octagonal. **Weight:** 10.57 lbs. with 32 in. barrel. **Lengths:** 48.9 in. with 32 in. barrel. **Stock:** Walnut. **Sights:** Dovetail front, Vernier tang rear. **Features:** Cut checkering, case-colored finish on frame, buttplate, and lever. Imported by Stoeger Industries.
Price: Standard Sharps $1,919.00
Price: Special Sharps...$2,019.00
Price: Deluxe Sharps...$3,269.00
Price: Down Under Sharps.......................................$2,719.00
Price: Long Range Sharps...$2,719.00
Price: Buffalo Hunter Sharps....................................$2,620.00
Price: Sharps Cavalry Carbine $2,020.00
Price: Sharps Extra Deluxe.......................................$5,400.00
Price: Sharps Hunter..$1,699.00

UBERTI 1885 HIGH-WALL SINGLE-SHOT
Calibers: .45-70 Govt., .45-90, .45-120. **Barrels:** 28–32 in. **Weights:** 9.3–9.9 lbs. **Lengths:** 44.5–47 in. overall. **Stock:** Walnut stock and fore-end. **Sights:** Blade front, fully adjustable open rear. **Features:** Based on Winchester High-Wall design by John Browning. Color casehardened frame and lever, blued barrel and buttplate. Imported by Stoeger Industries.
Price: From...............................$1,079.00–$1,279.00

UBERTI 1885 COURTENEY STALKING RIFLE
Caliber: .303 British. **Barrel:** 24 in., round blue steel. **Stock:** A-grade walnut, Prince of Wales. **Sights:** Hooded front, V-style express rear. **Weight:** 7.1 lbs. **Features:** Casehardened receiver, checkered pistol grip, rubber buttpad.
Price: $1,729.99

UBERTI SPRINGFIELD TRAPDOOR RIFLE/CARBINE
Caliber: .45-70 Govt., single shot **Barrel:** 22 or 32.5 in. **Features:** Blued steel receiver and barrel, casehardened breechblock and buttplate. **Sights:** Creedmoor style.
Price: Springfield Trapdoor Carbine, 22 in. barrel $1,749.00
Price: Springfield Trapdoor Army, 32.5 in. barrel $2,019.0

Prices given are believed to be accurate at time of publication however, many factors affect retail pricing so exact prices are not possible.

75TH EDITION, 2021   429

BERETTA S686/S689 O/U RIFLE SERIES
Calibers: .30-06, 9.3x74R. **Barrels:** 23 in. O/U boxlock action. Single or double triggers. EELL Grade has better wood, moderate engraving.
Price: ....$4,200.00–$9,000.00
Price: EELL Diamond Sable grade, From $12,750.00

BRNO MODEL 802 COMBO GUN
Calibers/Gauges: .243 Win., .308 or .30-06/12 ga. Over/Under. **Barrels:** 23.6 in. **Weight:** 7.6 lbs. **Length:** 41 in. **Stock:** European walnut. **Features:** Double trigger, shotgun barrel is improved-modified chokes. Imported by CZ USA.
Price: $2,087.00

BRNO EFFECT
Caliber: .30-06 Single Shot..$1,585.00

BRNO STOPPER
Caliber: .458 Win. Over/Under $5,554.00
Caliber: .458 Win. Over/Under hand engraved $8,072.00

FAUSTI CLASS EXPRESS
Calibers: .30-06, .30R Blaser, 8x57 JRS, 9.3x74R, .444 Marlin, .45-70 Govt. Over/Under. **Barrels:** 24 in. **Weight:** 7.5 lbs. **Length:** 41 in. **Stock:** Oil-finished Grade A walnut. Pistol grip, Bavarian or Classic. **Sights:** Folding leaf rear, fiber optic front adjustable for elevation. **Features:** Inertia single or double trigger, automatic ejectors. Made in Italy and imported by Fausti USA.
Price: $4,990.00
Price: SL Express w/hand engraving, AA wood..............................$7,600.00

HEYM MODEL 88B SXS DOUBLE RIFLE
Calibers/Gauge: .22 Hornet, .300 Win. Mag., .375 H&H Belted Mag., .375 H&H Flanged Mag., .416 Rigby, .416/500 NE, .450/400 NE 3-in., .450 NE 3.25-in., .470 NE, .500 NE, .577 NE, .600 NE, 20 gauge, and more. **Barrel:** Up to 26 in., Krupp steel, hammer-forged. **Stock:** Custom select European walnut. **Sights:** V rear, bead front. **Weight:** 9 to 13 lbs. **Features:** Automatic ejectors, articulated front trigger, stocked-to-fit RH or LH, cocking indicators, engraving available.
Price: From.. $18,000.00

HEYM MODEL 89B SXS DOUBLE RIFLE
Calibers/Gauge: .22 Hornet, .300 Win. Mag., .375 H&H Belted Mag., .375 H&H Flanged Mag., .416 Rigby, .416/500 NE, .450/400 NE 3-in., .450 NE 3.25-in., .470 NE, .500 NE, .577 NE, .600 NE, 20 gauge, and more. **Barrel:** Up to 26 in., Krupp steel, hammer-forged. **Stock:** Custom select European walnut. **Sights:** V rear, bead front. **Weight:** 9-13 lbs. **Features:** Five frame sizes, automatic ejectors, intercepting sears, stocked-to-fit RH or LH, engraving available.
Price: From.. $23,000.00

HOENIG ROTARY ROUND ACTION DOUBLE
Calibers: Most popular calibers. Over/Under design. **Barrels:** 22–26 in. **Stock:** English Walnut; to customer specs. **Sights:** Swivel hood front with button release (extra bead stored in trap door grip cap), express-style rear on quarter-rib adjustable for windage and elevation; scope mount. **Features:** Round action opens by rotating barrels, pulling forward. Inertia extractor system, rotary safety blocks strikers. Single lever quick-detachable scope mount. Simple takedown without removing fore-end. Introduced 1997. Custom rifle made in USA by George Hoenig.
Price: From.. $22,500.00

HOENIG ROTARY ROUND ACTION COMBINATION
Calibers: Most popular calibers and shotgun gauges. Over/Under design with rifle barrel atop shotgun barrel. **Barrel:** 26 in. **Weight:** 7 lbs. **Stock:** English Walnut to customer specs. **Sights:** Front ramp with button release blades. Foldable aperture tang sight windage and elevation adjustable. Quarter-rib with scope mount. **Features:** Round action opens by rotating barrels, pulling forward. Inertia extractor; rotary safety blocks strikers. Simple takedown without removing forend. Custom rifle made in USA by George Hoenig.
Price: From...$27,500.00

HOENIG VIERLING FOUR-BARREL COMBINATION
Calibers/gauges: Two 20-gauge shotgun barrels with one rifle barrel chambered for .22 Long Rifle and another for .223 Remington. Custom rifle made in USA by George Hoenig.
Price: $50,000.00

KRIEGHOFF CLASSIC DOUBLE
Calibers: 7x57R, 7x65R, .308 Win., .30-06, 8x57 JRS, 8x75RS, 9.3x74R, .375NE, .500/.416NE, .470NE, .500NE. **Barrel:** 23.5 in. **Weight:** 7.3–11 lbs. **Stock:** High grade European walnut. Standard model has conventional rounded cheekpiece, Bavaria model has Bavarian-style cheekpiece. **Sights:** Bead front with removable, adjustable wedge (.375 H&H and below), standing leaf rear on quarter-rib. **Features:** Boxlock action; double triggers; short opening angle for fast loading; quiet extractors; sliding, self-adjusting wedge for secure bolting; Purdey-style barrel extension; horizontal firing pin placement. Many options available. Introduced 1997. Imported from Germany by Krieghoff International.
Price: $10,995.00
Price: Engraved sideplates, add $4,000.00
Price: Extra set of rifle barrels, add.................................$6,300.00
Price: Extra set of 20-ga., 28 in. shotgun barrels, add....................$4,400.00

KRIEGHOFF CLASSIC BIG FIVE DOUBLE RIFLE
Similar to the standard Classic except available in .375 H&H, .375 Flanged Mag. N.E., .416 Rigby, .458 Win., 500/416 NE, 470 NE, 500 NE. Has hinged front trigger, nonremovable muzzle wedge, Universal Trigger System, Combi Cocking Device, steel trigger guard, specially weighted stock bolt for weight and balance. Many options available. Introduced 1997. Imported from Germany by Krieghoff International.
Price: $13,995.00
Price: Engraved sideplates, add $4,000.00
Price: Extra set of 20-ga. shotgun barrels, add..............................$5,000.00
Price: Extra set of rifle barrels, add.................................$6,300.00

MERKEL BOXLOCK DOUBLE
Calibers: 5.6x52R, .243 Winchester, 6.5x55, 6.5x57R, 7x57R, 7x65R, .308 Win., .30-06, 8x57 IRS, 9.3x74R. **Barrel:** 23.6 in. **Weight:** 7.7 oz. **Length:** NA. **Stock:** Walnut, oil finished, pistol grip. **Sights:** Fixed 100 meter. **Features:** Anson & Deeley boxlock action with cocking indicators, double triggers, engraved color casehardened receiver. Introduced 1995. Imported from Germany by Merkel USA.
Price: Model 140-2, From Approx.................................$13,255.00
Price: Model 141 Small Frame SXS Rifle; built on smaller frame, chambered for 7mm Mauser, .30-06, or 9.3x74R From Approx.. ....$11,825.00
Price: Model 141 Engraved; fine hand-engraved hunting scenes on silvered receiver From Approx. $13,500.00

BERGARA B-14 RIMFIRE
Caliber: .22 LR. **Capacity:** 10. **Barrel:** 18 in., 4140 Bergara. **Stock:** HMR composite. **Sights:** None. **Weight:** 9.25 lbs. **Features:** Threaded muzzle, B-14R action, Remington 700 accessories compatible.
Price: **$1,150.99**

BROWNING BUCK MARK SEMI-AUTO
Caliber: .22 LR. **Capacity:** 10+1. **Action:** A rifle version of the Buck Mark Pistol; straight blowback action; machined aluminum receiver with integral rail scope mount; manual thumb safety. **Barrel:** Recessed crowns. **Stock:** Stock and forearm with full pistol grip. **Features:** Action lock provided. Introduced 2001. Four model name variations for 2006, as noted below. **Sights:** FLD Target, FLD Carbon, and Target models have integrated scope rails. Sporter has Truglo/Marble fiber-optic sights. Imported from Japan by Browning.
Price: FLD Target, 5.5 lbs., bull barrel, laminated stock...................... **$720.00**
Price: Target, 5.4 lbs., blued bull barrel, wood stock **$700.00**
Price: Sporter, 4.4 lbs., blued sporter barrel w/sights **$700.00**

BROWNING SA-22 SEMI-AUTO 22
Caliber: .22 LR. **Capacity:** Tubular magazine in buttstock holds 11 rounds. **Barrel:** 19.375 in. **Weight:** 5 lbs. 3 oz. **Length:** 37 in. overall. **Stock:** Checkered select walnut with pistol grip and semi-beavertail fore-end. **Sights:** Gold bead front, folding leaf rear. **Features:** Engraved receiver with polished blue finish; crossbolt safety; easy takedown for carrying or storage. The Grade VI is available with either grayed or blued receiver with extensive engraving with gold-plated animals: right side pictures a fox and squirrel in a woodland scene; left side shows a beagle chasing a rabbit. On top is a portrait of the beagle. Stock and fore-end are of high-grade walnut with a double-bordered cut checkering design. Introduced 1956. Made in Belgium until 1974. Currently made in Japan by Miroku.
Price: Grade I, scroll-engraved blued receiver **$700.00**
Price: Grade II, octagon barrel **$1,000.00**
Price: Grade VI BL, gold-plated engraved blued receiver **$1,640.00**

CITADEL M-1 CARBINE
Caliber: .22LR. **Capacity:** 10-round magazine. **Barrel:** 18 in. **Weight:** 4.8 lbs. **Length:** 35 in. **Stock:** Wood or synthetic in black or several camo patterns. **Features:** Built to the exacting specifications of the G.I. model used by U.S. infantrymen in both WWII theaters of battle and in Korea. Used by officers as well as tankers, drivers, artillery crews, mortar crews, and other personnel. Weight, barrel length and OAL are the same as the "United States Carbine, Caliber .30, M1," its official military designation. Made in Italy by Chiappa. Imported by Legacy Sports.
Price: Synthetic stock, black. **$316.00**
Price: Synthetic stock, camo. **$368.00**
Price: Wood stock. **$400.00**

CZ MODEL 512
Calibers: .22 LR/.22 WMR. **Capacity:** 5-round magazines. **Barrel:** 20.5 in. **Weight:** 5.9 lbs. **Length:** 39.3 in. **Stock:** Beech. **Sights:** Adjustable. **Features:** The modular design is easily maintained, requiring only a coin as a tool for field stripping. The action of the 512 is composed of an aluminum alloy upper receiver that secures

the barrel and bolt assembly and a fiberglass reinforced polymer lower half that houses the trigger mechanism and detachable magazine. The 512 shares the same magazines and scope rings with the CZ 455 bolt-action rifle.
Price: .22 LR **$495.00**
Price: .22 WMR **$526.00**

H&K 416-22
Caliber: .22 LR. **Capacity:** 10- or 20-round magazine. **Features:** Blowback semi-auto rifle styled to resemble H&K 416 with metal upper and lower receivers; rail interface system; retractable stock; pistol grip with storage compartment; on-rail sights; rear sight adjustable for wind and elevation; 16.1-in. barrel. Also available in pistol version with 9-in. barrel. Made in Germany by Walther under license from Heckler & Koch and imported by Umarex.
Price: **$599.00**

H&K MP5 A5
Caliber: .22 LR. **Capacity:** 10- or 25-round magazine **Features:** Blowback semi-auto rifle styled to resemble H&K MP5 with metal receiver; compensator; bolt catch; NAVY pistol grip; on-rail sights; rear sight adjustable for wind and elevation; 16.1-in. barrel. Also available in pistol version with 9-in. barrel. Also available with SD-type fore-end. Made in Germany by Walther under license from Heckler & Koch. Imported by Umarex.
Price: **$499.00**
Price: MP5 SD... **$599.00**

HOWA GAMEPRO RIMFIRE
Calibers: .22 LR, .22 WMR, .17 HMR. **Capacity:** 10. **Barrel:** 18 in., threaded, blued. **Stock:** Composite Hogue over-molded. **Sights:** Picatinny rail. **Weight:** 9.35 lbs. **Features:** Guaranteed sub-MOA, two-stage HACT trigger.
Price: **$699.99**

KEL-TEC SU-22CA
Caliber: .22 LR. **Capacity:** 26-round magazine. **Barrel:** 16.1 in. **Weight:** 4 lbs. **Length:** 34 in. **Features:** Blowback action, crossbolt safety, adjustable front and rear sights with integral Picatinny rail. Threaded muzzle.
Price: **$547.00**

MARLIN MODEL 60
Caliber: .22 LR. **Capacity:** 14-round tubular magazine. **Barrel:** 19 in. round tapered. **Weight:** About 5.5 lbs. **Length:** 37.5 in. overall. **Stock:** Press-checkered, laminated Maine birch with Monte Carlo, full pistol grip; black synthetic or Realtree Camo. **Sights:** Ramp front, open adjustable rear. Matted receiver is grooved for scope mount. **Features:** Last-shot bolt hold-open. Available with factory mounted 4x scope.
Price: Laminate **$209.00**
Price: Model 60C camo **$246.00**
Price: Synthetic **$201.00**

MARLIN MODEL 60SS SELF-LOADING RIFLE
Same as the Model 60 except breech bolt, barrel and outer magazine tube are made of stainless steel; most other parts are either nickel-plated or coated to match the stainless finish. Monte Carlo stock is of black/gray Maine birch laminate, and has nickel-plated swivel studs, rubber buttpad. Introduced 1993.
Price: **$315.00**

MARLIN MODEL 795
Caliber: .22. **Capacity:** 10-round magazine. **Barrel:** 18 in. with 16-groove Micro-Groove rifling. **Sights:** Ramp front sight, adjustable rear. Receiver grooved for scope mount. **Stock:** Black synthetic, hardwood, synthetic thumbhole, solid pink, pink camo, or Mossy Oak New Break-up camo finish. **Features:** Last shot hold-open feature. Introduced 1997. SS is similar to Model 795 except stainless steel barrel. Most other parts nickel-plated. Adjustable folding semi-buckhorn rear sights, ramp front high-visibility post and removable cutaway wide scan hood. Made in USA by Marlin Firearms Co.
Price: **$183.00**
Price: Stainless **$262.00**

MOSSBERG BLAZE SERIES

Caliber: .22 LR. **Capacities:** 10 or 25 rounds. **Barrel:** 16.5 in. **Sights:** Adjustable. **Weights:** 3.5–4.75 lbs. **Features:** A series of lightweight polymer rifles with several finish options and styles. Green Dot Combo model has Dead Ringer greet dot sight. Blaze 47 has AK-profile with adjustable fiber optic rear and raised front sight, ambidextrous safety, and a choice of wood or synthetic stock.

Price:	$210.00
Price: Muddy Girl camo	$269.00
Price: Green Dot Combo	$281.00
Price: Wildfire camo	$269.00
Price: Kryptek Highlander camo	$283.00
Price: Blaze 47 wood stock	$420.00

MOSSBERG MODEL 702 PLINKSTER

Caliber: .22 LR. **Capacity:** 10-round magazine. **Barrel:** 18 in. free-floating. **Weights:** 4.1–4.6 lbs. **Sights:** Adjustable rifle. Receiver grooved for scope mount. **Stock:** Wood or black synthetic. **Features:** Ergonomically placed magazine release and safety buttons, crossbolt safety, free gun lock. Made in USA by O.F. Mossberg & Sons, Inc.

Price: From $190.00

MOSSBERG MODEL 715T SERIES

Caliber: .22 LR. **Capacity:** 10- or 25-round magazine. **Barrel:** 16.25 or 18 in. with A2-style muzzle brake. **Weight:** 5.5 lbs. **Features:** AR style offered in several models. Flattop or A2 style carry handle.

Price: Black finish	$326.00
Price: Black finish, Red Dot sight	$375.00
Price: Muddy Girl camo	$438.00

REMINGTON MODEL 552 BDL DELUXE SPEEDMASTER

Calibers: .22 Short (20 rounds), Long (17) or LR (15) tubular magazine. **Barrel:** 21-in. round tapered. **Weight:** 5.75 lbs. **Length:** 40 in. overall. **Stock:** Walnut. Checkered grip and fore-end. **Sights:** Adjustable rear, ramp front. **Features:** Positive crossbolt safety in trigger guard, receiver grooved for tip-off mount. Operates with .22 Short, Long or Long Rifle cartridges. Classic design introduced in 1957.

Price: $707.00

ROSSI RS22

Caliber: .22 LR. **Capacity:** 10-round detachable magazine. **Barrel:** 18 in. **Weight:** 4.1 lbs. **Length:** 36 in. **Stock:** Black synthetic with impressed checkering. **Sights:** Adjustable fiber optic rear, hooded fiber optic front. Made in Brazil, imported by Rossi USA.

Price: Standard model, synthetic stock $139.00

RUGER 10/22 AUTOLOADING CARBINE

Caliber: .22 LR. **Capacity:** 10-round rotary magazine. **Barrel:** 18.5 in. round tapered (16.12 in. compact model). **Weight:** 5 lbs. (4.5, compact). **Length:** 37.25 in., 34 in. (compact) overall. **Stock:** American hardwood with pistol grip and barrel band, or synthetic. **Sights:** Brass bead front, folding leaf rear adjustable for elevation. **Features:** Available with satin black or stainless finish on receiver and barrel. Detachable rotary magazine fits flush into stock, crossbolt safety, receiver tapped and grooved for scope blocks or tip-off mount. Scope base adaptor furnished with each rifle. Made in USA by Sturm, Ruger & Co.

Price: Wood stock	$309.00
Price: Synthetic stock	$309.00
Price: Stainless, synthetic stock	$339.00
Price: Compact model, fiber-optic front sight	$359.00
Price: Go Wild Rockstar Camo	$399.00
Price: Collector's Series Man's Best Friend	$399.00
Price: Weaver 3-9x Scope	$399.00

RUGER 10/22 TAKEDOWN RIFLE

Caliber: .22 LR. **Capacity:** 10-round rotary magazine. **Barrels:** 18.5 in. stainless, or 16.6 in. satin black threaded with suppressor. Easy takedown feature enables quick separation of the barrel from the action by way of a recessed locking lever, for ease of transportation and storage. **Stock:** Black synthetic. **Sights:** Adjustable rear, gold bead front. **Weight:** 4.66 pounds. Comes with backpack carrying bag.

Price: Stainless	$439.00
Price: Satin black w/flash suppressor	$459.00
Price: Threaded barrel	$629.00
Price: With Silent-SR suppressor	$1,078.00

RUGER 10/22 SPORTER

Same specifications as 10/22 Carbine except has American walnut stock with hand-checkered pistol grip and fore-end, straight buttplate, sling swivels, 18.9-in. barrel, and no barrel band.

Price: $419.00

RUGER 10/22 TARGET LITE

Features a 16 1/8-in. heavy, hammer-forged threaded barrel with tight chamber dimensions, black or red/black laminate stock with thumbhole and adjustable length-of-pull, BX Trigger with 2.5-3 lbs. pull weight, minimal overtravel and positive reset.

Price: $649.00

SAVAGE A17 SERIES

Calibers: .17 HMR, . **Capacity:** 10-round rotary magazine. **Barrel:** 22 in. **Weight:** 5.4–5.6 lbs. **Features:** Delayed blowback action, Savage AccuTrigger, synthetic or laminated stock. Target model has heavy barrel, sporter or thumbhole stock. Introduced in 2016.

Price: Standard model	$473.00
Price: Sporter (Gray laminate stock)	$574.00
Price: Target Sporter	$571.00
Price: Target Thumbhole	$631.00

SAVAGE A22 SERIES

Caliber: .22 LR, .22 WMR. **Capacity 10-round magazine.** Similar to A17 series except for caliber.

Price:	$284.00
Price: A22 SS stainless barrel	$419.00
Price: Target Thumbhole stock, heavy barrel	$449.00
Price: Pro Varmint w/Picatinny rail, heavy bbl., target stock	$409.00
Price: 22 WMR	$479.00

SAVAGE A22 BNS-SR

Caliber: .22 LR. **Capacity:** 10. **Barrel:** 18 in., carbon steel. **Stock:** Laminated wood. **Sights:** Two-piece Weaver bases, no scope included. **Weight:** 6.6 lbs. **Features:** Ergonomic stock, AccuTrigger, straight blowback semi-auto.

Price: $479.99

SMITH & WESSON M&P15-22 SERIES

Caliber: .22 LR. **Capacities:** 10- or 25-round magazine. **Barrel:** 15.5 in., 16 in. or 16.5 in. **Stock:** 6-position telescoping or fixed. **Features:** A rimfire version of AR-derived M&P tactical autoloader. Operates with blowback action. Quad-mount Picatinny rails, plain barrel or compensator, alloy upper and lower, matte black metal finish. Kryptek Highlander or Muddy Girl camo finishes available.

Price: Standard	$449.00
Price: Kryptek Highlander or Muddy Girl camo	$499.00
Price: MOE Model with Magpul sights, stock and grip	$609.00
Price: Performance Center upgrades, threaded barrel	$789.00
Price: M&P 15 Sport w/Crimson Trace Red Dot sight	$759.00

THOMPSON/CENTER T/CR22

Caliber: .22 LR. **Capacities:** 10-round rotary magazine. **Barrel:** 20 in. stainless steel, threaded muzzle. **Stock:** Hogue overmolded sculpted and ambidextrous thumbhole. **Features:** Picatinny top rail, sling swivel studs, push-button safety, fully machined aluminum receiver with hole to allow cleaning from rear. From the Smith & Wesson Performance Center.

Price: $497.00

VOLQUARTSEN ULTRALITE MODSHOT

Caliber: .22 LR. **Capacity:** 10. **Barrel:** Forward blow comp, anodized aluminum. **Stock:** Modshot. **Sights:** Picatinny rail. **Weight:** 3.8 lbs. **Features:** Ultralight design, 2.25-lb. trigger pull, uses Ruger magazines, made in the USA.

Price: $1,769.99

Prices given are believed to be accurate at time of publication however, many factors affect retail pricing so exact prices are not possible.

BROWNING BL-22

Caliber: .22 LR. **Capacity:** Tubular magazines, 15+1. **Action:** Short-throw lever action, side ejection. Rack-and-pinion lever. **Barrel:** Recessed muzzle. **Stock:** Walnut, two-piece straight-grip Western style. **Trigger:** Half-cock hammer safety; fold-down hammer. **Sights:** Bead post front, folding-leaf rear. Steel receiver grooved for scope mount. **Weight:** 5–5.4 lbs. **Length:** 36.75–40.75 in. overall. **Features:** Action lock provided. Introduced 1996. FLD Grade II Octagon has octagonal 24-in. barrel, silver nitride receiver with scroll engraving, gold-colored trigger. FLD Grade I has satin-nickel receiver, blued trigger, no stock checkering. FLD Grade II has satin-nickel receivers with scroll engraving; gold-colored trigger, cut checkering. Both introduced 2005. Grade I has blued receiver and trigger, no stock checkering. Grade II has gold-colored trigger, cut checkering, blued receiver with scroll engraving. Imported from Japan by Browning.
Price: BL-22 Grade I/II, From .... $620.00–$700.00
Price: BL-22 FLD Grade I/II, From .... $660.00–$750.00
Price: BL-22 FLD, Grade II Octagon $980.00

HENRY LEVER-ACTION RIFLES

Caliber: .22 Long Rifle (15 shot), .22 Magnum (11 shots), .17 HMR (11 shots). **Barrel:** 18.25 in. round. **Weight:** 5.5–5.75 lbs. **Length:** 34 in. overall (.22 LR). **Stock:** Walnut. **Sights:** Hooded blade front, open adjustable rear. **Features:** Polished blue finish; full-length tubular magazine; side ejection; receiver grooved for scope mounting. Introduced 1997. Made in USA by Henry Repeating Arms Co.
Price: H001 Carbine .22 LR $378.00
Price: H001L Carbine .22 LR, Large Loop Lever $394.00
Price: H001Y Youth model (33 in. overall, 11-round .22 LR) $378.00
Price: H001M .22 Magnum, 19.25 in. octagonal barrel, deluxe
     walnut stock $525.00
Price: H001V .17 HMR, 20 in. octagonal barrel,
     Williams Fire Sights $578.00

HENRY LEVER-ACTION OCTAGON FRONTIER MODEL

Same as lever rifles except chambered in .17 HMR, .22 Short/Long/LR, .22 Magnum. **Barrel:** 20 in. octagonal. **Sights:** Marble's fully adjustable semi-buckhorn rear, brass bead front. **Weight:** 6.25 lbs. Made in USA by Henry Repeating Arms Co.
Price: H001T Lever Octagon .22 S/L/R $473.00
Price: H001TM Lever Octagon .22 Magnum, .17 HMR $578.00

HENRY GOLDEN BOY SERIES

Calibers: .17 HMR, .22 LR (16-shot), .22 Magnum. **Barrel:** 20 in. octagonal. **Weight:** 6.25 lbs. **Length:** 38 in. overall. **Stock:** American walnut. **Sights:** Blade front, open rear. **Features:** Brasslite receiver, brass buttplate, blued barrel and lever. Introduced 1998. Made in USA from Henry Repeating Arms Co.
Price: H004 .22 LR $578.00
Price: H004M .22 Magnum $625.00
Price: H004V .17 HMR $641.00
Price: H004DD .22 LR Deluxe, engraved receiver $1,575.00-1,654.00

HENRY SILVER BOY

Calibers: 17 HMR, .22 S/L/LR, .22 WMR. **Capacities:** Tubular magazine. 12 rounds (.17 HMR and .22 WMR), 16 rounds (.22 LR), 21 rounds (.22 Short).

Barrel: 20 in. **Stock:** American walnut with curved buttplate. **Finish:** Nickel receiver, barrel band and buttplate. **Sights:** Adjustable buckhorn rear, bead front. Silver Eagle model has engraved scroll pattern from early original Henry rifle. Offered in same calibers as Silver Boy. Made in USA from Henry Repeating Arms Company.
Price: .22 S/L/LR $630.00
Price: .22 WMR $682.00
Price: .17 HMR $709.00
Price: Silver Eagle .... $892.00–$945.00

HENRY PUMP ACTION

Caliber: .22 LR. **Capacity:** 15 rounds. **Barrel:** 18.25 in. **Weight:** 5.5 lbs. **Length:** NA. **Stock:** American walnut. **Sights:** Bead on ramp front, open adjustable rear. **Features:** Polished blue finish; receiver grooved for scope mount; grooved slide handle; two barrel bands. Introduced 1998. Made in USA from Henry Repeating Arms Co.
Price: H003T .22 LR $578.00
Price: H003TM .22 Magnum $620.00

MOSSBERG MODEL 464 RIMFIRE

Caliber: .22 LR. **Capacity:** 14-round tubular magazine. **Barrel:** 20-in. round blued. **Weight:** 5.6 lbs. **Length:** 35.75 in. overall. **Features:** Adjustable sights, straight grip stock, plain hardwood straight stock and fore-end. Lever-action model.
Price: $503.00
Price: SPX Tactical model, adjustable synthetic stock $525.00

REMINGTON 572 BDL DELUXE FIELDMASTER PUMP

Calibers: .22 Short (20), .22 Long (17) or .22 LR (15), tubular magazine. **Barrel:** 21 in. round tapered. **Weight:** 5.5 lbs. **Length:** 40 in. overall. **Stock:** Walnut with checkered pistol grip and slide handle. **Sights:** Big game. **Features:** Crossbolt safety; removing inner magazine tube converts rifle to single shot; receiver grooved for tip-off scope mount. Another classic rimfire, this model has been in production since 1955.
Price: $723.00

ANSCHUTZ MODEL 64 MP

Caliber: .22 LR. **Capacity:** 5-round magazine. **Barrel:** 25.6-in. heavy match. **Weight:** 9 lbs. **Stock:** Multipurpose hardwood with beavertail fore-end. **Sights:** None. Drilled and tapped for scope or receiver sights. **Features:** Model 64S BR (benchrest) has 20-in. heavy barrel, adjustable two-stage match-grade trigger, flat beavertail stock. Imported from Germany by Steyr Arms.
Price: $1,399.00

ANSCHUTZ 1416D/1516D CLASSIC

Calibers: .22 LR (1416D888), .22 WMR (1516D). **Capacity:** 5-round magazine. **Barrel:** 22.5 in. **Weight:** 6 lbs. **Length:** 41 in. overall. **Stock:** European hardwood with walnut finish; classic style with straight comb, checkered pistol grip and fore-end. **Sights:** Hooded ramp front, folding leaf rear. **Features:** Uses Match 64 action. Adjustable single-stage trigger. Receiver grooved for scope mounting. Imported from Germany by Steyr Arms.
Price: 1416D .22 LR $1,199.00
Price: 1416D Classic left-hand $1,249.00
Price: 1516D .22 WMR $1,249.00
Price: 1416D, thumbhole stock $1,649.00

Prices given are believed to be accurate at time of publication however, many factors affect retail pricing so exact pricing is not possible.

75TH EDITION, 2021 ⊕ **433**

RIMFIRE RIFLES Bolt Action & Single Shot

ANSCHUTZ 1710D CUSTOM
Caliber: .22 LR. **Capacity:** 5-round magazine. **Barrels:** 23.75- or 24.25-in. heavy contour. **Weights:** 6.5–7.375 lbs. **Length:** 42.5 in. overall. **Stock:** Select European walnut. **Sights:** Hooded ramp front, folding leaf rear; drilled and tapped for scope mounting. **Features:** Match 54 action with adjustable single-stage trigger; roll-over Monte Carlo cheekpiece, slim fore-end with Schnabel tip, Wundhammer palm swell on pistol grip, rosewood grip cap with white diamond insert; skip-line checkering on grip and fore-end. Introduced 1988. Imported from Germany by Steyr Arms.
Price: From..**$2,195.00**

BROWNING T-BOLT RIMFIRE
Calibers: .22 LR, .17 HMR, .22 WMR. **Capacity:** 10-round rotary box double helix magazine. **Barrel:** 22-in. free-floating, semi-match chamber, target muzzle crown. **Weight:** 4.8 lbs. **Length:** 40.1 in. overall. **Stock:** Walnut, maple or composite. **Sights:** None. **Features:** Straight-pull bolt action, three-lever trigger adjustable for pull weight, dual action screws, sling swivel studs. Crossbolt lockup, enlarged bolt handle, one-piece dual extractor with integral spring and red cocking indicator band, gold-tone trigger. Top-tang, thumb-operated two-position safety, drilled and tapped for scope mounts. Varmint model has raised Monte Carlo comb, heavy barrel, wide forearm. Introduced 2006. Imported from Japan by Browning. Left-hand models added in 2009.
Price: .22 LR, From.............................. $750.00–$780.00
Price: Composite Target .... $780.00–$800.00
Price: .17 HMR/.22 WMR, From .... $790.00–$830.00

COOPER MODEL 57-M REPEATER
Calibers: .22 LR, .22 WMR, .17 HMR, .17 Mach. **Barrel:** 22 in. or 24 in. **Weight:** 6.5–7.5 lbs. **Stock:** Claro walnut, 22 LPI hand checkering. **Sights:** None furnished. **Features:** Three rear locking lug, repeating bolt-action with 5-round magazine for .22 LR; 4-round magazine for .22 WMR and 17 HMR. Fully adjustable trigger. Left-hand models add .... $150 to base rifle price. 0.250-in. group rimfire accuracy guarantee at 50 yards; 0.5-in. group centerfire accuracy guarantee at 100 yards. Options include wood upgrades, case-color metalwork, barrel fluting, custom LOP, and many others.
Price: Classic $2,495.00
Price: Custom Classic...$2,995.00
Price: Western Classic $3,795.00
Price: Schnabel $2,595.00
Price: Jackson Squirrel...$2,595.00
Price: Jackson Hunter $2,455.00
Price: Mannlicher $4,755.00

CZ 457 AMERICAN
Calibers: .17 HMR, .22 LR, .22 WMR. **Capacity:** 5-round detachable magazine. **Barrel:** 24.8 in. **Weight:** 6.2 lbs. **Stock:** Turkish walnut American style with high flat comb. **Sights:** None. Integral 11mm dovetail scope base. **Features:** Adjustable trigger, push-to-fire safety, interchangeable barrel system.
Price: $476.00
Price: .17 HMR .22 WMR $496.00
Price: Varmint model.............................. $660.00-$762.00

CHIPMUNK SINGLE SHOT
Caliber: .22 Short, Long and Long Rifle or .22 WMR. Manually cocked single-shot bolt-action youth gun. **Barrel:** 16.125 in. blued or stainless. **Weight:**

2.6 lbs. **Length:** 30 in., LOP 11.6 in. **Stock:** Synthetic, American walnut or laminate. Barracuda model has ergonomic thumbhole stock with raised comb, accessory rail. **Sights:** Adjustable rear peep, fixed front. From Keystone Sporting Arms.
Price: Synthetic...$163.00-$250.00
Price: Walnut ....$209.00-$270.00
Price: Barracuda ....$258.00-$294.00

CRICKETT SINGLE SHOT
Caliber: .22 Short, Long and Long Rifle or .22 WMR. Manually cocked single-shot bolt-action. Similar to Chipmunk but with more options and models. **Barrel:** 16.125 in. blued or stainless. **Weight:** 3 lbs. **Length:** 30 in., LOP 11.6 in. **Stock:** Synthetic, American walnut or laminate. Available in wide range of popular camo patterns and colors. **Sights:** Adjustable rear peep, fixed front. Drilled and tapped for scope mounting using special Chipmunk base. Alloy model has AR-style buttstock, XBR has target stock and bull barrel, Precision Rifle has bipod and fully adjustable thumbhole stock.
Price: Alloy $300.00
Price: XBR ....$380.00-$400.00
Price: Precision Rifle ....$316.00-$416.00
Price: Adult Rifle ....$240.00-$280.00

HENRY MINI BOLT YOUTH RIFLE
Caliber: .22 LR, single-shot youth gun. **Barrel:** 16 in. stainless, 8-groove rifling. **Weight:** 3.25 lbs. **Length:** 30 in., LOP 11.5 in. **Stock:** Synthetic, pistol grip, wraparound checkering and beavertail forearm. Available in black finish or bright colors. **Sights:** William Fire sights. **Features:** One-piece bolt configuration manually operated safety.
Price: $289.00

MARLIN MODEL XT-17 SERIES
Caliber: .17 HRM. **Capacity:** 4- and 7-round, two magazines included. **Barrel:** 22 in. **Weight:** 6 lbs. **Stock:** Black synthetic with palm swell, stippled grip areas, or walnut-finished hardwood with Monte Carlo comb. Laminated stock available. **Sights:** Adjustable rear, ramp front. Drilled and tapped for scope mounts. **Features:** Adjustable trigger. Blue or stainless finish.
Price: .... $269.00–$429.00

MARLIN MODEL XT-22 SERIES
Calibers: .22 Short, .22 Long, .22 LR. **Capacities:** Available with 7-shot detachable box magazine or tubular magazine (17 to 22 rounds). **Barrels:** 22 in. Varmint model has heavy barrel. **Weight:** 6 lbs. **Stock:** Black synthetic, walnut-finished hardwood, walnut or camo. Tubular model available with two-tone brown laminated stock. **Finish:** Blued or stainless. **Sights:** Adjustable rear, ramp front. Some models have folding rear sight with a hooded or high-visibility orange front sight. **Features:** Pro-Fire Adjustable Trigger, Micro-Groove rifling, thumb safety with red cocking indicator. The XT-22M series is chambered for .22 WMR. Made in USA by Marlin Firearms Co.
Price: From .... $221.00–$340.00
Price: XT-22M .... $240.00–$270.00

MEACHAM LOW-WALL
Calibers: Any rimfire cartridge. **Barrels:** 26–34 in. **Weight:** 7-15 lbs. **Sights:** none. Tang drilled for Win. base, .375 in. dovetail slot front. **Stock:** Fancy eastern walnut with cheekpiece; ebony insert in forearm tip. **Features:** Exact copy of 1885 Winchester. With most Winchester factory options available including double-set triggers. Introduced 1994. Made in USA by Meacham T&H Inc.
Price: From..$4,999.00

MOSSBERG MODEL 817
Caliber: .17 HMR. **Capacity:** 5-round magazine. **Barrel:** 21-in. free-floating bull barrel, recessed muzzle crown. **Weight:** 4.9 lbs. (black synthetic), 5.2 lbs. (wood). **Stock:** Black synthetic or wood; length of pull, 14.25 in. **Sights:** Factory-installed Weaver-style scope bases. **Features:** Blued or brushed chrome metal finishes, crossbolt safety, gun lock. Introduced 2008. Made in USA by O.F. Mossberg & Sons, Inc.
Price: .... $230.00–$274.00

Prices given are believed to be accurate at time of publication however, many factors affect retail pricing so exact prices are not possible.

MOSSBERG MODEL 801/802

Caliber: .22 LR **Capacity:** 10-round magazine. **Barrel:** 18 in. free-floating. Varmint model has 21-in. heavy barrel. **Weight:** 4.1–4.6 lbs. **Sights:** Adjustable rifle. Receiver grooved for scope mount. **Stock:** Black synthetic. **Features:** Ergonomically placed magazine release and safety buttons, crossbolt safety, free gun lock. 801 Half Pint has 12.25-in. LOP, 16-in. barrel and weighs 4 lbs. Hardwood stock; removable magazine plug.

Price: Plinkster **$242.00**
Price: Half Pint **$242.00**
Price: Varmint **$242.00**

NEW ULTRA LIGHT ARMS 20RF

Caliber: .22 LR, single-shot or repeater. **Barrel:** Douglas, length to order. **Weight:** 5.25 lbs. **Length:** Varies. **Stock:** Kevlar/graphite composite, variety of finishes. **Sights:** None furnished; drilled and tapped for scope mount. **Features:** Timney trigger, hand-lapped action, button-rifled barrel, hand-bedded action, recoil pad, sling-swivel studs, optional Jewell trigger. Made in USA by New Ultra Light Arms.

Price: 20 RF single shot **$1,800.00**
Price: 20 RF repeater **$1,850.00**

RUGER AMERICAN RIMFIRE RIFLE

Calibers: .17 HMR, .22 LR,.22 WMR. **Capacity:** 10-round rotary magazine. **Barrels:** 22-in., or 18-in. threaded. **Sights:** Williams fiber optic, adjustable. **Stock:** Composite with interchangeable comb adjustments, sling swivels. Adjustable trigger.

Price: **$359.00**

RUGER PRECISION RIMFIRE RIFLE

Calibers: .17 HMR, .22 LR, .22 HMR. **Capacity:** 9 to 15-round magazine. **Barrel:** 18 in. threaded. **Weight:** 6.8 lbs. **Stock:** Quick-fit adjustable with AR-pattern pistol grip, free-floated handguard with Magpul M-LOK slots. **Features:** Adjustable trigger, oversized bolt handle, Picatinny scope base.

Price: **$529.00**

SAVAGE MARK II BOLT-ACTION

Calibers: .22 LR, .17 HMR. **Capacity:** 10-round magazine. **Barrel:** 20.5 in. **Weight:** 5.5 lbs. **Length:** 39.5 in. overall. **Stock:** Camo, laminate, thumbhole or OD Green stock available **Sights:** Bead front, open adjustable rear. Receiver grooved for scope mounting. **Features:** Thumb-operated rotating safety. Blue finish. Introduced 1990. Made in Canada, from Savage Arms, Inc.

Price: .... **$228.00–$280.00**
Price: Varmint w/heavy barrel **$242.00**
Price: Camo stock **$280.00**
Price: OD Green stock... **$291.00**
Price: Multi-colored laminate stock **$529.00**
Price: Thumbhole laminate stock **$469.00**

SAVAGE MARK II-FSS STAINLESS RIFLE

Similar to the Mark II except has stainless steel barreled action and black synthetic stock with positive checkering, swivel studs, and 20.75-in. free-floating and button-rifled barrel with magazine. Weighs 5.5 lbs. Introduced 1997. Imported from Canada by Savage Arms, Inc.

Price: **$336.00**

SAVAGE MODEL 93G MAGNUM BOLT ACTION

Caliber: .22 WMR. **Capacity:** 5-round magazine. **Barrel:** 20.75 in. **Weight:** 5.75 lbs. **Length:** 39.5 in. overall. **Stock:** Walnut-finished hardwood with Monte Carlo-type comb, checkered grip and fore-end. **Sights:** Bead front, adjustable open rear. Receiver grooved for scope mount. **Features:** Thumb-operated rotary safety. Blue finish. Introduced 1994. Made in Canada, from Savage Arms.

Price: Model 93G **$285.00**
Price: Model 93F (as above with black graphite/fiberglass stock) **$364.00**
Price: Model 93 BSEV, thumbhole stock **$646.00**

SAVAGE MODEL 93FSS MAGNUM RIFLE

Similar to Model 93G except stainless steel barreled action and black synthetic stock with positive checkering. Weighs 5.5 lbs. Introduced 1997. Imported from Canada by Savage Arms, Inc.

Price: **$353.00**

SAVAGE MODEL 93FVSS MAGNUM

Similar to Model 93FSS Magnum except 21-in. heavy barrel with recessed target-style crown, satin-finished stainless barreled action, black graphite/fiberglass stock. Drilled and tapped for scope mounting; comes with Weaver-style bases. Introduced 1998. Imported from Canada by Savage Arms, Inc.

Price: **$364.00**

SAVAGE B-MAG

Caliber: .17 Win. Super Magnum. **Capacity:** 8-round rotary magazine. **Stock:** Synthetic. **Weight:** 4.5 pounds. Chambered for new Winchester .17 Super Magnum rimfire cartridge that propels a 20-grain bullet at approximately 3,000 fps. **Features:** Adjustable AccuTrigger, rear locking lugs, new and different bolt-action rimfire design that cocks on close of bolt. New in 2013.

Price: **$402.00**
Price: Stainless steel receiver and barrel **$440.00**
Price: Heavy Bbl. Laminate stock **$589.00**

SAVAGE BRJ SERIES

Similar to Mark II, Model 93 and Model 93R17 rifles but features spiral fluting pattern on a heavy barrel, blued finish and Royal Jacaranda wood laminate stock.

Price: Mark II BRJ, .22 LR **$519.00**
Price: Model 93 BRJ, .22 Mag.................................... **$542.00**
Price: Model 93 R17 BRJ, .17 HMR **$542.00**

SAVAGE TACTICAL RIMFIRE SERIES

Similar to Savage Model BRJ series semi-auto rifles but with matte finish and a tactical-style wood stock.

Price: Mark II TR, .22 LR **$533.00**
Price: Mark II TRR, .22 LR, three-way accessory rail **$627.00**
Price: Model 93R17 TR, .17 HMR **$558.00**
Price: Model 93R17 TRR, .17 HMR, three-way accessory rail **$654.00**

SAVAGE B SERIES

Calibers: .17 HMR, .22 LR, 22 WMR. **Capacity:** 10-round rotary magazine. **Barrel:** 21 in. (16.25 in. threaded heavy barrel on Magnum FV-SR Model). **Stock:** Black synthetic with target-style vertical pistol grip. **Weight:** 6 lbs. Features include top tang safety, Accutrigger. Introduced in 2017.

Price: From.. **$281.00–$445.00**

SAVAGE MODEL 42

Calibers/Gauges: Break-open over/under design with .22 LR or .22 WMR barrel over a .410 shotgun barrel. Under-lever operation. **Barrel:** 20 in. **Stock:** Synthetic black matte. **Weight:** 6.1 lbs. **Sights:** Adjustable rear, bead front. Updated variation of classic Stevens design from the 1940s.

Price **$509.00**

Prices given are believed to be accurate at time of publication however, many factors affect retail pricing so exact prices are not possible.

75TH EDITION, 2021 ✛ **435**

ANSCHUTZ 1903 MATCH
Caliber: .22 LR. **Capacity:** Single-shot. **Barrel:** 21.25 in. **Weight:** 8 lbs. **Length:** 43.75 in. overall. **Stock:** Walnut-finished hardwood with adjustable cheekpiece; stippled grip and fore-end. **Sights:** None furnished. **Features:** Uses Anschutz Match 64 action. A medium weight rifle for intermediate and advanced Junior Match competition. Available from Champion's Choice.
Price: Right-hand $1,195.00

ANSCHUTZ 1912 SPORT
Caliber: .22 LR. **Barrel:** 26 in. match. **Weight:** 11.4 lbs. **Length:** 41.7 in. overall. **Stock:** Non-stained thumbhole stock adjustable in length with adjustable buttplate and cheekpiece adjustment. Flat fore-end raiser block 4856 adjustable in height. Hook buttplate. **Sights:** None furnished. **Features:** in. Free rifle in. for women. Smallbore model 1907 with 1912 stock: Match 54 action. Delivered with: Hand stop 6226, fore-end raiser block 4856, screwdriver, instruction leaflet with test target. Available from Champion's Choice.
Price: $2,995.00

ANSCHUTZ 1913 SUPER MATCH RIFLE
Same as the Model 1911 except European walnut International-type stock with adjustable cheekpiece, or color laminate, both available with straight or lowered fore-end, adjustable aluminum hook buttplate, adjustable hand stop, weighs 13 lbs, 46 in. overall. Stainless or blued barrel. Available from Champion's Choice.
Price: Right-hand, blued, no sights, walnut stock............................. $3,799.00

ANSCHUTZ 1907 STANDARD MATCH RIFLE
Same action as Model 1913 but with 0.875-in. diameter 26-in. barrel (stainless or blues). **Length:** 44.5 in. overall. **Weight:** 10.5 lbs. **Stock:** Choice of stock configurations. Vented fore-end. Designed for prone and position shooting ISU requirements; suitable for NRA matches. Also available with walnut flat-forend stock for benchrest shooting. Available from Champion's Choice.
Price: Right-hand, blued, no sights................................... $2,385.00

ARMALITE M15 A4 CARBINE 6.8 & 7.62X39
Calibers: 6.8 Rem., 7.62x39. **Barrel:** 16 in. chrome-lined with flash suppressor. **Weight:** 7 lbs. **Length:** 26.6 in. **Features:** Front and rear picatinny rails for mounting optics, two-stage tactical trigger, anodized aluminum/phosphate finish.
Price: $1,107.00

CZ 457 VARMINT PRECISION CHASSIS
Caliber: .22 LR. **Capacity:** 5. **Barrel:** 16.5 or 24 in., suppressor ready, cold hammer-forged, heavy. **Stock:** Aluminum chassis. **Sights:** None, integral 11mm dovetail. **Weight:** 7 lbs. **Features:** Fully adjustable trigger, receiver mounted push-to-fire safety, swappable barrel system.
Price: $999.99

MASTERPIECE ARMS MPA BA PMR COMPETITION RIFLE
Calibers: .308 Win., 6mm Creedmoor, 6.5 Creedmoor. **Capacity:** 10. **Barrel:** 26 in., M24 stainless steel, polished. **Stock:** Aluminum chassis. **Sights:** None, optional package with MPA 30mm mount and Bushnell scope. **Weight:** 11.5 lbs. **Features:** Built-in inclinometer, MPA/Curtis action, match-grade chamber.
Price: .... $2,999.99-$3,459.99

REMINGTON 40-XB RANGEMASTER TARGET
Calibers: 15 calibers from .22 BR Remington to .300 Win. Mag. **Barrel:** 27.25 in. **Weight:** 11.25 lbs. **Length:** 47 in. overall. **Stock:** American walnut, laminated thumbhole or Kevlar with high comb and beavertail fore-end stop. Rubber nonslip buttplate. **Sights:** None. Scope blocks installed. **Features:** Adjustable trigger. Stainless barrel and action. Receiver drilled and tapped for sights. Model 40-XB Tactical (2008) chambered in .308 Win., comes with guarantee of 0.75-in. maximum 5-shot groups at 100 yards. **Weight:** 10.25 lbs. Includes Teflon-coated stainless button-rifled barrel, 1:14 in. twist, 27.25-in. long, three longitudinal flutes. Bolt-action repeater, adjustable 40-X trigger and precision machined aluminum bedding block. Stock is H-S Precision Pro Series synthetic tactical stock, black with green web finish, vertical pistol grip. From Remington Custom Shop.
Price: 40-XB KS, aramid fiber stock, single shot $2,863.00
Price: 40-XB KS, aramid fiber stock, repeater $3,014.00
Price: 40-XB Tactical .308 Win. $2,992.00

REMINGTON 40-XBBR KS
Calibers: Five calibers from .22 BR to .308 Win. **Barrel:** 20 in. (light varmint class), 24 in. (heavy varmint class). **Weight:** 7.25 lbs. (light varmint class); 12 lbs. (heavy varmint class). **Stock:** Aramid fiber. **Sights:** None. Supplied with scope blocks. **Features:** Unblued benchrest with stainless steel barrel, trigger adjustable from 1.5 lbs. to 3.5 lbs. Special 2-oz. trigger extra cost. Scope and mounts extra. From Remington Custom Shop.
Price: Single shot $3,950.00

REMINGTON 700 PCR ENHANCED
Calibers: .308 Win., .260 Rem., 6.5 Creedmoor. **Capacity:** 5. **Barrel:** 24 in., cold hammer-forged, 5R rifling, threaded. **Stock:** Anodized aluminum chassis, Magpul Gen 3 PRS. **Sights:** Picatinny rail. **Weight:** 11 lbs. **Features:** Aluminum handguard with square drop, X-Mark Pro adjustable trigger, tactical bolt knob.
Price: $1,199.99

ROCK RIVER ARMS RBG
Calibers: .308 Win., 7.62mm, 6.5 Creedmoor. **Capacity:** 6. **Barrel:** 20, 22, 24 in., stainless steel, fluted. **Stock:** KRG chassis. **Sights:** 20 MOA rail. **Weight:** 10 to 10.5 lbs. **Features:** Sub-MOA accuracy, oversized bolt handle, Trigger Tech trigger.
Price: $4,150.99

SEEKINS PRECISION HAVAK ELEMENT
Calibers: .308 Win., 6mm Creedmoor, 6.5 PRC, 6.5 Creedmoor. **Capacity:** 3 to 5. **Barrel:** 21 in., Mountain Hunter contour, spiral fluted, threaded. **Stock:** Carbon composite. **Sights:** 20 MOA picatinny rail. **Weight:** 5.5 lbs. **Features:** Timney Elite Hunter trigger, M16-style extractor, 7075 aerospace aluminum/stainless steel body.
Price: $2,795.99

SIG SAUER CROSS RIFLE
Calibers: .277 Sig Fury, .308 Win., 6.5 Creedmoor. **Capacity:** 5. **Barrel:** 16 to 18 in., stainless steel. **Stock:** Sig precision, polymer/alloy, folding. **Sights:** Picatinny rail. **Weight:** 6.5 to 6.8 lbs. **Features:** M-LOK rail, two-stage match trigger.
Price: $1,779.99

SAKO TRG-22 BOLT-ACTION
Calibers: .308 Win., .260 Rem, 6.5 Creedmoor, .300 Win Mag, .338 Lapua. **Capacity:** 5-round magazine. **Barrel:** 26 in. **Weight:** 10.25 lbs. **Length:** 45.25 in. overall. **Stock:** Reinforced polyurethane with fully adjustable cheekpiece and buttplate. **Sights:** None furnished. Optional quick-detachable, one-piece scope mount base, 1 in. or 30mm rings. **Features:** Resistance-free bolt, free-floating heavy stainless barrel, 60-degree bolt lift. Two-stage trigger is adjustable for length, pull, horizontal or vertical pitch. TRG-42 has similar features but has long action and is chambered for .338 Lapua. Imported from Finland by Beretta USA.
Price: TRG-22 .... $3,495.00
Price: TRG-22 with folding stock $6,400.00
Price: TRG-42 .... $4,445.00
Price: TRG-42 with folding stock $7,400.00

SPRINGFIELD ARMORY M1A/M-21 TACTICAL MODEL
Similar to M1A Super Match except special sniper stock with adjustable cheekpiece and rubber recoil pad. Weighs 11.6 lbs. From Springfield Armory.
Price: $3,619.00
Price: Krieger stainless barrel..$4,046.00

Prices given are believed to be accurate at time of publication however, many factors affect retail pricing so exact prices are not possible.

ACCU-TEK AT-380 II ACP
Caliber: 380 ACP. **Capacity:** 6-round magazine. **Barrel:** 2.8 in. **Weight:** 23.5 oz. **Length:** 6.125 in. overall. **Grips:** Textured black composition. **Sights:** Blade front,rear adjustable for windage. **Features:** Made from 17-4 stainless steel, has an exposed hammer, manual firing-pin safety block and trigger disconnect. Magazine release located on the bottom of the grip. American made, lifetime warranty. Comes with two 6-round stainless steel magazines and a California-approved cable lock. Introduced 2006. Made in USA by Excel Industries.
Price: Satin stainless **$289.00**

ACCU-TEK HC-380
Similar to AT-380 II except has a 13-round magazine.
Price: **$330.00**

ACCU-TEK LT-380
Similar to AT-380 II except has a lightweight aluminum frame. **Weight:** 15 ounces.
Price: **$324.00**

AMERICAN CLASSIC 1911-A1 II SERIES
Caliber: .45 ACP, 9mm, .38 Super. **Capacity:** 8+1 magazine **Barrel:** 5 in. **Grips:** Checkered walnut. **Sights:** Novak-style rear, fixed front. **Finish:** Blue or hard chromed. Other variations include Trophy model with checkered mainspring housing, fiber optic front sight, hard-chrome finish.
Price: .... **$627-$700.00**

AMERICAN CLASSIC AMIGO SERIES
Caliber: .45 ACP. **Capacity:** 7+1. Same features as Commander size with 3.6-in. bull barrel and Officer-style frame.
Price: .... **$714.00-$813.00**

AMERICAN CLASSIC BX SERIES
Calibers: .45 ACP, 9mm. **Capacity:** 14- or 17-round magazine. **Barrel:** 5 in. **Grips:** Checkered aluminum. **Sights:** Mil-Spec style. **Finish:** Blue.
Price: **$774.00**

AMERICAN CLASSIC COMMANDER
Caliber: .45 ACP. Same features as 1911-A1 model except is Commander size with 4.25-in. barrel.
Price: .... **$624.00–$795.00**

AMERICAN CLASSIC COMPACT COMMANDER SERIES
Caliber: .45 ACP. **Capacity:** 7-round magazine. **Barrel:** 4.25 in. **Grips:** Textured hardwood. **Sights:** Fixed Novak style. **Finish:** Blue, hard chrome, two-tone.
Price: .... **$714.00-$812.00**

AMERICAN CLASSIC TROPHY
Caliber: .45 ACP. **Capacity:** 8-round magazine. **Barrel:** 5 in. **Grips:** Textured hardwood. **Sights:** Fixed, fiber-optic front/Novak rear. **Finish:** Hard chrome. **Features:** Front slide serrations, ambidextrous thumb safety.
Price: **$819.00**

AMERICAN TACTICAL IMPORTS MILITARY 1911
Caliber: .45 ACP. **Capacity:** 7+1 magazine. **Barrel:** 5 in. **Grips:** Textured mahogany. **Sights:** Fixed military style. **Finish:** Blue. Also offered in Commander and Officer's sizes and Enhanced model with additional features.
Price: .... **$500.00–$899.00**

AMERICAN TACTICAL IMPORTS GSG 1911
Caliber: .22 LR. **Capacity:** 10+1 magazine. **Weight:** 34 oz. Other features and dimensions similar to centerfire 1911.
Price: **$299.95**

AUTO-ORDNANCE 1911A1
Caliber: 45 ACP. **Capacity:** 7-round magazine. **Barrel:** 5 in. **Weight:** 39 oz. **Length:** 8.5 in. overall. **Grips:** Brown checkered plastic with medallion. **Sights:** Blade front, rear drift-adjustable for windage. **Features:** Same specs as 1911A1 military guns-parts interchangeable. Frame and slide blued; each radius has non-glare finish. Introduced 2002. Made in USA by Kahr Arms.
Price: 1911BKO Parkerized, plastic grips **$673.00**
Price: 1911BKOW Black matte finish, wood grips **$689.00**
Price: 1911BKOWWC1 Victory Girls Special **$750.00**

BAER 1911 BOSS .45
Caliber: .45 ACP. **Capacity:** 8+1 capacity. **Barrel:** 5 in. **Weight:** 37 oz. **Length:** 8.5 in. overall. **Grips:** Premium Checkered Cocobolo Grips. **Sights:** Low-Mount LBC Adj. Sight, Red Fiber Optic Front. **Features:** Speed Trigger, Beveled Mag Well, Rounded for Tactical. Rear cocking serrations on the slide, Baer fiber optic front sight (red), flat mainspring housing, checkered at 20 LPI, extended combat safety, Special tactical package, chromed complete lower, blued slide, (2) 8-round premium magazines.
Price: **$2,636.00**

BAER 1911 CUSTOM CARRY
Caliber: .45 ACP. **Capacity:** 7- or 10-round magazine. **Barrel:** 5 in. **Weight:** 37 oz. **Length:** 8.5 in. overall. **Grips:** Checkered walnut. **Sights:** Baer improved ramp-style dovetailed front, Novak low-mount rear. **Features:** Baer forged NM frame, slide and barrel with stainless bushing. Baer speed trigger with 4-lb. pull. Partial listing shown. Made in USA by Les Baer Custom, Inc.
Price: Custom Carry 5, blued **$2,190.00**
Price: Custom Carry 5, stainless **$2,290.00**
Price: Custom Carry 5, 9mm or .38 Super **$2,625.00**
Price: Custom Carry 4 Commanche-length, blued **$2,190.00**
Price: Custom Carry 4 Commanche-length, .38 Super **$2,550.00**

BAER 1911 PREMIER II

Calibers: .38 Super, .45 ACP. **Capacity:** 7- or 10-round magazine. **Barrel:** 5 in. **Weight:** 37 oz. **Length:** 8.5 in. overall. **Grips:** Checkered rosewood, double diamond pattern. **Sights:** Baer dovetailed front, low-mount Bo-Mar rear with hidden leaf. **Features:** Baer NM forged steel frame and barrel with stainless bushing, deluxe Commander hammer and sear, beavertail grip safety with pad, extended ambidextrous safety; flat mainspring housing; 30 LPI checkered front strap. Made in USA by Les Baer Custom, Inc.
Price: 5 in. .45 ACP **$2,2,245.00**
Price: 5 in. .38 Super, 9mm.. **$2,968.00**
Price: 6 in. .45 ACP, .38 Super, 9mm................................ $2,461.00-**$2,925.00**
Price: Super-Tac, .45 ACP, .38 Super $2,729.00-**3,917.00**
Price: 6-in Hunter 10mm.. **$3090.00**

BAER 1911 S.R.P.

Caliber: .45 ACP. **Barrel:** 5 in. **Weight:** 37 oz. **Length:** 8.5 in. overall. **Grips:** Checkered walnut. **Sights:** Trijicon night sights. **Features:** Similar to the F.B.I. contract gun except uses Baer forged steel frame. Has Baer match barrel with supported chamber, complete tactical action. Has Baer Ultra Coat finish. Introduced 1996. Made in USA by Les Baer Custom, Inc.
Price: Government or Commanche Length **$2,925.00**

BAER 1911 STINGER

Calibers: .45 ACP or .38 Super. **Capacity:** 7-round magazine. **Barrel:** 5 in. **Weight:** 34 oz. **Length:** 8.5 in. overall. **Grips:** Checkered cocobolo. **Sights:** Baer dovetailed front, low-mount Bo-Mar rear with hidden leaf. **Features:** Baer NM frame. Baer Commanche slide, Officer's style grip frame, beveled mag well. Made in USA by Les Baer Custom, Inc.
Price: .45 ACP .... **$2,307.00–$2,379.00**
Price: .38 Super **$2,925.00**

BAER HEMI 572

Caliber: .45 ACP. Based on Les Baer's 1911 Premier I pistol and inspired by Chrysler 1970 Hemi Cuda muscle car. **Features:** Double serrated slide, Baer fiber optic front sight with green insert, VZ black recon grips with hex-head screws, hard chrome finish on all major components, Dupont S coating on barrel, trigger, hammer, ambi safety and other controls.
Price: **$2,770.00**

BAER ULTIMATE MASTER COMBAT

Calibers: .45 ACP or .38 Super. A full house competition 1911 offered in 8 variations including 5 or 6-inch barrel, PPC Distinguished or Open class, Bullseye Wadcutter class and others. Features include double serrated slide, fitted slide to frame, checkered front strap and trigger guard, serrated rear of slide, extended ejector, tuned extractor, premium checkered grips, blued finish and two 8-round magazines.
Price: Compensated .45 .... **$3,131.00**
Price: Compensated .38 Super........................... **$3,234.00**

BAER 1911 MONOLITH S

Calibers: .45 ACP, .38 Super, 9mm, .40 S&W. A full house competition 1911 offered in 14 variations. Unique feature is extra-long dust cover that matches the length of the slide and reduces muzzle flip. Features include flat-bottom double serrated slide, low mount LBC adjustable sight with hidden rear leaf, dovetail front sight, flat serrated mainspring housing, premium checkered grips, blued finish and two 8-round magazines.
Price: .45 ....**From $2,419.00**
Price: .38 Super, .40 S&W ....**From $2,790.00**

BAER KENAI SPECIAL

Caliber: 10mm. **Capacity:** 9-round magazine. **Barrel:** 5 in. **Features:** Hard-chrome finish, double serrated slide, Baer fiber optic front sight with green or red insert, low-mount LBC adjustable rear sight, Baer black recon grips, special bear paw logo, flat serrated mainspring housing, lowered and flared ejection port, extended safety.
Price: **$3,630.00**

BAER GUNSITE PISTOL

Calibers: .45 ACP. **Capacity:** 8-round magazine. **Barrel:** 5 in. **Features:** double serrated slide, fitted slide to frame, flat serrated mainspring housing, flared and lowered ejection port, extended tactical thumb safety, fixed rear sight, dovetail front sight with night sight insert, all corners rounded, extended ejector, tuned extractor, premium checkered grips, blued finish and two 8-round magazines. Gunsite Raven logo on grips and slide.
Price: **$2,255.00**

BERETTA M92/96 A1 SERIES

Calibers: 9mm, .40 S&W. **Capacities:** 15-round magazine; .40 S&W, 12 rounds (M96 A1). **Barrel:** 4.9 in. **Weight:** 33-34 oz. **Length:** 8.5 in. **Sights:** Fiber optic front, adjustable rear. **Features:** Same as other models in 92/96 family except for addition of accessory rail.
Price: **$775.00**

BERETTA MODEL 92FS

Caliber: 9mm. **Capacity:** 10-round magazine. **Barrels:** 4.9 in., 4.25 in. (Compact). **Weight:** 34 oz. **Length:** 8.5 in. overall. **Grips:** Checkered black plastic. **Sights:** Blade front, rear adjustable for windage. Tritium night sights available. **Features:** Double action. Extractor acts as chamber loaded indicator, squared trigger guard, grooved front and backstraps, inertia firing pin. Matte or blued finish. Introduced 1977. Made in USA
Price: **$699.00**
Price: Inox **$850.00**

BERETTA MODEL 92G ELITE

Calibers: 9mm. **Capacities:** 15-round magazine. **Barrel:** 4.7 in. **Weight:** 33 oz. **Length:** 8.5 in. **Sights:** Fiber optic front, square notch rear. **Features:** M9A1 frame with M9A3 slide, front and rear serrations, ultra-thin VZ/LTT G10 grips, oversized mag release button, skeletonized trigger, ships with three magazines.
Price: **$1,100.00**

BERETTA M9 .22 LR

Caliber: .22 LR. **Capacity:** 10 or 15-round magazine. **Features:** Black Brunitron finish, interchangeable grip panels. Similar to centerfire 92/M9 with same operating controls, lighter weight (26 oz.).
Price: **$430.00**

BERETTA MODEL PX4 STORM

Calibers: 9mm, 40 S&W. **Capacities:** 17 (9mm Para.); 14 (40 S&W). **Barrel:** 4 in. **Weight:** 27.5 oz. **Grips:** Black checkered w/3 interchangeable backstraps. **Sights:** 3-dot system coated in Superluminova; removable front and rear sights. **Features:** DA/SA, manual safety/hammer decocking lever (ambi) and automatic firing pin block safety. Picatinny rail. Comes with two magazines (17/10 in 9mm Para. and 14/10 in 40 S&W). Removable hammer unit. American made by Beretta. Introduced 2005.
Price: 9mm or .40.. **$650.00**
Price: .45 ACP **$700.00**
Price: .45 ACP SD (Special Duty)........................ **$1,150.00**

BERETTA MODEL PX4 STORM SUB-COMPACT
Calibers: 9mm, 40 S&W. **Capacities:** 13 (9mm); 10 (40 S&W). **Barrel:** 3 in. **Weight:** 26.1 oz. **Length:** 6.2 in. overall. **Grips:** NA. **Sights:** NA. **Features:** Ambidextrous manual safety lever, interchangeable backstraps included, lock breech and tilt barrel system, stainless steel barrel, Picatinny rail.
Price: **$650.00**

BERETTA MODEL APX SERIES
Calibers: 9mm, 40 S&W. **Capacities:** 10, 17 (9mm); 10, 15 (40 S&W). **Barrel:** 4.25 or 3.7 in. (Centurion). **Weight:** 28, 29 oz. **Length:** 7.5 in. **Sights:** Fixed. **Features:** Striker fired, 3 interchangeable backstraps included, reversible mag release button, ambidextrous slide stop. Centurion is mid-size with shorter grip and barrel. Magazine capacity is two rounds shorter than standard model.
Price: **$575.00**

BERETTA MODEL M9
Caliber: 9mm. **Capacity:** 15. **Barrel:** 4.9 in. **Weights:** 32.2-35.3 oz. **Grips:** Plastic. **Sights:** Dot and post, low profile, windage adjustable rear. **Features:** DA/SA, forged aluminum alloy frame, delayed locking-bolt system, manual safety doubles as decocking lever, combat-style trigger guard, loaded chamber indicator. Comes with two magazines (15/10). American made by Beretta. Introduced 2005.
Price: **$675.00**

BERETTA MODEL M9A1
Caliber: 9mm. **Capacity:** 15. **Barrel:** 4.9 in. **Weights:** 32.2-35.3 oz. **Grips:** Plastic. **Sights:** Dot and post, low profile, windage adjustable rear. **Features:** Same as M9, but also includes integral Mil-Std-1913 Picatinny rail, has checkered front and backstrap. Comes with two magazines (15/10). American made by Beretta. Introduced 2005.
Price: **$775.00**

BERETTA M9A3
Caliber: 9mm. **Capacity:** 10 or 15. **Features:** Same general specifications as M9A1 with safety lever able to be converted to decocker configuration. Flat Dark Earth finish. Comes with three magazines, Vertec-style thin grip.
Price: **$1,100.00**

BERETTA BU9 NANO
Caliber: 9mm. **Capacity:** 6- or 8-round magazine. **Barrel:** 3.07 in. **Weight:** 17.7 oz. **Length:** 5.7 in. overall. **Grips:** Polymer. **Sights:** 3-dot low profile. **Features:** Double-action only, striker fired. Replaceable grip frames. Polymer frames offered in black, RE Blue, FDE, Rosa or Sniper Grey colors.
Price: **$450.00**

BERETTA PICO
Caliber: .380 ACP. **Capacity:** 6-round magazine. **Barrel:** 2.7 in. **Weight:** 11.5 oz. **Length:** 5.1 in. overall. **Grips:** Integral with polymer frame. Interchangeable backstrap. **Sights:** White outline rear. **Features:** Adjustable, quick-change. Striker-fired, double-action only operation. Ambidextrous magazine release and slide release. Available with Black, RE Blue, FDE or Lavender frame. Ships with two magazines, one flush, one with grip extension. Made in the USA.
Price: **$300.00**

BERSA THUNDER 45 ULTRA COMPACT
Caliber: .45 ACP. **Barrel:** 3.6 in. **Weight:** 27 oz. **Length:** 6.7 in. overall. **Grips:** Anatomically designed polymer. **Sights:** White outline rear. **Features:** Double action; firing pin safeties, integral locking system. Available in matte or duo-tone. Introduced 2003. Imported from Argentina by Eagle Imports, Inc.
Price: Thunder 45, matte blue **$500.00**

BERSA THUNDER 380 SERIES
Caliber: .380 ACP. **Capacity:** 7 rounds. **Barrel:** 3.5 in. **Weight:** 23 oz. **Length:** 6.6 in. overall. **Features:** Otherwise similar to Thunder 45 Ultra Compact. 380 DLX has 9-round capacity. 380 Concealed Carry has 8-round capacity. Imported from Argentina by Eagle Imports, Inc.
Price: Thunder Matte **$335.00**
Price: Thunder Satin Nickel **$355.00**
Price: Thunder Duo-Tone **$355.00**
Price: Thunder Duo-Tone with Crimson Trace Laser Grips **$555.00**
Price: Thunder CC Duo-Tone with aluminum frame.......... **$346.00**

Prices given are believed to be accurate at time of publication however, many factors affect retail pricing so exact prices are not possible.

75TH EDITION, 2021 ⬥ **439**

BERSA THUNDER 9 ULTRA COMPACT/40 SERIES

Calibers: 9mm, 40 S&W. **Barrel:** 3.5 in. **Weight:** 24.5 oz. **Length:** 6.6 in. overall.
Features: Otherwise similar to Thunder 45 Ultra Compact. 9mm Para. High
Capacity model has 17-round capacity. 40 High Capacity model has 13-round
capacity. Imported from Argentina by Eagle Imports, Inc.
Price: $500.00

BROWNING 1911-22 BLACK LABEL

Caliber: .22 LR. **Capacity:** 10-round magazine. **Barrels:** 4.25 in. or 3.625 in.
(Compact model). **Weight:** 14 oz. overall. **Features:** Other features are similar
to standard 1911-22 except for this model's composite/polymer frame,
extended grip safety, stippled black laminated grip, skeleton trigger and
hammer. Available with accessory rail (shown). Suppressor Ready model has
threaded muzzle protector, 4.875-inch barrel.
Price: $640.00
Price: With Rail.. $720.00
Price: Suppressor Ready model.. $800.00

BERSA THUNDER 22

Caliber: .22 LR. **Capacity:** 10-round magazine. **Weight:** 19 oz. **Features:**
Similar to Thunder .380 Series except for caliber. Alloy frame and slide. Finish:
Matte black, satin nickel or duo-tone.
Price: $320.00

BERSA THUNDER PRO XT

Caliber: 9mm. **Capacity:** 17-round magazine. **Barrel:** 5 in. **Weight:** 34 oz.
Grips: Checkered black polymer. **Sights:** Adjustable rear, dovetail fiber optic
front. **Features:** Available with matte or duo-tone finish. Traditional double/
single action design developed for competition. Comes with five magazines.
Price: $923.00

BROWNING 1911-22 POLYMER DESERT TAN

Caliber: .22 LR. **Capacity:** 10-round magazine. **Barrels:** 4.25 in. or 3.625 in. **Weight:**
13–14 oz. overall. **Features:** Other features are similar to standard 1911-22 except
for this model's composite/polymer frame. Also available with pink composite grips.
Price: $580.00

BROWNING 1911-22 COMPACT

Caliber: .22 LR **Capacity:** 10-round magazine. **Barrel:** 3.625 in. **Weight:**
15 oz. **Length:** 6.5 in. overall. **Grips:** Brown composite. **Sights:** Fixed.
Features: Slide is machined aluminum with alloy frame and matte blue
finish. Blowback action and single action trigger with manual thumb
and grip safeties. Works, feels and functions just like a full-size 1911. It
is simply scaled down and chambered in the best of all practice rounds:
.22 LR for focus on the fundamentals.
Price: $600.00

BROWNING 1911-380

Caliber: .380 ACP. **Capacity:** 8-round magazine. **Barrels:** 4.25 in. or 3.625 in.
(Compact). **Weight:** 16 to 17.5 oz. **Features:** Aluminum or stainless slide,
polymer frame with or without rail. Features are virtually identical to those
on the 1911-22. 1911-380 Pro has three-dot combat or night sights, G10
grips, accessory rail. Medallion Pro has checkered walnut grips.
Price: $670.00
Price: Pro, Medallion Pro.................................... $800.00–$910.00

BROWNING 1911-22 A1

Caliber: .22 LR, **Capacity:** 10-round magazine. **Barrel:** 4.25 in. **Weight:** 16 oz.
Length: 7.0625 in. overall. **Grips:** Brown composite. **Sights:** Fixed. **Features:** Slide
is machined aluminum with alloy frame and matte blue finish. Blowback action
and single action trigger with manual thumb and grip safeties. Works, feels and
functions just like a full-size 1911. It is simply scaled down and chambered in the
best of all practice rounds: .22 LR for focus on the fundamentals.
Price: $600.00

BROWNING BUCK MARK CAMPER UFX
Caliber: .22 LR. **Capacity:** 10-round magazine. **Barrel:** 5.5-in. tapered bull. **Weight:** 34 oz. **Length:** 9.5 in. overall. **Grips:** Overmolded Ultragrip Ambidextrous. **Sights:** Pro-Target adjustable rear, ramp front. **Features:** Matte blue receiver, matte blue or stainless barrel.
Price: Camper UFX.. $390.00
Price: Camper UFX stainless $430.00

BROWNING BUCK MARK MEDALLION ROSEWOOD
Caliber: .22 LR. **Capacity:** 10-round magazine. **Barrel:** 5.5-in. **Grips:** Laminate rosewood colored with gold Buckmark. **Sights:** Pro-Target adjustable rear, TruGlo/Marble's fiber-optic front. **Finish:** Matte black receiver, blackened stainless barrel with polished flats. Gold-plated trigger.
Price: $510.00

BROWNING BUCK MARK HUNTER
Caliber: .22 LR. **Capacity:** 10-round magazine. **Barrel:** 7.25-in. heavy tapered bull. **Weight:** 38 oz. **Length:** 11.3 in. overall. **Grips:** Cocobolo target. **Sights:** Pro-Target adjustable rear, Tru-Glo/Marble's fiber-optic front. Integral scope base on top rail. Scope in photo not included. **Features:** Matte blue.
Price: $500.00

BROWNING BUCK MARK CONTOUR STAINLESS URX
Caliber: .22 LR. **Capacity:** 10-round magazine. **Barrel:** 5.5 or 7.25-in. special contour. **Grips:** Checkered, textured. **Sights:** Pro-Target adjustable rear, Pro-Target front. Integral scope base on top rail. **Finish:** Matte black receiver, blackened stainless barrel with polished flats. Gold-plated trigger.
Price: $550.00

BROWNING BUCK MARK FIELD TARGET SUPPRESSOR READY
Caliber: .22 LR. **Capacity:** 10-round magazine. **Barrel:** 5.5-in. heavy bull, suppressor ready. **Grips:** Cocobolo target. **Sights:** Pro-Target adjustable rear, Tru-Glo/Marble's fiber-optic front. Integral scope base on top rail. Scope in photo not included. **Features:** Matte blue.
Price: $600.00

BROWNING BUCK PRACTICAL URX
Caliber: .22 LR. **Capacity:** 10-round magazine. **Barrels:** 5.5-in. tapered bull or 4-in. slab-sided (Micro). **Weight:** 34 oz. **Length:** 9.5 in. overall. **Grips:** Ultragrip RX Ambidextrous. **Sights:** Pro-Target adjustable rear, Tru-Glo/Marble's fiber-optic front. **Features:** Matte gray receiver, matte blue barrel.
Price: $479.00
Price: Stainless $470.00
Price: Micro $470.00

CHIAPPA 1911-22
Caliber: .22 LR. **Capacity:** 10-round magazine. **Barrel:** 5 in. **Weight:** 33.5 oz. **Length:** 8.5 in. **Grips:** Two-piece wood. **Sights:** Fixed. **Features:** A faithful replica of the famous John Browning 1911A1 pistol. Fixed barrel design. Available in black, OD green or tan finish. Target and Tactical models have adjustable sights.
Price: From .... $269.00–$408.00

CHIAPPA M9-22 STANDARD
Caliber: .22 LR. **Barrel:** 5 in. **Weight:** 2.3 lbs. **Length:** 8.5 in. **Grips:** Black molded plastic or walnut. **Sights:** Fixed front sight and windage adjustable rear sight. **Features:** The M9 9mm has been a U.S. standard-issue service pistol since 1990. Chiappa's M9-22 is a replica of this pistol in 22 LR. The M9-22 has the same weight and feel as its 9mm counterpart but has an affordable 10-shot magazine for the .22 Long Rifle cartridge, which makes it a true rimfire reproduction. Comes standard with steel trigger, hammer assembly and a 1/2x28 threaded barrel.
Price: $339.00

CHIAPPA M9-22 TACTICAL
Caliber: .22 LR. **Barrel:** 5 in. **Weight:** 2.3 lbs. **Length:** 8.5 in. **Grips:** Black molded plastic. **Sights:** Fixed front sight and Novak-style rear sights. **Features:** The M9-22 Tactical model comes with a faux suppressor (this ups the "cool factor" on the range and extends the barrel to make it even more accurate). It also has a 1/2x28 thread adaptor that can be used with a legal suppressor.
Price: $419.00

CHRISTENSEN ARMS 1911 SERIES
Calibers: .45 ACP, 9mm. **Barrels:** 4.25 in., 5 or 5.5 in. **Features:** Models are offered with aluminum, stainless steel or titanium frame with hand-fitted slide, match-grade barrel, tritium night sights and G10 Operator grip panels.
Price: Aluminum frame... $1,995.00
Price: Stainless $2,895.00
Price: Titanium.. $4,795.00–$5,095.00

CITADEL M-1911
Calibers: .45 ACP, 9mm. **Capacity:** 7 (.45), 8 (9mm). **Barrels:** 5 or 3.5 in. **Weight:** 2.3 lbs. **Length:** 8.5 in. **Grips:** Cocobolo. **Sights:** Low-profile combat fixed rear, blade front. **Finish:** Matte black. **Features:** Extended grip safety, lowered and flared ejection port, beveled mag well, Series 70 firing system. Built by Armscor (Rock Island Armory) in the Philippines and imported by Legacy Sports.
Price: $599.00

CIMARRON MODEL 1911
Caliber: .45 ACP. **Barrel:** 5 in. **Weight:** 37.5 oz. **Length:** 8.5 in. overall. **Grips:** Checkered walnut. **Features:** A faithful reproduction of the original pattern of the Model 1911 with Parkerized finish and lanyard ring. Polished or nickel finish available.
Price: $571.00
Price: Polished blue or nickel..................................... $800.00

CIMARRON MODEL 1911 WILD BUNCH
Caliber: .45 ACP. **Barrel:** 5 in. **Weight:** 37.5 oz. **Length:** 8.5 in. overall. **Grips:** Checkered walnut. **Features:** Original WWI 1911 frame with flat mainspring housing, correct markings, polished blue finish, comes with tanker shoulder holster.
Price: $956.00

COBRA ENTERPRISES FS32, FS380
Calibers: .32 ACP or .380 ACP. **Capacity:** 7 rounds. **Barrel:** 3.5 in. **Weight:** 2.1 lbs. **Length:** 6.375 in. overall. **Grips:** Black molded synthetic integral with frame. **Sights:** Fixed. Made in USA by Cobra Enterprises of Utah, Inc.
Price: .... $138.00–$250.00

COBRA ENTERPRISES PATRIOT SERIES
Calibers: .380, 9mm or .45 ACP. **Capacities:** 6-, 7- or 10-round magazine. **Barrel:** 3.3 in. **Weight:** 20 oz. **Length:** 6 in. overall. **Grips:** Black polymer. **Sights:** Fixed. **Features:** Bright chrome, satin nickel or black finish. Made in USA by Cobra Enterprises of Utah, Inc.
Price: .... $349.00–$395.00

COBRA DENALI
Caliber: .380 ACP. **Capacity:** 5 rounds. **Barrel:** 2.8 in. **Weight:** 22 oz. **Length:** 5.4 in. **Grips:** Black molded synthetic integral with frame. **Sights:** Fixed. **Features:** Made in USA by Cobra Enterprises of Utah, Inc.
Price: $179.00

COLT 1903 RE-ISSUE SERIES
Caliber: .32 ACP. **Capacity:** 8-round magazine. **Barrel:** 3.9 in. **Grips:** Checkered walnut. **Sights:** Fixed, round front/retro rear. **Finish:** Parkerized, Royal Blue, Blued or Chrome. **Features:** Reproduction of Colt 1903 pistol, marked "U.S. PROPERTY" on right side of frame.
Price: (Blued) $1,338.00
Price: (Chrome) $1,647.00
Price: (Parkerized)... $1,211.00
Price: (Royal Blue).. $1,544.00

COLT 1911 CLASSIC
Caliber: .45 ACP. **Capacity:** 7-round magazine. **Barrel:** 5 in. **Grips:** Double diamond checkered rosewood. **Sights:** Fixed-post front/retro rear. **Finish:** Blue. **Features:** Series 70 firing system.
Price: $799.00

COLT 1911 BLACK ARMY
Caliber: .45 ACP. **Capacity:** 7-round magazine. **Barrel:** 5 in. **Grips:** Double diamond checkered rosewood. **Sights:** Fixed, round front/retro rear. **Finish:** Matte blue. **Features:** Series 70 firing system, lanyard loop, reproduction of WWI U.S. Military model.
Price: $999.00

COLT MODEL 1991 MODEL O
Caliber: .45 ACP. **Capacity:** 7-round magazine. **Barrel:** 5 in. **Weight:** 38 oz. **Length:** 8.5 in. overall. **Grips:** Checkered black composition. **Sights:** Ramped blade front, fixed square notch rear, high profile. **Features:** Matte finish. Continuation of serial number range used on original G.I. 1911A1 guns. Comes with one magazine and molded carrying case. Introduced 1991. Series 80 firing system.
Price: Blue $799.00
Price: Stainless $879.00

COLT XSE SERIES MODEL O COMBAT ELITE

Caliber: .45 ACP. **Capacity:** 8-round magazine. **Barrel:** 5 in. **Grips:** Checkered, double-diamond rosewood. **Sights:** Three white-dot Novak. **Features:** Brushed stainless receiver with blued slide; adjustable, two-cut aluminum trigger; extended ambidextrous thumb safety; upswept beavertail with palm swell; elongated slot hammer.
Price: $1,100.00

COLT LIGHTWEIGHT COMMANDER

Calibers: .45 ACP, 8-shot, 9mm (9 shot). **Barrel:** 4.25 in. **Weight:** 26 oz. alloy frame, 33 oz. (steel frame). **Length:** 7.75 in. overall. **Grips:** G10 Checkered Black Cherry. **Sights:** Novak White Dot front, Low Mount Carry rear. **Features:** Blued slide, black anodized frame. Aluminum alloy frame.
Price: $999.00
Price: Combat Commander w/steel frame............................ $949.00

COLT DEFENDER

Caliber: .45 ACP (7-round magazine), 9mm (8-round). **Barrel:** 3 in. **Weight:** 22.5 oz. **Length:** 6.75 in. overall. **Grips:** Pebble-finish rubber wraparound with finger grooves. **Sights:** White dot front, snag-free Colt competition rear. **Features:** Stainless or blued finish; aluminum frame; combat-style hammer; Hi-Ride grip safety, extended manual safety, disconnect safety. Introduced 1998. Made in USA by Colt's Mfg. Co., Inc.
Price: Stainless $999.00
Price: Blue $999.00

COLT SERIES 70

Caliber: .45 ACP. **Barrel:** 5 in. **Weight:** 37.5 oz. **Length:** 8.5 in. **Grips:** Rosewood with double diamond checkering pattern. **Sights:** Fixed. **Features:** Custom replica of the Original Series 70 pistol with a Series 70 firing system, original roll marks. Introduced 2002. Made in USA by Colt's Mfg. Co., Inc.
Price: Blued $899.00
Price: Stainless $979.00

COLT 38 SUPER CUSTOM SERIES

Caliber: .38 Super. **Barrel:** 5 in. **Weight:** 36.5 oz. **Length:** 8.5 in. **Grips:** Wood with double diamond checkering pattern. **Finish:** Bright stainless. **Sights:** 3-dot. **Features:** Beveled magazine well, standard thumb safety and service-style grip safety, flat mainspring housing. Introduced 2003. Made in USA. by Colt's Mfg. Co., Inc.
Price: $1,549.00

COLT MUSTANG POCKETLITE

Caliber: .380 ACP. **Capacity:** 6-round magazine. **Barrel:** 2.75 in. **Weight:** 12.5 oz. **Length:** 5.5 in. **Grips:** Black composite. **Finish:** Brushed stainless. **Features:** Thumb safety, firing-pin safety block. Introduced 2012.
Price: $699.00

COLT MUSTANG LITE

Caliber: .380 ACP. Similar to Mustang Pocketlite except has black polymer frame.
Price: $599.00

COLT MUSTANG XSP

Caliber: .380 ACP. **Features:** Similar to Mustang Pocketlite except has polymer frame, black diamond or bright stainless slide, squared trigger guard, accessory rail, electroless nickel finished controls.
Price: Bright Stainless....................................... $528.00
Price: Black Diamond-Like Carbon finish...................... $672.00

COLT RAIL GUN

Caliber: .45 ACP. **Capacity:** (8+1). **Barrel:** 5 in. **Weight:** 40 oz. **Length:** 8.5 in. **Grips:** Rosewood double diamond. **Sights:** White dot front and Novak rear. **Features:** 1911-style semi-auto. Stainless steel frame and slide, front and rear slide serrations, skeletonized trigger, integral accessory rail, Smith & Alexander upswept beavertail grip palm swell safety, tactical thumb safety, National Match barrel.
Price: $1,199.00

COLT M45A1 MARINE PISTOL

Caliber: .45 ACP. Variant of Rail Gun series with features of that model plus Decobond Brown Coating, dual recoil springs system, Novak tritium front and rear 3-dot sights. Selected by U.S. Marine Corps as their Close Quarters Battle Pistol (CQBP).
Price: $1,699.00

COLT DELTA ELITE

Caliber: 10 mm. **Capacity:** 8+1. **Barrel:** 5 in. **Grips:** Black composite with Delta Medallions. **Sights:** Novak Low Mount Carry rear, Novak White Dot front. **Finish:** Two-tone stainless frame, black matte slide. **Features:** Upswept beavertail safety, extended thumb safety, 3-hole aluminum trigger.
Price: $1,199.00

Prices given are believed to be accurate at time of publication however, many factors affect retail pricing so exact prices are not possible.

75TH EDITION, 2021 ◈ 443

COLT SPECIAL COMBAT GOVERNMENT CARRY MODEL
Calibers: .45 ACP (8+1), .38 Super (9+1). **Barrel:** 5 in. **Weight:** NA. **Length:** 8.5 in. **Grips:** Black/silver synthetic. **Sights:** Novak front and rear night sights. **Features:** 1911-style semi-auto. Skeletonized three-hole trigger, slotted hammer, Smith & Alexander upswept beavertail grip palm swell safety and extended magazine well, Wilson tactical ambidextrous safety. Available in blued, hard chrome, or blued/satin-nickel finish, depending on chambering. Marine pistol has desert tan Cerakote stainless steel finish, lanyard loop.
Price: $2,095.00

COLT GOVERNMENT MODEL 1911A1 .22
Caliber: .22 LR. **Capacity:** 12-round magazine. **Barrel:** 5 in. **Weight:** 36 oz.
Features: Made in Germany by Walther under exclusive arrangement with Colt Manufacturing Company. Blowback operation. All other features identical to original, including manual and grip safeties, drift-adjustable sights.
Price: $399.00

COLT COMPETITION PISTOL
Calibers: .45 ACP, .38 Super or 9mm Para. Full-size Government Model with 5-inch national match barrel, dual-spring recoil operating system, adjustable rear and fiber optic front sights, custom G10 Colt logo grips blued or stainless steel finish.
Price: Blued finish $949.00
Price: Stainless steel $999.00
Price: 38 Super $1,099.00

COLT SERIES 70 NATIONAL MATCH GOLD CUP
Caliber: .45 ACP. **Barrel:** 5 in. national match. **Weight:** 37 oz. **Length:** 8.5 in. **Grips:** Checkered walnut with gold medallions. **Sights:** Adjustable Bomar rear, target post front. **Finish:** blued. **Features:** Flat top slide, flat mainspring housing. Wide three-hole aluminum trigger.
Price: $1,299.00

COLT GOLD CUP TROPHY
Calibers: .45 ACP or 9mm. Updated version of the classic Colt target and service pistol first introduced in the late 1950s to give shooters a serious competition pistol out of the box. Features include an undercut trigger guard, upswept beavertail grip safety and dual-spring recoil system. Checkering on the front and rear of the grip strap is 25 LPI with blue G10 grips. The new Gold Cup Trophy is built on the Series 70 firing system. Re-introduced to the Colt catalog in 2017.
Price: .... $1,699.00.

CZ 75 B
Calibers: 9mm, .40 S&W. **Capacity:** 16-round magazine (9mm), 10-round (.40). **Barrel:** 4.7 in. **Weight:** 34.3 oz. **Length:** 8.1 in. overall. **Grips:** High impact checkered plastic. **Sights:** Square post front, rear adjustable for windage; 3-dot system. **Features:** Single action/double action; firing pin block safety; choice of black polymer, matte or high-polish blue finishes. All-steel frame. B-SA is a single action with a drop-free magazine. Imported from the Czech Republic by CZ-USA.
Price: 75 B $625.00
Price: 75 B, stainless $783.00
Price: 75 B-SA $661.00

CZ 75B 45TH ANNIVERSARY
Caliber: 9mm. **Capacity:** 16-round magazine. **Barrel:** 4.6 in. **Grips:** Engraved wood. **Sights:** Fixed, 3-dot tritium. **Length:** 8.1 in. overall. **Weight:** 35.2 oz. unloaded. **Finish:** Blued. **Features:** Limited edition pistol, only 1,000 produced. Engraved frame and slide.
Price: $1,720.00

CZ 75 BD DECOCKER
Similar to the CZ 75B except has a decocking lever in place of the safety lever. All other specifications are the same. Introduced 1999. Imported from the Czech Republic by CZ-USA.
Price: 9mm, black polymer $612.00

Prices given are believed to be accurate at time of publication however, many factors affect retail pricing so exact prices are not possible.

CZ 75 B COMPACT

Similar to the CZ 75 B except has 14-round magazine in 9mm, 3.9-in. barrel and weighs 32 oz. Has removable front sight, non-glare ribbed slide top. Trigger guard is squared and serrated; combat hammer. Introduced 1993. Imported from the Czech Republic by CZ-USA.
Price: 9mm, black polymer **$631.00**
Price: 9mm, dual tone or satin nickel **$651.00**
Price: 9mm. D PCR Compact, alloy frame **$651.00**

CZ P-07

Calibers: .40 S&W, 9mm. **Capacity:** 15 (9mm), 12 (.40). **Barrel:** 3.8 in. **Weight:** 27.2 oz. **Length:** 7.3 in. overall. **Grips:** Polymer black Polycoat. **Sights:** Blade front, fixed groove rear. **Features:** The ergonomics and accuracy of the CZ 75 with a totally new trigger system. The new Omega trigger system simplifies the CZ 75 trigger system, uses fewer parts and improves the trigger pull. In addition, it allows users to choose between using the handgun with a decocking lever (installed) or a manual safety (included) by a simple parts change. The polymer frame design and a new sleek slide profile (fully machined from bar stock) reduce weight, making the P-07 a great choice for concealed carry.
Price: **$524.00**

CZ P-09 DUTY

Calibers: 9mm, .40 S&W. **Capacity:** 19 (9mm), 15 (.40). **Features:** High-capacity version of P-07. Accessory rail, interchangeable grip backstraps, ambidextrous decocker can be converted to manual safety.
Price: **$544.00**
Price: Suppressor ready **$629.00**

CZ P-10 F

Caliber: 9mm. **Capacity:** 19-round magazine. **Barrel:** 4.5 in. **Weight:** 26 oz. **Length:** 8 in. overall. **Grips:** Textured polymer. **Sights:** Fixed, 3-dot. **Features:** Striker fire.
Price: **$524.00**

CZ 75 SP-01

Similar to NATO-approved CZ 75 Compact P-01 model. Features an integral 1913 accessory rail on the dust cover, rubber grip panels, black Polycoat finish, extended beavertail, new grip geometry with checkering on front and back straps, and double or single action operation. Introduced 2005. The Shadow variant designed as an IPSC "production" division competition firearm. Includes competition hammer, competition rear sight and fiber-optic front sight, modified slide release, lighter recoil and mainspring for use with "minor power factor" competition ammunition. Includes Polycoat finish and slim walnut grips. Finished by CZ Custom Shop. Imported from the Czech Republic by CZ-USA.
Price: SP-01 Standard **$680.00**
Price: SP-01 Shadow Target II **$1,638.00**

CZ 97 B

Caliber: .45 ACP. **Capacity:** 10-round magazine. **Barrel:** 4.85 in. **Weight:** 40 oz. **Length:** 8.34 in. overall. **Grips:** Checkered walnut. **Sights:** Fixed. **Features:** Single action/double action; full-length slide rails; screw-in barrel bushing; linkless barrel; all-steel construction; chamber loaded indicator; dual transfer bars. Introduced 1999. Imported from the Czech Republic by CZ-USA.
Price: Black polymer **$707.00**
Price: Glossy blue **$727.00**

CZ 97 BD DECOCKER

Similar to the CZ 97 B except has a decocking lever in place of the safety lever. Tritium night sights. Rubber grips. All other specifications are the same. Introduced 1999. Imported from the Czech Republic by CZ-USA.
Price: **$816.00**

CZ 2075 RAMI

Calibers: 9mm. **Barrel:** 3 in. **Weight:** 25 oz. **Length:** 6.5 in. overall. **Grips:** Rubber. **Sights:** Blade front with dot, white outline rear drift adjustable for windage. **Features:** Single action/double action; alloy frame, steel slide; has laser sight mount. Rami BD has decocking system. Imported from the Czech Republic by CZ-USA.
Price: Rami Standard **$632.00**
Price: Rami Decocker version **$699.00**

CZ P-01

Caliber: 9mm. **Capacity:** 14-round magazine. **Barrel:** 3.85 in. **Weight:** 27 oz. **Length:** 7.2 in. overall. **Grips:** Checkered rubber. **Sights:** Blade front with dot, white outline rear drift adjustable for windage. **Features:** Based on the CZ 75, except with forged aircraft-grade aluminum alloy frame. Hammer forged barrel, decocker, firing-pin block, M3 rail, dual slide serrations, squared trigger guard, re-contoured trigger, lanyard loop on butt. Serrated front and backstrap. Introduced 2006. Imported from the Czech Republic by CZ-USA.
Price: CZ P-01 .... **$680.00**

CZ SCORPION EVO

Caliber: 9mm. **Capacity:** 20-round magazine. **Features:** Semi-automatic version of CZ Scorpion Evo submachine gun. Ambidextrous controls, adjustable sights, accessory rails.
Price: **$849.00**

Prices given are believed to be accurate at time of publication however, many factors affect retail pricing so exact prices are not possible.

75TH EDITION, 2021 ✛ **445**

DAN WESSON DWX FULL SIZE
Calibers: 9mm, .40 S&W. **Capacity:** 19-round magazine (9mm), 15-round magazine (.40 S&W). **Barrel:** 5 in. **Grips:** Checkered red aluminum. **Sights:** Fixed fiber-optic front/adjustable rear. **Length:** 8.52 in. overall. **Weight:** 43 oz. unloaded. Finish: Black Duty Coat. **Features:** Hybrid pistol built using the single-action fire control group of a Dan Wesson 1911 and frame of a CZ 75 pistol. Compatible with CZ P-09 and CZ P-10 F magazines. Bull barrel and full dust cover with accessory rail. Flat red aluminum trigger. Oversized controls.
Price: $1,799.00

DAN WESSON DWX COMPACT
Caliber: 9mm. **Capacity:** 15-round magazine. **Barrel:** 5 in. **Grips:** Checkered red aluminum. **Sights:** Fixed, night-sight front/U-notch rear. **Length:** 7.47 in. overall. **Weight:** 28.5 oz. unloaded. Finish: Black Duty Coat. **Features:** Hybrid pistol built using the single-action fire control group of a Dan Wesson 1911 and frame of a CZ 75 pistol. With or without accessory rail. Full dust cover. Flat red aluminum trigger. Oversized controls.
Price: $1,799.00

DAN WESSON DW RZ-45 HERITAGE
Caliber: .45 ACP. **Capacity:** 7-round magazine. **Weight:** 36 oz. **Length:** 8.8 in. overall. Similar to the RZ-10 Auto except in .45 ACP.
Price: 10mm, 8+1 ....$1,428.00

DAN WESSON KODIAK
Caliber: 10mm. **Capacity:** 8-round magazine. **Barrel:** 6.03 in. **Grips:** Textured G10. **Sights:** Fixed, fiber-optic front/adjustable rear. **Length:** 9.7 in. overall. **Weight:** 47.1 oz. unloaded. Finish: Black or tri-tone. **Features:** 1911 platform with coarse slide serrations, mag well and ambidextrous safety. Black version has bronzed controls and barrel, and tri-tone with a matte gray slide.
Price: (tri-tone)..$2,349.00

DAN WESSON SPECIALIST
Caliber: .45 ACP. **Capacity:** 8-round magazine. **Barrel:** 5 in. **Grips:** G10 VZ Operator II. **Sights:** Single amber tritium dot rear, green lamp with white target ring front sight. **Features:** Integral Picatinny rail, 25 LPI frontstrap checkering, undercut trigger guard, ambidextrous thumb safety, extended mag release and detachable two-piece mag well.
Price: $1,701.00

DAN WESSON V-BOB
Caliber: .45 ACP. **Capacity:** 8-round magazine. **Barrel:** 4.25 in. **Weight:** 34 oz. **Length:** 8 in. **Grips:** Slim Line G10. **Sights:** Heinie Ledge Straight-Eight Night Sights. **Features:** Black matte or stainless finish. Bobtail forged grip frame with 25 LPI checkering front and rear.
Price: $2,077.00

DAN WESSON POINTMAN
Calibers: 9mm, .38 Super, .45 ACP. **Capacity:** 8 or 9-round magazine. **Barrel:** 5 in. **Length:** 8.5 in. **Grips:** Double-diamond cocobolo. **Sights:** Adjustable rear and fiber optic front. **Features:** Undercut trigger guard, checkered front strap, serrated rib on top of slide.
Price: .45, .38 Super $1,597.00
Price: 9mm $1,558.00

DAN WESSON A2
Caliber: .45 ACP. **Capacity:** 8-round magazine capacity. Limited production model based on traditional 1911A1 design. **Features:** Modern fixed combat sights, lowered/flared ejection port, double-diamond walnut grips. Introduced 2017.
Price: $1,363.00

DAN WESSON VALOR
Caliber: .45 ACP. **Capacity:** 8-round magazine. **Barrel:** 5 in. **Grips:** Textured G10. **Sights:** Fixed, night-sight front/U-notch rear. **Length:** 8.75 in. overall. **Weight:** 39.7 oz. unloaded. Finish: Matte stainless or black Duty Coat. **Features:** 1911 platform with GI style slide serrations, Stan Chen SI mag well, tapered grip and tactical ambidextrous safety.
Price: (stainless) $1,864.00

DAN WESSON VIGIL
Calibers: 9mm, .45 ACP. **Capacity:** 8 (.45) or 9 (9mm). **Barrel:** 4.25 or 5 in. **Features:** Forged aluminum frame with stainless round-top slide, serrated tactical rear and tritium front sight, checkered frontstrap and backstrap, walnut grips with rounded butt.
Price: $1,298.00

DAN WESSON WRAITH
Calibers: .45 ACP, 9m, 10mm. **Capacity:** 8 (.45), 9 (.40), 10 (9mm). **Barrel:** 5.75, threaded. **Finish:** Distressed Duty. **Features:** High profile fixed combat sights, lowered/flared ejection port, G10 grips, extended controls and grip safety.
Price: $2,077.00

DESERT EAGLE 1911 G

Caliber: .45 ACP. **Capacity:** 8-round magazine. **Barrels:** 5 in. or 4.33 in. (DE1911C Commander size), or 3.0 in. (DE1911U Undercover). **Grips:** Double diamond checkered wood. **Features:** Extended beavertail grip safety, checkered flat mainspring housing, skeletonized hammer and trigger, extended mag release and thumb safety, stainless full-length guide road, enlarged ejection port, beveled mag well and high-profile sights. Comes with two 8-round magazines.
Price: $904.00
Price: Undercover... $1,019.00

DESERT EAGLE MARK XIX

Calibers: .357 Mag., 9 rounds; .44 Mag., 8 rounds; .50 AE, 7 rounds. **Barrels:** 6 in., 10 in., interchangeable. **Weight:** 62 oz. (.357 Mag.); 69 oz. (.44 Mag.); 72 oz. (.50 AE) **Length:** 10.25-in. overall (6-in. bbl.). **Grips:** Polymer; rubber available. **Sights:** Blade-on-ramp front, combat-style rear. Adjustable available. **Features:** Interchangeable barrels; rotating three-lug bolt; ambidextrous safety; adjustable trigger. Military epoxy finish. Satin, bright nickel, chrome, brushed, matte or black-oxide finishes available. 10-in. barrel extra. Imported from Israel by Magnum Research, Inc.
Price: .... $1,572.00–$2,060.00

BABY DESERT EAGLE III

Calibers: 9mm, .40 S&W, .45 ACP. **Capacities:** 10-, 12- or 15-round magazines. **Barrels:** 3.85 in. or 4.43 in. **Weights:** 28–37.9 oz. **Length:** 7.25–8.25 overall. **Grips:** Ergonomic polymer. **Sights:** White 3-dot system. **Features:** Choice of steel or polymer frame with integral rail; slide-mounted decocking safety. Upgraded design of Baby Eagle II series.
Price: .... $646.00–$691.00

DESERT EAGLE L5/L6

Caliber: .357 Magnum, .44 Magnum, .50 AE. **Capacity:** 7, 8 or 9+1. **Barrel:** 5 in. or 6 in (L6). **Weight:** 50 to 70 oz. **Length:** 9.7 in. (L5), 10.8, (L6). **Features:** Steel barrel, aluminum frame and stainless steel slide with full Weaver-style accessory rail and integral muzzle brake. Gas-operated rotating bolt, single-action trigger, fixed sights.
Price: From $1,790.00

DIAMONDBACK DB380

Caliber: .380 ACP. **Capacity:** 6+1. **Barrel:** 2.8 in. **Weight:** 8.8 oz. **Features:** ZERO-Energy striker firing system with a mechanical firing pin block, steel magazine catch, windage-adjustable sights. Frames available with several color finish options.
Price: .... $290.00–$350.00

DIAMONDBACK DB9

Caliber: 9mm. **Capacity:** 6+1. **Barrel:** 3 in. **Weight:** 11 oz. **Length:** 5.60 in. **Features:** Other features similar to DB380 model.
Price: .... $290.00–$350.00

DIAMONDBACK DB FS NINE

Caliber: 9mm. **Capacity:** 15+1. **Barrel:** 4.75 in. **Weight:** 21.5 oz. **Length:** 7.8 in. **Features:** Double-action, striker-fired model with polymer frame and stainless steel slide. Flared mag well, extended magazine base pad, ergonomically contoured grip, fixed 3-dot sights, front and rear slide serrations, integral MIL-STD 1913 Picatinny rail.
Price: $483.00

DIAMONDBACK FIREARMS DBX

Caliber: 5.7x28mm. **Capacity:** 20-round magazine. **Barrel:** 8 in. **Grips:** Magpul MOE-K. **Sights:** Optic-ready, Picatinny rail. **Length:** 16.9 in. overall, brace folded. **Weight:** 3 lbs. unloaded. **Finish:** Black hard coat anodized. **Features:** DBX muzzle brake, compatible with FN Five-seveN, side-folding brace. Uses AR15 Mil-Spec trigger.
Price: $1,299.00

Prices given are believed to be accurate at time of publication however, many factors affect retail pricing so exact prices are not possible.

75TH EDITION, 2021 **447**

DIAMONDBACK FIREARMS DBAM29

Caliber: 9mm. **Capacity:** 12- or 17-round magazine. **Barrel:** 3.5 in. **Grips:** Textured grip. **Sights:** Fixed, 3-dot. **Length:** 6.6 in. overall. **Weight:** 21 oz. unloaded. Finish: Black.
Price: $350.00

DOUBLESTAR 1911 SERIES

Caliber: .45 ACP. **Capacity:** 8-round magazine. **Barrels:** 3.5 in., 4.25 in., 5 in. **Weights:** 33–40 oz. **Grips:** Cocobolo wood. **Sights:** Novak LoMount 2 white-dot rear, Novak white-dot front. **Features:** Single action, M1911-style with forged frame and slide of 4140 steel, stainless steel barrel machined from bar stock by Storm Lake, funneled mag well, accessory rail, black Nitride finish. Optional features include bobtail grip frame, accessory rail.
Price: .... $1,364.00–$2,242.00

EAA WITNESS FULL SIZE

Calibers: 9mm, .38 Super. **Capacity:** 18-round magazine; .40 S&W, 10mm, 15-round magazine; .45 ACP, 10-round magazine. **Barrel:** 4.5 in. **Weight:** 35.33 oz. **Length:** 8.1 in. overall. **Grips:** Checkered rubber. **Sights:** Undercut blade front, open rear adjustable for windage. **Features:** Double-action/single-action trigger system; round trigger guard; frame-mounted safety. Available with steel or polymer frame. Also available with interchangeable .45 ACP and .22 LR slides. Steel frame introduced 1991. Polymer frame introduced 2005. Imported from Italy by European American Armory.
Price: Steel frame $699.00
Price: Polymer frame $589.00

EAA WITNESS COMPACT

Caliber: 9mm. **Capacity:** 14-round magazine; .40 S&W, 10mm, 12-round magazine; .45 ACP, 8-round magazine. **Barrel:** 3.6 in. **Weight:** 30 oz. **Length:** 7.3 in. overall. **Features:** Available with steel or polymer frame (shown). All polymer frame Witness pistols are capable of being converted to other calibers. Otherwise similar to full-size Witness. Imported from Italy by European American Armory.
Price: Polymer frame $589.00
Price: Steel frame $699.00

EAA WITNESS-P CARRY

Caliber: 9mm. **Capacity:** 17-round magazine; 10mm, 15-round magazine; .45 ACP, 10-round magazine. **Barrel:** 3.6 in. **Weight:** 27 oz. **Length:** 7.5 in. overall. **Features:** Otherwise similar to full-size Witness. Polymer frame introduced 2005. Imported from Italy by European American Armory.
Price: $711.00

EAA WITNESS PAVONA COMPACT POLYMER

Calibers: .380 ACP (13-round magazine), 9mm (13) or .40 S&W (9). **Barrel:** 3.6 in. **Weight:** 30 oz. **Length:** 7 in. overall. **Features:** Designed primarily for women with fine-tuned recoil and hammer springs for easier operation, a polymer frame with integral checkering, contoured lines and in black, charcoal, blue, purple or magenta with silver or gold sparkle.
Price: .... $476.00–$528.00

EAA WITNESS ELITE 1911

Caliber: .45 ACP. **Capacity:** 8-round magazine. **Barrel:** 5 in. **Weight:** 32 oz. **Length:** 8.58 in. overall. **Features:** Full-size 1911-style pistol with either steel or polymer frame. Also available in Commander or Officer's models with 4.25- or 3.5-in. barrel, polymer frame.
Price: $580.00
Price: Commander or Officer's Model............................... $627.00
Price: Steel frame $895.00

Prices given are believed to be accurate at time of publication however, many factors affect retail pricing so exact prices are not possible.

EAA SAR B6P
Caliber: 9mm. Based on polymer frame variation of CZ 75 design. Manufactured by Sarsilmaz in Turkey. Features similar to Witness series.
Price: .... **$407.00–$453.00**

EAA SAR K2-45
Caliber: .45 ACP. **Barrel:** 4.7 in. **Weight:** 2.5 lbs. **Features:** Similar to B6P with upgraded features. Built by Sarsilmaz for the Turkish military. Features include a cocked and locked carry system, ergonomically designed grip, steel frame and slide construction, adjustable rear sight, extended beaver tail, serrated trigger guard and frame, removable dove-tail front sight, auto firing pin block and low barrel axis for reduced felt recoil.
Price: **$849.00**

EAA MC 1911 SERIES
Caliber: .45 ACP, 9mm. **Capacity:** 8-round magazine, 9+1 (9mm). **Barrel:** 5, 4.4, or 3.4 in. **Weight:** 26-39 oz. **Sights:** Novak-style rear, fixed front. **Features:** 1911-style pistol with either steel or polymer frame, ambidextrous safety, extended beavertail. Available in full-size, Commander or Officer's models. Manufactured by Girsan in Turkey.
Price: .... **$572.00-$694.00**

ED BROWN CLASSIC CUSTOM
Caliber: .45 ACP, 9mm, .38 Super. **Capacity:** 7-round magazine. **Barrel:** 5 in. **Weight:** 40 oz. **Grips:** Cocobolo wood. **Sights:** Bo-Mar adjustable rear, dovetail front. **Features:** Single action, M1911 style, custom made to order, stainless frame and slide available. Special mirror-finished slide.
Price: From **$3,695.00**

ED BROWN KOBRA CARRY
Caliber: .45 ACP. **Capacity:** 7-round magazine. **Barrels:** 4.25 in. **Weight:** 34 oz. **Grips:** Hogue exotic wood. **Sights:** Ramp, front; fixed Novak low-mount night sights, rear. **Features:** Snakeskin pattern serrations on forestrap and mainspring housing, dehorned edges, beavertail grip safety.
Price: .45 ACP From.. **$2,995.00**
Price: 9 mm From... **$3,095.00**
Price: .38 Super From... **$3,095.00**

ED BROWN KOBRA CARRY LIGHTWEIGHT
Caliber: .45 ACP, 9mm, .38 Super. **Capacity:** 7-round magazine. **Barrel:** 4.25 in. (Commander model slide). **Weight:** 27 oz. **Grips:** Hogue exotic wood. **Sights:** 10-8 Performance U-notch plain black rear sight with .156-in. notch for fast acquisition

of close targets. Fixed dovetail front night sight with high-visibility white outlines. **Features:** Aluminum frame and bobtail housing. Matte finished Gen III coated slide for low glare, with snakeskin on rear of slide only. Snakeskin pattern serrations on forestrap and mainspring housing, dehorned edges, beavertail grip safety. LW insignia on slide, which stands for Lightweight.
Price: Kobra Carry Lightweight **$3,495.00**

ED BROWN EXECUTIVE SERIES
Similar to other Ed Brown products, but with 25-LPI checkered frame and mainspring housing. Various finish, sight and grip options.
Price: .... **$3,170.00-$3,880.00**

ED BROWN SPECIAL FORCES
Similar to other Ed Brown products, but with ChainLink treatment on forestrap and mainspring housing. Entire gun coated with Gen III finish. Square cut serrations on rear of slide only. Dehorned. Introduced 2006. Available with various finish, sight and grip options.
Price: From .... **$2,770.00–$4,775.00**

ED BROWN CCO SERIES
Caliber: .45 ACP, 9mm, .38 Super. **Capacity:** 7-round magazine. **Barrel:** 4.25 in. Built on Officer's size frame with Commander slide. **Features:** Snakeskin metal treatment on mainspring housing, front strap and slide, round butt housing, concealed-carry beavertail grip safety, fixed black rear sight, high visibility fiber optic front. Lightweight aluminum version available.
Price: From .... **$3,070.00–$3,585.00**

EXCEL ARMS MP-22
Caliber: .22 WMR. **Capacity:** 9-round magazine. **Barrel:** 8.5-in. bull barrel. **Weight:** 54 oz. **Length:** 12.875 in. overall. **Grips:** Textured black composition. **Sights:** Fully adjustable target sights. **Features:** Made from 17-4 stainless steel, comes with aluminum rib, integral Weaver base, internal hammer, firing pin block. American made, lifetime warranty. Comes with two 9-round stainless steel magazines and a California-approved cable lock. .22 WMR Introduced 2006. Made in USA by Excel Arms.
Price: **$477.00**

EXCEL ARMS MP-5.7
Caliber: 5.7x28mm. **Capacity:** 9-round magazine. **Features:** Blowback action. Other features similar to MP-22. Red-dot optic sights, scope and rings are optional.
Price: **$615.00**
Price: With optic sights.. **$685.00**
Price: With scope and rings... **$711.00**

FIRESTORM 380
Caliber: .380 ACP. **Capacity:** 7+1. **Barrel:** 3.5 in. **Weight:** 20 oz. **Length:** 6.6 in. **Sights:** Fixed, white outline system. **Grips:** Rubber. **Finish:** Black matte. **Features:** Traditional DA/SA operation.
Price: **$270.00**

FMK 9C1 G2

Caliber: 9mm. **Capacity:** 10+1 or 14+1. **Barrel:** 4 in. **Overall length:** 6.85 in. **Weight:** 23.45 oz. **Finish:** Black, Flat Dark Earth or pink. **Sights:** Interchangeable Glock compatible. **Features:** Available in either single action or double action only. Polymer frame, high-carbon steel slide, stainless steel barrel. Very low bore axis and shock absorbing backstrap are said to result in low felt recoil. DAO model has Fast Action Trigger (FAT) with shorter pull and reset. Made in the USA.
Price: $409.95

FN 509 COMPACT MRD

Caliber: 9mm. **Capacity:** 10-, 12- or 15-round magazine. **Barrel:** 3.7 in. **Grips:** Textured grip, interchangeable backstraps. **Sights:** Fixed, tall co-witness; FN Low Profile Optics Mounting System. **Length:** 6.8 in. overall. **Weight:** 25.5 oz. unloaded. **Finish:** Black or FDE.
Price: $799.00

FN FNS SERIES

Caliber: 9mm. **Capacity:** 17-round magazine, .40 S&W (14-round magazine). **Barrels:** 4 in. or 3.6 in. (Compact). **Weights:** 25 oz. (9mm), 27.5 oz. (.40). **Length:** 7.25 in. **Grips:** Integral polymer with two interchangeable backstrap inserts. **Features:** Striker fired, double action with manual safety, accessory rail, ambidextrous controls, 3-dot night sights.
Price: $599.00

FN FNX SERIES

Calibers: 9mm, .40 S&W. **Capacities:** 17-round magazine, .40 S&W (14 rounds), .45 ACP (10 or 14 rounds). **Barrels:** 4 in. (9mm and .40), 4.5 in. .45. **Weights:** 22–32 oz. (.45). **Lengths:** 7.4, 7.9 in. (.45). **Features:** DA/SA operation with decocking/manual safety lever. Has external extractor with loaded-chamber indicator, front and rear cocking serrations, fixed 3-dot combat sights.
Price: 9mm, .40 .... $699.00
Price: .45 ACP $824.00

FN FNX .45 TACTICAL

Similar to standard FNX .45 except with 5.3-in. barrel with threaded muzzle, polished chamber and feed ramp, enhanced high-profile night sights, slide cut and threaded for red-dot sight (not included), MIL-STD 1913 accessory rail, ring-style hammer.
Price: $1,349.00

FN FIVE-SEVEN

Caliber: 5.7x28mm. **Capacity:** 10- or 20-round magazine. **Barrel:** 4.8 in. **Weight:** 23 oz. **Length:** 8.2 in. **Features:** Adjustable three-dot system. Single-action polymer frame, chambered for low-recoil 5.7x28mm cartridge.
Price: $1,435.00

GLOCK 17/17C

Caliber: 9mm. **Capacities:** 17/19/33-round magazines. **Barrel:** 4.49 in. **Weight:** 22.04 oz. (without magazine). **Length:** 7.32 in. overall. **Grips:** Black polymer. **Sights:** Dot on front blade, white outline rear adjustable for windage. **Features:** Polymer frame, steel slide; double-action trigger with Safe Action system; mechanical firing pin safety, drop safety; simple takedown without tools; locked breech, recoil operated action. ILS designation refers to Internal Locking System. Adopted by Austrian armed forces 1983. NATO approved 1984. Model 17L has 6-inch barrel, ported or non-ported, slotted and relieved slide, checkered grip with finger grooves, no accessory rail. Imported from Austria by Glock, Inc. USA.
Price: From $599.00
Price: 17L $750.00
Price: 17 Gen 4 .... $649.00
Price: 17 Gen 5 .... $699.99

GLOCK GEN4 SERIES

In 2010, a new series of Generation 4 pistols was introduced with several improved features. These included a multiple backstrap system offering three different size options, short, medium or large frame; reversible and enlarged magazine release; dual recoil springs; and RTF (Rough Textured Finish) surface. Some recent models are only available in Gen 4 configuration.

GEN 5 SERIES

A new frame design was introduced in 2017 named Generation 5. The finger grooves were removed for more versatility and the user can customize the grip by using different backstraps, as with the Gen 4 models. A flared mag well and a cutout at the front of the frame give the user more speed during reloading. There is a reversible and enlarged magazine catch, changeable by users, as well as the ambidextrous slide stop lever to accommodate left- and right-handed operators. The rifling and crown of the barrel are slightly modified for increased precision. As of 2019, Gen 5 variants are available in Glock Models 17, 19, 26, 34 and 45.

GLOCK 19/19C

Caliber: 9mm. **Capacities:** 15/17/19/33-round magazines. **Barrel:** 4.02 in. **Weight:** 20.99 oz. (without magazine). **Length:** 6.85 in. overall. Compact version of Glock 17. Imported from Austria by Glock, Inc.
Price: $599.00
Price: 19 Gen 4 .... $649.00
Price: 19 Gen 5 .... $749.00

GLOCK 20/20C 10MM

Caliber: 10mm. **Capacity:** 15-round magazine. **Barrel:** 4.6 in. **Weight:** 27.68 oz. (without magazine). **Length:** 7.59 in. overall. **Features:** Otherwise similar to Model 17. Imported from Austria by Glock, Inc. Introduced 1990.
Price: From $637.00
Price: 20 Gen 4 .... $687.00

Prices given are believed to be accurate at time of publication however, many factors affect retail pricing so exact prices are not possible.

GLOCK MODEL 20 SF SHORT FRAME
Caliber: 10mm. **Barrel:** 4.61 in. with hexagonal rifling. **Weight:** 27.51 oz. **Length:** 8.07 in. overall. **Sights:** Fixed. **Features:** Otherwise similar to the Model 20 but with short-frame design, extended sight radius.
Price: $637.00

GLOCK 21/21C
Caliber: .45 ACP. **Capacity:** 13-round magazine. **Barrel:** 4.6 in. **Weight:** 26.28 oz. (without magazine). **Length:** 7.59 in. overall. **Features:** Otherwise similar to the Model 17. Imported from Austria by Glock, Inc. Introduced 1991. SF version has tactical rail, smaller diameter grip, 10-round magazine capacity. Introduced 2007.
Price: From $637.00
Price: 21 Gen 4 .... $687.00

GLOCK 22/22C
Caliber: .40 S&W. **Capacities:** 15/17-round magazine. **Barrel:** 4.49 in. **Weight:** 22.92 oz. (without magazine). **Length:** 7.32 in. overall. **Features:** Otherwise similar to Model 17, including pricing. Imported from Austria by Glock, Inc. Introduced 1990.
Price: From $599.00
Price: 22C $649.00
Price: 22 Gen 4 .... $649.00

GLOCK 23/23C
Caliber: .40 S&W. **Capacities:** 13/15/17-round magazine. **Barrel:** 4.02 in. **Weight:** 21.16 oz. (without magazine). **Length:** 6.85 in. overall. **Features:** Otherwise similar to the Model 22, including pricing. Compact version of Glock 22. Imported from Austria by Glock, Inc. Introduced 1990.
Price: $599.00
Price: 23C Compensated $621.00
Price: 23 Gen 4 .... $649.00

GLOCK 24/24C
Caliber: .40 S&W. **Capacities:** 10/15/17 or 22-round magazine. **Features:** Similar to Model 22 except with 6.02-inch barrel, ported or non-ported, trigger pull recalibrated to 4.5 lbs.
Price: From $750.00

GLOCK 26
Caliber: 9mm. **Capacities:** 10/12/15/17/19/33-round magazine. **Barrel:** 3.46 in. **Weight:** 19.75 oz. **Length:** 6.29 in. overall. Subcompact version of Glock 17. Imported from Austria by Glock, Inc.
Price: $599.00
Price: 26 Gen 4 .... $649.00
Price: 26 Gen 5 .... $749.00

GLOCK 27
Caliber: .40 S&W. **Capacities:** 9/11/13/15/17-round magazine. **Barrel:** 3.46 in. **Weight:** 19.75 oz. (without magazine). **Length:** 6.29 overall. **Features:** Otherwise similar to the Model 22, including pricing. Subcompact version of Glock 22. Imported from Austria by Glock, Inc. Introduced 1996.
Price: From $599.00
Price: 27 Gen 4 .... $649.00

GLOCK 29 GEN 4
Caliber: 10mm. **Capacities:** 10/15-round magazine. **Barrel:** 3.78 in. **Weight:** 24.69 oz. (without magazine). **Length:** 6.77 in. overall. **Features:** Otherwise similar to the Model 20, including pricing. Subcompact version of the Glock 20. Imported from Austria by Glock, Inc. Introduced 1997.
Price: Fixed sight $637.00

GLOCK MODEL 29 SF SHORT FRAME
Caliber: 10mm. **Barrel:** 3.78 in. with hexagonal rifling. **Weight:** 24.52 oz. **Length:** 6.97 in. overall. **Sights:** Fixed. **Features:** Otherwise similar to the Model 29 but with short-frame design, extended sight radius.
Price: $637.00

GLOCK 30 GEN 4
Caliber: .45 ACP. **Capacities:** 9/10/13-round magazines. **Barrel:** 3.78 in. **Weight:** 23.99 oz. (without magazine). **Length:** 6.77 in. overall. **Features:** Otherwise similar to the Model 21, including pricing. Subcompact version of the Glock 21. Imported from Austria by Glock, Inc. Introduced 1997. SF version has tactical rail, octagonal rifled barrel with a 1:15.75 rate of twist, smaller diameter grip, 10-round magazine capacity. Introduced 2008.
Price: $637.00
Price: 30 SF (short frame)............................ $637.00

GLOCK 30S
Caliber: .45 ACP. **Capacity:** 10-round magazine. **Barrel:** 3.78 in. **Weight:** 20 oz. **Length:** 7 in. **Features:** Variation of Glock 30 with a Model 36 slide on a Model 30SF frame (short frame).
Price: $637.00

GLOCK 31/31C
Caliber: .357 Auto. **Capacities:** 15/17-round magazine. **Barrel:** 4.49 in. **Weight:** 23.28 oz. (without magazine). **Length:** 7.32 in. overall. **Features:** Otherwise similar to the Model 17. Imported from Austria by Glock, Inc.
Price: From $599.00
Price: 31 Gen 4 .... $649.00

GLOCK 32/32C
Caliber: .357 Auto. **Capacities:** 13/15/17-round magazine. **Barrel:** 4.02 in. **Weight:** 21.52 oz. (without magazine). **Length:** 6.85 in. overall. **Features:** Otherwise similar to the Model 31. Compact. Imported from Austria by Glock, Inc.
Price: $599.00
Price: 32 Gen 4 .... $649.00

GLOCK 33
Caliber: .357 Auto. **Capacities:** 9/11/13/15/17-round magazine. **Barrel:** 3.46 in. **Weight:** 19.75 oz. (without magazine). **Length:** 6.29 in. overall. **Features:** Otherwise similar to the Model 31. Subcompact. Imported from Austria by Glock, Inc.
Price: From $599.00
Price: 33 Gen 4 .... $614.00

Prices given are believed to be accurate at time of publication however, many factors affect retail pricing so exact prices are not possible.

75TH EDITION, 2021 ⊕ 451

GLOCK 34
Caliber: 9mm. **Capacities:** 17/19/33-round magazine. **Barrel:** 5.32 in. **Weight:** 22.9 oz. **Length:** 8.15 in. overall. **Features:** Competition version of Glock 17 with extended barrel, slide, and sight radius dimensions. Available with MOS (Modular Optic System).
Price: From $679.00
Price: MOS $840.00
Price: 34 Gen 4 .... $729.00
Price: 34 Gen 5 .... $899.00

GLOCK 35
Caliber: .40 S&W. **Capacities:** 15/17-round magazine. **Barrel:** 5.32 in. **Weight:** 24.52 oz. (without magazine). **Length:** 8.15 in. overall. **Sights:** Adjustable. **Features:** Otherwise similar to the Model 22. Competition version of the Glock 22 with extended barrel, slide and sight radius dimensions. Available with MOS (Modular Optic System). Introduced 1996.
Price: From $679.00
Price: MOS... $840.00
Price: 35 Gen 4 .... $729.00

GLOCK 36
Caliber: .45 ACP. **Capacity:** 6-round magazine. **Barrel:** 3.78 in. **Weight:** 20.11 oz. (without magazine). **Length:** 6.77 overall. **Sights:** Fixed. **Features:** Single-stack magazine, slimmer grip than Glock 21/30. Subcompact. Imported from Austria by Glock, Inc. Introduced 1997.
Price: $637.00

GLOCK 37
Caliber: .45 GAP. **Capacity:** 10-round magazine. **Barrel:** 4.49 in. **Weight:** 25.95 oz. (without magazine). **Length:** 7.32 overall. **Features:** Otherwise similar to the Model 17. Imported from Austria by Glock, Inc. Introduced 2005.
Price: $614.00
Price: 37 Gen 4 .... $664.00

GLOCK 38
Caliber: .45 GAP. **Capacities:** 8/10-round magazine. **Barrel:** 4.02 in. **Weight:** 24.16 oz. (without magazine). **Length:** 6.85 overall. **Features:** Otherwise similar to the Model 37. Compact. Imported from Austria by Glock, Inc.
Price: $614.00

GLOCK 39
Caliber: .45 GAP. **Capacities:** 6/8/10-round magazine. **Barrel:** 3.46 in. **Weight:** 19.33 oz. (without magazine). **Length:** 6.3 overall. **Features:** Otherwise similar to the Model 37. Subcompact. Imported from Austria by Glock, Inc.
Price: $614.00

GLOCK 40 GEN 4
Caliber: 10mm. **Features:** Similar features as the Model 41 except for 6.01-in. barrel. Includes MOS optics.
Price: $840.00

GLOCK 41 GEN 4
Caliber: .45 ACP. **Capacity:** 13-round magazine. **Barrel:** 5.31 in. **Weight:** 27 oz. **Length:** 8.9 in. overall. **Features:** This is a long-slide .45 ACP Gen4 model introduced in 2014. Operating features are the same as other Glock models. Available with MOS (Modular Optic System).
Price: $749.00
Price: MOS.. $840.00

GLOCK 42 GEN 4
Caliber: .380 ACP. **Capacity:** 6-round magazine. **Barrel:** 3.25 in. **Weight:** 13.8 oz. **Length:** 5.9 in. overall. **Features:** This single-stack, slimline sub-compact is the smallest pistol Glock has ever made. This is also the first Glock pistol made in the USA.
Price: $499.00

GLOCK 43 GEN 4
Caliber: 9mm. **Capacity:** 6+1. **Barrel:** 3.39 in. **Weight:** 17.95 oz. **Length:** 6.26 in. **Height:** 4.25 in. **Width:** 1.02 in. **Features:** Newest member of Glock's Slimline series with single-stack magazine.
Price: $599.00

GLOCK 43X
Caliber: 9mm. **Capacity:** 17+1. **Barrel:** 4.02 in. **Weight:** 24.5 oz. **Length:** 7.4 in. **Height:** 5.5 in. **Width:** 1.3 in. Combines compact slide with full-size frame.
Price: $580.00

GLOCK G44
Caliber: .22 LR. **Capacity:** 10-round magazine. **Barrel:** 4.02 in. **Grips:** Textured grip, interchangeable backstraps. **Sights:** Fixed, dot front/notch rear. **Length:** 7.28 in. overall. **Weight:** 14.6 oz. unloaded. Finish: Black. **Features:** Same size as Glock G19, hybrid slide of polymer and steel.
Price: $430.00

GLOCK 45
Caliber: 9mm. **Capacity:** 10+1. **Barrel:** 3.41 in. **Weight:** 18.7 oz. **Length:** 6.5 in. **Height:** 5.04 in. **Width:** 1.1 in. Combines Glock 43 short and slim dimensions with extended frame size of G48.
Price: $580.00

GLOCK 48 GEN 4
Caliber: 9mm. **Capacity:** 10. **Barrel:** 3.41 in. **Weight:** 18.7 oz. **Length:** 6.05 in. **Height:** 5.04 in. **Width:** 1.1 in. **Features:** Silver-colored PVD coated slide with front serrations. Similar length and height as Model 19 with width reduced to 1.1 inch.
Price: $580.00

GRAND POWER P-1 MK7
Caliber: 9mm. **Capacity:** 15+1 magazine. **Barrel:** 3.7 in. **Weight:** 26 oz. **Features:** Compact DA/SA pistol featuring frame-mounted safety, steel slide and frame and polymer grips. Offered in several variations and sizes. Made in Slovakia
Price: $449.99

GUNCRAFTER INDUSTRIES
Calibers: 9mm, .38 Super, .45 ACP or .50 GI. **Capacity:** 7- or 8-round magazine. **Features:** 1911-style series of pistols best known for the proprietary .50 GI chambering. Offered in approximately 30 1911 variations. No. 1 has 5-inch heavy match-grade barrel, Parkerized or hard chrome finish, checkered grips and frontstrap, numerous sight options. Other models include Commander-style, Officer's Model, Long Slide w/6-inch barrel and several 9mm and .38 Super versions.
Price: ....$2,795.00–$5,195.00

HECKLER & KOCH USP
Calibers: 9mm, .40 S&W, .45 ACP. **Capacities:** 15-round magazine; .40 S&W, 13-shot magazine; 45 ACP, 12-shot magazine. **Barrels:** 4.25–4.41 in. **Weight:** 1.65 lbs. **Length:** 7.64–7.87 in. overall. **Grips:** Non-slip stippled black polymer. **Sights:** Blade front, rear adjustable for windage. **Features:** New HK design with polymer frame, modified Browning action with recoil reduction system, single control lever. Special "hostile environment" finish on all metal parts. Available in SA/DA, DAO, left- and right-hand versions. Introduced 1993. .45 ACP Introduced 1995. Imported from Germany by Heckler & Koch, Inc.
Price: USP .45 ....$1,199.00
Price: USP .40 and USP 9mm $952.00

HECKLER & KOCH USP COMPACT
Calibers: 9mm, .357 SIG, .40 S&W, .45 ACP. **Capacities:** 13-round magazine; .40 S&W and .357 SIG, 12-shot magazine; .45 ACP, 8-shot magazine. **Features:** Similar to the USP except the 9mm, .357 SIG and .40 S&W have 3.58-in. barrels, measure 6.81 in. overall and weigh 1.47 lbs. (9mm). Introduced 1996. .45 ACP measures 7.09 in. overall. Introduced 1998. Imported from Germany by Heckler & Koch, Inc.
Price: USP Compact .45 ....$1,040.00
Price: USP Compact 9mm, .40 S&W $992.00

HECKLER & KOCH USP45 TACTICAL
Calibers: .40 S&W, .45 ACP. **Capacities:** 13-round magazine; .45 ACP, 12-round magazine. **Barrels:** 4.90-5.09 in. **Weight:** 1.9 lbs. **Length:** 8.64 in. overall. **Grips:** Non-slip stippled polymer. **Sights:** Blade front, fully adjustable target rear. **Features:** Has extended threaded barrel with rubber O-ring; adjustable trigger; extended magazine floorplate; adjustable trigger stop; polymer frame. Introduced 1998. Imported from Germany by Heckler & Koch, Inc.
Price: USP Tactical .45 ....$1,352.00
Price: USP Tactical .40 ....$1,333.00

HECKLER & KOCH USP COMPACT TACTICAL

Caliber: .45 ACP. **Capacity:** 8-round magazine. **Features:** Similar to the USP Tactical except measures 7.72 in. overall, weighs 1.72 lbs. Introduced 2006. Imported from Germany by Heckler & Koch, Inc.
Price: USP Compact Tactical **$1,352.00**

HECKLER & KOCH HK45

Caliber: .45 ACP. **Capacity:** 10-round magazine. **Barrel:** 4.53 in. **Weight:** 1.73 lbs. **Length:** 7.52 in. overall. **Grips:** Ergonomic with adjustable grip panels. **Sights:** Low profile, drift adjustable. **Features:** Polygonal rifling, ambidextrous controls, operates on improved Browning linkless recoil system. Available in Tactical and Compact variations. Tactical models come with threaded barrel, adjustable TruGlo high-profile sights, Picatinny rail.
Price: HK45 .... **$819.00**
Price: HK45 Tactical **$919.00-999.00**

HECKLER & KOCH MARK 23 SPECIAL OPERATIONS

Caliber: .45 ACP. **Capacity:** 12-round magazine. **Barrel:** 5.87 in. **Weight:** 2.42 lbs. **Length:** 9.65 in. overall. **Grips:** Integral with frame; black polymer. **Sights:** Blade front, rear drift adjustable for windage; 3-dot. **Features:** Civilian version of the SOCOM pistol. Polymer frame; double action; exposed hammer; short recoil, modified Browning action. Introduced 1996. Imported from Germany by Heckler & Koch, Inc.
Price: **$2,299.00**

HECKLER & KOCH P30 AND P30L

Calibers: 9mm, .40 S&W. **Capacities:** 13- or 15-round magazines. **Barrels:** 3.86 in. or 4.45 in. (P30L) **Weight:** 26–27.5 oz. **Length:** 6.95, 7.56 in. overall. **Grips:** Interchangeable panels. **Sights:** Open rectangular notch rear sight with contrast points. **Features:** Ergonomic features include a special grip frame with interchangeable backstrap inserts and lateral plates, allowing the pistol to be individually adapted to any user. Browning-type action with modified short recoil operation. Ambidextrous controls include dual slide releases, magazine release levers and a serrated decocking button located on the rear of the frame (for applicable variants). A Picatinny rail molded into the front of the frame. The extractor serves as a loaded-chamber indicator.
Price: P30 .... **$1,099.00**
Price: P30L Variant 2 Law Enforcement Modification
(LEM) enhanced DAO **$1,149.00**
Price: P30L Variant 3 Double Action/Single Action
(DA/SA) with Decocker **$1,108.00**

HECKLER & KOCH P2000

Calibers: 9mm, .40 S&W. **Capacities:** 13-round magazine; .40 S&W, 12-shot magazine. **Barrel:** 3.62 in. **Weight:** 1.5 lbs. **Length:** 7 in. overall. **Grips:** Interchangeable panels. **Sights:** Fixed Patridge style, drift adjustable for windage, standard 3-dot. **Features:** Incorporates features of HK USP Compact pistol, including Law Enforcement Modification (LEM) trigger, double-action hammer system, ambidextrous magazine release, dual slide-release levers, accessory mounting rails, recurved, hook trigger guard, fiber-reinforced polymer frame, modular grip with exchangeable backstraps, nitro-carburized finish, lock-out safety device. Introduced 2003. Imported from Germany by Heckler & Koch, Inc.
Price: **$799.00**

HECKLER & KOCH P2000 SK

Calibers: 9mm, .357 SIG, .40 S&W. **Capacities:** 10-round magazine; .40 S&W and .357 SIG, 9-round magazine. **Barrel:** 3.27 in. **Weight:** 1.3 lbs. **Length:** 6.42 in. overall. **Sights:** Fixed Patridge style, drift adjustable. **Features:** Standard accessory rails, ambidextrous slide release, polymer frame, polygonal bore profile. Smaller version of P2000. Introduced 2005. Imported from Germany by Heckler & Koch, Inc.
Price: **$799.00**

HECKLER & KOCH VP9/VP 40

Calibers: 9mm, .40 S&W. **Capacities:** 10- or 15-round magazine. .40 S&W (10 or 13). **Barrel:** 4.09 in. **Weight:** 25.6 oz. **Length:** 7.34 in. overall. **Sights:** Fixed 3-dot, drift adjustable. **Features:** Striker-fired system with HK enhanced light pull trigger. Ergonomic grip design with interchangeable backstraps and side panels. VP9SK is compact model with 3.4-in. barrel.
Price: **$719.00**

HI-POINT FIREARMS MODEL 9MM COMPACT

Caliber: 9mm. **Capacity:** 8-round magazine. **Barrel:** 3.5 in. **Weight:** 25 oz. **Length:** 6.75 in. overall. **Grips:** Textured plastic. **Sights:** Combat-style adjustable 3-dot system; low profile. **Features:** Single-action design; frame-mounted magazine release; polymer frame offered in black or several camo finishes. Scratch-resistant matte finish. Introduced 1993. Comps are similar except they have a 4-in. barrel with muzzle brake/compensator. Compensator is slotted for laser or flashlight mounting. Introduced 1998. Made in USA by MKS Supply, Inc.
Price: C-9 9mm **$199.00**

HI-POINT FIREARMS MODEL 380 POLYMER

Caliber: .380 ACP. **Capacities:** 10- and 8-round magazine. **Weight:** 25 oz. **Features:** Similar to the 9mm Compact model except chambered for adjustable 3-dot sights. Polymer frame with black or camo finish. Action locks open after last shot. Trigger lock.
Price: CF-380 .... **$179.00**

Prices given are believed to be accurate at time of publication however, many factors affect retail pricing so exact prices are not possible.

HI-POINT FIREARMS 40 AND 45 SW/POLYMER
Calibers: .40 S&W, .45 ACP. **Capacities:** .40 S&W, 8-round magazine; .45 ACP, 9 rounds. **Barrel:** 4.5 in. **Weight:** 32 oz. **Length:** 7.72 in. overall. **Sights:** Adjustable 3-dot. **Features:** Polymer frames, offered in black or several camo finishes, last round lock-open, grip-mounted magazine release, magazine disconnect safety, integrated accessory rail, trigger lock. Introduced 2002. Made in USA by MKS Supply, Inc.
Price: $219.00

ITHACA 1911
Caliber: .45 ACP. **Capacity:** 7-round capacity. **Barrels:** 4.25 or 5 in. **Weight:** 35 or 40 oz. **Sights:** Fixed combat or fully adjustable target. **Grips:** Checkered cocobolo with Ithaca logo. Classic 1911A1 style with enhanced features including match-grade barrel, lowered and flared ejection port, extended beavertail grip safety, hand-fitted barrel bushing, two-piece guide rod, checkered front strap.
Price: $1,575.00
Price: Hand fit $2,375.00

IVER JOHNSON EAGLE
Calibers: 9mm, .45 ACP, 10mm. **Features:** Series of 1911-style pistols made in typical variations including full-size (Eagle), Commander (Hawk), Officer's (Thrasher) sizes.
Price: .... $532.00–$959.00

KAHR 25TH ANNIVERSARY K9
Caliber: 9mm. **Capacity:** 7-round magazine. **Barrel:** 4.02 in. **Grips:** Hogue textured and engraved aluminum. **Sights:** Fixed, TruGlo tritium. **Length:** 6 in. overall. **Weight:** 23.1 oz. unloaded. Finish: Sniper Grey Cerakote. **Features:** Limited 25th year anniversary edition includes custom 1791 leather holster and three magazines. Ported slide with "25 Years" engraving.
Price: $1,649.00

KAHR CM SERIES
Calibers: 9mm, .40 S&W, .45 ACP. **Capacities:** 9mm (6+1), .40 S&W (6+1). .45 ACP (5+1). CM45 Model is shown. **Barrels:** 3 in., 3.25 in. (45) **Weights:** 15.9–17.3 oz. **Length:** 5.42 in. overall. **Grips:** Textured polymer with integral steel rails molded into frame. **Sights:** CM9093, Pinned in polymer sight; PM9093, drift-adjustable, white bar-dot combat. **Features:** A conventional rifled barrel instead of the match-grade polygonal barrel on Kahr's PM series; the CM slide stop lever is MIM (metal-injection-molded) instead of machined; the CM series slide has fewer machining operations and uses simple engraved markings instead of roll marking. The CM series are shipped with one magazine instead of two. The slide is machined from solid 416 stainless with a matte finish, each gun is shipped with one 6-round stainless steel magazine with a flush baseplate. Magazines are U.S.-made, plasma welded, tumbled to remove burrs and feature Wolff springs. The magazine catch in the polymer frame is all metal and will not wear out on the stainless steel magazine after extended use.
Price: $460.00

KAHR CT 9/40/45 SERIES
Calibers: 9mm, .40 S&W, .45 ACP. **Capacities:** 9mm (8+1), .40 S&W (6+1) .45 ACP (7+1). **Barrel:** 4 in. **Weights:** 20–25 oz. **Length:** 5.42 in. overall. **Grips:** Textured polymer with integral steel rails molded into frame. **Sights:** Drift adjustable, white bar-dot combat. **Features:** Same as Kahr CM Series.
Price: $460.00

Prices given are believed to be accurate at time of publication however, many factors affect retail pricing so exact prices are not possible.

75TH EDITION, 2021 ⊕ **455**

KAHR CT 380
Caliber: .380 ACP. **Capacity:** (7+1). **Barrel:** 3 in. **Weight:** 14 oz. Other features similar to CT 9/40/45 models.
Price: **$419.00**

KAHR K SERIES
Calibers: K9: 9mm, 7-shot; K40: .40 S&W, 6-shot magazine. **Barrel:** 3.5 in. **Weight:** 25 oz. **Length:** 6 in. overall. **Grips:** Wraparound textured soft polymer. **Sights:** Blade front, rear drift adjustable for windage; bar-dot combat style. **Features:** Trigger-cocking double-action mechanism with passive firing pin block. Made of 4140 ordnance steel with matte black finish. Contact maker for complete price list. Introduced 1994. Made in USA by Kahr Arms.
Price: K9093C K9, matte stainless steel **$855.00**
Price: K9093NC K9, matte stainless steel w/tritium
    night sights **$985.00**
Price: K9094C K9 matte blackened stainless steel **$891.00**
Price: K9098 K9 Elite 2003, stainless steel **$932.00**
Price: K4043 K40, matte stainless steel **$855.00**
Price: K4043N K40, matte stainless steel w/tritium
    night sights **$985.00**
Price: K4044 K40, matte blackened stainless steel **$891.00**
Price: K4048 K40 Elite 2003, stainless steel **$932.00**

KAHR MK SERIES MICRO
Similar to the K9/K40 except is 5.35 in. overall, 4 in. high, with a 3.08 in. barrel. Weighs 23.1 oz. Has snag-free bar-dot sights, polished feed ramp, dual recoil spring system, DAO trigger. Comes with 5-round flush baseplate and 6-shot grip extension magazine. Introduced 1998. Made in USA by Kahr Arms.
Price: M9093 MK9, matte stainless steel **$911.00**
Price: M9093N MK9, matte stainless steel, tritium
    night sights **$1,017.00**
Price: M9098 MK9 Elite 2003, stainless steel **$991.00**
Price: M4043 MK40, matte stainless steel **$911.00**
Price: M4043N MK40, matte stainless steel, tritium
    night sights **$1,115.00**
Price: M4048 MK40 Elite 2003, stainless steel **$991.00**

KAHR P SERIES
Calibers: .380 ACP, 9mm, .40 S&W, 45 ACP. **Capacity:** 7-shot magazine.
Features: Similar to K9/K40 steel frame pistol except has polymer frame, matte stainless steel slide. Barrel length 3.5 in.; overall length 5.8 in.; weighs 17 oz. Includes two 7-shot magazines, hard polymer case, trigger lock. Introduced 2000. Made in USA by Kahr Arms.
Price: KP9093 9mm **$762.00**
Price: KP4043 .40 S&W **$762.00**
Price: KP4543 .45 ACP **$829.00**
Price: KP3833 .380 ACP (2008)....................................... **$667.00**

KAHR KP GEN 2 PREMIUM SERIES
Calibers: 9mm, .45 ACP. **Capacities:** KP9 9mm (7-shot magazine), KP45 .45 ACP (6 shots). **Barrel:** 3.5 in. **Features:** Black polymer frame, matte stainless slide, Tru-Glo Tritium fiber optic sights, short trigger, accessory rail.
Price: .... **$833.00-$1,101.00**

KAHR TP GEN 2 PREMIUM SERIES
Calibers: 9mm, .45 ACP. **Capacities:** TP9 9mm (8-shot magazine), TP45 .45 ACP (7 or 8 shots). **Barrels:** 4, 5, or 6 in. **Features:** Model with 4-inch barrel has features similar to KP GEN 2. The 5-inch model has front and rear slide serrations, white 3-dot sights, mount for reflex sights. The 6-inch model has the same features plus comes with Leupold Delta Point Reflex sight.
Price: **$976.00**
Price: 5-inch bbl **$1,015.00**
Price: 6-inch bbl **$1,566.00**

KAHR PM SERIES
Calibers: 9mm, .40 S&W, .45 ACP. **Capacity:** 7-round magazine. **Features:** Similar to P-Series pistols except has smaller polymer frame (Polymer Micro). Barrel length 3.08 in.; overall length 5.35 in.; weighs 17 oz. Includes two 7-shot magazines, hard polymer case, trigger lock. Introduced 2000. Made in USA by Kahr Arms.
Price: PM9093 PM9 .... **$810.00**
Price: PM4043 PM40 .... **$810.00**
Price: PM4543 PM45.. **$880.00**

KAHR T SERIES
Calibers: 9mm, .40 S&W. **Capacities:** T9: 9mm, 8-round magazine; T40: .40 S&W, 7-round magazine. **Barrel:** 4 in. **Weight:** 28.1–29.1 oz. **Length:** 6.5 in. overall. **Grips:** Checkered Hogue Pau Ferro wood grips. **Sights:** Rear: Novak low-profile 2-dot tritium night sight, front tritium night sight. **Features:** Similar to other Kahr makes, but with longer slide and barrel upper, longer butt. Trigger cocking DAO; locking breech; Browning-type recoil lug; passive striker block; no magazine disconnect. Comes with two magazines. Introduced 2004. Made in USA by Kahr Arms.
Price: KT9093 T9 matte stainless steel **$857.00**
Price: KT9093-NOVAK T9, "Tactical 9," Novak night sight **$980.00**
Price: KT4043 40 S&W... **$857.00**

KAHR CW SERIES
Caliber: 9mm, .40 S&W, .45 ACP. **Capacities:** 9mm, 7-round magazine; .40 S&W and .45 ACP, 6-round magazine. **Barrels:** 3.5 and 3.64 in. **Weight:** 17.7–18.7 oz. **Length:** 5.9–6.36 in. overall. **Grips:** Textured polymer. Similar to P-Series, but CW Series have conventional rifling, metal-injection-molded slide stop lever, no front dovetail cut, one magazine. CW40 introduced 2006. Made in USA by Kahr Arms. Several optional finishes available.
Price: .... **$449.00-$495.00**

KAHR P380
Caliber: .380 ACP. **Capacity:** 6+1. **Features:** Very small DAO semi-auto pistol. Features include 2.5-in. Lothar Walther barrel; black polymer frame with stainless steel slide; drift adjustable white bar/dot combat/sights; optional tritium sights; two 6+1 magazines. Overall length 4.9 in., weight 10 oz. without magazine.
Price: Standard sights **$667.00**
Price: Night sights.. **$792.00**

KAHR CW380
Caliber: .380 ACP. **Capacity:** 6-round magazine. **Barrel:** 2.58 in. **Weight:** 11.5 oz. **Length:** 4.96 in. **Grips:** Textured integral polymer. **Sights:** Fixed white-bar combat style. **Features:** DAO. Black or purple polymer frame, stainless slide.
Price: **$419.00**

KAHR TIG SPECIAL EDITION
Caliber: 9mm. **Capacity:** 8 rounds. **Weight:** 18.5 oz. **Barrel:** 4 in. (Sub-compact model). **Features:** Limited Special Edition to support Beyond the Battlefield Foundation founded by John "Tig" Tiegen and his wife to provide support for wounded veterans. Tiegen is one of the heroes of the Benghazi attack in 2012. Kryptek Typhon finish on frame, black Teracote finish on slide engraved with Tiegen signature, Tig logo and BTB logo. Production will be limited to 1,000 pistols. Part of the proceeds from the sale of each firearm will be donated to the Beyond the Battlefield Foundation by Kahr Firearms Group.
Price: **$541.00**

KEL-TEC P-11
Caliber: 9mm. **Capacity:** 10-round magazine. **Barrel:** 3.1 in. **Weight:** 14 oz. **Length:** 5.6 in. overall. **Grips:** Checkered black polymer. **Sights:** Blade front, rear adjustable for windage. **Features:** Ordnance steel slide, aluminum frame. DAO trigger mechanism. Introduced 1995. Made in USA by Kel-Tec CNC Industries, Inc.
Price: From **$340.00**

KEL-TEC PF-9
Caliber: 9mm. **Capacity:** 7 rounds. **Weight:** 12.7 oz. **Sights:** Rear sight adjustable for windage and elevation. **Barrel:** 3.1 in. **Length:** 5.85 in. **Features:** Barrel, locking system, slide stop, assembly pin, front sight, recoil springs and guide rod adapted from P-11. Trigger system with integral hammer block and the extraction system adapted from P-3AT. Mil-Std-1913 Picatinny rail. Made in USA by Kel-Tec CNC Industries, Inc.
Price: From **$356.00**

KEL-TEC P17
Caliber: .22 LR. **Capacity:** 16-round magazine. **Barrel:** 3.8 in. **Grips:** Textured polymer. **Sights:** Fixed. **Length:** 6.7 in. overall. **Weight:** 11.2 oz. unloaded. **Finish:** Matte black.
Price: **$199.00**

KEL-TEC P-32
Caliber: .32 ACP. **Capacity:** 7-round magazine. **Barrel:** 2.68. **Weight:** 6.6 oz. **Length:** 5.07 overall. **Grips:** Checkered composite. **Sights:** Fixed. **Features:** Double-action-only mechanism with 6-lb. pull; internal slide stop. Textured composite grip/frame.
Price: From **$326.00**

KEL-TEC P-3AT
Caliber: .380 ACP. **Capacity:** 7-round magazine **Weight:** 7.2 oz. **Length:** 5.2. **Features:** Lightest .380 ACP made; aluminum frame, steel barrel.
Price: From **$331.00**

KEL-TEC PLR-16
Caliber: 5.56mm NATO. **Capacity:** 10-round magazine. **Weight:** 51 oz. **Sights:** Rear sight adjustable for windage, front sight is M-16 blade. **Barrel:** 9.2 in. **Length:** 18.5 in. **Features:** Muzzle is threaded 1/2x28 to accept standard attachments such as a muzzle brake. Except for the barrel, bolt, sights and mechanism, the PLR-16 pistol is made of high-impact glass fiber reinforced polymer. Gas-operated semi-auto. Conventional gas-piston operation with M-16 breech locking system. MIL-STD-1913 Picatinny rail. Made in USA by Kel-Tec CNC Industries, Inc.
Price: Blued **$682.00**

Prices given are believed to be accurate at time of publication however, many factors affect retail pricing so exact prices are not possible.

75TH EDITION, 2021 ⊕ **457**

KEL-TEC PLR-22

Caliber: .22 LR. **Capacity:** 26-round magazine. **Length:** 18.5 in. overall. 40 oz. **Features:** Semi-auto pistol based on centerfire PLR-16 by same maker. Blowback action. Open sights and Picatinny rail for mounting accessories; threaded muzzle.
Price: $400.00

KEL-TEC PMR-30

Caliber: .22 Magnum (.22WMR). **Capacity:** 30 rounds. **Barrel:** 4.3 in. **Weight:** 13.6 oz. **Length:** 7.9 in. overall. **Grips:** Glass reinforced Nylon (Zytel). **Sights:** Dovetailed aluminum with front & rear fiber optics. **Features:** Operates on a unique hybrid blowback/locked-breech system. It uses a double-stack magazine of a new design that holds 30 rounds and fits completely in the grip of the pistol. Dual opposing extractors for reliability, heel magazine release to aid in magazine retention, Picatinny accessory rail under the barrel, Urethane recoil buffer, captive coaxial recoil springs. The barrel is fluted for light weight and effective heat dissipation. PMR30 disassembles for cleaning by removal of a single pin.
Price: $455.00

KIMBER COLLECTOR EDITION RAPTOR

Calibers: 9mm (Micro 9 and EVO), .45 ACP (1911) **Capacity:** 7- or 8-round magazine. Barrels: 3.15, 3.16 or 5 in. **Weight:** 15.6–38 oz. **Grips:** G10 smooth/scaled texture. **Sights:** Low profile, tritium. **Finish:** Two-tone bronze. **Features:** Scale-style slide serrations. Made in the Kimber Custom Shop.
Price: (1911 model)....................................**$1,524.00**
Price: (Micro 9 model).................................**$951.00**
Price: (EVO SP model) **$999.00**

KIMBER MICRO CDP

Caliber: .380 ACP. **Capacity:** 6-round magazine. **Barrel:** 2.75 in. **Weight:** 17 oz. **Grips:** Double diamond rosewood. Mini 1911-style single action with no grip safety.
Price: $869.00

KIMBER MICRO CRIMSON CARRY

Caliber: .380 ACP. **Capacity:** 6-round magazine. **Barrel:** 2.75 in. **Weight:** 13.4 oz. **Length:** 5.6 in **Grips:** Black synthetic, double diamond. **Sights:** Fixed low profile. **Finish:** Matte black. **Features:** Aluminum frame with satin silver finish, steel slide, carry-melt treatment, full-length guide rod, rosewood Crimson Trace Lasergrips.
Price: $839.00

KIMBER MICRO TLE

Caliber: .380 ACP. **Features:** Similar to Micro Crimson Carry. **Features:** Black slide and frame. Green and black G10 grips.
Price: $734.00

KIMBER MICRO RAPTOR

Caliber: .380 ACP **Capacity:** 6-round magazine. **Sights:** Tritium night sights. **Finish:** Stainless. **Features:** Variation of Micro Carry with Raptor-style scalloped "feathered" slide serrations and grip panels.
Price: $842.00

KIMBER COVERT SERIES

Caliber: .45 ACP **Capacity:** 7-round magazine. **Barrels:** 3, 4 or 5 in. **Weight:** 25–31 oz. **Grips:** Crimson Trace laser with camo finish. **Sights:** Tactical wedge 3-dot night sights. **Features:** Made in the Kimber Custom Shop. **Finish:** Kimber Gray frame, matte black slide, black small parts. Carry Melt treatment. Available in three frame sizes: Custom, Pro and Ultra.
Price: $1,457.00

KIMBER CUSTOM II

Caliber: 9mm, .45 ACP. **Barrel:** 5 in. **Weight:** 38 oz. **Length:** 8.7 in. overall. **Grips:** Checkered black rubber, walnut, rosewood. **Sights:** Dovetailed front and rear, Kimber low profile adjustable or fixed sights. **Features:** Slide, frame and barrel machined from steel or stainless steel. Match-grade barrel, chamber and trigger group. Extended thumb safety, beveled magazine well, beveled front and rear slide serrations, high ride beavertail grip safety, checkered flat mainspring housing, kidney cut under trigger guard, high cut grip, match-grade stainless steel barrel bushing, polished breechface, Commander-style hammer, lowered and flared ejection port, Wolff springs, bead blasted black oxide or matte stainless finish. Introduced in 1996. Made in USA by Kimber Mfg., Inc.
Price: Custom II **$871.00**
Price: Two-Tone **$1,136.00**

KIMBER CUSTOM TLE II

Caliber: .45 ACP or 10mm. **Features:** TLE (Tactical Law Enforcement) version of Custom II model plus night sights, frontstrap checkering, threaded barrel, Picatinny rail.
Price: .45 ACP **$1,007.00**
Price: 10mm **$1,028.00**

KIMBER MICRO 9
Caliber: 9mm. **Capacity:** 7-round magazine. **Barrel:** 3.15 in. **Weight:** 15.6 oz. **Features:** The easily concealed Micro 9 features mild recoil, smooth trigger pull and the intuitive operation of a 1911 platform. Micro 9 slides are made to the tightest allowable tolerances, with barrels machined from stainless steel for superior resistance to moisture. All Micro 9 frames are shaped from the finest aluminum for integrity and strength. Lowered and flared ejection ports for flawless ejection and a beveled magazine well for fast, positive loading. In 2020, Kimber offered 15 different Micro 9 models with a total of 26 variations.
Prices:...$654.00-$1,061.00

KIMBER STAINLESS II
Same features as Custom II except has stainless steel frame.
Price: Stainless II .45 ACP $998.00
Price: Stainless II 9mm $1,016.00
Price: Stainless II .45 ACP w/night sights........................... $1,141.00
Price: Stainless II Target .45 ACP (stainless, adj. sight) $1,108.00

KIMBER PRO CARRY II
Calibers: 9mm, .45 ACP. **Features:** Similar to Custom II, has aluminum frame, 4-in. bull barrel fitted directly to the slide without bushing. Introduced 1998. Made in USA by Kimber Mfg., Inc.
Price: Pro Carry II, .45 ACP $837.00
Price: Pro Carry II, 9mm $857.00
Price: Pro Carry II w/night sights $977.00
Price: Two-Tone $1,136.00

KIMBER SAPPHIRE PRO II
Caliber: 9mm. **Capacity:** 9-round magazine. **Features:** Similar to Pro Carry II, 4-inch match-grade barrel. Striking two-tone appearance with satin silver aluminum frame and high polish bright blued slide. Grips are blue/black G-10 with grooved texture. Fixed Tactical Edge night sights. From the Kimber Custom Shop.
Price: $1,652.00

KIMBER RAPTOR II
Caliber: .45 ACP. **Capacities:** .45 ACP (8-round magazine, 7-round (Ultra and Pro models). **Barrels:** 3, 4 or 5 in. **Weight:** 25–31 oz. **Grips:** Thin milled rosewood. **Sights:** Tactical wedge 3-dot night sights. **Features:** Made in the Kimber Custom Shop. Matte black or satin silver finish. Available in three frame sizes: Custom (shown), Pro and Ultra.
Price: .... $1,192.00–$1,464.00

KIMBER ULTRA CARRY II
Calibers: 9mm, .45 ACP. **Features:** Lightweight aluminum frame, 3-in. match-grade bull barrel fitted to slide without bushing. Grips 0.4-in. shorter. Light recoil spring. Weighs 25 oz. Introduced in 1999. Made in USA by Kimber Mfg., Inc.
Price: Stainless Ultra Carry II .45 ACP $919.00
Price: Stainless Ultra Carry II 9mm $1,016.00
Price: Stainless Ultra Carry II .45 ACP with night sights $1,039.00
Price: Two-Tone $1,177.00

KIMBER GOLD MATCH II
Caliber: .45 ACP. **Features:** Similar to Custom II models. Includes stainless steel barrel with match-grade chamber and barrel bushing, ambidextrous thumb safety, adjustable sight, premium aluminum trigger, hand-checkered double diamond rosewood grips. Barrel hand-fitted for target accuracy. Made in USA by Kimber Mfg., Inc.
Price: Gold Match II .45 ACP..................................... $1,393.00
Price: Gold Match Stainless II .45 ACP $1,574.00

KIMBER CDP II SERIES
Calibers: 9mm, .45 ACP. **Features:** Similar to Custom II but designed for concealed carry. Aluminum frame. Standard features include stainless steel slide, fixed Meprolight tritium 3-dot (green) dovetail-mounted night sights, match-grade barrel and chamber, 30 LPI frontstrap checkering, two-tone finish, ambidextrous thumb safety, hand-checkered double diamond rosewood grips. Introduced in 2000. Made in USA by Kimber Mfg., Inc.
Price: Ultra CDP II 9mm (2008) $1,359.00
Price: Ultra CDP II .45 ACP $1,318.00
Price: Compact CDP II .45 ACP $1,318.00
Price: Pro CDP II .45 ACP $1,318.00
Price: Custom CDP II (5-in. barrel, full length grip) $1,318.00

KIMBER CDP
Calibers: 9mm, .45 ACP. **Barrel:** 3, 4 or 5 in. **Weight:** 25–31 oz. **Features:** Aluminum frame, stainless slide, 30 LPI checkering on backstrap and trigger guard, low profile tritium night sights, Carry Melt treatment. **Sights:** Hand checkered rosewood or Crimson Trace Lasergrips. Introduced in 2017.
Price: $1,173.00
Price: With Crimson Trace Lasergrips................................. $1,473.00

KIMBER ECLIPSE II SERIES
Calibers: .38 Super, 10 mm, .45 ACP. **Features:** Similar to Custom II and other stainless Kimber pistols. Stainless slide and frame, black oxide, two-tone finish. Gray/black laminated grips. 30 LPI frontstrap checkering. All models have night sights; Target versions have Meprolight adjustable Bar/Dot version. Made in USA by Kimber Mfg., Inc.
Price: Eclipse Ultra II (3-in. barrel, short grip) $1,350.00
Price: Eclipse Pro II (4-in. barrel, full-length grip) $1,350.00
Price: Eclipse Custom II 10mm $1,350.00
Price: Eclipse Target II (5-in. barrel, full-length grip,
     adjustable sight) $1,393.00

Prices given are believed to be accurate at time of publication however, many factors affect retail pricing so exact prices are not possible.

75TH EDITION, 2021 ⊕ **459**

KIMBER TACTICAL ENTRY II
Caliber: 45 ACP. **Capacity:** 7-round magazine. **Barrel:** 5 in. **Weight:** 40 oz. **Length:** 8.7 in. overall. **Features:** 1911-style semi-auto with checkered frontstrap, extended magazine well, night sights, heavy steel frame, tactical rail.
Price: $1,490.00

KIMBER TACTICAL CUSTOM HD II
Caliber: .45 ACP. **Capacity:** 7-round magazine. **Barrel:** 5 in. match-grade. **Weight:** 39 oz. **Length:** 8.7 in. overall. **Features:** 1911-style semiauto with night sights, heavy steel frame.
Price: $1,387.00

KIMBER ULTRA CDP II
Calibers: 9mm, .45 ACP. **Capacities:** 7-round magazine (9 in 9mm). **Features:** Compact 1911-style pistol; ambidextrous thumb safety; carry melt profiling; full-length guide rod; aluminum frame with stainless slide; satin silver finish; checkered frontstrap; 3-inch barrel; rosewood double diamond Crimson Trace laser grips; tritium 3-dot night sights.
Price: $1,603.00

KIMBER STAINLESS ULTRA TLE II
Caliber: .45 ACP. **Capacity:** 7-round magazine. **Features:** 1911-style semi-auto pistol. Features include full-length guide rod; aluminum frame with stainless slide; satin silver finish; checkered frontstrap; 3-in. barrel; tactical gray double diamond grips; tritium 3-dot night sights.
Price: $1,136.00

KIMBER ROYAL II
Caliber: .45 ACP. **Capacity:** 7-round magazine. **Barrel:** 5 in. **Weight:** 38 oz. **Length:** 8.7 in. overall. **Grips:** Solid bone-smooth. **Sights:** Fixed low profile. **Features:** A classic full-size pistol wearing a charcoal blue finish complimented with solid bone grip panels. Front and rear serrations. Aluminum match-grade trigger with a factory setting of approximately 4–5 pounds.
Price: $1,785.00

KIMBER MASTER CARRY SERIES
Caliber: .45 ACP. **Capacity:** 8-round magazine, 9mm (Pro only). **Barrels:** 5 in. (Custom), 4 in. (Pro), 3 in. (Ultra) **Weight:** 25–30 oz. **Grips:** Crimson Trace Laser. **Sights:** Fixed low profile. **Features:** Matte black KimPro slide, aluminum round heel frame, full-length guide rod.
Price: $1,497.00

KIMBER WARRIOR SOC
Caliber: .45 ACP. **Capacity:** 7-round magazine. **Barrel:** 5 in threaded for suppression. **Sights:** Fixed Tactical Wedge tritium. **Finish:** Dark Green frame, Flat Dark Earth slide. **Features:** Full-size 1911 based on special series of pistols made for USMC. Service melt, ambidextrous safety.
Price: $1,392.00

KIMBER SUPER JAGARE
Caliber: 10mm. **Capacity:** 8+1. **Barrel:** 6 in, ported. **Weight:** 42 oz. **Finish:** Stainless steel KimPro, Charcoal gray frame, diamond-like carbon coated slide. Slide is ported. **Sights:** Delta Point Pro Optic. **Grips:** Micarta. Frame has rounded heel, high cut trigger guard. Designed for hunting.
Price: $2,688.00

KIMBER KHX SERIES
Calibers: .45 ACP, 9mm. **Capacity:** 8+1. **Features:** This series is offered in Custom, Pro and Ultra sizes. **Barrels:** 5-, 4- or 3-inch match-grade stainless steel. **Weights:** 25–38 oz. **Finishes:** Stainless steel frame and slide with matte black KimPro II finish. Stepped hexagonal slide and top-strap serrations. **Sights:** Green and red fiber optic and Hogue Laser Enhanced MagGrip G10 grips and matching mainspring housings. Pro and Ultra models have rounded heel frames. Optics Ready (OR) models available in Custom and Pro sizes with milled slide that accepts optics plates for Vortex, Trijicon and Leupold red-dot sights.
Price: Custom OR .45 ACP $1,087.00
Price: Custom OR 9mm $1,108.00
Price: Custom, Pro or Ultra .45... $1,259.00
Price: Custom, Pro or Ultra 9mm $1,279.00

KIMBER AEGIS ELITE SERIES

Calibers: 9mm, .45 ACP. **Features:** Offered in Custom, Pro and Ultra sizes with 5-, 4.25- or 3-in. barrels. **Sights:** Green or red fiber optic or Vortex Venom red dot on OI (Optics Installed) models (shown). **Grips:** G10. **Features:** Satin finish stainless steel frame, matte black or gray slide, front and rear AEX slide serrations.

Price: .45 ACP **$1,021.00**
Price: 9mm **$1,041.00**
Price: .45 OI **$1,375.00**
Price: 9mm OI **$1,395.00**

KIMBER EVO SERIES

Caliber: 9mm. **Capacity:** 7 rounds. **Barrel:** 3.16 in. **Sights:** Tritium night sights. **Weight:** 19 oz. **Grips:** G10. **Features:** Offered in TLE, CDP, Two Tone variants with stainless slide, aluminum frame.

Price: TLE **$925.00**
Price: CDP **$949.00**
Price: Two Tone **$856.00**

LIONHEART LH9 MKII

Caliber: 9mm. **Capacities:** 15-round magazine. LH9C Compact, 10 rounds. **Barrel:** 4.1 in. **Weight:** 26.5 oz. **Length:** 7.5 in **Grips:** One-piece black polymer with textured design. **Sights:** Fixed low profile. Novak LoMount sights available. **Finish:** Cerakote Graphite Black or Patriot Brown. **Features:** Hammer-forged heat-treated steel slide, hammer-forged aluminum frame. Double-action PLUS action.

Price: **$695.00**
Price: Novak sights .... **$749.**

LLAMA MAX-1

Calibers: .38 Super, .45 ACP. **Barrel:** 5 in. **Weight:** 37 oz. **Sights:** Mil-spec. fixed. **Features:** Standard size and features of the 1911A1 full-size model. Lowered ejection port, matte blue or hard chrome finish. Imported from the Philippines by Eagle Imports. Introduced in 2016.

Price: **$565.00**

LLAMA MICRO MAX

Caliber: .380 ACP. **Capacity:** 7-round magazine. **Weight:** 23 oz. **Sights:** Novak style rear, fiber optic front. **Grips:** Wood or black synthetic. **Features:** A compact 1911-style pistol with 3.75-in. barrel. Skeletonized hammer and trigger, double slide serrations, comes with two 7-shot magazines. Imported from the Philippines by Eagle Imports.

Price: **$468.00**

MAC 1911 BOB CUT

Caliber: .45 ACP. **Capacity:** 8+1 magazine. **Barrel:** 4.25 in. Commander-size 1911 design. **Sights:** Novak-type fully adjustable rear, dovetail front. **Weight:** 34.5 oz. **Finish:** Blue or hard chrome. **Grips:** Custom hardwood. **Features:** Stippled frontstrap, skeletonized trigger and hammer, flared and lowered ejection port, bobtail grip frame. Imported from the Philippines by Eagle Imports.

Price: **$902.00**

MAC 1911 BULLSEYE

Caliber: .45 ACP **Capacity:** 8+1 magazine. **Barrel:** 6-in. match-grade bull. **Sights:** Bomar-type fully adjustable rear, dovetail front. **Weight:** 46 oz. **Finish:** Blue or hard chrome. **Grips:** Hardwood. **Features:** Checkered frontstrap, skeletonized trigger and hammer, flared and lowered ejection port, wide front and rear slide serrations. Imported from the Philippines by Eagle Imports.

Price: **$1,219.00**

MAC 1911 CLASSIC

Caliber: .45 ACP. **Capacity:** 8-round magazine. **Barrel:** 5-in., match-grade bull. **Sights:** Bomar-type fully adjustable rear, fiber-optic front. **Weight:** 40.5 oz. **Finish:** Blue, black chrome or hard chrome. **Grips:** Hardwood. **Features:** Checkered frontstrap, skeletonized trigger and hammer, flared and lowered ejection port, wide front and rear slide serrations. Imported from the Philippines by Eagle Imports.

Price: **$1,045.00**

Prices given are believed to be accurate at time of publication however, many factors affect retail pricing so exact prices are not possible.

75TH EDITION, 2021 ✛ **461**

MAC 3011 SLD TACTICAL

Calibers: 9mm, .40 S&W, .45 ACP. **Capacity:** 14-, 15- or 17-round magazines. **Barrel:** 5 in.-, match-grade bull. **Sights:** Bomar-type fully adjustable rear, fiber-optic front. **Weight:** 46.5 oz. **Finish:** Blue. **Grips:** Aluminum. **Features:** Checkered frontstrap serrations, skeletonized trigger and hammer, flared and lowered ejection port, ambidextrous safety, full dust cover. Imported from the Philippines by Eagle Imports.
Price: $1,136.00

MOSSBERG MC1SC

Caliber: 9mm **Capacity:** 6+1 magazine. **Barrel:** 3.4 in. **Sights:** Three white-dot, snag free. TruGlo tritium Pro sights or Viridian E-Series Red Laser available as option. **Weight:** 22 oz., loaded. **Grips:** Integral with aggressive texturing and with palm swell. **Features:** Glass-reinforced polymer frame, stainless steel slide with multi-angle front and rear serrations, flat-profile trigger with integrated blade safety, ships with one 6-round and one 7-round magazine. Optional cross-bolt safety. Centennial Limited Edition (1,000 units) has 24k gold accents, tritium nitride finish on barrel, polished slide.

Price:	**$421.00**
Price: Viridian laser sight....................	**$514.00**
Price: TruGlo tritium sights..................	**$526.00**
Price: Centennial Limited Edition	**$686.00**
Price: FDE	**$428.00**
Price: Two-Tone..................................	**$421.00**

MOSSBERG MC2C

Caliber: 9mm. **Capacity:** 13- or 15-round magazine. **Barrel:** 3.9 in. **Grips:** Textured polymer. **Sights:** Fixed, 3-dot. **Length:** 7.1 in. overall. **Weight:** 21 oz. unloaded. **Finish:** Matte black. **Features:** Accessory rail, forward-slide serrations.
Price: $490.00

NIGHTHAWK CUSTOM AGENT2 COMMANDER

Calibers: 9mm, .45 ACP. **Capacity:** 10-round magazine. **Barrel:** 4.25 in. **Grips:** G10 Railscale texture. **Sights:** Fixed, Heinie Ledge Black rear/gold-bead front. **Length:** 7.85 in. overall. **Weight:** 38.6 oz. unloaded. **Finish:** Smoke Cerakote. **Features:** Accessory rail, faceted slide with side windows, one-piece mainspring housing/mag well, ultra-high-cut front grip strap.
Price: $4,499.00

NIGHTHAWK CUSTOM BULL OFFICER

Caliber: 9mm. **Capacity:** 8-round magazine. **Barrel:** 3.8 in. **Grips:** Textured carbon fiber. **Sights:** Fixed, Heinie Ledge Black rear/fiber-optic front. **Length:** 7.85 in. overall. **Weight:** 38.2 oz. unloaded. **Finish:** Black nitride. **Features:** Bull nose and French border on slide, ultra-high-cut front grip strap, dehorned.
Price: $3,699.00

NIGHTHAWK CUSTOM COLT SERIES 70

Caliber: .45 ACP. **Capacity:** 7-round magazine. **Barrel:** 5 in. **Grips:** Textured linen micarta. **Sights:** Fixed, retro rear/gold-bead front. **Length:** 8.75 in. overall. **Weight:** 39 oz. unloaded. **Finish:** Smoked nitride. **Features:** Match-grade solid short trigger, fully machined disconnector, retro hammer, Nighthawk Custom beavertail grip safety, mainspring housing and match barrel bushing.
Price: $2,599.00

NIGHTHAWK CUSTOM GRP

Calibers: 9mm, 10mm, .45 ACP. **Capacity:** 8-round magazine. **Features:** Global Response Pistol (GRP). Black, Sniper Gray, green, Coyote Tan or Titanium Blue finish. Match-grade barrel and trigger, choice of Heinie or Novak adjustable night sights.
Price: $3,095.00

NIGHTHAWK CUSTOM T4

Calibers: 9mm, .45 ACP **Capacities:** .45 ACP, 7- or 8-round magazine; 9mm, 9 or 10 rounds; 10mm, 9 or 10 rounds. **Barrels:** 3.8, 4.25 or 5 in. **Weights:** 28–41 ounces, depending on model. **Features:** Manufacturer of a wide range of 1911-style pistols in Government Model (full-size), Commander and Officer's frame sizes. Shown is T4 model, introduced in 2013 and available only in 9mm.
Price: From .... $3,495.00–$3,695.00

NIGHTHAWK CUSTOM THUNDER RANCH

Caliber: 9mm, .45 ACP. **Capacity:** 8-round (.45 ACP), 10-round (9mm) magazine. **Barrel:** 5 in. **Grips:** Textured linen micarta. **Sights:** Fixed, Heinie Black Ledge rear/gold-bead front. **Length:** 8.6 in. overall. **Weight:** 41.3 oz. unloaded. **Finish:** Smoked nitride. **Features:** Custom front- and rear-cocking serrations, lanyard-loop mainspring housing, GI-Style nub thumb safety and custom engraving.
Price: $3,399.00

NIGHTHAWK CUSTOM SHADOW HAWK

Caliber: 9mm. **Barrels:** 5 in. or 4.25 in. **Features:** Stainless steel frame with black Nitride finish, flat-faced trigger, high beavertail grip safety, checkered frontstrap, Heinie Straight Eight front and rear titanium night sights.
Price: $3,795.00

NIGHTHAWK CUSTOM VICE PRESIDENT

Caliber: 9mm. **Capacity:** 10-round magazine. **Barrel:** 4.25 in. **Grips:** G10 Railscale Ascend texture. **Sights:** Fixed, Heinie Straight Eight Ledge rear/ tritium front. **Length:** 7.4 in. overall. **Weight:** 32 oz. unloaded. **Finish:** Black DLC. **Features:** Gold titanium nitride barrel, heavy angle slide-lightening cuts, one-piece mainspring housing/mag well, ultra-high-cut front grip strap, dehorned.
Price: $4,199.00

NIGHTHAWK CUSTOM WAR HAWK

Caliber: .45 ACP. **Barrels:** 5 in. or 4.25 in. **Features:** One-piece mainspring housing and mag well, Everlast Recoil System, Hyena Brown G10 grips.
Price: $3,895.00

NIGHTHAWK CUSTOM BOB MARVEL 1911

Calibers: 9mm or .45 ACP. **Barrel:** 4.25-in. bull barrel. **Features:** Everlast Recoil System, adjustable sights, match trigger, black Melonite finish.
Price: $4,395.00

Prices given are believed to be accurate at time of publication however, many factors affect retail pricing so exact prices are not possible.

NIGHTHAWK CUSTOM DOMINATOR
Caliber: .45 ACP. **Capacity:** 8-round magazine. **Features:** Stainless frame, black Perma Kote slide, cocobolo double-diamond grips,, front and rear slide serrations, adjustable sights.
Price: $3,699.00

NIGHTHAWK CUSTOM SILENT HAWK
Caliber: .45 ACP. **Capacity:** 8-round magazine. **Barrel:** 4.25 in. **Features:** Commander recon frame, G10 black and gray grips. Designed to match Silencerco silencer, not included with pistol.
Price: $4,295.00

NIGHTHAWK CUSTOM HEINIE LONG SLIDE
Calibers: 10mm, .45 ACP. **Barrel:** Long slide 6-in. **Features:** Cocobolo wood grips, black Perma Kote finish, adjustable or fixed sights, frontstrap checkering.
Price: $3,895.00

NIGHTHAWK CUSTOM BORDER SPECIAL
Caliber: .45 ACP **Capacity:** 8+1 magazine. **Barrel:** 4.25-in. match grade. **Weight:** 34 oz. **Sights:** Heinie Black Slant rear, gold bead front. **Grips:** Cocobolo double diamond. **Finish:** Cerakote Elite Midnight black. **Features:** Commander-size steel frame with bobtail concealed carry grip. Scalloped frontstrap and mainspring housing. Serrated slide top. Rear slide serrations only. Crowned barrel flush with bushing.
Price: $3,699.00

NIGHTHAWK VIP BLACK
Caliber: .45 ACP. **Capacity:** 8+1 magazine. Hand built with all Nighthawk 1911 features plus deep hand engraving throughout, black DLC finish, custom vertical frontstrap and mainspring serrations, 14k solid gold bead front sight, crowned barrel, giraffe bone grips, custom walnut hardwood presentation case.
Price: $7,999.00

NORTH AMERICAN ARMS GUARDIAN DAO
Calibers: .25 NAA, .32 ACP, .380 ACP, .32 NAA. **Capacity:** 6-round magazine. **Barrel:** 2.49 in. **Weight:** 20.8 oz. **Length:** 4.75 in. overall. **Grips:** Black polymer. **Sights:** Low-profile fixed. **Features:** DAO mechanism. All stainless steel construction. Introduced 1998. Made in USA by North American Arms. The .25 NAA is based on a bottle-necked .32 ACP case, and the .32 NAA is on a bottle-necked .380 ACP case. Custom model has roll-engraved slide, high-polish features, choice of grips.
Price: .25 NAA, .32 ACP $409.00
Price: .32 NAA, .380 ACP $486.00
Price: Engraved Custom Model .... $575.00-$625.00

PHOENIX ARMS HP22, HP25
Calibers: .22 LR, .25 ACP. **Capacities:** .22 LR, 10-shot (HP22), .25 ACP, 10-shot (HP25). **Barrel:** 3 in. **Weight:** 20 oz. **Length:** 5.5 in. overall. **Grips:** Checkered composition. **Sights:** Blade front, adjustable rear. **Features:** Single action, exposed hammer; manual hold-open; button magazine release. Available in satin nickel,matte blue finish. Introduced 1993. Made in USA by Phoenix Arms.
Price: With gun lock $162.00
Price: HP Range kit with 5-in. bbl., locking case and
      accessories (1 Mag) $207.00
Price: HP Deluxe Range kit with 3- and 5-in. bbls., 2 mags, case $248.00

REMINGTON R1
Caliber: .45 ACP. **Capacity:** 7-round magazine. **Barrels:** 5 in. (Full-size); 4.25 in. (Commander). **Weight:** 38.5 oz., 31 oz. (Ultralite). **Grips:** Double diamond walnut. **Sights:** Fixed, dovetail front and rear, 3-dot. **Features:** Flared and lowered ejection port. Comes with two magazines.
Price: Full-size or Commander $774.00
Price: Stainless $837.00
Price: Ultralite Commander... $849.00

REMINGTON R1 LIMITED
Calibers: 9mm, .40 S&W, .45 ACP (Double-stack only). **Capacity:** 19+1 magazine. **Barrel:** 5 in. **Grips:** G10 VZ Operator. **Weight:** 38 oz. **Features:** Stainless steel frame and slide. Double Stack Model has 19-shot capacity.
Price: $1,250.00
Price: Limited Double Stack.. $1,310.00

REMINGTON R1 RECON
Calibers: 9mm, .45 ACP. **Barrel:** 4.25-in. match grade. **Features:** Double-stack stainless steel frame and slide. G10 VZ Operator grips, skeletonized trigger, ambidextrous safety, PVD coating, Tritium night sights, wide front and rear serrations, checkered mainspring housing and frontstrap.
Price: $1,275.00

REMINGTON R1 TACTICAL
Caliber: .45 ACP. **Barrel:** 5-in. **Sights:** Trijicon night sights. **Features:** Single- or double-stack frame. Threaded barrel available on double-stack model. Adjustable trigger. Other features same as Recon.
Price: $1,250.00
Price: Threaded barrel.. $1,275.00

REMINGTON R1 HUNTER
Caliber: 10mm. **Capacity:** 8-round magazine. **Barrel:** 6-in. match grade. **Sights:** Fully adjustable. **Finish:** Stainless steel. Comes with two 8-shot magazines, Operator II VZ G10 grips.
Price: $1,310.00

REMINGTON R1 ENHANCED

Calibers: .45 ACP, 9mm. **Capacities:** Same features as standard R1 except 8-shot magazine (.45), 9-shot (9mm). Stainless satin black oxide finish, wood laminate grips and adjustable rear sight. Other features include forward slide serrations, fiber optic front sight. Available with threaded barrel.

Price:	**$903.00**
Price: Stainless	**$990.00**
Price: Threaded barrel..................	**$959.00**
Price: With Crimson Trace Laser Sight............	**$1,129.00**
Price: Enhanced Double Stack	**$999.00**

REMINGTON R1 CARRY

Caliber: .45 ACP. **Capacity:** 8-round magazine. **Barrel:** 5 in. or 4.25 in. (Carry Commander). **Weight:** 35–39 oz. **Grips:** Cocobolo. **Sights:** Novak-type drift-adjustable rear, tritium-dot front sight. **Features:** Skeletonized trigger. Comes with one 8- and one 7-round magazine.

Price: **$1,067.00**

REMINGTON RM380

Caliber: .380 ACP. **Capacity:** 6-round magazine. **Barrel:** 2.9 in. **Length:** 5.27 in. **Height:** 3.86 in. **Weight:** 12.2 oz. **Sights:** Fixed and contoured. **Grips:** Glass-filled nylon with replaceable panels. **Features:** Double-action-only operation, all-metal construction with aluminum frame, stainless steel barrel, light dual recoil spring system, extended beavertail. Executive has brushed stainless slide, black frame, laminate Macassar exotic ebony grips.

Price: Light blue/black two-tone	**$348.00**
Price: Executive	**$405.00**
Price: Black finish	**$436.00**
Price: With Crimson Trace Laser Sight............	**$638.00**

REMINGTON RP9/RP45

Calibers: 9mm, .45 ACP. **Capacities:** 10- or 18-round magazine. **Barrel:** 4.5 in. **Weight:** 26.4 oz. **Sights:** Drift adjustable front and rear. **Features:** Striker-fired polymer frame model with Picatinny rail. Interchangeable backstraps. Smooth, light trigger pull with short reset, trigger safety. Easy loading double-stack magazine.

Price: **$418.00**

REMINGTON R51

Caliber: 9mm. **Capacity:** 7-round magazine. **Barrel:** 3.4 in. **Sights:** Fixed low profile. **Weight:** 22 oz. **Features:** Skeletonized trigger with crisp, light pull. Aluminum frame with black stainless slide. Redesigned and improved variation of 2014 model, which was recalled. Reintroduced in 2017.

Price:	**$448.00**
Price: Smoke/Silver Two Tone finish..........	**$460.00**
Price: Crimson Trace Laser Grips	**$648.00**

REPUBLIC FORGE 1911

Calibers: .45 ACP, 9mm, .38 Super, .40 S&W, 10mm. **Features:** A manufacturer of custom 1911-style pistols offered in a variety of configurations, finishes and frame sizes, including single- and double-stack models with many options. Made in Texas.

Price: From **$2,795.00**

ROBERTS DEFENSE 1911 SERIES

Caliber: .45 ACP. **Capacity:** 8-round magazine. **Barrels:** 5, 4.25 or 3.5 in. **Weights:** 26–38 oz. **Sights:** Novak-type drift-adjustable rear, tritium-dot or fiber optic front sight. **Features:** Skeletonized trigger. Offered in four model variants with many custom features and options. Made in Wisconsin by Roberts Defense.

Price: Recon......................	**$2,370.00**
Price: Super Grade	**$2,270.00**
Price: Operator...................	**$2,350.00**

ROCK ISLAND ARMORY 1911A1-45 FSP

Calibers: 9mm, .38 Super, .45 ACP. **Capacities:**.45 ACP (8 rounds), 9mm Parabellum, .38 Super (9 rounds**). Features:** 1911-style semi-auto pistol. Hard rubber grips, 5-inch barrel, blued, Duracoat or two-tone finish, drift-adjustable sights. Nickel finish or night sights available.

Price: From **$592.00**

ROCK ISLAND ARMORY 1911A1-FS MATCH

Caliber: .45 ACP. **Barrels:** 5 in. or 6 in. **Features:** 1911 match-style pistol. Features fiber optic front and adjustable rear sights, skeletonized trigger and hammer, extended beavertail, double diamond checkered walnut grips.

Price: **$877.00**

ROCK ISLAND ARMORY 1911A1-.22 TCM

Caliber: .22 TCM. **Capacity:** 17-round magazine. **Barrel:** 5 in. **Weight:** 36 oz. **Length:** 8.5 in. **Grips:** Polymer. **Sights:** Adjustable rear. **Features:** Chambered for high velocity .22 TCM rimfire cartridge. Comes with interchangeable 9mm barrel.

Price: From **$806.00**

Prices given are believed to be accurate at time of publication however, many factors affect retail pricing so exact prices are not possible.

ROCK ISLAND ARMORY PRO MATCH ULTRA "BIG ROCK"
Caliber: 10mm. **Capacity:** 8- or 16-round magazine. **Barrel:** 6 in. **Weight:** 40 oz. **Length:** 8.5 in. **Grips:** VZ G10. **Sights:** Fiber optic front, adjustable rear. **Features:** Two magazines, upper and lower accessory rails, extended beavertail safety.
Price: $1,187.00
Price: High capacity model $1,340.00

ROCK ISLAND ARMORY MAP & MAPP
Caliber: 9mm, .22 TCM. **Capacity:** 16-round magazine. **Barrel:** 3.5 (MAPP) or 4 in (MAP). Browning short recoil action-style pistols with: integrated front sight; snag-free rear sight; single- & double-action trigger; standard or ambidextrous rear safety; polymer frame with accessory rail.
Price: From $429.00

ROCK ISLAND ARMORY XT22
Calibers: .22 LR, .22 Magnum. **Capacities:** 10- or 15-round magazine. **Barrel:** 5 in. **Weight:** 38 oz. **Features:** The XT-22 is the only .22 1911 with a forged 4140 steel slide and a one piece 4140 chrome moly barrel. Available as a .22/.45 ACP combo.
Price: $600.00
Price: .22 LR/.45 combo $900.00

ROCK ISLAND ARMORY BABY ROCK 380
Caliber: .380 ACP. **Capacity:** 7-round magazine. **Features:** Blowback operation. An 85 percent-size version of 1911-A1 design with features identical to full-size model.
Price: $460.00

ROCK RIVER ARMS LAR-15/LAR-9
Calibers: .223/5.56mm NATO, 9mm. **Barrels:** 7 in., 10.5 in. Wilson chrome moly, 1:9 twist, A2 flash hider, 1/2x28 thread. **Weights:** 5.1 lbs. (7-in. barrel), 5.5 lbs. (10.5-in. barrel). **Length:** 23 in. overall. **Stock:** Hogue rubber grip. **Sights:** A2 front. **Features:** Forged A2 or A4 upper, single stage trigger, aluminum free-float tube, one magazine. Similar 9mm Para. LAR-9 also available. From Rock River Arms, Inc.
Price: LAR-15 7 in. A2 AR2115 .... $1,175.00
Price: LAR-15 10.5 in. A4 AR2120 .... $1,055.00
Price: LAR-9 7 in. A2 9mm2115 .... $1,320.00

ROCK RIVER ARMS TACTICAL PISTOL
Caliber: .45 ACP. **Features:** Standard-size 1911 pistol with rosewood grips, Heinie or Novak sights, Black Cerakote finish.
Price: $2,200.00

ROCK RIVER ARMS LIMITED MATCH
Calibers: .45 ACP, 40 S&W, .38 Super, 9mm. **Barrel:** 5 in. **Sights:** Adjustable rear, blade front. **Finish:** Hard chrome. **Features:** National Match frame with beveled magazine well, front and rear slide serrations, Commander Hammer, G10 grips.
Price: $3,600.00

ROCK RIVER ARMS CARRY PISTOL
Caliber: .45 ACP. **Barrel:** 5 in. **Sights:** Heinie. **Finish:** Parkerized. **Grips:** Rosewood. **Weight:** 39 oz.
Price: $1,600.00

ROCK RIVER ARMS 1911 POLY
Caliber: .45 ACP. **Capacity:** 7-round magazine. **Barrel:** 5 in. **Weight:** 33 oz. **Sights:** Fixed. **Features:** Full-size 1911-style model with polymer frame and steel slide.
Price: $925.00

RUGER-57
Caliber: 5.7x28mm. **Capacity:** 20-round magazine. **Barrel:** 4.94 in. **Grips:** Textured polymer. **Sights:** Adjustable rear/fiber-optic front, optic ready. **Length:** 8.65 in. overall. **Weight:** 24.5 oz. unloaded. **Finish:** Black oxide. **Features:** 1911-style ambidextrous manual safety, Picatinny-style accessory rail, drilled and tapped for optics with optic-adapter plate. Made in the USA.
Price: $799.00

RUGER AR-556 PISTOL
Calibers: 5.56 NATO, .350 Legend, .300 BLK. **Capacity:** .350 Legend (5-round magazine), 5.56 NATO or .300 BLK (30-round magazine). **Barrels:** 9.5 - 10.5 in. **Weight:** 6.2 lbs. **Sights:** Optic-ready, Picatinny rail. **Grips:** AR15 A2 style. **Features:** SB Tactical SBA3 brace.
Price: .... $899.00-$949.00

RUGER AMERICAN PISTOL
Calibers: 9mm, .45 ACP. **Capacities:** 10 or 17 (9mm), 10 (.45 ACP). **Barrels:** 4.2 in. (9), 4.5 in. (.45). **Lengths:** 7.5 in or 8 in. **Weights:** 30–31.5 oz. **Sights:** Novak LoMount Carry 3-Dot. **Finish:** Stainless steel slide with black Nitride finish. **Grip:** One-piece ergonomic wrap-around module with adjustable palm swell and trigger reach. **Features:** Short take-up trigger with positive re-set, ambidextrous mag release and slide stop, integrated trigger safety, automatic sear block system, easy takedown. Introduced in 2016.
Price: $579.00

RUGER AMERICAN COMPACT PISTOL
Caliber: 9mm. **Barrel:** 3.5 in. **Features:** Compact version of American Pistol with same general specifications.
Price: $579.00

RUGER LITE RACK LCP II
Caliber: .22 LR. **Capacity:** 10-round magazine. **Barrel:** 2.75 in. **Grips:** Textured polymer. **Sights:** Integral-notch rear/post front. **Length:** 5.2 in. overall. **Weight:** 11.2 oz. unloaded. **Finish:** Black. **Features:** A good training/practice pistol for anyone who carries a Ruger LCP or LCP II. Lite Rack system with refined slide serrations, cocking ears and lighter recoil spring. Made in the USA.
Price: $349.00

Prices given are believed to be accurate at time of publication however, many factors affect retail pricing so exact prices are not possible.

75TH EDITION, 2021 ⊕ **465**

RUGER PC CHARGER

Caliber: 9mm. **Capacity:** 17-round magazine. **Barrel:** Threaded 6.5 in. **Grips:** AR15 A2 style. **Sights:** Optic-ready, Picatinny-style rail. **Length:** 16.5 in. overall. **Weight:** 5.2 lbs. unloaded. Finish: Blued. **Features:** Pistol version of the Ruger PC Carbine with a glass-filled polymer chassis system and M-LOK rail. Easy takedown system separates barrel/fore-end assembly from the action, and interchangeable magazine wells for Ruger American, Ruger Security-9 or Glock magazines. Made in the USA.
Price: $799.00

RUGER SECURITY-9 PRO

Caliber: 9mm. **Capacity:** 15-round magazine. **Barrel:** 4 in. **Grips:** Textured polymer. **Sights:** Fixed-steel tritium. **Length:** 7.24 in. overall. **Weight:** 23.8 oz. unloaded. Finish: Black oxide. **Features:** Rugged construction with black oxide, through-hardened, alloy-steel slide and barrel and high-performance, glass-filled nylon grip frame. Made in the USA.
Price: $549.00

RUGER SECURITY-9 COMPACT PRO

Caliber: 9mm. **Capacity:** 10-round magazine. **Barrel:** 3.42 in. **Grips:** Textured polymer. **Sights:** Fixed-steel tritium. **Length:** 6.52 in. overall. **Weight:** 21.9 oz. unloaded. Finish: Black oxide. **Features:** Similar to Ruger Security-9 Pro. Precision-machined, hard-coat, anodized-aluminum chassis with full-length guide rails. Made in the USA.
Price: $549.00

RUGER SR9 /SR40

Calibers: 9mm, .40 S&W. **Capacities:** 9mm (17-round magazine), .40 S&W (15). **Barrel:** 4.14 in. **Weights:** 26.25, 26.5 oz. **Grips:** Glass-filled nylon in two color options — black or OD Green, w/flat or arched reversible backstrap. **Sights:** Adjustable 3-dot, built-in Picatinny-style rail. **Features:** Semi-auto in six configurations, striker-fired, through-hardened stainless steel slide brushed or blackened stainless slide with black grip frame or blackened stainless slide with OD Green grip frame, ambidextrous manual 1911-style safety, ambi. mag release, mag disconnect, loaded chamber indicator, Ruger cam block design to absorb recoil, comes with two magazines. 10-shot mags available. Introduced 2008. Made in USA by Sturm, Ruger & Co.
Price: SR9 (17-Round), SR9-10 (SS) $569.00

RUGER SR9C/SR40C COMPACT

Calibers: 9mm, .40 S&W. **Capacities:** 10- and 17-round magazine. **Barrels:** 3.4 in. (SR9C), 3.5 in. (SR40C). **Weight:** 23.4 oz. **Features:** Features include 1911-style ambidextrous manual safety; internal trigger bar interlock and striker blocker; trigger safety; magazine disconnector; loaded chamber indicator; two magazines, one 10-round and the other 17-round; 3.5-in. barrel; 3-dot sights; accessory rail; brushed stainless or blackened allow finish.
Price: $569.00

RUGER SECURITY-9

Caliber: 9mm. **Capacity:** 10- or 15-round magazine. **Barrel:** 4 or 3.4 in. **Weight:** 21 oz. **Sights:** Drift-adjustable 3-dot. Viridian E-Series Red Laser available. Striker-fired polymer-frame compact model. Uses the same Secure Action as LCP II. Bladed trigger safety plus external manual safety.
Price: $379.00
Price: Viridian Laser sight $439.00

RUGER SR45

Caliber: .45 ACP. **Capacity:** 10-round magazine. **Barrel:** 4.5 in. **Weight:** 30 oz. **Length:** 8 in. **Grips:** Glass-filled nylon with reversible flat/arched backstrap. **Sights:** Adjustable 3-dot. **Features:** Same features as SR9.
Price: $569.00

RUGER LC9S

Caliber: 9mm. **Capacity:** 7+1. **Barrel:** 3.12 in. **Grips:** Glass-filled nylon. **Sights:** Adjustable 3-dot. **Features:** Brushed stainless slide, black glass-filled grip frame, blue alloy barrel finish. Striker-fired operation with smooth trigger pull. Integral safety plus manual safety. Aggressive frame checkering with smooth "melted" edges. Slightly larger than LCS380. LC9S Pro has no manual safety.
Price: $479.00

RUGER LC380
Caliber: .380 ACP. Other specifications and features identical to LC9.
Price: $479.00
Price: LaserMax laser grips $529.00
Price: Crimson Trace Laserguard $629.00

RUGER CHARGER
Caliber: .22 LR. **Capacity:** 15-round BX-15 magazine. **Features:** Based on famous 10/22 rifle design with pistol grip stock and fore-end, scope rail, bipod. Black laminate stock. Silent-SR Suppressor available. Add $449. NFA regulations apply. Reintroduced with improvements and enhancements in 2015.
Price: Standard $309.00
Price: Takedown $419.00

RUGER LCP
Caliber: .380. **Capacity:** 6-round magazine. **Barrel:** 2.75 in. **Weight:** 9.4 oz. **Length:** 5.16 in. **Grips:** Glass-filled nylon. **Sights:** Fixed, drift adjustable or integral Crimson Trace Laserguard.
Price: Blued $259.00
Price: Stainless steel slide.................................... $289.00
Price: Viridian-E Red Laser sight............................ $349.00
Price: Custom w/drift adjustable rear sight.......................... $269.00

RUGER MARK IV SERIES
Caliber: .22 LR. **Capacity:** 10-round magazine. **Barrels:** 5.5 in, 6.875 in. Target model has 5.5-in. bull barrel, Hunter model 6.88-in. fluted bull, Competition model 6.88-in. slab-sided bull. **Weight:** 33–46 oz. **Grips:** Checkered or target laminate. **Sights:** Adjustable rear, blade or fiber-optic front (Hunter). **Features:** Updated design of Mark III series with one-button takedown. Introduced 2016. Modern successor of the first Ruger pistol of 1949.
Price: Standard $449.00
Price: Target (blue) $529.00
Price: Target (stainless) $689.00
Price: Hunter ....$769.00–$799.00
Price: Competition $749.00

RUGER 22/45 MARK IV

RUGER LCP II
Caliber: .380. **Capacity:** 6-round magazine. **Barrel:** 2.75 in. **Weight:** 10.6 oz. **Length:** 5.16 in. **Grips:** Glass-filled nylon. **Sights:** Fixed. **Features:** Last round fired holds action open. Larger grip frame surface provides better recoil distribution. Finger grip extension included. Improved sights for superior visibility. Sights are integral to the slide, hammer is recessed within slide.
Price: $349.00

RUGER EC9S
Caliber: 9mm. **Capacity:** 7-shot magazine. **Barrel:** 3.125 in. Striker-fired polymer frame. **Weight:** 17.2 oz.
Price: $299.00

RUGER 22/45 MARK IV PISTOL
Caliber: .22 LR. **Features:** Similar to other .22 Mark IV autos except has Zytel grip frame that matches angle and magazine latch of Model 1911 .45 ACP pistol. Available in 4.4-, 5.5-in. bull barrels. Comes with extra magazine, plastic case, lock. Molded polymer or replaceable laminate grips. **Weight:** 25–33 oz. **Sights:** Adjustable. Updated design of Mark III with one-button takedown. Introduced 2016.
Price: $409.00
Price: 4.4-in. bull threaded barrel w/rails $529.00
Price: Lite w/aluminum frame, rails $549.00

Prices given are believed to be accurate at time of publication however, many factors affect retail pricing so exact prices are not possible.

75TH EDITION, 2021 ✛ **467**

RUGER SR22

Caliber: .22 LR. **Capacity:** 10-round magazine. **Barrel:** 3.5 in. **Weight:** 17.5 oz. **Length:** 6.4 in. **Sights:** Adjustable 3-dot. **Features:** Ambidextrous manual safety/decocking lever and mag release. Comes with two interchangeable rubberized grips and two magazines. Black or silver anodize finish. Available with threaded barrel.
Price: Black **$439.00**
Price: Silver **$459.00**
Price: Threaded barrel **$479.00**

RUGER SR1911

Caliber: .45. **Capacity:** 8-round magazine. **Barrel:** 5 in. (3.5 in. Officer Model) **Weight:** 39 oz. **Length:** 8.6 in., 7.1 in. **Grips:** Slim checkered hardwood. **Sights:** Novak LoMount Carry rear, standard front. **Features:** Based on Series 70 design. Flared and lowered ejection port. Extended mag release, thumb safety and slide-stop lever, oversized grip safety, checkered backstrap on the flat mainspring housing. Comes with one 7-round and one 8-round magazine.
Price: **$939.00**

RUGER SR1911 CMD

Caliber: .45 ACP. **Barrel:** 4.25 in. **Weight:** 29.3 (aluminum), 36.4 oz. (stainless). **Features:** Commander-size version of SR1911. Other specifications and features are identical to SR1911. Lightweight Commander also offered in 9mm.
Price: Low glare stainless **$939.00**
Price: Anodized aluminum two-tone.................................. **$979.00**

RUGER SR1911 TARGET

Calibers: 9mm, 10mm, .45 ACP. **Capacities:** .45 and 10mm (8-round magazine), 9mm (9 shot). **Barrel:** 5 in. **Weight:** 39 oz. **Sights:** Bomar adjustable. **Grips:** G10 Deluxe checkered. **Features:** Skeletonized hammer and trigger, satin stainless finish. Introduced in 2016.
Price: **$1,019.00**

RUGER SR1911 COMPETITION

Calibers: 9mm. **Capacities:** .10+1. **Barrel:** 5 in. **Weight:** 39 oz. **Sights:** Fiber optic front, adjustable target rear. **Grips:** Hogue Piranha G10 Deluxe checkered. **Features:** Skeletonized hammer and trigger, satin stainless finish, hand-fitted frame and slide, competition trigger, competition barrel with polished feed ramp. From Ruger Competition Shop. Introduced in 2016.
Price: **$2,499.00**

RUGER SR1911 OFFICER

Caliber: .45 ACP, 9mm. **Capacity:** 8-round magazine. **Barrel:** 3.6 in. **Weight:** 27 oz. **Features:** Compact variation of SR1911 Series. Black anodized aluminum frame, stainless slide, skeletonized trigger, Novak 3-dot Night Sights, G10 deluxe checkered G10 grips.
Price: **$979.00**

SCCY CPX

Caliber: 9mm. **Capacity:** 10-round magazine. **Barrel:** 3.1 in. **Weight:** 15 oz. **Length:** 5.7 in. overall. **Grips:** Integral with polymer frame. **Sights:** 3-dot system, rear adjustable for windage. **Features:** Zytel polymer frame, steel slide, aluminum alloy receiver machined from bar stock. DAO with consistent 9-pound trigger pull. Concealed hammer. Available with (CPX-1) or without (CPX-2) manual thumb safety. Introduced 2014. CPX-3 is chambered for .380 ACP. Made in USA by SCCY Industries.
Price: CPX-1 .... **$284.00**
Price: CPX-2 .... **$270.00**
Price: CPX-3 .... **$305.00**

SEECAMP LWS 32/380 STAINLESS DA

Calibers: .32 ACP, .380 ACP. **Capacity:** 6-round magazine. **Barrel:** 2 in., integral with frame. **Weight:** 10.5 oz. **Length:** 4.125 in. overall. **Grips:** Glass-filled nylon. **Sights:** Smooth, no-snag, contoured slide and barrel top. **Features:** Aircraft quality 17-4 PH stainless steel. Inertia-operated firing pin. Hammer fired DAO. Hammer automatically follows slide down to safety rest position after each shot, no manual safety needed. Magazine safety disconnector. Polished stainless. Introduced 1985. From L.W. Seecamp.
Price: .32 .... **$446.25**
Price: .380 .... **$795.00**

Prices given are believed to be accurate at time of publication however, many factors affect retail pricing so exact prices are not possible.

SIG SAUER 1911

Calibers: .45 ACP, .40 S&W. **Capacities:** .45 ACP, .40 S&W. 8- and 10-round magazine. **Barrel:** 5 in. **Weight:** 40.3 oz. **Length:** 8.65 in. overall. **Grips:** Checkered wood grips. **Sights:** Novak night sights. Blade front, drift adjustable rear for windage. **Features:** Single-action 1911. Hand-fitted dehorned stainless steel frame and slide; match-grade barrel, hammer/sear set and trigger; 25-LPI front strap checkering, 20-LPI mainspring housing checkering. Beavertail grip safety with speed bump, extended thumb safety, firing pin safety and hammer intercept notch. Introduced 2005. XO series has contrast sights, Ergo Grip XT textured polymer grips. STX line available from Sig Sauer Custom Shop; two-tone 1911, non-railed, Nitron slide, stainless frame, burled maple grips. Polished cocking serrations, flat-top slide, mag well. Carry line has Siglite night sights, lanyard attachment point, gray diamondwood or rosewood grips, 8+1 capacity. Compact series has 6+1 capacity, 7.7 OAL, 4.25-in. barrel, slim-profile wood grips, weighs 30.3 oz. Ultra Compact in 9mm or .45 ACP has 3.3-in. barrel, low-profile night sights, slim-profile gray diamondwood or rosewood grips. 6+1 capacity. 1911 C3 is a 6+1 compact .45 ACP, rosewood custom wood grips, two-tone and Nitron finishes. Weighs 30 oz. unloaded, lightweight alloy frame. Length is 7.7 in. Now offered in more than 30 different models with numerous options for frame size, grips, finishes, sight arrangements and other features. From SIG Sauer, Inc.

Price: Nitron	$1,174.00
Price: Tacops	$1,221.00
Price: XO Black	$1,010.00
Price: STX	$1,244.00
Price: Nightmare	$1,244.00
Price: Carry Nightmare	$1,195.00
Price: Compact C3	$1,010.00
Price: Ultra Compact	$1,119.00
Price: Max	$1,663.00
Price: Spartan	$1,397.00
Price: Super Target	$1,609.00
Price: Traditional Stainless Match Elite	$1,164.00
Price: We the People	$1,481.00
Price: Select	$1,234.00
Price: Stand Commemorative (Honored Veterans, C.O.P.S.)	$1,279.00

SIG SAUER P220

Caliber: .45 ACP, 10mm. **Capacity:** 7- or 8-round magazine. **Barrel:** 4.4 in. **Weight:** 27.8 oz. **Length:** 7.8 in. overall. **Grips:** Checkered black plastic. **Sights:** Blade front, drift adjustable rear for windage. Optional Siglite night sights. **Features:** Double action. Stainless steel slide, Nitron finish, alloy frame, M1913 Picatinny rail; safety system of decocking lever, automatic firing pin safety block, safety intercept notch, and trigger bar disconnector. Squared combat-type trigger guard. Slide stays open after last shot. Introduced 1976. P220 SAS Anti-Snag has dehorned stainless steel slide, front Siglite night sight, rounded trigger guard, dust cover, Custom Shop wood grips. Equinox line is Custom Shop

product with Nitron stainless slide with a black hard-anodized alloy frame, brush-polished flats and nickel accents. Truglo tritium fiber-optic front sight, rear Siglite night sight, gray laminated wood grips with checkering and stippling. From SIG Sauer, Inc.

Price:	$1,087.00
Price: P220 Elite Stainless	$1,450.00
Price: Hunter SAO	$1,629.00
Price: Legion 45 ACP	$1,413.00
Price: Legion 10mm	$1,904.00

SIG SAUER P225 A-1

Caliber: 9mm. **Capacity:** 8-round magazine. **Barrels:** 3.6 or 5 in. **Weight:** 30.5 oz. **Features:** Shorter and slim-profile version of P226 with enhanced short reset trigger, single-stack magazine.

Price:	$1,122.00
Price: Night sights	$1,236.00

SIG SAUER P226

Calibers: 9mm, .40 S&W. **Barrel:** 4.4 in. **Length:** 7.7 in. overall. **Features:** Similar to the P220 pistol except has 4.4-in. barrel, measures 7.7 in. overall, weighs 34 oz. DA/SA or DAO. Many variations available. Snap-on modular grips. Legion series has improved short reset trigger, contoured and shortened beavertail, relieved trigger guard, higher grip, other improvements. From SIG Sauer, Inc.

Price: From	$1,087.00
Price: Elite Stainless	$1,481.00
Price: Legion	$1,428.00
Price: Legion RX w/Romeo 1 Reflex sight	$1,685.00
Price: MK25 Navy Version	$1,187.00

SIG SAUER P227

Caliber: .45 ACP. **Capacity:** 10-round magazine. **Features:** Same general specifications and features as P226 except chambered for .45 ACP and has double-stack magazine.

Price:	$1,087.00–$1,350.00

SIG SAUER P229 DA

Caliber: Similar to the P220 except chambered for 9mm (10- or 15-round magazines), .40 S&W, (10- or 12-round magazines). **Barrels:** 3.86-in. barrel, 7.1 in. overall length and 3.35 in. height. **Weight:** 32.4 oz. **Features:** Introduced 1991. Snap-on modular grips. Frame made in Germany, stainless steel slide assembly made in U.S.; pistol assembled in U.S. Many variations available. Legion series has improved short reset trigger, contoured and shortened beavertail, relieved trigger guard, higher grip, other improvements. Select has Nitron slide, Select G10 grips, Emperor Scorpion has accessory rail, FDE finish, G10 Piranha grips.

Price: P229, From	$1,085.00
Price: P229 Emperor Scorpion	$1,282.00
Price: P229 Legion	$1,413.00

Prices given are believed to be accurate at time of publication however, many factors affect retail pricing so exact prices are not possible.

75TH EDITION, 2021 ⊕ **469**

Price: P229 Select.. **$1,195.00**

SIG SAUER SP2022
Calibers: 9mm, .40 S&W. **Capacities:** 10-, 12-, or 15-round magazines. **Barrel:** 3.9 in. **Weight:** 30.2 oz. **Length:** 7.4 in. overall. **Grips:** Composite and rubberized one-piece. **Sights:** Blade front, rear adjustable for windage. **Features:** Polymer frame, stainless steel slide; integral frame accessory rail; replaceable steel frame rails; left- or right-handed magazine release, two interchangeable grips.
Price: **$642.00**

SIG SAUER P238
Caliber: .380 ACP. **Capacity:** 6-round magazine. **Barrel:** 2.7 in. **Weight:** 15.4 oz. **Length:** 5.5 in. overall. **Grips:** Hogue G-10 and Rosewood grips. **Sights:** Contrast/Siglite night sights. **Features:** All-metal beavertail-style frame.
Price: **$723.00**
Price: Desert Tan **$738.00**
Price: Polished... **$798.00**
Price: Rose Gold **$932.00**
Price: Emperor Scorpion **$801.00**

SIG SAUER P320
Calibers: 9mm, .357 SIG, .40 S&W, .45 ACP. **Capacities:** 15 or 16 rounds (9mm), 13 or 14 rounds (.357 or .40). **Barrels:** 3.6 in. (Subcompact), 3.9 in. (Carry model) or 4.7 in. (Full size). **Weights:** 26–30 oz. **Lengths:** 7.2 or 8.0 in overall. **Grips:** Interchangeable black composite. **Sights:** Blade front, rear adjustable for windage. Optional Siglite night sights. **Features:** Striker-fired DAO, Nitron finish slide, black polymer frame. Frame size and calibers are interchangeable. Introduced 2014. Made in USA by SIG Sauer, Inc.
Price: Full size **$679.00**
Price: Carry (shown) **$679.00**

SIG SAUER P320 SUBCOMPACT
Calibers: 9mm, .40 S&W. **Barrel:** 3.6 in. **Features:** Accessory rail. Other features similar to Full-Size and Carry models.
Price: **$679.00**

SIG SAUER MODEL 320 RX
Caliber: 9mm. **Capacity:** 17-round magazine. **Barrels:** 4.7 in. or 3.9 in. **Features:** Full and Compact size models with ROMEO1 Reflex sight, accessory rail, stainless steel frame and slide. XFive has improved control ergonomics, bull barrel, 21-round magazines.
Price: **$952.00**
Price: XFive... **$1,005.00**

SIG SAUER P365
Caliber: 9mm. **Barrel:** 3.1 in. **Weight:** 17.8 oz. **Features:** Micro-compact striker-fired model with 10-round magazine, stainless steel frame and slide, XRAY-3 day and night sights fully textured polymer grip.
Price: **$599.00**

SIG SAUER P365 XL
Caliber: 9mm. **Capacity:** 12-round magazine. **Barrel:** 3.7 in. **Grips:** Textured polymer. **Sights:** Optic-ready, Day/Night sights. **Length:** 6.6 in. overall. **Weight:** 20.7 oz. unloaded. Finish: Nitron. **Features:** Grip with integrated carry mag well and extended beavertail, flat trigger and optic-ready slide.
Price: **$605.00**

SIG SAUER P365 XL ROMEOZERO
Caliber: 9mm. **Capacity:** 12-round magazine. **Barrel:** 3.7 in. **Grips:** Textured polymer. **Sights:** RomeoZero red dot, Xray3 front sight. **Length:** 6.6 in. overall. **Weight:** 20.7 oz. unloaded. Finish: Nitron. **Features:** Grip with integrated carry mag well and extended beavertail, and flat trigger.
Price: **$749.00**

SIG SAUER P365SAS
Caliber: 9mm. **Capacity:** 10-round magazine. **Barrel:** 3.1 in. **Grips:** Textured polymer. **Sights:** Flush-mounted FT Bullseye fiber-tritium night sight. **Length:** 5.8 in. overall. **Weight:** 17.8 oz. unloaded. Finish: Nitron. **Features:** Ported slide and barrel, Sig Anti Snag (SAS) treatment.
Price: **$599.99**

SIG SAUER P320-M18

Caliber: 9mm. **Capacity:** 17-round magazine. **Barrel:** 3.9 in. **Grips:** Textured polymer. **Sights:** Siglite front/night rear, optic ready. **Length:** 7.2 in. overall. **Weight:** 28.1 oz. unloaded. Finish: Coyote tan. **Features:** Commercial version of U.S. Military M18, manual thumb safety.
Price: $679.99

SIG SAUER P320 RXP FULL-SIZE

Caliber: 9mm. **Capacity:** 17-round magazine. **Barrel:** 4.7 in. **Grips:** Textured polymer. **Sights:** Romeo1Pro red dot, suppressor contrast 3-dot. **Length:** 8 in. overall. **Weight:** 30 oz. unloaded. Finish: Nitron.
Price: $899.99

SIG SAUER P320 RXP COMPACT

Caliber: 9mm. **Capacity:** 15-round magazine. **Barrel:** 3.9 in. **Grips:** Textured polymer. **Sights:** Romeo1Pro red dot, suppressor contrast 3-dot. **Length:** 7.2 in. overall. **Weight:** 26 oz. unloaded. Finish: Nitron.
Price: $899.99

SIG SAUER P320 RXP XFULL-SIZE

Caliber: 9mm. **Capacity:** 17-round magazine. **Barrel:** 4.7 in. **Grips:** Textured polymer. **Sights:** Romeo1Pro red dot, suppressor contrast 3-dot. **Length:** 8 in. overall. **Weight:** 30 oz. unloaded. Finish: Nitron.
Price: $899.99

SIG SAUER MPX

Calibers: 9mm, .357 SIG, .40 S&W. **Capacities:** 10, 20 or 30 rounds. **Barrel:** 8 in. **Weight:** 5 lbs **Features:** Semi-auto AR-style gun with closed, fully locked short-stroke pushrod gas system.
Price: From $2,016.00

SIG SAUER P938

Calibers: 9mm, .22 LR. **Capacities:** 9mm (6-shot mag.), .22 LR (10-shot mag.). **Barrel:** 3.0 in. **Weight:** 16 oz. **Length:** 5.9 in. **Grips:** Rosewood, Blackwood, Hogue Extreme, Hogue Diamondwood. **Sights:** Siglite night sights or Siglite rear with Tru-Glo front. **Features:** Slightly larger version of P238.
Price: .... $760.00–$1,195.00
Price: .22 LR $656.00

SMITH & WESSON M&P SERIES

Calibers: .22 LR, 9mm, .40 S&W. **Capacities, full-size models:** 12 rounds (.22), 17 rounds (9mm), 15 rounds (.40). **Compact models:** 12 (9mm), 10 (.40). **Barrels:** 4.25, 3.5 in. **Weights:** 24, 22 oz. **Lengths:** 7.6, 6.7 in. **Grips:** Polymer with three interchangeable palm swell grip sizes. **Sights:** 3 white-dot system with low-profile rear. **Features:** Zytel polymer frame with stainless steel slide, barrel and structural components. VTAC (Viking Tactics) model has Flat Dark Earth finish, VTAC Warrior sights. Compact models available with Crimson Trace Lasergrips. Numerous options for finishes, sights, operating controls.
Price: $569.00
Price: (VTAC) $799.00
Price: (Crimson Trace) .... $699.00–$829.00
Price: M&P 22 .... $389.00–$419.00

SMITH & WESSON M&P 45

Caliber: .45 ACP. **Capacity:** 8 or 10 rounds. **Barrel length:** 4 or 4.5 in. **Weight:** 26, 28 or 30 oz. **Features:** Available with or without thumb safety. **Finish:** Black or Dark Earth Brown. **Features:** M&P model offered in three frame sizes.
Price: .... $599.00–$619.00
Price: Threaded barrel kit $719.00

SMITH & WESSON M&P M2.0 SERIES

Calibers: 9mm, .40 S&W, .45 ACP. **Capacities:** 17 rounds (9mm), 15 rounds (.40), 10 rounds (.45). **Barrels:** 4.0 (Compact), 4.25, 4.5 or 4.6 in. (.45 only). **Weights:** 25 –27 oz. **Finishes:** Armornite Black or Flat Dark Earth. **Grip:** Textured polymer with 4 interchangeable modular inserts. Second Generation of M&P Pistol series. Introduced in 2017.
Price: $599.00
Price: Compact $569.00

SMITH & WESSON M&P 9/40 SHIELD

Calibers: 9mm, .40 S&W. **Capacities:** 7- and 8-round magazine (9mm); 6-round and 7-round magazine (.40). **Barrel:** 3.1 in. **Length:** 6.1 in. **Weight:** 19 oz. **Sights:** 3-white-dot system with low-profile rear. **Features:** Ultra-compact, single-stack variation of M&P series. Available with or without thumb safety. Crimson Trace Green Laserguard available.
Price: $449.00

Prices given are believed to be accurate at time of publication however, many factors affect retail pricing so exact prices are not possible.

75TH EDITION, 2021 ✦ **471**

Price: CT Green Laserguard **$589.00**

SMITH & WESSON M&P 45 SHIELD
Caliber: .45 ACP. **Barrel:** 3.3 in. Ported model available. **Weight:** 20–23 oz. **Sights:** White dot or tritium night sights. Comes with one 6-round and one 7-round magazine.
Price: **$479.00**
Price: Tritium night sights **$579.00**
Price: Ported barrel **$609.00**

SMITH & WESSON MODEL SD9 VE/SD40 VE
Calibers: .40 S&W, 9mm. **Capacities:** 10+1, 14+1 and 16+1 **Barrel:** 4 in. **Weight:** 39 oz. **Length:** 8.7 in. **Grips:** Wood or rubber. **Sights:** Front: Tritium Night Sight, Rear: Steel Fixed 2-Dot. **Features:** SDT (Self Defense Trigger) for optimal, consistent pull first round to last, standard Picatinny-style rail, slim ergonomic textured grip, textured finger locator and aggressive front and backstrap texturing with front and rear slide serrations.
Price: **$389.00**

SMITH & WESSON MODEL SW1911
Calibers: .45 ACP, 9mm. **Capacities:** 8 rounds (.45), 7 rounds (subcompact .45), 10 rounds (9mm). **Barrels:** 3, 4.25, 5 in. **Weights:** 26.5–41.7 oz. **Lengths:** 6.9–8.7 in. **Grips:** Wood, wood laminate or synthetic. Crimson Trace Lasergrips available. **Sights:** Low-profile white dot, tritium night sights or adjustable. **Finish:** Black matte, stainless or two-tone. **Features:** Offered in three different frame sizes. Skeletonized trigger. Accessory rail on some models. Compact models have round-butt frame. Pro Series have 30 LPI checkered frontstrap, oversized external extractor, extended mag well, full-length guide rod, ambidextrous safety.
Price: Standard Model E Series, From **$979.00**
Price: Crimson Trace grips **$1,149.00**
Price: Pro Series .... **$1,459.00–$1,609.00**
Price: Scandium Frame E Series **$1,449.00**

SMITH & WESSON BODYGUARD 380
Caliber: .380 Auto. **Capacity:** 6+1. **Barrel:** 2.75 in. **Weight:** 11.85 oz. **Length:** 5.25 in. **Grips:** Polymer. **Sights:** Integrated laser plus drift-adjustable front and rear. **Features:** The frame of the Bodyguard is made of reinforced polymer, as is the magazine base plate and follower, magazine catch and trigger. The slide, sights and guide rod are made of stainless steel, with the slide and sights having a Melonite hardcoating.
Price: **$449.00**

SMITH & WESSON PERFORMANCE CENTER M&P380 SHIELD EZ
Caliber: .380 ACP. **Capacity:** 8-round magazine. **Barrel:** 3.67 in. **Grips:** Textured polymer. **Sights:** Fixed, HI-VIZ Litewave H3 Tritium/Litepipe. **Length:** 6.8 in. overall. **Weight:** 23 oz. unloaded. **Finish:** Black Armornite frame and black, silver or gold accents. **Features:** Easy to rack slide, grip safety, manual thumb safety, accessory rail, reversible magazine release, ported barrel and lightening cuts in slide.
Price: **$517.00**

SMITH & WESSON PERFORMANCE CENTER M&P9 AND M&P40 M2.0 C.O.R.E. PRO SERIES
Calibers: 9mm, .40 S&W. **Capacity:** 17-round (9mm) or 15-round (.40 S&W) magazine. **Barrel:** 4.25 or 5 in. **Grips:** Four interchangeable palm-swell inserts. **Sights:** Fixed, tall 3-dot/C.O.R.E. optics-ready system. **Length:** 7.5-8.5 in. overall. **Weight:** 23-27.2 oz. unloaded. **Finish:** Black Armornite. **Features:** Accessory rail, reversible magazine release and tuned action with audible trigger reset.
Price: (4.25-in. barrel) **$700.00**
Price: (5-in. barrel) **$721.00**

SMITH & WESSON PERFORMANCE CENTER M&P9 AND M&P40 M2.0 PORTED SERIES
Calibers: 9mm, .40 S&W. **Capacity:** 17-round (9mm) or 15-round (.40 S&W) magazine. **Barrel:** 4.25 or 5 in. **Grips:** Four interchangeable palm-swell inserts. **Sights:** Fixed, fiber-optic front and rear. **Length:** 8.5 in. overall. **Weight:** 23 oz. unloaded. **Finish:** Black Armornite. **Features:** Accessory rail, reversible magazine release, ported barrel and slide and tuned action with audible trigger reset.
Price: (4.25-in. barrel) **$700.00**
Price: (5-in. barrel) **$721.00**

SMITH & WESSON PERFORMANCE CENTER M&P9 AND M&P40 M2.0 PORTED C.O.R.E. SERIES
Calibers: 9mm, .40 S&W. **Capacity:** 17-round (9mm) or 15-round (.40 S&W) magazine. **Barrel:** 4.25 or 5 in. **Grips:** Four interchangeable palm-swell inserts. **Sights:** Fixed, tall 3-dot/C.O.R.E. optics-ready system. **Length:** 8.5 in. overall. **Weight:** 23 oz. unloaded. **Finish:** Black Armornite. **Features:** Accessory rail, reversible magazine release, oversized slide release, ported barrel and slide, and tuned action with audible trigger reset.

Price: (4.25-in. barrel) **$714.00**
Price: (5-in. barrel) **$735.00**

SMITH & WESSON M&P9 SHIELD EZ M2.0

Caliber: 9mm. **Capacity:** 8-round magazine. **Barrel:** 3.67 in. **Grips:** Textured polymer. **Sights:** Fixed, 3-dot. **Length:** 6.8 in. overall. **Weight:** 23.2 oz. unloaded. Finish: Black Armornite. **Features:** Accessory rail and reversible magazine release, with or without manual thumb safety.
Price: **$479.00**
Price: (Crimson Trace Laserguard) **$575.00**

SMITH & WESSON M&P9 M2.0 COMPACT

Caliber: 9mm. **Capacity:** 15-round magazine. **Barrel:** 4 in. **Grips:** Four interchangeable palm-swell inserts. **Sights:** Fixed, steel 3-dot. **Length:** 7.3 in. overall. **Weight:** 26.6 oz. unloaded. Finish: FDE. **Features:** Accessory rail, with or without manual thumb safety.
Price: **$569.00**

SPHINX SDP

Caliber: 9mm. **Capacity:** 15-shot magazine. **Barrel:** 3.7 in. **Weight:** 27.5 oz. **Length:** 7.4 in. **Sights:** Defiance Day & Night Green fiber/tritium front, tritium 2-dot red rear. **Features:** DA/SA with ambidextrous decocker, integrated slide position safety, aluminum MIL-STD 1913 Picatinny rail, Blued alloy/steel or stainless. Aluminum and polymer frame, machined steel slide. Offered in several variations. Made in Switzerland and imported by Kriss USA.
Price: From **$999.00**

SPRINGFIELD ARMORY EMP ENHANCED MICRO

Calibers: 9mm, 40 S&W. **Capacity:** 9-round magazine. **Barrel:** 3-inch stainless steel match grade, fully supported ramp, bull. **Weight:** 26 oz. **Length:** 6.5 in. overall. **Grips:** Thinline cocobolo hardwood. **Sights:** Fixed low-profile combat rear, dovetail front, 3-dot tritium. **Features:** Two 9-round stainless steel magazines with slam pads, long aluminum match-grade trigger adjusted to 5 to 6 lbs., forged aluminum alloy frame, black hardcoat anodized finish; dual spring full-length guide rod, forged satin-finish stainless steel slide. Introduced 2007. Champion has 4-inch barrel, fiber optic front sight, three 10-round magazines, Bi-Tone finish.
Price: .... **$1,104.00–$1,249.00**
Price: Champion **$1,179.00**

SPRINGFIELD ARMORY XD SERIES

Calibers: 9mm, .40 S&W, .45 ACP. **Barrels:** 3, 4, 5 in. **Weights:** 20.5-31 oz. **Lengths:** 6.26-8 overall. **Grips:** Textured polymer. **Sights:** Varies by model; Fixed sights are dovetail front and rear steel 3-dot units. **Features:** Three sizes in X-Treme Duty (XD) line: Sub-Compact (3-in. barrel), Service (4-in. barrel), Tactical (5-in. barrel). Three ported models available. Ergonomic polymer frame, hammer-forged barrel, no-tool disassembly, ambidextrous magazine release, visual/tactile loaded chamber indicator, visual/tactile striker status indicator, grip safety, XD gear system included. Compact is shipped with one extended magazine (13) and one compact magazine (10). XD Mod.2 Sub-Compact has newly contoured slide and redesigned serrations, stippled grip panels, fiber-optic front sight. OSP has Vortex Venom Red Dot sight, and suppressor-height sights that co-witness with red dot. Non-threaded barrel is also included.

Price: Sub-Compact OD Green 9mm/40 S&W, fixed sights **$508.00**
Price: Compact .45 ACP, 4 barrel, Bi-Tone finish **$607.00**
Price: Service Black 9mm/.40 S&W, fixed sights **$541.00**
Price: Service Black .45 ACP, external thumb safety **$638.00**
Price: V-10 Ported Black 9mm/.40 S&W **$608.00**
Price: XD Mod.2 .... **$565.00**
Price: XD OSP w/Vortex Venom Red Dot Sight **$958.00**

Prices given are believed to be accurate at time of publication however, many factors affect retail pricing so exact prices are not possible.

75TH EDITION, 2021 ⊕ **473**

SPRINGFIELD ARMORY XD(M) SERIES
Calibers: 9mm, .40 S&W, .45 ACP. **Barrels:** 3.8 or 4.5 in. **Sights:** Fiber optic front with interchangeable red and green filaments, adjustable target rear. **Grips:** Integral polymer with three optional backstrap designs. **Features:** Variation of XD design with improved ergonomics, deeper and longer slide serrations, slightly modified grip contours and texturing. Black polymer frame, forged steel slide. Black and two-tone finish options.
Price: .... **$623.00–$779.00**

SPRINGFIELD ARMORY MIL-SPEC 1911A1
Caliber: .45 ACP. **Capacity:** 7-round magazine. **Barrel:** 5 in. **Weights:** 35.6–39 oz. **Lengths:** 8.5–8.625 in. overall. **Finish:** Stainless steel. **Features:** Similar to Government Model military .45.
Price: Mil-Spec Parkerized, 7+1, 35.6 oz. **$785.00**
Price: Mil-Spec Stainless Steel, 7+1, 36 oz. **$889.00**

SPRINGFIELD ARMORY 1911 LOADED
Caliber: .45 ACP. **Capacity:** 7-round magazine. **Barrel:** 5 in. **Weight:** 34 oz. **Length:** 8.6 in. overall. Similar to Mil-Spec 1911A1 with the following additional **features:** Lightweight Delta hammer, extended and ergonomic beavertail safety, ambidextrous thumb safety, and other features depending on the specific model. MC, Marine, LB and Lightweight models have match-grade barrels, low-profile 3-dot combat sights.
Price: Parkerized **$950.00**
Price: Stainless **$1,004.00**
Price: MC Operator (shown) **$1,308.00**
Price: Marine Operator **$1,308.00**
Price: LB Operator **$1,409.00**
Price: Lightweight Operator **$1,210.00**
Price: 10mm TRP (Trijicon RMR Red Dot sight **$2,238.00**

SPRINGFIELD ARMORY TACTICAL RESPONSE
Caliber: .45 ACP, 10mm. **Features:** Similar to 1911A1, except checkered frontstrap and main-spring housing, Novak Night Sight combat rear sight and matching dove-tailed front sight, tuned, polished extractor, oversize barrel link; lightweight speed trigger and combat action job, match barrel and bushing, extended ambidextrous thumb safety and fitted beavertail grip safety. Checkered Cocobolo wood grips, comes with two Wilson 7-shot magazines. Frame is engraved "Tactical" both sides of frame with "TRP" Introduced 1998. TRP-Pro Model meets FBI specifications for SWAT Hostage Rescue Team.
Price: **$1,646.00**
Price: Operator with adjustable Trijicon night sights **$1,730.00**

SPRINGFIELD ARMORY RANGE OFFICER
Calibers: 9mm, .45 ACP. **Barrels:** 5-in. stainless match grade. Compact model has 4 in. barrel. **Sights:** Adjustable target rear, post front. **Grips:** Double diamond checkered walnut. **Weights:** 40 oz., 28 oz. (compact). **Features:** Operator model has fiber optic sights.
Price: **$936.00**
Price: Compact **$899.00**
Price: Stainless finish **$1,045.00**
Price: Operator **$1,029.00**
Price: Elite Operator **$1,145.00**

SPRINGFIELD ARMORY RONIN OPERATOR
Calibers: 9mm, .45 ACP. **Capacity:** 7-round (.45 ACP) or 9-round (9mm) magazine. **Barrel:** 5 in. **Grips:** Checkered wood. **Sights:** Fiber-optic front, tactical-rack, white-dot rear. **Length:** 8.6 in. overall. **Weight:** 40 oz. unloaded. Finish: Two-tone, black slide/stainless frame.
Price: **$849.00**

SPRINGFIELD ARMORY CHAMPION OPERATOR LIGHTWEIGHT
Caliber: .45 ACP. **Barrel:** 4-in. stainless match-grade bull barrel. **Sights:** 3-dot Tritium combat profile. **Grips:** Double diamond checkered cocobolo with Cross Cannon logo. **Features:** Alloy frame with integral rail, extended ambi thumb safety and trigger, lightweight Delta hammer.
Price: **$1,050.00**

SPRINGFIELD ARMORY 911
Caliber: .380 ACP. **Barrel:** 2.7-in. stainless steel. **Sights:** 3-dot Tritium combat profile. Viridian Green Laser available. **Weight:** 12.6 oz. **Length:** 6.5 in. **Grips:** Grooved Hogue G10. **Features:** Alloy frame, stainless steel slide.
Price: $599.00
Price: Viridian Laser $809.00

SPRINGFIELD ARMORY 911 9MM
Caliber: 9mm. **Barrel:** 3-in. stainless steel. **Sights:** Pro-Glo Tritium/luminescent front, white-dot outlined Tritium rear. **Weight:** 15.3 oz. **Length:** 5.9 in. **Grips:** Thin-line G10. **Features:** Alloy frame, stainless steel slide.
Price: $659.00
Price: Viridian Laser $849.00

STANDARD MANUFACTURING 1911 SERIES
Caliber: .45 ACP. **Capacity:** 7-round magazine. **Barrel:** 5-inch stainless steel match grade. **Weight:** 38.4 oz. **Length:** 8.6 in. **Grips:** Checkered rosewood double diamond. **Sights:** Fixed, Warren Tactical blade front/U-notch rear. **Finish:** Blued, case color, or nickel. **Features:** Forged frame and slide, beavertail grip safety, extended magazine release and thumb safety, checkered mainspring housing and front grip strap.
Price: (blued)... $1,295.00
Price: (blued, engraved) $1,579.00
Price: (case color)... $1,599.00
Price: (case color, engraved).................................. $1,899.00
Price: (nickel).. $1,499.00

STEYR M-A1 SERIES
Calibers: 9mm, .40 S&W. **Capacities:** 9mm (15 or 17-round capacity) or .40 S&W (10-12). **Barrels:** 3.5 in. (MA-1), 4.5 in. (L-A1), 3 in. (C-A1). **Weight:** 27 oz. **Sights:** Fixed with white outline triangle. **Grips:** Black synthetic. Ergonomic low-profile for reduced muzzle lift. **Features:** DAO striker-fired operation.
Price: M-A1... $575.00
Price: C-A1 compact model...................................... $575.00
Price: L-A1 full-size model $575.00
Price: S-A1 subcompact model................................ $575.00

STOEGER STR-9 COMPACT
Caliber: 9mm. **Capacity:** 13-round magazine. **Barrel:** 3.8 in. **Grips:** Three interchangeable backstraps. **Sights:** 3-dot sights or tritium night sights. **Length:** 6.9 in. overall. **Weight:** 24 oz. unloaded. **Finish:** Matte black. **Features:** Compact version of the STR-9 striker-fire pistol. Aggressive forward and rear slide serrations and accessory rail. Made in Turkey.
Price: (depending on configuration)..................................... $329.00-$449.00

STOEGER COMPACT COUGAR
Caliber: 9mm. **Capacity:** 13+1. **Barrel:** 3.6 in. **Weight:** 32 oz. **Length:** 7 in. **Grips:** Wood or rubber. **Sights:** Quick read 3-dot. **Features:** DA/SA with a matte black finish. The ambidextrous safety and decocking lever is easily accessible to the thumb of a right- or left-handed shooter.
Price: $469.00

STI FIREARMS STACCATO SERIES
Calibers: 9mm, .40 S&W, .38 Super. **Capacity:** 9-, 17- or 21-round magazine. **Barrels:** 3.9- or 5-in., match-grade. **Sights:** Optic-ready, Dawson Precision Perfect Impact. **Weight:** 38 - 46.5 oz. **Finish:** Carbon black. **Grips:** Textured polymer. **Features:** 4-lb. trigger pull, ambidextrous safety levers, single- or double-stack magazine.
Price: .... $1,699.00-$4,299.00

TAURUS CURVE
Caliber: .380 ACP. **Capacity:** 6+1. **Barrel:** 2.5 in. **Weight:** 10.2 oz. **Length:** 5.2 in. **Features:** Unique curved design to fit contours of the body for comfortable concealed carry with no visible "printing" of the firearm. Double-action only. Light and laser are integral with frame.
Price: $404.00

TAURUS G2S
Caliber: 9mm. **Capacity:** 6+1. **Barrel:** 3.2 in. **Weight:** 20 oz. **Length:** 6.3 in. **Sights:** Adjustable rear, fixed front. **Features:** Double/Single Action, polymer frame in blue with matte black or stainless slide, accessory rail, manual and trigger safeties.
Price: $317.00
Price: Two tone with stainless slide...................................... $333.00

Prices given are believed to be accurate at time of publication however, many factors affect retail pricing so exact prices are not possible.

75TH EDITION, 2021 ⬩ **475**

TAURUS TH9

Caliber: 9mm. **Capacity:** 16+1. **Barrel:** 4.3 in. **Weight:** 28 oz. **Length:** 7.7 in. **Sights:** Novak drift adjustable. **Features:** Full-size 9mm double-stack model with SA/DA action. Polymer frame has integral grips with finger grooves and stippling panels. Compact model has 3.8-in barrel, 6.8-in overall length.
Price: $377.00

TAURUS MODEL 1911

Calibers: 9mm, .45 ACP. **Capacities:** .45 ACP 8+1, 9mm 9+1. **Barrel:** 5 in. **Weight:** 33 oz. **Length:** 8.5 in. **Grips:** Checkered black. **Sights:** Heinie straight 8. **Features:** SA. Blued, stainless steel, duotone blue and blue/gray finish. Standard/Picatinny rail, standard frame, alloy frame and alloy/Picatinny rail. Introduced in 2007. Imported from Brazil by Taurus International.
Price: 1911B, Blue $633.00
Price: 1911B, Walnut grips $685.00
Price: 1911SS, Stainless Steel $752.00
Price: 1911SS-1, Stainless Steel w/rail.................. $769.00
Price: 1911 DT, Duotone Blue $727.00

TAURUS MODEL 92

Caliber: 9mm. **Capacity:** 10- or 17-round magazine. **Barrel:** 5 in. **Weight:** 34 oz. **Length:** 8.5 in. overall. **Grips:** Checkered rubber, rosewood, mother of pearl. **Sights:** Fixed notch rear. 3-dot sight system. Also offered with micrometer-click adjustable night sights. **Features:** DA, ambidextrous 3-way hammer drop safety, allows cocked and locked carry. Blued, stainless steel, blued with gold highlights, stainless steel with gold highlights, forged aluminum frame, integral key-lock. .22 LR conversion kit available. Imported from Brazil by Taurus International.
Price: 92B $433.00
Price: 92SS $550.00

TAURUS SPECTRUM

Caliber: .380. **Barrel:** 2.8 in. **Weight:** 10 oz. **Length:** 5.4 in. **Sights:** Low-profile integrated with slide. **Features:** Polymer frame with stainless steel slide. Many finish combinations with various bright colors. Made in the USA. Introduced in 2017.
Price: .... $289.00–$305.00

TRISTAR 100 /120 SERIES

Calibers: 9mm, .40 S&W (C-100 only). **Capacities:** 15 (9mm), 11 (.40). **Barrels:** 3.7–4.7 in. **Weights:** 26–30 oz. **Grips:** Checkered polymer. **Sights:** Fixed. **Finishes:** Blue or chrome. **Features:** Alloy or steel frame. SA/DA. A series of pistols based on the CZ 75 design. Imported from Turkey.
Price: From .... $460.00–$490.00

TURNBULL MODEL 1911

Caliber: .45 ACP. **Features:** An accurate reproduction of 1918-era Model 1911 pistol. Forged slide with appropriate shape and style. Late-style sight with semi-circle notch. Early-style safety lock with knurled undercut thumb piece. Short, wide checkered spur hammer. Hand-checkered double-diamond American Black Walnut grips. Hand polished with period correct Carbonia charcoal bluing. Custom made to order with many options. Made in the USA by Doug Turnbull Manufacturing Co.
Price: From $2,625.00

WALTHER P99 AS

Calibers: 9mm, .40 S&W. **Capacities:** 15 or 10 rounds (9mm), 10 or 8 rounds (.40). **Barrels:** 3.5 or 4 in. **Weights:** 21–26 oz. **Lengths:** 6.6–7.1 in. **Grips:** Polymer with interchangeable backstrap inserts. **Sights:** Adjustable rear, blade front with three interchangeable inserts of different heights. **Features:** Offered in two frame sizes, standard and compact. DA with trigger safety, decocker, internal striker safety, loaded chamber indicator. Made in Germany.
Price: $629.00

WALTHER PK380

Caliber: .380 ACP. **Capacity:** 8-round magazine. **Barrel:** 3.66 in. **Weight:** 19.4 oz. **Length:** 6.5 in. **Sights:** Three-dot system, drift adjustable rear. **Features:** DA with external hammer, ambidextrous mag release and manual safety. Picatinny rail. Black frame with black or nickel slide.
Price: $399.00
Price: Nickel slide $449.00

Prices given are believed to be accurate at time of publication however, many factors affect retail pricing so exact prices are not possible.

WALTHER PPK, PPK/S
Caliber: .380 ACP. **Capacities:** 6+1 (PPK), 7+1 (PPK/s). **Barrel:** 3.3 in. **Weight:** 21-26 oz. **Length:** 6.1 in. **Grips:** Checkered plastic. **Sights:** Fixed. New production in 2019. Made in Fort Smith, AR with German-made slide.
Price: $749.00

WALTHER PPQ M2
Calibers: 9mm, .40 S&W, .45 ACP, .22 LR. **Capacities:** 9mm, (15-round magazine), .40 S&W (11). .45 ACP, 22 LR (PPQ M2 .22). **Barrels:** 4 or 5 in. **Weight:** 24 oz. **Lengths:** 7.1, 8.1 in. **Sights:** Drift-adjustable. **Features:** Quick Defense trigger, firing pin block, ambidextrous slidelock and mag release, Picatinny rail. Comes with two extra magazines, two interchangeable frame backstraps and hard case. Navy SD model has threaded 4.6-in. barrel. M2 .22 has aluminum slide, blowback operation, weighs 19 ounces.
Price: 9mm, .40 .... $649.00–$749.00
Price: M2 .22 .... $429.00
Price: .45 .... $699.00–$799.00

WALTHER CCP
Caliber: 9mm. **Capacity:** 8-round magazine. **Barrel:** 3.5 in. **Weight:** 22 oz. **Length:** 6.4 in. **Features:** Thumb-operated safety, reversible mag release, loaded chamber indicator. Delayed blowback gas-operated action provides less recoil and muzzle jump, and easier slide operation. Available in all black or black/stainless two-tone finish.
Price: From .... $469.00–$499.00

WALTHER PPS M2 SERIES
Caliber: 9mm. **Capacity:** 6-, 7- or 8-round magazine. **Barrel:** 3.2 in. **Sights:** Optic-ready, fixed 3-dot, fixed 3-dot tritium or Crimson Trace Laserguard. **Weight:** 19.4 oz. **Length:** 6.3 in. **Finish:** Carbon black. **Grips:** Textured polymer. **Features:** Striker-fire, 6.1-lb. trigger pull.
Price: .... $469.00-$560.00

WALTHER P22
Caliber: .22 LR. **Barrels:** 3.4, 5 in. **Weights:** 19.6 oz. (3.4), 20.3 oz. (5). **Lengths:** 6.26, 7.83 in. **Sights:** Interchangeable white dot, front, 2-dot adjustable, rear. **Features:** A rimfire version of the Walther P99 pistol, available in nickel slide with black frame, Desert Camo or Digital Pink Camo frame with black slide.
Price: From $379.00
Price: Nickel slide/black frame, or black slide/camo frame $449.00

WALTHER Q4 STEEL FRAME
Caliber: 9mm. **Capacity:** 15-round magazine. **Barrel:** 4 in. **Grips:** Textured polymer, wrap around. **Sights:** 3-dot night. **Length:** 7.4 in. overall. **Weight:** 39.7 oz. unloaded. **Finish:** Matte black Tenifer. **Features:** Duty optimized beaver tail, Quick Defense trigger, accessory rail, oversized controls.
Price: $1,399.00
Price: (optic-ready model)..$1,499.00

WILSON COMBAT ELITE SERIES
Calibers: 9mm, .38 Super, .40 S&W; .45 ACP. **Barrel:** Compensated 4.1-in. hand-fit, heavy flanged cone match grade. **Weight:** 36.2 oz. **Length:** 7.7 in. overall. **Grips:** Cocobolo. **Sights:** Combat Tactical yellow rear tritium inserts, brighter green tritium front insert. **Features:** High-cut frontstrap, 30 LPI checkering on frontstrap and flat mainspring housing, High-Ride Beavertail grip safety. Dehorned, ambidextrous thumb safety, extended ejector, skeletonized ultra light hammer, ultralight trigger, Armor-Tuff finish on frame and slide. Introduced 1997. Made in USA by Wilson Combat. This manufacturer offers more than 100 different 1911 models ranging in price from about $2,800 to $5,000. XTAC and Classic 6-in. models shown. Prices show a small sampling of available models.
Price: Classic, From...$3,300.00
Price: CQB, From $2,865.00
Price: Hackathorn Special...$3,750.00
Price: Tactical Carry $3,750.00
Price: Tactical Supergrade $5,045.00
Price: Bill Wilson Carry Pistol $3,850.00
Price: Ms. Sentinel...$3,875.00
Price: Hunter 10mm, .460 Rowland $4,100.00
Price: Beretta Brigadier Series, From...$1,195.00
Price: X-Tac Series, From $2,760.00
Price: Texas BBQ Special, From...$4,960.00

Prices given are believed to be accurate at time of publication however, many factors affect retail pricing so exact prices are not possible.

75TH EDITION, 2021 ✦ **477**

BAER 1911 ULTIMATE MASTER COMBAT

Calibers: .38 Super, 400 Cor-Bon, .45 ACP (others available). **Capacity:** 10-shot magazine. **Barrels:** 5, 6 in. Baer National Match. **Weight:** 37 oz. **Length:** 8.5 in. overall. **Grips:** Checkered cocobolo. **Sights:** Baer dovetail front, low-mount Bo-Mar rear with hidden leaf. **Features:** Full-house competition gun. Baer forged NM blued steel frame and double serrated slide; Baer triple port, tapered cone compensator; fitted slide to frame; lowered, flared ejection port; Baer reverse recoil plug; full-length guide rod; recoil buff; beveled magazine well; Baer Commander hammer, sear; Baer extended ambidextrous safety, extended ejector, checkered slide stop, beavertail grip safety with pad, extended magazine release button; Baer speed trigger. Made in USA by Les Baer Custom, Inc.

Price: .45 ACP Compensated $3,240.00
Price: .38 Super Compensated $3,390.00
Price: 5-in. Standard barrel $3,040.00
Price: 5-in. barrel .38 Super or 9mm $3,140.00
Price: 6-in. barrel $3,234.00
Price: 6-in. barrel .38 Super or 9mm $3,316.00

BAER 1911 NATIONAL MATCH HARDBALL

Caliber: .45 ACP. **Capacity:** 7-round magazine. **Barrel:** 5 in. **Weight:** 37 oz. **Length:** 8.5 in. overall. **Grips:** Checkered walnut. **Sights:** Baer dovetail front with under-cut post, low-mount Bo-Mar rear with hidden leaf. **Features:** Baer NM forged steel frame, double serrated slide and barrel with stainless bushing; slide fitted to frame; Baer match trigger with 4-lb. pull; polished feed ramp, throated barrel; checkered frontstrap, arched mainspring housing; Baer beveled magazine well; lowered, flared ejection port; tuned extractor; Baer extended ejector, checkered slide stop; recoil buff. Made in USA by Les Baer Custom, Inc.

Price: $2,379.00

BAER 1911 PPC OPEN CLASS

Caliber: .45 ACP, 9mm. **Barrel:** 6 in, fitted to frame. **Sights:** Adjustable PPC rear, dovetail front. **Grips:** Checkered Cocobola. **Features:** Designed for NRA Police Pistol Combat matches. Lowered and flared ejection port, extended ejector, polished feed ramp, throated barrel, frontstrap checkered at 30 LPI, flat serrated mainspring housing, Commander hammer, front and rear slide serrations. 9mm has supported chamber.

Price: $2,775.00
Price: 9mm w/supported chamber $3,187.00

BAER 1911 BULLSEYE WADCUTTER

Similar to National Match Hardball except designed for wadcutter loads only. Polished feed ramp and barrel throat; Bo-Mar rib on slide; full-length recoil rod; Baer speed trigger with 3.5-lb. pull; Baer deluxe hammer and sear; Baer beavertail grip safety with pad; flat mainspring housing checkered 20 LPI. Blue finish; checkered walnut grips. Made in USA by Les Baer Custom, Inc.

Price: From $2,461.00

COLT GOLD CUP NM SERIES

Caliber: .45 ACP, 9mm, .38 Super. **Capacity:** 8-round magazine. **Barrel:** 5-inch National Match. **Weight:** 37 oz. **Length:** 8.5. **Grips:** Checkered wraparound rubber composite with silver-plated medallions or checkered walnut grips with gold medallions. **Sights:** Target post dovetail front, Bomar fully adjustable rear. **Features:** Adjustable aluminum wide target trigger, beavertail grip safety, full-length recoil spring and target recoil spring, available in blued finish or stainless steel.

Price: (blued) $1,299.00
Price: (stainless) $1,350.00
Price: Gold Cup Lite $1,199.00
Price: Gold Cup Trophy $1,699.00

COLT COMPETITION PISTOL

Calibers: .45 ACP, 9mm or .38 Super. **Capacities:** 8 or 9-shot magazine. **Barrel:** 5 in. National Match. **Grips:** Custom Blue Colt G10. **Sights:** Novak adjustable rear, fiber optic front. A competition-ready pistol out of the box at a moderate price. Blue or satin nickel finish. Series 80 firing system. O Series has stainless steel frame and slide with Cerakote gray frame and black slide, competition trigger, gray/black G-10 grips, front and rear slide serrations.

Price: .... $949.00–$1,099.00
Price: Competition O series $2,499.00

CZ 75 TS CZECHMATE

Caliber: 9mm. **Capacity:** 20-round magazine. **Barrel:** 130mm. **Weight:** 1360 g **Length:** 266mm overall. **Features:** The handgun is custom built, therefore the quality of workmanship is fully comparable with race pistols built directly to IPSC shooters' wishes. Individual parts and components are excellently match fitted, broke-in and tested. Every handgun is outfitted with a four-port compensator, nut for shooting without a compensator, the slide stop with an extended finger piece, the slide stop without a finger piece, ergonomic grip panels from aluminum with a new type pitting and side mounting provision with the C-More red-dot sight. For shooting without a red-dot sight there is included a standard target rear sight of Tactical Sports type, package contains also the front sight.

Price: $3,416.00

CZ 75 TACTICAL SPORTS

Calibers: 9mm,.40 S&W. **Capacities:** 17-20-round magazines. **Barrel:** 114mm. **Weight:** 1270 g **Length:** 225mm overall. **Features:** Semi-automatic handgun with a locked breech. This model is designed for competition shooting in accordance with world IPSC (International Practical Shooting Confederation) rules and regulations. The CZ 75 TS pistol model design stems from the standard CZ 75 model. However, this model features a number of special modifications, which are usually required for competitive handguns: SA trigger mechanism, match trigger made of plastic featuring option for trigger travel adjustments before discharge (using upper screw), and for overtravel (using bottom screw). The adjusting screws are set by the manufacturer — sporting hammer specially adapted for a reduced trigger pull weight, an extended magazine catch, grip panels made of walnut, guiding funnel made of plastic for quick inserting of the magazine into pistol's frame. Glossy blued slide, silver Polycoat frame. Packaging includes 3 magazines.

Price: $1,837.00

Prices given are believed to be accurate at time of publication however, many factors affect retail pricing so exact prices are not possible.

CZ SHADOW 2 SA
Caliber: 9mm. **Capacity:** 17-round magazine. **Barrel:** 4.89 in. **Grips:** Textured blue aluminum. **Sights:** Fiber-optic front, HAJO rear. **Length:** 8.53 in. overall. **Weight:** 46.5 oz. unloaded. Finish: Nitride black. **Features:** Single-action-only trigger. Swappable magazine release with adjustable, extended button with three settings. Ambidextrous manual thumb safety.
Price: $1,349.00

DAN WESSON CHAOS
Caliber: 9mm. **Capacity:** 21-round magazine. **Barrel:** 5 in. **Weight:** 3.20 lbs. **Length:** 8.75 in. overall. **Features:** A double-stack 9mm designed for 3-Gun competition.
Price: $3,829.00

DAN WESSON HAVOC
Calibers: 9mm, .38 Super. **Capacity:** 21-round magazine. **Barrel:** 4.25 in. **Weight:** 2.20 lbs. **Length:** 8 in. overall. **Features:** The Havoc is based on an "All Steel" Hi-capacity version of the 1911 frame. It comes ready to compete in Open IPSC/USPSA division. The C-more mounting system offers the lowest possible mounting configuration possible, enabling extremely fast target acquisition. The barrel and compensator arrangement pair the highest level of accuracy with the most effective compensator available.
Price: $4,299.00

DAN WESSON MAYHEM
Caliber: .40 S&W. **Capacity:** 18-round magazine. **Barrel:** 6 in. **Weight:** 2.42 lbs. **Length:** 8.75 in. overall. **Features:** The Mayhem is based on an "All-Steel" Hi-capacity version of the 1911 frame. It comes ready to compete in Limited IPSC/USPSA division or fulfill the needs of anyone looking for a superbly accurate target-grade 1911. The 6-in. bull barrel and tactical rail add to the static weight, or "good weight." A 6-in. long slide for added sight radius and enhanced pointability, but that would add to the "bad weight" so the 6-in. slide has been lightened to equal the weight of a 5 in. The result is a 6 in. long slide that balances and feels like a 5 in. but shoots like a 6 in. The combination of the all-steel frame with industry leading parts delivers the most well-balanced, softest shooting 6-in. limited gun on the market.
Price: $3,899.00

DAN WESSON TITAN
Caliber: 10mm. **Capacity:** 21-round magazine. **Barrel:** 4.25 in. **Weight:** 1.62 lbs. **Length:** 8 in. overall. **Features:** The Titan is based on an "All Steel" Hi-capacity version of the 1911 frame. The rugged HD night sights are moved forward and recessed deep into the slide yielding target accuracy and extreme durability. The Snake Scale serrations' aggressive 25 LPI checkering, and the custom competition G-10 grips ensure controllability even in the harshest of conditions. The combination of the all-steel frame, bull barrel and tactical rail enhance the balance and durability of this formidable target-grade Combat handgun.
Price: $3,829.00

DAN WESSON DISCRETION
Caliber: .45 ACP. **Capacity:** 8-round magazine. **Barrel:** 5.75 in. Match-grade stainless extended and threaded. **Weight:** 2.6 lbs. **Features:** Ported slide, serrated trigger, competition hammer, high tritium sights for sighting over the top of most suppressors.
Price: $2,142.00

EAA WITNESS ELITE GOLD TEAM
Calibers: 9mm, 9x21, .38 Super, .40 S&W, .45 ACP. **Barrel:** 5.1 in. **Weight:** 44 oz. **Length:** 10.5 in. overall. **Grips:** Checkered walnut, competition-style. **Sights:** Square post front, fully adjustable rear. **Features:** Triple-chamber cone compensator; competition SA trigger; extended safety and magazine release; competition hammer; beveled magazine well; beavertail grip. Hand-fitted major components. Hard chrome finish. Match-grade barrel. From EAA Custom Shop. Introduced 1992. Limited designed for IPSC Limited Class competition. Features include full-length dust-cover frame, funneled magazine well, interchangeable front sights. Stock (2005) designed for IPSC Production Class competition. Match introduced 2006. Made in Italy, imported by European American Armory.
Price: Gold Team $2,406.00
Price: Stock, 4.5 in. barrel, hard-chrome finish $1,263.00
Price: Limited Custom Xtreme..................................... $2,502.00
Price: Witness Match Xtreme...................................... $2,335.00
Price: Witness Stock III Xtreme $2,252.00

FREEDOM ARMS MODEL 83 .22 FIELD GRADE SILHOUETTE CLASS
Caliber: .22 LR. **Capacity:** 5-round cylinder. **Barrel:** 10 in. **Weight:** 63 oz. **Length:** 15.5 in. overall. **Grips:** Black Micarta. **Sights:** Removable Patridge front blade; Iron Sight Gun Works silhouette rear click-adjustable for windage and elevation (optional adj. front sight and hood). **Features:** Stainless steel, matte finish, manual sliding-bar safety system; dual firing pins, lightened hammer for fast lock time, pre-set trigger stop. Introduced 1991. Made in USA by Freedom Arms.
Price: Silhouette Class $2,762.00

FREEDOM ARMS MODEL 83 CENTERFIRE SILHOUETTE MODELS
Calibers: 357 Mag., .41 Mag., .44 Mag. **Capacity:** 5-round cylinder. **Barrel:** 10 in., 9 in. (.357 Mag. only). **Weight:** 63 oz. (41 Mag.). **Length:** 15.5 in., 14.5 in. (.357 only). **Grips:** Pachmayr Presentation. **Sights:** Iron Sight Gun Works silhouette rear sight, replaceable adjustable front sight blade with hood. **Features:** Stainless steel, matte finish, manual sliding-bar safety system. Made in USA by Freedom Arms.
Price: Silhouette Models, From $2,460.00

Prices given are believed to be accurate at time of publication however, many factors affect retail pricing so exact prices are not possible.

75TH EDITION, 2021 ⊕ **479**

KIMBER SUPER MATCH II

Caliber: .45 ACP. **Capacity:** 8-round magazine. **Barrel:** 5 in. **Weight:** 38 oz. **Length:** 8.7 in. overall. **Grips:** Rosewood double diamond. **Sights:** Blade front, Kimber fully adjustable rear. **Features:** Guaranteed to shoot 1-in. groups at 25 yards. Stainless steel frame, black KimPro slide; two-piece magazine well; premium aluminum match-grade trigger; 30 LPI frontstrap checkering; stainless match-grade barrel; ambidextrous safety; special Custom Shop markings. Introduced 1999. Made in USA by Kimber Mfg., Inc.
Price: **$2,313.00**

MAC RAPIDO

Calibers: 9mm, .38 Super. **Capacity:** 17-round magazine. Barrels: 5- or 5.5-in., match-grade with compensator. **Sights:** Optic ready. **Weight:** 46.5 oz. **Finish:** Blue. **Grips:** Aluminum. **Features:** Checkered frontstrap serrations, combat trigger and hammer, flared and lowered ejection port, ambidextrous safety. Imported from the Philippines by Eagle Imports.
Price: **$1,725.00**

RUGER AMERICAN COMPETITION

Caliber: 9mm. **Capacity:** 17-round magazine. **Barrel:** 5 in. **Grips:** Three interchangeable grip inserts. **Sights:** Adjustable rear, fiber-optic front, optic ready. **Length:** 8.3 in. overall. **Weight:** 34.1 oz. unloaded. **Finish:** Black Nitrite. **Features:** Slide is drilled and tapped for mounting red-dot reflex optics, ported stainless steel slide. Made in the USA.
Price: **$579.00**

RUGER MARK IV TARGET

Caliber: .22 LR. **Capacity:** 10-round magazine. **Barrel:** 5.5-in. heavy bull. **Weight:** 35.6 oz. **Grips:** Checkered synthetic or laminate. **Sights:** .125 blade front, micro-click rear, adjustable for windage and elevation. **Features:** Loaded Chamber indicator; integral lock, magazine disconnect. Plastic case with lock included.
Price: (blued) **$529.00**
Price: (stainless) **$689.00**

SMITH & WESSON MODEL 41 TARGET

Caliber: .22 LR. **Capacity:** 10-round magazine. **Barrels:** 5.5 in., 7 in. **Weight:** 41 oz. (5.5-in. barrel). **Length:** 10.5 in. overall (5.5-in. barrel). **Grips:** Checkered walnut with modified thumb rest, usable with either hand. **Sights:** .125 in. Patridge on ramp base; micro-click rear-adjustable for windage and elevation. **Features:** .375 in. wide, grooved trigger; adjustable trigger stop drilled and tapped.
Price: .... **$1,369.00–$1,619.00**

SIG SAUER P320 XFIVE LEGION

Caliber: 9mm. **Capacity:** 17-round magazine. **Barrel:** 5 in. **Grips:** Textured polymer. **Sights:** Dawson Precision adjustable rear, fiber-optic front, optic ready. **Length:** 8.5 in. overall. **Weight:** 43.5 oz. unloaded. **Finish:** Legion gray. **Features:** TXG tungsten infused heavy XGrip module, slide has lightening cuts, Henning Group aluminum magazine basepads.
Price: **$999.99**

S.P.S. VISTA

Calibers: 9mm, .38 Super. **Capacity:** 17-round magazine. Barrels: 5- or 5.5-in., match-grade with compensator. **Sights:** Optic ready. **Weight:** 43 oz. **Finish:** Black chrome. **Grips:** Aluminum. **Features:** Polymer frame, checkered frontstrap serrations, skeletonized trigger and hammer, flared and lowered ejection port, ambidextrous safety, wide mag well. Imported from Spain by Eagle Imports.
Price: **$2,450.00**

S.P.S. PANTERA

Calibers: 9mm, .40 S&W, .45 ACP. **Capacity:** 12-, 16- or 18-round magazine. **Barrel:** 5-in., match-grade. **Sights:** Bomar-type, fully adjustable rear, fiber-optic front. **Weight:** 36.6 oz. **Finish:** Black, black chrome, chrome. **Grips:** Polymer. **Features:** Polymer frame, checkered frontstrap serrations, skeletonized trigger and hammer, flared and lowered ejection port, ambidextrous safety, wide mag well, full dust cover. Imported from Spain by Eagle Imports.
Price: **$1,730.00**

STI APEIRO

Calibers: 9mm, .40 S&W, .45 ACP. **Features:** 1911-style semi-auto pistol with Schuemann "Island" barrel; patented modular steel frame with polymer grip; high capacity double-stack magazine; stainless steel ambidextrous thumb safeties and knuckle relief high-rise beavertail grip safety; unique sabertooth rear cocking serrations; 5-inch fully ramped, fully supported "Island" bull barrel, with the sight milled in to allow faster recovery to point of aim; custom engraving on the polished sides of the (blued) stainless steel slide; stainless steel mag well; STI adjustable rear sight and Dawson fiber optic front sight; blued frame.
Price: **$2,999.00**

STI DVC P

Calibers: 9mm, .45 ACP. **Barrel:** 5.0 in., compensated. **Sights:** HOST rear with Fiber Optic front. **Grip:** Gen II 2011 Double Stack. **Features:** Diamond Like Carbon Black finish, Dawson Precision Tool-Less guide rod, railed frame.
Price: **$3,999.00**

STI DVC O

Calibers: 9mm, .38 Super. **Barrel:** 5.4 in., TX2 Compensated, TiN coated. **Sights:** Frame mounted C-More RTS2. **Grip:** Gen II 2011. **Finish:** Hard chrome with Black DLC Barrel. **Features:** 2.5-lb trigger, ambidextrous safety, Dawson Precision Tool-Less guide rod.
Price: **$3,999.00**

STI DVC S

Calibers: 9mm, .38 Super. **Barrel:** 4.15 in., TX1 Compensated. **Sights:** Frame mounted C-More RTS2. **Grip:** Gen II 2011. **Finish:** Hard chrome or Black DLC with TiN or DLC Barrel. **Features:** 2.5-lb trigger, ambidextrous safety, Dawson Precision Tool-Less guide rod.
Price: **$3,999.00**

STI TROJAN

Calibers: 9mm, .45 ACP. **Barrel:** 5 in. **Weight:** 36 oz. **Length:** 8.5 in. **Grips:** Rosewood. **Sights:** STI front with STI adjustable rear. **Features:** Stippled frontstrap, flat-top slide, one-piece steel guide rod.
Price: (Trojan 5) **$1,499.00**

CHARTER ARMS BOOMER
Caliber: .44 Special. **Capacity:** 5-round cylinder. **Barrel:** 2 in., ported. **Weight:** 20 oz. **Grips:** Full rubber combat. **Sights:** Fixed.
Price: Blued **$443.00**

CHARTER ARMS POLICE BULLDOG
Caliber: .38 Special. **Capacity:** 6-round cylinder. **Barrel:** 4.2 in. **Weight:** 26 oz. **Sights:** Blade front, notch rear. Large frame version of Bulldog design.
Price: Blued **$408.00**

CHARTER ARMS CHIC LADY & CHIC LADY DAO
Caliber: .38 Special. **Capacity:** 5-round cylinder. **Barrel:** 2 in. **Weight:** 12 oz. **Grip:** Combat. **Sights:** Fixed. **Features:** 2-tone pink or lavender & stainless with aluminum frame. American made by Charter Arms.
Price: Chic Lady **$473.00**
Price: Chic Lady DAO **$483.00**

CHARTER ARMS CRIMSON UNDERCOVER
Caliber: .38 Special +P. **Capacity:** 5-round cylinder. **Barrel:** 2 in. **Weight:** 16 oz. **Grip:** Crimson Trace. **Sights:** Fixed. **Features:** Stainless finish and frame. American made by Charter Arms.
Price: **$577.00**

CHARTER ARMS OFF DUTY
Caliber: .38 Special. **Barrel:** 2 in. **Weight:** 12.5 oz. **Sights:** Blade front, notch rear. **Features:** 5-round cylinder, aluminum casting, DAO with concealed hammer. Also available with semi-concealed hammer. American made by Charter Arms.
Price: Aluminum **$404.00**
Price: Crimson Trace Laser grip **$657.00**

CHARTER ARMS MAG PUG
Caliber: .357 Mag. **Capacity:** 5-round cylinder. **Barrel:** 2.2 in. **Weight:** 23 oz. **Sights:** Blade front, notch rear. **Features:** American made by Charter Arms.
Price: Blued or stainless **$400.00**
Price: 4.4-in. full-lug barrel **$470.00**
Price: Crimson Trace Laser Grip **$609.00**

CHARTER ARMS PITBULL
Calibers: 9mm, 40 S&W, .45 ACP. **Capacity:** 5-round cylinder. **Barrel:** 2.2 in. **Weights:** 20–22 oz. **Sights:** Fixed rear, ramp front. **Grips:** Rubber. **Features:** Matte stainless steel frame or Nitride frame. Moon clips not required for 9mm, .45 ACP.
Price: 9mm **$502.00**
Price: .40 S&W **$489.00**
Price: .45 ACP **$489.00**
Price: 9mm Black Nitride finish **$522.00**
Price: .40, .45 Black Nitride finish **$509.00**

CHARTER ARMS PATHFINDER
Calibers: .22 LR or .22 Mag. **Capacity:** 6-round cylinder. **Barrel:** 2 in., 4 in. **Weights:** 20 oz. (12 oz. Lite model). **Grips:** Full. **Sights:** Fixed or adjustable (Target). **Features:** Stainless finish and frame.
Price .22 LR **$365.00**
Price .22 Mag **$367.00**
Price: Lite **$379.00**
Price: Target **$409.00**

CHARTER ARMS SOUTHPAW
Caliber: .38 Special +P. **Capacity:** 5-round cylinder. **Barrel:** 2 in. **Weight:** 12 oz. **Grips:** Rubber Pachmayr style. **Features:** Snubnose, matte black aluminum alloy frame with stainless steel cylinder. Cylinder latch and crane assembly are on right side of frame for convenience of left-hand shooters.
Price: **$419.00**

CHARTER ARMS THE PINK LADY
Caliber: .38 Special. **Capacity:** 6-round cylinder. **Barrel:** 2.2 in. **Grips:** Full. **Sights:** Fixed rear, LitePipe front. **Weight:** 12 oz. **Features:** As the name indicates, the Pink Lady has a pink and stainless steel finish. This is an aluminum-framed revolver from the Undercover Lite series.
Price: **$357.00**

Prices given are believed to be accurate at time of publication however, many factors affect retail pricing so exact prices are not possible.

75TH EDITION, 2021 **481**

CHARTER ARMS TARGET MAGNUM
Caliber: .357 Magnum. **Capacity:** 6-round cylinder. **Barrel:** 6 in. **Grips:** Full. **Sights:** Fully adjustable rear, fixed front. **Features:** This revolver of the Mag Pug series is built on Charter's XL frame. The 6-inch barrel and fully adjustable sights make this a great target piece that can also be used for hunting. Like all Charters, this one is made in the USA.
Price: **$476.00**

CHARTER ARMS THE PROFESSIONAL II
Caliber: .357 Magnum. **Capacity:** 6-round cylinder. **Barrel:** 3 in. **Grips:** Wood. **Sights:** Fixed rear, LitePipe front. **Features:** Built on Charter's large frame, the PROFESSIONAL II is a member of the PROFESSIONAL series of revolvers that is finished in a tough and attractive Blacknitride finish.
Price: **$406.00**

CHARTER ARMS THE PROFESSIONAL III
Caliber: .357 Magnum. **Capacity:** 6-round cylinder. **Barrel:** 4.2 in. **Grips:** Wood. **Sights:** Fixed rear, LitePipe front. **Features:** The PROFESSIONAL III is also a member of the PROFESSIONAL series of American-made revolvers from Charter Arms. This one, however, is built on Charter's XL frame, with a wood grip and a Blacknitride finish.
Price: **$470.00**

CHARTER ARMS THE PROFESSIONAL IV
Caliber: .32 Magnum. **Capacity:** 7-round cylinder. **Barrel:** 3 in. **Grips:** Wood. **Sights:** Fixed rear, LitePipe front. **Features:** A member of the PROFESSIONAL series, the PROFESSIONAL IV is manufactured on the large frame and features a 7-shot cylinder chambered in .32 Magnum. The finish is stainless steel.
Price: **$420.00**

CHARTER ARMS THE PROFESSIONAL V
Caliber: .357 Magnum. **Capacity:** 6-round cylinder. **Barrel:** 3 in. **Grips:** Wood. **Sights:** Fixed rear, LitePipe front. **Features:** A member of the PROFESSIONAL series, the PROFESSIONAL V is manufactured on the large frame and features a 6-shot cylinder chambered in .357 Magnum. The finish is stainless steel.
Price: **$399.00**

CHARTER ARMS THE PROFESSIONAL VI
Caliber: .357 Magnum. **Capacity:** 6-round cylinder. **Barrel:** 4.2 in. **Grips:** Wood. **Sights:** Fixed rear, LitePipe front. **Features:** The final model in the PROFESSIONAL series, the PROFESSIONAL VI is manufactured on Charter Arms' XL frame and features a 6-shot cylinder. The finish is stainless steel.
Price: **$420.00**

CHARTER ARMS UNDERCOVER
Caliber: .38 Special +P. **Capacity:** 6-round cylinder. **Barrel:** 2 in. **Weight:** 12 oz. **Sights:** Blade front, notch rear. **Features:** American made by Charter Arms.
Price: Blued **$346.00**

CHARTER ARMS UNDERCOVER LITE
Caliber: .38 Special. **Capacity:** 6-round cylinder. **Barrel:** 2.2 in. **Grips:** Full. **Sights:** Fixed rear, LitePipe front. **Weight:** 12 oz. **Features:** Aluminum-framed lightweight revolver with anodized finish. Lots of power in a feather-weight package.
Price: **$357.00**

CHARTER ARMS UNDERCOVER SOUTHPAW
Caliber: .38 Spec. +P. **Capacity:** 5-round cylinder. **Barrel:** 2 in. **Weight:** 12 oz. **Sights:** NA. **Features:** Cylinder release is on the right side and the cylinder opens to the right side. Exposed hammer for both SA and DA. American made by Charter Arms.
Price: **$419.00**

CHIAPPA RHINO
Calibers: .357 Magnum, 9mm, .40 S&W. **Features:** 2-, 4-, 5- or 6-inch barrel; fixed or adjustable sights; visible hammer or hammerless design. **Weights:** 24–33 oz. Walnut or synthetic grips with black frame; hexagonal-shaped cylinder. Unique design fires from bottom chamber of cylinder.
Price: From .... $1,090.00-**$1,465.00**

COBRA SHADOW
Caliber: .38 Special +P. **Capacity:** 5 rounds. **Barrel:** 1.875 in. **Weight:** 15 oz. Aluminum frame with stainless steel barrel and cylinder. **Length:** 6.375 in. **Grips:** Rosewood, black rubber or Crimson Trace Laser. **Features:** Black anodized, titanium anodized or custom colors including gold, red, pink and blue.
Price: **$369.00**
Price: Rosewood grips **$434.00**
Price: Crimson Trace Laser grips **$625.00**

Prices given are believed to be accurate at time of publication however, many factors affect retail pricing so exact prices are not possible.

COLT COBRA
Caliber: .38 Special. **Capacity:** 6 rounds. **Sights:** Fixed rear, fiber optic red front. **Grips:** Hogue rubbed stippled with finger grooves. **Weight:** 25 oz. **Finish:** Matte stainless. Same name as classic Colt model made from 1950–1986 but totally new design. Introduced in 2017. King Cobra has a heavy-duty frame and 3-inch barrel.
Price: $699.00
Price: King Cobra $899.00

COLT NIGHT COBRA
Caliber; .38 Special. **Capacity:** 6 rounds. **Grips:** Black synthetic VC G10. **Sight:** Tritium front night sight. DAO operation with bobbed hammer. Features a linear leaf spring design for smooth DA trigger pull.
Price: $899.00

COLT PYTHON
Caliber: .357 Magnum. **Capacity:** 6-round cylinder. **Barrels:** 4.25 and 6 in. **Grips:** Walnut. **Sights:** Fully adjustable rear, fixed red ramp interchangeable front. **Weights:** 42 oz. (4.25 in.), 46 oz. (6 in.). **Features:** New and improved and available only in stainless steel. Has recessed target crown and user-interchangeable front sight.
Price: $1,499.00

COMANCHE II-A
Caliber: .38 Special. **Capacity:** 6-round cylinder. **Barrels:** 3 or 4 in. **Weights:** 33, 35 oz. **Lengths:** 8, 8.5 in. overall. **Grips:** Rubber. **Sights:** Fixed. **Features:** Blued finish, alloy frame. Distributed by SGS Importers.
Price: $220.00

DAN WESSON 715
Caliber: .357 Magnum. **Capacity:** 6-round cylinder. **Barrel:** 6-inch heavy barrel with full lug. **Weight:** 38 oz. **Lengths:** 8, 8.5 in. overall. **Grips:** Hogue rubber with finger grooves. **Sights:** Adjustable rear, interchangeable front blade. **Features:** Stainless steel. Interchangeable barrel assembly. Reintroduced in 2014. 715 Pistol Pack comes with 4-, 6- and 8-in. interchangeable barrels.
Price: From $1,558.00
Price: Pistol Pack.. $1,999.00

EAA WINDICATOR
Calibers: .38 Special, .357 Mag **Capacity:** 6-round cylinder. **Barrels:** 2 in., 4 in. **Weight:** 30 oz. (4 in.). **Length:** 8.5 in. overall (4 in. bbl.). **Grips:** Rubber with finger grooves. **Sights:** Blade front, fixed rear. **Features:** Swing-out cylinder; hammer block safety; blue or nickel finish. Introduced 1991. Imported from Germany by European American Armory.
Price: .38 Spec. from $354.00
Price: .357 Mag, steel frame from $444.00

KIMBER K6S
Caliber: .357 Magnum. **Capacity:** 6-round cylinder. **Barrel:** 2-inch full lug. **Grips:** Gray rubber. **Finish:** Satin stainless. Kimber's first revolver, claimed to be world's lightest production 6-shot .357 Magnum. DAO design with non-stacking match-grade trigger. Introduced 2016. CDP model has laminated checkered rosewood grips, Tritium night sights, two-tone black DLC/brushed stainless finish, match grade trigger.
Price: $878.00
Price: 3-in. Barrel... $899.00
Price: Deluxe Carry w/Medallion grips............................ $1,088.00
Price: Custom Defense Package $1,155.00
Price: Crimson Trace Laser Grips $1,177.00
Price: TLE $999.00
Price: DA/SA $949.00

Prices given are believed to be accurate at time of publication however, many factors affect retail pricing so exact prices are not possible.

75TH EDITION, 2021 **483**

KIMBER K6s DASA TARGET
Caliber: .357 Magnum. **Capacity:** 6-round cylinder. **Barrel:** 4 in. **Grips:** Walnut laminate, oversized. **Sights:** Fully adjustable rear, fiber-optic front. **Features:** The DASA is the next evolution of the K6s. The DASA is outfitted with a double- and single-action trigger mechanism. Kimber's K6s revolvers feature the purportedly smallest cylinder capable of housing 6 rounds of .357 Magnum at 1.39-inch diameter, making for a very slim and streamlined package.
Price: **$989.00**

KIMBER K6s DASA COMBAT
Caliber: .357 Magnum. **Capacity:** 6-round cylinder. **Barrel:** 4 in. **Grips:** Walnut laminate, oversized with finger grooves. **Sights:** Fixed front and rear with white dots. **Features:** The DASA Combat is outfitted with a double- and single-action trigger mechanism. Kimber's K6s DASA revolvers have a smooth no-stack double-action trigger and a crisp 3.25- to 4.25-lb. single-action pull. The K6s DASA revolvers are equipped with knurled hammer spur.
Price: **$989.00**

KIMBER K6s DASA TEXAS EDITION
Caliber: .357 Magnum. **Capacity:** 6-round cylinder. **Barrel:** 2 in. **Grips:** Ivory G10. **Sights:** Fixed front and rear with white dots. **Features:** The Texas Edition is adorned with ivory G10 grips with the state moto, name and flag on this special edition. The satin finish has American Western cut scroll engraving on the barrel, frame and cylinder. The K6s DASA Texas Edition revolvers are equipped with knurled hammer spur.
Price: **$1,359.00**

KIMBER K6s ROYAL
Caliber: .357 Magnum. **Capacity:** 6-round cylinder. **Barrel:** 2 in. **Grips:** Walnut. **Sights:** Fixed brass-bead front and rear with white dots. **Features:** The K6s Royal features a 2-inch barrel for easy concealment. The dovetailed white-dot rear sight complements the brass-bead front sight. The Royal's stainless steel is hand polished to a high shine and a Dark Oil DLC is applied for a unique look.
Price: **$1,699.00**

KORTH USA
Calibers: .22 LR, .22 WMR, .32 S&W Long, .38 Special, .357 Mag., 9mm. **Capacity:** 6-shot. **Barrels:** 3, 4, 5.25, 6 in. **Weights:** 36–52 oz. **Grips:** Combat, Sport: Walnut, Palisander, Amboina, Ivory. **Finish:** German Walnut, matte with oil finish, adjustable ergonomic competition style. **Sights:** Adjustable Patridge (Sport) or Baughman (Combat), interchangeable and adjustable rear w/Patridge front (Target) in blue and matte. **Features:** DA/SA, 3 models, over 50 configurations, externally adjustable trigger stop and weight, interchangeable cylinder, removable wide-milled trigger shoe on Target model. Deluxe models are highly engraved editions. Available finishes include high polish blued finish, plasma coated in high polish or matte silver, gold, blue or charcoal. Many deluxe options available. From Korth USA.
Price: From **$8,000.00**
Price: Deluxe Editions, from **$12,000.00**

KORTH SKYHAWK
Caliber: 9mm. **Barrels:** 2 or 3 in. **Sights:** Adjustable rear with gold bead front. **Grips:** Hogue with finger grooves. **Features:** Polished trigger, skeletonized hammer. Imported by Nighthawk Custom.
Price: **$1,699.00**

NIGHTHAWK CUSTOM/KORTH-WAFFEN NXR
Caliber: .44 Magnum. **Capacity:** 6-round cylinder **Barrel:** 6 in. **Grips:** Ivory G10. **Sights:** Adjustable rear, fast-changeable front. **Weight:** 3.05 lbs. **Features:** The NXR is a futuristic looking stainless steel double-action revolver that is black DLC finished. Comes equipped with a removable under-barrel balancing lug/weight. Picatinny rail on top of barrel and underneath for easy accessory mounting.
Price: $5,299.00

RUGER (CUSTOM SHOP) SUPER GP100 COMPETITION REVOLVER
Calibers: .357 Magnum, 9mm. **Capacity:** 8-round cylinder. **Barrels:** 5.5 and 6 in. **Grips:** Hogue hand-finished hardwood. **Sights:** Adjustable rear, fiber-optic front. **Weights:** 47 oz., 45.6 oz. **Features:** Designed for competition, the new Super GP100 is essentially a Super Redhawk with the frame extension removed and replaced by a shrouded, cold hammer-forged barrel. The Super GP utilizes the superior action of the Super Redhawk. The high-strength stainless steel cylinder has a PVD finish and is extensively fluted for weight reduction. Comes with high-quality, impact-resistant case.
Price: $1,549.00

RUGER GP-100
Calibers: .357 Mag., .327 Federal Mag., .44 Special **Capacities:** 6- or 7-round cylinder, .327 Federal Mag (7-shot), .44 Special (5-shot), .22 LR, (10-shot). **Barrels:** 3-in. full shroud, 4-in. full shroud, 6-in. full shroud. (.44 Special offered only with 3-in. barrel.) **Weights:** 36–45 oz. **Sights:** Fixed; adjustable on 4- and 6-in. full shroud barrels. **Grips:** Ruger Santoprene Cushioned Grip with Goncalo Alves inserts. **Features:** Uses action, frame features of both the Security-Six and Redhawk revolvers. Full-length, short ejector shroud. Satin blue and stainless steel.
Price: Blued $769.00
Price: Satin stainless $799.00
Price: .22 LR $829.00
Price: .44 Spl... $829.00
Price: 7-round cylinder, 327 Fed or .357 Mag $899.00

RUGER GP-100 MATCH CHAMPION
Calibers: 10mm Magnum, .357 Mag. **Capacity:** 6-round cylinder. **Barrel:** 4.2-in. half shroud, slab-sided. **Weight:** 38 oz. **Sights:** Fixed rear, fiber optic front. **Grips:** Hogue Stippled Hardwood. **Features:** Satin stainless steel finish.
Price: Blued $969.00

RUGER LCR
Calibers: .22 LR (8-round cylinder), .22 WMR, .327 Fed. Mag. .38 Special and .357 Mag., 5-round cylinder. **Barrel:** 1.875 in. **Weights:** 13.5–17.10 oz. **Length:** 6.5 in. overall. **Grips:** Hogue Tamer or Crimson Trace Lasergrips. **Sights:** Pinned ramp front, U-notch integral rear. **Features:** The Ruger Lightweight Compact Revolver (LCR), a 13.5 ounce, small frame revolver with a smooth, easy-to-control trigger and highly manageable recoil.
Price: .22 LR, .22 WMR, .38 Spl., iron sights $579.00
Price: 9mm, .327, .357, iron sights... $669.00
Price: .22 LR, .22WMR, .38 Spl. Crimson Trace Lasergrip $859.00
Price: 9mm, .327, .357, Crimson Trace Lasergrip $949.00

RUGER LCRX
Calibers: .38 Special +P, 9mm, .327 Fed. Mag., .22 WMR. **Barrels:** 1.875 in. or 3 in. **Features:** Similar to LCR except this model has visible hammer, adjustable rear sight. The 3-inch barrel model has longer grip. 9mm comes with three moon clips.
Price: $579.00
Price: .327 Mag., .357 Mag., 9mm $669.00

Prices given are believed to be accurate at time of publication however, many factors affect retail pricing so exact prices are not possible.

75TH EDITION, 2021 ◈ **485**

RUGER SP-101

Calibers: .22 LR (8 shot); .327 Federal Mag. (6-shot), 9mm, .38 Spl, .357 Mag. (5-shot). **Barrels:** 2.25, 3 1/16, 4.2 in (.22 LR, .327 Mag., .357 Mag). **Weights:** 25–30 oz. **Sights:** Adjustable or fixed, rear; fiber-optic or black ramp front. **Grips:** Ruger Cushioned Grip with inserts. **Features:** Compact, small frame, double-action revolver. Full-length ejector shroud. Stainless steel only.

Price: Fixed sights	**$719.00**
Price: Adjustable rear, fiber optic front sights	**$769.00**
Price: .327 Fed Mag 3-in bbl	**$769.00**
Price: .327 Fed Mag	**$749.00**

RUGER REDHAWK

Calibers: .44 Rem. Mag., .45 Colt and .45 ACP/.45 Colt combo. **Capacity:** 6-round cylinder. **Barrels:** 2.75, 4.2, 5.5, 7.5 in. (.45 Colt in 4.2 in. only.) **Weight:** 54 oz. (7.5 bbl.). **Length:** 13 in. overall (7.5-in. barrel). **Grips:** Square butt cushioned grip panels. TALO Distributor exclusive 2.75-in. barrel stainless model has round butt, wood grips. **Sights:** Interchangeable Patridge-type front, rear adjustable for windage and elevation. **Features:** Stainless steel, brushed satin finish, blued ordnance steel. 9.5 sight radius. Introduced 1979.

Price:	**$1,079.00**
Price: Hunter Model 7.5-in. bbl.	**$1,159.00**
Price: TALO 2.75 in. model	**$1,069.00**

RUGER SUPER REDHAWK

Calibers: 10mm, .44 Rem. Mag., .454 Casull, .480 Ruger. **Capacities:** 5- or 6-round cylinder. **Barrels:** 2.5 in. (Alaskan), 5.5 in., 6.5 in. (10mm), 7.5 in. or 9.5 in. **Weight:** 44–58 oz. **Length:** 13 in. overall (7.5-in. barrel). **Grips:**

Hogue Tamer Monogrip. **Features:** Similar to standard Redhawk except has heavy extended frame with Ruger Integral Scope Mounting System on wide topstrap. Wide hammer spur lowered for better scope clearance. Incorporates mechanical design features and improvements of GP-100. Ramp front sight base has Redhawk-style interchangeable insert sight blades, adjustable rear sight. Alaskan model has 2.5-inch barrel. Satin stainless steel and low-glare stainless finishes. Introduced 1987.

Price: .44 Magnum, 10mm	**$1,159.00**
Price: .454 Casull, .480 Ruger	**$1,199.00**
Price: Alaskan, .44 Mag, .454 Casull, .480 Ruger	**$1,189.00**

SMITH & WESSON GOVERNOR

Calibers: .410 Shotshell (2.5 in.), .45 ACP, .45 Colt. **Capacity:** 6 rounds. **Barrel:** 2.75 in. **Length:** 7.5 in., (2.5 in. barrel). **Grip:** Synthetic. **Sights:** Front: Dovetailed tritium night sight or black ramp, rear: fixed. **Grips:** Synthetic. **Finish:** Matte black or matte silver (Silver Edition). **Weight:** 29.6 oz. **Features:** Capable of chambering a mixture of .45 Colt, .45 ACP and .410 gauge 2.5-inch shotshells, the Governor is suited for both close and distant encounters, allowing users to customize the load to their preference. Scandium alloy frame, stainless steel cylinder. Packaged with two full moon clips and three 2-shot clips.

Price:	**$869.00**
Price: w/Crimson Trace Laser Grip	**$1,179.00**

SMITH & WESSON J-FRAME

The J-frames are the smallest Smith & Wesson wheelguns and come in a variety of chamberings, barrel lengths and materials as noted in the individual model listings.

SMITH & WESSON 60LS/642LS LADYSMITH

Calibers: .38 Special +P, .357 Mag. **Capacity:** 5-round cylinder. **Barrels:** 1.875 in. (642LS); 2.125 in. (60LS) **Weights:** 14.5 oz. (642LS); 21.5 oz. (60LS); **Length:** 6.6 in. overall (60LS). **Grips:** Wood. **Sights:** Black blade, serrated ramp front, fixed notch rear. 642 CT has Crimson Trace Laser Grips. **Features:** 60LS model has a Chiefs Special-style frame. 642LS has Centennial-style frame, frosted matte finish, smooth combat wood grips. Introduced 1996. Comes in a fitted carry/storage case. Introduced 1989. Made in USA by Smith & Wesson.

Price: (642LS)	**$499.00**
Price: (60LS)	**$759.00**
Price: (642 CT)	**$699.00**

SMITH & WESSON MODEL 63

Caliber: .22 LR **Capacity:** 8-round cylinder. **Barrel:** 3 in. **Weight:** 26 oz. **Length:** 7.25 in. overall. **Grips:** Black synthetic. **Sights:** Hi-Viz fiber optic front sight, adjustable black blade rear sight. **Features:** Stainless steel construction throughout. Made in USA by Smith & Wesson.

Price:	**$769.00**

Prices given are believed to be accurate at time of publication however, many factors affect retail pricing so exact prices are not possible.

SMITH & WESSON MODEL 442/637/638/642 AIRWEIGHT
Caliber: .38 Special +P. **Capacity:** 5-round cylinder. **Barrels:** 1.875 in., 2.5 in. **Weight:** 15 oz. **Length:** 6.375 in. overall. **Grips:** Soft rubber. **Sights:** Fixed, serrated ramp front, square notch rear. **Features:** A family of J-frame .38 Special revolvers with aluminum-alloy frames. Model 637; Chiefs Special-style frame with exposed hammer. Introduced 1996. Models 442, 642; Centennial-style frame, enclosed hammer. Model 638, Bodyguard style, shrouded hammer. Comes in a fitted carry/storage case. Introduced 1989. Made in USA by Smith & Wesson.
Price: From **$469.00**
Price: Laser Max Frame Mounted Red Laser sight **$539.00**

SMITH & WESSON MODELS 637 CT/638 CT
Similar to Models 637, 638 and 642 but with Crimson Trace Laser Grips.
Price: **$699.00**

SMITH & WESSON MODEL 340/340PD AIRLITE SC CENTENNIAL
Calibers: .357 Mag., 38 Special +P. **Capacity:** 5-round cylinder. **Barrel:** 1.875 in. **Weight:** 12 oz. **Length:** 6.375 in. overall (1.875-in. barrel). **Grips:** Rounded butt rubber. **Sights:** Black blade front, rear notch **Features:** Centennial-style frame, enclosed hammer. Internal lock. Matte silver finish. Scandium alloy frame, titanium cylinder, stainless steel barrel liner. Made in USA by Smith & Wesson.
Price: **$1,019.00**

SMITH & WESSON MODEL 351PD
Caliber: .22 Mag. **Capacity:** 5-round cylinder. **Barrel:** 1.875 in. **Weight:** 10.6 oz. **Length:** 6.25 in. overall (1.875-in. barrel). **Sights:** HiViz front sight, rear notch. **Grips:** Wood. **Features:** 7-shot, aluminum-alloy frame. Chiefs Special-style frame with exposed hammer. Nonreflective matte-black finish. Internal lock. Made in USA by Smith & Wesson.
Price: **$759.00**

SMITH & WESSON MODEL 360/360PD AIRLITE CHIEF'S SPECIAL
Calibers: .357 Mag., .38 Special +P. **Capacity:** 5-round cylinder. **Barrel:** 1.875 in. **Weight:** 12 oz. **Length:** 6.375 in. overall (1.875-in. barrel). **Grips:** Rounded butt rubber. **Sights:** Red ramp front, fixed rear notch. **Features:** Chief's Special-style frame with exposed hammer. Internal lock. Scandium alloy frame, titanium cylinder, stainless steel barrel. Model 360 has unfluted cylinder. Made in USA by Smith & Wesson.
Price: 360 .... **$770.00**
Price: 360PD **$1,019.00**

SMITH & WESSON MODEL 317 AIRLITE
Caliber: .22 LR. **Capacity:** 8-round cylinder. **Barrel:** 1.875 in. **Weight:** 10.5 oz. **Length:** 6.25 in. overall (1.875-in. barrel). **Grips:** Rubber. **Sights:** Serrated ramp front, fixed notch rear. **Features:** Aluminum alloy, carbon and stainless steels, Chiefs Special-style frame with exposed hammer. Smooth combat trigger. Clear Cote finish. Model 317 Kit Gun has adjustable rear sight, fiber optic front. Introduced 1997.
Price: **$759.00**

Prices given are believed to be accurate at time of publication however, many factors affect retail pricing so exact prices are not possible.

75TH EDITION, 2021 ✦ **487**

SMITH & WESSON BODYGUARD 38
Caliber: .38 Special +P. **Capacity:** 5-round cylinder. **Barrel:** 1.9 in. **Weight:** 14.3 oz. **Length:** 6.6 in. **Grip:** Synthetic. **Sights:** Front: Black ramp, Rear: fixed, integral with backstrap. Plus: Integrated laser sight. **Finish:** Matte black. **Features:** The first personal protection series that comes with an integrated laser sight.
Price: **$539.00**

SMITH & WESSON MODEL 640 CENTENNIAL DA ONLY
Calibers: .357 Mag., .38 Special +P. **Capacity:** 5-round cylinder. **Barrel:** 2.125 in. **Weight:** 23 oz. **Length:** 6.75 in. overall. **Grips:** Uncle Mike's Boot grip. **Sights:** Tritium Night Sights. **Features:** Stainless steel. Fully concealed hammer, snag-proof smooth edges. Internal lock.
Price: **$839.00**

SMITH & WESSON MODEL 649 BODYGUARD
Caliber: .357 Mag., .38 Special +P. **Capacity:** 5-round cylinder. **Barrel:** 2.125 in. **Weight:** 23 oz. **Length:** 6.625 in. overall. **Grips:** Uncle Mike's Combat. **Sights:** Black pinned ramp front, fixed notch rear. **Features:** Stainless steel construction, satin finish. Internal lock. Bodyguard style, shrouded hammer. Made in USA by Smith & Wesson.
Price: **$729.00**

SMITH & WESSON K-FRAME/L-FRAME
The K-frame series are mid-size revolvers and the L-frames are slightly larger.

SMITH & WESSON MODEL 10 CLASSIC
Caliber: .38 Special. **Capacity:** 6-round cylinder. **Features:** Bright blued steel frame and cylinder, checkered wood grips, 4-inch barrel and fixed sights. The oldest model in the Smith & Wesson line, its basic design goes back to the original Military & Police Model of 1905.
Price: **$739.00**

SMITH & WESSON MODEL 17 MASTERPIECE CLASSIC
Caliber: .22 LR. **Capacity:** 6-round cylinder. **Barrel:** 6 in. **Weight:** 40 oz. **Grips:** Checkered wood. **Sights:** Pinned Patridge front, micro-adjustable rear. Updated variation of K-22 Masterpiece of the 1930s.
Price: **$989.00**

SMITH & WESSON MODEL 19 CLASSIC
Caliber: .357 Magnum. **Capacity:** 6-round cylinder **Barrel:** 4.25 in. **Weight:** 37.2 oz. **Grips:** Walnut. **Sights:** Adjustable rear, red ramp front. **Finish:** Polished blue. Classic-style thumbpiece. Reintroduced 2019.
Price: **$826.00**

SMITH & WESSON MODEL 48 CLASSIC
Same specifications as Model 17 except chambered in .22 Magnum (.22 WMR) and is available with a 4- or 6-inch barrel.
Price: .... **$949.00–$989.00**

SMITH & WESSON MODEL 64/67
Caliber: .38 Special +P. **Capacity:** 6-round cylinder **Barrel:** 3 in. **Weight:** 33 oz. **Length:** 8.875 in. overall. **Grips:** Soft rubber. **Sights:** Fixed, .125-in. serrated ramp front, square notch rear. Model 67 is similar to Model 64 except for adjustable sights. **Features:** Satin finished stainless steel, square butt.
Price: From .... **$689.00–$749.00**

SMITH & WESSON MODEL 66
Caliber: .357 Magnum. **Capacity:** 6-round cylinder. **Barrel:** 4.25 in. **Weight:** 36.6 oz. **Grips:** Synthetic. **Sights:** White outline adjustable rear, red ramp front. **Features:** Return in 2014 of the famous K-frame "Combat Magnum" with stainless finish.
Price: **$849.00**

SMITH & WESSON MODEL 69
Caliber: .44 Magnum. **Capacity:** 5-round cylinder. **Barrel:** 4.25 in. **Weight:** 37 oz. **Grips:** Checkered wood. **Sights:** White outline adjustable rear, red ramp front. **Features:** L-frame with stainless finish, 5-shot cylinder, introduced in 2014.
Price: **$989.00**

SMITH & WESSON MODEL 610
Caliber: 10mm. **Capacity:** 6-round cylinder. Barrels: 4.25 and 6 in. **Grips:** Walnut. **Sights:** Fully adjustable rear, fixed red ramp interchangeable front. Weights: 42.6 oz. (4.25 in.), 50.1 oz (6 in.). **Features:** Built on Smith & Wesson's large N-frame in stainless steel only. Will also fire .40 S&W ammunition. Comes with three moon clips.
Price: **$987.00**

SMITH & WESSON MODEL 617
Caliber: .22 LR. **Capacity:** 10-round cylinder. **Barrel:** 6 in. **Weight:** 44 oz. **Length:** 11.125 in. **Grips:** Soft rubber. **Sights:** Patridge front, adjustable rear. Drilled and tapped for scope mount. **Features:** Stainless steel with satin finish. Introduced 1990.
Price: From **$829.00**

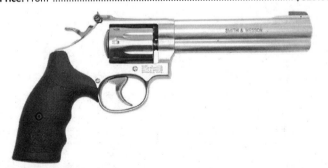

SMITH & WESSON MODEL 648
Caliber: .22 Magnum. **Capacity:** 8-round cylinder. **Barrel:** 6 in. **Grips:** Walnut. **Sights:** Fully adjustable rear, Patridge front. **Weight:** 46.2 oz. **Features:** This reintroduction was originally released in 1989 and produced until 2005. Ideal for target shooting or small-game hunting.
Price: **$752.00**

SMITH & WESSON MODEL 686/686 PLUS
Caliber: .357 Mag/.38 Special. **Capacity:** 6 (686) or 7 (Plus). **Barrels:** 6 in. (686), 3 or 6 in. (686 Plus), 4 in. (SSR). **Weight:** 35 oz. (3 in. barrel). **Grips:** Rubber. **Sights:** White outline adjustable rear, red ramp front. **Features:** Satin stainless frame and cylinder. Stock Service Revolver (SSR) has tapered underlug, interchangeable front sight, high-hold ergonomic wood grips, chamfered charge holes, custom barrel w/recessed crown, bossed mainspring.
Price: 686 .... **$829.00**
Price: Plus **$849.00**
Price: SSR **$999.00**

SMITH & WESSON MODEL 986 PRO
Caliber: 9mm. **Capacity:** 7-round cylinder **Barrel:** 5-in. tapered underlug. **Features:** SA/DA L-frame revolver chambered in 9mm. Features similar to 686 PLUS Pro Series with 5-inch tapered underlug barrel, satin stainless finish, synthetic grips, adjustable rear and Patridge blade front sight.
Price: **$1,149.00**

SMITH & WESSON M&P R8
Caliber: .357 Mag. **Capacity:** 8-round cylinder. **Barrel:** 5-in. half lug with accessory rail. **Weight:** 36.3 oz. **Length:** 10.5 in. **Grips:** Black synthetic. **Sights:** Adjustable v-notch rear, interchangeable front. **Features:** Scandium alloy frame, stainless steel cylinder.
Price: **$1,329.00**

SMITH & WESSON N-FRAME
These large-frame models introduced the .357, .41 and .44 Magnums to the world.

SMITH & WESSON MODEL 25 CLASSIC
Calibers: .45 Colt or .45 ACP. **Capacity:** 6-round cylinder. **Barrel:** 6.5 in. **Weight:** 45 oz. **Grips:** Checkered wood. **Sights:** Pinned Patridge front, micro-adjustable rear.
Price: **$1,019.00**

Prices given are believed to be accurate at time of publication however, many factors affect retail pricing so exact prices are not possible.

75TH EDITION, 2021 ◈ **489**

SMITH & WESSON MODEL 27 CLASSIC

Caliber: .357 Magnum. **Capacity:** 6-round cylinder. **Barrels:** 4 or 6.5 in. **Weight:** 41.2 oz. **Grips:** Checkered wood. **Sights:** Pinned Patridge front, micro-adjustable rear. Updated variation of the first magnum revolver, the .357 Magnum of 1935.

Price: (4 in.) **$1,019.00**
Price: (6.5 in.) **$1,059.00**

SMITH & WESSON MODEL 29 CLASSIC

Caliber: .44 Magnum **Capacity:** 6-round cylinder. **Barrel:** 4 or 6.5 in. **Weight:** 48.5 oz. **Length:** 12 in. **Grips:** Altamont service walnut. **Sights:** Adjustable white-outline rear, red ramp front. **Features:** Carbon steel frame, polished-blued or nickel finish. Has integral key lock safety feature to prevent accidental discharges. Original Model 29 made famous by "Dirty Harry" character played in 1971 by Clint Eastwood.

Price: .... **$999.00–$1,169.00**

SMITH & WESSON MODEL 57 CLASSIC

Caliber: .41 Magnum. **Capacity:** 6-round cylinder. **Barrel:** 6 in. **Weight:** 48 oz. **Grips:** Checkered wood. **Sights:** Pinned red ramp, micro-adjustable rear.

Price: **$1,009.00**

SMITH & WESSON MODEL 329PD ALASKA BACKPACKER

Caliber: .44 Magnum. **Capacity:** 6-round cylinder. **Barrel:** 2.5 in. **Weight:** 26 oz. **Length:** 9.5 in. **Grips:** Synthetic. **Sights:** Adj. rear, HiViz orange-dot front. **Features:** Scandium alloy frame, blue/black finish, stainless steel cylinder.

Price: From **$1,159.00**

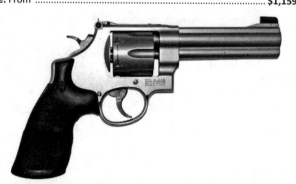

SMITH & WESSON MODEL 625/625JM

Caliber: .45 ACP. **Capacity:** 6-round cylinder. **Barrels:** 4 in., 5 in. **Weight:** 43 oz. (4-in. barrel). **Length:** 9.375 in. overall (4-in. barrel). **Grips:** Soft rubber; wood optional. **Sights:** Patridge front on ramp, S&W micrometer click rear adjustable for windage and elevation. **Features:** Stainless steel construction with .400-in. wide semi-target hammer, .312-in. smooth combat trigger; full lug barrel. Glass beaded finish. Introduced 1989. Jerry Miculek Professional (JM) Series has .265-in. wide grooved trigger, special wooden Miculek Grip, five full moon clips, gold bead Patridge front sight on interchangeable front sight base, bead blast finish. Unique serial number run. Mountain Gun has 4-in. tapered barrel, drilled and tapped, Hogue Rubber Monogrip, pinned black ramp front sight, micrometer click-adjustable rear sight, satin stainless frame and barrel weighs 39.5 oz.

Price: 625 or 625JM **$1,074.00**

SMITH & WESSON MODEL 629

Calibers: .44 Magnum, .44 S&W Special. **Capacity:** 6-round cylinder. **Barrels:** 4 in., 5 in., 6.5 in. **Weight:** 41.5 oz. (4-in. bbl.). **Length:** 9.625 in. overall (4-in. bbl.). **Grips:** Soft rubber; wood optional. **Sights:** .125-in. red ramp front, white outline rear, internal lock, adjustable for windage and elevation. Classic similar to standard Model 629, except Classic has full-lug 5-in. barrel, chamfered front of cylinder, interchangeable red ramp front sight with adjustable white outline rear, Hogue grips with S&W monogram, drilled and tapped for scope mounting. Factory accurizing and endurance packages. Introduced 1990. Classic Power Port has Patridge front sight and adjustable rear sight. Model 629CT has 5-in. barrel, Crimson Trace Hoghunter Lasergrips, 10.5 in. OAL, 45.5 oz. weight. Introduced 2006.

Price: From **$949.00**

SMITH & WESSON X-FRAME

These extra-large X-frame S&W revolvers push the limits of big-bore handgunning.

SMITH & WESSON MODEL 500

Caliber: 500 S&W Magnum. **Capacity:** 5-round cylinder. **Barrels:** 4 in., 6.5 in., 8.375 in. **Weight:** 72.5 oz. **Length:** 15 in. (8.375-in. barrel). **Grips:** Hogue Sorbothane Rubber. **Sights:** Interchangeable blade, front, adjustable rear. **Features:** Recoil compensator, ball detent cylinder latch, internal lock. 6.5-in.-barrel model has orange-ramp dovetail Millett front sight, adjustable black rear sight, Hogue Dual Density Monogrip, .312-in. chrome trigger with overtravel stop, chrome tear-drop hammer, glass bead finish. 10.5-in.-barrel model has red ramp front sight, adjustable rear sight, .312-in. chrome trigger with overtravel stop, chrome teardrop hammer with pinned sear, hunting sling. Compensated Hunter has .400-in. orange ramp dovetail front sight, adjustable black blade rear sight, Hogue Dual Density Monogrip, glass bead finish w/black clear coat. Made in USA by Smith & Wesson.

Price: From **$1,299.00**

SMITH & WESSON MODEL 460V

Caliber: 460 S&W Magnum (Also chambers .454 Casull, .45 Colt). **Capacity:** 5-round cylinder. **Barrels:** 7.5 in., 8.375-in. gain-twist rifling. **Weight:** 62.5 oz. **Length:** 11.25 in. **Grips:** Rubber. **Sights:** Adj. rear, red ramp front. **Features:** Satin stainless steel frame and cylinder, interchangeable compensator. 460XVR (X-treme Velocity Revolver) has black blade front sight with interchangeable green Hi-Viz tubes, adjustable rear sight. 7.5-in.-barrel version has Lothar-Walther barrel, 360-degree recoil compensator, tuned Performance Center action, pinned sear, integral Weaver base, non-glare surfaces, scope mount accessory kit for mounting full-size scopes, flashed-chromed hammer and trigger, Performance Center gun rug and shoulder sling. Interchangeable Hi-Viz green dot front sight, adjustable black rear sight, Hogue Dual Density Monogrip, matte-black frame and shroud finish with glass-bead cylinder finish, 72 oz. Compensated Hunter has teardrop chrome hammer, .312-in. chrome trigger, Hogue Dual Density Monogrip, satin/matte stainless finish, HiViz interchangeable front sight, adjustable black rear sight. XVR introduced 2006.

Price: 460V **$1,369.00**
Price: 460XVR, fr **$1,369.00**

Prices given are believed to be accurate at time of publication however, many factors affect retail pricing so exact prices are not possible.

STANDARD MANUFACTURING S333 THUNDERSTRUCK
Caliber: .22 Magnum. **Capacity:** 8-round cylinder. **Barrel:** 1.25 in. **Grips:** Polymer. **Sights:** Fixed front and rear. **Weight:** 18 oz. **Features:** Designed to be the ultimate in personal protection and featuring two-barrels that fire simultaneously with each trigger pull. The DA revolver has an 8-round, .22 Magnum capacity. Frame is constructed of 7075 aircraft-grade aluminum with anodized finish.
Price: $429.00

SUPER SIX CLASSIC BISON BULL
Caliber: .45-70 Government. **Capacity:** 6-round cylinder. **Barrel:** 10in. octagonal with 1:14 twist. **Weight:** 6 lbs. **Length:** 17.5 in. overall. **Grips:** NA. **Sights:** Ramp front sight with dovetailed blade, click-adjustable rear. **Features:** Manganese bronze frame. Integral scope mount, manual cross-bolt safety.
Price: $1,500.00

TAURUS 942
Caliber: .22 LR. **Capacity:** 8-round cylinder. **Barrels:** 2 and 3 in. **Grips:** Soft rubber. **Sights:** Drift-adjustable rear, serrated-ramp front. **Weight:** 17.8, 25 oz. **Features:** The 942 is based closely on the Taurus 856 revolver, but chambered in .22 LR with an 8-shot cylinder. Eight models are available: 2- and 3-inch-barrel models with a steel-alloy frame and cylinder in matte-black finish, 2- and 3-inch-barrel models with an ultralight aluminum-alloy frame in hard-coat, black-anodized finish, 2- and 3-inch-barrel models with a stainless steel frame and cylinder in a matte finish, and 2- and 3-inch-barrel models with an ultralight aluminum-alloy frame in a stainless-matte finish. Imported by Taurus International.
Prce: .... $369.52 - $384.97

TAURUS DEFENDER 856
Caliber: .38 Special +P. **Capacity:** 6-round cylinder. **Barrel:** 3 in. **Grips:** Hogue rubber, VZ black/gray, walnut. **Sights:** Fixed rear, tritium night sight with bright orange outline. **Features:** The Defender 856 is built on Taurus' small frame, making for a compact defensive revolver. Four standard models are available to include a stainless steel frame with matte finish, an ultralight aluminum-alloy frame with matte finish, stainless steel frame with black Tenifer finish, and an aluminum-alloy frame with hard-coat, black-anodized finish. Two upgrade versions are available with special grips and finish treatments. Imported by Taurus International.
Price: ....$429.00 - $477.00

TAURUS MODEL 17 TRACKER
Caliber: .17 HMR. **Capacity:** 7-round cylinder. **Barrel:** 6.5 in. **Weight:** 45.8 oz. **Grips:** Rubber. **Sights:** Adjustable. **Features:** Double action, matte stainless, integral key-lock.
Price: From $539.00

TAURUS MODEL 992 TRACKER
Calibers: .22 LR with interchangeable .22 WMR cylinder. **Capacity:** 9-round cylinder. **Barrel:** 4 or 6.5 in with ventilated rib. **Features:** Adjustable rear sight, blued or stainless finish.
Price: Blue $640.00
Price: Stainless $692.00

TAURUS MODEL 44SS
Caliber: .44 Magnum. **Capacity:** 5-round cylinder. **Barrel:** Ported, 4, 6.5, 8.4 in. **Weight:** 34 oz. **Grips:** Rubber. **Sights:** Adjustable. **Features:** Double action. Integral key-lock. Introduced 1994. Finish: Matte stainless. Imported from Brazil by Taurus International Manufacturing, Inc.
Price: From ....$648.00-$664.00

TAURUS MODEL 65
Caliber: .357 Magnum. **Capacity:** 6-round cylinder. **Barrel:** 4-in. full underlug. **Weight:** 38 oz. **Length:** 10.5 in. overall. **Grips:** Soft rubber. **Sights:** Fixed. **Features:** Double action, integral key-lock. Matte blued or stainless. Imported by Taurus International.
Price: Blued $539.00
Price: Stainless $591.00

TAURUS MODEL 66
Similar to Model 65, 4 in. or 6 in. barrel, 7-round cylinder, adjustable rear sight. Integral key-lock action. Imported by Taurus International.
Price: Blue $599.00
Price: Stainless $652.00

TAURUS MODEL 82 HEAVY BARREL
Caliber: .38 Special. **Capacity:** 6-round cylinder. **Barrel:** 4 in., heavy. **Weight:** 36.5 oz. **Length:** 9.25 in. overall. **Grips:** Soft black rubber. **Sights:** Serrated ramp front, square notch rear. **Features:** Double action, solid rib, integral key-lock. Imported by Taurus International.
Price: From $521.00

Prices given are believed to be accurate at time of publication however, many factors affect retail pricing so exact prices are not possible.

75TH EDITION, 2021 ✛ 491

TAURUS MODEL 85FS
Caliber: .38 Special. **Capacity:** 5-round cylinder. **Barrel:** 2 in. **Weights:** 17–24.5 oz., titanium 13.5–15.4 oz. **Grips:** Rubber, rosewood or mother of pearl. **Sights:** Ramp front, square notch rear. **Features:** Spurred hammer. Blued, matte stainless, blue with gold accents, stainless with gold accents; rated for +P ammo. Integral keylock. Some models have titanium frame. Introduced 1980. Imported by Taurus International.
Price: From **$379.00**

TAURUS MODEL 856 ULTRALIGHT
Caliber: .38 Special. **Capacity:** 6-round cylinder. **Barrel:** 2 in. Matte black or stainless. **Weights:** 15.7 oz., titanium 13.5–15.4 oz. **Grips:** Rubber, rosewood or mother of pearl. **Sights:** Serrated ramp front, square notch rear. **Features:** Aluminum frame, matte black or stainless cylinder, azure blue, bronze, burnt orange or rouge finish.
Price: .... **$364.00-$461.00**

TAURUS 380 MINI
Caliber: .380 ACP. **Capacity:** 5-round cylinder w/moon clip. **Barrel:** 1.75 in. **Weight:** 15.5 oz. **Length:** 5.95 in. **Grips:** Rubber. **Sights:** Adjustable rear, fixed front. **Features:** DAO. Available in blued or stainless finish. Five Star (moon) clips included.
Price: Blued **$478.00**
Price: Stainless **$514.00**

TAURUS MODEL 45-410 JUDGE
Calibers: 2.5-in. .410/.45 Colt, 3-in. .410/.45 Colt. **Barrels:** 3 in., 6.5 in. (blued finish). **Weights:** 35.2 oz., 22.4 oz. **Length:** 7.5 in. **Grips:** Ribber rubber. **Sights:** Fiber Optic. **Features:** DA/SA. Matte stainless and ultra-lite stainless finish. Introduced in 2007. Imported from Brazil by Taurus International.
Price: From **$511.00**

TAURUS JUDGE PUBLIC DEFENDER POLYMER
Caliber: .45 Colt/.410 (2.5 in.). **Capacity:** 5-round cylinder. **Barrel:** 2.5-in. **Weight:** 27 oz. **Features:** SA/DA revolver with 5-round cylinder; polymer frame; Ribber rubber-feel grips; fiber-optic front sight; adjustable rear sight; blued or stainless cylinder; shrouded hammer with cocking spur; blued finish.
Price: From **$469.00**

TAURUS RAGING HUNTER
Calibers: .357 Magnum, .44 Magnum, .454 Casull. **Capacity:** 7 (.357), 6 (.44) and 5 (.454) rounds. **Barrels:** 5.12, 6.75, 8.37 in. **Grips:** Cushioned rubber. **Sights:** Adjustable rear, fixed front. **Weight:** 49 - 59.2 oz. **Features:** This is a DA/SA big-game-hunting revolver, available in three calibers and three barrel lengths, each featuring a Picatinny rail for easy optic mounting without removing the iron sights. All Raging Hunter models come with factory porting and cushioned rubber grips. Two finishes are available: matte black and two-tone matte stainless. Imported by Taurus International.
Prce: **$919.55**

TAURUS MODEL 627 TRACKER
Caliber: .357 Magnum. **Capacity:** 7-round cylinder. **Barrels:** 4 or 6.5 in. **Weights:** 28.8, 41 oz. **Grips:** Rubber. **Sights:** Fixed front, adjustable rear. **Features:** Double-action. Stainless steel, Shadow Gray or Total Titanium; vent rib (steel models only); integral key-lock action. Imported by Taurus International.
Price: From **$577.00**

TAURUS MODEL 444 ULTRA-LIGHT
Caliber: .44 Magnum. **Capacity:** 5-round cylinder. **Barrels:** 2.5 or 4 in. **Weight:** 28.3 oz. **Grips:** Cushioned inset rubber. **Sights:** Fixed red-fiber optic front, adjustable rear. **Features:** UltraLite titanium blue finish, titanium/alloy frame built on Raging Bull design. Smooth trigger shoe, 1.760-in. wide, 6.280-in. tall. Barrel rate of twist 1:16, 6 grooves. Introduced 2005. Imported by Taurus International.
Price: **$944.00**

TAURUS MODEL 444/454 RAGING BULL SERIES
Calibers: .44 Magnum, .454 Casull. **Barrels:** 2.25 in., 5 in., 6.5 in., 8.375 in. **Weight:** 53–63 oz. **Length:** 12 in. overall (6.5 in. barrel). **Grips:** Soft black rubber. **Sights:** Patridge front, adjustable rear. **Features:** DA, ventilated rib, integral key-lock. Most models have ported barrels. Introduced 1997. Imported by Taurus International.
Price: 444 .... **$900.00**
Price: 454 .... **$1,204.00**

Prices given are believed to be accurate at time of publication however, many factors affect retail pricing so exact prices are not possible.

TAURUS RAGING HUNTER

Caliber: .44 Magnum. **Capacity:** 6-round cylinder. **Barrel:** 8.375 in. **Sights:** Adjustable rear, fixed front. **Grips:** Soft rubber with cushioned inset. **Weight:** 55 oz. **Features:** DA, ventilated rib. Imported by Taurus International.
Price: $919.00

TAURUS MODEL 605 PLY

Caliber: .357 Magnum. **Capacity:** 5-round cylinder. **Barrel:** 2 in. **Weight:** 20 oz. **Grips:** Rubber. **Sights:** Fixed. **Features:** Polymer frame steel cylinder. Blued or stainless. Introduced 1995. Imported by Taurus International.
Price: Blued $393.00
Price: Stainless $410.00

TAURUS MODEL 905

Caliber: 9mm. **Capacity:** 5-round cylinder. **Barrel:** 2 in. **Features:** Small-frame revolver with rubber boot grips, fixed sights, choice of exposed or concealed hammer. Blued or stainless finish.
Price: Blued $531.00
Price: Stainless $583.00

TAURUS MODEL 692

Calibers: .38 Special/.357 Magnum or 9mm. **Capacity:** 7-round cylinder. **Barrels:** 3 or 6.5 in, ported. **Sights:** Adjustable rear, fixed front. **Grip:** "Ribber" textured. **Finish:** Matte blued or stainless. **Features:** Caliber can be changed with a swap of the cylinders which are non-fluted.
Price: $659.00

Prices given are believed to be accurate at time of publication however, many factors affect retail pricing so exact prices are not possible.

75TH EDITION, 2021 ⬦ 493

CIMARRON 1872 OPEN TOP
Calibers: .38, .44 Special, .44 Colt, .44 Russian, .45 LC, .45 S&W Schofield. **Barrels:** 5.5 in. and 7.5 in. **Grips:** Walnut. **Sights:** Blade front, fixed rear. **Features:** Replica of first cartridge-firing revolver. Blued finish; Navy-style brass or steel Army-style frame. Introduced 2001 by Cimarron F.A. Co.
Price: Navy model $529.00
Price: Army $550.00

CIMARRON 1875 OUTLAW
Calibers: .357 Magnum, .38 Special, .44 W.C.F., .45 Colt, .45 ACP. **Barrels:** 5.5 in. and 7.5 in. **Weight:** 2.5–2.6 lbs. **Grip:** 1-piece walnut. **Features:** Standard blued finish with color casehardened frame. Replica of 1875 Remington model. Available with dual .45 Colt/.45 ACP cylinder.
Price: $578.00
Price: Dual Cyl. $686.00

CIMARRON MODEL 1890
Caliber: .357 Magnum, .38 Special, .44 W.C.F., .45 Colt, .45 ACP. **Barrel:** 5.5 in. **Weight:** 2.4-2.5 lbs. **Grip:** 1-piece walnut. **Features:** Standard blued finish with standard blue frame. Replica of 1890 Remington model. Available with dual .45 Colt/.45 ACP cylinder.
Price: $606.00
Price: Dual Cylinder $702.00

CIMARRON BISLEY MODEL SINGLE-ACTION
Calibers: .357 Magnum, .44 WCF, .44 Special, .45. **Features:** Similar to Colt Bisley, special grip frame and trigger guard, knurled wide-spur hammer, curved trigger. Introduced 1999. Imported by Cimarron F.A. Co.
Price: From $636.00

CIMARRON LIGHTNING SA
Calibers: .22 LR, .32-20/.32 H&R dual cyl. combo, .38 Special, .41 Colt. **Barrels:** 3.5 in., 4.75 in., 5.5 in. **Grips:** Smooth or checkered walnut. **Sights:** Blade front. **Features:** Replica of the Colt 1877 Lightning DA. Similar to Cimarron Thunderer, except smaller grip frame to fit smaller hands. Standard blued, charcoal blued or nickel finish with forged, old model, or color casehardened frame. Dual cylinder model available with .32-30/.32 H&R chambering. Introduced 2001. From Cimarron F.A. Co.
Price: From .... $503.00–$565.00
Price: .32-20/.32 H&R dual cylinder $649.00

CIMARRON MODEL P SAA
Calibers: .32 WCF, .38 WCF, .357 Magnum, .44 WCF, .44 Special, .45 Colt and .45 ACP. **Barrels:** 4.75, 5.5, 7.5 in. **Weight:** 39 oz. **Length:** 10 in. overall (4.75-in. barrel). **Grips:** Walnut. **Sights:** Blade front. **Features:** Old model black-powder frame with Bullseye ejector, or New Model frame. Imported by Cimarron F.A. Co.
Price: From $550.00

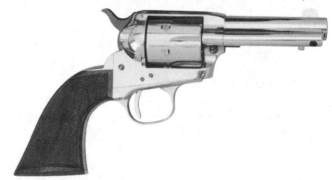

CIMARRON MODEL "P" JR.
Calibers: .22 LR, .32-20, .32 H&R, 38 Special **Barrels:** 3.5, 4.75, 5.5 in. **Grips:** Checkered walnut. **Sights:** Blade front. **Features:** Styled after 1873 Colt Peacemaker, except 20 percent smaller. Blue finish with color case-hardened frame; Cowboy action. Introduced 2001. From Cimarron F.A. Co.
Price: From $480.00

CIMARRON ROOSTER SHOOTER
Calibers: .357, .45 Colt and .44 W.C.F. **Barrel:** 4.75 in. **Weight:** 2.5 lbs. **Grip:** 1-piece orange finger grooved. **Features:** A replica of John Wayne's Colt Single Action Army model used in many of his great Westerns including his Oscar-winning performance in "True Grit," where he brings the colorful character Rooster Cogburn to life.
Price: $909.00

CIMARRON THUNDERER
Calibers: .357 Magnum, .44 WCF, .45 Colt. **Capacity:** 6-round cylinder. **Features:** Doc Holiday combo comes with leather shoulder holster, ivory handled dagger. Gun and knife have matching serial numbers. Made by Uberti.
Price: From .... $575.00–$948.00
Price: Combo $1,559.00

CIMARRON FRONTIER
Calibers: .357 Magnum, .44 WCF, .45 Colt. **Barrels:** 3.5, 4.75, 5.5 or 7.5 in. **Features:** Basic SAA design. Choice of Old Model or Pre-War frame. Blued or stainless finish. Available with Short Stroke action.
Price: Blued $530.00
Price: Stainless $723.00
Price: Short Stroke Action $598.00

Prices given are believed to be accurate at time of publication however, many factors affect retail pricing so exact prices are not possible.

CIMARRON U.S.V. ARTILLERY MODEL SINGLE-ACTION
Caliber: .45 Colt. **Barrel:** 5.5 in. **Weight:** 39 oz. **Length:** 11.5 in. overall. **Grips:** Walnut. **Sights:** Fixed. **Features:** U.S. markings and cartouche, casehardened frame and hammer. Imported by Cimarron F.A. Co.
Price: Blued finish.. **$594.00**
Price: Original finish **$701.00**

CIMARRON BAD BOY
Calibers: .44 Magnum, 10mm. **Capacity:** 6-round cylinder. **Barrel:** 8 in. **Grips:** Walnut. **Sights:** Fully adjustable rear, fixed front. **Features:** Built on a replica Single Action Army Pre-War frame with an 1860 Army-style, one-piece walnut grip. The carbon-alloy steel frame is covered in a classic blue finish and it is fitted with an 8-inch octagon barrel and adjustable sights, and chambered in the popular semi-auto 10mm round in 2020.
Price: **$726.05**

COLT NEW FRONTIER
Calibers: .357 Magnum, .44 Special and .45 Colt. **Barrels:** 4.75 in., 5.5 in., and 7.5 in. **Grip:** Walnut. **Features:** From 1890 to 1898, Colt manufactured a variation of the venerable Single Action Army with a uniquely different profile. The "Flattop Target Model" was fitted with an adjustable leaf rear sight and blade front sights. Colt has taken this concept several steps further to bring shooters a reintroduction of a Colt classic. The New Frontier has that sleek flattop design with an adjustable rear sight for windage and elevation and a target ready ramp-style front sight. The guns are meticulously finished in Colt Royal Blue on both the barrel and cylinder, with a case-colored frame. Additional calibers available through Colt Custom Shop.
Price: **$1,899.00**

COLT SINGLE ACTION ARMY
Calibers: .357 Magnum, .45 Colt. **Capacity:** 6-round cylinder. **Barrels:** 4.75, 5.5, 7.5 in. **Weight:** 40 oz. (4.75-in. barrel). **Length:** 10.25 in. overall (4.75-in. barrel). **Grips:** Black Eagle composite. **Sights:** Blade front, notch rear. **Features:** Available in full nickel finish with nickel grip medallions, or Royal Blue with color casehardened frame. Reintroduced 1992. Additional calibers available through Colt Custom Shop.
Price: Blued **$1,599.00**
Price: Nickel.. **$1,799.00**

EAA BOUNTY HUNTER SA
Calibers: .22 LR/.22 WMR, .357 Mag., .44 Mag., .45 Colt. **Capacities:** 6. 10-round cylinder available for .22LR/.22WMR. **Barrels:** 4.5 in., 7.5 in. **Weight:** 2.5 lbs. **Length:** 11 in. overall (4.625 in. barrel). **Grips:** Smooth walnut. **Sights:** Blade front, grooved topstrap rear. **Features:** Transfer bar safety; 3-position hammer; hammer-forged barrel. Introduced 1992. Imported by European American Armory
Price: Centerfire, blued or case-hardened **$478.00**
Price: Centerfire, nickel **$515.00**
Price: .22 LR/.22 WMR, blued **$343.00**
Price: .22LR/.22WMR, nickel **$380.00**
Price: .22 LR/.22WMR, 10-round cylinder **$465.00**

EMF 1875 OUTLAW
Calibers: .357 Magnum, .44-40, .45 Colt. **Barrels:** 7.5 in., 9.5 in. **Weight:** 46 oz. **Length:** 13.5 in. overall. **Grips:** Smooth walnut. **Sights:** Blade front, fixed groove rear. **Features:** Authentic copy of 1875 Remington with firing pin in hammer; color casehardened frame, blued cylinder, barrel, steel backstrap and trigger guard. Also available in nickel, factory engraved. Imported by E.M.F. Co.
Price: All calibers **$520.00**
Price: Laser Engraved **$800.00**

Prices given are believed to be accurate at time of publication however, many factors affect retail pricing so exact prices are not possible.

75TH EDITION, 2021 ⬦ **495**

EMF 1873 GREAT WESTERN II
Calibers: .357 Magnum, .45 Colt, .44/40. **Barrels:** 3.5 in., 4.75 in., 5.5 in., 7.5 in. **Weight:** 36 oz. **Length:** 11 in. (5.5-in. barrel). **Grips:** Walnut. **Sights:** Blade front, notch rear. **Features:** Authentic reproduction of the original 2nd Generation Colt single-action revolver. Standard and bone casehardening. Coil hammer spring. Hammer-forged barrel. Alchimista has case-hardened frame, brass backstrap, longer and wider 1860 grip.
Price: 1873 Californian .... **$545.00–$560.00**
Price: 1873 Custom series, bone or nickel, ivory-like grips **$689.90**
Price: 1873 Stainless steel, ivory-like grips **$589.90**
Price: 1873 Paladin **$560.00**
Price: Deluxe Californian with checkered walnut grips stainless.......... **$780.00**
Price: Buntline.. **$605.00**
Price: Alchimista... **$675.00**

EMF 1873 DAKOTA II
Caliber: .357 Magnum, 45 Colt. **Barrel:** 4.75 in. **Grips:** Walnut. **Finish:** black.
Price: **$460.00**

FREEDOM ARMS MODEL 97 PREMIER GRADE
Calibers: .17 HMR, .22 LR, .32 H&R, .327 Federal, .357 Magnum, 6 rounds; .41 Magnum, .44 Special, .45 Colt. **Capacity:** 5-round cylinder. **Barrels:** 4.25 in., 5.5 in., 7.5 in., 10 in. (.17 HMR, .22 LR, .32 H&R). **Weight:** 40 oz. (5.5 in. .357 Mag.). **Length:** 10.75 in. (5.5 in. bbl.). **Grips:** Impregnated hardwood; Micarta optional. **Sights:** Adjustable rear, replaceable blade front. Fixed rear notch and front blade. **Features:** Stainless steel construction, brushed finish, automatic transfer bar safety system. Introduced in 1997. Lifetime warranty. Made in USA by Freedom Arms.
Price: From **$2,148.00**

FREEDOM ARMS MODEL 83 PREMIER GRADE
Calibers: .357 Magnum, 41 Magnum, .44 Magnum, .454 Casull, .475 Linebaugh, .500 Wyo. Exp. **Capacity:** 5-round cylinder. **Barrels:** 4.75 in., 6 in., 7.5 in., 9 in. (.357 Mag. only), 10 in. (except .357 Mag. and 500 Wyo. Exp.) **Weight:** 53 oz. (7.5-in. bbl. in .454 Casull). **Length:** 13 in. (7.5 in. bbl.). **Grips:** Impregnatedhardwood. **Sights:** Adjustable rear with replaceable front sight. Fixed rear notch and front blade. **Features:** Stainless steel construction with brushed finish; manual sliding safety bar. Micarta grips optional. 500 Wyo. Exp. Introduced 2006. Lifetime warranty. Made in USA by Freedom Arms, Inc.
Price: From **$2,738.00**

HERITAGE ROUGH RIDER
Calibers: .22 LR, 22 LR/22 WMR combo, .357 Magnum .44-40, .45 Colt. **Capacity:** 6-round cylinder. **Barrels:** 3.5 in., 4.75 in., 5.5 in., 7.5 in. **Weights:** 31–38 oz. **Grips:** Exotic cocobolo laminated wood or mother of pearl; bird's head models offered. **Sights:** Blade front, fixed rear. Adjustable sight on 4.75 in. and 5.5 in. models. **Features:** Hammer block safety. Transfer bar with Big Bores. High polish blue, black satin, silver satin, casehardened and stainless finish. Introduced 1993. Made in USA by Heritage Mfg., Inc.
Price: Rimfire calibers, From **$200.00**
Price: Centerfire calibers, From.. **$450.00**

FREEDOM ARMS MODEL 83 FIELD GRADE
Calibers: .22 LR, .357 Magnum, .41 Magnum, .44 Magnum, .454 Casull, .475 Linebaugh, .500 Wyo. Exp. **Capacity:** 5-round cylinder. **Barrels:** 4.75 in., 6 in., 7.5 in., 9 in. (.357 Mag. only). **Weight:** 56 oz. (7.5-in. bbl. in .454 Casull). **Length:** 13.1 in. (7.5 in. bbl.). **Grips:** Pachmayr standard, impregnated hardwood or Micarta optional. **Sights:** Adjustable rear with replaceable front sight. Model 83 frame. All stainless steel. Introduced 1988. Made in USA by Freedom Arms Inc.
Price: From **$2,332.00**

MAGNUM RESEARCH BFR SINGLE ACTION

Calibers: .44 Magnum, .444 Marlin, .45-70, .45 Colt/.410, .450 Marlin, .454 Casull, .460 S&W Magnum, .480 Ruger/.475 Linebaugh, .500 Linebaugh, .500 JRH, .500 S&W, .30-30. **Barrels:** 6.5 in., 7.5 in. and 10 in. **Weights:** 3.6–5.3 lbs. **Grips:** Black rubber. **Sights:** Rear sights are the same configuration as the Ruger revolvers. Many aftermarket rear sights will fit the BFR. Front sights are machined by Magnum in four heights and anodized flat black. The four heights accommodate all shooting styles, barrel lengths and calibers. All sights are interchangeable with each BFR's. **Features:** Crafted in the USA, the BFR single-action 5-shot stainless steel revolver frames are CNC machined inside and out from a pre-heat treated investment casting. This is done to prevent warping and dimensional changes or shifting that occurs during the heat treat process. Magnum Research designed the frame with large calibers and substantial recoil in mind, built to close tolerances to handle the pressure of true big-bore calibers. The BFR is equipped with a transfer bar safety feature that allows the gun to be carried safely with all five chambers loaded.
Price: ....**$1,218.00-$1,302.00**

MAGNUM RESEARCH BFR SHORT FRAME

Caliber: .357 Magnum, .44 Magnum. **Capacity:** 6-round cylinder. Barrels: 5 and 7.5 in. **Grips:** Standard rubber, Bisley, white polymer or black micarta. **Sights:** Adjustable rear, fixed front. **Weights:** 3.5, 3.65 lbs. **Features:** Made entirely of super tough 17-4PH stainless steel, BFRs are made in the United States and were designed from the outset to handle powerful revolver cartridges. The pre-eminent single-action hunting revolver. Two grip frame options available: a standard plow handle with rubber grip, and Magnum Research iteration of a Bisley with white polymer or black micarta grips.
Price: **$1,302.00**

MAGNUM RESEARCH BFR LONG FRAME

Caliber: .350 Legend. **Capacity:** 6-round cylinder. Barrels: 7.5 and 10 in. **Grips:** Standard rubber, Bisley, white polymer or black micarta. **Sights:** Adjustable rear, fixed front. **Weights:** 4.8, 5 lbs. **Features:** Built on Magnum Research's long frame and made entirely of 17-4PH stainless steel. The first long frame in six-shot configuration. Two grip frame options available: a standard plow handle with rubber grip, and Magnum Research iteration of a Bisley with white polymer or black micarta grips.
Price:... ....**$1,302.00**

NORTH AMERICAN ARMS MINI

Calibers: .22 Short, 22 LR, 22 WMR. **Capacity:** 5-round cylinder. **Barrels:** 1.125 in., 1.625 in. **Weight:** 4–6.6 oz. **Length:** 3.625 in., 6.125 in. overall. **Grips:** Laminated wood. **Sights:** Blade front, notch fixed rear. **Features:** All stainless steel construction. Polished satin and matte finish. Engraved models available. From North American Arms.
Price: .22 Short, .22 LR **$226.00**
Price: .22 WMR **$236.00**

NORTH AMERICAN ARMS MINI-MASTER

Calibers: .22 LR, .22 WMR. **Capacity:** 5-round cylinder. **Barrel:** 4 in. **Weight:** 10.7 oz. **Length:** 7.75 in. overall. **Grips:** Checkered hard black rubber. **Sights:** Blade front, white outline rear adjustable for elevation, or fixed. **Features:** Heavy vented barrel; full-size grips. Non-fluted cylinder. Introduced 1989.
Price: .... **$284.00–$349.00**

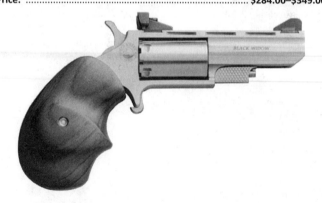

NORTH AMERICAN ARMS BLACK WIDOW

Similar to Mini-Master, 2-in. heavy vent barrel. Built on .22 WMR frame. Non-fluted cylinder, black rubber low-profile grips. Available with Millett low-profile fixed sights or Millett sight adjustable for elevation only. Overall length 5.875 in., weighs 8.8 oz. From North American Arms.
Price: Adjustable sight, .22 LR or .22 WMR **$352.00**
Price: Fixed sight, .22 LR or .22 WMR **$288.00**

NORTH AMERICAN ARMS "THE EARL" SINGLE-ACTION

Calibers: .22 Magnum with .22 LR accessory cylinder. **Capacity:** 5-round cylinder. **Barrel:** 4 in. octagonal. **Weight:** 6.8 oz. **Length:** 7.75 in. overall. **Grips:** Wood. **Sights:** Barleycorn front and fixed notch rear. **Features:** Single-action mini-revolver patterned after 1858-style Remington percussion revolver. Includes a spur trigger and a faux loading lever that serves as cylinder pin release.
Price: .... **$298.00,$332.00 (convertible)**

Prices given are believed to be accurate at time of publication however, many factors affect retail pricing so exact prices are not possible.

75TH EDITION, 2021 ◈ 497

RUGER NEW MODEL SINGLE-SIX SERIES
Calibers: .22 LR, .17 HMR. Convertible and Hunter models come with extra cylinder for .22 WMR. **Capacity:** 6. **Barrels:** 4.62 in., 5.5 in., 6.5 in. or 9.5 in. **Weight:** 35–42 oz. **Finish:** Blued or stainless. **Grips:** Black checkered hard rubber, black laminate or hardwood (stainless model only). Single-Six .17 Model available only with 6.5-in. barrel, blue finish, rubber grips. Hunter Model available only with 7.5-in. barrel, black laminate grips and stainless finish.
Price: (blued) $629.00
Price: (stainless) $699.00

RUGER SINGLE-TEN AND RUGER SINGLE-NINE SERIES
Calibers: .22 LR, .22 WMR. **Capacities:** 10 (.22 LR Single-Ten), 9 (.22 Mag Single-Nine). **Barrels:** 5.5 in. (Single-Ten), 6.5 in. (Single-Nine). **Weight:** 38–39 oz. **Grips:** Hardwood Gunfighter. **Sights:** Williams Adjustable Fiber Optic.
Price: $699.00

RUGER NEW MODEL BLACKHAWK/ BLACKHAWK CONVERTIBLE
Calibers: .30 Carbine, .357 Magnum/.38 Special, .41 Magnum, .44 Special, .45 Colt. **Capacity:** 6-round cylinder. **Barrels:** 4.625 in., 5.5 in., 6.5 in., 7.5 in. (.30 carbine and .45 Colt). **Weights:** 36–45 oz. **Lengths:** 10.375 in. to 13.5 in. **Grips:** Rosewood or black checkered. **Sights:** .125-in. ramp front, micro-click rear adjustable for windage and elevation. **Features:** Rosewood grips, Ruger transfer bar safety system, independent firing pin, hardened chrome-moly steel frame, music wire springs through-out. Case and lock included. Convertibles come with extra cylinder.
Price: (blued) $669.00
Price: (Convertible, .357/9mm) $749.00
Price: (Convertible, .45 Colt/.45 ACP) $749.00
Price: (stainless, .357 only) $799.00

RUGER BISLEY SINGLE ACTION
Calibers: .44 Magnum. and .45 Colt. **Barrel:** 7.5-in. barrel. **Length:** 13.5 in. **Weight:** 48–51 oz. Similar to standard Blackhawk, hammer is lower with smoothly curved, deeply checkered wide spur. The trigger is strongly curved with wide smooth surface. Longer grip frame. Adjustable rear sight, ramp-style front. Unfluted cylinder and roll engraving, adjustable sights. Plastic lockable case. Orig. fluted cylinder introduced 1985; discontinued 1991. Unfluted cylinder introduced 1986.
Price: $899.00

RUGER NEW MODEL SUPER BLACKHAWK
Caliber: .44 Magnum/.44 Special. **Capacity:** 6-round cylinder. **Barrel:** 4.625 in., 5.5 in., 7.5 in., 10.5 in. bull. **Weight:** 45–55 oz. **Length:** 10.5 in. to 16.5 in. overall. **Grips:** Rosewood. **Sights:** .125-in. ramp front, micro-click rear adjustable for windage and elevation. **Features:** Ruger transfer bar safety system, fluted or unfluted cylinder, steel grip and cylinder frame, round or square back trigger guard, wide serrated trigger, wide spur hammer. With case and lock.
Price: $829.00

RUGER NEW MODEL SUPER BLACKHAWK HUNTER
Caliber: .44 Magnum. **Capacity:** 6-round cylinder. **Barrel:** 7.5 in., full-length solid rib, unfluted cylinder. **Weight:** 52 oz. **Length:** 13.625 in. **Grips:** Black laminated wood. **Sights:** Adjustable rear, replaceable front blade. **Features:** Reintroduced Ultimate SA revolver. Includes instruction manual, high-impact case, set of medium scope rings, gun lock, ejector rod as standard. Bisley-style frame available.
Price: (Hunter, Bisley Hunter) $959.00

RUGER NEW VAQUERO SINGLE-ACTION
Calibers: .357 Magnum, .45 Colt. **Capacity:** 6-round cylinder. **Barrel:** 4.625 in., 5.5 in., 7.5 in. **Weight:** 39–45 oz. **Length:** 10.5 in. overall (4.625 in. barrel). **Grips:** Rubber with Ruger medallion. **Sights:** Fixed blade front, fixed notch rear. **Features:** Transfer bar safety system and loading gate interlock. Blued model color casehardened finish on frame, rest polished and blued. Engraved model available. Gloss stainless. Introduced 2005.
Price: $829.00

Prices given are believed to be accurate at time of publication however, many factors affect retail pricing so exact prices are not possible.

RUGER NEW MODEL BISLEY VAQUERO

Calibers: .357 Magnum, .45 Colt. **Capacity:** 6-round cylinder. **Barrel:** 5.5-in. **Length:** 11.12 in. **Weight:** 45 oz. **Features:** Similar to New Vaquero but with Bisley-style hammer and grip frame. Simulated ivory grips, fixed sights.
Price: $899.00

RUGER NEW BEARCAT SINGLE-ACTION

Caliber: .22 LR. **Capacity:** 6-round cylinder. **Barrel:** 4 in. **Weight:** 24 oz. **Length:** 9 in. overall. **Grips:** Smooth rosewood with Ruger medallion. **Sights:** Blade front, fixed notch rear. Distributor special edition available with adjustable sights. **Features:** Reintroduction of the Ruger Bearcat with slightly lengthened frame, Ruger transfer bar safety system. Available in blued finish only. Rosewood grips. Introduced 1996 (blued), 2003 (stainless). With case and lock.
Price: SBC-4, blued $639.00
Price: KSBC-4, satin stainless $689.00

TAYLOR'S CATTLEMAN SERIES

Calibers: .357 Magnum or 45 Colt. **Barrels:** 4.75 in., 5.5 in., or 7.5 in. **Features:** Series of Single Action Army-style revolvers made in many variations.
Price: Gunfighter w/blued & color case finish.................................... $556.00
Price: Stainless $720.00
Price: Nickel.. $672.00
Price: Charcoal blued $647.00
Price: Bird's Head 3.5- or 4.5-in. bbl., walnut grips $603.00
Price: Engraved (shown).. $925.00

UBERTI 1851–1860 CONVERSION

Calibers: .38 Special, .45 Colt. **Capacity:** 6-round engraved cylinder. **Barrels:** 4.75 in., 5.5 in., 7.5 in., 8 in. **Weight:** 2.6 lbs. (5.5-in. bbl.). **Length:** 13 in. overall (5.5-in. bbl.). **Grips:** Walnut. **Features:** Brass backstrap, trigger guard; color casehardened frame, blued barrel, cylinder. Introduced 2007.
Price: 1851 Navy $569.00
Price: 1860 Army $589.00

RUGER WRANGLER

Caliber: .22 LR. **Capacity:** 6-round cylinder. **Barrel:** 4.62 in. **Grips:** Checkered synthetic. **Sights:** Fixed front and rear. **Weight:** 30 oz. **Features:** Inexpensive to own and inexpensive to shoot, this SA revolver is built on an aluminum-alloy frame and fitted with a cold hammer-forged barrel. Available in three models with three different finishes: Black Cerakote, Silver Cerakote or Burnt Bronze Cerakote. Equipped with transfer-bar mechanism and a free-wheeling pawl, allowing for easy loading and unloading.
Price: $249.00

UBERTI 1871–1872 OPEN TOP

Calibers: .38 Special, .45 Colt. **Capacity:** 6-round engraved cylinder. **Barrels:** 4.75 in., 5.5 in., 7.5 in. **Weight:** 2.6 lbs. (5.5-in. bbl.). **Length:** 13 in. overall (5.5-in. bbl.). **Grips:** Walnut. **Features:** Blued backstrap, trigger guard; color casehardened frame, blued barrel, cylinder. Introduced 2007.
Price: .... $539.00–$569.00

STANDARD MANUFACTURING NICKEL SINGLE ACTION

Calibers: .38 Special, .45 Colt. **Capacity:** 6-round cylinder. Barrels: 4.75, 5.5 and 7.5 in. **Grips:** Walnut. **Sights:** Fixed front and rear. **Weight:** 40 oz. **Features:** This is one of the finest Single Action Army reproductions ever built, with great attention to detail. Made entirely from 4140 steel, the new nickel-plated revolvers are available in .38 special and the iconic .45 Colt. You can also opt for C-coverage engraving, making for a truly remarkable firearm. One- or two-piece walnut grips available.
Price: .... $1,995.00 - $3,495.00

Prices given are believed to be accurate at time of publication however, many factors affect retail pricing so exact prices are not possible.

75TH EDITION, 2021 ⊕ **499**

UBERTI 1873 CATTLEMAN SINGLE-ACTION

Caliber: .45 Colt. **Capacity:** 6-round cylinder. **Barrels:** 4.75 in., 5.5 in., 7.5 in. **Weight:** 2.3 lbs. (5.5-in. bbl.). **Length:** 11 in. overall (5.5-in. bbl.). **Grips:** Styles: Frisco (pearl styled); Desperado (buffalo horn styled); Chisholm (checkered walnut); Gunfighter (black checkered), Cody (ivory styled), one-piece walnut. **Sights:** Blade front, groove rear. **Features:** Steel or brass backstrap, trigger guard; color casehardened frame, blued barrel, cylinder. NM designates New Model plunger-style frame; OM designates Old Model screw cylinder pin retainer.

Price: 1873 Cattleman Frisco **$869.00**
Price: 1873 Cattleman Desperado (2006) **$889.00**
Price: 1873 Cattleman Chisholm (2006) **$599.00**
Price: 1873 Cattleman NM, blued 4.75 in. barrel **$669.00**
Price: 1873 Cattleman NM, Nickel finish, 7.5 in. barrel **$689.00**
Price: 1873 Cattleman Cody **$899.00**

UBERTI 1873 CATTLEMAN BIRD'S HEAD SINGLE ACTION

Calibers: .357 Magnum, .45 Colt. **Capacity:** 6-round cylinder. **Barrels:** 3.5 in., 4 in., 4.75 in., 5.5 in. **Weight:** 2.3 lbs. (5.5-in. bbl.). **Length:** 10.9 in. overall (5.5-in. bbl.). **Grips:** One-piece walnut. **Sights:** Blade front, groove rear. **Features:** Steel or brass backstrap, trigger guard; color casehardened frame, blued barrel, fluted cylinder.

Price: **$569.00**

UBERTI CATTLEMAN .22

Caliber: .22 LR. **Capacity:** 6- or 12-round cylinder. **Barrel:** 5.5 in. **Grips:** One-piece walnut. **Sights:** Fixed. **Features:** Blued and casehardened finish, steel or brass backstrap/trigger guard.

Price: (brass backstrap, trigger guard) **$539.00**
Price: (steel backstrap, trigger guard) **$559.00**
Price: (12-round model, steel backstrap, trigger guard) **$589.00**

UBERTI DALTON REVOLVER

Caliber: .45 Colt. **Capacity:** 6-round cylinder. **Barrel:** 5.5 in. **Grips:** Simulated pearl. **Sights:** Fixed front and rear. **Weight:** 2.3 lbs. **Features:** Uberti USA expands its Outlaws & Lawmen Series of revolvers with the addition of the Dalton Revolver, a faithful reproduction of the Colt Single Action Army revolver used by Dalton Gang leader Bob Dalton. Features hand-chased engraving from famed Italian engraving company, Atelier Giovanelli, on the receiver, grip frame and cylinder.

Price: **$1,109.00**

UBERTI 1873 BISLEY SINGLE-ACTION

Calibers: .357 Magnum, .45 Colt (Bisley); .22 LR and .38 Special. (Stallion), both with 6-round fluted cylinder. **Barrels:** 4.75 in., 5.5 in., 7.5 in. **Weight:** 2–2.5 lbs. **Length:** 12.7 in. overall (7.5-in. barrel). **Grips:** Two-piece walnut. **Sights:** Blade front, notch rear. **Features:** Replica of Colt's Bisley Model. Polished blued finish, color casehardened frame. Introduced 1997.

Price: 1873 Bisley, 7.5-in. barrel **$619.00**

UBERTI 1873 BUNTLINE AND REVOLVER CARBINE SINGLE-ACTION

Caliber: .357 Magnum, .44-40, .45 Colt. **Capacity:** 6. **Barrel:** 18 in. **Length:** 22.9–34 in. **Grips:** Walnut pistol grip or rifle stock. **Sights:** Fixed or adjustable.

Price: 1873 Revolver Carbine, 18-in. bbl., 34 in. OAL **$729.00**
Price: 1873 Cattleman Buntline Target, 18-in. bbl. 22.9 in. OAL **$639.00**

UBERTI OUTLAW, FRONTIER, AND POLICE

Caliber: .45 Colt. **Capacity:** 6-round cylinder. **Barrels:** 5.5 in., 7.5 in. **Weight:** 2.5–2.8 lbs. **Length:** 10.8 in. to 13.6 in. overall. **Grips:** Two-piece smooth walnut. **Sights:** Blade front, notch rear. **Features:** Cartridge version of 1858 Remington percussion revolver. Nickel and blued finishes. Fluted cylinder.

Price: 1875 Outlaw, nickel finish **$609.00**
Price: 1875 Frontier, blued finish **$609.00**
Price: 1890 Police, blued finish **$599.00**

UBERTI 1870 SCHOFIELD-STYLE TOP BREAK

Calibers: .38 Special, .44 Russian, .44-40, .45 Colt. **Capacity:** 6-round cylinder. **Barrels:** 3.5 in., 5 in., 7 in. **Weight:** 2.4 lbs. (5-in. barrel) **Length:** 10.8 in. overall (5-in. barrel). **Grips:** Two-piece smooth walnut or pearl. **Sights:** Blade front, notch rear. **Features:** Replica of Smith & Wesson Model 3 Schofield. Single-action, top break with automatic ejection. Polished blued finish (first model). Introduced 1994.

Price: .... **$1,189.00-$1,599.00**

UBERTI STAINLESS STEEL SHORT STROKE CMS PRO

Caliber: .45 Colt. **Capacity:** 6-round cylinder. **Barrel:** 3.5 in. **Grips:** Synthetic traditional. **Sights:** Fixed front and rear. **Weight:** 2.1 lbs. **Features:** Made specifically for the rigors of Cowboy Mounted Shooting competition, and built entirely of stainless steel. Good for quick, one-handed shooting while riding a horse. Features low-profile, short-stroke hammer with 20-percent less travel. Extra-wide, deeply grooved hammer, and chambered in the classic .45 Colt.
Price: **$909.00**

UBERTI STAINLESS STEEL SHORT STROKE CMS KL PRO

Caliber: .45 Colt. **Capacity:** 6-round cylinder. **Barrel:** 3.5 in. **Grips:** Synthetic bird's head. **Sights:** Fixed front and rear. **Weight:** 2.1 lbs. **Features:** Made specifically for the rigors of Cowboy Mounted Shooting competition, and built entirely of stainless steel. This model is the result of the partnership between Uberti USA and legendary Cowboy Mounted Shooter competitor Kenda Lenseigne, winner of multiple world and national mounted shooting championships. It features a modified bird's-head grip with Lenseigne's brand on the grip and her signature engraved on the barrel. Features low-profile, short-stroke hammer with 20-percent less travel. Extra-wide, deeply grooved hammer, and chambered in the classic .45 Colt.
Price: **$909.00**

Prices given are believed to be accurate at time of publication however, many factors affect retail pricing so exact prices are not possible.

75TH EDITION, 2021 ✛ 501

AMERICAN DERRINGER MODEL 1
Calibers: All popular handgun calibers plus .45 Colt/.410 Shotshell. **Capacity:** 2, (.45-70 model is single shot). **Barrel:** 3 in. **Overall length:** 4.82 in. **Weight:** 15 oz. **Features:** Manually operated hammer-block safety automatically disengages when hammer is cocked. Texas Commemorative has brass frame and is available in .38 Special, .44-40. or .45 Colt.
Price: .... $635.00–$735.00
Price: Texas Commemorative $835.00

AMERICAN DERRINGER MODEL 8
Calibers: .45 Colt/.410 shotshell. **Capacity:** 2. **Barrel:** 8 in. **Weight:** 24 oz.
Price: $915.00
Price: High polish finish $1,070.00

AMERICAN DERRINGER DA38
Calibers: .38 Special, .357 Magnum, 9mm Luger. **Barrel:** 3.3 in. **Weight:** 14.5 oz. **Features:** DA operation with hammer-block thumb safety. Barrel, receiver and all internal parts are made from stainless steel.
Price: .... $690.00–$740.00

BOND ARMS TEXAS DEFENDER DERRINGER
Calibers: Available in more than 10 calibers, from .22 LR to .45 LC/.410 shotshells. **Barrel:** 3 in. **Weight:** 20 oz. **Length:** 5 in. **Grips:** Rosewood. **Sights:** Blade front, fixed rear. **Features:** Interchangeable barrels, stainless steel firing pins, cross-bolt safety, automatic extractor for rimmed calibers. Stainless steel construction, brushed finish. Right or left hand.
Price: $543.00
Price: Interchangeable barrels, .22 LR thru .45 LC, 3 in. $139.00
Price: Interchangeable barrels, .45 LC, 3.5 in. .... $159.00–$189.00

BOND ARMS RANGER II
Caliber: .45 LC/.410 shotshells or .357 Magnum/.38 Special. **Barrel:** 4.25 in. **Weight:** 23.5 oz. **Length:** 6.25 in. **Features:** This model has a trigger guard. Intr. 2011. From Bond Arms.
Price: $673.00

BOND ARMS CENTURY 2000 DEFENDER
Calibers: .45 LC/.410 shotshells. or .357 Magnum/.38 Special. **Barrel:** 3.5 in. **Weight:** 21 oz. **Length:** 5.5 in. **Features:** Similar to Defender series.
Price: $517.00

BOND ARMS COWBOY DEFENDER
Calibers: From .22 LR to .45 LC/.410 shotshells. **Barrel:** 3 in. **Weight:** 19 oz. **Length:** 5.5 in. **Features:** Similar to Defender series. No trigger guard.
Price: $493.00

BOND ARMS GRIZZLY
Calibers: .45 Colt/.410 bore. **Capacity:** 2 rounds. **Barrel:** 3 in. **Grips:** Rosewood. **Sights:** Fixed front and rear. **Features:** Similar to other Bond Arms derringers, this model is chambered in .45 Colt and 2.5-inch, .410-bore shotshells. Vibrant rosewood grips with grizzly-bear artwork adorn the Grizzly. It includes a matching leather holster embossed with a grizzly bear.
Price: $377.00

BOND ARMS SNAKE SLAYER
Calibers: .45 LC/.410 shotshell (2.5 in. or 3 in.). **Barrel:** 3.5 in. **Weight:** 21 oz. **Length:** 5.5 in. **Grips:** Extended rosewood. **Sights:** Blade front, fixed rear. **Features:** Single-action; interchangeable barrels; stainless steel firing pin. Introduced 2005.
Price: $603.00

BOND ARMS ROUGHNECK
Calibers: 9mm, .357 Magnum, .45 ACP. **Capacity:** 2 rounds. **Barrel:** 2.5 in. **Grips:** Textured rubber. **Sights:** Fixed front and rear. **Weight:** 22 oz. **Features:** A member of the new Bond Arms Rough series of derringers that includes the premium features found in all Bond guns, including stainless steel barrel, cross-bolt safety, retracting firing pin, spring-loaded, cam-lock lever and rebounding hammer. Each gun of the new series undergoes a quick clean up and deburring and then is bead-blasted, giving it a rough finish. This lightweight tips the scales at 22 ounces.
Price: $269.00

BOND ARMS ROUGH N ROWDY
Calibers: .45 Colt/.410 bore. **Capacity:** 2 rounds. **Barrel:** 3 in. **Grips:** Black rubber. **Sights:** Fixed front and rear. **Features:** Similar to Bond Arms Roughneck, this model is chambered in .45 Colt and 2.5-inch, .410 bore shotshells.
Price: $299.00

BOND ARMS STINGER
Calibers: 9mm, .38 Special. **Capacity:** 2 rounds. **Barrel:** 2.5 in. **Grips:** Black rubber. **Sights:** Fixed front and rear. **Weight:** 12 oz. **Features:** An all-new offering from Bond Arms that redefines the term lightweight, the Stinger is a slim-line derringer with an aluminum frame and stainless steel barrels that tips the scales at a whopping 12 oz.
Price: $299.00

BOND ARMS SNAKE SLAYER IV
Calibers: .45 LC/.410 shotshell (2.5 in. or 3 in.). **Barrel:** 4.25 in. **Weight:** 22 oz. **Length:** 6.25 in. **Grips:** Extended rosewood. **Sights:** Blade front, fixed rear. **Features:** Single-action; interchangeable barrels; stainless steel firing pin. Introduced 2006.
Price: **$648.00**

Calibers: .22 WMR, .32 H&R Mag., .38 Special, 9mm Para., .380 ACP. **Barrel:** 2.75 in. **Weight:** 14 oz. **Length:** 4.65 in. overall. **Grips:** Textured black or white synthetic or laminated rosewood. **Sights:** Blade front, fixed notch rear. **Features:** Alloy frame, steel-lined barrels, steel breechblock. Plunger-type safety with integral hammer block. Black, chrome or satin finish. Introduced 2002. Made in USA by Cobra Enterprises of Utah, Inc.
Price: **$187.00**

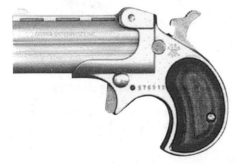

COBRA STANDARD SERIES DERRINGERS
Calibers: .22 LR, .22 WMR, .25 ACP, .32 ACP. **Barrel:** 2.4 in. **Weight:** 9.5 oz. **Length:** 4 in. overall. **Grips:** Laminated wood or pearl. **Sights:** Blade front, fixed notch rear. **Features:** Choice of black powder coat, satin nickel or chrome finish. Introduced 2002. Made in USA by Cobra Enterprises of Utah, Inc.
Price: **$169.00**

COBRA LONG-BORE DERRINGERS
Calibers: .22 WMR, .38 Special, 9mm. **Barrel:** 3.5. in. **Weight:** 16 oz. **Length:** 5.4 in. overall. **Grips:** Black or white synthetic or rosewood. **Sights:** Fixed. **Features:** Chrome, satin nickel, or black Teflon finish. Introduced 2002. Made in USA by Cobra Enterprises of Utah, Inc.
Price: **$187.00**

COBRA TITAN .45 LC/.410 DERRINGER
Calibers: .45 LC, .410 or 9mm, 2-round capacity. **Barrel:** 3.5 in. **Weight:** 16.4 oz. **Grip:** Rosewood. **Features:** Standard finishes include: satin stainless, black stainless and brushed stainless. Made in USA by Cobra Enterprises of Utah, Inc.
Price: **$399.00**

COMANCHE SUPER SINGLE-SHOT
Calibers: .45 LC/.410 **Barrel:** 10 in. **Sights:** Adjustable. **Features:** Blue finish, not available for sale in CA, MA. Distributed by SGS Importers International, Inc.
Price: **$240.00**

DOUBLETAP DERRINGER
Calibers: .45 Colt or 9mm **Barrel:** 3 in. **Weight:** 12 oz. **Length:** 5.5 in. **Sights:** Adjustable. **Features:** Over/under, two-barrel design. Rounds are fired individually with two separate trigger pulls. Tip-up design, aluminum frame.
Price: **$499.00**

Prices given are believed to be accurate at time of publication however, many factors affect retail pricing so exact prices are not possible.

75TH EDITION, 2021 ✦ **503**

HEIZER PS1 POCKET SHOTGUN

Calibers: .45 Colt or .410 shotshell. Single-shot. **Barrel:** Tip-up, 3.25 in. **Weight:** 22 oz. **Length:** 5.6 in. **Width:** .742 in **Height:** 3.81 in. **Features:** Available in several finishes. Standard model is matte stainless or black. Also offered in Hedy Jane series for the women in pink or in two-tone combinations of stainless and pink, blue, green, purple. Includes interchangeable AR .223 barrel. Made in the USA by Heizer Industries. **Price:** $499.00

HEIZER POCKET AR

Caliber: .223 Rem./5.56 NATO. Single shot. **Barrel:** 3.75 in., ported or non-ported. **Length:** 6.375 in. **Weight:** 23 oz. **Features:** Similar to PS1 pocket shotgun but chambered for .223/5.56 rifle cartridge. **Price:** $339.00

HEIZER PAK1

Caliber: 7.2x39. Similar to Pocket AR but chambered for 7.62x39mm. Single shot. **Barrel:** 3.75 in., ported or unported. **Length:** 6.375 in. **Weight:** 23 oz. **Price:** $339.00

HENRY MARE'S LEG

Calibers: .22 LR, .22 WMR, .357 Magnum, .44 Magnum, .45 Colt. **Capacities:** 10 rounds (.22 LR), 8 rounds (.22 WMR), 5 rounds (others). **Barrel:** 12.9 in. **Length:** 25 in. **Weight:** 4.5 lbs. (rimfire) to 5.8 lbs. (centerfire calibers). **Features:** Lever-action operation based on Henry rifle series and patterned after gun made famous in Steve McQueen's 1950s TV show, "Wanted: Dead or Alive." Made in the USA.
Price: .22 LR...$462.00
Price: .22 WMR $473.00
Price: Centerfire calibers $1,024.00

MAXIMUM SINGLE-SHOT

Calibers: .22 LR, .22 Hornet, .22 BR, .22 PPC, 223 Rem., .22-250, 6mm BR, 6mm PPC, .243, .250 Savage, 6.5mm-35M, .270 MAX, .270 Win., 7mm TCU, 7mm BR, 7mm-35, 7mm INT-R, 7mm-08, 7mm Rocket, 7mm Super-Mag., .30 Herrett, .30 Carbine, .30-30, .308 Win., 30x39, .32-20, .350 Rem. Mag., .357 Mag., .357 Maximum, .358 Win., .375 H&H, .44 Mag., .454 Casull. **Barrel:** 8.75 in., 10.5 in., 14 in. **Weight:** 61 oz. (10.5-in. bbl.); 78 oz. (14-in. bbl.). **Length:** 15 in., 18.5 in. overall (with 10.5- and 14-in. bbl., respectively). **Grips:** Smooth walnut stocks and fore-end. Also available with 17-finger-groove grip. **Sights:** Ramp front, fully adjustable open rear. **Features:** Falling block action; drilled and tapped for M.O.A. scope mounts; integral grip frame/receiver; adjustable trigger; Douglas barrel (interchangeable). Introduced 1983. Made in USA by M.O.A. Corp. **Price:** $1,062.00

ROSSI MATCHED PAIR, "DUAL THREAT PERFORMER"

Calibers: .22LR, .44 Magnum, .223, .243. .410, 20 gauge, single shot. Interchangeable rifle and shotgun barrels in various combinations. **Sights:** Fiber optic front sights, adjustable rear. **Features:** Two-in-one pistol system with single-shot simplicity. Removable choke and cushioned grip with a Taurus Security System. **Price:** .22/.410 from $345.00

Prices given are believed to be accurate at time of publication however, many factors affect retail pricing so exact prices are not possible.

THOMPSON/CENTER ENCORE PRO HUNTER

Calibers: .223, .308. Single shot, break-open design. **Barrel:** 15 in. **Weight:** 4.25–4.5 lbs. **Grip:** Walnut on blued models, rubber on stainless. Matching fore-end. **Sights:** Adjustable rear, ramp front. **Features:** Interchangeable barrels, adjustable trigger. Pro Hunter has "Swing Hammer" to allow reaching the hammer when the gun is scoped. Other Pro Hunter features include fluted barrel.
Price: From **$779.00**

THOMPSON/CENTER G2 CONTENDER

Calibers: .22 LR or .357 Magnum. A second generation Contender pistol maintaining the same barrel interchangeability with older Contender barrels and their corresponding forends (except Herrett fore-end). The G2 frame will not accept old-style grips due to the change in grip angle. Incorporates an automatic hammer block safety with built-in interlock. Features include trigger adjustable for overtravel, adjustable rear sight; ramp front sight blade, blued steel finish.
Price: From **$729.00**

Prices given are believed to be accurate at time of publication however, many factors affect retail pricing so exact prices are not possible.

75TH EDITION, 2021 ✛ **505**

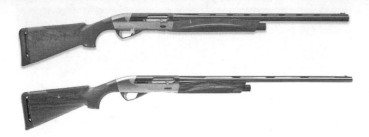

BENELLI ETHOS

Gauges: 12 ga., 20 ga., 28 ga. 3 in. **Capacity:** 4+1. **Barrel:** 26 in. or 28 in. (Full, Mod., Imp. Cyl., Imp. Mod., Cylinder choke tubes). **Weights:** 6.5 lbs. (12 ga.), 5.3–5.7 (20 & 28 ga.). **Length:** 49.5 in. overall (28 in. barrel). **Stock:** Select AA European walnut with satin finish. **Sights:** Red bar fiber optic front, with three interchangeable inserts, metal middle bead. **Features:** Utilizes Benelli's Inertia Driven system. Recoil is reduced by Progressive Comfort recoil reduction system within the buttstock. Twelve and 20-gauge models cycle all 3-inch loads from light 7/8 oz. up to 3-inch magnums. Also available with nickel-plated engraved receiver. Imported from Italy by Benelli USA, Corp.
Price: **$1,999.00**
Price: Engraved nickel-plated (shown)...............................**$2,149.00**
Price: 20 or 28 ga. (engraved, nickel plated only)............**$2,149.00**

BENELLI ETHOS BE.S.T.

Benelli expands its Ethos line with the new BE.S.T. model, so named for the Benelli Surface Treatment, a proprietary coating that protects steel from rust and corrosion and was tested over several months in saltwater with no signs of corrosion. Parts treated with BE.S.T. are backed with a 25-year warranty against rust and corrosion.
Price: From $2,199.00

BENELLI ETHOS SPORT

Gauges: 12 ga., 20 ga., 28 ga. 3 in. **Capacity:** 4+1. **Barrel:** Ported, 28 in. or 30 in. (12 ga. only). Full, Mod., Imp. Cyl., Imp. Mod., Cylinder extended choke tubes. Wide rib. Other features similar to Ethos model.
Price: $2,269.00

BENELLI ULTRA LIGHT

Gauges: 12 ga., 20 ga., 28 ga. 3 in. chamber (12, 20), 2 3/4 in. (28). **Barrels:** 24 in., 26 in. Mid-bead sight. **Weights:** 5.2–6 lbs. **Features:** Similar to Legacy line. Drop adjustment kit allows the stock to be custom fit without modifying the stock. WeatherCoat walnut stock. Lightened receiver, shortened magazine tube, carbon-fiber rib and grip cap. Introduced 2008. Imported from Italy by Benelli USA, Corp.
Price: 12 and 20 ga. **$1,699.00**
Price: 28 ga. **$1,799.00**

BENELLI M2 FIELD

Gauges: 20 ga., 12 ga., 3-in. chamber. **Barrels:** 21 in., 24 in., 26 in., 28 in. **Weights:** 5.4–7.2 lbs. **Length:** 42.5–49.5 in. overall. **Stock:** Synthetic, Advantage Max-4 HD, Advantage Timber HD, APG HD. **Sights:** Red bar. **Features:** Uses the Inertia Driven bolt mechanism. Vent rib. Comes with set of five choke tubes. Imported from Italy by Benelli USA.
Price: Synthetic stock 12 ga. **$1,499.00**
Price: Camo stock 12 ga. **$1,549.00**
Price: Synthetic stock 20 ga. **$1,499.00**
Price: Camo stock 20 ga. **$1,599.00**
Price: Rifled slug ....**$1,469.00–$1,589.00**
Price: Left-hand 12 ga. **$1,409.00**
Price: Left-hand model 20 ga. **$1,519.00**
Price: Tactical, from **$1,249.00**

BENELLI M2 TURKEY EDITION

Gauges: 12 ga. and 20 ga., Full, Imp. Mod, Mod., Imp. Cyl., Cyl. choke tubes. **Barrel:** 24 in. **Weight:** 6-7 lbs. **Stock:** 12 ga. model has ComfortTech with pistol grip, Bottomland/Cerakote finish. 20 ga. has standard stock with Realtree APG finish. **Features:** From the Benelli Performance Shop.
Price: 20 ga. standard stock **$3,199.00**
Price: 12 ga. pistol grip stock **$3,399.00**

BENELLI MONTEFELTRO

Gauges: 12 ga. and 20 ga. Full, Imp. Mod, Mod., Imp. Cyl., Cyl. choke tubes. **Barrels:** 24 in., 26 in., 28 in., 30 in. (Sporting). **Weights:** 5.3–7.1 lbs. **Stock:** Checkered walnut with satin finish. **Lengths:** 43.6–49.5 in. overall. **Features:** Burris FastFire II sight. Uses the Inertia Driven rotating bolt system with a simple inertia recoil design. Finish is blued. Introduced 1987.
Price: Standard Model **$1,129.00**
Price: Silver **$1,779.00**
Price: Sporting **$1,329.00**

BENELLI SUPER BLACK EAGLE III

Gauge: 12 ga., 3 1/2 inch. Latest evolution of Super Black Eagle. ComforTech stock with adjustable comb, 22 synthetic chevrons, gel recoil pad. Offered with several camo finishes, black synthetic or satin walnut. Left-hand model available. Introduced in 2017.
Price: **$1,899.00**
Price: Camo finish **$1,999.00**
Price: Rifle Slug **$1,499.00**
Price: Turkey Performance Shop, From........................**$2,999.00**
Price: Waterfowl Performance Shop, From **$3,199.00**

BENELLI SUPER BLACK EAGLE III BE.S.T.

Benelli expands its SBE III line with the new BE.S.T. model, so named for the Benelli Surface Treatment, a proprietary coating that protects steel from rust and corrosion and was tested over several months in saltwater with no signs of corrosion. Parts treated with BE.S.T. are backed with a 25-year warranty against rust and corrosion. The BE.S.T. package will be available on select SBE III models.
Price: From.. **$2,199.00**

BENELLI SUPERSPORT & SPORT II

Gauges: 20 ga., 12 ga., 3-in. chamber. **Capacity:** 4+1. **Barrels:** 28 in., 30 in., ported, 10mm sporting rib. **Weight:** 7.2–7.3 lbs. **Lengths:** 49.6–51.6 in. **Stock:** Carbon fiber, ComforTech (Supersport) or walnut (Sport II). **Sights:** Red bar front, metal midbead. Sport II is similar to the Legacy model except has nonengraved dual tone blued/silver receiver, ported wide-rib barrel, adjustable buttstock, and functions with all loads. Walnut stock with satin finish. Introduced 1997. **Features:** Designed for high-volume sporting clays. Inertia-driven action, Extended CrioChokes. Ported. Imported from Italy by Benelli USA.
Price: SuperSport **$2,199.00**
Price: Sport II **$1,899.00**

BENELLI VINCI

Gauge: 12 ga., 3-in. **Barrels:** 26- or 28-inch ribbed. Tactical model available with 18.5-in. barrel. **Finishes:** Black, MAX-4HD or APG HD; synthetic contoured stocks; optional Steady-Grip model. **Weight:** 6.7–6.9 lbs. **Features:** Gas-operated action. Modular disassembly; interchangeable choke tubes. Picatinny rail, pistol grip, ghost ring sight.
Price: ....**$1,349.00–$1,469.00**

BENELLI SUPER VINCI
Gauge: 12 ga.- 2 3/4 in., 3 in. and 3 1/2 in. **Capacity:** 3+1. **Barrels:** 26 in., 28 in. **Weights:** 6.9–7 lbs. **Lengths:** 48.5–50.5 in. **Stock:** Black synthetic, Realtree Max4 and Realtree APG. **Features:** Crio Chokes: C,IC,M,IM,F. Length of Pull: 14.375 in. Drop at Heel: 2 in. Drop at Comb: 1.375 in. **Sights:** Red bar front sight and metal bead mid-sight. Minimum recommended load: 3-dram, 1 1/8 oz. loads (12 ga.). Receiver drilled and tapped for scope mounting. Imported from Italy by Benelli USA., Corp.
Price: Black Synthetic Comfortech **$1,799.00**
Price: Camo **$1,899.00**

BERETTA A300 OUTLANDER
Gauge: 12 ga., 3-in. **Capacity:** 3+1. Operates with 2 3/4-in. shells. **Barrel:** 28 in. with Mobilechoke system. **Stock:** Synthetic, camo or wood. **Weight:** 7.1 pounds. **Features:** Based on A400 design but at a lower price.
Price: .... **$775.00–$850.00**

BERETTA A350 XTREMA
Gauge: 12 ga., 3 1/2-in. **Capacity:** 3+1. Operates with 3- and 2 3/4-in. shells. **Barrel:** 24 in. or 28 in. with Optima Choke HP system. **Stock:** Synthetic, camo or wood. **Weight:** 7-7 3/4 pounds. Adjustable buttstock.
Price: Max 5 Waterfowl **$1,150.00**
Price: Turkey w/Mossy Oak Obsession camo.................... **$1,365.00**

BERETTA A400 XTREME PLUS MAX
Gauge: 12 ga., 3 1/2-in. **Capacity:** 3+1. Also operates with 3- and 2 3/4-in. shells. **Barrel:** 26, 28 or 30 in. with five Black Edition Extended choke tubes. **Stock:** Kick-Off Mega and Kick-Off 3 with soft comb. **Finish:** Realtree Max-5. **Weight:** 7-7 3/4 pounds.
Price: **$1,900.00**

BERETTA A400 XPLOR UNICO
Gauge: 12 ga.. 2 3/4 to 3 1/2-inch shells. **Barrels:** 26- or 28-inch "Steelium" with interchangeable choke tubes. **Features:** Self-regulation gas-operated shotgun. Optional Kick-Off hydraulic damper. Anodized aluminum receiver; sculpted, checkered walnut buttstock and fore-end.
Price: **$1,755.00**
Price: With Kick-Off recoil reduction system................... **$1,855.00**

BERETTA A400 XCEL SPORTING
Gauge: 12 ga. 3-in. chamber. **Barrels:** 28 in., 30 in. 32 in. **Weight:** 7.5 lbs. **Stock:** Walnut and polymer. **Features:** Gas operated. In addition to A400 specifications and features, the Sporting model has aqua blue receiver. Optional Gun Pod electronic system gives digital readout of air temperature, ammunition pressure, number of rounds fired.
Price: **$1,745.00**
Price: With Kick-Off system.. **$1,845.00**

BERETTA A400 XPLOR ACTION
Gauges: 12 ga., 20 (3 in.) or 28 ga. (2 3/4-in. chamber). **Barrels:** 28 in., 30 in. **Weight:** 5.3 (28 ga.) to 6.7 lbs. **Stock:** Walnut and polymer combination. **Features:** Gas-operating Blink operating system can reportedly fire 4 rounds in less than one second. Kick-Off hydraulic recoil reduction system reduces felt recoil up to 70 percent.
Price: **$1,600.00**
Price: With Kick-Off system.. **$1,700.00**

BROWNING A5
Gauges: 12 ga., 3 or 3 1/2; 16 ga., 2 3/4 in. (Sweet Sixteen). **Barrels:** 26 in., 28 in. or 30 in. **Weights:** 5 3/4 to 7 lbs. **Lengths:** 47.25–51.5 in. **Stock:** Gloss finish walnut with 22 LPI checkering, black synthetic or camo. Adjustable for cast and

drop. **Features:** Operates on Kinematic short-recoil system, totally different than the classic Auto-5 long-recoil action manufactured from 1903–1999. Lengthened forcing cone, three choke tubes (IC, M, F), flat ventilated rib, brass bead front sight, ivory middle bead. Available in Mossy Oak Duck Blind or Break-up Infinity camo. Ultimate Model has satin finished aluminum alloy receiver with light engraving of pheasants on left side, mallards on the right. Gloss blued finish, Grade III oil-finished walnut stock. Wicked Wing has Cerakote Burnt Bronze finish on receiver and barrel, Mossy Oak Shadow Grass Blades camo on stock.
Price: A5 Hunter **$1,670.00**
Price: A5 Hunter 3 1/2 in. **$1,800.00**
Price: A5 Stalker (synthetic) **$1,540.00**
Price: A5 Stalker 3 1/2 in. **$1,670.00**
Price: A5 Ultimate **$2,030.00**
Price: A5 Sweet Sixteen **$1,740.00**
Price: A5 Wicked Wing **$1,870.00**
Price: A5 Wicked Wing 3 1/2 in.. **$2,000.00**

BROWNING MAXUS HUNTER
Gauges: 12 ga., 3 in. and 3 1/2 in. **Barrels:** 26 in., 28 in. and 30 in. Flat ventilated rib with fixed cylinder choke; stainless steel; matte finish. **Weight:** 7 lbs. 2 oz. **Length:** 40.75 in. **Stock:** Gloss finish walnut stock with close radius pistol grip, sharp 22 LPI checkering, Speed Lock Forearm, shim adjustable for length of pull, cast and drop. **Features:** Vector Pro-lengthened forcing cone, three Invector-Plus choke tubes, Inflex Technology recoil pad, ivory front bead sight, One 1/4 in. stock spacer. Strong, lightweight aluminum alloy receiver with durable satin nickel finish & laser engraving (pheasant on the right, mallard on the left). All-Purpose Hunter has Mossy Oak Break-Up Country Camo, Duratouch coated composite stock. Wicked Wing has Cerakote Burnt Bronze finish on receiver and barrel, Mossy Oak Shadow Grass Blades camo on stock.
Price: 3 in. **$1,590.00**
Price: 3 1/2 in. **$1,740.00**
Price: All-Purpose Hunter.. **$1,780.00**
Price: Maxus Wicked Wing... **$1,900.00**

BROWNING MAXUS SPORTING
Gauge: 12 ga., 3 in. **Barrels:** 28 in., 30 in. flat ventilated rib. **Weight:** 7 lbs. 2 oz. **Length:** 49.25 in.–51.25 in. **Stock:** Gloss finish high grade walnut stock with close radius pistol grip, Speed Lock forearm, shim adjustable for length of pull, cast and drop. **Features:** Laser engraving of game birds transforming into clay birds on the lightweight alloy receiver. Quail are on the right side, and a mallard duck on the left. The Power Drive Gas System reduces recoil and cycles a wide array of loads. It's available in a 28 in. or 30 in. barrel length. The high-grade walnut stock and forearm are generously checkered, finished with a deep, high gloss. The stock is adjustable and one .250-in. stock spacer is included. For picking up either clay or live birds quickly, the HiViz Tri-Comp fiber-optic front sight with mid-bead ivory sight does a great job, gathering light on the most overcast days. Vector Pro-lengthened forcing cone, five Invector-Plus choke tubes, Inflex Technology recoil pad, HiViz Tri-Comp fiber-optic front sight, ivory mid-bead sight, one .250-in. stock spacer.
Price: **$1,800.00**
Price: Golden Clays **$2,100.00**

Prices given are believed to be accurate at time of publication however, many factors affect retail pricing so exact prices are not possible.

75TH EDITION, 2021 ✛ **507**

BROWNING MAXUS SPORTING CARBON FIBER

Gauge: 12 ga., 3 in. **Barrels:** 28 in., 30 in. flat ventilated rib. **Weights:** 6 lbs. 15 oz.–7 lbs. **Length:** 49.25–51.25 in. **Stock:** Composite stock with close radius pistol grip, Speed Lock forearm, textured gripping surfaces, shim adjustable for length of pull, cast and drop, carbon fiber finish, Dura-Touch Armor Coating. **Features:** Strong, lightweight aluminum alloy, carbon fiber finish on top and bottom. The stock is finished with Dura-Touch Armor Coating for a secure, non-slip grip when the gun is wet. It has the Browning exclusive Magazine Cut-Off, a patented Turn-Key Magazine Plug and Speed Load Plus. Deeply finished look of carbon fiber and Dura-Touch Armor Coating. Vector Pro-lengthened forcing cone, five Invector-Plus choke tubes, Inflex Technology recoil pad, HiViz Tri-Comp fiber-optic front sight, ivory mid-bead sight, one .250-in. stock spacer.
Price: $1,590.00

BROWNING GOLD LIGHT 10 GAUGE

Gauge: 10 ga. 3 1/2 in. **Capacity:** 4 rounds. **Barrels:** 24 (NWTF), 26 or 28 in. **Stock:** Composite with Dura-Cote Armor coating. Mossy Oak camo (Break-Up Country or Shadow Grass Blades). **Weight:** Approx. 9.5 pounds. Gas operated action, aluminum receiver, three standard Invector choke tubes. Receiver is drilled and tapped for scope mount. National Wild Turkey Foundation model has Hi-Viz 4-in-1 fiber optic sight, NWTF logo on buttstock.
Price: Mossy Oak Camo finishes.. $1,780.00
Price: NWTF Model... $1,900.00

BROWNING SILVER

Gauges: 12 ga., 3 in. or 3 1/2 in.; 20 ga., 3 in. chamber. **Barrels:** 26 in., 28 in., 30 in. Invector Plus choke tubes. **Weights:** 7 lbs., 9 oz. (12 ga.), 6 lbs., 7 oz. (20 ga.). **Stock:** Satin finish walnut or composite. **Features:** Active Valve gas system, semi-humpback receiver. Invector Plus choke system, three choke tubes. Imported by Browning.
Price: Silver Field, 12 ga... $1,070.00
Price: Silver Field, 20 ga... $1,140.00
Price: Black Lightning, 12 ga.................................... $1,140.00
Price: Silver Field Composite, 12 ga., 3 in. $1,000.00
Price: Silver Field Composite, 12 ga., 3 1/2 in. $1,070.00
Price: Silver Field Rifled Deer Matte, 20 ga.............. $1,200.00

CHARLES DALY MODEL 600

Gauges: 12 ga. or 20 ga. (3 in.) or 28 ga. (2 3/4 in.). **Capacity:** 5+1. **Barrels:** 26 in., 28 in. (20 and 28 ga.), 26 in., 28 in. or 30 in. (12 ga.). Three choke tubes provided (Rem-Choke pattern). **Stock:** Synthetic, wood or camo. **Features:** Comes in several variants including Field, Sporting Clays, Tactical and Trap. Left-hand models available. Uses gas-assisted recoil operation. Imported from Turkey.
Price: Field 12, 20 ga... $480.00
Price: Field 28 ga.. $531.00
Price: Sporting $858.00
Price: Tactical $685.00

CHARLES DALY MODEL 635 MASTER MAG

Gauge: 12 ga., 3 1/2 in. **Barrels:** 24 in., 26 in., 28 in. Ported. **Stock:** Synthetic with full camo coverage. **Features:** Similar to Model 600 series.
Price: From.. $665.00

CZ MODEL 712/720

Gauges: 12 ga., 20 ga. **Capacity:** 4+1. **Barrel:** 26 in. **Weight:** 6.3 lbs. **Stock:** Turkish walnut with 14.5 in. length of pull. **Features:** Chrome-lined barrel with 3-inch chamber, ventilated rib, five choke tubes. Matte black finish.
Price: 712 12 ga. .... $499.00–$699.00
Price: 720 20 ga... $516.00–$599.00

CZ 1012

Gauge: 12 ga., 3 in. **Capacity:** 4+1. **Barrel:** 28 in., 8mm flat ventilated rib. **Weight:** 6.5-6.9 lbs. **Length:** 47 in. **Stock:** Options in either Turkish walnut or black synthetic. **Features:** The company's first gas-less, inertia-driven semi-automatic wears a gloss-black chrome barrel finish along with a choice of three receiver finishes: standard blued, bronze or gray. Oversized controls ideal for use when wearing gloves. Cross-bolt safety located at front of trigger guard. Includes five chokes (F, IM, M, IC, C).
Price: .... $659.00-$749.00

CZ 1012 ALL TERRAIN

Gauge: 12 ga., 3 in. **Capacity:** 4+1. **Barrel:** 28 in., 8mm flat ventilated rib. **Weight:** 6.5 lbs. **Length:** 47 in. **Stock:** Turkish walnut with checkering. **Features:** The company's first gas-less, inertia-driven semi-automatic joins the All-Terrain family, which means it includes OD Green Cerakote on all exterior metalwork. Includes installed magazine plug. Oversized controls ideal for use when wearing gloves, sling studs, rubber recoil pad. Cross-bolt safety located at front of trigger guard. Includes five extended black chokes (F, IM, M, IC, C) and ships in a hard case.
Price: $690.00

CZ 1012 BOTTOMLANDS

Gauge: 12 ga., 3 in. **Capacity:** 4+1. **Barrel:** 28 in., 8mm flat ventilated rib. **Weight:** 6.5 lbs. **Length:** 47 in. **Stock:** Synthetic with full Mossy Oak Bottomland camouflage. **Features:** The company's first gas-less, inertia-driven semi-automatic is now dressed for hunting with full camouflage coverage on furniture, receiver and barrels. Oversized controls, sling studs, rubber recoil pad. Cross-bolt safety located at front of trigger guard. Includes five extended chokes (F, IM, M, IC, C).
Price: $749.00

ESCORT WATERFOWL EXTREME SEMI-AUTO

Gauges: 12 ga. or 20 ga., 2 3/4 in. through 3 1/2 in. **Capacity:** 5+1. **Barrel:** 28 in. **Weight:** 7.4 lbs. **Length:** 48 in. **Stock:** Composite stock with close radius pistol grip; Speed Lock forearm; textured gripping surfaces; shim adjustable for length of pull, cast and drop; Realtree Max4 or AP camo finish; Dura-Touch Armor Coating. **Sights:** HiVis MagniSight fiber-optic, magnetic sight to enhance sight acquisition in lowlight conditions. **Features:** The addition of non-slip grip pads on the fore-end and pistol grip provide a superior hold in all weather conditions. Smart-Valve gas pistons regulate gas blowback to cycle every round — from 2 3/4-inch range loads through 3 1/2-inch heavy magnums. Escorts also have Fast-loading systems that allow one-handed round changes without changing aiming position. Left-hand models available at no increase in price.
Price: Black/Synthetic $551.00
Price: Realtree Camo $736.00
Price: 3 1/2-in. Black/Synthetic $649.00
Price: 3 1/2-in. Realtree Camo $815.00

EUROPEAN AMERICAN ARMORY (EAA) MC312 GOBBLER

Gauge: 12 ga., 3.5 in. **Barrel:** 24 in., with ventilated turkey rib. **Length:** 50 in. **Stock:** Synthetic camouflage with either straight or pistol-grip options. **Features:** The MC312 inertia-driven semi-auto produced by Girsan gets a turkey upgrade with a shorter barrel, mid-bead, Picatinny rail cut into the receiver, Cerakote finish receiver and barrel, cross-bolt safety, sling studs, rubber buttpad, fiber-optic front sight, and field-tested reflex optic. Includes flush mount choke tubes.
Price: $606.97

Prices given are believed to be accurate at time of publication however, many factors affect retail pricing so exact prices are not possible.

FABARM XLR5 VELOCITY AR

Gauge: 12 ga. **Barrels:** 30 or 32 in. **Weight:** 8.25 lbs. **Features:** Gas-operated model designed for competition shooting. Unique adjustable rib that allows a more upright shooting position. There is also an adjustable trigger shoe, magazine cap adjustable weight system. Five interchangeable choke tubes. Imported from Italy by Fabarm USA.

Price: From	$2,755.00–$3,300.00
Price: FR Sporting	$1,990.00–$2,165.00
Price: LR (Long Rib)	$2,260.00–$2,800.00

FRANCHI AFFINITY

Gauges: 12 ga., 20 ga. Three-inch chamber also handles 2 3/4-inch shells. **Barrels:** 26 in., 28 in., 30 in. (12 ga.), 26 in. (20 ga.). 30-in. barrel available only on 12-ga. Sporting model. **Weights:** 5.6–6.8 pounds. **Stocks:** Black synthetic or Realtree Camo. Left-hand versions available. Catalyst model has stock designed for women.

Price: Synthetic	$789.00
Price: Synthetic left-hand action	$899.00
Price: Camo	$949.00
Price: Compact	$849.00
Price: Catalyst	$969.00
Price: Sporting	$1,149.00
Price: Companion	$1,599.00

MOSSBERG 930

Gauge: 12 ga., 3 in. **Capacity:** 4-shell magazine. **Barrels:** 24 in., 26 in., 28 in., over-bored to 10-gauge bore dimensions; factory ported, Accu-Choke tubes. **Weight:** 7.5 lbs. **Length:** 44.5 in. overall (28-in. barrel). **Stock:** Walnut or synthetic. Adjustable stock drop and cast spacer system. **Sights:** Turkey Taker fiber-optic, adjustable windage and elevation. Front bead fiber-optic front on waterfowl models. **Features:** Self-regulating gas system, dual gas-vent system and piston, EZ-Empty magazine button, cocking indicator. Interchangeable Accu-Choke tube set (IC, Mod, Full) for waterfowl and field models. XX-Full turkey Accu-Choke tube included with turkey models. Ambidextrous thumb-operated safety, Uni-line stock and receiver. Receiver drilled and tapped for scope base attachment, free gun lock. Introduced 2008. From O.F. Mossberg & Sons, Inc.

Price: Turkey, From	$630.00
Price: Waterfowl, From	$619.00
Price: Combo, From	$693.00
Price: Field, From	$560.00
Price: Slugster, From	$678.00
Price: Turkey Pistolgrip; Mossy Oak Infinity Camo	$735.00
Price: Tactical; 18.5-in. tactical barrel, black synthetic stock and matte black finish	$878.00
Price: SPX; no muzzle brake, M16-style front sight, ghost ring rear sight, pistol grip stock, 8-shell extended magazine	$1,046.00
Price: Home Security/Field Combo; 18.5 in. Cylinder bore barrel and 28 in. ported Field barrel; black synthetic stock and matte black finish	$693.00
Price: High Performance (13-round magazine)	$974.00

MOSSBERG MODEL 935 MAGNUM

Gauge: 12 ga. 3 in. and 3 1/2-in., interchangeable. **Barrels:** 22 in., 24 in., 26 in., 28in. **Weights:** 7.25–7.75 lbs. **Lengths:** 45–49 in. overall. **Stock:** Synthetic. **Features:** Gas-operated semi-auto models in blued or camo finish. Fiber-optics sights, drilled and tapped receiver, interchangeable Accu-Mag choke tubes.

Price: 935 Magnum Turkey Pistol grip; full pistol grip stock	$924.00
Price: 935 Magnum Grand Slam: 22 in. barrel	$756.00
Price: 935 Magnum Waterfowl: 26 in. or 28 in. barrel	$660.00-$735.00
Price: 935 Pro Series Waterfowl	$875.00

MOSSBERG 940 JM PRO

Gauge: 12 ga., 3 in. **Capacity:** 9+1. **Barrel:** 24 in., ventilated rib. **Weight:** 7.75 lbs. **Length:** 44.75 in. **Stock:** Choice of either black synthetic or Black Multicam. **Features:** Created in conjunction with speed shooter Jerry Miculek, the new 940 JM Pro uses a redesigned gas system built for fast-cycling competition. Adjustable for length of pull, cast and drop. Hi-Viz green front fiber-optic sight, oversized controls. Nickel-boron coated internal parts and anodized receivers in either tungsten gray or black. Competition-level loading port allows for quad loading, elongated pinch-free elevator, and anodized bright orange follower. Black synthetic model uses gold finish appointments and a tungsten-gray

receiver. Multicam model wears black-anodized receiver. Ships with Briley Extended choke tube set.

Price:	$1,015.00

MOSSBERG SA-20

Gauge: 20 or 28 ga. **Barrels:** 20 in. (Tactical), 26 in. or 28 in. **Weight:** 5.5–6 lbs. **Stock:** Black synthetic. Gas operated action, matte blue finish. Tactical model has ghost-ring sight, accessory rail.

Price: 20 ga. From	$592.00–$664.00
Price: 28 ga. From	$588.00–$675.00

MOSSBERG SA-410 FIELD

Gauge: .410 bore, 3 in. **Capacity:** 4+1. **Barrel:** 26 in., ventilated rib. **Weight:** 6.5 lbs. **Length:** 46 in. **Stock:** Black synthetic. **Features:** Mossberg offers the baby bore for small-game and field hunters as well as light recoiling plinking with this lightweight gas-driven autoloader. Metalwork is finished in matte blue. Brass front bead, fixed 13.75 in. length of pull, ventilated rubber buttpad. Cross-bolt safety, easy-load elevator. Includes Sport Set flush fit chokes (F, IM, M, IC, C).

Price:	$616.00

MOSSBERG SA-410 TURKEY

Gauge: .410 bore, 3 in. **Capacity:** 4+1. **Barrel:** 26 in., ventilated rib. **Weight:** 6.5 lbs. **Length:** 46 in. **Stock:** Synthetic stock with Mossy Oak Bottomland camouflage. **Features:** Mossberg expands its baby-bore turkey lineup with this gas-driven semi-automatic. Both the stocks and metalwork wear full camouflage coverage. Rear fiber-optic ghost-ring sight and front green fiber-optic. Top Picatinny rail for easy optics mounting. Cross-bolt safety, easy-load elevator. Ships with an XX-Full Extended Turkey choke.

Price:	$735.00

RETAY GORDION

Gauge: 12 ga., 3 in. **Barrels:** 26 in., 28 in., ventilated rib. **Weight:** 6.5-6.75 lbs. **Stock:** Choice of black synthetic, several Realtree camo patterns, or Turkish walnut. **Features:** The Turkish-made Gordion line of semi-automatics uses an inertia-plus action and bolt system. Oversized SP controls, quick unload system, TruGlo red front sight. Choice of matte or polished black receiver and barrel, or full camouflage coverage. Easy-Load port as well as Easy Unload system that allows the magazine tube to be emptied without racking the action. Includes a stock adjustment ship kit, TSA airline-approved hard case, and five flush choke tubes (F, IM, M, IC, S).

Price:	$799.00-$899.00
Price: Gordion Turkey 24-in. barrel, Realtree or Mossy Oak camo	$925.00

RETAY MASAI MARA

Gauges: 12 ga., 3.5 in., 20 ga., 3 in. **Barrels:** 26 in., 28 in., ventilated rib. **Weight:** 6.5-6.75 lbs. **Stock:** Choice of synthetic in black or numerous camouflage patterns or two grades of Turkish walnut. **Features:** The Turkish-made Masai Mara line of semi-automatics uses an inertia-plus action and bolt system. Oversized controls, Easy Unload system, TruGlo red fiber-optic front sight. Options in Cerakote metalwork or anodized finishes. Push-button removeable trigger group for both safety and easy field cleaning. Microcell rubber recoil pad. Includes a TSA airline-approved hard case and ships with five flush choke tubes (F, IM, M, IC, S).

Price: From	$1,099.00
Price: Upland Grade 2	$1,399.00
Price: Upland Grade 3	$1,900.00
Price: Comfort Grade 2	$1,399.00
Price: Comfort Grade 4	$1,999.00
Price: SP Air King Waterfowl Camo/Cerakote	$1,600.00
Price: SP Air King Waterfowl Cerakote	$1,600.00

REMINGTON MODEL 11-87 SPORTSMAN

Gauges: 12 ga., 20 ga., 3 in. **Barrels:** 26 in., 28 in., RemChoke tubes. Standard contour, vent rib. **Weights:** 7.75–8.25 lbs. **Lengths:** 46–48 in. overall. **Stock:** American walnut with satin finish. **Sights:** Single bead front. **Features:** Matte-black metal finish, magazine cap swivel studs.

Price:	$816.00
Price: Mossy Oak New Break-Up camo	$88.00

Prices given are believed to be accurate at time of publication however, many factors affect retail pricing so exact prices are not possible.

75TH EDITION, 2021 ◆ **509**

REMINGTON MODEL 1100 CLASSIC
Gauges: 12 ga., 20 ga. or 28 ga. **Barrels:** 28 in. (12 ga.), 26 in. (20), 25 in. (28). **Features:** Part of the Remington American Classics Collection honoring Remington's most enduring firearms. American walnut B-grade stock with classic white line spacer and grip caps, ventilated recoil pad the white line spacer and white diamond grip cap. Machine-cut engraved receiver has tasteful scroll pattern with gold inlay retriever and "American Classic" label. Limited availability.
Price: **$1,686.00**

REMINGTON MODEL 1100 200TH YEAR ANNIVERSARY
Gauge: 12 ga. **Barrel:** 28 in. **Features:** C-grade American walnut stock with *fleur-de-lis* checkering. Receiver has classic engraving pattern, gold inlay. Limited edition of 2,016 guns to honor the Remington company's 200th anniversary — the oldest firearms manufacturer in the USA. Limited availability.
Price: **$1,999.00**

REMINGTON MODEL 1100 COMPETITION MODELS
Gauges: .410 bore, 28 ga., 20 ga., 12 ga. **Barrels:** 26 in., 27 in., 28 in., 30 in. light target contoured vent rib barrel with twin bead target sights. **Stock:** Semi-fancy American walnut stock and fore-end, cut checkering, high gloss finish. **Features:** Classic Trap has 30-inch barrel and weighs approximately 8.25 pounds. Sporting Series is available in all four gauges with 28-inch barrel in 12 and 20 gauge, 27 in. in 28 and .410. **Weights:** 6.25–8 pounds. Competition Synthetic model has synthetic stock with adjustable comb, case and length. Five Briley Target choke tubes. High-gloss blued barrel, Nickel-Teflon finish on receiver and internal parts. **Weight:** 8.1 pounds.
Price: Classic Trap **$1,334.00**
Price: Sporting Series, From **$1,252.00**
Price: Competition Synthetic: **$1,305.00**

REMINGTON VERSA MAX SERIES
Gauge: 12 ga., 2 3/4 in., 3 in., 3 1/2 in. **Barrels:** 26 in. and 28 in. flat ventilated rib. **Weights:** 7.5–7.7 lbs. **Length:** 40.25 in. **Stock:** Synthetic. **Features:** Reliably cycles 12-gauge rounds from 2 3/4 in. to 3 1/2 in. magnum. Versaport gas system regulates cycling pressure based on shell length. Reduces recoil to that of a 20-gauge. Self-cleaning. Continuously cycled thousands of rounds in torture test. Synthetic stock and fore-end with grey overmolded grips. Drilled and tapped receiver. Enlarged trigger guard opening and larger safety for easier use with gloves. TriNyte Barrel and Nickel Teflon plated internal components offer extreme corrosion resistance. Includes 5 Flush Mount Pro Bore Chokes (Full, Mod, Imp Mod Light Mod, IC)
Price: Sportsman, From **$1,066.00**
Price: Synthetic, From **$1,427.00**
Price: Tactical, From **$1,456.00**
Price: Waterfowl, From **$1,765.00**
Price: Camo, From **$1,664.00**
Price: Sportsman, MO Bottomland or Realtree Edge, 26 in. **$1,247.00**

REMINGTON MODEL V3
Gauge: 12 ga., 3 in. **Capacity:** 3+1 magazine. **Barrels:** 26 or 28 in. **Features:** The newest addition to the Remington shotgun family operates on an improved VersaPort gas system, claimed to offer the least recoil of any 12-ga. autoloader. Operating system is located in front of the receiver instead of the fore-end, resulting in better weight distribution than other autoloaders, and improved handling qualities. **Stock:** Walnut, black synthetic, or camo. Designed to function with any 2 3/4- or 3-in. ammo. Made in the USA by Remington.
Price: Synthetic black...**$895.00**
Price: Walnut or camo...**$995.00**
Price: Field Sport NWTF, Mossy Oak Obsession, 26 in. **$1,025.00**

SAVAGE RENEGAUGE
Gauge: 12 ga., 3 in. **Capacity:** 4+1. **Barrels:** 26 in., 28 in., fluted with steel

ventilated rib. **Weight:** 7.9-8 lbs. **Length:** 47.5-49.5 in. **Stock:** Black synthetic stock with Monte Carlo style cheekpiece, adjustable for length of pull, comb height, drop and cast. **Features:** American-made D.R.I.V. (Dual Regulating Inline Valve) gas system. Single-piece, chrome-plated action-bar assembly and chrome-plated reciprocating components. Melonite-finished external metalwork. Stock rod buffer to reduce felt recoil. Red fiber-optic sight, competition-ready easy-loading port, oversized controls. Includes three Beretta/Benelli-style chokes (IC, M, F) and hard case.
Price: **$1,449.00**

SAVAGE RENEGAUGE TURKEY
Gauge: 12 ga., 3 in. **Capacity:** 4+1.**Barrel:** 24 in., fluted with steel ventilated rib. **Weight:** 7.8 lbs. **Length:** 49.5 in. **Stock:** Camouflage synthetic stock with Monte Carlo style cheekpiece, adjustable for length of pull, comb height, drop and cast. Choice of Mossy Oak Bottomland or Mossy Oak Obsession. **Features:** American-made D.R.I.V. (Dual Regulating Inline Valve) gas system. Single-piece, chrome-plated action-bar assembly and chrome-plated reciprocating components. Stock rod buffer to reduce felt recoil. Melonite finished external metalwork. Red fiber-optic sight, competition-ready easy-loading port, oversized controls. Includes four Beretta/Benelli-style chokes (EF, F, IC, M) and hard case.
Price: **$1,549.00**

SAVAGE RENEGAUGE WATERFOWL
Gauge: 12 ga., 3 in. **Capacity:** 4+1. **Barrels:** 26 in., 28 in., fluted with steel ventilated rib. **Weight:** 7.8 lbs. **Lengths:** 47.5-49.5 in. **Stock:** Camouflage synthetic stock with Monte Carlo style cheekpiece, adjustable for length of pull, comb height, drop and cast. Mossy Oak Shadow Grass Blades pattern. **Features:** American-made D.R.I.V. (Dual Regulating Inline Valve) gas system. Single-piece, chrome-plated action-bar assembly and chrome-plated reciprocating components. Stock rod buffer to reduce felt recoil. Melonite-finished external metalwork. Red fiber-optic sight, competition-ready easy-loading port, oversized controls. Includes three Beretta/Benelli-style chokes (IC, M, F) and hard case.
Price: **$1,549.00**

SKB MODEL IS300
Gauge: 12 ga., 2-3/4- and 3-in. loads. **Capacity:** 4+1 magazine. **Barrels:** 26 in., 28 in. or 30 in. with 3 choke tubes IC, M, F. **Stock:** Black synthetic, oil-finished walnut or camo. **Weight:** 6.7–7.3 pounds. **Features:** Inertia-driven operating system. Target models have adjustable stock dimensions including cast and drop. Made in Turkey and imported by GU, Inc.
Price: Synthetic **$625.00**
Price: Walnut or Camo Field **$715.00**
Price: Walnut Target...**$870.00**
Price: RS300 Target with adjustable stock......................**$1,000.00**

SKB MODEL HS 300
Gauges: 12 ga. or 20 ga. **Barrel:** 26 or 28 in. **Stock:** Checkered walnut or camo finish. **Weight:** 7 lbs. **Features:** Gas-operated design. Introduced in 2017.
Price: Walnut stock..**$750.00**
Price: Camo stock **$780.00**

STANDARD MANUFACTURING SKO-12
Gauge: 12 ga., 3 in. **Capacity:** 5-round magazine. **Barrel:** 18-7/8-in. **Weight:** 7 lbs., 10 oz. **Length:** 38 in. **Stock:** Synthetic with six-position buttstock and will accept any Mil-Spec buttstock. **Features:** Gas-operated semi-automatic. Receivers machined from aircraft-grade aluminum and Mil-Spec hard anodized. Extended 22-inch Picatinny rail. Ambidextrous safety, AR-style mag and bolt release. MOE slots on fore-end. Tru-Choke thread pattern.
Price: **$1,100.00**

STANDARD MANUFACTURING SKO SHORTY
Gauge: 12 ga., 3 in. **Capacity:** 5-round magazine. **Barrel:** 18-7/8-in. **Weight:** 7.14 lbs. **Length:** 28.75 in. **Stock:** Black synthetic with forward vertical grip, but without a buttstock. **Features:** Gas-operated semi-automatic. Receivers machined from aircraft-grade aluminum and Mil-Spec hard anodized. Ambidextrous safety, AR-style mag and bolt release. MOE slots on fore-end. No sights or top rail. Tru-Choke thread pattern. Buttstock conversion kit available from manufacturer.
Price: **$599.00**

STOEGER M3500 PREDATOR/TURKEY
Gauge: 12 ga., 3.5 in. **Capacity:** 4+1. **Barrel:** 24 in., ventilated rib. **Length:** 46 in. **Weight:** 7.5 lbs. **Stock:** Synthetic Mossy Oak Overwatch. **Features:**

Prices given are believed to be accurate at time of publication however, many factors affect retail pricing so exact prices are not possible.

Stoeger expands its M3500 line of inertia-driven autoloaders with a predator- and turkey-specific model with a shorter barrel and rubber pistol grip. Red bar fiber-optic front sight. Receiver drilled and tapped for optics mounting. Ships with a paracord sling and five extended chokes, including MOJO Predator and MOJO Turkey tubes.
Price: **$929.00**

STOEGER M3500 WATERFOWL
Gauge: 12 ga., 3.5 in. **Barrel:** 28 in., ventilated rib. **Length:** 50 in. **Weight:** 7.8 lbs. **Stock:** Synthetic Realtree Max-5, Mossy Oak Shadow Grass Blades, or True Timber DRT. **Features:** Stoeger expands its M3500 line of inertia-driven autoloaders with a waterfowl-specific model. Red bar fiber-optic front sight. Flat Dark Earth Cerakote finish, enlarged trigger guard, drilled and tapped for optics mounting. Ships with a paracord sling and five extended choke tubes.
Price: **$849.00**

STOEGER MODEL 3000
Gauge: 12 ga., 2 3/4- and 3-in. loads. Minimum recommended load 3-dram, 1 1/8 ounces. **Capacity:** 4+1 magazine. Inertia-driven operating system. **Barrels:** 26 or 28 in. with 3 choke tubes IC, M, XF. **Weights:** 7.4–7.5 lbs. **Finish:** Black synthetic or camo (Realtree APG or Max-4). M3K model is designed for 3-Gun competition and has synthetic stock, 24-in. barrel, modified loading port.
Price: Synthetic **$599.00**
Price: Walnut or Camo **$649.00**
Price: M3K.. **$699.00**
Price: 3000R rifled slug model **$649.00**

STOEGER MODEL 3020
Gauge: 20 ga., 2 3/4- or 3-in. loads. **Features:** This model has the same general specifications as the Model 3000 except for its chambering and weight of 5.5 to 5.8 pounds.
Price: Synthetic...................................... **$599.00**
Price: Camo.. **$649.00**

STOEGER MODEL 3500
Gauge: 12 ga. 2 3/4-, 3- and 3 1/2-in. loads. Minimum recommended load 3-dram, 1-1/8 ounces. **Barrels:** 24 in., 26 in. or 28 in. Choke tubes for IC, M, XF. **Weights:** 7.4–7.5 pounds. **Finish:** Satin walnut, black synthetic or camo (Realtree APG or Max-4). **Features:** Other features similar to Model 3000.
Price: Synthetic **$679.00**
Price: Camo.. **$799.00**
Price: Satin Walnut (shown) **$769.00**

TRISTAR VIPER G2
Gauges: 12 ga., 20 ga. 2 3/4 in. or 3 in. interchangeably. **Capacity:** 5-round magazine. **Barrels:** 26 in., 28 in. (carbon fiber only offered in 12-ga. 28 in. and 20-ga. 26 in.). **Stock:** Wood, black synthetic, Mossy Oak Duck Blind camouflage, faux carbon fiber finish (2008) with the new Comfort Touch technology. **Features:** Magazine cutoff, vent rib with matted sight plane, brass front bead (camo models have fiber-optic front sight), shot plug included, and 3 Beretta-style choke tubes (IC, M, F). Viper synthetic, Viper camo have swivel studs. Five-year warranty. Viper Youth models have shortened length of pull and 24 in. barrel. Sporting model has ported barrel, checkered walnut stock with adjustable comb. Imported by Tristar Sporting Arms Ltd.
Price: From... **$549.00**
Price: Camo models, From **$640.00**
Price: Silver Model...................... **$670.00–$715.00**
Price: Youth Model.................................. **$565.00**
Price: Sporting Model.............................. **$825.00**

TRISTAR VIPER MAX
Gauge: 12. 3 1/2 in. **Barrel:** 24–30 in., threaded to accept Benelli choke tubes. Gas-operated action. Offered in several model variants. Introduced in 2017.
Price: .... **$630.00–$730.00**

WEATHERBY SA-SERIES
Gauges: 12 ga., 20 ga., 3 in. **Barrels:** 26 in., 28 in. flat ventilated rib. **Weight:** 6.5 lbs. **Stock:** Wood and synthetic. **Features:** The SA-08 is a reliable workhorse that lets you move from early season dove loads to late fall's heaviest waterfowl loads in no time. Available with wood and synthetic stock options in 12- and 20-gauge models, including a scaled-down youth model to fit 28 ga. Comes with 3 application-specific choke tubes (SK/IC/M). Made in Turkey.
Price: SA-08 Synthetic **$649.00**
Price: SA-08 Synthetic Youth...................... **$649.00**
Price: SA-08 Deluxe **$849.00**

WEATHERBY SA-459
Gauges: 12 ga., 20 ga., 3 in. **Capacities:** 5 or 8 round. **Barrels:** 18.5 in. (Tactical) or 21.25 in. (Turkey). **Features:** Tactical model has Picatinny rail, pistol grip synthetic stock, ghost ring rear and M16-type front sight. Turkey model has fiber optic front sight, Realtree Xtra Green camo finish full coverage.
Price: Tactical model................................ **$699.00**
Price: Turkey model **$799.00**

WEATHERBY 18-I
Gauges: 12 ga., 20 ga., 3 in. **Capacities:** 4+1. **Barrels:** 26 or 28 in. **Stock:** Synthetic, camo or walnut. **Features:** Inertia-operated system. Mossy Oak Shadow Grass or Realtree Max-5 camo full coverage.
Price: Synthetic.................................... **$1,099.00**
Price: Waterfowler camo **$1,199.00**
Price: Deluxe model walnut stock........... **$1,899.00**

WINCHESTER SUPER X3
Gauge: 12 ga., 3 in. and 3 1/2 in. **Barrels:** 26 in., 28 in., .742-in. back-bored; Invector Plus choke tubes. **Weights:** 7–7.25 lbs. **Stock:** Composite, 14.25 in. x 1.75 in. x 2 in. Mossy Oak New Break-Up camo with Dura-Touch Armor Coating. Pachmayr Decelerator buttpad with hard heel insert, customizable length of pull. **Features:** Alloy magazine tube, gunmetal grey Perma-Cote UT finish, self-adjusting Active Valve gas action, lightweight recoil spring system. Electroless nickel-plated bolt, three choke tubes, two length-of-pull stock spacers, drop and cast adjustment spacers, sling swivel studs. Introduced 2006. Made in Belgium, assembled in Portugal.
Price: Field **$1,140.00**
Price: Sporting, adj. comb **$1,700.00**
Price: Long Beard, pistol grip camo stock.... **$1,270.00**
Price: Composite Sporting...................... **$1,740.00**

WINCHESTER SUPER X4
Gauge: 12 ga., 3 in. and 3 1/2 in. **Capacity:** 4-round magazine. **Barrels:** 22 in., 24 in., 26 in. or 28 in. Invector Plus Flush choke tubes. **Weight:** 6 lbs. 10 oz. **Stock:** Synthetic with rounded pistol grip and textured gripping surfaces, or satin finished checkered grade II/III Turkish walnut. Length-of-pull spacers. Several camo finishes available. **Features:** TruGlo fiber optic front sight, Inflex Technology recoil pad, active valve system, matte blue barrel, matte black receiver. Offered in Standard, Field, Compact, Waterfowl, Cantilever Buck, Cantilever Turkey models.
Price: Synthetic.. **$940.00**
Price: Field, From .... **$940.00–$1,070.00**
Price: Upland Field **$1,100.00**
Price: Waterfowl Hunter .... **$940.00–$1,070.00**
Price: Hybrid Hunter.............................. **$1,040.00**
Price: NWTF Cantilever Turkey, Mossy Oak Obsession **$1,070.00**
Price: 20-gauge, 3-inch models, From **$939.99**
Price: Universal Hunter in MOBU camo, From........... **$1,069.99**

Prices given are believed to be accurate at time of publication however, many factors affect retail pricing so exact prices are not possible.

75TH EDITION, 2021 ◈ **511**

BENELLI SUPERNOVA
Gauge: 12 ga. 3 1/2 in. **Capacity:** 4-round magazine. **Barrels:** 24 in., 26 in., 28 in. **Lengths:** 45.5–49.5 in. **Stock:** Synthetic; Max-4, Timber, APG HD (2007). **Sights:** Red bar front, metal midbead. **Features:** 2 3/4 in., 3 in. chamber (3 1/2 in. 12 ga. only). Montefeltro rotating bolt design with dual action bars, magazine cutoff, synthetic trigger assembly, adjustable combs, shim kit, choice of buttstocks. Introduced 2006. Imported from Italy by Benelli USA.
Price: $549.00
Price: Camo stock $669.00
Price: Rifle slug model .... $829.00–$929.00
Price: Tactical model.......................... $519.00–$549.00

BENELLI NOVA
Gauges: 12 ga., 20 ga. **Capacity:** 4-round magazine. **Barrels:** 24 in., 26 in., 28 in. **Stock:** Black synthetic, Max-4, Timber and APG HD. **Sights:** Red bar. **Features:** 2 3/4 in., 3 in. (3 1/2 in. 12 ga. only). Montefeltro rotating bolt design with dual action bars, magazine cut-off, synthetic trigger assembly. Introduced 1999. Field & Slug Combo has 24 in. barrel and rifled bore; open rifle sights; synthetic stock; weighs 8.1 lbs. Imported from Italy by Benelli USA.
Price: Field Model.. $449.00
Price: Max-5 camo stock $559.00
Price: H20 model, black synthetic, matte nickel finish $669.00
Price: Tactical, 18.5-in. barrel, Ghost Ring sight $459.00
Price: Black synthetic youth stock, 20 ga. $469.00

BROWNING BPS
Gauges: 10 ga., 12 ga., 3 1/2 in.; 12 ga., 16 ga., or 20 ga., 3 in. (2 3/4 in. in target guns), 28 ga., 2 3/4 in., 5-shot magazine, .410, 3 in. chamber. **Barrels:** 10 ga. 24 in. Buck Special, 28 in., 30 in., 32 in. Invector; 12 ga., 20 ga. 22 in., 24 in., 26 in., 28 in., 30 in., 32 in. (Imp. Cyl., Mod. or Full), .410 26 in. (Imp. Cyl., Mod. and Full choke tubes.) Also available with Invector choke tubes, 12 or 20 ga. Upland Special has 22-in. barrel with Invector tubes. BPS 3 in. and 3 1/2 in. have back-bored barrel. **Weight:** 7 lbs., 8 oz. (28 in. barrel). **Length:** 48.75 in. overall (28 in. barrel). **Stock:** 14.25 in. x 1.5 x 2.5 in. Select walnut, semi-beavertail fore-end, full pistol grip stock. **Features:** All 12 ga. 3 in. guns except Buck Special and game guns have back-bored barrels with Invector Plus choke tubes. Bottom feeding and ejection, receiver top safety, high post vent rib. Double action bars eliminate binding. Vent rib barrels only. All 12 and 20 ga. guns with 3 in. chamber available with fully engraved receiver flats at no extra cost. Each gauge has its own unique game scene. Introduced 1977. Stalker is same gun as the standard BPS except all exposed metal parts have a matte blued finish and the stock has a black finish with a black recoil pad. Available in 10 ga. (3 1/2 in.) and 12 ga. with 3 in. or 3 1/2 in. chamber, 22 in., 28 in., 30 in. barrel with Invector choke system. Introduced 1987. Rifled Deer Hunter is similar to the standard BPS except has newly designed receiver/magazine tube/barrel mounting system to eliminate play, heavy 20.5-in. barrel with rifle-type sights with adjustable rear, solid receiver scope mount, "rifle" stock dimensions for scope or open sights, sling swivel studs. Gloss or matte finished wood with checkering, polished blue metal. Medallion model has additional engraving on receiver, polished blue finish, AA/AAA grade walnut stock with checkering. All-Purpose model has Realtree AP camo on stock and fore-end, HiVis fiber optic sights. Introduced 2013. Imported from Japan by Browning.
Price: Field, Stalker models, From........... $600.00–$700.00
Price: Camo coverage $820.00
Price: Deer Hunter $830.00
Price: Deer Hunter Camo................................ $870.00
Price: Field Composite..................... $659.99-$679.99
Price: Field Composite Camo $779.99
Price: Magnum Hunter (3 1/2 in.)........... $800.00–$1,030.00
Price: Medallion $830.00
Price: Trap $840.00

BROWNING BPS 10 GAUGE SERIES
Similar to the standard BPS except completely covered with Mossy Oak Shadow Grass camouflage. Available with 26- and 28-in. barrel. Introduced

1999. Imported by Browning
Price: Mossy Oak camo $950.00
Price: Synthetic stock, Stalker $800.00

BROWNING BPS NWTF TURKEY SERIES
Similar to the standard BPS except has full coverage Mossy Oak Break-Up Infinity camo finish on synthetic stock, fore-end and exposed metal parts. Offered in 12 ga., 3 in. or 3 1/2 in., or 10 ga. 24-in. bbl. has extra-full choke tube and HiViz fiber-optic sights. Introduced 2001. From Browning.
Price: 12 ga., 3 in. $950.00
Price: 3 1/2 in. $1,030.00

BROWNING BPS MICRO MIDAS
Gauges: 12 ga, 20 ga, 28 ga. or .410 bore. **Barrels:** 24 or 26 in. Three Invector choke tubes for 12 and 20 ga., standard tubes for 28 ga. and .410. **Stock:** Walnut with pistol grip and recoil pad. Satin finished and scaled down to fit smaller statured shooters. Length of pull is 13.25 in. Two spacers included for stock length adjustments. **Weights:** 7–7.8 lbs.
Price: .... $700.00–$740.00

BROWING BPS HIGH CAPACITY
Gauge: .410 bore. 3 in. **Capacity:** 5-round magazine. **Barrel:** 20 in. fixed Cylinder choke; stainless Steel; Matte finish. **Weight:** 6 lbs. **Length:** 40.75 in. **Stock:** Black composite on All Weather with matte finish. **Features:** Forged and machined steel; satin nickel finish. Bottom ejection; dual steel action bars; top tang safety. HiViz Tactical fiber-optic front sight; stainless internal mechanism; swivel studs installed.
Price: Synthetic $800.00

CHARLES DALY 300 SERIES
Gauges: 12 ga., 20 ga. or 28 ga. 3 in. and 2 3/4-in. shells (12 ga. and 20 ga.), 2 3/4 in. (28 ga.). Model 335 Master Mag is chambered for 12-ga. 3 1/2-inch shells. **Barrels:** 24 in., 26 in., 28 in. and 30 in., depending upon specific model. Ventilated rib. Three choke tubes (REM-Choke pattern) are provided. **Stock:** Synthetic, walnut or camo. **Weights:** 7–8 lbs. Left-hand models available. Imported from Turkey.
Price: Field .... $365.00–$495.00
Price: Tactical.. $354.00–$503.00
Price: Turkey $553.00

CZ 612
Gauge: 12 ga. Chambered for all shells up to 3 1/2 in. **Capacity:** 5+1, magazine plug included with Wildfowl Magnum. **Barrels:** 18.5 in. (Home Defense), 20 in. (HC-P), 26 in. (Wildfowl Mag). **Weights:** 6–6.8 pounds. **Stock:** Polymer. **Finish:** Matte black or full camo (Wildfowl Mag.) HC-P model has pistol grip stock, fiber optic front sight and ghost-ring rear. Home Defense Combo comes with extra 26-in. barrel.
Price: Wildfowl Magnum $428.00
Price: Home Defense .... $304.00–$409.00
Price: Target $549.00

CZ MODEL 620/628 Field Select
Gauges: 20 ga. or 28 ga. **Barrel:** 28 inches. **Weight:** 5.4 lbs. **Features:** Similar to Model 612 except for chambering. Introduced in 2017.
Price: $429.00

ESCORT FIELDHUNTER TURKEY
Gauges: 12 ga., 3 in., 20 ga., 3 in., .410 bore, 3 in. **Capacity:** 4+1. **Barrels:** 22 in., 24 in., 26 in., ventilated rib. **Length:** 42-46 in. **Weight:** 6.0-6.9 lbs. **Stock:** Synthetic with camo finish. **Features:** The pump-action Turkey model addition to the FieldHunter family is built of aircraft alloy with a black chrome-finished steel barrel that is camo coated. Cantilever Weaver optics rail, fully adjustable green rear fiber-optic sight with windage-adjustable front red fiber-optic sight. Cross-bolt safety, rubber butt pad, sling studs. Includes three chokes (Ext Turkey, F, IM).
Price: $399.99

ESCORT PUMP SERIES
Gauges: 12 ga., 20 ga.; 3 in. **Barrels:** 18 in. (AimGuard, Home Defense and MarineGuard), 22 in. (Youth Pump), 26 in., and 28 in. lengths. **Weight:** 6.7-7.0 lbs. **Stock:** Polymer in black, Shadow Grass camo or Obsession camo finish. Two adjusting spacers included. Youth model has Trio recoil pad.

Prices given are believed to be accurate at time of publication however, many factors affect retail pricing so exact prices are not possible.

Sights: Bead or Spark front sights, depending on model. AimGuard and MarineGuard models have blade front sights. **Features:** Black-chrome or dipped camo metal parts, top of receiver dovetailed for sight mounts, gold plated trigger, trigger guard safety, magazine cutoff. Three choke tubes (IC, M, F) except AimGuard/MarineGuard which are cylinder bore. Models include: FH, FH Youth, AimGuard and Marine Guard. Introduced in 2003. Imported from Turkey by Legacy Sports International.

Price: $379.00
Price: Youth model $393.00
Price: Model 87 w/wood stock $350.00
Price: Home Defense (18-in. bbl.) $400.00

ESCORT SLUGGER
Gauge: 12 ga., 3 in. **Capacity:** 5+1. **Barrels:** 26 in., 28 in., ventilated rib. **Length:** 38 in. **Weight:** 6.4-6.5 lbs. **Stock:** Black synthetic. Slugger Tactical has pistol grip. **Features:** The pump-action Slugger is built of black-anodized aircraft alloy with a black chrome-finished steel barrel. Fixed cylinder bore choke, cross-bolt safety, fiber-optic front sight, rubber butt pad, sling studs.
Price: .... $209.99-$219.99

HARRINGTON & RICHARDSON (H&R) PARDNER PUMP
Gauges: 12 ga., 20 ga. 3 in. **Barrels:** 21–28 in. **Weight:** 6.5–7.5 lbs. **Stock:** Synthetic or hardwood. Ventilated recoil pad and grooved fore-end. **Features:** Steel receiver, double action bars, cross-bolt safety, easy takedown, ventilated rib, screw-in choke tubes.
Price: From... $231.00–$259.00

IAC MODEL 97T TRENCH GUN
Gauge: 12 ga., 2 3/4 in. **Barrel:** 20 in. with cylinder choke. **Stock:** Hand rubbed American walnut. **Features:** Replica of Winchester Model 1897 Trench Gun. Metal handguard, bayonet lug. Imported from China by Interstate Arms Corp.
Price: $465.00

IAC HAWK SERIES
Gauge: 12, 2 3/4 in. **Barrel:** 18.5 in. with cylinder choke. **Stock:** Synthetic. **Features:** This series of tactical/home defense shotguns is based on the Remington 870 design. 981 model has top Picatinny rail and bead front sight. 982 has adjustable ghost ring sight with post front. 982T has same sights as 982 plus a pistol grip stock. Imported from China by Interstate Arms Corporation.
Price: 981 .... $275.00
Price: 982 .... $285.00
Price: 982T $300.00

ITHACA MODEL 37 FEATHERLIGHT
Gauges: 12 ga., 20 ga., 16 ga., 28 ga. **Capacity:** 4+1. **Barrels:** 26 in., 28 in. or 30 in. with 3-in. chambers (12 and 20 ga.), plain or ventilated rib. **Weights:** 6.1–7.6 lbs. **Stock:** Fancy-grade black walnut with Pachmayr Decelerator recoil pad. Checkered fore-end made of matching walnut. **Features:** Receiver machined from a single block of steel or aluminum. Barrel is steel shot compatible. Three Briley choke tubes provided. Available in several variations including turkey, home defense, tactical and high-grade.
Price: 12 ga., 16 ga. or 20 ga. From $895.00
Price: 28 ga. From.. $1,149.00
Price: Turkey Slayer w/synthetic stock, From $925.00
Price: Trap Series 12 ga.................................. $1,020.00
Price: Waterfowl.. $885.00
Price: Home Defense 18- or 20-in. bbl.................. $784.00

ITHACA DEERSLAYER III SLUG
Gauges: 12 ga., 20 ga. 3 in. **Barrel:** 26 in. fully rifled, heavy fluted with 1:28 twist for 12 ga. 1:24 for 20 ga. **Weights:** 8.14–9.5 lbs. with scope mounted.

Length: 45.625 in. overall. **Stock:** Fancy black walnut stock and fore-end. **Sights:** NA. **Features:** Updated, slug-only version of the classic Model 37. Bottom ejection, blued barrel and receiver.
Price: $1,350.00

MAVERICK ARMS MODEL 88
Gauges: 12 ga., 20 ga. 3 in. **Barrels:** 26 in. or 28 in., Accu-Mag choke tubes for steel or lead shot. **Weight:** 7.25 lbs. **Stock:** Black synthetic with recoil pad. **Features:** Crossbolt safety, aluminum alloy receiver. Economy model of Mossberg Model 500 series. Available in several variations including Youth, Slug and Special Purpose (home defense) models.
Price: .... $231.00-$259.00

MOSSBERG MODEL 835 ULTI-MAG
Gauge: 12 ga., 3 1/2 in. **Barrels:** Ported 24 in. rifled bore, 24 in., 28 in., Accu-Mag choke tubes for steel or lead shot. Combo models come with interchangeable second barrel. **Weight:** 7.75 lbs. **Length:** 48.5 in. overall. **Stock:** 14 in. x 1.5 in. x 2.5 in. Dual Comb. Cut-checkered hardwood or camo synthetic; both have recoil pad. **Sights:** White bead front, brass mid-bead; fiber-optic rear. **Features:** Shoots 2 3/4-, 3- or 3 1/2-in. shells. Back-bored and ported barrel to reduce recoil, improve patterns. Ambidextrous thumb safety, twin extractors, dual slide bars. Mossberg Cablelock included. Introduced 1988.
Price: Turkey .... $601.00–$617.00
Price: Waterfowl .... $518.00–$603.00
Price: Turkey/Deer combo .... $661.00–$701.00
Price: Turkey/Waterfowl combo $661.00
Price: Tactical Turkey $652.00

MOSSBERG MODEL 500 SPORTING SERIES
Gauges: 12 ga., 20 ga., .410 bore, 3 in. **Barrels:** 18.5 in. to 28 in. with fixed or Accu-Choke, plain or vent rib. Combo models come with interchangeable second barrel. **Weight:** 6.25 lbs. (.410), 7.25 lbs. (12). **Length:** 48 in. overall (28-in. barrel). **Stock:** 14 in. x 1.5 in. x 2.5 in. Walnut-stained hardwood, black synthetic, Mossy Oak Advantage camouflage. Cut-checkered grip and fore-end. **Sights:** White bead front, brass mid-bead; fiber-optic. **Features:** Ambidextrous thumb safety, twin extractors, disconnecting safety, dual action bars. Quiet Carry fore-end. Many barrels are ported. FLEX series has many modular options and accessories including barrels and stocks. From Mossberg. Left-hand versions (L-series) available in most models.
Price: Turkey, From $486.00
Price: Waterfowl, From $537.00
Price: Combo, From $593.00
Price: FLEX Hunting $702.00
Price: FLEX All Purpose $561.00
Price: Field, From $419.00
Price: Slugster, From $447.00
Price: FLEX Deer/Security combo...................... $787.00
Price: Home Security 410 .... $477.00
Price: Tactical...................................... $486.00-$602.00

MOSSBERG MODEL 500 SUPER BANTAM PUMP
Same as the Model 500 Sporting Pump except 12 or 20 ga., 22-in. vent rib Accu-Choke barrel with choke tube set; has 1 in. shorter stock, reduced length from pistol grip to trigger, reduced fore-end reach. Introduced 1992.
Price: $419.00
Price: Combo with extra slug barrel, camo finish $549.00

Prices given are believed to be accurate at time of publication however, many factors affect retail pricing so exact prices are not possible.

75TH EDITION, 2021 ⊕ **513**

MOSSBERG 510 MINI BANTAM

Gauges: 20 ga., .410 bore, 3 in. **Barrel:** 18.5 in. vent-rib. **Weight:** 5 lbs. **Length:** 34.75 in. **Stock:** Synthetic with optional Mossy Oak Break-Up Infinity, Muddy Girl pink/black camo. **Features:** Available in either 20 ga. or .410 bore, the Mini features an 18.5-in. vent-rib barrel with dual bead sights. Parents don't have to worry about their young shooter growing out of this gun too quick, the adjustable classic stock can be adjusted from 10.5 to 11.5-in. length of pull so the Mini can grow with your youngster. This adjustability also helps provide a proper fit for young shooters and allowing for a more safe and enjoyable shooting experience.
Price: From .... $419.00–$466.00

MOSSBERG SHOCKWAVE SERIES

Gauges: 12, 20 ga. or .410 cylinder bore, 3-inch chamber. **Barrel:** 14 3/8, 18.5 in. **Weight:** 5 – 5.5 lbs. **Length:** 26.4 - 30.75 in. **Stock:** Synthetic or wood. Raptor bird's-head type pistol grip. Nightstick has wood stock and fore-end.
Price: From $455.00
Price: CTC Laser Saddle Model $613.00
Price: Ceracote finish $504.00
Price: Nightstick (shown $539.00
Price: Mag-Fed $721.00
Price: SPX w/heatshield $560.00

REMINGTON MODEL 870 WINGMASTER

Gauge: 12 ga., 20 ga., 28 ga., .410 bore. **Barrel:** 25 in., 26 in., 28 in., 30 in. (RemChokes). **Weight:** 7.25 lbs. **Lengths:** 46–48 in. **Stock:** Walnut, hardwood. **Sights:** Single bead (Twin bead Wingmaster). **Features:** Light contour barrel. Double action bars, cross-bolt safety, blue finish. LW is 28 ga. and .410 bore only, 25-in. vent rib barrel with RemChoke tubes, high-gloss wood finish. Gold-plated trigger, American B Grade or Claro walnut stock and fore-end, high-gloss finish, *fleur-de-lis* checkering. A classic American shotgun first introduced in 1950.
Price: From $847.00

REMINGTON MODEL 870 TAC-14

Similar to 870 Wingmaster except has Raptor pistol grip, synthetic or hardwood grip fore-end. Has 18-in. plain barrel (cyl.), bead front sight, 7-round magazine. Marine Magnum has electroless nickel-plated finish on all metal parts including inside receiver and barrel. Special Purpose model has full-length synthetic stock.
Price: $443.00
Price: DM Detachable magazine model $559.00
Price: Marine Magnum $841.00
Price: Marine Magnum Special Purpose $841.00

REMINGTON MODEL 870 CLASSIC TRAP

Similar to Model 870 Wingmaster except has 30-in. vent rib barrel, singles, mid- and long-handicap choke tubes, semi-fancy American walnut stock, high-polish blued receiver with engraving. Chamber 2.75 in. From Remington Arms Co.
Price: $1,120.00

REMINGTON MODEL 870 EXPRESS

Similar to Model 870 Wingmaster except laminate, synthetic black, or camo stock with solid, black recoil pad and pressed checkering on grip and fore-end. Outside metal surfaces have black oxide finish. Comes with 26- or 28-in. vent rib barrel with mod. RemChoke tube. ShurShot Turkey (2008) has ShurShot synthetic pistol-grip thumbhole design, extended fore-end, Mossy Oak Obsession camouflage, matte black metal finish, 21-in. vent rib barrel, twin beads, Turkey Extra Full Rem Choke tube. Receiver drilled and tapped for mounting optics. ShurShot FR CL (Fully Rifled Cantilever, 2008) includes compact 23-in. fully rifled barrel with integrated cantilever scope mount. New (in 2020) 870 Express Trap, 12 ga., 3 in., 30-in. barrel. Hardwood Monte Carlo stock with raised comb, mid-bead, ivory front target sight, gold trigger. Ships with three choke tubes.
Price: Trap, ... $609.00
Price: .... $417.00–$629.00

REMINGTON MODEL 870 EXPRESS SUPER MAGNUM

Similar to Model 870 Express except 28-in. vent rib barrel with 3 1/2-in. chamber, vented recoil pad. Introduced 1998. Model 870 Express Super Magnum Waterfowl (2008) is fully camouflaged with Mossy Oak Duck Blind pattern, 28-inch vent rib Rem Choke barrel, "Over Decoys" Choke tube (.007 in.) fiber-optic HiViz single bead front sight; front and rear sling swivel studs, padded black sling.
Price: $469.00
Price: Waterfowl, Mossy Oak Duck Blind camo $660.86

REMINGTON MODEL 870 EXPRESS TACTICAL

Similar to Model 870 but in 12 ga. only (2 3/4 in. and 3 in. interchangeably) with 18.5-in. barrel, Tactical RemChoke extended/ported choke tube, black synthetic buttstock and fore-end, extended magazine tube, gray powder coat finish overall. 38.5 in. overall length. Weighs 7.5 lbs.
Price: $601.00
Price: Model 870 TAC Desert Recon; desert camo stock and sand-toned metal surfaces $692.00
Price: Tactical Magpul $898.00

REMINGTON 870 DM SERIES

Gauge: 12 ga. (2 3/4 in. and 3 in. interchangeably). **Capacity:** Detachable 6-round magazine. **Barrel:** 18.5-in. cylinder bore. **Stock:** Hardwood or black synthetic with textured gripping surfaces. Tac-14 DM model features short pistol grip buttstock and 14-inch barrel.
Price: $559.00

REMINGTON MODEL 870 SPS SHURSHOT SYNTHETIC SUPER SLUG
Gauge: 12 ga.; 2 3/4 in. and 3 in. interchangeable. **Barrel:** 25.5-in. extra-heavy, fully rifled pinned to receiver. **Weight:** 7.875 lbs. **Length:** 47 in. overall. **Features:** Pump-action model based on 870 platform. SuperCell recoil pad. Drilled and tapped for scope mounts with Weaver rail included. Matte black metal surfaces, ShurShot pistol grip buttstock with Mossy Oak Treestand camo.
Price: **$829.00**
Price: 870 SPS ShurShot Synthetic Turkey; adjustable
    sights and APG HD camo buttstock and fore-end **$681.00**

REMINGTON 870 EXPRESS SYNTHETIC SUPER MAG TURKEY-WATERFOWL CAMO
Gauge: 12 ga., 2 3/4 to 3 1/2 in. **Features:** Pump-action shotgun. Full Mossy Oak Bottomland camo coverage; 26-inch barrel with HiViz fiber-optics sights; Wingmaster HD Waterfowl and Turkey Extra Full RemChokes; SuperCell recoil pad; drilled and tapped receiver.
Price: **$629.00**

REMINGTON 870 EXPRESS SYNTHETIC TURKEY CAMO
Gauge: 12 ga., 2 3/4 and 3 in. **Features:** Pump-action shotgun. 21-inch vent rib bead-sighted barrel; standard Express finish on barrel and receiver; Turkey Extra Full RemChoke; synthetic stock with integrated sling swivel attachment.
Price: **$492.00**

REMINGTON 870 SUPER MAG TURKEY-PREDATOR CAMO WITH SCOPE
Gauge: 12 ga., 2 3/4 to 3 1/2 in. **Features:** Pump-action shotgun. 20-in. barrel; TruGlo red/green selectable illuminated sight mounted on pre-installed Weaver-style rail; black padded sling; Wingmaster HDTurkey/Predator RemChoke; full Mossy Oak Obsession camo coverage; ShurShot pistol grip stock with black overmolded grip panels; TruGlo 30mm Red/Green Dot Scope pre-mounted.
Price: **$710.00**

STANDARD MANUFACTURING DP-12
Gauge: 12 ga., 3 in. **Capacity:** 14+2. **Barrels:** 18-7/8 in. **Weight:** 9 lbs., 12oz. **Length:** 29.5 in. **Stock:** Black synthetic. **Features:** Double-barrel bullpup pump design. Single trigger, inline shell feeding. Machined from aircraft-grade aluminum with thermal-coated receiver. Ambidextrous safety and pump-slide release. Composite front vertical grip, sling attachments, fore-end MOE rails. Rubber recoil pad with dual-spring shock absorbing mechanism. Includes spreader choke tubes with Tru-Choke thread pattern.
Price: **$1,395.00**

STEVENS MODEL 320
Gauges: 12 ga., or 20 ga. with 3-in. chamber. **Capacity:** 5+1. **Barrels:** 18.25 in., 20 in., 22 in., 26 in. or 28 in. with interchangeable choke tubes. Features include all-steel barrel and receiver; bottom-load and ejection design; black synthetic stock.
Price: Security Model **$276.00**
Price: Field Model 320 with 28-inch barrel......................... **$251.00**
Price: Combo Model with Field and Security barrels **$307.00**

STOEGER P3000
Gauge: 12 ga. 3-in. **Barrels:** 18.5 in., 26 in., 28 in., with ventilated rib. **Weight:** 6.5–7 lbs. **Stock:** Black synthetic. Camo finish available. Defense Model available with or without pistol grip.
Price: **$299.00**
Price: Camo finish **$399.00**
Price: Defense model w/pistol grip **$349.00**

TRISTAR COBRA III CAMO
Gauges: 12 ga., 3 in., 20 ga., 3 in. **Barrels:** 24 in., 26 in., 28 in., ventilated rib. **Weight:** 6.7-6.9 lbs. **Length:** 44.5-48.5 in. **Stock:** Synthetic camo with either Realtree Max-5 or Realtree Advantage Timber. **Features:** Third model upgrade to the Cobra pump action with extended fore-end. Solid rubber buttpad, cross-bolt safety, chrome-lined barrel, sling studs. Realtree camo coverage. Includes three Beretta Mobil-style choke tubes (IC, M, F).
Price: .... **$365.00-$395.00**

TRISTAR COBRA III FIELD
Gauges: 12 ga., 3 in., 20 ga., 3 in. **Barrels:** 26 in., 28 in., ventilated rib. **Weight:** 6.7-7.0 lbs. **Length:** 46.5-48.5 in. **Stock:** Field models available with either Turkish walnut or black synthetic furniture. **Features:** Third model upgrade to the Cobra pump-action line with extended fore-end. Rubber buttpad, cross-bolt safety, chrome-lined barrel, high-polish blue metalwork, sling studs. Includes three Beretta Mobil-style choke tubes (IC, M, F).
Price: .... **$305.00-$335.00**

TRISTAR COBRA III YOUTH
Gauge: 20 ga., 3 in. **Barrel:** 24 in., ventilated rib. **Weight:** 5.4-6.5 lbs. **Length:** 37.7 in. **Stock:** Version III youth models available with black synthetic, Realtree Max-5 camo or Turkish-walnut furniture. **Features:** Third iteration of the Cobra pump-action with extended fore-end. Ventilated rubber buttpad, cross-bolt safety, chrome-lined barrel, sling studs. Shorter length of pull on Youth model. Includes three Beretta Mobil-style choke tubes (IC, M, F).
Price: .... **$305.00-$365.00**

WINCHESTER SUPER X (SXP)
Gauges: 12 ga., 3 in. or 3 1/2 in. chambers; 20 ga., 3 in. **Barrels:** 18 in., 26 in., 28 in. Barrels .742-in. back-bored, chrome plated; Invector Plus choke tubes. **Weights:** 6.5–7 lbs. **Stocks:** Walnut or composite. **Features:** Rotary bolt, four lugs, dual steel action bars. Walnut Field has gloss-finished walnut stock and forearm, cut checkering. Black Shadow Field has composite stock and forearm, non-glare matte finish barrel and receiver. SXP Defender has composite stock and forearm, chromed plated, 18-in. cylinder choked barrel, non-glare metal surfaces, five-shot magazine, grooved forearm. Some models offered in left-hand versions. Reintroduced 2009. Made in USA by Winchester Repeating Arms Co.
Price: Black Shadow Field, 3 in. **$380.00**
Price: Black Shadow Field, 3 1/2 in. **$430.00**
Price: SXP Defender.................................... **$350.00–$400.00**
Price: Waterfowl Hunter 3 in. **$460.00**
Price: Waterfowl Hunter 3 1/2 in. **$500.00**
Price: Turkey Hunter 3 1/2 in. **$520.00**
Price: Black Shadow Deer **$520.00**
Price: Trap **$480.00**
Price: Field, walnut stock.............................. **$400.00–$430.00**
Price: 20-ga., 3-in. models, from **$379.99**

WINCHESTER SUPER X (SXP) BUCK/BIRD COMBO
The Winchester SXP Buck/Bird combo expands on the Super-X pump lineup with options in both 12 and 20 gauge. Choice of vent-rib bird barrel in either 26- or 28-in., along with a 22-in. rifled deer barrel with sights. Black synthetic stock, matte-finish metalwork.
Price: **$629.99-659.99**

Prices given are believed to be accurate at time of publication however, many factors affect retail pricing so exact pricing is not possible.

75TH EDITION, 2021 ✦ **515**

AMERICAN TACTICAL INC (ATI) CRUSADER
Gauges: 12 ga., 3 in., 20 ga., 3 in., 28 ga., 2.75 in, .410 bore, 3 in. **Barrels:** 26 in., 28 in., 30 in., ventilated rib. **Weight:** 6.0-6.5 lbs. **Stock:** Turkish walnut with oil finish. **Features:** ATI's new O/U line has both Field and Sport models. Made from 7075 aluminum with laser engraving on the receiver. Single selective trigger, fiber-optic front sight, extractors, chrome-moly steel barrel. Ships with five chokes: flush on the Field, extended on the Sport.
Price: Crusader Field **$499.95**
Price: Crusader Sport **$549.95**

BERETTA 686 SILVER PIGEON I
Gauges: 12 ga., 3 in., 20 ga., 3 in., 28 ga., 2.75 in., .410 bore. **Barrels:** 26 in., 28 in, 30 in., with 6x6 rib. **Weight:** 6.2-7.25 lbs. **Stock:** Selected walnut in either left- or right-handed versions with a choice of Schnabel or rounded fore-end. **Features:** The improved version of the Silver Pigeon features upgraded Steelium Optima HP barrels, deeper laser engraving of floral motifs, and oil-finished stocks. MicroCore recoil pad, dual conical locking lugs, tang safety and barrel selector, single gold-plated trigger. Includes five interchangeable Mobil chokes and a fitted hard carrying case. Available in both Field and Sporting models.
Price: From **$2,350.00**

BERETTA 694
Gauge: 12 ga., 3 in. **Barrels:** 28 in., 30 in., 32 in., with either 10x8 or 10x10 ventilated rib. **Weight:** 7.8-8.1 lbs. **Stock:** Walnut with 35/50 and 35/55 B-Fast options. **Features:** Designed specifically for competition shooting, the 694 has a slim, modern design. Steelium Plus barrels for dense, uniform patterns. Fore-end iron system with adjustable opening. MicroCore 18mm recoil pad, single centrally positioned adjustable trigger, 1.5 pitch checkering, 2.5-plus grade wood. Matte gray Nistan finish with blue inlay trim. Balance weights of 20g and 40g available separately. Both Sporting and Trap models available.
Price: From **$4,500.00**

BARRETT SOVEREIGN ALBANY
Gauges: 12 ga., 20 ga., 28 ga. 3 in. (2 3/4 for 28 ga.) **Barrels:** 26 in., 28 in. or 30 in. **Stock:** Checkered grade AAA Turkish walnut with rounded Prince of Wales pistol grip. **Features:** Receiver scaled to individual gauges. Round body boxlock design, ornamental sideplates, coin-finished receiver. Introduced in 2016. Imported from Italy by Barrett Firearms.
Price: 12 or 20 ga. **$5,700.00**
Price: 28 ga. **$6,150.00**

BARRET SOVEREIGN BX-PRO
Gauge: 12 ga. **Barrels:** 30 in., 32 in. with 6 extended choke tubes. Ventilated rib tapered from 10mm to 7mm. **Stock:** A+ grade walnut with rounded Prince of Wales pistol grip. Cast-off comb and toe for right-handed shooters Length of pull: 14.5 inches. Adjustable comb. Right-hand palm swell. **Features:** Automatic ejectors, single selective trigger, coin finished and engraved receiver. Imported from Fausti of Italy by Barrett Firearms.
Price: **$3,075.00**

BARRET SOVEREIGN RUTHERFORD
Gauges: 12 ga., 16 ga., 20 ga., 28 ga. **Barrels:** 26 in., 28 in. with 5 choke tubes. Chamber lengths are 3-in. for 12 and 20 ga., 2 ¾ in. for 16 ga. and 28 ga. **Stock:** A+ grade with cut checkering, red recoil pad, and rounded Prince of Wales pistol grip. **Features:** Receivers are sized to individual gauge, automatic ejectors, single selective trigger, coin finished receiver. Imported from Fausti of Italy by Barrett Firearms.
Price: 12, 20 ga. **$2,200.00**
Price: 16, 28 ga. **$2,520.00**

BENELLI 828U
Gauges: 12 ga. 3 in. **Barrels:** 26 in., 28 in. **Weights:** 6.5–7 lbs. **Stock:** AA-grade satin walnut, fully adjustable for both drop and cast. **Features:** New

patented locking system allows use of aluminum frame. Features include carbon fiber rib, fiber-optic sight, removable trigger group, and Benelli's Progressive Comfort recoil reduction system.
Price: Matte black **$2,699.00**
Price: Nickel **$3,199.00**
Price: 20-gauge Nickel **$3,199.00**

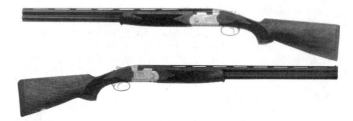

BERETTA 686/687 SILVER PIGEON SERIES
Gauges: 12 ga., 20 ga., 28 ga., 3 in. (2 3/4 in. 28 ga.). .410 bore, 3 in. **Barrels:** 26 in., 28 in. **Weight:** 6.8 lbs. **Stock:** Checkered walnut. **Features:** Interchangeable barrels (20 ga. and 28 ga.), single selective gold-plated trigger, boxlock action, auto safety, Schnabel fore-end.
Price: 686 Silver Pigeon Grade I **$2,350.00**
Price: 686 Silver Pigeon Grade I, Sporting **$2,400.00**
Price: 687 Silver Pigeon Grade III **$3,430.00**
Price: 687 Silver Pigeon Grade V **$4,075.00**

BERETTA MODEL 687 EELL
Gauges: 12 ga., 20 ga., 28 ga., 410 bore. **Features:** Premium-grade model with decorative sideplates featuring lavish hand-chased engraving with a classic game scene enhanced by detailed leaves and flowers that also cover the trigger guard, trigger plate and fore-end lever. Stock has high-grade, specially selected European walnut with fine-line checkering. Offered in three action sizes with scaled-down 28 ga. and .410 receivers. Combo models are available with extra barrel sets in 20/28 or 28/.410.
Price: **$7,995.00**
Price: Combo model **$9,695.00**

BERETTA MODEL 690
Gauge: 12 ga. 3 in. **Barrels:** 26 in., 28 in., 30 in. with OptimaChoke HP system. **Features:** Similar to the 686/687 series with minor improvements. Stock has higher grade oil-finished walnut. Re-designed barrel/fore-end attachment reduces weight.
Price: .... **$2,650.00–$3,100.00**

BERETTA MODEL 692 SPORTING
Gauge: 12 ga., 3 in. **Barrels:** 30 in. with long forcing cones of approximately 14 in.. Skeet model available with 28- or 30-in. barrel, Trap model with 30 in or 32 in. Receiver is .50-in. wider than 682 model for improved handling. **Stock:** Hand rubbed oil finished select walnut with Schnabel fore-end. Features include selective single adjustable trigger, manual safety, tapered 8mm to 10mm rib.
Price: **$4,800.00**
Price: Skeet **$5,275.00**
Price: Trap **$5,600.00**

BERETTA DT11
Gauge: 12 ga. 3 in. **Barrels:** 30 in., 32 in., 34 in. Top rib has hollowed bridges. **Stock:** Hand-checkered buttstock and fore-end. Hand-rubbed oil, Tru-Oil or wax finish. Adjustable comb on skeet and trap models. **Features:** Competition model offered in Sporting, Skeet and Trap models. Newly designed receiver, top lever, safety/selector button.
Price: Sporting, From **$8,650.00**
Price: Skeet, From **$8,650.00**
Price: Trap, From **$8,999.00**

Prices given are believed to be accurate at time of publication however, many factors affect retail pricing so exact prices are not possible.

BLASER F3 SUPERSPORT
Gauge: 12 ga., 3 in. **Barrel:** 32 in. **Weight:** 9 lbs. **Stock:** Adjustable semi-custom, Turkish walnut wood grade: 4. **Features:** The latest addition to the F3 family is the F3 SuperSport. The perfect blend of overall weight, balance and weight distribution make the F3 SuperSport the ideal competitor. Briley Spectrum-5 chokes, free-floating barrels, adjustable barrel hanger system on o/u, chrome plated barrels full length, revolutionary ejector ball system, barrels finished in a powder coated nitride, selectable competition trigger.

Price: SuperSport, From $9,076.00
Price: Competition Sporting.................................... $7,951.00
Price: Superskeet... $9,076.00
Price: American Super Trap $9,530.00

BROWNING CYNERGY
Gauges: .410 bore, 12 ga., 20 ga., 28 ga. **Barrels:** 26 in., 28 in., 30 in., 32 in. **Stocks:** Walnut or composite. **Sights:** White bead front most models; HiViz Pro-Comp sight on some models; mid bead. **Features:** Mono-Lock hinge, recoil-reducing interchangeable Inflex recoil pad, silver nitride receiver; striker-based trigger, ported barrel option. Imported from Japan by Browning.

Price: Field Grade Model, 12 ga. $1,910.00
Price: CX composite.. $1,710.00
Price: CX walnut stock... $1,780.00
Price: Field, small gauges..................................... $1,940.00
Price: Ultimate Turkey, Mossy Oak Breakup camo $2,390.00
Price: Micro Midas $1,979.99
Price: Feather $2,269.99
Price: Wicked Wing $2,339.99

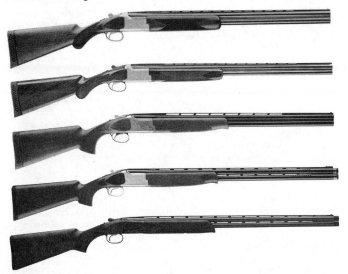

BROWNING CITORI SERIES
Gauges: 12 ga., 20 ga., 28 ga., .410 bore. **Barrels:** 26 in., 28 in. in 28 ga. and .410 bore. Offered with Invector choke tubes. All 12- and 20-ga. models have back-bored barrels and Invector Plus choke system. **Weights:** 6 lbs., 8 oz. (26 in. .410) to 7 lbs., 13 oz. (30 in. 12 ga.). **Length:** 43 in. overall (26-in. bbl.). **Stock:** Dense walnut, hand checkered, full pistol grip, beavertail fore-end. Field-type recoil pad on 12 ga. field guns and trap and skeet models. **Sights:** Medium-raised beads, German nickel silver. **Features:** Barrel selector integral with safety, automatic ejectors, three-piece takedown. Imported from Japan by Browning.

Price: White Lightning $2,670.00
Price: Feather Lightning....................................... $2,870.00
Price: Gran Lightning $3,300.00
Price: Crossover (CX) $2,140.00
Price: Crossover (CX) w/adjustable comb $2,560.00
Price: Crossover (CXS)... $2,140.00
Price: Crossover Target (CXT) $2,260.00
Price: Crossover Target (CXT) w/adjustable comb......... $2,660.00
Price: Crossover (CXS)... $2,190.00
Price: Crossover (CXS) w/adjustable comb $2,590.00
Price: Crossover (CXS Micro) $2,140.00
Price: White Lightning .410 bore and 28 ga. .... $2,669.99-$2,739.99
Price: CX White... $2,379.99
Price: CX White Adjustable.................................... $2,939.99
Price: CX Micro... $2,469.99
Price: CXS 20/28 Ga. Combo $3,939.99
Price: CXS White.. $2,439.99
Price: CXT White.. $2,499.99

BROWNING CITORI FIELD SPORTING GRADE VII
Gauge: 12 ga., 3 in. **Barrels:** 30 in., 32 in., with 3/8 to 1/2 ventilated rib. **Weight:** 8 lbs.-8.2 lbs. **Length:** 47.5-49.5 in. **Stock:** Grade VI/VII black walnut with gloss-oil finish and nameplate inlay for owner's initials. **Features:** This top-end shotgun from the Browning High Grade Program offers silver bird-dog engraving. Inflex recoil pad. Triple Trigger System with three trigger shoes and gold-plated trigger, and trigger guard engraving. Silver-Nitride receiver finish, cut checkering at 20 LPI. Polished blued barrels with chrome-plated chambers. Hi-Viz Pro Comp sight and ivory mid-bead. Includes five extended black Midas Grade choke tubes (F, IM, M, IC, SK). Ideal for sporting clays, skeet and hunting.
Price: $6,269.99

BROWNING CITORI TRAP MAX
Gauge: 12 ga., 2.75 in. **Barrels:** 30 in., 32 in., ported with 5/16 to 7/16 adjustable ventilated rib. **Weight:** 9.0-9.2 lbs. **Length:** 47.75-49.75 in. **Stock:** Grade V/VI black walnut with gloss-oil finish. **Features:** Graco adjustable Monte Carlo comb. Buttplate adjusts for location and angle. GraCoil recoil reduction system increases comfort and offers length-of-pull adjustment. Adjustable rib allows for 50/50 or 90/10 POI. Semi-beavertail forearm with finger grooves, Pachmayr Decelerator XLT recoil pad. Close radius grip and palm swell. Triple Trigger System with three trigger shoes, gold-plated trigger, Hi-Viz Pro Comp sight, ivory mid-bead, polished blue barrels, Silver-Nitride receiver, chrome-plated chamber. Five Invector DS Extended choke tubes ideal for trap (F, LF, M, IM, IM).
Price: $5,859.99

BROWNING 725 CITORI
Gauges: 12 ga., 20 ga., 28 ga. or .410 bore. **Barrels:** 26 in., 28 in., 30 in. **Weights:** 5.7-7.6 lbs. **Length:** 43.75-50 in. **Stock:** Gloss oil finish, grade II/III walnut. **Features:** New receiver that is significantly lower in profile than other 12-gauge Citori models. Mechanical trigger, Vector Pro lengthened forcing cones, three Invector-DS choke tubes, silver nitride finish with high relief engraving.

Price: 725 Field (12 ga. or 20 ga.) $2,560.00
Price: 725 Field (28 ga. or .410 bore)...................... $2,590.00
Price: 725 Field Grade VI $6,000.00
Price: 725 Feather (12 ga. or 20 ga.)....................... $2,670.00
Price: 725 Sporting, From $3,270.00
Price: 725 Sporting w/adjustable comb $3,600.00
Price: 725 Sporting Golden Clays $5,440.00
Price: 725 Trap, From... $3,400.00

BROWNING 725 FEATHER
Gauges: 12 ga., 3 in., 20 ga., 3 in. **Barrels:** 26 in., 28 in., with 0.25-in. ventilated rib. **Weight:** 5 lbs., 12 oz.-6 lbs., 9 oz. **Length:** 43.75-45.75 in. **Stock:** Grade II/III walnut with gloss-oil finish. **Features:** Lightweight aluminum-alloy receiver with steel breech face and hinge pin, Silver-Nitride finish. New accented engraving. Inflex recoil pad, ivory bead sight, gold-plated trigger. Ideal for hunting and sporting clays. Includes three Invector DS flush-mount choke tubes (F, M, IC).
Price: $2,739.99

CAESAR GUERINI

Gauges: 12 ga., 20 ga., 28 ga., also 20/28 gauge combo. Some models are available in .410 bore. **Barrels:** All standard lengths from 26–32 inches. **Weights:** 5.5–8.8 lbs. **Stock:** High-grade walnut with hand-rubbed oil finish. **Features:** A wide range of over/under models designed for the field, sporting clays, skeet and trap shooting. The models listed below are representative of some of the different models and variants. Many optional features are offered including high-grade wood and engraving, and extra sets of barrels. Made it Italy and imported by Caesar Guerini USA.

Price: Summit Sporting..$3,995.00
Price: Summit Limited $4,895.00
Price: Summit Ascent $5,135.00
Price: Tempio $4,325.00
Price: Ellipse $4,650.00
Price: Ellipse Curve $7,500.00
Price: Ellipse EVO Sporting $6,950.00
Price: Magnus, from $5,075.00
Price: Maxum, from $6,825.00
Price: Forum, from..$11,500.00
Price: Woodlander $3,795.00
Price: Invictus Sporting, from..................................$7,400.00
Price: Maxum Trap...$9,295.00
Price: Maxum Sporting...$7,150.00

CAESAR GUERINI REVENANT

Addition of a new combo set to the high-grade 2019 Revenant O/U with a tapered, solid rib and highly engraved maple leaf and branch design receiver. Now with a 20/28-gauge combo barrel set.

Price: From $13,495.00

CHARLES DALY 202

Gauges: 12 ga., 3 in., 20 ga., 3 in., .410 bore, 3 in. **Barrels:** 26 in., 28 in., ventilated rib. **Length:** 43-45 in. **Weight:** 6.2-7.3 lbs. **Stock:** Checkered walnut. **Features:** The new Charles Daly 202 line of O/U shotguns are built of aluminum alloy. Silver receivers are engraved with a dog scene. Single selective mechanical reset trigger, fixed fiber-optic front sight, extractors, rubber buttpad. Includes five extended Mobil style chokes (SK, IC, M, IM, F).
Price: From $499.00

CONNECTICUT SHOTGUN A10 AMERICAN

Gauges: 12 ga., 20 ga., 28 ga., .410 bore. 2 3/4, 3 in. Sidelock design. **Barrels:** 26 in., 28 in., 30 in. or 32 in. with choice of fixed or interchangeable chokes. **Weight:** 6.3 lbs. **Stock:** Hand rubbed oil finish, hand checkered at 24 LPI. Black, English or Turkish walnut offered in numerous grades. Pistol or Prince of Wales grip, short or long tang. **Features:** Low-profile, shallow frame full sidelock. Single-selective trigger, automatic ejectors. Engraved models available. Made in the USA by Connecticut Shotgun Mfg. Co.
Price: 12 ga., From $9,999.00
Price: Smaller ga., From...$11,900.00
Price: Sporting Clays $14,950.00

CONNECTICUT SHOTGUN MODEL 21 O/U

Gauge: 20 ga., 3 in. **Barrels:** 26–32 in. chrome-lined, back-bored with extended forcing cones. **Weight:** 6.3 lbs. **Stock:** A Fancy (2X) American walnut, standard point checkering, choice of straight or pistol grip. Higher grade walnut is optional. **Features:** The over/under version of Conn. Shotgun's replica of the Winchester Model 21 side-by-side, built

CZ ALL TERRAIN SERIES

Gauges: 12 ga., 3 in., 20 ga., 3 in. **Barrels:** 28 in., 30 in. **Stock:** Walnut, various styles. **Features:** CZ's new All-Terrain series encompasses five existing shotgun models. The new package includes upgraded wood, OD Green Cerakote finish on all metalwork, as well as a set of rare earth magnets added to the extractor/ejectors of the SxS and O/U models to keep shells from dropping out while handling a dog or working in the blind.

Price: Upland Ultralight All-Terrain 12 ga. or 20 ga. $890.00
Price: Redhead Premier All-Terrain 12 ga. or 20 ga. $1,123.00
Price: Drake All-Terrain 12 ga. or 20 ga. $791.00

CZ REDHEAD PREMIER

Gauges: 12 ga., 20 ga., (3 in. chambers), 28 ga. (2 3/4 in.). **Barrel:** 28 in. **Weight:** 7.4 lbs. **Length:** NA. **Stock:** Round-knob pistol grip, Schnabel fore-end, Turkish walnut. **Features:** Single selective triggers and extractors (12 & 20 ga.), screw-in chokes (12 ga., 20 ga., 28 ga.) choked IC and Mod (.410), coin-finished receiver, multi chokes. From CZ-USA.
Price: Deluxe $953.00
Price: Mini (28 ga., .410 bore) $1,057.00
Price: Target $1,389.00
Price: 16 ga., 28 in. barrel...................................$988.00

CZ SUPER SCROLL COMBO

Gauges: 20 and 28 combo. **Barrels:** 30 in. for both gauges with five choke tubes for each set. **Stock:** Grave V Turkish walnut with Schnabel fore-end, rounded grip. **Weight:** 6.7 pounds. **Features:** Ornate hand-engraved scrollwork on receiver, faux sideplates, trigger guard and mono-block. Comes in a custom-fitted aluminum case.
Price: $3,899.00

CZ UPLAND STERLING

Gauge: 12 ga., 3 in. **Barrels:** 28 in. with ventilated rib, fiber optic sight, five choke tubes. **Stock:** Turkish walnut with stippled gripping surfaces. **Weight:** 7.5 pounds. Lady Sterling has smaller stock dimensions.
Price: $999.00
Price: Lady Sterling $1,321.00

CZ WINGSHOOTER ELITE

Gauge: 12 ga., 20 ga., 2 3/4 in. **Barrel:** 28 in. flat ventilated rib. **Weight:** 6.3 lbs. **Length:** 45.5 in. **Stock:** Turkish walnut. **Features:** This colorful Over/Under shotgun has old world craftsmanship but with a new stylish look. This elegant hand engraved work of art is available in four gauges and its eye-catching engraving will stand alone in the field or range. 12- and 20-ga. models have auto ejectors, while the 28 ga. and .410 have extractors only. Heavily engraved scroll work with special side plate design, mechanical selective triggers, box Lock frame design, 18 LPI checkering, coil spring operated hammers, chrome lined, 5 interchangeable choke tubes and special engraved skeleton butt plate.
Price: 12 ga. or 20 ga. $1,059.00

FAUSTI CLASS ROUND BODY

Gauges: 16 ga., 20 ga., 28 ga.. **Barrels:** 28 or 30 in. **Weights:** 5.8–6.3 lbs. **Lengths:** 45.5–47.5 in. **Stock:** Turkish walnut Prince of Wales style with oil finish. Features include automatic ejectors, single selective trigger, laser-engraved receiver.
Price: From...$4,199.00

FAUSTI CALEDON

Gauges: 12 ga., 16 ga., 20 ga., 28 ga. and .410 bore. **Barrels:** 26 in., 28 in., 30 in. **Weights:** 5.8–7.3 lbs. **Stock:** Turkish walnut with oil finish, round pistol grip. **Features:** Automatic ejectors, single selective trigger, laser-engraved receiver. Coin finish receiver with gold inlays.
Price: 12 ga. or 20 ga. $1,999.00
Price: 16 ga., 28 ga., .410 bore $2,569.00

FAUSTI MAGNIFICENT

Gauges: 12 ga., 16 ga., 20 ga., 28 ga., .410 bore. **Barrels:** 26 in., 28 in., 30 in. **Stock:** AAA-Grade oil finished walnut. **Features:** Frame size scaled to gauge. Laser deep sculpted engraving coin finished receiver with gold inlays. Automatic ejectors, single selective trigger.
Price: 12 ga. $4,999.00
Price: Smaller ga. $5,559.00

FRANCHI INSTINCT SERIES

Gauges: 12 ga., 16 ga., 20 ga., 28 ga., .410 bore, 2 1/5 in. 2 3/4 in, 3 in." **Barrels:** 26 in., 28 in. **Weight:** 5.3–6.4 lbs. **Lengths:** 42.5–44.5 in. **Stock:** AA-grade satin walnut (LS), A-grade (L) with rounded pistol grip and recoil pad. Single trigger, automatic ejectors, tang safety, choke tubes. L model has steel receiver, SL has aluminum alloy receiver. Sporting model has higher grade wood, extended choke tubes. Catalyst model is designed for women, including stock dimensions for cast, drop, pitch, grip and length of pull.

Price: L **$1,299.00**
Price: SL **$1,599.00**
Price: Sporting **$1,999.00**
Price: Catalyst **$1,469.00**
Price: SL 28 ga. and .410 bore **$1,699.00**

FRANCHI INSTINT SLX

Gauges: 12 ga., 3 in., 16 ga., 2.75 in., 20 ga., 3 in. **Barrel:** 28 in., ventilated rib. **Length:** 46.25 in. **Weight:** 5.6-6.3 lbs. **Stock:** AA-grade walnut. **Features:** Similar to the SL family of O/Us, but with both reduced weight and the addition of deluxe aesthetics. Floral engraving on the receiver along with a gold trigger and inlays. Upgraded wood, Prince of Wales grip and Schnabel fore-end. Auto ejectors, barrel select switch, red fiber-optic front sight, gloss-blued barrels, tang safety. Includes five extended choke tubes and a hard case.

Price: .... **$1,999.00-$2,099.00**

KOLAR SPORTING CLAYS

Gauge: 12 ga., 2 3/4 in. **Barrels:** 30 in., 32 in., 34 in.; extended choke tubes. **Stock:** 14.625 in. x 2.5 in. x 1.875 in. x 1.375 in. French walnut. Four stock versions available. **Features:** Single selective trigger, detachable, adjustable for length; overbored barrels with long forcing cones; flat tramline rib; matte blue finish. Made in U.S. by Kolar.

Price: Standard **$11,995.00**
Price: Prestige **$14,190.00**
Price: Elite Gold **$16,590.00**
Price: Legend **$17,090.00**
Price: Select **$22,590.00**
Price: Custom .... **Price on request**

KOLAR AAA COMPETITION TRAP

Gauge: 12 ga. Similar to the Sporting Clays gun except has 32 in. O/U 34 in. Unsingle or 30 in. O/U 34 in. Unsingle barrels as an over/under, unsingle, or combination set. Stock dimensions are 14.5 in. x 2.5 in. x 1.5 in.; American or French walnut; step parallel rib standard. Contact maker for full listings. Made in USA by Kolar.

Price: Single bbl., From **$8,495.00**
Price: O/U, From **$11,695.00**

KOLAR AAA COMPETITION SKEET

Similar to the Sporting Clays gun except has 28 in. or 30 in. barrels with Kolarite AAA sub-gauge tubes; stock of American or French walnut with matte finish; flat tramline rib; under barrel adjustable for point of impact. Many options available. Contact maker for complete listing. Made in USA by Kolar.

Price: Max Lite, From **$13,995.00**

KRIEGHOFF K-80 SPORTING CLAYS

Gauge: 12 ga. **Barrels:** 28 in., 30 in., 32 in., 34 in. with choke tubes. **Weight:** About 8 lbs. **Stock:** #3 Sporting stock designed for gun-down shooting. **Features:** Standard receiver with satin nickel finish and classic scroll engraving. Selective mechanical trigger adjustable for position. Choice of tapered flat or 8mm parallel flat barrel rib. Free-floating barrels. Aluminum case. Imported from Germany by Krieghoff International, Inc.

Price: Standard grade with five choke tubes, From **$12,395.00**

KRIEGHOFF K-80 SKEET

Gauge: 12 ga., 2 3/4 in. **Barrels:** 28 in., 30 in., 32 in., (skeet & skeet), optional choke tubes. **Weight:** About 7.75 lbs. **Stock:** American skeet or straight skeet stocks, with palm-swell grips. Walnut. **Features:** Satin gray

receiver finish. Selective mechanical trigger adjustable for position. Choice of ventilated 8mm parallel flat rib or ventilated 8–12mm tapered flat rib. Introduced 1980. Imported from Germany by Krieghoff International, Inc.

Price: Standard, skeet chokes **$11,795.00**

KRIEGHOFF K-80 TRAP

Gauge: 12 ga., 2 3/4 in. **Barrels:** 30 in., 32 in. (Imp. Mod. & Full or choke tubes). **Weight:** About 8.5 lbs. **Stock:** Four stock dimensions or adjustable stock available; all have palm-swell grips. Checkered European walnut. **Features:** Satin nickel receiver. Selective mechanical trigger, adjustable for position. Ventilated step rib. Introduced 1980. Imported from Germany by Krieghoff International, Inc.

Price: K-80 O/U (30 in., 32 in., Imp. Mod. & Full), From............... **$11,795.00**
Price: K-80 Unsingle (32 in., 34 in., Full), standard, From **$13,995.00**
Price: K-80 Combo (two-barrel set), standard, From **$17,995.00**

KRIEGHOFF K-20

Similar to the K-80 except built on a 20-ga. frame. Designed for skeet, sporting clays and field use. Offered in 20 ga., 28 ga. and .410; **Barrels:** 28 in., 30 in. and 32 in. Imported from Germany by Krieghoff International Inc.

Price: K-20, 20 ga., From **$11,695.00**
Price: K-20, 28 ga., From **$12,395.00**
Price: K-20, .410, From **$12,395.00**
Price: From K-20 Sporting or Parcours **$12,395.00**
Price: K-20 Victoria... **$12,395.00**

LEBEAU-COURALLY BOSS-VEREES

Gauges: 12 ga., 20 ga., 2 3/4 in. **Barrels:** 25–32 in. **Weight:** To customer specifications. **Stock:** Exhibition-quality French walnut. **Features:** Boss-type sidelock with automatic ejectors; single or double triggers; chopper lump barrels. A custom gun built to customer specifications. Imported from Belgium by Wm. Larkin Moore.

Price: From **$96,000.00**

MERKEL MODEL 2001EL O/U

Gauges: 12 ga., 20 ga., 3 in., 28 ga. 2-3/4 in. chambers. **Barrels:** 12 ga. 28 in.; 20 ga., 28 ga. 26.75 in. **Weight:** About 7 lbs. (12 ga.). **Stock:** Oil-finished walnut; English or pistol grip. **Features:** Self-cocking Blitz boxlock action with cocking indicators; Kersten double cross-bolt lock; silver-grayed receiver with engraved hunting scenes; coil spring ejectors; single selective or double triggers. Imported from Germany by Merkel USA.

Price: **$13,255.00**

MERKEL MODEL 2000CL

Similar to Model 2001EL except scroll-engraved casehardened receiver; 12 ga., 20 ga., 28 ga. Imported from Germany by Merkel USA.

Price: **$12,235.00**

MOSSBERG SILVER RESERVE II

Gauge: 12 ga., 3 in. **Barrels:** 28 in. with ventilated rib, choke tubes. **Stock:** Select black walnut with satin finish. **Sights:** Metal bead. Available with extractors or automatic ejectors. Also offered in Sport model with ported barrels with wide rib, fiber optic front and middle bead sights. Super Sport has extra wide high rib, optional adjustable comb.

Price: Field **$773.00**
Price: Sport **$950.00**
Price: Sport w/ejectors.. **$1,070.00**
Price: Super Sport w/ejectors **$1,163.00**
Price: Super Sport w/ejectors, adj. comb **$1,273.00**

PERAZZI HIGH TECH 2020

Gauge: 12 ga., 3 in. **Barrels:** 27-9/16 in., 28-3/8 in., 29-1/2 in., 30-3/4 in., 31-1/2 in., flat ramped stepped 9/32 x 3/8 in. rib. **Weight:** 8 lbs.-8 lbs., 8 oz. **Stock:** Oil-finish, high-grade walnut, HT design standard or custom adjustable. **Features:** The competition grade High Tech 2020 is made in Italy. Logo engraving across silver-finish receiver. Hand-cut checkering, blued-steel barrels. Removeable trigger group with coil or flat springs and selector. Ventilated mid-rib. Interchangeable chokes available on demand.

Price: From **$21,075.00**

Prices given are believed to be accurate at time of publication however, many factors affect retail pricing so exact prices are not possible.

75TH EDITION, 2021 ⬦ **519**

PERAZZI MX8/MX8 TRAP/SKEET
Gauge: 12 ga., 20 ga. 2 3/4 in. **Barrels:** Trap: 29.5 in. (Imp. Mod. & Extra Full), 31.5 in. (Full & Extra Full). Choke tubes optional. Skeet: 27.625 in. (skeet & skeet). **Weights:** About 8.5 lbs. (trap); 7 lbs., 15 oz. (skeet). **Stock:** Interchangeable and custom made to customer specs. **Features:** Has detachable and interchangeable trigger group with flat V springs. Flat .4375 in. vent rib. Many options available. Imported from Italy by Perazzi USA, Inc.
Price: Trap, From $11,760.00
Price: Skeet, From $11,760.00

PERAZZI MX8
Gauge: 12 ga., 20 ga. 2 3/4 in. **Barrels:** 28.375 in. (Imp. Mod. & Extra Full), 29.50 in. (choke tubes). **Weight:** 7 lbs., 12 oz. **Stock:** Special specifications. **Features:** Has single selective trigger; flat .4375 in. x .3125 in. vent rib. Many options available. Imported from Italy by Perazzi USA, Inc.
Price: Standard, From $11,760.00
Price: Sporting, From $11,760.00
Price: SC3 Grade (variety of engraving patterns), From $21,000.00
Price: SCO Grade (more intricate engraving/inlays), From $36,000.00

PERAZZI MX12 HUNTING
Gauge: 12 ga., 2 3/4 in. **Barrels:** 26.75 in., 27.5 in., 28.375 in., 29.5 in. (Mod. & Full); choke tubes available in 27.625 in., 29.5 in. only (MX12C). **Weight:** 7 lbs., 4 oz. **Stock:** To customer specs; interchangeable. **Features:** Single selective trigger; coil springs used in action; Schnabel fore-end tip. Imported from Italy by Perazzi USA, Inc.
Price: From $12,700.00
Price: MX12C (with choke tubes), From $12,700.00

PERAZZI MX20 HUNTING
Gauges: 20 ga., 28 ga., .410 with 2 3/4 in. or 3 in. chambers. **Barrel:** 26 in. standard barrel choked Mod. & Full. **Weight:** 6 lbs., 6 oz. **Features:** Similar to the MX12 except 20 ga. frame size. Non-removable trigger group. Imported from Italy by Perazzi USA, Inc.
Price: From $12,700.00
Price: MX20C (with choke tubes), From $13,700.00

PERAZZI MX2000S
Gauges: 12 ga., 20 ga. **Barrels:** 29.5 in., 30.75 in., 31.5 in. with fixed I/M and Full chokes, or interchangeable. Competition model with features similar to MX8.
Price: $13,200.00

PERAZZI MX15 UNSINGLE TRAP
Gauge: 12 ga. **Barrel:** 34 in. with fixed Full choke. **Features:** Bottom single barrel with 6-notch adjustable rib, adjustable stock, drop-out trigger or interchangeable. Competition model with features similar to MX8.
Price: $9,175.00

PIOTTI BOSS
Gauges: 12 ga., 16 ga., 20 ga., 28 ga., .410 bore. **Barrels:** 26–32 in., chokes as specified. **Weight:** 6.5–8 lbs. **Stock:** Dimensions to customer specs. Best quality figured walnut. **Features:** Essentially a custom-made gun with many options. Introduced 1993. SportingModel is production model with many features of custom series Imported from Italy by Wm. Larkin Moore.
Price: From $78,000.00
Price: Sporting Model..$27,200.00

RIZZINI AURUM
Gauges: 12 ga., 16 ga., 20 ga., 28 ga., .410 bore. **Barrels:** 26, 28, 29 and 30, set of five choke tubes. **Weight:** 6.25 to 6.75 lbs. (Aurum Light 5.5 to 6.5 lbs.) **Stock:** Select Turkish walnut with Prince of Wales grip, rounded fore-end. Hand checkered with polished oil finish. **Features:** Boxlock low-profile action, single selective trigger, automatic ejectors, engraved game scenes in relief, light coin finish with gold inlay. Aurum Light has alloy receiver.
Price: 12, 16, 20 ga..$3,425.00
Price: 28, .410 bore...$3,625.00
Price: Aurum Light 12, 16, 20 ga..$3,700.00
Price: Aurum Light 28, .410 bore..$3,900.00

RIZZINI ARTEMIS
Gauges: 12 ga., 16 ga., 20 ga., 28 ga., .410 bore. Same as Upland EL model except dummy sideplates with extensive game scene engraving. Fancy European walnut stock. Fitted case. Introduced 1996. Imported from Italy by Fierce Products and by Wm. Larkin Moore & Co.
Price: From $3,975.00
Price: Artemis Light $4,395.00

RIZZINI BR 460
Gauge: 12 ga., 3 in. **Barrels:** 30 in., 32 in., with 10mm x 6mm ventilated rib. **Length:** 43-45 in. **Weight:** 8.3 lbs. **Stock:** Walnut with hand-rubbed oil finish and adjustable comb. **Features:** These Rizzini O/U Competition guns are produced in Skeet, Sporting, Trap, and Double Trap, each with different characteristics. Choice of fixed or interchangeable chokes and fixed, adjustable or ramped rib. Stock checkered at 28 LPI. White rounded style front sight with silver mid-bead. Rubber buttpad. Either standard or long forcing cones depending on model. Ships with hard case and velvet stock sleeve.
Price: From $7,045.00

RIZZINI FIERCE 1 COMPETITION
Gauges: 12 ga., 20 ga., 28 ga. **Barrels:** 28, 30 and 32 in. Five extended completion choke tubes. **Weight:** 6.6 to 8.1 lbs. **Stock:** Select Turkish walnut, hand checkered with polished oil finish. **Features:** Available in trap, skeet or sporting models. Adjustable stock and rib available. Boxlock low-profile action, single selective trigger, automatic ejectors, engraved game scenes in relief, light coin finish with gold inlay. Aurum Light has alloy receiver.
Price: From..$4,260.00

SKB 590 FIELD
Gauges: 12 ga., 20 ga., 3 in. **Barrels:** 26 in., 28 in., 30 in. Three SKB Competition choke tubes (IC, M, F). Lengthened forcing cones. **Stock:** Oil finished walnut with Pachmayr recoil pad. **Weight:** 7.1–7.9 lbs. **Sights:** NA. **Features:** Boxlock action, bright blue finish with laser engraved receiver. Automatic ejectors, single trigger with selector switch incorporated in thumb-operated tang safety. Youth Model has 13 in. length of pull. Imported from Turkey by GU, Inc.
Price: $1,300.00

SKB 90TSS
Gauges: 12 ga., 20 ga., 2 3/4 in. **Barrels:** 28 in., 30 in., 32 in. Three SKB Competition choke tubes (SK, IC, M for Skeet and Sporting Models; IM, M, F for Trap). Lengthened forcing cones. **Stock:** Oil finished walnut with Pachmayr recoil pad. **Weight:** 7.1–7.9 lbs. **Sights:** Ventilated rib with target sights. **Features:** Boxlock action, bright blue finish with laser engraved receiver. Automatic ejectors, single trigger with selector switch incorporated in thumb-operated tang safety. Sporting and Trap models have adjustable comb and buttpad system. Imported from Turkey by GU, Inc.
Price: Skeet $1,470.00
Price: Sporting Clays, Trap...$1,800.00

Prices given are believed to be accurate at time of publication however, many factors affect retail pricing so exact prices are not possible.

STEVENS MODEL 555
Gauges: 12 ga., 20 ga., 28 ga., .410; 2 3/4 and 3 in. **Barrels:** 26 in., 28 in. **Weights:** 5.5–6 lbs. **Features:** Five screw-in choke tubes with 12 ga., 20 ga., and 28 ga.; .410 has fixed M/IC chokes. Turkish walnut stock and Schnabel fore-end. Single selective mechanical trigger with extractors.
Price: **$705.00**
Price: Enhanced Model **$879.00**

STOEGER CONDOR
Gauge: 12 ga., 20 ga., 2 3/4 in., 3 in.; 16 ga., .410. **Barrels:** 22 in., 24 in., 26 in., 28 in., 30 in. **Weights:** 5.5-7.8 lbs. **Sights:** Brass bead. **Features:** IC, M, or F screw-in choke tubes with each gun. Oil finished hardwood with pistol grip and fore-end. Auto safety, single trigger, automatic extractors.
Price: From .... **$449.00–$669.00**
Price: Combo with 12 and 20 ga. barrel sets **$899.00**
Price: Competition **$669.00**

TRISTAR HUNTER EX
Gauge: 12 ga., 20 ga., 28 ga., .410. **Barrels:** 26 in., 28 in. **Weights:** 5.7 lbs. (.410); 6.0 lbs. (20, 28), 7.2–7.4 lbs. (12). Chrome-lined steel mono-block barrel, five Beretta-style choke tubes (SK, IC, M, IM, F). **Length:** NA. **Stock:** Walnut, cut checkering. 14.25 in x 1.5 in. x 2.375 in. **Sights:** Brass front sight. **Features:** All have extractors, engraved receiver, sealed actions, self-adjusting locking bolts, single selective trigger, ventilated rib. 28 ga. and .410 built on true frames. Five-year warranty. Imported from Italy by Tristar Sporting Arms Ltd.
Price: From .... **$640.00-$670.00**

TRISTAR HUNTER MAG CAMO
Gauge: 12 ga., 3.5 in. **Barrels:** 26 in., 28 in., 30 in., ventilated rib. **Length:** 44-48 in. **Weight:** 7.3-7.9 lbs. **Stock:** Synthetic, with choice of black or numerous Mossy Oak patterns. **Features:** The 3.5-inch magnum chambered Hunter Mag O/U expands with the addition of Cerakote/Mossy Oak combination models. Steel mono-block construction, extractors, rubber recoil pad, fiber-optic front sight, single selective trigger, chrome-lined barrel, swivel studs. Includes five Mobil-style choke tubes (SK, IC, M, IM, F).
Price: .... **$655.00-$760.00**

TRISTAR SETTER
Gauge: 12 ga., 20 ga., 3-in. **Barrels:** 28 in. (12 ga.), 26 in. (20 ga.) with ventilated rib, three Beretta-style choke tubes. **Weights:** 6.3–7.2 pounds. **Stock:** High gloss wood. Single selective trigger, extractors.
Price: .... **$535.00-$565.00**
Price: Sporting Model .... **$824.00-$915.00**

TRISTAR TT-15 FIELD
Gauges: 12 ga., 3 in., 20 ga., 3 in., 28 ga., 2.75 in., .410 bore, 3 in. **Barrel:** 28 in., ventilated rib. **Length:** 45 in. **Weight:** 5.7-7.0 lbs. **Stock:** Turkish walnut. **Features:** Field hunting O/U model with steel mono-block construction, mid-rib, top-tang barrel selector and safety. Chrome-lined barrel and chamber, engraved silver receiver, single selective trigger, fiber-optic front sight, auto ejectors. Includes five Mobil-style extended, color-coded chokes (SK, IC, M, IM, F).
Price: **$855.00**

TRISTAR TRINITY
Gauges: 12 ga., 3 in., 16 ga., 2.75 in., 20 ga., 3 in. Barrels: 26 in., 28 in., steel ventilated rib. **Weight:** 6.3-6.9 lbs. **Length:** 43.5-45.5 in. **Stock:** Oil-finished Turkish walnut with checkering. **Features:** The CNC-machined all-steel receiver Trinity wears 24-karat gold inlay on the silver-finish engraved receiver. Barrels are blued steel. Single selective trigger, red fiber-optic front sight, rubber buttpad, dual extractors. Includes five Beretta Mobil-style chokes (SK, IC, M, IM, F).
Price: **$685.00**

TRISTAR TRINITY LT
Gauges: 12 ga., 3 in., 20 ga., 3 in., 28 ga., 2.75 in., .410 bore, 3 in. **Barrels:** 26 in., 28 in, ventilated rib. **Weight:** 5.3-6.3 lbs. **Length:** 43.5-45.5 in. **Stock:** Oil-finished Turkish walnut with checkering. **Features:** The CNC-machined lightweight aluminum-alloy receiver Trinity LT is engraved and wears a silver finish. Barrels are blued steel. Single selective trigger, red fiber-optic front sight, rubber buttpad, dual extractors. Includes five Beretta Mobil-style chokes (SK, IC, M, IM, F).
Price: .... **$685.00-$700.00**

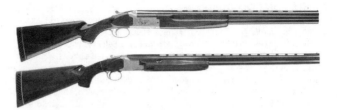

WINCHESTER MODEL 101
Gauge: 12 ga., 2 3/4 in., 3 in. **Barrels:** 28 in., 30 in., 32 in., ported, Invector Plus choke system. **Weights:** 7 lbs. 6 oz.–7 lbs. 12. oz. **Stock:** Checkered high-gloss grade II/III walnut stock, Pachmayr Decelerator sporting pad. **Features:** Chrome-plated chambers; back-bored barrels; tang barrel selector/safety; Signature extended choke tubes. Model 101 Field comes with solid brass bead front sight, three tubes, engraved receiver. Model 101 Sporting has adjustable trigger, 10mm runway rib, white mid-bead, Tru-Glo front sight, 30 in. and 32 in. barrels. Model 101 Pigeon Grade Trap has 10mm steel runway rib, mid-bead sight, interchangeable fiber-optic front sight, porting and vented side ribs, adjustable trigger shoe, fixed raised comb or adjustable comb, Grade III/IV walnut, 30 in. or 32 in. barrels, molded ABS hard case. Reintroduced 2008. Made in Belgium by FN. Winchester 150th Anniversary Commemorative model has grade IV/V stock, deep relief scrolling on a silver nitride finish receiver.
Price: Field **$1,900.00**
Price: Sporting **$2,380.00**
Price: Pigeon Grade Trap **$2,520.00**
Price: Pigeon Grade Trap w/adj. comb **$2,680.00**

WINCHESTER 101 LIGHT
Gauge: 12 ga., 3 in. **Barrels:** 26 in., 28 in., ventilated rib. **Length:** 43-45 in. **Weight:** 6 lbs.-6 lbs., 4 oz. **Stock:** Grade II/III Turkish walnut. **Features:** Similar to the Model 101, but weighs 1 pound less with its aluminum-alloy receiver; adorned with quail on the right and flushing pheasants on the left. Pachmayr Decelerator buttpad with white-line spacer, chrome-plated back-bored barrels, cut checkering, steel grip cap, brass front bead. Includes three Invector Plus chokes (F, M, IC).
Price: **$1,869.99**

WINCHESTER 101 DELUXE FIELD
Gauge: 12 ga., 3 in. **Barrels:** 26 in., 28 in., ventilated rib. **Length:** 43-45 in. **Weight:** 6 lbs., 12 oz. **Stock:** Grade III European walnut. **Features:** Classic field gun design on the proven 101 line of O/U shotguns. Detailed engraving on the sides of the steel receiver. Blued metalwork. Pachmayr Decelerator recoil pad, hard-chrome-plated chamber and bore, steel grip cap, brass bead front, white mid-bead. Includes three Invector Plus chokes (F, M, IC).
Price: **$1,999.99**
Price: Deluxe Field Maple **$1,999.99**

Prices given are believed to be accurate at time of publication however, many factors affect retail pricing so exact prices are not possible.

75TH EDITION, 2021 ⊕ 521

ARRIETA SIDELOCK DOUBLE

Gauges: 12 ga., 16 ga., 20 ga., 28 ga., .410 bore. **Barrels:** Length and chokes to customer specs. **Weight:** To customer specs. **Stock:** To customer specs. Straight English with checkered butt (standard), or pistol grip. Select European walnut with oil finish. **Features:** Essentially custom gun with myriad options. H&H pattern hand-detachable sidelocks, selective automatic ejectors, double triggers (hinged front) standard. Some have self-opening action. Finish and engraving to customer specs. Imported from Spain by Quality Arms, Wm. Larking Moore and others.

Price: Model 557 .... **$6,970.00**
Price: Model 570 .... **$7,350.00**
Price: Model 578 .... **$12,200.00**
Price: Model 600 Imperial **$14,125.00**
Price: Model 803 .... **$17,000.00**
Price: Model 931 .... **$40,000.00**

AYA MODEL 4/53

Gauges: 12 ga., 16 ga., 20 ga., 28 ga., 410 bore. **Barrels:** 26 in., 27 in., 28 in., 30 in. **Weights:** To customer specifications. **Length:** To customer specifications. **Features:** Hammerless boxlock action; double triggers; light scroll engraving; automatic safety; straight grip oil finished walnut stock; checkered butt. Made in Spain. Imported by New England Custom Gun Service.

Price: **$5,500.00**
Price: No. 2 .... **$7,000.00**
Price: No. 2 Rounded Action **$7,400.00**

AYA MODEL ADARRA

Gauges: 12 ga., 16 ga., 20 ga., 28 ga., 410 bore. **Barrel:** 26 in., 28 in. **Weight:** Approx. 6.7 lbs. **Features:** Hammerless boxlock action; double triggers; light scroll engraving; automatic safety; straight grip oil finished walnut stock; checkered butt. Made in Spain. Imported by New England Custom Gun Service.

Price: **$6,000.00**

BARRETT SOVEREIGN BELTRAMI

Gauges: 12 ga., 20 ga. or 28 ga. 3 in. (2 3/4 for 28 ga.). **Barrels:** 26 in., 28 in. or 30 in. **Stock:** Checkered grade AAA Turkish walnut with straight grip. **Features:** Boxlock design, ornamental sideplates, coin-finished receiver. Receiver scaled to individual gauges. Imported from Italy by Barrett Firearms.

Price: 12 ga. or 20 ga. **$6,150.00**
Price: 28 ga. **$6,550.00**

BERETTA 486 PARALELLO

Gauges: 12 ga., 20 ga., 3 in., or 28 ga. 2 3/4 in. **Barrels:** 26 in., 28 in., 30 in. **Weight:** 7.1 lbs. **Stock:** English-style straight grip, splinter fore-end. Select European walnut, checkered, oil finish. **Features:** Round action, Optima-Choke Tubes. Automatic ejection or mechanical extraction. Firing-pin block safety, manual or automatic, open top-lever safety. Imported from Italy by Beretta USA

Price: From **$5,350.00**

CHARLES DALY 500

Gauge: .410 bore, 3 in. **Barrel:** 28 in. **Length:** 43.25 in. **Weight:** 4.4 lbs. **Stock:** Checkered walnut English-style buttstock. **Features:** Charles Daly's new pair of baby-bore SxS Model 500 includes two versions, both steel, one with a black engraved receiver and the other black engraved with gold accents. Double triggers, extractors, manual safety, brass front bead. Includes five Mobil-style chokes (SK, IC, M, IM, F).

Price: .... **$725.00-$875.00**

CIMARRON 1878 COACH GUN

Gauge: 12 ga. 3 in. **Barrels:** 20 in., 26 in. **Weights:** 8–9 lbs. **Stock:** Hardwood. External hammers, double triggers. **Finish:** Blue, Cimarron "USA", Cimarron "Original."

Price: Blue .... **$597.00 (20 in.)–$623.00 (26 in.)**

CIMARRON DOC HOLLIDAY MODEL

Gauge: 12 ga. **Barrels:** 20 in., cylinder bore. **Stock:** Hardwood with rounded pistol grip. **Features:** Double triggers, hammers, false sideplates.

Price: **$1,581.00**

CONNECTICUT SHOTGUN MANUFACTURING CO. RBL

Gauges: 12 ga., 16 ga., 20 ga.. **Barrels:** 26 in., 28 in., 30 in., 32 in. **Weight:** NA. **Length:** NA. **Stock:** NA. **Features:** Round-action SxS shotguns made in the USA. Scaled frames, five TruLock choke tubes. Deluxe fancy grade walnut buttstock and fore-end. Quick Change recoil pad in two lengths. Various dimensions and options available depending on gauge.

Price: 12 ga. **$3,795.00**
Price: 16 ga. **$3,795.00**
Price: 20 ga. Special Custom Model **$7,995.00**

CONNECTICUT SHOTGUN MANUFACTURING CO. MODEL 21

Gauges: 12 ga., 16 ga., 20 ga., 28 ga., .410 bore. **Features:** A faithful re-creation of the famous Winchester Model 21. Many options and upgrades are available. Each frame is machined from specially produced proof steel. The 28 ga. and .410 guns are available on the standard frame or on a newly engineered small frame. These are custom guns and are made to order to the buyer's individual specifications, wood, stock dimensions, barrel lengths, chokes, finishes and engraving.

Price: 12 ga., 16 ga. or 20 ga., From **$15,000.00**
Price: 28 ga. or .410, From **$18,000.00**

CZ ALL TERRAIN SERIES

Gauges: 12 ga., 3 in., 20 ga., 3 in. **Barrels:** 28 in., 30 in. **Stock:** Walnut, various styles. **Features:** CZ's new All-Terrain series encompasses five existing shotgun models. The new package includes upgraded wood, OD Green Cerakote finish on all metalwork, as well as a set of rare earth magnets added to the extractor/ejectors of the SxS and O/U models to keep shells from dropping out while handling a dog or working in the blind.

Price: Bobwhite G2 All-Terrain 12 ga. or 20 ga. **$828.00**

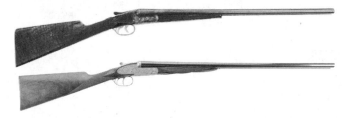

CZ SHARP-TAIL

Gauges: 12 ga., 20 ga., 28 ga., .410. (5 screw-in chokes in 12 and 20 ga. and fixed chokes in IC and Mod in .410). **Barrels:** 26 in. or 28 in. **Weight:** 6.5 lbs. **Stock:** Hand-checkered Turkish walnut with straight English-style grip and single selective trigger.

Price: Sharp-Tail **$1,022.00**
Price: Sharp-Tail Target **$1,298.00**

CZ HAMMER COACH

Gauge: 12 ga., 3 in. **Barrel:** 20 in. **Weight:** 6.7 lbs. **Features:** Following in the tradition of the guns used by the stagecoach guards of the 1880s, this cowboy gun features double triggers, 19th-century color casehardening and fully functional external hammers.

Price: **$922.00**
Price: Classic model w/30-in. bbls. **$963.00**

EMF MODEL 1878 WYATT EARP

Gauge: 12. **Barrel:** 20 in.. **Weight:** 8 lbs. **Length:** 37 in. overall. **Stock:** Smooth walnut with steel butt place. **Sights:** Large brass bead. **Features:** Colt-style exposed hammers rebounding type; blued receiver and barrels; cylinder bore. Based on design of Colt Model 1878 shotgun. Made in Italy by Pedersoli.

Price: **$1,590.00**
Price: Hartford Coach Model **$1,150.00**

SHOTGUNS Side-by-Side

EUROPEAN AMERICAN ARMORY (EAA) CHURCHILL 512
Gauges: 12 ga., 3in., 20 ga., 3 in., 28 ga., 3 in., .410 bore. **Barrels:** 26 in., 28 in. **Length:** 45-47 in. **Stock:** Standard Turkish walnut. **Features:** These Turkish made Akkar side-by-sides have a Nitride-silver receiver, rubber buttpad, checkered stock, single selective gold-plated trigger, front bead, manual safety, chrome-lined barrels, extractors. Ships with three choke tubes.
Price: **$1,355.00**

FAUSTI DEA SERIES
Gauges: 12 ga., 16 ga., 20 ga., 28 ga., .410. **Barrels:** 26 in., 28 in., 30 in. **Weight:** 6-6.8 lbs. **Stock:** AAA walnut, oil finished. Straight grip, checkered butt, classic fore-end. **Features:** Automatic ejectors, single non-selective trigger. Duetto model is in 28 ga. with extra set of .410 barrels. Made in Italy and imported by Fausti, USA.
Price: 12 ga. or 20 ga. **$3,718.00**
Price: 16 ga., 28 ga., .410 .... **$4,990.00**
Price: Duetto **$5,790.00**

FOX, A.H.
Gauges: 16 ga., 20 ga., 28 ga., .410. **Barrels:** Length and chokes to customer specifications. Rust-blued Chromox or Krupp steel. **Weight:** 5.5-6.75 lbs. **Stock:** Dimensions to customer specifications. Hand-checkered Turkish Circassian walnut with hand-rubbed oil finish. Straight, semi or full pistol grip; splinter, Schnabel or beavertail fore-end; traditional pad, hard rubber buttplate or skeleton butt. **Features:** Boxlock action with automatic ejectors; double or Fox single selective trigger. Scalloped, rebated and color case-hardened receiver; hand finished and hand-engraved. Grades differ in engraving, inlays, grade of wood, amount of hand finishing. Introduced 1993. Made in U.S. by Connecticut Shotgun Mfg.
Price: CE Grade **$19,500.00**
Price: XE Grade **$22,000.00**
Price: DE Grade **$25,000.00**
Price: FE Grade **$30,000.00**
Price: 28 ga./.410 CE Grade **$21,500.00**
Price: 28 ga./.410 XE Grade **$24,000.00**
Price: 28 ga./.410 DE Grade **$27,000.00**
Price: 28 ga./.410 FE Grade............................. **$32,000.00**

GARBI MODEL 101
Gauges: 12 ga., 16 ga., 20 ga., 28 ga. **Barrels:** 26 in., 28 in., choked to customer specs. **Weights:** 5.5-7.5 lbs. **Stock:** 14.5 in. x 2.25 in. x 1.5 in. Select European walnut. Straight grip, checkered butt, classic fore-end. **Features:** Sidelock action, automatic ejectors, double triggers standard. Color casehardened action, coin finish optional. Single trigger; beavertail fore-end, etc. optional. Hand engraved with scroll engraving. Imported from Spain by Wm. Larkin Moore.
Price: From **$17,000.00**

GARBI MODEL 103A, 103B
Similar to the Garbi Model 101 except has Purdey-type fine scroll and rosette engraving. Model 103B has nickel-chrome steel barrels, H&H-type easy opening mechanism; other mechanical details remain the same. Imported from Spain by Wm. Larkin Moore.
Price: Model 103A, From **$23,000.00**
Price: Model 103B, From **$26,500.00**

GARBI MODEL 200
Similar to the Garbi Model 101 except has heavy-duty locks, magnum proofed. Very fine Continental-style floral and scroll engraving, well figured walnut stock. Other mechanical features remain the same. Imported from Spain by Wm. Larkin Moore.
Price: **$27,000.00**

MERKEL MODEL 147SL
H&H style sidelock action with cocking indicators, ejectors. Silver-grayed receiver and sideplates have arabesque engraving, fine hunting scene engraving. Limited edition. Imported from Germany by Merkel USA.
Price: Model 147SL **$13,255.00**

MERKEL MODEL 280EL, 360EL
Similar to Model 47E except smaller frame. Greener crossbolt with double under-barrel locking lugs, fine engraved hunting scenes on silver-grayed receiver, luxury-grade wood, Anson and Deeley boxlock action. H&H ejectors, single-selective or double triggers. Introduced 2000. Imported from Germany by Merkel USA.
Price: Model 280EL (28 ga., 28 in. barrel, Imp. Cyl. and Mod. chokes) **$8,870.00**
Price: Model 360EL (.410, 28 in. barrel, Mod. and Full chokes).......**$8,870.00**

MERKEL MODEL 280SL AND 360SL
Similar to Model 280EL and 360EL except has sidelock action, double triggers, English-style arabesque engraving. Introduced 2000. Imported from Germany by Merkel USA.
Price: Model 280SL (28 ga., 28 in. barrel, Imp. Cyl. and Mod. chokes) **$13,255.00**
Price: Model 360SL (.410, 28 in. barrel, Mod. and Full chokes) **$13,255.00**

MERKEL MODEL 1620
Gauge: 16 ga. **Features:** Greener crossbolt with double under-barrel locking lugs, scroll-engraved casehardened receiver, Anson and Deeley boxlock action, Holland & Holland ejectors, English-style stock, single selective or double triggers, or pistol grip stock with single selective trigger. Imported from Germany by Merkel USA.
Price: Model 1620EL **$8,870.00**
Price: Model 1620EL Combo; 16- and 20-ga. two-barrel set **$13,255.00**

MERKEL MODEL 40E
Gauges: 12 ga., 20 ga. **Barrels:** 28 in. (12 ga.), 26.75 in. (20 ga.). **Weight:** 6.2 lbs. **Features:** Anson & Deeley locks, Greener-style crossbolt, automatic ejectors, choice of double or single trigger, blue finish, checkered walnut stock with cheekpiece.
Price: **$4,795.00**

PIOTTI KING NO. 1
Gauges: 12 ga., 16 ga., 20 ga., 28 ga., .410. **Barrels:** 25-30 in. (12 ga.), 25-28 in. (16 ga., 20 ga., 28 ga., .410). To customer specs. Chokes as specified. **Weight:** 6.5-8 lbs. (12 ga. to customer specs.). **Stock:** Dimensions to customer specs. Finely figured walnut; straight grip with checkered butt with classic splinter fore-end and hand-rubbed oil finish standard. Pistol grip, beavertail fore-end. **Features:** Holland & Holland pattern sidelock action, automatic ejectors. Double trigger; non-selective single trigger optional. Coin finish standard; color case-hardened optional. Top rib; level, file-cut; concave, ventilated optional. Very fine, full coverage scroll engraving with small floral bouquets. Imported from Italy by Wm. Larkin Moore.
Price: From...**$42,800.00**

PIOTTI LUNIK SIDE-BY-SIDE SHOTGUN
Similar to the Piotti King No. 1 in overall quality. Has Renaissance-style large scroll engraving in relief. Best quality Holland & Holland-pattern sidelock ejector double with chopper lump (demi-bloc) barrels. Other mechanical specifications remain the same. Imported from Italy by Wm. Larkin Moore.
Price: From...**$46,000.00**

PIOTTI PIUMA
Gauges: 12 ga., 16 ga., 20 ga., 28 ga., .410. **Barrels:** 25-30 in. (12 ga.), 25-28 in. (16 ga., 20 ga., 28 ga., .410). **Weights:** 5.5-6.25 lbs. (20 ga.). **Stock:** Dimensions to customer specs. Straight grip stock with walnut checkered butt, classic splinter fore-end, hand-rubbed oil finish are standard; pistol grip, beavertail fore-end, satin luster finish optional. **Features:** Anson & Deeley boxlock ejector double with chopper lump barrels. Level, file-cut rib, light scroll and rosette engraving, scalloped frame. Double triggers; single non-selective optional. Coin finish standard, color case-hardened optional. Imported from Italy by Wm. Larkin Moore.
Price: From...**$25,000.00**

Prices given are believed to be accurate at time of publication however, many factors affect retail pricing so exact prices are not possible.

75TH EDITION, 2021 ⊕ **523**

SAVAGE FOX A-GRADE

Gauge: 12 or 20. **Barrels:** 26 or 28 in. with solid rib and IC, M, and F choke tubes. **Features:** Straight-grip American walnut stock with splinter fore-end, oil finish and cut checkering. Anson & Deeley-style boxlock action, Holland & Holland-style ejectors, double triggers and brass bead sight. A re-creation of the famous Fox double gun, presented by Savage and made at the Connecticut Shotgun Manufacturing Co. plant.
Price: From...$5,375.00

SKB 200 SERIES

Gauges: 12 ga., 20 ga., .410, 3 in.; 28 ga., 2 3/4 in. **Barrels:** 26 in., 28 in. Five choke tubes provided (F, IM, M, IC, SK). **Stock:** Hand checkered and oil finished Turkish walnut. Prince of Wales grip and beavertail fore-end. **Weight:** 6–7 lbs. **Sights:** Brass bead. **Features:** Boxlock with platform lump barrel design. Polished bright blue finish with charcoal color case hardening on receiver. Manual safety, automatic ejectors, single selective trigger. 200 HR target model has high ventilated rib, full pistol grip. 250 model has decorative color casehardened sideplates. Imported from Turkey by GU, Inc.
Price: 12 ga., 20 ga. $2,100.00
Price: 28 ga., .410..$2,250.00
Price: 200 28 ga./.410 Combo $3,300.00
Price: 200 HR 12 ga., 20 ga. $2,500.00
Price: 200 HR 28 ga., .410...................................$2,625.00
Price: 200 HR 28 ga./.410 combo $3,600.00
Price: 250 12 ga., 20 ga. $2,600.00
Price: 250 28 ga., .410...$2,725.00
Price: 250 28 ga./.410 Combo................................$3,700.00

SKB 7000SL SIDELOCK

Gauges: 12 ga., 20 ga. **Barrels:** 28 in., 30 in. Five choke tubes provided (F, IM, M, IC, SK). **Stock:** Premium Turkish walnut with hand-rubbed oil finish, fine-line hand checkering, Prince of Wales grip and beavertail fore-end. **Weights:** 6–7 lbs. **Sights:** Brass bead. **Features:** Sidelock design with Holland & Holland style seven-pin removable locks with safety sears. Bison Bone Charcoal casehardening, hand engraved sculpted sidelock receiver. Manual safety, automatic ejectors, single selective trigger. Available by special order only. Imported from Turkey by GU, Inc.
Price: From...$6,500.00

STOEGER UPLANDER

Gauges: 12 ga., 20 ga., .410, 3 in.; 28 ga., 2 3/4. **Barrels:** 22 in., 24 in., 26 in., 28 in. **Weights:** 6.5–7.3 lbs. **Sights:** Brass bead. **Features:** Double trigger, IC & M choke tubes included with gun. Other choke tubes available. Tang auto safety, extractors, black plastic buttplate. Imported by Benelli USA.
Price: Standard $449.99
Price: Supreme (single trigger, AA-grade wood) $549.99
Price: Longfowler (12 ga., 30-in. bbl.) $449.99
Price: Home Defense (20 or 12 ga., 20-in. bbl., tactical sights) $499.00
Price: Double Defense (20 ga.) fiber-optic sight, accessory rail $499.00

STOEGER COACH GUN

Gauges: 12 ga., 20 ga., 2 3/4 in., 3 in., .410 bore, **Barrel:** 20 in. **Weight:** 6.5 lbs. **Stock:** Brown hardwood, classic beavertail fore-end. **Sights:** Brass bead. **Features:** Double or single trigger, IC & M choke tubes included, others available. Tang auto safety, extractors, black plastic buttplate. Imported by Benelli USA.
Price: From..$549.00
Price: $449.00
Price: .410 bore, 3-inch, 20-in. barrel...............................$449.00
Price: Black-finished hardwood/polished-nickel model $549.00

YILDIZ ELEGANT

Gauge: .410 bore, 3 in. **Barrels:** 26 in., 28 in., 30 in., with 7mm or 8mm rib. **Weight:** 4.8-6.0 lbs. **Stock:** Oil-finish selected walnut from standard through Grades 3 and 5, some pistol grip and others straight English-style. **Features:** Built of 4140 Steel, with varying degrees of receiver engraving. Manual or automatic safety, extractors or ejectors, depending on model. Single selective trigger, front bead, full black rubber recoil pad. Models include: A1, A3, A4, A5, and Special Lux. Includes five Mobil chokes. Manufactured in Turkey and imported/sold through Academy.
Price: From $479.99

BROWNING BT-99 TRAP
Gauge: 12 ga. **Barrels:** 30 in., 32 in., 34 in. **Stock:** Walnut; standard or adjustable. **Weights:** 7 lbs. 11 oz.–9 lbs. **Features:** Back-bored single barrel; interchangeable chokes; beavertail forearm; extractor only; high rib.
Price: BT-99 w/conventional comb, 32- or 34-in. barrel.................. **$1,470.00**
Price: BT-99 w/adjustable comb, 32- or 34-in. barrel..................... **$1,840.00**
Price: BT-99 Max High Grade w/adjustable comb, 32- or
    34-in. barrel... **$5,340.00**
Price: Micro Adjustable LOP Model.................................... **$1,669.99**

CHARLES DALY 101
Gauges: 12 ga., 3 in., 20 ga., 3in., .410 bore. **Barrels:** 26 in., 28 in. **Weight:** 5.0-8.1 lbs. **Length:** 41.75-43.75 in. **Stock:** Choice of either checkered walnut or black synthetic stocks. **Features:** These updated break-action single shots have become more affordable than ever. Though built of steel, they're still quite light. Brass front bead, manual safety, single trigger, extractor, rubber butt pad. Includes a Modified Beretta/Benelli Mobil choke tube.
Price: ....**$119.00-$129.00**

HENRY .410 LEVER-ACTION SHOTGUN
Gauge: .410, 2 1/2 in. **Capacity:** 5. **Barrels:** 20 or 24 in. with either no choke (20 in.) or full choke (24 in.). **Stock:** American walnut. **Sights:** Gold bead front only. **Finish:** Blued. Introduced in 2017. **Features:** Design is based on the Henry .45-70 rifle.
Price: 20-in. bbl.. **$893.00**
Price: 24-in. bbl.. **$947.00**

HENRY SINGLE-SHOT SHOTGUN
Gauges: 12 ga., 20 ga. or .410 bore, 3 1/2 in. (12 ga.), 3 in. (20 ga. and 410). **Barrels:** 26 or 28 in. with either modified choke tube (12 ga., 20 ga., compatible with Rem-Choke tubes) or fixed full choke (.410). **Stock:** American walnut, straight or pistol grip. **Sights:** Gold bead front only. **Weight:** 6.33 lbs. **Finish:** Blued or brass receiver. **Features:** Break-open single-shot design. Introduced in 2017.
Price: **$448.00**
Price: Brass receiver, straight grip.................................... **$576.00**

KRIEGHOFF K-80 SINGLE BARREL TRAP GUN
Gauge: 12 ga., 2 3/4 in. **Barrel:** 32 in., 34 in. Unsingle. Fixed Full or choke tubes. **Weight:** About 8.75 lbs. **Stock:** Four stock dimensions or adjustable stock available. All hand-checkered European walnut. **Features:** Satin nickel finish. Selective mechanical trigger adjustable for finger position. Tapered step vent rib. Adjustable point of impact.
Price: Standard Grade Full Unsingle, From **$12,995.00**

KRIEGHOFF KX-6 SPECIAL TRAP GUN
Gauge: 12 ga., 2 3/4 in. **Barrel:** 32 in., 34 in.; choke tubes. **Weight:** About 8.5 lbs. **Stock:** Factory adjustable stock. European walnut. **Features:** Ventilated tapered step rib. Adjustable position optional, optional release trigger. Fully adjustable rib. Satin gray electroless nickel receiver. Fitted aluminum case. Imported from Germany by Krieghoff International, Inc.
Price: **$5,995.00**

LJUTIC MONO GUN SINGLE BARREL
Gauge: 12 ga. **Barrel:** 34 in., choked to customer specs; hollow-milled rib, 35.5-in. sight plane. **Weight:** Approx. 9 lbs. **Stock:** To customer specs. Oil finish, hand checkered. **Features:** Custom gun. Pull or release trigger; removable trigger guard contains trigger and hammer mechanism; Ljutic pushbutton opener on front of trigger guard. From Ljutic Industries.
Price: Std., med. or Olympic rib, custom bbls., fixed choke. **$7,495.00**
Price: Stainless steel mono gun..................................... **$8,495.00**

LJUTIC LTX PRO 3 DELUXE MONO GUN
Deluxe, lightweight version of the Mono gun with high-quality wood, upgrade checkering, special rib height, screw-in chokes, ported and cased.
Price: **$8,995.00**
Price: Stainless steel model....................................... **$9,995.00**

ROSSI CIRCUIT JUDGE
Revolving shotgun chambered in .410 (2 1/2- or 3-in./.45 Colt. Based on Taurus Judge handgun. Features include 18.5-in. barrel; fiber-optic front sight; 5-round cylinder; hardwood Monte Carlo stock.
Price: From.. **$689.00**

SAVAGE 212/220
Gauges: 12 ga., 3 in., 20 ga., 3 in. **Barrel:** 22 in., carbon steel. **Weight:** 7.34-7.75 lbs. **Length:** 43 in. **Stock:** Synthetic AccuFit stock with included LOP and comb inserts. Thumbhole model uses gray wood laminate. **Features:** The bolt-action Savage models 212 and 220, so named for their chamberings, are available in Slug, Slug Camo, Thumbhole, Left-Handed and Turkey models. Choice of button-rifled slug barrels or smoothbore. Detachable box magazine, thread-in barrel headspacing. User adjustable AccuTrigger and AccuStock internal chassis. Oversized bolt handle, Picatinny optics rail, sling studs, rubber buttpad.
Price: ....**$629.00-$799.00**
Price: 212 Turkey w/extended X-Full choke........................ **$779.00**
Price: 220 Turkey w/extended X-Full choke........................ **$695.00**

STEVENS 301 TURKEY XP
Gauges: 20 ga., 3 in., .410 bore, 3 in. **Barrel:** 26 in., black matte. **Weight:** 5.07 lbs. **Length:** 41.5 in. **Stock:** Camouflage synthetic stock and fore-end with either Mossy Oak Obsession or Mossy Oak Bottomland pattern. **Features:** Single-shot break action with removable one-piece rail. XP variant includes mounted and bore-sighted 1x30 red-dot optic. Barrel optimized for Federal Premium TSS Heavyweight turkey loads. Swivel studs, front bead, manual hammer block safety, rubber recoil pad. Includes Winchoke pattern Extra Full turkey choke.
Price: **$239.00**

STEVENS 555 TRAP
Gauges: 12 ga., 3 in., 20 ga., 3 in. **Barrel:** 30 in., raised ventilated rib. **Weight:** 6.6-6.8 lbs. **Length:** 47.5 in. **Stock:** Turkish walnut stock and fore-end with adjustable comb and oil finish. **Features:** Lightweight silver aluminum receiver scaled to gauge with steel breech reinforcement. Top single barrel with shell extractor. Manual tang safety, front bead, chrome-lined barrel, semi-gloss metalwork finish. Includes three chokes.
Price: **$689.00**

STEVENS 555 TRAP COMPACT
Gauges: 12 ga., 3 in., 20 ga., 3 in. **Barrel:** 26 in., raised ventilated rib. **Weight:** 7.3-7.5 lbs. **Length:** 42.5 in. **Stock:** Turkish walnut stock and fore-end with adjustable comb and oil finish. **Features:** Lightweight silver aluminum receiver scaled to gauge with steel breech reinforcement. Top single barrel with shell extractor. Manual tang safety, front bead, chrome-lined barrel, semi-gloss metalwork finish. Compact 13.5 in. length of pull. Includes three chokes.
Price: **$689.00**

TAR-HUNT RSG-12 PROFESSIONAL RIFLED SLUG GUN
Gauge: 12 ga., 2 3/4 in., 3 in. **Capacity:** 1-round magazine. **Barrel:** 23 in., fully rifled with muzzle brake. **Weight:** 7.75 lbs. **Length:** 41.5 in. overall. **Stock:** Matte black McMillan fiberglass with Pachmayr Decelerator pad. **Sights:** None furnished; comes with Leupold windage or Weaver bases. **Features:** Uses rifle-style action with two locking lugs; two-position safety; Shaw barrel; single-stage, trigger; muzzle brake. Many options available. All models have area-controlled feed action. Introduced 1991. Made in U.S. by Tar-Hunt Custom Rifles, Inc.
Price: 12 ga. Professional model **$3,495.00**
Price: Left-hand model **$3,625.00**

TAR-HUNT RSG-20 MOUNTAINEER SLUG GUN
Similar to the RSG-12 Professional except chambered for 20 ga. (2 3/4 in. and 3 in. shells); 23 in. Shaw rifled barrel with muzzle brake; two-lug bolt; one-shot blind magazine; matte black finish; McMillan fiberglass stock with Pachmayr Decelerator pad; receiver drilled and tapped for Rem. 700 bases. Right- or left-hand versions. Weighs 6.5 lbs. Introduced 1997. Made in USA by Tar-Hunt Custom Rifles, Inc.
Price: **$3,495.00**

Prices given are believed to be accurate at time of publication however, many factors affect retail pricing so exact prices are not possible.

75TH EDITION, 2021 ⊕ **525**

BENELLI M2 TACTICAL
Gauge: 12 ga., 2 3/4 in., 3 in. **Capacity:** 5-round magazine. **Barrel:** 18.5 in. IC, M, F choke tubes. **Weight:** 6.7 lbs. **Length:** 39.75 in. overall. **Stock:** Black polymer. Standard or pistol grip. **Sights:** Rifle type ghost ring system, tritium night sights optional. **Features:** Semi-auto inertia recoil action. Cross-bolt safety; bolt release button; matte-finish metal. Introduced 1993. Imported from Italy by Benelli USA.
Price: From..**$1,239.00–$1,359.00**

BENELLI M3 TACTICAL
Gauge: 12 ga., 3 in. **Barrel:** 20 in. **Stock:** Black synthetic w/pistol grip. **Sights:** Ghost ring rear, ramp front. Convertible dual-action operation (semi-auto or pump).
Price: **$1,599.00**

BENELLI M4 TACTICAL
Gauge: 12 ga., 3 in. **Barrel:** 18.5 in. **Weight:** 7.8 lbs. **Length:** 40 in. overall. **Stock:** Synthetic. **Sights:** Ghost Ring rear, fixed blade front. **Features:** Auto-regulating gas-operated (ARGO) action, choke tube, Picatinny rail, standard and collapsible stocks available, optional LE tactical gun case. Introduced 2006.
Price: From..**$1,999.00**
Price: M4 H20 Cerakote Finish **$2,269.00**

BENELLI NOVA TACTICAL
Gauge: 12 ga., 3 in. **Barrel:** 18.5 in. **Stock:** Black synthetic standard or pistol grip. **Sights:** Ghost ring rear, ramp front. Pump action.
Price: From..**$439.00**

BENELLI VINCI TACTICAL
Gauge: 12 ga., 3 in. **Barrel:** 18.5 in. Semi-auto operation. **Stock:** Black synthetic. **Sights:** Ghost ring rear, ramp front.
Price: **$1,349.00**
Price: ComforTech stock **$1,469.00**

IVER JOHNSON STRYKER-12
Gauge: 12 ga., 3 in. **Barrel:** 20 in., smoothbore with muzzle brake. **Length:** 43 in. **Stock:** Black synthetic two-piece, pistol-grip stock. **Features:** This AR15-style semi-auto shotgun uses a standard AR15 bolt and mag release. A2-style detachable carry handle with adjustable sight, fiber-optic front sight. Light rails on both sides and bottom of fore-end. Push button releases the stock and leaves the pistol grip for a modular platform. Cross-bolt safety, thick rubber buttpad. Ships with two MKA 1919 5-round box magazines.
Price: **$495.00**

KEL-TEC KSG BULL-PUP TWIN-TUBE
Gauge: 12 ga. **Capacity:** 13+1. **Barrel:** 18.5 in. **Overall Length:** 26.1 in. **Weight:** 8.5 lbs. (loaded). **Features:** Pump-action shotgun with two magazine tubes. The shotgun bears a resemblance to the South African designed Neostead pump-action gun. The operator is able to move a switch located near the top of the grip to select the right or left tube, or move the switch to the center to eject a shell without chambering another round. Optional accessories include a factory installed Picatinny rail with flip-up sights and a pistol grip. KSG-25 has 30-in. barrel and 20-round capacity magazine tubes.
Price: **$990.00**
Price: KSG-25 ....**$1400.00**

KEL-TEC KS7 BULLPUP
Gauge: 12 ga., 3 in. **Capacity:** 6+1. **Barrel:** 18.5 in. **Length:** 26.1 in. **Weight:** 5.9 lbs. **Stock:** Black synthetic bullpup. **Features:** The pump-action KS7 Bullpup is a compact self-defense shotgun. Carry handle, Picatinny rail, M-LOK mounting points. Rear loading, downward ejection, ambidextrous controls. Cylinder choke.
Price from: **$495.00**

MOSSBERG MAVERICK 88 CRUISER
Gauges: 12 ga., 3 in., 20 ga., 3in. **Capacity:** 5+1 or 7+1 capacity. Barrels: 18.5 in., 20 in. **Length:** 28.125-30.375 in. **Weight:** 5.5-6.0 lbs. **Stock:** Black synthetic pistol grip. **Features:** Fixed cylinder bore choke, blued metalwork, bead front sight, cross-bolt safety.
Price: **$231.00**

MOSSBERG MODEL 500 SPECIAL PURPOSE
Gauges: 12 ga., 20 ga., .410, 3 in. **Barrels:** 18.5 in., 20 in. (Cyl.). **Weight:** 7 lbs. **Stock:** Walnut-finished hardwood or black synthetic. **Sights:** Metal bead front. **Features:** Slide-action operation. Available in 6- or 8-round models. Top-mounted safety, double action slide bars, swivel studs, rubber recoil pad. Blue, Parkerized, Marinecote finishes. Mossberg Cablelock included. The HS410 Home Security model chambered for .410 with 3 in. chamber; has pistol grip fore-end, thick recoil pad, muzzle brake and has special spreader choke on the 18.5-in. barrel. Overall length is 37.5 in. Blued finish; synthetic field stock. Mossberg Cablelock and video included. Mariner model has Marinecote metal finish to resist rust and corrosion. Synthetic field stock; pistol grip kit included. 500 Tactical 6-shot has black synthetic tactical stock. Introduced 1990.
Price: 500 Mariner...**$636.00**
Price: HS410 Home Security...**$477.00**
Price: Home Security 20 ga. **$631.00**
Price: FLEX Tactical **$672.00**
Price: 500 Chainsaw pistol grip only; removable top handle **$547.00**
Price: JIC (Just In Case)..**$500.00**
Price: Thunder Ranch **$553.00**

MOSSBERG MODEL 590 SPECIAL PURPOSE
Gauges: 12 ga., 20 ga., .410 3 in. **Capacity:** 9-round magazine. **Barrel:** 20 in. (Cyl.). **Weight:** 7.25 lbs. **Stock:** Synthetic field or Speedfeed. **Sights:** Metal bead front or Ghost Ring. **Features:** Slide action. Top-mounted safety, double slide action bars. Comes with heat shield, bayonet lug, swivel studs, rubber recoil pad. Blue, Parkerized or Marinecote finish. Shockwave has 14-inch heavy walled barrel, Raptor pistol grip, wrapped fore-end and is fully BATFE compliant. Magpul model has Magpul SGA stock with adjustable comb and length of pull. Mossberg Cablelock included. From Mossberg.
Price: From **$559.00**
Price: Flex Tactical **$672.00**
Price: Tactical Tri-Rail Adjustable **$879.00**
Price: Mariner..**$756.00**
Price: Shockwave...**$455.00-$721.00**
Price: MagPul 9-shot **$836.00**

MOSSBERG 930 SPECIAL PURPOSE SERIES
Gauge: 12 ga., 3 in. **Barrel:** 18.5-28 in. flat ventilated rib. **Weight:** 7.3 lbs. **Length:** 49 in.. **Stock:** Composite stock with close radius pistol grip; Speed Lock forearm; textured gripping surfaces; shim adjustable for length of pull, cast and drop; Mossy Oak Bottomland camo finish; Dura-Touch Armor Coating. **Features:** 930 Special Purpose shotguns feature a self-regulating gas system that vents excess gas to aid in recoil reduction and eliminate stress on critical components. All 930 autoloaders chamber both 2 3/4 inch and 3-in. 12-ga. shotshells with ease — from target loads, to non-toxic magnum loads, to the latest sabot slug

ammo. Magazine capacity is 7+1 on models with extended magazine tube, 4+1 on models without. To complete the package, each Mossberg 930 includes a set of specially designed spacers for quick adjustment of the horizontal and vertical angle of the stock, bringing a custom-feel fit to every shooter. All 930 Special Purpose models feature a drilled and tapped receiver, factory-ready for Picatinny rail, scope base or optics installation. 930 SPX models conveniently come with a factory-mounted Picatinny rail and LPA/M16-Style Ghost Ring combination sight right out of the box. Other sighting options include a basic front bead, or white-dot front sights. Mossberg 930 Special Purpose shotguns are available in a variety of configurations; 5-round tactical barrel, 5-round with muzzle brake, 8-round pistol-grip, and even a 5-round security/field combo.

Price: Tactical 5-Round..$612.00
Price: Home Security...$662.00
Price: Standard Stock...$787.00
Price: Pistol Grip 8-Round $1,046.00
Price: 5-Round Combo w/extra 18.5-in. barrel $693.00
Price: Chainsaw..$564.00

REMINGTON 870 DM SERIES
Gauge: 12 ga. (2 3/4 in., 3 in. interchangeably) **Barrel:** 18.5-in. cylinder bore. Detachable 6-round magazine. **Stock:** Hardwood or black synthetic with textured gripping surfaces. Tac-14 DM model features short pistol grip buttstock and 14-in. barrel.
Price: $529.00

REMINGTON MODEL 870 PUMP TACTICAL SHOTGUNS
Gauges: 12 ga., 2 3/4 or 3 in. **Barrels:** 18 in., 20 in., 22 in. (Cyl or IC). **Weight:** 7.5–7.75 lbs. **Length:** 38.5–42.5 in. overall. **Stock:** Black synthetic, synthetic Speedfeed IV full pistol-grip stock, or Knoxx Industries SpecOps stock w/recoil-absorbing spring-loaded cam and adjustable length of pull (12 in. to 16 in., 870 only). **Sights:** Front post w/dot. **Features:** R3 recoil pads, LimbSaver technology to reduce felt recoil, 2-, 3- or 4-round extensions based on barrel length; matte-olive-drab barrels and receivers. Standard synthetic-stocked version is equipped with 22-in. barrel and four-round extension. Introduced 2006. From Remington Arms Co.
Price: 870 Express Tactical Knoxx 20 ga. $555.00
Price: 870 Express Magpul $898.00
Price: 870 Special Purpose Marine (nickel)...........................$841.00

REMINGTON 870 EXPRESS TACTICAL
Gauge: 12 ga., 2 3/4 and 3 in. **Features:** Pump-action shotgun; 18.5-in. barrel; extended ported Tactical RemChoke; SpeedFeed IV pistol-grip stock with SuperCell recoil pad; fully adjustable XS Ghost Ring Sight rail with removable white bead front sight; 7-round capacity with factory-installed 2-shot extension; drilled and tapped receiver; sling swivel stud.
Price: From..$600.00

REMINGTON 887 NITRO MAG TACTICAL
Gauge: 12 ga., 2 3/4 to 3 1/2 in. **Features:** Pump-action shotgun,18.5-in. barrel with ported, extended tactical RemChoke; 2-shot magazine extension; barrel clamp with integral Picatinny rails; ArmorLokt coating; synthetic stock and fore-end with specially contour grip panels.
Price: $534.00

REMINGTON V3 TACTICAL
Addition of two tactical models to the V3 lineup with the same VersaPort self-regulating gas system that works with any shotshell from 2.75 in. to 3 in. Capacity: 6+1. Both wear an 18.5 in. barrel and oversized controls. One model with rifle sights, the other with a vent rib and bead sights.
Price: ....$1,024.85-$1,076.35

REMINGTON V3 COMPETITION TACTICAL
Addition of competition tactical model to the exiting V3 lineup. This 12 ga. uses the same Versa-Port technology to self-regulate for any shotshell from 2.75 in. to 3in. Capacity: 8+1. **Features:** 22-inch barrel with Hi-Viz front sight and low-profile, dovetail-rib mounting rear sight and oversized controls.
Price: $1,128.00

RETAY MASAI MARA WARDEN
Gauge: 12 ga., 3 in. **Barrel:** 18.5 in. **Weight:** 6.6 lbs. **Stock:** Black Synthetic. **Features:** The Turkish-made Masai Mara line of semi-automatics uses an inertia-plus action and bolt system. Oversized controls, quick unload system, Picatinny rail, extended charging handle, ghost-ring sights. Push-button removeable trigger group. Microcell rubber recoil pad. Includes a hard case and ships with five MaraPro choke tubes.
Price: $1,099.00

ROCK ISLAND ARMORY/ARMSCOR VRBP-100
Gauge: 12 ga., 3 in. **Capacity:** 5+1. **Barrel:** 20 in. contoured. **Length:** 32 in. **Weight:** 7.94 lbs. **Stock:** Black polymer bullpup design with pistol grip. **Features:** Semi-automatic bullpup design. Compatible with all VR Series magazines. Matte-black anodized finish. Includes rubber spacers to adjust length of pull. Full length top rail with flip-up sights, right-sided Picatinny accessory rail. Ships with three interchangeable chokes.
Price: $774.00

ROCK ISLAND ARMORY/ARMSCOR VRPA-40
Gauge: 12 ga., 3 in. **Capacity:** 5+1. **Barrel:** 20 in., contoured. **Length:** 55.11 in. **Weight:** 6.9 lbs. **Stock:** Black synthetic. **Features:** The VRPA40 marks the more affordable pump action addition to the VR family of shotguns. Magazine fed, aluminum heat shield, fiber-optic front sight, adjustable rear sight, Picatinny rail. Marine black anodized, compatible with VR series 9-round magazines. Mobil chokes.
Price: $399.99

TACTICAL RESPONSE STANDARD MODEL
Gauge: 12 ga., 3 in. **Capacity:** 7-round magazine. **Barrel:** 18 in. (Cyl.). **Weight:** 9 lbs. **Length:** 38 in. overall. **Stock:** Fiberglass-filled polypropylene with non-snag recoil absorbing butt pad. Nylon tactical fore-end houses flashlight. **Sights:** Trak-Lock ghost ring sight system. Front sight has Tritium insert. **Features:** Highly modified Remington 870P with Parkerized finish. Comes with nylon three-way adjustable sling, high visibility non-binding follower, high-performance magazine spring, Jumbo Head safety, and Side Saddle extended 6-shotshell carrier on left side of receiver. Introduced 1991. From Scattergun Technologies, Inc.
Price: Standard model, From..$1,540.00
Price: Border Patrol model, From $1,135.00
Price: Professional Model 13-in. bbl. (Law enf., military only)........$1,550.00

WINCHESTER SXP EXTREME DEFENDER
Gauge: 12 ga., 3 in. **Barrel:** 18 in., with Heat Shield. **Length:** 38.5 in. **Weight:** 7.0 lbs. **Stock:** Flat Dark Earth composite with textured grip panels and pistol grip. **Features:** Aluminum-alloy receiver, hard-chrome chamber and bore, Picatinny rail with ghost-ring sight, blade front sight. Two interchangeable comb pieces and two quarter-inch length-of-pull spacers for custom fit. Side-mounted Picatinny accessory rails, sling studs, Inflex recoil pad. Includes one Invector Plus cylinder choke and one Door Breacher choke.
Price: $529.99

Prices given are believed to be accurate at time of publication however, many factors affect retail pricing so exact prices are not possible.

75TH EDITION, 2021 ⟡ **527**

CHIAPPA LE PAGE PERCUSSION DUELING PISTOL
Caliber: .45. **Barrel:** 10 in. browned octagon, rifled. **Weight:** 2.5 lbs. **Length:** 16.6 in. overall. **Stock:** Walnut, rounded, fluted butt. **Sights:** Blade front, open-style rear. **Features:** Double set trigger. Bright barrel, silver-plated brass furniture. External ramrod. Made by Chiappa.
Price: Chiappa 940.001 ....$779.00

CVA OPTIMA PISTOL
Caliber: .50. **Barrel:** 14 in., 1:28-in. twist, Cerakote finish. **Weight:** 3.7 lbs. **Length:** 19 in. **Stock:** Black synthetic, Realtree Xtra Green. **Sights:** Scope base mounted. **Features:** Break-open action, all stainless construction, aluminum ramrod, quick-removal breech plug for 209 primer. From CVA.
Price: PP222SM Stainless/Realtree Xtra, rail mount $354.00
Price: PP221SM Stainless/black, rail mount...$307.00

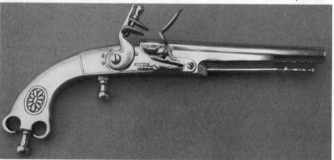

DIXIE MURDOCK SCOTTISH HIGHLANDER'S PISTOL
Caliber: .352. **Barrel:** 7.5 in., blued steel finish, round. **Weight:** 3.75 lbs. **Length:** 18.25 in. overall. **Stock:** Steel frame. **Sights:** None. **Features:** Flintlock, steel ramrod. An exact copy of an Alexander Murdock Scottish pistol of the 1770s. Made in India. Imported by Dixie Gun Works.

Price: Dixie Gun Works FH1040..$425.00

DIXIE MODEL 1855 U.S. DRAGOON PISTOL
Caliber: .58. **Barrel:** 12 in., bright finish, round. **Weight:** 2.25 lbs. **Length:** 16.75 in. overall. **Stock:** Walnut. **Sights:** Fixed rear and front sights. **Features:** Percussion, swivel-style, steel ramrod. Made by Palmetto Arms. Imported by Dixie Gun Works.
Price: Dixie Gun Works PH1000 ....$650.00

LYMAN PLAINS PISTOL
Caliber: .50 or .54. **Barrel:** 8 in.; 1:30-in. twist, both calibers. **Weight:** 3.1 lb. **Length:** 15 in. overall. **Stock:** Walnut. **Sights:** Blade front, square-notch rear adjustable for windage. **Features:** Polished brass triggerguard and ramrod tip, color case-hardened coil spring lock, spring-loaded trigger, stainless steel nipple, blackened iron furniture. Hooked patent breech, detachable belt hook. Introduced 1981. From Lyman Products.
Price: 6010608 .50-cal. $426.95
Price: 6010609 .54-cal...$426.95
Price: 6010610 .50-cal Kit $349.95
Price: 6010611 .54-cal. Kit...$349.95

PEDERSOLI CARLETON UNDERHAMMER MATCH PERCUSSION PISTOL
Caliber: .36. **Barrel:** 9.5 in., browned octagonal, rifled. **Weight:** 2.25 lbs. **Length:** 16.75 in. overall. **Stock:** Walnut. **Sights:** Blade front, open rear, adjustable for elevation. **Features:** Percussion, under-hammer ignition, adjustable trigger, no half cock. No ramrod. Made by Pedersoli. Imported by Dixie Gun Works.
Price: Dixie Gun Works FH0332..$925.00

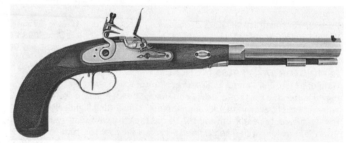

PEDERSOLI CHARLES MOORE ENGLISH DUELING PISTOL
Caliber: .45. **Barrel:** 11 in., 1:18 twist **Weight:** 2.5 lbs. **Length:** 16.5 in. overall. **Stock:** Walnut. **Sights:** Fixed. **Features:** Flintlock or percussion. Single set, adjustable trigger. Blued barrel and lock, steel furniture left in the white. Wooden ramrod. Replica of a fine British dueling pistol made by Charles Moore in London. Made by Pedersoli. Imported by Dixie Gun Works.
Price: Dixie Gun Works Flintlock FH0237 .... $795.00
Price: Dixie Gun Works Percussion PH0501 .... $610.00

PEDERSOLI FRENCH AN IX NAPOLEONIC PISTOL
Caliber: .69. **Barrel:** 8.25 in. **Weight:** 3 lbs. **Length:** 14 in. overall. **Stock:** Walnut. **Sights:** None. **Features:** Flintlock, case-hardened lock, brass furniture, buttcap, lock marked "Imperiale de S. Etienne." Steel ramrod. Made by Pedersoli. Imported by Dixie Gun Works.
Price: Dixie Gun Works FH0890.. $740.00

PEDERSOLI FRENCH AN IX GENDARMERIE NAPOLEONIC PISTOL
Caliber: .69. **Barrel:** 5.25 in. **Weight:** 3 lbs. **Length:** 14 in. overall. **Stock:** Walnut. **Sights:** None. **Features:** Flintlock, case-hardened lock, brass furniture, buttcap, lock marked "Imperiale de S. Etienne." Steel ramrod. Imported by Dixie Gun Works.
Price: Dixie Gun Works Gendarmerie FHO954...................................$725.00

Prices given are believed to be accurate at time of publication however, many factors affect retail pricing so exact prices are not possible.

PEDERSOLI FRENCH AN XIII NAPOLEONIC PISTOL

Caliber: .69. **Barrel:** 8.25 in. **Weight:** 3 lbs. **Length:** 14 in. overall. **Stock:** Walnut half-stock. **Sights:** None. **Features:** Flintlock, case-hardened lock, brass furniture, butt cap, lock marked "Imperiale de S. Etienne." Steel ramrod. Made by Pedersoli. Imported by Dixie Gun Works.
Price: Dixie Gun Works AN XIII FHO895 .... **$725.00**

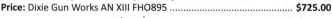
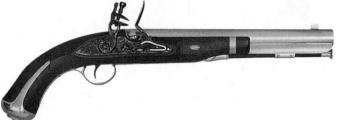

PEDERSOLI HARPER'S FERRY 1805 PISTOL

Caliber: .58. **Barrel:** 10 in. **Weight:** 2.5 lbs. **Length:** 16 in. overall. **Stock:** Walnut. **Sights:** Fixed. **Features:** Flintlock or percussion. Case-hardened lock, brass-mounted German silver-colored barrel. Wooden ramrod. Replica of the first U.S. government made flintlock pistol. Made by Pedersoli. Imported by Dixie Gun Works.
Price: Dixie Gun Works Flint RH0225 .... **$565.00**
Price: Dixie Gun Works Flint Kit RH0411 .... **$450.00**
Price: Dixie Gun Works Percussion RH0951 .... **$565.00**
Price: Dixie Gun Works Percussion Kit RH0937 .... **$395.00**

PEDERSOLI HOWDAH HUNTER PISTOLS

Caliber: .50, 20 gauge, .58. **Barrels:** 11.25 in., blued, rifled in .50 and .58 calibers. **Weight:** 4.25 to 5 lbs. **Length:** 17.25 in. **Stock:** American walnut with checkered grip. **Sights:** Brass bead front sight. **Features:** Blued barrels, swamped barrel rib, engraved, color case-hardened locks and hammers, captive steel ramrod. Available with detachable shoulder stock, case, holster and mold. Made by Pedersoli. Imported by Dixie Gun Works, Cabela's, Taylor's and others.
Price: Dixie Gun Works, 50X50, PH0572 .... **$895.00**
Price: Dixie Gun Works, 58XD58, PH09024 .... **$895.00**
Price: Dixie Gun Works, 20X20 gauge, PH0581 .... **$850.00**
Price: Dixie Gun Works, 50X20 gauge, PH0581 .... **$850.00**
Price: Dixie Gun Works, 50X50, Kit, PK0952 .... **$640.00**
Price: Dixie Gun Works, 50X20, Kit, PK1410........................ **$675.00**
Price: Dixie Gun Works, 20X20, Kit, PK0954........................ **$640.00**

PEDERSOLI KENTUCKY PISTOL

Caliber: .45, .50, .54. **Barrel:** 10.33 in. **Weight:** 2.5 lbs. **Length:** 15.4 in. overall. **Stock:** Walnut with smooth rounded birds-head grip. **Sights:** Fixed. **Features:** Available in flint or percussion ignition in various calibers. Case-hardened lock, blued barrel, drift-adjustable rear sights, blade front. Wooden ramrod. Kit guns of all models available from Dixie Gun Works. Made by Pedersoli. Imported by Dixie Gun Works, EMF and others.
Price: Dixie Gun Works .45 Percussion, PH0440 .... **$395.00**
Price: Dixie Gun Works.45 Flint, PH0430 .... **$437.00**
Price: Dixie Gun Works .45 Flint, Kit FH0320 .... **$325.00**

Price: Dixie Gun Works .50 Flint, PH0935 .... **$495.00**
Price: Dixie Gun Works .50 Percussion, PH0930 .... **$450.00**
Price: Dixie Gun Works. 54 Flint, PH0080 .... **$495.00**
Price: Dixie Gun Works .54 Percussion, PH0330 .... **$450.00**
Price: Dixie Gun Works .54 Percussion, Kit PK0436 .... **$325.00**
Price: Dixie Gun Works .45, Navy Moll, brass buttcap, Flint PK0436 ...... **$650.00**
Price: .45, Navy Moll, brass buttcap, Percussion PK0903 ....**$595.00**

PEDERSOLI LE PAGE PERCUSSION DUELING PISTOL

Caliber: .44. **Barrel:** 10 inches, browned octagon, rifled. **Weight:** 2.5 lbs. **Length:** 16.75 inches overall. **Stock:** Walnut, rounded checkered butt. **Sights:** Blade front, open-style rear. **Features:** Single set trigger, external ramrod. Made by Pedersoli. Imported by Dixie Gun Works.
Price: Dixie, Pedersoli, PH0431 ....$950.00
Price: Dixie, International, Pedersoli, PH0231..................................$1,250.00

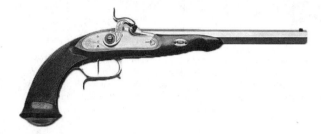

PEDERSOLI MAMELOUK

Caliber: .57. **Barrel:** 7-5/8 in., bright. **Weight:** 1.61 lbs. **Length:** 13 in. overall. **Stock:** Walnut, with brass end cap and medallion. **Sights:** Blade front. **Features:** Flint, lanyard ring, wooden ramrod. Made by Pedersoli. Available on special order from IFG (Italian Firearms Group)
Price: .... **TBD at time of order**

PEDERSOLI MANG TARGET PISTOL

Caliber: .38. **Barrel:** 11.5 in., octagonal, browned; 1:15-in. twist. **Weight:** 2.5 lbs. **Length:** 17. in. overall. **Stock:** Walnut with fluted grip. **Sights:** Blade front, open rear adjustable for windage. **Features:** Browned barrel, polished breech plug, remainder color case-hardened. Made by Pedersoli. Imported by Dixie Gun Works.
Price: PH0503 .... **$1,795.00**

PEDERSOLI MORTIMER TARGET PISTOL

Caliber: .44. **Barrel:** 10 in., bright octagonal on Standard, browned on Deluxe, rifled. **Weight:** 2.55 lbs. **Length:** 15.75 in. overall. **Stock:** Walnut, checkered saw-handle grip on Deluxe. **Sights:** Blade front, open-style rear. **Features:** Percussion or flint, single set trigger, sliding hammer safety, engraved lock on Deluxe. Wooden ramrod. Made by Pedersoli. Imported by Dixie Gun Works.
Price: Dixie, Flint, FH0316 ....$1,175.00
Price: Dixie, Percussion, PH0231 ....$1,095.00
Price: Dixie, Deluxe, FH0950 ....$2,220.00

TRADITIONS KENTUCKY PISTOL

Caliber: .50. **Barrel:** 10 in., 1:20 in. twist. **Weight:** 2.75 lbs. **Length:** 15 in. **Stock:** Hardwood full stock. **Sights:** Brass blade front, square notch rear adjustable for windage. **Features:** Polished brass finger spur-style trigger guard, stock cap and ramrod tip, color case-hardened leaf spring lock, spring-loaded trigger, No. 11 percussion nipple, brass furniture. From Traditions, and as kit from Bass Pro and others.
Price: P1060 Finished **$244.00**
Price: KPC50602 Kit **$209.00**

PEDERSOLI PHILADELPHIA DERRINGER

Caliber: .45. **Barrel:** 3.1 in., browned, rifled. **Weight:** 0.5 lbs. **Length:** 6.215 in. **Stock:** European walnut checkered. **Sights:** V-notch rear, blade front. **Features:** Back-hammer percussion lock with engraving, single trigger. Made by Pedersoli. Imported by Dixie Gun Works.
Price: Dixie, PH0913 . ...**$550.00**
Price: Dixie, Kit PK0863 . ...**$385.00**

PEDERSOLI QUEEN ANNE FLINTLOCK PISTOL

Caliber: .50. **Barrel:** 7.5 in., smoothbore. **Stock:** Walnut. **Sights:** None. **Features:** Flintlock, German silver-colored steel barrel, fluted brass triggerguard, brass mask on butt. Lockplate left in the white. No ramrod. Introduced 1983. Made by Pedersoli. Imported by Dixie Gun Works.
Price: Dixie, RH0211 ....**$495.00**
Price: Dixie, Kit, FH0421 ....**$375.00**

PEDERSOLI REMINGTON RIDER DERRINGER

Caliber: 4.3 mm (BB lead balls only). **Barrel:** 2.1 in., blued, rifled. **Weight:** 0.25 lbs. **Length:** 4.75 in. **Grips:** All-steel construction. **Sights:** V-notch rear, bead front. **Features:** Fires percussion cap only – no powder. Available as case-hardened frame or polished white. Made by Pedersoli. Imported by Dixie Gun Works.
Price: Dixie, Case-hardened PH0923. ....**$210.00**

PEDERSOLI SCREW BARREL PISTOL

Caliber: .44. **Barrel:** 2.35 in., blued, rifled. **Weight:** 0.5 lbs. **Length:** 6.5 in. **Grips:** European walnut. **Sights:** None. **Features:** Percussion, boxlock with center hammer, barrel unscrews for loading from rear, folding trigger, external hammer, combination barrel and nipple wrench furnished. Made by Pedersoli. Imported by Dixie Gun Works.
Price: Dixie, PH0530. ....**$225.00**
Price: Dixie, PH0545. ....**$175.00**

TRADITIONS TRAPPER PISTOL

Caliber: .50. **Barrel:** 9.75 in., octagonal, blued, hooked patent breech, 1:20 in. twist. **Weight:** 2.75 lbs. **Length:** 15.5 in. **Stock:** Hardwood, modified saw-handle style grip, halfstock. **Sights:** Brass blade front, rear sight adjustable for windage and elevation. **Features:** Percussion or flint, double set triggers, polished brass triggerguard, stock cap and ramrod tip, color case-hardened leaf spring lock, spring-loaded trigger, No. 11 percussion nipple, brass furniture. From Traditions and as a kit from Bass Pro and others.
Price: P1100 Finished, percussion **$329.00**
Price: P1090 Finished, flint **$369.00**
Price: KPC51002 Kit, percussion **$299.00**
Price: KPC50902 Kit, flint **$359.00**

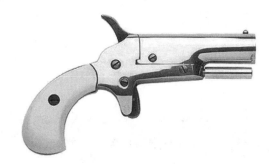

TRADITIONS VEST POCKET DERRINGER

Caliber: .31. **Barrel:** 2.35 in., round brass, smoothbore. **Weight:** .75 lbs. **Length:** 4.75 in. **Grips:** Simulated ivory. **Sights:** Front bead. **Features:** Replica of riverboat gambler's derringer. No. 11 percussion cap nipple, brass frame and barrel, spur trigger, external hammer. From Traditions.
Price: P1381, Brass **$194.00**
Price: Dixie, White, PH0920. ....**$175.00**

DANCE AND BROTHERS PERCUSSION REVOLVER
Caliber: .44. **Barrel:** 7.4 in., round. **Weight:** 2.5 lbs. **Length:** 13 in. overall. **Grips:** One-piece walnut. **Sights:** Brass blade front, hammer notch rear. **Features:** Reproduction of the C.S.A. revolver. Brass trigger guard. Color case-hardened frame Made by Pietta. Imported by Dixie Gun Works and others.
Price: Dixie Gun Works RH0344 .... **$350.00**

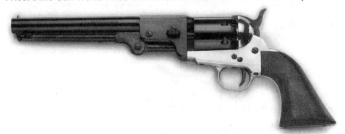

GRISWOLD AND GUNNISON PERCUSSION REVOLVER
Caliber: .36. **Barrel:** 7.5 in., round. **Weight:** 2.5 lbs. **Length:** 13.25 in. **Grips:** One-piece walnut. **Sights:** Fixed. **Features:** Reproduction of the C.S.A. revolver. Brass frame and triggerguard. Made by Pietta. Imported by EMF, Cabela's and others.
Price: EMF PF51BRGG36712 .... **$235.00**

NORTH AMERICAN COMPANION PERCUSSION REVOLVER
Caliber: .22. **Barrel:** 1-1/8 in. **Weight:** 5.1 oz. **Length:** 4 in. overall. **Grips:** Laminated wood. **Sights:** Blade front, notch rear. **Features:** All stainless steel construction. Uses No. 11 percussion caps. Comes with bullets, powder measure, bullet seater, leather clip holster, gun rag. Long Rifle frame. Introduced 1996. Made in U.S. by North American Arms.
Price: NAA-22LR-CB Long Rifle frame **$251.00**

NORTH AMERICAN SUPER COMPANION PERCUSSION REVOLVER
Caliber: .22. **Barrel:** 1-5/8 in. **Weight:** 7.2 oz. **Length:** 5-1/8 in. **Grips:** Laminated wood. **Sights:** Blade font, notched rear. **Features:** All stainless steel construction. No. 11 percussion caps. Comes with bullets, powder measure, bullet seater, leather clip holster, gun rag. Introduced 1996. Larger "Magnum" frame. Made in U.S. by North American Arms.
Price: NAA-Mag-CB Magnum frame **$296.00**

PEDERSOLI REMINGTON PATTERN TARGET REVOLVER
Caliber: .44. **Barrel:** 8 in., tapered octagon progressive twist. **Weight:** 2.75 lbs. **Length:** 13-3/4 in. overall. **Grips:** One-piece hardwood. **Sights:** V-notch on top strap, blued steel blade front. **Features:** Brass trigger guard, Non-reflective coating on the barrel and a wear resistant coating on the cylinder, blued steel frame, case-hardened hammer, trigger and loading lever. Made by Pedersoli. Imported by EMF, Dixie Gun Works, Cabela's and others.
Price: EMF Steel Frame PF58ST448 .... **$1,010.00**

PIETTA TEXAS PATTERSON PERCUSSION REVOLVER
Caliber: .36. **Barrel:** 9 in. tapered octagon. **Weight:** 2.75 lbs. **Length:** 13.75 in. **Grips:** One-piece walnut. **Sights:** Brass pin front, hammer notch rear. **Features:** Folding trigger, blued steel furniture, frame and barrel; engraved scene on cylinder. Ramrod: Loading tool provided. **Made by Pietta.** Imported by E.M.F, Dixie Gun Works.
Price: EMF PF36ST36712 .... **$610.00**

PIETTA 1851 NAVY MODEL PERCUSSION REVOLVER
Caliber: .36, .44, 6-shot. **Barrel:** 7.5 in. **Weight:** 44 oz. **Length:** 13 in. overall. **Grips:** Walnut. **Sights:** Post front, hammer notch rear. **Features:** Available in brass-framed and steel-framed models. Made by Pietta. Imported by EMF, Dixie Gun Works, Cabela's, Cimarron, Taylor's, Traditions and others.
Price: Brass frame EMF PF51BR36712 ....**$230.00**
Price: Steel frame EMF PF51CH36712...............................**$275.00**

PIETTA 1851 NAVY LONDON MODEL PERCUSSION REVOLVER
Caliber: .36, 6-shot. **Barrel:** 7.5 in. **Weight:** 44 oz. **Length:** 13 in. overall. **Grips:** Walnut. **Sights:** Post front, hammer notch rear. **Features:** steel frame and steel trigger guard and back strap. Available with oval trigger guard or squared back trigger guard. Made by Pietta. Imported by EMF, Dixie, Gun Works, Cabela's, Cimarron, Taylor's, Traditions and others.
Price: EMF PF51CHS36712 ....**$275.00**

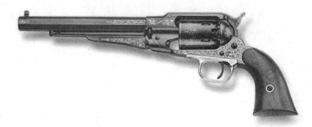

PIETTA 1851 NAVY SHERIFF'S MODEL PERCUSSION REVOLVER
Caliber: .44, 6-shot. **Barrel:** 5.5 in. **Weight:** 40 oz. **Length:** 11 in. overall. **Grips:** Walnut. **Sights:** Post front, hammer notch rear. **Features:** Available in brass-framed and steel-framed models. Made by Pietta. Imported by EMF, Dixie, Gun Works, Cabela's.
Price: Brass frame EMF PF51BR44512 .... $235.00
Price: Steel frame EMF PF51CH44512... $275.00

PIETTA 1851 NAVY CAPTAIN SCHAEFFER MODEL PERCUSSION REVOLVER
Caliber: .36, 6-shot. **Barrel:** 4 in. **Weight:** 40 oz. **Length:** 9.5 in. overall. **Grips:** Grips Ultra-ivory (polymer). **Sights:** Post front, hammer notch rear. **Features:** Polished steel finish, completely laser engraved. Made by Pietta. Imported by EMF
Price: EMF PF51LESS36312UI.. $395.00

PIETTA 1851 NAVY YANK PEPPERBOX MODEL PERCUSSION REVOLVER
Caliber: .36, 6-shot. **Barrel:** No Barrel. **Weight:** 36 oz. **Length:** 7 in. overall. **Grips:** One-piece walnut. **Sights:** Post front, hammer notch rear. **Features:** There is no barrel. Rounds fire directly out of the chambers of the elongated cylinder. Made by Pietta. Imported by EMF, Dixie Gun Works and Taylor's & Co.
Price: EMF PF51PEPPER36 .... $235.00

PIETTA 1851 NAVY BUNTLINE MODEL PERCUSSION REVOLVER
Caliber: .44, 6-shot. **Barrel:** 12 in. **Weight:** 36 oz. **Length:** 18.25 in. overall. **Grips:** Walnut. **Sights:** Post front, hammer notch rear. **Features:** Available in brass-framed and steel-framed models. Made by Pietta. Imported by EMF, Dixie Gun Works (Brass only).
Price: Brass frame EMF PF51BR4412 .... $245.00
Price: Steel frame EMF PF51CH4412... $295.00

PIETTA 1851 NAVY SNUBNOSE MODEL PERCUSSION REVOLVER
Caliber: .44, 6-shot. **Barrel:** 3 in. **Weight:** 36 oz. **Length:** 8.25 in. overall. **Grips:** Birds-head grip frame, one-piece checkered walnut. **Sights:** Post front, hammer notch rear. **Features:** Color case-hardened, steel-frame. Made by Pietta. Imported by Dixie Gun Works.
Price: Dixie SS1249 .... $395.00

PIETTA 1858 GENERAL CUSTER
Caliber: .44, 6-shot. Barrel: 8 in., blued. Grips: Two-piece wood. Sights: Open. Weight: 2.7 lbs. Features: Nickel-plated trigger guard, color case-hardened hammer, laser engraving.
Price: $360.00

PIETTA 1860 ARMY MODEL PERCUSSION REVOLVER
Caliber: .44. **Barrel:** 8 in. **Weight:** 2.75 lbs. **Length:** 13.25 in. overall. **Grips:** One-piece walnut. **Sights:** Brass blade front, hammer notch rear. **Features:** Models available with either case-hardened, steel frame, brass trigger guard, or brass frame, trigger guard and backstrap. EMF also offers a model with a silver finish on all the metal. Made by Pietta. Imported by EMF, Cabela's, Dixie Gun Works, Taylor's and others.
Price: EMF Brass Frame PF60BR448.................................... $260.00
Price: EMF Steel Frame PF60CH448...................................... $295.00
Price: EMF Steel Frame Old Silver finish PF60OS448 .... $325.00
Price: EMF Steel Frame Old Silver finish Deluxe Engraved PF60CHES448 ....$350.00

PIETTA 1860 ARMY SHERIFF'S MODEL PERCUSSION REVOLVER
Caliber: .44. **Barrel:** 5.5in. **Weight:** 40 oz. **Length:** 11.5 in. overall. **Grips:** One-piece walnut. **Sights:** Brass blade front, hammer notch rear. **Features:** Case-hardened, steel frame, brass trigger guard. Made by Pietta. Imported by EMF, Cabela's, Dixie Gun Works and others.
Price: EMF PF60CH44512.. $295.00

PIETTA 1860 ARMY SNUBNOSE MODEL PERCUSSION REVOLVER
Caliber: .44. **Barrel:** 3 in. **Weight:** 36 oz. **Length:** 8.25 in. overall. **Grips:** Birds-head grip frame, one-piece, checkered walnut. **Sights:** Brass blade front, hammer notch rear. **Features:** Fluted cylinder, case-hardened, steel frame, brass trigger guard, Made by Pietta. Imported by EMF.
Price: EMF PF51CHLG44212CW $385.00

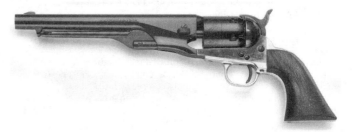

PIETTA NAVY 1861 PERCUSSION REVOLVER
Caliber: .36. **Barrel:** 8 in. **Weight:** 2.75 lbs. **Length:** 13.25 in. overall. **Grips:** One-piece walnut. **Sights:** Brass blade front, hammer notch rear. **Features:** Steel, case-hardened frame, brass-grip frame, or steel-grip frame (London Model), case-hardened creeping loading lever. Made by Pietta. Imported by EMF, Dixie Gun Works, Cabela's and others.
Price: EMF with brass triggerguard PF61CH368CIV $300.00
Price: EMF with steel triggerguard PF61CH368................................. $300.00

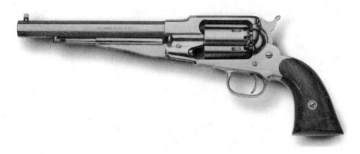

PIETTA 1858 REMINGTON ARMY REVOLVER

Caliber: .44. **Barrel:** 8 in., tapered octagon. **Weight:** 2.75 lbs. **Length:** 13.5 in. overall. **Grips:** Two-piece walnut. **Sights:** V-notch on top strap, blued steel blade front. **Features:** Brass triggerguard, blued steel backstrap and frame, case-hardened hammer and trigger. Also available, a brass-framed model, and an all stainless steel model. Made by Pietta. Imported by EMF, Dixie Gun Works, Cabela's and others.
Price: EMF Steel Frame PF58ST448 .... **$290.00**
Price: EMF Brass Frame PF58BR448 .... **$250.00**
Price: EMF Stainless Steel PF58SS448 .... **$430.00**

PIETTA 1858 REMINGTON TARGET REVOLVER

Caliber: .44. **Barrel:** 8 in., tapered octagon. **Weight:** 2.75 lbs. **Length:** 13.5 in. overall. **Grips:** Two-piece walnut. **Sights:** Adjustable rear, ramped blade front. **Features:** Brass triggerguard, blued steel frame, case-hardened hammer, and trigger. Also available, a brass-framed model. Made by Pietta. Imported by EMF, Dixie Gun Works, Cabela's and others.
Price: EMF PF58STT448 .... **$350.00**

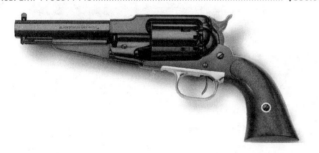

PIETTA 1858 REMINGTON SHIRIFF'S MODEL REVOLVER

Caliber: .36 and .44. **Barrel:** 5.5in., tapered octagon. **Weight:** 2.75 lbs. **Length:** 11.5 in. overall. **Grips:** Two-piece checkered walnut. **Sights:** V-notch on top strap, blued steel blade front. **Features:** Brass triggerguard, blued steel backstrap and frame, case-hardened hammer and trigger. Also available in a color case-hardened-framed model, and in an all stainless steel model. Made by Pietta. Imported by EMF, and others.
Price: EMF Blued Steel Frame PF58ST36612 .... **$290.00**
Price: EMF Color Case-Hardened frame PF58CH44512CW **$395.00**
Price: EMF Stainless Steel PF58SS44512CW **$490.00**

PIETTA 1858 REMINGTON BUFFALO BILL COMMEMORATIVE REVOLVER

Caliber: .44. **Barrel:** 8 in., tapered octagon. **Weight:** 2.75 lbs. **Length:** 13-3/4 in. overall. **Grips:** Two-piece walnut. **Sights:** V-notch on top strap, blued steel blade front. **Features:** Gold-filled engraving over dark blue steel. A higher-grade gun commemorating the life of Buffalo Bill Cody. Made by Pietta. Imported by EMF.
Price: EMF PF58BB448 .... **$695.00**

PIETTA REMINGTON BELT MODEL REVOLVER

Caliber: .36. **Barrel:** 6.5 in., octagon. **Weight:** 44 oz. **Length:** 12.5 in. overall. **Grips:** Two-piece walnut. **Sights:** V-notch on top strap, blued steel blade front. **Features:** Brass triggerguard, blued steel backstrap and frame, case-hardened hammer and trigger. Made by Pietta. Imported by Dixie Gun Works.
Price: Dixie RH0214 .... **$295.00**

PIETTA 1863 REMINGTON POCKET MODEL REVOLVER

Caliber: .31, 5-shot. **Barrel:** 3.5 in. **Weight:** 1 lb. **Length:** 7.6 in. **Grips:** Two-piece walnut. **Sights:** Pin front, groove-in-frame rear. **Features:** Spur trigger, iron-, brass- or nickel-plated frame. Made by Pietta. Imported by EMF (Steel Frame), Dixie Gun Works, Taylor's and others.
Price: Brass frame, Dixie PH0407 .... **$260.00**
Price: Steel frame, Dixie PH0370 .... **$295.00**
Price: Nickel-plated, Dixie PH0409 .... **$315.00**

PIETTA LEMATT REVOLVER

Caliber: .44/20 Ga. **Barrel:** 6.75 in. (revolver); 4-7/8 in. (single shot). **Weight:** 3 lbs. 7 oz. **Length:** 14 in. overall. **Grips:** Hand-checkered walnut. **Sights:** Post front, hammer notch rear. **Features:** Exact reproduction with all-steel construction; 44-cal., 9-shot cylinder, 20-gauge single barrel; color case-hardened hammer with selector; spur triggerguard; ring at butt; lever-type barrel release. Made by Pietta. Imported by EMF, Dixie Gun Works and others.
Price: EMF Navy PFLMSTN44634 .... **$1,075.00**
Price: EMF Cavalry PFLMST44712 .... **$1,100.00**
Price: EMF Army PFLMSTA44634 .... **$1,100.00**

PIETTA SPILLER & BURR PERCUSSION REVOLVER

Caliber: .36. **Barrel:** 7 in., octagon. **Weight:** 2.5 lbs. **Length:** 12.5 in. overall. **Grips:** Two-piece walnut. **Sights:** V-notch on top strap, blued steel blade front. **Features:** Reproduction of the C.S.A. revolver. Brass frame and trigger guard. Also available as a kit. Made by Pietta. Imported by Dixie Gun Works, Traditions, Midway USA and others.
Price: Dixie RH0120 .... **$275.00**
Price: Dixie kit RH0300 .... **$235.00**

PIETTA STARR DOUBLE-ACTION ARMY REVOLVER

Caliber: .44. **Barrel:** 6 in. tapered round. **Weight:** 3 lbs. **Length:** 11.75 in. **Grips:** One-piece walnut. **Sights:** Hammer notch rear, dovetailed front. **Features:** Double-action mechanism, round tapered barrel, all blued frame and barrel. Made by Pietta. Imported by Dixie Gun Works and others.
Price: Dixie RH460 .... **$565.00**

PIETTA STARR SINGLE-ACTION ARMY REVOLVER

Caliber: .44. **Barrel:** 8 in. tapered round. **Weight:** 3 lbs. **Length:** 13.5 in. **Grips:** One-piece walnut. **Sights:** Hammer notch rear, dovetailed front. **Features:** Single-action mechanism, round tapered barrel, all blued frame and barrel. Made by Pietta. Imported by Cabela's, Dixie Gun Works and others.
Price: Dixie RH460 .... **$550.00**

PIETTA 1873 PERCUSSION REVOLVER

Caliber: .44. **Barrel:** 5.5 in. **Weight:** 40 oz. **Length:** 11.25 in. overall. **Grips:** One-piece walnut. **Sights:** V-notch on top strap, blued steel blade front. **Features:** A cap-and-ball version of the Colt Single Action Army revolver. Made by Pietta. Imported by EMF, Cabela's, Dixie Gun Works and others.
Price: EMF PF73CHS434NM **$360.00**

TRADITIONS U.S. MARSHAL

Caliber: .36, 6-shot. **Barrel:** 8 in., blued. **Grips:** One-piece walnut. **Sights:** Open, hammer/blade. **Weight:** 2.61 lbs. **Features:** Case-hardened frame, single action, U.S. Marshal logo on grips.
Price: **$351.99**

Prices given are believed to be accurate at time of publication however, many factors affect retail pricing so exact prices are not possible.

75TH EDITION, 2021 ⊕ **533**

TRADITIONS WILDCARD
Caliber: .36, 6-shot. **Barrel:** 7.375 in., blued octagon. **Grips:** Simulated stag. **Sights:** Open, hammer/blade. **Weight:** 2.5 lbs. **Features:** 1851 "Gunfighter," 13.5-in. overall length, case-hardened frame.
Price: **$409.99**

UBERTI 1847 WALKER PERCUSSION REVOLVER
Caliber: .44. **Barrel:** 9 in. **Weight:** 4.5 lbs. **Length:** 15.7 in. overall. **Grips:** One-piece hardwood. **Sights:** Brass blade front, hammer notch rear. **Features:** Copy of Sam Colt's first U.S. contract revolver. Engraved cylinder, case-hardened hammer and loading lever. Blued finish. Made by Uberti. Imported by Cabela's, Cimarron, Dixie Gun Works, EMF, Taylor's, Uberti U.S.A. and others.
Price: Uberti USA, standard model, blued steel 340200 .... **$429.00**

UBERTI DRAGOON PERCUSSION REVOLVERS
Caliber: .44. **Barrel:** 7.5 in. **Weight:** 4.1 lbs. **Grips:** One-piece walnut. **Sights:** Brass blade front, hammer notch rear. **Features:** Four models of the big .44 caliber revolvers that followed the massive Walker model and pre-dated the sleek 1860 Army model. Blued barrel, backstrap and trigger guard. Made by Uberti. Imported by Uberti USA, Dixie Gun Works, Taylor's and others.
Price: Uberti USA, Whitneyville Dragoon 340830 .... **$429.00**
Price: Uberti USA, First Model Dragoon 340800 .... **$429.00**
Price: Uberti USA, Second Model Dragoon 340810 .... **$429.00**
Price: Uberti USA, Third Model Dragoon 340860................................ **$429.00**

UBERTI 1849 POCKET MODEL WELLS FARGO PERCUSSION REVOLVER
Caliber: .31. **Barrel:** 4 in., seven-groove, RH twist. **Weight:** About 24 oz. **Grips:** One-piece walnut. **Sights:** Brass pin front, hammer notch rear. **Features:** Unfluted cylinder with stagecoach holdup scene, cupped cylinder pin, no grease grooves, one safety pin on cylinder and slot in hammer face. Made by Uberti. Imported by Uberti USA, Cimarron, Dixie Gun Works and others.
Price: Uberti USA 340350... **$349.00**

UBERTI 1849 WELLS FARGO PERCUSSION REVOLVER
Caliber: .31. **Barrel:** 4 in.; seven-groove; RH twist. **Weight:** About 24 oz. **Grips:** One-piece walnut. **Sights:** Brass pin front, hammer notch rear. **Features:** No loading lever, Unfluted cylinder with stagecoach holdup scene, cupped cylinder pin, no grease grooves, one safety pin on cylinder and slot in hammer face. Made by Uberti. Imported by Uberti USA, Cimarron, Dixie Gun Works and others.
Price: Uberti USA 340380... **$349.00**

UBERTI NAVY MODEL 1851 PERCUSSION REVOLVER
Caliber: .36, 6-shot. **Barrel:** 7.5 in. **Weight:** 44 oz. **Length:** 13 in. overall. **Grips:** One-piece walnut. **Sights:** Post front, hammer notch rear. **Features:** Brass backstrap and trigger guard, or steel backstrap and trigger guard (London Model), engraved cylinder with navy battle scene; case-hardened hammer, loading lever. Made by Uberti and Pietta. Imported by Uberti USA, Cabela's, Cimarron, and others.
Price: Uberti USA Brass grip assembly 340000 .... **$329.00**
Price: Uberti USA London Model 340050 .... **$369.00**

UBERTI 1860 ARMY REVOLVER
Caliber: .44. **Barrel:** 8 in. **Weight:** 44 oz. **Length:** 13.25 in. overall. **Grips:** One-piece walnut. **Sights:** Brass blade front, hammer notch rear. **Features:** Steel or case-hardened frame, brass triggerguard, case-hardened creeping loading lever. Many models and finishes are available for this pistol. Made by Uberti. Imported by Cabela's, Cimarron, Dixie Gun Works, EMF, Taylor's, Uberti U.S.A. and others.
Price: Uberti USA, roll engraved cylinder 340400 .... **$349.00**
Price: Uberti USA, full fluted cylinder 340410 .... **$369.00**

UBERTI 1861 NAVY PERCUSSION REVOLVER
Caliber: .36 **Barrel:** 7.5 in. **Weight:** 44 oz. **Length:** 13.25 in. overall. **Grips:** One-piece walnut. **Sights:** Brass blade front, hammer notch rear. **Features:** Brass backstrap and trigger guard, or steel backstrap and trigger guard (London Model), engraved cylinder with navy battle scene; case-hardened hammer, loading lever. Made by Uberti. Imported by Uberti USA, Cabela's, Cimarron, Dixie Gun Works, Taylor's and others.
Price: Uberti USA Brass grip assembly 340630 .... **$349.00**
Price: Uberti USA London Model 340500 .... **$349.00**

UBERTI 1862 POLICE PERCUSSION REVOLVER
Caliber: .36, 5-shot. **Barrel:** 5.5 in., 6.5 in., 7.5 in. **Weight:** 26 oz. **Length:** 12 in. overall (6.5 in. bbl.). **Grips:** One-piece walnut. **Sights:** Fixed. **Features:** Round tapered barrel; half-fluted and rebated cylinder; case-hardened frame, loading lever and hammer; brass trigger guard and backstrap. Made by Uberti. Imported by Cimarron, Dixie Gun Works, Taylor's, Uberti U.S.A. and others.
Price: Uberti USA 340700... **$369.00**

UBERTI 1862 POCKET NAVY PERCUSSION REVOLVER
Caliber: .36, 5-shot. **Barrel:** 5.5 in., 6.5 in. **Weight:** 26 oz. **Length:** 12 in. overall (6.5 in. bbl.). **Grips:** One-piece walnut. **Sights:** Fixed. **Features:** Octagon barrel; case-hardened frame, loading lever and hammer; silver or brass trigger guard and backstrap; also available in an all stainless steel version. Made by Uberti. Imported by Uberti USA, Cimarron, Dixie Gun Works, Taylor's and others.
Price: Uberti USA 340750.. **$369.00**

UBERTI LEACH AND RIGDON PERCUSSION REVOLVER
Caliber: .36. **Barrel:** 7.5 in., octagon to round. **Weight:** 2.75 lbs. **Length:** 13 in. **Grips:** One-piece walnut. **Sights:** Hammer notch and pin front. **Features:** Steel frame. Reproduction of the C.S.A. revolver. Brass backstrap and trigger guard. Made by Uberti. Imported by Uberti USA, Dixie Gun Works and others.
Price: Uberti USA 340030.. **$349.00**

UBERTI NEW ARMY REMINGTON PERCUSSION REVOLVER
Caliber: .44, 6-shot. **Barrel:** Tapered octagon 8 in. **Weight:** 32 oz. **Length:** Standard 13.5 in. **Grips:** Two-piece walnut. **Sights:** Standard blade front, groove-in-frame rear; adjustable on some models. **Features:** Many variations of this gun are available. Target Model (Uberti U.S.A.) has fully adjustable target rear sight, target front, .36 or .44. Made by Uberti. Imported by Uberti USA, Cimarron F.A. Co., Taylor's and others.
Price: Uberti USA Steel frame, 341000 .... **$369.00**
Price: Uberti USA Stainless, 341020.................................... **$449.00**

Prices given are believed to be accurate at time of publication however, many factors affect retail pricing so exact prices are not possible.

75TH EDITION, 2021 ◈ **535**

ARMI SPORT ENFIELD THREE-BAND P1853 RIFLE

Caliber: .58. **Barrel:** 39 in. **Weight:** 10.25 lbs. **Length:** 52 in. overall. **Stock:** European walnut. **Sights:** Blade front, flip-up rear with elevator marked to 800 yards. **Features:** Reproduction of the original three-band rifle. Percussion musket-cap ignition. Blued barrel with steel barrelbands, brass furniture. Case-hardened lock. Lockplate marked "London Armory Co. and Crown." Made by Euro Arms, Armi Sport (Chiappa). Imported by Dixie Gun Works and others.
Price: Dixie Gun Works rifled bore PR1130 ....**$895.00**
Price: Dixie Gun Work smooth bore PR1052....................**$750.00**

CVA ACCURA IN-LINE BREAK-ACTION RIFLE

Caliber: .50. **Barrel:** 28 in. fluted. **Weight:** 7.5 lbs. **Length:** Standard 45 in. **Stock:** Ambidextrous solid composite in standard or thumbhole. **Sights:** Adj. fiber-optic. **Features:** Break-action, quick-release breech plug, aluminum loading rod, cocking spur, lifetime warranty. By CVA.
Price: CVA PR3120NM (Accura MR Nitride with Black Stocks
 and Scope Mount)...**$493.00**

CVA ACCURA V2 LR NITRIDE "SPECIAL EDITION" IN-LINE BREAK-ACTION RIFLE

Caliber: .50. **Barrel:** 30 in. fluted. **Weight:** 7.5 lbs. **Length:** Standard 45 in. **Stock:** Ambidextrous solid composite. **Sights:** Adj. fiber-optic. **Features:** Break-action, quick-release breech plug, aluminum loading rod, cocking spur, equipped with a genuine, Nitride treated, 30-inch Bergara Barrel, and a deep pistol grip stock decorated in APG camo. Lifetime warranty. By CVA.
Price: CVA PR6124NM **$449.95**

CVA ACCURA LR

Caliber: .45, .50. **Barrel:** 30 in., Nitride-treated, 416 stainless steel Bergara. Stock: Ambidextrous thumbhole camo. **Sights:** DuraSight Dead-On one-piece scope mount, scope not included. **Weight:** 6.75 lbs. **Features:** Reversible hammer spur, CrushZone recoil pad, quick-release breech plug.
Price: **$605.95**

CVA ACCURA MR (MOUNTAIN RIFLE) IN-LINE BREAK-ACTION RIFLE

Caliber: .50. **Barrel:** 25 in. **Weight:** 6.35 lbs. **Length:** Standard 45 in. **Stock:** Ambidextrous solid composite. **Sights:** DuraSight DEAD-ON One-Piece Scope Mount. **Features:** Break-action, quick-release breech plug, aluminum loading rod, cocking spur, and a deep pistol grip stock decorated in Realtree APG camo. Lifetime warranty. By CVA.
Price: CVA PR3121SNM **$546.00**

CVA PLAINS RIFLE

Caliber: .50. **Barrel:** 28 in., Nitride, fluted, stainless steel Bergara. **Stock:** Ambidextrous composite Realtree MAX-1 XT. **Sights:** DuraSight Dead-On one-piece scope mount, scope not included. **Weight:** 7.2 lbs. **Features:** Solid aluminum PalmSaver ramrod, reversible cocking spur, Quake Claw sling.
Price: **$593.95**

CVA PARAMOUNT PRO

Caliber: .45, magnum. **Barrel:** Fluted Bergara free-floating, Cerakote/Nitride stainless steel/camo. **Stock:** Grayboe fiberglass. **Sights:** Threaded 3/4x20, scope not included. **Weight:** 8.75 lbs. **Features:** TriggerTech trigger, VariFlame breech plug, accessory trap door, self-deploying ramrod.
Price: **$1,667.95**

CVA PARAMOUNT PRO COLORADO

Caliber: .50, magnum. **Barrel:** Fluted Bergara free-floating, Cerakote/Nitride stainless steel/camo. **Stock:** Grayboe fiberglass. **Sights:** Williams peep sight. **Weight:** 8.75 lbs. **Features:** TriggerTech trigger, VariFlame breech plug, accessory trap door, self-deploying ramrod.
Price: **$1,667.95**

CVA OPTIMA IN-LINE BREAK-ACTION RIFLE

Caliber: .50. **Barrel:** 26 in., stainless steel. **Weight:** 6.65 lbs. **Length:** 41in. **Stock:** Ambidextrous solid composite. Available in pistol grip or thumbhole configurations. **Sights:** DuraSight DEAD-ON One-Piece Scope Mount. **Features:** Ambidextrous with rubber grip panels in black or Realtree APG camo, crush-zone recoil pad, reversible hammer spur, quake claw sling. Lifetime warranty. By CVA.
Price: CVA PR2020SM... **$371.00**

CVA WOLF IN-LINE BREAK-ACTION RIFLE

Caliber: .50 **Barrel:** 24 in. **Weight:** 6.23 lbs. **Stock:** Ambidextrous composite. **Sights:** Dead-On Scope Mounts or Fiber Optic. **Features:** Break-action, quick-release breech plug for 209 primer, aluminum loading road, cocking spur. Lifetime warranty. By CVA.
Price: CVA PR2112SM (.50-cal, stainless/Realtree Hardwoods HD,
 scope mount)..**$289.50**
Price: CVA PR2112S (50-cal, stainless/Realtree Hardwoods HD,
 fib. opt. sight) **$289.50**
Price: CVA PR2110SM (.50-cal, stainless/black, scope mount) **$240.50**

DIXIE DELUXE CUB RIFLE

Caliber: .32, .36. **Barrel:** 28 in. octagonal. **Weight:** 6.5 lbs. **Length:** 44 in. overall. **Stock:** Walnut. **Sights:** Fixed. **Features:** Each gun available in either flint or percussion ignition. Short rifle for small game and beginning shooters. Brass patchbox and furniture. Made by Pedersoli for Dixie Gun Works.
Price: Dixie Gun Works (.32-cal. flint) PR3130....................**$890.00**
Price: Dixie Gun Works (.36-cal. flint) FR3135...................... **$890.00**
Price: Dixie Gun Works (.32-cal. Percussion kit) PK3360 .... **$690.00**
Price: Dixie Gun Works (.36-cal. Percussion kit) PK3365................. **$690.00**
Price: Dixie Gun Works (.32-cal. Flint kit) PK3350 .... **$710.00**
Price: Dixie Gun Works (.36-cal. Flint kit) PK335 .... **$710.00**
Price: Dixie Gun Works (.32-cal. percussion) PR3140................. **$850.00**
Price: Dixie Gun Works (.36-cal. percussion) PR3145.................. **$850.00**

DIXIE PENNSYLVANIA RIFLE

Caliber: .45 and .50. **Barrel:** 41.5 in. octagonal, .45/1:48, .50/1:56 in. twist. **Weight:** 8.5, 8.75 lbs. **Length:** 56 in. overall. **Stock:** European walnut, full-length stock. **Sights:** Notch rear, blade front. **Features:** Flintlock or percussion, brass patchbox, double-set triggers. Also available as kit guns for both calibers and ignition systems. Made by Pedersoli for Dixie Gun Works.
Price: Dixie Gun Works (.45-cal. flint) FR1060..................**$1,100.00**
Price: Dixie Gun Works (.50-cal. flint) FR3200.................. **$1,100.00**
Price: Dixie Gun Works (.45-cal. Percussion kit) PR1075.................... **$910.00**
Price: Dixie Gun Works (.50-cal. Percussion kit) PK3365..................... **$910.00**
Price: Dixie Gun Works (.45-cal. Flint kit) FR1065 .... **$910.00**
Price: Dixie Gun Works (.50-cal. Flint kit) FK3420 .... **$910.00**
Price: Dixie Gun Works (.45-cal. percussion) FR1070...................... **$1,050.00**
Price: Dixie Gun Works (.50-cal. percussion) PR3205...................... **$1,050.00**

Prices given are believed to be accurate at time of publication however, many factors affect retail pricing so exact pricing is not possible.

EUROARMS 1803 HARPER'S FERRY FLINTLOCK RIFLE
Caliber: .54. **Barrel:** 35.5 in., smoothbore. **Weight:** 9.5 lbs. **Length:** 50.5 in. overall. **Stock:** Half-stock, walnut w/oil finish. **Sights:** Blade front, notched rear. **Features:** Color case-hardened lock, browned barrel, with barrel key. Made by Euroarms. Imported by Dixie Gun Works.
Price: Dixie Gun Works FR0171 ....$795.00

EUROARMS J.P. MURRAY ARTILLERY CARBINE
Caliber: .58. **Barrel:** 23.5 in. **Weight:** 8 lbs. **Length:** 39.5 in. **Stock:** European walnut. **Sights:** Blade front, fixed notch rear. **Features:** Percussion musket-cap ignition. Reproduction of the original Confederate carbine. Lock marked "J.P. Murray, Columbus, Georgia." Blued barrel. Made by Euroarms. Imported by Dixie Gun Works and others.
Price: Dixie, Gun Works PR0173..$1,100.00

EUROARMS ENFIELD MUSKETOON P1861
Caliber: .58. **Barrel:** 24 in. **Weight:** 9 lbs. **Length:** 40 in. overall. **Stock:** European walnut. **Sights:** Blade front, flip-up rear with elevator marked to 700 yards. **Features:** Reproduction of the original cavalry version of the Enfield rifle. Percussion musket-cap ignition. Blued barrel with steel barrelbands, brass furniture. Case-hardened lock. Euroarms version marked London Armory with crown. Pedersoli version has Birmingham stamp on stock and Enfield and Crown on lockplate. Made by Euroarms. Imported by Dixie Gun Works and others.
Price: Dixie Gun Works PR0343..$1,050.00

KNIGHT 500 IN-LINE RIFLE
Caliber: .50. **Barrel:** 28 in., custom Green Mountain. **Weight:** 10 lbs. **Length:** 46 in. overall. **Stock:** Boyd's custom stock with integrated aluminum bedding **Sights:** Not included. **Features:** Competition-grade muzzleloader that can be used as a hunting rifle, handcrafted Green Mountain barrel, the stock also features an adjustable cheek piece that gives you a clear view down range. Made in U.S. by Knight Rifles.
Price: Muzzleloaders.com MMTE758TAR...................... **Starting at $2,080.99**

KNIGHT BIGHORN IN-LINE RIFLE
Caliber: .50. **Barrel:** 26 in., 1:28 in. twist. **Weight:** 7 lbs. 3 oz. **Length:** 44.5 in. overall. **Stock:** G2 straight or thumbhole, Carbon Knight straight or thumbhole or black composite thumbhole with recoil pad, sling swivel studs. **Ramrod:** Carbon core with solid brass extendable jag. **Sights:** Fully adjustable metallic fiber optic. **Features:** Uses four different ignition systems (included): #11 nipple, musket nipple, bare 208 shotgun primer and 209 Extreme shotgun primer system (Extreme weatherproof full plastic jacket system); vented breech plug, striker fired with one-piece removable hammer assembly. With recommended loads, guaranteed to have 4-inch, three-shot groups at 200 yards. Also available as Western gun with exposed ignition. Made in U.S. by Knight Rifles.
Price: Muzzleloaders.com MBH706C $646.99

KNIGHT DISC EXTREME
Caliber: .50, .52. **Barrel:** 26 in., fluted stainless, 1:28 in. twist. **Weight:** 7 lbs. 14 oz. to 8 lbs. **Length:** 45 in. overall. **Stock:** Carbon Knight straight or thumbhole with blued or SS; G2 thumbhole; left-handed Nutmeg thumbhole. Ramrod: Solid brass extendable jag. **Sights:** Fully adjustable metallic fiber optics. **Features:** Bolt-action rifle, full plastic jacket ignition system, #11 nipple, musket nipple, bare 208 shotgun primer. With recommended loads, guaranteed to have 4-inch, three-shot groups at 200 yards. Also available as Western gun with exposed ignition. Made in U.S. by Knight Rifles.
Price: Muzzleloaders.com MDE706SMX ....**Starting at $721.99**

KNIGHT LITTLEHORN IN-LINE RIFLE
Caliber: .50. **Barrel:** 22 in., 1:28 in. twist. **Weight:** 6.7 lbs. **Length:** 39 in. overall. **Stock:** 12.5-in. length of pull, G2 straight or pink Realtree AP HD. **Ramrod:** Carbon core with solid brass extendable jag. **Sights:** Fully adjustable Williams fiber optic. **Features:** Uses four different ignition systems (included): Full Plastic Jacket, #11 nipple, musket nipple or bare 208 shotgun primer; vented breech plug, striker-fired with one-piece removable hammer assembly. **Finish:** Stainless steel. With recommended loads, guaranteed to have 4-inch, three-shot groups at 200 yards. Also available as Western gun with exposed ignition. Made in U.S. by Knight Rifles.
Price: Muzzleloaders.com MLHW702C ....**Starting at $390.00**

KNIGHT MOUNTAINEER IN-LINE RIFLE
Caliber: .45, .50, .52. **Barrel:** 27 in. fluted stainless steel, free floated. **Weight:** 8 lbs. (thumbhole stock), 8.3 lbs. (straight stock). **Length:** 45.5 inches. **Sights:** Fully adjustable metallic fiber optic. **Features:** Bolt-action rifle, adjustable match-grade trigger, aluminum ramrod with carbon core, solid brass extendable jag, vented breech plug. Ignition: Full plastic jacket, #11 nipple, musket nipple, bare 208 shotgun primer. With recommended loads, guaranteed to have 4-inch, three-shot groups at 200 yards. Also available as Western gun with exposed ignition. Made in U.S. by Knight Rifles.
Price: Muzzleloaders.com MMT707SNMNT ....**Starting at $1,016.99**

KNIGHT TK-2000 IN-LINE SHOTGUN
Gauge: 12. **Barrel:** 26 inches. **Choke:** Extra-full and improved cylinder available. **Stock:** Realtree Xtra Green straight or thumbhole. **Weight:** 7.7 pounds. **Sights:** Williams fully adjustable rear, fiber-optic front. **Features:** Striker-fired action, receiver is drilled and tapped for scope, adjustable trigger, removable breech plug, double-safety system. Ignition: #209 primer with Full Plastic Jacket, musket cap or No. 11. Striker-fired with one-piece removable hammer assembly. Made in U.S. by Knight Rifles.
Price: Muzzleloaders.com MTK2000SXG............................**Starting at $742.99**

KNIGHT ULTRA-LITE IN-LINE RIFLE
Caliber: .45 or .50. **Barrel:** 24 in. **Stock:** Black, tan or olive-green Kevlar spider web. **Weight:** 6 lbs. **Features:** Bolt-action rifle. Ramrod: Carbon core with solid brass extendable jag. **Sights:** With or without Williams fiber-optic sights, drilled and tapped for scope mounts. **Finish:** Stainless steel. Ignition: 209 Primer with Full Plastic Jacket, musket cap or #11 nipple, bare 208 shotgun primer; vented breech plug. With recommended loads, guaranteed to have 4-inch, three-shot groups at 200 yards. Also available as Western version with exposed ignition. Made in U.S. by Knight Rifles.
Price: Muzzleloaders.com MULE704TNT ....**Starting at $1,217.99**

KNIGHT VISION IN-LINE RIFLE
Caliber: .50. **Barrel:** 24 in. **Length:** 44 in. **Stock:** Black composite. **Weight:** 7.9 lbs. **Features:** Break-open rifle with carbon-steel barrel and all-new machined steel action. With recommended loads, guaranteed to have 4-inch, three-shot groups at 200 yards. Ramrod: Carbon core with solid brass extendable jag. Ignition: Full Plastic Jacket. **Sights:** Weaver sight bases attached, and Williams fiber-optic sights provided. **Finish:** Blued steel. Made in U.S. by Knight Rifles.
Price: Muzzleloaders.com MKVE04XT...............................**Starting at $346.99**

KNIGHT WOLVERINE IN-LINE RIFLE
Caliber: .50. **Barrel:** 22 in. stainless steel, 1:28 in. twist. **Weight:** 6.9 lbs. **Length:** 40.5 overall. **Stock:** Realtree Hardwoods straight, CarbonKnight straight. Ramrod: Carbon core with solid brass extendable jag. **Sights:** Fully adjustable Williams fiber optic. **Features:** Ignition systems (included): #11 nipple, musket nipple, bare 208 shotgun primer; vented breech plug, striker-fired with one-piece removable hammer assembly. **Finish:** Stainless steel. With recommended loads, guaranteed to have 4-inch, three-shot groups at 200 yards. Also available as Western gun with exposed ignition. Made in U.S. by Knight Rifles.
Price: Muzzleloaders.com MWS702XT...............................**Starting at $395.99**

Prices given are believed to be accurate at time of publication however, many factors affect retail pricing so exact prices are not possible.

75TH EDITION, 2021 ◈ 537

LYMAN DEERSTALKER RIFLE
Caliber: .50, .54. **Barrel:** 28 in. octagon, 1:48 in. twist. **Weight:** 10.8 lbs. **Length:** 45 in. overall. **Stock:** European walnut with black rubber recoil pad. **Sights:** Lyman's high visibility, fiber-optic sights. **Features:** Fast-twist rifling for conical bullets. Blackened metal parts to eliminate glare, stainless steel nipple. Hook breech, single trigger, coil spring lock. Steel barrel rib and ramrod ferrules. From Lyman.
Price: Muzzleloaders.com 6033146/7. 50-cal /.54-cal. flint............... $448.00
Price: Muzzleloaders.com 6033140/7 .50-cal /.54-cal. percussion $398.00

LYMAN GREAT PLAINS RIFLE
Caliber: .50, .54. **Barrel:** 32 in., 1:60 in. twist. **Weight:** 11.6 lbs. **Stock:** Walnut. **Sights:** Steel blade front, buckhorn rear adjustable for windage and elevation, and fixed notch primitive sight included. **Features:** Percussion or flint ignition. Blued steel furniture. Stainless steel nipple. Coil spring lock, Hawken-style triggerguard and double-set triggers. Round thimbles recessed and sweated into rib. Steel wedge plates and toe plate. Introduced 1979. From Lyman.
Price: 6031102/3 .50-cal./.54-cal percussion.......................................$784.95
Price: 6031105/6 .50-cal./.54-cal flintlock $839.95
Price: 6031125/6 .50-ca./.54-cal left-hand percussion $824.95
Price: 6031137 .50-cal. left-hand flintlock $859.95
Price: 6031111/2 .50/.54-cal. percussion kit..................... ....$639.95
Price: 6031114/5 .50/.54-cal. flintlock kit..$689.95

LYMAN GREAT PLAINS HUNTER MODEL
Similar to Great Plains model except 1:32 in. twist, shallow-groove barrel for conicals or sabots, and comes drilled and tapped for Lyman 57GPR peep sight.
Price: 6031120/1 .50-cal./.54-cal percussion.......................................$791.95
Price: 6031148/9 .50-cal./.54-cal flintlock $839.95
Price: 6031112 .50-cal/.54-cal percussion kit $669.95
Price: 6031115 .50-cal/.54-cal flintlock kit..$729.95

LYMAN TRADE RIFLE
Caliber: .50, .54. **Barrel:** 28 in. octagon, 1:48 in. twist. **Weight:** 10.8 lbs. **Length:** 45 in. overall. **Stock:** European walnut. **Sights:** Blade front, open rear adjustable for windage, or optional fixed sights. **Features:** Fast-twist rifling for conical bullets. Polished brass furniture with blue steel parts, stainless steel nipple. Hook breech, single trigger, coil spring percussion lock. Steel barrel rib and ramrod ferrules. Introduced 1980. From Lyman.
Price: 6032125/6 .50-cal./.54-cal. percussion.................................... $565.00
Price: 6032129/30 .50-cal./.54-cal. flintlock $583.00

PEDERSOLI 1777 CHARLEVILLE MUSKET
Caliber: .69. **Barrel:** 44.75 in. round, smoothbore. **Weight:** 10.5 lbs. **Length:** 57 in. **Stock:** European walnut, fullstock. **Sights:** Steel stud on upper barrelband. **Features:** Flintlock using one-inch flint. Steel parts all polished armory bright, brass furniture. Lock marked Charleville. Made by Pedersoli. Imported by Cabela's, Dixie Gun Works, others.
Price: Dixie Gun Works FR0930 .... $1,450.00

PEDERSOLI 1795 SPRINGFIELD MUSKET
Caliber: .69. **Barrel:** 44.75 in., round, smoothbore. **Weight:** 10.5 lbs. **Length:** 57.25 in. **Stock:** European walnut, fullstock. **Sights:** Brass stud on upper barrelband. **Features:** Flintlock using one-inch flint. Steel parts all polished armory bright, brass furniture. Lock marked US Springfield. Made by Pedersoli. Imported by Cabela's, Dixie Gun Works, others.
Price: Dixie Gun Works FR3210 .... $1,495.00

PEDERSOLI POTSDAM 1809 PRUSSIAN MUSKET
Caliber: .75. **Barrel:** 41.2 in. round, smoothbore. **Weight:** 9 lbs. **Length:** 56 in. **Stock:** European walnut, fullstock. **Sights:** Brass lug on upper barrelband. **Features:** Flintlock using one-inch flint. Steel parts all polished armory bright, brass furniture. Lock marked "Potsdam over G.S." Made by Pedersoli. Imported by Dixie Gun Works.
Price: Dixie Gun Works FR3175 .... $1,575.00

PEDERSOLI 1816 FLINTLOCK MUSKET
Caliber: .69. **Barrel:** 42 in., smoothbore. **Weight:** 9.75 lbs. **Length:** 56-7/8 in. overall. **Stock:** Walnut w/oil finish. **Sights:** Blade front. **Features:** All metal finished in "National Armory Bright," three barrel bands w/springs, steel ramrod w/button-shaped head. Made by Pedersoli. Imported by Dixie Gun Works.
Price: Dixie Gun Works PR3180, Percussion conversion $1,495.00

PEDERSOLI 1841 MISSISSIPPI RIFLE
Caliber: .54, .58. **Barrel:** 33 inches. **Weight:** 9.5 lbs. **Length:** 48.75 in. overall. **Stock:** European walnut. **Sights:** Blade front, notched rear. **Features:** Percussion musket-cap ignition. Reproduction of the original one-band rifle with large brass patchbox. Color case-hardened lockplate with browned barrel. Made by Pedersoli. Imported by Dixie Gun Works, Cabela's and others.
Price: Dixie Gun Works PR0870 (.54 caliber)...................................$1,200.00
Price: Dixie Gun Works PR3470 (.58 caliber)...................................$1,100.00

PEDERSOLI 1854 LORENZ RIFLE
Caliber: .54. **Barrel:** 37 in. **Weight:** 9 lbs. **Length:** 49 in. overall. **Stock:** European walnut. **Sights:** Blade front, rear steel open, flip-up style. **Features:** Percussion musket-cap ignition. Armory bright lockplate marked "Konigi. Wurt Fabrik." Armory bright steel barrel. Made by Pedersoli. Imported by Dixie Gun Works.
Price: Dixie Gun Works PR3156...$1,500.00

PEDERSOLI 1857 MAUSER RIFLE
Caliber: .54. **Barrel:** 39.75 in. **Weight:** 9.5 lbs. **Length:** 52 in. overall. **Stock:** European walnut. **Sights:** Blade front, rear steel adjustable for windage and elevation. **Features:** Percussion musket-cap ignition. Color case-hardened lockplate marked "Konigi. Wurt Fabrik." Armory bright steel barrel. Made by Pedersoli. Imported by Dixie Gun Works.
Price: Dixie Gun Works PR1330...$1,695.00

PEDERSOLI 1861 RICHMOND MUSKET
Caliber: .58. **Barrel:** 40 inches. **Weight:** 9.5 lbs. **Length:** 55.5 in. overall. **Stock:** European walnut. **Sights:** Blade front, three-leaf military rear. **Features:** Reproduction of the original three-band rifle. Percussion musket-cap ignition. Lock marked C. S. Richmond, Virginia. Armory bright. Made by Pedersoli. Imported by Dixie Gun Works and others.
Price: Dixie Gun Works PR4095..$1,150.00

PEDERSOLI 1861 SPRINGFIELD RIFLE
Caliber: .58. **Barrel:** 40 inches. **Weight:** 10 lbs. **Length:** 55.5 in. overall. **Stock:** European walnut. **Sights:** Blade front, three-leaf military rear. **Features:** Reproduction of the original three-band rifle. Percussion musket-cap ignition. Lockplate marked 1861 with eagle and U.S. Springfield. Armory bright steel. Made by Armi Sport/Chiappa, Pedersoli. Imported by Cabela's, Dixie Gun Works, others.
Price: Cabela's $1,199.99

PEDERSOLI BAKER CAVALRY SHOTGUN
Gauge: 20. **Barrels:** 11.25 inches. **Weight:** 5.75 pounds. **Length:** 27.5 in. overall. **Stock:** American walnut. **Sights:** Bead front. **Features:** Reproduction of shotguns carried by Confederate cavalry. Single non-selective trigger, back-action locks. No. 11 percussion musket-cap ignition. Blued barrel with steel furniture. Case-hardened lock. Pedersoli also makes a 12-gauge coach-length version of this back-action-lock shotgun with 20-inch barrels, and a full-length version in 10, 12 and 20 gauge. Made by Pedersoli. Imported by Cabela's and others.
Price: Cabela's $1,099.99

Prices given are believed to be accurate at time of publication however, many factors affect retail pricing so exact prices are not possible.

PEDERSOLI BRISTLEN MORGES AND WAADTLANDER TARGET RIFLES
Caliber: .44, .45. **Barrel:** 29.5 in. tapered octagonal, hooked breech. **Weight:** 15.5 lbs. **Length:** 48.5 in. overall. **Stock:** European walnut, halfstock with hooked buttplate and detachable palm rest. **Sights:** Creedmoor rear on Morges, Swiss Diopter on Waadtlander, hooded front sight notch. **Features:** Percussion back-action lock, double set, double-phase triggers, one barrel key, muzzle protector. Specialized bullet molds for each gun. Made by Pedersoli. Imported by Dixie Gun Works and others.
Price: Dixie Gun Works, .44 Bristlen Morges PR0165 .... **$2,995.00**
Price: Dixie Gun Works, .45 Waadtlander PR0183 .... **$2,995.00**

PEDERSOLI BROWN BESS
Caliber: .75. **Barrel:** 42 in., round, smoothbore. **Weight:** 9 lbs. **Length:** 57.75 in. **Stock:** European walnut, fullstock. **Sights:** Steel stud on front serves as bayonet lug. **Features:** Flintlock using one-inch flint with optional brass flash guard (SCO203), steel parts all polished armory bright, brass furniture. Lock marked Grice, 1762 with crown and GR. Made by Pedersoli. Imported by Cabela's, Dixie Gun Works, others.
Price: Dixie Gun Works Complete Gun FR0810 .... **$1,350.00**
Price: Dixie Gun Works Kit Gun FR0825 .... **$1,050.00**
Price: Dixie Gun Works Trade Gun, 30.5-in. barrel FR0665 .... **$1,495.00**
Price: Dixie Gun Works Trade Gun Kit FR0600 .... **$975.00**

PEDERSOLI COOK & BROTHER CONFEDERATE CARBINE/ARTILLERY/RIFLE
Caliber: .58 **Barrel:** 24/33/39 inches. **Weight:** 7.5/8.4/8.6 lbs. **Length:** 40.5/48/54.5 in. **Stock:** Select oil-finished walnut. **Features:** Percussion musket-cap ignition. Color case-hardened lock, browned barrel. Buttplate, triggerguard, barrelbands, sling swivels and nose cap of polished brass. Lock marked with stars and bars flag on tail and Athens, Georgia. Made by Pedersoli. Imported by Dixie Gun Works, others.
Price: Dixie Gun Works Carbine PR0830 .... **$995.00**
Price: Dixie Gun Works Artillery/Rifle PR32165 .... **$995.00**

PEDERSOLI COUNTRY HUNTER
Caliber: .50. **Barrel:** 26 in. octagonal. **Weight:** 6 lbs. **Length:** 41.75 in. overall. **Stock:** European walnut, halfstock. **Sights:** Rear notch, blade front. **Features:** Percussion, one barrel key. Made by Pedersoli. Imported by Dixie Gun Works.
Price: Cherry's Fine Guns Percussion, .50 .... **$675.00**
Price: Cherry's Fine Guns Flint, .50 .... **$688.00**

PEDERSOLI ENFIELD MUSKETOON P1861
Caliber: .58. **Barrel:** 33 in. **Weight:** 9 lbs. **Length:** 35 in. overall. **Stock:** European walnut. **Sights:** Blade front, flip-up rear with elevator marked to 700 yards. **Features:** Reproduction of the original cavalry version of the Enfield rifle. Percussion musket-cap ignition. Blued barrel with steel barrelbands, brass furniture. Case-hardened lock. Euroarms version marked London Armory with crown. Pedersoli version has Birmingham stamp on stock and Enfield and Crown on lockplate. Made by Euroarms, Pedersoli. Imported by Cabela's and others.
Price: Cabela's **$1,099.99**

PEDERSOLI FRONTIER RIFLE
Caliber: .32, .36, .45, .50, .54. **Barrel:** 39 in., octagon, 1:48 twist. **Weight:** 7.75 lbs. **Length:** 54.5 in. overall. **Stock:** American black walnut. **Sights:** Blade front, rear drift adjustable for windage. **Features:** Color case-hardened lockplate and cock/hammer, brass triggerguard and buttplate; double set, double-phased triggers. Made by Pedersoli. Imported by Dixie Gun Works, and by Cabela's (as the Blue Ridge Rifle).
Price: Cabela's Percussion **$599.99**
Price: Cabela's Flintlock **$649.99**

PEDERSOLI ENFIELD THREE-BAND P1853 RIFLE
Caliber: .58. **Barrel:** 39 in. **Weight:** 10.25 lbs. **Length:** 52 in. overall. **Stock:** European walnut. **Sights:** Blade front, flip-up rear with elevator marked to 800 yards. **Features:** Reproduction of the original three-band rifle. Percussion musket-cap ignition. Blued barrel with steel barrelbands, brass furniture. Case-hardened lock. Lockplate marked "London Armory Co. and Crown." Made by Pedersoli. Imported by Cabela's.
Price: Cabela's **$1,149.99**

PEDERSOLI INDIAN TRADE MUSKET
Gauge: 20. **Barrel:** 36 in., octagon to round, smoothbore. **Weight:** 7.25 lbs. **Length:** 52 in. overall. **Stock:** American walnut. **Sights:** Blade front sight, no rear sight. **Features:** Flintlock. Kits version available. Made by Pedersoli. Imported by Dixie Gun Works.
Price: Dixie Gun Works, FR3170 .... **$1,095.00**
Price: Dixie Gun Works Kit, FK3370 .... **$995.00**

PEDERRSOLI JAEGER RIFLE
Caliber: .54. **Barrel:** 27.5 in. octagon, 1:24 in. twist. **Weight:** 8.25 lbs. **Length:** 43.5 in. overall. **Stock:** American walnut; sliding wooden patchbox on butt. **Sights:** Notch rear, blade front. **Features:** Flintlock or percussion. Conversion kits available, and recommended converting percussion guns to flintlocks using kit LO1102 at $209.00. Browned steel furniture. Made by Pedersoli. Imported by Dixie Gun Works.
Price: Dixie Gun Works Percussion, PR0835 .... **$1,350.00**
Price: Dixie Gun Works Flint, PR0835 .... **$1,450.00**
Price: Dixie Gun Works Percussion, kit gun, PK0146 .... **$1,075.00**
Price: Dixie Gun Works Flint, kit gun, PKO143 .... **$1,100.00**

PEDERSOLI KENTUCKY RIFLE
Caliber: .32, .45 and .50. **Barrel:** 35.5 in. octagonal. **Weight:** 7.5 (.50 cal.) to 7.75 lbs. (.32 cal.) **Length:** 51 in. overall. **Stock:** European walnut, full-length stock. **Sights:** Notch rear, blade front. **Features:** Flintlock or percussion, brass patchbox, double-set triggers. Also available as kit guns for all calibers and ignition systems. Made by Pedersoli. Imported by Dixie Gun Works.
Price: Dixie Gun Works Percussion, .32, PR3115 .... **$750.00**
Price: Dixie Gun Works Flint, .32, FR3100 .... **$775.00**
Price: Dixie Gun Works Percussion, .45, FR3120 .... **$750.00**
Price: Dixie Gun Works Flint, .45, FR3105 .... **$775.00**
Price: Dixie Gun Works Percussion, .50, FR3125 .... **$750.00**
Price: Dixie Gun Works Flint, .50, FR3110 .... **$775.00**

PEDERSOLI KODIAK DOUBLE RIFLES AND COMBINATION GUN.
Caliber: .50, .54 and .58. **Barrel:** 28.5 in.; 1:24/1:24/1:48 in. twist. **Weight:** 11.25/10.75/10 lbs. **Stock:** Straight grip European walnut. **Sights:** Two adjustable rear, steel ramp with brass bead front. **Features:** Percussion ignition, double triggers, sling swivels. A .72-caliber express rifle and a .50-caliber/12-gauge shotgun combination gun are also available. Blued steel furniture. Stainless steel nipple. Made by Pedersoli. Imported by Dixie Gun Works and some models by Cabela's and others.
Price: Dixie Gun Works Rifle 50X50 PR0970 .... **$1,525.00**
Price: Dixie Gun Works Rifle 54X54 PR0975 .... **$1,525.00**
Price: Dixie Gun Works Rifle 58X58 PR0980 .... **$1,525.00**
Price: Dixie Gun Works Combo 50X12 gauge PR0990 .... **$1,350.00**
Price: Dixie Gun Works Express Rifle .72 caliber PR0916 .... **$1,550.00**

PEDERSOLI MAGNUM PERCUSSION SHOTGUN & COACH GUN
Gauge: 10, 12, 20 **Barrel:** Chrome-lined blued barrels, 25.5 in. Imp. Cyl. and Mod. **Weight:** 7.25, 7, 6.75 lbs. **Length:** 45 in. overall. **Stock:** Hand-checkered walnut, 14-in. pull. **Features:** Double triggers, light hand engraving, case-hardened locks, sling swivels. Made by Pedersoli. From Dixie Gun Works, others.
Price: Dixie Gun Works 10-ga. PS1030 .... **$1,250.00**
Price: Dixie Gun Works 10-ga. kit PS1040 .... **$975.00**
Price: Dixie Gun Works 12-ga. PS0930 .... **$1,175.00**
Price: Dixie Gun Works 12-ga. Kit PS0940 .... **$875.00**
Price: Dixie Gun Works 12-ga. Coach gun, CylXCyl, PS0914 .... **$1,150.00**
Price: Dixie Gun Works 20-ga. PS0334 .... **$1,175.00**

Prices given are believed to be accurate at time of publication however, many factors affect retail pricing so exact prices are not possible.

75TH EDITION, 2021 ✦ **539**

PEDERSOLI MORTIMER RIFLE & SHOTGUN
Caliber: .54, 12 gauge. **Barrel:** 36 in., 1:66 in. twist, and cylinder bore. **Weight:** 10 lbs. rifle, 9 lbs. shotgun. **Length:** 52.25 in. **Stock:** Halfstock walnut. **Sights:** Blued steel rear with flip-up leaf, blade front. **Features:** Percussion and flint ignition. Blued steel furniture. Single trigger. Lock with hammer safety and "waterproof pan" marked Mortimer. A percussion .45-caliber target version of this gun is available with a peep sight on the wrist, and a percussion shotgun version is also offered. Made by Pedersoli. Imported by Dixie Gun Works.
Price: Dixie Gun Works Flint Rifle, FR0151 ....$1,575.00
Price: Dixie Gun Works Flint Shotgun FS0155 ....$1,525.00

PEDERSOLI OLD ENGLISH SHOTGUN
Gauge: 12 **Barrels:** Browned, 28.5 in. Cyl. and Mod. **Weight:** 7.5 lbs. **Length:** 45 in. overall. **Stock:** Hand-checkered American maple, cap box, 14-in. pull. **Features:** Double triggers, light hand engraving on lock, cap box and tang, swivel studs for sling attachment. Made by Pedersoli. From Dixie Gun Works, others.
Price: Dixie Gun Works PR4090 .... $1,750.00

PEDERSOLI ROCKY MOUNTAIN & MISSOURI RIVER HAWKEN RIFLES
Caliber: .54 Rocky Mountain, .45 and .50 in Missouri River. **Barrel:** 34.75 in. octagonal with hooked breech; Rocky Mountain 1:65 in. twist; Missouri River 1:47 twist in .45 cal., and 1:24 twist in .50 cal. **Weight:** 10 lbs. **Length:** 52 in. overall. **Stock:** Maple or walnut, halfstock. **Sights:** Rear buckhorn with push elevator, silver blade front. **Features:** Available in Percussion, with brass furniture and double triggers. Made by Pedersoli. Imported by Dixie Gun Works and others.
Price: Dixie Gun Works Rocky Mountain, Maple PR3430 .... **$1,395.00**
Price: Dixie Gun Works Rocky Mountain, Walnut PR3435 .... **$1,195.00**
Price: Dixie Gun Works Missouri River, .50 Walnut PR3415 .... **$1,275.00**
Price: Dixie Gun Works Missouri River, .45 Walnut PR3405 .... **$1,275.00**

PEDERSOLI PENNSYLVANIA RIFLE
Caliber: .32, .45 and .50. **Barrel:** 41.5 in. browned, octagonal, 1:48 in. twist. **Weight:** 8.25 lbs. **Length:** 56 in. overall. **Stock:** American walnut. **Sights:** Rear semi-buckhorn with push elevator, steel blade front. **Features:** Available in flint or percussion, with brass furniture, and double triggers. Also available as a kit. Made by Pedersoli. Imported by Dixie Gun Works and others.
Price: Dixie Gun Works Flint .32 FR3040 .... **$950.00**
Price: Dixie Gun Works Percussion .32 PR3055....................... **$900.00**
Price: Dixie Gun Works Flint .45 PR3045 .... **$950.00**
Price: Dixie Gun Works Percussion .45 PR3060....................... **$900.00**
Price: Dixie Gun Works Flint .50 PR3050.............................. **$950.00**
Price: Dixie Gun Works Percussion .50 PR3065....................... **$900.00**
Price: Dixie Gun Works Flint Kit .32 FK3260 .... **$750.00**
Price: Dixie Gun Works Percussion kit .32 PK3275 .... **$695.00**
Price: Dixie Gun Works Flint kit .45 FK3265 .... **$750.00**
Price: Dixie Gun Works Percussion kit .45 PR3280................... **$695.00**
Price: Dixie Gun Works Flint kit .50 FK3270 .... **$750.00**
Price: Dixie Gun Works Percussion kit .50 PK3285.................. **$695.00**

PEDERSOLI SHARPS NEW MODEL 1859 MILITARY RIFLE AND CARBINE
Caliber: .54. **Barrel:** 30 in., 6-groove, 1:48 in. twist. **Weight:** 9 lbs. **Length:** 45.5 in. overall. **Stock:** Oiled walnut. **Sights:** Blade front, ladder-style rear. **Features:** Blued barrel, color case-hardened barrelbands, receiver, hammer, nose cap, lever, patchbox cover and buttplate. Introduced in 1995. Rifle made by Pedersoli. Rifle imported from Italy by Dixie Gun Works and others.
Price: Dixie Gun Work Rifle PR0862 .... $1,650.00
Price: Dixie Gun Work Carbine (22-in. barrel) PR0982.................... $1,400.00

PEDERSOLI SHARPS MODEL 1863 SPORTING RIFLE
Caliber: .45. **Barrel:** 32 in., octagon, 6-groove, 1:18 in. twist. **Weight:** 10.75 lbs. **Length:** 49 in. overall. **Stock:** Oiled walnut. **Sights:** Silver blade front, flip-up rear. **Features:** Browned octagon barrel, color case-hardened receiver, hammer and buttplate. Rifle made by Pedersoli. Imported by Dixie Gun Works and others.
Price: Dixie Gun Work Rifle PR5001 .... $1,500.00

PEDERSOLI SHARPS CONFEDERATE CARBINE
Caliber: .54. **Barrel:** 22 in., 6-groove, 1:48 in. twist. **Weight:** 8 lbs. **Length:** 39 in. overall. **Stock:** Oiled walnut. **Sights:** Blade front, dovetailed rear. **Features:** Browned barrel, color case-hardened receiver, hammer, and lever. Brass buttplate and barrel bands. Rifle made by Pedersoli. Imported by Dixie Gun Works and others.
Price: Dixie Gun Work Carbine PR3380................................ $1,395.00

PEDERSOLI TRADITIONAL HAWKEN TARGET RIFLE
Caliber: .50 and .54. **Barrel:** 29.5 in. octagonal, 1:48 in. twist. **Weight:** 9 or 8.5 lbs. **Length:** 45.5 in. overall. **Stock:** European walnut, halfstock. **Sights:** Rear click adjustable for windage and elevation, blade front. **Features:** Percussion and flintlock, brass patchbox, double-set triggers, one barrel key. Flint gun available for left-handed shooters. Both flint and percussion guns available as kit guns. Made by Pedersoli. Imported by Dixie Gun Works.
Price: Dixie Gun Works Percussion, .50 PR0502...................................**$650.00**
Price: Dixie Gun Works Percussion, .54 PR0507..............................**$650.00**
Price: Dixie Gun Works Flint, .50 FR1332 ....**$725.00**
Price: Dixie Gun Works Flint, .54 FR3515 ....**$725.00**

PEDERSOLI TRYON RIFLE
Caliber: .50. **Barrel:** 32 in. octagonal, 1:48 in. twist. **Weight:** 9.5 lbs. **Length:** 49 in. overall. **Stock:** European walnut, halfstock. **Sights:** Elevation-adjustable rear with stair-step notches, blade front. **Features:** Percussion, brass patchbox, double-set triggers, two barrel keys. Made by Pedersoli. Imported by Dixie Gun Works.
Price: Percussion, PR0860 .... **$1,100.00**

PEDERSOLI VOLUNTEER RIFLE
Caliber: .451. **Barrel:** 33 in., round interior bore 1:21 in. twist. **Weight:** 9.5 lbs. **Length:** 49 in. **Stock:** Oiled Grade 1 American walnut. **Sights:** Blade front, ladder-style rear. **Features:** Checkered stock wrist and fore-end. Blued barrel, steel ramrod, bone charcoal case-hardened receiver and hammer. Designed for .451 conical bullets. Compare to hexagonal-bored Whitworth Rifle below. Hand-fitted and finished.
Price: Dixie Gun Works PR3150...... .... **$1,295.00**

PEDERSOLI WHITWORTH RIFLE
Caliber: .451. **Barrel:** 36 in., hexagonal interior bore 1:20 in. twist. **Weight:** 9.6 lbs. **Length:** 52.5 in. **Stock:** Oiled Grade 1 American walnut. **Sights:** Blade front, ladder-style rear. **Features:** Checkered stock wrist and fore-end. Blued barrel, steel ramrod, bone charcoal case-hardened receiver and hammer. Designed for .451 conical hexagonal bullet. Compare to round-bored Volunteer Rifle above. Hand-fitted to original specifications using original Enfield arsenal gauges.
Price: Dixie Gun Works PR3256...... .... **$1,750.00**

PEDERSOLI ZOUAVE RIFLE
Caliber: .58 percussion. **Barrel:** 33 inches. **Weight:** 9.5 lbs. **Length:** 49 inches. **Stock:** European walnut. **Sights:** Blade front, three-leaf military rear. **Features:** Percussion musket-cap ignition. One-piece solid barrel and bolster. Brass-plated patchbox. Made in Italy by Pedersoli. Imported by Dixie Gun Works, others.
Price: Dixie Gun Works PF0340. ....**$975.00**

REMINGTON MODEL 700 ULTIMATE MUZZLELOADER
Caliber: .50 percussion. **Barrel:** 26 in., 1:26 in. twist, satin stainless steel, fluted. **Length:** 47 in. **Stock:** Bell & Carlson black synthetic. **Sights:** None on

Prices given are believed to be accurate at time of publication however, many factors affect retail pricing so exact prices are not possible.

synthetic-stocked model. Ramrod: Stainless steel. **Weight:** 8.5 lbs. **Features:** Remington single shot Model 700 bolt action, re-primable cartridge-case ignition using Remington Magnum Large Rifle Primer, sling studs.
Price: 86960 Starting at **$1,015.00**

THOMPSON/CENTER IMPACT MUZZLELOADING RIFLE
Caliber: .50. **Barrel:** 26 in., 1:28 twist, Weather Shield finish. **Weight:** 6.5 lbs. **Length:** 41.5 in. **Stock:** Straight Realtree Hardwoods HD or black composite. **Features:** Sliding-hood, break-open action, #209 primer ignition, removable breech plug, synthetic stock adjustable from 12.5 to 13.5 in., adjustable fiber-optic sights, aluminum ramrod, camo, QLA relieved muzzle system.
Price: .50-cal Stainless/Realtree Hardwoods, Weather Shield **$324.00**
Price: .50-cal Blued/Black/scope, case..**$263.99**

THOMPSON/CENTER PRO HUNTER FX
Caliber: .50 as muzzleloading barrel. **Barrel:** 26 in., Weather Shield with relieved muzzle on muzzleloader; interchangeable with 14 centerfire calibers. **Weight:** 7 lbs. **Length:** 40.5 in. overall. **Stock:** Interchangeable American walnut butt and fore-end, black composite, FlexTech recoil-reducing camo stock as thumbhole or straight, rubber over-molded stock and fore-end. **Ramrod:** Solid aluminum. **Sights:** Tru-Glo fiber-optic front and rear. **Features:** Blue or stainless steel. Uses the frame of the Encore centerfire pistol; break-open design using triggerguard spur; stainless steel universal breech plug; uses #209 shotshell primers. Made in U.S. by Thompson/Center Arms.
Price: .50-cal Stainless/Black FlexTech Stock Model 5800................... **$649.00**
Price: .50-cal Stainless/Engraved frame FlexTech RT-AP camo.............**$709.00**

THOMPSON/CENTER TRIUMPH BONE COLLECTOR
Caliber: .50. **Barrel:** 28 in., Weather Shield coated. **Weight:** 6.5 lbs. Overall: 42 in. **Stock:** FlexTech recoil-reducing. Black composite or Realtree AP HD camo straight, rubber over-molded stock and fore-end. **Sights:** Fiber optic. **Ramrod:** Solid aluminum. **Features:** Break-open action, Quick Detachable Speed Breech XT plug, #209 shotshell primer ignition, easy loading QLA relieved muzzle. Made in U.S. by Thompson/Center Arms. Available from Cabela's, Bass Pro.
Price: .50-cal Synthetic Realtree AP, fiber optics.... .... **$720.00**
Price: .50-cal Synthetic/Weather Shield Black....................................... **$638.00**
Price: .50-cal. Weather Shield/AP Camo.. **$679.00**
Price: .50 cal. Silver Weather Shield/AP Camo.......................................**$689.00**

THOMPSON/CENTER STRIKE
Caliber: .50. **Barrel:** 24 or 20 in., nitride finished, tapered barrel. **Weight:** 6.75 or 6.25 lbs. **Length:** 44 in. or 40 in. **Stock:** Walnut, black synthetic, G2-Vista Camo. **Finish:** Armornite nitride. **Features:** Break-open action, sliding hammerless cocking mechanism, optional pellet or loose powder primer holders, easily removable breech plugs retained by external collar, aluminum frame with steel mono-block to retain barrel, recoil pad. **Sights:** Williams fiber-optic sights furnished, drilled and tapped for scope. Made in the U.S. by Thompson/Center.
Price: .50 cal. 24-in. barrel, black synthetic stock **$499.00**
Price: .50 cal. 24-in. barrel, walnut stock **$599.00**
Price: .50 cal. 24-in. barrel, G2 camo stock **$549.00**

TRADITIONS BUCKSTALKER IN-LINE RIFLE
Caliber: .50. **Barrel:** 24 in., Cerakote finished, Accelerator Breech Plug. **Weight:** 6 lbs. **Length:** 40 in. **Stock:** Synthetic, G2 Vista camo or black. **Sights:** Fiber-optic rear. **Features:** Break-open action, matte-finished action and

barrel. Ramrod: Solid aluminum. Imported by Traditions.
Price: R72003540 .50-cal. Youth Synthetic stock/blued.....................**$219.00**
Price: R72103540 .50-cal. Synthetic stock/Cerakote **$329.00**
Price: R5-72003540 .50-cal. Synthetic stock/blued, scope.................**$294.00**
Price: R5-72103547 .50-cal. Synthetic stock/Cerakote, scope **$369.00**

TRADITIONS CROCKETT RIFLE
Caliber: .32. **Barrel:** 32 in., 1:48 in. twist. **Weight:** 6.75 lbs. **Length:** 49 in. overall. **Stock:** Beech, inletted toe plate. **Sights:** Blade front, fixed rear. **Features:** Set triggers, hardwood halfstock, brass furniture, color case-hardened lock. Percussion. Imported by Traditions.
Price: R26128101 .32-cal. Percussion, finished **$543.00**
Price: RK52628100 .32-cal. Percussion, kit... **$479.00**

TRADITIONS EVOLUTION BOLT-ACTION BLACKPOWDER RIFLE
Caliber: .50 percussion. **Barrel:** 26 in., 1:28 in. twist, Cerakote finished barrel and action. **Length:** 39 in. **Sights:** Steel Williams fiber-optic sights. **Weight:** 7 to 7.25 lbs. **Length:** 45 in. overall. **Features:** Bolt action, cocking indicator, thumb safety, shipped with adaptors for No. 11 caps, musket caps and 209 shotgun-primer ignition, sling swivels. Ramrod: Aluminum, sling studs. Available with exposed ignition as a Northwest gun. Imported by Traditions.
Price: R67113350 .50-cal. synthetic black, Cerakote.......................... **$250.00**
Price: R67113353 .50-cal. synthetic Realtree AP camo...... ....**$299.00**

TRADITIONS HAWKEN WOODSMAN RIFLE
Caliber: .50. **Barrel:** 28 in., blued, 15/16 in. flats. **Weight:** 7 lbs., 11 oz. **Length:** 44.5 in. overall. **Stock:** Walnut stained hardwood. **Sights:** Beaded blade front hunting-style open rear adjustable for windage and elevation. **Features:** Brass patchbox and furniture. Double-set triggers. Flint or percussion. Imported by Traditions.
Price: R2390801 .50-cal. Flintlock **$544.00**
Price: R24008 .50-cal. Percussion **$499.00**

TRADITIONS KENTUCKY DELUXE
Caliber: .50. **Barrel:** 33.5 in., blued octagon. **Stock:** Walnut-finished select hardwood. **Sights:** Fixed blade. **Weight:** 7 lbs. **Features:** Double set trigger, brass patch box, available as a kit, authentic wooden ramrod.
Price: .... **$379.00-$485.00**

TRADITIONS KENTUCKY RIFLE
Caliber: .50. **Barrel:** 33.5 in., 7/8 in. flats, 1:66 in. twist. **Weight:** 7 lbs. **Length:** 49 in. overall. **Stock:** Beech, inletted toe plate. **Sights:** Blade front, fixed rear. **Features:** Full-length, two-piece stock; brass furniture; color case-hardened lock. Flint or percussion. Imported by Traditions.
Price: R2010 .50-cal. Flintlock,1:66 twist **$509.00**
Price: R2020 .50-cal. Percussion, 1:66 twist...................................... **$449.00**
Price: KRC52206 .50-cal. Percussion, kit... **$343.00**

Prices given are believed to be accurate at time of publication however, many factors affect retail pricing so exact prices are not possible.

75TH EDITION, 2021 ✦ **541**

TRADITIONS MOUNTAIN RIFLE

Caliber: .50. **Barrel:** 32 in., octagon with brown Cerakote finish. **Stock:** Select hardwoods. **Sights:** Primitive, adjustable rear. **Weight:** 8.25 lbs. **Features:** Available in percussion or flintlock, case-hardened lock, wooden ramrod, available as a kit.
Price: .... **$494.00-$649.00**

TRADITIONS NITROFIRE

Caliber: .50. **Barrel:** 26 in., ultralight chromoly steel, tapered and fluted, premium Cerakote finish. **Stock:** Synthetic black or camo. **Sights:** Drilled and tapped, optional 3-9x40 scope. **Weight:** 6.5 lbs. **Features:** Several stock color options, Federal FireStick ignition system, no breech plug required, aluminum ramrod, sling swivel studs.
Price: .... **$549.00-$699.00**

TRADITIONS PA PELLET FLINTLOCK

Caliber: .50. **Barrel:** 26 in., blued, 1:28 in. twist., Cerakote. **Weight:** 7 lbs. **Length:** 45 in. **Stock:** Hardwood, synthetic and synthetic break-up, sling swivels. Fiber-optic sights. **Features:** New flintlock action, removable breech plug, available as left-hand model with hardwood stock. Imported by Traditions.
Price: R3800501 .50-cal. Hardwood, blued, fib. opt **$519.00**
Price: R3890501 .50-cal. Hardwood, left-hand, blued **$529.00**
Price: R3800550 .50-cal. Synthetic/blued, fib. opt **$497.00**

TRADITIONS PENNSYLVANIA RIFLE

Caliber: .50. **Barrel:** 40.25 in., 7/8 in. flats, 1:66 in. twist, octagon. **Weight:** 9 lbs. **Length:** 57.5 in. overall. **Stock:** Walnut. **Sights:** Blade front, adjustable rear. **Features:** Single-piece walnut stock, brass patchbox and ornamentation. Double-set triggers. Flint or percussion. Imported by Traditions.
Price: R2090 .50-cal. Flintlock **$865.00**
Price: R2100 .50-cal. Percussion... **$834.00**

TRADITIONS PURSUIT ULTRALIGHT MUZZLELOADER

Caliber: .50. **Barrel:** 26 in., chromoly tapered, fluted barrel with premium Cerakote finish, Accelerator Breech Plug. **Weight:** 5.5 lbs. **Length:** 42 in. **Stock:** Rubber over-molded Soft Touch camouflage, straight and thumbhole stock options. **Sights:** Optional 3-9x40 scope with medium rings and bases, mounted and bore-sighted by a factory-trained technician. **Features:** Break-open action, Williams fiber-optic sights. Imported by Traditions.
Price: Pursuit G4 Ultralight .50 Cal. Select Hardwoods/
     Cerakote R741101NS...**$469.00**
Price: Pursuit G4 Ultralight .50 Cal. Mossy Oak Break Up Country Camo/
     Cerakote R7411416..**$404.00**
Price: Pursuit G4 Ultralight .50 Cal. Mossy Oak Break Up Country/Cerakote/
     Scope/Carrying Case..... ....**$479.00**

TRADITIONS TRACKER IN-LINE RIFLE

Caliber: .50. **Barrel:** 24 in., blued or Cerakote, 1:28 in. twist. **Weight:** 6 lbs., 4 oz. **Length:** 43 in. **Stock:** Black synthetic. **Ramrod:** Synthetic, high-impact polymer. **Sights:** Lite Optic blade front, adjustable rear. **Features:** Striker-fired action,

thumb safety, adjustable trigger, rubber buttpad, sling swivel studs. Takes 150 grains of Pyrodex pellets, one-piece musket cap and 209 ignition systems. Drilled and tapped for scope. Legal for use in Northwest. Imported by Traditions.
Price: R44003470 .50-cal. Synthetic/blued **$184.00**

TRADITIONS VORTEK STRIKERFIRE

Caliber: .50 **Barrel:** 28 in., chromoly, tapered, fluted barrel. **Weight:** 6.25 lbs. **Length:** 44 in. **Stock:** Over-molded soft-touch straight stock, removable buttplate for in-stock storage. **Finish:** Premium Cerakote and Realtree Xtra. **Features:** Break-open action, sliding hammerless cocking mechanism, drop-out trigger assembly, speed load system, Accelerator Breech Plug, recoil pad. **Sights:** Optional 3-9x40 muzzleloader scope. Imported by Traditions.
Price: Vortek StrikerFire with Nitride Coating Mossy Oak
     Break-Up Country Camo..... ....**$583.00**
Price: Vortek StrikerFire with 3-9x40 Sig Sauer Whisky 3 Scope,
     Sling & Case...**$756.00**

TRADITIONS VORTEK STRIKERFIRE LDR

Caliber: .50. **Barrel:** 30 in., chromoly, tapered, fluted barrel. **Weight:** 6.8 lbs. **Length:** 46 in. **Stock:** Over-molded soft-touch straight stock, removable buttplate for in-stock storage. **Finish:** Premium Cerakote and Realtree Xtra. **Features:** Break-open action, sliding hammerless cocking mechanism, drop-out trigger assembly, speed load system, Accelerator Breech Plug, recoil pad. **Sights:** Optional 3-9x40 muzzleloader scope. Imported by Traditions.
Price: R491140WA Synthetic/black Hogue Over-mold,
     Cerakote barrel, no sights..**$499.00**

WOODMAN ARMS PATRIOT

Caliber: .45, .50. **Barrel:** 24 in., nitride-coated, 416 stainless, 1:24 twist in .45, 1:28 twist in .50. **Weight:** 5.75 lbs. **Length:** 43-in. **Stocks:** Laminated, walnut or hydrographic dipped, synthetic black, over-molded soft-touch straight stock. **Finish:** Nitride black and black anodized. **Features:** Break-open action, hammerless cocking mechanism, match-grade patented trigger assembly, speed load system, recoil pad. **Sights:** Picatinny rail with built-in rear and 1-inch or 30 mm scope mounts, red fiber-optic front bead.
Price: Patriot .45 or .50-cal..**$899.00**

UBERTI 1858 NEW ARMY REMINGTON TARGET CARBINE REVOLVER

Caliber: .44, 6-shot. **Barrel:** Tapered octagon, 18 in. **Weight:** 70.4 oz. **Length:** Standard 35.3 in. **Stock:** Walnut. **Sights:** Standard blade front, adjustable rear. **Features:** Replica of Remington's revolving rifle of 1866. Made by Uberti. Imported by Uberti USA, Cimarron F.A. Co., Taylor's and others.
Price: Uberti USA, 341200... **$559.00**

Prices given are believed to be accurate at time of publication however, many factors affect retail pricing so exact prices are not possible.

AIRFORCE TALON P PCP AIR PISTOL
Caliber: .25. **Barrel:** Rifled 12.0 in. **Weight:** 3.5 lbs. **Length:** 24.2 in. **Sights:** None, grooved for scope. **Features:** Quick-detachable air tank with adjustable power. Match-grade Lothar Walther, massive power output in a highly compact size, two-stage trigger. **Velocity:** 400-900 fps.
Price: $479.95

AIR VENTURI V10 MATCH AIR PISTOL
Caliber: .177 pellets. **Barrel:** Rifled. **Weight:** 1.95 lbs. **Length:** 12.6 in. **Power:** Single stroke pneumatic. **Sights:** Front post, fully adjustable rear blade, **Features:** 10-Meter competition class pistol, fully adjustable trigger, 1.5-lb. trigger pull **Velocity:** 400 fps.
Price: $300.00

ALFA PROJ COMPETITION PCP PISTOL
Caliber: .177 pellets. **Barrel:** Rifled. **Weight:** 1.94 lbs. **Length:** 15.5 inches. **Power:** Pre-charged pneumatic. **Sights:** Front post, fully adjustable rear blade. **Features:** 10-meter competition class pistol, highly adjustable trigger, Velocity: 500 fps.
Price: $879.99

ASG STI DUTY ONE CO2 BB PISTOL
Caliber: .177 steel BBs. **Barrel:** Smoothbore **Weight:** 1.82 lbs. **Length:** 8.66 in. **Power:** CO2. **Sights:** Fixed. **Features:** Blowback, accessory rail, and metal slide. **Velocity:** 383 fps.
Price: $120.00

ATAMAN AP16 REGULATED COMPACT AIR PISTOL, SILVER
Caliber: .22 pellets. **Barrel:** Rifled Match Barrel **Weight:** 1.76 lbs. **Length:** 12.0 in. **Power:** Pre-Charged Pneumatic. **Sights:** Fixed Front Ramp, Adjustable Rear Notch. **Features:** 7-round Rotary Magazine, 300 Bar Max Fill, Regulated for hunting power, exceptional build quality, available in satin and blued finishes **Velocity:** 590 fps.
Price: $1,049.99

ATAMAN AP16 REGULATED STANDARD AIR PISTOL
Caliber: .22 pellets. **Barrel:** Rifled Match Barrel **Weight:** 2.2 lbs. **Length:** 14.37 in. **Power:** Pre-Charged Pneumatic. **Sights:** Fixed Front Ramp, Adjustable Rear Notch. **Features:** 7-round Rotary Magazine, 300 Bar Max Fill, Regulated for hunting power, exceptional build quality, **Velocity:** 656 fps.
Price: $1,049.99

BEEMAN P17 AIR PISTOL
Caliber: .177 pellets. **Barrel:** Rifled. **Weight:** 1.7 lbs. **Length:** 9.6 in. **Power:** Single stroke pneumatic. **Sights:** Front and rear fiber-optic sights, rear sight fully adjustable. **Features:** Exceptional trigger, grooved for scope mounting with dry-fire feature for practice. **Velocity:** 410 fps.
Price: $44.99

BEEMAN P1 MAGNUM AIR PISTOL
Caliber: .177, .20, .22. pellets. **Barrel:** Rifled. **Weight:** 2.5 lbs. **Length:** 11 in. **Power:** Single stroke, spring-piston. **Grips:** Checkered walnut. **Sights:** Blade front, square notch rear with click micrometer adjustments for windage and elevation. Grooved for scope mounting. **Features:** Dual power for .177 and 20 cal.; Compatible with all Colt 45 auto grips. Dry-firing feature for practice. **Velocity:** varies by caliber and power setting.
Price: .... $455.99–$549.99

BEEMAN P3 PNEUMATIC AIR PISTOL
Caliber: .177. pellets. **Barrel:** Rifled **Weight:** 1.7 lbs. **Length:** 9.6 in. **Power:** Single-stroke pneumatic. **Sights:** Front and rear fiber-optic sights, rear sight fully adjustable. **Features:** Grooved for scope mounting, exceptional trigger, automatic safety. **Velocity:** 410 fps.
Price: $249.95

BEEMAN P11 AIR PISTOL
Caliber: .177, .22. **Barrel:** Rifled. **Weight:** 2.6 lbs. **Length:** 10.75 in. **Power:** Single-stroke pneumatic with high and low settings. **Sights:** Front ramp sight, fully adjustable rear sight. **Features:** 2-stage adjustable trigger and automatic safety. **Velocity:** Up to 600 fps in .177 caliber and Up to 460 fps in .22 caliber.
Price: .... $525.95–$634.95

BENJAMIN MARAUDER PCP PISTOL
Caliber: .22 **Barrel:** Rifled. **Weight:** 2.7-3 lbs. **Length:** Pistol length 18 in./ Carbine length 29.75 in. **Power:** Pre-charged pneumatic **Sights:** None. Grooved for optics. **Features:** Multi-shot (8-round rotary magazine) bolt action, shrouded steel barrel, two-stage adjustable trigger, includes both pistol grips and a carbine stock and is built in America. **Velocity:** 700 fps.
Price: $419.99

Prices given are believed to be accurate at time of publication however, many factors affect retail pricing so exact prices are not possible.

75TH EDITION, 2021 ◈ 543

BENJAMIN MARAUDER WOODS WALKER PCP PISTOL
Caliber: .22 **Barrel:** Rifled. **Weight:** 2.7 lbs. **Length:** Pistol length 18 in./Carbine length 29.75 in. **Power:** Pre-charged pneumatic **Sights:** Includes CenterPoint Multi-TAC Quick Aim Sight. **Features:** Multi-shot (8-round rotary magazine) bolt action, shrouded steel barrel, two-stage adjustable trigger, includes both pistol grips and a carbine stock and is built in America. **Velocity:** 700 fps.
Price: $550.00

BENJAMIN TRAIL MARK II NP AIR PISTOL
Caliber: .177 pellets. **Barrel:** Rifled. **Weight:** 3.43 lbs. **Length:** 16 in. **Power:** Single cock, nitro piston. **Sights:** Fiber-optic front, fully adjustable rear. **Features:** Grooved for scope, **Velocity:** To 625 fps.
Price: $130.99

BERETTA APX BLOWBACK AIR PISTOL
Caliber: .177 steel BBs. **Barrel:** Smoothbore. **Weight:** 1.47 lbs. **Length:** 7.48 in. **Power:** CO2. **Sights:** Fixed. **Features:** Highly accurate replica action pistol, 19-shot capacity, front accessory rail, metal and ABS plastic construction. **Velocity:** 400 fps.
Price: $69.95

BERETTA MODEL 84FS

BERETTA M84FS AIR PISTOL
Caliber: .177 steel BBs. **Barrel:** Smoothbore **Weight:** 1.4 lbs. **Length:** 7 in. **Power:** CO2. **Sights:** Fixed. **Features:** Highly realistic replica action pistol, blowback operation, full metal construction. **Velocity:** To 360 fps.
Price: $119.95

BERETTA PX4 STORM CO2 PISTOL
Caliber: .177 pellet /.177 steel BBs. **Barrel:** Rifled **Weight:** 1.6 lbs. **Length:** 7.6 in. **Power:** CO2. **Sights:** Blade front sight and fixed rear sight. **Features:** Semi-automatic, 16-shot capacity with maximum of 40-shots per fill, dual ammo capable. **Velocity:** To 380 fps.
Price: $119.99

BERETTA ELITE II CO2 PISTOL
Caliber: .177 steel BBs. **Barrel:** Smoothbore **Weight:** 1.5 lbs. **Length:** 8.5 in. **Power:** CO2. **Sights:** Blade front sight and fixed rear sight. **Features:** Semi-automatic, 19-shot capacity. **Velocity:** Up to 410 fps.
Price: $54.95

BERETTA M9A3 FULL AUTO BB PISTOL
Caliber: .177 steel BBs. **Barrel:** Smoothbore **Weight:** NA. **Length:** NA. **Power:** CO2. **Sights:** Blade front sight and fixed rear sight. **Features:** Can operate as semi-automatic or fully automatic, full size 18-shot magazine, blowback slide, single/double action, ambidextrous safety. **Velocity:** To 380 fps.
Price: $124.99

BERETTA 92A1 CO2 FULL AUTO BB PISTOL
Caliber: .177 steel BBs. **Barrel:** Smoothbore **Weight:** 2.4 lbs. **Length:** 8.5 in. **Power:** CO2. **Sights:** Fixed. **Features:** Highly realistic replica action pistol, 18-shot semi-automatic, full metal construction, selectable fire semi-automatic & full-automatic. **Velocity:** To 330 fps.
Price: $139.99

BERETTA 92FS CO2 PELLET GUN
Caliber: .177 pellets. **Barrel:** Rifled **Weight:** 2.75 lbs. **Length:** 8.0 in. **Power:** CO2. **Sights:** Fixed front sight, rear adjustable for windage. **Features:** Highly realistic replica-action pistol, 8-shot semi-automatic, full metal construction, available in various finishes and grips. **Velocity:** To 425 fps.
Price: .... $225.00-$289.00

BERSA THUNDER 9 PRO BB PISTOL
Caliber: .177 steel BBs. **Barrel:** Smoothbore. **Weight:** 1.17 lbs. **Length:** 7.56 in. **Power:** CO2. **Sights:** Fixed, three-white-dot system. **Features:** Highly realistic replica action pistol, 19-shot semi-automatic, composite/synthetic construction. **Velocity:** To 400 fps.
Price: $64.95

BERSA BP9CC DUAL TONE BLOWBACK AIR PISTOL
Caliber: .177 steel BBs. **Barrel:** Smoothbore. **Weight:** 1.35 lbs. **Length:** 6.61 in. **Power:** CO2. **Sights:** Fixed three-dot system. **Features:** Blowback, metal slide, weaver accessory rail. **Velocity:** 350 fps.
Price: $104.95

BROWNING 800 EXPRESS AIR PISTOL
Caliber: .177 pellets. **Barrel:** Rifled. **Weight:** 3.9 lbs. **Length:** 18 in. **Power:** Single cock, spring-piston. **Sights:** Fiber-optic front sight and adjustable fiber-optic rear sight. **Features:** Automatic safety, 11mm dovetail rail scope mounting possible. **Velocity:** 700 fps.
Price: $168.00

Prices given are believed to be accurate at time of publication however, many factors affect retail pricing so exact prices are not possible.

BROWNING BUCK MARK URX

COLT DEFENDER

BROWNING BUCK MARK URX AIR PISTOL BROWNING BUCK MARK AIR PISTOL
Caliber: .177 pellets. **Barrel:** Rifled **Weight:** 1.5 lbs. **Length:** 12.0 in. **Power:** Single cock, spring-piston. **Sights:** Front ramp sight, fully adjustable rear notch sight. **Features:** Weaver rail for scope mounting, light cocking force. **Velocity:** 360 fps.
Price: **$50.00**

CHIAPPA FAS 6004 PNEUMATIC PISTOL
Caliber: .177 pellets. **Barrel:** Rifled. **Weight:** 2 lbs. **Length:** 11.0 in. **Power:** Single stroke pneumatic. **Sights:** Fully adjustable target rear sight. **Features:** Walnut ambidextrous grip, fully adjustable trigger. **Velocity:** 330 fps.
Price: **$443.00**

COBRAY INGRAM M11 CO2 BB SUBMACHINE GUN
Caliber: .177 BBs. **Barrel:** Smoothbore. **Weight:** 1.2 lbs. **Length:** 10.0 in. **Power:** CO2. **Sights:** Fixed sights. **Features:** Semiautomatic, 39-shot capacity, folding metal stock. **Velocity:** 394 fps.
Price: **$59.95**

COLT PYTHON

COLT PYTHON CO2 PISTOL
Caliber: .177 steel BBs. **Barrel:** Smoothbore **Weight:** 2.6 lbs. **Length:** 11.25 in. **Power:** CO2. **Sights:** Fixed. **Features:** High-quality replica, swing-out cylinder, removable casings and functioning ejector, multiple finishes. **Velocity:** To 400 fps.
Price: **$149.99**

COLT DEFENDER BB PISTOL
Caliber: .177 steel BBs. **Barrel:** Smoothbore **Weight:** 1.6 lbs. **Length:** 6.75 in. **Power:** CO2. **Sights:** Fixed with blade ramp front sight. **Features:** Semi-automatic, 16-shot capacity, all metal construction, realistic weight and feel. **Velocity:** 410 fps.
Price: **$75.00**

COLT 1911 SPECIAL COMBAT CLASSIC BB PISTOL
Caliber: .177 steel BBs. **Barrel:** Smoothbore. **Weight:** 2.05 lbs. **Length:** 8.58 in. **Power:** CO2. **Sights:** Blade front sight and adjustable rear sight. **Features:** Semi-automatic, 20-shot capacity, realistic action, weight and feel. **Velocity:** 400 fps.
Price: **$120.00**

COLT 1911 A1 CO2 PELLET PISTOL
Caliber: .177 pellets. **Barrel:** Rifled **Weight:** 2.4 lbs. **Length:** 9.0 in. **Power:** CO2. **Sights:** Blade ramp front sight and adjustable rear sight. **Features:** Semi-automatic, 8-shot capacity, all metal construction, realistic weight and feel. **Velocity:** 425 fps.
Price: **$279.95**

COLT COMMANDER CO2 PISTOL
Caliber: .177 steel BBs. **Barrel:** Smoothbore. **Weight:** 2.1 lbs. **Length:** 8.5 in. **Power:** CO2. **Sights:** Blade front sight and fixed rear sight. **Features:** Semi-automatic, blowback action, 18-shot capacity, highly realistic replica pistol. **Velocity:** 325 fps.
Price: **$119.99**

COLT SAA CO2 PELLET REVOLVER, NICKEL
Caliber: .177 pellets. **Barrel:** Rifled. **Weight:** 2.1 lbs. **Length:** 11 in. **Power:** CO2. **Sights:** Blade front sight and fixed rear sight. **Features:** Full metal revolver with manual safety, realistic loading, 6 individual shells, highly accurate, full metal replica pistol, multiple finishes and grips available. **Velocity:** 380 fps.
Price: **$179.99**

JOHN WAYNE "DUKE" COLT SINGLE ACTION ARMY CO2 PELLET REVOLVER
Caliber: .177 steel BBs. **Barrel:** Smoothbore. **Weight:** 2.1 lbs. **Length:** 11 in. **Power:** CO2. **Sights:** Blade front sight and fixed rear sight. **Features:** Officially licensed "John Wayne Duke" imagery and signature, full metal revolver with manual safety, realistic loading, 6 individual shells, highly accurate, full metal replica pistol, multiple finishes and grips available. **Velocity:** 380 fps.
Price: **$189.99**

Prices given are believed to be accurate at time of publication however, many factors affect retail pricing so exact prices are not possible.

75TH EDITION, 2021 ⟡ **545**

COMETA INDIAN AIR PISTOL, NICKEL/BLACK
Caliber: .177 pellets. **Barrel:** Rifled. **Weight:** 2.43 lbs. **Length:** 10.43 in. **Power:** Spring Powered. **Sights:** Blade front sight and adjustable rear sight. **Features:** Single shot, cold-hammered forged barrel, textured grips. **Velocity:** 492 fps.
Price: ....$199.95–$219.95

CROSMAN 2240 CO2 PISTOL
Caliber: .22. **Barrel:** Rifled. **Weight:** 1.8 lbs. **Length:** 11.13 in. **Power:** CO2. **Sights:** Blade front, rear adjustable. **Features:** Single shot bolt action, ambidextrous grip, all metal construction. **Velocity:** 460 fps.
Price: $79.99

CROSMAN 2300S TARGET PISTOL
Caliber: .177 pellets. **Barrel:** Rifled. **Weight:** 2.66 lbs. **Length:** 16 in. **Power:** CO2. **Sights:** Front fixed sight and Williams notched rear sight. **Features:** Meets IHMSA rules for Production Class Silhouette Competitions. Lothar Walter match-grade barrel, adjustable trigger, adjustable hammer, stainless steel bolt, 60 shots per CO2 cartridge. **Velocity:** 520 fps.
Price: $340.00

CROSMAN 2300T CO2 PISTOL
Caliber: .177 pellets. **Barrel:** Rifled. **Weight:** 2.66 lbs. **Length:** 13.25 in. **Power:** CO2. **Sights:** fixed front sight and LPA rear sight. **Features:** Single-shot, bolt action, adjustable trigger, designed for shooting clubs and organizations that teach pistol shooting and capable of firing 40 shots per CO2 cartridge. **Velocity:** 420 fps.
Price: $229.99

CROSMAN 1701P SILHOUETTE PCP AIR PISTOL
Caliber: .177 pellets. **Barrel:** Rifled Lothar Walther Match. **Weight:** 2.5 lbs. **Length:** 14.75 in. **Power:** Pre-charged Pneumatic. **Sights:** fixed front sight rear sight not included **Features:** Adjustable trigger, designed for shooting silhouette competition, 50 shots per fill. **Velocity:** 450 fps.
Price: $429.95

CROSMAN 1720T PCP TARGET PISTOL
Caliber: .177 pellets. **Barrel:** Rifled Lothar Walther Match. **Weight:** 2.96 lbs. **Length:** 18.00 in. **Power:** Pre-charged Pneumatic. **Sights:** Not included **Features:** Adjustable trigger, designed for shooting silhouettes, fully shrouded barrel, 50 shots per fill. **Velocity:** 750 fps.
Price: $559.99

CROSMAN SNR.357S DUAL AMMO CO2 REVOLVER
Caliber: .177 steel BBs/.177 pellets. **Barrel:** Smoothbore **Weight:** 2.00 lbs. **Length:** 11.73 in. **Power:** CO2. **Sights:** Adjustable rear sight, Fixed Front Blade. **Features:** Full metal revolver in "stainless steel" finish. Comes with shells for BBs and .177 lead pellets **Velocity:** 400 fps. with steel BBs.
Price: $84.95

CROSMAN TRIPLE THREAT CO2 REVOLVER
Caliber: .177 steel BBs/.177 pellets. **Barrel:** Rifled. **Weight:** Variable. **Length:** Variable. **Power:** CO2. **Sights:** Adjustable rear sight. **Features:** Comes with three barrels (3 in., 6 in., and 8 in.) and six-shot BB clip and 10-shot .177 lead pellet clip, single/double action, die cast full metal frame. **Velocity:** Up to 425 fps. with steel BBs.
Price: $99.99

CROSMAN C11 CO2 BB GUN
Caliber: .177 steel BBs. **Barrel:** Smoothbore **Weight:** 1.4 lbs. **Length:** 7.0 in. **Power:** CO2. **Sights:** Fixed. **Features:** Compact semi-automatic BB pistol, front accessory rail. **Velocity:** 480 fps.
Price: $49.99

CROSMAN WILDCAT CO2 BB Pistol
Caliber: .177 steel BBs. **Barrel:** Smoothbore. **Weight:** 1.4 lbs. **Length:** 8.5 in. **Power:** CO2. **Sights:** Fixed. **Features:** 18-round drop-out magazine, accessory rail. **Velocity:** 480 fps.
Price: $59.99

CROSMAN MK45 BB PISTOL
Caliber: .177 steel BBs. **Barrel:** Smoothbore. **Weight:** 1.1 lbs. **Length:** 7.5 in. **Power:** CO2. **Sights:** Fixed. **Features:** 20-round drop-out magazine, accessory rail. **Velocity:** 480 fps.
Price: $49.99

CROSMAN CM9B MAKO BB PISTOL
Caliber: .177 BBs. **Barrel:** Smoothbore. **Weight:** 1.7 lbs. **Length:** 8.6 in. **Power:** CO2. **Sights:** Fiber optic. Blowback action, tricolor, accessory rail. **Velocity:** 425 fps.
Price: $79.99

CROSMAN PFM16 FULL METAL CO2 BB PISTOL
Caliber: .177 steel BBs. **Barrel:** Smoothbore. **Weight:** 1.6 lbs. **Length:** 6.5 in. **Power:** CO2. **Sights:** Fixed. **Features:** Compact semi-automatic BB pistol, full metal construction, 20-shot capacity, kit includes: co2, BBs, and holster. **Velocity:** 400 fps.
Price: $49.99

CROSMAN PFAM9B FULL AUTO PISTOL
Caliber: .177 steel BBs. **Barrel:** Smoothbore. **Weight:** 1.6 lbs. **Length:** 6.5 in. **Power:** CO2. **Sights:** Fixed. **Features:** Full metal construction, full, auto, blowback slide, 20-shot capacity. **Velocity:** 400 fps.
Price: $129.99

CROSMAN PSM45 SPRING POWERED AIR PISTOL
Caliber: .177 steel BBs. **Barrel:** Smoothbore. **Weight:** 1.3 lbs. **Length:** 8.25 in. **Power:** Spring powered. **Sights:** Fixed. **Features:** Metal slide, polymer frame, 20-shot capacity, Picatinny accessory rail. **Velocity:** 190 fps.

Price: **$34.95**

CROSMAN AMERICAN CLASSIC 1377C / PC77, BLACK
Caliber: .177 pellets. **Barrel:** Rifled **Weight:** 2 lbs. **Length:** 13.63 in. **Power:** Multi-pump pneumatic. **Sights:** Front fixed sight and adjustable rear sight. **Features:** Single shot, bolt action. **Velocity:** 600 fps.
Price: **$76.95**

CROSMAN AMERICAN CLASSIC 1322 AIR PISTOL, BLACK
Caliber: .22. **Barrel:** Rifled **Weight:** 2 lbs. **Length:** 13.63 in. **Power:** Multi-pump pneumatic. **Sights:** Front Blade & Ramp. **Features:** Single shot, bolt action. **Velocity:** To 460 fps.
Price: **$79.99**

CROSMAN VIGILANTE CO2 REVOLVER
Caliber: .177 steel BBs/.177 pellets. **Barrel:** Rifled. **Weight:** 2 lbs. **Length:** 11.38 in. **Power:** CO2. **Sights:** Blade front, rear adjustable. **Features:** Single- and double-action revolver (10-shot pellet/6-shot BBs) synthetic frame and finger-molded grip design. **Velocity:** 465 fps.
Price: **$79.99**

CROSMAN GI MODEL 1911 CO2 BLOWBACK BB PISTOL
Caliber: .177 steel BBs. **Barrel:** Smoothbore. **Weight:** 1.88 lbs. **Length:** 8.63 in. **Power:** CO2. **Sights:** Rear Fixed sights **Front Blade**. **Features:** Full metal replica with realistic blowback, 20-round capacity, double-action only. **Velocity:** 450 fps.
Price: **$99.99**

CZ P-09 DUTY CO2 PISTOL
Caliber: .177 BBs/.177 flat-head pellets. **Barrel:** Rifled. **Weight:** 1.6 lbs. **Length:** 8.2 in. **Power:** CO2. **Sights:** Three-dot fixed sights. **Features:** Blowback action, manual safety, double-action-only trigger, 16-round capacity in a 2x8 shot stick magazine, Weaver-style accessory rail, threaded muzzle, blue or two-tone finish, ambidextrous safety with decocker. **Velocity:** 492 fps.
Price: **$104.95**

CZ-75 CO2 PISTOL
Caliber: .177 BBs. **Barrel:** Smooth. **Weight:** 2.1 lbs. **Length:** 8.2 in. **Power:** CO2. **Sights:** Fixed sights. **Features:** Blowback action, manual safety, full metal construction, single-action trigger, removable 17-round BB magazine, Weaver-style accessory rail, also available as a non-blowback compact version. **Velocity:** 312 fps.
Price: **$159.95**

CZ 75 SP-01 SHADOW CO2 BB PISTOL
Caliber: .177 steel BBs. **Barrel:** Smoothbore threaded for barrel extension. **Power:** CO2. **Weight:** 1.3 lbs. **Length:** 8.4 in. **Sights:** Fiber-optic front and rear. **Features:** Non-blowback, double action, accessory rail, 21-round capacity, also available in a heavier-weight, blowback version. **Velocity:** 380 fps.
Price: **$59.95**

CZ 75 P-07 DUTY PISTOL
Caliber: .177 steel BBs. **Barrel:** Smoothbore. **Weight:** 1.81 lbs. **Length:** 7.5 in. **Power:** CO2. **Sights:** Fixed. **Features:** Full metal construction, accessory rail, blowback, 20-round dropout magazine, threaded barrel, blue or two-tone finish, also available in a non-blowback, lower-priced version. **Velocity:** 342 fps.
Price: **$109.95**

CZ 75D COMPACT CO2 BB PISTOL
Caliber: .177 steel BBs. **Barrel:** Smoothbore. **Weight:** 1.5 lbs. **Length:** 7.4 in. **Power:** CO2. **Sights:** Adjustable rear sight and blade front sight. **Features:** Compact design, non-blowback action, blue or two-tone finish, accessory rail. **Velocity:** 380 fps.
Price: **$79.95**

DAISY POWERLINE 340 AIR PISTOL
Caliber: .177 steel BBs. **Barrel:** Smoothbore. **Weight:** 1.0 lbs. **Length:** 8.5 in. **Power:** Single cock, spring-piston. **Sights:** Rear sight Fixed **Front blade**. **Features:** Spring-air action, 200-shot BB reservoir with a 13-shot Speed-load Clip located in the grip. **Velocity:** 240 fps.
Price: **$24.99**

DAISY 408 CO2 PISTOL
Caliber: .177 steel BBs. **Barrel:** Rifled. **Weight:** 1.3 lbs. **Length:** 7.75 in. **Power:** CO2. **Sights:** Front blade, fixed open rear. **Features:** Semi-automatic, 8-shot removable clip, lower accessory rail. **Velocity:** 485 fps.
Price: **$64.99**

DAISY POWERLINE 415 CO2 BB PISTOL
Caliber: .177 steel BBs. **Barrel:** Smoothbore. **Weight:** 1 lb. **Length:** 8.6 in. **Power:** CO2. **Sights:** Front blade, fixed open rear. **Features:** Semi-automatic 21-shot BB pistol. **Velocity:** 500 fps.
Price: **$35.99**

DAISY 426 PISTOL
Caliber: .177 steel BBs. **Barrel:** Smoothbore. **Weight:** 1 lb. **Length:** 6.8 in. **Power:** CO2. **Sights:** Front blade, fixed open rear. **Features:** Semi-automatic, 8-shot removable clip, lower accessory rail. **Velocity:** 430 fps.
Price: **$29.99**

DAISY POWERLINE 5170

DAISY POWERLINE 5170 AIRSTRIKE PISTOL
Caliber: .177 steel BBs. **Barrel:** Smoothbore. **Weight:** 1.0 lbs. **Length:** 9.5 in. **Power:** CO2. **Sights:** Blade and ramp front, Fixed rear. **Features:** Semi-automatic, 21-shot capacity, upper and lower weaver rails for mounting sights and other accessories. **Velocity:** 520 fps.
Price: **$47.99**

DAISY POWERLINE 5501 CO2 PISTOL
Caliber: .177 steel BBs. **Barrel:** Smoothbore. **Weight:** 1.0 lbs. **Length:** 6.8 in. **Power:** CO2. **Sights:** Blade and ramp front, Fixed rear. **Features:** CO2 semi-automatic blowback action. 15-shot clip. **Velocity:** 430 fps.
Price: **$79.99**

Prices given are believed to be accurate at time of publication however, many factors affect retail pricing so exact prices are not possible.

75TH EDITION, 2021 **547**

DAN WESSON 2.5 in./4 in./6 in./8 in. PELLET REVOLVER
Caliber: .177 BBs or .177 pellets. **Barrel:** Smoothbore (BB version) or Rifled (Pellet version). **Weights:** 1.65–2.29 lbs. **Lengths:** 8.3–13.3 in. **Power:** CO2. **Sights:** Blade front and adjustable rear sight. **Features:** Highly realistic replica revolver with swing-out, six-shot cylinder, Weaver-style scope rail, multiple finishes and grip configurations, 6 realistic cartridges, includes a speed loader. **Velocities:** 318–426 fps.
Price: ....$159.95–$199.95

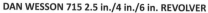

DAN WESSON 715 2.5 in./4 in./6 in. REVOLVER
Caliber: .177 BBs or .177 pellets. **Barrel:** Smoothbore (BB Version) or Rifled (Pellet version). **Weights:** 2.2–2.7 lbs. **Lengths:** 8.3–11.7 in. **Power:** CO2. **Sights:** Blade front and adjustable rear sight. **Features:** Highly realistic replica revolver, accessory rail, multiple finishes and grip configurations, six realistic cartridges, includes a speed loader. **Velocities:** 318–426 fps.
Price: ....$150.00–$199.95

DAN WESSON VALOR 1911 PISTOL
Caliber: .177 pellets. **Barrel:** Rifled. **Weight:** 2.2 lbs. **Length:** 8.7 in. **Power:** CO2. **Sights:** Fixed. **Features:** Non-blowback, full metal construction, 12-round capacity in two six-round drum magazines. **Velocities:** 332 fps.
Price: $99.99

FEINWERKBAU P11 PICCOLO AIR PISTOL
Caliber: .177 pellets. **Barrel:** Rifled. **Weight:** 1.6 lbs. **Length:** 13.58 in. **Power:** Pre-charged pneumatic. **Sights:** Front post, fully adjustable rear blade, **Features:** 10-Meter competition class pistol, meets ISSF requirements, highly adjustable match trigger, **Velocity:** 492 fps.
Price: $1,600.00

FEINWERKBAU P8X PCP 10-METER AIR PISTOL
Caliber: .177 pellets. **Barrel:** Rifled. **Weight:** 2.09 lbs. **Length:** 16.33 in. **Power:** Pre-charged pneumatic. **Sights:** Front post, fully adjustable rear blade. **Features:** 10-Meter competition class pistol with highly customizable grip system, meets ISSF requirements, highly adjustable match trigger. **Velocity:** 508 fps.
Price: $2,399.99

GAMO C-15 BONE COLLECTOR CO2 Pistol
Caliber: .177 BB/.177 pellets. **Barrel:** Smooth. **Weight:** 1.5 lbs. **Length:** 10 in. **Power:** CO2. **Sights:** Fixed. **Features:** Blowback action, approximately 80 shots per CO2 cylinder, single/double action, manual safety, has two side-by-side eight-shot magazines **Velocity:** 450 fps with PBA pellets.
Price: $118.95

GAMO P-900 IGT AIR PISTOL
Caliber: .177 pellets. **Barrel:** Rifled. **Weight:** 1.3 lbs. **Length:** 12.6 in. **Power:** Single cock, gas-pistol. **Sights:** Fiber-optic front and fully adjustable fiber-optic rear sight. **Features:** Break-barrel single-shot, ergonomic design, rubberized grip. **Velocity:** 508 fps.
Price: $79.95

GAMO P-900 IGT AIR PISTOL
Caliber: .177 pellets. **Barrel:** Rifled. **Weight:** 1.3 lbs. **Length:** 12.6 in. **Power:** Single-cock, gas-pistol. **Sights:** Fiber-optic front and fully adjustable fiber-optic rear. **Features:** Break-barrel single-shot, ergonomic design, rubberized grip. **Velocity:** 508 fps.
Price: $79.95

GAMO P-25 AIR PISTOL
Caliber: .177 pellets. **Barrel:** Rifled. **Weight:** 1.5 lbs. **Length:** 7.75 in. **Power:** CO2. **Sights:** Fixed. **Features:** Semi-automatic, 16-shot capacity, realistic blowback action. **Velocity:** 450 fps.
Price: $109.95

GAMO PR-776 CO2 REVOLVER
Caliber: .177 pellets. **Barrel:** Rifled. **Weight:** 2.29 lbs. **Length:** 11.5 in. **Power:** CO2. **Sights:** Fixed front sight with fully adjustable rear sight. **Features:** All metal frame, comes with two 8-shot clips, double- and single-action **Velocity:** 438 fps.
Price: $120.00

GAMO PT-85 CO2 PISTOL
Caliber: .177 pellets. **Barrel:** Rifled. **Weight:** 1.5 lbs. **Length:** 7.8 in. **Power:** CO2. **Sights:** Fixed. **Features:** Semi-automatic, 16-shot capacity, realistic blowback action **Velocity:** 450 fps.
Price: $119.95

GLETCHER STECHKIN APS GOLD BLOWBACK CO2 BB PISTOL
Caliber: .177 steel BBs. **Barrel:** Smoothbore. **Weight:** 2.3 lbs. **Length:** 8.88 in. **Power:** CO2. **Sights:** Fixed **Features:** Full metal gold-colored frame, highly realistic replica of the Soviet Stechkin pistol, 22-round magazine, double action and single action. **Velocities:** 361 fps.
Price: $259.95

GLETCHER NGT F CO2 BB REVOLVER
Caliber: .177 steel BBs. **Barrel:** Smoothbore. **Weight:** 1.54 lbs. **Length:** 9.00 in. **Power:** CO2. **Sights:** Fixed **Features:** Full metal frame, highly realistic replica, 7-shot cylinder with realistic "shells," double action and single action, available in blued and polished silver finishes. **Velocity:** 403 fps..
Price: ....$134.99-$179.99

GLOCK 17 GEN3/GEN 4 CO2 PISTOL
Caliber: .177 BBs. **Barrel:** Smoothbore. **Weight:** 1.6 lbs. **Length:** 7.75 in. **Power:** CO2. **Sights:** Fixed **Features:** Blowback action, metal slide and magazine, 18 BB capacity, manual safety, double-action trigger, replica of the Glock 17 firearm. **Velocity:** 365 fps..
Price: $109.99-129.99

GLOCK 19 GEN3 CO2 PISTOL
Caliber: .177 BBs. **Barrel:** Smoothbore. **Weight:** 1.6 lbs. **Length:** 7.25 in. **Power:** CO2. **Sights:** Fixed **Features:** Non-blowback action, manual safety, 16 BB capacity, integrated Weaver-style accessory rail, double-action trigger, replica of the Glock 19 firearm. **Velocity:** 410 fps.
Price: $79.95

Prices given are believed to be accurate at time of publication however, many factors affect retail pricing so exact prices are not possible.

HAMMERLI AP-20 AIR PISTOL
Caliber: .177 pellets. **Barrel:** Rifled. **Weight:** 1.92 lbs. **Length:** 16.34 in. **Power:** Pre-charged pneumatic. **Sights:** Fully adjustable micrometer. **Features:** 2-stage adjustable trigger factory set to 500 grams pull weight, single shot, bolt action, up to 120 shots per fill. **Velocity:** 492 fps.
Price: $999.99

HATSAN USA AT P1 QUIET ENERGY
PCP PISTOL

HATSAN USA AT P1 QUIET ENERGY PCP PISTOL
Calibers: .177, .22, .25. **Barrel:** Rifled. **Weight:** 4.7 lbs. **Length:** 23.2 in. **Power:** Pre-charged pneumatic. **Sights:** N/A. Grooved for scope mounting. **Features:** Multi-shot magazine feed, integrated suppressor, muzzle energy suitable for pest control and small game hunting. **Velocity:** .177, 870 fps/.22, 780 fps/.25, 710 fps.
Price: $479.99

HATSAN USA AT P2 QUIET ENERGY TACT PCP PISTOL
Caliber: .25. **Barrel:** Rifled, 10.4 in. **Weight:** 6.6 lbs. **Length:** 36 in. **Power:** Pre-charged pneumatic. **Sights:** N/A. Grooved for scope mounting. **Features:** Side-lever action, multi-shot magazine feed, integrated suppressor, muzzle energy suitable for pest control and small-game hunting, comes with shoulder stock. **Velocity:** 710 fps.
Price: $549.99

HATSAN SORTIE AIR PISTOL
Caliber: .177, .22, or .25 pellets. **Barrel:** Rifled. **Weight:** 4.4 lbs. **Length:** 15.5 in. **Power:** Pre-charged pneumatic. **Sights:** Fiber-optic front and fully adjustable rear sight. **Features:** Polymer grips, semi-automatic action, fully shrouded barrel, rotary magazine, Picatinny rail. Velocity with lead pellets: 850 fps (.177), 700 fps (.22), 625 fps (.25).
Price: $649.99

H&K VP9 BB CO2 PISTOL
Caliber: .177 steel BBs. **Barrel:** Smoothbore. **Weight:** 1.42 lbs. **Length:** 7.2 in. **Power:** CO2. **Sights:** Fixed. **Features:** Highly realistic replica, blowback action, integrated front weaver accessory rail, 18-round magazine. **Velocity:** 350 fps.
Price: $89.99

H&K P30 BB CO2 PISTOL
Caliber: .177 BB/.177 pellet. **Barrel:** Rifled. **Weight:** 1.7 lbs. **Length:** 7.1 in. **Power:** CO2. **Sights:** Front and rear windage adjustable. **Features:** Highly realistic replica, blowback action, integrated front weaver accessory rail, eight-pellet rotary magazine, drop out 15-BB magazine, double/single action. **Velocity:** 360 fps.
Price: $249.99

H&K USP CO2 BB PISTOL
Caliber: .177 steel BBs. **Barrel:** Smoothbore. **Weight:** 1.35 lbs. **Length:** 7.5 in. **Power:** CO2. **Sights:** Fixed **Features:** Highly realistic replica, integrated front weaver accessory rail, 22-round magazine, double action only. **Velocity:** 360 fps.
Price: $60.00

H&K HK45 CO2 BB PISTOL
Caliber: .177 steel BBs. **Barrel:** Smoothbore. **Weight:** 1.4 lbs. **Length:** 8.0 in. **Power:** CO2. **Sights:** Fixed. **Features:** Highly realistic replica, integrated front weaver accessory rail, 20-shot capacity, double-action only. **Velocity:** 400 fps.
Price: $54.99

Prices given are believed to be accurate at time of publication however, many factors affect retail pricing so exact pricing are not possible.

75TH EDITION, 2021 ◈ **549**

MORINI MOR-162EL AIR PISTOL
Caliber: .177 pellets. **Barrel:** Rifled. **Weight:** 2.25 lbs. **Length:** 16.14 in. **Power:** Pre-charged pneumatic. **Sights:** Front post, rear adjustable for windage. **Features:** Adjustable electronic trigger, single-shot bolt action, extreme match grade accuracy, over 200 regulated shots per 200 bar fill. **Velocity:** 500 fps.
Price: $2,200.00

MORINI CM 200EI AIR PISTOL
Caliber: .177 pellets. **Barrel:** Rifled, Lothar Walther. **Weight:** 2.17 lbs. **Length:** 15.75 in. **Power:** Pre-charged pneumatic. **Sights:** Front post, rear diopter/micrometer adjustable. **Features:** Adjustable electronic trigger, single-shot bolt action, digital manometer, battery life of 15,000 shots, match-grade accuracy, available with medium or large grip size, muzzle compensator, 150 regulated shots per 200 bar fill, comes with two air cylinders. **Velocity:** 492 fps.
Price: $2,439.49

SIG SAUER X-FIVE ASP .177 CO2 PISTOL
Caliber: .177 pellets. **Barrel:** Smoothbore. **Weight:** 2.75 lbs. **Length:** 9.75 in. **Power:** CO2. **Sights:** Fixed. **Features:** Realistic replica action pistol, 18-shot capacity, front accessory rail, full metal construction, metal slide with blowback action. **Velocity:** 300 fps.
Price: $159.95

REMINGTON 1875 CO2 REVOLVER
Caliber: .177 steel BBs/.177 pellet. **Barrel:** Smoothbore. **Weight:** 2.3 lbs. **Length:** 13.1 in. **Power:** CO2. **Sights:** Fixed. **Features:** Metal construction, nickel finish, faux ivory grip, single action, functional load gate, hammer and extractor. **Velocity:** Up to 450 fps.
Price: $149.99

SIG SAUER 1911 METAL BLOWBACK CO2 BB PISTOL
Caliber: .177 steel BBs. **Barrel:** Smoothbore. **Weight:** 2.0 lbs. **Length:** 8.75 in. **Power:** CO2. **Sights:** Adjustable. **Features:** Extremely Realistic replica action pistol, 20-shot capacity, front accessory rail, black or silver finish, full metal construction, metal slide with blowback action. **Velocity:** 430 fps.
Price: $139.95

REMINGTON 1911 RAC
CO2 BB PISTOL

REMINGTON 1911 RAC CO2 BB PISTOL
Caliber: .177 steel BBs. **Barrel:** Smoothbore. **Weight:** 2.0 lbs. **Length:** 8.0 in. **Power:** CO2. **Sights:** Fixed. **Features:** All metal, blowback, extremely realistic replica pistol, bottom weaver/picatinny accessory rail. **Velocity:** 320 fps.
Price: $109.99

SIG SAUER P226 CO2 PELLET PISTOL
Caliber: .177 pellets. **Barrel:** Rifled. **Weight:** 2.35 lbs. **Length:** 8.25 in. **Power:** CO2. **Sights:** Fixed. **Features:** Highly detailed replica action pistol, 16-shot capacity, front accessory rail, full metal construction, metal slide with blowback action, available in dark earth and black. **Velocity:** 450 fps.
Price: $109.99

RWS LP 8 PISTOL
Caliber: .177 pellets. **Barrel:** Rifled. **Weight:** 3.20 lbs. **Length:** 7 in. **Power:** Spring powered. **Sights:** Fixed front with fully adjustable rear. **Features:** Powerful spring-powered air pistol, single cock delivers full power, exceptional design and build quality. **Velocity:** 700 fps.
Price: $349.95

SCHOFIELD NO. 3 REVOLVER, FULL METAL
Caliber: .177 steel BBs or .177 pellets. **Barrel:** Smoothbore. **Weight:** 2.4 lbs. **Length:** 12.5 in. **Power:** CO2. **Sights:** Fixed. **Features:** Highly detailed replica revolver, 6-shot capacity, realistic reusable cartridges, available in black and nickel finishes. **Velocity:** 430 fps.
Price: .... $159.95–$169.95

SIG SAUER P320 CO2 PISTOL
Caliber: .177 BBs/.177 pellets. **Barrel:** Rifled. **Weight:** 2.2 lbs. **Length:** 9.6 in. **Power:** CO2. **Sights:** Fixed, white dot. **Features:** 30-round belt-fed magazine, front accessory rail, polymer frame, metal slide with blowback action, black or coyote tan finish. **Velocity:** 430 fps.
Price: $119.99

Prices given are believed to be accurate at time of publication however, many factors affect retail pricing so exact prices are not possible.

SMITH & WESSON 586 & 686
Caliber: .177 pellets. **Barrel:** Rifled. **Weights:** Model 586 4 in. 2.50 lbs. / Model 586 & 686 6 in. 2.8 lbs. **Length:** Model 586 4-in. barrel - 9.5 in. - Model 586, 6 in. barrel - 11.50 in. / Model 686 6 in. barrel - 11.5 in. **Power:** CO2. **Sights:** Fixed front, adjustable rear **Features:** Extremely accurate, full metal, replica revolvers.
Price: 586 4-in. barrel. Velocity - 400 fps **$300.00**
Price: 586 6-in. barrel. Velocity - 425 fps **$295.95**
Price: 686 6-in. barrel. Velocity - 425 fps **$329.95**

SMITH & WESSON M&P CO2 PISTOL
Caliber: .177 steel BBs. **Barrel:** Smoothbore. **Weight:** 1.5 lbs. **Lengths:** 7.5 in. **Power:** CO2. **Sights:** Blade front and ramp rear fiber optic. **Features:** Integrated accessory rail, removable 19-shot BB magazine, double-action only, synthetic frame available in dark earth brown or black color. **Velocity:** 300–480 fps.
Price: **$50.00**

SMITH & WESSON M&P 45 CO2 PISTOL
Caliber: .177 steel BBs, .177 pellets. **Barrel:** Rifled. **Weight:** 1.35 lbs. **Length:** 8.1 in. **Power:** CO2. **Sights:** Fixed front sight, fully adjustable rear sight. **Features:** Double and single action, 8-shot semi-automatic. **Velocity:** 370 fps.
Price: **$80.00**

SMITH & WESSON 327 TRR8 CO2 BB PISTOL
Caliber: .177 steel BBs. **Barrel:** Smoothbore. **Weight:** 2.0 lbs. **Length:** 12 in. **Power:** CO2. **Sights:** Fiber-optic front sight, fully adjustable fiber-optic rear sight. **Features:** High-quality replica, top-mounted weaver scope rail, weaver accessory rail under the barrel, swing-out cylinder, removable casings and functioning ejector. **Velocity:** 400 fps.
Price: **$120.00**

STEYR M9-A1 PISTOL
Caliber: .177 BBs. **Barrel:** Smoothbore. **Weight:** 1.2 lbs. **Length:** 7.5 in. **Power:** CO2. **Sights:** Fixed. **Features:** Non-blowback, accessory rail, metal slide, two-tone or blue finish, 19-round capacity. **Velocity:** 449 fps.
Price: .... **$59.95 (blue); 99.95 (two-tone)**

STI DUTY ONE CO2 BB PISTOL
Caliber: .177 steel BBs. **Barrel:** Smoothbore. **Weight:** 1.8 lbs. **Length:** 8.8 in. **Power:** CO2. **Sights:** Fixed. **Features:** Blowback, accessory rail, metal slide, threaded barrel, 20-round magazine. **Velocity:** 397 fps.
Price: **$99.95**

STEYR M9-A1 CO2 PISTOL
Caliber: .177 steel BBs. **Barrel:** Smoothbore. **Weight:** 2.4 lbs. **Length:** 7.4 in. **Power:** CO2. **Sights:** Fixed. **Features:** Non-blowback, accessory rail, metal slide, removable 19-round magazine. Velocity: 449 fps.
Price: **$99.95**

TANFOGLIO WITNESS 1911 CO2 BB PISTOL, BROWN GRIPS
Caliber: .177 steel BBs. **Barrel:** Smoothbore. **Weight:** 1.98 lbs. **Length:** 8.6 in. **Power:** CO2. **Sights:** Fixed. **Features:** Often recognized as the "standard" for 1911 replica action pistols, 18-shot capacity, full metal construction with metal slide with blowback action. **Velocity:** 320 fps.
Price: **$119.99**

UMAREX LEGENDS MAKAROV ULTRA BLOWBACK CO2 BB PISTOL
Caliber: .177 steel BBs. **Barrel:** Smoothbore. **Weight:** 1.40 lbs. **Length:** 6.38 in. **Power:** CO2. **Sights:** Fixed. **Features:** Highly realistic replica, all-metal construction with blowback action, semi-automatic and fully-automatic capable, 16-round capacity. **Velocity:** 350 fps.
Price: **$90.99**

UMAREX LEGENDS M712 BROOM HANDLE FULL-AUTO CO2 BB PISTOL
Caliber: .177 steel BBs. **Barrel:** Smoothbore. **Weight:** 3.10 lbs. **Length:** 12.00 in. **Power:** CO2. **Sights:** Fixed front sight with rear sight adjustable for elevation. **Features:** Highly realistic replica that functions as the original, all-metal construction with blowback action, semi-automatic and fully-automatic capable, 18-round capacity. **Velocity:** 360 fps.
Price: **$149.99**

UMAREX LEGENDS P08 BLOWBACK CO2 BB PISTOL
Caliber: .177 steel BBs. **Barrel:** Smoothbore. **Weight:** 1.90 lbs. **Length:** 8.75 in. **Power:** CO2. **Sights:** Fixed. **Features:** Highly realistic replica that functions as the original, all-metal construction with blowback action, 21-round capacity. **Velocity:** 300 fps.
Price: **$149.99**

UMAREX BRODAX BB
Caliber: .177 steel BBs. **Barrel:** Smoothbore. **Weight:** 1.52 lbs. **Length:** 10.0 in. **Power:** CO2. **Sights:** Fixed. **Features:** Aggressively styled BB revolver, 10-shot capacity, top accessory rail, front accessory rail, synthetic construction. **Velocity:** 375 fps.
Price: $42.99

UMAREX SA10 CO2 PISTOL
Caliber: .177 pellet or steel BBs. **Barrel:** Rifled. **Weight:** 2.05 lbs. **Length:** 9.25 in. **Power:** CO2. **Sights:** Fixed. **Features:** Full metal slide with polymer grips, blowback action, ported slide with gold-look barrel and breech block, threaded muzzle, magazine holds the CO2 cylinder, an 8-shot rotary clip, and three additional clips, under-muzzle accessory rail. **Velocity:** 420 fps.
Price: $129.99

UMAREX STRIKE POINT PELLET MULTI-PUMP AIR PISTOL
Caliber: .177 pellets. **Barrel:** Rifled. **Weight:** 2.6 lbs. **Length:** 14.00 in. **Power:** Multi-pump pneumatic. **Sights:** Adjustable rear sight, fixed fiber-optic front sight. **Features:** Variable power based on number of pumps, bolt action, includes integrated "silenceair" moderator for quite shooting. **Velocity:** Up to 650 fps.
Price: $59.99

UMAREX TREVOX AIR PISTOL
Caliber: .177 pellets. **Barrel:** Rifled. **Weight:** 3.5 lbs. **Length:** 18.25 in. **Power:** Gas Piston. **Sights:** Adjustable rear sight, fixed fiber-optic front sight. **Features:** full power from a single cock, suitable for target practice and plinking, includes integrated "silenceair" moderator for quite shooting. **Velocity:** 540 fps.
Price: $89.95

UMAREX XBG CO2 PISTOL
Caliber: .177 steel BBs. **Barrel:** Smoothbore. **Weight:** 0.7 lbs. **Length:** 6.75 in. **Power:** CO2. **Sights:** Fixed. **Features:** 19-shot capacity, under barrel accessory rail, double-action only. **Velocity:** 410 fps.
Price: $40.00

UZI MINI CARBINE
Caliber: .177 steel BBs. **Barrel:** Smoothbore. **Weight:** 2.45 lbs. **Length:** 23.5 in. **Power:** CO2. **Sights:** Fixed. **Features:** Realistic replica airgun, 28-shot capacity, foldable stock, semi-automatic with realistic blowback system, heavy bolt provides realistic "kick" when firing. **Velocity:** 390 fps.
Price: $120.95

UZI CO2 BB SUBMACHINE GUN
Caliber: .177 steel BBs. **Barrel:** Smoothbore. **Weight:** 4.85 lbs. **Length:** 23.5 in. **Power:** CO2. **Sights:** Fixed. **Features:** Realistic replica airgun, 25-shot capacity, foldable stock, semi-automatic and fully-automatic selectable fire, realistic blowback system. **Velocity:** 360 fps.
Price: $199.99

WALTHER CP88, BLUED, 4-INCH BARREL
Caliber: .177 pellets. **Barrel:** Rifled. **Weight:** 2.3 lbs. **Length:** 7 in. **Power:** CO2. **Sights:** Blade ramp front sight and adjustable rear sight. **Features:** Manual safety, semi-auto repeater, single or double action, available in multiple finishes and grip materials, 8-shot capacity. **Velocity:** 400 fps.
Price: ....$229.99–$300.00

WALTHER CP88, BLUED, 6-INCH BARREL
Caliber: .177 pellets. **Barrel:** Rifled. **Weight:** 2.5 lbs. **Length:** 9 in. **Power:** CO2. **Sights:** Blade ramp front sight and adjustable rear sight. **Features:** Manual safety, Semi-auto repeater, single or double action, available in multiple finishes and grip materials, 8-shot capacity. **Velocity:** 450 fps.
Price: ....$229.95–$329.99

WALTHER CP99 CO2 GUN, BLACK
Caliber: .177 pellets. **Barrel:** Rifled **Weight:** 1.6 lbs. **Length:** 7.1 in. **Power:** CO2. **Sights:** Fixed front and fully adjustable rear sight. **Features:** Extremely realistic replica pistol, single and double action, 8-shot rotary magazine. **Velocity:** 360 fps.
Price: $200.00

Prices given are believed to be accurate at time of publication however, many factors affect retail pricing so exact prices are not possible.

WALTHER CP99 COMPACT

WALTHER PPS

WALTHER CP99 COMPACT & COMPACT NICKEL
Caliber: .177 steel BBs. **Barrel:** Smoothbore. **Weight:** 1.7 lbs. **Length:** 6.6 in. **Power:** CO2. **Sights:** Fixed front and rear. **Features:** Extremely realistic replica pistol, semi-automatic 18-shot capacity, available in various configurations including a nickel slide. **Velocity:** 345 fps.
Price: ....$99.95–$105.99

WALTHER PPQ

WALTHER PPQ / P99 Q CO2 PISTOL
Caliber: .177 steel BBs, .177 pellets. **Barrel:** Rifled **Weight:** 1.37 lbs. **Length:** 7.0 in. **Power:** CO2. **Sights:** Fixed front and fully adjustable rear sight. **Features:** Extremely realistic replica pistol, semi-automatic 8-shot rotary magazine. **Velocity:** 360 fps.
Price: $70.00

WALTHER P38 CO2 BB PISTOL
Caliber: .177 steel BBs. **Barrel:** Smoothbore. **Weight:** 1.9 lbs. **Length:** 8.5 in. **Power:** CO2. **Sights:** Fixed. **Features:** Authentic replica action pistol, blowback action, semi-automatic 20-shot magazine. **Velocity:** 400 fps.
Price: $120.00

WALTHER PPK/S CO2 PISTOL
Caliber: .177 steel BBs. **Barrel:** Smoothbore. **Weight:** 3.7 lbs. **Length:** 6.1 in. **Power:** CO2. **Sights:** Fixed. **Features:** Authentic replica action pistol, blowback slide locks back after last shot, stick-style magazine with 15-shot capacity. **Velocity:** 295 fps.
Price: $129.95

WALTHER PPS M BLOWBACK COMPACT CO2 PISTOL
Caliber: .177 steel BBs. **Barrel:** Smoothbore. **Weight:** 1.2 lbs. **Length:** 6.38 in. **Power:** CO2. **Sights:** Fixed. **Features:** Authentic replica action pistol, blowback action, semi-automatic 18-shot capacity. **Velocity:** 390 fps.
Price: $99.95

WEBLEY AND SCOTT MKVI REVOLVER
Caliber: .177 pellets. **Barrel:** Rifled. **Weight:** 2.4 lbs. **Length:** 11.25 in. **Power:** CO2. **Sights:** Fixed. **Features:** Authentic replica pistol, single/double action, can be field-stripped, full metal construction, six-shot capacity, available in silver or distressed finish. **Velocity:** 430 fps.
Price: $199.99

WEIHRAUCH HW 75
Caliber: .177 pellets. **Barrel:** Rifled. **Weight:** 2.34 lbs. **Length:** 11.0 in. **Power:** Spring-powered. **Sights:** Fixed front sight with fully adjustable rear sight. **Features:** Single shot, designed precision shooting, beautifully crafted German airgun, two-stage adjustable trigger. **Velocity:** 410 fps.
Price: $482.99

WEIHRAUCH HW 40 AIR PISTOL
Caliber: .177, .20, .22. **Barrel:** Rifled. **Weight:** 1.7 lbs. **Length:** 9.5 in. **Power:** Single-stroke spring piston. **Sights:** Fiber-optic, fully adjustable. **Features:** Automatic safety, two-stage trigger, single shot. **Velocity:** 400 fps..
Price: $252.00

WEIHRAUCH HW 44 AIR PISTOL, FAC VERSION
Caliber: .177, .22. **Barrel:** Rifled. **Weight:** 2.9 lbs. **Length:** 19 in. **Power:** Pre-charged pneumatic. **Sights:** None. **Features:** Ambidextrous safety, two-stage adjustable match trigger, built in suppressor, Weaver-style scope rail, 10-shot magazine, built-in air cartridge with quick fill, internal pressure gauge. **Velocity:** 750 (.177), 570 (.22) fps.
Price: $1,049.99

WEIHRAUCH HW 45 AIR PISTOL
Caliber: .177, .20, .22. **Barrel:** Rifled. **Weight:** 2.5 lbs. **Length:** 10.9 in. **Power:** Single-stroke spring piston. **Sights:** Fiber-optic, fully adjustable. **Features:** Automatic safety, two-stage trigger, single shot, two power levels, blued or two tone. **Velocity:** 410/558 (.177), 394/492 (.20), 345/427 (.22) fps.
Price: $516.00

WEIHRAUCH HW 75 AIR PISTOL
Caliber: .177. **Barrel:** Rifled. **Weight:** 2.3 lbs. **Length:** 11 in. **Power:** Single-stroke spring piston. **Sights:** Micrometer adjustable rear. **Features:** Ambidextrous, adjustable match-type trigger, single shot. **Velocity:** 410 fps.
Price: $482.99

WINCHESTER MODEL 11

WINCHESTER MODEL 11 BB PISTOL
Caliber: .177 steel BBs. **Barrel:** Smoothbore. **Weight:** 1.9 lbs. **Length:** 8.5 in.
Power: CO2. **Sights:** Fixed. **Features:** All-metal replica action pistol, blowback action, 4-lb. 2-stage trigger, semi-automatic 15-shot capacity. **Velocity:** 410 fps.
Price: **$149.99**

AIR ARMS TX200 MKIII AIR RIFLE
Calibers: .177, .22. **Barrel:** Rifled, Lothar Walter match-grade, 13.19 in. **Weight:** 9.3 lbs. **Length:** 41.34 in. **Power:** Single cock, spring-piston. **Stock:** Various; right- and left-handed versions, multiple wood options. **Sights:** 11mm dovetail. **Features:** Fixed barrel, heirloom quality craftsmanship, holds the record for the most winning spring powered airgun in international field target competitions. **Velocities:** .177, 930 fps/.22, 755 fps.
Price: ....$699.99–$829.99

AIR ARMS PRO-SPORT RIFLE
Calibers: .177, .22. **Barrel:** Rifled, Lothar Walter match-grade, 9.5 in. **Weight:** 9.03 lbs. **Length:** 40.5 in. **Power:** Single cock, spring-piston **Stock:** Various; right-and left-handed versions, multiple wood options. **Sights:** 11mm dovetail. **Features:** Fixed barrel, Heirloom quality craftsmanship, unique inset cocking arm. **Velocities:** .177, 950 fps/.22, 750 fps.
Price: $824.99–879.99

AIR ARMS S510 XTRA FAC PCP AIR RIFLE
Calibers: .177, .22, .25. **Barrel:** Rifled, Lothar Walter match-grade, 19.45 in. **Weight:** 7.55 lbs. **Length:** 43.75 in. **Power:** Pre-charged pneumatic. **Stock:** Right-handed, multiple wood options. **Sights:** 11mm dovetail. **Features:** Side-lever action, 10-round magazine, shrouded barrel, variable power, Heirloom quality craftsmanship **Velocities:** .177, 1,050 fps/.22, 920 fps/.25, 850 fps.
Price: $1,299.99

AIR ARMS S510 ULTIMATE SPORTER
Calibers: .177, .22, .25. **Barrel:** Rifled, Lothar Walter match-grade, 19.5 in. **Weight:** 8.6 lbs. **Length:** 44.25 in. **Power:** Pre-charged pneumatic. **Stock:** Fully adjustable, ambidextrous laminate stock. **Sights:** 11mm dovetail. **Features:** Side-lever action, 10-shot magazine, integrated suppressor, variable power, Heirloom quality craftsmanship. **Velocities:** .177, 1,050 fps/.22, 920 fps/.25, 850 fps.
Price: $1,699.99

AIR ARMS T200 SPORTER
Caliber: .177 pellets. **Barrel:** Hammer-forged, rifled 19.1 in. **Weight:** 6.6 lbs. **Length:** 35.5 in. **Power:** Pre-charged pneumatic. **Stock:** Hardwood. **Sights:** Globe front sight, fully adjustable diopter rear sight. **Features:** Aluminum muzzle brake, two-stage adjustable trigger, removable air tank, single shot, grooved receiver, made by CZ. **Velocity:** 575 fps.
Price: $650.00

AIR ARMS FTP 900 FIELD TARGET PCP AIR RIFLE
Caliber: .177. **Barrel:** Rifled, Lothar Walter match-grade, 19.0 in. **Weight:** 11.00 lbs. **Length:** 42.50 in. **Power:** Pre-charged pneumatic **Stock:** Fully adjustable competition style, available in right- or left-handed laminate stock. **Sights:** 11mm dovetail. **Features:** Side-lever action, single shot for maximum accuracy, integrated muzzle break, heirloom quality craftsmanship, regulated for supreme shot consistency, delivers up to 100 shots per fill. **Velocity:** 800 fps.
Price: $3,029.99

AIR ARMS GALAHAD RIFLE REG FAC
Calibers: .22, .25. **Barrel:** Rifled, Lothar Walter match-grade, 19.4 in. **Weight:** 8.6 lbs. **Length:** 35.5 in. **Power:** Pre-charged pneumatic. **Stock:** Ambidextrous bullpup stock available in "soft touch" synthetic over beech or walnut. **Sights:** 11mm dovetail. **Features:** Moveable side-lever action, 10-shot magazine, available with integrated moderator, variable power with integrated regulator, Heirloom quality craftsmanship. **Velocity:** .22, 900 fps/.25, 800 fps.
Price: ....$1699.99–$1849.00

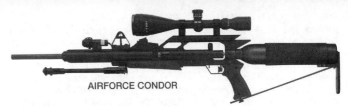

AIRFORCE CONDOR

AIRFORCE CONDOR/CONDOR SS RIFLE
Calibers: .177, .20, .22, .25. **Barrel:** Rifled, Lothar Walther match-grade, 18 or 24 in. **Weight:** 6.1 lbs. **Length:** 38.1-38.75 in. **Power:** Pre-charged pneumatic. **Stock:** Synthetic pistol grip, tank acts as buttstock. **Sights:** Grooved for scope mounting. **Features:** Single shot, adjustable power, automatic safety, large 490cc tank volume, extended scope rail allows easy mounting of the largest air-gun scopes, optional CO_2 power system available, manufactured in the USA by AirForce Airguns. **Velocities:** .177, 1,450 fps/.20, 1,150 fps/.22, 1,250 fps/.25, 1,100 fps.
Price: $744.95

AIRFORCE EDGE 10-METER AIR RIFLE
Caliber: .177. **Barrel:** Rifled, Lothar Walther match-grade, 12 in. **Weight:** 6.1 lbs. **Length:** 40.00 in. **Power:** Pre-charged pneumatic. **Stock:** Synthetic pistol grip, tank acts as buttstock. **Sights:** Front sight only or match front globe and rear micrometer adjustable diopter sight. **Features:** Single shot, automatic safety, two-stage adjustable trigger, accepted by CMP for completive shooting, available in multiple colors and configurations, manufactured in the USA. **Velocity:** .530 fps.
Price: ....$640.00–$799.95

AIRFORCE ESCAPE/SS/UL AIR RIFLE
Calibers: .22, .25. **Barrel:** Rifled, Lothar Walther match-grade, 12, 18 or 24 in. **Weight:** 4.3-5.3 lbs. **Length:** 32.3-39.00 in. **Power:** Pre-charged pneumatic. **Stock:** Synthetic pistol grip, tank acts as buttstock. **Sights:** Grooved for scope mounting. **Features:** Single shot, adjustable power, automatic safety, extended scope rail allows easy mounting of the largest airgun scopes, manufactured in the USA by AirForce Airguns. **Velocities:** .22, 1,300 fps/.25, 1,145 fps.
Price: ....$642.95-$694.95

AIRFORCE TALON PCP AIR RIFLE
Calibers: .177, .22, .25. **Barrel:** Rifled, Lothar Walther match-grade, 18 in. **Weight:** 5.5 lbs. **Length:** 32.6 in. **Power:** Pre-charged pneumatic. **Stock:** Synthetic pistol grip, tank acts as buttstock. **Sights:** Grooved for scope mounting. **Features:** Single shot, adjustable power, automatic safety, large 490cc tank volume, extended scope rail allows easy mounting of the largest airgun scopes, optional CO_2 power system available, manufactured in the USA by AirForce Airguns. **Velocities:** .177, 1,100 fps/.22, 950 fps/.25, 850 fps.
Price: $609.95

AIRFORCE TALON P PCP CARBINE
Caliber: .25. **Barrel:** Rifled, Lothar Walther match-grade, 12 in. **Weight:** 4.3 lbs. **Length:** 27.75-32.35 in. **Power:** Pre-charged pneumatic. **Stock:** Synthetic pistol grip. **Sights:** Grooved for scope mounting. **Features:** Single shot, removable moderator to reduce noise, adjustable power, can be easily broken down for compact transport, automatic safety, two-stage adjustable trigger, 213cc air tank, up to 50 foot-pounds of energy. **Velocity:** 500-900 fps.
Price: $749.95

AIRFORCE TALON SS PCP AIR RIFLE
Calibers: .177, .20, .22, .25. **Barrel:** Rifled, Lothar Walther match-grade, 12 in. **Weight:** 5.25 lbs. **Length:** 32.75 in. **Power:** Pre-charged pneumatic. **Stock:** Synthetic pistol grip, tank acts as buttstock. **Sights:** Grooved for scope mounting. **Features:** Fully shrouded barrel with integrated suppressor, single shot, adjustable power, automatic safety, large 490cc tank volume, extended scope rail allows easy mounting of the largest airgun scopes, multiple color options available, optional CO_2 power system available, manufactured in the USA by AirForce Airguns. **Velocities:** .177, 1,000 fps/.20, 800 fps/.22, 800 fps/.25, 665 fps.
Price: $652.95

Prices given are believed to be accurate at time of publication however, many factors affect retail pricing so exact prices are not possible.

75TH EDITION, 2021 ✦ **555**

AIRFORCE TEXAN / TEXAN SS AIR RIFLE
Calibers: .30, .35, .45. **Barrel:** Rifled, 34.00 in. **Weight:** 7.65 lbs. **Length:** 48.00 in. **Power:** Pre-charged pneumatic. **Stock:** Synthetic pistol grip, tank acts as buttstock. **Sights:** Grooved for scope mounting. **Features:** Delivers massive energy and long-range accuracy, two-stage non-adjustable trigger, very easy to cock, open receiver accepts a vast selection of off the shelf or custom cast ammunition, available in a fully shrouded suppressed model, manufactured in the USA by AirForce Airguns. **Velocities:** .30, 1,100 fps, 300 ft-lbs/.35, 1,000 fps, 350 ft-lbs/.45, 1,000 fps 500 ft-lbs.
Price: .... $1,054.95–$1210.95

AIRFORCE INTERNATIONAL LYNX V10 AIR RIFLE
Calibers: .177, .22. **Barrel:** Rifled, hammer forged barrel, 18.5 in. **Weight:** 7.25 lbs. **Length:** 41.30 in. **Power:** Pre-charged pneumatic. **Stock:** Natural or black hardwood stock. **Sights:** 11mm dovetail for scope mounting. **Features:** Multi-shot magazine varies on caliber, side-lever action, adjustable power and adjustable trigger, Spanish made. **Velocities:** .177, 1,000 fps/.22, 700 fps.
Price: $599.95

AIRFORCE INTERNATIONAL ORION AIR RIFLE
Calibers: .177, .22, .25. **Barrel:** Hammer forged barrel, 18.5 in. **Weight:** 7.25 lbs. **Length:** 41.00 in. **Power:** Pre-charged pneumatic. **Stock:** Right-handed hardwood stock with adjustable cheek riser. **Sights:** 11mm dovetail for scope mounting. **Features:** Multi-shot magazine varies on caliber, side-lever action, adjustable power and adjustable trigger. **Velocities:** .177, 1,000 fps/.22, 800 fps/.25, 600 fps.
Price: $629.95

AIRFORCE INTERNATIONAL MODEL 94 SPRING AIR RIFLE
Calibers: .177, .22, 25. **Barrel:** Rifled, hammer forged, 18.75 in. **Weight:** 7.5 lbs. **Length:** 44.9 in. **Power:** Spring piston. **Stock:** Synthetic with textured grip and forearm. **Sights:** Fixed fiber-optic front and fully adjustable fiber-optic rear. **Features:** Single shot, adjustable two-stage trigger, 32-pound cocking effort, integral muzzle brake. **Velocities:** 1100 fps (.177)/900 fps (.22)/700 fps (.25).
Price: $249.95

AIRFORCE INTERNATIONAL MODEL 95 SPRING AIR RIFLE
Calibers: .177, .22. **Barrel:** Rifled, hammer forged. **Weight:** 7.25 lbs. **Length:** 44.9 in. **Power:** Spring piston. **Stock:** Hardwood stock with checkering on grip and forearm. **Sights:** None, 11mm dovetail for scope mounting. **Features:** Single shot, adjustable trigger, 32-pound cocking effort. **Velocities:** .177, 980 fps/.22, 835 fps.
Price: $315.95

AIRGUN TECHNOLOGY VULCAN 2 BULLPUP RIFLE
Calibers: .22, .25. **Barrel:** 19.6 in. **Weight:** 7.25 lbs. **Length:** 29.75 in. **Power:** Pre-charged pneumatic. **Stock:** Ambidextrous walnut bullpup stock with polymer cheekpiece. **Sights:** Picatinny rail for scope mounting. **Features:** Has a biathlon side lever, comes with two 12-shot magazines, includes a hard case, side-lever action, shrouded barrel with M14 adapter, up to 60 shots per fill. **Velocities:** .22, 800 fps/.25, 600 fps.
Price: $1,799.99

AIR VENTURI WING SHOT II SHOTGUN
Caliber: .50. **Barrel:** Smoothbore 22.5 in. **Weight:** 7.4 lbs. **Length:** 43.0 in. **Power:** Pre-charged pneumatic. **Stock:** Ambidextrous wood stock. **Sights:** Fixed bead shotgun-style sight. **Features:** 244cc reservoir delivers several powerful shots, shoots shot cartridges and round balls, exceptionally reliable. Use as a shotgun to hunt birds or small game or as a slug gun to hunt larger game. **Velocity:** 760 fps (with slug), 1,130 fps.
Price: $849.99

AMERICAN AIR ARMS EVOL CLASSIC CARBINE
Calibers: .22, .25, .30. **Barrel:** Hammer forged, rifled, threaded, 15 in. (.22), 18 in. (.25, .30). **Weight:** 7-7.2 lbs. **Length:** 36-39 in. with moderator. **Power:** Pre-charged pneumatic. **Stock:** Walnut. **Sights:** None, Picatinny rail. **Features:** Upper and lower chassis made from aluminum, titanium air cylinder, Picatinny underside accessory rail, adjustable two-stage trigger set to 10 ounces, 9- to 13-shot rotary magazine, Magpul stock and grip, manufactured in very limited quantities. **Velocity:** Adjustable.
Price: $2,895.99

AMERICAN AIR ARMS SLAYER HI-POWER BULLPUP RIFLE
Calibers: .308, .357. **Barrel:** Rifled, threaded, 24 in. (.357), 26 in. (.308). **Weight:** 7.2 lbs. **Length:** 36-40 in. with moderator. **Power:** Pre-charged pneumatic. **Stock:** Synthetic adjustable-length stock. **Sights:** None, Picatinny rail. **Features:** Titanium reservoir, 3-pound cocking effort, 6 (.357 caliber) or 7 (.308 caliber) round rotary magazine, adjustable two-stage trigger, underside accessory rail, rear velocity adjuster, available in right or left hand, manufactured in very limited quantities. **Velocity:** 950 fps.
Price: $2,795.99

ANSCHUTZ 9015 AIR RIFLE
Caliber: .177. **Barrel:** Rifled, 16.5 in. **Weight:** Variable from 8.1 to 11 pounds. **Length:** Variable from 39.0 to 47 in. **Power:** Pre-charged pneumatic. **Stock:** Fully adjustable variable composition. **Sights:** Fully adjustable target sights with interchangeable inserts. **Features:** Single shot, ambidextrous grip, adjustable match trigger, exchangeable air cylinder with integrated manometer, approximately 200 shots per fill, available with a bewildering array of options. **Velocity:** 560 fps.
Price: .... $2,545.00 - $5,350.00

ASG TAC-4.5 CO2 BB RIFLE
Caliber: .177 steel BBs. **Barrel:** Smoothbore. **Weight:** 3.5 lbs. **Length:** 36.0 in. **Power:** CO2 **Stock:** Synthetic thumbhole stock. **Sights:** Fixed fiber-optic front sight and fully adjustable fiber-optic rear sight/weaver rail for optics. **Features:** Semi-automatic action, includes bi-pod, 21-shot capacity. **Velocity:** 417 fps.
Price: $119.99

ATAMAN M2R TACT CARBINE TYPE 2 AIR RIFLE
Calibers: .177, .22, .25, .30, .35. **Barrel:** Lothar Walther rifled match-grade, 20.47 in. **Weight:** 8.82 lbs. **Length:** 43.31 in. **Power:** Pre-charged pneumatic. **Stock:** Ambidextrous stock available in various configurations and finishes. **Sights:** weaver rails for scope mounting. **Features:** Multi-shot side-lever action, shot capacity varies on caliber, adjustable match trigger, finely tuned regulator matched to optimal velocity in each caliber for maximum accuracy. **Velocities:** .177, 980 fps/.22, 980 fps/.25, 980 fps/.30, 984 fps/.35, 900 fps.
Price: .... $1,499.99-$1,999.99

ATAMAN M2R BULLPUP TYPE 1 & 2 AIR RIFLE
Calibers: .22, .25, .35. **Barrel:** Lothar Walther rifled match-grade free-floating, 20.47 in. **Weight:** 8.81 lbs. **Length:** 32.12 in. **Power:** Pre-charged pneumatic. **Stock:** Ambidextrous bullpup stock available in walnut or "soft touch" synthetic. **Sights:** Integrated Picatinny rails for scope mounting. **Features:** Multi-shot side level action, shot capacity varies on caliber, adjustable match trigger, side-lever action, finely tuned regulator matched to optimal velocity in each caliber for maximum accuracy. **Velocities:** .22, 980 fps/.25, 980 fps/.35, 900 fps.
Price: $1,429.99–1,899.99

ATAMAN M2R CARBINE ULTRA COMPACT AIR RIFLE
Caliber: .22. **Barrel:** Lothar Walther rifled match-grade, 15.39 in. **Weight:** 6.17 lbs. **Length:** 36.48 in. **Power:** Pre-charged pneumatic. **Stock:** Ambidextrous adjustable/foldable stock available in walnut or "soft touch" synthetic. **Sights:** Weaver rails for scope mounting. **Features:** Multi-shot side-lever action, 10-shot capacity, adjustable match trigger, finely tuned regulator matched to optimal velocity. **Velocity:** 850 fps.
Price: $1,319.99

Prices given are believed to be accurate at time of publication however, many factors affect retail pricing so exact prices are not possible.

BEEMAN RS-2 DUAL-CALIBER GAS RAM AIR RIFLE COMBO
Calibers: .177, .22. **Barrel:** Rifled. **Weight:** 6.9 lbs. **Length:** 45.5 in. **Power:** Break-barrel, gas-piston. **Stock:** Ambidextrous hardwood stock. **Sights:** Fiber-optic front and rear, includes 4x32 scope and rings. **Features:** Single-shot, easily exchangeable .177 and .22 cal. barrels, two-stage trigger. **Velocities:** .177, 1,000 fps/.22, 830 fps.
Price: $179.99

BEEMAN QUIET TEK DC DUAL CALIBER GAS RAM AIR RIFLE COMBO
Calibers: .177, .22. **Barrel:** Rifled. **Weight:** 6.7 lbs. **Length:** 47 in. **Power:** Break-barrel, spring-piston. **Stock:** Ambidextrous synthetic stock. **Sights:** None, grooved for scope mounting, includes 4x32 scope and rings. **Features:** Integrated suppressor, single shot, easily exchangeable .177- and .22-cal. barrels, two-stage trigger. **Velocities:** .177, 1,000 fps/.22, 830 fps.
Price: $179.99

BEEMAN R7 AIR RIFLE
Calibers: .177, .20. **Barrel:** Rifled 13.5 in. **Weight:** 6.1 lbs. **Length:** 37 in. **Power:** Break-barrel, spring-piston. **Stock:** Ambidextrous walnut-stained beech, cut-checkered pistol grip, Monte Carlo comb and rubber buttpad. **Sights:** None, grooved for scope. **Features:** German quality, limited lifetime warranty, highly adjustable match-grade trigger, very easy to cock and shoot, extremely accurate. **Velocities:** .177, 700 fps/.20, 620 fps.
Price: ....$329.99–$379.99

BEEMAN R9 AIR RIFLE
Calibers: .177, .20, .22. **Barrel:** Rifled 16.33 in. **Weight:** 7.3 lbs. **Length:** 43 in. **Power:** Break-barrel, spring-piston. **Stock:** Ambidextrous walnut-stained beech, cut-checkered pistol grip, Monte Carlo comb and rubber buttpad. **Sights:** None, grooved for scope. **Features:** German quality, limited lifetime warranty, highly adjustable match-grade trigger, extremely accurate. **Velocities:** .177, 935 fps/.20, 800 fps/.22, 740 fps.
Price: ....$439.99–$479.99

BEEMAN RAM AIR RIFLE COMBO, RS2 TRIGGER
Calibers: .177, .22. **Barrel:** Rifled 20 in. **Weight:** 7.9 lbs. **Length:** 46.5 in. **Power:** Break-barrel, spring-piston. **Stock:** Ambidextrous hardwood stock. **Sights:** None, grooved for scope mounting, includes 3-9x32 scope and rings. **Features:** Muzzle brake for extra cocking leverage, single-shot, adjustable two-stage trigger. **Velocities:** .177, 1,000 fps/.22, 850 fps.
Price: $220.00

BEEMAN SILVER KODIAK X2 COMBO AIR RIFLE
Calibers: .177, .22. **Barrel:** Rifled. **Weight:** 8.75 lbs. **Length:** 47.75 in. **Power:** Break-barrel, spring-piston. **Stock:** Ambidextrous synthetic stock. **Sights:** None includes 4x32 scope and rings. **Features:** Satin finish nickel plated receiver and barrels, single-shot, easily exchangeable .177 and .22 cal barrels, two-stage trigger. **Velocities:** .177, 1,000 fps/.22, 830 fps.
Price: $169.99

BENJAMIN 392 / 397 AIR RIFLE
Calibers: .177, .22. **Barrel:** Rifled 19.25 in. **Weight:** 5.5 lbs. **Length:** 36.25 in. **Power:** Multi-pump Pneumatic. **Stock:** Ambidextrous wood or synthetic stock. **Sights:** Front ramp and adjustable rear sight. **Features:** Multi-pump system provides variable power, single-shot bolt action. **Velocities:** .177, 800 fps/.20, 685 fps.
Price: $172.99

BENJAMIN ARMADA, BASE, TACTICAL, & MAGPUL EDITION AIR RIFLE

BENJAMIN ARMADA
Calibers: .177, .22, .25. **Barrel:** Rifled, 20 in. **Weight:** 7.3 lbs. (10.3 lbs. with scope and bipod). **Length:** 42.8 in. **Power:** Pre-charged pneumatic. **Stock:** Adjustable mil-spec AR-15-style buttstock, all metal M-LOK compatible handguard with 15 in. of picatinny rail space. **Sights:** None, weaver/Picatinny rail for scope mounting. **Features:** Fully shrouded barrel with integrated suppressor, dampener device, bolt action, multi shot, choked barrel for maximum accuracy. **Velocities:** .177, 1,100 fps/.22, 1,000 fps/.25, 900 fps.
Price: $649.99

BENJAMIN AKELA PCP AIR RIFLE
Caliber: .22. **Barrel:** Rifled. **Weight:** 7.7 lbs. **Length:** 32.9 in. **Power:** Pre-charged pneumatic. **Stock:** Bullpup-style Turkish walnut. **Sights:** None, Picatinny rail for scope mounting. **Features:** Side-cocking lever, adjustable trigger shoe, 3,000-psi pressure, up to 60 shots per fill, 12-shot rotary magazine. **Velocity:** 1,000 fps.
Price: $649.99

BENJAMIN BULLDOG .357 BULLPUP

BENJAMIN BULLDOG .357 BULLPUP
Caliber: .357. **Barrel:** Rifled 28 in. **Weight:** 7.7 lbs. **Length:** 36 in. **Power:** Pre-charged pneumatic. **Stock:** Synthetic bullpup stock with pistol grip. **Sights:** Full top Picatinny rail. **Features:** Innovative bullpup design, massive power output of up to 180 ft-lbs, 5-shot magazine, shrouded barrel for noise reduction, large cylinder delivers up to 10 usable shots, available in multiple bundled configurations and stock finishes. **Velocity:** Up to 900 fps based on the weight of the projectile.
Price: ....$849.99-$1,099.99

BENJAMIN CAYDEN PCP AIR RIFLE
Caliber: .22. **Barrel:** Rifled. **Weight:** 7.95 lbs. **Length:** 40.8 in. **Power:** Pre-charged pneumatic. **Stock:** Turkish walnut stock with adjustable cheekpiece. **Sights:** None, grooved 11mm dovetail for scope mounting. **Features:** Side-cocking lever, adjustable trigger shoe, 3,000-psi pressure, up to 60 shots per fill, 12-shot rotary magazine. **Velocity:** 1,000 fps.
Price: $599.99

Prices given are believed to be accurate at time of publication however, many factors affect retail pricing so exact prices are not possible.

75TH EDITION, 2021 ◈ **557**

BENJAMIN FORTITUDE GEN 2 PCP RIFLE
Calibers: .177 or .22. **Barrel:** Rifled 24.25 in. **Weight:** 5.3 lbs. **Length:** 42.6 in. **Power:** Pre-charged pneumatic. **Stock:** Synthetic, ambidextrous. **Sights:** None, grooved 11mm dovetail for scope mounting. **Features:** Shrouded barrel with integrated suppressor, 10-shot rotary magazine, 3,000 PSI pressure gauge with regulator, 60 to 200 shots per fill, adjustable hammer spring. **Velocity:** 950 fps (.177), 850 fps (.22).
Price: **$319.99**

BENJAMIN IRONHIDE AIR RIFLE
Calibers: .177, .22. **Barrel:** Rifled, 15.75 in. **Weight:** 7.8 lbs. **Length:** 45.5 in. **Power:** Nitro Piston Elite break-barrel. **Stock:** Synthetic thumbhole stock. **Sights:** Fixed front and adjustable rear, includes CenterPoint 4x32 scope and mounts. **Features:** Single shot, sound suppression, adjustable two-stage trigger. **Velocity:** 1,400 fps (.177), 1,100 fps (.22).
Price: **$199.95**

BENJAMIN KRATOS PCP AIR RIFLE
Calibers: .22, .25. **Barrel:** Rifled. **Weight:** 8.26 lbs. **Length:** 43.35 in. **Power:** Pre-charged pneumatic. **Stock:** Turkish walnut stock with adjustable cheekpiece. **Sights:** None, Picatinny rail for scope mounting. **Features:** Side-cocking lever, adjustable trigger shoe, 3,000-psi pressure, up to 60 shots per fill, 12-shot rotary magazine in .22, 10-shot rotary magazine in .25. **Velocities:** 1,000 fps (.22), 900 fps (.25).
Price: **$699.99**

BENJAMIN MARAUDER PCP AIR RIFLE
Caliber: .177, .22, .25. **Barrel:** Rifled 20 in. **Weight:** Synthetic 7.3 lbs./ Hardwood 8.2 lbs. **Length:** 42.8 in. **Power:** Pre-charged pneumatic. **Stock:** Ambidextrous stock available in hardwood or synthetic, adjustable cheek riser. **Sights:** None, grooved for scope mounting. **Features:** Multi-shot bolt action, 10-shot in .177 and .22, 8-shot in .25, user-adjustable performance settings for power and shot count, reversible bolt handle. Also available with options such as an integrated regulator for shot-to-shot consistency, a Picatinny rail and a Lothar Walther barrel. **Velocities:** .177, 1,100 fps/.22, 1,000 fps/.25, 900 fps.
Price: ....**$579.99–$599.99**

BENJAMIN MARAUDER SEMIAUTOMATIC PCP AIR RIFLE
Caliber: .22. **Barrel:** Rifled, 20 in. **Weight:** 8.2 lbs. **Length:** 42.8 in. **Power:** Pre-charged pneumatic. **Stock:** Hardwood ambidextrous with adjustable cheek riser. **Sights:** None, grooved for scope mounting. **Features:** Multi-shot semi-automatic action, 10-shot, regulated, up to 60 shots per fill, ambidextrous charging handle, shrouded barrel with integrated resonance dampener. **Velocity:** 950 fps.
Price: **$729.99**

BENJAMIN PROWLER BREAK BARREL RIFLE
Calibers: .177, .22. **Barrel:** Rifled. **Weight:** 6.4 lbs. **Length:** 45 in. **Power:** Break-barrel, Nitro-Piston. **Stock:** Ambidextrous synthetic. **Sights:** None, comes with a CenterPoint 4x32 scope. **Features:** Reduced recoil, 35-pound cocking effort, single-shot, adjustable two-stage trigger. **Velocities:** 1,200 fps (.177), 950 fps (.22).
Price: **$149.95**

BENJAMIN TRAIL STEALTH NITRO PISTON 2 (NP2) BREAK BARREL AIR RIFLE
Calibers: .177, .22. **Barrel:** Rifled 15.75 in. **Weight:** 8.3 lbs. **Length:** 46.25 in. **Power:** Break-barrel, 2nd generation gas-piston. **Stock:** Ambidextrous thumbhole stock available in wood and synthetic options as well as multiple finishes and patterns. **Sights:** None, picatinny rail for scope mounting, multiple Crosman CenterPoint scope options available as factory bundles. **Features:** Very quiet due to the shrouded barrel with integrated suppressor, extremely easy cocking, single-shot, advanced adjustable two-stage trigger, innovative sling mounts for optional Benjamin break-barrel rifle sling. **Velocities:** .177, 1,400 fps/.22, 1,100 fps.
Price: ....**$295.95–$349.95**

BENJAMIN TRAIL NITRO PISTON 2 (NP2) SBD BREAK BARREL AIR RIFLE
Calibers: .177, .22. **Barrel:** Rifled 15.75 in. **Weight:** 8.3 lbs. **Length:** 45.6 in. **Power:** Break-barrel, 2nd generation gas-piston. **Stock:** Ambidextrous thumbhole stock available in wood and synthetic options as well as multiple finishes and patterns. **Sights:** None, Picatinny rail for scope mounting, multiple Crosman CenterPoint scope options available as factory bundles. **Features:** Newly introduced SBD integrated suppressor

does not interfere with scope sight picture, extremely easy cocking, single-shot, advanced adjustable two-stage trigger, innovative sling mounts for optional Benjamin break-barrel rifle sling. **Velocities:** .177, 1,400 fps/.22, 1,100 fps.
Price: ....**$299.95–$339.99**

BENJAMIN MAXIMUS PCP AIR RIFLE
Calibers: .177, .22. **Barrel:** Rifled 26.25 in. **Weight:** 5.0 lbs. **Length:** 41.7 in. **Power:** Pre-Charged Pneumatic. **Stock:** Ambidextrous synthetic stock. **Sights:** Front Fiber-optic and adjustable rear fiber-optic sight/grooved 11mm dovetail for scope mounting. **Features:** HPA required only 2000 psi to operate, built in pressure gauge. **Velocities:** .177, 1,000 fps/.22, 850 fps.
Price: **$219.99**

BENJAMIN VARMINT POWER PACK
Caliber: .22. **Barrel:** Rifled. **Weight:** 7.38 lbs. **Length:** 44.5 in. **Power:** Break-barrel, gas-piston. **Stock:** Ambidextrous synthetic stock. **Sights:** none, Weaver rail for scope mounting, includes a Crosman CenterPoint 4x32 scope with laser and light attachments complete with intermittent pressure switches. **Features:** Shrouded barrel, easy cocking, single-shot, adjustable two-stage trigger. **Velocity:** 950 fps.
Price: **$249.95**

BENJAMIN WILDFIRE SEMI-AUTOMATIC PCP AIR RIFLE
Caliber: .177. **Barrel:** Rifled 20.39 in. **Weight:** 3.69 lbs. **Length:** 36.88 in. **Power:** Pre-Charged Pneumatic. **Stock:** Ambidextrous synthetic stock. **Sights:** Front fiber- optic and adjustable rear sight/grooved 11mm dovetail for scope mounting. **Features:** HPA required only 2000 psi to operate, built in pressure gauge, 12-shot semi-automatic system, double-action only. **Velocity:** .177, 800 fps.
Price: **$149.99**

BERETTA CX4 STORM

BERETTA CX4 STORM RIFLE
Caliber: .177 pellets. **Barrel:** Rifled 17.5 in. **Weight:** 5.25 lbs. **Length:** 30.75 in. **Power:** CO2. **Stock:** Synthetic thumbole. **Sights:** Adjustable front and rear. **Features:** Multi-shot semi-automatic with 30-round belt-fed magazine, highly realistic replica, utilizes large 88/90 gram disposable CO2 canisters for high shot count and uninterrupted shooting sessions. Available bundled with a Walther red-dot optics. **Velocity:** 600 fps.
Price: ....**$375.95–$400.00**

BLACK OPS TACTICAL SNIPER GAS-PISTON AIR RIFLE
Calibers: .177, .22. **Barrel:** Rifled. **Weight:** 9.6 in. **Length:** 44.0 in. **Power:** Break-barrel, gas-piston. **Stock:** Ambidextrous pistol grip synthetic stock. **Sights:** none, Weaver rail for scope mounting, includes a 4x32 scope. **Features:** Muzzle break helps with cocking force, single-shot, single cock delivers maximum power, adjustable single-stage trigger. **Velocity:** .177, 1,250 fps/.22, 1,000 fps.
Price: ....**$179.99–$199.99**

Prices given are believed to be accurate at time of publication however, many factors affect retail pricing so exact prices are not possible.

BROCOCK BANTAM HI-LITE PCP RIFLE
Caliber: .25. **Barrel:** Rifled, Lothar Walther barrel. **Weight:** 6.4 lbs. **Length:** 34 in. **Power:** Pre-charged pneumatic. **Stock:** Semi-bullpup, beech wood. **Sights:** None, grooved for scope mounting. **Features:** 10-shot magazine, 480cc carbon-fiber air bottle, adjustable cheek piece and buttpad, three-step power adjuster. **Velocities:** NA.
Price: $1,554.99

BROWNING LEVERAGE AIR RIFLE
Calibers: .177, .22. **Barrel:** Rifled 18.9 in. **Weight:** 8.6 lbs. **Length:** 44.8 in. **Power:** Under-lever cock, spring-piston **Stock:** Hardwood right handed with raised cheekpiece. **Sights:** Front fiber-optic sight and fully adjustable rear fiber-optic sight, Weaver/Picatinny rail for scope mounting, includes 3-9x40 scope. **Features:** Fixed barrel accuracy, easy cocking, two-stage trigger. **Velocities:** .177, 1,000 fps/.22, 800 fps.
Price: $230.00

BSA R-10 SE PCP AIR RIFLE
Calibers: .177, .22. **Barrel:** Rifled, BSA-made cold hammer forged precision barrel, 19 in. **Weight:** 7.3 lbs. **Length:** 44 in. **Power:** Pre-charged pneumatic. **Stock:** Available right- or left-hand, walnut, laminate, camo or black synthetic. **Sights:** None, grooved for scope mounting. **Features:** Multi-shot bolt action, 10-shot magazine (eight-shot for .25 caliber), fully regulated valve for maximum accuracy and shot consistency, free-floating, shrouded barrel, also available with lower power/velocity and as a shorter carbine. **Velocities:** 1,000 fps (.177)/980 fps (.22).
Price: 1,299.99-1,495.99

BSA BUCCANEER SE AIR RIFLE
Calibers: .177, .22. **Barrel:** Rifled, BSA-made cold hammer forged precision barrel, 24 in. **Weight:** 7.7 lbs. **Length:** 42.5 in. **Power:** Pre-charged pneumatic. **Stock:** Ambidextrous beech stock or hardwood stock wrapped in innovative black soft-touch. **Sights:** None, grooved for scope mounting. **Features:** Multi-shot bolt action, 10-shot magazine, enhanced valve system for maximum shot count and consistency, integrated suppressor, adjustable two-stage trigger. **Velocities:** .177, 1,000 fps/.22, 800 fps.
Price: ....$649.99–$749.99

BSA DEFIANT BULLPUP AIR RIFLE
Calibers: .177, .22. **Barrel:** Rifled, cold hammer forged precision barrel, 18.5 in. **Weight:** 9 lbs. **Length:** 31 in. **Power:** Pre-charged pneumatic. **Stock:** Ambidextrous walnut, black soft-touch or black pepper laminate with adjustable buttpad. **Sights:** None, grooved for scope mounting. **Features:** Multi-shot bolt action, two 10-shot magazines, enhanced valve system for maximum shot count and consistency, integrated suppressor, adjustable two-stage trigger. **Velocities:** .177, 825 fps /.22. 570 fps.
Price: .... $NA

BSA GOLD STAR SE HUNTER FIELD TARGET PCP AIR RIFLE
Caliber: .177. **Barrel:** Rifled, BSA-made enhanced cold hammer forged precision barrel, 15.2 in. **Weight:** 7 lbs. **Length:** 35.8 in. **Power:** Pre-charged pneumatic. **Stock:** Highly adjustable gray laminate field target competition stock. **Sights:** None, grooved for scope mounting. **Features:** Multi-shot boltaction, 10-shot magazine, fully regulated valve for maximum accuracy and shot consistency, 70 consistent shots per charge, free-floating barrel with 1/2 UNF threaded muzzle, includes adjustable air stripper, adjustable match-grade trigger. **Velocity:** 800 fps.
Price: $1,499.99

BSA SCORPION PCP AIR RIFLE
Caliber: .177. **Barrel:** Rifled, free-floated match-grade barrel, 18.5 in. **Weight:** 7.7 lbs. **Length:** 36.5 in. **Power:** Pre-charged pneumatic. **Stock:** Monte Carlo wood stock with checkered grip and forearm. **Sights:** None, 11 mm scope rail. **Features:** Single-shot bolt action, bolt can be swapped from right hand to left hand, sling swivel studs, approximately 25 shots per fill, two-stage adjustable trigger. **Velocity:** 1000 fps.
Price: $900.00

BSA ULTRA XL AIR RIFLE
Calibers: .177, .22. **Barrel:** Rifled, BSA-made cold hammer forged precision barrel, 15.2 in. **Weight:** 7.3 lbs. **Length:** 35.4 in. **Power:** Pre-charged pneumatic. **Stock:** Ambidextrous, thumbhole, adjustable cheek piece, wood. **Sights:** None, grooved for scope mounting. **Features:** 10-shot magazine, fully regulated valve for maximum accuracy and shot consistency, free-floating, shrouded barrel, single-stage adjustable trigger, removable muzzle brake, also available as the JSR version for smaller framed shooters. **Velocities:** .177, 700 fps/.22, 570 fps.
Price: $750.00

CROSMAN CHALLENGER PCP COMPETITION

CROSMAN CHALLENGER PCP COMPETITION AIR RIFLE
Caliber: .177. **Barrel:** Match-grade Lothar Walther rifled barrel. **Weight:** 7.3 lbs. **Length:** 41.75 in. **Power:** Pre-charged pneumatic/CO2. **Stock:** Highly adjustable synthetic competition stock. **Sights:** Globe front sight and Precision Diopter rear sight. **Features:** Innovative dual fuel design allows this rifle to run on HPA or CO2, single-shot, adjustable match-grade trigger, approved by the Civilian Marksmanship Program (CMP) for 3-position air rifle Sporter Class competition. **Velocity:** 530 fps.
Price: $700.00-900.00

CROSMAN GENESIS NP AIR RIFLE
Caliber: .22. **Barrel:** Rifled. **Weight:** 7.44 lbs. **Length:** 44.5 in. **Power:** Break-barrel, gas-piston. **Stock:** Ambidextrous wood stock with dual raised cheekpieces and checkered grip and forearm. **Sights:** None, Weaver/Picatinny rail for scope mounting, includes 4x32 scope and rings. **Features:** Shrouded barrel with integrated suppressor, extremely easy cocking, single-shot, adjustable two-stage trigger, innovative sling mounts for optional Benjamin break-barrel rifle sling. **Velocity:** 950 fps**Price:** $229.99

CROSMAN FULL AUTO AK1 RIFLE
Caliber: .177 BBs. **Barrel:** Rifled. **Weight:** NA. **Length:** NA. **Power:** CO2. **Stock:** Synthetic adjustable/folding 5-position buttstock. **Sights:** Open. **Features:** Releasable magazine holds two CO2 cartridges and spring-feeds 28 BBs, shoots full- or semi-auto with blowback, AK compatible pistol grip, quad-rail forearm for accessory mounting. **Velocity:** 430 fps.
Price: $375.00

CROSMAN M4-177

CROSMAN M4-177 RIFLE (various styles and kits available)
Caliber: .177 steel BBs, .177 pellets. **Barrel:** Rifled 17.25 in. **Weight:** 3.75 lbs. **Length:** 33.75 in. **Power:** Multi-pump pneumatic. **Stock:** M4-style adjustable plastic stock. **Sights:** Weaver/Picatinny rail for scope mounting and flip-up sights. Bundled packages include various included sighting options. **Features:** Single-shot bolt action, lightweight and very accurate, multiple colors available. "Ready to go" kits available complete with ammo, safety glasses, targets and extra 5-shot pellet magazines. **Velocity:** 660 fps.
Price: ....$89.99-$149.99

Prices given are believed to be accurate at time of publication however, many factors affect retail pricing so exact prices are not possible.

75TH EDITION, 2021 ⊕ **559**

CROSMAN MODEL 760 PUMPMASTER AIR RIFLE
Caliber: .177 steel BBs, .177 pellets. **Barrel:** Rifled 16.75 in. **Weight:** 2.75 lbs. **Length:** 33.5 in. **Power:** Multi-pump pneumatic. **Stock:** Ambidextrous plastic stock. **Sights:** Blade and ramp, rear sight adjustable for elevation, grooved for scope mounting. **Features:** Single-shot pellet, BB repeater, bolt action, lightweight, accurate and easy to shoot. Multiple colors available and configurations available. "Ready to go" kits available complete with ammo, safety glasses, targets and extra 5-shot pellet magazines. **Velocity:** 625 fps.
Price: ....$50.00–$60.00

CROSMAN DIAMONDBACK SBD AIR RIFLE
Caliber: .22. **Barrel:** Rifled. **Weight:** 8.5 lbs. **Length:** 46.5 in. **Power:** Break-barrel, Nitro-piston. **Stock:** Synthetic with pistol grip. **Sights:** Open sights, dovetail for scope mounting, includes CenterPoint 4x32 scope and rings. **Features:** SBD sound-suppression system, sling mounts, single-shot, adjustable two-stage trigger. **Velocities:** 1,100 fps.
Price: $189.95

CROSMAN FIRE NITRO PISTON AIR RIFLE
Caliber: .177. **Barrel:** Rifled. **Weight:** 6 lbs. **Length:** 43.5 in. **Power:** Break-barrel, Nitro-piston. **Stock:** Synthetic thumbhole style. **Sights:** None, dovetail for scope mounting, includes CenterPoint 4x32 scope and rings. **Features:** Integrated muzzle brake for reduced recoil and noise, single-shot, adjustable two-stage trigger. **Velocities:** 1,200 fps.
Price: $149.95

CROSMAN OPTIMUS AIR RIFLE COMBO
Caliber: .177, .22. **Barrel:** Rifled. **Weight:** 6.5 lbs. **Length:** 43 in. **Power:** Break-barrel. **Stock:** Ambidextrous wood. **Sights:** Fiber-optic with adjustable rear sight, dovetail for scope mounting, includes CenterPoint 4x32 scope and rings. **Features:** Single-shot, adjustable two-stage trigger. **Velocities:** 1,200 fps (.177)/950 fps (.22).
Price: $149.99

CROSMAN QUEST SBD AIR RIFLE, NP ELITE
Caliber: .177, .22. **Barrel:** Rifled 15.75 in. **Weight:** 7.8 lbs. **Length:** 45.5 in. **Power:** Break-barrel, Nitro-Piston. **Stock:** Synthetic. **Sights:** None, dovetail for scope mounting, includes CenterPoint 4x32 scope and rings. **Features:** SBD sound suppression, single-shot, adjustable two-stage trigger. **Velocities:** 1,400 fps (.177)/1,100 fps (.22) with alloy pellet.
Price: $184.99

CROSMAN REPEATAIR 1077/1077 FREESTYLE AIR RIFLE
Caliber: .177 pellets. **Barrel:** Rifled 20.38 in. **Weight:** 3.75 lbs. **Length:** 36.88 in. **Power:** CO2. **Stock:** Ambidextrous plastic stock. **Sights:** Blade and ramp, rear sight adjustable for windage and elevation, grooved for scope mounting. **Features:** Multi-shot, semi-automatic, 12-shot magazine, lightweight, fun and easy to shoot. "Ready to go" kits available complete with ammo, CO2, targets, target trap, etc. **Velocity:** 625 fps.
Price: ....$94.99-$129.99

CROSMAN 2100B CLASSIC AIR RIFLE
Caliber: .177 steel BBs, .177 pellets. **Barrel:** Rifled 20.84 in. **Weight:** 4.81 lbs. **Length:** 39.75 in. **Power:** Multi-pump pneumatic. **Stock:** Ambidextrous plastic stock with simulated wood grain. **Sights:** Blade and ramp, rear sight adjustable for windage and elevation, grooved for scope mounting. **Features:** Adult-size inexpensive airgun, single-shot, bolt action, lightweight, accurate and easy to shoot. **Velocity:** 755 fps.
Price: $79.95

CROSMAN SHOCKWAVE NP AIR RIFLE
Calibers: .177, .22. **Barrel:** Rifled 15.00 in. **Weight:** 6.0 lbs. **Length:** 43.5 in. **Power:** Break-barrel, gas-piston. **Stock:** Ambidextrous synthetic with dual raised cheekpieces. **Sights:** Front fiber-optic sight and fully adjustable fiber-

optic rear sight, Weaver/Picatinny rail for scope mounting, includes 4x32 scope and rings. **Features:** Single-shot, includes bipod, adjustable two-stage trigger. **Velocities:** .177, 1,200 fps/.22, 950 fps.
Price: $169.99

CROSMAN TYRO AIR RIFLE
Calibers: .177. **Barrel:** Rifled. **Weight:** 4.9 lbs. **Length:** 37.5 in. **Power:** Break-barrel, spring-piston. **Stock:** Synthetic thumbhole with spacers to adjust length of pull. **Sights:** Front fiber-optic sight and adjustable rear sight. **Features:** Single shot, sized for smaller shooters. **Velocities:** 720 fps with alloy pellet.
Price: $105.99

DAISY 1938 RED RYDER

DAISY 1938 RED RYDER AIR RIFLE
Caliber: .177 steel BBs. **Barrel:** Smoothbore 10.85 in. **Weight:** 2.2 lbs. **Length:** 35.4 in. **Power:** Single-cock, lever action, spring-piston. **Stock:** Solid wood stock and fore-end. **Sights:** Blade front sight, adjustable rear sight. **Features:** 650 BB reservoir, single-stage trigger, designed for all day fun and backyard plinking, exceptional first airgun for young shooters. **Velocity:** 350 fps.
Price: $56.99

DAISY ADULT RED RYDER BB RIFLE
Caliber: .177 steel BBs. **Barrel:** Smoothbore, 10.85 in. **Weight:** 2.95 lbs. **Length:** 36.75 in. **Power:** Single-cock, lever-action, spring-piston. **Stock:** Solid wood stock and fore-end. **Sights:** Blade front sight, adjustable rear sight. **Features:** A larger, adult-size version of the classic youth Red Ryder with 650-shot reservoir. 18-pound cocking effort. **Velocity:** 350 fps.
Price: $52.99

DAISY MODEL 887 GOLD MEDALIST COMPETITION
Caliber: .177 pellets. **Barrel:** Rifled, match-grade Lothar Walther barrel, 20.88 in. **Weight:** 6.9 lbs. **Length:** 38.5 in. **Power:** CO2. **Stock:** Ambidextrous laminated wood stock. **Sights:** Globe front sight and Precision Diopter rear sight. **Features:** Precision bored and crowned barrel for match accuracy, bulk fill CO2 is capable of up to 300 shots, additional inserts available for front sight, ideal entry level rifle for all 10-meter shooting disciplines. **Velocity:** 500 fps.
Price: $563.99

DAISY MODEL 499B CHAMPION COMPETITION RIFLE
Caliber: .177 BBs. **Barrel:** Smoothbore, 20.88 in. **Weight:** 3.1 lbs. **Length:** 36.25. **Power:** Lever-action spring piston. **Stock:** Hardwood. **Sights:** Hooded front with aperture inserts and adjustable rear peep sight. **Features:** Single-shot, 5-meter competition rifle. **Velocity:** 240 fps.
Price: $164.99

DAISY MODEL 599 COMPETITION AIR RIFLE
Caliber: .177 pellets. **Barrel:** Rifled, cold hammer forged BSA barrel, 20.88 in. **Weight:** 7.1 lbs. **Length:** 34.35-37.25 in. **Power:** Pre-charged pneumatic. **Stock:** Ambidextrous beech wood stock with vertical and length-of-pull adjustment, adjustable comb. **Sights:** Hooded front and diopter rear sight. **Features:** Trigger weight adjustable down to 1.5 lbs., rotating trigger adjustment for positioning right or left, straight pull T-bolt handle, removable power cylinder. **Velocity:** 520 fps.
Price: $595.00

DAISY MODEL 25 PUMP GUN
Caliber: .177 steel BBs. **Barrel:** Smoothbore. **Weight:** 3 lbs. **Length:** 37 in. **Power:** pump action, spring-air. **Stock:** Solid wood buttstock. **Sights:** Fixed front and rear sights. **Features:** 50 shot BB reservoir, removable screw out shot tube, decorative engraving on receiver, rear sight can be flipped over to change from open to peep sight. **Velocity:** 350 fps.
Price: $47.99

DAISY MODEL 105 BUCK AIR RIFLE
Caliber: .177 steel BBs. **Barrel:** Smoothbore 7.97 in. **Weight:** 1.6 lbs. **Length:** 29.8 in. **Power:** Single-cock, lever action, spring-piston. **Stock:** Solid wood buttstock. **Sights:** Fixed front and rear sights. **Features:** 400 BB reservoir, single-stage trigger, designed for all day fun and backyard plinking. **Velocity:** 275 fps.
Price: $35.99

DAISY MODEL 753 ELITE

DAISY MODEL 753S MATCH GRADE AVANTI
Caliber: .177 pellets. **Barrel:** Rifled, Lothar Walther, 19.5 in. **Weight:** 7.3 lbs. **Length:** 38.5 in. **Power:** Single-stroke pneumatic. **Stock:** Ambidextrous wood stock & Synthetic stock available **Sights:** Globe front sight and Precision Diopter rear sight. **Features:** Full-size wood stock, additional inserts available for front sight, fully self-contained power system, excellent "first" rifle for all 10-meter shooting disciplines. **Velocity:** 495 fps.
Price: ....$300.00–$469.99

DAISY PINK 1998 BB GUN
Caliber: .177, steel BBs. **Barrel:** Smoothbore 10.85 in. **Weight:** 2.2 lbs. **Length:** 35.4 in. **Power:** Single-cock, lever action, spring-piston. **Stock:** Solid wood stock and forearm painted pink. **Sights:** Blade front sight, adjustable rear sight. **Features:** 650 BB reservoir, single-stage trigger, designed for all day fun and backyard plinking, great option for young ladies just starting out. **Velocity:** 350 fps.
Price: $47.99

DAISY POWERLINE MODEL 880 AIR RIFLE
Caliber: .177 steel BBs, .177 pellets. **Barrel:** Rifled, 21 in. **Weight:** 3.1 lbs. **Length:** 37.6 in. **Power:** Multi-pump pneumatic. **Stock:** Synthetic. **Sights:** Fiber-optic front sight, rear sight adjustable for elevation, grooved for scope mounting. **Features:** Single-shot pellet, 50 shot BB, lightweight, accurate and easy to shoot. **Velocity:** 800 fps (BBs), 665 fps (pellets).
Price: $55.99

DAISY POWERLINE MODEL 35 AIR RIFLE
Caliber: .177 steel BBs, .177 pellets. **Barrel:** Smoothbore. **Weight:** 2.25 lbs. **Length:** 34.5 in. **Power:** Multi-pump pneumatic. **Stock:** Ambidextrous plastic stock, available in black and pink camo. **Sights:** Blade and ramp, rear sight adjustable for elevation, grooved for scope mounting. **Features:** Single-shot pellet, BB rep, lightweight, accurate and easy to shoot. **Velocity:** 625 fps.
Price: ....$41.99-$69.95

DAISY POWERLINE 901 AIR RIFLE
Caliber: .177 steel BBs, .177 pellets. **Barrel:** Rifled 20.8 in. **Weight:** 3.2 lbs. **Length:** 37.75 in. **Power:** Multi-pump pneumatic **Stock:** Ambidextrous black wood grain plastic stock. **Sights:** Front fiber-optic sight, rear blade sight adjustable for elevation, grooved for scope mounting. **Features:** Full-size adult airgun, single-shot pellet, BB repeater, bolt action, lightweight, accurate and easy to shoot. "Ready to go" kit available complete with ammo, safety glasses, shatterblast targets, 4x15 scope and mounts. **Velocity:** 750 fps.
Price: ....$71.99–$95.99

DAYSTATE DELTA WOLF RIFLE
Calibers: .177, .22, .25, .30. **Barrel:** Rifled, 43 cm (.177 or .22) or 60 cm (.177, .22, .25, .30). **Weight:** 6.8 lbs. **Length:** 34 in. **Power:** Pre-charged pneumatic. **Stock:** AR-style. **Sights:** None, 22mm Picatinny rail. **Features:** Advanced Velocity Technology with display touch screen, multi-caliber with fast-change barrel system, factory set power profiles for each caliber, built-in chronoscope that allows the shooter to dial in the preferred velocity, OEM Huma-Air regulated, large-capacity (813-shot) magazine, Bluetooth connectivity, switchable side-lever action, carbon-fiber shroud and optional silencer, removable air tank. **Velocity:** NA.
Price: $2,999.99

DAYSTATE HUNTSMAN REGAL XL AIR RIFLE
Calibers: .177, .22, .25. **Barrel:** Rifled 17 in. **Weight:** 6.17 lbs. **Length:** 40.0 in. **Power:** Pre-charged pneumatic. **Stock:** Right-handed Monte Carlo hardwood. **Sights:** None, 11mm grooved dovetail for scope mounting. **Features:** Features the exceptional pedigree of the finest European airguns, 10-shot rotary magazine, rear bolt action, adjustable trigger, fully moderated barrel. **Velocity:** (not provided).
Price: $1,499.99

DAYSTATE RED WOLF RIFLE
Calibers: .177, .22, .25. **Barrel:** Match grade rifled Lothar Walther 17 in. **Weight:** 7.5 lbs. **Length:** 39 in. **Power:** Pre-charged pneumatic. **Stock:** Fully adjustable walnut. **Sights:** None, 11mm grooved dovetail for scope mounting. **Features:** Three individual programmed energy and velocity settings, computer controlled state-of-the-art MCT firing system, LCD screen displays air pressure, battery state, number of shots fired. Ten-shot magazine, fully adjustable trigger from ounces to pounds, stock provides cheek-piece adjustments for height, left and right canting as well as buttpad adjustment for up, down, left and right. **Velocity:** NA.
Price: $2,899.99

DAYSTATE TSAR TARGET RIFLE
Calibers: .177 pellet. **Barrel:** Match grade rifled Lothar Walther 20.5 in. **Weight:** 9.9 lbs. **Length:** 39 in. **Power:** Pre-charged pneumatic. **Stock:** Laminate. **Sights:** None, 11mm grooved dovetail for scope mounting. **Features:** Adjustable cheek rest and buttpad, five-level adjustable multi-sear trigger, fully moderated barrel, designed for field target competition, side lever cocking system allows for dry-firing practice. **Velocity:** (not provided).
Price: $2,935.90

DIANA AR8 N-TEC AIR RIFLE
Calibers: .177, .22. **Barrel:** Rifled 19.5 in. **Weight:** 8.45 lbs. **Length:** 48.0 in. **Power:** Break-barrel, German gas-piston. **Stock:** Ambidextrous synthetic thumbhole stock. **Sights:** Front post and fully adjustable rear sight, grooved for scope mounting. **Features:** European quality, exceptional two-stage adjustable match trigger, single-shot, German manufactured to stringent quality control and testing, limited lifetime warranty. The new N-TEC gas-piston power plant boasts smoother cocking and shooting, making the N-TEC line of Diana guns the most refined Diana airguns to date. **Velocities:** .177, 1,320 fps/.22, 975 fps.
Price: $399.99

DIANA 240 CLASSIC AIR RIFLE
Caliber: .177. **Barrel:** Rifled 16.5 in. **Weight:** 5.0 lbs. **Length:** 40 in. **Power:** Break-barrel, spring-piston. **Stock:** Ambidextrous beech stock. **Sights:** Front fiber-optic sight and fully adjustable rear fiber-optic sight, grooved for scope mounting. **Features:** European quality, exceptional two-stage adjustable trigger, single-shot, German manufactured to stringent quality control and testing, limited lifetime warranty. Various bundled configurations available. **Velocity:** .177, 580 fps.
Price: $219.99

DIANA Mauser K98 AIR RIFLE
Calibers: .177, .22. **Barrel:** Rifled 18.0 in. **Weight:** 9.5 lbs. **Length:** 44 in. **Power:** Break-barrel, spring-piston. **Stock:** Authentic Mauser K98 hardwood stock. **Sights:** Front post and fully adjustable rear sight, 11mm dovetail grooved for scope mounting. **Features:** European quality, fixed barrel with underlever cocking, exceptional two-stage adjustable match trigger, single-shot, German manufactured to stringent quality control and testing, limited lifetime warranty. **Velocities:** .177, 1,150 fps/.22, 850 fps.
Price: $469.99

DIANA RWS 34P STRIKER COMBO
Calibers: .177, .22. **Barrel:** Rifled 19.0 in. **Weight:** 7.75 lbs. **Length:** 46 in. **Power:** Break-barrel, spring-piston. **Stock:** Ambidextrous beech or synthetic stock. **Sights:** Front fiber-optic sight and fully adjustable rear fiber-optic sight, grooved for scope mounting. **Features:** European quality, exceptional two-stage adjustable match trigger, single-shot, German manufactured to stringent quality control and testing, limited lifetime warranty. Various bundled configurations available. **Velocity:** .177, 1,000 fps/.22, 800 fps.
Price: $399.99

DIANA MODEL 340
AIR RIFLE

DIANA 340 N-TEC PREMIUM AIR RIFLE
Calibers: .177, .22. **Barrel:** Rifled 19.5 in. **Weight:** 7.9 lbs. **Length:** 46 in. **Power:** Break-barrel, German gas-piston. **Stock:** Ambidextrous beech stock. **Sights:** Front fiber-optic sight and fully adjustable rear fiber-optic sight, grooved for scope mounting. **Features:** European quality, exceptional two-stage adjustable match trigger, single-shot, German manufactured to stringent quality control and testing, limited lifetime warranty. The new N-TEC gas-piston power plant boasts smoother cocking and shooting, making the N-TEC line of Diana guns the most refined Diana airguns to date. Various bundled configurations available. **Velocities:** .177, 1,000 fps/.22, 800 fps.
Price: $449.99

DIANA RWS 350 MAGNUM
Calibers: .177, .22. **Barrel:** Rifled 19.25 in. **Weight:** 8.2 lbs. **Length:** 48 in. **Power:** Break-barrel, spring-piston. **Stock:** Right handed beech stock with grip and forearm checkering. **Sights:** Post and globe front sight and fully adjustable rear sight, grooved for scope mounting. **Features:** European quality, exceptional two-stage adjustable match trigger, single-shot, German manufactured to stringent quality control and testing, limited lifetime warranty. Various bundled configurations available. **Velocities:** .177, 1,250 fps/.22, 1,000 fps.
Price: $429.95

DIANA 350 N-TEC MAGNUM PREMIUM AIR RIFLE
Calibers: .177, .22. **Barrel:** Rifled 19.5 in. **Weight:** 6.7 lbs. **Length:** 48.5 in. **Power:** Break-barrel, German gas-piston. **Stock:** Ambidextrous stock, available in beech and synthetic options. **Sights:** Front post and fully adjustable rear sight, grooved for scope mounting. **Features:** European quality, exceptional two-stage adjustable match trigger, single-shot, German manufactured to stringent quality control and testing, limited lifetime warranty. The new N-TEC gas-piston power plant boasts smoother cocking and shooting, making the N-TEC line of Diana guns the most refined Diana airguns to date. **Velocities:** .177, 1,250 fps/.22, 1,000 fps.
Price: $499.99

DIANA MODEL 48 AIR RIFLE

DIANA MODEL RWS 48 AIR RIFLE, T06 TRIGGER
Calibers: .177, .22. **Barrel:** Rifled 17 in. **Weight:** 8.5 lbs. **Length:** 42.13 in. **Power:** Single-cock, side-lever, spring-piston. **Stock:** Ambidextrous beech thumbhole stock. **Sights:** Blade front sight, fully adjustable rear sight, grooved for scope mounting. **Features:** European quality, exceptional two-stage match trigger, single-shot, German manufactured to stringent quality control and testing, limited lifetime warranty. **Velocities:** .177, 1,100 fps/.22, 900 fps.
Price: $398.95

DIANA 460 MAGNUM
Calibers: .177, .22. **Barrel:** Rifled 18.44 in. **Weight:** 8.3 lbs. **Length:** 45 in. **Power:** Under-lever, spring-piston. **Stock:** Right-hand hardwood stock with grip and fore-end checkering. **Sights:** Post front sight and fully adjustable rear sight, grooved for scope mounting. **Features:** European quality, exceptional two-stage adjustable match trigger, single-shot, German manufactured to stringent quality control and testing, limited lifetime warranty. Various bundled configurations available. **Velocity:** .177, 1,200 fps/.22, 1,000 fps.
Price: $419.99

DIANA 56 TARGET HUNTER AIR RIFLE
Calibers: .177, .22. **Barrel:** Rifled 17.3 in. **Weight:** 11.1 lbs. **Length:** 44 in. **Power:** Single-cock, side-lever, spring-piston. **Stock:** Ambidextrous beech thumbhole stock. **Sights:** None, grooved for scope mounting. **Features:** European quality, exceptional two-stage match trigger, single-shot, German manufactured to stringent quality control and testing. **Velocities:** .177, 1,100 fps/.22, 890 fps.
Price: ....$799.99-$999.99

DIANA STORMRIDER GEN 2 PCP RIFLE
Calibers: .177, .22. **Barrel:** Rifled 19 in. **Weight:** 5.0 lbs. **Length:** 40.5 in. **Power:** Pre-charged pneumatic. **Stock:** Checkered beech stock. **Sights:** Blade front, fully adjustable rear, 11 mm dovetail grove. **Features:** Entry level PCP rifle, nine-shot (.177) or seven-shot (.22) capacity, adjustable two-stage trigger, built-in muzzle brake, integrated pressure gauge. **Velocities:** 1,050 fps (.177)/900 fps (.22).
Price: $219.99

DPMS CLASSIC A4 NITRO PISTON AIR RIFLE
Caliber: .177 pellets. **Barrel:** Rifled 15 in. **Weight:** 7 lbs. **Length:** 40 in. **Power:** Break-barrel, gas-piston. **Stock:** Ambidextrous AR-15-styled stock. **Sights:** none, Weaver/Picatinny rail for flip-up sights and scope mounting, includes 4x32 scope and rings. **Features:** Aggressive and realistic AR-15 styling. Sling mounts, single-shot, adjustable two-stage trigger. **Velocity:** 1,200 fps.
Price: $229.95

Prices given are believed to be accurate at time of publication however, many factors affect retail pricing so exact prices are not possible.

DPMS SBR FULL AUTO BB RIFLE
Caliber: .177 BB. **Barrel:** Smoothbore. **Weight:** 6.2 lbs. **Length:** 26.5 in. **Power:** CO2. **Stock:** Adjustable six-position buttstock with AR compatible pistol grip. **Sights:** Folding BUIS front and rear with Picatinny rail. **Features:** Blowback action, quad rail forearm for accessory mounting, 25-round drop-out magazine, fully auto with up to 1,400 rounds per minute. **Velocity:** 430 fps.
Price: $199.99

EDGUN LESHIY GEN2 PCP RIFLE
Calibers: .177, .22, .25. **Barrel:** Rifled, Lothar Walther, 10-14 in. **Weight:** 4.25 lbs. **Length:** 25 in., (without moderator) overall. **Power:** Pre-charged pneumatic. **Stock:** Ambidextrous adjustable. **Sights:** None, Weaver-style rail for scope mounting. **Features:** Single shot, folds in the center to cock the action, can be stored while folded making it compact to carry, chassis CNC machined out of aluminum, easily switchable between calibers with replacement barrels, up to 40 shots per fill depending on caliber. **Velocities:** Approximately 950 fps (adjustable).
Price: $1,395.99

EVANIX RAINSTORM II PCP AIR RIFLE
Calibers: .22, .25, .30, .35 (9mm). **Barrel:** Rifled, 17.00 in. **Weight:** 7.2 lbs. **Length:** 39.00 in. overall. **Power:** Pre-charged Pneumatic. **Stock:** Ambidextrous beech thumbhole stock. **Sights:** None, grooved 11mm dovetail for scope mounting **Features:** Multi-shot side-lever action, shot count varies based on caliber, very well made and versatile hunting airgun. **Velocities:** .22, 1,176 fps/.25, 910 fps/.30, 910 fps/.35, 800 fps.
Price: $799.99-999.99

EVANIX REX AIR RIFLE
Calibers: .22, .25, .35 (9mm), .45. **Barrel:** Rifled, 19.68 in. **Weight:** 5.51 lbs. **Length:** 35.82 in. overall. **Power:** Pre-charged Pneumatic. **Sights:** weaver rail for scope mounting **Features:** Lightweight, compact and massively powerful, single shot, capable of putting out well over 200 foot pounds at the muzzle in .45 caliber, truly effective hunting power in a compact package **Velocities:** .22, 1,080 fps/.25, 970 fps/.35, 860 fps/.45, 700 fps.
Price: $699.99-799.99

FEINWERKBAU 500 AIR RIFLE
Caliber: .177. **Barrel:** Rifled 13.8 in. **Weight:** 7.05 lbs. **Length:** 43.7 in. **Power:** Pre-charged pneumatic. **Stock:** Ambidextrous beech stock with adjustable cheekpiece and buttstock. **Sights:** Globe front sight and diopter rear. **Features:** Meets requirements for ISSF competition, trigger-pull weight adjusts from 3.9 to 7.8 ounces, bolt action, competition grade airgun. **Velocity:** 574 fps.
Price: $1,650

FEINWERKBAU 800X FIELD TARGET AIR RIFLE
Caliber: .177. **Barrel:** Rifled 16.73 in. **Weight:** 11.7–15.05 lbs. **Length:** 49.76 in. **Power:** Pre-charged pneumatic. **Stock:** Highly adaptable field target competition stock **Sights:** None, 11mm grooved for scope mounting. **Features:** Designed from airguns featuring Olympic accuracy, this field target variant is designed to win., 5-way adjustable match trigger, bolt action, competition grade airgun **Velocity:** 825 fps.
Price: $3,799.99

FEINWERKBAU P75 BIATHLON AIR RIFLE
Caliber: .177. **Barrel:** Rifled 16.73 in. **Weight:** 9.26 lbs. **Length:** 42.91 in. **Power:** Pre-charged pneumatic. **Stock:** Highly adaptable laminate wood competition stock **Sights:** Front globe with aperture inserts and diopter micrometer rear. **Features:** 5-shot bolt action, competition grade airgun, inspired from airguns featuring Olympic accuracy, 5-way adjustable match trigger. **Velocity:** 564 fps.
Price: $3,254.95

FEINWERKBAU SPORT AIR RIFLE
Caliber: .177. **Barrel:** Rifled 18.31 in. **Weight:** 8.27 lbs. **Length:** 44.84 in. **Power:** Spring-piston break barrel. **Stock:** Ambidextrous wood stock with dual raised cheekpieces. **Sights:** Front globe, fully adjustable rear sight, grooved for scope mounting. **Features:** Lightweight, single-shot, easy cocking, adjustable two-stage trigger. **Velocity:** .177, 850 fps.
Price: $999.99

FX CROWN AIR RIFLE
Calibers: .177, .22, .25, .30. **Barrel:** Rifled 19-23.5 in. **Weight:** 6.5 - 7.5 lbs. **Length:** 38.5 - 43 in. **Power:** Pre-charged pneumatic. **Stock:** Ambidextrous stock in walnut, laminate or synthetic. **Sights:** None, 11mm grooved for scope mounting. **Features:** Smooth Twist X barrels can be swapped to change not only caliber but also twist rate, adjustable 15-ounce two-stage trigger, externally adjustable regulator, adjustable power wheel and hammer spring, removable carbon fiber tank, dual air-pressure gauges, multiple-shot magazine (14 to 18 shots depending on caliber). **Velocities:** .177, 1,000 fps/.22, 920 fps/.25, 900 fps/.30, 870 fps.
Price: $1,799.99-2,199.99

FX IMPACT AIR RIFLE
Calibers: .25, .30. **Barrel:** Rifled 24.4 in. **Weight:** 7.0 lbs. **Length:** 34.0 in. **Power:** Pre-charged pneumatic. **Stock:** Compact bullpup stock in various materials and finishes **Sights:** None, 11mm grooved for scope mounting. **Features:** Premium airgun brand known for exceptional build quality and accuracy, regulated for consistent shots, adjustable two-stage trigger, FX smooth twist barrel, multi-shot side lever action, fully moderated barrel, highly adjustable and adaptable air rifle system. **Velocities:** .25, 900 fps/.30, 870 fps.
Price: $2,198.99

FX WILDCAT AIR RIFLE
Calibers: .22, .25. **Barrel:** Rifled 19.7 in. **Weight:** 6.1 lbs. **Length:** 26.5 in. **Power:** Pre-charged pneumatic. **Stock:** Compact bullpup stock in various materials and finishes. **Sights:** None, 11mm grooved for scope mounting. **Features:** Premium airgun brand known for exceptional build quality and accuracy, regulated for consistent shots, adjustable two-stage trigger, FX smooth twist barrel, multi-shot side lever action, fully moderated barrel. **Velocity:** .22, 1,200 fps/.25, 900 fps.
Price: $1,499.99–1,899.99

FX .30 BOSS AIR RIFLE
Caliber: .30. **Barrel:** Rifled 24.4 in. **Weight:** 7.0 lbs. **Length:** 47.5 in. **Power:** Pre-charged pneumatic. **Stock:** Right-handed Monte Carlo Stock available in various materials and finishes. **Sights:** None. 11mm grooved for scope mounting. **Features:** Premium airgun brand known for exceptional build quality and accuracy, regulated for consistent shots, adjustable two-stage trigger, FX smooth twist barrel, multi-shot side lever action, fully moderated barrel. **Velocities:** .22, 1,200 fps/.25, 900 fps.
Price: .... $1,949.99–$2,399.99

Prices given are believed to be accurate at time of publication however, many factors affect retail pricing so exact prices are not possible.

75TH EDITION, 2021 ✦ **563**

GAMO COYOTE WHISPER PCP AIR RIFLE
Calibers: .177, .22. **Barrel:** Cold hammer-forged match-grade rifled barrel, 24.5 in. **Weight:** 6.6 lbs. **Length:** 42.9 in. **Power:** Pre-charged pneumatic. **Stock:** Ambidextrous hardwood stock. **Sights:** None, grooved for scope mounting, **Features:** European class airgun, highly accurate and powerful, adjustable two-stage trigger, integrated moderator, 10-shot bolt action. **Velocities:** .177, 1,200 fps/.22, 1,000 fps.
Price: $559.99

GAMO SWARM MAXXIM MULTI-SHOT AIR RIFLE
Calibers: .177, .22. **Barrel:** Rifled 19.9 in. **Weight:** 5.64 lbs. **Length:** 45.3 in. **Power:** Break-barrel, gas-piston. **Stock:** Ambidextrous lightweight composite stock. **Sights:** None, grooved for scope mounting, includes recoil-reducing rail, 3-9x32 scope and mounts. **Features:** New for 2017, loaded with patented features including an ingenious 10-shot multi-shot system allows for automatic loading with each cock of the barrel, easy cocking, adjustable two-stage trigger, all-weather fluted barrel, features integrated suppressor technology. **Velocities:** .177, 1,300 fps/.22, 975 fps.
Price: $249.99

GAMO SWARM MAGNUM MULTI-SHOT AIR RIFLE
Caliber: .22. **Barrel:** Rifled 21.3 in. **Weight:** 6.88 lbs. **Length:** 49.2 in. **Power:** Break-barrel, gas-piston. **Stock:** Ambidextrous lightweight composite stock. **Sights:** None, grooved for scope mounting, includes recoil-reducing rail, 3-9x32 scope and mounts. **Features:** New for 2018, loaded with patented features including an ingenious 10-shot multi-shot system allows for automatic loading with each cock of the barrel, easy cocking, adjustable two-stage trigger, steel barrel, features integrated suppressor technology. **Velocity:** 1,300 fps.
Price: $279.99

GAMO URBAN PCP AIR RIFLE
Caliber: .22. **Barrel:** Cold hammer forged match grade rifled barrel. **Weight:** 6.7 lbs. **Length:** 42.0 in. **Power:** Pre-charged pneumatic. **Stock:** Ambidextrous composite thumbhole stock. **Sights:** None, grooved for scope mounting, **Features:** European class airgun, highly accurate and powerful, adjustable two-stage trigger, integrated moderator, 10-shot bolt action. **Velocity:** 800 fps.
Price: $450.00

GAMO TC35 AIR RIFLE
Caliber: .35. **Barrel:** rifled, 14.96 in. **Weight:** 6.0 lbs. **Length:** 35.88 in. **Power:** Pre-charged pneumatic. **Stock:** Ambidextrous. **Sights:** None, weaver rail for scope mounting, **Features:** Very light and yet very powerful producing up to 170 ft-lbs of muzzle energy, adjustable trigger, two power settings, shrouded barrel, single-shot action allows for an extremely wide range of ammo choices.
Price: $1,099.99

GAMO BIG BORE TC45 AIR RIFLE
Caliber: .45. **Barrel:** rifled, 24.24 in. **Weight:** 8.0 lbs. **Length:** 47.13 in. **Power:** Pre-charged pneumatic. **Stock:** Ambidextrous. **Sights:** None, weaver rail for scope mounting. **Features:** Very light and yet very powerful producing over 400 ft-lbs of muzzle energy shooting 350-grain cast slugs, adjustable trigger, two power settings, shrouded barrel, single shot action allows for an extremely wide range of ammo choices.
Price: $1,099.99

GAMO VARMINT HUNTER HP AIR RIFLE
Caliber: .177 pellets. **Barrel:** Rifled 18 in. **Weight:** 6.61 lbs. **Length:** 43.78 in. **Power:** Break-barrel, spring-piston. **Stock:** Ambidextrous lightweight composite with dual raised cheekpieces. **Sights:** None, grooved for scope mounting, includes recoil-reducing rail, 4x32 scope and mounts, laser and light with intermittent pressure switches included. **Features:** Lightweight, single-shot, easy cocking, adjustable two-stage trigger, all-weather fluted barrel. **Velocity:** 1,400 fps.
Price: $309.99

GAMO WHISPER FUSION MACH 1 AIR RIFLE, IGT
Calibers: .177, .22. **Barrel:** Rifled, 20.5 in. **Weight:** 6.6 lbs. **Length:** 46 in. **Power:** Break-barrel, Inert Gas Technology gas-piston. **Stock:** Lightweight composite stock with ambidextrous cheek piece. **Sights:** Globe fiber-optic front sight and fully adjustable fiber-optic rear sight, grooved for scope mounting, includes Shock Wave Absorber recoil reducing pad, 3-9x40 scope and heavy-duty mount. **Features:** Integrated Gamo "Whisper" noise-dampening system and bull barrel noise-suppression system for maximum stealth, single-shot, 32-pound cocking effort, adjustable two-stage trigger. **Velocities:** .177, 1,420 fps/.22, 1,020 fps.
Price: $299.99

HAMMERLI 850 AIR MAGNUM
Calibers: .177, .22. **Barrel:** Rifled 23.62 in. **Weight:** 5.65 lbs. **Length:** 41 in. **Power:** CO2. **Stock:** Ambidextrous lightweight composite stock with dual raised cheekpieces. **Sights:** Globe fiber-optic front sight and fully adjustable fiber-optic rear sight, grooved for scope mounting. **Features:** Multi-shot bolt action, 8-shot rotary magazine, utilizes 88-gram disposable CO2 canisters delivering up to 200 shots per cartridge. Extremely accurate, very easy to shoot. German manufacturing. **Velocities:** .177, 760 fps/.22, 655 fps.
Price: $349.99

HAMMERLI AR20 SILVER AIR RIFLE
Calibers: .177. **Barrel:** Rifled Lothar Walther 19.7 in. **Weight:** 8.75 lbs. **Length:** 41.65-43.66 in. **Power:** Pre-charged pneumatic. **Stock:** Ambidextrous aluminum stock with vertically adjustable buttpad and spacers for adjusting length. **Sights:** Globe front sight and fully adjustable diopter rear sight, grooved for scope mounting. **Features:** Single shot, ambidextrous cocking piece, removable aluminum air cylinder, meets ISSF requirements, stock is available in several colors. **Velocity:** 557 fps.
Price: $995.95

Prices given are believed to be accurate at time of publication however, many factors affect retail pricing so exact prices are not possible.

HATSAN USA EDGE CLASS AIRGUNS

Calibers: .177, .22, .25. **Barrel:** Rifled 17.7 in. **Weight:** 6.4–6.6 lbs. **Length:** 43 in. **Power:** Break-barrel, spring-piston and gas-spring variations. **Stock:** Multiple synthetic and synthetic skeleton stock options. Available in different colors such as black, muddy girl camo, moon camo, etc. **Sights:** Fiber-optic front sight and fully adjustable fiber-optic rear sight, grooved for scope mounting, includes 3-9x32 scope and mounts. **Features:** European manufacturing with German steel, single-shot, adjustable two-stage trigger, performance tested at the factory with lead pellets for accurate velocity specifications. **Velocities:** .177, 1,000 fps/.22, 800 fps/.25, 650 fps.
Price: ....$150.00–$180.00

HATSAN USA AIRMAX PCP AIR RIFLE

Calibers: .177, .22, .25. **Barrel:** Rifled 23.0 in. **Weight:** 10.8 lbs. **Length:** 37 in. **Power:** Pre-charged pneumatic. **Stock:** Ambidextrous wood bullpup stock. **Sights:** None, combination Picatinny rail and 11mm dovetail for scope mounting. **Features:** Multi-shot side-lever action, 10-shot .177 and .22 magazines/9-shot .25 magazine, "Quiet Energy" barrel shroud with integrated suppressor, removable air cylinder, fully adjustable two-stage "Quattro" trigger, "EasyAdjust" elevation comb, sling swivels, includes two magazines. **Velocities:** .177, 1,170 fps/.22, 1,070 fps/.25, 970 fps.
Price: $799.99

HATSAN USA BULLBOSS QE AIR RIFLE

Calibers: .177, .22, .25. **Barrel:** Rifled 23.0 in. **Weight:** 8.6 lbs. **Length:** 36.8 in. **Power:** Pre-charged pneumatic. **Stock:** Ambidextrous synthetic or hardwood bullpup stock. **Sights:** None, innovative dual rail 11mm dovetail and Weaver compatible for scope mounting. **Features:** Multi-shot side-lever action, 10-shot .177 and .22 magazines/9-shot .25 magazine, "Quiet Energy" barrel shroud with integrated suppressor, European manufacturing with German steel, removable air cylinder, fully adjustable two-stage "Quattro" trigger, performance tested at the factory with lead pellets for accurate velocity specifications. **Velocities:** .177, 1,170 fps/.22, 1,070 fps/.25, 970 fps.
Price: ....$649.99–$799.99

HATSAN USA BARRAGE SEMI-AUTOMATIC PCP AIR RIFLE

Calibers: .177, .22 .25. **Barrel:** Rifled 19.7 in. **Weight:** 10.1 lbs. **Length:** 40.9 in. **Power:** Pre-charged pneumatic. **Stock:** Ambidextrous adjustable synthetic thumbhole stock with integrated magazine storage. **Sights:** None, innovative dual rail 11mm dovetail and Weaver compatible for scope mounting. **Features:** Air-driven true semi-automatic action, 14 shots in .177 and 12 shots in .22, "Quiet Energy" barrel shroud with integrated suppressor, 500 cc cylinder with 250BAR capacity, European manufacturing with German steel, performance tested at the factory with lead pellets for accurate velocity specifications. **Velocities:** .177, 1,100 fps/.22, 1,000 fps/.25, 900 fps.
Price: .... $1,099.99–$1,199.99

HATSAN USA BULLMASTER SEMI-AUTOMATIC PCP AIR RIFLE

Calibers: .177, .22, .25. **Barrel:** Rifled 19.7 in. **Weight:** 10.3 lbs. **Length:** 30.9 in. **Power:** Pre-charged pneumatic. **Stock:** Ambidextrous adjustable synthetic bullpup stock with integrated magazine storage. **Sights:** None, innovative dual rail 11mm dovetail and Weaver compatible for scope mounting. **Features:** Air-driven true semi-automatic action, 14 shots in .177 and 12 shots in .22, "Quiet Energy" barrel shroud with integrated suppressor, 500 cc cylinder with 250BAR capacity, European manufacturing with German steel, performance tested at the factory with lead pellets for accurate velocity specifications. **Velocities:** .177, 1,100 fps/.22, 1,000 fps/.25 900 fps.
Price: $1,099.99–1,199.99

HATSAN USA HERCULES BULLY PCP AIR RIFLE

Calibers: .177, .22, .25, .30, .35, .45. **Barrel:** Rifled 23 in. **Weight:** 13 lbs. **Length:** 48.4 in. **Power:** Pre-charged pneumatic. **Stock:** Adjustable synthetic all-weather bullpup stock with, sling mounts. **Sights:** None, innovative dual rail 11mm dovetail and Weaver compatible for scope mounting. **Features:** Available in 6 calibers, 500cc of air via carbon fiber reservoir, multi-shot side-lever action, 17-shot .177 magazine, 14-shot .22 magazine, 13-shot .25 magazine, 10-shot .30 magazine, 9-shot .35 magazine, 7-shot .45 magazine. "Quiet Energy" barrel shroud with integrated suppressor, European manufacturing with German steel, fully adjustable two-stage "Quattro" trigger, performance tested at the factory with lead pellets for accurate velocity specifications. **Velocities:** .177, 1,450 fps/.22, 1,300 fps/.25, 1,200 fps/.30, 1,070 fps/.35, 910 fps/.45, 850 fps.
Price: $899.99

HATSAN USA FLASH QE PCP

Calibers: .177, .22, .25. **Barrel:** Rifled, 17.7 in. **Weight:** 5.9 lbs. **Length:** 42.3 in. **Power:** Pre-charged pneumatic. **Stock:** Ambidextrous synthetic or hardwood thumbhole stock. **Sights:** None, innovative dual rail 11mm dovetail and Weaver compatible for scope mounting. **Features:** Very lightweight, multi-shot side-lever action, multi-shot magazine (shot count varies by caliber). "Quiet Energy" barrel shroud with integrated suppressor, European manufacturing with German steel, fully adjustable two-stage "Quattro" trigger, performance tested at the factory with lead pellets for accurate velocity specifications. **Velocities:** .177, 1,250 fps/.22, 1,100 fps/.25, 900 fps.
Price: ....$329.99-$399.99

HATSAN USA FLASHPUP QE PCP

Calibers: .177, .22, .25. **Barrel:** Rifled, 19.4 in. **Weight:** 6.1 lbs. **Length:** 32.0 in. **Power:** Pre-charged pneumatic. **Stock:** Ambidextrous hardwood bullpup stock. **Sights:** None, innovative dual rail 11mm dovetail and Weaver compatible for scope mounting. **Features:** Very lightweight, multi-shot side-lever action, multi-shot magazine (shot count varies by caliber). "Quiet Energy" barrel shroud with integrated suppressor, European manufacturing with German steel, fully adjustable two-stage "Quattro" trigger, performance tested at the factory with lead pellets for accurate velocity specifications. **Velocity:** .177, 1,250 fps/.22, 1,100 fps/.25, 900 fps.
Price: ....$399.99-$439.99

HATSAN USA GLADIUS AIRGUN

Calibers: .177, .22, .25. **Barrel:** Rifled, 23.0 in. **Weight:** 10.6 lbs. **Length:** 38 in. **Power:** Pre-charged pneumatic. **Stock:** Ambidextrous adjustable synthetic bullpup stock with integrated magazine storage. **Sights:** None, innovative dual rail 11mm dovetail and Weaver compatible for scope mounting. **Features:** 6 way variable power, multi-shot side-lever action, 10-shot .177 and .22 magazines / 9-shot .25 magazine, "Quiet Energy" barrel shroud with integrated suppressor, European manufacturing with German steel, removable air cylinder, fully adjustable two-stage "Quattro" trigger, performance tested at the factory with lead pellets for accurate velocity specifications. **Velocities:** .177, 1,070 fps/.22, 970 fps/.25, 870 fps.
Price: $999.99

HATSAN USA MOD 87 QE VORTEX AIRGUN

HATSAN USA MOD 87 QE VORTEX AIR RIFLE
Calibers: .22 **Barrel:** Rifled 10.6 in. **Weight:** 7.4 lbs. **Length:** 44.5 in. **Power:** Break-barrel, gas-spring. **Stock:** Synthetic all-weather stock with adjustable cheekpiece. **Sights:** Fiber-optic front sight and fully adjustable fiber-optic rear sight, grooved for scope mounting, includes 3-9x32 scope and mounts. **Features:** "Quiet Energy" barrel shroud with integrated suppressor, European manufacturing with German steel, single-shot, fully adjustable two-stage "Quattro" trigger, performance tested at the factory with lead pellets for accurate velocity specifications. **Velocities:** .177, 1,000 fps/.22, 800 fps/.25, 650 fps.
Price: $219.99

HATSAN USA MOD 125 SNIPER VORTEX AIRGUN

HATSAN USA MOD 125 SNIPER VORTEX AIR RIFLE
Calibers: .177, .22, .25. **Barrel:** Rifled 19.6 in. **Weight:** 9 lbs. **Length:** 48.8 in. **Power:** Break-barrel, gas-spring. **Stock:** Synthetic all-weather stock with adjustable cheekpiece, available in black or camo options. **Sights:** Fiber-optic front sight and fully adjustable fiber-optic rear sight, grooved for scope mounting, includes 3-9x32 scope and mounts. **Features:** Integrated suppressor, European manufacturing with German steel, single-shot, fully adjustable two-stage "Quattro" trigger, performance tested at the factory with lead pellets for accurate velocity specifications. **Velocities:** .177, 1,250 fps/.22, 1,000 fps/.25, 750 fps.
Price: ....$320.99-$379.99

HATSAN USA MOD 135
QE VORTEX AIRGUN

HATSAN USA MOD 135 QE VORTEX AIR RIFLE
Calibers: .177, .22, .25, .30. **Barrel:** Rifled 10.6 in. **Weight:** 9.9 lbs. **Length:** 47.2 in. **Power:** Break-barrel, gas-spring. **Stock:** Turkish walnut stock with grip and fore-end checkering, adjustable buttplate and cheekpiece. **Sights:** Fiber-optic front sight and fully adjustable fiber-optic rear sight, innovative dual rail 11mm dovetail and Weaver compatible for scope mounting. **Features:** The most powerful break barrel in the world. Worlds first "big-bore" break-barrel airgun, "Quiet Energy" barrel shroud with integrated suppressor, European manufacturing with German steel, single-shot, fully adjustable two-stage "Quattro" trigger, performance tested at the factory with lead pellets for accurate velocity specifications. **Velocities:** .177, 1,250 fps/.22, 1,000 fps/.25, 750 fps/.30, 550 fps.
Price: $329.99

HATSAN USA MOD "TORPEDO" 150 SNIPER VORTEX AIRGUN
Calibers: .177, .22, .25. **Barrel:** Rifled 13 in. **Weight:** 9.4 lbs. **Length:** 48.4 in. **Power:** Under-lever, gas-spring. **Stock:** Synthetic all-weather stock with adjustable cheekpiece. **Sights:** Fiber-optic front sight and fully adjustable fiber-optic rear sight, innovative dual rail 11mm dovetail and Weaver compatible for scope mounting. **Features:** Integrated suppressor, enhanced fixed barrel accuracy, European manufacturing with German steel, single-shot, fully adjustable two-stage "Quattro" trigger, performance tested at the factory with lead pellets for accurate velocity specifications. **Velocities:** .177, 1,250 fps/.22, 1,000 fps/.25, 750 fps.
Price: $359.99

HATSAN USA AT44 QE PCP AIRGUN

HATSAN USA AT44 QE PCP AIRGUN
Calibers: .177, .22, .25. **Barrel:** Rifled 19.5 in. **Weight:** 8 lbs. **Length:** 45.4 in. **Power:** Pre-charged pneumatic. **Stock:** Various configurations, synthetic all-weather stock with front accessory rail and sling mounts. Turkish hardwood with sling mounts, full tactical stock with soft rubber grip inserts, adjustable buttstock and cheek riser. **Sights:** None, innovative dual rail 11mm dovetail and Weaver compatible for scope mounting. **Features:** Multi-shot side-lever action, 10-shot .177 and .22 magazines / 9-shot .25 magazine. "Quiet Energy" barrel shroud with integrated suppressor, European manufacturing with German steel, removable air cylinder, fully adjustable two-stage "Quattro" trigger, performance tested at the factory with lead pellets for accurate velocity specifications. **Velocities:** .177, 1,070 fps/.22, 970 fps/.25, 870 fps.
Price: $599.00

HATSAN USA ALPHA YOUTH QE AIR RIFLE
Caliber: .177. **Barrel:** Rifled, 15.4 in. **Weight:** 5.3 lbs. **Length:** 37.8 in. **Power:** Spring piston. **Stock:** Synthetic ambidextrous. **Sights:** Fiber-optic front sight and fully adjustable fiber-optic rear sight, dual-rail 11mm dovetail and Weaver compatible for scope mounting. **Features:** Easy cocking, designed for smaller, younger shooters, single-shot, integrated Quiet Energy sound-reducing moderator, adjustable trigger. Velocity: 600 fps with lead-free pellet.
Price: $99.99

HATSAN USA BT BIG BORE CARNIVORE BIG BORE QE AIR RIFLE
Calibers: .30, .35. **Barrel:** Rifled 23 in. **Weight:** 9.3 lbs. **Length:** 48.9 in. **Power:** Pre-charged pneumatic. **Stock:** Synthetic all-weather stock with sling mounts, front accessory rail, adjustable cheekpiece and buttpad. **Sights:** None, innovative dual rail 11mm dovetail and Weaver compatible for scope mounting. **Features:** Multi-shot bolt action, 6-shot .35 magazine / 7-shot .30 magazine. "Quiet Energy" barrel shroud with integrated suppressor, European manufacturing with German steel, removable air cylinder, fully adjustable two-stage "Quattro" trigger, performance tested at the factory with lead pellets for accurate velocity specifications. **Velocities:** .30, 860 fps/.35, 730 fps.
Price: $800.00

HATSAN USA GALATIAN QE AIR RIFLE
Calibers: .177, .22, .25. **Barrel:** Rifled 17.7 in. **Weight:** 8.6 lbs. **Length:** 43.3 in. **Power:** Pre-charged pneumatic. **Stock:** Synthetic all-weather stock with extra mag storage, sling mounts, tri-rail front accessory rails, adjustable cheek riser and buttstock. **Sights:** None, innovative dual rail 11mm dovetail and Weaver compatible for scope mounting. **Features:** Multi-shot side-lever action, 17-shot .177 magazine, 14-shot .22 magazine, 13-shot .25 magazine. "Quiet Energy" barrel shroud with integrated suppressor, European manufacturing with German steel, removable air cylinder, fully adjustable two-stage "Quattro" trigger, performance tested at the factory with lead pellets for accurate velocity specifications. **Velocities:** .177, 1,130 fps/.22, 1,050 fps/.25, 950 fps.
Price: $999.99

Prices given are believed to be accurate at time of publication however, many factors affect retail pricing so exact prices are not possible.

HATSAN USA HERCULES QE AIR RIFLE
Calibers: .177, .22, .25, .30, .35, .45. **Barrel:** Rifled 23 in. **Weight:** 13 lbs. **Length:** 48.4 in. **Power:** Pre-charged pneumatic. **Stock:** Fully adjustable synthetic all-weather stock with, sling mounts. **Sights:** None, innovative dual rail 11mm dovetail and Weaver compatible for scope mounting. **Features:** Available in 6 calibers, 1000cc of air on board provides industry leading shot count and energy on target. Multi-shot side-lever action, 17-shot .177 magazine, 14-shot .22 magazine, 13-shot .25 magazine, 10-shot .30 magazine, 9-shot .35 magazine, 7-shot .45 magazine. "Quiet Energy" barrel shroud with integrated suppressor, European manufacturing with German steel, fully adjustable two-stage "Quattro" trigger, performance tested at the factory with lead pellets for accurate velocity specifications. **Velocities:** .177, 1,300 fps/.22, 1,230 fps/.25, 1,200 fps/.30, 1,070 fps/.35, 930 fps/.45, 810 fps.
Price: **$1,399.99**

HATSAN USA HYDRA QE AIR RIFLE
Calibers: .177, .22, .25. **Barrel:** Rifled, 17.7 in. **Weight:** 6.8 lbs. **Length:** 42.7 in. **Power:** Pre-charged pneumatic. **Stock:** Turkish walnut. **Sights:** None, dual-rail 11mm dovetail and Weaver compatible for scope mounting. **Features:** Multi-caliber platform with Versi-Cal technology, swap calibers with a single thumb screw, extra barreled receivers sold separately, Quiet Energy fully shrouded barrel, fully adjustable two-stage "Quattro" trigger, multishot (14 rounds, .177; 12 rounds, .22; 10 rounds, .25). **Velocities:** .177, 1,250 fps/.22, 1,120 fps/.25, 900 fps (with lead-free pellets).
Price: **$449.99**

HATSAN USA PILEDRIVER BIG BORE PCP AIR RIFLE
Calibers: .45, .50. **Barrel:** Rifled, 33 in. **Weight:** 10 lbs. **Length:** 46.5 in. **Power:** Pre-charged pneumatic. **Stock:** Bullpup-style synthetic thumbhole stock with adjustable cheek piece. **Sights:** None, dual-rail 11mm dovetail and Weaver compatible for scope mounting. **Features:** 480cc carbon-fiber tank, long sidelever for easy cocking, three Picatinny accessory rails, 4 to 6 shots in .45 caliber, 3 to 5 shots in 50 caliber, fully adjustable two-stage "Quattro" trigger. **Velocities:** .45, 900 fps/.50, 850 fps.
Price: **$1,199.99**

HATSAN USA PROXIMA MULTISHOT UNDERLEVER AIR RIFLE
Calibers: .177, .22, .25. **Barrel:** Rifled, 15.5 in. **Weight:** 9.3 lbs. **Length:** 45.4 in. **Power:** Gas piston. **Stock:** Turkish walnut ambidextrous stock with thumbhole and elevation-adjustable comb. **Sights:** Hooded TruGlo fiber-optic front sight, micro-adjustable rear sight. **Features:** Fixed barrel, underlever cocking system, shock-absorber system, fully adjustable two-stage "Quattro" trigger, 45-pound cocking effort. **Velocities:** .177, 820 fps/.22, 720 fps/.25, 620 fps.
Price: **$449.99**

HATSAN USA VECTIS LEVER ACTION PCP AIR RIFLE
Calibers: .177, .22, .25. **Barrel:** Rifled 17.7 in. **Weight:** 7.1 lbs. **Length:** 41.3 in. **Power:** Pre-charged pneumatic. **Stock:** Synthetic all-weather stock. **Sights:** Fiber-optic front and rear, combination dual 11mm dovetail and Weaver compatible for scope mounting. **Features:** Multi-shot lever action, 14-shot .177 magazine, 12-shot .22 magazine, 10-shot .25 magazine. "Quiet Energy" barrel shroud with integrated suppressor, fully adjustable two-stage "Quattro" trigger, Picatinny under barrel accessory rail. **Velocities:** .177, 1,150 fps/.22, 1,000 fps/.25, 900 fps.
Price: **$399.99**

KALIBR CRICKET BULLPUP PCP AIR RIFLE
Caliber: .22. **Barrel:** Rifled 17.5 in. **Weight:** 6.95 lbs. **Length:** 27.0 in. **Power:** Pre-charged pneumatic. **Stock:** Ambidextrous bullpup stock available in various materials. **Sights:** None, weaver rail for scope mounting. **Features:** Multi-shot side-lever action, 14-shot magazine, shrouded barrel with integrated suppression technology, adjustable two-stage trigger. **Velocity:** .22, 925 fps.
Price: .... **$1,629.00–$1,835.00**

KRAL ARMS PUNCHER MEGA WALNUT SIDELEVER PCP AIR RIFLE
Calibers: .177, .22, .25. **Barrel:** Rifled 21.0 in. **Weight:** 8.35 lbs. **Length:** 42.0 in. **Power:** Pre-charged pneumatic. **Stock:** Ambidextrous stock available in synthetic with adjustable cheek piece, and Turkish walnut. **Sights:** None, 11mm grooved dovetail for scope mounting. **Features:** Multi-shot side-lever action, 14-shot .177 magazine, 12-shot .22 magazine, 10-shot .25 magazine, half shrouded barrel with integrated suppression technology, available in blue and satin marine finish, adjustable two-stage trigger. **Velocities:** .177, 1,070 fps/.22, 975 fps/.25, 825 fps.
Price: **$599.99**

KRAL ARMS PUNCHER PRO PCP AIR RIFLE
Calibers: .177, .22, .25. **Barrel:** Rifled 22.8 in. **Weight:** 8.6 lbs. **Length:** 41.3 in. **Power:** Pre-charged pneumatic. **Stock:** Monte Carlo hardwood right-handed stock. **Sights:** None, 11mm grooved dovetail for scope mounting. **Features:** Multi-shot rear bolt action, 14-shot .177 magazine, 12-shot .22 magazine, 10-shot .25 magazine, half shrouded barrel with integrated suppression technology, two-stage adjustable trigger. **Velocities:** .177, 1,070 fps/.22, 975 fps/.25, 825 fps.
Price: **$599.99**

KRAL ARMS PUNCHER BREAKER SILENT SYNTHETIC SIDELEVER PCP AIR RIFLE
Calibers: .177, .22, .25. **Barrel:** Rifled 21.0 in. **Weight:** 7.4 lbs. **Length:** 29.0 in. **Power:** Pre-charged pneumatic. **Stock:** Ambidextrous bullpup stock available in synthetic and Turkish walnut. **Sights:** None, 11mm grooved dovetail for scope mounting. **Features:** Multi-shot side-lever action, 14-shot .177 magazine, 12-shot .22 magazine, 10-shot .25 magazine, half shrouded barrel with integrated suppression technology, available in blue and satin marine finish, adjustable two-stage trigger. **Velocities:** .177, 1,100 fps/.22, 975 fps/.25, 825 fps.
Price: **$549.99**

KRAL ARMS PUNCHER BIG MAX PCP AIR RIFLE
Calibers: .177, .22, .25. **Barrel:** Rifled 22.0 in. **Weight:** 9.5 lbs. **Length:** 42.1 in. **Power:** Pre-charged pneumatic. **Stock:** Ambidextrous Turkish walnut pistol grip. **Sights:** None, 11mm grooved dovetail for scope mounting. **Features:** Multi-shot side-lever action, 14-shot .177 magazine, 12-shot .22 magazine, 10-shot .25 magazine, shrouded barrel, adjustable two-stage trigger, massive dual air reservoirs with total of 850 CC. **Velocities:** .177, 1,070 fps/.22, 975 fps/.25, 825 fps.
Price: **$779.99**

KRAL ARMS PUNCHER PITBULL PCP AIR RIFLE
Calibers: .177, .22, .25. **Barrel:** Rifled 23.0 in. **Weight:** 8.65 lbs. **Length:** 42.3 in. **Power:** Pre-charged pneumatic. **Stock:** Ambidextrous Turkish walnut pistol grip.

Prices given are believed to be accurate at time of publication however, many factors affect retail pricing so exact prices are not possible.

75TH EDITION, 2021 ⊕ **567**

Sights: None, 11mm grooved dovetail for scope mounting. **Features:** Multi-shot side-lever action, 14-shot .177 magazine, 12-shot .22 magazine, 10-shot .25 magazine, shrouded barrel, adjustable two-stage trigger, massive dual air reservoirs with total of 755 CC. **Velocities:** .177, 1,070 fps/.22, 975 fps/.25, 825 fps.
Price: $749.99

LCS AIR ARMS SK19 FULL AUTO AIRGUN
Calibers: .22, .25. **Barrel:** Lothar Walther match grade, 23 in. **Weight:** 7.75 lbs. **Length:** 35 in. **Power:** Pre-charged pneumatic. **Stock:** Laminate with adjustable cheek piece. **Sights:** None, Picatinny rail for scope mounting. **Features:** Made in USA, selector for semi-auto or full-auto rate of fire, tunable regulated action, carbon-fiber barrel shroud, 480cc removable tank, optional 580cc tank available, hard case, 19-shot magazine. Velocity: 890-910 fps.
Price: $2,089.00

RAPID AIR WEAPONS RAW HM1000X LRT RIFLE
Calibers: .22, .25, .30, .357. **Barrel:** Lothar Walther match grade with polygonal rifling, 24 in. **Weight:** 7 lbs., 13 oz. **Length:** 45.4 in. **Power:** Pre-charged pneumatic. **Stock:** Laminate with adjustable cheek piece. **Sights:** Grooved for scope mounting. **Features:** Picatinny rail and M-LOK mounting slots, match-grade trigger, multi-shot rotary magazine, adjustable power, side-lever cocking, regulated, quick-fill system, available with right- or left-hand actions. **Velocities:** .22, 950 fps/.25, 900 fps/.30, NA/.357, NA.
Price: $2,199.95

RAPID AIR WEAPONS RAW HM1000X CHASSIS RIFLE
Calibers: .22, .25. **Barrel:** Lothar Walther match grade with polygonal rifling, 24 in. **Weight:** 7 lbs., 13 oz. **Length:** 43-47 in. **Power:** Pre-charged pneumatic. **Stock:** Synthetic AR-15 style. **Sights:** Grooved for scope mounting. **Features:** Chassis constructed from aluminum, designed to accept all AR-15 buttstocks, buffer tubes and pistol grips, Picatinny rail and M-LOK mounting slots, match-grade trigger, 12-shot rotary magazine, adjustable power, side-lever cocking, regulated, quick-fill system. **Velocities:** .22, 950 fps/.25, 920 fps.
Price: $2,199.99

REMINGTON EXPRESS

REMINGTON EXPRESS HUNTER AIR RIFLE W/SCOPE COMBOS
Caliber: .177 or .22. **Barrel:** Rifled, 19 in. **Weight:** 8 lbs. **Length:** 45 in. **Power:** Break-barrel, spring-piston **Stock:** Available in ambidextrous wood with grip and fore-end checkering and textured synthetic options. **Sights:** Fiber-optic front sight and fully adjustable fiber-optic rear sight, grooved for scope mounting, includes 4x32 scope and mounts. **Features:** Single-shot, two-stage trigger. **Velocity:** 1,000 fps (.177), 800 fps (.22).
Price: $159.99

REMINGTON 725 VTR AIR RIFLE
Caliber: .25. **Barrel:** Rifled. **Weight:** 10.5 lbs. **Length:** 48 in. **Power:** Break-barrel, spring-piston. **Stock:** Ambidextrous, synthetic. **Sights:** None, grooved for scope mounting, includes 4x32 scope and mounts. **Features:** Single-shot, bull barrel, Picatinny rail. **Velocity:** 900 fps with alloy pellet.
Price: $249.99

REMINGTON 1100 AIR RIFLE
Caliber: .177 BB or pellet. **Barrel:** Smooth bore. **Weight:** 3.25 lbs. **Length:** 33.9 in. **Power:** Multi-pump pneumatic. **Stock:** Synthetic. **Sights:** Fixed front and adjustable rear. **Features:** Single-shot pellet, 1,000 shot BB, youth rifle. **Velocity:** 645 fps with BB.
Price: $59.99

RUGER 10/22 CO2 RIFLE
Calibers: .177 pellets. **Barrel:** Rifled 18 in. **Weight:** 4.5 lbs. **Length:** 37.1 in. **Power:** Two 12-gram CO2 cylinders. **Stock:** Synthetic stock. **Sights:** Rear sight adjustable for elevation, accepts aftermarket rail. **Features:** 10-shot Ruger-style rotary magazine, bolt cocks rifle, 3-pound single-action trigger pull, sling attachments. **Velocity:** 650 fps.
Price: $149.95

RUGER AIR MAGNUM COMBO

RUGER AIR MAGNUM COMBO
Calibers: .177, .22. **Barrel:** Rifled 19.5 in. **Weight:** 9.5 lbs. **Length:** 48.5 in. **Power:** Break-barrel, spring-piston. **Stock:** Ambidextrous Monte Carlo synthetic stock with textured grip and fore-end. **Sights:** Fiber-optic front sight and fully adjustable fiber-optic rear sight, Weaver scope rail, includes 4x32 scope and mounts. **Features:** Single-shot, two-stage trigger. **Velocities:** .177, 1,400 fps/.22, 1,200 fps.
Price: $220.00

RUGER EXPLORER
Caliber: .177 pellets. **Barrel:** Rifled 15 in. **Weight:** 4.45 lbs. **Length:** 37.12 in. **Power:** Break-barrel, spring-piston **Stock:** Ambidextrous synthetic skeleton stock. **Sights:** Fiber-optic front sight and fully adjustable fiber-optic rear sight, grooved for scope mounting. **Features:** Designed as an entry level youth break-barrel rifle, easy to shoot and accurate, single-shot, two-stage trigger. **Velocity:** 495 fps.
Price: $89.99

RUGER TARGIS HUNTER MAX AIR RIFLE COMBO
Caliber: .22. **Barrel:** Rifled 18.7 in. **Weight:** 9.85 lbs. **Length:** 44.85 in. **Power:** Break-barrel, spring-piston. **Stock:** Ambidextrous synthetic stock with texture grip and fore-end, includes rifle sling. **Sights:** Fiber-optic front sight and fully adjustable fiber-optic rear sight, picatinny optics rail, includes scope and mounts. **Features:** Integrated "SilencAIR" suppressor, single-shot, two-stage trigger. **Velocity:** 1,000 fps.
Price: $229.95

RUGER TARGIS AIR RIFLE
Caliber: .177. **Barrel:** Rifled 18.7 in. **Weight:** 9.85 lbs. **Length:** 44.85 in. **Power:** Break-barrel, spring-piston, single-shot. **Stock:** Black colored synthetic with ventilated comb. **Sights:** Fiber-optic front sight and adjustable rear sight with Weaver/Picatinny rail system. **Features:** Two-stage trigger with 3.3-lb. trigger pull weight and rubber buttplate. **Velocities:** 1,200 fps with alloy pellets and 1,000 fps with lead pellets.
Price: $175.95

Prices given are believed to be accurate at time of publication however, many factors affect retail pricing so exact prices are not possible.

SENECA BIG BORE 44 909 LIGHT HUNTER 500CC TANK
Caliber: .45. **Barrel:** Rifled 21.65 in. **Weight:** 8.5 lbs. **Length:** 42.1 in. **Power:** Pre-charged pneumatic. **Stock:** Right-handed wood stock. **Sights:** Fixed front sight with fully adjustable rear sight. **Features:** Massive 500cc reservoir delivers several powerful shots, delivers well over 200 ft-lbs at the muzzle, long-range hunting accuracy, exceptionally reliable. **Velocity:** 730 fps.
Price: **$729.99**

SENECA DRAGON CLAW PCP AIR RIFLE
Caliber: .50. **Barrel:** Rifled, 21.65 in. **Weight:** 8.5 lbs. **Length:** 42.1 in. **Power:** Pre-charged pneumatic. **Stock:** Right-handed wood stock. **Sights:** Fixed front sight with fully adjustable rear sight. **Features:** Massive 500cc reservoir delivers several powerful shots, 230 ft-lbs energy at the muzzle on high setting, two power levels, dual air chambers, built-in manometer, 11mm scope rail. Velocity: 639 fps.
Price: **$729.99**

SENECA DRAGON FLY MULTI-PUMP AIR RIFLE
Calibers: .177, .22. **Barrel:** Rifled 21.7 in. **Weight:** 6.65 lbs. **Length:** 38.5 in. **Power:** Multi-Pump pneumatic. **Stock:** Ambidextrous wood stock. **Sights:** Fixed front sight with fully adjustable rear sight. **Features:** No recoil for maximum precision, variable power based on number of pumps, bolt action, single shot and multi-shot capability. **Velocities:** .177, 800 fps/.22 630 fps.
Price: **$219.99**

SENECA RECLUSE AIR RIFLE
Caliber: .35 (9mm). **Barrel:** Rifled 21.60 in. **Weight:** 7.5 lbs. **Length:** 42.1 in. **Power:** Pre-charged pneumatic. **Stock:** Right-handed wood stock. **Sights:** Fixed front sight with fully adjustable rear sight. **Features:** Massive 500cc reservoir delivers several powerful shots, delivers well over 150 ft-lbs at the muzzle, long-range hunting accuracy, exceptionally reliable. **Velocity:** 983 fps.
Price: **$699.95**

SIG SAUER MCX CO2 RIFLE & SCOPE, BLACK
Caliber: .177. **Barrel:** Rifled 17.7 in. **Weight:** 7.9 lbs. **Length:** 34.7 in. **Power:** CO2. **Stock:** Synthetic stock, various color options. **Sights:** Varies with model, weaver rail system for iron sight systems, red dot systems, and traditional scope mounting. **Features:** 30-round semi-auto, reliable belt fed magazine system, available in various colors and sighting combination, very realistic replica. **Velocity:** 700 fps.
Price: **$269.99**

SIG SAUER MPX CO2 RIFLE, DOT SIGHT, BLACK
Caliber: .177. **Barrel:** Rifled 8 in. **Weight:** 6.6 lbs. **Length:** 25.8 in. **Power:** CO2. **Stock:** Synthetic stock, various color options. **Sights:** Varies with model, weaver rail system for iron sight systems, red dot systems, and traditional scope mounting. **Features:** 30-round semi-auto, reliable belt fed magazine system, available in various colors and sighting combination, very realistic replica. **Velocity:** 575 fps.
Price: **$245.95**

SIG SAUER ASP20 RIFLE
Caliber: .177 or .22 pellets. **Barrel:** Rifled 13.8 in. **Weight:** 8.5 pounds. **Length:** 45.6 in. **Power:** Break barrel. **Stock:** Black synthetic or black-stained beech wood. **Sights:** None, Picatinny rail. **Features:** Two-stage Matchlite trigger adjustable from 2.5 to 4 pounds, integrated suppressor, 33-pound cocking effort. **Velocity:** 1,021 fps (.177), 841 fps (.22).
Price: ....**$399.99-$489.99**

SPRINGFIELD ARMORY M1A UNDERLEVER RIFLE
Calibers: .177, .22. **Barrel:** Rifled, 18.9 in. **Weight:** 9.9 lbs. **Length:** 45.6 in. **Power:** Spring-piston underlever. **Stock:** Ambidextrous wood. **Sights:** Fixed front sight, rear peep sight adjustable for windage and elevation. **Features:** Fixed barrel, single shot, realistic replica of the National Match firearm, threaded holes on the left-hand side accept a traditional M1A/M14 mount for a scope, 35-pound cocking effort, two-stage nonadjustable trigger. Velocity: 1,000 fps (.177), 750 fps (.22).
Price: **$219.99**

UMAREX EMBARK AIR RIFLE
Caliber: .177. **Barrel:** Rifled 15 in. **Weight:** 4.45 **Length:** 37.25 in. **Power:** Spring piston. **Stock:** Ambidextrous neon green thumbhole synthetic. **Sights:** Fully adjustable micrometer rear, grooved 11mm dovetail for scope mounting. **Features:** Official air rifle for the Student Air Rifle program, 12-inch length of pull, muzzle brake, 16.5-pound cocking effort, 4.25-pound trigger pull, automatic safety. **Velocity:** 510 fps.
Price: **$109.95**

UMAREX GAUNTLET PCP AIR RIFLE, SYNTHETIC STOCK
Caliber: .177, .22., .25 **Barrel:** Rifled 23.5 in. **Weight:** 8.5 lbs. **Length:** 46 in. **Power:** Pre-charged pneumatic. **Stock:** Ambidextrous synthetic. **Sights:** None, grooved 11mm dovetail for scope mounting. **Features:** Removable regulated bottle, multi-shot bolt action, fully shrouded and moderated, adjustable two-stage trigger, first production PCP with these high-end features at this low price point. **Velocities:** .177, 1,000 fps/.22, 900 fps.
Price: **$329.99**

Prices given are believed to be accurate at time of publication however, many factors affect retail pricing so exact prices are not possible.

75TH EDITION, 2021 ⟐ **569**

UMAREX HAMMER AIR RIFLE
Caliber: .50. **Barrel:** Rifled 29.5 in. **Weight:** 8.5 **Length:** 43.75 in. **Power:** Precharged pneumatic. **Stock:** Nymax synthetic. **Sights:** None, Picatinny rail for scope mounting. **Features:** Fires three full-power shots, 2-pound straight pull bolt cocks rifle and advances the magazine, 4,500-psi. built-in carbon-fiber tank with quick disconnect Foster fitting, trigger-block safety, will not fire without magazine, Magpul AR grip, full-length composite barrel shroud, comes with two double-chamber magazines. **Velocities:** 1,130 fps (180-grain non-lead bullet), 760 fps (550-grain lead slug).
Price: $849.99

UMAREX LEGENDS COWBOY LEVER ACTION RIFLE
Caliber: .177 BBs. **Barrel:** Smoothbore, 19.25 in. **Weight:** 7.75 lbs. **Length:** 38 in. **Power:** CO2. **Stock:** Faux wood polymer. **Sights:** Blade front sight with rear sight adjustable for elevation. **Features:** Lever-action, 10-shot capacity, ejectable cartridges, full metal frame, powered by two CO2 capsules, saddle ring. Velocity: 600 fps.
Price: $219.95

UMAREX LEGENDS M1A1 FULL AUTO BB GUN
Caliber: .177 BBs. **Barrel:** Rifled, 12 in. **Weight:** 7.75 lbs. **Length:** 31.75 in. **Power:** CO2. **Stock:** Synthetic. **Sights:** Fixed. **Features:** Semi-auto and full-auto fire capability, 30-round, drop-free magazine with two CO2 cartridges, full metal frame, faux-wood polymer stock, blowback action, sling mounts. Velocity: 435 fps.
Price: $249.95

UMAREX MORPH 3X CO2 PISTOL & RIFLE COMBO
Caliber: .177 BBs. **Barrel:** Rifled, 4.5 in. (pistol), 12 in. (rifle). **Weight:** 1.5 lbs. (pistol), 2.5 lbs. (rifle). **Length:** 11.5 in. (pistol), 38.5 in. (rifle). **Power:** CO2. **Stock:** Synthetic. **Sights:** Fixed, fiber-optic. **Features:** Converts from pistol, to carbine, to rifle, nonremovable 30-round BB magazine, double-action only, integral Weaver/Picatinny rail. Includes pistol, detachable, skeletonized shoulder stock, forearm and barrel extender. Velocity: 380 fps (pistol), 600 fps (rifle).
Price: $90.00

UMAREX SYNERGIS UNDER LEVER AIR RIFLE, COMBO
Caliber: .177 pellets. **Barrel:** Rifled, 18.5 in. **Weight:** 8.3 lbs. **Length:** 45.3 in. **Power:** Gas piston under lever. **Stock:** Synthetic. **Sights:** None, Picatinny rail for scope mounting. **Features:** 3-9x32 scope, two magazines, 12-shot repeater, fixed barrel, removable magazine, integrated suppressor, 2-stage nonadjustable trigger. **Velocity:** 1,000 fps.
Price: $199.95

UMAREX THROTTLE AIR RIFLE COMBO, GAS PISTON
Calibers: .177, .22. **Barrel:** Rifled 15.9 in. **Weight:** 8.3 lbs. **Length:** 45.3 in. **Power:** Break-barrel, gas-piston. **Stock:** Ambidextrous synthetic. **Sights:** None, Weaver rail for scope mounting, includes 3-9x32 AO scope and mounts. **Features:** Single shot, includes integrated suppressor, features new "STOPSHOX" anti-recoil feature. **Velocities:** .177, 1,200 fps/.22, 1,000 fps.
Price: $229.95

WALTHER LG400 UNIVERSAL AIR RIFLE, AMBI GRIP
Caliber: .177. **Barrel:** Advanced match-grade rifled barrel 16.53 in. **Weight:** 8.6 lbs. **Length:** 43.7 in. **Power:** Pre-charged pneumatic. **Stock:** Ambidextrous competition, highly adjustable wood stock. **Sights:** Olympic-grade, match Diopter/Micrometer adjustable sights. **Features:** True professional class 10-meter target rifle, meets ISSF requirements. **Velocity:** 557 fps.
Price: $1,800.00

WALTHER MAXIMATHOR AIR RIFLE
Calibers: .22, .25. **Barrel:** Advanced match-grade rifled barrel, 23.5 in. **Weight:** 9.6 lbs. **Length:** 41.75 in. **Power:** Pre-charged pneumatic. **Stock:** Ambidextrous wood stock. **Sights:** None, grooved 11mm dovetail for scope mounting. **Features:** Bolt action 8-shot magazine, pure hunting PCP with range and accuracy. **Velocities:** .22, 1,260 fps/.25, 1,000 fps.
Price: $799.99

WALTHER LEVER ACTION

WALTHER LEVER ACTION CO2 RIFLE, BLACK
Caliber: .177. **Barrel:** Rifled 18.9 in. **Weight:** 6.2 lbs. **Length:** 39.2 in. **Power:** CO2 **Stock:** Ambidextrous wood stock. **Sights:** Blade front sight, adjustable rear sight. **Features:** Lever-action repeater, 8-shot rotary magazine, great wild west replica airgun. **Velocity:** 600 fps.
Price: $499.99

WALTHER 1250 DOMINATOR COMBO AIR RIFLE
Calibers: .177, .22. **Barrel:** Rifled 23.62 in. **Weight:** 8 lbs. **Length:** 40.94 in. **Power:** Pre-charged pneumatic. **Stock:** Ambidextrous synthetic stock with dual raised cheekpieces. **Sights:** None, grooved for scope mounting, includes 8-32x56 side focus mil-dot scope and mounts. **Features:** German-engineered and manufactured, bolt-action repeater, 8-shot rotary magazine, adjustable two-stage trigger. Ships with hard case, bipod and muzzle brake. **Velocities:** .177, 1,200 fps/.22, 1,000 fps.
Price: $949.99

WALTHER LG400 JUNIOR AIR RIFLE
Caliber: .177. **Barrel:** Advanced match-grade rifled barrel, 16.53 in. **Weight:** 7.7 lbs. **Length:** 39.8 in. **Power:** Pre-charged pneumatic. **Stock:** Ambidextrous highly adjustable competition laminate wood stock. **Sights:** Olympic-grade, match Diopter/Micrometer adjustable sights. **Features:** 10-meter competition target rifle, meets ISSF requirements, removable air cylinder delivers up to 400 shots per fill. **Velocity:** 570 fps.
Price: $1,800.00

Prices given are believed to be accurate at time of publication however, many factors affect retail pricing so exact prices are not possible.

WALTHER ROTEK AIR RIFLE
Calibers: .177, .22. **Barrel:** Rifled Lothar Walther 19.7 in. **Weight:** 8 lbs. **Length:** 41 in. **Power:** Pre-charged pneumatic. **Stock:** Ambidextrous Minelli beech with checkered forearm and grip. **Sights:** None, 11 mm dovetail grooved for scope mounting. **Features:** 1/2 UNF threaded muzzle, eight-shot rotary clip, vibration reduction system, two-stage adjustable match trigger. **Velocities:** 1,000 fps (.177)/900 fps (.22).
Price: **$759.99**

WALTHER TERRUS AIR RIFLE
Calibers: .177, .22. **Barrel:** Rifled 17.75 in. **Weight:** 7.52 lbs. **Length:** 44.25 in. **Power:** Single-cock, spring-piston. **Stock:** Ambidextrous beech and synthetic stock options available. **Sights:** Front fiber-optic sight and fully adjustable rear fiber-optic sight, grooved for scope mounting. **Features:** German engineered and manufactured, very easy cocking and shooting, 1/2 UNF threaded muzzle, single-shot, two-stage target trigger, limited lifetime warranty. **Velocities:** .177, 1,050 fps /.22, 800 fps.
Price: **$299.99**

WEIHRAUCH HW50S SPRING PISTON RIFLE
Calibers: .177, .22. **Barrel:** Rifled, 15.5 in. **Weight:** 6.8 lbs. **Length:** 40.5 in. **Power:** Spring-piston. **Stock:** Checkered beech wood. **Sights:** Front globe and adjustable rear. **Features:** Single shot, 24-pound cocking effort, two-stage adjustable Rekord trigger. **Velocity:** 820 fps (.177), 574 fps (.22).
Price: **$367.99**

WEIHRAUCH HW90 SPRING PISTON RIFLE
Calibers: .177, .22, .25. **Barrel:** Rifled, 19.7 in. **Weight:** 6.8 lbs. **Length:** 45.3 in. **Power:** Spring-piston. **Stock:** Checkered beech wood. **Sights:** Front globe and adjustable rear, 11 mm dovetail for scope mounting. **Features:** Single shot, 46-pound cocking effort, two-stage adjustable Rekord trigger. **Velocity:** 1,050 fps (.177), 853 fps (.22), 625 fps (.25).
Price: **$682.99**

WEIHRAUCH HW97K/KT AIR RIFLE
Calibers: .177, .20, .22, **Barrel:** Rifled, 11.81 in. **Weight:** 8.8 lbs. **Length:** 40.1 in. **Power:** Under-lever, spring-piston. **Stock:** Various, beech wood, blue-gray laminated, or synthetic, with or without thumbhole. **Sights:** None, grooved for scope. **Features:** Silver or blue finish, highly adjustable match-grade trigger. Extremely accurate fixed-barrel design. **Velocity:** 820 fps (.177), 755 fps (.22).
Price: .... **$749.95-$890.00**

WEIHRAUCH HW100 SK PCP RIFLE
Calibers: .177, .22. **Barrel:** Rifled, 16.2 in. **Weight:** 7.65 lbs. **Length:** 38.4 in. **Power:** Pre-charged pneumatic. **Stock:** Monte Carlo walnut stock with raised cheek piece. **Sights:** Grooved for scope mounting. **Features:** Multi-shot side lever, includes two 14-round magazines, shrouded barrel, two-stage adjustable match trigger. **Velocity:** 1,135 fps (.177), 870 fps (.22).
Price: **$1,700.00**

WINCHESTER 77XS MULTI-PUMP AIR RIFLE
Caliber: .177 steel BBs, .177 Pellet. **Barrel:** Rifled 20.8 in. **Weight:** 3.1 lbs. **Length:** 37.6 in. **Power:** Multi-pump pneumatic. **Stock:** Ambidextrous synthetic thumbhole stock. **Sights:** Blade front sight, adjustable rear sight, grooved for scope mounting, includes 4x32 scope and mounts. **Features:** Single-shot pellet, 50-round BB repeater, bolt action, lightweight, accurate and easy to shoot. **Velocity:** 800 fps.
Price: **$95.45**

WINCHESTER 1400CS AIR RIFLE, MOSSY OAK CAMO
Caliber: .177. **Barrel:** Rifled. **Weight:** 9 lbs. **Length:** 51.2 in. **Power:** Break-barrel, spring-piston. **Stock:** Ambidextrous synthetic thumbhole Mossy Oak camo pattern stock. **Sights:** None, grooved for scope mounting, includes 3-9x32 scope and mounts. **Features:** Single-shot, includes web sling, integrated bipod. **Velocity:** 1,400 fps.
Price: **$229.99**

WINCHESTER 1052SS AIR RIFLE COMBO
Caliber: .22. **Barrel:** Rifled. **Weight:** 8.2 lbs. **Length:** 46.25 in. **Power:** Break-barrel, spring-piston. **Stock:** Ambidextrous synthetic thumbhole stock. **Sights:** None, grooved for scope mounting, includes 3-9x32 scope and mounts. **Features:** Single-shot, includes web sling, all-weather fluted barrel jacket. **Velocity:** 1,000 fps.
Price: **$199.99**

WINCHESTER MODEL 70
Calibers: .35, .45. **Barrel:** Rifled, 20.87 in. **Weight:** 9.0 lbs. **Length:** 41.75 in. **Power:** Pre-charged pneumatic. **Stock:** Right handed hardwood. **Sights:** None, grooved for scope mounting. **Features:** Multi-Shot big bore (6 shots .35 / 5 shots .45), highly stable shot strings for maximum accuracy, traditional Winchester styling, .35 produces up to 134 ft-lbs, .45 produces over 200 ft-lbs. **Velocities:** .35, 865 fps/.45, 803 fps.
Price: **$849.99**

ZBROIA HORTIZIA PCP RIFLE
Calibers: .177, .22. **Barrel:** Rifled. **Power:** Pre-charged pneumatic. **Stock:** Black stained ash, Monte-Carlo style wood stock. **Sights:** None, grooved for scope mounting. **Features:** Up to 100 shots per fill in .177 caliber or 60 shots in .22 caliber, free-floated barrel with 12 grooves, two-stage adjustable trigger that is detachable, side-lever cocking, 10- or 12-shot repeater, built-in manometer with 4,351-psi fill, made in the Ukraine. **Velocities:** .177, 1,000 fps/.22, 980 fps.
Price: **$849.99**

ZBROIA KOZAK TACTICAL PCP RIFLE
Calibers: .177, .22. **Barrel:** Rifled. **Power:** Pre-charged pneumatic. **Stock:** Black stained ash wood stock, semi-bullpup design with adjustable cheek piece. **Sights:** None, grooved for scope mounting. **Features:** Up to 100 shots per fill (.22 caliber), free-floated barrel with 12 grooves, two-stage adjustable trigger, side-lever cocking, 10- or 12-shot repeater, built-in manometer with 4,351-psi fill, made in the Ukraine. **Velocities:** .177, 1,000 fps/.22, 980 fps.
Price: **$869.99**

Many manufacturers do not supply suggested retail prices. Others did not get their pricing to us before press time. All pricing can vary dependent on the exact brand and style of ammo selected and/or the retail outlet from which you make your purchase. Pricing has been rounded to the nearest dollar and represents our best estimate of average pricing.
An * after the cartridge means these loads are available with Nosler Partition or Swift A-Frame bullets. Listed pricing may or may not reflect this bullet type.
** = these are packed 50 to box, all others are 20 to box. Wea. Mag.= Weatherby Magnum. Spfd. = Springfield. A-Sq. = A-Square. N.E.=Nitro Express.

Cartridge	Bullet Wgt. Grs.	VELOCITY (fps)					ENERGY (ft. lbs.)					TRAJ. (in.)				Est. Price/box
		Muzzle	100 yds.	200 yds.	300 yds.	400 yds.	Muzzle	100 yds.	200 yds.	300 yds.	400 yds.	100 yds.	200 yds.	300 yds.	400 yds.	
17, 22																
17 Hornet	15.5	3860	2924	2159	1531	1108	513	294	160	81	42	1.4	0	-9.1	-33.7	NA
17 Hornet	20	3650	3078	2574	2122	1721	592	421	294	200	131	1.1	0	-6.4	-20.6	NA
17 Hornet	25	3375	2842	2367	1940	1567	632	448	311	209	136	1.4	0	24.8	56.3	NA
17 Remington Fireball	20	4000	3380	2840	2360	1930	710	507	358	247	165	1.6	1.5	-2.8	-13.5	NA
17 Remington Fireball	25	3850	3280	2780	2330	1925	823	597	429	301	206	0.9	0	-5.4	NA	NA
17 Remington	20	4200	3544	2978	2477	2029	783	558	394	272	183	0	-1.3	-6.6	-17.6	NA
17 Remington	25	4040	3284	2644	2086	1606	906	599	388	242	143	2	1.7	-4	-17	$17
4.6x30 H&K	30	2025	1662	1358	1135	1002	273	184	122	85	66	0	-12.7	-44.5	—	NA
4.6x30 H&K	40	1900	1569	1297	1104	988	320	218	149	108	86	0	-14.3	-39.3	—	NA
204 Ruger (Hor)	24	4400	3667	3046	2504	2023	1032	717	494	334	218	0.6	0	-4.3	-14.3	NA
204 Ruger (Fed)	32 Green	4030	3320	2710	2170	1710	1155	780	520	335	205	0.9	0	-5.7	-19.1	NA
204 Ruger	32	4125	3559	3061	2616	2212	1209	900	666	486	348	0	-1.3	-6.3	—	NA
204 Ruger	32	4225	3632	3114	2652	2234	1268	937	689	500	355	0.6	0	-4.2	-13.4	NA
204 Ruger	40	3900	3451	3046	2677	2336	1351	1058	824	636	485	0.7	0	-4.5	-13.9	NA
204 Ruger	45	3625	3188	2792	2428	2093	1313	1015	778	589	438	1	0	-5.5	-16.9	NA
5.45x39mm	60	2810	2495	2201	1927	1677	1052	829	645	445	374	1	0	-9.2	-27.7	NA
221 Fireball	40	3100	2510	1991	1547	1209	853	559	352	212	129	0	-4.1	-17.3	-45.1	NA
221 Fireball	50	2800	2137	1580	1180	988	870	507	277	155	109	0	-7	-28	0	$14
22 Hornet (Fed)	30 Green	3150	2150	1390	990	830	660	310	130	65	45	0	-6.6	-32.7	NA	NA
22 Hornet	34	3050	2132	1415	1017	852	700	343	151	78	55	0	-6.6	-15.5	-29.9	NA
22 Hornet	35	3100	2278	1601	1135	929	747	403	199	100	67	2.75	0	-16.9	-60.4	NA
22 Hornet	40	2800	2397	2029	1698	1413	696	510	366	256	177	0	-4.6	-17.8	-43.1	NA
22 Hornet	45	2690	2042	1502	1128	948	723	417	225	127	90	0	-7.7	-31	0	$27**
218 Bee	46	2760	2102	1550	1155	961	788	451	245	136	94	0	-7.2	-29	0	$46**
222 Rem.	35	3760	3125	2574	2085	1656	1099	759	515	338	213	1	0	-6.3	-20.8	NA
222 Rem.	50	3345	2930	2553	2205	1886	1242	953	723	540	395	1.3	0	-6.7	-20.6	NA
222 Remington	40	3600	3117	2673	2269	1911	1151	863	634	457	324	1.07	0	-6.13	-18.9	NA
222 Remington	50	3140	2602	2123	1700	1350	1094	752	500	321	202	2	-0.4	-11	-33	$11
222 Remington	55	3020	2562	2147	1773	1451	1114	801	563	384	257	2	-0.4	-11	-33	$12
222 Rem. Mag.	40	3600	3140	2726	2347	2000	1150	876	660	489	355	1	0	-5.7	-17.8	NA
222 Rem. Mag.	50	3340	2917	2533	2179	1855	1238	945	712	527	382	1.3	0	-6.8	-20.9	NA
222 Rem. Mag.	55	3240	2748	2305	1906	1556	1282	922	649	444	296	2	-0.2	-9	-27	$14
22 PPC	52	3400	2930	2510	2130	NA	1335	990	730	525	NA	2	1.4	-5	0	NA
223 Rem.	35	3750	3206	2725	2291	1899	1092	799	577	408	280	1	0	-5.7	-18.1	NA
223 Rem.	35	4000	3353	2796	2302	1861	1243	874	607	412	269	0.8	0	-5.3	-17.3	NA
223 Rem.	64	2750	2368	2018	1701	1427	1074	796	578	411	289	2.4	0	-11	-34.1	NA
223 Rem.	75	2790	2562	2345	2139	1943	1296	1093	916	762	629	1.5	0	-8.2	-24.1	NA
223 Remington	40	3650	3010	2450	1950	1530	1185	805	535	340	265	2	1	-6	-22	$14
223 Remington	40	3800	3305	2845	2424	2044	1282	970	719	522	371	0.84	0	-5.34	-16.6	NA
223 Remington (Rem)	45 Green	3550	2911	2355	1865	1451	1259	847	554	347	210	2.5	2.3	-4.3	-21.1	NA
223 Remington	50	3300	2874	2484	2130	1809	1209	917	685	504	363	1.37	0	-7.05	-21.8	NA
223 Remington	52/53	3330	2882	2477	2106	1770	1305	978	722	522	369	2	0.6	-6.5	-21.5	$14
223 Remington (Win)	55 Green	3240	2747	2304	1905	1554	1282	921	648	443	295	1.9	0	-8.5	-26.7	NA
223 Remington	55	3240	2748	2305	1906	1556	1282	922	649	444	296	2	-0.2	-9	-27	$12
223 Remington	60	3100	2712	2355	2026	1726	1280	979	739	547	397	2	0.2	-8	-24.7	$16
223 Remington	62	3000	2700	2410	2150	1900	1240	1000	800	635	495	1.6	0	-7.7	-22.8	NA
223 Remington	64	3020	2621	2256	1920	1619	1296	977	723	524	373	2	-0.2	-9.3	-23	$14
223 Remington	69	3000	2720	2460	2210	1980	1380	1135	925	750	600	2	0.8	-5.8	-17.5	$15
223 Remington	75	2790	2554	2330	2119	1926	1296	1086	904	747	617	2.37	0	-8.75	-25.1	NA
223 Rem. Super Match	75	2930	2694	2470	2257	2055	1429	1209	1016	848	703	1.2	0	-6.9	-20.7	NA
223 Remington	77	2750	2584	2354	2169	1992	1293	1110	948	804	679	1.93	0	-8.2	-23.8	NA
223 WSSM	55	3850	3438	3064	2721	2402	1810	1444	1147	904	704	0.7	0	-4.4	-13.6	NA
223 WSSM	64	3600	3144	2732	2356	2011	1841	1404	1061	789	574	1	0	-5.7	-17.7	NA
5.56 NATO	55	3130	2740	2382	2051	1750	1196	917	693	514	372	1.1	0	-7.3	-23	NA
5.56 NATO	75	2910	2676	2543	2242	2041	1410	1192	1002	837	693	1.2	0	-7	-21	NA
224 Wea. Mag.	55	3650	3192	2780	2403	2057	1627	1244	943	705	516	2	1.2	-4	-17	$32

Cartridge	Bullet Wgt. Grs.	VELOCITY (fps)					ENERGY (ft. lbs.)					TRAJ. (in.)				Est. Price/box
		Muzzle	100 yds.	200 yds.	300 yds.	400 yds.	Muzzle	100 yds.	200 yds.	300 yds.	400 yds.	100 yds.	200 yds.	300 yds.	400 yds.	
22 Nosler	55	3350	2965	2615	2286	1984	1370	1074	833	638	480	0	-2.5	-10.1	-24.4	
22 Nosler	77	2950	2672	2410	2163	1931	1488	1220	993	800	637	0	-3.4	-12.8	-29.7	
224 Valkyrie	90	2700	2542	2388	2241	2098	1457	1291	1140	1003	880	1.9	0	-8.1	-23.2	NA
224 Valkyrie	75	3000	2731	2477	2237	2010	1499	1242	1022	833	673	1.6	0	-7.3	-21.5	NA
224 Valkyrie	60	3300	2930	2589	2273	1797	1451	1144	893	688	522	1.3	0	-6.5	-19.8	NA
225 Winchester	55	3570	3066	2616	2208	1838	1556	1148	836	595	412	2	1	-5	-20	$19
22-250 Rem.	35	4450	3736	3128	2598	2125	1539	1085	761	524	351	6.5	0	-4.1	-13.4	NA
22-250 Rem.	40	4000	3320	2720	2200	1740	1420	980	660	430	265	2	1.8	-3	-16	$14
22-250 Rem.	40	4150	3553	3033	2570	2151	1530	1121	817	587	411	0.6	0	-4.4	-14.2	NA
22-250 Rem.	45 Green	4000	3293	2690	2159	1696	1598	1084	723	466	287	1.7	1.7	-3.2	-15.7	NA
22-250 Rem.	50	3725	3264	2641	2455	2103	1540	1183	896	669	491	0.89	0	-5.23	-16.3	NA
22-250 Rem.	52/55	3680	3137	2656	2222	1832	1654	1201	861	603	410	2	1.3	-4	-17	$13
22-250 Rem.	60	3600	3195	2826	2485	2169	1727	1360	1064	823	627	2	2	-2.4	-12.3	$19
22-250 Rem.	64	3425	2988	2591	2228	1897	1667	1269	954	705	511	1.2	0	-6.4	-20	NA
220 Swift	40	4200	3678	3190	2739	2329	1566	1201	904	666	482	0.51	0	-4	-12.9	NA
220 Swift	50	3780	3158	2617	2135	1710	1586	1107	760	506	325	2	1.4	-4.4	-17.9	$20
220 Swift	50	3850	3396	2970	2576	2215	1645	1280	979	736	545	0.74	0	-4.84	-15.1	NA
220 Swift	50	3900	3420	2990	2599	2240	1688	1298	992	750	557	0.7	0	-4.7	-14.5	NA
220 Swift	55	3800	3370	2990	2630	2310	1765	1390	1090	850	650	0.8	0	-4.7	-14.4	NA
220 Swift	55	3650	3194	2772	2384	2035	1627	1246	939	694	506	2	2	-2.6	-13.4	$19
220 Swift	60	3600	3199	2824	2475	2156	1727	1364	1063	816	619	2	1.6	-4.1	-13.1	$19
22 Savage H.P.	70	2868	2510	2179	1874	1600	1279	980	738	546	398	0	-4.1	-15.6	-37.1	NA
22 Savage H.P.	71	2790	2340	1930	1570	1280	1225	860	585	390	190	2	-1	-10.4	-35.7	NA
6mm (24)																
6mm BR Rem.	100	2550	2310	2083	1870	1671	1444	1185	963	776	620	2.5	-0.6	-11.8	0	$22
6mm Norma BR	107	2822	2667	2517	2372	2229	1893	1690	1506	1337	1181	1.73	0	-7.24	-20.6	NA
6mm Creedmoor	108	2786	2618	2456	2299	2149	1861	1643	1446	1267	1106	1.5	0	-6.6	-18.9	$26
6mm PPC	70	3140	2750	2400	2070	NA	1535	1175	895	665	NA	2	1.4	-5	0	NA
243 Winchester	55	4025	3597	3209	2853	2525	1978	1579	1257	994	779	0.6	0	-4	-12.2	NA
243 Win.	58	3925	3465	3052	2676	2330	1984	1546	1200	922	699	0.7	0	-4.4	-13.8	NA
243 Winchester	60	3600	3110	2660	2260	1890	1725	1285	945	680	475	2	1.8	-3.3	-15.5	$17
243 Win.	70	3400	3020	2672	2350	2050	1797	1418	1110	858	653	0	-2.5	-9.7	—	NA
243 Winchester	70	3400	3040	2700	2390	2100	1795	1435	1135	890	685	1.1	0	-5.9	-18	NA
243 Winchester	75/80	3350	2955	2593	2259	1951	1993	1551	1194	906	676	2	0.9	-5	-19	$16
243 Win.	80	3425	3081	2763	2468	2190	2984	1686	1357	1082	852	1.1	0	-5.7	-17.1	NA
243 Win.	87	2800	2574	2359	2155	1961	1514	1280	1075	897	743	1.9	0	-8.1	-23.8	NA
243 Win.	95	3185	2908	2649	2404	2172	2140	1784	1480	1219	995	1.3	0	-6.3	-18.6	NA
243 W. Superformance	80	3425	3080	2760	2463	2184	2083	1684	1353	1077	847	1.1	0	-5.7	-17.1	NA
243 Winchester	85	3320	3070	2830	2600	2380	2080	1770	1510	1280	1070	2	1.2	-4	-14	$18
243 Winchester	90	3120	2871	2635	2411	2199	1946	1647	1388	1162	966	1.4	0	-6.4	-18.8	NA
243 Winchester*	100	2960	2697	2449	2215	1993	1945	1615	1332	1089	882	2.5	1.2	-6	-20	$16
243 Winchester	105	2920	2689	2470	2261	2062	1988	1686	1422	1192	992	2.5	1.6	-5	-18.4	$21
243 Light Mag.	100	3100	2839	2592	2358	2138	2133	1790	1491	1235	1014	1.5	0	-6.8	-19.8	NA
243 WSSM	55	4060	3628	3237	2880	2550	2013	1607	1280	1013	794	0.6	0	-3.9	-12	NA
243 WSSM	95	3250	3000	2763	2538	2325	2258	1898	1610	1359	1140	1.2	0	-5.7	-16.9	NA
243 WSSM	100	3110	2838	2583	2341	2112	2147	1789	1481	1217	991	1.4	0	-6.6	-19.7	NA
6mm Remington	80	3470	3064	2694	2352	2036	2139	1667	1289	982	736	2	1.1	-5	-17	$16
6mm R. Superformance	95	3235	2955	2692	2443	3309	2207	1841	1528	1259	1028	1.2	0	-6.1	-18	NA
6mm Remington	100	3100	2829	2573	2332	2104	2133	1777	1470	1207	983	2.5	1.6	-5	-17	$16
6mm Remington	105	3060	2822	2596	2381	2177	2105	1788	1512	1270	1059	2.5	1.1	-3.3	-15	$21
240 Wea. Mag.	87	3500	3202	2924	2663	2416	2366	1980	1651	1370	1127	2	2	-2	-12	$32
240 Wea. Mag.	100	3150	2894	2653	2425	2207	2202	1860	1563	1395	1082	1.3	0	-6.3	-18.5	NA
240 Wea. Mag.	100	3395	3106	2835	2581	2339	2559	2142	1785	1478	1215	2.5	2.8	-2	-11	$43
25-20 Win.	86	1460	1194	1030	931	858	407	272	203	165	141	0	-23.5	0	0	$32**
25-45 Sharps	87	3000	2677	2385	2112	1859	1739	1384	1099	862	668	1.1	0	-7.4	-22.6	$25
25-35 Win.	117	2230	1866	1545	1282	1097	1292	904	620	427	313	2.5	-4.2	-26	0	$24
250 Savage	100	2820	2504	2210	1936	1684	1765	1392	1084	832	630	2.5	0.4	-9	-28	$17
257 Roberts	100	2980	2661	2363	2085	1827	1972	1572	1240	965	741	2.5	-0.8	-5.2	-21.6	$20
257 Roberts	122	2600	2331	2078	1842	1625	1831	1472	1169	919	715	2.5	0	-10.6	-31.4	$21
257 Roberts+P	100	3000	2758	2529	2312	2105	1998	1689	1421	1187	984	1.5	0	-7	-20.5	NA
257 Roberts+P	117	2780	2411	2071	1761	1488	2009	1511	1115	806	576	2.5	-0.2	-10.2	-32.6	$18
257 Roberts+P	120	2780	2560	2360	2160	1970	2060	1750	1480	1240	1030	2.5	1.2	-6.4	-23.6	$22

Cartridge	Bullet Wgt. Grs.	VELOCITY (fps)					ENERGY (ft. lbs.)					TRAJ. (in.)				Est. Price/box
		Muzzle	100 yds.	200 yds.	300 yds.	400 yds.	Muzzle	100 yds.	200 yds.	300 yds.	400 yds.	100 yds.	200 yds.	300 yds.	400 yds.	
257 R. Superformance	117	2946	2705	2478	2265	2057	2253	1901	1595	1329	1099	1.1	0	-5.7	-17.1	NA
25-06 Rem.	87	3440	2995	2591	2222	1884	2286	1733	1297	954	686	2	1.1	-2.5	-14.4	$17
25-06 Rem.	90	3350	3001	2679	2378	2098	2243	1790	1434	1130	879	1.2	0	-6	-18.3	NA
25-06 Rem.	90	3440	3043	2680	2344	2034	2364	1850	1435	1098	827	2	1.8	-3.3	-15.6	$17
25-06 Rem.	100	3230	2893	2580	2287	2014	2316	1858	1478	1161	901	2	0.8	-5.7	-18.9	$17
25-06 Rem.	117	2990	2770	2570	2370	2190	2320	2000	1715	1465	1246	2.5	1	-7.9	-26.6	$19
25-06 Rem.*	120	2990	2730	2484	2252	2032	2382	1985	1644	1351	1100	2.5	1.2	-5.3	-19.6	$17
25-06 Rem.	122	2930	2706	2492	2289	2095	2325	1983	1683	1419	1189	2.5	1.8	-4.5	-17.5	$23
25-06 R. Superformance	117	3110	2861	2626	2403	2191	2512	2127	1792	1500	1246	1.4	0	-6.4	-18.9	NA
25 WSSM	85	3470	3156	2863	2589	2331	2273	1880	1548	1266	1026	1	0	-5.2	-15.7	NA
25 WSSM	115	3060	2844	2639	2442	2254	2392	2066	1778	1523	1398	1.4	0	-6.4	-18.6	NA
25 WSSM	120	2990	2717	2459	2216	1987	2383	1967	1612	1309	1053	1.6	0	-7.4	-21.8	NA
257 Wea. Mag.	87	3825	3456	3118	2805	2513	2826	2308	1870	1520	1220	2	2.7	-0.3	-7.6	$32
257 Wea. Mag.	90	3550	3184	2848	2537	2246	2518	2026	1621	1286	1008	1	0	-5.3	-16	NA
257 Wea. Mag.	100	3555	3237	2941	2665	2404	2806	2326	1920	1576	1283	2.5	3.2	0	-8	$32
257 Wea. Mag.	110	3330	3069	2823	2591	2370	2708	2300	1947	1639	1372	1.1	0	-5.5	-16.1	NA
257 Scramjet	100	3745	3450	3173	2912	2666	3114	2643	2235	1883	1578	2.1	2.77	0	-6.93	NA
6.5																
6.5 Grendel	123	2590	2420	2256	2099	1948	1832	1599	1390	1203	1037	1.8	0	-8.6	-25.1	NA
6.5x47 Lapua	123	2887	NA	2554	NA	2244	2285	NA	1788	NA	1380	NA	4.53	0	-10.7	NA
6.5x50mm Jap.	139	2360	2160	1970	1790	1620	1720	1440	1195	985	810	2.5	-1	-13.5	0	NA
6.5x50mm Jap.	156	2070	1830	1610	1430	1260	1475	1155	900	695	550	2.5	-4	-23.8	0	NA
6.5x52mm Car.	139	2580	2360	2160	1970	1790	2045	1725	1440	1195	985	2.5	0	-9.9	-29	NA
6.5x52mm Car.	156	2430	2170	1930	1700	1500	2045	1630	1285	1005	780	2.5	-1	-13.9	0	NA
6.5x52mm Carcano	160	2250	1963	1700	1467	1271	1798	1369	1027	764	574	3.8	0	-15.9	-48.1	NA
6.5x55mm Swe.	93	2625	2350	2090	1850	1630	1425	1140	905	705	550	2.4	0	-10.3	-31.1	NA
6.5x55mm Swe.	123	2750	2570	2400	2240	2080	2065	1810	1580	1370	1185	1.9	0	-7.9	-22.9	NA
6.5x55mm Swe.*	139/140	2850	2640	2440	2250	2070	2525	2170	1855	1575	1330	2.5	1.6	-5.4	-18.9	$18
6.5x55mm Swe.	140	2550	NA	NA	NA	NA	2020	NA	NA	NA	NA	0	0	0	0	$18
6.5x55mm Swe.	140	2735	2563	2397	2237	2084	2325	2041	1786	1556	1350	1.9	0	-8	-22.9	NA
6.5x55mm Swe.	156	2650	2370	2110	1870	1650	2425	1950	1550	1215	945	2.5	0	-10.3	-30.6	NA
260 Rem.	100	3200	2917	2652	2402	2165	2273	1889	1561	1281	1041	1.3	0	-6.3	-18.6	NA
260 Rem.	130	2800	2613	2433	2261	2096	2262	1970	1709	1476	1268	1.8	0	-7.7	-22.2	NA
260 Remington	125	2875	2669	2473	2285	2105	2294	1977	1697	1449	1230	1.71	0	-7.4	-21.4	NA
260 Remington	140	2750	2544	2347	2158	1979	2351	2011	1712	1448	1217	2.2	0	-8.6	-24.6	NA
6.5 Creedmoor	120	3020	2815	2619	2430	2251	2430	2111	1827	1574	1350	1.4	0	-6.5	-18.9	NA
6.5 Creedmoor	120	3050	2850	2659	2476	2300	2479	2164	1884	1634	1310	1.4	0	-6.3	-18.3	NA
6.5 Creedmoor	130															
6.5 Creedmoor	140	2550	2380	2217	2060	1910	2021	1761	1527	1319	1134	2.3	0	-9.4	-27	NA
6.5 Creedmoor	140	2710	2557	2410	2267	2129	2283	2033	1805	1598	1410	1.9	0	-7.9	-22.6	NA
6.5 Creedmoor	140	2820	2654	2494	2339	2190	2472	2179	1915	1679	1467	1.7	0	-7.2	-20.6	NA
6.5 C. Superformance	129	2950	2756	2570	2392	2221	2492	2175	1892	1639	1417	1.5	0	-6.8	-19.7	NA
6.5x52R	117	2208	1856	1544	1287	1104	1267	895	620	431	317	0	-8.7	-32.2	—	NA
6.5x57	131	2543	2295	2060	1841	1638	1882	1532	1235	986	780	0	-5.1	-18.5	-42.1	NA
6.5 PRC	143	2960	2808	2661	2519	2381	2782	2503	2248	2014	1800	1.5	0	-6.4	-18.2	NA
6.5 PRC	147	2910	2775	2645	2518	2395	2764	2514	2283	2069	1871	1.5	0	-6.5	-18.4	NA
6.5-284 Norma	142	3025	2890	2758	2631	2507	2886	2634	2400	2183	1982	1.13	0	-5.7	-16.4	NA
6.5-284 Norma	156	2790	2531	2287	2056	-	2697	2220	1812	1465	-	1.9	0	-8.6	-	NA
6.5 Weatherby RPM	127	3225	3011	2809	2615	2429	2933	2554	2224	1928	1664	3	3.7	0	-8.8	$65
6.5 Weatherby RPM	140	2975	2772	2579	2393	2215	2751	2389	2067	1780	1525	3.8	4.5	0	-10.6	$50
6.5 Weatherby RPM	140	3075	2885	2703	2529	2361	2939	2587	2272	1988	1766	3.4	4.1	0	-9.5	$65
6.71 (264) Phantom	120	3150	2929	2718	2517	2325	2645	2286	1969	1698	1440	1.3	0	-6	-17.5	NA
6.5 Rem. Mag.	120	3210	2905	2621	2353	2102	2745	2248	1830	1475	1177	2.5	1.7	-4.1	-16.3	Disc.
264 Win. Mag.	100	3400	3104	2828	2568	2322	2566	2139	1775	1464	1197	1.1	0	-5.4	-16.1	NA
264 Win. Mag.	125	3200	2978	2767	2566	2373	2841	2461	2125	1827	1563	1.2	0	-5.8	-16.8	NA
264 Win. Mag.	130	3100	2900	2709	2526	2350	2773	2427	2118	1841	1594	1.3	0	-6.1	-17.6	NA
264 Win. Mag.	140	3030	2782	2548	2326	2114	2854	2406	2018	1682	1389	2.5	1.4	-5.1	-18	$24
6.5 Nosler	129	3400	3213	3035	2863	2698	3310	2957	2638	2348	2085	0.9	0	-4.7	-13.6	NA
6.5 Nosler	140	3300	3118	2943	2775	2613	3119	2784	2481	2205	1955	1	0	-5	-14.6	NA
6.71 (264) Blackbird	140	3480	3261	3053	2855	2665	3766	3307	2899	2534	2208	2.4	3.1	0	-7.4	NA
6.8 REM SPC	90	2840	2444	2083	1756	1469	1611	1194	867	616	431	2.2	0	-3.9	-32	NA
6.8 REM SPC	110	2570	2338	2118	1910	1716	1613	1335	1095	891	719	2.4	0	-6.3	-20.8	NA

Cartridge	Bullet Wgt. Grs.	VELOCITY (fps)					ENERGY (ft. lbs.)					TRAJ. (in.)				Est. Price/box
		Muzzle	100 yds.	200 yds.	300 yds.	400 yds.	Muzzle	100 yds.	200 yds.	300 yds.	400 yds.	100 yds.	200 yds.	300 yds.	400 yds.	
6.8mm Rem.	115	2775	2472	2190	1926	1683	1966	1561	1224	947	723	2.1	0	-3.7	-9.4	NA
27																
270 Win. (Rem.)	115	2710	2482	2265	2059	NA	1875	1485	1161	896	NA	0	4.8	-17.3	0	NA
270 Win.	120	2675	2288	1935	1619	1351	1907	1395	998	699	486	2.6	0	-12	-37.4	NA
270 Win.	140	2940	2747	2563	2386	2216	2687	2346	2042	1770	1526	1.8	0	-6.8	-19.8	NA
270 Win. Supreme	130	3150	2881	2628	2388	2161	2865	2396	1993	1646	1348	1.3	0	-6.4	-18.9	NA
270 Win. Supreme	150	2930	2693	2468	2254	2051	2860	2416	2030	1693	1402	1.7	0	-7.4	-21.6	NA
270 W. Superformance	130	3200	2984	2788	2582	2393	2955	2570	2228	1924	1653	1.2	0	-5.7	-16.7	NA
270 Winchester	100	3430	3021	2649	2305	1988	2612	2027	1557	1179	877	2	1	-4.9	-17.5	$17
270 Winchester	130	3060	2776	2510	2259	2022	2702	2225	1818	1472	1180	2.5	1.4	-5.3	-18.2	$17
270 Winchester	135	3000	2780	2570	2369	2178	2697	2315	1979	1682	1421	2.5	1.4	-6	-17.6	$23
270 Winchester*	140	2940	2700	2480	2260	2060	2685	2270	1905	1590	1315	2.5	1.8	-4.6	-17.9	$20
270 Winchester*	150	2850	2585	2336	2100	1879	2705	2226	1817	1468	1175	2.5	1.2	-6.5	-22	$17
277 Fury	140	3000														
270 WSM	130	3275	3041	2820	2609	2408	3096	2669	2295	1564	1673	1.1	0	-5.5	-16.1	NA
270 WSM	140	3125	2865	2619	2386	2165	3035	2559	2132	1769	1457	1.4	0	-6.5	-19	NA
270 WSM	150	3000	2795	2599	2412	2232	2997	2601	2250	1937	1659	1.5	0	-6.6	-19.2	NA
270 WSM	150	3120	2923	2734	2554	2380	3242	2845	2490	2172	1886	1.3	0	-5.9	-17.2	NA
270 Wea. Mag.	100	3760	3380	3033	2712	2412	3139	2537	2042	1633	1292	2	2.4	-1.2	-10.1	$32
270 Wea. Mag.	130	3375	3119	2878	2649	2432	3287	2808	2390	2026	1707	2.5	-2.9	-0.9	-9.9	$32
270 Wea. Mag.	130	3450	3194	2958	2732	2517	3435	2949	2525	2143	1828	1	0	-4.9	-14.5	NA
270 Wea. Mag.*	150	3245	3036	2837	2647	2465	3507	3070	2681	2334	2023	2.5	2.6	-1.8	-11.4	$47
27 Nosler	150	3300	3143	2983	2828	2676	3638	3289	2964	2663	2385	1	0	-4.9	-14.2	$81
7mm																
7mm BR	140	2216	2012	1821	1643	1481	1525	1259	1031	839	681	2	-3.7	-20	0	$23
275 Rigby	140	2680	2455	2242	2040	1848	2233	1874	1563	1292	1062	2.2	0	-9.1	-26.5	NA
7mm Mauser*	139/140	2660	2435	2221	2018	1827	2199	1843	1533	1266	1037	2.5	0	-9.6	-27.7	$17
7mm Mauser	139	2740	2556	2379	2209	2046	2317	2016	1747	1506	1292	1.9	0	-8.1	-23.3	NA
7mm Mauser	154	2690	2490	2300	2120	1940	2475	2120	1810	1530	1285	2.5	0.8	-7.5	-23.5	$17
7mm Mauser	175	2440	2137	1857	1603	1382	2313	1774	1340	998	742	2.5	-1.7	-16.1	0	$17
7x30 Waters	120	2700	2300	1930	1600	1330	1940	1405	990	685	470	2.5	-0.2	-12.3	0	$18
7x30 Waters	120	2700	2425	2167	1926	1702	1942	1567	1251	988	772	2.2	0	-9.7	-28.8	$36
7mm-08 Rem.	120	2675	2435	2207	1992	1790	1907	1579	1298	1057	854	2.2	0	-9.4	-27.5	NA
7mm-08 Rem.	120	3000	2725	2467	2223	1992	2398	1979	1621	1316	1058	2	0	-7.6	-22.3	$18
7mm-08 Rem.	139	2840	2608	2387	2177	1978	2489	2098	1758	1463	1207	1.8	0	-7.9	-23.2	NA
7mm-08 Rem.*	140	2860	2625	2402	2189	1988	2542	2142	1793	1490	1228	2.5	0.8	-6.9	-21.9	$18
7mm-08 Rem.	154	2715	2510	2315	2128	1950	2520	2155	1832	1548	1300	2.5	1	-7	-22.7	$23
7-08 R. Superformance	139	2950	2857	2571	2393	2222	2686	2345	2040	1768	1524	1.5	0	-6.8	-19.7	NA
7x64mm	173	2526	2260	2010	1777	1565	2452	1962	1552	1214	941	0	-5.3	-19.3	-44.4	NA
7x64mm Bren.	140	2950	2710	2483	2266	2061	2705	2283	1910	1597	1320	1.5	0	-2.9	-7.3	$24.50
7x64mm Bren.	154	2820	2610	2420	2230	2050	2720	2335	1995	1695	1430	2.5	1.4	-5.7	-19.9	NA
7x64mm Bren.*	160	2850	2669	2495	2327	2166	2885	2530	2211	1924	1667	2.5	1.6	-4.8	-17.8	$24
7x64mm Bren.	175	2650	2445	2248	2061	1883	2728	2322	1964	1650	1378	2.2	0	-9.1	-26.4	$24.50
7x65mmR	173	2608	2337	2082	1844	1626	2613	2098	1666	1307	1015	0	-4.9	-17.9	-41.9	NA
275 Rigby	139	2680	2456	2242	2040	1848	2217	1861	1552	1284	1054	2.2	0	-9.1	-26.5	NA
284 Winchester	150	2860	2595	2344	2108	1886	2724	2243	1830	1480	1185	2.5	0.8	-7.3	-23.2	$24
280 R. Superformance	139	3090	2890	2699	2516	2341	2946	2578	2249	1954	1691	1.3	0	-6.1	-17.7	NA
280 Rem.	139	3090	2891	2700	2518	2343	2947	2579	2250	1957	1694	1.3	0	-6.1	-17.7	NA
280 Remington	140	3000	2758	2528	2309	2102	2797	2363	1986	1657	1373	2.5	1.4	-5.2	-18.3	$17
280 Remington*	150	2890	2624	2373	2135	1912	2781	2293	1875	1518	1217	2.5	0.8	-7.1	-22.6	$17
280 Remington	160	2840	2637	2442	2556	2078	2866	2471	2120	1809	1535	2.5	0.8	-6.7	-21	$20
280 Remington	165	2820	2510	2220	1950	1701	2913	2308	1805	1393	1060	2.5	0.4	-8.8	-26.5	$17
280 Ack. Imp.	140	3150	2946	2752	2566	2387	3084	2698	2354	2047	1772	1.3	0	-5.8	-17	NA
280 Ack. Imp.	150	2900	2712	2533	2360	2194	2800	2450	2136	1855	1603	1.6	0	-7	-20.3	NA
280 Ack. Imp.	160	2950	2751	2561	2379	2205	3091	2686	2331	2011	1727	1.5	0	-6.9	-19.9	NA
7x61mm S&H Sup.	154	3060	2720	2400	2100	1820	3200	2520	1965	1505	1135	2.5	1.8	-5	-19.8	NA
7mm Dakota	160	3200	3001	2811	2630	2455	3637	3200	2808	2456	2140	2.1	1.9	-2.8	-12.5	NA
7mm Rem. Mag.	139	3190	2986	2791	2605	2427	3141	2752	2405	2095	1817	1.2	0	-5.7	-16.5	NA
7mm Rem. Mag. (Rem.)	140	2710	2482	2265	2059	NA	2283	1915	1595	1318	NA	0	-4.5	-1.57	0	NA
7mm Rem. Mag.*	139/140	3150	2930	2710	2510	2320	3085	2660	2290	1960	1670	2.5	2.4	-2.4	-12.7	$21
7mm Rem. Mag.	150/154	3110	2830	2568	2320	2085	3221	2667	2196	1792	1448	2.5	1.6	-4.6	-16.5	$21
7mm Rem. Mag.*	160/162	2950	2730	2520	2320	2120	3090	2650	2250	1910	1600	2.5	1.8	-4.4	-17.8	$34

Cartridge	Bullet Wgt. Grs.	VELOCITY (fps)					ENERGY (ft. lbs.)					TRAJ. (in.)				Est. Price/box
		Muzzle	100 yds.	200 yds.	300 yds.	400 yds.	Muzzle	100 yds.	200 yds.	300 yds.	400 yds.	100 yds.	200 yds.	300 yds.	400 yds.	
7mm Rem. Mag.	165	2900	2699	2507	2324	2147	3081	2669	2303	1978	1689	2.5	1.2	-5.9	-19	$28
7mm Rem Mag.	175	2860	2645	2440	2244	2057	3178	2718	2313	1956	1644	2.5	1	-6.5	-20.7	$21
7 R.M. Superformance	139	3240	3033	2836	2648	2467	3239	2839	2482	2163	1877	1.1	0	-5.5	-15.9	NA
7 R.M. Superformance	154	3100	2914	2736	2565	2401	3286	2904	2560	2250	1970	1.3	0	-5.9	-17.2	NA
7mm Rem. SA ULTRA MAG	140	3175	2934	2707	2490	2283	3033	2676	2277	1927	1620	1.3	0	-6	-17.7	NA
7mm Rem. SA ULTRA MAG	150	3110	2828	2563	2313	2077	3221	2663	2188	1782	1437	2.5	2.1	-3.6	-15.8	NA
7mm Rem. SA ULTRA MAG	160	2850	2676	2508	2347	2192	2885	2543	2235	1957	1706	1.7	0	-7.2	-20.7	NA
7mm Rem. SA ULTRA MAG	160	2960	2762	2572	2390	2215	3112	2709	2350	2029	1743	2.6	2.2	-3.6	-15.4	NA
7mm Rem. WSM	140	3225	3008	2801	2603	2414	3233	2812	2438	2106	1812	1.2	0	-5.6	-16.4	NA
7mm Rem. WSM	160	2990	2744	2512	2081	1883	3176	2675	2241	1864	1538	1.6	0	-7.1	-20.8	NA
7mm Wea. Mag.	139	3300	3091	2891	2701	2519	3361	2948	2580	2252	1958	1.1	0	-5.2	-15.2	NA
7mm Wea. Mag.	140	3225	2970	2729	2501	2283	3233	2741	2315	1943	1621	2.5	2	-3.2	-14	$35
7mm Wea. Mag.	140	3340	3127	2925	2732	2546	3467	3040	2659	2320	2016	0	-2.1	-8.2	-19	NA
7mm Wea. Mag.	150	3175	2957	2751	2553	2364	3357	2913	2520	2171	1861	0	-2.5	-9.6	-22	NA
7mm Wea. Mag.	154	3260	3023	2799	2586	2382	3539	3044	2609	2227	1890	2.5	2.8	-1.5	-10.8	$32
7mm Wea. Mag.*	160	3200	3004	2816	2637	2464	3637	3205	2817	2469	2156	2.5	2.7	-1.5	-10.6	$47
7mm Wea. Mag.	165	2950	2747	2553	2367	2189	3188	2765	2388	2053	1756	2.5	1.8	-4.2	-16.4	$43
7mm Wea. Mag.	175	2910	2693	2486	2288	2098	3293	2818	2401	2033	1711	2.5	1.2	-5.9	-19.4	$35
7.21(.284) Tomahawk	140	3300	3118	2943	2774	2612	3386	3022	2693	2393	2122	2.3	3.2	0	-7.7	NA
7mm STW	140	3300	3086	2889	2697	2513	3384	2966	2594	2261	1963	0	-2.1	-8.5	-19.6	NA
7mm STW	140	3325	3064	2818	2585	2364	3436	2918	2468	2077	1737	2.3	1.8	-3	-13.1	NA
7mm STW	150	3175	2957	2751	2553	2364	3357	2913	2520	2171	1861	0	-2.5	-9.6	-22	NA
7mm STW	175	2900	2760	2625	2493	2366	3267	2960	2677	2416	2175	0	-3.1	-11.2	-24.9	NA
7mm STW Supreme	160	3150	2894	2652	2422	2204	3526	2976	2499	2085	1727	1.3	0	-6.3	-18.5	NA
7mm Rem. Ultra Mag.	140	3425	3184	2956	2740	2534	3646	3151	2715	2333	1995	1.7	1.6	-2.6	-11.4	NA
7mm Rem. Ultra Mag.	160	3225	3035	2854	2680	2512	3694	3273	2894	2551	2242	0	-2.3	-8.8	-20.2	NA
7mm Rem. Ultra Mag.	174	3040	2896	2756	2621	2490	3590	3258	2952	2669	2409	0	-2.6	-9.9	-22.2	NA
7mm Firehawk	140	3625	3373	3135	2909	2695	4084	3536	3054	2631	2258	2.2	2.9	0	-7.03	NA
7.21 (.284) Firebird	140	3750	3522	3306	3101	2905	4372	3857	3399	2990	2625	1.6	2.4	0	-6	NA
.28 Nosler	160	3300	3114	2930	2753	2583	3883	3444	3049	2693	2371	1.1	0	-5.1	-14.9	$78
30																
300 ACC Blackout	110	2150	1886	1646	1432	1254	1128	869	661	501	384	0	-8.3	-29.6	-67.8	NA
300 AAC Blackout	125	2250	2031	1826	1636	1464	1404	1145	926	743	595	0	-7	-24.4	-54.8	NA
300 AAC Blackout	220	1000	968	-	-	-	488	457	-	-	-	0	-	-	-	-
30 Carbine	110	1990	1567	1236	1035	923	977	600	373	262	208	0	-13.5	0	0	$28**
30 Carbine	110	2000	1601	1279	1067	—	977	626	399	278	—	0	-12.9	-47.2	—	NA
300 Whisper	110	2375	2094	1834	1597	NA	1378	1071	822	623	NA	3.2	0	-13.6	NA	NA
300 Whisper	208	1020	988	959	NA	NA	480	451	422	NA	NA	0	-34.1	NA	NA	NA
303 Savage	190	1890	1612	1327	1183	1055	1507	1096	794	591	469	2.5	-7.6	0	0	$24
30 Remington	170	2120	1822	1555	1328	1153	1696	1253	913	666	502	2.5	-4.7	-26.3	0	$20
7.62x39mm Rus.	123	2360	2049	1764	1511	1296	1521	1147	850	623	459	3.4	0	-14.7	-44.7	NA
7.62x39mm Rus.	123/125	2300	2030	1780	1550	1350	1445	1125	860	655	500	2.5	-2	-17.5	0	$13
30-30 Win.	55	3400	2693	2085	1570	1187	1412	886	521	301	172	2	0	-10.2	-35	$18
30-30 Win.	125	2570	2090	1660	1320	1080	1830	1210	770	480	320	-2	-2.6	-19.9	0	$13
30-30 Win.	140	2500	2198	1918	1662	—	1943	1501	1143	858	—	2.9	0	-12.4	—	NA
30-30 Win.	150	2390	2040	1723	1447	1225	1902	1386	989	697	499	0	-7.5	-27	-63	NA
30-30 Win. Supreme	150	2480	2095	1747	1446	1209	2049	1462	1017	697	487	0	-6.5	-24.5	0	NA
30-30 Win.	160	2300	1997	1719	1473	1268	1879	1416	1050	771	571	2.5	-2.9	-20.2	0	$18
30-30 Win. Lever Evolution	160	2400	2150	1916	1699	NA	2046	1643	1304	1025	NA	3	0.2	-12.1	NA	NA
30-30 PMC Cowboy	170	1300	1198	1121	—	—	638	474	—	—	—	0	-27	0	0	NA
30-30 Win.*	170	2200	1895	1619	1381	1191	1827	1355	989	720	535	2.5	-5.8	-23.6	0	$13
300 Savage	150	2630	2354	2094	1853	1631	2303	1845	1462	1143	886	2.5	-0.4	-10.1	-30.7	$17
300 Savage	150	2740	2499	2272	2056	1852	2500	2081	1718	1407	1143	2.1	0	-8.8	-25.8	NA
300 Savage	180	2350	2137	1935	1754	1570	2207	1825	1496	1217	985	2.5	-1.6	-15.2	0	$17
30-40 Krag	180	2430	2213	2007	1813	1632	2360	1957	1610	1314	1064	2.5	-1.4	-13.8	0	$18
7.65x53mm Arg.	180	2590	2390	2200	2010	1830	2685	2280	1925	1615	1345	2.5	0	-27.6	0	NA
7.5x53mm Argentine	150	2785	2519	2269	2032	1814	2583	2113	1714	1376	1096	2	0	-8.8	-25.5	NA
308 Marlin Express	140	2800	2532	2279	2040	1818	2437	1992	1614	1294	1207	2	0	-8.7	-25.8	NA
308 Marlin Express	160	2660	2430	2226	2026	1836	2513	2111	1761	1457	1197	3	1.7	-6.7	-23.5	NA
307 Winchester	150	2760	2321	1924	1575	1289	2530	1795	1233	826	554	2.5	-1.5	-13.6	0	Disc.
307 Winchester	160	2650	2386	2137	1904	1688	2494	2022	1622	1287	1688	2.3	0	-10	-29.6	NA
7.5x55 Swiss	180	2650	2450	2250	2060	1880	2805	2390	2020	1700	1415	2.5	0.6	-8.1	-24.9	NA

Cartridge	Bullet Wgt. Grs.	VELOCITY (fps)					ENERGY (ft. lbs.)					TRAJ. (in.)				Est. Price/box
		Muzzle	100 yds.	200 yds.	300 yds.	400 yds.	Muzzle	100 yds.	200 yds.	300 yds.	400 yds.	100 yds.	200 yds.	300 yds.	400 yds.	
7.5x55mm Swiss	165	2720	2515	2319	2132	1954	2710	2317	1970	1665	1398	2	0	-8.5	-24.6	NA
30 Remington AR	123/125	2800	2465	2154	1867	1606	2176	1686	1288	967	716	2.1	0	-9.7	-29.4	NA
308 Winchester	55	3770	3215	2726	2286	1888	1735	1262	907	638	435	-2	1.4	-3.8	-15.8	$22
308 Win.	110	3165	2830	2520	2230	1960	2447	1956	1551	1215	938	1.4	0	-6.9	-20.9	NA
308 Win. PDX1	120	2850	2497	2171	NA	NA	2164	1662	1256	NA	NA	0	-2.8	NA	NA	NA
308 Winchester	150	2820	2533	2263	2009	1774	2648	2137	1705	1344	1048	2.5	0.4	-8.5	-26.1	$17
308 W. Superformance	150	3000	2772	2555	2348	1962	2997	2558	2173	1836	1540	1.5	0	-6.9	-20	NA
308 Win.	155	2775	2553	2342	2141	1950	2650	2243	1887	1577	1308	1.9	0	-8.3	-24.2	NA
308 Win.	155	2850	2640	2438	2247	2064	2795	2398	2047	1737	1466	1.8	0	-7.5	-22.1	NA
308 Winchester	165	2700	2440	2194	1963	1748	2670	2180	1763	1411	1199	2.5	0	-9.7	-28.5	$20
308 Winchester	168	2680	2493	2314	2143	1979	2678	2318	1998	1713	1460	2.5	0	-8.9	-25.3	$18
308 Win. Super Match	168	2870	2647	2462	2284	2114	3008	2613	2261	1946	1667	1.7	0	-7.5	-21.6	NA
308 Win. (Fed.)	170	2000	1740	1510	NA	NA	1510	1145	860	NA	NA	0	0	0	0	NA
308 Winchester	178	2620	2415	2220	2034	1857	2713	2306	1948	1635	1363	2.5	0	-9.6	-27.6	$23
308 Win. Super Match	178	2780	2609	2444	2285	2132	3054	2690	2361	2064	1797	1.8	0	-7.6	-21.9	NA
308 Winchester*	180	2620	2393	2178	1974	1782	2743	2288	1896	1557	1269	2.5	-0.2	-10.2	-28.5	$17
30-06 Spfd.	55	4080	3485	2965	2502	2083	2033	1483	1074	764	530	2	1.9	-2.1	-11.7	$22
30-06 Spfd. (Rem.)	125	2660	2335	2034	1757	NA	1964	1513	1148	856	NA	0	-5.2	-18.9	0	NA
30-06 Spfd.	125	2700	2412	2143	1891	1660	2023	1615	1274	993	765	2.3	0	-9.9	-29.5	NA
30-06 Spfd.	125	3140	2780	2447	2138	1853	2736	2145	1662	1279	953	2	1	-6.2	-21	$17
30-06 Spfd.	150	2910	2617	2342	2083	1853	2820	2281	1827	1445	1135	2.5	0.8	-7.2	-23.4	$17
30-06 Superformance	150	3080	2848	2617	2417	2216	3159	2700	2298	1945	1636	1.4	0	-6.4	-18.9	NA
30-06 Spfd.	152	2910	2654	2413	2184	1968	2858	2378	1965	1610	1307	2.5	1	-6.6	-21.3	$23
30-06 Spfd.*	165	2800	2534	2283	2047	1825	2872	2352	1909	1534	1220	2.5	0.4	-8.4	-25.5	$17
30-06 Spfd.	168	2710	2522	2346	2169	2003	2739	2372	2045	1754	1497	2.5	0.4	-8	-23.5	$18
30-06 M1 Garand	168	2710	2523	2343	2171	2006	2739	2374	2048	1758	1501	2.3	0	-8.6	-24.6	NA
30-06 Spfd. (Fed.)	170	2000	1740	1510	NA	NA	1510	1145	860	NA	NA	0	0	0	0	NA
30-06 Spfd.	178	2720	2511	2311	2121	1939	2924	2491	2111	1777	1486	2.5	0.4	-8.2	-24.6	$23
30-06 Spfd.*	180	2700	2469	2250	2042	1846	2913	2436	2023	1666	1362	-2.5	0	-9.3	-27	$17
30-06 Superformance	180	2820	2630	2447	2272	2104	3178	2764	2393	2063	1769	1.8	0	-7.6	-21.9	NA
30-06 Spfd.	220	2410	2130	1870	1632	1422	2837	2216	1708	1301	988	2.5	-1.7	-18	0	$17
30-06 High Energy	180	2880	2690	2500	2320	2150	3315	2880	2495	2150	1845	1.7	0	-7.2	-21	NA
30 T/C	150	2920	2696	2483	2280	2087	2849	2421	2054	1732	1450	1.7	0	-7.3	-21.3	NA
30 T/C Superformance	150	3000	2772	2555	2348	2151	2997	2558	2173	1836	1540	1.5	0	-6.9	-20	NA
30 T/C Superformance	165	2850	2644	2447	2258	2078	2975	2560	2193	1868	1582	1.7	0	-7.6	-22	NA
300 Rem SA Ultra Mag	150	3200	2901	2622	2359	2112	3410	2803	2290	1854	1485	1.3	0	-6.4	-19.1	NA
300 Rem SA Ultra Mag	165	3075	2792	2527	2276	2040	3464	2856	2339	1898	1525	1.5	0	-7	-20.7	NA
300 Rem SA Ultra Mag	180	2960	2761	2571	2389	2214	3501	3047	2642	2280	1959	2.6	2.2	-3.6	-15.4	NA
300 Rem. SA Ultra Mag	200	2800	2644	2494	2348	2208	3841	3104	2761	2449	2164	0	-3.5	-12.5	-27.9	NA
7.82 (308) Patriot	150	3250	2999	2762	2537	2323	3519	2997	2542	2145	1798	1.2	0	-5.8	-16.9	NA
300 RCM	150	3265	3023	2794	2577	2369	3550	3043	2600	2211	1870	1.2	0	-5.6	-16.5	NA
300 RCM Superformance	150	3310	3065	2833	2613	2404	3648	3128	2673	2274	1924	1.1	0	-5.4	-16	NA
300 RCM Superformance	165	3185	2964	2753	2552	2360	3716	3217	2776	2386	2040	1.2	0	-5.8	-17	NA
300 RCM Superformance	180	3040	2840	2649	2466	2290	3693	3223	2804	2430	2096	1.4	0	-6.4	-18.5	NA
300 WSM	150	3300	3061	2834	2619	2414	3628	3121	2676	2285	1941	1.1	0	-5.4	-15.9	NA
300 WSM	180	2970	2741	2524	2317	2120	3526	3005	2547	2147	1797	1.6	0	-7	-20.5	NA
300 WSM	180	3010	2923	2734	2554	2380	3242	2845	2490	2172	1886	1.3	0	-5.9	-17.2	NA
300 WSM	190	2875	2729	2588	2451	2319	3486	3142	2826	2535	2269	0	3.2	-11.5	-25.7	NA
308 Norma Mag.	180	2975	2787	2608	2435	2269	3536	3105	2718	2371	2058	0	-3	-11.1	-25	NA
308 Norma Mag.	180	3020	2820	2630	2440	2270	3645	3175	2755	2385	2050	2.5	2	-3.5	-14.8	NA
300 Dakota	200	3000	2824	2656	2493	2336	3996	3542	3131	2760	2423	2.2	1.5	-4	-15.2	NA
300 H&H Mag.	180	2870	2678	2494	2318	2148	3292	2866	2486	2147	1844	1.7	0	-7.3	-21.6	NA
300 H&H Magnum*	180	2880	2640	2412	2196	1990	3315	2785	2325	1927	1583	2.5	0.8	-6.8	-21.7	$24
300 H&H Mag.	200	2750	2596	2447	2303	2164	3357	2992	2659	2355	2079	1.8	0	-7.6	-21.8	NA
300 H&H Magnum	220	2550	2267	2002	1757	NA	3167	2510	1958	1508	NA	-2.5	-0.4	-12	0	NA
300 Win. Mag.	150	3290	2951	2636	2342	2068	3605	2900	2314	1827	1424	2.5	1.9	-3.8	-15.8	$22
300 WM Superformance	150	3400	3150	2914	2690	2477	3850	3304	2817	2409	2043	1	0	-5.1	-15	NA
300 Win. Mag.	165	3100	2877	2665	2462	2269	3522	3033	2603	2221	1897	2.5	2.4	-3	-16.9	$24
300 Win. Mag.	178	2900	2760	2568	2375	2191	3509	3030	2606	2230	1897	2.5	1.4	-5	-17.6	$29
300 Win. Mag.	178	2960	2770	2588	2413	2245	3463	3032	2647	2301	1992	1.5	0	-6.7	-19.4	NA
300 WM Super Match	178	2960	2770	2587	2412	2243	3462	3031	2645	2298	1988	1.5	0	-6.7	-19.4	NA
300 Win. Mag.*	180	2960	2745	2540	2344	2157	3501	3011	2578	2196	1859	2.5	1.2	-5.5	-18.5	$22

Cartridge	Bullet Wgt. Grs.	VELOCITY (fps)					ENERGY (ft. lbs.)					TRAJ. (in.)				Est. Price/box
		Muzzle	100 yds.	200 yds.	300 yds.	400 yds.	Muzzle	100 yds.	200 yds.	300 yds.	400 yds.	100 yds.	200 yds.	300 yds.	400 yds.	
300 WM Superformance	180	3130	2927	2732	2546	2366	3917	3424	2983	2589	2238	1.3	0	-5.9	-17.3	NA
300 Win. Mag.	190	2885	1691	2506	2327	2156	3511	3055	2648	2285	1961	2.5	1.2	-5.7	-19	$26
300 Win. Mag.	195	2930	2760	2596	2438	2286	3717	3297	2918	2574	2262	1.5	0	-6.7	-19.4	NA
300 Win. Mag.*	200	2825	2595	2376	2167	1970	3545	2991	2508	2086	1742	-2.5	1.6	-4.7	-17.2	$36
300 Win. Mag.	220	2680	2448	2228	2020	1823	3508	2927	2424	1993	1623	2.5	0	-9.5	-27.5	$23
300 Rem. Ultra Mag.	150	3450	3208	2980	2762	2556	3964	3427	2956	2541	2175	1.7	1.5	-2.6	-11.2	NA
300 Rem. Ultra Mag.	150	2910	2686	2473	2279	2077	2820	2403	2037	1716	1436	1.7	0	-7.4	-21.5	NA
300 Rem. Ultra Mag.	165	3350	3099	2862	2938	2424	4110	3518	3001	2549	2152	1.1	0	-5.3	-15.6	NA
300 Rem. Ultra Mag.	180	3250	3037	2834	2640	2454	4221	3686	3201	2786	2407	2.4	0	-3	-12.7	NA
300 Rem. Ultra Mag.	180	2960	2774	2505	2294	2093	3501	2971	2508	2103	1751	2.7	2.2	-3.8	-16.4	NA
300 Rem. Ultra Mag.	200	3032	2791	2562	2345	2138	4083	3459	2916	2442	2030	1.5	0	-6.8	-19.9	NA
300 Rem. Ultra Mag.	210	2920	2790	2665	2543	2424	3975	3631	3311	3015	2740	1.5	0	-6.4	-18.1	NA
30 Nosler	180	3200	3004	2815	2635	2462	4092	3606	3168	2774	2422	0	-2.4	-9.1	-20.9	NA
30 Nosler	210	3000	2868	2741	2617	2497	4196	3836	3502	3193	2906	0	-2.7	-10.1	-22.5	NA
300 Wea. Mag.	100	3900	3441	3038	2652	2305	3714	2891	2239	1717	1297	2	2.6	-0.6	-8.7	$32
300 Wea. Mag.	150	3375	3126	2892	2670	2459	3794	3255	2786	2374	2013	1	0	-5.2	-15.3	NA
300 Wea. Mag.	150	3600	3307	3033	2776	2533	4316	3642	3064	2566	2137	2.5	3.2	0	-8.1	$32
300 Wea. Mag.	165	3140	2921	2713	2515	2325	3612	3126	2697	2317	1980	1.3	0	-6	-17.5	NA
300 Wea. Mag.	165	3450	3210	3000	2792	2593	4360	3796	3297	2855	2464	2.5	3.2	0	-7.8	NA
300 Wea. Mag.	178	3120	2902	2695	2497	2308	3847	3329	2870	2464	2104	2.5	-1.7	-3.6	-14.7	$43
300 Wea. Mag.	180	3330	3110	2910	2710	2520	4430	3875	3375	2935	2540	1	0	-5.2	-15.1	NA
300 Wea. Mag.	190	3030	2830	2638	2455	2279	3873	3378	2936	2542	2190	2.5	1.6	-4.3	-16	$38
300 Wea. Mag.	220	2850	2541	2283	1964	1736	3967	3155	2480	1922	1471	2.5	0.4	-8.5	-26.4	$35
300 Pegasus	180	3500	3319	3145	2978	2817	4896	4401	3953	3544	3172	2.28	2.89	0	-6.79	NA
300 Norma Magnum	215	3017	2881	2748	2618	2491	4346	3963	3605	3272	2963	NA	NA	NA	NA	$85
300 Norma Magnum	230	2934	2805	2678	2555	2435	4397	4018	3664	3334	3028	NA	NA	NA	NA	$85
300 Norma Magnum	225	2850	2731	2615	2502	2392	4058	3726	3417	3128	2859	1.6	0	-6.7	-18.9	NA
300 PRC	212	2860	2723	2589	2849	2565	3850	3489	3156	2849	2565	1.6	0	-6.8	-19.3	NA
300 PRC	225	2810	2692	2577	2465	2356	3945	3620	3318	3036	2773	1.7	0	-6.9	-19.5	NA
31																
32-20 Win.	100	1210	1021	913	834	769	325	231	185	154	131	0	-32.3	0	0	$23**
303 British	150	2685	2441	2211	1993	1789	2401	1985	1628	1323	1066	2.2	0	-9.3	-27.4	NA
303 British	180	2460	2124	1817	1542	1311	2418	1803	1319	950	687	2.5	-1.8	-16.8	0	$18
303 Light Mag.	150	2830	2570	2325	2094	1884	2667	2199	1800	1461	1185	2	0	-8.4	-24.6	NA
7.62x54mm Rus.	146	2950	2730	2520	2320	NA	2820	2415	2055	1740	NA	2.5	2	-4.4	-17.7	NA
7.62x54mm Rus.	174	2800	2607	2422	2245	2075	3029	2626	2267	1947	1664	1.8	0	-7.8	-22.4	NA
7.62x54mm Rus.	180	2580	2370	2180	2000	1820	2650	2250	1900	1590	1100	2.5	0	-9.8	-28.5	NA
7.7x58mm Jap.	150	2640	2399	2170	1954	1752	2321	1916	1568	1271	1022	2.3	0	-9.7	-28.5	NA
7.7x58mm Jap.	180	2500	2300	2100	1920	1750	2490	2105	1770	1475	1225	2.5	0	-10.4	-30.2	NA
8mm																
8x56 R	205	2400	2188	1987	1797	1621	2621	2178	1796	1470	1196	2.9	0	-11.7	-34.3	NA
8x57mm JS Mau.	165	2850	2520	2210	1930	1670	2965	2330	1795	1360	1015	2.5	1	-7.7	0	NA
32 Win. Special	165	2410	2145	1897	1669	NA	2128	1685	1318	1020	NA	2	0	-13	-19.9	NA
32 Win. Special	170	2250	1921	1626	1372	1175	1911	1393	998	710	521	2.5	-3.5	-22.9	0	$14
8mm Mauser	170	2360	1969	1622	1333	1123	2102	1464	993	671	476	2.5	-3.1	-22.2	0	$18
8mm Mauser	196	2500	2338	2182	2032	1888	2720	2379	2072	1797	1552	2.4	0	-9.8	-27.9	NA
325 WSM	180	3060	2841	2632	2432	2242	3743	3226	2769	2365	2009	1.4	0	-6.4	-18.7	NA
325 WSM	200	2950	2753	2565	2384	2210	3866	3367	2922	2524	2170	1.5	0	-6.8	-19.8	NA
325 WSM	220	2840	2605	2382	2169	1968	3941	3316	2772	2300	1893	1.8	0	-8	-23.3	NA
8mm Rem. Mag.	185	3080	2761	2464	2186	1927	3896	3131	2494	1963	1525	2.5	1.4	-5.5	-19.7	$30
8mm Rem. Mag.	220	2830	2581	2346	2123	1913	3912	3254	2688	2201	1787	2.5	0.6	-7.6	-23.5	Disc.
33																
338 Federal	180	2830	2590	2350	2130	1930	3200	2670	2215	1820	1480	1.8	0	-8.2	-23.9	NA
338 Marlin Express	200	2565	2365	2174	1992	1820	2922	2484	2099	1762	1471	3	1.2	-7.9	-25.9	NA
338 Federal	185	2750	2550	2350	2160	1980	3105	2660	2265	1920	1615	1.9	0	-8.3	-24.1	NA
338 Federal	210	2630	2410	2200	2010	1820	3225	2710	2265	1880	1545	2.3	0	-9.4	-27.3	NA
338 Federal MSR	185	2680	2459	2230	2020	1820	2950	2460	2035	1670	1360	2.2	0	-9.2	-26.8	NA
338-06	200	2750	2553	2364	2184	2011	3358	2894	2482	2118	1796	1.9	0	-8.22	-23.6	NA
330 Dakota	250	2900	2719	2545	2378	2217	4668	4103	3595	3138	2727	2.3	1.3	-5	-17.5	NA
338 Lapua	250	2900	2685	2481	2285	2098	4668	4002	2416	2899	2444	1.7	0	-7.3	-21.3	NA
338 Lapua	250	2963	2795	2640	2493	NA	4842	4341	3881	3458	NA	1.9	0	-7.9	0	NA
338 Lapua	285	2745	2616	2491	2369	2251	4768	4331	3926	3552	3206	1.8	0	-7.4	-21	NA
338 Lapua	300	2660	2544	2432	2322	-	4715	4313	3940	3592	-	1.9	0	-7.8	-	NA

Cartridge	Bullet Wgt. Grs.	VELOCITY (fps)					ENERGY (ft. lbs.)					TRAJ. (in.)				Est. Price/box
		Muzzle	100 yds.	200 yds.	300 yds.	400 yds.	Muzzle	100 yds.	200 yds.	300 yds.	400 yds.	100 yds.	200 yds.	300 yds.	400 yds.	
338 RCM Superformance	185	2980	2755	2542	2338	2143	3647	3118	2653	2242	1887	1.5	0	-6.9	-20.3	NA
338 RCM Superformance	200	2950	2744	2547	2358	2177	3846	3342	2879	2468	2104	1.6	0	-6.9	-20.1	NA
338 RCM Superformance	225	2750	2575	2407	2245	2089	3778	3313	2894	2518	2180	1.9	0	-7.9	-22.7	NA
338 WM Superformance	185	3080	2850	2632	2424	2226	3896	3337	2845	2413	2034	1.4	0	-6.4	-18.8	NA
338 Win. Mag.	200	3030	2820	2620	2429	2246	4077	3532	3049	2621	2240	1.4	0	-6.5	-18.9	NA
338 Win. Mag.*	210	2830	2590	2370	2150	1940	3735	3130	2610	2155	1760	2.5	1.4	-6	-20.9	$33
338 Win. Mag.*	225	2785	2517	2266	2029	1808	3871	3165	2565	2057	1633	2.5	0.4	-8.5	-25.9	$27
338 WM Superformance	225	2840	2758	2582	2414	2252	4318	3798	3331	2911	2533	1.5	0	-6.8	-19.5	NA
338 Win. Mag.	230	2780	2573	2375	2186	2005	3948	3382	2881	2441	2054	2.5	1.2	-6.3	-21	$40
338 Win. Mag.*	250	2660	2456	2261	2075	1898	3927	3348	2837	2389	1999	2.5	0.2	-9	-26.2	$27
338 Ultra Mag.	250	2860	2645	2440	2244	2057	4540	3882	3303	2794	2347	1.7	0	-7.6	-22.1	NA
338 Lapua Match	250	2900	2760	2625	2494	2366	4668	4229	3825	3452	3108	1.5	0	-6.6	-18.8	NA
338 Lapua Match	285	2745	2623	2504	2388	2275	4768	4352	3966	3608	3275	1.8	0	-7.3	-20.8	NA
33 Nosler	225	3025	2856	2687	2525	2369	4589	4074	3608	3185	2803	0	-2.8	-10.4	-23.4	NA
33 Nosler	265	2775	2661	2547	2435	2326	4543	4167	3816	3488	3183	0	-3.4	-12.2	-26.8	NA
33 Nosler	300	2550	2445	2339	2235	2134	4343	3981	3643	3327	3033	0	-4.3	-15	-32.6	NA
8.59(.338) Galaxy	200	3100	2899	2707	2524	2347	4269	3734	3256	2829	2446	3	3.8	0	-9.3	NA
340 Wea. Mag.*	210	3250	2991	2746	2515	2295	4924	4170	3516	2948	2455	2.5	1.9	-1.8	-11.8	$56
340 Wea. Mag.*	250	3000	2806	2621	2443	2272	4995	4371	3812	3311	2864	2.5	2	-3.5	-14.8	$56
338 A-Square	250	3120	2799	2500	2220	1958	5403	4348	3469	2736	2128	2.5	2.7	-1.5	-10.5	NA
338-378 Wea. Mag.	225	3180	2974	2778	2591	2410	5052	4420	3856	3353	2902	3.1	3.8	0	-8.9	NA
338 Titan	225	3230	3010	2800	2600	2409	5211	4524	3916	3377	2898	3.07	3.8	0	-8.95	NA
338 Excalibur	200	3600	3361	3134	2920	2715	5755	5015	4363	3785	3274	2.23	2.87	0	-6.99	NA
338 Excalibur	250	3250	2922	2618	2333	2066	5863	4740	3804	3021	2370	1.3	0	-6.35	-19.2	NA
34, 35																
348 Winchester	200	2520	2215	1931	1672	1443	2820	2178	1656	1241	925	2.5	-1.4	-14.7	0	$42
348 Winchester LeveRevolution	200	2560	2294	2044	1811	1597	2910	2336	1855	1456	1133	2.6	0	-10.9	-32.6	na
357 Magnum	158	1830	1427	1138	980	883	1175	715	454	337	274	0		-33.1	0	$25**
350 Legend	145	2350	1916	1539	1241	n/a	1778	1182	763	496	n/a	0	-8.1	-31.2	NA	na
350 Legend	150	2325	1968	1647	1373	na	4800	1289	903	628	na	0	-7.6	-28.1	na	na
350 Legend	160	2225	1843	1509	1243	na	1759	1206	809	548	na	0	-8.9	-33.2	na	na
350 Legend	180	2100	1762	1466	1230	na	1762	1240	859	604	na	0	-9.8	-36	na	na
350 Legend	265	1060	990	936	890	na	661	577	515	466	na	0	-34.1	-107.4	na	na
35 Remington	150	2300	1874	1506	1218	1039	1762	1169	755	494	359	2.5	-4.1	-26.3	0	$16
35 Remington	200	2080	1698	1376	1140	1001	1921	1280	841	577	445	2.5	-6.3	-17.1	-33.6	$16
35 Remington	200	2225	1963	1722	1505	—	2198	1711	1317	1006	—	3.8	0	-15.6	—	NA
35 Rem. Lever Evolution	200	2225	1963	1721	1503	NA	2198	1711	1315	1003	NA	3	-1.3	-17.5	NA	NA
356 Winchester	200	2460	2114	1797	1517	1284	2688	1985	1434	1022	732	2.5	-1.8	-15.1	0	$31
356 Winchester	250	2160	1911	1682	1476	1299	2591	2028	1571	1210	937	2.5	-3.7	-22.2	0	$31
358 Winchester	200	2475	2180	1906	1655	1434	2720	2110	1612	1217	913	2.9	0	-12.6	-37.9	NA
358 Winchester	200	2490	2171	1876	1619	1379	2753	2093	1563	1151	844	2.5	-1.6	-15.6	0	$31
358 STA	275	2850	2562	2292	2039	NA	4958	4009	3208	2539	NA	1.9	0	-8.6	0	NA
350 Rem. Mag.	200	2710	2410	2130	1870	1631	3261	2579	2014	1553	1181	2.5	-0.2	-10	-30.1	$33
35 Whelen	200	2675	2378	2100	1842	1606	3177	2510	1958	1506	1145	2.5	-0.2	-10.3	-31.1	$20
35 Whelen	200	2910	2585	2283	2001	1742	3760	2968	2314	1778	1347	1.9	0	-8.6	-25.9	NA
35 Whelen	225	2500	2300	2110	1930	1770	3120	2650	2235	1870	1560	2.6	0	-10.2	-29.9	NA
35 Whelen	250	2400	2197	2005	1823	1652	3197	2680	2230	1844	1515	2.5	-1.2	-13.7	0	$20
358 Norma Mag.	250	2800	2510	2230	1970	1730	4350	3480	2750	2145	1655	2.5	1	-7.6	-25.2	NA
358 STA	275	2850	2562	2292	2039	1764	4959	4009	3208	2539	1899	1.9	0	-8.58	-26.1	NA
9.3mm																
9.3x57mm Mau.	232	2362	2058	1778	1528	NA	2875	2182	1630	1203	NA	0	-6.8	-24.6	NA	NA
9.3x57mm Mau.	286	2070	1810	1590	1390	1110	2710	2090	1600	1220	955	2.5	-2.6	-22.5	0	NA
370 Sako Mag.	286	3550	2370	2200	2040	2880	4130	3570	3075	2630	2240	2.4	0	-9.5	-27.2	NA
9.6x62mm	232	2625	2302	2002	1728	-	2551	2731	2066	1539	-	2.6	0	-11.3	-	NA
9.3x62mm	250	2550	2376	2208	2048	—	3609	3133	2707	2328	—	0	-5.4	-17.9	—	NA
9.3x62mm	286	2360	2155	1961	1778	1608	3537	2949	2442	2008	1642	0	-6	-21.1	-47.2	NA
9.3x62mm	286	2400	2163	1941	1733	—	3657	2972	2392	1908	—	0	-6.7	-22.6	—	NA
9.3x64mm	286	2700	2505	2318	2139	1968	4629	3984	3411	2906	2460	2.5	2.7	-4.5	-19.2	NA
9.3x72mmR	193	1952	1610	1326	1120	996	1633	1112	754	538	425	0	-12.1	-44.1	—	NA
9.3x74mmR	250	2550	2376	2208	2048	—	3609	3133	2707	2328	—	0	-5.4	-17.9	—	NA
9.3x74Rmm	286	2360	2136	1924	1727	1545	3536	2896	2351	1893	1516	0	-6.1	-21.7	-49	NA
375																
375 Winchester	200	2200	1841	1526	1268	1089	2150	1506	1034	714	527	+2.5	-4.0	-26.2	0.0	$27
375 Winchester	250	1900	1647	1424	1239	1103	2005	1506	1126	852	676	+2.5	-6.9	-33.3	0.0	$27
376 Steyr	225	2600	2331	2078	1842	1625	3377	2714	2157	1694	1319	2.5	0.0	-10.6	-31.4	NA

Cartridge	Bullet Wgt. Grs.	VELOCITY (fps)					ENERGY (ft. lbs.)					TRAJ. (in.)				Est. Price/box
		Muzzle	100 yds.	200 yds.	300 yds.	400 yds.	Muzzle	100 yds.	200 yds.	300 yds.	400 yds.	100 yds.	200 yds.	300 yds.	400 yds.	
376 Steyr	270	2600	2372	2156	1951	1759	4052	3373	2787	2283	1855	2.3	0.0	-9.9	-28.9	NA
375 Dakota	300	2600	2316	2051	1804	1579	4502	3573	2800	2167	1661	+2.4	0.0	-11.0	-32.7	NA
375 N.E. 2-1/2"	270	2000	1740	1507	1310	NA	2398	1815	1362	1026	NA	+2.5	-6.0	-30.0	0.0	NA
375 Flanged	300	2450	2150	1886	1640	NA	3998	3102	2369	1790	NA	+2.5	-2.4	-17.0	0.0	NA
375 Ruger	250	2890	2675	2471	2275	2088	4636	3973	3388	2873	2421	1.7	0	-7.4	-21.5	NA
375 Ruger	260	2900	2703	2514	2333	—	4854	4217	3649	3143	—	0	-4.0	-13.4	—	NA
375 Ruger	270	2840	2600	2372	2156	1951	4835	4052	3373	2786	2283	1.8	0.0	-8.0	-23.6	NA
375 Ruger	300	2660	2344	2050	1780	1536	4713	3660	2800	2110	1572	2.4	0.0	-10.8	-32.6	NA
375 Flanged NE	300	2400	2103	1829	NA	NA	3838	2947	2228	NA	NA	0	-6.4	-	-	NA
375 H&H Magnum	250	2890	2675	2471	2275	2088	4636	3973	3388	2873	2421	1.7	0	-7.4	-21.5	NA
375 H&H Magnum	250	2670	2450	2240	2040	1850	3955	3335	2790	2315	1905	+2.5	-0.4	-10.2	-28.4	NA
375 H&H Magnum	270	2690	2420	2166	1928	1707	4337	3510	2812	2228	1747	+2.5	0.0	-10.0	-29.4	$28
375 H&H Mag.	270	2800	2562	2337	2123	1921	4700	3936	3275	2703	2213	1.9	0	-8.3	-24.3	NA
375 H&H Magnum*	300	2530	2245	1979	1733	1512	4263	3357	2608	2001	1523	+2.5	-1.0	-10.5	-33.6	$28
375 H&H Mag.	300	2660	2345	2052	1782	1539	4713	3662	2804	2114	1577	2.4	0	-10.8	-32.6	NA
375 H&H Hvy. Mag.	270	2870	2628	2399	2182	1976	4937	4141	3451	2150	1845	+1.7	0.0	-7.2	-21.0	NA
375 H&H Hvy. Mag.	300	2705	2386	2090	1816	1568	4873	3793	2908	2195	1637	+2.3	0.0	-10.4	-31.4	NA
375 H&H Mag.	350	2300	2052	1821	-	-	4112	3273	2578	-	-	0	-6.7	-	-	NA
375 Rem. Ultra Mag.	270	2900	2558	2241	1947	1678	5041	3922	3010	2272	1689	1.9	2.7	-8.9	-27.0	NA
375 Rem. Ultra Mag.	260	2950	2750	2560	2377	—	5023	4367	3783	3262	—	0	-3.8	-12.9	—	NA
375 Rem. Ultra Mag.	300	2760	2505	2263	2035	1822	5073	4178	3412	2759	2210	2.0	0.0	-8.8	-26.1	NA
375 Wea. Mag.	260	3000	2798	2606	2421	—	5195	4520	3920	3384	—	0	-3.6	-12.4	—	NA
375 Wea. Mag.	300	2700	2420	2157	1911	1685	4856	3901	3100	2432	1891	+2.5	-.04	-10.7	0.0	NA
378 Wea. Mag.	260	3100	2894	2697	2509	—	5547	4834	4199	3633	—	0	-4.2	-14.6	—	NA
378 Wea. Mag.	270	3180	2976	2781	2594	2415	6062	5308	4635	4034	3495	+2.5	+2.6	-1.8	-11.3	$71
378 Wea. Mag.	300	2929	2576	2252	1952	1680	5698	4419	3379	2538	1881	+2.5	+1.2	-7.0	-24.5	$77
375 A-Square	300	2920	2626	2351	2093	1850	5679	4594	3681	2917	2281	+2.5	+1.4	-6.0	-21.0	NA
38-40 Win.	180	1160	999	901	827	764	538	399	324	273	233	0.0	-33.9	0.0	0.0	$42**
40, 41																
400 A-Square DPM	400	2400	2146	1909	1689	NA	5116	2092	3236	2533	NA	2.98	0	-10	NA	NA
400 A-Square DPM	170	2980	2463	2001	1598	NA	3352	2289	1512	964	NA	2.16	0	-11.1	NA	NA
408 CheyTac	419	2850	2752	2657	2562	2470	7551	7048	6565	6108	5675	-1.02	0	1.9	4.2	NA
405 Win.	300	2200	1851	1545	1296		3224	2282	1589	1119		4.6	0	-19.5	0	NA
450/400-3"	400	2050	1815	1595	1402	NA	3732	2924	2259	1746	NA	0	NA	-33.4	NA	NA
416 Ruger	400	2400	2151	1917	1700	NA	5116	4109	3264	2568	NA	0	-6	-21.6	0	NA
416 Dakota	400	2450	2294	2143	1998	1859	5330	4671	4077	3544	3068	2.5	-0.2	-10.5	-29.4	NA
416 Taylor	375	2350	2021	1722	na	na	4600	3403	2470	NA	NA	0	-7	NA	NA	NA
416 Taylor	400	2350	2117	1896	1693	NA	4905	3980	3194	2547	NA	2.5	-1.2	15	0	NA
416 Hoffman	400	2380	2145	1923	1718	1529	5031	4087	3285	2620	2077	2.5	-1	-14.1	0	NA
416 Rigby	350	2600	2449	2303	2162	2026	5253	4661	4122	3632	3189	2.5	-1.8	-10.2	-26	NA
416 Rigby	400	2370	2210	2050	1900	NA	4990	4315	3720	3185	NA	2.5	-0.7	-12.1	0	NA
416 Rigby	400	2400	2115	1851	1611	—	5115	3973	3043	2305	—	0	-6.5	-21.8	—	NA
416 Rigby	400	2415	2156	1915	1691	—	5180	4130	3256	2540	—	0	-6	-21.6	—	NA
416 Rigby	410	2370	2110	1870	1640	NA	5115	4050	3165	2455	NA	2.5	-2.4	-17.3	0	$110
416 Rigby No. 2	400	2400	2115	1851	1611	—	5115	3973	3043	2305	—	0	-6.5	-21.8	—	NA
416 Rem. Mag.*	350	2520	2270	2034	1814	1611	4935	4004	3216	2557	2017	2.5	-0.8	-12.6	-35	$82
416 Rem. Mag.	400	2400	2142	1901	1679	—	5116	4076	3211	2504	—	3.1	0	-12.7	—	NA
416 Rem. Mag	450	2150	1925	1716	-	-	4620	3702	2942	-	-	0	-7.8	-	-	NA
416 Wea. Mag.*	400	2700	2397	2115	1852	1613	6474	5104	3971	3047	2310	2.5	0	-10.1	-30.4	$96
10.57 (416) Meteor	400	2730	2532	2342	2161	1987	6621	5695	4874	4147	3508	1.9	0	-8.3	-24	NA
500/416 N.E.	400	2300	2092	1895	1712	—	4697	3887	3191	2602	—	0	-7.2	-24	—	NA
404 Jeffrey	400	2150	1924	1716	1525	NA	4105	3289	2614	2064	NA	2.5	-4	-22.1	0	NA
404 Jeffrey	400	2300	2053	1823	1611	—	4698	3743	2950	2306	—	0	-6.8	-24.1	—	NA
404 Jeffery	400	2350	2020	1720	1458	—	4904	3625	2629	1887	—	0	-6.5	-21.8	—	NA
404 Jeffery	450	2150	1946	1755	-	-	4620	3784	3078	-	-	0	-7.6	-	-	NA
425, 44																
425 Express	400	2400	2160	1934	1725	NA	5115	4145	3322	2641	NA	2.5	-1	-14	0	NA
44-40 Win.	200	1190	1006	900	822	756	629	449	360	300	254	0	-33.3	0	0	$36**
44 Rem. Mag.	210	1920	1477	1155	982	880	1719	1017	622	450	361	0	-17.6	0	0	$14
44 Rem. Mag.	240	1760	1380	1114	970	878	1650	1015	661	501	411	0	-17.6	0	0	$13
444 Marlin	240	2350	1815	1377	1087	941	2942	1753	1001	630	472	2.5	-15.1	-31	0	$22
444 Marlin	265	2120	1733	1405	1160	1012	2644	1768	1162	791	603	2.5	-6	-32.2	0	Disc.
444 Mar. Lever Evolution	265	2325	1971	1652	1380	NA	3180	2285	1606	1120	NA	3	-1.4	-18.6	NA	NA
444 Mar. Superformance	265	2400	1976	1603	1298	NA	3389	2298	1512	991	NA	4.1	0	-17.8	NA	NA

Cartridge	Bullet Wgt. Grs.	VELOCITY (fps)					ENERGY (ft. lbs.)					TRAJ. (in.)				Est. Price/box
		Muzzle	100 yds.	200 yds.	300 yds.	400 yds.	Muzzle	100 yds.	200 yds.	300 yds.	400 yds.	100 yds.	200 yds.	300 yds.	400 yds.	

45

Cartridge	Bullet Wgt. Grs.	Muzzle	100	200	300	400	Muzzle	100	200	300	400	100	200	300	400	Est. Price/box
45-70 Govt.	250	2025	1616	1285	1068	—	2276	1449	917	634	—	6.1	0	-27.2	—	NA
45-70 Govt.	300	1810	1497	1244	1073	969	2182	1492	1031	767	625	0	-14.8	0	0	$21
45-70 Govt. Supreme	300	1880	1558	1292	1103	988	2355	1616	1112	811	651	0	-12.9	-46	-105	NA
45-70 Govt.	325	2000	1685	1413	1197	—	2886	2049	1441	1035	—	5.5	0	-23	—	NA
45-70 Lever Evolution	325	2050	1729	1450	1225	NA	3032	2158	1516	1083	NA	3	-4.1	-27.8	NA	NA
45-70 Govt. CorBon	350	1800	1526	1296			2519	1810	1307			0	-14.6	0	0	NA
45-70 Govt.	405	1330	1168	1055	977	918	1590	1227	1001	858	758	0	-24.6	0	0	$21
45-70 Govt. PMC Cowboy	405	1550	1193	—	—	—	1639	1280	—	—	—	0	-23.9	0	0	NA
45-70 Govt. Garrett	415	1850	—	—	—	—	3150	—	—	—	—	3	-7	0	0	NA
45-70 Govt. Garrett	530	1550	1343	1178	1062	982	2828	2123	1633	1327	1135	0	-17.8	0	0	NA
450 Bushmaster	250	2200	1831	1508	1480	1073	2686	1860	1262	864	639	0	-9	-33.5	0	NA
450 Marlin	325	2225	1887	1587	1332	—	3572	2570	1816	1280	—	4.2	0	-18.1	—	NA
450 Marlin	350	2100	1774	1488	1254	1089	3427	2446	1720	1222	922	0	-9.7	-35.2	0	NA
450 Mar. Lever Evolution	325	2225	1887	1585	1331	NA	3572	2569	1813	1278	NA	3	-2.2	-21.3	NA	NA
457 Wild West Magnum	350	2150	1718	1348	NA	NA	3645	2293	1413	NA	NA	0	-10.5	NA	NA	NA
450/500 N.E.	400	2050	1820	1609	1420	—	3732	2940	2298	1791	—	0	-9.7	-32.8	—	NA
450 N.E. 3-1/4"	465	2190	1970	1765	1577	NA	4952	4009	3216	2567	NA	2.5	-3	-20	0	NA
450 N.E.	480	2150	1881	1635	1418	—	4927	3769	2850	2144	—	0	-8.4	-29.8	—	NA
450 N.E. 3-1/4"	500	2150	1920	1708	1514	NA	5132	4093	3238	2544	NA	2.5	-4	-22.9	0	NA
450 No. 2	465	2190	1970	1765	1577	NA	4952	4009	3216	2567	NA	2.5	-3	-20	0	NA
450 No. 2	500	2150	1920	1708	1514	NA	5132	4093	3238	2544	NA	2.5	-4	-22.9	0	NA
450 Ackley Mag.	465	2400	2169	1950	1747	NA	5947	4857	3927	3150	NA	2.5	-1	-13.7	0	NA
450 Ackley Mag.	500	2320	2081	1855	1649	NA	5975	4085	3820	3018	NA	2.5	-1.2	-15	0	NA
450 Rigby	500	2350	2139	1939	1752	—	6130	5079	4176	3408	—	0	-6.8	-22.9	—	NA
450 Rigby	550	2100	1866	1651	-	-	5387	4256	3330	-	-	-	-	-	-	NA
458 Win. Magnum	400	2380	2170	1960	1770	NA	5030	4165	3415	2785	NA	2.5	-0.4	-13.4	0	$73
458 Win. Magnum	465	2220	1999	1791	1601	NA	5088	4127	3312	2646	NA	2.5	-2	-17.7	0	NA
458 Win. Magnum	500	2040	1823	1623	1442	1237	4620	3689	2924	2308	1839	2.5	-3.5	-22	0	$61
458 Win. Mag.	500	2140	1880	1643	1432	—	5084	3294	2996	2276	—	0	-8.4	-29.8	—	NA
458 Win. Magnum	510	2040	1770	1527	1319	1157	4712	3547	2640	1970	1516	2.5	-4.1	-25	0	$41
458 Lott	465	2380	2150	1932	1730	NA	5848	4773	3855	3091	NA	2.5	-1	-14	0	NA
458 Lott	500	2300	2029	1778	1551	—	5873	4569	3509	2671	—	0	-7	-25.1	—	NA
458 Lott	500	2300	2062	1838	1633	NA	5873	4719	3748	2960	NA	2.5	-1.6	-16.4	0	NA
460 Short A-Sq.	500	2420	2175	1943	1729	NA	6501	5250	4193	3319	NA	2.5	-0.8	-12.8	0	NA
460 Wea. Mag.	500	2700	2404	2128	1869	1635	8092	6416	5026	3878	2969	2.5	0.6	-8.9	-28	$72

475

Cartridge	Bullet Wgt. Grs.	Muzzle	100	200	300	400	Muzzle	100	200	300	400	100	200	300	400	Est. Price/box
500/465 N.E.	480	2150	1917	1703	1507	NA	4926	3917	3089	2419	NA	2.5	-4	-22.2	0	NA
470 Rigby	500	2150	1940	1740	1560	NA	5130	4170	3360	2695	NA	2.5	-2.8	-19.4	0	NA
470 Nitro Ex.	480	2190	1954	1735	1536	NA	5111	4070	3210	2515	NA	2.5	-3.5	-20.8	0	NA
470 N.E.	500	2150	1885	1643	1429	—	5132	3945	2998	2267	—	0	-8.9	-30.8	—	NA
470 Nitro Ex.	500	2150	1890	1650	1440	1270	5130	3965	3040	2310	1790	2.5	-4.3	-24	0	$177
475 No. 2	500	2200	1955	1728	1522	NA	5375	4243	3316	2573	NA	2.5	-3.2	-20.9	0	NA

50, 58

Cartridge	Bullet Wgt. Grs.	Muzzle	100	200	300	400	Muzzle	100	200	300	400	100	200	300	400	Est. Price/box
50 Alaskan	450	2000	1729	1492	NA	NA	3997	2987	2224	NA	NA	0.0	-11.25	NA	NA	NA
500 Jeffery	570	2300	1979	1688	1434	—	6694	4958	3608	2604	—	0	-8.2	-28.6	—	NA
505 Gibbs	525	2300	2063	1840	1637	NA	6166	4922	3948	3122	NA	+2.5	-3.0	-18.0	0.0	NA
505 Gibbs	570	2100	1893	1701	-	-	5583	4538	3664	-	-	0	-8.1	-	-	NA
505 Gibbs	600	2100	1899	1711	-	-	5877	4805	3904	-	-	0	-8.1	-	-	NA
500 N.E.	570	2150	1889	1651	1439	—	5850	4518	3450	2621	—	0	-8.9	-30.6	—	NA
500 N.E.-3"	570	2150	1928	1722	1533	NA	5850	4703	3752	2975	NA	+2.5	-3.7	-22.0	0.0	NA
500 N.E.-3"	600	2150	1927	1721	1531	NA	6158	4947	3944	3124	NA	+2.5	-4.0	-22.0	0.0	NA
495 A-Square	570	2350	2117	1896	1693	NA	5850	4703	3752	2975	NA	+2.5	-1.0	-14.5	0.0	NA
495 A-Square	600	2280	2050	1833	1635	NA	6925	5598	4478	3562	NA	+2.5	-2.0	-17.0	0.0	NA
500 A-Square	600	2380	2144	1922	1766	NA	7546	6126	4920	3922	NA	+2.5	-3.0	-17.0	0.0	NA
500 A-Square	707	2250	2040	1841	1567	NA	7947	6530	5318	4311	NA	+2.5	-2.0	-17.0	0.0	NA
500 BMG PMC	660	3080	2854	2639	2444	2248	13688			500 yd. zero		+3.1	+3.9	+4.7	+2.8	NA
577 Nitro Ex.	750	2050	1793	1562	1360	NA	6990	5356	4065	3079	NA	+2.5	-5.0	-26.0	0.0	NA
577 Tyrannosaur	750	2400	2141	1898	1675	NA	9591	7633	5996	4671	NA	+3.0	0.0	-12.9	0.0	NA

600, 700

Cartridge	Bullet Wgt. Grs.	Muzzle	100	200	300	400	Muzzle	100	200	300	400	100	200	300	400	Est. Price/box
600 N.E.	900	1950	1680	1452	NA	NA	7596	5634	4212	NA	NA	+5.6	0.0	0.0	0.0	NA
700 N.E.	1200	1900	1676	1472	NA	NA	9618	7480	5774	NA	NA	+5.7	0.0	0.0	0.0	NA

50 BMG

Cartridge	Bullet Wgt. Grs.	Muzzle	100	200	300	400	Muzzle	100	200	300	400	100	200	300	400	Est. Price/box
50 BMG	624	2952	2820	2691	2566	2444	12077	11028	10036	9125	8281	0	-2.9	-10.6	-23.5	NA
50 BMG Match	750	2820	2728	2637	2549	2462	13241	12388	11580	10815	10090	1.5	0.0	-6.5	-18.3	NA

Notes: Blanks are available in 32 S&W, 38 S&W and 38 Special. "V" after barrel length indicates test barrel was vented to produce ballistics similar to a revolver with a normal barrel-to-cylinder gap. Ammo prices are per 50 rounds except when marked with an ** which signifies a 20 round box; *** signifies a 25-round box. Not all loads are available from all ammo manufacturers. Listed loads are those made by Remington, Winchester, Federal, and others. DISC. is a discontinued load. Prices are rounded to the nearest whole dollar and will vary with brand and retail outlet.

Cartridge	Bullet Wgt. Grs.	VELOCITY (fps)			ENERGY (ft. lbs.)			Mid-Range Traj. (in.)		Bbl. Lgth. (in).	Est. Price/ box
		Muzzle	50 yds.	100 yds.	Muzzle	50 yds.	100 yds.	50 yds.	100 yds.		
22, 25											
221 Rem. Fireball	50	2650	2380	2130	780	630	505	0.2	0.8	10.5"	$15
25 Automatic	35	900	813	742	63	51	43	NA	NA	2"	$18
25 Automatic	45	815	730	655	65	55	40	1.8	7.7	2"	$21
25 Automatic	50	760	705	660	65	55	50	2	8.7	2"	$17
30											
7.5mm Swiss	107	1010	NA	NA	240	NA	NA	NA	NA	NA	NEW
7.62x25 Tokarev	85	1647	1458	1295	512	401	317	0	-3.2	4.75	
7.62mm Tokarev	87	1390	NA	NA	365	NA	NA	0.6	NA	4.5"	NA
7.62 Nagant	97	790	NA	NA	134	NA	NA	NA	NA	NA	NEW
7.63 Mauser	88	1440	NA	NA	405	NA	NA	NA	NA	NA	NEW
30 Luger	93	1220	1110	1040	305	255	225	0.9	3.5	4.5"	$34
30 Carbine	110	1790	1600	1430	785	625	500	0.4	1.7	10"	$28
30-357 AeT	123	1992	NA	NA	1084	NA	NA	NA	NA	10"	NA
32											
32 NAA	80	1000	933	880	178	155	137	NA	NA	4"	NA
32 S&W	88	680	645	610	90	80	75	2.5	10.5	3"	$17
32 S&W Long	98	705	670	635	115	100	90	2.3	10.5	4"	$17
32 Short Colt	80	745	665	590	100	80	60	2.2	9.9	4"	$19
32 H&R	80	1150	1039	963	235	192	165	NA	NA	4"	NA
32 H&R Magnum	85	1100	1020	930	230	195	165	1	4.3	4.5"	$21
32 H&R Magnum	95	1030	940	900	225	190	170	1.1	4.7	4.5"	$19
327 Federal Magnum	85	1400	1220	1090	370	280	225	NA	NA	4-V	NA
327 Federal Magnum	100	1500	1320	1180	500	390	310	-0.2	-4.5	4-V	NA
32 Automatic	60	970	895	835	125	105	95	1.3	5.4	4"	$22
32 Automatic	60	1000	917	849	133	112	96			4"	NA
32 Automatic	65	950	890	830	130	115	100	1.3	5.6	NA	NA
32 Automatic	71	905	855	810	130	115	95	1.4	5.8	4"	$19
8mm Lebel Pistol	111	850	NA	NA	180	NA	NA	NA	NA	NA	NEW
8mm Steyr	112	1080	NA	NA	290	NA	NA	NA	NA	NA	NEW
8mm Gasser	126	850	NA	NA	200	NA	NA	NA	NA	NA	NEW
9mm, 38											
380 Automatic	60	1130	960	NA	170	120	NA	1	NA	NA	NA
380 Automatic	75	950	NA	NA	183	NA	NA	NA	NA	3"	$33
380 Automatic	85/88	990	920	870	190	165	145	1.2	5.1	4"	$20
380 Automatic	90	1000	890	800	200	160	130	1.2	5.5	3.75"	$10
380 Automatic	95/100	955	865	785	190	160	130	1.4	5.9	4"	$20
38 Super Auto +P	115	1300	1145	1040	430	335	275	0.7	3.3	5"	$26
38 Super Auto +P	125/130	1215	1100	1015	425	350	300	0.8	3.6	5"	$26
38 Super Auto +P	147	1100	1050	1000	395	355	325	0.9	4	5"	NA
38 Super Auto +P	115	1130	1016	938	326	264	225	1	-9.5	-	NA
9x18mm Makarov	95	1000	930	874	211	182	161	NA	NA	4"	NEW
9x18mm Ultra	100	1050	NA	NA	240	NA	NA	NA	NA	NA	NEW
9x21	124	1150	1050	980	365	305	265	NA	NA	4"	NA
9x21 IMI	123	1220	1095	1010	409	330	281	-3.15	—	5	NA
9x23mm Largo	124	1190	1055	966	390	306	257	0.7	3.7	4"	NA
9x23mm Win.	125	1450	1249	1103	583	433	338	0.6	2.8	NA	NA
9mm Steyr	115	1180	NA	NA	350	NA	NA	NA	NA	NA	NEW
9mm Luger	88	1500	1190	1010	440	275	200	0.6	3.1	4"	$24
9mm Luger	90	1360	1112	978	370	247	191	NA	NA	4"	$26
9mm Luger	92	1325	1117	991	359	255	201	-3.2	—	4	NA
9mm Luger	95	1300	1140	1010	350	275	215	0.8	3.4	4"	NA
9mm Luger	100	1180	1080	NA	305	255	NA	0.9	NA	4"	NA
9mm Luger Guard Dog	105	1230	1070	970	355	265	220	NA	NA	4"	NA
9mm Luger	115	1155	1045	970	340	280	240	0.9	3.9	4"	$21
9mm Luger	123/125	1110	1030	970	340	290	260	1	4	4"	$23

Cartridge	Bullet Wgt. Grs.	VELOCITY (fps)			ENERGY (ft. lbs.)			Mid-Range Traj. (in.)		Bbl. Lgth. (in).	Est. Price/ box
		Muzzle	50 yds.	100 yds.	Muzzle	50 yds.	100 yds.	50 yds.	100 yds.		
9mm Luger	124	1150	1040	965	364	298	256	-4.5	—	4	NA
9mm Luger	135	1010	960	918	306	276	253	—	—	4	NA
9mm Luger	140	935	890	850	270	245	225	1.3	5.5	4"	$23
9mm Luger	147	990	940	900	320	290	265	1.1	4.9	4"	$26
9mm Luger +P	90	1475	NA	NA	437	NA	NA	NA	NA	NA	NA
9mm Luger +P	115	1250	1113	1019	399	316	265	0.8	3.5	4"	$27
9mm Federal	115	1280	1130	1040	420	330	280	0.7	3.3	4"V	$24
9mm Luger Vector	115	1155	1047	971	341	280	241	NA	NA	4"	NA
9mm Luger +P	124	1180	1089	1021	384	327	287	0.8	3.8	4"	NA
9mm Luger +P	124	1180	1089	1021	384	327	287	0.8	3.8	4"	NA
38											
38 S&W	146	685	650	620	150	135	125	2.4	10	4"	$19
38 S&W Short	145	720	689	660	167	153	140	-8.5	—	5	NA
38 Short Colt	125	730	685	645	150	130	115	2.2	9.4	6"	$19
39 Special	100	950	900	NA	200	180	NA	1.3	NA	4"V	NA
38 Special	110	945	895	850	220	195	175	1.3	5.4	4"V	$23
38 Special	110	945	895	850	220	195	175	1.3	5.4	4"V	$23
38 Special	130	775	745	710	175	160	120	1.9	7.9	4"V	$22
38 Special Cowboy	140	800	767	735	199	183	168			7.5" V	NA
38 (Multi-Ball)	140	830	730	505	215	130	80	2	10.6	4"V	$10**
38 Special	148	710	635	565	165	130	105	2.4	10.6	4"V	$17
38 Special	158	755	725	690	200	185	170	2	8.3	4"V	$18
38 Special +P	95	1175	1045	960	290	230	195	0.9	3.9	4"V	$23
38 Special +P	110	995	925	870	240	210	185	1.2	5.1	4"V	$23
38 Special +P	125	975	929	885	264	238	218	1	5.5	4"	NA
38 Special +P	125	945	900	860	250	225	205	1.3	5.4	4"V	#23
38 Special +P	129	945	910	870	255	235	215	1.3	5.3	4"V	$11
38 Special +P	130	925	887	852	247	227	210	1.3	5.5	4"V	NA
38 Special +P	147/150	884	NA	NA	264	NA	NA	NA	NA	4"V	$27
38 Special +P	158	890	855	825	280	255	240	1.4	6	4"V	$20
357											
357 SIG	115	1520	NA	NA	593	NA	NA	NA	NA	NA	NA
357 SIG	124	1450	NA	NA	578	NA	NA	NA	NA	NA	NA
357 SIG	125	1350	1190	1080	510	395	325	0.7	3.1	4"	NA
357 SIG	135	1225	1112	1031	450	371	319	—	—	4	NA
357 SIG	147	1225	1132	1060	490	418	367	—	—	4	NA
357 SIG	150	1130	1030	970	420	355	310	0.9	4	NA	NA
356 TSW	115	1520	NA	NA	593	NA	NA	NA	NA	NA	NA
356 TSW	124	1450	NA	NA	578	NA	NA	NA	NA	NA	NA
356 TSW	135	1280	1120	1010	490	375	310	0.8	3.5	NA	NA
356 TSW	147	1220	1120	1040	485	410	355	0.8	3.5	5"	NA
357 Mag., Super Clean	105	1650									NA
357 Magnum	110	1295	1095	975	410	290	230	0.8	3.5	4"V	$25
357 (Med.Vel.)	125	1220	1075	985	415	315	270	0.8	3.7	4"V	$25
357 Magnum	125	1450	1240	1090	585	425	330	0.6	2.8	4"V	$25
357 Magnum	125	1500	1312	1163	624	478	376	—	—	8	NA
357 (Multi-Ball)	140	1155	830	665	420	215	135	1.2	6.4	4"V	$11**
357 Magnum	140	1360	1195	1075	575	445	360	0.7	3	4"V	$25
357 Magnum FlexTip	140	1440	1274	1143	644	504	406	NA	NA	NA	NA
357 Magnum	145	1290	1155	1060	535	430	360	0.8	3.5	4"V	$26
357 Magnum	150/158	1235	1105	1015	535	430	360	0.8	3.5	4"V	$25
357 Mag. Cowboy	158	800	761	725	225	203	185				NA
357 Magnum	165	1290	1189	1108	610	518	450	0.7	3.1	8-3/8"	NA
357 Magnum	180	1145	1055	985	525	445	390	0.9	3.9	4"V	$25
357 Magnum	180	1180	1088	1020	557	473	416	0.8	3.6	8"V	NA
357 Mag. CorBon F.A.	180	1650	1512	1386	1088	913	767	1.66	0		NA
357 Mag. CorBon	200	1200	1123	1061	640	560	500	3.19	0		NA
357 Rem. Maximum	158	1825	1590	1380	1170	885	670	0.4	1.7	10.5"	$14**
40, 10mm											
40 S&W	120	1150	-	-	352	-	-	-	-	-	$38
40 S&W	125	1265	1102	998	444	337	276	-3	—	4	NA

Cartridge	Bullet Wgt. Grs.	VELOCITY (fps)			ENERGY (ft. lbs.)			Mid-Range Traj. (in.)		Bbl. Lgth. (in).	Est. Price/ box
		Muzzle	50 yds.	100 yds.	Muzzle	50 yds.	100 yds.	50 yds.	100 yds.		
40 S&W	135	1140	1070	NA	390	345	NA	0.9	NA	4"	NA
40 S&W Guard Dog	135	1200	1040	940	430	325	265	NA	NA	4"	NA
40 S&W	155	1140	1026	958	447	362	309	0.9	4.1	4"	$14***
40 S&W	165	1150	NA	NA	485	NA	NA	NA	NA	4"	$18***
40 S&W	175	1010	948	899	396	350	314	—	—	4	NA
40 S&W	180	985	936	893	388	350	319	1.4	5	4"	$14***
40 S&W	180	1000	943	896	400	355	321	4.52	—	4	NA
40 S&W	180	1015	960	914	412	368	334	1.3	4.5	4"	NA
400 Cor-Bon	135	1450	NA	NA	630	NA	NA	NA	NA	5"	NA
10mm Automatic	155	1125	1046	986	436	377	335	0.9	3.9	5"	$26
10mm Automatic	155	1265	1118	1018	551	430	357	—	—	5	NA
10mm Automatic	170	1340	1165	1145	680	510	415	0.7	3.2	5"	$31
10mm Automatic	175	1290	1140	1035	650	505	420	0.7	3.3	5.5"	$11**
10mm Auto. (FBI)	180	950	905	865	361	327	299	1.5	5.4	4"	$16**
10mm Automatic	180	1030	970	920	425	375	340	1.1	4.7	5"	$16**
10mm Auto H.V.	180	1240	1124	1037	618	504	430	0.8	3.4	5"	$27
10mm Auto	200	1100	1015	951	537	457	402	-1.1	-9.6	NA	NA
10mm Automatic	200	1160	1070	1010	495	510	430	0.9	3.8	5"	$14**
10.4mm Italian	177	950	NA	NA	360	NA	NA	NA	NA	NA	NEW
41 Action Exp.	180	1000	947	903	400	359	326	0.5	4.2	5"	$13**
41 Rem. Magnum	170	1420	1165	1015	760	515	390	0.7	3.2	4"V	$33
41 Rem. Magnum	175	1250	1120	1030	605	490	410	0.8	3.4	4"V	$14**
41 (Med. Vel.)	210	965	900	840	435	375	330	1.3	5.4	4"V	$30
41 Rem. Magnum	210	1300	1160	1060	790	630	535	0.7	3.2	4"V	$33
41 Rem. Magnum	240	1250	1151	1075	833	706	616	0.8	3.3	6.5V	NA
44											
44 S&W Russian	247	780	NA	NA	335	NA	NA	NA	NA	NA	NA
44 Special	210	900	861	825	360	329	302	5.57	—	6	NA
44 Special FTX	165	900	848	802	297	263	235	NA	NA	2.5"	NA
44 S&W Special	180	980	NA	NA	383	NA	NA	NA	NA	6.5"	NA
44 S&W Special	180	1000	935	882	400	350	311	NA	NA	7.5"V	NA
44 S&W Special	200	875	825	780	340	302	270	1.2	6	6"	$13**
44 S&W Special	200	1035	940	865	475	390	335	1.1	4.9	6.5"	$13**
44 S&W Special	240/246	755	725	695	310	285	265	2	8.3	6.5"	$26
44-40 Win.	200	722	698	676	232	217	203	-3.4	-23.7	4	NA
44-40 Win.	205	725	689	655	239	216	195	—	—	7.5	NA
44-40 Win.	210	725	698	672	245	227	210	-11.6	—	5.5	NA
44-40 Win.	225	725	697	670	263	243	225	-3.4	-23.8	4	NA
44-40 Win. Cowboy	225	750	723	695	281	261	242				NA
44 Rem. Magnum	180	1610	1365	1175	1035	745	550	0.5	2.3	4"V	$18**
44 Rem. Magnum	200	1296	1193	1110	747	632	548	-0.5	-6.2	6	NA
44 Rem. Magnum	200	1400	1192	1053	870	630	492	0.6	NA	6.5"	$20
44 Rem. Magnum	200	1500	1332	1194	999	788	633	—	—	7.5	NA
44 Rem. Magnum	210	1495	1310	1165	1040	805	635	0.6	2.5	6.5"	$18**
44 Rem. Mag. FlexTip	225	1410	1240	1111	993	768	617	NA	NA	NA	NA
44 (Med. Vel.)	240	1000	945	900	535	475	435	1.1	4.8	6.5"	$17
44 R.M. (Jacketed)	240	1180	1080	1010	740	625	545	0.9	3.7	4"V	$18**
44 R.M. (Lead)	240	1350	1185	1070	970	750	610	0.7	3.1	4"V	$29
44 Rem. Magnum	250	1180	1100	1040	775	670	600	0.8	3.6	6.5"V	$21
44 Rem. Magnum	250	1250	1148	1070	867	732	635	0.8	3.3	6.5"V	NA
44 Rem. Magnum	275	1235	1142	1070	931	797	699	0.8	3.3	6.5"	NA
44 Rem. Magnum	300	1150	1083	1030	881	781	706	—	—	7.5	NA
44 Rem. Magnum	300	1200	1100	1026	959	806	702	NA	NA	7.5"	$17
44 Rem. Magnum	330	1385	1297	1220	1406	1234	1090	1.83	0	NA	NA
44 Webley	262	850	—	—	—	—	—	—	—	—	NA
440 CorBon	260	1700	1544	1403	1669	1377	1136	1.58	NA	10"	NA
45, 50											
450 Short Colt/450 Revolver	226	830	NA	NA	350	NA	NA	NA	NA	NA	NEW
45 S&W Schofield	180	730	NA	NA	213	NA	NA	NA	NA	NA	NA
45 S&W Schofield	230	730	NA	NA	272	NA	NA	NA	NA	NA	NA
45 G.A.P.	165	1007	936	879	372	321	283	-1.4	-11.8	5	NA

Cartridge	Bullet Wgt. Grs.	VELOCITY (fps)			ENERGY (ft. lbs.)			Mid-Range Traj. (in.)		Bbl. Lgth. (in.)	Est. Price/ box
		Muzzle	50 yds.	100 yds.	Muzzle	50 yds.	100 yds.	50 yds.	100 yds.		
45 G.A.P.	185	1090	970	890	490	385	320	1	4.7	5"	NA
45 G.A.P.	230	880	842	NA	396	363	NA	NA	NA	NA	NA
45 Automatic	150	1050	NA	NA	403	NA	NA	NA	NA	NA	$40
45 Automatic	165	1030	930	NA	385	315	NA	1.2	NA	5"	NA
45 Automatic Guard Dog	165	1140	1030	950	475	390	335	NA	NA	5"	NA
45 Automatic	185	1000	940	890	410	360	325	1.1	4.9	5"	$28
45 Auto. (Match)	185	770	705	650	245	204	175	2	8.7	5"	$28
45 Auto. (Match)	200	940	890	840	392	352	312	2	8.6	5"	$20
45 Automatic	200	975	917	860	421	372	328	1.4	5	5"	$18
45 Automatic	230	830	800	675	355	325	300	1.6	6.8	5"	$27
45 Automatic	230	880	846	816	396	366	340	1.5	6.1	5"	NA
45 Automatic +P	165	1250	NA	NA	573	NA	NA	NA	NA	NA	NA
45 Automatic +P	185	1140	1040	970	535	445	385	0.9	4	5"	$31
45 Automatic +P	200	1055	982	925	494	428	380	NA	NA	5"	NA
45 Super	185	1300	1190	1108	694	582	504	NA	NA	5"	NA
45 Win. Magnum	230	1400	1230	1105	1000	775	635	0.6	2.8	5"	$14**
45 Win. Magnum	260	1250	1137	1053	902	746	640	0.8	3.3	5"	$16**
45 Win. Mag. CorBon	320	1150	1080	1025	940	830	747	3.47			NA
455 Webley MKII	262	850	NA	NA	420	NA	NA	NA	NA	NA	NA
45 Colt FTX	185	920	870	826	348	311	280	NA	NA	3"V	NA
45 Colt	200	1000	938	889	444	391	351	1.3	4.8	5.5"	$21
45 Colt	225	960	890	830	460	395	345	1.3	5.5	5.5"	$22
45 Colt + P CorBon	265	1350	1225	1126	1073	884	746	2.65	0		NA
45 Colt + P CorBon	300	1300	1197	1114	1126	956	827	2.78	0		NA
45 Colt	250/255	860	820	780	410	375	340	1.6	6.6	5.5"	$27
454 Casull	250	1300	1151	1047	938	735	608	0.7	3.2	7.5"V	NA
454 Casull	260	1800	1577	1381	1871	1436	1101	0.4	1.8	7.5"V	NA
454 Casull	300	1625	1451	1308	1759	1413	1141	0.5	2	7.5"V	NA
454 Casull CorBon	360	1500	1387	1286	1800	1640	1323	2.01	0		NA
460 S&W	200	2300	2042	1801	2350	1851	1441	0	-1.6	NA	NA
460 S&W	260	2000	1788	1592	2309	1845	1464	NA	NA	7.5"V	NA
460 S&W	250	1450	1267	1127	1167	891	705	NA	NA	8.375-V	NA
460 S&W	250	1900	1640	1412	2004	1494	1106	0	-2.75	NA	NA
460 S&W	300	1750	1510	1300	2040	1510	1125	NA	NA	8.4-V	NA
460 S&W	395	1550	1389	1249	2108	1691	1369	0	-4	NA	NA
475 Linebaugh	400	1350	1217	1119	1618	1315	1112	NA	NA	NA	NA
480 Ruger	325	1350	1191	1076	1315	1023	835	2.6	0	7.5"	NA
50 Action Exp.	300	1475	1251	1092	1449	1043	795	-	-	6"	NA
50 Action Exp.	325	1400	1209	1075	1414	1055	835	0.2	2.3	6"	$24**
500 S&W	275	1665	1392	1183	1693	1184	854	1.5	NA	8.375	NA
500 S&W	300	1950	1653	1396	2533	1819	1298	—	—	8.5	NA
500 S&W	325	1800	1560	1350	2340	1755	1315	NA	NA	8.4-V	NA
500 S&W	350	1400	1231	1106	1523	1178	951	NA	NA	10"	NA
500 S&W	400	1675	1472	1299	2493	1926	1499	1.3	NA	8.375	NA
500 S&W	440	1625	1367	1169	2581	1825	1337	1.6	NA	8.375	NA
500 S&W	500	1300	1178	1085	1876	1541	1308	—	—	8.5	NA
500 S&W	500	1425	1281	1164	2254	1823	1505	NA	NA	10"	NA

Rimfire Ammunition Ballistics

Note: The actual ballistics obtained with your firearm can vary considerably from the advertised ballistics.
Also, ballistics can vary from lot to lot with the same brand and type load.

Cartridge	Bullet Wt. Grs.	Velocity (fps) 22-1/2" Bbl.		Energy (ft. lbs.) 22-1/2" Bbl.		Mid-Range Traj. (in.)	Muzzle Velocity
		Muzzle	100 yds.	Muzzle	100 yds.	100 yds.	6" Bbl.
17 Aguila	20	1850	1267	NA	NA	NA	NA
17 Hornady Mach 2	15.5	2050	1450	149	75	NA	NA
17 Hornady Mach 2	17	2100	1530	166	88	0.7	NA
17 HMR Lead Free	15.5	2550	1901	NA	NA	0.9	NA
17 HMR TNT Green	16	2500	1642	222	96	NA	NA
17 HMR	17	2550	1902	245	136	NA	NA
17 HMR	17	2650	na	na	na	na	NA
17 HMR	20	2375	1776	250	140	NA	NA
17 Win. Super Mag.	15	3300	2496	363	207	0	NA
17 Win. Super Mag.	20 Tipped	3000	2504	400	278	0	NA
17 Win. Super Mag.	20 JHP	3000	2309	400	237	0	NA
17 Win. Super Mag.	25 Tipped	2600	2230	375	276	0	NA
5mm Rem. Rimfire Mag.	30	2300	1669	352	188	NA	24
22 Short Blank	—	—	—	—	—	—	—
22 Short CB	29	727	610	33	24	NA	706
22 Short Target	29	830	695	44	31	6.8	786
22 Short HP	27	1164	920	81	50	4.3	1077
22 Colibri	20	375	183	6	1	NA	NA
22 Super Colibri	20	500	441	11	9	NA	NA
22 Long CB	29	727	610	33	24	NA	706
22 Long HV	29	1180	946	90	57	4.1	1031
22 LR Pistol Match	40	1070	890	100	70	4.6	940
22 LR Shrt. Range Green	21	1650	912	127	NA	NA	NA
CCI Quiet 22 LR	40	710	640	45	36	NA	NA
22 LR Sub Sonic HP	38	1050	901	93	69	4.7	NA
22 LR Segmented HP	40	1050	897	98	72	NA	NA
22 LR Standard Velocity	40	1070	890	100	70	4.6	940
22 LR AutoMatch	40	1200	990	130	85	NA	NA
22 LR HV	40	1255	1016	140	92	3.6	1060
22 LR Silhoutte	42	1220	1003	139	94	3.6	1025
22 SSS	60	950	802	120	86	NA	NA
22 LR HV HP	40	1280	1001	146	89	3.5	1085
22 Velocitor GDHP	40	1435	0	0	0	NA	NA
22 LR Segmented HP	37	1435	1080	169	96	2.9	NA
22 LR Hyper HP	32/33/34	1500	1075	165	85	2.8	NA
22 LR Expediter	32	1640	NA	191	NA	NA	NA
22 LR Stinger HP	32	1640	1132	191	91	2.6	1395
22 LR Lead Free	30	1650	NA	181	NA	NA	NA
22 LR Hyper Vel	30	1750	1191	204	93	NA	NA
22 LR Shot #12	31	950	NA	NA	NA	NA	NA
22 WRF LFN	45	1300	1015	169	103	3	NA
22 Win. Mag. Lead Free	28	2200	NA	301	NA	NA	NA
22 Win. Mag.	30	2200	1373	322	127	1.4	1610
22 Win. Mag. V-Max BT	33	2000	1495	293	164	0.6	NA
22 Win. Mag. JHP	34	2120	1435	338	155	1.4	NA
22 Win. Mag. JHP	40	1910	1326	324	156	1.7	1480
22 Win. Mag. FMJ	40	1910	1326	324	156	1.7	1480
22 Win. Mag. Dyna Point	45	1550	1147	240	131	2.6	NA
22 Win. Mag. JHP	50	1650	1280	300	180	1.3	NA
22 Win. Mag. Shot #11	52	1000	—	NA	—	—	NA

Shotshell Loads & Prices

NOTES: * = 10 rounds per box. ** = 5 rounds per box. Pricing variations and number of rounds per box can occur with type and brand of ammunition. Listed pricing is the average nominal cost for load style and box quantity shown. Not every brand is available in all shot size variations. Some manufacturers do not provide suggested list prices. All prices rounded to nearest whole dollar. The price you pay will vary dependent upon outlet of purchase. # = new load spec this year; "C" indicates a change in data.

Dram Equiv.	Shot Ozs.	Load Style	Shot Sizes	Brands	Avg. Price/box	Velocity (fps)
10 Gauge 3-1/2" Magnum						
Max	2-3/8	magnum blend	5, 6, 7	Hevi-shot	NA	1200
4-1/2	2-1/4	premium	BB, 2, 4, 5, 6	Win., Fed., Rem.	$33	1205
Max	2	premium	4, 5, 6	Fed., Win.	NA	1300
4-1/4	2	high velocity	BB, 2, 4	Rem.	$22	1210
Max	18 pellets	premium	00 buck	Fed., Win.	$7**	1100
Max	1-7/8	bismuth	BB, 2, 4	Bis.	NA	1225
Max	1-3/4	high density	BB, 2	Rem.	NA	1300
4-1/4	1-3/4	steel	TT, T, BBB, BB, 1, 2, 3	Win., Rem.	$27	1260
Mag	1-5/8	steel	T, BBB, BB, 2	Win.	$27	1285
Max	1-5/8	bismuth	BB, 2, 4	Bismuth	NA	1375
Max	1-1/2	hypersonic	BBB, BB, 2	Rem.	NA	1700
Max	1-1/2	heavy metal	BB, 2, 3, 4	Hevi-Shot	NA	1500
Max	1-1/2	steel	T, BBB, BB, 1, 2, 3	Fed.	NA	1450
Max	1-3/8	steel	T, BBB, BB, 1, 2, 3	Fed., Rem.	NA	1500
Max	1-3/8	steel	T, BBB, BB, 2	Fed., Win.	NA	1450
Max	1-3/4	rifled slug	slug	Fed.	NA	1280
Max	24 pellets	buckshot	1 Buck	Fed.	NA	1100
Max	54 pellets	Super-X	4 Buck	Win.	NA	1150
12 Gauge 3-1/2" Magnum						
Max	2-1/4	premium	4, 5, 6	Fed., Rem., Win.	$13*	1150
Max	2	lead	4, 5, 6	Fed.	NA	1300
Max	2	copper plated turkey	4, 5	Rem.	NA	1300
Max	18 pellets	premium	00 buck	Fed., Win., Rem.	$7**	1100
Max	1-7/8	Wingmaster HD	4, 6	Rem.	NA	1225
Max	1-7/8	heavyweight	5, 6	Fed.	NA	1300
Max	1-3/4	high density	BB, 2, 4, 6	Rem.		1300
Max	1-7/8	bismuth	BB, 2, 4	Bis.	NA	1225
Max	1-5/8	blind side	Hex, 1, 3	Win.	NA	1400
Max	1-5/8	Hevi-shot	T	Hevi-shot	NA	1350
Max	1-5/8	Wingmaster	T	Rem.	NA	1350
Max	1-5/8	high density	BB, 2	Fed.	NA	1450
Max	1-5/8	blind side	Hex, BB, 2	Win.	NA	1400
Max	1-3/8	heavyweight	2, 4, 6	Fed.	NA	1450
Max	1-3/8	steel	T, BBB, BB, 2, 4	Fed., Win., Rem.	NA	1450
Max	1-1/2	FS steel	BBB, BB, 2	Fed.	NA	1500
Max	1-1/2	Supreme H-V	BBB, BB, 2, 3	Win.	NA	1475
Max	1-3/8	H-speed steel	BB, 2	Rem.	NA	1550
Max	1-1/4	steel	BB, 2	Win.	NA	1625

Dram Equiv.	Shot Ozs.	Load Style	Shot Sizes	Brands	Avg. Price/box	Velocity (fps)
12 Gauge 3-1/2" Magnum (cont.)						
Max	24 pellets	premium	1 Buck	Fed.	NA	1100
Max	54 pellets	Super-X	4 Buck	Win.	NA	1050
12 Gauge 3" Magnum						
4	2	premium	BB, 2, 4, 5, 6	Win., Fed., Rem.	$9*	1175
4	1-7/8	premium	BB, 2, 4, 6	Win., Fed., Rem.	$19	1210
4	1-7/8	duplex	4x6	Rem.	$9*	1210
Max	1-3/4	turkey	4, 5, 6	Fed., Fio., Win., Rem.	NA	1300
Max	1-3/4	high density	BB, 2, 4	Rem.	NA	1450
Max	1-5/8	high density	BB, 2	Fed.	NA	1450
Max	1-5/8	Wingmaster HD	4, 6	Rem.	NA	1227
Max	1-5/8	high velocity	4, 5, 6	Fed.	NA	1350
4	1-5/8	premium	2, 4, 5, 6	Win., Fed., Rem.	$18	1290
Max	1-1/2	Wingmaster HD	T	Rem.	NA	1300
Max	1-1/2	Hevi-shot	T	Hevi-shot	NA	1300
Max	1-1/2	high density	BB, 2, 4	Rem.	NA	1300
Max	1-1/2	slug	slug	Bren.	NA	1604
Max	1-5/8	bismuth	BB, 2, 4, 5, 6	Bis.	NA	1250
4	24 pellets	buffered	1 buck	Win., Fed., Rem.	$5**	1040
4	15 pellets	buffered	00 buck	Win., Fed., Rem.	$6**	1210
4	10 pellets	buffered	000 buck	Win., Fed., Rem.	$6**	1225
4	41 pellets	buffered	4 buck	Win., Fed., Rem.	$6**	1210
Max	1-3/8	heavyweight	5, 6	Fed.	NA	1300
Max	1-3/8	high density	B, 2, 4, 6	Rem. Win.	NA	1450
Max	1-3/8	slug	slug	Bren.	NA	1476
Max	1-3/8	blind side	Hex, 1, 3, 5	Win.	NA	1400
Max	1-1/4	rifled slug	slug	Fed.	NA	1600
Max	1-3/16	saboted slug	copper slug	Rem.	NA	1500
Max	7/8	rifled slug	slug	Rem.	NA	1875
Max	1-1/8	low recoil	BB	Fed.	NA	850
Max	1-1/8	steel	BB, 2, 3, 4	Fed., Win., Rem.	NA	1550
Max	1-1/16	high density	2, 4	Win.	NA	1400
Max	1	steel	4, 6	Fed.	NA	1330
Max	1-3/8	buckhammer	slug	Rem.	NA	1500
Max	1	TruBall slug	slug	Fed.	NA	1700
Max	1	rifled slug	slug, magnum	Win., Rem.	$5**	1760
Max	1	saboted slug	slug	Rem., Win., Fed.	$10**	1550

12 Gauge 3" Magnum (cont.)

Dram Equiv.	Shot Ozs.	Load Style	Shot Sizes	Brands	Avg. Price/box	Velocity (fps)
Max	385 grs.	Partition Gold	slug	Win.	NA	2000
Max	1-1/8	Rackmaster	slug	Win.	NA	1700
Max	300 grs.	XP3	slug	Win.	NA	2100
3-5/8	1-3/8	steel	BBB, BB, 1, 2, 3, 4	Win., Fed., Rem.	$19	1275
Max	1-1/8	snow goose FS	BB, 2, 3, 4	Fed.	NA	1635
Max	1-1/8	steel	BB, 2, 4	Rem.	NA	1500
Max	1-1/8	steel	T, BBB, BB, 2, 4, 5, 6	Fed., Win.	NA	1450
Max	1-1/8	steel	BB, 2	Fed.	NA	1400
Max	1-1/8	FS lead	3, 4	Fed.	NA	1600
Max	1-3/8	blind side	Hex, BB, 2	Win.	NA	1400
4	1-1/4	steel	T, BBB, BB, 1, 2, 3, 4, 6	Win., Fed., Rem.	$18	1400
Max	1-1/4	FS steel	**BBB, BB, 2**	Fed.	NA	1450

12 Gauge 2-3/4"

Dram Equiv.	Shot Ozs.	Load Style	Shot Sizes	Brands	Avg. Price/box	Velocity (fps)
Max	1-5/8	magnum	4, 5, 6	Win., Fed.	$8*	1250
Max	1-3/8	lead	4, 5, 6	Fiocchi	NA	1485
Max	1-3/8	turkey	4, 5, 6	Fio.	NA	1250
Max	1-3/8	steel	4, 5, 6	Fed.	NA	1400
Max	1-3/8	bismuth	BB, 2, 4, 5, 6	Bis.	NA	1300
3-3/4	1-1/2	magnum	BB, 2, 4, 5, 6	Win., Fed., Rem.	$16	1260
Max	1-1/4	blind side	Hex, 2, 5	Win.	NA	1400
Max	1-1/4	Supreme H-V	4, 5, 6, 7-1/2	Win.	NA	1400
NA		1400	BB, 2, 4, 5, 6, 7-1/2, 8, 9	Win., Fed., Rem., Fio.	$13	1330
3-3/4	1-1/4	high velocity	BB, 2, 4, 5, 6, 7-1/2, 8, 9	Win., Fed., Rem., Fio.	$13	1330
Max	1-1/4	high density	B, 2, 4	Win.	NA	1450
Max	1-1/4	high density	4, 6	Rem.	NA	1325
3-1/4	1-1/4	standard velocity	6, 7-1/2, 8, 9	Win., Fed., Rem., Fio.	$11	1220
Max	1-1/8	Hevi-shot	5	Hevi-shot	NA	1350
3-1/4	1-1/8	standard velocity	4, 6, 7-1/2, 8, 9	Win., Fed., Rem., Fio.	$9	1255
Max	1-1/8	steel	2, 4	Rem.	NA	1390
Max	1	steel	BB, 2	Fed.	NA	1450
3-1/4	1	Standard velocity	6, 7-1/2, 8	Rem., Fed., Fio., Win.	$6	1290
3-1/4	1-1/4	target	7-1/2, 8, 9	Win., Fed., Rem.	$10	1220
3	1-1/8	spreader	7-1/2, 8, 8-1/2, 9	Fio.	NA	1200
3	1-1/8	target	7-1/2, 8, 9, 7-1/2x8	Win., Fed., Rem., Fio.	$7	1200
2-3/4	1-1/8	target	7-1/2, 8, 8-1/2, 9, 7-1/2x8	Win., Fed., Rem., Fio.	$7	1145

12 Gauge 2-3/4" (cont.)

Dram Equiv.	Shot Ozs.	Load Style	Shot Sizes	Brands	Avg. Price/box	Velocity (fps)
2-3/4	1-1/8	low recoil	7-1/2, 8	Rem.	NA	1145
2-1/2	26 grams	low recoil	8	Win.	NA	980
2-1/4	1-1/8	target	7-1/2, 8, 8-1/2, 9	Rem., Fed.	$7	1080
Max	1	spreader	7-1/2, 8, 8-1/2, 9	Fio.	NA	1300
3-1/4	28 grams (1 oz)	target	7-1/2, 8, 9	Win., Fed., Rem., Fio.	$8	1290
3	1	target	7-1/2, 8, 8-1/2, 9	Win., Fio.	NA	1235
2-3/4	1	target	7-1/2, 8, 8-1/2, 9	Fed., Rem., Fio.	NA	1180
3-1/4	24 grams	target	7-1/2, 8, 9	Fed., Win., Fio.	NA	1325
3	7/8	light	8	Fio.	NA	1200
3-3/4	8 pellets	buffered	000 buck	Win., Fed., Rem.	$4**	1325
4	12 pellets	premium	00 buck	Win., Fed., Rem.	$5**	1290
3-3/4	9 pellets	buffered	00 buck	Win., Fed., Rem., Fio.	$19	1325
3-3/4	12 pellets	buffered	0 buck	Win., Fed., Rem.	$4**	1275
4	20 pellets	buffered	1 buck	Win., Fed., Rem.	$4**	1075
3-3/4	16 pellets	buffered	1 buck	Win., Fed., Rem.	$4**	1250
4	34 pellets	premium	4 buck	Fed., Rem.	$5**	1250
3-3/4	27 pellets	buffered	4 buck	Win., Fed., Rem., Fio.	$4**	1325
		PDX1	1 oz. slug, 3-00 buck	Win.	NA	1150
Max	1 oz	segmenting,	slug	Win.	NA	1600
Max	1-1/4	rifled slug	slug	Fed.	NA	1520
Max	1-1/4	slug	slug	Lightfield		1440
Max	1-1/4	saboted slug	attached sabot	Rem.	NA	1550
Max	1	rifled slug	slug, magnum	Rem., Fio.	$5**	1680
Max	1	rifled slug	slug	Win., Fed., Rem.	$4**	1610
Max	1	saboted slug	slug	Sauvestre		1640
Max	1	sabot slug	slug	Sauvestre		1640
Max	7/8	rifled slug	slug	Rem.	NA	1800
Max	400	plat. tip	sabot slug	Win.	NA	1700
Max	385 grains	Partition Gold Slug	slug	Win.	NA	1900
Max	385 grains	Core-Lokt bonded	sabot slug	Rem.	NA	1900
Max	325 grains	Barnes Sabot	slug	Fed.	NA	1900
Max	300 grains	SST Slug	sabot slug	Hornady	NA	2050

12 Gauge 2-3/4" (cont.)

Dram Equiv.	Shot Ozs.	Load Style	Shot Sizes	Brands	Avg. Price/box	Velocity (fps)
Max	3/4	Tracer	#8 + tracer	Fio.	NA	1150
Max	130 grains	less lethal	.73 rubber slug	Lightfield	NA	600
Max	3/4	non-toxic	zinc slug	Win.	NA	NA
3	1-1/8	steel target	6-1/2, 7	Rem.	NA	1200
2-3/4	1-1/8	steel target	7	Rem.	NA	1145
3	1	steel	7	Win.	$11	1235
3-1/2	1-1/4	steel	T, BBB, BB, 1, 2, 3, 4, 5, 6	Win., Fed., Rem.	$18	1275
3-3/4	1-1/8	steel	BB, 1, 2, 3, 4, 5, 6	Win., Fed., Rem., Fio.	$16	1365
3-3/4	1	steel	2, 3, 4, 5, 6, 7	Win., Fed., Rem., Fio.	$13	1390
Max	7/8	steel	7	Fio.	NA	1440

16 Gauge 2-3/4"

Dram Equiv.	Shot Ozs.	Load Style	Shot Sizes	Brands	Avg. Price/box	Velocity (fps)
3-1/4	1-1/4	magnum	2, 4, 6	Fed., Rem.	$16	1260
3-1/4	1-1/8	high velocity	4, 6, 7-1/2	Win., Fed., Rem., Fio.	$12	1295
Max	1-1/8	bismuth	4, 5	Bis.	NA	1200
2-3/4	1-1/8	standard velocity	6, 7-1/2, 8	Fed., Rem., Fio.	$9	1185
2-1/2	1	dove	6, 7-1/2, 8, 9	Fio., Win.	NA	1165
2-3/4	1		6, 7-1/2, 8	Fio.	NA	1200
Max	1-5/16	steel	2, 4	Fed., Rem.	NA	1300
Max	7/8	steel	2, 4	Win.	$16	1300
3	12 pellets	buffered	1 buck	Win., Fed., Rem.	$4**	1225
Max	4/5	rifled slug	slug	Win., Fed., Rem.	$4**	1570
Max	.92	saboted slug	slug	Sauvestre	NA	1560

20 Gauge 3" Magnum

Dram Equiv.	Shot Ozs.	Load Style	Shot Sizes	Brands	Avg. Price/box	Velocity (fps)
3	1-1/4	premium	2, 4, 5, 6, 7-1/2	Win., Fed., Rem.	$15	1185
Max	1-1/4	Wingmaster HD	4, 6	Rem.	NA	1185
3	1-1/4	turkey	4, 6	Fio.	NA	1200
Max	1-1/4	Hevi-shot	2, 4, 6	Hevi-shot	NA	1250
Max	1-1/8	high density	4, 6	Rem.	NA	1300
Max	18 pellets	buckshot	2 buck	Fed.	NA	1200
Max	24 pellets	buffered	3 buck	Win.	$5**	1150

20 Gauge 3" Magnum (cont.)

Dram Equiv.	Shot Ozs.	Load Style	Shot Sizes	Brands	Avg. Price/box	Velocity (fps)
2-3/4	20 pellets	buck	3 buck	Rem.	$4**	1200
Max	1	hypersonic	2, 3, 4	Rem.	NA	Rem.
3-1/4	1	steel	1, 2, 3, 4, 5, 6	Win., Fed., Rem.	$15	1330
Max	1	blind side	Hex, 2, 5	Win.	NA	1300
Max	7/8	steel	2, 4	Win.	NA	1300
Max	7/8	FS lead	3, 4	Fed.	NA	1500
Max	1-1/16	high density	2, 4	Win.	NA	1400
Max	1-1/16	bismuth	2, 4, 5, 6	Bis.	NA	1250
Mag	5/8	saboted slug	275 gr.	Fed.	NA	1900
Max	3/4	TruBall slug	slug	Fed.	NA	1700

20 Gauge 2-3/4"

Dram Equiv.	Shot Ozs.	Load Style	Shot Sizes	Brands	Avg. Price/box	Velocity (fps)
2-3/4	1-1/8	magnum	4, 6, 7-1/2	Win., Fed., Rem.	$14	1175
2-3/4	1	high velocity	4, 5, 6, 7-1/2, 8, 9	Win., Fed., Rem., Fio.	$12	1220
Max	1	bismuth	4, 6	Bis.	NA	1200
Max	1	Hevi-shot	5	Hevi-shot	NA	1250
Max	1	Supreme H-V	4, 6, 7-1/2	Win. Rem.	NA	1300
Max	1	FS lead	4, 5, 6	Fed.	NA	1350
Max	7/8	steel	2, 3, 4	Fio.	NA	1500
2-1/2	1	Standard velocity	6, 7-1/2, 8	Win., Rem., Fed., Fio.	$6	1165
2-1/2	7/8	clays	8	Rem.	NA	1200
2-1/2	7/8	promotional	6, 7-1/2, 8	Win., Rem., Fio.	$6	1210
2-1/2	1	target	8, 9	Win., Rem.	$8	1165
Max	7/8	clays	7-1/2, 8	Win.	NA	1275
2-1/2	7/8	target	8, 9	Win., Fed., Rem.	$8	1200
Max	3/4	steel	2, 4	Rem.	NA	1425
2-1/2	7/8	steel - target	7	Rem.	NA	1200
1-1/2	7/8	low recoil	8	Win.	NA	980
Max	1	buckhammer	slug	Rem.	NA	1500
Max	5/8	saboted slug	Copper Slug	Rem.	NA	1500
Max	20 pellets	buffered	3 buck	Win., Fed.	$4	1200
Max	5/8	saboted slug	slug	Win.,	$9**	1400

Dram Equiv.	Shot Ozs.	Load Style	Shot Sizes	Brands	Avg. Price/ box	Velocity (fps)
20 Gauge 2-3/4" (cont.)						
2-3/4	5/8	rifled slug	slug	Rem.	$4**	1580
Max	3/4	saboted slug	copper slug	Fed., Rem.	NA	1450
Max	3/4	rifled slug	slug	Win., Fed., Rem., Fio.	$4**	1570
Max	.9	saboted slug	slug	Sauvestre		1480
Max	260 grains	Partition Gold Slug	slug	Win.	NA	1900
Max	260 grains	Core-Lokt Ultra	slug	Rem.	NA	1900
Max	260 grains	saboted slug	platinum tip	Win.	NA	1700
Max	3/4	steel	2, 3, 4, 6	Win., Fed., Rem.	$14	1425
Max	250 grains	SST slug	slug	Hornady	NA	1800
Max	1/2	rifled slug	slug	Rem.	NA	1800
Max	67	SST slug	slug	Hornady	NA	1800
28 Gauge 3"						
Max	7/8	tundra tungsten	4, 5, 6	Fiocchi	NA	TBD
28 Gauge 2-3/4"						
2	1	high velocity	6, 7-1/2, 8	Win.	$12	1125
2-1/4	3/4	high velocity	6, 7-1/2, 8, 9	Win., Fed., Rem., Fio.	$11	1295
2	3/4	target	8, 9	Win., Fed., Rem.	$9	1200
Max	3/4	sporting clays	7-1/2, 8-1/2	Win.	NA	1300
Max	5/8	bismuth	4, 6	Bis.	NA	1250
Max	5/8	steel	6, 7	NA	NA	1300
Max	5/8	slug		Bren.	NA	1450

Dram Equiv.	Shot Ozs.	Load Style	Shot Sizes	Brands	Avg. Price/ box	Velocity (fps)
410 Bore 3"						
Max	11/16	high velocity	4, 5, 6, 7-1/2, 8, 9	Win., Fed., Rem., Fio.	$10	1135
Max	9/16	bismuth	4	Bis.	NA	1175
Max	3/8	steel	6	NA	NA	1400
		judge	5 pellets 000 Buck	Fed.	NA	960
		judge	9 pellets #4 Buck	Fed.	NA	1100
Max	Mixed	Per. Defense	3DD/12BB	Win.	NA	750
410 Bore 2-1/2"						
Max	1/2	high velocity	4, 6, 7-1/2	Win., Fed., Rem.	$9	1245
Max	1/5	rifled slug	slug	Win., Fed., Rem.	$4**	1815
1-1/2	1/2	target	8, 8-1/2, 9	Win., Fed., Rem., Fio.	$8	1200
Max	1/2	sporting clays	7-1/2, 8, 8-1/2	Win.	NA	1300
Max		buckshot	5-000 Buck	Win.	NA	1135
		judge	12-bb's, 3 disks	Win.	NA	TBD
Max	Mixed	Per. Defense	4DD/16BB	Win.	NA	750
Max	42 grains	less lethal	4/.41 rubber balls	Lightfield	NA	1150